The New York Times
Twentieth Century in Review

THE COLD WAR

VOLUME II: 1964–1992

Other Titles in
The New York Times 20th Century in Review

The Gay Rights Movement

Forthcoming

Political Censorship
The Balkans

The New York Times
Twentieth Century in Review

THE COLD WAR

VOLUME II: 1964–1992

Editor
Francis J. Gavin

Introduction by Craig R. Whitney

FITZROY DEARBORN PUBLISHERS
CHICAGO • LONDON

For information write to:

FITZROY DEARBORN PUBLISHERS
919 North Michigan Avenue, Suite 760
Chicago IL 60611
USA

or

FITZROY DEARBORN PUBLISHERS
310 Regent Street
London W1B 3AX
England

British Library and Library of Congress Cataloging in Publication Data are available.

ISBN 1-57958-321-0

First published in the USA and UK 2001

Typeset by Print Means Inc., New York, New York

Printed by Edwards Brothers, Ann Arbor, Michigan

Cover Design by Peter Aristedes, Chicago Advertising and Design, Chicago, Illinois

CONTENTS

VOLUME I
1918–1963

VOLUME II
1964–1992

PART VI

VIETNAM AND AMERICAN RETREAT

June 2, 1964

U.S. AIDES CHART AN 'UPHILL' FIGHT IN SOUTHEAST ASIA

Lull in Laos War Tempers Attitude of Urgency as Hawaii Talks Open

BASIC TASKS REVIEWED

Rusk, McNamara and Top Staff Consider How to Press Saigon Plans

By MAX FRANKEL
Special to The New York Times.

HONOLULU, June 1—High Administration officials began a two-day strategy conference on Southeast Asia today with a somewhat diminished sense of urgency about the situation in Laos.

A lull in the military sparring among the rival Laotian factions, at least for the moment, has tended to reduce the officials' interest in hasty countermeasures, none of which had been contemplated with much enthusiasm.

The officials hope now to stretch over a longer period of time a program of less dramatic political and military moves designed to combat doubts about Washington's commitment to the region and especially to South Vietnam.

Concurrently they hope to prepare themselves and President Johnson for a faster reaction to any further deterioration of non-Communist positions there.

Rusk and McNamara Lead

The nation's highest diplomatic and military officials, led by Secretary of State Dean Rusk and Secretary of Defense Robert S. McNamara, have gathered here for the talks.

They arrived yesterday from all over the world aboard three giant Air Force jets with a logistic commotion that fairly expressed the anxiety that produced the call for the conference last Thursday. Equally symbolic was their circuitous drive up a little volcanic mountain here to the opening meeting this morning.

"Uphill" is the word most often used now to describe the United States battle in Southeast Asia. The momentary calm in Laos has not diminished the difficulty of the problem, officials assert, but it has begun to refocus attention on more basic tasks.

Mr. Rusk, Mr. McNamara, the principal military, intelligence and propaganda officials of the Administration and two dozen specialists in Southeast Asian affairs assembled in the conference rooms of the Pacific Command Headquarters at Camp H. M. Smith on the Aiea Heights, overlooking Pearl Harbor.

They sat literally over a sea of oil, stored inside the mountain lest there be another attack on this Pacific outpost. But the discussions covered a political and military conflict wholly different from the kind that followed the Japanese attack on Pearl Harbor on Dec. 7, 1941.

The subtle, complex and frustrating nature of the present warfare was evident in the reports about Laos and South Vietnam.

The crisis in Laos resulted from two assaults on the neutralist coalition Government of Prince Souvanna Phouma, established by a 14-nation Geneva conference two years ago. First came a coup by right-wing military leaders in April. Their ascendant influence was countered two weeks ago by a military offensive by the leftist Pathet Lao forces.

In what was by modern military standards a pathetic and primitive series of battles, the Pathet Lao forces evicted the Neutralist forces from the Plaine des Jarres and challenged the coalition Government whose authority they had never really recognized.

The major powers, including the Soviet Union, Communist China, Britain and France, were propelled by this modest resumption of civil war into complex diplomatic maneuvers. But the main problem was Washington's, because the collapse in Laos coincided with even more serious Communist challenges to the United States-backed Government of South Vietnam.

The Administration responded by talking tough and by casting about for ways of proving its determination. Spokesmen say it remains eager, however, to avoid direct military involvement on the Asian mainland.

One form of retaliation in Laos is said to have been reasonably successful by the standards of warfare there.

Main Issue Untouched

United States jet planes undertook reconnaissance flights over Pathet Lao territory and non-Communist Laotians were sent on modest bombing raids in T-28 propeller planes. The noise from these sorties and a few successful detonations were said to have frightened some Pathet Lao forces into retreat.

But this barely touched the real political and psychological crisis. It seems doubtful that the United States is willing to marshal the military or diplomatic force needed to re-establish a viable coalition Government or to restore the neutralists to the Plaine des Jarres.

Officials here insist that they will not resume international negotiations over Laos if the Communists insist on digesting their recent gains of territory. However, no one has yet been willing to say that recapture of that ground is now a major objective for Washington and at least one proposal—by Poland for limited negotiations—is regarded as a possible basis for a counterproposal.

A return of American troops to Thailand is advocated by some as a significant demonstration. But others, including the Thais, are said to believe that Washington must be more assertive than it was two years ago.

The Thais want a promise of direct intervention and have threatened to strike at Laotian territory themselves if the Pathet Lao forces approach their frontier.

Proxy Plan Ruled Out

Counteraction by proxy—by Laotian and South Vietnamese forces—is also being examined. The non-Communists of both countries, however, are under severe political pressure and neither group is considered to be capable yet of a sustained and complex program of aerial warfare or counterinsurgency.

These considerations force the officials here to return to familiar problems, to the shoring up of the South Vietnamese Government and the improvement of its economic life and propaganda as well as its military programs. Small groups of officials reviewed these questions at the afternoon session.

Whether all this will be enough to warn Communist adversaries in Asia and to reassure wavering governments in Cambodia, Burma and elsewhere is a question that is not likely to be answered here.

* * *

July 1, 1964

THANT IS GLOOMY ON CONGO FUTURE

Voices Fears as U.N. Force Leaves After 4 Years—Adoula Quits as Premier

By THOMAS J. HAMILTON
Special to The New York Times.

UNITED NATIONS, N. Y., June 30—The Secretary General, U Thant, warned the Security Council today that "the immediate outlook" for the Congo after the withdrawal of the United Nations force was "none too promising."

The last United Nations troops left the Congo today.

[Cyrille Adoula resigned as Premier of the Congo. President Joseph Kasavubu named him head of a caretaker regime pending the appointment of a government of transition and a national election.]

Mr. Thant said that the situation in the Congo had greatly improved from the "collapse and chaos" that followed Belgium's grant of independence to the Congo four years ago.

U.N. the 'Sole Prop'

But he emphasized that the Congo still needed "wise, imaginative, strong and courageous leadership, effective government and some measure of understanding from the people." He added that "failure to overcome present dangers would no doubt bring disintegration and ruin."

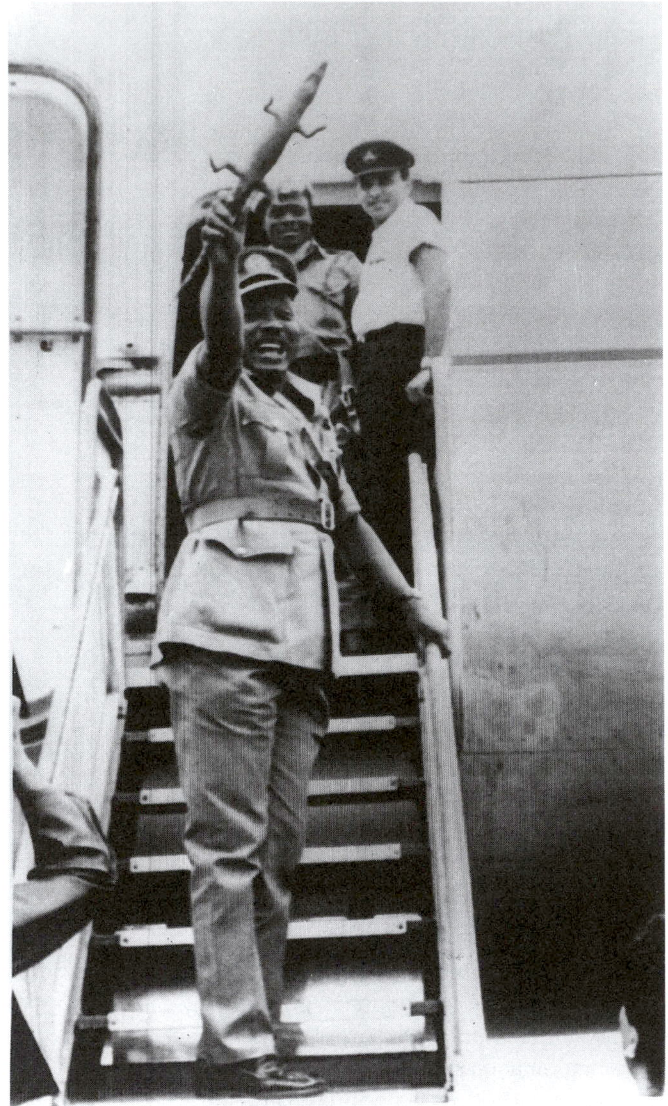

Associated Press Cablephoto

LAST TO LEAVE: General Aguiyi Iromsi of Nigeria, the last United Nations soldier to leave the Congo, boards aircraft. He is waving a crocodile-shaped stick.

The Secretary General said that the Congo had been "unprepared" for independence and that the United Nations had become the country's "sole prop and hope."

The following, he said, are the "two major and indispensable conditions" for hope for the Congo:

"(A) The training and reorganization of the national army, including the training of a substantial officer corps.

"(B) The achievement of national reconciliation—amongst the contending political leaders and factions of the country."

The Secretary General declared that, despite the withdrawal of the troops, United Nations economic and technical assistance to the Congo would continue on a larger scale than in any other country, and he emphasized the need for additional voluntary contributions.

He said that $1.5 million would be needed to maintain the civilian program for the remainder of 1964 and that $7 million would be required for 1965. The United Nations civilian program has placed about 2,000 experts and officials in the Congo, including 800 school teachers.

Discussing the outlook, Mr. Thant emphasized that the Congolese Army, which has a strength of 29,000, "is still insufficiently trained and officered to cope with any major crisis."

The Secretary General said that the situation in South Katanga, where United Nations troops smashed the forces of Moise Tshombe, the former provincial President, in January, 1963, presented "a query for the future."

In his discussion of the political situation Mr. Thant emphasized that Mr. Tshombe, who took refuge in Europe after the United Nations victory over his forces, had recently returned and was "understood to be carrying on talks in Leopoldville."

The report, which was written before Mr. Tshombe emerged as the principal candidate to succeed Premier Cyrille Adoula, noted that the late Secretary General, Dag Hammarskjold, was killed in September, 1961, while on his way to try to arrange talks between Mr. Tshombe and Mr. Adoula on a cease-fire.

New Approach on Tshombe

In July, 1962, before Mr. Tshombe's downfall, Mr. Thant described him and other members of the Katanga Government as "a bunch of clowns." He made this remark in a news conference in Helsinki, Finland, in a discussion of Katanga's claim to independence.

Mr. Thant, who was then acting Secretary General, said that he had been trying to arrange negotiations between Mr. Tshombe and the Congolese Government but had not succeeded.

He added that "in the light of what I have just explained, I really do not know whether I can do serious business with such a bunch of clowns in Katanga." Later, Mr. Thant repeated his description of the Katanga leaders as "clowns."

In his report today, however, Mr. Thant implied that he hoped that Mr. Tshombe would be successful in his current attempt to reconcile differences among Congolese leaders of all shades of opinion.

* * *

August 3, 1964

RED PT BOATS FIRE AT U.S. DESTROYER ON VIETNAM DUTY

Maddox and Four Aircraft Shoot Back After Assault 30 Miles Off Coast

ATTACKERS DRIVEN OFF

American Units Undamaged—Rusk Says 'Other Side Got a Sting Out of This'

By ARNOLD H. LUBASCH
Special to The New York Times.

WASHINGTON, Aug. 2—Three North Vietnamese PT boats fired torpedoes and 37-mm. shells at a United States destroyer in international waters about 30 miles off North Vietnam today.

The destroyer and four United States aircraft fired back, damaged them and drove them off.

The incident was announced here in an official statement by the Defense Department. It said that neither the destroyer nor the aircraft sustained casualties or damage.

The statement said that the destroyer, the 3,300-ton Maddox, was on a routine patrol when an unprovoked attack took place in the Gulf of Tonkin.

Cautious on Identification

At first Government officials were cautious in commenting that the attacking boats presumably came from North Vietnam, but Secretary of State Dean Rusk said in New York tonight that the attackers were North Vietnamese.

"The other side got a sting out of this," the Secretary said. "If they do it again, they'll get another sting."

Reports received here, apparently based on close air surveillance of the attacking boats, indicated there was no doubt that they were from North Vietnam.

President Johnson was informed immediately and received reports from top Government officials at a 45-minute White House meeting. He issued no statement.

Not Regarded as Crisis

Government officials said later that the attack was not regarded as a major crisis. They said the United States Seventh Fleet had been patrolling the area for some time, would continue its patrols and had sufficient strength on hand.

Adm. U. S. Grant Sharp Jr., Commander in Chief in the Pacific, was advised of the incident by radio as he flew back to his Pearl Harbor headquarters from a visit to South Vietnam.

The Defense Department statement on the attack, issued also by the Pacific Command, said that the boats were damaged by gunfire from the Maddox and the four carrier-based jet aircraft. The statement said:

"While on routine patrol in international waters at 4:08 A.M., E.D.T., the United States destroyer Maddox underwent an unprovoked attack by three PT-type boats at latitude 19-40 north, longitude 106-34 east, in Tonkin Gulf. The attacking boats launched three torpedoes and used 37-mm. gunfire.

"The Maddox answered with 5-inch gunfire. Shortly thereafter, four F-8 aircraft from the U.S.S. Ticonderoga joined in the defense of Maddox, using Zuni rockets and 20-MM. strafing attacks.

"The PT boats were driven off with one seen to be badly damaged and not moving and the other two damaged and retreating slowly. No casualties or damage was sustained by the Maddox or the aircraft."

The Zuni rocket-propelled missile, designed for firing from launchers carried on aircraft, has a non-nuclear warhead said to be almost as destructive as a nuclear weapon.

Defense Department officials described the incident as unwelcome but not especially serious. They observed that the most effective protest possible was made by the destroyer and four fighter planes.

The attacking boats, which displayed no flags or other identifying marks, were picked up on the destroyer's radar, kept coming and opened fire, according to the Defense Department officials.

After the attackers were driven off, they said, the United States forces resumed their patrol. No effort was made to sink the PT boats, because the fleet was not at war, they said.

The Maddox was apparently carrying out a surveillance mission, according to officials here. They said there was no ready explanation why the PT boats would in effect attack the powerful Seventh Fleet.

State Department officials noted that Seventh Fleet patrols in the area were nothing new and would continue, although shooting incidents could not be precluded. They indicated that the United States did not plan an immediate diplomatic protest as a result of the incident.

The White House declined to make any comment and would not even acknowledge that the high-level briefing for the President had taken place.

The White House meeting was attended by Secretary of State Rusk, Under Secretary of State George W. Ball, Deputy Defense Secretary Cyrus R. Vance, Gen. Earle G. Wheeler, Chairman of the Joint Chiefs of Staff, and other top military and diplomatic representatives, officials said.

Later, Mr. Rusk went to New York to make a speech.

One reason the Seventh Fleet patrols the area of the incident is that it attempts to maintain surveillance on supplies that might be moving by sea from ports in Communist North Vietnam to Communist guerrillas in South Vietnam.

* * *

August 6, 1964

U.S. PLANS NO NEW VIETNAM RAID AFTER HITTING 25 PATROL BOATS; TELLS U.N. OF HANOI AGGRESSION

4 BASES BOMBED

Oil Depot Also Target of 5-Hour Attack—2 Planes Lost

By JACK RAYMOND
Special to The New York Times.

WASHINGTON, Aug. 5—United States aircraft bombed North Vietnam bases, naval craft and an oil storage depot in a five-hour raid along 100 miles of coast early today.

Secretary of Defense Robert S. McNamara said that 25 North Vietnam patrol boats had been destroyed or damaged and that the oil installation had been 90 per cent destroyed.

He declared that unless the United States was further provoked, no new American attacks were planned.

The Defense Secretary also announced that strong reinforcements had been dispatched to the Southeast Asia crisis area. He said certain Army and Marine Corps units had been alerted.

Two of the attacking American planes were lost and two returned damaged from the raids, the Defense Secretary said. He attributed the casualties to antiaircraft fire in the vicinity of the bases.

Success Reported

In a second announcement, made before Columbia Broadcasting System television cameras tonight, the Defense Secretary reported that the air strikes had been "very successful."

Reconnaissance flights have confirmed initial reports of success, the Defense Secretary said.

The reconnaissance planes, unlike the attacking aircraft, did not encounter any antiaircraft fire, Mr. McNamara added. The planes took off from the same carrier from which the original attack was launched against the coastal bases.

Told of a North Vietnamese claim that one of the two lost Navy pilots had been captured, the Defense Secretary said that was "possible."

One Plane Lost at Sea

One of the lost planes may have been downed in North Vietnam although the other was believed to have been lost at sea, he said.

Mr. McNamara did not accept the entire claim of the North Vietnam Army High Command that five United States planes were downed and two returned damaged from the raids.

A United States spokesman said that the figures given by Mr. McNamara that two United States planes were lost "still hold."

The Defense Secretary reported on the hostilities at a news conference at the Pentagon this morning.

The atmosphere in the press conference room was reminiscent of the Cuba missile crisis of 1962. The Secretary, as in that earlier crisis, had slept in his office. He seemed confident and relaxed as he discussed the first American military attack since the Korean war.

The United States has supported the Government of South Vietnam and its neighbor, Laos, against Communist invasion threats and actual insurgency since 1954 when the French were driven out of Indochina. The sea patrols in the Gulf of Tonkin had been carried out peacefully for nearly two years until the North Vietnamese gunboat attacks prompted United States retaliation.

Asked whether he thought that the air strike had accomplished its objectives, Mr. McNamara replied that it "made clear to the North Vietnamese our intention to maintain our right to operate on the high seas. That was the objective. I think that has been accomplished."

Today's raids, Mr. McNamara said, began at about noon, Vietnamese time, and lasted until nearly 5 P.M. That would be from midnight to 5 A.M. today, Eastern daylight time.

The Secretary said the weather was bad and the sky heavily overcast.

64 Attack Sorties

He reported that warplanes from the aircraft carriers Ticonderoga and Constellation in the Gulf of Tonkin flew 64 attack sorties against four PT boat bases and an important oil storage depot.

The bases were identified as Hongay, Loc Chao, Phuc Loi and Quang Khe, all on the North Vietnamese coast. The oil storage facility was at Vinh, near Phuc Loi.

The destruction of the Vinh oil depot appeared to be especially important because, as Mr. McNamara pointed out, it was a support facility for the North Vietnamese Navy's Russian-built Swatow-type motor gunboats.

This type of vessel was said to be among the PT boats that attacked the American destroyers and precipitated the coastal raids.

The Vinh depot represented 10 per cent of the entire oil storage capacity of North Vietnam, Mr. McNamara said.

Other sources indicated that the destruction or damage of 25 North Vietnamese patrol boats represented about half of the North Vietnamese Navy.

The North Vietnamese Navy is understood to have consisted of about 50 patrol boats of various types, including modernized junks. According to Jane's Fighting Ships, the standard reference, North Vietnam's fleet includes 16 Russian-built torpedo boats that were turned over to the Hanoi regime in 1961.

Linked to Attacks

Pentagon officials indicated that the North Vietnamese used the Russian-built craft in the attacks upon the American destroyers Maddox and C. Turner Joy.

The Maddox, which was the target of the first North Vietnamese attack, carries the flag of Capt. John J. Herrick, commander of the destroyer squadron.

Secretary McNamara, this morning, emphasized that the two destroyers were "continuing their patrol in international waters in the Gulf of Tonkin."

The New York Times (by Patrick A. Burns)

EXPLAINS U.S. ACTION: Adlai E. Stevenson, U.S. delegate to U.N., addressing Security Council meeting on the Vietnamese crisis. At top is Platon D. Morozov, Deputy Soviet Representative. Center is R. W. Jackling, British Deputy Permanent Representative.

The Secretary did not identify the types of airplanes used in the United States attacks, but mostly single and double-engined jet fighters and fighter bombers were believed to have been involved.

The Constellation, a modern 60,000-ton supercarrier of the Forrestal class, carries 100 planes, including jet-powered F-4 Phantoms, twin-jet A-4 and A-3 heavy attack bombers and propeller-driven Skyraiders.

The Ticonderoga, a 30,000-ton carrier of the Essex class, normally carries 60 airplanes, including F-8 jet Crusaders and the Skyraiders.

Heavy Antiaircraft Fire

Mr. McNamara, in response to questions, said that the North Vietnamese had mounted "heavy antiaircraft fire" over several of the targets.

He indicated that the antiaircraft weapons were not modern. They were "guns rather than missiles," he said in answer to a question.

The PT boat base at Hongay, the northernmost of the targets, provided the heaviest antiaircraft fire, he said.

He withheld the names of the lost pilots until their families could be notified.

The lost pilots, he disclosed under additional questioning, had been flying single-seater planes and had been lost "at sea."

The answer appeared to confirm the belief that the reconnaissance missions were carried out to ascertain the extent of the damage.

Mr. McNamara described the four bases that were attacked as the "main bases" of the North Vietnamese PT boat fleet.

"There were no civilian centers close to the bases which were attacked," he said.

No attempts were made to silence the antiaircraft batteries, he added, stating that the attack was directed solely against the patrol boat bases and the associated facilities.

* * *

August 8, 1964

CONGRESS BACKS PRESIDENT ON SOUTHEAST ASIA MOVES; KHANH SETS STATE OF SIEGE

RESOLUTION WINS

Senate Vote is 88 to 2 After House Adopts Measure, 416-0

By E. W. KENWORTHY
Special to The New York Times.

WASHINGTON, Aug. 7—The House of Representatives and the Senate approved today the resolution requested by President Johnson to strengthen his hand in dealing with Communist aggression in Southeast Asia.

After a 40-minute debate, the House passed the resolution, 416 to 0. Shortly afterward the Senate approved it, 88 to 2. Senate debate, which began yesterday afternoon, lasted nine hours.

The resolution gives prior Congressional approval of "all necessary measures" that the President may take "to repel any armed attack" against United States forces and "to prevent further aggression."

The resolution, the text of which was printed in The New York Times Thursday, also gives advance sanction for "all necessary steps" taken by the President to help any nation covered by the Southeast Asia collective defense treaty that requests assistance "in defense of its freedom."

Johnson Hails Action

President Johnson said the Congressional action was "a demonstration to all the world of the unity of all Americans."

"The votes prove our determination to defend our forces, to prevent aggression and to work firmly and steadily for peace and security in the area," he said.

"I am sure the American people join me in expressing the deepest appreciation to the leaders and members of both parties in both houses of Congress for their patriotic, resolute and rapid action."

The debates in both houses, but particularly in the Senate, made clear, however, that the near-unanimous vote did not reflect a unanimity of opinion on the necessity or advisability of the resolution.

Except for Senators Wayne L. Morse, Democrat of Oregon, and Ernest Gruening, Democrat of Alaska, who cast the votes against the resolution, members in both houses uniformly praised the President for the retaliatory action he had ordered against North Vietnamese torpedo boats and their bases after the second torpedo boat attack on United States destroyers in the Gulf of Tonkin.

There was also general agreement that Congress could not reject the President's requested resolution without giving an impression of disunity and nonsupport that did not, in fact, exist.

There was no support for the thesis on which Senators Morse and Gruening based their opposition—that the resolution was "unconstitutional" because it was "a predated declaration of war power" reserved to Congress.

Nevertheless, many members said the President did not need the resolution because he had the power as Commander in Chief to order United States forces to repel attacks.

Several members thought the language of the resolution was unnecessarily broad and they were apprehensive that it would be interpreted as giving Congressional support for direct participation by United States troops in the war in South Vietnam.

Expansion Held Inevitable

Representative of these doubts and reservations were the brief remarks by Senator George D. Aiken, Republican of Vermont. Senator Aiken, a member of the Foreign Relations Committee, said:

"It has been apparent to me for some months that the expansion of the war in Southeast Asia was inevitable. I felt that it shouldn't occur, but the decision wasn't mine.

"I am still apprehensive of the outcome of the President's decision, but he felt that the interests of the United States required prompt action. As a citizen I feel I must support our President whether his decision is right or wrong.

"I hope the present action will prove to be correct. I support the resolution with misgivings."

In the House, Eugene Siler, Republican of Kentucky, who was absent, was paired against the resolution, but his opposition was not counted. His office said he regarded the resolution as "buck-passing" by the President with the intent of silencing any later criticism.

Reservations about the resolution took two principal forms. The first was that it might be interpreted as giving advance approval of a change in the United States mission in South Vietnam of providing a training cadre and matériel.

Senator Gaylord Nelson, Democrat of Wisconsin, made much of this question yesterday. Today he proposed an amendment to resolve all doubts about the meaning of the resolution.

Conflicting Views Noted

Mr. Nelson noted that some members had welcomed the resolution as authorizing the President "to act against the privileged sanctuary" of the Communists in North Vietnam while other members thought it did not envisage an extension of the present mission.

His amendment stated: "Our continuing policy is to limit our role to the provision of aid, training assistance, and military advice, and it is the sense of Congress that, except when provoked to a greater response, we should continue to attempt to avoid a direct military involvement in the Southeast Asian conflict."

Mr. Nelson asked Senator J. W. Fulbright, Democrat of Arkansas, whether as chairman of the Foreign Relations Committee and floor manager of the resolution he would accept the amendment. If not, Mr. Nelson said, he could not support the resolution.

Mr. Fulbright replied that he could not accept the amendment because the House had already voted and adoption of the amendment would require that the resolution go to conference with resulting delay.

'An Accurate Reflection'

However, Mr. Fulbright added at the amendment was "unobjectionable" as a statement of policy and was "an accurate reflection of what I believe is the President's policy."

With this reassurance, Mr. Nelson was satisfied that he had made a "legislative record" of Administration intent. He did not offer his amendment and voted for the resolution.

The second reservation arose from the possibility that Premier Nguyen Khanh of South Vietnam might extend the war into North Vietnam and that the United States would lose control of its freedom of action.

Senator Jacob K. Javits, Republican of New York, asked Fulbright: "Suppose that South Vietnam should be jeopardized by its own extension of struggle beyond its own capacity to wage a successful war in North Vietnam. Then what would happen in terms of commitment and the commitment which the President is empowered to undertake?"

Mr. Fulbright declared that he did not believe South Vietnam "could involve us beyond the point where we ourselves wished to be involved."

* * *

September 4, 1964

CRISIS IN VIETNAM: HOW IT DEVELOPED

By PETER GROSE

Special to The New York Times.

SAIGON, South Vietnam, Sept. 3—South Vietnam lost another Government last week, a situation that Premier Nguyen Khanh was trying to repair today.

Divisive forces in this troubled land had gained the upper hand, setting back months of patient effort to erect a stable national structure and to rebuild a society in disarray.

The shrewd and jaunty army commander, who had been leading the effort, and the United States, which had been supporting it, lost control. Both acknowledge they have yet to be sure of regaining it.

A tortuous train of events, starting with a muffled pistol shot on a night in January, reached a climax last Friday in an uprising in which the Communist enemy played a leading role.

The South Vietnamese people challenged the entire war effort of their shaky Government and the United States aimed at preventing a Communist victory in South Vietnam.

For better or worse, independent observers have concluded, the Vietnam war as it had been fought in the last three years seems to be drawing to a close.

To replace it by a costly new effort with more direct American participation or to cut losses in a negotiated peace—that is the larger policy question. The setback to the United States policy of leading South Vietnam to internal stability was the third in 10 months.

Unlike the overthrow of President Ngo Dinh Diem last November and the lightning seizure of power by General Khanh Jan. 30, last week's upheaval was not planned. None of the forces contributing to it expected it to go so far.

Thus, when the Government fell Aug. 25, there was no alternative regime waiting to take over. There was only anarchy at the top to deal with anarchy in the streets.

Although General Khanh has resumed his role as Premier, the weaknesses in the Government he tried to are build exposed so vividly that they cannot again be concealed.

Few people took notice of that single pistol shot in a Saigon backyard about 9 o'clock the night of Jan. 31. There was general relief that a coup d'état had been accomplished the day before without bloodshed; compared with the battle to oust President Diem three months earlier, General Khanh's accession to power was virtually painless.

The man who died was Nguyen Van Nhung, a 44-year-old major in the Vietnamese Army with more than 20 years of service. He was not well known except as a loyal aide for his entire army career to Maj. Gen. Duong Van Minh, "Big Minh," who stepped into power as the leader of the military junta the day of Mr. Diem's downfall.

To a small group of people involved on both sides in the November coup, however, Major Nhung had become a symbol. He was the man credited, or blamed, for killing President Diem and Ngo Dinh Nhu, his equally hated brother, the morning of Nov. 2 while his beloved chief was strengthening the army's position as the head of revolutionary government.

General's Ties to Diem Caused Apprehension

Major Nhung had killed President Diem. Then the major himself was dead, either a suicide in captivity or murdered by an unknown hand. Why was this little known major the sole victim of General Khanh's coup d'état?

Two important men asked this question. One was General Minh himself, despairing, according to his confidants, at the loss of a faithful aide.

The other important man who wondered about Major Nhung's death was a man of religion, a Buddhist bonze, or monk, for whom things had not gone well since the Buddhist uprisings that had led to Mr. Diem's ouster and death.

This bonze was in the process of gathering funds to go abroad, to leave Vietnam and to "bury his life" as he told his few intimates. Hearing of Major Nhung's death, his ambitions for political power revived and he canceled his travel plans.

The fear of both these men was that Major Nhung had died in the settlement of an old score, that with General

Associated Press

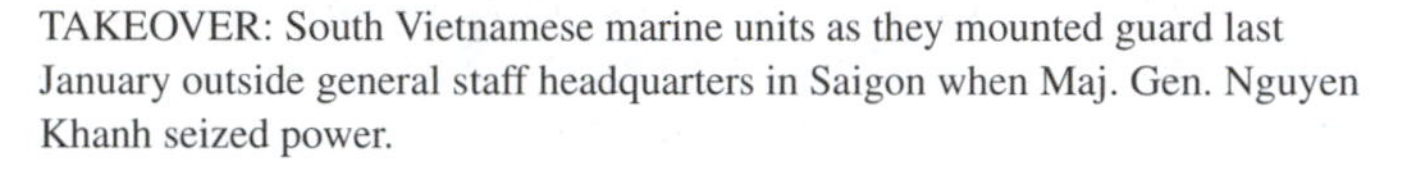

TAKEOVER: South Vietnamese marine units as they mounted guard last January outside general staff headquarters in Saigon when Maj. Gen. Nguyen Khanh seized power.

United Press International

ANARCHY: Buddhist demonstrators as they regrouped their forces after ransacking Roman Catholic homes and setting fire to furnishings in the streets of Danang last week.

Khanh's accession to power the partisans of Mr. Diem were given their chance to avenge the President's death.

In the months that followed and up to last week, General Khanh was unable to dispel the notion that somehow his Government was serving as the cover for a revival of pro-Diem forces.

At his first news conference, on Jan. 31, the new leader dealt at length with his role in an attempted coup in November, 1960, when, as a young brigadier, he was believed to have saved President Diem's life.

General Khanh insisted that his role had been merely one of mediator to help moderate that crisis. Yet afterward President Diem gave him command of troops in the then critical Second Army Corps region in central Vietnam.

Repeatedly General Khanh has denied adherence to the insidious Can Lao or "Personalist" party led by Mr. Nhu. Less a political party than a secret society, the Can Lao was instrumental at all levels of the Government for enforcing the Ngo family rule.

As for the people around him, the general could not deny that many army officers in high positions had served in responsible jobs under Mr. Diem, perhaps had even been members of the Can Lao.

General Khanh gave two explanations: First, he said not everyone who had served under Mr. Diem had believed in his practices, especially the more oppressive measures of the later months. General Minh himself, General Khanh would note, had been military adviser in the Presidential Palace.

Second, General Khanh said, if all the Government employes of the nine years of Mr. Diem's rule were eliminated from service, few with experience would be left to run the complicated affairs of administration.

But fears lingered among certain civilian politicians, among the Buddhists and among both groups' army adherents. These fears flared to the surface in the critical days just passed.

Dead 10 months Mr. Diem seemed, nevertheless, to be one of the most powerful forces in the country.

General Khanh had moved quickly to set up his Government in the first two weeks of February. His intention was to rely heavily on civilian politicians, representatives of old-time nationalist political parties banned under Mr. Diem.

As one senior diplomat said:

"Khanh wanted to have different shades of opinion in his Government—well, he got them, with disastrous results."

Chief among the returned exiles was a deceptively mild and unassuming man named Nguyen Ton Hoan, leader of the predominant faction of the old Dai Viet, or Greater Vietnam movement. Mr. Hoan closed his Vietnamese restaurant on the Left Bank in Paris to return to Saigon after a nine-year absence.

He did so expecting to be Premier, for some of his army contacts in the Dai Viet, a nationalist party, had been with General Khanh from the start of the planning for the January coup.

General Khanh saw, however, that rivalry and infighting among the splintered political parties were so great that one faction could gain support from the others. The general became Premier himself, leaving to Mr. Hoan the post of First Deputy Premier.

It was still a post from which the Dai Viet thought it could extend its party power. Government appointments promptly were handed out to party regulars and General Khanh found himself having to spend as much time holding reins on Mr. Hoan as he did in fighting the war—the activity he said he really wanted to pursue.

"It did not seem fair to the other parties for the Dai Viet to take everything," General Khanh said, with what was viewed as a certain political naiveté last week in reviewing the last seven months.

Early in April, the general succeeded in squeezing out one of the main Dai Viet manipulators, Ha Thuc Ky, Interior Minister, who had tried to put party members in key jobs of province chiefs.

Long afterward General Khanh said Mr. Ky had been plotting a coup to overthrow the Khanh Government for the Dai

Viets. It was one of countless coup scares that plagued General Khanh during his rule.

With Mr. Hoan's resignation, the uncomfortable alliance of General Khanh and the Dai Viet was finally broken.

Army Was Both Friend And Foe for Khanh

For his first seven months, the army was at once General Khanh's greatest strength and his major burden.

He succeeded in splitting potential enemies, a signal achievement in itself, with the help of certain colleagues tied to him by one means or another.

By his side, though not always on his side, was Maj. Gen. Tran Thien Khiem, Defense Minister and commander in chief of the armed forces. If any coup were to have been pulled off, General Khiem's adherence would have been crucial. It was eagerly sought by the Dai Viet in particular, informed sources said.

But General Khiem apparently stood by his military school classmate, though General Khanh had to promote the silent, humorless Khiem to the rank of lieutenant general, meaning that General Khiem outranks both Generals Khanh and Minh.

Across the countryside General Khanh moved to put his own key men in key command positions as much as possible. Provincial chiefs, field commanders and staff officers became the general's backbone of local support—he had little among the population.

The resulting dislocations, following so soon the first junta's changes after Mr. Diem, aroused concern among Vietnamese and American officers alike. But General Khanh maintained that it would seem that this was the only way to insure effective control over the war effort.

Americans reluctantly saw his point and eventually the command structure was stabilized.

General Minh remained a central problem. The husky and slow-moving officer seemed to do little during General Khanh's seven-month tenure, though he was retained in the honorific role of head of state.

One day, in a good mood, General Minh dropped in unannounced at General Khanh's office where the Premier was poring through stocks of daily governmental papers. The senior general sat at his side and helped him for the morning. General Khanh was so delighted he talked about it for days afterward. But it never seemed to happen again.

Persons close to General Minh say he never got over Major Nhung's death; the major's portrait still hangs over a private Buddhist shrine in the general's staff office.

Perhaps it was because he could not forgive the man he held responsible for his faithful aide's death, perhaps it was because General Khanh had arrested General Minh's colleagues in the first junta, perhaps it was because he saw General Khanh as only a brash upstart—probably for all three reasons prestigious "Big Minh" refused to lift a finger on General Khanh's behalf.

Premier Khanh had other trump cards, however. He was clever and energetic, willing to work harder than any general the Vietnamese had seen in recent years. He seemed not to mind responsibility, though he asserted that he followed a majority vote of his mixed civilian-military Cabinet on most policy decisions.

Furthermore, General Khanh had the personal support of the United States from the day Secretary of Defense Robert S. McNamara threw his arm around the beaming general and shouted to a crowd "Vietnam muon nam!" ("Long live Vietnam!")

There once was a time when the United States was just assisting the Vietnamese Government, standing on the outside and offering its money and men when requested. This was under President Diem's rule.

Under Premier Khanh the United States became involved in the Vietnamese Government at all levels. The Premier and the United States Ambassador met in planning sessions three times weekly or more. American captains went into the field as advisers to local authorities in the districts, the lowest rung on the central Government's administrative ladder.

American aid was increased—it is now approaching $2 million a day—and Mr. McNamara promised Premier Khanh "a blank check." United States military personnel, who someone had said, would be phased out by the end of next year were increased, now totaling 18,000 men in that country.

With Premier Khanh many Americans began to hope. In a more honest and open atmosphere than the year before there was little downright optimism, but good things started to happen. Plans to pacify the country were agreed upon and Americans considered them good plans.

The army performed well against the Vietcong, sometimes.

Vietcong Seized Initiative After Major Build-up

Field workers were trained and some of them started their jobs in hamlets. Premier Khanh seemed to react to problems in a way satisfying to his American co-workers—so satisfying in fact that he seemed to have lost touch with the Vietnamese ways of working.

This was to prove his weak point, observers judge, for in the crisis of August he came up with an American kind of solution rather than a gentler, more obscure Vietnamese answer.

In July, things began going wrong. Military progress in the field was all but wiped out by a Vietcong offensive before the rainy season. The insurgents' build-up during the quiet months of spring gave them a capacity to strike hard at widely separated points, keeping the initiative from wore unwieldy Government forces.

Military analysis concluded that in tactics, in surprise and in determination, the Vietcong outclassed the understrength Vietnamese Army.

General Khanh grew openly tired of the pacification strategy and his responses to American pressure became more reluctant as he saw that this method of fighting could not work fast enough to keep the population from growing restive under the increased demands of war.

Picking up public hints of American policy-makers, Premier Khanh came out in July for an expansion of the effort and attacks on Communist North Vietnam, the command point of the Vietcong insurgency. In advocating his "march to the North," General Khanh acknowledged later, he did so against the advice of his Cabinet—one of the only two times he said he had acted like a dictator.

American policy-makers apparently did not mean for their hints to be taken literally at that time. As Premier Khanh saw it, his stanch friends the Americans had slapped him down and he was left alone to face new threats and a war in countryside that apparently could not be won.

A stroke of luck for him was the North Vietnamese attacks on United States destroyers in the Gulf of Tonkin and the retaliatory United States air strikes early in August. Premier Khanh grasped at a last straw and rushed into new actions that brought everything to a tragic climax.

Meanwhile, another element had been at work.

The Buddhists of South Vietnam, five million of whom are said to practice the religion, had shown their force during their six-month protest that led to the downfall of the Diem Government, which they accused of favoring the Roman Catholic minority.

After the November revolution they seemed to fade away from active participation in politics. They appeared to be torn by internal dissension and incapable of any united movement such as they had launched against Mr. Diem; presumably the leaders were quietly at work trying to set up tight organization over the sects of Vietnamese Buddhism.

On Jan. 3, a unified Buddhist organization came into being. Religious and secular affairs were clearly separated, with the highly centralized secular affairs section being organized into a cabinet or "institute" and "general offices" resembling a shadow government paralleling the national governmental structure.

Buddhist Charter Drafted by Monk, 42

Vietnamese Buddhism had never advanced so boldly into temporal affairs before. The man who drafted the charter, confidently expecting to be head of the secular institute, equivalent to a Buddhist Premier, was a 42-year-old monk named Thich Tri Quang.

Tri Quang (Thich is a Buddhist title translatable as "the venerable") had sought refuge in the United States Embassy at the height of President Diem's repressive measures against Buddhist defiance.

His name and appeal were well known, but his thoughts remained a closed book to foreigners—even, or perhaps especially, to his American hosts, who treated him with care and courtesy.

Now a year later, Tri Quang looks back upon his days with Americans with a mixture of fondness and embarrassment: fondness directed particularly at the embassy's marine guards who brought him food, but embarrassment at having had to turn to foreigners at a moment of need.

For Tri Quang, according to those who know him well, is nothing so much as a chauvinist, a proud and insistent Vietnamese to whom anything foreign is inferior to his national heritage.

With the formation of a unified Buddhist faith by 11 of the country's 14 sects, elections were held for key posts. It was a power struggle and when the votes were counted Tri Quang found himself defeated.

The direction of Buddhist secular affairs went to Thich Tam Chau, a North Vietnamese refugee, an outspoken anti-Communist who threw full support to the ruling military junta.

The Shadow Government Assumes Substance

Tri Quang said he considered his useful work at an end. In despair, he told friends he was going on a pilgrimage to India, Ceylon and Japan to "bury his life." He started raising private funds for his travels.

So deep was the suspicion among the Buddhist leaders that Tam Chau found it necessary to make a public statement that Tri Quang would be traveling only in a private capacity and should not be considered abroad as a spokesman for the Vietnamese Buddhists.

Through January Tam Chau organized the Buddhist structure, training representatives down to lowest levels of the country. The shadow government assumed substance.

Now there are seven senior monks, each controlling affairs in several provinces—roughly comparable to Government's four army corps commanders. Each province has one Buddhist representative and two deputies comparable to the Government's province chief and deputies. All these field officials are appointed by and are responsible to the Buddhist cabinet, the Secular Affairs Institute.

With religion and organization, Buddhism, it was recognized, could claim intense loyalty among a larger bloc of the nation's population than any other organized force.

When General Khanh seized power Jan. 30, Tam Chau did not hesitate. He promptly threw Buddhist support to the new Government.

Tri Quang had other ideas. The personalities around General Khanh, the sudden reappearance of men known and hated during the Diem years and, most puzzlingly, the shooting of Major Nhung gave him hope for a resumed Buddhist campaign.

He abruptly canceled his travel plans and moved to Hue to prepare for a new bid for power, first within the Buddhist organization and then in the country at large.

Even with Tri Quang inactive, Buddhists had noted new incidents of repressive measures reminiscent, they said, of the Diem days. With many of the lower-level civil servants necessarily held over from the former governments, it was inevitable that some hard feelings would remain.

During December and January, religious incidents were reported in land development centers of Long An Province and elsewhere. These were peacefully resolved through mediation by two Buddhists sent to the scene by Tam Chau.

When later alleged incidents blew up in central Vietnam, it was one of Tri Quang's partisans, Trich Thien Minh, Buddhist Commissioner for Youth, who went to investigate. His conclusions were disastrous for the struggling Government of General Khanh, who was trying to placate the fears of both the Buddhists and Catholics.

There can be little doubt that religious rivalries brought injustices in many incidents; there is also a clear indication that Tri Quang and his associates used these incidents to inflate their case against Can Lao elements in the Khanh Government.

Into April, Tam Chau and Tri Quang were quietly jockeying for power, according to Buddhist sources.

Tri Quang, in Hue, had encouraged his followers at the university there to publish a weekly journal. It became an advocate for his brand of politically aggressive Buddhism.

In April, Tri Quang returned to Saigon carrying with him copies of the journal for free distribution. Face to face with Tam Chau, he apparently won over the more moderate monk with his warnings of new Diemist threats to Buddhism.

The Buddhist lines were now sharply drawn. The fence-sitting Khanh Government was the target; only the pretext was lacking.

Worry Over Diem Aides Contributed to Unrest

These are the strains that led up to crisis last week:

- Widespread belief that under General Khanh the Diemists had regained an upper hand.
- Political parties, mainly the Catholic-inclined Dai Viet, working through military and civilian adherents to enlarge their own power.
- Close American participation in the internal affairs of South Vietnam and a Premier often thinking more like an American than a Vietnamese.
- An army stalemated in the field and asked to pursue a pacification policy that seemed to lead only to a long, drawn-out war of attrition. Students were being asked to leave the comforts of the city and join the army to plod through the mud and jungles.
- Communist insurgents aware that a military victory was beyond their grasp as long as American air power and matériel were available to the Government but confident of victory through political agitation.
- A massive Buddhist movement under aggressive leadership determined to gain a voice in the country's affairs commensurate with its numbers among the population.

General Khanh, according to reliable sources, saw the United States air strikes on North Vietnam as the excuse he needed to usher in emergency decrees tightening his authority over the divisive elements that had been troubling him. This he did on Aug. 7.

But imbued with the American ideas of a strong war government, he went further. Nine days later the Premier forced through a drastic new Constitution, installing himself as President, ousting General Minh, abandoning the Military Revolutionary Council and assuming virtually dictatorial powers.

American diplomats now say they were frightened at the speed with which General Khanh moved. But their public statements at the time supported the moves, which were considered necessary to lead a nation under a grave war threat.

Buddhists Saw Constitution As Work of Khanh

In the Constitution, the Buddhists saw the pretext they had been seeking—they deduced that the man who had drafted the document was none other than General Khanh, a man whose legal talents had served President Diem. The General never said who had written the Constitution.

For their part, Dai Viet adherents, fearing they were being edged out, unleashed their student supporters to denounce General Khanh's moves toward a dictatorship. The Buddhists did the same, using the occasion of the Aug. 20 anniversary of last year's police attacks on Buddhist shrines.

General Khanh and his aides made a risky decision. Aware of the dangers of looking like a new Diem, General Khanh ordered the law enforcement authorities not to resist the agitators in the streets.

"Let them demonstrate," a Khanh aide said early last week. "They will quickly see that we are not repressing them."

But as General Khanh acknowledged, "We believed it was a small-scale movement—only later did we see it was vast movement across the country."

Banner-waving demonstrators turned to violence against a radio station and the Ministry of Information. In centers of tension such as Danang, long-simmering Buddhist-Catholic hatred flared into a fury of street fighting.

Abruptly, the Vietcong leadership reduced its terrorism and attacks in the provinces, according to field reports, and sent trained agitators by the busload into Saigon.

From Thursday evening witness saw country buses full of young men but no women driving to the central market square where the Buddhists had demonstrated earlier. The Buddhist ceremony had broken down into an unofficial gathering of back-street youths.

The new arrivals disappeared into the crowd, the independent witnesses said, and by Friday the market square was barricaded against the police.

It took a military and police assault to clear up pockets of defiance Friday night. The Government troops fired shots mostly into air—but there were deaths and the hope of building popular support through leniency was lost.

General Khanh had already capitulated. Late Monday night he met with Thich Tam Chau and Thich Tri Quang to try to reach a settlement. Almost point by point a communiqué he issued when he stepped down answered the Buddhists' demands that the Aug. 16 Constitution be revoked, that action be taken against "impure" Diemist remnants and that preparations be made for a government more favorable to Buddhism.

The author of these demands was Tri Quang. According to reliable sources, he drafted them Monday night on rough sheet of paper in his air-conditioned room in a pagoda.

General Khanh met Tri Quang's demands, but they were only the start.

What does this enigmatic monk want? American officials who have been in touch with him since last year admit ignorance on this crucial point.

Because they do not understand him, some observers call Tri Quang a Communist—a matter on which there are firm indications to the contrary. General Khanh insists that the Buddhist leaders are strongly anti-Communist.

The American trouble has been that Tri Quang is not a man to place his cards on the table before a foreigner. This reluctance does not carry over to Vietnamese friends whom he trusts.

Violence of Communism Alien to the Buddhists

From detailed probing of these conversations over the months, there emerges the political program of the man who appeared to observers last week as the most powerful single person in South Vietnam.

Buddhism has been the unofficial religion of the mass of Vietnamese people for 10 centuries. It has deep roots in the nation's society. It is not a false ideology such as Mr. Nhu's "Personalism," but it can motivate millions of Vietnamese citizens at all levels.

Communism is not a Vietnamese ideology. The violence, cruelty and treachery it has brought to Vietnam are in sharp contrast with the compassion, pity and peace of Buddha's teachings.

Roman Catholicism, brought to Vietnam by European colonialists but more recently identified with the oppressive rule of Mr. Diem, is seen by Buddhists as a more immediate threat than Communism.

Tri Quang is well aware of the unhappy fate of Buddhists under the North Vietnam Communist regime. He blames Vietnam's age-old enemies, the Chinese, for forcing Communism on the Vietnamese people.

But he asks how an ideology only two or three decades old in Vietnam can triumph over the weight of 10 centuries.

Speaking as a Vietnamese, Tri Quang hopes and expects both the Chinese and the Americans to leave his country alone. He wants to use the mass strength of Buddhism to achieve this end, presumably under his own leadership. Foreigners, in his view, have turned Vietnamese against Vietnamese.

If the United States were to withdraw from Vietnam, he acknowledges, there would be several years of troubles and violence for Buddhists trying to coexist with Communists. But his faith is unwavering that Buddhism would emerge as the stronger of the two ideologies.

A Western analyst could pick countless holes in this contention. So indeed do some Vietnamese Buddhists and Tri Quang's position at the head of the movement is far from secure: he won Tam Chau's support once but he may not keep it.

It seems clear that the rising influence of Thich Tri Quang is not helpful to the present United States policy of fighting the Communists through military pacification measures, leaving the formation of the ideal government to later.

But the events of the last week have shown nothing so much as the frailty of American policy for an Asian society.

* * *

September 4, 1964

KHANH RESUMES POST OF PREMIER IN SAIGON REGIME

He Ends Triumvirate's Rule and Reinstates Minh as the Chief of State

DEFENSE CHIEF QUITS

Khiem, Catholic Among Top Three, Resigns—U.S. Sees Steps Toward Stability

By JACK LANGGUTH
Special to The New York Times.

SAIGON, South Vietnam, Sept. 3—Maj. Gen. Nguyen Khanh resumed the Premiership today and began attempting to patch together a Government for South Vietnam.

His first actions, after his return from a period of rest in Dalat, were to dissolve the military triumvirate set up last week and to restore Maj. Gen. Duong Van Minh to the position of chief of state.

These moves suggested General Khanh's desire to return to the type of government he headed before Aug. 16, when he ousted General Minh, assumed the title of President and greatly expanded his own powers under a new constitution.

> [Lieut. Gen. Tran Thien Khiem, a Roman Catholic, member of the triumvirate and Defense Minister, resigned Friday, The Associated Press reported. In Washington, officials regarded the return of General Khanh as Premier as pointing to a new stability in Saigon.]

Opponents Are Warned

In Hue, General Minh sternly warned Buddhist and student groups today that they must support the central Government.

"We must have unity to avert a catastrophe," he said, "and we must unite before the country falls to the Communists."

United States observers in Hue, a university city that is a center of dissatisfaction with the military Government, were impressed by the grim and urgent note sounded by General Minh.

He also urged the Buddhists to put aside their distrust and end their harassment of the Can Lao, a predominantly Roman Catholic political party formed by supporters of President Ngo Dinh Diem, who was killed Nov. 2 after the overthrow of his regime.

"Not all members of the Can Lao are criminals," the general said. "Those who are should be tried for their acts. The others should be let alone."

Citizen Group Pledged

Nguyen Xuan Oanh, who has been acting Premier during General Khanh's absence, promised gatherings in Hue that a 15-member citizens' committee, representative of the diverse Vietnamese population, would soon be named.

The return of General Khanh and his apparent willingness to compromise seemed to mark the end of his shortlived one-man rule.

After his assumption of full power Aug. 16, protest demonstrations began almost at once. Buddhist and student leaders were quick to denounce General Khanh and to liken him to President Diem.

General Khanh did not attempt to suppress the protests. But as they spread throughout the country, bringing bloodshed and vandalism, he announced Aug. 27 the formation of triumvirate of generals.

General Khanh, General Minh and Lieut. Gen. Tran Van Khiem, the Defense Minister and armed forces commander, were to have led the country for two months until a new government could be devised.

When the street rioting persisted, however, General Khanh went north Saturday to Dalat.

He indicated that he would return only with full powers. It was believed here that the resignation Tuesday night of the First Deputy Premier, one of General Khanh's chief political rivals, hurried his return.

The deputy, Nguyen Ton Hoan, is a leader of the nationalist Dai Viet movement. Another Dai Viet member, Brig. Gen. Nguyen Van Thieu, has been an enigmatic figure to the Khanh supporters.

They feared that General Thieu, as army chief of staff, might lead a coup against the Government. But an ally of General Khanh said today that the Premier was now convinced that General Thieu would not jeopardize his position by engaging in Dai Viet politics.

The spokesman said that General Khanh was resuming complete command immediately. But he might return to Dalat for the weekend.

Combat Action Drops

At a monthly briefing this afternoon, officers of the United States Military Assistance Command displayed no optimism as they discussed military operations during August against the Vietcong guerrillas.

Although patrols by the Government forces increased substantially, actual contact with the Vietcong declined.

In almost 63,000 movements last month, the army encountered the Communist guerrillas on only 360 occasions.

A United States officer said much of the patrolling had been in villages cleared of rebel troops.

"However," he added, "there was still very little contact and one would think there ought to be more."

One of General Khanh's first acts on returning to Saigon was to persuade Thich Tam Chou, one of the most influential Buddhist leaders, to call off a threatened 48-hour fast. Buddhist monks then began a two-day prayer session in the headquarters in Saigon.

The general also won his agreement to reconsider a general strike the Buddhists had threatened if their demands were not met.

KHIEM CITES BUDDHIST PRESSURE

SAIGON, Friday, Sept. 4 (AP)—One of South Vietnam's top military leaders resigned today, a day after the war-torn country's caretaker Government reverted to Maj. Gen. Nguyen Khanh's control.

A Government spokesman said that the Defense Minister Lieut. Gen. Tran Thien Khiem, one of three generals in the triumvirate that had ruled for the last week, had quit because he "had had enough of the Buddhists running the country."

General Khiem, the only Roman Catholic in the triumvirate appeared to be making his resignation apply not only to his post as Defense Minister but also to any governmental position.

As a lieutenant general, he has been the highest ranking active officer in the nation.

General Khiem's resignation came after Buddhist leaders demanded the ouster of seven high officers of the Vietnamese army, including General Khiem.

The others on the Buddhist blacklist were Brig. Gen. Nguyen Van Thieu, chief of staff; Brig. Gen. Do Cau Tri, II Corps commander; Brig. Gen. Duong Ngoc Lam, prefect of Saigon and commander of the Vietnamese paramilitary forces; Maj. Gen. Lam Van Phat, Interior Minister; Brig. Gen. Nguyen Cao, and Col. Tran Ngoc Huyen, Deputy Minister of Information.

Colonel Huyen resigned yesterday, without giving a reason.

Triumvirate Members Meet

This morning, the members of the dissolved triumvirate, Generals Khanh, Khiem and Minh, held their first session together since General Khanh returned from his "temporary retirement" in the mountain resort of Dalat.

Immediately after the meeting, members of the Government gathered at the Premier's office for an emergency session of the Cabinet.

Yesterday, the Buddhist leader, Thich Tam Chau, arrived at General Khanh's palace in a chauffeur-driven limousine and conferred with the Premier for more than three hours. Thich Tam Chau was armed with threats of a nationwide Buddhist fast and general strikes, renewed street demonstrations and general insurrection if Buddhist demands were not met.

But the Buddhists called off a scheduled 48-hour strike after discussions with General Khanh in Saigon later yesterday and replaced it with a 48-hour prayer session. Subsequently they called off the prayer session. Activity at Buddhist national headquarters in Saigon, at a frantic pitch for a few days, quieted this morning.

U. S. OFFICIALS ENCOURAGED

Special to The New York Times.

WASHINGTON, Sept. 3—Administration officials indicated today that they saw General Khanh's return to the Premiership as an encouraging step toward restoring political stability in South Vietnam.

Considerable uncertainty and concern remain, however.

Powerful pressure applied by the United States this week on military and civilian groups in and around the Saigon regime was said to have made it possible for General Khanh to return to office on what appeared to be his own terms.

But the Administration was under no illusions that its influence could alone force the rival factions into enough harmony to assure an effective Government in the long run.

Although no complete analysis of the latest events has yet reached here from the embassy in Saigon, officials here fully realized how tenuous was the whole Vietnamese structure and how easily it could be upset again.

It was understood that Ambassador Maxwell D. Taylor had not yet seen Premier Khanh since the latter's return from Dalat. It was expected, however, that they would confer tomorrow and that this meeting would throw additional light on the over-all situation.

The immediate concern here was whether Vietnam's three key military figures—General Khanh, General Minh and General Khiem—could really work together against the background of their rivalries.

The judgment here was that, at least temporarily, General Minh had been set aside in terms of real power.

* * *

September 27, 1964

MAN AND THE BOMB

'Fail Safe' Is Less Devastating Than 'Dr. Strangelove,' Anyhow

By BOSLEY CROWTHER

The odd situation of Columbia Pictures releasing two important films within eight months on the subject of the perilous possibility of an accidental start of nuclear war puts that company in the position of reiterating the darkest dread of our times and giving the public some cogent, if not particularly consoling, food for thought.

The first was, of course, "Dr. Strangelove or How I Learned to Stop Worrying and Love the Bomb," which touched off quite an intellectual ruckus when it was released early in the year. And the second is the upcoming "Fail Safe," which was given its world premiere the other night at the New York Film Festival and opens here at Loew's State and in neighborhood theaters on Oct. 7.

What is most interesting about them, from a strictly intellectual point of view, is that they give diametrically opposing estimations of the capacity of man to control the deadly instrument that his ingenuity has wrought. And it is this fundamental difference in their regard for the capacity of man—or of the men who are in command of our destinies—that separates their moral attitudes.

Incompetent Man

"Dr. Strangelove" states quite boldly that man is not able to control the nuclear bomb—which, incidentally, is recognized at the beginning of both films as a menace of cosmic consequence.

It is a madman, a blood-curdling specimen of the lunatic fringe, that starts things going by ordering a flight of Strategic Air Force bombers to fly to Moscow and drop nuclear bombs. And it is a group of top-level bunglers—a bigoted head of the Joint Chiefs of Staff, a maniacal scientific expert and even a pitiful President of the United States—that futilely fumbles with this problem until the bombers get through and the Russians retaliate and the world is blown to smithereens.

It is a dismal, depressing, "sick" picture of the state of man and of government that this film gives, and it is not very much alleviated by the fact that it is presented as a howling joke. Although partisans of the film have been writing to me, in the light of recent political developments in this country, with the cryptic query, "Well?", I still cannot accept its pessimism, its unmitigated mockery of man.

On the other hand, "Fail Safe," which follows a similar melodramatic line, has a more realistic premise and gives man a better break. It is also a cliff-hanging drama of what happens in high places during the terrible hours—or minutes—between the time a flight of nuclear-charged American bombers are dispatched to Moscow and the time they arrive on target.

Mad Machine

But here the hideous mission is dispatched not by a single willful man but by an inexplicable malfunction in a complicated man-made computer machine. A highly sophisticated mechanism that sends signals to in-flight aircraft from the SAC base in Omaha goes haywire and sends an irrevocable order to a flight of bombers to proceed to Moscow and drop their bombs. The only fault of man in this concept—though, of course a grave fault it is—is that he has put too much responsibility and reliance in the efficiency of a machine.

From here on, however, the premise is that man has the will and the wits to correct or do something about the error. At SAC base, a group of officers (Frank Overton, Fritz Weaver and others) take all the rational steps to get the bombers off the mission. In Washington, at the Pentagon, a group of top-level security people offers conflicting advice. And in a subbasement of the White House, the President (Henry Fonda) listens in to the sizzling exchanges between the bombers and SAC base and makes the command decisions after conferring with Moscow on the "hot line."

Of course, it is just a movie—a highly suspenseful one—and the ultimate resolution is not encouraging. But, at least, it leaves an audience with a shred of respect for man and a realization that wise ones must control the bomb.

* * *

October 16, 1964

KHRUSHCHEV OUSTED FROM TOP POSTS; BREZHNEV GETS CHIEF PARTY POSITION AND KOSYGIN IS NAMED NEW PREMIER

MOSCOW IS QUIET

Pravda Says Change Won't Bring Return of Harsh Policies

By HENRY TANNER
Special to The New York Times.

MOSCOW, Friday, Oct. 16—Premier Khrushchev has been deprived of political power in the Soviet Union.

He was replaced by Leonid I. Brezhnev, 57 years old, as First Secretary of the Communist party and by Aleksei N. Kosygin, 60, as Premier.

Mr. Khrushchev, who is 70, even lost his seat in the Presidium of the Central Committee of the party, the third most important position he held in the leadership.

This indicated that he had fallen into disgrace.

Dispatches did not mention if Mr. Khrushchev had been removed from the Central Committee itself. Under normal procedure such action would come at a meeting of the Soviet Communist party Congress.

Adzhubei Reported Ousted

The changes were announced by Tass, the Soviet press agency, a few minutes after midnight.

The Tass statement did not contain a single word of praise for the ousted leader.

Unofficial but reliable sources later reported that Aleksei I. Adzhubei, Mr. Khrushchev's son-in-law, had been deposed as chief editor of the Government newspaper Izvestia.

Mr. Khrushchev's whereabouts was not known. Nor was it known whether he was at liberty or under surveillance. Western diplomats assumed, however, that the changeover had been made peacefully.

Diplomats Voice Assurance

Moscow's streets were quiet. There were no signs of movements by either the army or police. Some of the smaller Western embassies, which had been without a police guard for the last several months, reported yesterday that the policemen were back in front of the gates.

Western diplomats said they did not expect the new leaders to change basic Soviet policy toward the West.

Mr. Brezhnev and Mr. Kosygin can be expected to continue Mr. Khrushchev's policy of "peaceful coexistence" with the United States, the diplomats said.

The Soviet Communist party newspaper Pravda indicated today that the party would continue to carry out policies of de-Stalinization and economic improvements under its new leadership.

The paper printed the same bare announcement that had been carried in the English-language version of Tass. There were one-column pictures of Mr. Kosygin and Mr. Brezhnev but no comment.

Pravda printed the following statement:

"The Communist party of the Soviet Union firmly and positively translates into reality the Leninist general line worked out at the 20th and 22d congresses of the party."

This could be construed as an assurance that there would be no return to Stalin's dictatorial policies.

Informed sources expressed the conviction that it was the Chinese-Soviet conflict that had led to Mr. Khrushchev's fall.

Mr. Brezhnev and Mr. Kosygin can be expected to put an end to the drive toward a showdown with the Chinese Communists which has been the foremost trait of the last few months of the Khrushchev regime, the sources said.

December Meeting in Doubt

The sources said the new leadership might well have decided even before coming to power to call off the meeting of 26 Communist parties that was to begin here Dec. 15.

The meeting was to make preparations for a full-scale conference of the world Communist parties.

Mr. Khrushchev had staked his own prestige and that of the Communist party of the Soviet Union and the Soviet Government on this project for a conference.

But the response of the invited parties had been deeply disappointing. With Mr. Khrushchev's continued presence at the helm, the sources said, the Soviet leadership would have been committed to go through with a potentially disastrous project, while without him it would feel free to change plans and avoid a showdown.

Mr. Khrushchev has been under vitriolic personal attack by the Chinese leaders.

The two new Soviet leaders have consistently echoed the Khrushchev line on the Chinese-Soviet conflict and other issues. But this was not regarded as preventing them from adopting different policies now.

In the past Mr. Khrushchev had also been under attack for his agricultural policies. But this was not thought to have been a central issue in his fall.

This year's crop has been good, especially in the virgin lands, which was Mr. Khrushchev's special pride.

Removal Took Two Days

The maneuvering to bring about Mr. Khrushchev's fall from power covered two days, according to Tass. The meeting of the Central Committee, which took the party leadership from him Wednesday, was followed by a meeting of the Presidium of the Supreme Soviet (Parliament), which stripped him of the Premiership yesterday, the press agency reported.

Mikhail A. Suslov, a spokesman in the Kremlin's dispute with Communist China, was reported to have delivered the

Associated Press

Nikita S. Khrushchev—Relieved of political posts

Leonid I. Brezhnev—Named as the leader of the party

Aleksei N. Kosygin—Appointed as the Soviet Premier

key address. Mr. Suslov had appeared at times to be lukewarm in his support of Mr. Khrushchev.

It was President Anastas I. Mikoyan, Mr. Khrushchev's closest and oldest friend in the leadership, who presided over the session of the Presidium.

Mr. Mikoyan lived up to his reputation of being adept at surviving political upheavals. He is the only man left who has been near the center of Soviet power continuously since the middle nineteen-twenties and all through Stalin's rule.

The Tass announcement emphasized that Mr. Khrushchev had been relieved of his duties at his own "request." If that was true he was the first Soviet leader since the revolution to have taken such a step.

Tass Report of Action

The Tass report said:

"The Presidium of the Supreme Soviet of the U.S.S.R. met Oct. 15 this year with Comrade A. I. Mikoyan, the President of the Presidium of the Supreme Soviet of the U.S.S.R. in the chair.

"The Presidium of the Supreme Soviet of the U.S.S.R. discussed the question of the Chairman of the Council of Ministers of the U.S.S.R."

The Tass announcement said:

"The Presidium of the Supreme Soviet of the U.S.S.R. granted the request of Nikita Sergeyevich Khrushchev on his relief from the duties of Chairman of the Council of Ministers of the U.S.S.R. in view of his advanced age and deterioration of health.

The Presidium of the Supreme Soviet of the U.S.S.R. appointed Comrade Aleksei Nikolayevich Kosygin as Chairman of the Council of Ministers of the U.S.S.R, releasing him from his duties of First Vice Chairman of the Council of Ministers of the U.S.S.R.

"The decrees by the Presidium of the Supreme Soviet of the U.S.S.R. on the relief of Comrade N. S. Khrushchev from his duties as Chairman of the Council of Ministers of the U.S.S.R. and on the appointment of Comrade A. N. Kosygin as Chairman of the Council of Ministers of the U.S.S.R were adopted unanimously by the members of the Presidium of the Supreme Soviet of the U.S.S.R.

"The members of the Presidium of the Supreme Soviet of the U.S.S.R. warmly congratulated Comrade A. N. Kosygin on his appointment to the post of Chairman of the Council of Ministers of the U.S.S.R.

"Comrade A. N. Kosygin heartily thanked the Central Committee of the Communist party of the Soviet Union and the Presidium of the Supreme Soviet of the U.S.S.R for the confidence shown him and gave the assurance that he would do his utmost to discharge his duties."

The transformation of the Soviet regime came virtually without warning. Rumors that a major political event was imminent was started in the early evening.

Communist correspondents from Western countries were told, apparently by party officials, to keep their radios tuned in for an announcement.

All through the day there had been a series of small but unusual events that caught the attention of correspondents and warned them that an upheaval might be in the making.

Mr. Khrushchev's name was not mentioned in any of yesterday's newspapers except in the published text of a speech made at the airport yesterday by President Osvaldo Dorticós Terrado of Cuba.

Last night, President Mikoyan accompanied President Dorticós to a concert in the Kremlin's Palace of Congresses as if nothing had happened.

Mr. Khrushchev's picture should have gone up in many places around the city in preparation for the big homecoming celebration and parade for the crew of the spaceship Voskhod.

The celebration is expected tomorrow or Sunday, but observers noted that in several places the familiar picture was absent.

Then Tass announced that there had been a luncheon at the Kremlin for President Dorticós. It listed virtually all members of the party leadership as present but not Mr. Khrushchev.

The absence was all the more striking since Mr. Khrushchev had been reliably reported to have returned to Moscow from the Black Sea coast yesterday.

In the afternoon, the Russians gave a reception for Gaston Palewski, the French Minister of Atomic Research who is here on a visit.

President Mikoyan, Mr. Brezhnev, Mr. Kosygin and other Soviet leaders were present, but Mr. Khrushchev again was absent.

A luncheon for the visiting Foreign Trade Minister of Italy, which was scheduled for 1:30 P.M., was delayed for two hours without an explanation.

A large number of black limousines were parked most of yesterday morning in front of the downtown building that houses the headquarters of the Central Committee of the party.

This seemed to indicate that a meeting of the Central Committee was being held.

To cap it all, the Government newspaper Izvestia failed to appear at its usual time last night. It is usually available at 6 P.M.

Members of the staff said by telephone that the paper would not appear till early morning, together with Pravda, the party newspaper. Such a delay occurs on occasions when the party and the Government want to issue a major statement.

The last time Mr. Khrushchev was in the news was Monday when he had a cheerful radio conversation with Dr. Boris B. Yegorov, a member of the crew of the Voskhod shortly after the spaceship had gone into orbit.

He told Dr. Yegorov to keep himself and the other crew members in good shape for the huge "reception we are organizing for you [in Moscow] when you get back."

* * *

October 17, 1964

PRAVDA SAYS KHRUSHCHEV IS HAREBRAINED SCHEMER; GIVES WEST PEACE PLEDGE

POLICIES OUTLINED

New Chiefs Promise to Continue Efforts for 'Coexistence'

By HENRY TANNER
Special to The New York Times.

MOSCOW, Saturday, Oct. 17—Without naming the deposed Soviet leader, Nikita S. Khrushchev, the new regime accused him today of "harebrained scheming," "bragging and phrase-mongering" and "armchair methods."

In its first declaration of a program the Soviet leadership at the same time pledged to continue its policy of peaceful coexistence with the West.

The new leadership, headed by Leonid I. Brezhnev and Aleksei N. Kosygin, said that it would press for a conference of world Communist parties next year to deal with the ideological challenge of the Chinese Communists.

In the ouster of Mr. Khrushchev, announced yesterday, Mr. Brezhnev took over the post of party First Secretary and Mr. Kosygin became Premier.

The program was defined in an editorial in Pravda, the party newspaper. A text of the editorial was made public by Tass, the Soviet press agency.

The Pravda editorial was clearly a devastating attack on Mr. Khrushchev by his former associates.

Pretenses Removed

Western observers felt that it did away with any pretense that Mr. Khrushchev's departure might have been voluntary on the grounds of old age and health, as yesterday's official announcement said.

The charges against Mr. Khrushchev seemed to center on his domestic economic policies.

This was contrary to the expectations of Western diplomats who had been convinced that the Soviet-Chinese conflict was the pivotal issue in his downfall. They still did not rule out the possibility that Mr. Khrushchev would be castigated on this issue later.

The editorial said:

"The Leninist party is an enemy of subjectivism and drifting in Communist construction.

"Harebrained scheming, immature conclusions and hasty decisions and actions divorced from reality, bragging and phrase-mongering, commandism, unwillingness to take into account the achievements of science and practical experience are alien to it.

"The construction of Communism is a live, creative undertaking that does not tolerate armchair methods, personal decisions and disregard for the practical experience of the masses."

'Cult of Personality'

These accusations appeared to include the charge that Mr. Khrushchev had been guilty of building up a "cult of personality" of his own while attacking similar practices of Stalin.

This impression was heightened by the fact that the editorial declared that "collective leadership" was the "most important Leninist principle of the life and activity of the party" and the "greatest political asset" of the Soviet Communist party.

What the new leaders and the others seemed to say in today's editorial, in other words, was that Mr. Khrushchev had departed from the principle of "collective leadership" instituted after Stalin's death.

The implication was that his successors would restore true "collective leadership."

The Communist party is irreconcilably opposed to the "ideology and practice of the personality cult," the editorial said.

Parley May Be Broadened

After having reiterated the Soviet leadership's determination to call for an international conference of Communist parties, the editorial said this conference should discuss "problems of peace" and of "national independence" as well as those of the unity of the international Communist movement.

This appeared to give the proposed conference a broader frame of reference than it had under the plans worked out by the Khrushchev regime. Such a broadening might serve to reduce opposition to the conference by other parties.

The Chinese Communists were not specifically named in the editorial.

Last Aug. 10 the Soviet leadership sent out invitations for a preliminary meeting of 26 Communist parties to begin here Dec. 15. The preliminary meetings would have the task of preparing for a full conference of all the parties some time next year.

This Soviet project ran into strong opposition from many foreign Communist parties. Even some of the Kremlin's closest allies, such as the Polish and Italian Communists, declared they would accept the invitation only with great misgivings.

The new leadership made its first public appearance at a Kremlin reception while Mr. Khrushchev was being pushed into oblivion.

The Government newspaper Izvestia failed to mention the former Premier's name in a long article on the liberation of the Ukraine from Nazi occupation 20 years ago.

This was in sharp contrast with the way Ukrainian history had been written while Mr. Khrushchev was in power. He had invariably been described as having played a heroic, indispensable role.

Shoppers who bought a portfolio of photographs of Soviet leaders early this morning found that Mr. Khrushchev's picture had already been removed.

Close Associates Ousted

At least four close associates of the deposed Premier are known to have been removed from their posts.

They are Mikhail A. Kharlamov, who was head of Soviet radio and television; Vladimir S. Lebedev, Grigori T. Shuisky and Oleg A. Troyanovsky. The latter three were personal aides to Mr. Khrushchev.

These men along with Aleksei I. Adzhubei, Mr. Khrushchev's son-in-law who was the editor of Izvestia, were the key members of the "brain trust" of the former Premier.

Pravda was believed to be under new editorial direction.

Pavel A. Satyukov, editor of the newspaper during Mr. Khrushchev's rule, was unofficially reported yesterday as having been ousted. Today this report was amended to the effect that Mr. Satyukov was in Paris, would return to Moscow today and would "probably" be dismissed.

The scene at the big Kremlin reception given by the new leadership President Osvaldo Dorticós Torrado of Cuba was almost exactly the same as at all similar receptions in the past. The only difference was that Mr. Khrushchev was absent.

Among those at the reception was Mikhail A. Suslov, who was reliably reported to have played a key role in the crucial session of the Communist party's Central Committee that deposed Mr. Khrushchev.

It was he, according to authoritative sources, who delivered the principal accusing speech against Mr. Khrushchev.

Specialists explained that this did not necessarily mean that Mr. Suslov, a party secretary, had been the principal instigator and engineer of Mr. Khrushchev's overthrow. It was possible that he had been chosen merely as a spokesman by the anti-Khrushchev majority and assigned the most unpleasant part of the task.

Mr. Suslov charged that Mr. Khrushchev had made grave errors in the Chinese-Soviet conflict, that he had mishandled Soviet agriculture and that he was guilty of nepotism and of creating a "cult of personality," the sources said.

Brezhnev Absent

Mr. Brezhnev, the man believed to be the strongest figure in the new leadership, at least for the time being, was not at the reception. Officials said he was too busy to attend.

Anastas I. Mikoyan, the 69-year-old chief of state who had been Mr. Khrushchev's close personal friend, acted as host.

If Mr. Mikoyan's emotions had been touched at all by the events of the last few days, it did not register on his dark face. His voice was firm and controlled as he proposed a toast for President Dorticós. Mr. Mikoyan ate heartily and conversed with gusto with his guests.

Premier Kosygin looked wan, his face more deeply lined than usual.

The most poignant moment was at the very beginning. About 10 of the leading members of the party and Government were standing in two rows waiting for President Mikoyan to bring President Dorticós up to them.

Then the orchestra struck up the Cuban anthem and all movement stopped.

The 10 men did not look like conquering heroes who had just taken over one of the world's most powerful governments.

They looked drab, tired and pensive as they stood rigidly staring into space, each alone with his thoughts.

Then the orchestra stopped abruptly and they burst into seemingly forced activity, smiling and shaking the hands of their Cuban guest.

Mr. Khrushchev was present at the Central Committee meeting and defended himself in a lengthy speech, sources said.

Western observers noted that yesterday's Tass announcement, which is still the only official explanation of the shake-up, did not say that the Central Committee had been unanimous in its decision to oust Mr. Khrushchev.

It was widely concluded from this that there had been discussion and probably dissension. The announcement mentioned, by contrast, that the action of the Presidium of the Supreme Soviet (Parliament) to depose Mr. Khrushchev as Premier had been unanimous.

The whereabouts of Mr. Khrushchev was not known today.

Soviet officials who were asked this question at the Kremlin reception answered either abruptly or in embarrassment that they did not know.

In the Western community here, it was assumed that he and his family were at home in a building near the center of the city where many members of the regime, past and present, have apartments.

Ironically, the same building is also home to Vyacheslav M. Molotov, the former Foreign Minister whom Mr. Khrushchev ousted from power seven years ago.

Like Mr. Molotov, Mr. Khrushchev is believed to be an ordinary private citizen now.

By depriving him of his seat in the Presidium of the Central Committee of the party, as well as of his key positions as Government and party leader, his successors have removed from him a chance to continue in the role of an honored if inactive elder statesman.

* * *

October 17, 1964

CHINA TESTS ATOMIC BOMB, ASKS SUMMIT TALK ON BAN; JOHNSON MINIMIZES PERIL

U.S. IS DENOUNCED

Peking Says Purpose of Test Is to Defend Peace of World

By SEYMOUR TOPPING
Special to The New York Times.

HONG KONG, Oct. 16—Communist China announced tonight that it had exploded its first atom bomb. Peking pledged that it would never be the first to use nuclear weapons in the future.

A communiqué stated that a nuclear test was successfully conducted at 3 P.M. Peking time (3 A.M., Eastern daylight time) in the western region of China. No details were disclosed. [In Washington, the test site was reported to be in Sinkiang, a province bordering the Soviet Union.]

"The success of China's nuclear test is a major achievement of the Chinese people in the strengthening of their national defense and the safeguarding of their motherland as well as a major contribution by the Chinese people to the cause of the defense of world peace," the communiqué asserted.

An accompanying Government statement declared that the purpose of developing nuclear weapons was to protect the Chinese people "from the danger of the United States launching a nuclear war."

Excesses Ruled Out

"On the question of nuclear weapons, China will commit neither the error of adventurism nor the error of capitulation," the statement said. "The Chinese people can be trusted."

The Peking statement formally proposed to the governments of the world that a universal summit conference be convened to discuss the question of a complete prohibition on and the thorough destruction of nuclear weapons.

It said that as a first step the summit conference "should reach agreement to the effect that the nuclear powers and those countries which will soon become nuclear powers undertake not to use nuclear weapons, neither to use them against nonnuclear countries and nuclear-free zones nor against each other."

The proposal was dismissed by Western observers here as propaganda. The terms do not allow for practical negotiations with a view to reaching specific agreements, they commented.

Although Communist China became the world's fifth nuclear nation, following the United States, the Soviet Union, Britain and France, specialists here doubted that it had the capability of becoming a first-class military power during this decade.

The principal advantage accruing to it immediately is psychological and political. The entry of the first nonwhite nation into the exclusive "nuclear club" was regarded here as certain to have a strong impact on the peoples of Asia and

Africa despite United States efforts to prepare them for Peking's accomplishment.

Western experts have estimated that it will take several years before the Chinese can build a delivery system. The withdrawal of Soviet military aid in 1960 disrupted Peking's program to develop ballistic missiles and left its air force largely obsolescent.

Altogether, this has been a triumphant day for Communist China.

The nuclear test was successfully carried out less than 12 hours after the announcement that Nikita S. Khrushchev, ideological arch-enemy of Peking, had been ousted from the leadership of the Soviet party and Government.

Greetings Sent to Brezhnev

Mao Tse-tung, chairman of the Chinese Communist party, and other top leaders, extended "warm greetings" in a message to Leonid I. Brezhnev, the new Soviet party leader; Aleksei N. Kosygin, the new Premier, and Anastas I. Mikoyan, President, who retained his office.

A cautiously worded Chinese message avoided mentioning Mr. Khrushchev or any outstanding issues. However, it concluded with a series of exhortations that analysts here viewed as an invitation to a new attempt at some kind of rapprochement. The message said:

"May the Chinese and Soviet parties and the two countries unite on the basis of Marxism-Leninism and proletarian internationalism!

"May the fraternal, unbreakable friendship between the Chinese and Soviet peoples continuously develop."

"May the Chinese and Soviet peoples win one victory after another in their common struggle against imperialism headed by the United States and for the defense of world peace."

Wishes for Soviet Success

The message also expressed the hope that the Soviet party and Government "will achieve new successes in their construction work in all fields and in the struggle for the defense of world peace."

The signers of the message were Mr. Mao; Liu Shao-chi, President; Marshal Chu Teh, chairman of the Standing Committee of the National Peoples' Congress, and Chou En-lai, Premier.

Specialists on Soviet relations believe that the imminence of the detonation of the Chinese bomb was a factor in the decision by the Central Committee Wednesday to remove Mr. Khrushchev. A majority of the Soviet leadership evidently decided, for tactical reasons, at least, to adopt a more flexible attitude toward Communist China.

The Italian and Rumanian and many other parties have been opposed to any move to exclude the Chinese from the international movement. The imminent nuclear test was certain to give more weight to their views.

The analysts said that a formal split in the international Communist movement had been postponed and possibly averted by the ouster of Mr. Khrushchev.

The texts of the Moscow announcements were published this morning in Peking newspapers without comment. Jenmin Jih Pao, official organ, which carried the announcements under the headline "Kruschev Steps Down," subordinated them to a report on the cotton industry.

There was no expectation among analysts here that the change in Moscow would lead to any early settlement of the fundamental issues between Moscow and Peking. Divergences of both ideological and national interests have become so profound that no quick solution is regarded as possible.

As part of the day's triumphs, the Labor victory in Britain was certain to please the Chinese Communists. Harold Wilson, the new British Prime Minister, has favored an improvement of relations with Peking and detonation of its bomb was thought likely to reinforce his attitude.

The United States has opposed any disarmament agreement that would ban nuclear weapons without concurrent restrictions on conventional arms. Confronted by a Chinese Communist Army of two and a half million men, the United States, in defending Southeast Asia or Taiwan, would have to depend on its nuclear arsenal to curb aggression.

The Chinese statement obviously was intended to reassure the nonaligned nations, which have expressed misgivings about Peking's failure to adhere to the nuclear test ban treaty signed in Moscow last summer by the United States, Britain and the Soviet Union.

The statement described the treaty as a "big fraud" to fool the world about attempts by the signatories to consolidate their nuclear monopoly.

The statement reiterated the thesis of Mao Tse-tung, chairman of the Chinese Communist party, that the "atom bomb is a paper tiger" and that people, not weapons, decide wars. It said the aim of Communist China in developing nuclear weapons was "to break the nuclear monopoly of the nuclear powers and to eliminate nuclear weapons."

Hsinhua, the Chinese Communist press agency, reported that Mr. Mao and other leaders received more than a thousand young people, who sang and danced in a performance entitled "The East Glows Red."

* * *

December 2, 1964

JOHNSON DIRECTS TAYLOR TO PRESS VIETNAM ON WAR

President Is Said to Defer Decision on Question of Extending Conflict

By CHARLES MOHR
Special to The New York Times.

WASHINGTON, Dec. 1—President Johnson discussed today proposals for expanding the war in Vietnam, then directed Ambassador Maxwell D. Taylor to "consult urgently"

Associated Press Wirephoto

TOPIC IS SOUTH VIETNAM: President Johnson conferring with Secretary of Defense Robert S. McNamara at White House meeting yesterday. Others are Secretary of State Rusk, left, and Ambassador Maxwell D. Taylor.

with the Government of South Vietnam on measures to improve the anti-Communist struggle within that nation.

Priority was said to have been given to the question of strengthening the Government of Premier Tran Van Huong or making it more acceptable to the many dissident factions in Saigon.

In a two-and-one-half-hour meeting with the President, Mr. Taylor discussed the question of American air strikes on Communist supply routes and depots in Laos and in North Vietnam. But it was indicated that Mr. Johnson took no immediate decision on this point.

Aid to Vietcong Reviewed

It was understood Mr. Johnson felt that steps toward a more stable civilian government in Saigon should be explored before committing the United States to a wider war.

At the same time, a White House statement issued after the conference, in which Mr. Taylor reported to the President, said they had "reviewed the accumulating evidence of continuing and increased North Vietnamese support" for the Vietcong guerrillas in South Vietnam.

The statement said that Mr. Taylor had "reported that the political situation in Saigon was still difficult but that the new Government under Prime Minister Huong was making a determined effort to strengthen national unity."

Qualified sources reported that Mr. Taylor's assessment of the political and military situation in Vietnam was one of marked pessimism.

News Parley Barred

Newsmen entered the Cabinet room after the meeting. President Johnson was apparently considering allowing a news conference with Mr. Taylor, but Secretary of Defense Robert S. McNamara, who was sitting at the President's left, was overheard to say softly: "It would be impossible for Max to talk to these people without leaving the impression the situation is going to hell."

The meeting was also attended by Vice President-elect Hubert H. Humphrey; Secretary of State Dean Rusk; the Central Intelligence Agency Director, John A. McCone; Gen. Earle G. Wheeler, chairman of the Joint Chiefs of Staff; McGeorge Bundy, Special Assistant to the President for National Security Affairs; his brother, William P. Bundy, Assistant Secretary of State for Eastern Affairs, and John T. McNaughton, Assistant Secretary of Defense for International Security Affairs.

The White House statement said Ambassador Taylor had reported that "security problems have increased over the past few months in the northern provinces of South Vietnam" and that uneven progress had been made elsewhere.

He also said that "the strength of the armed forces of the Government was being increased by improved recruiting and conscription, and by the nearly 100 per cent increase in the combat strength of the Vietnamese Air Force."

The statement added that "Government forces were continuing to inflict heavy losses on the Vietcong."

Nonetheless, it is known that Mr. Taylor has expressed support for the idea of air attacks on supply routes to the Vietcong, which extend from North Vietnam through Communist-controlled eastern Laos to the South Vietnamese border.

The White House statement said that "the President reaffirmed the basic United States policy of providing all possible and useful assistance" to South Vietnam and "noted that this policy accords with the terms of the Congressional Joint Resolution of Aug. 10, 1964, which remains in full force and effect."

Aid to Asians Pledged

That resolution, passed after North Vietnamese torpedo boats had attacked United States destroyers in the Gulf of Tonkin, said that the United States "regards as vital to its national interest" the security of Southeast Asia and was prepared "to take all necessary steps, including the use of armed force" to assist nations in that area.

Observers have noted that the resolution could be used as authorization to begin hostilities against North Vietnam or against military installations the North Vietnamese control in Laos.

Qualified sources indicated that Mr. Taylor also discussed proposals for improving "civic action" programs designed to win peasant support for the Government and for military reforms aimed at a more vigorous prosecution of the war.

Premier Huong's Government has been under mounting attack from Buddhists and others, primarily on the ground that ambitious political forces, long frustrated under the regime of Ngo Dinh Diem, were excluded from the Cabinet of civil servants chosen by Mr. Huong.

* * *

December 12, 1964

VERSATILE REVOLUTIONIST

Ernesto Che Guevara

The bearded man in the olive green fatigue uniform paused outside the General Assembly of the United Nations yesterday, took out a knife and cut the hot end off his half-smoked Havana. Then he stuffed the unsmoked part into his pocket before going into the Assembly to make a speech against "colonialism and imperialism" and the United States. He was Maj. Ernesto Che Guevara, Cuba's Minister of Industry and head of the Cuban delegation to the new Assembly session.

He is the rare "complete revolutionary." He was one of the key guerrilla leaders who brought Fidel Castro to power and he has since played a dominant role in Cuba as self-taught economist, diplomat and author of a book on guerrilla warfare.

At 36 years of age he is widely regarded as the chief brain of the Cuban revolution and there is no doubt of his great versatility.

This soft-spoken son of an Argentine architect and builder started out studying medicine, then moved on to Marxist revolutionary doctrine.

His nickname, Che, is a common Argentine slang word, means "Mac" or, sometimes, "Hey listen," and he has now made it his formal middle name.

Of Spanish and Irish descent, he was born June 14, 1928, in Rosario, Argentina's big grain port, the oldest of five children in a relatively well-to-do family. His paternal grandmother, born in California, was a United States citizen. It is frequently said that her suffering while dying of cancer led him to seek a medical education. He himself was puny as a youth, suffering, as he still does, from asthma.

His father, seeking a better climate for young Ernesto, moved the family to the mountain town of Alta Gracia and saw to it that the boy participated actively in sports.

Ernesto swam, played golf and rugby and learned to shoot but he was also an avid consumer of leftist and Marxist literature. As a teen-ager he took part in street fights against backers of Juan D. Perón, then Argentina's dictator.

In 1952 he and a friend undertook a hiking and motorcycle tour of vast areas of South America.

Returning to Argentina, the young Guevara got his degree in medicine and surgery in 1953. He then decided to leave the country permanently to avoid compulsory service in the Perón army.

He was associated with left-wing movements in Bolivia, Peru, Ecuador, Panama and Costa Rica before joining up with the Castro brothers—Fidel and Raul—in Mexico in 1956. In Guatemala he held a minor post in the agrarian-reform program of the Communist-dominated regime of President Jacobo Arbenz Guzmán.

During this period he married Hilda Gadea, a Peruvian leftist.

Mrs. Guevara introduced Fidel Castro to her husband and later said she had lost him to the revolution. The Guevaras had a daughter but after the Cuban revolution Dr. Guevara divorced his wife and married a Cuban, Aleida Marsh.

Dr. Guevara was one of the 12 survivors of the 80-man force in Mr. Castro's ill-fated invasion attempt on the south coast of Cuba in December, 1956.

The survivors escaped to the mountains, where they made their headquarters, built up their forces and began the campaigns that overthrew the Fulgencio Batista Government.

After Mr. Castro took power in January, 1959, Dr. Guevara took on a wide range of new duties without giving up his military life. He was a major by then. He was sent to neutralist and Communist countries as a trade envoy; he worked in the agrarian reform program, and at the end of 1959 he became president of the National Bank. All the while he trained a large civilian militia against the possibility of invasion and wrote a book, "Guerrilla Warfare."

Major Guevara is credited with having established Cuba's close economic ties with the Communist bloc. He also became closely identified with attempts to spread the Cuban revolution throughout Latin America.

He seized American-owned property and declared "the only way to carry out an agrarian revolution is to take land first and worry about compensation later."

In 1961 he became Minister of Industry and announced a four-year plan to build up industry. But economic conditions and harvests worsened and, despite some industrial gains, over-all production declined. Last January he announced a cutback in industrial investment to concentrate more on consumer goods.

Major Guevara's extensive travels in recent years have included Moscow and Peking.

* * *

December 12, 1964

U.S. GIVING SAIGON MORE HELP TO CUT RED SUPPLY LINES

Acts to Finance Build-up of Army for Action Against Groups of Infiltrators

AIR RAIDS ARE WEIGHED

Washington Says Aid Step Does Not Mean Extension of Conflict to the North

By PETER GROSE

Special to The New York Times.

SAIGON, South Vietnam, Dec. 11—The United States has decided to increase its military assistance to South Vietnam for new action against the infiltration routes from Communist North Vietnam.

According to a communiqué issued today, joint planning is under way between the South Vietnamese Government and American military and diplomatic representatives here "to achieve greater effectiveness against the infiltration threat."

The nature of the new military measures was not confirmed, "for security reasons," but moves under discussion include air and ground attacks against Communist staging areas in the mountains of southern Laos, where the so-called Ho Chi Minh trail enters South Vietnam.

Briefing on Decisions

The attacks would be carried out by the South Vietnamese armed forces assisted by American advisory personnel and matériel support.

[Washington officials emphasized that the increased military and economic aid to South Vietnam did not foreshadow a move to expand the war to Communist North Vietnam.]

The Saigon announcement followed five days of consultations between the two Governments in which Ambassador Maxwell D. Taylor briefed the Vietnamese leaders on decisions taken by President Johnson during a recent Vietnam policy review in Washington.

The United States also promised additional aid to strengthen Vietnamese air defenses, to increase the size of the country's armed forces and the police and to speed up economic and rural development.

Vietnam's Plans Less Clear

American and Vietnamese officials declined to disclose the type or value of the new increase in aid. The United States is spending $700 million a year in military and economic aid to help the Saigon Government crush the Communist insurgency. There are more than 22,000 American military advisers on duty in Vietnam.

The commitments undertaken by the Government of Premier Tran Van Huong were less clearly spelled out in the communiqué. The 200-word statement was approved by Premier Huong and Ambassador Taylor at a conference this afternoon.

"For its part," the communiqué said, "the Government of Vietnam is reviewing ways of increasing the scope and effectiveness of its programs related to the development of security and local government in the rural areas."

Buddhists Seek Ouster

In accepting American aid to support larger armed forces, the Vietnamese Government tacitly agreed to one of Mr. Taylor's prime requirements: that more people be mobilized to fight actively against the mounting power of the insurgents.

The Vietnamese armed forces, including paramilitary units and the police, now total 615,000 men. The Americans have urged an increase of at least 100,000 to insure security in the areas of the country under the Government's control.

The communiqué also put the United States squarely behind the present South Vietnamese Government in the face of rising opposition.

"In the course of the discussions the United States representatives expressed full support for the duly constituted Government of Prime Minister Huong," the communiqué said.

This seemed to defy a new Buddhist campaign launched officially today to oust Mr. Huong for allegedly committing "crimes" similar to those of the late President Ngo Dinh Diem who was overthrown after five months of Buddhist-led pressure last year.

Holding back from the vehement anti-American statements expressed by Buddhist leaders lately, the chief political spokesman for the church organization, Thich Tam Chau, nevertheless wrote to Mr. Taylor today holding him "responsible before the Vietnamese and American peoples for the continuation of the Huong Government."

In a five-point communiqué and a letter to the chief of state, Phan Khac Suu, the Buddhist leaders emphasized what they considered the American Ambassador's responsibility for maintaining Mr. Huong in power against "the just desires of the Vietnamese people and the Buddhist Church."

Several hundred monks, including the top leaders, moved into their heavily guarded Buddhist headquarters today to hold fast against feared Government reprisals.

The effect of the new American commitment on the Budhist campaign could not be predicted with any certainty, but Mr. Taylor's hope of insuring Government stability before undertaking any new military actions has clearly been abandoned.

Rather, the view that new American activities could be a useful element in lining up support behind Premier Huong seems to have been accepted. This contention, which remains controversial, has been rejected up to now as too great a risk.

No time element was cited in today's Government communiqué for actions against the infiltration routes or other increases in American aid.

The American spokesman said that consultations between American and Vietnamese officials would be continued to work out details of how the new measures, both military and economic, would be implemented.

"Some programs will probably be announced," he said. "Others will just happen."

Up to now action against infiltration has been a primary mission of Vietnamese and American special forces operating from isolated outposts high in the Annamite Mountains. Theoretically, their patrols through the jungle operate only on the South Vietnamese side of the poorly marked frontier.

Air Attacks Reported

There have also been reports of air attacks in Laos by the Royal Laotian Air Force. So far, neither of these types of actions has been successful in interdicting what the communiqué called "mounting" infiltration of Communist men and matériel.

Official documentation of the extent of this infiltration and its effect on the South Vietnamese counterinsurgency operation has been prepared by American intelligence officials but has not yet been released.

Informed sources said that the number of troops believed to have entered South Vietnam through the mountain trails this year was nearly 10,000—five times greater than in previous years.

* * *

January 7, 1965

SENATORS DIVIDED ON VIETNAM STAND

Frustration and Uncertainty Prevail as Debate Nears

By The Associated Press

WASHINGTON, Jan. 6—On the threshold of renewed Congressional debate over South Vietnam, many Senators share a sense of frustration and uncertainty over the course of the United States-backed war on Communism in Southeast Asia.

Eighty-three Senators spoke out in an Associated Press survey today as Congress prepared to review the situation in South Vietnam. Senator Mike Mansfield of Montana, the Democratic majority leader, has forecast a full-scale debate in the Senate.

"The problem is tragically difficult," said Senator Alan Bible, Democrat of Nevada, "but I believe we must continue to do everything possible under the present policy—increasing the emphasis on a stable and responsible Vietnamese Government."

Thirty-one of the Senators, ready to prescribe a course, voiced generally similar views, many of them suggesting negotiations later if the anti-Communist forces are in a better bargaining position.

"It's a mistake to negotiate when losing," said Senator William Proxmire, Democrat of Wisconsin.

Ten Senators favored moving for negotiations now, some suggesting United Nations guidance toward a settlement based on neutrality.

Only three took an unqualified stand for expansion of the struggle into Communist North Vietnam. However, five others mentioned commitment of United States combat troops or action against North Vietnam as possible steps toward an end to the struggle.

Senator George D. Aiken, Republican of Vermont, said the United States should not take either step unless the nation was ready to face an all-out war that would include nuclear weapons.

Senator Mansfield said:

"Expansion will not resolve the problem. It is more likely to enlarge it, and in the end we may find ourselves engaged all over Asia in full-scale war."

Three Senators called for the withdrawal of United States advisers and military aid from South Vietnam.

Raising the specter of a new Korea, Senator Allen J. Ellender, Democrat of Louisiana, said it was time for the United States to get out "without any ifs or ands."

Eight at a Loss What to Do

Three Senators urged steps to strengthen the South Vietnamese Government without specifically endorsing a United States course.

Eight said they simply did not know what should be done.

"I don't know how you get off a tiger's back," said one Senator, who declined to be identified.

Others refused to comment on the situation, at least for the present. Some said they would await the outcome of two Senate inquiries, one already under way by the Foreign Relations Committee, the other planned by the Armed Services Committee.

Representative of the wide range of views expected in the forthcoming Senate debate were the demands made by Strom Thurmond, Republican of South Carolina, and Wayne Morse, Democrat of Oregon. Senator Thurmond called on the United

States to step up the battle and stop "providing sanctuaries for the Communists," while Senator Morse demanded that the United States "stop making an American puppet out of South Vietnam."

The survey showed that many Senators shared the "sense of frustration" voiced recently by Secretary of State Dean Rusk "that things are not somehow moving more rapidly toward a conclusion."

One Republican Senator who asked to remain unidentified complained that Congress and the nation had not been given the facts.

"The situation in Vietnam is impossible unless a more stable government can be established," Senator Aiken said. "I don't know how long we can wait on this."

Senator Frank Church, Democrat of Idaho, saw disaster ahead for United States policy. He called for an international agreement that would guarantee the independence and neutrality of South Vietnam—and possibly Cambodia and Laos as well.

Mr. Church said such an agreement should be administered by the United Nations or a special international commission.

Calling for a similar course, Senator Ernest Gruening, Democrat of Alaska, commented, "It's Asians against Asians, and white intervention will not solve the problem by arms."

Mr. Gruening added that he would support the use of American troops in Vietnam but under United Nations auspices.

Buffer Zone Suggested

Senator Olin D. Johnston, Democrat of South Carolina, said, "I suggest the United Nations handle it, set up a buffer zone between North and South Vietnam and police it."

Other Senators saw no answer in neutralization.

Senators Robert C. Byrd, Democrat of West Virginia, and Frank Lausche, Democrat of Ohio, warned that neutralization could lead to Communist domination.

Offering the toughest formula, Senator Thurmond said, "Give the South Vietnamese all the supplies they need and whatever aid they need to bomb the North Vietnamese but, if necessary, bomb them with United States troops, planes and ammunition."

Also calling for action against North Vietnam, Senator John G. Tower, Republican of Texas, said, "Continuation of the present policy means continuation of a policy that is losing the war."

He advised against intervention by United States combat troops but said the only way to "reverse the gradual defeat of freedom" was to move against Communist supply lines from the North.

"If a stalemate situation develops or the Vietnamese achieve a momentum toward victory," he added, "then meaningful negotiations might result in an acceptable solution."

Senator Jack Miller, Republican of Iowa, said: "Under this present policy, the situation has deteriorated. The United States has already bombed North Vietnamese military installations, pursuant to orders of President Johnson, in response to attacks on our destroyers in the Bay of Tonkin.

"We should assist the South Vietnamese in doing the same thing in response to attacks on their country supplied, controlled and directed from North Vietnam."

Senator John Sparkman, Democrat of Alabama, was among the Senators who expressed a qualified call for expansion of the struggle.

"I am not in favor of expanding the war to the Communist North, except to the extent as may be necessary to destroy the supply lines from North Vietnam to the Communists in South Vietnam," he said. "This might necessitate the bombing of supply bases inside North Vietnam."

Senator Wallace F. Bennett, Republican of Utah, asserted that United States policy should be designed to win the war and added, "This may involve sending in combat units, or it may involve crossing into the North using Vietnamese units."

Senator Harrison A. Williams Jr., Democrat of New Jersey, said it might be time to consider sending in United States combat troops but with the proviso that they "be kept strictly within the borders in South Vietnam."

Clifford P. Case, Republican of New Jersey, said the situation was so delicate he did not want to comment. The Senators from New York and Connecticut were not reached.

RUSK BRIEFS HOUSE UNIT

WASHINGTON, Jan. 6 (UPI)—Secretary of State Dean Rusk briefed the House Foreign Affairs Committee today on the Vietnam crisis. In a session similar to yesterday's briefing of the Senate Foreign Relations Committee, he painted what one Representative described as a "sobering" picture.

The Secretary told the House committee that the State Department was currently more concerned about the political difficulties in South Vietnam than in how the war against the Communists was going.

Also today, Senator Morse said in the Senate that the Johnson Administration would leave office as "the most discredited Administration" in history if it continued its current South Vietnam policy.

* * *

January 7, 1965

U.S. VOICES A HOPE SAIGON IS NEARING ACCORD ON REGIME

Barring Last-Minute Hitch, Agreement Would Resolve Civilian-Military Rift

CONCESSIONS REPORTED

Each Side Said to Win Point but Officers Are Expected to Retain Their Power

Special to The New York Times.

WASHINGTON, Jan. 6—Administration officials expressed guarded optimism tonight that a solution of the South Vietnamese political crisis was imminent, with restoration of a unified government under civilian control.

The military and civilian factions were reported to be near an agreement to end their three-week struggle for power. There is a possibility that an announcement of the political compromise they have worked out will be made tomorrow.

If American officials were being guarded in their optimism, it was because they could not be certain, in the current situation in Saigon, where tempers are frayed and personality clashes are intense, that a settlement was reached until the agreement was signed and announced. There was concern, therefore, that some last-minute hitch might develop.

Facade of Civil Rule

Even if the agreement were signed, the officials acknowledge, only the facade of civilian government will have been patched together. It is recognized that the military will continue to wield substantial power and that, at best, it can be prevailed upon only to keep this in the background.

Basically, it was reported here, the agreement calls for military recognition of the authority of the civilian Government, with the Chief of State, Phan Khac Suu, and Premier Tran Van Huong remaining in power.

As a concession to the military, it was said, the High National Council, now in abeyance, would be abolished. In its place some form of national congress would be established to provide the legal basis for the Government's continuation.

The council has become, at the least, the symbolic issue in the political dispute that has kept Saigon in turmoil and Washington in uncertainty for three weeks. The 17-man council was set up last Nov. 1, as a provisional legislature to carry out the transition from military to civilian control:

On Dec. 20 a clique of younger generals staged a virtual coup d'état by forcing the dissolution of the council, accusing it of unspecified acts that interfered with the war effort against the Vietcong guerrillas.

The effect of the military action was to undermine the legal basis of the Government, which traced its authority back to the council's appointment of Mr. Suu as Chief of State.

More important, in the eyes of Washington, the military action, following a series of upheavals, undermined efforts to establish a stable government that could serve as a rallying point for the political-military struggle against the Communists.

Threats Were Hinted

Another basic provision of the agreement, this a concession to the civilian faction, calls for the release of some of the prisoners, many of them members of the council, who were arrested by the military Dec. 20.

The tentative agreement was reported to have been worked out primarily by Premier Huong and Air Vice Marshal Nguyen Cao Ky, a leader of the young generals, with Ambassador Maxwell D. Taylor and his deputy, U. Alexis Johnson, serving as intermediaries. The two Americans have taken an active role in attempting to resolve the crisis.

The argument has repeatedly been made to the generals, it was said, that a stable, unified government could not exist if the military saw fit to intervene every time they disagreed with governmental actions. The American officials have also stressed the adverse effect on the war effort.

The arguments have been backed up by thinly veiled threats from Washington that unless a unified government was restored, the United States might be forced to curtail its extensive military and economic assistance.

In the behind-the-scenes-negotiations, the United States apparently succeeded in its tactical objective of isolating Lieut. Gen. Nguyen Khanh, commander in chief of the armed forces, from his military subordinates in the political power struggle.

General Khanh, who had been Premier until establishment of the civilian government in November, supported the young generals and emerged as the principal antagonist of Ambassador Taylor in his efforts to further a resolution of the crisis.

It has never been clear to American officials to what extent General Khanh was a participant in the Dec. 20 power play or could count on their political support. There has been a growing belief that General Khanh was capitalizing on their action in a bid to reassert his own role.

As seen by some experts here on Vietnamese affairs, the generals, in turn, were using General Khanh as a focus of American ire and to win concessions.

There has been some recent optimism about a solution in Saigon. A week ago Secretary of State Dean Rusk expressed it when he reviewed the international situation with President Johnson. A week earlier Mr. Rusk had suggested a cut in assistance as a means of effecting a government supported by most Vietnamese factions.

SOME EASING IN SAIGON

Special to The New York Times.

SAIGON, South Vietnam, Jan. 6—Although there were no tangible political developments today, private conferences continued and the prevailing feeling of constraint seemed somewhat diminished.

Mr. Johnson, the Deputy United States Ambassador, met twice with Vice Premier Nguyen Xuan Oanh, the former Harvard economist who served briefly as Premier last fall.

Air Vice Marshal Ky, who is the head of the newly formed military liaison commission, has met with Thich Tam Chau, the principal Buddhist leader, and the Rev. Hoang Quynh, a leading Roman Catholic official.

* * *

January 7, 1965

STALIN HID AS NAZI ATTACK BEGAN, EX-ENVOY RECALLS

MOSCOW, Jan. 6 (UPI)—Stalin went into hiding for the first four days of the Soviet German war in 1941 and refused to see anyone or make any decisions on the conduct of the war, according to Ivan M. Maisky, Moscow's wartime Ambassador to London.

In a new chapter of his memoirs, published today by the monthly magazine Novy Mir, Mr. Maisky said he sat for four days beginning June 21, 1941, in his London embassy office waiting in vain for instructions from Moscow.

The former Ambassador sharply criticized Stalin for having ignored early British and American warnings of an impending Nazi invasion and for having failed to prepare the country to meet the onslaught, which resulted in enormous initial reverses.

* * *

February 5, 1965

JOHNSON STRESSES U.S. COMMITMENT TO GUARD VIETNAM

Bars Speculation on Pullout at His News Conference—Bundy Trip 'Routine'

By JOHN W. FINNEY
Special to The New York Times.

WASHINGTON, Feb. 4—President Johnson declared today that the Administration was determined to continue its policy of "helping the people of South Vietnam preserve their freedom."

Discussing the Vietnamese problem at his news conference, the President conveyed no indication of any change in policy, such as an expansion of the anti-Communist war, and no feeling of crisis brought on by deterioration in the political and military situation.

He declined to speculate on the implications of the visit of the Soviet Premier, Aleksei N. Kosygin, to North Vietnam. He also insisted that the current Saigon visit of McGeorge Bundy, his special assistant for national security affairs, was a routine consultation.

Bars Talk of Withdrawal

Mr. Johnson refused to consider any suggestion that the United States might be forced to withdraw from South Vietnam.

If a potentially significant theme emerged in the President's replies, it was in his relatively narrow justification for the extensive American commitment there.

Repeatedly Mr. Johnson said that the United States was in South Vietnam in response to a commitment made 10 years ago under President Dwight D. Eisenhower "to try to help the people of Vietnam help themselves to preserve their freedom."

In asserting that the Administration intended to abide by this commitment, he added that its attention was focused on making this assistance "more effective and efficient."

One Argument Dropped

Mr. Johnson declined to present a further argument that had been offered: that the commitment in South Vietnam was in the long-range strategic and diplomatic interest of the United States to prevent Chinese Communist expansion through Southeast Asia.

It was not clear whether the limitation of Mr. Johnson's explanation was due to the impromptu nature of his comments and to a reluctance to discuss Vietnam, or to an intent to leave the door open for change in the United States commitment.

Some Administration officials said the purpose might have been to soften the psychological defeat in any eventual withdrawal from South Vietnam, either at the request of the South Vietnamese or because of a negotiated settlement.

The Administration could then argue, according to these officials, that the withdrawal was prompted by an end of need or desire for American assistance in preserving the freedom of South Vietnam. The strategic implications would not then have to be emphasized.

Although a negotiated settlement has been suggested by some members of his party in Congress, Mr. Johnson refused to discuss such an eventuality. Similarly he refused to consider "crossing any such bridge" as withdrawal from South Vietnam. He said he did not foresee such a request from the South Vietnamese Government.

The President also commented on reports from Paris that North and South Vietnamese officials were secretly exploring the possibility of a negotiated settlement. He said this was "completely untrue."

The President disposed of one question that the State Department had refused to answer: whether the United States would extend diplomatic recognition to the South Vietnamese Government that emerged from the military coup d'état of Jan. 27.

"We are working with the existing Government as we have been right along," he said, and he suggested that the question of diplomatic recognition did not demand an answer.

KHANH CANCELS MEETING

SAIGON, Friday, Feb. 5 (UPI)—South Vietnam's military Commander in Chief, Lieut. Gen. Nguyen Khanh, canceled his scheduled meeting today with McGeorge Bundy. The cancellation appeared to be General Khanh's second rebuff to Mr. Bundy in two days.

Yesterday General Khanh sent last-minute word that he would not attend a reception for Vietnamese military leaders at the home of Gen. William C. Westmoreland, commander of United States forces in Vietnam. General Khanh has been cool to American officials since August, when they began voicing opposition to military rule.

A United States spokesman said the embassy hoped Mr. Bundy's appointment with General Khanh could be rescheduled.

SAIGON NOTES COINCIDENCES

SAIGON, South Vietnam, Feb 4 (AP)—McGeorge Bundy began a round of fact-finding conferences with United States officials today amid speculation in some Vietnamese quarters that a Washington-Moscow deal might be in the offing.

Mr. Bundy's arrival coincided with the departure of Premier Kosygin from Moscow for talks in Hanoi, North Vietnam. Mr. Bundy denied that his trip was related to the Kosygin visit.

Several Vietnamese took particular notice of White House overtures toward an exchange of visits by President Johnson and the Soviet leaders.

"How can we interpret this?" a Vietnamese official asked.

He added: "Johnson is trying to make friends with Kosygin at the very time when Kosygin and one of his generals are visiting Hanoi, our enemy to the death. American policy is sometimes very difficult to understand, unless a deal is being made. The Americans and the Russians made a deal on Laos, which is still in effect. Would it be that they have something like that in mind for Vietnam?"

* * *

February 8, 1965

U.S. JETS ATTACK NORTH VIETNAM IN REPRISAL FOR VIETCONG RAIDS; JOHNSON ORDERS FAMILIES HOME

CAPITAL IS TENSE

But President Asserts Nation Still Opposes Widening of War

By TOM WICKER
Special to The New York Times.

WASHINGTON, Feb. 7—United States aircraft struck at North Vietnam early today in response to what President Johnson called "provocations ordered and directed by the Hanoi regime."

Mr. Johnson made it clear, however, that the air strike was a limited response rather than a signal for a general expansion of the guerrilla warfare in South Vietnam.

In what appeared to be the most threatening crisis in Southeast Asia since the Gulf of Tonkin clash last August, Washington replied to severe Vietcong attacks.

The guerrillas had struck without warning against major American installations at Pleiku in the central plateau of South Vietnam, at an airstrip in Tuyhoa and at villages near Nhatrang.

49 Aircraft in Action

At the President's order, 49 carrier-based fighter planes bombed and strafed barracks and staging areas of the Vietcong guerrillas in the vicinity of Donghoi, just north of the border between North and South Vietnam.

The raid occurred swiftly about 2 P.M. Sunday, Vietnamese time (1 A.M., Eastern standard time). Secretary of Defense Robert S. McNamara said one American plane had gone down in the South China Sea. The Hanoi radio in the North Vietnamese capital said four aircraft had been knocked out.

Today, amid tension, President Johnson ordered the evacuation of about 1,800 dependents of United States military and civilian personnel stationed in South Vietnam.

Missile Unit Dispatched

He also ordered into the Danang area of South Vietnam an air-defense battalion equipped with Hawk ground-to-air missiles.

In the Vietcong attack at Pleiku, 8 Americans were killed and 108 wounded, but first reports did not indicate American casualties in the two other attacks.

Tension in Washington was heightened, and the United States response appeared conditioned to some extent by the Hanoi visit of Premier Aleksei N. Kosygin of the Soviet Union. Mr. Kosygin said in a speech to a Hanoi group that Moscow would assist North Vietnam against any nation that encroached on its territory.

Johnson Repeats Pledge

Administration officials insisted that the air attack had been carried out without regard to Mr. Kosygin's visit to Hanoi and would have been staged even if he had not been there.

In a White House statement announcing the retaliatory attack, Mr. Johnson repeated the pledge, given at the time of the Tonkin incident, that "we seek no wider war."

But the President cautioned that "whether or not this course can be maintained lies with the North Vietnamese aggressors."

The response to the Vietcong attacks, he said, "was carefully limited to military areas which are supplying men and arms for attacks in South Vietnam." Thus, he said, "the response is appropriate and fitting."

Mr. McNamara, at a news conference with George Ball, the Under Secretary of State, emphasized the same point. He refused to say, however, that the Donghoi attacks closed the United States' response, and he declined to comment on "future military operations."

Associated Press Radiophoto

RESULT OF VIETCONG ATTACK: Wreckage of U.S. helicopter at Camp Holloway air base, which was shelled early yesterday by mortars in a surprise attack by guerrillas.

Informed sources indicated that the United States had made private approaches to the Soviet Union with an assurance that "no wider war" was intended.

The Administration wrote the same assurances into a report delivered to the United Nations tonight by Adlai E. Stevenson, the United States delegate.

In his statement announcing the attack on Donghoi, and in a later White House statement directing the withdrawal of the dependents, Mr. Johnson asserted that the Vietcong attacks on Saturday made it clear that "Hanoi" had ordered more aggressive action against South Vietnam and the American forces there.

In the second statement, Mr. Johnson said: "We have no choice now but to clear the decks and make absolutely clear our continued determination to back South Vietnam in its fight to maintain its independence."

Intelligence Data Cited

No information was put on the public record to explain the Administration's insistence that the attack on Pleiku had been specifically ordered by Hanoi as a direct challenge to the United States.

But informed sources said secret intelligence information confirmed the accusation.

Mr. McNamara said at his news conference that the attacks had been "ordered and directed and masterminded" from Hanoi.

Mr. Ball added that the United States and South Vietnam had had no choice but to respond as they did. To have refrained, he said, would have been to give a "misleading signal" to the North Vietnamese about American purposes in the South.

Official sources said it was the severity of the Vietcong attack on Pleiku, primarily, that convinced the Administration that it had been directly challenged. Others suggested that additional motives were involved.

One was apparently the presence of Mr. Kosygin in Hanoi. Most sources here suggest that he probably knew nothing of the Vietcong attacks but that they were ordered by Hanoi during his visit, either to show him that the American force in South Vietnam was "a paper tiger" or, possibly foreseeing a sharp American response, to press to aid North Vietnam against United States "imperialism."

Psychological Motive

Washington sources believe Mr. Kosygin and his Government do not welcome being put on such a spot by the North Vietnamese. But they add that if Washington had made no response to the Vietcong attacks, it would have strengthened North Vietnamese and perhaps Chinese Communist arguments for a stronger military effort in South Vietnam.

Another motivation may have been the Administration's desire to reassert its determination to remain in South Vietnam, in the face of increasing political unrest there and increasing talk at home about the possibility of negotiations or withdrawal.

Informed sources also suggested that United States officials had wanted to bomb the Donghoi area on military grounds, and the Pleiku attack had provided a reason for doing so.

Mr. McNamara described the Donghoi area as the starting point for infiltration of men and supplies for the Vietcong through Laos and into South Vietnam, on a direct route to the Pleiku area.

One official, asked why the Pleiku raid had been considered more of a challenge than a similar severe Vietcong action last year against Bienhoa air base, replied, "There is a limit to America's patience."

"When the attack was repeated, and repeated under these circumstances," he said there was no alternative to a strong response.

This response was similar to the one ordered by President Johnson after North Vietnamese patrol vessels attacked United States destroyer patrolling the Gulf of Tonkin.

Carrier-based planes then attacked the coastal anchorages and bases of the North Vietnamese craft.

Congress Chiefs Informed

President Johnson's decision to strike back after the Pleiku attack was made at a meeting of the National Security Council during the night. Representative John W. McCormack of Massachusetts, Speaker of the House, and Senator Mike Mansfield of Montana, the majority leader, were also present.

The Senate Republican leader, Everett McKinley Dirksen of Illinois, was consulted later by telephone. He said today that he approved of the President's actions and pointed out that no Congressional approval had been required.

Mr. Johnson was up and down during most of the night, keeping track of the situation, the White House said. He conferred early in the morning with a somewhat larger group of officials—this time including Representative Gerald R. Ford of Michigan, the House Republican leader.

At that meeting, the White House statement announcing the Donghoi attacks was approved. The McNamara-Ball news conference, which took place at the Pentagon at 1:30 P.M., was also approved.

One high Congressional source expressed doubt that Mr. Johnson's action would meet with complete Congressional approval. A number of members have spoken recently for a change of policy or for withdrawal from South Vietnam.

Several members questioned whether defenses had been adequate at Pleiku and why the American forces had been taken by surprise.

Mr. McNamara said there was no sure defense against sneak guerrilla attacks at night.

Among those questioning the circumstances of the Pleiku raid were Senators Clifford P. Case of New Jersey, Thomas H. Kuchel of California, and Hugh Scott of Pennsylvania, all Republicans.

Senator Ernest Gruening, Democrat of Alaska, repeated his call for a United States withdrawal from South Vietnam.

* * *

February 18, 1965

WASHINGTON STILL REJECTS ANY VIETNAM NEGOTIATIONS

By MAX FRANKEL

Special to The New York Times.

WASHINGTON, Feb. 17—In Congress, in the diplomatic corps and in mail reaching Washington, there is more and more talk in favor of "negotiation" over Vietnam. But the Administration continued today to shun that word or any other suggestion that it might wish to bargain for peace.

"You're right," a prominent official remarked. "We trip over the word. And yet we hate to appear so stringent. It's a real dilemma."

Foreign Minister Maurice Couve de Murville of France arrived this evening. His visit is likely to produce even more public discussion about taking the problems of Southeast Asia back to the conference table.

The French have been the most persistent advocates of a diplomatic solution rather than a military one and have tried to bring Washington and Peking toward a conversation.

Policy Is Reiterated

President Johnson and Vice President Humphrey indicated in brief public comments, however, what their associates have been reiterating in private: that they see no alternative at the moment to standing militarily at the side of the South Vietnamese Government and that a call for negotiations or any other specific commitment to future tactics would further weaken the position of anti-Communist forces in Asia.

The reasoning behind this position has not been made explicit. A number of high State Department officials have described themselves as embarrassed by uncertainty in conversations with colleagues in allied embassies.

Members of Congress who oppose negotiations have joined those who favor them in urging the President to explain at length his objective and tactics.

Some of the Administration's reticence has been ascribed to differences among Mr. Johnson's closest advisers about the extent to which retaliatory attacks upon North Vietnam should continue. But fear of displaying an interest in negotiation has long been virtually unanimous.

The private response of officials to the appeals for negotiation has been the question "When, and with whom?"

It is based on a belief that the non-Communist forces of South Vietnam are too weak politically and militarily to negotiate anything except the surrender of their country to the Vietcong.

The question is based, too, on a belief that even if the Soviet Union, Communist China and North Vietnam were interested in guaranteeing the "neutrality" of South Vietnam, they could not persuade the Vietcong to lay down their arms without assuring them a dominant position in future Saigon governments—the equivalent, in Washington's eyes, of defeat.

Morale Effect Feared

Even a vague commitment to negotiations is feared here because officials suspect that it would destroy the morale of South Vietnam's Army and further undermine the coalition, already shaky, of military, civilian and religious leaders.

Such a commitment would ignite rumors of secret deals and sellouts, officials predict, and could well bring to power Vietnamese "neutralists" who would force the United States to withdraw and who would attempt their own negotiations.

A face-saving American withdrawal or the admission of the Vietcong to seats of power in Saigon is a frank objective of some of those urging negotiations. But all the evidence here suggests that the Administration remains determined to deny South Vietnam to the Communists and would contemplate negotiations only if they promised to do so.

Thus the objective of the United States is still defined officially as a return to the "essentials" of the 1954 Geneva accord on Indochina, meaning the partition of Vietnam into Communist and non-Communist sectors.

Partition Now Doubted

There is strong doubt here that either Communist China or North Vietnam is willing any longer to assure such a division. There is even greater doubt that the rebels in South Vietnam, having fought so long and feeling themselves successful, would abandon their fight for the sake of some larger regional settlement of no direct value to them.

President de Gaulle and many others have urged the Administration to disengage itself from ground combat in Vietnam and to think instead of using its superior air and sea power to guarantee an agreement. Others have urged persistent attacks on North Vietnam or even on China to strengthen Washington's bargaining position.

The answer here remains that the "main problem" lies in South Vietnam. By retaliatory bombing of North Vietnam, the Administration has begun to try to discourage major rebel attacks, especially on American forces, and to stem the flow of men and supplies from North Vietnam.

But even military leaders who favor the bombings believe that the Vietcong could fight effectively for a long time without further outside help. While officials believe that North Vietnam has planned and directed most rebel activities, they doubt that Hanoi would be able to call off the guerrilla war and they see no sign that it wishes to.

RED CROSS AT GENEVA OFFERS TO AID VIETCONG WOUNDED

GENEVA, Feb. 17 (UPI)—The International Red Cross said today it has offered to aid the North Vietnamese Red Cross in helping wounded Vietcong fighters.

The offer was made on the basis of the first Geneva Convention of 1949, which provides for "easing the condition of the wounded and sick among armed forces in battle." North Vietnam signed this convention in 1957, the statement said.

* * *

February 18, 1965

JOHNSON ASSERTS U.S. WILL PERSIST IN VIETNAM POLICY

President Declares 'Justified and Necessary' Actions Will Be Continued

CONSULTS EISENHOWER

Some Democratic Senators Press for a Negotiated Settlement of Crisis

By CHARLES MOHR

Special to The New York Times.

WASHINGTON, Feb. 17—President Johnson said today the United States would persist in the defense of South Vietnam and would continue actions that are justified and necessary.

The President spoke as debate on Vietnam began again in Congress. The Republican leadership strongly supported his policy of retaliatory air strikes against North Vietnam, while some Democrats urged a negotiated withdrawal from Vietnam.

Mr. Johnson also held a surprise meeting with former President Dwight D. Eisenhower on policy in Vietnam.

General Eisenhower made no statement after the meeting. The White House press secretary, George E. Reedy, said the two men talked for more than two hours during the morning and then had lunch together just before Mr. Johnson's speech.

Eisenhower Has Check-up

Mr. Reedy said the general, who has been vacationing in Palm Desert, Calif., had come to Washington for a medical check-up at Walter Reed Army Hospital.

President Johnson's statements on Vietnam were made at the conclusion of what was primarily an economic address before the National Industrial Conference Board.

He neither threatened to continue air strikes against North Vietnam nor gave the Asian Communist capitals any assurance that they would stop.

The President declared that "we seek no wider war," but he also added:

"We will persist in the defense of freedom and our continuing actions will be those which are justified and those that are made necessary by the continuing aggression of others. Those actions will be measured, fitting and adequate. Our stamina and the stamina of the American people is equal to the task."

The Administration believes that high priority should again be given to vigorous anti-guerrilla warfare in South Vietnam, some informed sources said. But they did not rule out further air strikes if provocation from North Vietnam made them necessary.

Mr. Johnson was believed to have put deliberate stress on the need for stamina, since even successful combat against the Vietcong would be protracted.

Meanwhile, two Democratic Senators called for an end of the American commitment through negotiation.

Senator George McGovern of South Dakota said his mail was running 15 to 1 in favor of a negotiated settlement in Vietnam. He added that military victory in Vietnam appeared impossible.

Senator Frank Church of Idaho also called for negotiations and said that "systematic and sustained bombing of North Vietnam," unattended by any offer of recourse to the bargaining table, "can only lead us into war."

A number of Democratic Senators replied in strong terms, expressing support for President Johnson's policy.

A statement by the joint Senate-House Republican leadership said "there can be no negotiations" in Vietnam so long as there is infiltration of South Vietnam from the Communist North.

"We urge the President to make this clear to the world," said the group, headed by the Senate Republican leader, Everett McKinley Dirksen of Illinois, and the House Republican leader, Gerald R. Ford of Michigan.

Full Support From G.O.P.

The Republicans expressed full support for the recent United States air assaults on North Vietnam. They said that if they had any differences, "it is the belief that these measures might have been applied more frequently." They noted that North Vietnam was first bombed last August in response to a North Vietnamese attack on United States destroyers in the Gulf of Tonkin.

Former President Harry S. Truman issued a statement yesterday in support of the Johnson policy in Vietnam.

The White House said Mr. Johnson had not discussed the statement with Mr. Truman by phone until after it was written. But it appeared that the President welcomed such support and might be seeking it to forestall a growing public disagreement that could cloud American intentions in foreign capitals.

The current debate on Vietnam comes at a time when the exact limits of United States policy on Vietnam are somewhat unclear, evidently on the ground that too much clarity might be a comfort to Hanoi and Peking.

The Administration has not specified what sort of provocations by the Vietcong would bring new air action against the guerrillas main supporter, North Vietnam.

Mr. Johnson said today that the United States' objective in Vietnam was clear—"the defense and protection of freedom of a brave people who are under attack that is controlled and directed from outside their country."

"We have no ambition there for ourselves," he went on. "We seek no dominion. We seek no conquest."

Some Government sources indicated that the Administration was not so much opposed to negotiations as unable to see what kind of settlement could possibly satisfy both the Communists and the United States.

Senators McGovern and Church were met with forceful language from many of their fellow Democrats.

Both Senators Church and McGovern said that the public supported President Johnson's decision to bomb North Vietnam but that the public now desired a negotiated peace.

Both men suggested that the loss of a toehold in Southeast Asia would not be catastrophic on the ground that United States sea and air power would still be felt in Asia.

* * *

February 21, 1965

WE MUST CHOOSE—(1) 'BUG OUT' (2) NEGOTIATE (3) FIGHT

A military commentator argues for a greater use of our power in Vietnam: 'We must fight a war to prevent an irreparable defeat.'

By HANSON W. BALDWIN

What should we do—"bug out" or fight? Should we be "Hawks" or "Doves"? Or is there a third choice—negotiations now?

Recent events in Vietnam indicate that "the war that is not a war" has reached a crossroads. Washington's policy of the past four years, based on the polite fiction that we were not fighting a war but merely helping the Vietnamese to defeat the Vietcong insurgents within their own territory, has reached a point of no return.

Compromise and consensus—perhaps applicable to some of the nation's great domestic problems—cannot be guideposts to foreign policy. There must be a clear-cut and courageous decision. And though in Vietnam we face the hard problem of risking much to gain little, the risk must be taken: we must fight a war to prevent an irreparable defeat. We must use what it takes to win.

Our policy should not be "unconditional surrender" or unlimited victory. Our goal of victory should be the defeat of Communist attempts to conquer South Vietnam and extend their control deep into Southeast Asia.

The reasons we must fight for Vietnam have little to do with making Saigon safe for "democracy" or "freedom." There has been far too much cant on this point, far too much effort devoted to trying to establish a politically legitimate South Vietnamese Government after our own image. Nor does it do much good to argue the past, debating whether or not we should have become involved in Vietnam in the first place. The facts are that Communist expansionism in Asia has been consistent, related and progressive, that the end of the Korean war, without a simultaneous settlement in Vietnam, gave Peking and North Vietnam's Ho Chi Minh the opportunity in Southeast Asia they have so well exploited.

Belatedly, but nevertheless clearly, the United States became aware of the threat. Our commitments to Saigon began in the Eisenhower Administration and were enormously amplified after the Kennedy Administration took power four years ago. Today, we are committed—fully committed—by the words of Presidents and Cabinet members, by the actions of the Government, by the deep involvement of United States military forces.

United States global prestige and power is intimately bound up with the outcome of the Vietnamese struggle. In Vietnam, we are attempting to formulate an answer to the Communist strategy of creeping aggression, of subversion and insurgency, of what Khrushchev called "wars of national liberation." If the might and will of the United States cannot evolve a victorious answer to such tactics, we are undone; the map of the world will gradually become red. And if we will not fight in Vietnam, where—after the series of Communist conquests in the past 20 years—will we fight? Where will we draw the line?

The psychological and political consequences of a United States defeat in Vietnam, a United States withdrawal, or a negotiated peace likely to lead to a Communist takeover, would be disastrous in much of Asia. It would undermine Thailand (already openly threatened by Peking), Laos (even now half-conquered by Communism), Malaya, the Philippines (with its growing anti-Americanism), Burma, India, Japan and even Taiwan, Okinawa and Australia.

For a long time after the politically stalemated end of the Korean war, Peking was successfully depicting the United States to the peoples of Asia as a "paper tiger." The defeat of the French—backed heavily by American aid—in Indochina, enhanced this image of a windy, weak-willed, feeble Uncle Sam. That image has since been dispelled by United States actions in and around the Taiwan Straits, during the Cuban missile crisis and, recently, by President Johnson's retaliatory air attacks upon North Vietnamese objectives. But the portrait of flabby indecision could be easily revived if the United States loses in Vietnam.

Strategically, South Vietnam is too important to be allowed to go by default. North Vietnam badly needs the rice of the South. More important, the area is the traditional rice bowl of the continent. Geographically, Vietnam is a long appendix pointing toward the rich archipelago of Indonesia and abutting strategic sea passages. Whoever dominates it will eventually control most of the Indonesian archipelago.

The strategic importance of the area is similar to the so-called "rimlands," or maritime nations, of Western Europe which represent a powerful bastion against the "heartland" of Soviet Russia. In Asia, the non-Communist strategic position vis-à-vis Red China is based upon mainland positions—Pakistan, India, Southeast Asia and the island bastions of the Philippines, Taiwan, Okinawa and Japan. If the "rimlands" of Asia fall to Communism, the island positions will be doomed sooner or later. Ultimately the Communists will challenge us upon what is now our unchallenged domain—the oceans.

In a word, we must remain in Southeast Asia for our own security needs. South Vietnam is in itself not "vital" in the sense that the United States cannot live without it. But if lost we would be forced to commence the next chapter of the world conflict in retreat, and at a disadvantage.

Despite the admitted importance of South Vietnam to the United States global position, the current breed of neo-isolationists and the "Doves" who believe we must cut our losses and get out advance many arguments against deeper involvement and in favor of withdrawal.

Most of the arguments represent the voices of defeat and despair, caution and fear.

"Why not negotiate now?"

Any negotiations opened now would lead from weakness, not strength. If we want to negotiate and not to surrender, we shall have to raise our ante considerably. And "meaningful" negotiations are "meaningful" to the Communists only if they are faced with superior power and a position of strength.

We must "aim to parley." Personally, I seriously doubt whether talks can guarantee peace in Vietnam and Southeast Asia, as some quarters have suggested, by neutralizing the area politically and militarily, in short, by eliminating the struggle for influence between Communists and non-Communists. Nevertheless, we need not fear negotiations if we speak from strength, by really putting up a fight for Vietnam.

Continuing U.S. air and sea attacks on North Vietnam would serve notice on Hanoi, Peking and Moscow that the United States will no longer tolerate "sanctuary warfare." They might—hopefully—force Hanoi to the conference table. Indeed, such a policy would appear to be the minimum necessary to open any kind of negotiations. Yet even such a program will not "win" the war in the South.

"If the French couldn't win, how can the United States achieve victory?"

The implication of this argument is twofold: (1) we have donned the colonial mantle of the French, and (2) our power is no greater than that of Paris. Both suggestions are absurd.

As some of our diplomats have found to their discomfort, South Vietnam is distinctly an independent country—not, as in France's day, part of a colonial empire. In fact, the fear of Chinese Communist colonialism is probably greater in all of Vietnam, and in North Vietnam in particular, than the fear of United States "imperialism." As for a comparison between the political, economic and military power of the United States and France, there is none. Particularly in the air and at sea we can mobilize power completely unavailable to

France, backed up by the ultimate force which France did not possess—a nuclear arsenal.

"You can't win a war against guerrillas."

Not true. We have dressed up the fighting in Vietnam with a fancy name—"counterinsurgency," but some of its basic military elements resemble the kind of war Americans have fought successfully many times in the past in Nicaragua, Haiti and behind the main fighting fronts during the Korean War. Other anti-Communist guerrilla wars were won in Greece, the Philippines and Malaya. The Portuguese seem to have done a pretty good job of stamping out the rebellion in Angola. Guerrillas can be defeated, but it takes careful organization, special training and security forces than should be from 10 to 30 times larger than the guerrillas. It takes infinite determination and patience.

"Continued fighting or expanded U.S. involvement will mean higher U.S. casualties and greater risks of broadening the war."

Of course. You cannot win a war without spilling blood. We must pay the price of power. Risks are unavoidable in any foreign policy worthy of its name. The question is not whether there will be risks, but the degree of risk. For against the perils of action must be weighed the perils of inaction. Political and military history clearly reveal that compromise, hesitancy or appeasement merely lead to ultimate disaster. In Vietnam, the longer we wait, the greater the price we shall have to pay for even partial victory (as we are now discovering), and the more restricted our choice of options.

"We have no moral right to be in Vietnam, or to attack North Vietnam."

Neither do the Vietcong. Nor does North Vietnam have the right to support the civil war in the South. Our involvement was a response to Communist aggression. Since the beginning, Hanoi has organized, supplied and directed the Vietcong insurgency. We were invited by the South Vietnamese Government to come to its aid. A high moral purpose is an essential element of our foreign policy but we can be left with no purpose—moral or otherwise—if we are conquered by the doctrine that the ends justify the means. If we are inhibited from action by Hamlet-like indecision over legalistic concepts of international law, we shall lose the world.

"What's the use of further military involvement when the political instability of South Vietnam pulls the rug from under our feet?"

Here is one of the more cogent objections to greater involvement. But in the long history of Vietnam there have always been feuding sects and factions. Moreover, the French left behind them a people still unequipped for self-government. Yet somehow or other the war has gone on and somewhat better in some respects recently. Greater United States involvement—above all, a tangible determination to win—may well do more for Saigon's political stability than any amount of diplomatic pressures.

"Isn't the real danger that escalation might involve us in a larger war? Wouldn't the Chinese come in?"

This is the $64 million question. It is quite clear that if the United States becomes more involved we must be prepared for greater effort by the enemy. Escalation in some form would be not only possible, but likely. But we have advantages. We are fighting as we did in Korea, on a peninsula where our superior sea and air power can be most effective. North Vietnam's few power plants and industries are vulnerable to destruction. The Gulf of Tonkin is easily blockaded. And China itself, with an obsolete air force and minimal naval power, could not defend itself effectively against a determined air and sea attack.

Nevertheless, an expanded effort by the United States in Vietnam may well be answered by an increased flow of supplies and men from North Vietnam, perhaps by an all-out attack by the North Vietnamese Army, and perhaps ultimately by aid from China into South Vietnam. Though the flow could be hampered and reduced by air attacks it could not be completely halted. It is quite possible that the United States might become involved in a new kind of Korean war. But this would not be hopeless by any means. In fact, some well-informed authorities believe the United States could win a Korean type of war in South Vietnam-Laos against the best that the Chinese Communists could throw against us.

"What about the specter of nuclear weapons? Wouldn't Russia join in, even if China didn't have enough A-bombs to do us any harm?"

There is no certain answer to these questions, but a full scale nuclear war is highly unlikely. The United States has scared itself to death by its own nuclear propaganda. The fear of a nuclear exchange—never probable, or even likely—has been the greatest single restraint upon a positive and firm United States diplomacy since World War II.

Presidents and public alike have been inhibited by the nightmare of the mushroom cloud. Yet the lessons of the Cuban missile crisis should be remembered. Is it in any way probable that the Kremlin would risk for Vietnam what it would not risk for Cuba? Moscow knows our nuclear power. Would Russia invite its own destruction as a nation by invoking the use of nuclear weapons in any cause except the defense of its own soil? The questions answer themselves.

We must also remember the risks of delay. If there is a danger of nuclear retaliation today by Peking, how much greater will it be tomorrow when China will have accumulated a stockpile of weapons? Time is restricting our options.

Clearly, then, the stakes in Vietnam are large enough to warrant the risks of greater United States involvement. Whether or not we raise our ante, the energy will. The Communists are implacably determined to triumph and the only factor that can prevent their victory is superior power in all its forms. "More of the same" on our part will no longer serve any purpose, save slow defeat.

What should we do? First and foremost, we must recognize as a Government and as a people that we are fighting a war in Vietnam, not merely "advising" how to fight one. Such a recognition would awaken a greater sense of national and military determination, inspire a Presidential and Congressional enunciation of purpose, and create a more streamlined military operation in Vietnam.

Second, the United States itself must provide maximum possible security in Vietnam to major United States installations, such as airfields, supply depots and headquarters. Secretary McNamara's statement that it was impossible to guard against such attacks as those recently made by the Vietcong against United States airfields and barracks is no answer. Of course, 100 per cent security is impossible in any war defense against terrorism and sabotage is especially difficult. But there is no doubt whatsoever that we can provide better security to key installations than the South Vietnamese, who have been responsible for the job in the past.

We need United States ground tactical units in South Vietnam to defend our installations. We need infantry battalions, military police companies, Army engineers and Navy Seabees to build aircraft revetments, dugouts and protected barracks. Yet all this is purely defensive; it should reduce United States casualties but it will not "win" the war.

Another essential measure is simplification and streamlining of both the high military command and the "country team" units, composed of representatives from various government agencies, that support our aid effort in Vietnam. We must get more Americans and more Vietnamese out of the bistros of Saigon and into the bush. The coordination between the military, the Central Intelligence Agency, the State Department, the United States Information Agency and the Agency for International Development is far better than it once was. But it is still far from perfect, in Saigon or in Washington. The war has shown, for instance, that South Vietnamese-United States teams have been able in many instances to carry out the military portion of the "clear-and-hold" prescription for victory. But AID—not the military—is responsible for police and internal security forces in Vietnam, and these cadres rarely have been able to hold an area once it has been cleared of the Vietcong. Perhaps military troops should be charged with the "hold," as well as the "clear," part of the operations. Certainly internal policing needs a major overhaul.

A basic change in the prescription for victory demands a United States-South Vietnamese unified command such as now exists in South Korea.

Continuous and heavy air and sea attacks against staging areas, supply routes, training fields, camps and recuperation centers of the Vietcong in North and South Vietnam and Laos will be necessary for any appreciable diminution in the flow of men and supplies to the Communists. The one-shot retaliatory raids have only temporary and minimum military importance; viewed as political and psychological warnings, they are likely to provoke the Vietcong and North Vietnam to a redoubled war effort.

The history of air power dictates the need for unrelenting massive attacks. Bombing targets in North Vietnam probably would have to be broadened to include power plants, bridges, industries, road junctions, docks and oil storage facilities. A naval blockade and naval gunfire may well supplement the air bombardment. To carry out effectively any such program as this United States air and naval forces in the Western Pacific would require material strengthening.

Meanwhile, it would take years of effort inside South Vietnam itself to reduce the Vietcong to manageable proportions. Much larger, and better led, South Vietnamese forces would be necessary. They would have to be supplemented by United States ground troops—perhaps in small numbers at first, but more later, particularly if North Vietnamese regular forces and Chinese soldiers joined the Vietcong.

How many United States soldiers would be needed is uncertain—probably a minimum of three to six divisions (utilized chiefly in battalion or brigade-size units), possibly as many as 10 or 12 divisions. Including Air Force, Navy and supporting units perhaps 200,000 to 1,000,000 Americans would be fighting in Vietnam.

Obviously, this would mean a Korea-type conflict, a major war, no matter what euphemisms would be used. Nor could we wage it in the present "business-as-usual" economy. We would require partial mobilization, vastly beefed-up military production. Many weaknesses in our military structure would need strengthening. Even so, we could not anticipate quick success. The war would be long, nasty and wearing.

No one could relish such a prospect as this; the stark statistics of war explain the President's reluctance to embark upon a path that has no turning.

Vietnam is a nasty place to fight. But there are no neat and tidy battlefields in the struggle for freedom; there is no "good" place to die. And it is far better to fight in Vietnam—on China's doorstep—than fight some years hence in Hawaii, on our own frontiers.

Hanson W. Baldwin has been The Times military editor for many years.

* * *

March 1, 1965

U.S. SAID TO PLAN LIMITED AIR WAR AS LEVER ON HANOI

'Virtual Certainty' Is Voiced by Top American Officials and Vietnamese Aides

WORD AWAITED IN SAIGON

Washington Was Reported Ready to Order Assaults Before Feb. 19 Coup

By ROBERT KLEIMAN.
Special to The New York Times.

SAIGON, South Vietnam, Feb. 28—The highest American and South Vietnamese officials here say they are "virtually certain" that President Johnson has decided to open a continuing, limited air war against North Vietnam to bring about a negotiated settlement of the Vietnam problem on honorable terms.

They say the air war would be unrelated to specific provocation.

Their virtual certainty on a Presidential decision is based in part on instructions from Washington in the middle of February to prepare for the first air strike of the new series. This was to be a joint American and South Vietnamese attack. It was postponed during the abortive coup d'état of Feb. 19, and new orders are now awaited daily.

[In Washington, Administration sources said the United States was stepping up air surveillance of the Vietnamese coast to curtail sea-borne aid from the North to the Vietcong.]

Past Wavering Cited

In discussing the President's plans, United States and South Vietnamese officials say their certainty is "virtual" rather than absolute because earlier Presidential avoidance of a decision has distorted and perhaps rendered inoperative key elements of the original "peace through pressure" plan.

The latest version of this plan, officials say, was submitted to the President in December. Earlier last year, the project was known as the McNamara-Bundy plan, after the Secretary of Defense and Mr. George Bundy, special assistant to President Johnson.

A later variant was drafted by John T. McNaughton, Assistant Secretary of Defense for International Security Affairs.

Way Cleared by Election

No decision was made on these proposals during the long Presidential campaign despite deterioration of the political and military situation in South Vietnam. But as soon as the election was over, two of the State Department's young experts on Asian affairs were known to have prepared a new draft.

This, for the first time, won unanimous agreement among agencies both in Washington and in Saigon.

The December plan proposed that North Vietnam be given indications that there could be a better route to economic viability, to the rice of South Vietnam and to independence from China than the reunification of Vietnam by force.

This alternative to aggression—including trade with the West, increased diplomatic recognition, possible food-for-peace aid, and international-development assistance—was to be made even more attractive by the opening of a low-intensity air war against North Vietnam.

The aim was not to bomb North Vietnam into submission, a high official said, but "to do something we could stop doing to them, in return for equivalent concessions."

The idea was to reply to Hanoi's continuing surreptitious, undeclared ground war against South Vietnam not with tit-for-tat blows set-off only when Americans were injured but with a continuing, surreptitious undeclared war against North Vietnam. Already this was under way in Laos.

The attacks would be neither announced nor officially admitted. The raids, two or three a week, were to start near the 17th Parallel, North Vietnam's border, with South Vietnam. They were to be restricted initially to a few planes—a 24-plane raid is by far the biggest yet employed in Laos—and were to strike at the southern third of North Vietnam, below the 19th Parallel.

The participating South Vietnamese propeller-driven Skyraider fighter-bombers would thus remain beyond the range of Hanoi-based MIG interceptors.

Assurances to Reds

More important, it was said, the 19th-parallel limit would support assurances to Moscow and to Peking that the raids were aimed neither at China nor at the destruction of the Hanoi Government.

This small, semiclandestine type of offensive was favored because of major disadvantages of large-scale, publicized raids. Some of these had been demonstrated by the 64-plane retaliation for the Tonkin Gulf strike in August.

Large-scale, publicly announced raids, it was felt, might provoke Chinese intervention. They would put the Soviet Union on the spot, forcing gestures of solidarity with Hanoi and possibly Peking. They would make it more difficult for North Vietnamese leaders to back down without a loss of prestige.

They would, moreover, place Washington under pressure from its allies and American opinion to enter prematurely into talks—"the wrong conference with the wrong people at the wrong time," in the words of an official here.

Plan Is Revived

Officials maintain that all but the first of these disadvantages have been brought upon Washington by the three February strikes, which involved as many as 160 planes.

It was only after the Feb. 11 raid that the December plan, in the President's bottom drawer for two months, was pulled out.

American commanders in Saigon were instructed to prepare for a continuing aerial offensive, but publicly and with announcements.

Ambassador Maxwell D. Taylor argued for silence, but was overruled by the argument that clandestine raids would be politically unpopular in the United States.

On the other hand, the attack profile prepared in Saigon for White House approval—President Johnson's authorization would be required for each strike—also departed from the December plan by yielding to Air Force preference for a 100-plane raid that would obviate a dangerous second trip to the target.

No Final Approval

Most important, officials say, is the continuing absence of the "diplomatic track" of the December plan. Apparently the President has not yet entirely approved this and last week it was still being reworked in Washington.

The December plan assumed that sooner or later Hanoi would ask for talks, even if only after the raids were increased in intensity, frequency, importance of targets and proximity to the capital.

At that time, direct private talks between Hanoi and Saigon—rather than a big international conference, initially—were to be preferred.

A cease-fire before negotiations was not considered feasible on either side. But Hanoi would be expected to show good faith by accepting, probably tacitly, a progressive reduction in military activity on both sides, similar to the one that paved the way for French-Algerian peace negotiations in March, 1962.

The chief objective of the negotiations, it is reported, would be to get Hanoi to agree to a cease-fire accompanied by the evacuation of Communist guerrillas, as in 1954 and 1955, when 120,000 were moved to the North.

In return, Saigon would agree to a phased reduction of American troops to the original 680-man military-aid mission.

* * *

March 21, 1965

MOSCOW ACCUSES PEKING OF FRAUD

Says Students Who Clashed With Police in Soviet Were Made Heroes of 'Farce'

By HENRY TANNER
Special to The New York Times.

MOSCOW, March 20—The Soviet Union accused Communist China today of fraud and lies in the case of Chinese students involved in clashes with Soviet policemen in front of the United States Embassy here March 4.

Moscow dismissed as an anti-Soviet "propaganda farce" the heroes' welcome given by Peking last Sunday to four students who alleged they had been injured by Soviet policemen. A violent demonstration by foreign students against United States policy in Vietnam was repressed by the policemen and troops.

The latest Soviet denunciations came a day after Communist China condemned the recent Moscow meeting of 19 pro-Soviet Communist parties as an illegal move intended to deepen the schism in the Communist world.

Hsinhua, the Chinese Communist press agency, in the first official comment on the conference, said it had been attended by such "notorious renegades" as the Indian party secretary, S. A. Dange, and "splinter revisionist groups" from other countries.

Crew Members Quoted

The Soviet statement today was in the form of three long dispatches by Tass, the official press agency.

It quoted crew members of the Soviet airliner that carried the four students to Peking as having said that they were in perfect health before they arrived in the Chinese capital but that once there nurses rubbed make-up on their faces to make them look pale and then carried them off on stretchers though they were able to walk.

The second report quoted physicians from the Botkin Hospital here to the effect that one of the students involved simulated "convulsions" and then inflicted a slight wound inside his mouth so he was able to spit blood on the floor.

The third dispatch quoted African and non-Chinese students as having condemned "provocations" by the Chinese.

Previously Moscow reported accusations against the Chinese students by personnel at the hospital.

The Moscow leadership has pledged, the last time during the meeting of the 19 pro-Soviet parties, that it will not resume public polemics against Peking in their dispute over the Kremlin line of peaceful coexistence with capitalist countries.

It has honored this pledge to the extent that its recent attacks on Peking have been confined to the issue of the Chinese attitude in the clash between the Soviet policemen and the Asian students. The attacks did not extend to the ideological conflict.

Another aspect of the dispute within the international Communist movement was reflected in front-page announcements here of the death of Gheorghe Gheorghiu-Dej, Rumanian Communist leader, who had led his regime into a position of independence from Moscow.

A black-bordered box, containing a message of condolence addressed to the Rumanian party by the Soviet leadership, was the only item on the front pages not related to the Soviet spaceship from which a man floated on a tether.

According to custom, there should also have been a large photograph of the deceased leader and a sketch glorifying him. It was thought possible that these had been omitted for lack of room in the newspapers and would be printed shortly.

Some of the leading members of the Soviet Government and party are expected to fly to Bucharest next week for the state funeral of Mr. Gheorghiu-Dej. This will be the first encounter between Soviet and Chinese leaders since Premier Aleksei N. Kosygin's visit to Peking last month.

The death of Mr. Gheorghiu-Dej is not thought to have brought any great change in Soviet-Rumanian relations. Premier Ion Georghe Maurer, second-ranking man in the

Rumanian regime, and other leaders are expected to continue the policy of silent defiance of Moscow.

* * *

April 18, 1965

'WE ARE DELUDING OURSELVES IN VIETNAM'

By HANS J. MORGENTHAU

The address which President Johnson delivered on April 7 at Johns Hopkins University is important for two reasons. On the one hand, the President has shown for the first time a way out of the impasse in which we find ourselves in Vietnam. By agreeing to negotiations without preconditions he has opened the door to negotiations which those preconditions had made impossible from the outset.

By proposing a project for the economic development of Southeast Asia—with North Vietnam a beneficiary and the Soviet Union a supporter—he has implicitly recognized the variety of national interests in the Communist world and the need for varied American responses tailored to those interests. By asking "that the people of South Vietnam be allowed to guide their own country in their own way," he has left all possibilities open for the future evolution of relations between North and South Vietnam.

On the other hand, the President reiterated the intellectual assumptions and policy proposals which brought us to an impasse and which make it impossible to extricate ourselves. The President has linked our involvement in Vietnam with our war of independence and has proclaimed the freedom of all nations as the goal of our foreign policy. He has started from the assumption that there are two Vietnamese nations, one of which has attacked the other, and he sees that attack as an integral part of unlimited Chinese aggression. Consistent with this assumption, the President is willing to negotiate with China and North Vietnam but not with the Vietcong.

Yet we cannot have it both ways. We cannot at the same time embrace these false assumptions and pursue new sound policies. Thus we are faced with a real dilemma. This dilemma is by no means of the President's making.

We are militarily engaged in Vietnam by virtue of a basic principle of our foreign policy that was implicit in the Truman Doctrine of 1947 and was put into practice by John Foster Dulles from 1954 onward. This principle is the military containment of Communism. Containment had its origins in Europe; Dulles applied it to the Middle East and Asia through a series of bilateral and multilateral alliances. Yet what was an outstanding success in Europe turned out to be a dismal failure elsewhere. The reasons for that failure are twofold.

First, the threat that faced the nations of Western Europe in the aftermath of the Second World War was primarily military. It was the threat of the Red Army marching westward. Behind the line of military demarcation of 1945 which the policy of containment declared to be the westernmost limit of the Soviet empire, there was an ancient civilization, only temporarily weak and able to maintain itself against the threat of Communist subversion.

The situation is different in the Middle East and Asia. The threat there is not primarily military but political in nature. Weak governments and societies provide opportunities for Communist subversion. Military containment is irrelevant to that threat and may even be counterproductive. Thus the Baghdad Pact did not protect Egypt from Soviet influence and SEATO has had no bearing on Chinese influence in Indonesia and Pakistan.

Second, and more important, even if China were threatening her neighbors primarily by military means, it would be impossible to contain her by erecting a military wall at the periphery of her empire. For China is, even in her present underdeveloped state, the dominant power in Asia. She is this by virtue of the quality and quantity of her population, her geographic position, her civilization, her past power remembered and her future power anticipated. Anybody who has traveled in Asia with his eyes and ears open must have been impressed by the enormous impact which the resurgence of China has made upon all manner of men, regardless of class and political conviction, from Japan to Pakistan.

The issue China poses is political and cultural predominance. The United States can no more contain Chinese influence in Asia by arming South Vietnam and Thailand than China could contain American influence in the Western Hemisphere by arming, say, Nicaragua and Costa Rica.

If we are convinced that we cannot live with a China predominant on the mainland of Asia, then we must strike at the heart of Chinese power—that is, rather than try to contain the power of China, we must try to destroy that power itself. Thus there is logic on the side of that small group of Americans who are convinced that war between the United States and China is inevitable and that the earlier that war comes, the better will be the chances for the United States to win it.

Yet, while logic is on their side, practical judgment is against them. For while China is obviously no match for the United States in overall power, China is largely immune to the specific types of power in which the superiority of the United States consists—that is nuclear, air and naval power. Certainly, the United States has the power to destroy the nuclear installations and the major industrial and population centers of China, but this destruction would not defeat China; it would only set her development back. To be defeated, China has to be conquered.

Physical conquest would require the deployment of millions of American soldiers on the mainland of Asia. No American military leader has ever advocated a course of action so fraught with incalculable risks, so uncertain of outcome, requiring sacrifices so out of proportion to the interests at stake and the benefits to be expected. President Eisenhower declared on Feb. 10, 1954, that he "could conceive of no greater tragedy than for the United States to become involved in an all-out war in Indochina." General MacArthur, in the Congressional hearings concerning his dismissal and in personal conversation with President

Kennedy, emphatically warned against sending American foot soldiers to the Asian mainland to fight China.

If we do not want to set ourselves goals which cannot be attained with the means we are willing to employ, we must learn to accommodate ourselves to the predominance of China on the Asian mainland. It is instructive to note that those Asian nations which have done so—such as Burma and Cambodia—live peacefully in the shadow of the Chinese giant.

This *modus vivendi,* composed of legal independence and various degrees of actual dependence, has indeed been for more than a millennium the persistent pattern of Chinese predominance on the mainland of Asia. The military conquest of Tibet is the sole exception to that pattern. The military operations at the Indian border do not diverge from it, since their purpose was the establishment of a frontier disputed by both sides.

On the other hand, those Asian nations which have allowed themselves to be transformed into outposts of American military power—such as Laos a few years ago, South Vietnam and Thailand—have become the actual or prospective victims of Communist aggression and subversion. Thus it appears that peripheral military containment is counterproductive. Challenged at its periphery by American military power at its weakest—that is, by the proxy client-states—China or its proxies respond with locally superior military and political power.

In specific terms, accommodation means four things: (1) recognition of the political and cultural predominance of China on the mainland of Asia as a fact of life; (2) liquidation of the peripheral military containment of China; (3) strengthening of the uncommitted nations of Asia by nonmilitary means; (4) assessment of Communist governments in Asia in terms not of Communist doctrine but of their relation to the interests and power of the United States.

In the light of these principles, the alternative to our present policies in Vietnam would be this: a face-saving agreement which would allow us to disengage ourselves militarily in stages spaced in time; restoration of the status quo of the Geneva Agreement of 1954, with special emphasis upon all-Vietnamese elections; cooperation with the Soviet Union in support of a Titoist all-Vietnamese Government, which would be likely to emerge from such elections.

This last point is crucial, for our present policies not only drive Hanoi into the waiting arms of Peking, but also make it very difficult for Moscow to pursue an independent policy. Our interests in Southeast Asia are identical with those of the Soviet Union: to prevent the expansion of the military power of China. But while our present policies invite that expansion, so do they make it impossible for the Soviet Union to join us in preventing it. If we were to reconcile ourselves to the establishment of a Titoist government in all of Vietnam, the Soviet Union could successfully compete with China in claiming credit for it and surreptitiously cooperate with us in maintaining it.

Testing the President's proposals by these standards, one realizes how far they go in meeting them. These proposals do not preclude a return to the Geneva agreement and even assume the existence of a Titoist government in North Vietnam. Nor do they preclude the establishment of a Titoist government for all of Vietnam, provided the people of South Vietnam have freely agreed to it. They also envision the active participation of the Soviet Union in establishing and maintaining a new balance of power in Southeast Asia. On the other hand, the President has flatly rejected a withdrawal "under the cloak of a meaningless agreement." The controlling word is obviously "meaningless," and only the future can tell whether we shall consider any face-saving agreement as "meaningless" regardless of its political context.

However, we are under a psychological compulsion to continue our military presence in South Vietnam as part of the peripheral military containment of China. We have been emboldened in this course of action by the identification of the enemy as "Communist," seeing in every Communist party and regime an extension of hostile Russian or Chinese power. This identification was justified 20 or 15 years ago when Communism still had a monolithic character. Here, as elsewhere, our modes of thought and action have been rendered obsolete by new developments.

It is ironic that this simple juxtaposition of "Communism" and "free world" was erected by John Foster Dulles's crusading moralism into the guiding principle of American foreign policy at a time when the national Communism of Yugoslavia, the neutralism of the third world and the incipient split between the Soviet Union and China were rendering that juxtaposition invalid.

Today, it is belaboring the obvious to say that we are faced not with one monolithic Communism whose uniform hostility must be countered with equally uniform hostility, but with a number of different Communisms whose hostilities, determined by different national interests, vary. In fact, the United States encounters today less hostility from Tito, who is a Communist, than from de Gaulle, who is not.

We can today distinguish four different types of Communism in view of the kind and degree of hostility to the United States they represent: a Communism identified with the Soviet Union—e.g., Poland; a Communism identified with China—e.g., Albania; a Communism that straddles the fence between the Soviet Union and China—e.g., Rumania, and independent Communism—e.g., Yugoslavia. Each of these Communisms must be dealt with in terms of the bearing its foreign policy has upon the interests of the United States in a concrete instance.

It would, of course, be absurd to suggest that the officials responsible for the conduct of American foreign policy are unaware of these distinctions and of the demands they make for discriminating subtlety. Yet it is an obvious fact of experience that these officials are incapable of living up to these demands when they deal with Vietnam.

Thus they maneuver themselves into a position which is antirevolutionary per se and which requires military opposition to revolution wherever it is found in Asia, regardless of how it affects the interests—and how susceptible it is to the power—of the United States. There is a historic precedent for this kind of policy: Metternich's military opposition to liberalism after the Napoleonic Wars, which collapsed in 1848. For better or for worse, we live again in an age of revolution. It is the task of statesmanship not to oppose what cannot be opposed with a chance of success, but to bend it to one's own interests. This is what the President is trying to do with his proposal for the economic development of Southeast Asia.

Why do we support the Saigon Government in the civil war against the Vietcong? Because the Saigon Government is "free" and the Vietcong are "Communist." By containing Vietnamese Communism, we assume that we are really containing the Communism of China.

Yet this assumption is at odds with the historic experience of a millennium and is unsupported by contemporary evidence. China is the hereditary enemy of Vietnam, and Ho Chi Minh will become the leader of a Chinese satellite only if the United States forces him to become one.

Furthermore, Ho Chi Minh, like Tito and unlike the Communist governments of the other states of Eastern Europe, came to power not by courtesy of another Communist nation's victorious army but at the head of a victorious army of his own. He is, then, a natural candidate to become an Asian Tito, and the question we must answer is: How adversely would a Titoist Ho Chi Minh, governing all of Vietnam, affect the interests of the United States? The answer can only be: not at all. One can even maintain the proposition that, far from affecting adversely the interests of the United States, it would be in the interest of the United States if the western periphery of China were ringed by a chain of independent states, though they would, of course, in their policies take due account of the predominance of their powerful neighbor.

The roots of the Vietnamese civil war go back to the very beginning of South Vietnam as an independent state. When President Ngo Dinh Diem took office in 1954, he presided not over a state but over one-half of a country arbitrarily and, in the intentions of all concerned, temporarily severed from the other half. He was generally regarded as a caretaker who would establish the rudiments of an administration until the country was united by nationwide elections to be held in 1956 in accordance with the Geneva accords.

Diem was confronted at home with a number of private armies which were politically, religiously or criminally oriented. To the general surprise, he subdued one after another and created what looked like a viable government. Yet in the process of creating it, he also laid the foundations for the present civil war. He ruthlessly suppressed all opposition, established concentration camps, organized a brutal secret police, closed newspapers and rigged elections. These policies inevitably led to a polarization of the politics of South Vietnam—on one side, Diem's family, surrounded by a Pretorian guard; on the other, the Vietnamese people, backed by the Communists, declaring themselves liberators from foreign domination and internal oppression.

Thus, the possibility of civil war was inherent in the very nature of the Diem regime. It became inevitable after Diem refused to agree to all-Vietnamese elections and, in the face of mounting popular alienation, accentuated the tyrannical aspects of his regime. The South Vietnamese who cherished freedom could not help but oppose him. Threatened by the secret police, they went either abroad or underground where the Communists were waiting for them.

Until the end of last February, the Government of the United States started from the assumption that the war in South Vietnam was a civil war, aided and abetted—but not created—from abroad, and spokesmen for the Government have made time and again the point that the key to winning the war was political and not military and was to be found in South Vietnam itself. It was supposed to lie in transforming the indifference or hostility of the great mass of the South Vietnamese people into positive loyalty to the Government.

To that end, a new theory of warfare called "counterinsurgency" was put into practice. Strategic hamlets were established, massive propaganda campaigns were embarked upon, social and economic measures were at least sporadically taken. But all was to no avail. The mass of the population remained indifferent, if not hostile, and large units of the army ran away or went over to the enemy.

The reasons for this failure are of general significance, for they stem from a deeply ingrained habit of the American mind. We like to think of social problems as technically self-sufficient and susceptible of simple, clear-cut solutions. We tend to think of foreign aid as a kind of self-sufficient, technical economic enterprise subject to the laws of economics and divorced from politics, and of war as a similarly self-sufficient, technical enterprise, to be won as quickly, as cheaply, as thoroughly as possible and divorced from the foreign policy that preceded and is to follow it. Thus our military theoreticians and practitioners conceive of counterinsurgency as though it were just another branch of warfare like artillery or chemical warfare, to be taught in special schools and applied with technical proficiency wherever the occasion arises.

This view derives of course from a complete misconception of the nature of civil war. People fight and die in civil wars because they have a faith which appears to them worth fighting and dying for, and they can be opposed with a chance of success only by people who have at least as strong a faith.

Magsaysay could subdue the Huk rebellion in the Philippines because his charisma, proven in action, aroused a faith superior to that of his opponents. In South Vietnam there is nothing to oppose the faith of the Vietcong and, in consequence, the Saigon Government and we are losing the civil war.

A guerrilla war cannot be won without the active support of the indigenous population, short of the physical extermination of that population. Germany was at least consistent when, during the Second World War, faced with unmanageable guerrilla warfare throughout occupied Europe, she tried to master the situation through a deliberate policy of extermination. The French tried "counterinsurgency" in Algeria and failed; 400,000 French troops fought the guerrillas in Indochina for nine years and failed.

The United States has recognized that it is failing in South Vietnam. But it has drawn from this recognition of failure a most astounding conclusion.

The United States has decided to change the character of the war by unilateral declaration from a South Vietnamese civil war to a war of "foreign aggression." "Aggression from the North: The Record of North Vietnam's Campaign to Conquer South Vietnam" is the title of a white paper published by the Department of State on the last day of February, 1965. While normally foreign and military policy is based upon intelligence—that is, the objective assessment of facts—the process is here reversed: a new policy has been decided upon, and intelligence must provide the facts to justify it.

The United States, stymied in South Vietnam and on the verge of defeat, decided to carry the war to North Vietnam not so much in order to retrieve the fortunes of war as to lay the groundwork for "negotiations from strength." In order to justify that new policy, it was necessary to prove that North Vietnam is the real enemy. It is the white paper's purpose to present that proof.

Let it be said right away that the white paper is a dismal failure. The discrepancy between its assertions and the factual evidence adduced to support them borders on the grotesque. It does nothing to disprove, and tends even to confirm, what until the end of February had been official American doctrine: that the main body of the Vietcong is composed of South Vietnamese and that 80 per cent to 90 per cent of their weapons are of American origin.

This document is most disturbing in that it provides a particularly glaring instance of the tendency to conduct foreign and military policy not on their own merits, but as exercises in public relations. The Government fashions an imaginary world that pleases it, and then comes to believe in the reality of that world and acts as though it were real.

It is for this reason that public officials are so resentful of the reporters assigned to Vietnam and have tried to shut them off from the sources of news and even to silence them. They resent the confrontation of their policies with the facts. Yet the facts are what they are, and they take terrible vengeance on those who disregard them.

However, the white paper is but the latest instance of a delusionary tendency which has led American policy in Vietnam astray in other respects. We call the American troops in Vietnam "advisers" and have assigned them by and large to advisory functions, and we have limited the activities of the marines who have now landed in Vietnam to guarding American installations. We have done this for reasons of public relations, in order to spare ourselves the odium of open belligerency.

There is an ominous similarity between this technique and that applied to the expedition in the Bay of Pigs. We wanted to overthrow Castro, but for reasons of public relations we did not want to do it ourselves. So it was not done at all, and our prestige was damaged far beyond what it would have suffered had we worked openly and single-mindedly for the goal we had set ourselves.

Our very presence in Vietnam is in a sense dictated by considerations of public relations; we are afraid lest our prestige would suffer were we to retreat from an untenable position.

One may ask whether we have gained prestige by being involved in a civil war on the mainland of Asia and by being unable to win it. Would we gain more by being unable to extricate ourselves from it, and by expanding it unilaterally into an international war? Is French prestige lower today than it was 11 years ago when France was fighting in Indochina, or five years ago when she was fighting in Algeria? Does not a great power gain prestige by mustering the wisdom and courage necessary to liquidate a losing enterprise? In other words, is it not the mark of greatness, in circumstances such as these, to be able to afford to be indifferent to one's prestige?

The peripheral military containment of China, the indiscriminate crusade against Communism, counterinsurgency as a technically self-sufficient new branch of warfare, the conception of foreign and military policy as a branch of public relations—they are all misconceptions that conjure up terrible dangers for those who base their policies on them.

One can only hope and pray that the vaunted pragmatism and common sense of the American mind—of which the President's new proposals may well be a manifestation—will act as a corrective upon those misconceptions before they lead us from the blind alley in which we find ourselves today to the rim of the abyss. Beyond the present crisis, however, one must hope that the confrontation between these misconceptions and reality will teach us a long-overdue lesson to rid ourselves of these misconceptions altogether.

Hans J. Morgenthau is Michelson Distinguished Service Professor of Political Science and Modern History at the University of Chicago and serves as a consultant to the State and Defense Departments.

* * *

April 30, 1965

U.S. SENDS AIRBORNE UNITS INTO DOMINICAN REPUBLIC; O.A.S. SUMMONS MINISTERS

2,500 MEN FLY IN

Two Battalions to Aid 1,700 Marines in Anti-Red Move

By TAD SZULC
Special to The New York Times

SANTO DOMINGO, Friday, April 30—United States airborne troops began landing here early today as a further step under President Johnson's policy of using American forces to protect American lives and restore order in the Dominican Republic.

Associated Press Wirephoto

U.S. CITIZENS EVACUATED IN DOMINICAN REPUBLIC: Women and children assisted by U.S. marines prepare to board helicopter near Haiti for the carrier Beker.

The Army airborne troops landed at 12:30 A.M., Eastern daylight time, at San Isidro Air Force Base where the two-day-old Dominican military junta has its headquarters.

[The State Department announced Friday that two battalions of the United States 82d Airborne Division—about 2,500 men—were landing at San Isidro to reinforce 1,700 marines already in the Dominican Republic, The Associated Press reported.]

Quick Action Expected

It was expected that both the marines, which are based in the southern section of the city, and the airborne troops, which were arriving on the eastern bank of the Ozamo River, would enter into action later today. They would support the forces of the Dominican military junta in their attempts to smash a Communist-infiltrated revolt that had already brought heavy casualties.

The hard-pressed military junta was reported last night to have requested direct intervention by the United States to restore law and order to this embattled capital.

A quickly deteriorating civil war situation added to the pressures for intervention.

The marines were ordered here Wednesday to protect the evacuation of Americans and other nationals. More than 500 landed that day, and other landings began yesterday.

Marines were drawn into action already yesterday to repulse a series of rebel sniping raids on the American Embassy. The marines killed six of the snipers.

[Similar sniping attacks were reported by the embassies of El Salvador, Peru, Mexico and Ecuador, The Associated Press reported.]

1,000 Dead Reported

Fighting raged throughout this war-torn city most of the day and an official estimate said that as many as 1,000 persons may have been killed since the outbreak of the revolution last Saturday.

At that time, rebel forces favoring the return to power of the exiled former President, Juan Bosch, deposed the civilian junta that had succeeded him in 1963.

The current three-man military junta, backed by the counter-revolutionary forces of Brig. Gen. Elias Wessin y Wessin, was named Wednesday.

A high-ranking United States Navy officer declared that the function of the marines was not only to protect the continuing evacuation but also "to see that no Communist government is established in the Dominican Republic."

Last night, American sources here described the situation as nearing anarchy. It was in view of this that it appeared that active participation by American troops was required to bolster the junta's efforts to control the rebellion.

In the course of the afternoon, two Vampire jets and a number of P-51 fighters hurled rockets at rebel positions and strafed them in the northern part of Santo Domingo in an effort to hit at their new concentrations.

An attack by the rebel forces on the Ozama Fortress, the headquarters of the riot control police, was reported to have failed. The rebels apparently had attempted to break in to capture the large quantity of weapons stored there.

Earlier in the day, the diplomatic corps, meeting under the chairmanship of the Papal Uuncio, was reported to have expressed satisfaction at the presence of United States Marines here.

The foreign diplomats sought to mediate for a cease-fire. But it appeared impossible to determine who precisely constituted the rebel leadership, and if one existed, whether it indeed exercised full control over the city.

Reports spoke of some executions of civilians and junta troops captured by the rebels. One report said that 20 captured navy men were marched to a prison, lined against a wall and machine-gunned.

Complete Power Failure

Reports from hospitals told of large numbers of injured persons who could not be cared for because of lack of water and medical supplies.

An eyewitness who visited a military hospital told of 90 dying persons, left to their fate with flies on their wounds and doctors and nurses unable to assist them.

With a complete power failure in the city, Santo Domingo was a ghost town.

American sources indicated last night that at least 50 known Communists, sympathizers of Premier Fidel Castro of Cuba or other leftwing extremists, were deeply engaged in the rebellion.

It appeared that these Communists or extreme leftist elements had wrested control of the revolution from democratic elements that had sought the return of former President

Bosch, and turned this movement into what American sources described as an attempt to create a pro-Communist Government here.

Although a number of ranking officers who had been originally involved in the attempt to return to power former President Bosch were still involved in the fighting, it appeared that the situation had reached the point at which they could no longer dissociate themselves from their extremist co-fighters.

One American source said that the situation was one of "a madness of killing" in which ideology played less of a role than the need to go on with a forward thrust that could no longer be arrested.

* * *

June 16, 1965

FULBRIGHT URGES A HOLDING ACTION IN VIETNAM WAR

Says U.S. Must Stay Till Reds Realize Cause Is Hopeless and Agree to Negotiate

WITHDRAWAL IS OPPOSED

Senator Also Rules Out Any Escalation—Sees Need for Concession on Each Side

By E. W. KENWORTHY
Special to The New York Times.

WASHINGTON, June 15—Senator J. W. Fulbright proposed today that the United States conduct a "resolute but restrained" holding action in Vietnam until the Communists see the futility of trying to win a complete military victory and agree to negotiate.

In a Senate speech, the Chairman of the Foreign Relations Committee said a negotiated settlement must involve "major concessions by both sides."

The terms of such a settlement cannot now be foreseen, Mr. Fulbright said, but he suggested that they might include "a return to the Geneva accords of 1954, not just in their 'essentials' but in all their specifications."

Border Called Temporary

The Geneva accords specified that the 17th Parallel, the line dividing North and South Vietnam, was a temporary demarcation and not a national boundary. They also provided for unification of the two regions after elections to have been held in 1956.

Former President Ngo Dinh Diem of South Vietnam, with the support of the United States, refused to hold elections at that time because of a well-founded fear that the popularity of Ho Chi Minh, the North Vietnamese leader, would secure a victory for the Communists.

[In Saigon a Vietcong terrorist bomb exploded at the civilian airport terminal Wednesday morning. At least 32 persons were wounded, including 20 United States servicemen.]

Opposed to Withdrawal

Senator Fulbright also said that he was equally opposed to unconditional withdrawal of American forces and to escalation of the war.

Unconditional withdrawal, the Arkansas Democrat said, would have "disastrous consequences" extending beyond South Vietnam. He said it would "betray our obligation to a country we promised to defend," destroy the credibility of other American guarantees and encourage Peking to believe that guerrilla warfare was "a relatively safe and inexpensive way of expanding Communist power."

On the other hand, Mr. Fulbright said, it is now apparent that the forces of South Vietnam and the United States can win a complete victory only "at a cost far exceeding the requirements of our interest and honor."

The bombing of North Vietnam has failed to weaken the Vietcong's war-making capacity, the Senator said, and further escalation would invite the intervention of a large number of North Vietnamese troops and draw the United States into either a jungle war or an expanded air war, with the attendant risks of massive intervention by the Chinese and general nuclear war.

In this situation, Mr. Fulbright said, the United States must sustain the South Vietnamese Army "so as to persuade the Communists that Saigon cannot be crushed and that the United States will not be driven from South Vietnam."

'Reasonable Alternative' Urged

At the same time, despite repeated Communist rejections of President Johnson's offer of unconditional negotiations, the United States "must continue to offer the Communists a reasonable and attractive alternative to military victory," Mr. Fulbright declared.

Mr. Fulbright's speech aroused considerable interest here for two reasons. First, he has made no secret of his fears that President Johnson would be driven by the pressure of events, and the urgings of his military advisers, into escalating the war. Second, Mr. Fulbright had a long conversation with the President yesterday on the Vietnam situation.

Resistance to Pressure

The Senator was said to be considerably heartened by what Mr. Johnson told him about the resistance he and Secretary of Defense Robert S. McNamara were putting up to the pressures from the Pentagon and some parts of the State Department for expanding the war.

The President, according to informed sources, told Mr. Fulbright that it would be helpful if he made a speech emphasizing that the Administration was committed to the goal of ending the war as soon as possible by negotiations without preconditions.

The President believes that much of the criticism directed at his Vietnam policy is unjustified and that many of the critics, even in the academic community, are not sufficiently informed on the lengths to which the United States has gone to induce Hanoi, Peking and Moscow to agree to negotiations.

Republicans and Democrats alike are divided on Vietnam policy. Among those who have shared, Mr. Fulbright's misgivings are Senators George McGovern of South Dakota, Albert Gore of Tennessee and Frank Church of Idaho, all Democrats, and Senators John Sherman Cooper of Kentucky, Jacob K. Javits of New York and George Aiken of Vermont, Republicans.

Two other Democratic Senators, Wayne Morse of Oregon and Ernest Gruening of Alaska, have been the most outspoken critics. Both have repeatedly called on the President to take the conflict to the United Nations.

In a speech today, Mr. Gruening said that the President's visit to San Francisco June 26 for the 20 anniversary of the founding of the United Nations would provide "a dramatic opportunity to revitalize the sagging United Nations and to help solve our dilemma in Vietnam."

Mr. Johnson should use the occasion, Mr. Gruening said, "to fulfill the pledge of the United States when it signed the Charter to use the peace-keeping machinery of the United Nations and to foresake unilateral action."

Mr. Morse and Mr. Gruening got support from an unexpected quarter today when Senator A. Willis Robertson, Democrat of Virginia, said that, despite past rebuffs to U Thant by Peking and Hanoi, "we would have nothing to lose by taking the issue of North Vietnamese aggression to the United Nations."

* * *

January 6, 1966

U.S. IS REPORTED OFFERING TO EXTEND VIETNAM LULL

By HEDRICK SMITH

Special to The New York Times.

CAIRO, Jan. 5—United States envoys have told neutralist leaders that Washington is ready to extend indefinitely the pause in the bombings of North Vietnam if Hanoi will respond with a gesture of peace, diplomatic sources said today.

The diplomatic sources quoted Ambassador at Large W. Averell Harriman, who conferred last night with President Gamel Abdel Nasser, as having said that the most important gesture would be for Hanoi to stop the infiltration of troops into South Vietnam.

Mr. Harriman, departing on the next leg of his peace mission, declined to indicate how long the bombing pause would be continued.

"There has to be a response from North Vietnam indicating their desire for peace," he said at the airport. "Any result from the bombing pause will have to come from North Vietnam."

Informed sources said that Mr. Harriman had asked President Nasser to undertake new diplomatic soundings with Communist and other powers and that President Nasser had agreed largely because the suspension had convinced him that President Johnson genuinely desired peace in Vietnam.

"In our discussions President Nasser has shown considerable interest in Vietnam and offered to be helpful," Mr. Harriman said. He said discussions here had been "constructive and contributed to the friendship" between the United States and the United Arab Republic.

The disclosure that the United Arab Republic would put out new peace feelers in North Vietnam, Communist China, the Soviet Union and other countries was made this morning in the newspaper Al Ahram, which often presents the Government's views.

Officials said contacts would begin tomorrow but emphasized that the new initiatives should not be described as mediation.

In a comment that was considered to be a reflection of President Nasser's thinking, Al Ahram said that it would be "a hopeful sign that the suspension of American air raids on North Vietnam should continue and that there should be no escalation of the war by increasing the number of American troops involved there."

Jan. 20-24 Fine Prospect

Neutral diplomats reported that both President Nasser and President Tito of Yugoslavia had been impressed with the sincerity of President Johnson's latest efforts for peace.

These diplomats said that the forthcoming Vietnamese Lunar New Year holiday, when the Vietcong have proposed a four-day cease-fire, appeared to be the most suitable time for Hanoi, with minimum loss of face, to stop sending fresh troops into South Vietnam. The holiday will be celebrated Jan. 20 to Jan. 24. The diplomats emphasized that so far there had been no indication that Hanoi was prepared to take any such step toward peace.

Ambassador Harriman, who arrived here yesterday after visiting Poland, Yugoslavia, India, Pakistan and Iran, is going to Thailand and Japan.

According to diplomatic informants, Mr. Harriman encouraged several countries to put forth peace feelers but the Indian and Yugoslav Governments recommended that the approaches be made by Cairo because it is on a better footing with Hanoi and Peking.

Cairo is one of few world capitals with resident representatives of Communist China, North Vietnam and the Vietcong as well as of the Soviet Union and Western powers. This makes it a natural channel for diplomatic contacts.

Action for U.S. Captives Sought

This position was pointed up today by a report that the United States had asked Cairo to act as protecting power for American military prisoners in North Vietnam. Cairo is checking whether this arrangement is acceptable to Hanoi before replying.

The quickness of Cairo's agreement to check with the North Vietnamese has been interpreted as indication that President Nasser is favorably disposed to undertake the task.

Well-placed informants said that the arrangement, if accepted, would not cover any American prisoners held by the Vietcong.

The Pentagon lists "25 Army and Air Force" men as detained by all enemy forces in Vietnam. The Marines and Navy have no such category, just listing all unaccounted-for men as missing. The total "missing" for all services is 149.

Last spring President Nasser was reluctant to be drawn into a role as an intermediary in the Vietnamese conflict because he was reported to have regarded the prospects for peace as poor.

* * *

January 8, 1966

DIRKSEN BREAKS WITH PRESIDENT ON VIETNAM WAR

Calls for Full Military Victory—
Mansfield Sees All-Out Conflict if Talks Fail

By E. W. KENWORTHY
Special to The New York Times.

WASHINGTON, Jan. 7—Senator Everett McKinley Dirksen of Illinois, in his first break with President Johnson on the Vietnam war, said today that the United States should achieve a complete military victory before entering peace negotiations.

An opposite view of the Vietnam war was given by Senator Mike Mansfield of Montana, the Democratic leader. In a report on a global tour he had taken, which included Vietnam, he said that negotiations at this time, "if they are accompanied by a cease-fire and stand-fast, would serve to stabilize the situation" in South Vietnam.

He warned, however, that if peace efforts failed the war could escalate until it became a "general war on the Asian mainland."

MacArthur Quoted

Mr. Mansfield's report was drafted before President Johnson launched his global peace offensive in an effort to bring about negotiations to end the Vietnam war. The Senator said in his report that the chances of a negotiated settlement were "very slim."

Mr. Dirksen, the Senate Republican leader, told reporters: "When MacArthur said, 'There is no substitute for victory,' he planted a phrase that is never to be forgotten."

The Illinois Senator was referring to a remark by the late General of the Army Douglas MacArthur in a letter to Representative Joseph W. Martin Jr., Republican of Massachusetts, in April 1951. The general was alluding to his opposition to orders barring him from extending the Korean war outside Korea, in order to get at the Chinese Communists, who had intervened on the side of North Korea.

When Mr. Dirksen was asked whether he did not subscribe to President Johnson's reiterated offer of "negotiations without prior conditions" on Vietnam, he replied: "How much negotiations are you going to get unless they are beaten?"

Senator Dirksen defined victory as "when the Vietcong lay down their arms."

"We must have capitulation before there is peace," he said.

Senator Dirksen's call for "victory before negotiations" immediately aroused speculation that the Republicans were getting ready to make Vietnam a campaign issue in this Congressional election year, as they made Korea an issue in the Presidential elections of 1952.

The first intimations that Mr. Dirksen was preparing to make a political issue of the war came in a speech last Dec. 10 to a party rally in Des Moines, Iowa, when he said: "Far too many young Americans are coming back from Vietnam in wooden caskets. Peace is the real issue."

Offer Not Questioned Before

But this was interpreted as indicating he was simply preparing to join the House Republican leaders, Gerald R. Ford of Michigan and Melvin R. Laird of Wisconsin in their repeated calls for intensified air bombing of North Vietnam and less investment of American ground forces in the war.

Never before has Mr. Dirksen questioned the President's offer of unconditional negotiations, first put forward in his speech last April at Johns Hopkins University.

Nor has Mr. Dirksen criticized the President's conduct of the war. In fact, last February, he noted:

"President Johnson has been disturbed at his own party leaders' questioning his action in Vietnam. I was the only one who would hold up his hand in Congress and in the media in favor of his action on the Vietnam situation."

And last summer, when Mr. Ford, the House minority leader, proposed expansion of the bombing to North Vietnam and criticized Democrats who urged a negotiated settlement, Mr. Dirksen took indirect issue with him, saying:

"We try to avoid military judgment here. We are not trying to run the war. We pray that the national security decisions of the President may always be wise."

Blockade Advocated

Yet today, at a news conference, Mr. Dirksen advocated a blockade of North Vietnam and apparently advocated air bombing of the port of Haiphong if the Vietcong continued the fighting.

He said he would not sit in Judgment on how long the pause in the bombing should continue. But, he said, there is talk of putting 400,000 American troops into South Vietnam. He then raised the question of "how much of Hanoi may be regarded as an open city" and how much a military center.

"Haiphong is different," he said, pointing out that it is a port of entry for war supplies for the North Vietnamese and Vietcong and that its shallow canal, which must be constantly dredged, makes it highly vulnerable.

He was extremely critical of allies of the United States who continue shipments to North Vietnam. He said the United States had committed itself to defend its North Atlantic allies. "What help has de Gaulle been?" He asked, "and Britain and Turkey? That's great cooperation."

The blockading of Haiphong "is the just, proper and necessary thing to do," he said.

There comes a time, he added, "when you don't care whether you make your allies mad."

It was believed that Mr. Dirksen's statements would cause deep distress at the White House and State Department, coming as they did at the very climax of President Johnson's "peace offensive" in capitals around the world.

W. Averell Harriman, his principal envoy, is in Japan, where there is great concern about further escalation of the war. G. Mennen Williams, Assistant Secretary of State for African Affairs, returned from his African trip tonight. He will see President Johnson tomorrow.

Senator Mansfield may also be expected to be concerned by Mr. Dirksen's call for complete victory. Mr. Mansfield has always doubted the effectiveness of bombing of North Vietnam.

Mr. Mansfield said today that both sides were using the pause in the bombing to build up forces and supplies. He added that if the infiltration from North Vietnam continued at the present rate, the United States would have to land additional troops in South Vietnam.

Unlike Mr. Dirksen, he thought the sealing off of Haiphong would not accomplish "anything effective," because he believed North Vietnam was getting much more material by railroad from Communist China than through Haiphong.

Altogether, the report by Senator Mansfield presented a gloomy picture of the military, political and economic situation within South Vietnam, it offered slight hope that other nations in Asia, with the exception of Korea, would provide much more than moral support, and very little of that, to the United States effort in South Vietnam.

Despite the fact that United States troops in Vietnam have been increased from 10,000 in 1962 to 170,000 last December, the Mansfield report said that "the overall control of the country remains about the same as it was at the beginning of 1965," when there were fewer than 30,000 American troops in the embattled country.

About 22 per cent of the population is still under Vietcong control and 18 per cent more inhabits "contested areas," the report said.

The report said the Government of Air Vice Marshal Nguyen Cao Ky, which is made up largely of military officers, was "young and hopeful" but had "little knowledge of politics." The new leaders speak of their intention to form a representative democracy, beginning with a consultative assembly to prepare a constitution, and a referendum on the constitution and elections for a legislative body by the end of 1967, providing that elections by that time can be held in two-thirds of the country without intimidation, Mr. Mansfield reported.

But his report noted that if an election were held at the present time, not more than 25 per cent of the villages under Government control would be free of intimidation. The report suggested that the situation was not likely to improve within two years.

The ravages of war and terrorism, the report said, have taken a heavy toll of productive capacity. Despite a resources control program instituted by the South Vietnamese Government, the Vietcong have been able to restrict the flow of food into the cities or make the peasants pay a tax for their movement. Consequently, Saigon lives largely "on the sufferance of the Vietcong," it said.

The report says that Asian countries nearest to Vietnam saw in the escalation of the war "a heightened danger of a spillover into their territory."

The fighting within Laos "is now a closely interwoven part of the Vietnamese struggles," Senator Mansfield reported. As for Cambodia, he wrote, the overwhelming concern is "the preservation of its national integrity."

Mr. Mansfield reported that Burma, the Philippines and Japan were all preoccupied with their internal problems and wanted to avoid "direct involvement in the Vietnamese conflict."

No Quick Solution Seen

Even Korea, he said, which had 20,000 soldiers and marines in South Vietnam, is presented with "new problems of military balance" along the 38th Parallel, the dividing line with North Korea, as a result of withdrawal of forces for Vietnam.

Mr. Mansfield apparently agrees with Senator George Aiken, Republican of Vermont, who accompanied him on the tour, that "Communist China is winning this war."

The Chinese Communists have not introduced their own manpower, he says, though they may have "begun to make preliminary preparations for that eventuality."

So far Peking takes the view, he suggests, that intervention is not necessary since the Vietcong are winning with the help of North Vietnam and the United States will become discouraged as its casualties mount.

Mr. Mansfield sees no immediate solution to the problem, either militarily or through negotiations if they occur.

The introduction of large United States forces has blunted but not turned back the Vietcong drive, and lines remain substantially as they were when Washington stepped up its commitment, he reported. All that is changed, he said, is the scope and intensity of the battle.

Any hope of negotiations, Mr. Mansfield believes, is largely dependent on the initiatives of the combatants and not third parties.

Mr. Mansfield was also accompanied on his tour by Senator Edmund S. Muskie, Democrat of Maine, Daniel B. Inouye, Democrat of Hawaii, and J. Caleb Boggs, Republican of Delaware.

* * *

January 9, 1966

8,000 G.I.'S OPEN BIGGEST ATTACK OF VIETNAM WAR

Australians Join in a Drive on Vietcong 20 Miles Northwest of Saigon

HEAVY GUNS IN ACTION

Start of Operation Withheld From South Vietnamese to Bar a Leak to Foe

By United Press International

SAIGON, Sunday, Jan. 9—United States forces have launched their largest offensive operation of the Vietnam war to sweep clean the Communists' Hobo Forest stronghold 20 miles north-northwest of Saigon, military officials said today.

About 8,000 American troops, aided by Australians and New Zealanders, converged on the Vietcong's Iron Triangle yesterday morning in the wake of a strike by B-52 strategic bombers and an artillery barrage unprecedented in this war.

Military sources said the operation was kept secret from the South Vietnamese Army command and the Government for fear of an intelligence leak.

Headquarters of the South Vietnamese Army's III Corps here is known to be riddled with Vietcong agents. For that reason word of the operation was confined to the allies involved. It was believed to have been the first such operation kept secret from the South Vietnamese command.

Copters Take in Troops

American military authorities at the forward command post at Trunglay, in Haunghia Province, 24 miles northwest of Saigon, said at least five United States Army helicopters were saddled with machinegun fire as elements of the First Infantry Division and the 173d Airborne Brigade were lifted into landing zones both north and south of the forest.

Artillerymen said that never in the history of the Vietnamese war had so much artillery been used to soften up suspected Vietcong positions.

Howitzers and cannons of all sizes, ranging up to 8-inch guns, began pounding the landing zones 90 minutes before the 100 troop-carrying helicopters appeared from the directions of Bienhoa and Laikhe, the bases of the 173d Airborne Brigade and the First Infantry Division's Third Brigade.

After a brief but furious skirmish with United States armored elements, the Vietcong withdrew into the forest. The heavy machineguns of the American armored vehicles chewed down small trees as the United States troops returned the fire of the retreating Vietcong.

Three of the damaged helicopters flew out under their own power, according to Maj. Gen. Jonathan N. Seaman, commander of the First Division, who has over-all control of the operation.

The remaining two copters and their crews were lifted out of the operation area by huge H-37 helicopters.

Most of the battalions thrown into the offensive—600 to 800 men in each battalion—had clashes with the Vietcong.

The Australians briefly were pinned down by more than 100 Communist troops, who raked the Australians' landing zone with fire from three sides.

With artillery and air support, however, the Australians managed to overcome Vietcong resistance to their airborne landing. The mangled bodies of at least six Vietcong were found when Australians drove the Communists from their defensive trenches and foxholes.

The Australians also reported capturing about 5,000 rounds of ammunition, along with 12 machinegun barrels, 35 grenades, three individual weapons and a quantity of assorted military equipment.

United States and Australian casualties were light throughout the first day of the operation, according to the military command.

Combined armored-infantry elements were attempting to trap the Vietcong in a giant horseshoe. The points of the horseshoe were to extend to the Saigon River. The eastern boundary was being patrolled by both fighter-bombers and rocket-firing helicopters to prevent the trapped Communist units from escaping.

The target of the massive offensive, the Hobo or Anson Forest, lies astride the major jungle trail connecting the Vietcong's Zones C and D. American military sources said the forest region is the operational base of at least a battalion of Communist troops. Vietcong regiments of 1,500 to 2,000 men have been known to be in the region from time to time.

More than 1,000 Vietnamese villagers herded about 500 head of livestock out of the general area of the attack. Peasants stoically squatted in newly harvested rice paddies around Trunglap while artillery rounds whistled overhead and fighter-bombers pounded the forest. Trunglap is the site of the Saigon Government's Ranger training center.

VIETCONG SLAY MISSIONARY

Special to The New York Times.

SAIGON, Jan. 8—Terrorists killed a British missionary this morning 380 miles northeast of Saigon and exploded a bomb tonight near a floating restaurant, one of the capital's landmarks.

The bomb attack, at the My Canh Cafe, slightly injured a South Vietnamese policeman and two South Vietnamese civilians on the street. It did not harm the 60-odd diners on board.

Last June 25, the My Canh was attacked with two claymore mines, devices that hurl half-inch steel balls in directed arcs; 42 persons were killed and 80 injured then.

The missionary, 31-year-old John Haywood of Birmingham, England, was machine-gunned about 8 A.M. on a highway between the cities of Danang and Hue. He had been following a South Vietnamese civilian rice convoy in his blue microbus when Vietcong guerrillas ambushed the column and halted it by detonating a mine under the leading truck.

A missionary for the World Wide Evangelization Crusade, Mr. Haywood had been in South Vietnam for three years and had been in charge of a Danang leper colony devoted to the treatment of terminal leprosy cases.

The My Canh, moored in the Saigon River, is connected by a gangplank to a busy pier in the downtown area. Near the gangplank stands a small green kiosk that during the day sells souvenirs, curios, cigarettes and other articles.

This evening a Vietnamese woman approached the area and suddenly put down a paper sack behind the kiosk. A policeman immediately sounded an alarm on his whistle and the woman fled.

* * *

February 1, 1966

JOHNSON ASKS U.N. TO SUMMON A VIETNAM PEACE CONFERENCE AS BOMBING IN NORTH RESUMES

U. S. SCORES REDS

President and Rusk Term Response to Offers Negative

By TOM WICKER
Special to The New York Times.

WASHINGTON, Jan. 31—President Johnson announced today the resumption of the bombing of North Vietnam, but said he would ask the United Nations Security Council to help in a continuing "pursuit of peace."

That pursuit, the President insisted in a seven-and-one-half-minute nationally televised address, would be "as determined and as unremitting as the pressure of our military strength on the field of battle."

Mr. Johnson spoke at 10 A.M., several hours after American warplanes carried out the first of the new series of attacks. Reports from Saigon indicated that they struck roads, bridges and other key points on the North Vietnamese supply routes to the south.

'Denunciation and Rejection'

The new attacks came after 37 days of a pause in the American bombing, which began last February. During the pause, Mr. Johnson directed a world-wide diplomatic "peace offensive" that he said had met with "understanding and support" everywhere but in Hanoi and Peking.

"From those two capitals," he said, "have come only denunciation and rejection."

Mr. Johnson's announcement was followed by a news conference by Secretary of State Dean Rusk, and by a concentrated effort by high Administration officials to explain the President's decision and to win public support for it.

Late today, Democratic Congressional leaders met with the President at the White House.

Bombing Again Limited

From these activities the strong impression emerged that a primary reason for the resumption of bombing was the fear here of a "miscalculation" by Hanoi in interpreting the pause as a sign of weakness and anxiety to quit the war.

Government officials said the bombing of North Vietnam would be limited to military targets, as in the past, but that every other aspect of the American war effort would be intensified.

Mr. Johnson and Mr. Rusk emphasized also, however, that the bombing was being resumed because there had been no reply from Hanoi to the peace offensive, either through diplomatic channels or by slackening activity on the battlefield.

Mr. Rusk said the only indications from Hanoi had been "negative, harsh and unyielding." In the war itself, he said, Vietcong activity was at approximately the levels preceding the pause and in the first week of the pause the number of incidents had reached an all-time high.

Official sources said there had been 745 "incidents" in that week alone.

In New York, Arthur J. Goldberg, the United States delegate to the United Nations, requested an immediate meeting of the Security Council. He will propose a resolution calling upon the Council to seek an international conference on Vietnam.

The Council will meet at 10 A.M. tomorrow, it was announced late today.

Few here expressed optimism that much could be accomplished through the United Nations. For one thing, the Soviet Union has a veto in the Security Council and officials said there had been no indication that the Russians were prepared to go along with an American resolution on Vietnam.

Mr. Rusk said the time had come to seek United Nations action because "quiet diplomacy" had not "yielded any result."

In the past, he said, the United States had believed that United Nations debate might "get in the way of private explorations of the possibility of peace."

Quiet diplomacy would not now be abandoned, he said, "but nevertheless there is not the same obstacle to a full discussion in the Security Council as was apparent, say, four or five weeks ago."

Hope for Private Talks

Some high officials said that one hope for the United Nations discussions was that it might lead to unofficial conversations between diplomats that might prove helpful.

Mr. Rusk said the Council's attention would be called to the appeal of Pope Paul VI for arbitration by neutral nations.

"I am not at all sure that His Holiness was talking in the most technical sense when he used the term 'arbitration,' " Mr. Rusk said. "But a role for neutral countries to explore the possibilities of peace would be entirely agreeable and welcome by the United States."

Arbitration usually refers to a procedure by which impartial arbiters of a dispute make recommendations for its settlement, with the understanding that the disputing parties will accept them.

Mr. Johnson made it plain that he was not abandoning his peace efforts.

"The end of the pause," he said, "does not mean the end of our own pursuit of peace. That pursuit will be as determined and as unremitting as the pressure of our military strength on the field of battle."

All the "processes of diplomacy," Mr. Rusk added, "will continue in full operation, publicly and privately, directly and indirectly, in order that any possibility of peace can be explored and tested."

It could not be determined whether the resumption of bombing meant that Mr. Johnson and his advisers had decided upon a broad expansion of the war, including a major build-up of ground forces in South Vietnam. The United States already has about 200,000 troops in that country, many of them in combat with Vietcong and North Vietnamese forces.

Selective Bombing

First indications, confirmed by the statements of officials, were that the resumption of the bombing would be confined, as before, to careful and controlled attacks on supply routes and other military targets.

Mr. Rusk said that from the military point of view the resumption meant that "we are approximately where we were in December before the suspension occurred."

Mr. Johnson specified that the planes had struck only "lines of supply" from North Vietnam to South Vietnam and said "our air strikes on North Vietnam from the beginning have been aimed at military targets and controlled with great care. Those who direct and supply the aggression have no claim to immunity from military reply."

High officials said, however, that these statements could not be taken as commitments that the raids would never be extended to other targets—industrial complexes, for instance, or such population centers as Hanoi. Nor had another pause in the bombing been precluded, they said, if the situation warranted it.

Government officials indicated that other aspects of the war would be intensified and that more combat troops would be sent to South Vietnam.

In general, the resumption of the bombing was taken here to indicate that hopes for a slackening of the war or for a diplomatic settlement have all but vanished and that the Johnson Administration now is preparing for a lengthy military contest.

"It is possible," Mr. Rusk said, "that one of the obstacles to peace has been a failure on the part of Hanoi to understand that the United States will in fact meet its commitment. The way to shorten this war is to make it very clear to Hanoi that the course upon which they are embarked is futile and that if they are prepared to sit down and talk like reasonable men, answers can be found which will relieve both themselves and their brothers in the South of the violence, of which there has been more than enough."

Other high officials said that Hanoi's unwillingness to reply favorably to the peace offensive meant that the North Vietnamese had not yet concluded that they could not win on the battlefield and impose a Communist regime on South Vietnam.

In this view, the National Liberation Front, the parent organization of the Vietcong, was believed to be even more militantly opposed to negotiating a settlement than Hanoi itself.

These officials said it was important that both Hanoi and the National Liberation Front should be convinced that they could not win militarily, something that can only be accomplished, they believe, by countering military force.

Mr. Rusk put it this way:

"If they are relying upon a military victory in the South, they must abandon that hope. If they are relying on international opinion to divert the United States from its commitment, they must recognize that the world community does not support their aggression. If they are relying upon domestic differences among us to save their cause, they must understand that that will not occur."

Peace Pursuit Continues

This was a primary reason high officials advanced for coupling the approach to the United Nations with a resumption of the bombing. They said American determination to pursue the war had to be demonstrated even though the "pursuit of peace" continued.

It also appeared likely that the Administration hoped that the United Nations move would help to hold down an expected blast of criticism from many nations at the resumption of the bombing, which a number of governments had sought to delay.

Mr. Johnson described the apparent failure of his "peace offensive" as follows:

"In these 37 days, the efforts of our allies have been rebuffed. The efforts of neutral nations have come to nothing. We have sought without success to learn of any response to efforts made by the governments of Eastern Europe. There has been no answer to the enlightened efforts of the Vatican. Our own direct private approaches have all been in vain. The answer of Hanoi to all is the answer that was published three days ago—they persist in aggression and they insist on the surrender of South Vietnam to the Communists.

"It is therefore very plain that there is no readiness for peace in that regime today."

Mr. Rusk added that Hanoi had been informed "at an early stage" that the suspension of bombing might be extended if North Vietnam "would reciprocate by making a serious contribution toward peace."

But no such contribution had been made, he said, either through diplomatic suggestion or a slackening of battlefield activity.

* * *

February 18, 1966

TAYLOR ASSERTS A 'LIMITED' WAR IS INTENT OF U.S.

Ex-Chairman of Joint Chiefs Refuses to Describe Scope of Vietnam Commitment

TESTIMONY IS TELEVISED

General Tells Senate Panel Troop Needs Are Not an 'Endless Requirement'

By E. W. KENWORTHY
Special to The New York Times.

WASHINGTON, Feb. 17—Gen. Maxwell D. Taylor repeatedly assured the Senate Foreign Relations Committee today that the Administration intended to wage only a "limited" war in Vietnam, but he refused to be pinned down on the limits.

Testifying in the large, ornate caucus room of the old Senate Office Building before batteries of television cameras, the former chairman of the Joint Chiefs of Staff and Ambassador to Saigon said that the Administration's strategy was limited in objective, in geographical scope, in weapons and forces employed and in targets attacked.

Troop Information Sought

But what the committee members wanted particularly to know was the limit that the Administration intended to put on the investment of United States ground forces, and whether there was any accuracy to reports that the present force of 205,000 men might be doubled or tripled.

Senator Albert Gore, Democrat of Tennessee, said that as the war had widened, so had the gap between the Executive and the Congress and the people. One of the troubles, Mr. Gore said, had been "the creeping escalation."

Most members of Congress, Mr. Gore went on, were "in the dark," and he cited a recent prediction by Senator John Stennis, Mississippi Democrat, who is chairman of the Preparedness Subcommittee, that American ground forces would reach 600,000 men.

'The Highest Authority'

He noted that Senator Stuart Symington, Missouri Democrat, a member of the Armed Services Committee, had said that this figure did not originate with Mr. Stennis but "came from the highest military authority in a hearing before the Armed Services Committee."

"What is the limit of forces you have in mind?" Senator Gore asked General Taylor, who is now an adviser to President Johnson.

The general declined to state a figure. But he insisted that the "growing requirement" would not be "an endless requirement in an open-ended war."

General Taylor gave three reasons for rejecting the estimate of Senator Mike Mansfield, Democrat of Montana, the majority leader, in his recent report, that the conflict might well become "open-ended" and that all mainland Southeast Asia "cannot be ruled out as a potential battlefield."

First, the General said, the United States was not setting as an objective the occupation of all of South Vietnam or the hunting down of every guerrilla, but the securing of "a high proportion of the population" through attacks on "main line enemy units."

Second, he said, there was "a finite number" of enemy troops which could be sustained by North Vietnam under air attacks on supply lines and increased ground attacks on their units. He said he wished he knew "where that ceiling is," but the "data on Vietcong logistics are too uncertain to permit precision."

Third, the general questioned whether the enemy could long find replacements for losses now estimated at 17,000 a month. These, he said, were made up of an estimated 3,800 killed, 11,000 wounded and 2,400 defections.

General Taylor was the third Administration witness and the first with distinguished military credentials. The other two were David E. Bell, Director of Foreign Aid, and Secretary of State Dean Rusk, who will appear again tomorrow.

President an Interested Viewer

Today's hearings, like those last week when Lieut. Gen. James M. Gavin and George F. Kennan, former Ambassador to Moscow, expressed concern over the Administration's policy, were broadcast over national television. One of the most interested viewers was President Johnson.

The chamber was crowded, with spectators lining the walls three deep. Several wives of Senators and high Administration officials were on hand, including Mrs. Robert S. McNamara, wife of the Secretary of Defense, and Mrs. J. W. Fulbright, wife of the committee chairman.

There were many college-age spectators and, judging from one short burst of applause that Mr. Fulbright quickly silenced, the "doves" outnumbered the "hawks."

The applause came during an exchange between the general and Senator Wayne Morse, Democrat of Oregon, who has been a severe critic of Vietnam policy for the last four years.

The exchange was occasioned by a statement by General Taylor that the leaders of North Vietnam still hoped for "some kind of victory in the South," apparently because they were convinced the United States could be detached from support of South Vietnam.

Reference to Paris

The general said that these leaders had not forgotten that they had "won more in Paris than in [the battle of] Dienbienphu [in 1954] and believed that the Vietcong might be as fortunate in Washington."

Senator Morse reminded the general that in the spring of 1954 Pierre Mendes-France ran for Premier on a pledge to bring the Vietnam war to an end, and that he regarded his election as a mandate to carry out the pledge and that he did so at the Geneva conference.

Associated Press Wirephotos

Senator J. W. Fulbright, left, Arkansas Democrat who is chairman of the Foreign Relations Committee, and Senator Wayne Morse, center, Oregon Democrat, listen to Gen. Maxwell D. Taylor, right, as he explains Administration's policy in Vietnam. Senator Morse, a severe critic of the policy, engaged in sharp exchange with General Taylor.

"Now," the Senator said to the general, "when the people of a country demonstrate an opposition to a foreign policy of that country and make clear that they wanted the Indochina war stopped, do you interpret that as a weakness on the home front?"

The general said that he would regard it as weakness "if one attaches importance to success in Southeast Asia," but he conceded the right of a people to change a policy of their government.

Mr. Morse then said that he thought the American people, before too long, "will repudiate our war in Southeast Asia."

"That, of course, is good news to Hanoi, Senator," the general replied.

Smear Is Charged

"I know that is the smear artist that you militarists give to those of us who have honest differences of opinion, but I don't intend to get down in the gutter with you and engage in that kind of debate," Mr. Morse snapped.

"All I am asking is if the people decided that this war should be stopped in Southeast Asia, are you going to take the position that is weakness on the home front in a democracy?"

"I would feel that our people were badly misguided and did not understand the consequences of such a disaster," General Taylor said, his temper visibly rising.

"Well, we agree on one thing, that they can be badly misguided," Mr. Morse said, "and you and the President in my judgment have been misguiding them for a long time in this war."

It was then that the applause broke out. Mr. Fulbright shut it off with his gavel and reminded the spectators that they were guests of the committee and would remain silent.

Other Senators, however, were plainly upset by the general's implication that the Communists were counting on winning more of the war in Washington than on the battlefield. And some of them did not think much of the general's history.

Questioned by Aiken

Senator George D. Aiken, Republican of Vermont, asked him if he really thought that the French would have won in Vietnam "had it not been for the weakening will in Paris."

"I doubt it, Senator," the general replied. "I think colonialism was doomed in Vietnam, but I think they could have lasted longer and could have had better terms."

Later, Senator Fulbright asked the general whether he was intimating "a reflection upon the validity on the value of these hearings" by suggesting the war might be lost in Washington.

General Taylor said, no, he was simply expressing a personal feeling about the hopes of Hanoi's leaders "that the same kind of situation will arise here" as in France.

Senator Russell Long, who has been the Administration's most impassioned defender, in two floor speeches yesterday and in the committee today also drew an analogy between criticism of the Indochina war in France in 1954 and the Vietnam war in Washington now.

Some Senators believed today that this comparison had become an Administration "line" against the committee hearings.

Stennis Hits 'Carping'

On the floor today Senator Stennis said that the Congress and the people were entitled to know "what our policy is and where we are headed." However, he said, he opposed the "carping and divisive criticism which gives to the world and our troops in the field the impression that the United States is a divided nation."

Mr. Stennis said that the debate and criticism had not so far presented any effective alternative "to the course we have followed recently and proposed to follow in the future."

The Senate is debating authorization of $4.8-billion of the $12.3-billion requested by President Johnson as supplemental funds in the current fiscal year for Vietnam fighting needs. All but $4.8-billion of the $12.3-billion is already authorized by law.

While Senator Stennis and others were debating the bill on the Senate floor, the House Armed Services Committee unanimously approved the $4.8-billion authorization, sending it to the House floor.

Senator Stennis predicted larger draft calls and a partial call-up of National Guardsmen and military reservists.

The Senator also predicted that United States forces in Vietnam would be built up beyond the 400,000 level—a prediction that has been made in many quarters frequently but not officially confirmed. Present strength in Vietnam is about 205,000.

Mr. Stennis said that a reserve and National Guard call-up would particularly involve units with specialized skills.

He called for passage of the authorization measure "with dispatch" and also said that if the war continues "increased taxes are urgent."

General Taylor said, in response to questions, that he did not believe the Chinese Communists would enter the conflict for several reasons. He cited their food problems, their vulnerability to air attack and their reluctance to get engaged in a war with the West while they were also embroiled with the Soviet Union for leadership of the Communist world.

Concedes the Risk

But he conceded there was "always the risk" of Chinese intervention, a risk which must be accepted.

He also said repeatedly that the United States did not seek a complete military victory over North Vietnam but was simply trying to convince Hanoi that it could not win and that it must permit "freedom and self-determination" in South Vietnam.

The United States would not insist on unconditional surrender or the dismantling of the Communist Government in the North. Nor would it retain bases in South Vietnam, he said.

These limited objectives, he thought, would induce Hanoi to make peace when it became convinced, through attrition of manpower and "the loss and pain" of bombing, that it could not win.

* * *

February 22, 1966

DE GAULLE INSISTS ON RULE OF BASES OF NATO IN FRANCE

Says Allied Units Must Be Under the Jurisdiction of Paris by April 4, 1969

PROCESS TO BE GRADUAL

President Indicates He Will Withdraw His Last Forces From Alliance by Deadline

By HENRY TANNER
Special to The New York Times.

PARIS, Feb. 21—President de Gaulle declared today that France would claim control of foreign military bases on her soil by April 4, 1969, the day the North Atlantic Treaty Organization may be renounced by its 15 members.

He also warned in effect that the last remaining French forces in NATO—two divisions and about 400 planes in West Germany—would be withdrawn from control by the integrated allied command by that time.

Speaking at a news conference, General de Gaulle said that by April 4, 1969, when the treaty is open for revision, "a normal sovereignty" would have to be restored.

This means, he said, that "everything that is French on the ground, in the air and on the seas and every foreign element stationed in France must be under the sole control of French authorities."

The general thus spelled out in concrete terms the principle he had announced at his last news conference five months ago. At that time, he had stated that "at the expiration of our present commitments, in 1969 at the latest, we shall end the subordination [within NATO] that is called integration."

Statement to Ball Cited

Today's news conference marked the first time that President de Gaulle had said in a public statement that France would claim control of the foreign bases on her soil. However, he is known to have done so privately on many occasions.

He is understood, for instance, to have told Under Secretary of State George W. Ball last summer that American military bases could remain on French soil only if they were put under French control.

NATO installations in France include several large bases of the United States Air Force, a small United States Navy shore headquarters near Nice and a number of supply and communications centers of the United States Army.

Supreme Headquarters Allied Powers Europe (SHAPE) at Roquencourt in the Paris suburbs and the headquarters of Allied Forces Central Europe at Fontainebleau, south of Paris, are the two major integrated NATO headquarters on French soil.

United States European Command headquarters is in Saint-Germain-en-Laye, northwest of Paris.

The United States has about 60,000 military personnel in France. Other members of the alliance are represented in the various integrated commands but otherwise have practically no forces in France.

Western diplomats regarded today's news conference statement not as a new departure but as part of a continual process by which President de Gaulle is gradually filling in the details in a basic concept that has been known for a long time. This is his way, it is believed, of building up the French negotiating position.

High-ranking French officials have been saying that the de Gaulle Government did not intend to initiate negotiations on NATO reorganization in the near future.

The time is not ripe for such basic negotiations involving the future of the relations between the United States and Europe because the Johnson Administration is too deeply absorbed in the Vietnam crisis, these authorized sources have said.

Tonight French sources said that this view was borne out by the general's statement.

After having set the April, 1969, deadline, President de Gaulle declared that France would act in such a way that the changes in the alliance would come "progressively" and that her "allies would not find themselves suddenly inconvenienced."

'Protectorate' Charged

At one point, however, he described United States policies in harsh terms.

The United States, he said, established an "American protectorate in Europe" after the war "under the cover of NATO."

Since then, he added, conditions have changed. He asserted that the threat of aggression from the East had waned and noted that the United States had lost its monopoly of nuclear weapons.

"Nothing can be done to make a treaty completely valid when its objective has changed," the general said, "and nothing can be done to make an alliance stay as is when the conditions in which it was concluded have changed. In that case, it is necessary to adapt the law, the treaty, the alliance to the new conditions."

President de Gaulle charged that the American involvement in local "conflicts" such as Korea, Cuba and Vietnam was a danger to Europe.

By virtue of "the famous escalation," he said, Europe could find herself drawn "automatically" into such a conflict unless she managed to have a "European strategy" of her own as distinct from the strategy that the United States now imposed on her through NATO.

This, he said, is the reason why integration within the alliance is no longer acceptable, although the alliance as such remains valid.

A Glittering Performance

The general's news conference in the grand ballroom of the Presidential Elysée Palace was, as always, a glittering and painstakingly formal affair.

More than a thousand French and foreign reporters had assembled under the eight huge crystal chandeliers, crowded elbow to elbow on gilded cane chairs or leaning against the tapestried walls.

When the great moment came, a heavy purple curtain parted, and the President, flanked by ushers wearing silver chains and swallow tails, stepped up to a small dais.

"I have the honor to greet you," he said.

Then he announced the topics he intended to cover—the Presidential election of last December, the internal economic situation, the "Ben Barka affair," NATO, Europe and Vietnam.

He invited questions to each topic. But his responses were carefully pondered, memorized speeches. Each of them, with the exception of the final brief one on Vietnam, lasted precisely 15 minutes. It was as always a remarkable performance.

The 75-year-old general delivered his text without a single false step, without once referring to notes, like a great actor in a role written especially for him. He was in turn solemn, sarcastic and even humorous.

When a reporter wanted to know why he had not given the country during the election campaign an account of the kidnapping in Paris of Mehdi Ben Barka, a Moroccan leftist Opposition leader, the President slumped forward, as if in utter dejection, his eyes downcast, and shot back, "It was because of my inexperience."

The treatment of Vietnam was unexpectedly short and general, lasting barely five minutes.

"Short of wiping out all resistance to the far corners of the earth," the general declared, there is no way to end this war except by negotiation.

He called for a return to the Geneva agreements of 1954 and said that both the conditions and the potential signers of a peaceful solution were known.

To start with, what is needed, he said, is contact between the five great world powers. He made it clear that these included Communist China.

France, he said in a reference to recognition of Peking, has already oriented her foreign relations in that sense.

Conciliatory on Trade Bloc

The President also made the following points:

- He was more conciliatory than in the past in his references to France's partners in the European Economic Community, or Common Market. He offered to attend a conference of its leaders if it were proposed by one of the other partners—West Germany, Italy, Belgium, the Netherlands or Luxembourg.

• He accused Interior Minister Mohammed Oufkir of Morocco of having played the principal role in the Ben Barka kidnapping and of having thus provoked a dangerous deterioration of French-Moroccan relations.

At the same time, he cleared all members of his Government as well as "high-ranking" officials in general of any involvement in the crime that was committed on the French side by what he described as "vulgar and subaltern" elements.

• He described France's economy as strong and getting ever stronger.

He declared also that, because the December election gave him a second term in the Presidency, France could hope to live and develop in "conditions that, in the memory of man, she had never known before."

* * *

Associated Press

President Sukarno Lieut. Gen. Suharto

March 12, 1966

SUKARNO YIELDS POWERS TO ARMY TO CURB UNREST; COMMUNIST PARTY BANNED

TROOPS ACCLAIMED

Jakarta Is Reported Calm—President to Retain His Title

By Reuters

JAKARTA, Indonesia, Saturday, March 12—Army leaders under Lieut. Gen. Suharto staged a peaceful take-over of power in Indonesia today after all-night talks with President Sukarno lasting into the early hours.

Crack troops and paracommandos moved into the city and took up positions under cover of the predawn darkness. The moves followed days of mounting unrest by students engaged in anti-Communist demonstrations.

Early this morning the Jakarta radio announced that President Sukarno had transferred his powers to General Suharto.

The army's orders were being issued in the name of President Sukarno and he was evidently keeping the formal title of the office.

Victory Parade Held

Heavy armor and armed troops of the Indonesian Army held a massive victory parade today, wildly cheered by hundreds of thousands of students and citizens.

While the parade was going on General Suharto issued in President Sukarno's name a decree banning the Indonesian Communist party.

The ban applied to the party and its affiliates.

General Suharto ordered "immediate, precise and correct" action against the Communists. He said this was necessary because remnants of the Sept. 30 Movement, which staged the abortive coup d'etat last fall, were still active.

The order said that the Communists were conducting underground activities, including slander, aggravation, threats, rumors and armed activity, which seriously threatened the peoples' peace and security.

Grave Threat Seen

General Suharto said the party's underground activities posed a grave threat to the Indonesian Revolution in general and prevented it from continuing its course, especially in the economic field and in crushing Malaysia.

A particular target of the sweeping moves by General Suharto and the army leadership has been Foreign Minister Subandrio, who has shown strong leanings toward Communist Chinese policies.

The political fate of the unpopular Ministers, Dr. Subandrio and the Minister of Basic Education, Dr. Sumardjo, was not yet known officially.

Unofficial reports said the pro-Communist Ministers were already in army custody.

General Suharto is expected to announce a new Cabinet shortly.

An official announcement signed by General Suharto in the President's name said the Army chief had the power to take any steps necessary to insure security, calm and stability and to guarantee President Sukarno's personal safety and authority.

At hand and on alert in Jakarta are the Army Strategic Reserves, the crack Siliwangi Division, a popular paratroop commando regiment, Jakarta garrison troops, tank and armored car units and artillery and cavalry units. These units will be taking part in the parade, led by Col. Sarwo Eddy, commander of the paratroop regiment.

General Suharto's announcement said that he was empowered to take control "for the sake of the integrity of the nation and state of the Republic of Indonesia and the implementation of all the teachings" of President Sukarno.

Students Pledge Backing

The Jakarta radio said that the anti-Communist students and political parties immediately pledged themselves to give General Suharto every help he needed in carrying out his new responsibilities.

President Sukarno gave over authority to General Suharto after the 100-member Indonesian Cabinet met yesterday to discuss the crisis caused by nearly two weeks of increasingly violent student demonstrations.

High school and university students have been demonstrating against Communist China, which has been accused of involvement in the abortive Oct. 1 coup, for a ban on the Communist party, and for cabinet changes and lower commodity prices.

General Suharto was formerly army commander under Gen. Abdul Haris Nasution, the chief of staff of the armed forces and Defense Minister who was recently dismissed by President Sukarno.

General Nasution is understood to be giving his support to General Suharto as his military successor.

* * *

March 15, 1966

PUBLIC BACKS NEGOTIATIONS WITH VIETCONG, POLL SAYS

By WALLACE TURNER
Special to The New York Times.

SAN FRANCISCO, March 14—A poll showing that Americans are willing to have their Government negotiate with the Vietcong to settle the Vietnam war was released today by a group of Stanford University political scientists.

The poll also showed that, confronted with the choice of withdrawal or all-out war in Vietnam, 60 per cent of those questioned favored all-out war.

The Johnson Administration has indicated that the Vietcong could enter into negotiations by speaking through the North Vietnamese. It has not conceded that the National Liberation Front, the political organization of the Vietcong, could be a direct party in negotiations.

Poll Cost $10,000

About 200 individual contributors, mostly academics from Stanford, paid approximately half the $10,000 cost of the poll. The rest of the cost was paid by the National Opinion Research Center at the University of Chicago. The center conducted the polling in late February and early March.

Dr. Sidney Verba, a professor of political science at Stanford, said the survey was taken because "we felt as professional students of public opinion that this was a foreign policy question in which polls were being importantly used."

"We felt that the polls we saw reported in newspapers did not go deeply enough into public attitudes. We were curious to see what the deeper attitudes were," he said.

The poll was conducted among 1,474 persons selected by the National Opinion Research Center as a national cross-section in age, sex and employment status. Thirty questions were asked.

Following are examples of questions and answers in the survey:

Would you favor negotiations with the Vietcong if they were willing to negotiate? Yes, 88 per cent. No, 8 per cent.

Would you favor a truce negotiated by the United Nations or a neutral power, with each side holding territory it now holds? Yes, 70 per cent. No, 22 per cent.

Would you favor a new government in which the Vietcong took some part? Yes, 52 per cent. No, 36 per cent.

Would you favor free elections, even if the Vietcong might win? Yes, 54 per cent. No, 34 per cent.

However, other answers showed the public opposed to abandoning the defense of Southeast Asia. For example:

Would you approve of withdrawing American troops immediately from South Vietnam? Yes, 15 per cent. No, 81 per cent.

Would you favor gradual withdrawal? Yes, 39 per cent. No, 56 per cent.

Would you withdraw even if meant the loss of Laos and Thailand? Yes, 13 per cent. No, 77 per cent.

Offered a choice of continuing the present situation, fighting a major war or withdrawing, 49 per cent said they would continue, while 23 per cent said they would fight a major war and 19 per cent said they would withdraw. The remaining 9 per cent declined to choose.

When the alternative of continuing the present situation was withdrawn, 60 per cent chose a major war and 31 per cent favored withdrawal.

The first question sought to determine general support of the Administration's handling of the Vietnam war. Mr. Johnson's actions were endorsed by 61 per cent and disapproved by 29 per cent, while 10 per cent would not choose.

The poll, released today at Palo Alto, Calif., also explored attitudes toward paying for the Vietnam war.

There was opposition to cutting aid to education (78 per cent), increasing taxes (67 per cent), economic controls (53 per cent) and reducing medicare payments (66 per cent). But while 50 per cent were opposed to cutting back the poverty program, 46 per cent would accept it.

The degree of opposition to sacrifice to meet war costs varied with the attitude toward Mr. Johnson's decisions. Those who approved them opposed increased taxes by a margin of 59-to-39 per cent, but those who disapproved opposed tax increases by 81 to 18 per cent.

Other questions explored attitudes on enlarging the war:

Would you support calling up the National Guard and reserves? Yes, 60 per cent. No, 32 per cent. Support all-out mobilization? Yes, 40 per cent. No, 51 per cent.

Would you have 500,000 troops in South Vietnam? Yes, 45 per cent. No, 46 per cent. Bomb cities in North Vietnam? Yes, 38 per cent. No, 55 per cent. Fight a ground war in China? Yes, 32 per cent. No, 60 per cent. An atomic war with

China? Yes, 30 per cent. No, 64 per cent. With the Soviet Union? Yes, 22 per cent. No, 71 per cent.

Questions also were asked about attitudes toward Cuba, China and the Soviet Union. About 90 per cent either approved United States policies toward these nations or thought they were "too soft."

The poll analysts said the answers knocked down the theory that opposition to Mr. Johnson's policies was building among the "hawks." His opposition is from those who want to cut back, negotiate or somehow end the war without further escalation, it was argued.

The analysts said that only 6 per cent of the sample appeared to take consistent "hawk" positions in favor of stronger American action and against any negotiation or accommodation with the Vietcong.

The "doves," who took the opposite position in all instances, amounted to 14 per cent of the sample.

These "real hawks" approve of Mr. Johnson's actions by 72 to 23 per cent, while the "real doves" disapproved by 48 to 44 per cent.

The results of the survey were analyzed by Dr. Verba; Gordon Black, a graduate student; Richard Brody, assistant professor; Paul Ekman, research associate; Norman Nie, graduate student; Edwin B. Parker, associate professor, and Nelson W. Polsby, a fellow at the Stanford Center for Advanced Study in the Behavioral Sciences.

Peter H. Rossi and Paul Sheatsley of the Chicago center supervised the sampling and field work.

* * *

April 12, 1966

VIETNAM TURMOIL NOW SLOWS WAR, WASHINGTON SAYS

Cut in Ground Attacks and in Air Sorties in the South Conceded in Capital

BOMB SHORTAGE CITED

Both Civilians and Soldiers in Danang Port Refuse to Unload U.S. Vessels

By MAX FRANKEL
Special to The New York Times.

WASHINGTON, April 11—The Johnson Administration acknowledged today that the political turmoil in Vietnam had begun to disrupt the war effort. Officials were sparing, however, with facts that would portray the degree of disruption.

South Vietnamese ground troops were said to be "mounting fewer attacks" on the Vietcong in many parts of the country and especially in the rebellious northern provinces.

In addition, military and civilian Vietnamese workers at the huge American base at Danang were reported to have refused to unload American ships, thus causing a "temporary" shortage of bombs.

Sorties Cut a Third

Together, these developments were said to have reduced by at least a third the number of American air sorties in South Vietnam. The reduction was ascribed in part to the reduced number of ground actions requiring air support and in part to the ammunition shortage.

The Defense Department acknowledged the disruption in confirming reports from Saigon. It thus reversed the judgment of high Administration officials, made as recently as yesterday, that the political crisis had caused "no particular reduction" in military operations.

Pentagon spokesmen declined to give any general account of the reduced activity, saying they did not wish to go beyond information obtained by reporters in Vietnam. They said that United States forces were operating in normal patterns against the Vietcong and that the bombing of North Vietnam had not been affected.

The first use of Guam-based B-52's over North Vietnam that was announced later was said by officials here to have no relation to the shortage of bombs at Danang. Increased use of the planes, reconverted recently to carry larger loads of conventional bombs than previously, had been planned for some time, the officials said.

Pentagon spokesmen would not explain the nature of the dock workers' boycott. At least some of the workers were thought to have been organized to support Buddhist agitation against Premier Nguyen Cao Ky and the military junta.

"There has been a temporary problem in distribution of bombs within the country," Arthur S. Sylvester, Assistant Secretary of Defense, said. "The distribution problem has resulted primarily from disorders at Danang, which caused diversion of ordnance-carrying vessels to other unloading areas. Steps are being taken to alleviate the distribution problem."

There appeared to be a serious political problem behind the "distribution" difficulties. South Vietnamese troops as well as civilians were reported to have rejected appeals that they help unload the American vessels.

Hitherto, Washington thought that of the two South Vietnamese Army divisions stationed in the northern area around Danang, only one regiment and some individual officers and men had thrown their support to the Buddhists. When faced with trouble on the docks, however, Americans on the scene called for American troops to begin unloading, and diverted some ships to other ports.

The references to distribution problems also raised the possibility that supply lines beyond the dock area had somehow been disrupted.

The extent of the cutback in South Vietnamese actions requiring air support was even more difficult to determine from the information made available here. One source said the reduction was not confined to the northern, more rebellious provinces.

An Air Force spokesman in Saigon was reported to have said that the number of air sorties in South Vietnam Sunday declined to 300 from the usual total of 450 or 500. In acknowledging the cutback, spokesmen said a reduction of one-third was a fair estimate. They did not say how much was due to the dock strike and how much to reduced ground action.

Before today, the State and Defense Departments had reported a reduction in Vietcong activity, but took considerable comfort from the belief that the South Vietnamese army had not let up its "search and destroy" efforts against the guerillas.

In fact, the political crisis as a whole had been publicly described here as a "healthy" manifestation of political maneuvering.

"I would not regard this as anything that needs to be deplored, so long as it doesn't interfere with the conduct of the military operations or with the conduct of the operations that must inevitably accompany the military operations toward improving the society and building a stronger base for democracy in the future."

In unofficial conversation, however, there is no longer any doubt here that political and social as well as military activities have been gravely set back by the crisis, regardless of its outcome. The most serious consequence, it is thought, is the hope and encouragement that the Communists will draw from the dissension and that they will use to sustain their efforts for many months.

* * *

April 26, 1966

HUMPHREY URGES HARD LINE IN WAR

Calls for Endurance to Meet Frustrations and Scolds Vietnam Policy Critics

By HOMER BIGART

Vice President Humphrey preached a hard line on Vietnam yesterday and called for a display of national endurance to surmount "frustrating and at times heartbreaking" times ahead.

He talked for an hour and two minutes to newspaper executives here without once mentioning the prospect of peace negotiations.

On the contrary, he warned against proposals for a coalition government in Saigon that would include the National Liberation Front, the political arm of the Vietcong. Such proposals, he said, come right out of the book of Communist conquest.

It is a waste of time to debate whether the United States should or should not be in South Vietnam, Mr. Humphrey said at the annual luncheon meeting of The Associated Press at the Waldorf-Astoria Hotel.

Won't Argue With History

"We are there," he said. "I'm not going to argue about that, because that's ancient history and can't be repealed."

He was also impatient with critics who recalled the French defeat in Indochina.

"Well, we're not the French, with all respect to that fine nation," he said. "We are not colonialists. We have no empire to save. We are not fighting against a whole people. We are fighting for the freedom of that people."

Critics who call it a civil war "ought to know better," scolded the Vice President. His version: "The war is being waged by the National Liberation Front. The N.L.F. is a front. That's the only honest word in it. It's a front for Hanoi."

Despite the implication of blood, sweat and tears ahead, Mr. Humphrey said he'd be willing to "bet" President Johnson would not ask for a tax increase.

Even without a tax rise, the nation would have both guns and butter, he promised.

"Guns and butter, foreign aid or domestic aid . . . are tied together and you cannot separate them," he declared.

Two days before, speaking in Washington at the annual dinner of the Americans for Democratic Action, the militantly liberal wing of the Democratic party with which he was formerly identified, Mr. Humphrey stressed President Johnson's avowed desire for a peace conference. There was no mention of a peace conference yesterday.

Instead, Mr. Humphrey called for dual victories in Vietnam against "poverty, disease and despair" and "the classic power tactics of Communism."

"We must not lose the peace in either struggle," he said.

Warning that "it won't be easy, it will be frustrating and at times heartbreaking," Mr. Humphrey added: "We must stay and see it through. And the free nations of the world need to know that we have the vision and the endurance to do so."

He said the United States was willing to abide by the results of the coming election in South Vietnam. "We support that election, with all its uncertainties," he said. He challenged North Vietnam to hold free elections.

In support of the Administration's foreign aid request, he noted that it was only about one-fourth of 1 per cent of the gross national product and 2 per cent of the budget.

"If someone has a substitute for foreign aid, I'd like to hear about it," he said. "The investment we make in foreign aid ... is certainly less than that necessary to treat the symptoms of massive economic crisis and disorder and, yes, of war."

A.P. Elects Directors

Ten members of Youth Against War and Fascism picketed near the Park Avenue entrance of the hotel as Mr. Humphrey spoke. One carried a sign: "H. H. Humphrey—Johnson's war salesman."

The board of directors of The Associated Press released their annual report at a business meeting preceding the luncheon. The report noted that two A.P. men had been killed and four others wounded in Vietnam, and that the financial cost of coverage was also heavy.

Restrictions on the coverage of the Vietnam war, deplored in last year's report, have been eased, the directors reported. The report said there were now 1,226 daily newspaper members of the A.P. in the United States. Broadcast membership was 2,828. There were 4,515 subscribers to the A.P. service abroad in 103 countries and territories.

Four new directors were elected at the annual meeting of The Associated Press, and three were re-elected.

Paul Miller of The Rochester Times-Union and The Democrat and Chronicle, who is president of the A.P., was re-elected to the board. Elected with him were James L. Knight of The Miami Herald; John Cowles Jr. of The Minneapolis Tribune, and Martin S. Hayden of The Detroit News and Sunday News.

Max E. Nussbaum of The Moultrie (Ga.) Observer was re-elected a director from cities of less than 50,000 population; Gene Robb of The Albany Knickerbocker News and Times-Union was re-elected as a director who is a resident of New York State, and Fred A. Seaton of The Hastings (Neb.) Daily Tribune was elected a director to fill the unexpired term of Harry F. Byrd Jr., resigned.

* * *

May 5, 1966

PEKING PRESSES CULTURAL PURGE; ARMY JOINS IN CALL FOR VIGILANCE

By SEYMOUR TOPPING
Special to The New York Times.

HONG KONG, May 4—A widespread cultural purge with clearly stated political overtones is under way within the Chinese Communist party.

The extent of the purge, and the seriousness with which it is being conducted, have been made clear in recent days by some of the most authoritative journals of the Chinese party.

The Army joined today in spreading the call for vigilance against "antiparty, anti-Socialist" intellectuals. An editorial in Jiefangjun Pao, the official army newspaper, asserted:

"Activities of these antiparty, anti-Socialist elements are not an accidental phenomenon. They are responding to the great international anti-Chinese chorus of imperialists, modern revisionists and various reactionaries to revive the Chinese reactionary class, which has been struck down."

The army newspaper accused certain intellectuals, whom it did not name, of being linked to "right-wing opportunists" within the Communist party. The editorial asserted that the debate developing on the cultural front was not simply an academic dispute but a "struggle to the death" to eliminate bourgeois ideology.

[American analysts of Chinese affairs viewed the editorial's reference to "revisionists" as a thinly veiled charge that links had been established by Soviet Communists with some Chinese Communists. The Chinese leadership has scorned the Soviet leadership as "revisionists" since their ideological break.]

The paper's view reflected the mounting intensity of the cultural purge in China, which is directed at compelling strict adherence to the dogmas of Mao Tse-tung, chairman of the Communist party, in literature, art, education and journalism. Political commissars have been accusing leading members of the intelligentsia of pretending to follow the party line while resisting the regime's efforts to "remold their thinking."

'Lordly Attitude' Condemned

Hurrg Chi, the ideological journal of the Central Committee, warned intellectuals that they would have to shed their "lordly attitude" and bow to the criticism of the masses.

"Workers, peasants and soldiers who are armed with Mao Tse-tung's thinking have a most acute sense for distinguishing flowers from poisonous weeds," the journal asserted.

Reports from China said that leading intellectuals had been jolted by the public humiliation of Kuo Mo-jo, the country's most prominent scholar and the regime's spokesman on cultural affairs for many years.

The 78-year-old scholar has conceded that he failed in his voluminous published works to apply correctly the teachings of Mao Tse-tung.

"Strictly speaking, according to the standards of today, all that I have written should be burned," Mr. Kuo said in a speech made on April 14 and published last week in the Peking press.

Intellectuals have interpreted the confession as a warning that no one in the cultural fields is safe from the party purge.

Mr. Kuo has been a literary and political collaborator of Chairman Mao. It was not known what part, if any, Mr. Mao took in impelling his old associate to make his unexpected speech of self-criticism. Mr. Kuo is president of the Chinese Academy of Sciences and chairman of the All-China Federation of Literary and Art Workers, and holds more than 20 other official positions.

Mr. Mao has been absent from public activities for five months and is believed to be ill. However, today's Hung Chi article asserted: "Mao Tse-tung's ideas are the supreme directive for all our work."

Hsinhua, the Government press agency, reported that Mr. Kuo had spent May Day with factory workers in Chengtu, Szechuan, his native province. Mr. Kuo has been a prominent participant in national celebrations in Peking, particularly in his capacity as chairman of the China Peace Committee.

Observers said Mr. Kuo might have returned to Szechuan to undergo "molding of thinking among the masses." In his speech of self-criticism, he concluded by saying: "Now I must learn from the workers, peasants and soldiers."

The army newspaper asserted that a distinction should be made between antiparty intellectuals and those whose heart was with the party and Socialism and whose errors in writing poor works could be corrected.

There was no indication how Mr. Kuo or other prominent intellectuals known to be in trouble with the party were being catalogued.

There was an ominous tone in the attack of the army newspaper on intellectuals. The party's policy has been generally to remold disgraced intellectuals through persuasion rather than violent retaliation.

Hsinhua also distributed the text of a speech made Saturday in Peking by Premier Chou En-lai in which he stated: "A

Socialist cultural revolution of great historic significance is being launched in our country. This is a fierce and protracted struggle as to who will win, the proletariat or bourgeoisie in the ideological field."

Calling for the eradication of bourgeois ideology from all cultural fields, the Premier declared: "This is a key question in the development in depth of our Socialist revolution at the present stage, a question concerning the situation as a whole and a matter of the first magnitude affecting the destiny and future of our party and country."

Bourgeois Bent Seen

Analysis said that the cultural purge was a manifestation of the sense of insecurity Mr. Mao and other leaders felt about the evolution of Chinese Communist society.

Despite lip service paid to Maoist philosophy by intellectuals, the party is complaining that many of them have failed to remold themselves inwardly and have retained bourgeois leanings that could endanger the revolution.

Many of the country's intellectuals are portrayed in reports from the Chinese mainland as "frightened men" who feel that they may be denounced at any time. Party ideologists are rereading literary and scholarly works that date from 1959 to find evidence of heresy.

* * *

May 12, 1966

PRESIDENT URGES SCHOLARS TO BACK WAR IN VIETNAM

Replies to Fulbright Charge of 'Arrogance of Power'— Speaks at Princeton

300 PICKET ON CAMPUS

Plea for Understanding by 'Responsible' Intellectuals Is Heard by 3,000

By RONALD SULLIVAN

Special to The New York Times.

PRINCETON, N. J., May 11—President Johnson appealed today to the nation's scholars and intellectuals for understanding and support of his policies in Vietnam.

In replying to a charge by Senator J. W. Fulbright, chairman of the Senate Foreign Relations Committee, that the United States was "succumbing to the arrogance of power," the President declared in a speech here at Princeton University:

"The exercise of power in this century has meant for all of us in the United States not arrogance but agony. We have used our power not willingly and recklessly ever, but always reluctantly and with restraint."

Demonstrators March

Nearby, about 300 demonstrators protesting United States policy in Vietnam quietly marched back and forth carrying antiwar signs.

Wearing a black and purple academic robe, the President spoke at dedication ceremonies for the new Woodrow Wilson School of Public and International Affairs.

Before an audience of about 3,000 students and faculty members Mr. Johnson was awarded an honorary Doctor of Laws degree by the university. The audience was separated from the President by a shimmering shallow lagoon.

Mr. Johnson asked "responsible" intellectuals, "in the language of the current generation, to 'cool it'—to bring what my generation called 'not heat but light' to public affairs."

The President said, "Surely it is not a paranoid vision of America's place in the world to recognize that freedom is still indivisible, still has adversaries whose challenge must be answered."

"Today, of course, as we meet here," he said "that challenge is sternest at the moment in Southeast Asia. Yet there, as elsewhere, our great power is also tempered by great restraint."

He asked, "What nation has announced such limited objectives or such willingness to remove its military presence once those objectives are secured and achieved? What nation has spent the lives of its sons and vast sums of its fortune to provide the people of a small, striving country the chance to elect a course that we ourselves might not ourselves choose?"

The President was keeping a date he was forced to cancel last October when he underwent surgery for a gall bladder attack. His visit here today, which was kept secret until shortly before he left Washington, also represented an effort by Mr. Johnson to strengthen ties with the academic community, particularly in the area of foreign policy.

Pickets Oppose Policy

Shortly before he arrived at Princeton Airport aboard a small, two-engine Air Force jet, the demonstrators—students, faculty members and wives carrying small children—began to picket about a block away from where the President was to speak.

The President left Washington at 9:43 A.M. and landed here at 10:28 A.M. He arrived at the school about 20 minutes before the ceremonies began promptly at 11 A.M. He returned to Washington two hours later, landing there at 1:56 P.M.

John W. Gardner, Secretary of Health, Education and Welfare, who was originally scheduled to speak but did not, came from Washington, too. He and the President were greeted by Gov. Richard J. Hughes of New Jersey and President Robert F. Goheen of Princeton.

Then, precisely at 11 o'clock, the university trustees and faculty members, wearing bright orange and black robes and floppy black hats, emerged from Corwin Hall, the old Woodrow Wilson School building, and marched in a procession across the courtyard to the main entrance of the new $4-million white concrete structure.

Accompanied by Bodyguard

To the applause of the audience and the flourish of "Hail to the Chief" from the Princeton Band, the President came out into the bright sun; Governor Hughes in front of him, Dr.

The New York Times (by Neal Boenzi)

PICKETS AT PRINCETON: Opponents of U.S. policy in Vietnam march during campus visit by President Johnson.

Goheen beside him, and a Secret Service agent in a black robe and a black mortar marching behind him.

After short speeches by President Goheen and Governor Hughes, James F. Oates Jr., charter trustee and University Orator, read the citation as Dr. Goheen conferred the honorary degree upon the President.

Then, with the stark, slender, tapered columns of the building behind him, the President spoke for 28 minutes, reading from a prepared text. Not once was he interrupted by applause, which came politely at the end.

Nowhere did the President refer to Senator Fulbright by name. But the Arkansas Democrat's speech April 21 at the Johns Hopkins University School of Advanced International Studies and the continuing debate over American policy in Vietnam, particularly in the universities, were clearly the President's target today when he declared that the "intellectual today is very much an inside man" even though "he has not always been the partner of government."

'Affluence of Power'

But he said, "This affluence of power for an intellectual community that once walked on the barren fringes of authority has not been won without some pain."

"An uneasy conscience is the price any concerned man pays, whether politician or professor, for a share in the nuclear age," he said.

The President asked his critics to accept the fact that "security and aggression, as well as peace and war, must be the concerns of foreign policy; that a great power influences the world just as surely when it withdraws its strength as when it exercises its strength; that aggression must be deterred where possible and met early when undertaken; that the application of military force, when it becomes necessary, must be for limited purposes and must be tightly controlled."

Finally, the President took the occasion to announce that he would ask Congress next year to expand opportunities for students to prepare for public service.

The President delayed his departure to chat for a few minutes with his nephew, Philip Dobbitt, a 17-year-old freshman from Austin, Tex. University officials found the student after a flurry of telephone calls to several dormitories.

* * *

May 16, 1966

KY FORCES HOLD DANANG; BUDDHISTS FEAR CIVIL WAR; U.S. APPEALS FOR ACCORD

FIGHT LASTS A DAY

10 Are Reported Dead in Wild Shooting—Rebels Hole Up

By NEIL SHEEHAN
Special to The New York Times.

DANANG, South Vietnam, May 15—The ruling junta appeared tonight to have seized control of most of this city after a day of wild shooting between troops loyal to the Government and rebel military units allied with Buddhist insurgents.

In a surprise move, Premier Nguyen Cao Ky and the other junta leaders flew 1,000 Vietnamese marines to the air base on the outskirts of this port and garrison city in the hours before dawn.

At dawn the marines, supported by tanks and Vietnamese Air Force planes, which buzzed the town, moved into the city and began systematically seizing vital points.

Marines Are Reinforced

The marines were later reinforced by 500 paratroopers and Rangers. They met disorganized resistance from a force estimated to number 300 to 500 soldiers, but succeeded in occupying the I Army Corps headquarters, the civilian and military police stations, the radio station and other major installations.

There was a great deal of shooting today in Danang, including one strafing attack by air force planes on rebels in the central market.

Most of the shooting was apparently wild and inaccurate and casualties were reported to be light. Although estimates varied, it appeared that about 10 people on both sides, including civilians, had been killed and at least a dozen wounded.

[In Saigon, Buddhist monks denounced the Government move on Danang as an "act of treachery" that would "surely lead to civil war."]

Danang settled into an uneasy quiet at night, with only an occasional stray shot breaking the silence. Vietnamese Air Force C-47's kept the city illuminated with flares and observation planes circled overhead. Premier Ky, who has designated himself Air Vice Marshal, is head of the air force as well as Premier.

Rebels Retreat to Pagodas

The streets were deserted except for patrols of Vietnamese marines and paratroopers. The thousands of United States marines stationed here were confined to camps on the outskirts of the city.

The remaining rebel soldiers, estimated at 150, were holed up in and around two Buddhist pagodas that have served as headquarters for opposition to the Government junta. Several hundred Buddhist layman, as well as Buddhist priests, have taken shelter in the pagodas.

Rebel soldiers said they intended to defend the pagodas to the death.

Danang had been in the hands of Buddhists and rebel military units since mid-March, when Buddhist leaders began agitation to displace the military-dominated junta with a civilian government.

In Hue, 50 miles north of here, the Buddhist and rebel military units that hold the town were reported to be preparing to resist any attempt at occupation by the junta. Hue is the principal Buddhist strong-hold in central Vietnam.

Reports from Hue said that troops of the First Vietnamese Army Division, which supports the Buddhist cause, had taken up positions at vital points in the town and had set up road blocks on the routes leading into it from both north and south. [Unconfirmed reports said the anti-Ky troops had seized control of the Hue airfield, The Associated Press said.]

At a demonstration in Hue by 3,000 people, Buddhist student leaders denounced the junta's seizure of Danang and accused Premier Ky of "killing innocent people." Later over the Hue Radio, the student leaders called on the population to resist if Premier Ky sent troops to seize the city.

Lieut. Gen. Nguyen Chanh Thi, the former I Army Corps commander, whose dismissal by the junta March 10 brought the start of the campaign, said in Hue that rebel troops would defend the town.

In the provincial capital of Hoian, 18 miles south of here, Lieut. Col. Dam Quang Yeu, provincial military commander and a bitter opponent of the junta, was reported to be attempting to rally troops to resist any attempt to occupy Hoian.

Ky Backed Down in April

Early in April, Premier Ky announced that he was going to seize Danang to reassert Government authority. But he then retreated on the assertion and three battalions of Vietnamese marines that had been flown to the air base here were removed.

This time the Premier and his supporters acted in secrecy and apparently caught almost everyone by surprise.

American officials here learned of some impending move when South Vietnamese Air Force planes began landing at the air base after 2:30 A.M., but the first alarm Buddhist leaders apparently received was when the marines occupied the Army Corps headquarters compound near the air base at 6:30 A.M.

Mayor Vanishes

Dr. Nguyen Van Man, Mayor of Danang and a principal local opponent of the junta, has disappeared. Premier Ky in April vowed to have Dr. Man executed on charges of treason.

Premier Ky, Lieut. Gen. Nguyen Huu Co, Defense Minister and Deputy Premier, and Lieut. Gen Cao Van Vien, Chairman of the Vietnamese Joint General Staff, flew here early in the morning. Late in the afternoon Premier Ky and General Co returned to Saigon.

Associated Press Radiophoto

TROOPS MOVE IN DANANG: South Vietnamese soldiers and tanks in city in northern part of the country. Forces had been sent in to take over by Premier Nguyen Cao Ky.

It was evident from the disorganized resistance that the Buddhists and their supporting military units had not had sufficient warning to prepare an effective defense.

The marines swept aside a large number of primitive roadblocks on the way from the air base to town and did not run into any resistance until they seized the radio station at 9:30 A.M.

A dozen rebels there resisted for a short time.

The marines had to take the radio station again later after they had moved elsewhere and 50 rebel soldiers took positions in and around the building. They were driven off again by the marines and tanks and the pro-Ky troops then occupied the station.

The heaviest and last fighting took place early in the evening at the central market, which was defended by 25 rebel soldiers armed with two .50-caliber machine guns and other automatic weapons. About 300 youths and curiosity-seekers also gathered there, shaking their fists at the buzzing planes and shouting encouragement to the rebels.

When the rebels began firing at the planes, two fighter-bombers swooped and raked the market place with a burst from their machine guns.

A column of pro-Government troops led by two tanks then moved up the street and a fierce fight began that lasted about an hour and 45 minutes. The tanks and troops finally cleared the rebels from the market place.

While this battle was in progress, 150 Buddhist youths and priests and girl and boy scouts sat praying on the pavement in front of a major pagoda 800 yards up an adjacent street.

Some of the girls wept as a priest harangued them over a loudspeaker and bullets crackled through the treetops and splattered into the walls and roof of the pagoda.

Troops wearing saffron-colored arm bands to show adherence to the Buddhist cause took up positions inside the pagoda and set up mortars.

Witnesses said many soldiers on both sides appeared reluctant to kill each other and fired into the air or into trees and buildings.

* * *

May 29, 1966

NUN'S FIERY DEATH IN HUE SETS OFF CLASH IN SAIGON

Protest Suicide of Buddhist Leads to March by 20,000 and Battle With Troops

ANTI-KY FORCES IN RIFT

Key Military Leaders Move Toward Reconciliation, but Civilian Obduracy Grows

By R. W. APPLE Jr.
Special to The New York Times.

HUE, South Vietnam, May 29—A 55-year-old Buddhist nun burned herself to death before dawn today to protest the policies of the ruling military junta.

[The nun's suicide touched off a violent clash in Saigon between 20,000 demonstrators and Government troops, The Associated Press reported. South Vietnamese marines fired tear gas to prevent the crowd from reaching the center of the capital.]

The immolation, the first since the current political crisis began almost 11 weeks ago, was carried out as the Government demonstrated a new determination to restore order to this rebellious university city 400 miles northeast of Saigon.

Split in Anti-Ky Ranks

Lieut. Gen. Phan Van Khoa, chief of Thuathien Province and Mayor of Hue, told the leaders of the anti-Government student group yesterday that he intended to re-establish control over the radio station which the students have held for two months.

A split appeared to be developing within the Buddhist-led Struggle Movement, with key military men moving toward a reconciliation with Premier Nguyen Cao Ky and the students and militant monks growing more obdurately opposed to the Premier.

It was thought unlikely that the anti-Government civilians could maintain their hold without the support of the soldiers with whom they have been closely allied.

Others Surround Her

At the same time, there appeared to be a division in the Buddhist leadership in Saigon. Informed sources said a showdown was developing between militants and moderates in the Unified Buddhist Church, which has led the effort to displace the junta headed by Air Vice Marshal Ky.

The nun's suicide occurred in the courtyard in front of the Dieu De Pagoda. Squatting on the ground, she poured the contents of a five-gallon can of gasoline over her head and lit it with a match. She sat stolidly for 9 seconds and then collapsed.

The nun, Thanh Quang, had been taking part in a 48-hour hunger strike. She left behind two letters, one attacking Premier Ky and the other asking President Johnson to renounce American support of the Ky regime.

Other nuns and monks, who had been sleeping or praying, rushed from the pagoda and formed a circle around the blazing body. They were joined later by Thich Tri Quang, the leader of the rebellion against the Government here.

More than 2,000 Buddhist faithful stood shoulder to shoulder in and outside of the courtyard, many of them dabbing at their eyes. Powerful loudspeakers amplified the shrill funeral lamentations of nuns and the sobs of women in the crowd.

Immolations were a principal weapon of the Buddhists in their successful campaign to bring down the Government of the late Ngo Dinh Diem in November, 1963. Thanh Quang was reported to have volunteered to burn herself at the time but had been denied permission by the church's senior monk.

A French doctor in Hue said a representative of the Buddhists had called at his office yesterday and asked for a quantity of morphine, a pain-killing drug. He said he refused to provide it.

Colonel Ordered to Stay On

Colonel Khoa, who submitted his resignation Friday because he felt that he had lost control of the situation, was ordered to stay on the job by Saigon, informed sources said. He has steadfastly avoided any anti-Government action.

The colonel told the students that they would be permitted to use the station for an hour a day after his troops had occupied it. But he said they would have to submit the text of their broadcasts for censorship and to give him the names of speakers.

In a broadcast last night an unidentified speaker said he and his friends would "fight to the last drop of our blood" for the station.

To show his determination, Colonel Khoa brought a second battalion of troops from the Third Regiment of the First Vietnamese Division into the city. A battalion arrived Thursday after students had sacked and burned the American cultural center and library.

It was the ouster of General Tri from the command of the I Army Corps and from the junta that precipitated the series of events that led to the present crisis in the South Vietnamese political scene. A popular officer in the northern provinces of South Vietnam that had been his domain, he became a central figure in the anti-Government movement, which combined Buddhist and army elements.

When Marshal Ky suppressed the dissidents in Danang, the Unified Buddhist Church redoubled its efforts to force him out and install a civilian government. Before the Danang incident the Buddhists had professed themselves content with the Premier's pledge that the first steps toward civilian rule would be taken in September.

* * *

June 8, 1966

U.S. PLANS A VIETNAM DRIVE USING 100,000 MORE G.I.'S

Offensive Is Designed to Open Roads—Troops Due by End of Year

By WILLIAM M. BEECHER
Special to The New York Times.

WASHINGTON, June 7—A major United States offensive in South Vietnam to open principal highways and the north-south railroad is awaiting the new scheduled arrival by the end of the year of about 100,000 more American troops.

That would bring the number of United States troops there to nearly 400,000.

The offensive would entail pushing North Vietnamese and Vietcong battalions out of the coastal provinces astride arteries into the interior.

"We'll never persuade the South Vietnamese peasant we offer some hope for the future while we continue to hop over troubled areas in our airplanes and helicopters, leaving him to contend on the ground with persistent armed harassment," a Pentagon official commented.

The timetable for the new effort is dependent on two factors—the speed of the buildup of United States military forces over the next several months and the ferocity of enemy attacks during the same period.

Current plans call for adding before the end of the year about 100,000 American troops to the approximately 260,000 now in Vietnam. The freedom of American and South Vietnamese forces to take on the proposed assignments will depend in large part on whether the Vietcong actually initiate anticipated assaults to take advantage of the monsoon rains that have begun to lash the central and southern areas of South Vietnam.

"If they do, our road clearing operation will get a slower start," one planner explained, "but we'll press ahead with it in any case. We consider this a priority effort."

Pressure on U.S. Mounts

The military has been under rising pressure to open up the main roads Vietnamese farmers use to get to their markets. The pressure mounted after the Honolulu conference in February at which President Johnson promised Premier Nguyen Cao Ky increased assistance in pursuing a program of economic and social reform, particularly in rural Vietnam.

But Gen. William C. Westmoreland, commander of American forces in Vietnam, apparently has felt until now that the limited forces he had available would be better employed on search-and-destroy missions to keep the enemy off balance than on an ancillary road-clearing campaign.

There have been only sporadic attempts recently to escort farmers to local markets with their rice harvests and to open Highway 19, from the coastal city of Quinhon through Ankhe to Pleiku in the Central Highlands, to military convoys.

Progress Is Seen

"The fact that Westmoreland thinks we've progressed to the point where we can try a massive effort is a welcome sign in itself," a defense official commented.

The principal objective will be to clear out Vietcong forces operating in and around Route 1, the major highway from Saigon along the coast to Hue. "Actually," said one officer with tongue in cheek, "Route 1 goes all the way to Hanoi, but we have no current plans to clear it north of the 17th Parallel." The cease-fire line of 1954, dividing North and South Vietnam, is roughly on the 17th Parallel.

Attendant to the effort to secure Route 1 will be a drive to open the only north-south railroad that parallels the highway along much of its course. Secondary efforts will involve clearing operations along important lateral east-west roadways, such as Highway 21, which runs from the coast about 200 miles northeast of Saigon to Banmethuot, and Highway 19.

That will require cleaning out some coastal provinces that have harbored major Communist troop concentrations for some time, a defense official noted. The provinces include Quangngay, south of Danang, Phuyen, along the central coast, and Phuoctuy, east of Saigon.

Task Is Formidable

The job will be a tough one. In Phuyen, for example, Route 1 runs through a series of mountain defiles. "It's ideal guerrilla country," said one specialist on Vietnam. "It's a series of setups for ambush."

The planners have in mind a number of air-land-sea pincer movements in which large ground forces on foot and helicopters will go into position as blocking forces while Marine landing units sweep in from the sea to drive Communist units inland into waiting American and South Vietnamese forces. Air Force and Navy fighter-bombers will be used liberally, it is said.

It is hoped that once some of the enemy strongholds have been cleared out, South Vietnamese forces will stay behind to discourage the enemy from returning in force and to keep pressure on whatever guerrillas remain.

* * *

July 31, 1966

47 CONGRESSMEN BID U.S. REBUKE KY

Urge the Administration to Dissociate Itself From 'Spirit of Escalation'

By JOHN W. FINNEY
Special to The New York Times.

WASHINGTON, July 30—Forty-seven Representatives called upon the Johnson Administration today to dissociate itself from the "spirit of escalation" being advocated by Premier Nguyen Cao Ky of South Vietnam.

A statement by 44 Democrats and three Republicans urged the Administration to take "new initiatives" to reach a negotiated settlement. The Congressmen warned that the war was showing increasing danger of spreading.

Indirectly, they also suggested that the United States take steps to bring the Vietcong into a civilian government. They did so by urging American support of "fair and free elections open to all parties" in South Vietnam.

Background of Statement

The statement was prompted by recent proposals by Premier Ky for a military confrontation with Communist China and an armed invasion of North Vietnam and by the Johnson Administration's failure thus far to repudiate directly the suggestions by the South Vietnamese leader.

In an interview in the current issue of U. S. News & World Report, Premier Ky called for an allied invasion of North Vietnam to crush the aggression from the North, even at the risk of bringing Communist China into the war.

Describing the Communist Chinese as the "real enemy" in Southeast Asia, the Premier said, "It is better to face them now than in 5 or 10 years."

Apparently because of a desire not to offend the South Vietnamese leader, the White House and the State Department this week have declined to comment directly on Premier Ky's statements.

Only by indirection has the State Department repudiated the suggestions by emphasizing that the United States position remains one of "not seeking any wider war" and not threatening any regime.

The statement by the 47 Representatives said that the "recent statements by Premier Ky suggesting an invasion of North Vietnam and eventual war with China indicate that he and other South Vietnamese generals have ambitions that extend far beyond and contradict the limited aims stated by President Johnson in seeking self-determination for the Vietnamese people."

"The spiral of escalation now being advocated by General Ky must be opposed and new initiatives attempted for negotiated settlement," the statement added.

The statement said Premier Ky's declarations "dramatize the necessity for the American Government to redirect its energies more forcefully in pursuit of a peaceful political settlement of the war."

"The danger that the war will spread is increasing daily," it continued. "Extension of the conflict may embroil the major powers of the world in a destructive and brutal confrontation that would shatter all hopes of world peace."

A Possible New Initiative

As one possible "new initiative," the statement suggested that the United States "should use its great influence to assure that fair and free elections open to all parties will be held in the South so that a truly representative government may be established."

"The granting of political rights to all would offer a peaceful alternative to those who now pursue the path of armed rebellion," it added.

The statement was initiated by Representative Don Edwards, Democrat of California, who is national chairman of Americans for Democratic Action.

One unusual feature of the statement was that it drew far wider support among House members than past statements drafted by a small group of liberal Democrats opposed to Administration policy in Vietnam.

According to its drafters, the statement probably would have had even more signers if it had not been for the implicit suggestion that the Vietcong be included in any eventual civilian government in Saigon.

In addition to Mr. Edwards, those Representatives signing the statement were:

DEMOCRATS

Joseph P. Addabbo, New York; John A. Blatnik, Minnesota; Jonathan B. Bingham, New York; George E. Brown Jr., California; Phillip Burton, California; Ronald Brooks Cameron, California; Jeffery Cohelan, California; John Conyers Jr., Michigan; John Dow, New York; Ken W. Dyal, California; Leonard Farbstein, New York; Donald Fraser, Minnesota; Jacob H. Gilbert, New York; Bernard B. Grabowski, Connecticut; Henry B. Gonzalez, Texas; Augustus Hawkins, California; Ken Hechler, West Virginia; Henry Helstoski, New Jersey; Robert W. Kastenmeier, Wisconsin Robert Leggett, California; John C. Mackie, Michigan; Spark M. Matsunaga, Hawaii; Richard M. McCarthy, New York.

Also Patsy T. Mink, Hawaii; William S. Moorhead, Pennsylvania; Robert N. C. Nix, Pennsylvania; Barrett O'Hara, Illinois; Edward J. Patten, New Jersey; Thomas Rees, California; Joseph Y. Resnick, New York; Henry S. Reuss, Wisconsin; Benjamin S. Rosenthal, New York; Edward Roybal, California; William F. Ryan, New York; James H. Scheuer, New York; John R. Schmidhauser, Iowa; William L. St. Onge, Connecticut; Herbert Tenzer, New York; Lionel van Deerlin, California; Weston Vivian, Michigan; Jerome R. Waldie, California; Lester Wolff, New York; Sydney R. Yates, Illinois.

REPUBLICANS

Seymour Halpern, New York; Theodore R. Kupferman, New York; Ogden Reid, New York.

* * *

July 31, 1966

U.S. PLANES BOMB BUFFER TERRITORY DIVIDING VIETNAM

Blow at Demilitarized Zone, First in War, Is Ordered to Counter Infiltration

AIRCRAFT STRIKE TWICE

Washington Says Move Does Not Necessarily Portend Ground Attack on Area

By R. W. APPLE Jr.
Special to The New York Times.

SAIGON, South Vietnam, July 30—United States warplanes bombed the demilitarized zone between North and South Vietnam today for the first time.

A United States military spokesman said the attack had been ordered because North Vietnamese troops had used the six-mile-wide buffer strip as an avenue of infiltration and as a sanctuary. No American troops have fought in the zone.

[A second United States air attack in the zone was carried out Sunday, according to The Associated Press.]

[In Washington, officials said the bombing was intended as a warning to North Vietnam against further infiltration through the buffer area and did not necessarily portend extension of the ground war into the zone.]

The 1954 Geneva accord that ended the French-Indochinese war banned all military activity in the zone. North Vietnam signed the accord, but the United States did not. It associated itself with the goals of the agreement.

Attackers From Guam

Although the latest bombing was expected to produce protest, other articles of the accord have been violated repeatedly—for example, a provision barring the introduction of jet aircraft into North or South Vietnam. The International Control Commission, composed of India, Poland and Canada, has tacitly admitted its inability to enforce the provisions of the accord.

In today's attack, 15 eight-engine B-52 Stratofortresses each carrying up to 60,000 pounds of bombs, swept over the target at 5:10 A.M. They had flown from Andersen Air Force Base on Guam, more than 2,500 miles away.

The spokesman described the target area as a complex of ammunition dumps, gun positions and weapons storage areas from which American planes had been fired upon in recent days. It is about 15 miles inland from the South China Sea and less than a mile south of the Benhai River, which forms

Associated Press

RESCUE OPERATION: A member of a U.S. Marine Corps evacuation crew adjusts a sling around a wounded man as another marine signals a helicopter to pick up the victim. The scene occurred last week in course of Operation Hastings, in Quangtri Province.

the demarcation line between North and South, roughly at the 17th Parallel.

United States marines have been fighting North Vietnam's 324-B Division in Quangtri Province, the northernmost in South Vietnam, for 16 days. Through yesterday, the marines reported having killed 818 enemy troops.

Informed sources said there had been a dramatic acceleration in Communist infiltration across the demilitarized zone since the onset of the monsoon rains in Laos last month made the maze of tracks known as the Ho Chi Minh Trail nearly impassable.

The entire 324-B Division, estimated at 8,000 to 10,000 men, is believed to have entered South Vietnam through the zone. Prisoners taken by the Americans during heavy fighting last week said many of their comrades had retreated into that area.

Marines engaged in Operation Hastings, the code name for the campaign in Quangtri Province have maneuvered to within 500 yards of the demilitarized zone. But the spokesman said no American troops were within six miles of the target of the B-52 raid.

Brig. Gen. Lowell E. English, assistant commander of the Third Marine Division and chief of the Hastings task force, said last week that his men had been ordered to shoot back if they were fired upon from the demilitarized zone.

The United States spokesman here said reconnaissance reports had shown "large enemy troop concentrations" in the demilitarized zone.

Other military sources said a large buildup had also taken place just across the North Vietnamese border, where intensive air raids in the last two weeks have produced hundreds of secondary explosions from gasoline and ammunition dumps.

There was apparently some reluctance on the part of the United States to disclose the attack. The communiqué distributed at the American military briefing here said only that the B-52's had "struck a major base camp in northern Quangtri Province." The fact that the target was in that part of Quangtri inside the demilitarized zone was elicited by correspondents' questions.

Three times in the past, United States planes have mistakenly bombed the buffer strip, and each time the American command has taken pains to indicate that the action was unintentional.

In the first two raids, on Sept. 16 and 17, 1965, about 40 South Vietnamese policemen and their families were killed. The policemen guard the bridge across the Benhai River. In the third raid, on Nov. 13, a civilian was killed.

Before the latest raid, United States pilots dropped a million leaflets over the area just north of the zone, warning residents to stay away. It was reasonably certain that wind current carried a number of the leaflets into the zone.

In North Vietnam, United States pilots flew 100 missions yesterday, striking 11 fuel dumps.

* * *

August 29, 1966

STRATEGISTS SEE NEED IN VIETNAM FOR 600,000 G.I.'S

Would Double U.S. Strength in Next 18 Months Even if Hanoi Changes Tactics

PACIFICATION IS AN AIM

Effort at 'Nation Building' Would Accompany a Drive on Vietcong Strongholds

By WILLIAM M. BEECHER
Special to The New York Times.

SAIGON, South Vietnam, Aug. 28—Top military strategists here, engaged in long-range planning of the war effort, are thinking in terms of building American forces in Vietnam to about 600,000 over the next 18 months.

That would double the number of United States troops here.

The planners are looking toward a two-part effort.

A third to a half of the American troops would devote most of their efforts to ambitious "nation building" projects in the densely populated areas of Vietnam.

The rest would attack harder and in greater numbers the principal enemy base areas, in which the Vietcong have traditionally trained men, stored supplies, planned attacks and then recuperated after each fight.

Bigger Force Held Necessary

Significantly larger forces are required, the thinking goes, regardless of whether the enemy continues to form division-size units and seek big victories or decides to break up into smaller elements and revert to hit-and-run harassing attacks.

Concurrent with the projected buildup of ground forces, the Air Force would add about five new squadrons of tactical fighter-bombers to the 18 it now operates in South Vietnam and would vastly expand its airlift capacity to haul daily thousands of tons of ammunition, food and other supplies from coastal ports to combat units in the interior.

The Navy would add a number of coastal surveillance craft and river patrol boats.

The deployment of 200,000 to 300,000 G.I.'s to help South Vietnamese military and civilian teams build up the country from the hamlet level would constitute a significant shift in emphasis. The Marines devote a substantial part of their effort in the northern provinces of South Vietnam to civic action projects, and Army units, to a lesser degree, are also involved in pacification programs.

But to date the military effort has concentrated on searching for and engaging the enemy's main combat elements.

That was long regarded as the proper emphasis because of the nearness of an enemy victory in the spring and summer of 1965, before the commitment of major American combat units.

But no responsible official, military or civilian, American or South Vietnamese, now says the Vietcong appear preeminent in the field. On the contrary, in battle after battle for several months, enemy forces have consistently come off second best.

They no longer have the initiative to pick the time and place for each battle. Their infrequent surprise attacks are now costly because of the speed with which American and allied forces can rush reinforcements and firepower into the battle.

Victories Are Not Enough

But ranking officials here, as in Washington, believe that military victories are not enough.

Unless the 10 million or more peasants can be persuaded that the Saigon Government will provide security and improve their living conditions, the long-range prospects of defeating the enemy are considered bleak.

The Vietcong have planted well-indoctrinated, highly motivated cells in the hamlets and villages. They have been able to exact taxes, food and military recruits from the generally apathetic peasantry by promising a better life and threatening to call in guerrilla bands or Vietcong army units if their demands are not met.

One high United States official commented:

"The only way to uproot this Communist infrastructure is to get into each village and win over the peasants by providing them some peace from marauders, by building schools and dispensaries, providing teachers for their children, fertilizer for their crops, market roads, some voice in their government, local and national.

"Where this has been done, in some cases at least, the peasants have started to point out the Vietcong agents in their midst. They've told us about booby traps, arms caches and enemy hideouts in some cases."

Troops to Destroy Caches

American forces that sweep into enemy base areas will not pull out after a couple of weeks as they have done, the planners say. The troops will stay for a month or more, searching out weapons caches in caves and tunnels and blowing up the hiding places so they cannot be reused.

The enemy is expected to stand and defend many of his vital installations, which have been built up by years of labor.

The planners intend to concentrate more men and more helicopters in these base-area campaigns.

New tactics are being devised to stress more patrolling on foot, with assistance from fighter-bombers and tanks, for the units that will concentrate on pacification efforts along the coastline. It is believed that these units will encounter mostly smaller enemy forces.

* * *

August 30, 1966

SOVIET IS REVILED BY PEKING THRONG IN ALL-DAY RALLY

Marchers Set Up Din Near Embassy but Are Kept at Distance by Police

RUSSIANS CLOSE GATES

Youthful Red Guards Erect Portraits of Their Heroes to Block Car Passage

By Reuters

PEKING, Aug. 29—Thousands of demonstrators paraded today in a street near the Soviet Embassy in a rally against "revisionism"—China's name for Soviet Communism.

No incidents were reported and the well-disciplined marchers never went nearer than 100 yards from the embassy in a demonstration that lasted all day.

[Japanese reports from Peking said further demonstrations planned for Tuesday apparently had been canceled by the Chinese leadership to avoid a possible diplomatic break with the Soviet Union, The Associated Press reported from Tokyo.]

Associated Press Radiophoto

GUARDING SOVIET EMBASSY: Communist Chinese soldiers at Soviet Embassy in Peking to control demonstrations by Red Guards, youth group backing party head Mao Tse-tung. Device, center, broadcasts voice instructions and displays images on screen.

United Press International Radiophoto

ON 'ANTI-REVISIONISM STREET': Chinese Communist youths cluster around sign bearing new name given to street leading to Soviet Embassy in Peking as they take part in massive demonstration outside the embassy building. Being held up at center is a picture of Mao Tse-tung, party chairman, who is ardently backed by Red Guards.

The embassy was guarded by about 200 Chinese troops and policemen. Foreign diplomats and correspondents, who received printed invitations to attend, moved freely among the marchers.

Compound's Gates Shut

The main gates of the walled embassy compound remained closed. Soldiers and policemen formed a double row to guard the gates. But the embassy was subjected to a din of amplified drumming and shouted slogans from the marchers.

The demonstration began with a formal ceremony changing the name of the Street of Growing Prestige to Anti-Revisionism Street.

The demonstration seemed to some observers to be partly a defiant reply from the militant Red Guards to a Soviet note last week complaining about their "hooligan pranks" outside the embassy.

The Red Guard, loose bands consisting mostly of teenagers, are the vanguard of China's continuing "great proletarian cultural revolution" aimed at removing all old and foreign influences from Chinese life.

Restraint Is Urged

Although the youths have government approval for their activities, excesses in recent days have prompted official admonishment that reasoning, not violence, is the path to success.

In the demonstration, young Red Guards placed huge portraits of the party chairman, Mao Tse-tung, and of Marx, Engels, Lenin and Stalin a few paces in front of the green-domed embassy's gates. The spot is near where foreign diplomats and newsmen were taunted and threatened last week.

The portraits blocked the passage of any car that might try to leave or enter the embassy.

Most of the demonstrators crowding the streets around the embassy were Red Guards. Each demonstrator carried a red booklet of quotations from Chairman Mao's works, and shouted in unison slogans attacking Soviet "revisionism."

It was a well-organized rally and the demonstrators lined the neighboring streets in orderly fashion.

Reporting generally on the progress of the revolution, Hsinhua, the official press agency, said the young Red Guards had responded well to the call for more discipline and civility in pressing their crusade.

"They are determined to become model workers in applying mass discipline and carrying out the policies of the party and the state and to build the Red Guard into highly organized and disciplined ranks of revolutionary young people," it said.

The agency reported in another dispatch that the revolution had swept through every city in China.

During the ceremony in which the street was renamed, Red Guards gave a series of speeches denouncing Soviet revisionism at the top of their voices from a platform, built on the boulevard on the opposite end of the street from the embassy. Then the demonstrators marched out of the street leading to the embassy, but continued to stream past the platform beating drums, gongs and cymbals and shouting slogans all day.

Every column of marchers was led by a big garlanded gilt-framed portrait of Chairman Mao, followed by a percussion band. Pairs of loudspeakers were placed every few yards along the embassy street, making it impossible to be heard except by shouting loudly.

Behind the embassy walls there was no sign of activity, but Soviet sources said a side gate was being used for embassy business.

Guards Seem Less Active

Meanwhile, the Red Guards continued their activities in the city center, but there appeared to be fewer than last week.

Diplomats and correspondents have seen several cases of rough treatment of Chinese adults, mostly in the night before the mass rally. Others involved young people, probably about the same age as some of the Red Guards.

In one case a girl, about 16, was seen being driven off in a Red Guard truck with older people, presumably members of her family. The girl wore a tall, pointed hat with inscriptions denouncing her. The adults wore placards around their necks.

There was still no word on what had become of about 16 Chinese nuns believed to have been in a convent occupied by the Red Guards last week.

Eight foreign nuns who were also in the convent when it was taken over have been expelled from China for "illegal espionage activities."

* * *

October 11, 1966

HANOI BARS PART OF THANT'S PLAN

It Rules Out De-escalation of Ground War, but Backs Call for End of Bombing

By DREW MIDDLETON
Special to The New York Times.

UNITED NATIONS, N. Y., Oct. 10—Nhan Dan, the organ of the North Vietnamese Communist party, has rejected Secretary General Thant's proposal for de-escalation of the ground war while endorsing his call for a cessation of United States bombing.

The article in the Communist newspaper was regarded by United Nations officials as the first authoritative response by President Ho Chi Minh's Government to Mr. Thant's three steps to peace.

[In Peking, the Chinese denounced the recent peace proposals of the United States, Britain, the Vatican and Mr. Thant and asserted that American troops "must be withdrawn immediately and completely."]

A report on the North Vietnamese article was received at the United Nations shortly after Torsten Nilsson, Sweden's Foreign Minister, proposed to the General Assembly that the United States take the lead in reducing ground operations in addition to halting air strikes in an effort to bring North Vietnam to the conference table.

The general tone of the Communist statement on peace moves is intransigent.

The peace plea of Pope Paul VI was dismissed as "nothing but an appeal to the Vietnamese people" to surrender that "will never be heeded."

The United Nations was told it "must" condemn American aggression and force the United States to respect the organization's Charter and the Geneva agreements of 1954 that ended the Indochina war and set up North and South Vietnam.

Jean Raffaelli, the French Press Agency's correspondent in Hanoi, in a dispatch dated Oct. 6, characterized the article as comparable to an official reply.

Only one approach, the article indicated, is acceptable to Hanoi: international condemnation of American "aggression" with the United States accepting the consequences in the form of a withdrawal from South Vietnam.

Mr. Thant's three steps to peace, proposed early this year, are an end to the bombing of North Vietnam, a scaling down of military activities by both sides and the participation of the Vietcong in a settlement. Sources close to the Secretary General noted that he had never called for a simultaneous de-escalation of the ground operations but only a "scaling down of all military operations by all sides."

Nhan Dan accepted the first point as a self-evident step to peace but was highly critical of the second. The Secretary General, it said, in general has voiced "relatively objective opinions" and "revealed the bellicose nature of American imperialism."

But his second point was considered "passive" and contradictory.

"Thant has not made the necessary distinction," the article said, "namely that American imperialism is the aggressor and the Vietnamese people is the victim of aggression. He demands that this people should curb its struggle for independence and freedom."

The Secretary General's proposal for the reduction of military operations by both sides, Nhan Dan said, differs little from American "trumpetings" about simultaneous de-escalation.

The Communist paper warmly welcomed Mr. Thant's proposal for Vietcong representation at the peace conference. It called the National Liberation Front, which is the political arm of the Vietcong, the only authentic spokesman of the South Vietnamese people.

Pope Paul's appeal was dismissed as that of "certain religious powers" which "chant in unison with American imperialism." These powers, Nhan Dan said, have launched "moving appeals" about peace while "keeping up an orchestral accompaniment to the ditty composed by Goldberg for the United Nations."

This was a reference to the proposal by Arthur J. Goldberg, the chief United States delegate to the United Nations, that the United States would stop bombing the North if Hanoi indicated it would scale down its activity in South Vietnam.

Nhan Dan's admonition to the United Nations to condemn the United States went beyond anything the General Assembly seems prepared to do now. Mr. Nilsson's proposals also went beyond anything thus far put forward by a non-Communist, or nonaligned Government.

Both actions reinforced the pressure in what Mr. Nilsson called "a veritable poll of international public opinion" for unilateral action by the United States to promote negotiations.

The Assembly's concentration on a settlement in Southeast Asia also encouraged an unorthodox proposal on membership for Communist China. Frank Aiken, Ireland's Minister for External Affairs, suggested that the Communists take Nationalist China's seat in the Security Council while Nationalist China remains a member with a place in the General Assembly.

These proposals by leading neutrals reflected, diplomats said, a general uneasiness over the stalemate on peace talks and the absence of Communist China from any settlement here that might guarantee the future stability of the Indochinese peninsula.

Poland contributed the major attack on United States policy in today's debate. Josef Winiewicz, Deputy Foreign Minister, discussing the growing opposition to that policy, cited a New York Times editorial as evidence. Present American policy, he said, "leads nowhere" and "certainly closes the door" to a peaceful settlement.

* * *

October 28, 1966

RED CHINA SAYS A-BOMB BORNE BY GUIDED MISSILE EXPLODED ON TEST TARGET

BIG ADVANCE SEEN

Peking's Fourth Bomb May Have Put It On Par With France

Special to The New York Times.

HONG KONG, Friday, Oct. 28—Communist China announced today that it had exploded on target a nuclear weapon carried by a guided missile.

Peking gave no details of either the extent of the explosion or the distance the missile had traveled in the test, conducted yesterday.

A communiqué issued by Hsinhua, the Chinese Communist press agency, said:

"On Oct. 27, 1966, China successfully conducted over its own territory a guided missile-nuclear weapon test. The guided missile flew normally and the nuclear warhead accurately hit the target at the appointed distance, effecting a nuclear explosion."

The test, the fourth in a series of nuclear explosions begun just over two years ago, marks a giant Chinese stride toward operational nuclear capability. With each of its last two tests Peking has progressed faster than was generally predicted.

Estimate by McNamara

The test may have put China on a par with France in nuclear development. The French say they have tested a warhead for a medium-range ballistic missile they are developing. The United States, the Soviet Union and Britain have exploded hydrogen bombs.

[In Washington, United States officials suggested that the test might increase worldwide pressure for the signing of a treaty barring the spread of atomic weapons. But other sources speculated that such large nonnuclear powers as Japan and India, on China's periphery, might now make greater demands before agreeing to forgo developing their own nuclear weapons. At the United Nations, many delegates viewed China's successful test as strengthening the case for its admission.]

The impact of the latest test, with its implication that Communist China is close to achieving a missile-delivery system, is expected to be especially unsettling in Asia, where, despite Peking's cautious reluctance to involve itself in the Vietnamese war, it appears as a belligerent, unpredictable and threatening power.

Earlier this year Secretary of Defense Robert S. McNamara estimated that China would be capable of launching a nuclear attack on countries within 500 miles of its borders within two or three years and against the United States within a decade or more.

The test's success was insured, the Peking communiqué said, by "the Chinese People's Liberation Army and China's scientists, technicians and broad sections of workers and functionaries, who, enthusiastically responding to the call of Comrade Lin Piao and holding high the great red banner of Mao Tse-tung's thought, put politics in the forefront."

The communiqué said they were "propelled by the great proletarian cultural revolution," which is Peking's term for the current purge of people and ideas out of favor with Mr. Mao and Mr. Lin.

Analysts in Hong Kong said Mr. Mao and Mr. Lin appeared to be capitalizing on the test to raise their prestige and strengthen their hand in continuing the purge.

The announcement said that the test marked the fact that China's science technology and defense capabilities were "advancing at an even greater speed under the brilliant illumination of Mao Tse-tung's thought." China has attributed all its major scientific advancements to the thought of Mr. Mao, Chairman of the Chinese Communist party's Central Committee.

Credit Given to Lin Piao

"This is a great victory for Mao Tse-tung's thought," the communiqué said. "It fully testifies to the fact that once Mao Tse-tung's thought is grasped by the masses, it generates a tremendous material force and displays incomparably great power."

"It is another new important achievement scored by the Chinese people in further strengthening their national defense and safeguarding the security of their country, and the peace of the world," it added.

Lin Piao, Defense Minister and heir apparent to Mr. Mao, and the military establishment he guides, were among those given credit for the test's success.

The first Chinese atomic device, detonated Oct. 15, 1964, had an explosive force equivalent to that of the United States bomb dropped on Hiroshima—or about 20,000 tons of TNT.

The second blast, which appeared to have been somewhat larger, took place May 14, 1965.

On May 8 last the Chinese conducted what they described as a "nuclear explosion that contained thermonuclear material."

The United States Atomic Energy Commission twice upgraded its estimate of the size of this explosion, finally stating that it had a yield exceeding 200 kilotons, or more than 200,000 tons of TNT—about 10 times the original estimate.

Many analysts had believed that the Chinese were capable of delivering their bombs only with obsolete Soviet-made aircraft. However, they have been test-firing missiles of many types for several years and are known to have received from the Russians a small number of missiles with a range of more than 1,000 miles.

Studied in the U.S.

The man believed to be most responsible for Chinese missile development is Tsien Hsue-shen, who received his master's degree in aeronautical engineering from the Massachusetts Institute of Technology and his doctorate from the California Institute of Technology.

Many Asian leaders have tended to play down China's growing nuclear strength and have allowed themselves to be convinced by Western estimates that the Chinese were still a long way from attaining full membership in the "nuclear club."

The Chinese reflected their expectation of an unfavorable reaction in Asia by declaring, as they had on the occasion of previous tests, that they were developing nuclear weapons "entirely for the purpose of defense," with the ultimate aim of destroying them.

The communiqué stated:

"We solemnly declare once again that at no time and in no circumstances will China be the first to use nuclear weapons. As in the past, the Chinese people and Government will continue to carry on an unswerving struggle, together with all other peace-loving people, and countries of the world, for the noble aim of completely prohibiting and thoroughly destroying nuclear weapons."

Peking has taken a stand against the treaty for a partial nuclear test ban. It declined an invitation from the United Nations General Assembly to participate in a world disarmament conference and has also spurned a suggestion by Secretary General Thant that Chinese Communist delegates take part in disarmament talks in Geneva.

Periodically Communist China has proposed the holding of a world summit conference to discuss the prohibition and destruction of nuclear weapons. This proposal, viewed by observers as a propaganda gesture, was not mentioned in the communiqué today.

The communiqué also included a sharp denunciation of the United States and the Soviet Union, which it said were "stepping up their collaboration and contriving to strike a bargain on the question of the so-called prevention of nuclear proliferation so as to maintain their nuclear monopoly and sabotage the revolutionary struggle of the people of various countries."

"China's purpose in developing nuclear weapons," the communiqué added, "is precisely to oppose the nuclear monopoly and nuclear blackmail by the United States and the Soviet Union, acting in collusion."

While professing that its nuclear weapons were for the purpose of defense, Communist China did not hestitate to hint that they might be used for other purposes. It declared:

"The possession by the Chinese people of guided missiles and nuclear weapons is a great encouragement to the heroic Vietnamese people, who are waging a war of resistance against U.S. aggression and for national salvation, and to all revolutionary peoples of the world who are now engaged in heroic struggle as well as a new contribution to the defense of world peace."

* * *

October 28, 1966

FREE DEMOCRATS QUIT BONN REGIME, ENDING COALITION

Four Ministers Resign in Fight on Tax-Rise Plan—Erhard Future in Doubt

By PHILIP SHABECOFF
Special to The New York Times.

BONN, Oct. 27—West Germany's government coalition disintegrated today.

The four Cabinet Ministers belonging to the Free Democratic party, minority partner in the coalition, resigned, ostensibly in protest against plans by Chancellor Ludwig Erhard and his ruling Christian Democrats to raise some taxes to meet an estimated $1-billion budgetary deficit next year.

The Ministers are Vice Chancellor Erich Mende, who is the leader of the Free Democrats; Dr. Rolf Dahlgrün, the Finance Minister; Ewald Bucher, Housing Minister, and Walter Scheel, Minister for Economic Cooperation.

Chancellor Erhard now rules West Germany as head of a minority government. His hold on the Chancellorship is considered tenuous at best.

Erhard Planned to Remain

However, the rotund, cigar-smoking Bavarian politician has stated repeatedly that he intends to remain in office until the next regular election in 1969. This week a Government spokesman denied rumors that Dr. Erhard was planning to step down for the good of his party.

The present line-up in the Bundestag, or lower house of Parliament, includes 245 Christian Democrats, including their Bavarian wing, the Christian Social party, 202 Social Democrats and 49 Free Democrats.

After a 10-hour meeting yesterday it appeared that a government crisis over the budget issue had been avoided. The four Free Democratic Ministers seemingly had conceded that taxes might have to be raised to balance the 1967 federal budget.

However, at a stormy morning meeting of the party's Parliamentary group, a heterogeneous collection of old-line liberals, big business men, some right-wing nationalists and some individualists, the Ministers reverted to their adamant position.

Campaign Issue Needed

The Free Democrats, who followed more or less a classic liberal economic policy, insisted that the budget be balanced by other means than tax increases, including reduced federal expenditure and cuts in government subsidies.

It is widely believed here, however, that the budget issue was seized on by the Free Democrats as a pretext for a calculated, well-dramatized withdrawal from the Erhard Government.

With important elections coming up in Bavaria and Hesse next month, the Free Democrats were badly in need of a dramatic campaign issue.

They have been losing ground at the polls steadily in recent years and in Bavaria they stand in danger of falling below the 10 per cent of the vote a party must achieve to be entitled to Parliamentary seats.

More significant is the fact that the Free Democratic party has lost its liking for Chancellor Erhard's leadership in recent months and has been increasingly at odds with him on vital policy matters.

By breaking the present coalition the Free Democrats have cleared the way for cooperation with a new Chancellor in a new government altogether, of course.

Ratner Barzel, leader of the Christian Democrats in the Bundestag, placed the entire blame for the coalition's collapse on the Free Democrats. Their Ministers, he said, refused further cooperation "in the responsible conduct of government."

The collapse of the coalition has pushed the political situation in Bonn into a state of extreme fluidity. At least half a dozen possibilities for a new government are open.

Statement by Government

A Government spokesman said tonight that Chancellor Erhard would seek a tenable majority for his Government as soon as possible.

Dr. Erhard was reported to have asked Minister of Economics Kurt Schmücker to take over the Finance Ministry and Minister for Refugees Johann-Baptist Gradl to take over the Ministry for All-German Affairs, which was held by Dr. Mende.

The Chancellor was also said to have asked Werner Dollinger, Minister for Federal Assets, to take over the Economic Cooperation Portfolio and Dr. Bruno Heck, Minister for Family Affairs, to look after the Housing Ministry.

At the moment, it seems most likely that Dr. Erhard will continue as head of a minority government for a while. That period could be very short, but the Chancellor will be difficult to dislodge if he makes a fight of it.

The West German Constitution, whose electoral provisions were designed to prevent the fatal instability that characterized the Weimar Republic after World War I, stacks the odds against the removal of a Chancellor between elections.

Article 67 of the Constitution provides that a Chancellor can be unseated only by a "constructive vote of no confidence", that is, Parliament must elect a successor to the Chancellorship by a majority vote at the same time that it votes no confidence in the incumbent.

The Chancellor can himself call for a vote of confidence. If he fails to get it, he can ask the federal President to dissolve the Bundestag and call a new election within the next 21 days.

With the political tide in West Germany running in favor of the Opposition Social Democratic party in recent months, however, the ruling Christian Democrats would be very reluctant to call a new national election.

Dr. Erhard has been under constant attack almost since the day he took over the Chancellorship from Dr. Konrad Adenauer Oct. 15, 1963. In recent months he has been assailed with increasing frequency for alleged lack of leadership.

At 69 he may be willing to withdraw from the tremendous pressures of the Chancellorship.

There is no dearth of Christian Democrats waiting in the wings if the Chancellor does step down.

Among those considered available for the job are Mr. Barzel, Dr. Eugen Gerstenmaier, president of the Bundestag; Paul Lücke, the Interior Minister; Dr. Gerhard Schröder, the Foreign Minister, and Kurt-Georg Kiesinger, Minister-President of Baden-Wurttemberg.

Former Defense Minister Franz Josef Strauss, leader of the Christian Socialist party, also is known to aspire to the Chancellorship.

* * *

November 14, 1966

PRESTIGE OF RED CHINA PLUMMETS

Fellow Communists in Asia Are Upset by Upheavals

REPUTATION IN WEST MARRED BY PURGE AND RED GUARDS

By MAX FRANKEL
Special to The New York Times.

HONG KONG, Nov. 13—Whatever urgent domestic requirements inspired Communist China's "cultural revolution," the spectacle of yet another convulsion in the world's most populous nation has done great damage to its prestige and influence around the world.

A journey around the western Pacific and reports by correspondents of The New York Times throughout the world not only support this conclusion; they show no significant doubt about it.

In just a year the upheavals inside China have changed its reputation from that of a formidable challenger of the United States throughout Asia and of the Soviet Union inside the Communist world to that of a hobbled giant riddled by dissent and thus incapable of sustained growth and self-assertion.

Startled, bemused or just plain confused by strife among the Chinese leaders and their inability to settle the conflict within the institutions of their Government and party, the non-Communists of Asia have become less awed by their giant neighbor, Communists have become more ashamed, and Russians and Americans have been moved in Asia and elsewhere to try to exploit Peking's loss of glamour.

Prestige, of course, is often a transitory attribute, especially in international politics, where governments tend to judge others only through distorting lenses of their own interests. Nevertheless, officials and diplomats sense particular significance in the fact that China's reputation has discernibly diminished, not only among non-Communist nations but among communities of Chinese living outside China and among parties and front organizations of the Communist world.

From Nathan Road here in Hong Kong, where the sentimental attachment of the Chinese to their homeland has always been formidable, to Leninallee in East Berlin, where there has always been a modicum of admiration for the Spartans of Peking, there are now signs of deep disappointment and disaffection.

The overseas Chinese, often feared by their host countries as a potential fifth column responsive to Peking, are said to have been dismayed by the sacrifices of economic progress and orderly government to the drive for ideological purity and the purge.

The spectacle of weakness and division in China has more than vitiated the pride and encouragement these same communities derived only recently from Chinese development of nuclear weapons and other attributes of big-power status.

The Communists of most nations are described as dismayed by the fact that China is contributing so vividly to the reputation of all Communists as dogmatic, totalitarian, violent and even irrational. At a time when most Communists had decided to concentrate on providing a better life for the people of their own countries and avoiding military conflict, Peking is found to be an embarrassing liability.

In the world at large the turmoil in Peking is thought also to have damaged the Communist cause in two specific ways.

First, by aggravating their conflict with Moscow and straining relations even with North Vietnam, the Chinese have blocked all chances of international Communist cooperation for either military or diplomatic support of North Vietnam.

And by their own militant conduct and refusal to coexist even with Communist nations the Chinese are thought to have given greater credence to the American argument that Peking is a threat to stability and peace and therefore a proper object of containment.

Non-Communists in Asia such as the Japanese, who have sought to find their own path to good relations with China, have been particularly startled by the emotional extremism unleashed in Peking.

Asians Turn to Soviet

For Asian Communists the "cultural revolution," the stridency of Peking's propaganda and the spectacle of Red Guard excesses appear to have been taken as yet another indication that the Soviet Union, though white and European, makes a better claim to leadership of the Communist movement.

The Japanese Communists, already alienated by Chinese nuclear tests and opposition to joining the treaty forbidding most nuclear tests, have broken sharply with Peking recently. The North Koreans have continued their swing away from association with China and back toward alignment with Moscow.

And the North Vietnamese, though dependent on Chinese support in their war, have firmly rejected Peking's contention that the Soviet Union is acting in collusion with the United States. By their neutrality in the dispute between their bigger allies they have greatly strained relations with the Chinese and made themselves increasingly dependent upon Soviet assistance.

The decline in China's prestige began last year after the failure of the coup by the pro-Chinese Indonesian Communist party and after the expulsion of Peking's envoys from several African countries.

Yet China's test of nuclear weapons and its encouragement of the guerrilla war against the United States in Vietnam tended to offset the damage. At least in its own sphere in Asia, China continued to loom as a great power, demanding not only recognition but subservience by other nations. Small countries such as Cambodia still felt that their safety depended more upon the Chinese than on the Americans or anyone else.

Today, with the war in Vietnam no longer so one-sided—indeed, with the Communist drive blunted—with the United States increasingly committed to containment of Chinese influence and, above all, with the Chinese proving themselves deeply divided about their own future course, the pendulum has clearly swung the other way.

Not one report from Times correspondents found the Chinese to be enhancing their position. Following is a digest of some of those reports.

JAPAN

Chinese Communist prestige began to decline among Japanese intellectuals when well-known figures such as Kuo Mo-jo, the intellectual leader, and Peng Chen, the mayor of Peking, were struck down by the cultural revolution. The activities of the Red Guards have appalled the Japanese, who compare their juvenile excesses and the general atmosphere in China to those produced by Japanese Fascism in the late thirties. China's refusal to support negotiations on Vietnam and its insistence on developing nuclear weapons are other sources of disaffection, although the Japanese still want to expand trade with China both for its own sake and for its ameliorating effect on the Chinese.

AUSTRALIA

Communist China has long been regarded as an aggressive revolutionary force and a long-term threat. But it still seems far away to South Pacific nations and thus events inside China do not significantly affect day-to-day judgments. Nevertheless, recent signs of factional conflict in China and failure of the North Vietnamese to make progress in the war have brought a feeling of relief. The Chinese nuclear tests always produce shudders of alarm, but Peking's nuclear power is generally seen only as part of its long-range bid for power.

INDONESIA

Peking is viewed as an inevitable source of agitation and friction by the new Indonesian Government but not as a direct military threat now. Recent events in China have disturbed Chinese intellectuals and their attachment to the homeland, but the Chinese are being treated so harshly by the Indonesians that many young people who are being repatriated go with a strong commitment to Peking's ideology.

SINGAPORE

China's prestige, which had soared among the largely Chinese population, seems to have fallen as a result of the "cultural revolution" and the Red Guard movement. These events have plainly nullified the effects that China's fourth nuclear test and announcement of a guided missile last month would have had otherwise. The Singapore Chinese look on the upheaval as a reversal of all previous progress and believed it is damaging China's reputation more than anything that has happened in the 17 years since the Communists achieved power. China's stock, so far as the Vietnam war is concerned, is also thought to have dropped sharply. At least there is a marked diminution in the demands for a halt in the bombing of North Vietnam and withdrawal of American troops. Most people would prefer that Asians settle the conflict by themselves, but they plainly do not want the Chinese Communists to settle it in their way.

MALAYSIA

The Government fears China less than it fears its own Chinese population. Malaysian officials insist that the local Chinese have remained loyal to Peking and that therefore the American efforts in Vietnam and commitments to all Southeast Asia are essential to their own survival. The Malaysians say that Peking's prestige among the Chinese is so great that nothing short of civil war will shake it. But they do not consider China a direct military threat in the foreseeable future.

SOUTH VIETNAM

Few South Vietnamese look far beyond their war to events in Communist China, but Dr. Tran Van Do, the Foreign Minister, finds comfort in what he calls a conflict of the generations in Peking. He believes the Red Guard revolution has eroded China's standing in Asia. "She is more and more isolated and her 700 million people are not so great a threat as we have all been taught to think," he says. He doubts that China will enter the war unless the United States adopts altogether different tactics toward North Vietnam. He also believes that North Vietnam is now in a position to resist Chinese pressure against negotiations if it wishes.

THAILAND

The Thai Government regards China as a long-term threat to itself and other Asian nations unless the United States provides a counterforce. While there is a certain amount of cheering in the press for Peking's internal difficulties, the Government's basic view has not been influenced by either the problems or the achievements of the Chinese Communists.

INDIA

Chinese credibility suffered heavily last fall after Peking's threat to intervene in the war over Kashmir on Pakistan's side turned out to be idle. The recent Chinese nuclear test with a guided missile, however, forced the Indians to take stock again and recognize China's potential as a threat. Yet, the general belief is that China is unlikely to move soon against India or elsewhere in Southeast Asia, and now it is expected that China will concentrate on internal problems for some time.

SOVIET UNION

The Russians have sensed a serious loss of China's prestige since the collapse of the attempted coup in Indonesia and especially during the last year's cultural revolution. They appear to have decide in mid-August to take the offensive to exploit the disillusion in other Communist parties. In this effort the Russians are emphasizing Peking's refusal to join in the common front in Vietnam. But they are also concentrating on portraying internal unrest, which the Russians picture as action hostile to the mass of Chinese Communists and to party institutions. The Chinese nuclear tests contribute to the apprehensions of the average Soviet citizen. The Government takes the line that the current Chinese leadership is a transitory aberration from the Communist family and will change for the better after Chairman Mao Tse-tung is replaced.

WEST GERMANY

There have been no official assessments of events in China because of a feeling that the situation is too confused. There is some concern, however, about Chinese progress in nuclear weaponry and about the effect this will have in diverting American attention to Asia. The Germans feel that Washington already is too preoccupied with the Far East to attend to the problem of German reunification.

FRANCE

Chinese prestige has undoubtedly slipped during the recent excesses, but some of the ridicule has abated recently. It is still, however, the domestic turmoil in China, and not the atomic bomb or Vietnam, that dominates French thinking about the Chinese. However, the French Government, eager to play up its own burgeoning nuclear arsenal, has attached greater importance than others to Chinese strides in nuclear technology.

AFRICA

The Soviet Union has been doing better diplomatically than Communist China in the last year, virtually supplanting Chinese influence in Algeria and Somalia and profiting elsewhere from Chinese excesses. Peking, which has diplomatic relations with 14 of the 38 independent African nations, has opened no new embassies on the continent in more than a year. In the meantime, Dahomey and the Central African Republic have broken off relations and Peking pulled out of Ghana only last week. Even in the half-dozen countries that receive aid from China officials prefer to retain the Soviet presence as competition and insurance.

LATIN AMERICA

Communist parties throughout the continent have been split for some time into pro-Soviet and pro-Chinese factions. The latter profited somewhat from the prestige of Chinese nuclear tests, but are still clearly in a minority everywhere. Chinese extremism has aroused fear in some places that pro-Soviet Communists might become more active to compete with pro-Chinese factions. Ironically, the Cubans, though in many ways following an analogous party line, have had their own troubles with the Chinese. Because they, too, tried to strike a balance between Peking and Moscow, the Chinese have denounced Premier Fidel Castro as a revisionist and Cubans have scolded the Chinese for making fools of themselves and trying to subvert the Cuban armed forces.

UNITED STATES

Washington analysts stress the inconclusiveness of their theories about what is going on in China. They believe that China's nuclear advances have, in the short run, been nullified by the internal dissention but will, nonetheless, present a serious challenge to China's neighbors in the long run. And if the internal troubles are resolved as most observers expect, short of civil war or collapse of the regime, it is thought that China's stature will rise again. The real damage done by the current upheaval, it is thought, depends on how much more serious the situation becomes—whether the top leadership is irreparably split or whether Mr. Mao is simply trying to shake up the bureaucracy and instill a more revolutionary spirit, and whether the Red Guards will get out of hand or split into rival groups.

* * *

January 1, 1967

DE GAULLE URGES U.S. TO QUIT WAR

Asks Ending of 'Detestable' Intervention—Russians Scorn British Peace Bid

By JOHN L. HESS
Special to The New York Times.

PARIS, Dec. 31—President de Gaulle called upon the United States tonight to end what he called its "detestable" intervention in Vietnam.

In a frankly political New Year's message to the French nation by television, the President hailed the peace and prosperity of France and the easing of tensions in Europe. Then, in words blunter than he had used before on the Vietnamese war, he declared:

"But while Europe takes the road to peace, war rages in Southeast Asia. Unjust war, for it results, in fact, from the armed intervention of the United States upon the territory of Vietnam. Detestable war, since it leads a great nation to ravage a small one.

Old Friendship Invoked

"In the name of good sense, of the attachment we retain with regard to Indochina, of the two-century-old friendship we bear for America, we hold it necessary that she put an end to the ordeal by bringing her forces back to her soil."

[In Moscow, Izvestia, the Government newspaper, scorned as a political maneuver the appeal by Foreign Secretary George Brown of Britain for immediate cease-fire talks by the United States, North Vietnam and South Vietnam.]

President de Gaulle again refrained in his address from offering his services in arranging a Vietnamese settlement; he has stated that such an offer would be vain.

But he said that on the day—"however distant it be"—that the United States did decide to withdraw, France would devote herself enthusiastically to "open wide the doors to world peace."

He did not elaborate, but did add a pledge of more "aid to backward peoples," in which, he commented, France is "the champion today." The allusion was apparently to the fact that France spends a larger part of her income on aid than does any other country.

The 76-year-old President gave his message easily from memory speaking in strong, clear tones, seated behind the desk in an ornate room of the Elysée Palace. From time to time he waved his arms or raised has bushy eyebrows to emphasize a point.

On the European scene, the general placed all his emphasis on East-West rapprochement. After a passing reference to "the German question," he promised a continuing building of friendship with each of the Communist countries of East Europe. They were the only other countries he mentioned by name.

He promised also to nurture France's contacts with each of her neighbors and in working to build the economic and perhaps one day political grouping of the Western Six.

There was no allusion to Britain's desire to enter the European Common Market whose six members are France, West Germany, Italy, the Netherlands, Belgium and Luxembourg.

Most of the 10-minute talk was a frank appeal for the reelection of a Gaullist National Assembly in March.

In spite of a few human shortcomings, the President said, France is ending a year of highly satisfactory results in the field of population, economics, science and sports.

All this he, said, has resulted in peace and stability, which he contrasted with the political, social and economic upheavals that had riven the nation in other their times.

Will the French voters, he demanded, keep or destroy "so obviously effective and salutary a regime? "

"How can it be doubted," he replied, "that the future will triumph over the past?"

Since most French newspapers do not publish on Sunday the Opposition had no immediate opportunity to retort to the President's New Year's greeting. The state-owned broadcast network will grant all parties time, but only when the campaign begins officially, two months from now.

WHITE HOUSE SILENT ON TALK

JOHNSON CITY, Tex., Dec. 31 (UPI)—The Texas White House said today that it had no comment on President de Gaulle's remarks in his New Year's message.

* * *

January 4, 1967

HANOI PREMIER TELLS VIEW

Pham Van Dong Places Stress, in Discussion, on End of Fighting

By HARRISON E. SALISBURY
Special to The New York Times.

HANOI, North Vietnam, Jan. 3—In a detailed discussion of North Vietnam's views on the war in Vietnam, Premier Pham Van Dong emphasized that once hostilities were brought to an end, it would be possible to "speak of other things."

"The moment the United States puts an end to the war, we will respect each other and settle every question," he said. "Why don't you [the United States] think that way?"

At another point, he said that with a cessation of hostilities, "we can speak about other things." He added: "After this there will be no lack of generosity on our part—you may be sure of that."

The Premier, who conducted the four-hour conversation in a reception room of the Presidential Palace, spoke vivaciously, swinging around in his chair to face his interviewer directly.

He said that he did not care for interviews because he thought they hampered a free exchange of opinions. He took as a framework for his remarks a series of questions put to him by the correspondent in advance, but these were merely take-off points in a wide-ranging discussion.

The Premier also took the occasion to discuss proposals from various quarters for bringing the war to an end by discussion. He appeared thoroughly aware of the wide variety of proposals that have been advanced, and did not hesitate to express his views on some questions privately.

The discussion closed on an optimistic note. Mr. Dong said that frank talk was a good thing and was essential to understanding.

"If we do not agree today we will agree tomorrow," he said. "Otherwise the day after tomorrow."

At the same time the Premier stressed again and again that North Vietnam was prepared to fight 10 years, 20 years, or any number of years in support of its sovereignty and independence in its "sacred war."

"We are determined to fight on until our sacred rights are recognized," he said, stressing Vietnam's valiant history in resisting invaders.

Three times the Vietnamese drove the Mongols out of their country, he recalled, and he asked how many times the Pentagon wanted to fight.

"We are an independent country," he said. "We have our policy of independence and sovereignty. We are masters of our destiny, of our affairs, of our policy, of our policy both major and minor. If we were not independent we could not wage such a war as we are now waging. We are independent and sovereign in all our foreign policy. That is the situation up to the present, and so it will be in the future."

He stressed Vietnam's independence, he said, because in the United States "there has been so much misunderstanding on this point."

One question submitted to him was: Under what circumstances North Vietnam would accept volunteers? The Premier replied:

"This depends on the situation. We have made preparations. Volunteers are not lacking—volunteers for the armed forces and civilians as well. If we need them, many will come. This is an important point on which we rely. This point also shows the independence of our foreign policy."

By this he presumably meant that volunteers would come only if North Vietnam asked for them and set the conditions for their coming.

Premier Dong entered into an extended discussion of Hanoi's four-points for ending the war, which are as follows:

Recognition of the independence, sovereignty, unity and territorial integrity of Vietnam and the withdrawal of United States forces from the area; pending reunification of Vietnam, respect for the military provisions of the Geneva agreements barring foreign forces; settlement of South Vietnam's internal affairs by the South Vietnamese under the guidance of the National Liberation Front and peaceful reunification of Vietnam by the peoples of North and South without foreign interference.

The Premier stressed that the four points were not to be considered as "conditions" for peace talks. He described them as providing a "basis of settlement of the Vietnam problem." He said they were to be understood as "valid conclusions for discussion."

"The big question," he added, "is to reach a settlement which can be enforced."

"The party which has to make first steps is Washington," he continued. "We have no doubt on this point. We cannot press history forward. If this does not come about today, it will come tomorrow. It's no use to make haste. If we show haste, the question will be put wrongly and we will have to wait again. So let the situation ripen."

Mr. Dong said he thought the most difficult of Hanoi's points for the United States to accept was the third, concerning South Vietnam. On this, he said, the North fully supports the Communist-led Liberation Front, the political arm of the Vietcong, and nothing can divide the two parts of the country. However, he thought actual reunification would not be a sudden process and he said there was no intention in the North to annex the South.

"We will consider this among ourselves," he said. "We will settle it by the most convenient means. There is no rush about it."

As to how long the war might go on if unresolved by negotiation, he said:

"We are prepared for a long war because a people's war must be a long war, a war against aggression has to be a long war. Nobody knows how long it will be. It lasts until there is no more aggression.

"We are preparing for that kind of war. Everyone of our citizens thinks like that. This is the kind of question often put to us by foreigners because they don't understand."

"This kind of question surprises us," the Premier commented. "How many years? What I used to tell our friends was that the younger generation will fight better than we—even kids just so high. They are preparing themselves. That's the situation.

"I'm not telling that to impress anyone. It's the truth. It's the logical consequence of the situation. Our Vietnam nation is a very proud nation. Our history is one of a very proud nation."

"How many years the war goes on depends on you and not on us," he added.

A repeatedly emphasized point was that the determining aspect lay not in American material superiority but in the fact that the Vietnamese fought for "independence, freedom, for life itself." The Premier said that the war "stands for everything for this generation and for future generations."

He conceded that this determination on the part of the Vietnamese was difficult to understand, not only for Americans but for many of North Vietnam's friends in Europe who did not see how the North Vietnamese could withstand an American expeditionary force well equipped with weapons and the nearby Seventh Fleet.

Now, however, he said, the North Vietnamese are able to demonstrate to their friends their ability to stand up to American material force.

"I have no hope of convincing you on this point," he added, "but I must tell it to you because it is very important."

Premier Dong based his presentation on an analysis that found the North Vietnamese position one of strength, not weakness. He said Saigon and Washington did not agree with this analysis, but suggested that perhaps they would in the future. The bombing of the North, in his view, has on balance proved a military failure.

It has caused severe damage, he said, but it has not compelled the North to capitulate. On the contrary, he indicated, northern military strength has increased and will continue to do so after passing through a most difficult period.

The key factor in this, Mr. Dong said, is the courageous strength of North Vietnamese youth. He said three million had volunteered for the army.

The economic aspects of bombing have been overcome, he said, and the country is in a position to continue the war and expand its potential.

He insisted that the situation in the South had turned very favorably for the Vietcong and he particularly stressed political weakness in Saigon where, he said, intensification of the political struggle against the regime was to be expected.

* * *

January 4, 1967

SOME IN U.S. DETECT A SHIFT

'4 Points' Not Condition to Talks, Aides Note—Others Doubt Change

By HEDRICK SMITH
Special to The New York Times.

WASHINGTON, Jan. 3—Some American officials saw signs tonight of a possibly significant shift in Hanoi's position toward Vietnam peace talks in remarks by the North Vietnamese Premier, Pham Van Dong.

These officials expressed considerable interest in a dispatch from Hanoi to The New York Times quoting the Premier as having stressed that Hanoi's four-point peace program did not constitute "conditions" for peace talks.

Other officials took a more cautious view. They noted that diplomatic intermediaries, as well as European critics of the Johnson Administration, had long maintained that the four-point program had never been intended as a condition to peace talks but merely as the Communist proposals to be laid before peace negotiators.

The interpretations grew out of a dispatch by Harrison E. Salisbury, an assistant managing editor of The New York Times, reporting his discussion with Premier Dong. The dispatch said:

"The Premier stressed that the four points were not to be considered as 'conditions' for peace talks. He described them as providing a 'basis for settlement of the Vietnam problem.'

He said they were to be understood as 'valid conclusions for discussions.' "

According to some United States experts on Southeast Asia, Hanoi had previously asserted "unmistakably" that its four points had to be accepted as a basis for settlement in advance of the opening of any peace negotiations.

As a consequence, these officials tentatively interpreted Premier Dong's comments as a new departure and were inclined to attach considerable significance to them.

Hanoi's four points are:

Recognition of the independence, sovereignty, unity and territorial integrity of Vietnam, and the withdrawal of United States forces from the area; pending reunification of Vietnam, respect for the military provisions of the Geneva agreement barring foreign forces; settlement of South Vietnam's internal affairs by the South Vietnamese under the guidance of the National Liberation Front and peaceful reunification of Vietnam by the peoples of North and South without foreign interference.

The four-point plan, as first reported in April 1965, was part of a policy declaration by the North Vietnamese Premier. An English-language report on it distributed by Hsinhua, the Chinese Communist press agency, was silent on whether the points were advanced as conditions to peace talks.

The Hsinsua dispatch, as reported in The Times on April 13, 1965, said that Hanoi regarded the four-point program as "the basis for the soundest political settlement of the Vietnamese problem." It added that in the view of the North Vietnamese Government, "any approach contrary to the above-mentioned stand is inappropriate."

In the past, Washington has regarded Hanoi's position on its four-point peace program as a major stumbling block to peace talks. The United States has refused to agree to the program in advance to peace talks though President Johnson has repeatedly offered to enter into unconditional peace negotiations.

Even in the face of a possible shift in Hanoi's position, American officials declined to speculate on what steps might follow.

In the past the United States has rejected Hanoi's four points as a conditions to negotiations because of its objections to the first and third points—withdrawal of all American forces and the recognition of the National Liberation Front, the political arm of the Vietcong, as the sole legitimate representative of the Vietnamese people.

While Washington is prepared to accept withdrawal of American forces from Vietnam as the result of a compromise worked out through negotiations, it refuses to withdraw from Vietnam prior to any talks because that would mean leaving the Saigon regime "at the mercy of the Communists," as officials have put it.

Earlier Dispatch Criticized

The Defense Department, meanwhile, in a letter made public today, again charged inaccuracies in a dispatch sent by Mr. Salisbury from North Vietnam on Christmas Day, which reported extensive damage from American bombs to civilian areas in the city of Namdinh.

The letter, dated Dec. 30 and signed by Phil G. Goulding, a Deputy Assistant Secretary of Defense for Public Affairs, was addressed to Representative Ogden Reid, Republican of Westchester.

In a prior telephone conversation with Mr. Goulding, Mr. Reid, a member of the Government information subcommittee of the House Committee on Government Operations, had requested, among other matters, that the Defense Department explain the apparent discrepancy between Mr. Salisbury's dispatches and Administration statements that it is American policy to bomb only military targets in North Vietnam.

In the letter, Mr. Goulding termed as "without accuracy" a statement in Mr. Salisbury's dispatch that "no American communiqué has asserted that Namdinh contains some facility that the United States regards as a military objective."

Mr. Goulding then repeated the essence of a statement made Thursday by Arthur Sylvester, Assistant Secretary of Defense for Public Affairs, that attacks on military targets in Namdinh had been announced three times in American military communiqués released in Saigon each day.

The Saigon military communiqué mentioned an attack on targets in Namdinh in April and twice in May, Mr. Goulding said. Mr. Sylvester said that targets in and around the city have been attacked 64 times since the middle of 1965.

"The New York Times simply did not take the time to research the matter themselves or, indeed, to ask our assistance," Mr. Goulding asserted.

Before it was published last Tuesday, Mr. Salisbury's dispatch was read to Defense Department officials. In a statement printed in the same issue of The New York Times, Administration officials conceded for the first time that American bombing raids against North Vietnam were accidentally causing damage to civilian areas.

The officials also said that there were military targets in Namdinh and the American aircraft had repeatedly bombed them.

* * *

February 14, 1967

U.S. RENEWS RAIDS IN NORTH, BUT PLEDGES PEACE EFFORT, AS DO MOSCOW AND LONDON

JOHNSON EXPLAINS

Says Foe Used Pause to Send Supplies to Troops in South

By JOHN W. FINNEY
Special to The New York Times.

WASHINGTON, Feb. 13—The United States resumed the bombing of North Vietnam today after a pause of nearly six days.

In explaining his decision to resume the attacks, President Johnson said the United States had "no alternative but to resume full-scale hostilities" in view of the use of the truce by the North Vietnamese for "major resupply efforts of their troops in South Vietnam" rather than to seek a peaceful settlement of the war.

The President emphasized, however, that "the door is open and will remain open" to a negotiated settlement.

The President's statement was issued about four hours after the bombing was resumed at 12:07 P.M. Eastern standard time (1:07 A.M. Tuesday, Saigon time) with strikes against targets in the southern section of North Vietnam.

The United States suspended the bombing at 6 P.M. Eastern standard time last Tuesday for the four-day Tet truce marking the lunar new year. On Presidential orders, the pause was extended until today.

White House Statement

Through the White House press secretary, George Christian, Mr. Johnson issued the following statement:

"It had been our hope that the truce periods connected with Christmas, New Year's and Tet might lead to some abatement of hostilities and to moves toward peace. Unfortunately, the only response we have had from the Hanoi Government was to use the periods for major resupply efforts of their troops in South Vietnam.

"Despite our efforts and those of third parties, no other response has yet come from Hanoi. Under these circumstances, in fairness to our own troops and those of our allies, we had no alternative but to resume full-scale hostilities after the cease-fire period. But the door is open and will remain open and we are prepared at any time to go more than halfway to meet any equitable overture from the other side."

The bombing resumption was announced at 12:45 P.M. by the Defense Department, which for the first time acknowledged that the United States had extended the pause beyond the originally scheduled four-day period.

As the Pentagon was making its announcement, the State Department was declining at a regular briefing to confirm that an extended pause was in effect, saying that this was "an operational matter."

The Defense Department also acknowledged that there had been a political motivation behind the extension of the bombing pause.

It said the pause had been extended so as not to interfere with the talks in London between Prime Minister Wilson and the Soviet Premier, Aleksei N. Kosygin.

The following statement was issued by the Defense Department:

"Combat operations against military targets in North Vietnam have now been resumed. The suspension of the operations, initiated at the beginning of Tet, was continued beyond the end of Tet for a short additional time in order to avoid any possibility that earlier resumption would be misconstrued in relation to Mr. Kosygin's visit to London."

Administration officials said the Kosygin-Wilson talks had not been the only factor in the decision to extend the bombing pause.

Assurance Was Sought

During the cease-fire, as indicated in the President's statement, the United States, through diplomatic channels, sought to ascertain if Hanoi was willing to modify its terms for discussions. It was decided to extend the bombing pause to give encouragement to Hanoi to ease its position, unacceptable to the United States, that there must be a permanent, unconditional cessation of American bombing before North Vietnam would consider negotiations.

Prime Minister Wilson was reported to have been in repeated contact by trans-Atlantic telephone with President Johnson and to have made the point that an extension of the bombing pause would give him greater latitude in his attempt to find an opening to negotiations.

There were also indications that at one point the United States offered a further extension in the bombing pause if North Vietnam would give a commitment to reduce its infiltration of men and supplies into South Vietnam.

Administration officials, however, declined to comment except to say that they were "not completely correct," on reports from London that at one point as the Kosygin-Wilson efforts were drawing to an end, the British Government, with United States approval, sent a message to Hanoi proposing an extension in the bombing pause in return for reduced infiltration.

According to reports from London, the failure of Hanoi to respond to the offer within a time limit led to the resumption of bombing. There was no confirmation of this by Johnson Administration officials.

It was indicated that the Administration would have been willing to extend the pause if Hanoi had indicated a willingness to reduce its infiltration.

As one official put it: "We were looking for even just a hint."

No signal was received from Hanoi, officials said.

The increased flow of supplies was confirmed, according to officials, by reconnaissance flights during the truce.

At the same time it was privately acknowledged by officials that the United States and South Vietnam had taken advantage of the cease-fire in ground fighting to resupply their forces in the field.

Decision Made Saturday

The decision to extend the four-day pause, it was learned, was made Saturday morning several hours before the end of the four-day Tet truce, although it had been under active consideration Friday evening.

The Administration realized it would be under considerable pressure, both at home and abroad, to extend the pause indefinitely. Starting early last week, therefore, the Administration began laying the groundwork for the resumption of the bombing.

On Wednesday President Johnson, in replying to an appeal from Pope Paul VI for an extension of the Tet truce, emphasized that the United States should not be expected to reduce its military activity "unless the other side is willing to do likewise."

Then at a televised news conference on Thursday, Secretary of State Dean Rusk ruled out any cessation of American bombing unless there was a reciprocal military response from the other side.

Arthur J. Goldberg, chief United States delegate to the United Nations, reported the theme on Friday in a speech in which he said the United States would be prepared to stop bombing only after there were assurances that this step would be "answered promptly by a tangible response toward peace from North Vietnam."

Despite these attempts to explain the administration's case, including the President's statement today, officials are resigned to the likelihood that the United States will encounter considerable criticism, both at home and abroad, for its decision to resume the bombing.

* * *

March 7, 1967

KOSYGIN DECLARES U.S. STEP-UP SPURS MORE AID TO HANOI

Soviet Leader Also Assails Rejection of North's Peace Offer Based on Bomb Halt

IT IS CALLED VITAL MOVE

Americans Are Accused of Hiding Aggressive Intention Behind New Ultimatums

By RAYMOND H. ANDERSON
Special to The New York Times.

MOSCOW, March 6—Premier Aleksei N. Kosygin declared today that United States escalation of the Vietnamese war would bring retaliatory increases in Communist aid to North Vietnam.

The Soviet leader denounced Washington's rejection of Hanoi's offer of peace talks in exchange for an unconditional halt in the United States bombing raids.

Hanoi's gesture, made Jan. 28 by Foreign Minister Nguyen Duy Trinh, was described by Premier Kosygin as "an extremely important peace initiative."

The United States refused to respond to the proposal unless Hanoi indicated that it would reciprocate for a bombing halt by a curtailment of military operations against South Vietnam.

Opportunity Called Genuine

Mr. Kosygin, speaking at a rally for candidates in the election Sunday of members of the Supreme Soviet (parliament) of the Russian Republic, reiterated Moscow's insistence that Foreign Minister Trinh's proposal had opened a genuine opportunity for settling the conflict.

"The American Government, however, did not avail itself of this opportunity," he said. "On the contrary, trying to camouflage its aggressive intentions, it hastened to set forth ultimatums that were absolutely unacceptable to the Vietnamese people."

Instead of responding to the peace overtures, Mr. Kosygin declared, the United States violated the lunar new year truce last month by redeploying troops and preparing to step up the war.

The escalation followed, he continued, with the resumption of bombing raids on North Vietnam, artillery attacks on the demilitarized zone between North Vietnam and South Vietnam, naval bombardment of the North Vietnamese coastline and the mining of rivers in North Vietnam to obstruct arms shipments.

"Perhaps the United States is hoping that the mining of the rivers and the shelling of the shoreline will lead to the isolation of North Vietnam," Mr. Kosygin said.

"One must say that their hopes are in vain. They obviously do not understand the people's feelings of internationalism. The people will find a way, by united efforts, to assure the necessary aid and support to the heroic, embattled Vietnamese people."

Mr. Kosygin charged that statements by the United States of its desire for settlement were "only words intended to delude public opinion."

"In such conditions, everyone who sides with the Vietnamese people's just cause should draw the appropriate conclusions," he added. "The new step escalating the aggression will encounter new efforts to put an end to it."

Denouncing the leadership of Communist China for having criticized the peace proposal by the North Vietnamese Foreign Minister, the Soviet leader said:

"In this case, as has been the case more than once in the past, the position of the present Chinese leadership has, in effect, coincided with the position of the imperialist circles of the United States."

Although Mr. Kosygin pledged that the Communist bloc's aid to North Vietnam would be increased if necessary, he did not reiterate recent Soviet allegations of Chinese obstruction of aid shipments moving to Vietnam by rail and air.

Little Hope for Accord

Premier Kosygin outlined the Soviet Government's position on domestic and foreign policy in a speech to an audience of selected constituents gathered in the ornate Bolshoi Theater. He is the unopposed candidate from the capital's Frunze District.

Although the bitter Soviet-Chinese dispute has been less apparent in recent days, the Premier made it clear that Moscow had little hope for a rapprochement with Peking as long as Mao Tse-tung remained as Chairman of the Chinese Communist party. Mr. Kosygin noted with a hopeful tone, however, that Chairman Mao's actions were meeting resistance and said that "we are convinced" that the ideas of Marx and Lenin and of the Bolshevik Revolution would triumph in China.

He reiterated Soviet accusations that a Neo-Fascist threat was arising in West Germany, but he pledged an "appropriate response" by Moscow if the Government of Chancellor Kurt Georg Kiesinger showed "a serious intention of marching in step with other European states."

* * *

March 16, 1967

JOHNSON DEFENDS BOMBING BUT INVITES PEACE TALKS; BUNKER TO REPLACE LODGE

POLICY AFFIRMED

President, in Nashville Talk, Says U.S. Will 'Stay the Course'

By ROY REED
Special to The New York Times.

NASHVILLE, Tenn., March 15—President Johnson chose this Upper South capital, with its long tradition of patriotism and military pride, for a strong defense and reassertion of his Vietnam policy today.

"America is committed to the defense of South Vietnam until an honorable peace can be negotiated," he said with emphasis, adding that if this point got through to the other side, peace talks could start at once.

He made a lengthy justification of the bombing of North Vietnam, repeated his willingness to end the war if the other side would show the same willingness and expressed his firm determination to "stay the course."

Guam Parley Broadened

Mr. Johnson used his address to the Tennessee Legislature for a surprise announcement of the replacement of Henry Cabot Lodge by Ellsworth Bunker as Ambassador to South Vietnam.

He also declared:

The leaders of South Vietnam will join him and his advisers for the discussion of the war scheduled this weekend on Guam, Premier Nguyen Cao Ky of South Vietnam had announced this earlier in the day.

Representatives of all the nations fighting with the United States in Vietnam will meet in Washington April 20-21 for "a general appraisal of the situation."

"Additional top-flight military personnel," none of them specified, will be sent to help Gen. William C. Westmoreland, the American commander, "in the intense operations that he will be conducting in the months ahead."

Mr. Johnson departed from his advance text to make these statements as the capstone to one of his strongest affirmations of his position on Vietnam.

Mr. Johnson got his warmest response of the day when he told the legislators of his determination to stay the course. Their applause was one of the few really warm demonstrations of support during his day of speaking, touring and visiting the people of middle Tennessee.

The crowds that came to see and hear him were large—although not so large as might have been expected, some observers said—and they were friendly but not noticeably enthusiastic. Many young people, especially, seemed restrained.

A group of young Negro pickets carried signs in front of the Capitol saying, "Tell the truth about Vietnam" and "Negotiate, y'all."

The President went to some length to defend the bombing of North Vietnam. It has proved its military usefulness, he said, by causing such disruption that half a million North Vietnamese are being kept busy repairing the damage.

"I also want to say categorically that it is not the position of the American Government that the bombing will be decisive in getting Hanoi to abandon aggression," he said. "It has, however, created very serious problems for them. The best indication of how substantial is the fact that they are working so hard around the world, with all their friends, to try to get us to stop."

As for bombing civilians, he said, the United States was making an unprecedented effort to hit military targets only.

"Any civilian casualties that result from our operations are inadvertent, in stark contrast to the calculated Vietcong policy of systematic terror," he said.

Once again answering critics who suggest a halt in the bombing, Mr. Johnson said three past pauses had been ignored by the North.

He repeated his willingness to try to end the war when North Vietnam showed its willingness, but he stressed the necessity for reciprocity.

'Fundamental Principle'

"Reciprocity must be the fundamental principle of any reduction in hostilities," he said. "The United States cannot and will not reduce its activities unless and until there is some reduction on the other side....

"We will negotiate a reduction of the bombing whenever the Government of North Vietnam is ready, and there are almost innumerable avenues of communication by which the government of North Vietnam can make their readiness known."

"To this date and this hour there has been no sign of that readiness," he added.

At another point he said: "It takes two to negotiate at a peace table."

If the war was settled, Mr. Johnson said, then American soldiers could come home and the Vietnamese could begin building a decent life.

"That is what we are working and fighting for," he concluded. "And we must not, we shall not, we will not fail."

The President's trip appeared to be part political and part personal. He clearly enjoyed it all, beginning with the moment when he stepped from his jet airplaine at 8 A.M., kissed his wife on the checks and was patted affectionately on the chin by her.

Mrs. Johnson arrived yesterday on a tour of educational institutions. He decided, apparently on short notice, to join her.

In the company of their longtime personal friends, Gov. and Mrs. Buford Ellington, they went first to the Hermitage, the home of Andrew Jackson a few miles from here, then to the Capitol, then to Columbia, 50 miles away, for the dedication of a new college, and finally back to Nashville for a reception and a forum on education.

Mr. Johnson winked at the girls, shook hands with the men and spread great smiles on everyone. The weather was overcast and uncomfortably cool and the President, usually the last to put on a coat, finally donned a light raincoat.

At one point he stopped the whole procession of dignitaries, Secret Service cars and press buses to buy ice-cream cones for the people in his car. A little later he stopped to look at a young horse of his that is being cared for on Governor Ellington's farm.

Mr. Ellington, who used to swap cattle with Mr. Johnson, is considered the President's best link to Tennessee Democrats in a state where the Democratic party is in trouble.

If the trip was designed to patch up political difficulties, there is some doubt that it was effective on all fronts. Political observers report that several Democratic Congressmen are grumbling over not having been informed of plans for the visit until it had been publicized.

Popular With Legislators

The speech was obviously popular with the legislators who only a week ago adopted a resolution supporting the Johnson policy.

Their support could not be taken for granted, however. In neighboring Arkansas, where the political climate is similar, the Legislature adopted a resolution last month asking the Administration to find a way to end the war. Senator J. W. Fulbright, the Arkansas Democrat who is a chief critic of the Vietnam policy, thought enough of the resolution to have it inserted in The Congressional Record.

Several thousand people watched the Presidential procession weave through the hilly downtown Nashville. Two of the demonstrators sat down in front of the Presidential car as Mr. Johnson was leaving the Capitol grounds, but highway patrolmen removed them. Three persons were taken into custody.

* * *

April 26, 1967

M'GOVERN LEADS A SENATE ATTACK UPON ESCALATION

Assault on Johnson Policy Joined by Kennedy, Church and Fulbright on Floor

WESTMORELAND SCORED

His Stand on Dissent Seen as Part of All-Out Drive—Holland Upholds Him

By E. W. KENWORTHY
Special to The New York Times.

WASHINGTON, April 25—Several Democratic Senators sharply attacked President Johnson's policy in Vietnam on the Senate floor today.

The attack—by George McGovern, Robert F. Kennedy, J. W. Fulbright and Frank—Church came a day after United States planes bombed air bases in North Vietnam. It also came a day after Gen. William C. Westmoreland, commander of United States forces in Vietnam, said that critics of the war were encouraging the enemy to believe "he can win politically that which he cannot accomplish militarily."

Some Senators came briefly to the defense of President Johnson and General Westmoreland.

Senator McGovern, of South Dakota, told the Senate that he knew "full well the political danger to my own career of challenging the President in wartime." The Senator will seek re-election next year.

Sees Step to World War

However, Senator McGovern said, he is convinced "that the new level of escalation marked by our bombing of the North Vietnamese airfields has brought us one step closer to World War III involving the limitless legions of China backed by the enormous firepower of Soviet Russia."

"So I do not intend to remain silent in the face of what I regard as a policy of madness," he said, "which sooner or later will envelop my son and American youth by the millions for years to come."

Senator Kennedy, of New York, interrupted Mr. McGovern to say that inevitably, after the steps taken by the United States in Asia in the last few weeks, "our adversaries in that part of the world will have to take other steps themselves."

"As surely as we are standing here, the Soviet Union, Communist China and North Vietnam will have to react to what we have done by acting themselves," Mr. Kennedy said.

Then, Mr. Kennedy asked:

"If we trace the history of the world, is it not a fact that that is how the destruction of mankind is ultimately arrived at?"

Senator Fulbright, of Arkansas, Chairman of the Foreign Relations Committee, said he believed that bringing General Westmoreland to Washington to speak before a joint session of Congress on Friday "is a final drive for a vastly enlarged manpower and a great drive for a military victory."

Mr. Fulbright said that as the tempo of the war increased, so would the pressure against dissent. Indeed, he suggested, the Senate might even be witnessing the beginning of the end of dissent, and that Mr. McGovern might be voicing "a final warning."

Future criticism, he said, will lead first to charges of disloyalty and then to charges of "muddle-headedness and then to treason."

Senator Church, of Idaho, recalled that the Administration had steadily expanded the air war since February, 1965, and increased American participation in the ground war since July, 1965. None of these steps, he said, achieved their declared objectives of interrupting the flow of supplies and troops from North Vietnam and bringing Hanoi to the conference table.

The spate of criticism was inspired by Senator McGovern's speech. There was no real debate between hawks and doves because the Senate met early and there were only about eight Senators, mostly doves, on the floor.

Senator McGovern began drafting the speech about two weeks ago when the first published reports appeared that the Soviet Union and Communist China, despite their ideological conflict, had agreed last March, at the urging of Hanoi, to cooperate in moving supplies into North Vietnam.

As a result of yesterday's bombing and General Westmoreland's strictures on war critics in a speech to newspaper executives in New York, the Senator added an introduction to his speech.

In this he recalled that for years the critics and "most of our best generals" had warned against setting "the stage for a larger and bloodier war on the Asian mainland." They have been proved right, he said, and "the glittering military solutions of the war hawks have proved to be wrong." He continued:

"Now, in their frustration, the hawks are trying to blame the failure of their policy on their critics."

"I do not blame General Westmoreland for his speech in New York because he is obviously doing both in Vietnam or in New York exactly what he is told to do by his Commander in Chief, the President."

"In trying to imply that it is American dissent which is causing the Vietnamese to continue the war," he went on, "the Administration is only confessing the weakness of its own case by trying to silence its critics and confuse the American people."

It was the statement about General Westmoreland that provoked the only extended exchange with defenders of the President's policy.

Senator Spessard L. Holland, Democrat of Florida, said he agreed with General Westmoreland's views on the effect of criticism. He said the general was on the scene and was therefore probably the best-equipped to make a judgment. He strongly rejected the idea that the general was "a Charlie McCarthy." It was incomprehensible, he said, that anyone would accuse the critics of "disloyalty or treason."

"They're already doing it," Mr. Fulbright interrupted.

Mr. McGovern amended this, saying, "They're coming pretty close."

Mr. Holland replied that he hoped that Congress and the country would pay attention to the general, and suggested that he testify before the Foreign Relations and Armed Services Committees.

"I think he will say what he believes," Mr. Holland said.

"And he is not running for re-election," snapped Senator Frank J. Lausche, Democrat of Ohio, who has advocated an intensification of the war.

Mr. Lausche charged Mr. McGovern with advocating pulling out the United States forces. Mr. McGovern said he had specifically not advocated this. What he has advocated for three years, Mr. McGovern said, is that the United States "quit widening this war."

Senator Russell B. Long of Louisiana, the Democratic whip, told Senator McGovern:

"Some of us think that there is more to fear than a bloodier war; that a Communist victory, a Communist take-over in Southeast Asia, particularly if it led to a Communist expansion elsewhere, would be a much greater disaster than a bloodier war in Vietnam."

Senator Stephen M. Young, Democrat of Ohio, said the Administration would do better to intensify peace efforts rather than calling General Westmoreland home "to lobby for further escalation."

Meanwhile, Barry Goldwater, Republican Presidential nominee in 1964, said he agreed with General Westmoreland's strictures on the war critics. Mr. Goldwater, who has urged expanded bombing, said General Westmoreland was justified in saying he was "delighted" at the beginning of the bombing of MIG fields.

Mr. Goldwater, who retires Thursday as a major general in the Air Force reserve, was here to receive a certificate of appreciation for 35 years of active and civilian duty.

Senator Kennedy backed the warnings of Senators McGovern and Fulbright about the effect of expansion of the war, saying:

"I had a visitor, a rather important visitor, from the Soviet Union during the last week, and he spoke about the Berlin crisis of 1961 and the Cuban crisis of 1962.

"He admitted quite frankly that those two efforts by the Soviet Union had driven the allies and NATO countries—France, Germany, the United States and England and other countries—very closely together in a way that they had not been in the past.

"He said that is what is happening in Southeast Asia today. He said: 'Through the efforts of the United States, you are accomplishing what we thought impossible, because you are bringing Communist China and Russia back together again.' "

Mr. Kennedy said he agreed with Mr. McGovern that four Administrations must share the blame for the situation, "including myself."

But, he went on, civilian casualties in South Vietnam alone were now running about 50,000 a year. "This is a terrible responsibility on our consciences," he said.

* * *

May 18, 1967

16 SENATORS WARN HANOI ON THE WAR

Say Far More in U.S. Back Conflict Than Criticize It

By JOHN HERBERS
Special to The New York Times.

WASHINGTON, May 17—Sixteen Senators critical of the United States military effort in Vietnam warned Hanoi today that their supporters were far outnumbered by Americans who either support the Administration or call for even greater escalation of the war.

In a signed statement, the substance of which was reported last night, the 16 Senators said a negotiated peace was "the last and only remaining alternative to a prolonged and intensified war."

The statement, initiated by Senator Frank Church, Democrat of Idaho, and directed to the Government of North Vietnam, said that despite the 16 Senators' opposition to President Johnson's policies the Senators also "remain steadfastly opposed to any unilateral withdrawal of American troops from South Vietnam."

They insisted that the statement was in no way a softening of their position on the war or a signal for lessening of dissent. Instead, they said, it should increase expression of opposition to the conflict.

One of the signers, George McGovern, Democrat of South Dakota, said the statement "should remove a haunting anxiety about dissent and ought to let us speak out with less inhibition against the mistake of continued escalation."

In the House, 18 Democrats who have been critical of the Administration's handling of the war endorsed the Senators' statement. Vice President Humphrey, attending a White House reception in honor of high military officials, also voiced approval.

Emphasize U.S. Resolve

The Senators pointed out that they had been accused by some supporters of the Administration's policy of prolonging the war by leaving a false impression with Hanoi that the United States did not have the will to persist in Vietnam.

Their statement sought to remove any such doubt about American resolve and to persuade North Vietnam to seek a negotiated peace.

"There are no doubt many citizens of the United States who share our expressed misgivings about the growing American involvement in Vietnam," the statement said. "But there are many more who either give their full endorsement to our Government's policy in Vietnam, or who press for even greater military action there."

The statement, entitled "A Plea for Realism," was cleared with Secretary of State Dean Rusk prior to its release. Both Senator Church and the State Department agreed that it was submitted to Mr. Rusk only for the purpose of making sure that it did not interfere with any diplomatic initiative toward settling the war.

Senator Church, who worked on the statement for two months, released it at a crowded news conference in a hearing room of the new Senate Office Building and later read it into the Congressional Record on the Senate floor.

There he was congratulated by several of the signers and by Senator Charles H. Percy, Republican of Illinois, who said he had been disturbed by public opinion polls showing that a number of Americans would support unilateral withdrawal.

Senator Percy, who also has been critical of Administration policy in Vietnam, said the Senate had the responsibility to point out that withdrawl from Vietnam would be "disastrous."

Mr. Church said the statement would not be communicated directly to Hanoi because that would violate the President's constitutional prerogative of dealing with a foreign power.

"We hope the statement will come to the attention of the Government of North Vietnam, and that it will be thoughtfully considered by all other foreign governments having influence in Hanoi," Senator Church said.

"Our objective is the settlement of the war at the conference table, not the repudiation of American commitments already made to South Vietnam, or the unilateral withdrawal of American forces from that embattled country," he said.

Senator Church, a member of the Foreign Relations Committee, said he had obtained the signatures of the 15 others. He pointed out that they constituted the majority of about 25 Senators who have in one way or another opposed increased use of military power in Vietnam.

Some, he said, did not sign because they have a policy against signing joint statements with other Senators, and others did not agree with some aspect of the wording.

The signers included the two best-known critics of President Johnson's war policy—J. W. Fulbright, Democrat of Arkansas, chairman of the Foreign Relations Committee, and Robert F. Kennedy, Democrat of New York.

Two of the signers were Republicans, John Sherman Cooper of Kentucky and Mark O. Hatfield of Oregon.

The others, all Democrats, were Wayne Morse of Oregon, Frank E. Moss of Utah, E. L. Bartlett of Alaska, Lee Metcalf of Montana, Vance Hartke of Indiana, Gaylord Nelson of Wisconsin, Quentin Burdick of North Dakota, Joseph S. Clark of Pennsylvania, Stephen M. Young of Ohio and Claiborne Pell of Rhode Island.

The House members who supported the statement were George E. Brown Jr., Phillip Burton, Jeffery Cohelan, Don Edwards, Augustus F. Hawkins, Thomas M. Rees and

Edward R. Roybal, all of California; Jonathan B. Bingham of the Bronx; Leonard Farbstein of Manhattan; Benjamin S. Rosenthal of Queens; James H. Scheuer of the Bronx; John Conyers Jr. of Michigan; Donald M. Fraser of Minnesota; Edith Green of Oregon; Henry Helstoski of New Jersey; Robert W. Kastenmeier of Wisconsin; Patsy T. Mink of Hawaii and Sidney R. Yates of Illinois.

The Senators' statement pointed up the change that has taken place in Senate dissent from that of last year, when Mr. Church and other members of the Foreign Relations Committee tried to arouse public opinion against the war as one means of persuading the President to change his policy.

The statement was acknowledgement that public opinion has gone the other way. Some of those who have opposed the President's policies and are up for re-election in 1968 are reported to be in political trouble because of their stand on the war.

Senator Church was asked if the statement had any bearing on the Senators' own political interests. He said he did not know.

In Idaho, he said, a recall move against him has been started "by elements of the John Birch Society." He said they objected to his vote earlier this year for the consular treaty with the Soviet Union and to his opposition to the bombing of North Vietnam.

Secretary Rusk was said to favor the Senators' statement for its possible effect in convincing North Vietnam of American resolve in the conflict and thus of the advisability of negotiation. He was said to believe that a statement several months ago by a similar group, warning Hanoi not to put captured American pilots on trial, had helped persuade the North Vietnamese not to hold such trials.

A number of the Senators who signed today's statement were also backers of the earlier statement, and Senator Church was a prime mover in the earlier one.

* * *

June 5, 1967

ISRAELI-EGYPTIAN BATTLE ERUPTS; PLANES AND TANKS ARE IN ACTION; CAIRO REPORTS ATTACKS FROM AIR

FIGHTING IS HEAVY

Each Side Accuses Other of Making First Assault

By TERENCE SMITH
Special to The New York Times.

TEL AVIV, Monday, June 5—Heavy fighting broke out early this morning between Israeli and Egyptian forces along the Sinai border, according to a statement issued by an army spokesman here.

The communiqué issued at 8 A.M. (2 A.M. Eastern Daylight time) read as follows:

"Since the early hours of this morning, heavy fighting has been taking place on the southern front between Egyptian armored and aerial forces which moved against Israel and our forces which went into action in order to check them."

The Government refused any further comment. However Kol Israel, the state broadcasting service, reported at 9 A.M. that there had been two Egyptian attempts to penetrate Israeli air space and that these attempts had been turned back by Israeli planes.

Despite the announcement of apparent warning, Jerusalem remained quiet. Traffic moved freely through the streets of the capital. There was no sound or sign of attack from the Jordanian section.

> [The Cairo radio, monitored in Beirut, reported that Israeli planes had raided Cairo and other areas, Reuters said. The radio said that 42 Israeli planes had been shot down.]

ARMY AND PLANES IN ACTION

By The Associated Press

TEL AVIV, Monday, June 5—Heavy fighting broke out early today between Israeli and Egyptian forces in Southern Israel, the Israeli Army announced.

The army said Egyptian armored and air forces "moved against Israel, and our forces went into action in order to check them."

The announcement said there was heavy fighting on the southern front.

The southern front is the flank facing the 80,000 Egyptian troops in the Gaza Strip and the Sinai Desert.

The fighting was the first serious clash reported since the new Arab-Israeli crisis developed three weeks ago. President Gamal Abdel Nasser of the United Arab Republic had said previously that Egypt would not make the first move against Israel but would meet any Israeli attack.

Cairo Radio asserted that Israeli forces had invaded Egypt and that Egyptian forces were resisting.

Air raid sirens were sounded for practice alarms in several Israeli cities this morning, sending people hurrying to the shelters.

Kol Israel, the government radio, said people were more surprised than frightened since there had been no indication that war was imminent.

A second Israeli Army communiqué, issued at 8:45 A.M. (2:45 A.M. Eastern Daylight time) said:

"A large number of Egyptian aircraft were seen approachin the Israel coast as well as toward the Negev. Israeli aircraft rose to engage them. Heavy fighting is going on."

The Negev is Israel's southern desert facing Egypt.

CAIRO REPORTS ATTACK

BEIRUT, Monday, June 5 (Reuters)—Egypt said today that Israel had launched land and air attacks on her territory, including air raids on Cairo and other parts of the country.

Syria broadcast an announcement that "we are now in the heart of the battle."

CAIRO RADIO REPORTS

CAIRO, Monday, June 5 (UPI)—The Cairo radio interrupted programs today to report that Israeli forces had attacked Egyptian forces.

At 3:35 A.M. New York time Cairo said in an alert to Egyptian armed forces in Gaza and Sinai and particularly near the Israeli port of Elath:

"The time has come to revenge, attack and liberate Palestine from Zionist gangs."

The message also was directed to "our brothers in Jordan and Syria."

42 PLANES CLAIMED

BEIRUT, Lebanon, Monday, June 5 (Reuters)—The Cario radio said today that 42 Israeli planes had been shot down so far in raids on Cairo and other Egyptian targets.

A broadcast from Syria appealed to the people to "rise for fighting ... the hour of victory has come." It did not make clear whether Syrian troops were actually in combat.

The Israeli radio said that Egyptian armored forces moved at dawn towards the Negev.

At the same time, radar screens showed numerous jet aircraft approaching the Israeli coast and coming from the south towards the Negev, the radio said.

"Egypt has launched this morning an air and ground offensive," the radio added.

* * *

June 11, 1967

CEASE-FIRE IN SYRIA ACCEPTED; ISRAELIS HOLD BORDER HEIGHTS; SOVIET BREAKS TIES TO ISRAEL

U.N.'S TERMS MET

But an Air Raid Near Damascus Sets Off a Bitter Debate

By DREW MIDDLETON
Special to The New York Times.

UNITED NATIONS, N. Y., Sunday, June 11—Syria and Israel have accepted United Nations arrangements for a cease-fire, but a heated Security Council debate over alleged truce violations continued into this morning.

At 2:40 A.M., when the Council finally adjourned, no action had been taken on the charges, or on three draft resolutions dealing with the cease-fire and the disposition of Arab refugees.

Secretary General Thant first announced the cease-fire at a morning session of the Council, informing the members that the peace had come to the last Middle Eastern battleground.

Syrian and Israeli representatives said they considered that the cease-fire was effective. But during the evening session, convened at the Soviet Union's request, Mr. Thant disclosed that United Nations observers reported bombing in the area of Damascus 17 minutes after the truce deadline.

Shelling Also Reported

Quoting a report from Lieut. Gen. Odd Bull, Chief of Staff of the United Nations Truce Supervision Organization, Mr. Thant also cited other reports of shelling from Syria into Israel and of Israeli occupation of El Quneitra, in Syrian territory.

General Bull informed the Secretary General that no Israeli troops were closer to Damascus than those at El Quneitra. But the Israeli-Syrian Mixed Armistice Commission reported that Israeli paratroops had been dropped at Tsil, about 20 miles east of Lake Tiberias (the Sea of Galilee), and at Rafid, 12 miles south-southeast of El Quneitra.

The Secretary General later read to the Security Council a cablegram from Foreign Minister Abba Eban of Israel. It said that truce orders had been issued in accordance with the Council's cease-fire resolution yesterday "at 1830 hours local time" (12:30 P.M., New York time, or 1630 Greenwich mean time), and that the cease-fire was "effectively enforced" and had continued uninterrupted.

A few minutes before this information reached the Council, Arthur J. Goldberg of the United States presented a new draft resolution demanding compliance with the Council's cease-fire order.

The United States resolution condemned "any and all violations," requested the Secretary General to make a full investigation of all violations. demanded respect for the cease-fire and called on the governments concerned to issue categorical cease-fire instructions to their forces.

The United States, Mr. Goldberg told the Council, believes that both Israel and Syria are obligated to comply strictly with the cease-fire orders and to stop all military action.

The United States resolution was a focus of acid debate.

Nikolai T. Fedorenko of the Soviet Union said the resolution came too late, "only after the Israeli aggressor" had seized the territory they desired. He also questioned the right of the Israeli delegate, Gideon Rafael, to address the council. He said Mr. Rafael lied already "had enough."

Mr. Rafael was allowed to speak, however, and he remarked that the Soviet delegate sounded like a prosecutor at the Moscow treason trials.

The report of the air raids prompted a harsh attack on Israel by Mr. Fedorenko. Denouncing "most brutal violations" of the cease-fire arranged at the demand of the Security Council, Mr. Fedorenko said the attacks made an "open mockery of the Security Council decisions."

Mr. Fedorenko had insisted on the emergency meeting though most Council members were exhausted by the long period of tension, capped by a protracted session that began at 4:30 A.M. yesterday and lasted until late morning. The night meeting was called for 9 o'clock but did not get started until 9:30.

Israeli Statements Assailed

Mr. Fedorenko bitterly assailed statements by Moshe Dayan, Israel's Minister of Defense, and by Yisrael Gailille, Minister of Information, that Israel would never go back to her former boundaries.

By what right, the Soviet representative asked, does "banditry expect reward at the expense of the lands of its neighbors?"

The Soviet representative said there must be a "resolute condemnation of Israeli aggression by the Security Council." Gopalaswami Parthasarathi of India joined Mr. Fedorenko in his denunciation of Israel. That country's defiance of Security Council decisions must not be allowed to continue, Mr. Parthasarathi declared.

Difficulties for U.N. Teams

General Bull's report to the Secretary General stressed the difficulties he was encountering in placing United Nation observer teams on the battlefront.

Nevertheless, the report on the bombing of Damascus struck diplomats as fairly circumstantial. The report noted bombing by two delta-wing aircraft 7 to 10 kilometers (4 to 6 miles) south of Damascus at 1647 G.M.T. and bombing by two unidentified aircraft at 1649 G.M.T. in the Damascus area.

These two attacks were seized upon by Mr. Fedorenko and the representatives of Syria and the United Arab Republic as signifying an air raid of major proportions.

In an earlier report to Mr. Thant on the cease-fire arrangements, General Bull had said his observers would be in position with liaison officers of the local Israeli and Syrian commands this morning.

The Syrians and Israelis have charged infringements of the cease-fire arrangements in the areas of El Quneitra, in Syria, and Tiberias, in Israel.

The gist of General Bull's cease-fire proposals, as reported by Mr. Thant, was as follows:

The cessation of all firing and troop movement at 1630 G.M.T. A United Nations spokesman in Jerusalem said that the cease-fire became effective at 1830 G.M.T., two-hours after the time set by General Bull, Reuters reported. The spokesman said the chairman of the Syrian-Israeli Mixed Armistice Commission had reported that firing had died down on both sides.

The chairman of the Israeli-Syrian Mixed Armistice Commission was to re-establish the control center at El Quneitra with observers positioned on the Syrian side in company with representatives of the Syrian command by this morning.

The officer in charge of the United Nations control center at Tiberias was to contact the senior Israeli delegate there to prepare for the stationing of observers on the Israeli side in liaison with representatives of the local command this morning.

Mr. Thant announced the Israeli and Syrian acceptances of the cease-fire arrangements in midafternoon, a few hours after the Security Council ended its long morning session.

The dispute began Friday after the Council had adopted unanimously a resolution calling upon Syria and Israel to cease fire forthwith. Two earlier resolutions this week had demanded a general cease-fire throughout the Middle East.

* * *

June 24, 1967

JOHNSON, KOSYGIN TALK 5 HOURS ABOUT MIDEAST, VIETNAM, ARMS, AND AGREE TO MEET TOMORROW

A CORDIAL SESSION

But There Is No Sign of Substantive Gains on Major Issues

By MAX FRANKEL
Special to The New York Times.

GLASSBORO, N. J., June 23—President Johnson and Premier Aleksei N. Kosygin talked for five and a half hours here today about the Middle East, Vietnam and arms control, and ran out of time before they ran out of things to say.

Emerging arm in arm and with broad smiles, the two leaders announced that they had agreed to meet here again at 1:30 P.M. on Sunday.

They appeared to have gotten along extremely well on a personal level but it appeared doubtful that they had made any significant progress on the most troublesome issues in the Middle East and in Vietnam.

Mr. Johnson, characterizing the meeting as "very good and very useful," placed particular emphasis on his agreement with the Soviet leader that it was "now" very important to reach international accord on a treaty to prevent the spread of nuclear weapons.

'Very Correctly Drawn Up'

Mr. Kosygin, expressing warm appreciation for the meeting, said he had nothing essential to add to Mr. Johnson's statement, "which was very correctly drawn up."

The two leaders summarized their views for the news media after their conversations, held at the residence of Dr. Thomas E. Robinson on the campus of Glassboro State College, of which he is president. The meeting was arranged unexpectedly yesterday after several days of pulling and hauling between the two sides on acceptable conditions.

United States officials said afterward that aside from noting the obvious fact that "Israel does exist," the two delegations had familiar and divergent views on the causes of and possible solutions to the problems between Israel and her Arab neighbors.

Hope for Some Consensus

The Russians have accused Israel of aggression in the six-day war early this month and have pledged full support to the Arab cause—a position that they apparently reiterated today.

Secretary of State Dean Rusk was said to have concluded at the meeting that "serious problems" remained in the Middle East but he also passed along an expression of hope that some consensus might yet be reached between Moscow and Washington on at least some policy objectives in that region.

Before the conference, President Johnson proposed a limitation on arms shipments to the Middle East, direct negotiations between Israel and the Arab countries, justice for Arab refugees, respect for maritime rights and better border arrangements.

The Russians were described as particularly tough in their argument that Israel must withdraw from occupied territories before there can be talk of peace settlements. Mr. Kosygin was said to have been unyielding on this point of apparent importance to his relations with the Arabs and unwilling even to link it with the known Soviet interest in according to all nations the right, demanded by Israel, to sail into the Gulf of Aqaba.

On Vietnam, too, there appeared little real agreement. Mr. Johnson said only that it was useful to "at least explore" the Southeast Asian situation.

But the stiffness of the past week appeared to have been dispelled by the face-to-face encounter.

Main Theme of the Day

The Soviet leader left no doubt that he endorsed Mr. Johnson's main theme of the day, which the President uttered in a luncheon toast; that the Soviet Union and the United States had a special responsibility to behave "reasonably and constructively" and a special obligation "that we make it possible for other countries to live in peace with each other if this can be done."

Mr. Johnson added the hope that the meeting had "contributed to getting us to know each other better and therefore to like each other better, just as our ambassadors in Moscow and Washington have become more acquainted and liked by the people they deal with."

The display of good fellowship persisted as each man moved from the college president's home past a long, patient crowd of several thousand Glassboro residents after the conference.

After driving only about 50 yards, Mr. Kosygin jumped from his limousine and stood atop an embankment to acknowledge the cheers. He shook a few hands and finally signaled the people into silence for a few words that the Soviet Ambassador to Washington, Anatoly F. Dobrynin, translated and shouted through cupped hands.

'I Want Friendship . . .'

Most of the words were lost in the tumult but they included the following: "I want friendship with the American people and I can assure you we want nothing but peace with the American people."

There were more cheers.

Fifteen minutes later Mr. Johnson emerged and he, too, went before the crowd, which was by now chanting, "We want Johnson, we want Johnson!"

"We had a good meeting today," he said, "and we liked things here so well we're coming here again on Sunday. You people have served your nation well by having us here."

In his brief statement summarizing the meeting, the President also announced that whatever business was left unfinished Sunday would be carried on by Secretary Rusk and the Soviet Foreign Minister, Andrei A. Gromyko, in New York next week.

Soviet sources said that the decision to resume the discussions Sunday was made "at the last minute" after most of the talks had been wound up.

President Johnson said he and Premier Kosygin had agreed that they had made "some small contribution" to the cease fire in the Middle East war and were only sorry that they were unable to prevent it altogether—"although we tried."

Fifth Postwar Meeting

The Johnson-Kosygin conference was the fifth postwar meeting between an American President and a Soviet Premier. It was the second in this country and, like the first, between President Dwight D. Eisenhower and Premier Nikita S. Khrushchev at Camp David, Md., in 1959, appeared destined to create at least a momentary sense of a "new spirit" in relations between the two countries.

Not only were the difficult questions between them not resolved but there appeared to have been no subsidiary agreements in relation to them. Nor had any such agreement been anticipated by the members of the American delegation as they arrived for this conference.

The President remarked at lunch, after the two men had spent two hours alone with their interpreters, Viktor M. Sukhodrev, the Russian, and William D. Krimer, that the real results of their conference "will be judged by what we can achieve in the future in order to achieve peace."

It was as they were winding up their talks that the idea of a further meeting was broached by the Soviet leader. Mr. Johnson was outlining the brief statement he proposed to make to the press and Mr. Kosygin subscribed to it, officials recalled.

The Soviet leader then disclosed that he now planned to remain in the United States until Sunday night and that if the President wished to discuss matters further he was prepared to do so. They then quickly agreed to return to the college campus.

Though there were sharp disagreements about the Middle East and other questions, there appeared to have been none of the table-thumping or warnings that marked Premier Khrushchev's confrontations with President Eisenhower in Paris in 1960 and with President Kennedy in Vienna in 1961.

This first meeting in six years between a United States President and a Soviet Premier appeared to get under way in an extremely pleasant atmosphere. If there was any annoyance left from the week-long wrangle over the terms and site for the conference, it was well hidden.

Mr. Johnson had been waiting at the 118-year-old house for 35 minutes, alternately conferring with his advisers inside and waving to the large and enthusiastic crowd outside.

The New York Times (by Patrick A. Burns)

AFTER THE MEETING: Premier Kosygin takes leave of President Johnson. Between them is Secretary of State Rusk.

Then, at 11:19 A.M., 19 minutes after the appointed hour, Mr. Kosygin's black Cadillac limousine, following four state police cars, came up through the woods behind the house. The Premier's window was open and he was inspecting the setting while tugging—much as Mr. Johnson often does—at the lobe of his left ear.

Llewellyn E. Thompson, the United States Ambassador to Moscow, who has been home for consultations, was the first to greet the Soviet leader, but the President was a few steps behind, arm extended for an elaborately negotiated handshake.

Until that moment they had known each other only as signatures at the foot of private communications. But the most recent of these—the first exchanges on their Hot Line teletypewriter connection at the start of the Arab-Israeli war 18 days ago—had set the mood for their encounter. The moment shooting began, Mr. Johnson and Mr. Kosygin exchanged pledges to stay out of the conflict, avoiding a direct clash despite their rivalry in the situation.

The symbolism of that agreement to compete without a confrontation was what Mr. Johnson most wished to preserve and enhance in discussions with Mr. Kosygin. The President has long spoken respectfully of the Soviet leader as a man who was not likely to be rash but who also was not easy to budge once committed. Furthermore, Mr. Johnson thought that he had registered the same impression in Moscow.

In any case, the handshake was warm and friendly. If anything, the small group of Soviet officials was even more forthcoming than the Americans in the first moments, but there soon were big smiles and expansive greetings all around.

Premier Kosygin shook hands with Secretary of State Rusk and Defense Secretary Robert S. McNamara, and all the Americans renewed their acquaintance with Foreign Minister Gromyko and Ambassador Dobrynin.

The two leaders posed for pictures and the President introduced his guests to Gov. and Mrs. Richard J. Hughes of New Jersey and to Dr. and Mrs. Robinson, who were evicted from their home without notice last night to provide a site for the meeting.

There was much cordial banter, the two principals chatting through their interpreters.

Only one comment was overheard, Mr. Kosygin's compliment to the President: "You chose a nice place."

Despite the swarm of people and the tangle of wires and the hum of huge air-conditioning units hurriedly installed during the night, Mr. Johnson agreed with the Premier that it was a nice place, cradled his elbow and led him inside.

Inside the rambling old two-story house topped by a belfry-like tower and faced with white, wrought-iron grillwork they entered the family sitting room. The furniture had been removed during the night to make room for a boat-shaped teak conference table from the college president's office and 20 straight-backed chairs to match.

Mr. Johnson and Mr. Kosygin remained in the sitting room for a few moments for official photographs.

The Soviet leader, noting that he had been a grandfather for 20 years, used time to congratulate the President on the birth two days ago of his grandson, Patrick Lyndon Nugent. Mr. Johnson is 58 and Mr. Kosygin is 63.

The President, who was heard to express appreciation for the welcome into the grandparents club, offered his guest some ice water and then lead him into Dr. Robinson's private study behind the sitting room.

It had been especially arranged for the more private part of the conference, with the Robinson family's pedestal rocker placed opposite two large, upholstered easy chairs alongside a three-seat sofa. Pictures, apparently family portraits, had been removed from the room, which had a dark green carpet and light brown drapes.

The President and the Premier met alone in this room with their interpreters for two hours while the rest of the delegates gathered around the conference table room, exchanging views in English, at least at the start.

In the family dining room, a hastily constructed table had been set for a lunch for 17 at 1:30 P.M. The meal, prepared by the White House mess and flown up this morning, consisted of shrimp, roast beef, rice pilaf, asparagus, dinner rolls and Cabernet Sauvignon red wine. A choice of pineapple sherbet or butter pecan ice cream in caramel sauce was offered for dessert.

Mr. Johnson's luncheon toast, the text of which was made public by the White House staff, expressed a strong desire to continue high-level discussions between the two countries. He indicated doubt that anything could be resolved with regard to Vietnam but said he wanted to go on exploring that situation as well as questions of mutual interest in Europe and the Western Hemisphere and the other topics he had listed.

Substantive discussions continued at the lunch table and the American side used this opportunity to press again its interest in continuing talks on placing a limit on the deployment of costly antimissile defense systems. The results of this exploration were not disclosed.

Mr. Kosygin made a brief toast on his own but it has not been made public.

Mr. Johnson middle of one side of the luncheon table, with Mr. Kosygin at his right and an interpreter crouched between them. They were observed at the start of the meal in animated discussion, each leaning toward the interpreter while repeatedly checking facial expressions to make certain he was understood. Mr. Rusk, with Mr. Gromyko on his right, sat at the middle of the other side of the table.

After lunch, Mr. Johnson and Mr. Kosygin ahd another hour by themselves with their interpreters before joining the larger group for the closing remarks.

The President was said to have repeatedly expressed his dreams for the future in terms of what he would like to leave for his newborn grandson, and Mr. Kosygin apparently took up the theme as the day progressed. At one point the President said, "You don't want my grandson fighting you and I don't want you shooting at him."

Mr. Johnson pointed out at several points that the two nations were really in basic agreement on the generalities of the kind of world they would like to build and that their differences emerged only when they dealt in specific and immediate world problems.

Mentions Consular Accord

In this connection, the President mentioned the number of specific issues that had been susceptible to negotiation between them since he and Mr. Kosygin came to lead their respective governments, and he went into some detail to demonstrate to Mr. Kosygin the effort he personally invested in getting the Senate finally to approve a consular agreement between the two countries.

The larger conference was said to have been dominated by Mr. Rusk and Mr. Gromyko, setting forth their views primarily on the Middle East and the proposed treaty against proliferation of nuclear weapons.

The other members of the American delegation were Walt W. Rostow and Marvin W. Watson, special assistants to the President; McGeorge Bundy, who is on leave as president of the Ford Foundation to manage White House coordination of Middle Eastern policy during the current crises; and George Christian, the White House press secretary.

The Soviet delegation included Leonid M. Zamyatin, head of the Foreign Ministry's press department; Yuri Voronstov, counselor of the Soviet Embassy in Washington; and Y. Firsov and B. Batsanov, assistants to Premiere Kosygin.

* * *

August 4, 1967

JOHNSON ASKS FOR 10% SURCHARGE ON PERSONAL AND BUSINESS TAXES; 45,000 MORE MEN TO GO TO VIETNAM

GOAL NOW 525,000

Troop Action Reflects Compromise—Rise in Spending Seen

By WILLIAM BEECHER
Special to The New York Times.

WASHINGTON, Aug. 3—President Johnson announced plans today to dispatch 45,000 to 50,000 more American troops to Vietnam, beyond the number already committed. This will bring the total to 525,000 by June 30, he said.

The decision, disclosed in Mr. Johnson's budget and tax message to Congress, represents a compromise between the 70,000 men sought by Gen William C. Westmoreland and the

15,000 to 30,000 men suggested by Secretary of Defense Robert S. McNamara.

[South Korea's President, Chung Hee Park, proposed to send 3,000 military reservists to Vietnam to free Korean and American support troops for combat duty.]

President Johnson also declared that military spending for the fiscal year ending next June might rise as much as $4-billion over the $73.1-billion that was foreseen in January, when he presented his budget request. But he asked Mr. McNamara to defer as many nonessential military expenditures as possible to absorb some of this increase, he said.

Plane Purchases Deferred

It is understood that Secretary McNamara has already pressed the services to eliminate or postpone at least $3-billion in spending. Pentagon sources say, for example, that because aircraft losses in Vietnam have been lower than expected, purchases of replacements will probably be slowed.

Mr. Johnson's action countered any suggestion that he was seriously thinking of reverting to a holding position while seeking a quick solution that would allow him to liquidate the burdensome war effort.

His intentions were indicated by the size of the troop increase, by the reports that he had assured the military that he was not foreclosing further reinforcements and by the language used in justifying the increase in troops.

Mr. Johnson repeated a passage from his State of the Union address conceding that the end of the war was not in sight and that the enemy could not be allowed to believe he could outlast the United States.

"These words are even more true today," he said. "The test before us as a people is not whether our commitments match our will and our courage; but whether we have the will and courage to match our commitments."

There are about 454,000 American servicemen in South Vietnam, including 55,000 Air Force men and 29,000 Navy men. In addition the Navy has an offshore contingent of 40,000, and there are about 35,000, mostly Air Force men, in Thailand.

Before the new announcement, the force in Vietnam was scheduled to reach 480,000 men by June, 1968.

It is understood that General Westmoreland urged, beyond that strength, 70,000 men by the end of 1968. Thus the new plan falls 25,000 men short of his request for 1968. The general asked for a much larger number, well over 100,000, by the end of 1969, qualified sources report.

Decision to Be Reviewed

Officials said the troop decision would be reviewed in a few months to determine whether the increase was large enough. The decision does not rule out further increases, they said.

The officials noted that General Westmoreland, the commander of American forces in Vietnam, had received authority to spend substantial funds to hire civilians—South Vietnamese, South Koreans, Americans and others—to take over some noncombat functions.

For example, some Army engineer battalions are building barracks and arms depots; if civilian construction teams take over some of these assignments, the engineers can build fortifications and roads in combat zones.

In addition, increases of nearly 65,000 men are projected in the South Vietnamese regular and militia forces. The United States will provide weapons and additional advisers for the new units.

3 Brigades Indicated

While defense officials were reluctant to specify which units were being considered for Vietnam service, they agreed that the most likely candidates were the newly formed 11th Infantry Brigade in Hawaii and the two remaining brigades of the 101st Airborne Division at Fort Campbell, Ky., one of which recently saw riot-control duty in Detroit.

The 101st Division's Third Brigade—about 5,000 men—is already in Vietnam.

When artillery and a few other combat-support units are added, the three indicated brigades will fill out most of the 45,000-man increase, the sources reported.

Before the new announcement, the largest single unit scheduled to go to Vietnam was the 198th Infantry Brigade, now at Fort Hood, Tex. The brigade is expected to be ready for movement by December.

Pentagon officials said no decision had been made on whether to form major units in the United States to take the place of those destined for Vietnam. If additional units are established, they said, higher draft calls will result.

Guard's Role Might Shift

There is speculation, in the wake of race riots in Detroit and other cities, that an effort will be made to increase the readiness of some National Guard units to handle domestic trouble.

One planner said it might be advisable to increase the alert status of these Guard units, a step that would make them more readily available for backup assignments if fighting suddenly erupted in the Middle East, in the Caribbean or elsewhere.

* * *

August 26, 1967

M'NAMARA DOUBTS BOMBING IN NORTH CAN END THE WAR

Differs With Military Chiefs on Escalation in Testimony Before Panel of Senate

OPPOSES NEW TARGETS

But Secretary Expects More Attacks to Be Authorized—Reaction Is Critical

By HEDRICK SMITH
Special to The New York Times.

WASHINGTON, Aug. 25—Secretary of Defense Robert S. McNamara said today that, on the basis of "past reaction," there was no reason to believe that North Vietnam "can be bombed to the negotiating table."

The Defense Secretary argued vigorously against recommendations of Congressional critics and military commanders who have urged that the air war be widened with attacks against such new types of targets as North Vietnamese ports and air defense and control centers in populated areas, or a sweeping air offensive against North Vietnam's entire industrial infrastructure.

Would Not 'Shorten War'

Such attacks, he declared, would "not materially shorten the war" in Vietnam.

His testimony to the Senate Preparedness Investigations Subcommittee brought a broadside of sharp criticism from both Democrats and Republicans, indicating that they sided with military leaders against Mr. McNamara on the conduct of the air war.

After six hours of hearings in closed session, Mr. McNamara told newsmen that he expected "additional targets" in North Vietnam "to be authorized in the future."

But the general thrust of his opening statement to the committee, released to the press in a censored version, indicated that he disagreed with the Joint Chiefs of Staff over the kind of targets to be attacked. Several Senators said this was the gist of the secret testimony as well.

Extensive Defense of Policy

In the Administration's most extensive and detailed public defense to date of its bombing policy, Mr. McNamara specifically opposed for the present recommendations from military commanders that the port of Haiphong be mined and that other North Vietnamese ports be subjected to systematic bombing.

"It seems obvious," his prepared statement said, "that cutting off seaborne imports would not prevent North Vietnam from continuing its present level of military operations in the South."

In spite of "growing signs of war weariness" in Hanoi, he asserted, "there is no basis to believe that any bombing campaign, short of one which had population as its target, would by itself force Ho Chi Minh's regime into submission." Mr. McNamara said he and the military commanders all opposed this type of attack.

"There is also nothing in the past reaction of the North Vietnamese leaders," he said, "that would provide any confidence that they can be bombed to the negotiating table." The fate of the war, he argued, will be decided by the fighting in South Vietnam.

The Defense Secretary also warned of the risks of provoking Communist China and the Soviet Union into direct intervention in the war by attacking certain targets. But military commanders, in testimony since the current hearings began on Aug. 9, were reported by committee members to have discounted these risks.

All members of the subcommittee who later spoke with the press disagreed with the Defense Secretary and made clear their endorsement of recommendations from military commanders. These were for raids against North Vietnamese MIG airfields, ports, air defense command and control centers and more targets in the buffer zone along North Vietnam's frontier with Communist China.

Symington Comments

Senator Stuart Symington, Democrat of Missouri, said that if Mr. McNamara's assessment of the bombing were correct and the service chiefs' wrong, "the United States should get out of Vietnam at the earliest possible time and on the best possible basis."

"With Mr. McNamara's premises," said the former Air Force Secretary, "there would be no chance for any true 'success' in this long war."

Senator Strom Thurmond, Republican of South Carolina, told newsmen the Defense Secretary had advocated a position "of stalemate, appeasement and no-win."

Senator John Stennis, the subcommittee chairman, warned of the risks of not attacking "vital targets" in North Vietnam before the fall monsoon season imposed practical limits on bombing operations. The Mississippi Democrat said he hoped "other vital targets" would be "released" by the President soon.

"The military are unanimous that there is need for hitting more targets," he declared.

Senator Jack R. Miller, Republican of Iowa, said he disagreed with Secretary McNamara's intimation that the United States cannot be "substanially more effective" in the bombing than at present.

"I think we can be more effective," he said. "If it might shorten the war, even by one day, then we ought to take the risks."

Mr. Miller said it was not a question of striking more targets but "more meaningful, more effective targets."

Central Themes

Repeatedly in his statement and in comments to the press later, Mr. McNamara came back to the central themes that adding more targets would not materially affect the course of the war, that his critics were trying to substitute more pressure in the air war against the North for successes in the ground war in South Vietnam, and that the outcome of the over-all conflict would be decided in the South.

He acknowledged that there were 57 targets in North Vietnam that the Joint Chiefs of Staff favored attacking but that the President had not approved.

"Whatever the merits of striking the targets may be," he said, "I believe it is clear that strikes against them will not materially shorten the war."

Although the Senators repeatedly spoke of a sharp disagreement between Mr. McNamara and the military commanders, he insisted to newsmen that there was no fundamental difference on over-all strategy.

Under questioning by newsmen, he acknowledged that there were differences between his position and that of the Joint Chiefs of Staff on bombing tactics. But he termed them "very narrow."

Although in his testimony Mr. McNamara had argued against bombing of North Vietnam's ports, in comments to the press at day's end he said that there could be changes in the values of various targets and the risks of attacking them that "could lead to a change in the decision to strike or not to strike targets" including Haiphong and other ports.

Ironically, committee sources noted, the controversy over air escalation comes at a time when President Johnson recently approved military requests for permission to hit more targets in North Vietnam.

In his testimony today, Mr. McNamara said the bombing campaign had so far been successful in fulfilling its limited objectives. He listed these as, first, "reducing the flow and/or increasing the cost of North Vietnamese movement of men and supplies into the South;" second, raising the morale of the South Vietnamese; and third, making it clear to Hanoi's leaders "they would have to pay a price in the North" for the war in the South.

But he emphasized that he believed the "final decision" in Vietnam "will not come until we and our allies prove to North Vietnam she cannot win in the South."

"The tragic and long drawn-out character of that conflict in the South makes very tempting the prospect of replacing it with some new kind of air campaign against the North. But however tempting, such an alternative seems to me completely illusory," he said.

"To pursue this objective would not only be futile but would involve risks to our personnel and to our nation that I am unable to recommend."

* * *

September 2, 1967

PRESIDENT DENIES RIFT ON BOMBING; DEFENDS POLICIES

Replies at News Conference to Senate Panel's Call for Wider War in Air

DIFFERENCES BELITTLED

Johnson Blames the Press for Reports of Division Among His Advisers

By ROY REED
Special to The New York Times.

WASHINGTON, Sept. 1—President Johnson defended today his policy of controlled bombing of North Vietnam and denied the existence of any serious rift between his military and civilian advisers.

Speaking at an unscheduled news conference in his office, the President offered a low-key, cautiously worded reply to those who have demanded that he widen the air war.

The Senate Preparedness Investigation Subcommittee, headed by Senator John Stennis of Mississippi, urged him yesterday to expand the air war, abandon "carefully controlled" bombing and pay more attention to his top-level military advisers in selecting targets.

Calls Policy Sound

Mr. Johnson said he did not want to argue with the subcommittee. Then he added:

"I believe our policy is a sound one. It is based on the best judgment that we have. Every decision is going to be made after we get all the facts and then we are going to do what we think is in the national interest. I am sure the committee wants to do the same thing."

Mr. Johnson conceded that the military and civilian chiefs running the war did not agree on everything, but he said there were "no deep divisions."

"There are no quarrels, no antagonisms," he said.

He said that in his 36 years in Washington he had never seen "more harmony, more general agreement and a more cooperative attitude" from the armed services.

Right Is Defended

Responding to a later question, the President defended the right of the military commanders to take their case to the public, even when it conflicted with their civilian chiefs.

Once again, Mr. Johnson cautioned against seeing too great a conflict between the military and civilian spokesmen of the Government. He suggested that the current conflict was mainly the work of an overzealous press.

"I think you would be doing the country a disservice if you felt for a moment that there were any deep divisions between us," he said.

"I think you make a little copy out of it and you blow it up," he said, directly addressing the 50 or so reporters around his desk. "I don't detect any fire, except from what I read."

The differences of opinion that the President sought to minimize have existed for some time. They came to light again during hearings on the bombing conducted by the Stennis subcommittee during the last several weeks.

The Joint Chiefs of Staff, testifying individually, told the subcommittee that United States planes should close the port of Haiphong, strike all meaningful military targets in North Vietnam and increase interdiction of the lines of communication from Communist China.

Secretary of Defense Robert S. McNamara, while calling his differences with the Joint Chiefs "very narrow," told the subcommittee during the same hearings that he saw no reason to believe that North Vietnam could be "bombed to the negotiating table."

Senator Mike Mansfield, the Democratic leader in the Senate, and George Christian, White House press secretary, said Mr. McNamara was speaking for the Administration.

Still In Charge

Mr. Johnson left no doubt that if any controversy existed between military and civilian thinkers, then, he, as the No. 1 civilian, was still in charge.

Asked if he saw a challenge of civilian control in the recommendations of the generals and the Stennis subcommittee, Mr. Johnson replied:

"No, we have gone through these things in every period of hostility that this nation has engaged in. We speak our minds freely. We have differences and we express them.

"But as President Truman used to say, in the last analysis, decisions will have to be made, and are made."

He jabbed his green-topped desk with his right hand to show precisely where the decisions finally were made.

"I try to give proper weight to the recommendations made to me and then do what I think is best for our country," he said.

Mr. Johnson replied to a question prompted by a Columbia Broadcasting System report that friends of Secretary McNamara had contended that he has considered resigning over expansion of the air war in Vietnam.

Asked if Mr. McNamara had suggested that he would resign if the bombing were stepped up, Mr. Johnson said:

"Absolutely not. That is the most ridiculous, nonsensical report that I have seen, I think, since I have been President. Anyone who knows Secretary McNamara would know that on the face that was not true. He doesn't go around threatening anything or anyone."

Without commenting directly on demands for a widened air war, Mr. Johnson noted that he already had authorized the bombing of about 300 of some 350 targets listed by the Joint Chiefs.

"The 50 left are in very strategic areas, primarily the port of Haiphong, Hanoi and the buffer zone," he said. "The decisions to bomb those other 50 targets have not been made.

Consider the Views

"Before the President acts on them he will carefully consider the views of his principal military advisers, such as the Joint Chiefs, and his principal political advisers, the Secretary of State, his principal deputy in military matters, the Secretary of Defense."

The President emphasized that bombing strategy was worked out by a number of military and civilian officials. Noting that they sometimes have varying opinions, he said:

"Some of them don't have the viewpoint on how it might affect our over-all political situation in the world, and so forth. All of those things are considered."

The President was asked if he agreed with a statement by Gen. Harold K. Johnson, Army Chief of Staff, that the United States might be able to begin slowly withdrawing troops from Vietnam in 18 months if present progress continued.

"That is General Johnson's opinion," the President said. "I have made no prediction and wouldn't care to at this time. General Johnson is a very competent military officer and he has been out there and reached some conclusions. He expreseed those to me. But I haven't made any prediction."

* * *

September 2, 1967

A PUZZLE OVER BOMBING

Johnson Leaves Questions Unresolved On Civilian-Military Debate About War

By TOM WICKER
Special to The New York Times.

WASHINGTON, Sept. 1—Two questions were left unresolved today when President Johnson denied that there was a "deep division" between him and the Joint Chiefs of Staff on the bombing of North Vietnam.

If there really is no major dispute, why did the chiefs give members of Congress the strong impression that "civilian authority consistently overruled the unanimous recommendation of the military commanders" and that the chiefs and Secretary of Defense Robert S. McNamara held "diametrically opposite views"?

And, if there is a serious difference despite Mr. Johnson's denial, does it threaten civilian control of the military, as Senator Mike Mansfield of Montana asked?

Mr. Johnson tried to qualify the extent of the dispute at a news conference today. He said that there were approximately 350 useful targets in North Vietnam, that military and civilians had agreed that about 300 of them would be hit, and that the other 50 had not yet been authorized for bombing.

These unbombed targets, he said, were "in very strategic areas" near Haiphong, Hanoi and the demilitarized zone, and a decision to hit them would have to be carefully weighed.

This obviously does not deal with the seriousness of the disagreement. The unauthorized targets, in military terms, could conceivably be more important than all the other 300. Even if in sum they were only half as important as those being bombed, this would still suggest a deep and serious division of military-civilian opinion.

Nor does the comment of George Christian, the White House news secretary, cover the situation. "You cannot expect uniform views," he said. "In a free society, you are not going to end debate."

Issue of Civilian Control

True enough, but the question is not whether there is debate but how serious it is. This, in its turn, raises the question of civilian control of the military.

What Senator Mansfield apparently fears is not that the military now dominates President Johnson; the very fact that some dispute exists makes it clear that that is not yet the case.

Mr. Mansfield suggested, rather, that the joint chiefs might now be conducting themselves in such a way as to threaten President Johnson's political ability to follow his policy of controlled bombing instead of theirs of virtually unrestricted bombing.

Mr. Johnson gave no indication today that he would retreat before the stroig statement of the Senate Preparedness Investigation subcommittee, which was based on the chiefs' secret testimony.

But the chiefs made public summaries of their testimony, suggesting that their military judgment was being overruled to the detriment of the war effort. Some of them have said the same thing in speeches. The subcommittee report gave even more authority to their views.

To the extent that this builds up Congressional and public pressure on the President and Mr. McNamara to follow the military advice, it undermines their ability to control the conduct of the war.

It was for precisely such activities, carried to a further extreme, that President Harry S. Truman removed Gen. Douglas MacArthur from command of the forces in Korea in 1951.

Another puzzling aspect of the apparent dissension was touched upon when President Johnson said that a recent speech by Gen. Wallace M. Greene, the Marine Commandant, had not been cleared at the White House. "None of the Chiefs of Staff clear [their speeches] here," he said.

The chiefs "express their opinion from time to time," the President said. "They can do so without any approval from here, and they do."

Kennedy Altered Policy

In 1961, President Kennedy precipitated a serious dispute with Congress and the military by insisting on strict policy review of speeches by high military officers. This led to charges that he was "muzzling" the military. But he and Mr. McNamara made their policy stick, even after former President Dwight D. Eisenhower criticized it.

Richard C. Fryklund, a Defense Department spokesman, said that this policy was still in effect and that the department had cleared General Greene's speech—in which he asked the American Legion to help promote the priority of the war in Vietnam as the nation's "most pressing problem."

Mr. Fryklund added that the generals did not always submit their speeches for review, but that they had to take responsibility for them if they exceeded the bounds of Administration policy. General Greene's speech did not do so, he said.

This suggests that the Marine Commandant expressed, if not the Administration's view, at least a sentiment not distasteful to the Department of Defense.

Mr. Johnson's comment at the news conference suggested, however, that General Greene had a perfect right to say what he wanted, whether the President approved or not. National security laws do make it clear that members of the joint chiefs have the right to carry dissenting views to Congress (a provision that President Eisenhower protested in 1958 as "legalized insubordination").

But that does not apply to public speeches, and Mr. Johnson's attitude seems considerably different from the Kennedy-McNamara position of 1961, that military leaders' public statements had to conform to Administration policy.

All of this has raised in the minds of more than one member of Congress the question whether the Administration is deliberately permitting the public dissent of the Chiefs of Staf in order to prepare public and world opinion for an extension of the bombing attacks in North Vietnam.

Even if that is not the case, with a Presidential campaign coming up and with at least two potential Republican opponents—Richard M. Nixon and Ronald Reagan—already advocating more bombing, the chiefs' differences with their civilian masters could become a more serious matter than Mr. Johnson conceded today.

Ultimately, he may have to yield to them or silence them, and as Mr. Truman found out, the latter course can raise a storm.

* * *

October 8, 1967

CRITICISM OF WAR MOUNTS; JOHNSON DEFENDS POLICIES

Survey Finds Discontent

Special to The New York Times.

WASHINGTON, Oct. 7—Public support for the Administration's conduct of the war in Vietnam has declined measurably in recent weeks, with increased sentiment for less military action and more negotiation.

This is the conclusion from a survey of Governors and Congressmen who were asked by The New York Times to gauge any shift in opinion on the Vietnam issue among their constituents.

More than two-thirds of the public officials replying to the questions reported rising criticism of the war as it is now being prosecuted, some of it from people who favor further intensification but the preponderance from those who want a more limited commitment or an end to the conflict.

The survey was taken against a background of mounting American commitment in Vietnam.

That commitment has increased United States forces there by 150,000 troops in the last year, to a total of 500,000. Total American casualties now exceed 100,000, including 13,643 dead—many of them in the last six months. The defense budget has risen to the neighborhood of $70-billion a year, and the budget's impact on the economy has caused President Johnson to request a 10 per cent surcharge on the income tax, which Congress is resisting.

Discouragement Found

Many of the replies to the Times survey reflected discouragement that this investment of men and money did not seem to be achieving visible progress rather than any basic quarrel with the aims of the investment.

The survey indicated the seriousness of the political problem Vietnam poses for the Democratic party's national ticket a year before President Johnson will seek re-election to a second full term.

Unless the public sentiment shown by the survey changes materially in 1968, Mr. Johnson will clearly be running in the face of criticism from two directions: those who think his policy is too belligerent and those who do not think it is belligerent enough. Dwindling support can be expected between these extremes.

All 50 Governors, 100 Senators and 433 Representatives were asked if there had been any change in sentiment on the war.

Anonymity Option

The officials were given the option of responding anonymously. Replies were received from 33 Governors, 64 Senators and 146 Representatives.

While reporting a marked shift in public reaction, few of the officials questioned said that they had changed their views on Vietnam. Of 243 interviewed, only 40 said that they had switched, 30 of them to a stronger peace posture and 10 to insistence on further intensification.

None of the men who reported shifts in their personal positions on the war were major political figures, with the exception of Senator Thruston H. Morton, Republican of Kentucky, the former Republican national chairman, who has moved from supporting the President to advocating disengagement.

A significant number of those interviewed reported a discernible polarization of Vietnam sentiment, with the large middle group that formerly accepted the war tending to split into two vocal critical factions, one advocating every possible peace effort and the other an all-out offensive for victory.

Administration officials said they had been receiving similar reports of growing concern over the war. Cabinet officers, who report regularly to President Johnson on findings in their travels, have told him that there is growing disgruntlement about Vietnam.

Some of these officials attribute the decline in support for the President to a lack of progress in the war, to weariness and disillusionment, to resentment because the war prevents important domestic spending and to unhappiness over the proposed 10 per cent tax surcharge.

There was no indication, however, that these Cabinet officers were moving away from strong support of the President's policies.

Three of the five leading Republican Presidential possibilities responded to the survey. Gov. George Romney of Michigan and Senator Charles H. Percy of Illinois provided direct statements, and the views of Gov. Ronald Reagan of California were described by aides.

Governor Rockefeller of New York did not respond. There have been recent reports that he is preparing to move away from his long-held position of full support for President Johnson's Vietnam policies.

Former Vice President Richard M. Nixon was not included in the survey, which was restricted to current officeholders.

'Never a Popular War'

Senator Percy said the Southeast Asian conflict "has never been a popular war, but it has never been as unpopular as it is today." He said he was particularly disturbed by the decision to bomb so close to China because "I do not believe the risks are worth the possible gain."

Governor Romney said he believed that "people are taking a more searching look at Vietnam than ever before," citing the increasing number of Republicans like Senator Morton who are speaking out against Administration policy.

According to aides, Governor Reagan believes military prosecution of the war should be pushed more strongly, with more military and less civilian control.

A typical comment on the erosion of the formerly large bloc of opinion in general support of the President came from Representative Donald M. Fraser, a Minnesota Democrat.

"In recent months there has been a noticeable polarization of views in my district," he said.

"Fewer and fewer people seem to support the Administration's policy. The mood appears increasingly to be one of 'win or get out.' But even the 'win' outlook seems to be losing supporters in favor of more determined efforts to get out."

The public officials that responded to the survey were about 3-to-2 Democratic. Of the 243, 145 identified themselves as general supporters of the President and 52 as clear-cut critics with the remaining 44 somewhere in the middle.

Their findings fell into the following categories:

- 69 of the officials did not detect any recent weakening of support for the war.
- 64 reported broad general opposition.

- 80 discerned a strong sentiment for negotiation or withdrawal.
- 30 reported criticism that military action had been too limited to win.

The public opinion polls also indicate a growing lack of confidence in the way President Johnson is handling the war. His most recent approval rating was 33 per cent in the Gallup Poll and 31 in the Harris Poll.

The word that appeared most often in explanations of declining Vietnam support was "frustration," a combination of shame that American military might was unavailing, a feeling of helplessness to affect events and a growing conviction that the President had not been entirely frank about the war.

"At the White House they gave a group of us Governors a thousand reasons why they couldn't bomb Haiphong Harbor," Gov. David E. Cargo of New Mexico, a Republican, recalled.

"Yet four days later it was done. I just about died when I heard that."

A number of the Congressmen reported a kind of merger between the hawks and doves in their districts, the hawks arguing the "win or get out" thesis but beginning to recognize that the first alternative appeared increasingly unachievable.

The single specific factor most often cited as a basis for the shift of opinion against the war was the growing casualty list. This appears to be particularly true in the smaller states and communities where combat fatalities have more personal impact.

"I fly the flag at half-mast for all the soldiers whenever they're buried here," Gov. Tim Babcock of Montana observed. "I see it down the pole quite a bit. Of course, this is not encouraging at all; the longer it goes, the more discouraging it becomes."

Both Senators and Representatives said they believed that President Johnson's request for a tax increase had crystallized sentiment against the war, although as the men who must vote such an increase, they are probably more conscious of such resistance than the Governors.

Representative William F. Ryan, Democrat of Manhattan, summed up the frustration complaint as follows:

"Everyone is frustrated. The 'why not win' group is frustrated by failure to achieve an easy and immediate victory. Those who have generally tended to support the Administration's policy are frustrated by the complicated nature of the war and its seeming endlessness.

"Those who have consistently opposed the war, frustrated and angry, now feel that protests and demonstrations have had little or no effect and see the only recourse to be the defeat of President Johnson."

Some of the Congressmen said that they believed the shift in sentiment against the war began last spring, when the American troop commitment was stepped up again and control of the pacification program was largely shifted to American personnel.

Party affiliation did not seem to have any direct correlation with reports of growing opposition to the war. Of the House members interviewed, about a third of both the Democrats and Republicans reported such sentiment.

* * *

October 8, 1967

JOHNSON DEFENDS POLICIES

President Firm in Speech

By MAX FRANKEL
Special to The New York Times.

WASHINGTON, Oct. 7—President Johnson vowed tonight that he would not play for popularity in the opinion polls by abandoning any of his major policies at home or abroad.

Surveying his low estate in the polls before an audience of party contributors, the President said that he was getting much advice on how to escape his troubles "cheaply and fast."

But his plan, he said, is to hold firm in Vietnam, to keep asking for a tax increase, to go on fighting discrimination and working for the poor.

"I have made my choice," Mr. Johnson asserted. "And I pray that I—and we—will have enough of that bravery, unselfishness and wisdom Jack Kennedy said we would need to see it through all the way."

As a politician, the President said, he values popularity and support as much as any man and he knows he can increase it—temporarily—by abandoning some of his policies, especially "by softening or renouncing the struggle in Vietnam, or escalating it to the red line of danger."

He said he would do neither, though he also knew better than anyone except the soldiers in Vietnam that this was a rough road to travel.

"But the road does lead to a free Asia and it does lead in my opinion a freer and happier and more secure Untied States," he said. "I believe the American people will follow its course—not blithely, not cheerfully—for they lament the waste of war, but with a firm determination, now that we have begun it, to see it through all the way."

Mr. Johnson did not discuss the factors that would go into his decision on whether to stand for re-election next year.

But few men around the White House doubt that he will run. They found his speech consistent with his privately expressed view that he was doing the right and responsible things and that he could in the end so persuade the nation's voters.

But the speech at the President's Ball, a $1,000-a-couple fund-raising dinner and dance at the Washington Hilton Hotel before more than 2,000 persons, began with a candid acknowledgement of the turn against him in the opinion polls.

Kennedy Ahead in Polls

Those polls have recently shown that Senator Robert F. Kennedy, democrat of New York, was preferred by a majority over Mr. Johnson as the Democratic parties candidate for President next year. They have also shown Governor Rockefeler of New York as running at least even and in some cases ahead of Mr. Johnson.

Moreover, general support for the President's policy in Vietnam has slipped in the polls from 72 per cent of the public last July to 58 per cent last month.

Mr. Johnson said that private polls still showed him running far ahead of William E. Miller, the defeated Republican candidate for Vice President in 1964, and of Harold E. Stassen, the perennially unsuccessful candidate for the Republican nomination for President, now a lawyer in Philadelphia.

Without directly challenging the accuracy of the polls, the President recalled their fallability with a reference to The Literary Digest, which had forecast that Alf M. Landon would defeat President Franklin D. Roosevelt in 1936.

He alluded to former President Harry S. Truman's definition of Presidential stoicism—"If you can't stand the heat, get out of the kitchen."

Then, admittedly simplifying the criticism, Mr. Johnson characterized most of it as advice to deny his responsibilities.

He is being asked, he said, to behave as if he is leading a small nation with few interests, behind oceans twice as wide as they are, indifferent to people of other races and cultures "so long as they aren't shooting at your house just now."

Subtle Advice

At home, he said, he is being asked to behave as if all babies are born with equal opportunities, as if health and education are some one else's concern and as if the inflation that he will arrest with a tax increase in inevitable.

Usually, he said, that advice is made to appear more subtle and reasonable, but it comes down to that.

"It is the voice, not of the dove or the hawk," the President said, "but of the ostrich. Be certain of this. In the time I have been given to lead this country, I shall not follow that advice."

The Democratic party, he said, has reason to be proud because it has set the agenda for action by which every succeeding Administration will be judged.

"Let them say that we have aroused expectations," he asserted. "Let them say we have not accomplished our goals entirely."

The main question in next year's election, Mr. Johnson suggested, will be whether the nation goes on building or becomes discouraged, impatient and ready to bury all that has been begun "in a shroud of inaction and reaction."

His first and last business until that election will be to try "to win and secure the peace," the President went on. He cannot predict when the issue will be resolved, he said, but is confident that he has chosen the road of responsibility in Vietnam.

* * *

October 10, 1967

BOLIVIAN ARMY SAYS GUEVARA WAS KILLED IN A GUERRILLA CLASH

By The Associated Press

LA PAZ, Bolivia, Oct. 9—Official army dispatches reported today that Ernesto Che Guevara, reputed mastermind of Latin-American Communist guerrillas, was killed in a clash in southeastern Bolivia yesterday. The army high command declined to confirm the report immediately.

Mr. Guevara, 39 years old, has been reported killed or captured before. Once Premier Fidel Castro's right-hand man, he has been reported active in a number of countries since he vanished from Cuba in April, 1965.

A hunt was intensified for him in Bolivia recently and the army reported at one time that it believed he and a small band had been trapped.

Col. Joaquin Zenteno Anaya, commander of the Eighth Army, said today that Mr. Guevara was one of a few guerrillas killed in the clash, at Higueras, about 300 miles southeast of La Paz.

The army chief of staff, Col. Marcos Vasquez Sempertegui, said that "official reports from Valle Grande affirm Guevara was killed and that his body is now with the Bolivian Army."

He emphasized, however, that the high command did not want to confirm the reports yet.

The army invited newsmen to fly tomorrow to Valle Grande, near Higueras. The invitation led to speculation that the high command wanted to display the body reported to be that of Mr. Guevara and that it was withholding an announcement until then.

It was also believed that the high command was proceeding cautiously because of problems in identifying the body positively.

Five Casualties Reported

At a meeting of the Organization of American States in Washington last month, Bolivian diplomats displayed photographs that they contended proved that Mr. Guevara had been leading the guerrillas in Bolivia. The photographs showed a man resembling him in the company of Bolivian and Cuban guerrillas.

Reports earlier today said that he was dead, wounded or captured.

An army communiqué issued in La Paz reported a fight between soldiers and guerrillas in the mountains and added: "The rebels put up desperate resistance and suffered five casualties, among them being presumably Ernesto Che Guevara."

Some military sources said Mr. Guevara had been mortally wounded and that he had talked with his captors before he died.

In 1965 after vanishing from Cuba, Mr. Guevara was said to have been killed in a leftist revolt in the Dominican Republic.

Later he was reported captured in Peru. Another report said he was hiding out in Argentina. After the Bolivian Army got what it said was convincing evidence that he was leading

This photo, issued recently by Bolivia, is said to show Ernesto Che Guevara in the field.

a guerrilla movement in Bolivia, it denied a report Sept. 26 that he had been killed.

The army communiqué issued today said the army had suffered four killed and four wounded in the clash four miles northwest of the town of Higueras.

It added that "operations continue in the Higueras zone."

Five-Hour Fight

Press reports from Valle Grande said the fighting began at about 1 PM and lasted about five or six hours. These accounts said that two of the guerrillas had been wounded and that if Mr. Guevara was not killed, he might be one of the wounded.

Mr. Guevara was believed sighted in the Valle Grande area 10 days ago. Two Bolivian guerrillas captured last week said he had been sick and had been traveling on a mule.

Army sources said he suffered from arthritis and asthma. They said Mr. Guevara and his fellow rebels were feeling dispirited after having suffered heavy casualties in a clash two weeks ago.

An Argentine who turned revolutionary after having received a medical degree, Mr. Guevara fought with Premier Castro in his revolution in the Sierra Maestra of Cuba. Afterward he played an active role in the Cuban Communist Government before he dropped out of sight.

He has been variously reported in Communist China, North Vietnam and the Congo as well as in several Latin-American countries.

* * *

October 22, 1967

GUARDS REPULSE WAR PROTESTERS AT THE PENTAGON

6 Break Through Line Into Building—
Mailer and Dellinger Are Arrested

250 SEIZED IN CLASHES

Spock Tells Demonstrators at Lincoln Memorial
That Johnson Is Real 'Enemy'

By JOSEPH A. LOFTUS
Special to The New York Times.

WASHINGTON, Oct. 21—Thousands of demonstrators stormed the Pentagon today after a calm rally and march by some 50,000 persons opposed to the war in Vietnam.

The protesters twice breached the lines of deputy Federal marshals backed by soldiers armed with bayonet-tipped rifles. But they were quickly driven back by the rifle butts of the soldiers and the marshals' nightsticks.

Six demonstrators succeed in entering a side door at the main Mall entrance of the building but were pushed out immediately by marshals.

There were no reports of serious injuries but the Pentagon steps were spattered with blood.

Soldiers and marshals arrested at least 250 persons at the Pentagon, including David Dellinger, chairman of the National Mobilization Committee to End the War in Vietnam, which organized the rally and march.

Mailer Arrested

Also arrested were Norman Mailer, the novelist, who was seized for technical violation of a police line; the Rev. John Boyles, an assistant Episcopal chaplain at Yale University, and Mrs. Dagmar Wilson, a founder of the Women's Strike for Peace organization. Two military policemen arrested Mrs. Wilson when she sat amid a group of about 50 persons in an off-limits area at the Pentagon.

Mr. Boyles was charged with unruly and disorderly conduct, breaking police lines and refusing to retreat. He pleaded guilty, was fined $25 and received a suspended five-day jail sentence.

The surging disorderly crowd that milled about the vast Pentagon shouted obscenities and taunted the forces on guard there. Some threw eggs and bottles as darkness fell, built bonfires and waved what they said were burning draft cards.

They clashed with the guards several times.

Several tear gas canisters exploded outside the building at various times. The Defense Department announced that the Army had not used tear gas at any time and charged that the demonstrators had.

Two soldiers were reported to have been injured, one by tear gas and one by a missile that struck him in the eye.

As darkness fell, the demonstrators settled down to what some said would be an all-night vigil.

However, at midnight, United States marshals began systematically picked up demonstrators encamped at the east entrance of the Mall entrance steps and carried them to waiting vans. At that point it was estimated that the troops outnumbered the demonstrators on the Mall who had dwindled to about 1,000.

At the Lincoln Memorial and elsewhere, the police reported ten persons arrested, most of them for demonstrations against the demonstrators.

A police and military consensus put the size of the crowd at the Lincoln Memorial, where the demonstrators first gathered, at 50,000 to 55,000. A warm autumn sun lighted the crowds that filled the corridor stretching from the Lincoln statue to the east end of the reflecting pool nearly halfway to the Washington Monument.

John B. Layton, chief of the Metropolitan police, returned to his office at 5:30 P.M. and pronounced the demonstration "well controlled and orderly." His force was responsible only for the territory on the District of Columbia side of the Potomac.

As 2:15 the march leaders stepped off for the Pentagon, across the Potomac River. For three hours the trek continued across Memorial Bridge. The test of strength at the Pentagon began well before the stragglers arrived.

About 4 P.M., some 2,000 demonstrators pushed up the steps in front of the Mall entrance, which faces a spacious lawn and a big parking lot that the demonstrators had permission to use.

A rope at the top of the steps at the mall side separated the demonstrators from United States marshals, who were backed up by military policemen.

Blue and red flags with a yellow flag in the middle, identified by some as Vietcong emblems, were carried on poles by some of these demonstrators. One marshal was struck on the head by one of the poles. Eight or ten others in the crowd pushed over the rope and the marshals hit them with night sticks.

About 20 young persons started to crawl under a flat-bed press truck near the top of the steps. Marshals dived after them with, whacking at hands and bodies. Helmeted military policemen carrying M-14 rifles, with bayonets fixed but sheathed, rushed out at that point to assist the marshals.

A few minutes later a second wave of military policemen carrying tear gas grenades emerged from the building and set up a third defense line. The confrontation lasted nearly a half-hour.

About 5:40 P.M., another crowd of 3,000 who had been outside the outer police lines around the highway got through a hole unopposed and dashed to an entrance used by the press. It was unguarded outside.

About a half-dozen got inside the door. Marshals used clubs to push them back. About 20 minutes before that about 300 military policemen had been brought up from the lower levels of the building and lined up in the corridor.

The M.P.'s, using rifle butts, pushed the intruders back and outside. Some of the demonstrators fell down the steps and

Associated Press Wirephotos

U.S. marshals clubbing antiwar demonstrators who tried to storm the Pentagon yesterday.

Demonstrators shouting at a military policeman at barrier.

left patches of blood behind. Some threw electric lamps, soft-drink cans, and sticks. It took the troops two to four minutes to expel the group.

Negroes Undecided

As darkness fell, the demonstrators settled down to what some said would be an all-night vigil. They made little bonfires with their posters on the Pentagon Mall and steps. The temperature, which had been 55 degrees in the afternoon, was expected to fall to 40 overnight.

Some began drifting away, but shortly before 8 P.M., the official Pentagon estimate of the throng was still 15,000 persons in the parking lot and grassy spaces. The atmosphere way from the building was "like a picnic," one observer said.

The military, which had refused to identify the units brought to Washington for the demonstration, reported tonight that 2,500 soldiers had been used on the Pentagon grounds and that an undisclosed number had remained in reserve.

The units that saw service were:

503d M.P. battalion, Fort Bragg; 91st Engineer Battalion, Fort Belvoir, Va.; First Squadron of Sixth Cavalry Regiment, Fort Meade, Md.; 714th Transportation Battalion, Fort Eustis, Va; four military police companies (one from Fort Dix, N. J.; one from the Presidio, San Francisco, and two from Fort Hood, Tex.).

The Pentagon troops were under the command of Maj. Gen. Charles S. O'Malley, commanding general of the Washington Military District. He said:

"No tear gas has been used by our troops. There is no evidence that any tear gas has been used by our side."

Lieut. Gen. John Throckmorton, commanding general of the Third Army, who commanded troops in the Detroit riot a few months ago, was at the Pentagon as a special assistant to the Army Chief of Staff. Officials did not say what his duties were.

Robert S. McNamara, Secretary of Defense, was at his office in the Pentagon all day except for a helicopter trip to the White House to help brief Souvanna Phouma, the Laotian Premier. A heavily protected heliport is close to the Pentagon.

The vast majority of the demonstrators at the Lincoln Memorial were white.

The sprinkling of Negroes at the rally gathered in a special section and debated whether to join the march. About a hundred decided to go to a Negro rally in Banneker Park,

AT THE PENTAGON: Deputy Federal Marshals and Military Police form security cordon against war protesters demonstrating at building yesterday.

across the street from Howard University, a few miles north of the Capitol.

A lesser number joined the march to the Pentagon.

John Wilson of New York, director of the Students Nonviolent Coordinating Committee, who had spoken at the first rally, joined the Banneker Park crowd.

At the memorial, Mr. Wilson led the crowd in a chant of "Hell, no, we won't go." He later asked for a moment of silence to mark the death of Ernesto Che Guevera, the Cuban revolutionary.

The trees around the basin, still untouched by frost, were in full leaf, though much of the green had turned to golden yellows and browns.

The mobilization committee, a loose confederation of perhaps 150 groups, established its platform at the top of the steps that rise from the basin to the circular drive around the Lincoln Memorial. The drive was closed to all motor traffic except police vehicles.

Mr. Dellinger, the chairman, said in his opening speech that "this is a beginning of a new stage in the American peace movement in which the cutting edge becomes active resistance."

Dr. Benjamin Spock, the pediatrician, said "we are convinced that this war which Lyndon Johnson is waging is disastrous to our country in every way, and that we, the protesters, are the ones who may help to save our country if we can persuade enough of our fellow citizens to think and vote as we do."

The enemy, "we believe in all sincerity," Dr. Spock went on, "is Lyndon Johnson, whom we elected as a peace candidate in 1964, and who betrayed us within three months, who has stubbornly led us deeper and deeper into a bloody quagmire in which uncounted hundreds of thousands of Vietnamese men, women and children have died, and 13,000 young Americans, too."

President Johnson worked in the White House, a few blocks east of the peace rally, and Mr. McNamara arrived at his Pentagon office at his usual hour of 8 A.M. Attorney General Ramsey Clark joined Mr. McNamara and other officials later at a command post inside the Pentagon's main entrance.

Hundreds of newsmen were admitted to the building but their movement was more restricted than on normal work days.

The mobilization committee, while agreed on the objective peace in Vietnam, did not attempt to agree on methods and approaches to the objective. The participating groups reflected many shades of political and social philosophies.

The nominal leadership included, by their own acknowledgment, Communists and Communist sympathizers, but an authorized Government official said there was no evidence that the Communists were in charge or that there were more than "a very, very few" of them in influential roles.

Many youths carried United States flags; one carried a North Vietnam flag.

A small plane trailed a banner: "The Fallen Angels Love You."

At the Lincoln memorial rally, the crowd was orderly and the leaders seemed determined to maintain that order. The only disorderly occurrence there was an attack by three members of the American Nazi party who overturned the lectern and microphones.

Banners identified students from schools ranging from the Harvard Divinity School to colleges in California and Texas. A group of 37 came from the High School of Music and Art in New York City.

Three youths who said they were members of the American Nazi party tried to break up the program at the memorial at noon. Coming from behind, they rushed the lectern while Clive Jenkins of the British Labor party was speaking. The podium and a dozen microphones spilled down the stone steps leading to the reflection pool.

Young men from the mobilization group rushed the interrupters. Punches were exchanged and the three youths were hauled away to a patrol wagon shouting—"Heil Hitler."

The demonstrators had assigned marshals, coordinators, and controllers from their own group around the speakers' platform. As soon as the lectern tumbled, they linked arms and shouted "stay back," as newsmen tried to get closer. There were no uniformed policemen or soldiers in the platform area or on the steps.

The lectern and microphones were replaced within a few minutes, and Mr. Jenkins continued his speech.

The three youths who were taken away were arrested on disorderly conduct charges. They identified themselves as William G. Kirstein, 19 years old; Frank A. Drager, 27, and Christopher Vidnjevich, 24. All gave the address of the American Nazi party in Arlington, Va. The police called the three "storm troopers."

Mr. Dellinger made light of it all.

"I was just signing the last check for the sound system," he said. "I thought he was after the check."

* * *

November 2, 1967

JOHNSON ASSERTS WAR PROTESTERS DO NOT AID PEACE

At Impromptu News Parley, He Calls Them No Help in Search for Solution

BACKS CRITICS' RIGHTS

But He Urges Courage and Stability on Home Front to Hasten a Settlement

By HEDRICK SMITH
Special to The New York Times.

WASHINGTON, Nov. 1—President Johnson said today that antiwar demonstrators in the United States were not helping to bring peace in Vietnam closer.

At an impromptu news conference this afternoon, the President said that if the demonstrators knew about Communist propaganda based on the protest against the war, they would see that they "have not contributed a great deal to the solution that we so eagerly seek."

On the contrary, Mr. Johnson contended, peace will come sooner if the American people are united rather than divided.

"If we can manifest on the home front the same courage, the same stability and the same good judgment [that American servicemen] are manifesting out there," the President declared, "I have not the slightest doubt that we will find the solution—and find it much earlier united than we will divided."

Stresses the Positive

The President, acknowledging the right of war critics to put forward alternatives to the Administration's policy, said he "preferred not to be negative."

Then, referring to last weekend's mass demonstrations at the Pentagon and other activities of war critics, he added, "I don't think they have really helped our marines a whole lot up there on the DMZ [demilitarized zone on either side of the border between North and South Vietnam] or made contributions to a solution" of the war.

He said that yesterday's mortar attack by the Vietcong on Independence Palace in Saigon during ceremonies for the new South Vietnamese President "ought to revolt the civilized world."

Shells Injured 3

The Vietcong lobbed three shells toward the palace during a party attended by 2,000 dignitaries, including Vice President Humphrey. The shells exploded on the lawn, injuring three persons.

The President restated his willingness to "go the last mile" in the search for peace in Vietnam. He said the United States would continue to be willing to "negotiate now, to stop the bombing now, if they [North Vietnam] will talk promptly, productively and not take advantage of us." This was a reaffirmation of a similar offer made in San Antonio, Tex., on Sept. 29.

But, with a shrug of his shoulders, he said there had been no favorable response from Hanoi and that, in the absence of such a response, he would continue struggling for from widening the war, to deter aggression and to permit self-determination in South Vietnam.

"We are doing what we believe and what we know, to the best of our knowledge, to be the right and proper thing to do," he said in answer to a question about bombing policy. "We are going to continue to do what we believe is right."

When a questioner suggested that the President had shifted from a policy statement made in his 1964 Presidential campaign to the effect that American soldiers were not going to be used to do the "job of Asians," Mr. Johnson took vigorous exception.

"There has not been a change of policy," the President said emphatically. "We always have said and we repeat now that we do not want American boys to do the fighting that South Vietnamese boys ought to do or that Asian boys ought to do."

"We are asking them all to do all they can," the President added. "But that did not imply then and does not imply now that we would not do what we needed to do to deter aggression."

The President's Position

The questioner was apparently referring to a statement made by the President on Oct. 21, 1964, that "we are not about to send American boys nine or ten thousand miles away from home to do what Asian boys ought to be doing for themselves."

The first American combat units were sent to Vietnam in February, 1965, but the major build-up of American forces began in June, 1965. The Administration has contended that by then the nature of the war had been changed by the North Vietnamese infiltration of regular army units into South Vietnam in November and December, 1964. Today, the United States has 467,000 troops in South Vietnam.

Asked whether he thought the newly established Government in Saigon should negotiate directly with the National Liberation Front, the political arm of the Vietcong, Mr. Johnson replied that he did not think "it would be helpful for me to tell you to tell them what they ought to do."

Earlier in the day, the State Department rejected as "nonsense" North Vietnam's latest charges that the United States was engaged in a deliberate campaign of attacking civilian areas.

In a statement yesterday, Hanoi said that American attacks in the Hanoi area in the last few days had killed or wounded more than 200 civilians and destroyed or set afire more than 150 homes.

* * *

November 3, 1967

M'CARTHY PRESSES FIGHT ON JOHNSON

May Enter Primaries in Bid to Repudiate War Policy

By JOHN HERBERS
Special to The New York Times.

WASHINGTON, Nov. 2—Senator Eugene J. McCarthy has committed himself to the difficult role of trying to persuade the Democratic party to repudiate President Johnson's Vietnam policy before next year's election.

In an interview, the Minnesota Democrat said he was weighing the possibility of offering himself in opposition to Mr. Johnson in some of the preferential primaries.

Even if he does, however, Mr. McCarthy thinks the antiwar dissent against the President should involve more than this. He says it should include attempts to obtain an antiwar plank in the 1968 party platform, to instruct delegates to the 1968 convention to oppose the present Vietnam policy and to send favorite-son candidates to the convention to challenge the President.

No other Democrat in Congress has gone so far in opposing Mr. Johnson's policy in Vietnam. But Mr. McCarthy said he considered such action a proper use of the party's political machinery and believed that it might be the only way the party can hold the support of academicians, religious leaders and youth.

"It is what the Democrats did in 1948 on the issue of civil rights, which was a highly divisive issue," he said. "There were those at that time that said, 'don't divide the party, don't split the party, we can work this out, let's have a moderate plank.'

"Some of these today who are calling for unity in the party were most active in the civil rights effort in 1948, which was a thoroughly divisive proposition to bring before a Democratic convention, and though there is no direct comparison between this issue and civil rights, the basic principle of facing up to it within the framework of the political party, I think, still is entirely valid."

In 1948, liberals, led by Hubert H. Humphrey, now Vice President and then Mayor of Minneapolis, pushed through a strong civil rights plank in the Philadelphia convention, precipitating a Southern walkout and formation of the States' Rights party headed by Strom Thurmond of South Carolina, now a Republican Senator. President Truman was re-elected without the South.

Opposes Unity Pleas

Senator McCarthy created a good deal of interest on a recent speaking tour in which he made a number of provocative statements. In Berkeley, Calif., he suggested the resignation of Secretary of State Dean Rusk and Democratic opposition to President Johnson's re-election, for which he was wildly applauded.

In the quiet of his office Tuesday, Senator McCarthy's language was more restrained but his resolve to open up the party for dissent on the war was clear.

"If the war continues to go pretty much as it has, which means badly, then I think the time has come to begin already—that the war in Vietnam should be made some kind of issue, and subject to the processes that the political parties go through on the way to national conventions in which they determine their platforms and pick their candidates.

"So I have objected to the cries and demands for unity in the Democratic party as they have come from John Bailey (chairman of the Democratic National Committee) and from the Administration spokesmen," he continued.

"Unless you want to encourage people to set up conditions which will move them to organize some kind of abortive third party movement I think the issue should be considered within the framework of the established political party; in my case it is the Democratic party.

"And I said I thought it should be met at a number of levels—one of resolutions and recommendations for the platform and consideration of instructing the delegations and favorite sons in certain cases; and there is always a possibility there might be a confrontation even with the President in some of the Presidential primaries."

* * *

November 19, 1967

BRITAIN DEVALUES POUND TO $2.40 TO AVERT A NEW ECONOMIC CRISIS; SEVERE RESTRAINTS ARE IMPOSED

REDUCTION IS 14.3%

Curbs Include a Basic Interest Rate of 8% and Spending Cuts

By ANTHONY LEWIS
Special to The New York Times.

LONDON, Nov. 18—Britain devalued the pound tonight.

The official value was lowered 14.3 per cent, from $2.80 to $2.40. The announcement was made at 9:30 P.M. (4:30 P.M., New York time) and the new rate was effective immediately.

The devaluation meant that a long struggle to maintain a chronically weak currency at the rate set in 1949 had ended in defeat for the Labor party Government. The consequences for the British people and for the world monetary system just began to be sensed tonight.

The move was made in an attempt to lower the cost of British goods in foreign countries in the hope that exports would rise, and to increase the price of imports in the hope that they would be reduced. The result would be a better balance between exports and imports.

Rumors a Factor

A secondary consideration in the decision to devalue the pound was the hope that the move would end the uncertainty and talk of devaluation that have been common in financial circles recently.

The politics as well as the economics of Britain will be shaken by the decision. It represents a devastating blow to the Government, and especially to Prime Minister Wilson and his Chancellor of the Exchequer, James Callaghan.

Along with the devaluation the Government ordered all banks and stock exchanges to remain closed Monday. It also outlined stringent measures designed to slow the economy: higher interest rates and taxes and reductions in Government spending.

At the same time Britain sought huge new international credits totaling $3-billion. The money will be used to replenish her depleted reserves of gold and dollars and to give strength to sterling in the days of readjustment ahead.

Of the total borrowing, $1.6-billion has been pledged by some of the world's leading central banks. The United States is in the pool, but it was not known tonight whether France had agreed to join.

The remaining $1.4-billion has been requested from the International Monetary Fund. A statement from the fund tonight said that Britain had been assured of "prompt and sympathetic consideration" and that a "favorable decision" was expected in a few days.

The lending arrangement was worked out with central bankers in the Group of Ten—the leading countries in world monetary affairs—who were meeting in Paris this week.

The urgent effort was to stop the deterioration of confidence in a major world trading currency. The pound is second only to the dollar in its use for international transactions and its place in many national reserves.

The pound was weak, basically, because Britain continued to import more than she exported.

Drain Turns to Panic

In the last week, events turned the chronic drain into panic. A record trade gap of $300-million was reported for October. As rumors of loans and devaluation circulated without official action, large amounts of Britain's reserves of gold and foreign currencies were poured out in an effort to keep the pound up to the official rate despite selling pressure.

The United States and Britain's friends in Europe were informed a few hours before the devaluation announcement. Their reactions quickly began to indicate what would happen in the world monetary system.

Ireland announced that she would devalue as Britain had, and Israel said she would make an announcement tomorrow. Denmark and Finland said they would devalue to some extent, and Norway may follow suit.

The countries in the sterling area, those that use the pound for trading, will differ in their reactions. In the old days they would have devalued almost automatically with Britain. Now such countries as South Africa and the rich Arab states are economically stronger than Britain.

No Market Devaluation

The Common Market's six members—France, West Germany, Italy, Belgium, the Netherlands and Luxembourg—will not devalue, demonstrating the very strength that makes Britain want to join the market.

The devaluation announcement was a sudden and dramatic turn after days of official silence in the midst of chaos in the financial markets.

Although the experts knew that devaluation was a real possibility after years of abstract discussion, the actual news came as a surprise. The British Broadcasting Corporation continued for an hour with a Doris Day movie on television. Early editions of Sunday newspapers had such headlines as "Why Are We Waiting?"

For three years, since the Labor party took over the Government, it has asked the British people for sacrifice to maintain the value of the pound. In a moment tonight, all the sacrifice—unemployment, lagging wages and a stagnant economy—seemed a wasted effort.

Devaluation Rejected

Moreover, Mr. Wilson and Mr. Callaghan had repeatedly rejected the prospect of devaluation.

On July 24 the Prime Minister said that those who started rumors about devaluation were "wasting their time." The same day the Chancellor said that to devalue would be to "break faith" with governments abroad and "bring down the standard of life of our own people."

The possibility that the Labor party itself would turn against the authors of the old policy could not be excluded. Under the parliamentary system Mr. Wilson could be forced from office by losing the support of his own party.

Edward Heath, the Conservative leader, was quick to denounce the Government tonight. He pointed out that the last devaluation of the pound, from $4.03 to $2.80 in 1949, also took place under a Labor government.

Move Is Condemned

"I utterly condemn the Government for devaluating the pound," Mr. Heath said. "Twice in 20 years disastrous Socialist policies and incompetent Labor ministers have brought about devaluation, created hardship at home and discredited Britain abroad."

A Liberal member of Parliament, Richard Wainwright, called for a new Chancellor of the Exchequer. He said devaluation had come about "in the worst possible way—in a great scramble, surrounded by something close to panic."

The Sunday Express, a Conservative newspaper, said in an editorial: "What should Mr. Wilson do next? Just one thing. Quit."

The pro-Labor Sunday Mirror said devaluation stood for "disaster and disillusion."

The other measures announced by the Government tonight made it clear that the public would have to suffer as part of the price of economic readjustment. These were the major directives:

• The country's basic interest rate, the bank rate, will rise to an extraordinary 8 per cent from 6 ½ per cent in an effort to slow down economic activity. In addition, banks will have to limit their loans except for such urgent needs as exports.

• The Government will cut defense spending next year by more than £100-million, or $240-million at the new rate. Domestic public expenditure will be slashed by the same amount.

• A large rebate now given to all manufacturing industry on the Selective Employment Tax, a flat tax on every worker employed, will be canceled except in distressed regions. A special export rebate will also be dropped.

• The corporation tax, the Government warned, will be increased in April from 40 to 42.5 per cent. It said a "strict watch" would be maintained to prevent undue increases in dividends.

Freeze Omitted

The one glaring omission from the list of measures was a freeze on wages. Experts have long warned that any devaluation would produce great pressures for higher wages to match the inevitably rising cost of living. But wage increases would kill the aim of keeping exports less expensive in foreign currencies.

The Treasury statement tonight said only that it was "essential" to avoid large wage claims and settlements lest "industrial costs go up once more and the competitive benefits of devaluation be frittered away." It said talks on this matter with labor and industry would begin at once.

At present there is no legal freeze on wages. The Trades Union Congress, parent body of British unions, is supposed to keep some control on increases, though its ability to do so seems doubtful. The Government's Prices and Incomes Board can delay rises briefly while investigating them.

Some thought the Government would inevitably move toward a wage freeze like the one it imposed for six months after the crisis in July, 1966. The theory was that it was merely trying tonight to avoid too much bad news for its union supporters at once.

One of the agonizing questions for the Government was what effect the debilitating drama of the last week, ending in the humiliation of tonight, would have on its already tattered hopes of entering the Common Market.

A Foreign Office spokesman said tonight that devaluation would "not affect our determination to join" and would "put beyond doubt our ability to accept the obligations of membership."

French Opposition

To say that France will not agree with that appraisal is to understate the situation. The French, who have been using all possible means to block the British application, can be expected to say that the devaluation shows that Britain is in much too weak an economic position to be considered.

Others in the community will argue, however, that Britain has taken the painful step urged on her by the market's economists.

The Council of Foreign Ministers of the market is meeting on Monday to consider the British application. From London's point of view the timing could hardly be worse.

Mr. Callaghan will appear in the House of Commons Monday to discuss the devaluation. On Tuesday Mr. Wilson is expected to appear at a long-scheduled meeting of Labor Parliamentary members of economic policy.

* * *

November 28, 1967

M'NAMARA IS NAMED BY U.S. TO HEAD THE WORLD BANK; JOHNSON MOVE A SURPRISE

SHIFT DUE IN 1968

Capital Sees No Hint of Any Change in Policy on War

By EDWIN L. DALE Jr.
Special to The New York Times.

WASHINGTON, Nov. 27—President Johnson has nominated Secretary of Defense Robert S. McNamara as the new president of the World Bank. The nomination has been submitted to the 107 member governments of the bank for their approval.

Although Mr. McNamara has played a key role in the Vietnam war, and has sometimes differed with the views of the Joint Chiefs of Staff, there was no indication that his shift to a new post would involve any change in the Government's policy on the war.

The news of Mr. McNamara's appointment was not formally announced today but became known on unimpeachable authority.

The White House and the Pentagon said officially that they had "no information" on the subject.

Surprise in Capital

Word of the shift, expected to take place next year, caused stunned surprise in Washington. There was no official hint of Mr. McNamara's successor as chief of the Pentagon, but early speculation centered on the recently elevated Deputy Secretary of Defense Paul H. Nitze.

Other possibilities mentioned here included John B. Connally Jr., the President's old friend who recently announced that he would not seek re-election as Governor of Texas; Cyrus R. Vance, another trusted associate who recently resigned as Deputy Secretary of Defense; Robert B. Anderson, also a close associate, who is a former Secretary of the Treasury, former Secretary of the Navy and former Deputy Secretary of Defense, and Harold Brown, Secretary of the Air Force.

Speculation on Republican

There was speculation, too, that the President might seek a prominent Republican for the post, as protection against attack in the 1968 election campaign, or that he would perpetuate the image of a highly successful industrial manager that Mr. McNamara made while president of the Ford Motor Company by naming Charles B. Thornton, chairman of the board of Litton Industries.

Senator Mike Mansfield of Montana, the Senate majority leader, said tonight that he had not heard of Secretary McNamara's nomination until informed by the press.

"I think it's a serious loss for this country," he said. "I think he is by far the best man in the Cabinet and the best Secretary of Defense we have ever had. I know of no one who can replace him and keep civilian control of the Defense Department as he did."

The post to which Mr. McNamara has been named has world-wide prestige. He would replace George D. Woods as president of the bank, the formal name of which is the International Bank for Reconstruction and Development. It is a multibillion-dollar lending institution whose primary function is to aid the economic development of poor countries.

An American has always been president of the bank, and the United States Government has known for several months that it would have to name a successor to Mr. Woods. He is 65 years old and does not desire reappointment to the presidency, which runs for a term of five years.

His term expires at the end of this year, but it has been extended for "up to one year," pending the naming of a successor. Thus the date of Mr. McNamara's taking office, if he is approved, is not certain. But it was reliably reported that the date would be next spring or earlier—in any case well before the Presidential election.

Mr. McNamara has frequently expressed a profound interest in the problems of the less developed countries. He devoted an entire speech in Montreal last year to the subject.

The formal decision on the new president of the bank will be made by its 20 executive directors, who represent the member countries. They are expected to vote on Wednesday, assuming they receive the approval of their governments.

Mr. McNamara's name was presented to the directors last week by the United States director, Livingston Merchant. A cable promptly went out to the member governments.

Nothing in the articles of agreement of the bank says that the president must be an American. But this has been the tradition in the bank's 22-year history, just as a European has always been managing director of the bank's sister institution, the International Monetary Fund.

The fund makes short-term loans in different currencies to nations experiencing difficulties with their balance of international payments.

It was expected that the member governments of the bank, respecting the tradition that the United States name the bank president, would not object to Mr. McNamara's nomination. However, after he became president his major role in the Vietnam war might create difficult problems for him in dealing with some of the bank's member countries.

The salary of the president of the World Bank is $40,000 a year. This is free of United States tax because of the international status of the bank. The salary of the Secretary of Defense is $30,000.

The White House has consistently said there has been no major disagreement over the conduct of the war between the President and Mr. McNamara. There has been an impression that Mr. McNamara was overruled by the President in the latest decisions to add more bombing targets in North Vietnam, but even this is denied.

In testimony before the Senate Preparedness Investigation Subcommittee last summer, Mr. McNamara presented a series of arguments against substantially extended bombing, but he emphasized that the situation could change. The Joint Chiefs and other military witnesses strongly supported expanded bombing, and the subcommittee adopted their view in its report.

The chief criticism of Mr. McNamara earlier was that he was too optimistic about how the war was going. But in the last year he has carefully avoided optimistic statements, although he has left no doubt of his view that the Allied forces were gradually gaining the upper hand.

As president of the World Bank, Mr. McNamara would have the decisive hand in its operations, although decisions on loans must be formally approved by the executive directors.

Since 1945, when it began operations, the bank has made loans totaling more than $12-billion. In the early years after World War II, these were "reconstruction" loans to Europe, but for a number of years now the emphasis has been on the less developed countries.

The bank has two kinds of loan operations and raises funds for each in a different manner.

Its ordinary loans carry an interest rate of 6 per cent, with 20 to 30 years to repay. The funds for these are raised through sale of the bank's bonds in the world's financial markets, chiefly in New York. The bonds now have a good reputation in all the main markets. No loan by the bank to a less developed country has ever been in default.

The loans go mainly for projects such as dams, electric power production, highway systems, port improvement and railways. Lately there have been loans in the fields of education and agriculture. The bank lends very little for industry.

The second loan operation is handled by an affiliate of the bank called the International Development Association. It has the same president and staff as the bank. Its loans carry no interest, and borrowers have 50 years to repay. The funds are raised by contributions from 21 relatively rich countries.

These loans go to the very poorest countries, such as India, which cannot absorb much debt.

This is the only operation of the bank that affects the United States taxpayer—the United States contribution comes out of the Federal Treasury.

The United States share in the first two rounds of contributions has been a little more than 40 per cent, or $112-million a year for the last three years.

* * *

December 11, 1967

SOVIET WARNS U.S. ON SPREADING WAR BEYOND VIETNAM

Cites Hints That Washington Is Weighing Move in Laos or Cambodian Blockade

VOWS 'STRONG REBUFF'

Statement Believed to Show Concern Over the Effects of McNamara Departure

By HENRY KAMM
Special to The New York Times.

MOSCOW, Dec. 10—The Soviet Union warned the United States today against extending its military action from Vietnam to neighboring Cambodia and Laos.

In a statement issued through Tass, the official press agency, Moscow charged that "officials and the United States military command" had called for a blockade of the Cambodian coast or an invasion of Cambodian territory.

At the same time, the statement continued, there have been reports that the United States plans to send troops into southern Laos to create a passageway linking Thailand and South Vietnam.

"In this way," the statement declared, "by pursuing the piratic line to further aggravation of the war in Vietnam, the United States' aggressive circles are by all indications preparing to spread the fire of that war to other countries of Southeast Asia."

Geneva Accords Cited

The statement, couched in a form that marked it as an authoritative expression of the Soviet leadership's position, concluded with this warning:

"The leading circles of the Soviet Union closely follow the developments in Southeast Asia. The Soviet Union proceeds from the belief that all states must respect the independence and neutrality of Cambodia and Laos and that the Geneva agreements guaranteeing the interests of these states must be unswervingly observed and respected.

"United States attempts to cause further aggravation of the situation in Southeast Asia will be strongly rebuffed by the peace-loving states of the world, and the United States will naturally bear the complete responsibility for the consequences of its actions."

Articles Express Concern

The statement followed a number of articles in the Soviet press expressing concern over increasing mention in the United States of the concept of "hot pursuit" of an enemy force across the South Vietnamese border into Laos or Cambodia. President Dwight D. Eisenhower's televised statement to that effect on Nov. 28 provided the impetus for a number of such articles.

Prince Norodom Sihanouk, the Chief of State of Cambodia, has repeatedly denied that the Vietcong or the North Vietnamese use his country as a sanctuary. He has demanded that the United States respect Cambodia's borders with South Vietnam.

There were indications here that the Soviet declaration was linked to the impending departure of Secretary of Defense Robert S. McNamara from the Pentagon.

Reports published in the United States suggest that McNamara successfully counseled President Johnson to reject recommendations from the Joint Chiefs of Staff to carry the war across South Vietnam's western borders. With Mr. McNamara out of the way, it is suggested here, Moscow may have thought it opportune to put Mr. Johnson on notice against yielding to military pressure for action in Laos and Cambodia.

Military supplies are reaching the enemy forces in South Vietnam through both countries. More effective American action to close the Ho Chi Minh Trail of supply paths through Laos and a partial naval blockade of Cambodia have been called for in the United States.

The Soviet statement also reflects Moscow's unhappiness with Premier Souvanna Phouma of Laos, whom the Soviet Union accuses of eroding his country's neutrality.

In recent days, Soviet-sponsored clandestine broadcasts heard in Laos have pointedly reminded the Premier of his obligation to maintain strict neutrality.

* * *

December 20, 1967

14 SCHOLARS WARN A VIETNAM DEFEAT MEANS BIGGER WAR

American 'Moderates' Say a Red Victory Would Spur Revolutionary Activity

By DREW MIDDLETON

Fourteen eminent American scholars and specialists on Asian affairs have concluded that the acceptance by the United States of a Communist victory in Vietnam would be likely to lead to larger, more costly wars rather than to a lasting peace.

A Communist victory, they warn in a report made public yesterday, would encourage those who advocate violence as the best instrument of change.

But they also view Vietnam as a crucial test of American political maturity as represented in a willingness to fight a limited war for limited but important objectives rather than to expand the war into a "ruinous" regional or global conflict involving other major powers.

In this context, they urge limited experimental steps toward de-escalation of the conflict, primarily to show that "there is no inevitable progression upwards."

Freedom House Played Role

The report is the result of the first conference sponsored by the new Freedom House Public Affairs Institute.

The participants, in the words of one of their number, Prof. Robert A. Scalapino of the University of California at Berkeley, are basically "moderates" whose views are based on both practical experience and study.

North Vietnam, the scholars maintain, hopes that a combination of internal political considerations and external pressures will force the United States Administration to end the war. "As long as the Communists believe this," the statement adds, "they will take their present hard-line position."

"In this sense," it says, "the outcome is being decided on the streets and in the homes of America as much as in the jungles of Vietnam."

The authors in addition to Professor Scalapino, are:

A. Doak Barnett, professor of government, Columbia University; Leo Cherne, executive director, Research Institute of America; Harry D. Gideonse, chancellor, New School for Social Research; Oscar Handlin, Charles Warren Professor of History, Harvard; and William W. Lockwood, professor of politics and international affairs, Princeton.

Also Richard L. Park, professor of political science, University of Michigan; Guy J. Pauker, the Rand Corporation; Lucian Pye, professor of political science, Massachusetts Institute of Technology; and Edwin O. Reischauer, University Professor, Harvard.

Also J. Milton Sacks, professor of political science, Brandeis University; Paul Seabury, professor of political science, Berkeley; Fred Von Der Mehden, professor of political science, University of Wisconsin; and Robert E. Ward, professor of political, science. Michigan.

National Debate Noted

Against the background of the national debate over Vietnam and Asia, the object of the report is to establish a middle ground for American opinion between the increasingly rigid positions of the left and the right.

In a short introduction, the authors say it is their feeling "that the moderate segment of the academic community must now be heard, lest other voices be mistaken for majority sentiment." Their statement, they add, "seeks to present a rational, moderate position as forcefully as possible."

The 6,700 word text is being sent to 3,600 scholars. The introduction concludes:

"If you find yourself sufficiently in accord with the major themes, we hope you would be willing to associate yourself with the statement and help promote its circulation for purposes of broader discussion."

3-Day Meeting in Tuxedo

Freedom House, a nonpartisan educational institution, brought the experts together at Tuxedo, N. Y., recently for a three-day discussion of American policy in Asia.

Leonard R. Sussman, executive director of the institute, said that the conference was financed by contributions.

The section of the report dealing with the war in Vietnam and its effect in Southeast Asia—especially the consequences of an American defeat—tends to support the policies of the present and previous Administrations.

Through these, the report notes the United States has "bought time" for 200 million people to develop politically and economically without ceaseless internal and external Communist pressures.

The report also deals with the policies of Japan, now the world's third industrial power, and with the events in Asia that "summon her increasingly to a position of leadership."

The most urgent item on the agenda between the United States and Japan from the Japanese viewpoint, the report says, is the recovery of Okinawa. The report suggests that the United States, which has retained control of the island since World War II for military reasons, "be sensitive" to the politics involved.

On Japan's Vietnam policy the panel notes that although the United States is, in general, the foreign nation most respected by Japanese as indicated by opinion polls, the polls also show that the Japanese are either against the American Vietnam policy or neutral.

The panel concludes that United States efforts to press for positive support on Vietnam "could only provoke a crisis." Continuation of the United States-Japan security treaty, up for review in 1970, is essential for the security of both nations, the panel said.

The report deals extensively with Communist China.

The panel concludes that the most likely outcome of the Cultural Revolution in China is a turn to political compromise and pragmatism—solutions rather than ideology. In this sense, it says, "Maoism—as apart from Mao—seems destined for significant revision with only the timing and the principal actors obscure."

Noting China's emphasis on "people's wars," the scholars report that the "potential threat of her revolutionary aspirations for Asia" is now "recognized by every non-Communist state in the region." But China has exercised "great prudence" in avoiding a direct confrontation with America or the Soviet Union, they note.

The United States, the report says, must continue to "deter, restrain and counter balance" Chinese power to avoid a major war in the Asian-Pacific area.

These efforts, the report maintains, should be accompanied by a concerted campaign to increase the openings toward international amity that pragmatic forces in China now, or in the future, may wish to exploit.

"We must establish an elaborate structure of inducements to moderation, even as we maintain a firm and explicit set of deterrents to extremism," it advises.

These should include proposals for "exchange, discussion and interaction" that challenge Chinese "isolationist fanaticism." Membership in the United Nations and participation in international conferences would be included.

Basic Themes Expounded

The panel expounds these basic themes in its conclusions:

The American record in the Asian Pacific area since 1943 is one "of which we can be proud," but in the near future new styles of operation, new techniques and new emphases" will be essential.

A study of policies for Asia requires an examination of American issues, procedures and cultural attitudes that affect foreign policy. To argue that the United States must choose between "the quest for some meaningful order in Asia and the quest for racial justice and urban development at home" is "false and dangerous," the report said. It adds that the United States "need not revert to the isolationist policies that precipitated World War I and World War II in order to solve our domestic problems."

"In many respects, the war in Vietnam will be won or lost in the South." This, the report explained, involves pressing policies that will draw popular support and emphasizing "seize and hold" rather than "search and destroy" operations.

The report looks critically at the role of mass media in relation to foreign policy. When Americans should be thinking in "complex, dispassionate, long-range terms," the report asserts, a large proportion of the mass media concentrates on "the most sensationalist and extreme events," inducing the "fears and stereotypes that inhibit national thought."

* * *

December 29, 1967

SIHANOUK EASES STAND OPPOSING INCURSION BY U.S.

CITES HOT PURSUIT

Says Units of Vietcong Entered Cambodia but Were Ousted

By Agence France-Presse

PNOMPENH, Cambodia, Dec. 28—Prince Norodom Sihanouk, the Cambodian chief of state, said today that under certain conditions Cambodian troops would not try to stop United States troops from entering the country in hot pursuit of Vietcong or North Vietnamese forces.

The Prince added that he would take such a position only if he was convinced that Vietcong or North Vietnamese troops had entered Cambodia illegally and were in an "uninhabited outlying region difficult to control."

Prince Sihanouk took that position in repy to questions submitted to him by The Washington Post. The main points of his reply were made public by Cambodian Information Services.

[In Washington, State Department officials said they would have no comment on the Prince's statements until they could study a complete text. The United States is widening its diplomatic efforts to keep the enemy from using Cambodian territory as a sanctuary. Washington has tried repeatedly to convince Prince Sihanouk that the enemy is doing so.]

Prince Adds a Warning

The Prince coupled his statement with a sharp warning that if there were "serious raids or bombings" against frontier areas inhabited by Cambodians or Vietnamese who had been living there a long time, Cambodian troops would strike back as strongly as possible.

He also warned the United States against sending South Vietnamese troops onto Cambodian soil, maintaining that once they came it would "become impossible to make them leave."

In the wide-ranging interview, Prince Sihanouk acknowledged that "small Vietnamese resistance units" had entered Cambodia "a number of times."

He insisted, however, that such infiltrators were expelled "a few hours later under the order of Cambodian officers."

He also said that while he would not take the initiative in inviting United States officials here for talks he would be willing to receive a personal envoy from President Johnson.

The Cambodian ruler chose to make his remarks at a time when reports are circulating that Washington is seriously considering allowing either American or South Vietnamese troops to enter countries around South Vietnam in "hot pursuit" of a retreating enemy.

Cambodia has maintained that there are no Vietcong or North Vietnamese bases on its soil, but United States officials have insisted to the contrary.

The Prince said there were two types of aggression possible.

Limited Combat

The first would involve a "limited combat between American and Vietnamese forces" in an uninhabited, outlying area. The presumption would be that either North Vietnamese or Vietcong had entered Cambodia illegally, as the United States says they do.

In such a case, he said, Cambodia would not intervene militarily but would protest to both parties involved.

The second type of aggression, he said, would involve military action against regions where Cambodians or Vietnamese live.

Prince Sihanouk said Cambodia's response in such a case would be much as he had outlined it in an announcement yesterday—a full military counter-attack, requests for aid from China and the Soviet Union, a call for volunteers from "friendly" Communist countries and a demand for an emergency meeting of the United Nations General Assembly.

The Prince warned the United States that if it used the "Saigon army" against Cambodian territory it would cause an "irreparable" breach between Washington and Pnompenh and that there would no longer be a "measured response."

He said it was "out of the question" that Cambodia "would ever appeal to Vietnamese to protect its territorial integrity," and added:

"We know only too well that if they come here in force it will become impossible to make them leave.

"We are not in the least enemies of the American Government and people. We are a country caught between the hammer and the anvil, a country that would very much like to remain the last haven of peace in Southeast Asia."

The Prince denied that there were any Vietcong or North Vietnamese "divisions, headquarters, bases or hospitals" on Cambodian territory.

He asked the Americans to understand that his army, which defends three frontiers with 34,000 men, could hardly do better shutting off the Vietnamese border than the Americans and their allies do with more than a million men.

Although the Prince emphasized that he could not invite American officials to confer with him, he added:

"If President Johnson, who has never accused or threatened us and who knows how to keep his sang-froid despite certain warmonger pressures, wishes to send me a representative accredited by him, I will gladly receive him."

The Prince also expressed a desire for "strict inspection" of Cambodian "frontiers, ports and airports" by the International Control Commission manned by India, Canada and Poland.

He said he hoped the United States would help strengthen the commission in Cambodia, but he expressed "deep regret" that the Soviet Union and Poland refused to go along.

* * *

January 6, 1968

SPOCK AND COFFIN INDICTED FOR ACTIVITY AGAINST DRAFT

U.S. Says Five Conspired to Counsel Young Men to Resist Service

By FRED P. GRAHAM
Special to The New York Times.

WASHINGTON, Jan. 5—Five men, including Dr. Benjamin Spock, the author and pediatrician, and the Rev. William Sloane Coffin Jr., chaplain of Yale University, were indicted today on charges of conspiring to counsel young men to violate the draft laws.

The others indicted are Michael Ferber, a 23-year-old Harvard University graduate student; Mitchell Goodman, 44, of New York and Temple, Me., an author, and Marcus Raskin, 33, of Washington, co-director of the Institute for Policy Studies, a private research organization.

In New York Dr. Spock said tonight that he hoped "100,000, 200,000 or even 500,000 young Americans either refuse to be drafted or to obey orders if in military service."

Attorney General Ramsey Clark announced the indictment, which was handed up this afternoon by a Federal grand jury in Boston.

If convicted, the men could receive maximum penalties of five years in prison and $10,000 fines.

Mr. Clark's announcement said the men would not be arrested but would be notified when to appear for arraignment in Federal District Court in Boston after a date had been set.

The indictment represents the strongest countermove by the Government so far to the antidraft movement that has sprung up among opponents of the United States' Vietnam war policy.

Dr. Spock, 64, is one of the best-known figures in the antiwar movement and has been mentioned as a possible independent candidate for President on a peace platform.

Mr. Coffin, who is 43, was a prominent figure in the series of antiwar demonstrations here late last October.

On Oct. 20 he turned in a briefcase full of what he said were draft cards to officials at the Justice Department building here and later accused one of them of being "derelict in his duty" for not having arrested him. He said he wanted to be arrested in order to precipitate a "moral, legal confrontation" with the Government over the draft.

Justice Department officials said later that the briefcase had contained draft cards and other matter.

The indictment accused the five men of conspiring to counsel, aid and abet young men to refuse to serve in the armed forces and perform other duties—such as carrying draft registration cards at all times—that are required by the Selective Service law.

Boston Rally Cited

Justice Department sources said the men had been indicted in Boston apparently because the first overt act of the conspiracy, as charged in the indictment, took place there. This was a rally at the Arlington Street Church on Oct. 16, at which a number of draft cards were collected to be turned over to the Justice Department. Several other acts of the alleged conspiracy were also said to have occurred in Boston.

According to the indictment, Dr. Spock, Mr. Coffin, Mr. Raskin and Mr. Goodman agreed to sponsor a nationwide draft-resistance program that would include disrupting the induction processes at various induction centers, making public appeals for young men to resist the draft and to refuse to serve in the military services and issuing calls for registrants to turn in their draft cards.

Mr. Ferber was accused of having acted with unnamed persons to collect the draft cards at the Boston rally.

Other specific acts alleged included the distribution in New York last August by Dr. Spock and Mr. Coffin of a statement entitled "A Call to Resist Illegitimate Authority" and a speech by Mr. Ferber at the Boston rally entitled "A Time to Say No."

The men were accused of having violated Title 50, Section 462(A) of the United States Code Appendix, a section of the Universal Military Training and Service Act that dates to World War I.

It declares that any person is guilty of violating the law if he "knowingly counsels, aids, or abets another to refuse or evade registration or service in the armed forces" or if he "shall knowingly hinder or interfere or attempt to do so in any way, by force or violence or otherwise," with the administration of the draft. It also makes it a crime to conspire to commit these acts.

Until today the antidraft controversy had centered on the insistence of Lieut. Gen. Lewis B. Hershey, director of Selective Service, that young men should be subject to draft reclassification if they staged illegal protests against Selective Service.

HERSHEY LAUDS INDICTMENT

WASHINGTON, Jan. 5 (AP)—General Hershey, informed by newsmen of the indictments, commented: "I don't know if they're guilty or not and I take no pleasure in seeing anybody get indicted, but if they are not guilty they ought to get a chance to show it and if they are, they ought to be punished."

"I think the Department of Justice has done a fine job in getting them indicted, and it's a job that ought to be done," he continued.

SPOCK HOPES 500,000 WILL REFUSE TO BE DRAFTED

By EDWARD C. BURKS

Dr. Benjamin Spock said last night he hoped "that 100,000, 200,000 or even 500,000 young Americans either refuse to be drafted or to obey orders if in military service."

That was the reaction of the tall 64-year-old author and pediatrician to the news from Boston that he was one of five persons indicted on a Federal charge of conspiring to counsel young men to violate draft laws.

Calm and in good spirits during a news conference at his small, unpretentious apartment at 135 East 83d Street, he cited the "Nuremberg laws" as justification for his antidraft activities.

The 'Higher Law'

"I certainly don't feel myself guilty," he said.

He referred to the "higher law" brought out at the time of the Nuremberg postwar trials of Nazi leaders. That law, he said, made it morally necessary to disobey when "your government is up to crimes against humanity."

He insisted that he was not afraid of going to jail but would fight it all the way to the Supreme Court.

"The Government is not going to quit easily and neither are we," he said.

Policy Called Illegal

One reason, he said, for the indictments is that "Lyndon Johnson and the Administration are feeling more desperate all the time because the war is still going against them."

He conceded that he had been giving moral and financial support to young war resisters for some time.

"I'm not a pacifist," he said. "I was very much for the war against Hitler and I also supported the intervention in Korea, but in this war we went in there to steal Vietnam."

He repeatedly described the American intervention in Vietnam as "illegal," "detrimental" and "disastrous."

Dr. Spock, a large-boned man who wears heavy horn-rimmed glasses, looked hale as he stood in front of a bookcase containing his "Baby and Child Care" volume in many languages and told how he would continue to do everything he could to stop the war.

He defended his conduct as "legal in the highest sense." The defiance of the anti-draft youths, he said, was "a very patriotic endeavor requiring enormous amounts of courage—the most effective way of opposing the war."

He then expressed the hope that hundreds of thousands would refuse induction in order to create "a very awkward position for the Government." Or, he said, the American people "can rise up and throw Lyndon Johnson out."

But while praising the peace campaign of Senator Eugene J. McCarthy, Democrat of Minnesota, Dr. Spock saw scant chance of denying the Democratic renomination to Mr. Johnson this summer and declined to endorse any candidate.

Immaculate in "television blue"—a blue suit, blue tie and blue shirt—Dr. Spock repeated his story for an array of cameras and other newsmen.

Did he feel that his antiwar activities were a disservice to American fighting men in Vietnam?

"No," he said, "I never feel any guilt about servicemen, although I know about half of the people in the country are on the other side, supporting the war.

"But soldiers don't have the best opportunity to judge the war. After all they only hear one side of it."

Mrs. Spock sat quietly at one end of the living room. Her husband, asked to pose with a copy of his book, of which 20 million copies have been sold, quipped:

"I don't want to be reading my own book. It's easier to go to jail for five years than to hold this."

Then he said that he was willing to go to jail if necessary to prove his point.

Indicted with him were Mitchell Goodman, a New York novelist; the Rev. William S. Coffin Jr., Yale University chaplain; Michael K. Ferber, Harvard graduate student, and Marcus Raskin, director of the Institute for Policy Studies in Washington.

"Since I preached a sermon at Arlington Street Church here on Oct. 16," Mr. Ferber said in Boston, "I appear to have been implicated in the demonstration that followed a few days later in Boston.

"I gather they have moved against the big shots, although I do not consider myself one of those but rather a middleman."

Mr. Goodman said: "I'm going to get a lawyer and fight this thing to the Supreme Court.

"I consider it very important to test the legality of the draft law and the constitutionality of Mr. Johnson's war. I suppose that the only way they can be tested is if people of some repute are arrested and tried.

"The United States Government is involved in illegalities and that's what we're fighting. People like me believe the Government has committed atrocities in Vietnam. We are attempting to save the moral integrity of this country."

Mr. Goodman questioned why the Government did not take legal action against all 2,000 signers of a statement entitled "A Call to Resist Illegitimate Authority."

The statement, signed by Dr. Linus Pauling, the Right Rev. James A. Pike and Robert Lowell, pledged the signers to raise money for youths who resisted the draft.

"Is the Government afraid to arrest some of these people?" Mr. Goodman said. "Why has the Government been selective? Have they begun a picking off process?

"I intend to continue my antiwar activities. My conscience forces me to do that."

Mr. Coffin and Mr. Raskin said in Washington that they would not comment until they had read the charges against him.

A spokesman at Yale refused to comment on Mr. Coffin's indictment.

* * *

January 24, 1968

NORTH KOREA SEIZES NAVY SHIP, HOLDS 83 ON BOARD AS U.S. SPIES; ENTERPRISE IS ORDERED TO AREA

---

4 CREWMEN HURT

Rusk Says Efforts Are Under Way to Obtain Vessel's Release

By NEIL SHEEHAN
Special to The New York Times.

WASHINGTON, Jan. 23—North Korean patrol boats seized a United States Navy intelligence ship off Wonsan today and took the vessel and her 83 crew members into the North Korean port.

The Defense Department, reporting the incident, said the ship had been in international waters about 25 miles off the eastern coast of North Korea when she was boarded by armed North Korean sailors at 1:45 P.M. (11:45 P.M. Monday, Eastern Standard time).

But North Korea, in a Pyongyang radio broadcast, asserted that the Pueblo had "intruded into the territorial waters of the republic and was carrying out hostile activities." The broadcast called the Pueblo "an armed spy boat of the United States imperialist aggressor force."

Matter of 'Utmost Gravity'

Secretary of State Dean Rusk called the seizure of the Pueblo "a matter of the utmost gravity." He said the United States was negotiating with North Korea "through the channels that are available to us to obtain the immediate release of the vessel and her crew."

The incident forced a sudden confrontation between the United States and an Asian Communist government that has long been calling for diversionary assaults against "United States imperialism" to distract American energies from the war in Vietnam.

The Defense Department said four crewmen of the Pueblo had been wounded, one critically. One report said a crew member had lost a leg. The Pentagon declined to say how the men had been wounded.

North Korean Report

Later—on Wednesday morning, Korean time—the North Vietnamese said at an armistice meeting in Panmunjom that several of the Pueblo's crew were "killed or wounded" in the incident, and a North Vietnamese broadcast monitored in Tokyo said the vessel resisted seizure. The Pentagon declined to comment.

The Pueblo carried 6 officers, 75 enlisted men and 2 civilians, whom the Defense Department identified as Navy civilian hydrographers performing oceanographic research.

Military sources said that the nuclear-powered aircraft carrier Enterprise and two destroyers were diverted toward Korea earlier in the day.

The Enterprise had just ended a visit in Sasebo, Japan, and was headed south toward the Gulf of Tonkin to join other carriers of the Seventh Fleet in staging air raids against North Vietnam when she and her escorting destroyers received orders to head for Korea.

There were also reports that the United States' Eighth Army in Korea and South Korean military forces had been placed on alert as a result of the Pueblo incident as well as the clash in Seoul on Sunday between South Korean policemen and a group of 31 armed North Korean infiltrators. The 31 were said to have planned to attack the presidential palace.

The Defense Department declined to confirm the alert reports but alerts by American and South Korean forces are normal in such circumstances.

The State Department spokesman, Robert J. McCloskey, said that an "urgent request" for the release of the Pueblo and her crew had been sent to South Korea through the Soviet Union.

Secret Devices Aboard

According to the Defense Department, the Pueblo is a 906-ton vessel that carries highly secret electronics equipment designed to intercept radar and other electronic signals and gather information for intelligence.

The details given by the Pentagon on the ship's position when it was boarded—127 degrees 54.3 minutes east longitude and 30 degrees 25 minutes north latitude—would have put her about 20 miles from the peninsula that forms the northern arm of Wonsan Bay and about 30 miles from the Port of Wonsan, where the Pueblo was taken.

Associated Press

Pueblo, seized off North Korea and taken to Wonsan, is an intelligence collection vessel of the United States Navy.

Defense Department officials did not, however, give the position of the Pueblo when she was first accosted by a North Korean gunboat at noon, nearly two hours before she was boarded. Some military sources said the ship had been closer than 25 miles to the coast. But they said they believed the Pueblo had been outside the 12-mile limit that North Korea claims for its territorial waters.

At the Panmunjom meeting, Rear Adm. John V. Smith, an American and the senior representative of the United Nations Command in Korea, said the Pueblo was 16 nautical miles—more than 18 statute miles—from the Coast when the overall confrontation began. A Pentagon spokesman would not comment on that report.

U.S. Version 'Categorical'

Mr. McCloskey said he could state "categorically" that the Pueblo had remained outside the 12-mile limit at all times.

Military sources said that the North Koreans opened fire on the Pueblo at one point before boarding. But other officers said they were not certain the North Koreans had fired upon the Pueblo, and that the injuries of the crewmen might have been wounded on attempts to blow up the ship's secret electronics equipment.

The Defense Department declined to comment on either report.

The Pentagon said the Pueblo had not used any weapons during the incident. The ship carries only two .50-caliber machine guns as well as small arms for the officers and men.

President Johnson was awakened at 2 A.M. and notified of the incident by Walt W. Rostow, special Presidential assistant. Secretary of Defense Robert S. McNamara and the Joint Chiefs of Staff were also notified.

George Christian, the Presidential press secretary, said Mr. Johnson discussed the seizure at his regular Tuesday strategy luncheon with Secretary McNamara, Secretary Rusk and other senior officials.

The Joint Chiefs also held a special meeting on the incident.

Military sources said the four North Korean patrol craft that surrounded the Pueblo were Soviet-made. Each was armed with four 25-mm. automatic antiaircraft guns.

The North Korean craft—one conventional patrol boat and three other craft of motor torpedo types—were capable of speeds of 28 to 40 knots, while the Pueblo had a top speed of 12.5 knots.

According to the Defense Department account, a North Korean patrol craft first approached the Pueblo about noon, Korean time, and, with international flag signals, asked the Pueblo to identify herself.

When the Pueblo replied that she was an American ship, the North Korean ship answered, "Heave to or I will open fire on you," the Defense Department said. The Pueblo replied, "I am in international waters."

Accounts of Action Differ

At this point, some military sources said, the Pueblo's captain, Comdr. Lloyd M. Bucher, tried to move farther from the coast and the North Korean vessel opened fire, wounding at least one of the crew. The Pentagon account said only that at this point "the patrol boat circled the Pueblo."

About an hour later, the Pentagon said, three other patrol craft appeared and one ordered in international signals: "Follow in my wake, I have a pilot aboard."

The four patrol boats "closed in" on the Pueblo, the Pentagon said, "taking different positions on her bow, beam and quarter."

One patrol craft then began backing toward the bow of the Pueblo "with fenders rigged" and "an armed boarding party" on her bow, the Pentagon said. Fenders are ropes or rubber bumpers used by ships to avoid damaging each other when they pull alongside.

Ship Apparently Halted

Although the Defense Department did not say so, its account gives the impression at this point that the Pueblo was stationary.

At 1:45 P.M., the Pentagon said, the Pueblo radioed that she was being boarded, and at 2:10 she said she had been "requested" to follow the North Korean vessels into Wonsan and that "she had not used any weapons."

The final message from the Pueblo came at 2:32, the Defense Department said. It reported that the Pueblo had come to "all stop" and that her radio was "going off the air."

Military sources said Commander Bucher had radioed earlier that he was destroying his secret electronic equipment, but it is unknown how much he succeeded in destroying. The equipment, if captured, would be valuable to North Korean and Soviet intelligence men.

Nevertheless, in declining to comment on whether the North Koreans had opened fire on the Pueblo on naval and ground alerts and on other unexplained circumstances surrounding the incident, the Administration appeared to be trying to avoid arousing Congressional and public opinion while there might still be time to negotiate the release of the ship and the crew.

Mr. McCloskey, the State Department spokesman, said American diplomats were using any channels "which might be helpful" in trying to negotiate the release of the ship and her crew. He did not specify the channels. Japan, an ally of the United States, has representation in North Korea.

* * *

January 30, 1968

NORWALK SCHOOL SUSPENDS 53 IN HAIRLINE DISPUTE

By WILLIAM BORDERS
Special to The New York Times.

NORWALK, Conn., Jan. 29—The principal of the Brien McMahon High School made a class-by-class inspection of haircuts today and then suspended 53 boys whose hair he said was too long.

"They are out until they get their hair cut," Carl H. Peterson, Norwalk's Director of Secondary Education, said.

The suspensions came amid a continuing controversy across the country between parents and their children, teachers and their pupils, and among youngsters themselves over the propriety of the teenage fad of long hair and long sideburns.

The 53 boys suspended today were believed to constitute the largest group in the country suspended en masse in the controversy.

The students, some of whom wear their hair at the shoulder or below, were sent home this morning after Dr. Luther A. Howard, the principal, made his room-to-room inspection tour.

Deadline Announced

Dr. Howard announced last week that today, the opening of the second semester, was the deadline for haircuts.

"He was completely within his rights, and we're backing him all the way," Mr. Peterson said.

Although individual students have been sent home for haircuts in the past here, the mass suspensions surprised many residents of this suburban community.

"When I pay my taxes to support the school, no one cares about hair," said Paul Good, whose 15-year-old son, Sean, was suspended because his blond hair curls over his ears.

Mr. Good, a 38-year-old freelance writer whose own hair covers his collar in the back, said that he was hoping to take the case to court.

"Of course, I don't like my boy's hair all the time, but what's it got to do with his education?" he asked.

At Mr. Good's request, the Fairfield County chapter of the American Civil Liberties Union will decide at an executive board meeting tomorrow whether to defend the suspended boys.

"I would certainly expect that we'd take the case, arguing that the suspensions were capricious and discriminatory," said Burton M. Weinstein, a Bridgeport lawyer and a member of the county chapter's executive board.

Mr. Weinstein said that in the case he was considering, "the school board would have to show that long hair interfered with the process of schooling."

Under Connecticut law, school authorities have a relatively free hand in determining grounds for suspending students from public schools, while conditions for expulsion are more narrowly defined. Mr. Weinstein argued that suspending a student until he got a haircut amounted to expulsion.

Other parents in Norwalk supported the principal's action, and three boys got haircuts during the day and returned to class.

"Of course, they have the right to set rules—they should have done it long ago," said one housewife who asked not to be identified, "so I won't get nutty phone calls."

In barring the boys from the student body of 1,700, Dr. Howard was acting on the strength of a dress code adopted in 1964 by the Board of Education.

Sweatshirts Banned

It bans such garb as blue jeans, sweatshirts and heavy boots, as well as "hair fashions and styles which are excessive and detract from a healthy atmosphere conducive to good educational practices."

Dr. Howard sent a note to the parents of the suspended boys, detailing the rules on hair style. The note said:

"Hair must be away from the eyes, and away from the collar line. Hair must be neat (not bushy) around the ears and must not overlap the ears. Sideburns are not to extend beyond the midpoint of the ears.

"The administration hopes that you will impress upon your son the importance of living within a society based on rules and regulations."

"Your son may return to school as soon as he has a haircut acceptable to board policy."

As the suspended boys left the brick school building this morning, some were neatly dressed in clean clothes and others were garbed in the style associated with hippies.

"I haven't gone to a barber this year, but my sister has trimmed the sides for me twice," said a senior with straight hair to the shoulder, a style known as a Prince Valiant haircut.

Another boy, who had long curls, said he had spent more time in barber shops since changing from a crewcut last year, and he added: "I also wash my hair three times a week now, and what guy with short hair does that?"

This afternoon several of the boys who had been suspended met voluntarily with Mr. Peterson at the Board of Education office.

"They still seem to think they have the right to set their own standards," the school official said later.

Some Expected Back

But he said that some of the boys had indicated they would get haircuts and be back in class tomorrow, joining the three who returned today.

One of the youths said, "I don't see their point about short hair, but I guess it's not worth missing school for."

Among the rest of the student body, the suspensions aroused a mixed reaction. A number of girls and boys said they admired the long hair.

But others apparently thought, as one boy with medium-length hair put it, that "those guys really do look pretty much like creeps."

There have been isolated cases of girl students at Norwalk high schools being sent home for wearing miniskirts that were considered too short or sweaters that were considered too tight, but their hair lengths have not been challenged by school authorities.

The Brien McMahon High School, built seven years ago, is in the Rowayton section of Norwalk, a largely upper-middle-class suburban neighborhood of well-kept, relatively new private homes on the south side of the city.

* * *

January 31, 1968

FOE INVADES U.S. SAIGON EMBASSY; RAIDERS WIPED OUT AFTER 6 HOURS; VIETCONG WIDEN ATTACK ON CITIES

AMBASSADOR SAFE

Guerrillas Also Strike Presidential Palace and Many Bases

By TOM BUCKLEY

Special to The New York Times.

SAIGON, South Vietnam, Wednesday, Jan. 31—A 17-man Vietcong squad seized parts of the United States Embassy in the center of Saigon and held them for six hours early today.

The Vietcong, wearing South Vietnamese Army uniforms, held off American military policemen firing machine guns and rocket launchers. Finally the invaders were routed by squads of American paratroopers who landed by helicopter on the roof of the building.

[Ambassador Ellsworth Bunker was taken from his residence about five blocks from the embassy to what was described as a secure area, The Associated Press reported. He returned to the embassy at 11 A.M. about two hours after the last enemy resistance was wiped out. Others of the embassy staff were also said to be safe. The American flag was raised in front of the embassy at 11:45 A.M., almost five hours later than normal.]

The daring raid was the most dramatic of scores of attacks launched by enemy commando units that carried the Vietcong's Lunar New Year offensive to the capital.

Fighting was continuing in Saigon at 2 P.M. local time (1 A.M., New York time.) A Vietcong squad, armed with a captured American machine gun and rocket launchers, was firing from among the concrete beams and pillars of a half-completed hotel across the street from the Presidential Palace.

Only scattered reports of American losses were available by midafternoon. The total was perhaps 40 men killed and twice as many wounded. The guerrillas' forces were believed to number no more than 500.

Elsewhere in the country, heavy fighting was reported in the capitals of the five provinces of the I Corps area, the north-

United Press International

Helicopter carrying blood to a military aid station lands in downtown Saigon in the midst of a sniper attack.

ernmost section of the country, and in several district towns there and in the Central Highlands cities of Banmethuot, Pleiku and Kontum.

Targets Widespread

The raiders in Saigon, besides attacking the embassy, fought their way onto the grounds of the Presidential Palace.

Waves of helicopters raked them with rockets and machinegun fire.

The palace houses the executive offices of President Nguyen Van Thieu and Vice President Nguyen Cao Ky. The United States Embassy said the President was safe at an undisclosed place. The whereabouts of the Vice President was said to be unknown.

As the fighting raged, this correspondent was pinned down for 15 minutes behind a military police jeep as tracer bullets arched a few feet overhead.

The bodies of at least two American military policemen lay perhaps 50 yards away. Vietcong and civilian dead also sprawled on the sidewalk.

Heavy fighting was also reported near the runway at Tansonnhut Airport, where an enemy company of about 100 men was making a suicide stand against a larger force of Vietnamese troops and American military policemen. The field was closed to all but emergency flights.

A handful of commandos held out in the building housing the Saigon radio, only a few blocks from the embassy. Part of the structure was burning.

The attacks began at 3 A.M. today. Eleven hours later, only fragmentary reports could be obtained of many of the guerrilla assaults that turned Saigon, a relatively placid island in a widening sea of war for the past two and a half years, into a battle ground.

Three American officers billets were attacked, as was the Philippine Embassy, the headquarters of the Vietnamese Navy, the Vietnamese Joint General Staff compound adjoining the airport, and the Gialong Palace, which houses government offices.

Associated Press

The U.S. Embassy Compound in Saigon, which was invaded by Vietcong,c in a photo taken recently as a copter landed on the roof. Building was designed to resist minor attacks.

The embassy attack capped a night of terror unmatched since the overthrow of President Ngo Dinh Diem on Nov. 1, 1963.

Beginning at 3 A.M. with mortar fire and a rocket barrage, guerrillas also struck three American billets for officers, the Tansonnhut air base on the edge of the city, the compound of the South Vietnamese General Staff adjoining the airport, the Philippine Embassy, South Vietnamese Navy headquarters and the studios of the Saigon radio.

While early reports said the Vietcong had taken over the main embassy building, or chancery, Marine officers denied that this had occurred. The raiders rampaged through the consular section, still housed in prefabricated buildings on the ground through the lower floors of a Villa occupied by Col. George Jacobson, the mission coordinator.

Gen. William C. Westmoreland, the American commander in Vietnam, visited the embassy grounds a few minutes after the American troops had taken control. He said: "The enemy's well-laid plans went afoul. All the enemy in the compound have been killed."

Heavy fighting was reported elsewhere in the country.

Fighting was reported throughout the former imperial capital, Hue. The Vietcong continued the attack begun yesterday in Hoian, with two battalions dug in around the provincial hospital and in an adjoining Vietnamese army compound. Six companies of Korean marines were reported moving to the attack.

The attacks occurred on the second day of Tet, the Lunar New Year.

Despite public warnings by the Saigon police that a terrorist assault could be expected last night in the aftermath of the enemy's attacks on major cities, the raids seemed to have caught both the Americans and the South Vietnamese by surprise.

Associated Press

Two G.I.'s seeking cover during the fighting at the U.S. Embassy compound in Saigon early today. The Vietcong invaders were driven out of compound after about six hours.

An American military-police battalion and the Saigon city police found themselves out gunned.

Not until the arrival of the first helicopters at the embassy were any infantry troops, American or South Vietnamese, seen in the center of the city. There were no tanks or heavy weapons to meet the enemy.

Safety Was Key Aim

The embassy compound, covering four acres, opened last September. The primary consideration in its construction was security—even down to the helicopter landing pad installed atop the Chancery, the compound's main structure, so Ambassador Bunker would not have to travel through crowds that might sometimes be hostile.

While Saigon was being attacked, reports of raids elsewhere were flooding into the American mission. Targets included the Bienhoa airbase and the headquarters of the American II Field Force at Longbinh, northeast of the city.

Danang, the second-largest city in South Vietnam, came under heavy attack, a day after it was rocked by rocket and mortar barrages.

The South Vietnamese police had warned yesterday afternoon that attacks by guerrilla "suicide squads" were expected. American civilians had been told to remain indoors. Service men were already under orders to remain indoors to leave the streets clear for the celebration of Tet.

The downtown streets were quiet and deserted when the first mortar rounds exploded on the block-square grounds of the Presidential Palace.

New Assaults Reported

Small-arms fire crackled in a dozen places. As the cannonade continued, allied helicopter gunships swung overhead, sweeping enormous lights over the area.

The fresh wave of attacks was viewed by some officers as the start of a general offensive intended to force the United

States to the bargaining table or make it face the likelihood of a greatly expanded and more costly war.

The new raids came as coherent reports of yesterday's sweeping raids became available.

Ground attacks, following mortar and rocket barrages had struck eight major cities—Danang, Nhatrang, Quinhon, Kontum, Holan, Pleiku, Banmethout and Tuyhoa—between midnight and 4 A.M.

Then, instead of slipping away in the darkness, enemy formations continued to hold positions in all of them except Danang and Tuyhoa, with fighting reported continuing this morning.

In the case of Kontum and Banmethuot, new assaults from outside the city were reported.

At Danang, South Vietnamese rangers and United States marines, supported by waves of helicopter gunships, pursued the retreating enemy through the southern outskirts of the city.

North Vietnamese snipers roamed the streets of Nhatrang 24 hours after attacking an American compound. Lieut Gen. William R. Rosson, commander of the I Field Force, and Lieut. Gen. Myung Shin Chae, commander of South Korean ground forces, had narrowly escaped the raid.

The situation remained unclear in Tuyhoa, the capital of Phuyen Province on the central coast, and Banmethuot, the capital of Darlac Province in the Central Highlands, where the enemy also mounted apparently successful assaults.

In all the raids, the enemy displayed coordination and offensive strength without precedent in the war.

While South Vietnamese military and governmental installations bore the brunt of the attacks, the American command disclosed that several American installations had also been hit. These included an Army airfield nine miles north of Camranh Bay, the vast supply base that had been visited twice by President Johnson. It was regarded as the most secure area in the country.

While casualty reports were incomplete and often contradictory, it appeared that American forces had escaped fairly lightly, with fewer than 50 men killed and perhaps 100 men wounded.

South Vietnamese losses were probably heavier.

Although the enemy units generally achieved surprise they took heavy casualties in the prolonged fighting that followed.

The figure may reach a total of more than 500 enemy dead. Informed sources in Saigon regarded this as a bargain price for the enemy to have paid for the enormous blow scored against Government prestige.

In response to the wave of attacks, the South Vietnamese Government canceled the 36-hour cease-fire it had ordered throughout the country for the Lunar New Year.

American forces at Khesanh and elsewhere along the demilitarized zone, in the Dakto region and in the border areas northwest of Saigon, had gone on full alert as soon as word of the attacks in the rear areas was received. But there was no attempt by the North Vietnamesse units opposing them to stage coordinated assaults.

An especially heavy enemy attack was directed at Danang in Quangnam Province, 370 miles northeast of Saigon.

Gene Roberts, chief of the New York Times bureau in Saigon, reported from Danang that four Phantom jets and two Marine Corps Intruder jets, all-weather aircraft equipped with radar navigation systems, had been destroyed in a rocket barrage.

At Pleiku, the major air base and supply terminal for the Central Highlands, at least 50 buildings were reported afire by Army officials early in the morning. Hundreds of refugees were said to be roaming the streets.

At Kontum, a province capital 50 miles north of Pleiku on Highway 14, a Vietcong force estimated at two battalions, striking about 3 A.M., fired mortars at the airfield, seized the post office and other Government buildings and attacked the Soviet Vietnamese Army's headquarters.

At Nhatrang the brunt of an attack by a North Vietnamese and a Vietcong battalion apparently fell on two adjoining American compounds, one housing senior officers and the other a military police company and a sector headquarters near the center of the city.

An interim report on casualties said that 12 Americans had been killed and 10 wounded, 7 Vietnamese soldiers killed and 23 irregulars wounded in the ambush. Sixty of the enemy were said to have died in the assault and 15 to have been taken prisoner.

* * *

February 2, 1968

STREET CLASHES GO ON IN VIETNAM, FOE STILL HOLDS PARTS OF CITIES; JOHNSON PLEDGES NEVER TO YIELD

ENEMY TOLL SOARS

Offensive Is Running 'Out of Steam,' Says Westmoreland

By CHARLES MOHR
Special to The New York Times.

SAIGON, South Vietnam, Friday, Feb. 2—Vicious street fighting continued today in many South Vietnamese towns and cities, and the Vietcong attacked three more province capitals.

The United States military commander, Gen. William C. Westmoreland, said yesterday that there was some evidence that the enemy's general offensive was "about to run out of steam," but he also conceded that the enemy had the capability to continue "this phase of their campaign for several more days."

[The United States command announced that 10,593 enemy soldiers had been killed since 6 P.M. Monday, by far the heaviest losses ever inflicted by the allies in Vietnam, United Press International reported. American losses were put at 281 killed and 1,195 wounded and South Vietnamese losses at 632 killed and 1,588 wounded.]

GUERRILLA DIES: Brig. Gen Nguyen Ngoc Loan, national police chief, executes man identified as a Vietcong terrorist in Saigon. Man wore civilian dress and had a pistol.

Some Question Totals

The assertion today that more than 10,000 of the enemy had died in the outbreaks was viewed with reserve by some observers. One, a press release, said that in a fight near Pleiku in the central highlands, 208 of the enemy were killed and one Vietnamese militiaman wounded.

Since Monday, the Vietcong have attacked 26 of the country's 44 province capitals, penetrating some of them deeply.

New attacks were reported yesterday and today on the towns of Baria, Muchoa and Phucuong, all province capitals. Other important cities, such as Danang, have also been attacked in the Vietcong drive.

Five battalions of Vietcong and North Vietnamese troops were still fighting heavily within the walls of the ancient citadel at Hue, the former imperial capital.

Strong Government forces had broken into the citadel to relieve troops who had held out in the South Vietnamese First Division compound within its confines.

Tenacious guerrilla forces were holding out in the important Mekong Delta towns of Mytho and Bentre, 40 and 55 miles south of Saigon. Vietnamese sources said the guerrillas were using the girls' high school as a command post in Mytho and that there was heavy fighting at the bus station this morning.

The United States Navy river patrol base near the delta town of Vinhlong had to be abandoned after Vietcong units overran that province capital.

One battalion of South Vietnamese troops was reported to be holding out in its compound in the city but was said to be "heavily engaged." Rescue forces were on their way.

Attacks Repulsed

Government sources said the attacks on the towns of Baria, east of Saigon, and Phucuong, to the northwest, had been repulsed eventually. But two Government tanks were destroyed in Baria and two armored cars in Phucuong.

Thirty Government soldiers died and 57 were wounded in the battle for Phucuong yesterday. They said they had killed 80 Vietcong.

On the outskirts of Saigon, two platoons of regional-force militia fled their post at an important bridge on the highway to nearby Bienhoa, the site of a major United States base, when guerrillas attacked.

The 38th South Vietnamese Ranger Battalion counterattacked and retook the bridge, Government sources said.

Sniping continued on a scattered scale in parts of Saigon and its Chinese quarter, Cholon. The Vietcong entered some houses in Cholon last night and sent the residents out to bring back food.

At 4 A.M. today a mortar and rocket attack was made on a United States supply company depot near the Saigon dock area. There was no immediate damage or casualty report.

Khesanh Attack Predicted

General Westmoreland said at his news conference yesterday that the enemy's "main effort" would be a big attack at or near the United States Marine outpost at Khesanh, near the borders of Laos and North Vietnam.

Discussing the enemy, who has massed 20,000 to 40,000 troops opposite the 5,000 marines, General Westmoreland commented, "I give him the capability of attacking in force at any time in the Khesanh area." But except for sporadic shelling from enemy guns and rockets, Khesanh remained quiet, as it had for several days.

The fighting in Saigon was aimed at wiping out the remnants of some five battalions—2,000 to 2,500 men—that entered the city Wednesday. Some of the sharper Saigon fighting occurred near the city's Tansonnhut air base.

In one incident yesterday, Government troops in Saigon broke into the An Quang pagoda, headquarters of the anti-Government faction of Vietnamese Buddhism, after getting reports that a sizable force of infiltrated guerrillas was inside. Only nuns, monks and children were found, witnesses said, but guerrillas were killed and captured in nearby residential buildings.

The Vietcong had occupied the compound of a South Vietnamese Army tank unit in the city and had beheaded one officer. They executed several women and children among the families of officers.

One South Vietnamese major, who helped retake his living quarters in fierce fighting, wept as he carried one of his dead children out of the area.

The Vietcong and the North Vietnamese are believed to have about 100 "combat effective" battalions, totaling 50,000 riflemen, in South Vietnam. A military official said that most of these units had been committed to the offensive that began Monday and that the rest were ready for quick use.

The total does not include the troops around Khesanh.

M.P. Billet Seized

Dalat, a mountain resort that is a favorite hideaway of South Vietnamese generals, was entered by the Vietcong. They seized an American military-police billet and controlled the central market, firing at "targets of opportunity," a military spokesman reported.

Troops of the United States' First Cavalry Division (Airmobile) were reported to have retaken Quangtri, the northernmost province capital in South Vietnam, after two battalions of enemy troops had overrun part of it.

Kontum, a mountain town near the border with Laos, was still partly in the hands of enemy forces, but the Vietcong troops had apparently eased their pressure on another mountain town, Banmethuot, the capital of Darlac Province.

"This is a terrible loss of face for the Government," an informed Vietnamese said. "Many people are very discouraged."

Premier Nguyen Van Loc announced that censorship would be imposed on South Vietnamese newspapers. In a reversal of an earlier decision, workers in Saigon were told to stay home today. A nationwide state of martial law was declared yesterday.

General Westmoreland said the Vietcong were paying a very heavy price for the political and psychological impact of their offensive.

The general said it would take "many, many weeks" and "in some cases months" for enemy units to regain full fighting strength.

General Westmoreland made it clear that he believed the wave of attacks on populated areas was only a phase of a general enemy strategy that would culminate with a large attack on Khesanh and on the whole of the two northernmost provinces, Quangtri and Thuathien.

The general indicated that he believed the campaign had been planned in Hanoi. He said it signaled an abandonment of the usual principle of protracted warfare followed by Communist guerrillas.

According to Lieut. Gen. Fred C. Weyand, commander of American forces in the 11 provinces surrounding Saigon, Vietcong prisoners captured in Saigon had been told to take objectives in the city and hold out for 48 hours, "until relieved" by reinforcements.

General Weyand, who is considered one of the most thoughtful students of the war in Vietnam, suggested that the offensive grew out of a basic change of the Vietcong's strategy aimed at correcting what he called "the degradation of their influence among the population."

For much of last year, he said, the Vietcong tried to avoid heavy, costly fighting with American and South Vietnamese units. But the national election in the fall, he said, "convinced them they had to do something about their slipping influence with the population."

Putting forth an opinion shared by General Westmoreland, General Weyand recalled that the Vietcong first staged a series of dramatic attacks in such isolated border areas as Locninh and Dakto late last year. One aim, he said, was to force American commanders to deploy troops away from populated areas.

Soon afterward, General Weyand asserted, the Vietcong began reinforcing their "regional" units near Saigon and other cities and reorganized their diffuse command structure around the capital into five pie-shaped units, all pointed toward coordinated attacks.

General Weyand said that he had become aware of this reorientation of enemy thinking and that, to meet it, by the middle of January he had withdrawn American units from search-and-destroy missions in remote areas. At least 85 per cent of the American troops under his command were then returned to duty in populated areas, the general said.

Intelligence reports indicated a strong likelihood of a Vietcong attack on towns during the period of Tet, the Lunar New Year, and on Monday night General Weyand ordered all units into a "maximum alert posture."

Nonetheless by Tuesday morning, large enemy forces had infiltrated Saigon. In a guerrilla war such infiltration can never be prevented, General Weyand said. While the population did not stage an uprising to welcome the Vietcong, General Weyand conceded that local guerrilla units had "performed an invaluable service" in guiding main units through the thin screen of South Vietnamese security forces around Saigon.

While saying that the Vietcong had failed to capture almost all of their military objectives in the attacks, General Weyand conceded that the Vietcong had concentrated on "remunerative" objectives of political and psychological warfare. This is the point of the new strategy, he said.

* * *

February 2, 1968

OFFENSIVE IS SAID TO PINPOINT ENEMY'S STRENGTHS

By TOM BUCKLEY

Special to The New York Times.

SAIGON, South Vietnam, Feb. 1—"Well, they can't stand many more days like that," an American general said yesterday, glancing up from an early report that said the Vietcong had lost more than 700 men on the first day of the latest wave of attacks throughout South Vietnam.

The enemy death toll for three days was tabulated at 5,800 men, as against 535 allied dead. If correct, the figure on enemy losses would equal the toll usually claimed for three weeks of fighting. [On Friday morning the announced death tolls were 10,593 of the enemy, 281 Americans and 632 South Vietnamese.]

Whatever price the guerrillas paid, the results were viewed in Saigon as incalculable in several respects: the effect on the Vietnamese civilians who may be regarded as loyal to the South Vietnamese Government; the stiffening of morale in Hanoi and guerrilla strongholds in the South; the reflection on American assertions that large sections of the country are "pacified," and the degree of belief with which such estimates are received around the world.

The Vietcong attacks have hit nearly every important province capital in the country, scores of district capitals, and many airfields, helicopter landing zones and military installations.

Surprise Is Achieved

In almost every case, the attackers appeared to have reached the centers of the cities and to have remained there, repulsing American and South Vietnamese troops for hours or days.

The apparent success of the first night's attacks in surprising the South Vietnamese troops, who have the primary responsibility for guarding the cities, is to some degree understandable in view of the gusto with which the arrival of the Lunar New Year is celebrated and the fact that a truce was in effect in three of the four corps areas.

What is difficult to understand is how the second night's attacks, including the one on Saigon, where an alert had been issued the previous afternoon, also succeeded.

Among the points that the attacks may have demonstrated are these:

- Despite official statistics to the contrary, no part of the country is secure either from terrorist bombs or from organized military operations.
- Even local guerrilla battalions, as distinct from the main force, still possess highly efficient communications, leadership and coordination. Despite the prevalence of Government informers and security agents, the battalions are able to carry out their preparations in secrecy. They have an arsenal of excellent weapons.
- Most important, after years of fighting and tens of thousands of casualties, the Vietcong can still find thousands of men who are ready not only to strike at night and slip away but also to undertake missions in which death is the only possible outcome.

As a result, only a relative handful of American troops could be brought in quickly to reinforce the hard-pressed South Vietnamese policemen and militiamen, few of them as well armed as the attackers.

By and large the South Vietnamese armed forces have not clearly demonstrated such an extreme dedication to duty. And the tactics of the American forces are calculated to keep casualties at a minimum.

Some observers feel that the attacks may put into doubt the wisdom of the American military policy of sending tens of thousands of the most effective combat troops into the empty border regions to hunt, almost always unsuccessfully, for North Vietnamese units while leaving the defense of populated areas to the South Vietnamese Army, militia and police.

All eyes were fixed on Khesanh, the marine outpost on the Laotian border, when the blow fell against every capital in the northern provinces of South Vietnam. Some 5,000 marines were in the fortress, still waiting for an attack by two divisions or more of North Vietnamese reported to be in the hills, and a large, powerful and highly mobile force was rushed into positions from which the fortress could quickly be reinforced.

Some Units Moved Back

While enemy units fought their way to the center of Pleiku, the two brigades of the Fourth Infantry Division assigned to the area—some 12,000 men—were patrolling the ridges and jungle to the west within 15 miles of the Cambodian border.

Lieut. Gen. Fred C. Weyand, commander of the II Field Force, which operates in the area, said that certain of these units had been moved back when the enemy threat became apparent, but he declined to go into details.

Major units of the First and 25th Divisions and the 199th Light Infantry Brigade, which until November had been within 15 or 20 miles of Saigon, were drawn 60 to 90 miles north of the capital by a series of North Vietnamese and Vietcong attacks.

In Saigon itself, the nerve center of American military, diplomatic and civilian aid activities, almost the only American forces on duty when the blow came at 3 A.M. yesterday were 300 military policemen, at least half of them assigned to individual guard posts.

These men performed well, by all accounts, in the fighting that followed. They possessed only rifles and light machine guns, which they were unaccustomed to using in combat, and they lacked armored vehicles and heavier weapons that could have made short work of the guerrillas.

The reserve battalions of South Vietnamese paratroops and marines near the center of the city seemed slow to react. It was understood that despite the alert in the city, only 50 per cent of them—the same figure as with the national police—had been in their barracks. The rest were out on holiday leave.

American forces from Bienhoa and Longbinh, themselves under Vietcong attack, were unable to help until 8:30 A.M., when a platoon of paratroops landed on the roof of the embassy.

These men, as far as could be determined, were the only American reinforcements who arrived in the city throughout the day and into the night, when the Vietcong struck again at two police stations and blew up a power plant in the Cholon section.

Effect of Embassy Raid

The Vietcong's choice of the new American Embassy as a major target appeared to indicate an attempt at humiliation. To the extent that the guerrillas blasted their way through the stone wall and fought from the compound for six hours, the attempt succeeded.

Whether the guerrillas entered the building itself seems of relatively little importance to anyone except members of the mission and the State Department. Despite the rush of official denials, statements from witnesses indicate that the guerrillas did temporarily take part of the main building's first floor.

"I don't know why they did it," an American officer said this morning. "They didn't achieve anything militarily. It was obviously just a propaganda thing."

More important than allied casualties, in the view of many officials, is the effect among the four million people—nearly 25 per cent of the South Vietnamese—who have enjoyed a high degree of security in this war-torn country for more than two years.

The reasoning may be incorrect, motivated by a sudden rush of fear, but it can be speculated that many people in scores of cities and towns are less certain now than they were two days ago that the allies are winning the war.

For the Americans and the South Vietnamese, the problem is to try, in the popular phrase here, "to get the ducks back in a row," to pick up the pieces, to make another effort to reorganize the South Vietnamese Army and to win back the ground that has been lost.

* * *

February 5, 1968

ENEMY ARTILLERY AND GROUND FORCE ASSAULT KHESANH

U.S. Marines at Strongpoint Near Demilitarized Zone Report Heavy Barrage

HILL ATTACK REPULSED

Westmoreland Aide Asserts the Vietcong Could Mount a Big New Offensive

By TOM BUCKLEY

Special to The New York Times.

SAIGON, South Vietnam, Monday, Feb. 5—North Vietnamese infantry and artillery units staged a heavy ground attack this morning against Hill 861, the isolated American strongpoint northeast of the outpost at Khesanh.

United States officers had speculated for weeks that the enemy was preparing for an offensive against the marines at Khesanh, in the northwestern corner of South Vietnam. There was no immediate indication whether the new attack was a prelude to such a drive.

The North Vietnamese assault teams broke through an outer ring of barbed wire on Hill 861 after an hour and a half of fighting but were driven out in 25 minutes by a determined counterattack.

While the attack was going on, American spokesmen reported a barrage of rockets and artillery and mortar fire hit the central camp at Khesanh, where 5,000 marines are facing an enemy force, estimated at 20,000 to 40,000 men, across the borders of Laos and North Vietnam.

[More than 100 North Vietnamese dead were found after the Khesanh clash, United Press International reported. In Saigon, according to Reuters, sharp fighting broke out Monday near the central market between government troops and Vietcong armed with rocket launchers.]

General Gives Warning

The strike near the demilitarized zone came less than 12 hours after the intelligence chief of the United States command warned that a second nationwide offensive by the Vietcong against population centers might start "at almost any time."

He said the offensive might be even more severe than the wave of attacks that has struck at least 35 population centers since Tuesday.

"The enemy has not expended his full capacity," said the officer, Brig. Gen. Philip B. Davidson Jr., at a news briefing.

Reports on the situation in the capital were contradictory. General Davidson said it was generally quiet, with only 600 to 700 Vietcong stragglers still in the city.

Late yesterday afternoon, however, the American mission reported new attacks on one of its warehouses in the southern end of the Chinese district, Cholon. The warehouse was first hit on Saturday.

The city police headquarters, a 10-minute ride from the United States Embassy, and four district police stations were also attacked.

Revised casualty figures were issued by the American command this morning. A total of 16,976 enemy soldiers were reported to have been killed since 6 P.M. last Monday. The command said that 4,131 people had been detained as suspected Vietcong.

Total allied deaths rose to 1,477 during the period. The number of wounded was put at 6,075. Of these, American losses were put at 471 dead and 2,744 wounded. South Vietnamese fighting forces reported having lost 993 dead and 3,229 wounded.

The number of deaths is higher than the totals for any full week of fighting in the war. The highest American toll had been 337, for the week ended May 20, 1967, and the South Vietnamese 380, for the week ended Dec. 9, 1967.

Throughout the country 3,498 enemy rifles and pistols and 722 crew-served weapons were said to have been captured. In some informed quarters, these figures were believed to provide a better indication of enemy losses than did the announced casualty figures.

Saigon appeared to be recovering somewhat this morning from the five days of terror that began early Wednesday and coincided with the celebration of the Lunar New Year.

Most stores remained closed, though, and sharp fighting was reported in some sections of the city.

Curfew Is Enforced

The curfew from 2 P.M. to 8 A.M. remained in effect for all Vietnamese last night, and for the first time, a strict curfew was also enforced on American civilians. They were forbidden to be on the streets between 7 P.M. and 8 A.M.

As the curfew hour fell last night, quiet hung over the city. As pedestrians and cars vanished, hundreds of rats appeared, burrowing into mounds of refuse that had accumulated in the gutters.

There were reports, apparently being given credence by senior South Vietnamese intelligence officials, that the raids on the United States Embassy and the Presidential Palace, as well as prolonged fighting on the outskirts of Saigon, might have been only a diversion to shield the infiltration of a large force of guerrillas into the southernmost parts of Cholon.

Two regiments of the Vietcong's Ninth Division—one of their most seasoned units, totaling 2,000 men—were reported within a night's march of the capital. Only a small part of this force was committed to the fighting that began on Tuesday.

General Davidson said that besides possible additional units, there were survivors of the nine or more battalions that made the initial assault.

Reinforcements Possible

He did not rule out the arrival of additional units, including North Vietnamese, from the belt of enemy-controlled jungle 30 to 40 miles north of the city.

One point that obviously concerns the American command is the possibility of a heavy rocket and mortar attack on Tansonnhut Airport and other targets of military importance around the capital.

Lending some weight to the view that the earlier attacks may have been both a warning and a diversion for the infiltration of forces into Cholon was the fact that the enemy units committed to battle near the airfield fought in place. They did not make a serious effort to overrun the field, which is the hub of military and civilian flights throughout the country as well as being an important fighter base.

Clustered around the airport are the headquarters of the American command and the Vietnamese Joint General Staff and other important military targets.

General Davidson said of the enemy, "He hasn't used rockets where the temptation must be well nigh unbearable—at Tansonnhut."

Through yesterday and last night, the American command made hurried efforts to strengthen its defenses there. Additional battalions of the First and 25th Divisions were being redeployed on the edge of the city.

Military officials at the highest level did not rule out a bombardment of Saigon itself in the next few nights, and it was known that foreign embassies and civilian concerns were already making plans for the rapid evacuation of their employes.

There are about 12,000 American civilians in Vietnam. About 7,000 live in Saigon.

As fighting continued in Hue, on the coast near North Vietnam, officials reported that "small pockets of enemy resistance" were holding out in the Citadel—the ancient seat of imperial power—and opposite it on the southern side of the Huong (Perfume) River.

General Davidson reported that in Hue as well as Quangtri, capital of the country's northernmost province, the guerrillas had set up revolutionary committees to rule the areas they held. South Vietnamese intelligence officials have reported the establishment of a similar committee in Saigon.

Two new clashes were reported about eight miles south of Danang, where on Tuesday guerrillas fired rockets at the major American air base and fought in the streets. In one new outbreak, United States marines grappled with an enemy battalion of 300 men. In the other, about a mile away, no esti-

United Press International

FIRE COVER was provided by a U.S. marine, left, as his comrades dragged a wounded buddy to safety in Hue, where fighting continued. An American general said that the enemy had been fighting at a rate far below maximum effort.

mate was made of the size of the enemy force. There was no immediate report of casualties.

Also in Quangtri Province, the Third Marine Amphibious Force announced that 156 enemy soldiers had been killed since Jan. 30 by a battalion of the Seventh Fleet's Ready Amphibious Group, which waded ashore four miles southeast of the artillery base at Giolinh, just south of the demilitarized zone. Marine casualties were listed as 30 killed and 133 wounded.

Early yesterday, the South Vietnamese command reported a rocket attack on the airfield at Phubai, five miles south of Hue, and assaults against infantry battalions at Lavang, in Quangtri Province, and Nghiahanh, in Quangngai Province.

In the II Corps area, comprising the Central Highlands and Lowlands, the major coastal cities of Quinhon and Nhatrang and the highland center of Pleiku were said to be quiet. It was in this region that the first wave of Vietcong attacks occurred.

Heavy fighting was still reported in Kontum, the capital of Kontum Province, and it appeared that three battalions of enemy troops, including North Vietnamese regulars, had taken a stronghold there.

In Banmethuot, hit hard early Tuesday and a scene of continuous fighting since, the guerrillas were said to have fired rockets at South Vietnamese installations Saturday night.

In the III Corps area, forming a sort of outer ring around Saigon, 43 American soldiers were reported wounded in a five-and-a-half-hour mortar attack on the First Infantry Division's forward headquarters at Laikhe.

An attack Friday on Xuanloc, the capital of Longkhanh Province northeast of Saigon, was reported to have been repulsed. In Binhduong Province to the west, 6 Americans were reported killed and 24 wounded in a fight 23 miles northwest of Saigon.

Closer to Saigon, new clashes were reported in the Thuduc and Goyap districts of Giadinh Province.

In the Mekong Delta, where the enemy has assaulted many province capitals, the situation was said to have been "stabilized," but details on specific actions were lacking.

General Davidson, in his review of the situation throughout the country, noted that the enemy had "carefully husbanded his principal resources" while leaving initial attacks largely to local battalions and hamlet platoons.

Among the units available for the second onslaught, he said, are the following North Vietnamese divisions, each numbering about 8,000 men:

The First, on the border of Cambodia and Laos in the Central Highlands, near Dakto; the Seventh, in the border area around Binhduong and Tayninh provinces; the Second, in Quangnam in the southern part of the I Corps area, and the Third and Fifth in Binhdinh and Phuyen provinces respectively, in the Central Lowlands.

General Davidson said that the interrogation of two prisoners, one of them an officer, suggested that a fifth North Vietnamese division, the 308th, might also have appeared in the border area.

"It's a famous unit," the general said, "a sort of spearhead outfit that participated in the battle of Dienbienphu."

He referred to the battle in 1954, in which the Communist-led Vietminh army, led by Gen. Vo Nguyen Giap, besieged and then overran a force of 12,500 French troops in an isolated strongpoint in what is now western North Vietnam.

General Giap, now the North Vietnamese Defense Minister, is reported by the American command to be personally directing the current South Vietnamese offensive.

Four North Vietnamese divisions supporting artillery regiments—in all, 35,000 to 40,000 men—have massed in this region, General Davidson said.

General Davidson, who arrived in Vietnam about four months ago, mentioned "enormous enemy losses" in the attacks that have been staged so far, but he appeared to qualify the statement by adding "by all counts available to us."

This was taken to be an allusion to the fact that the total of enemy dead had been complied largely by South Vietnamese officials. The accuracy of these reports has been a subject of debate.

Informed sources suggested that the briefing—unusually frank for a military figure and particularly so for a member of the intelligence community—was meant to prepare American public opinion for the likelihood of costly battles to come.

Reports on the fighting throughout the country, as presented by General Davidson, were veiled, heavily qualified and sketchy in view of the fact that many of the actions have been going on for four days or more. As a result, the presentation left the impression that the situation in many provinces might be graver than previous reports had indicated.

* * *

April 1, 1968

JOHNSON SAYS HE WON'T RUN

SURPRISE DECISION

President Steps Aside in Unity Bid—Says 'House' Is Divided

By TOM WICKER

Special to The New York Times.

WASHINGTON, March 31—Lyndon Baines Johnson announced tonight: "I shall not seek and I will not accept the nomination of my party as your President."

Later, at a White House news conference, he said his decision was "completely irrevocable."

The President told his nationwide television audience:

"What we have won when all our people were united must not be lost in partisanship. I have concluded that I should not permit the Presidency to become involved in partisan decisions."

Mr. Johnson, acknowledging that there was "division in the American house," withdrew in the name of national unity, which he said was "the ultimate strength of our country."

"With American sons in the field far away," he said, "with the American future under challenge right here at home, with our hopes and the world's hopes for peace in the balance every day, I do not believe that I should devote an hour or a day of my time to any personal partisan causes or to any duties other than the awesome duties of this office, the Presidency of your country."

Humphrey Race Possible

Mr. Johnson left Senator Robert F. Kennedy of New York and Senator Eugene J. McCarthy of Minnesota as the only two declared candidates for the Democratic Presidential nomination.

Vice President Humphrey, however, will be widely expected to seek the nomination now that his friend and political benefactor, Mr. Johnson, is out of the field. Mr. Humphrey indicated that he would have a statement on his plans tomorrow.

The President informed Mr. Humphrey of his decision during a conference at the latter's apartment in southwest Washington today before the Vice President flew to Mexico City. There, he will represent the United States at the signing of a treaty for a Latin-American nuclear-free zone.

Surprise to Aides

If Mr. Humphrey should become a candidate, he would find most of the primaries foreclosed to him. Only those in the District of Columbia, New Jersey and South Dakota remain open.

Therefore, he would have to rely on collecting delegates in states without primaries and on White House support if he were to head off Mr. Kennedy and Mr. McCarthy.

Former Vice President Richard M. Nixon is the only announced major candidate for the Republican nomination, although Governor Rockefeller has said that he would accept the nomination if drafted.

Mr. Johnson's announcement tonight came as a stunning surprise even to close associates. His main political strategists, James H. Rowe of Washington, White House Special Assistant Marvin W. Watson, and Postmaster General Lawrence F. O'Brien, spent much of today conferring on campaign plans.

They were informed of what was coming just before Mr. Johnson went on national television at 9 P.M. with a prepared speech on the war in Vietnam.

As the speech unfolded, it appeared to be a strong political challenge to Mr. Kennedy and Mr. McCarthy, announcing measures that they had been advocating.

The President thus seemed to be acting in the political tradition of his office—demonstrating that his was the power to act while his critics had only the power to propose.

But Mr. Johnson was really getting ready to place himself in a more obscure tradition—that Vice Presidents who succeed to the Presidency seek only one term of their own. Before him in this century, Theodore Roosevelt, Calvin Coolidge and Harry S. Truman followed that pattern.

'Willing to Pay Any Price'

Mr. Johnson ended his prepared speech and then launched into a peroration that had not been included in the printed text and that White Home sources said he had written himself.

He began by quoting Franklin D. Roosevelt: "Of those to whom much is given—much is asked."

He could not say that no more would be asked of Americans, he continued, but he believed that "now, no less than when the decade began, this generation of Americans is willing to pay any price, bear any burden, meet any hardship, support any friend, oppose any foe, to assure the survival and the success of liberty."

This quotation from a celebrated passage of John F. Kennedy's inaugural address of Jan. 20, 1961, appeared to be a jab at Senator Robert F. Kennedy, who now is campaigning against the war in Vietnam.

The ultimate strength of America, Mr. Johnson continued, in the rather funereal voice and with the solemn expression that he had maintained throughout his 40-minute speech, is not powerful weapons, great resources or boundless wealth but "the unity of our people."

He asserted again a political philosophy he has often expressed—that he was "a free man, an American, a public servant and a member of my party—in that order—always and only."

In his 37 years of public service, he said, he had put national unity ahead of everything because it was as true now as it had ever been that "a house divided against itself by the spirit of faction, of party, of region, of religion, of race, is a house that cannot stand."

Mr. Johnson spoke proudly of what he had accomplished in the "52 months and 10 days" since he took over the Presidency, after the assassination of John F. Kennedy in Dallas, Tex., on Nov. 22, 1963.

"Through all time to come," he said, "I think America will be a stronger nation, a more just society, a land of greater opportunity and fulfillment because of what we have all done together in these years of unparalleled achievement."

"Our reward," he said, "will come in a life of freedom and peace and hope that our children will enjoy through ages ahead."

But these gains, Mr. Johnson said, "must not now be lost in suspicion and distrust and selfishness and politics.... I have concluded that I should not permit the Presidency to become involved in the partisan divisions that are developing."

And so it was that the man who won the biggest political landslide in American history, when he defeated Senator Barry Goldwater of Arizona in the Presidential election of 1964, renounced the idea of a second term.

In American politics, a "draft" could override even words as strong as Mr. Johnson's, and he did stop short of the ultimate denial—the assertion that he would not run if nominated nor serve if elected.

But the first reaction of close associates and of other political observers here was that he meant what he said. Moreover, the candidacies of Senator Kennedy and Senator McCarthy would make a draft even of an incumbent President virtually impossible.

Roosevelt Move Recalled

Still, if Vice President Humphrey does not enter the race, suspicion will undoubtedly be voiced that Mr. Johnson is only trying to stimulate a draft.

Some observers with long memories recall that in 1940, President Franklin D. Roosevelt had Senator Alben W. Barkley of Kentucky read the Democratic National Convention a message in which Mr. Roosevelt said that he had "never had, and has not today, any desire or purpose to continue in the office of President, to be a candidate for that office, or to be nominated by the convention for that office."

The convention nevertheless nominated Mr. Roosevelt for a third term, and he won.

Mr. Roosevelt was not opposed for nomination by any candidate considered as powerful as Senator Robert Kennedy, however. In addition Senator McCarthy appears likely to win the Wisconsin primary on Tuesday, after having made a strong showing in New Hampshire.

The low point to which Mr. Johnson's political fortunes have fallen was dramatized in a Gallup Poll published today. It showed that his conduct of his office had the approval of only 36 per cent of those polled, while his handling of the war in Vietnam was approved by only 26 per cent.

The war was unquestionably the major factor in Mr. Johnson's slump in public esteem. He began a major escalation in February, 1965, by ordering the bombing of North Vietnam, just a few months after waging a Presidential campaign in which he had convinced most voters that he would not expand what was then a conflict involving only about 16,000 noncombatant American troops.

Over the years since then, the war has required a commitment of more than half a million combat troops, an expenditure of about $30-billion a year and heavy American casualties.

It limited Mr. Johnson's expenditures for domestic programs, alienated many of his supporters in Congress and provoked a widespread and sometimes violent dissent—including draft card burnings, a march of thousands on the Pentagon last year, and ultimately the candidacies of Senators Kennedy and McCarthy.

'A Nasty Fight' Seen

Nevertheless, a close political associate of the President said tonight that Mr. Johnson had by no means been "forced" out of the race by his opponents, nor was it yet clear that he would fail to win renomination.

"It was going to be a nasty fight but he had a good chance to win it," was his summation of the political situation. He said that one factor in Mr. Johnson's decision probably was that "this war's upset the hell out of him" and as a result he "really didn't have his mind on his politics."

There was some speculation tonight that Mr. Johnson might believe he could work more effectively for peace in Vietnam if he were not a partisan candidate for re-election—despite the "lame duck" status that would confer on him.

Senator Albert Gore, Democrat of Tennessee, an old antagonist of Mr. Johnson, said the withdrawal was "the greatest contribution toward unity and possible peace that President Johnson could have made."

To achieve peace, he said, will require "concessions and compromises which would subject a candidate for public office to the charge of appeasement, surrender and being soft on the Communists."

In support of this thesis, Mr. Johnson's speech on Vietnam—which came before his withdrawal announcement—was notably conciliatory, although Senator Gore pointed out that "the President did not reveal a change in war policy tonight. He discussed only tactics—a partial bombing halt."

In the wake of the President's announcement, some observers here were recalling signals that they had failed to recognize.

Theodore White the journalist interviewed Mr. Johnson earier this week and is reported to have said later that the President's remarks had a "valedictory" tone.

Others who have talked with the president lately have detected a note of "they can't take this away from me" when he discussed his domestic and other achievements.

There was little insight here tonight on why Mr. Johnson chose to announce a withdrawal rather than to fight for renomination. One clue may have been in the theme of national unity on which he chose to base his announcement.

Almost since he took office, and at least until the political pressures generated by the war in Vietnam became intense, Mr. Johnson had sounded that same theme of unity.

Early in his Presidency, he seemed to have built a "consensus" of Americans that was reflected in the more than 60 per cent of the vote he won in 1964.

As a reflection of that vote, he could work in 1965 and 1966 with a heavily Democratic, remarkably liberal Congress that passed some of the most far-reaching social legislation of the post-war era—medical care for the aged, voting rights for Southern Negroes, Federal aid to education, and a sweeping civil rights package.

Unity Theme Recalled

Mr. Johnson campaigned on a unity theme in 1964 and as far back as when he was the Democratic leader in the Senate, from 1952 to 1960, he frequently appealed for "closing ranks" and for "working together."

In 1964, typically, he appealed to the voters to gather in "one great tent" to work together for progress and prosperity and peace.

Thus he was eminently qualified to say, as he did tonight, that "as President of all the people, I cannot disregard the peril to the progress of the American people and the hope and the prospect of peace for all people. So I would ask all Americans whatever their personal interest or concern to guard against divisiveness and all of its ugly consequences."

On that note, Mr. Johnson took his own personal step to "guard against divisiveness."

He surprised everybody, the way he always likes to do, and it probably pleased him most that the news did not leak out before he announced it himself.

* * *

April 1, 1968

JOHNSON HALTS NORTH VIETNAM RAIDS; BIDS HANOI JOIN PEACE MOVES

DMZ IS EXEMPTED

Johnson Sets No Time Limit on Halting of Air and Sea Blows

By MAX FRANKEL
Special to The New York Times.

WASHINGTON, March 31—President Johnson announced tonight that he had ordered a halt in the air and naval bombardment of most of North Vietnam and invited the Hanoi Government to join him in a "series of mutual moves toward peace."

The President said:

"Tonight, in the hope that this action will lead to early talks, I am taking the first step to de-escalate the conflict. We are reducing—substantially reducing—the present level of hostilities. And we are doing so unilaterally and at once."

The President said that attacks would continue only in the area just north of the demilitarized zone, which separates North Vietnam from South Vietnam, and where, he said, the "continuing enemy build-up directly threatens allied forward positions and where movements of troops and supplies are clearly related to that threat."

Hanoi's Stand Recalled

The President set no time limit for his restraint order. Until now, North Vietnam has demanded an "unconditional"—apparently meaning permanent—halt in the bombing of all its territory and all other acts of war against it.

North Vietnam's restraint and other unspecified events, the President indicated, can make possible an early end of "even this limited bombing."

The areas to be spared, he said, include almost 90 per cent of North Vietnam's population and "most of its territory."

The White House refused to give a more specific geographical delineation.

[In Saigon, the United States command said that the order went into effect at 9 P.M. Sunday, New York time, when President Johnson began his address, The Associated Press reported.]

At the same time, Mr. Johnson used a televised address to the nation to urge the Soviet Union and Britain to do everything possible to move from his "unilateral act of de-escalation" toward a genuine peace.

He designated Ambassador at Large W. Averell Harriman and the American Ambassador to Moscow, Llewellyn Thompson, as his representatives to be available in Geneva or any other suitable place just as soon as Hanoi agreed to a conference.

Both men have enjoyed positions of special trust in Moscow and other parts of the Communist world.

But if peace does not come through negotiations, Mr. Johnson asserted, it will come when Hanoi understands that "our common resolve is unshakable and our common strength is invincible."

Mr. Johnson urged Hanoi to cooperate in arranging negotiations and did not repeat his statement of last month that Hanoi had had no interest in peace talks in recent weeks.

He cautioned the Vietnamese not to be misled by the "pressures" in the United States in this election year—meaning the criticism of his policy in Vietnam.

No 'Fake Solution'

He also warned that the United States would not "accept a fake solution" to the war and would hold out until North Vietnam understood that it could not take over South Vietnam by force.

Mr. Johnson placed heavy emphasis on the responsibility of the South Vietnamese to do more than they were doing in their own defense but offered a moderate increase of about 13,500 American troops over the next five months.

A part of this build-up will be met by the call-up of some Reserve units.

How this further shipment of troops will affect the total American force in Vietnam was not made clear by Mr. Johnson. He implied that the previously authorized force level of about 525,000 men by June would be met. He also cited the hurried dispatch of 11,000 Marine and Army airborne troops last month.

Officials said that these figures could not automatically be added because it was not yet clear how many of the 11,000 would remain in the war zone after the current emergency passed.

Defense Budgets To Rise

Mr. Johnson said that the troop build-ups, new equipment for the expanding South Vietnamese forces, price increases, equipment needs among the American forces and additional aid to South Korea would raise the defense budgets for the current fiscal year, ending June 30, by $2.5-billion and for the next year, starting July 1, by $2.6-billion above his previous estimates.

Most of these additional expenditures will be added to the designated costs of $24.5-billion for Vietnam in the current fiscal year and $25.8-billion in the fiscal year 1969.

Citing these increased costs and the threat of inflation and the threat to the dollar as the standard of international exchange, the President also renewed his appeal for early action in Congress on his proposal for a surcharge on personal and corporate income taxes.

He said that he would cut his 1969 expenditure budget of $186-billion by as much as Congress decreed in order to get the tax increase but did not make any specific proposals toward that end.

Before reaching the surprise political announcement at the end of his speech, Mr. Johnson made only one direct reference to the current election campaign—the word of caution that Hanoi not misinterpret the debates here.

Rebuttal Is Implicit

But his critics' charges of his refusal to seek peace appeared clearly on his mind as he outlined how far he was willing to go to curb the bombing and to assure North Vietnam of his good faith.

Such a halt in the bombing of most of North Vietnam had been urged upon the President last fall at the approach of the traditional Christmas and New Year truces in the war zone, but he rejected it then.

The reason appeared to be that he felt he would be incurring a disadvantage on the battlefield.

Some of his advisers also warned, as Gen. Maxwell D. Taylor did again in a television broadcast today, that certain efforts to limit the fighting might be misunderstood and taken as a sign of weakness in Hanoi.

More recently, however, the President and his advisers appeared to have reached the conclusion that the divisive debate in the United States could be taken as a sign of even greater weakness, and an effort to appease his critics plainly lay behind tonight's order and address to the nation.

Mr. Johnson recalled that he had offered Hanoi in secret last August, and made public in September, a proposal to halt all bombardment of North Vietnam when this would lead promptly to productive discussions, and that he would assume that North Vietnam "would not take military advantage" of such restraint.

Hanoi, he said, denounced this offer both privately and publicly and went on to rush preparations for what he called a "savage assault" on the people, Government and allies of South Vietnam during the lunar New Year holiday in January and February.

These attacks failed to achieve their principal objectives, he said, by not toppling the South Vietnamese Government or shattering its army and caused the Communists very heavy casualties.

But they did compel partial retreat of allied forces from the countryside and did cause disruption and suffering, he said.

The Communists may renew this attack, he warned. Nonetheless, he said that he was taking his "first step" to de-escalate the conflict so as to reduce the level of violence, to save the lives of brave men, of innocent women and children, and to permit the contending forces to move closer to a political settlement.

He specifically called upon President Ho Chi Minh of North Vietnam to "respond positively and favorably to this new step toward peace."

Moreover, Mr. Johnson reiterated past offers to permit North Vietnam after peace to profit from the economic development of all Southeast Asia that the United States expected to help finance after the war.

Manila Plan Reiterated

No one can foretell the precise terms of an eventual settlement, Mr. Johnson said, but he also reiterated the offer by the United States and its six allies first made at their Manila summit meeting in October, 1966—a promise to withdraw their forces from South Vietnam "as the other side withdraws its forces to the north, stops infiltration and the level of violence thus subsides."

The original Manila declaration said that the allied withdrawal could be achieved within six months. Mr. Johnson did not repeat that time limit tonight, but his spokesman said that he stood by the original Manila formulation.

The President went out of his way to pay tribute to the "great courage and endurance" of the South Vietnamese people.

But he reminded them that further efforts were required to expand their army, to move back into the countryside after the enemy offensive, to increase their taxes, to choose the very best men for responsible office, to develop political unity among themselves under their new constitution and to give a place to "all those groups" who wish to preserve South Vietnam's control over its own destiny.

This appeared to be as close as the President came to a suggestion that members of the National Liberation Front might be given a peaceful political role in a future South Vietnam.

The Saigon Government has bitterly resisted any role for the front and has only yielded reluctantly to American pressure to offer political participation to individual members of the Vietcong's political parent body.

Peace One Day

Mr. Johnson ended his talk from his office with a personal note, saying that one day there would be peace in Southeast Asia, though he could not yet tell when.

Mr. Johnson took indirect issue also with other criticisms by Mr. Kennedy by defending the exertions of the South Vietnamese in their own defense.

Moreover, he emphasized his interest in seeing "all" South Vietnamese participate in the future political life of their country, apparently a comment on Mr. Kennedy's plea that the Vietcong be given a "share" of the power in a future government.

The President spoke from his White House office for 40 minutes and then joined his family in the living quarters of the Executive Mansion. Earlier today he had gone with his daughter and son-in-law, Mr. and Mrs. Patrick J. Nugent, to St. Dominick's Roman Catholic Church here.

Thereafter, Mr. Johnson took the text of his speech—presumably including the portion announcing his refusal to run again—to the apartment of Vice President Humphrey on the banks of the Potomac. They spent about an hour together over breakfast.

* * *

May 21, 1968

FRANCE IS NEAR PARALYSIS AS MILLIONS JOIN STRIKE; REDS PRESS FOR COALITION

DE GAULLE SILENT

Leaders of Movement and Regime Strive to Avoid Force

By JOHN L. HESS
Special to The New York Times.

PARIS, May 20—France headed toward virtual paralysis today as millions more of her workers occupied factories, mines and offices.

The de Gaulle regime and the strike leaders challenging it were striving to avoid a test of force. But the threat of violence remained as hardship for the populace was growing.

Housewives stocked up on food, motorists formed lines at gasoline stations and depositors staged a run on banks.

Estimates of the number of strikers at nightfall ranged from 6 million to 10 million. The higher figure would encompass half the country's wage earners.

Test of Power Emerges

The strike movement began last week as a spontaneous expression of the French worker's feeling that he had not had his fair share of his country's growing prosperity, that his wage increases had been wiped out by price increases and that his greater productivity was resulting in unemployment.

Today, the movement was developing into a direct political test of power.

The Communists, now clearly in the leadership of the movement, pressed their election allies, the Federation of the Democratic and Socialist Left, to join them in a program for a coalition government. Their allies hesitated.

President de Gaulle, who is scheduled to address the nation Friday, kept his silence.

Production Sharply Cut

Most of the nation's productive industry came to a stop. Ports fell silent and barge traffic halted. No trains ran, few planes took off, and in the cities, 80 per cent of public transportation was down.

The Government-owned power network was occupied by employes, but current was maintained for the time being. Union leaders encouraged continued movement of food by truck, especially to hospitals, nurseries and factories. Immense traffic jams clogged Paris.

No mail was delivered here, and little moved elsewhere. Automatic telephone service was maintained, but manual calls, abroad and to rural areas, could not be made.

Staffs of the state radio and television networks were in permanent session in studios. Filmed programs, records and news broadcasts were permitted, but nothing more.

The unions also generally managed to keep newspapers publishing as a public service, but one of the largest provincial dailies, Daupiné Libéré in the Lyons area, was occupied and closed down.

The strike movement hit in unexpected places. Bet takers at the St. Cloud track halted this afternoon's flat races and marched to Vincennes, where the eveing's trotting program was canceled.

This ended the odd juxtaposition of strike news with racing results on the airwaves. Most athletic events were postponed indefinitely.

The student revolt, which led to the workers' movement, was totally eclipsed. At the Sorbonne, an assembly of student and teacher delegates, taking the name States General from the Parliament of the French Revolution, had to be postponed because most provincial delegates could not get there. They lacked transportation.

Students Hold Universities

Most of the nation's universities remained in control of students, however. In Paris primary and high schools, teachers met with classes when they could, but did no teaching. Their national federation called a full strike to begin Wednesday.

The Communist-led General Confederation of Labor appealed to workers to avoid provocations. To reduce the risk of violence, it banned parades and demonstrations outside the plants, and in nearly all cases it obtained the release of plant managers sequestered by enthusiastic workers.

The Government also seemed to be avoiding clashes. The police were reported to have ousted strikers from three telephone bureaus during the early hours this morning. Elsewhere, they remained conspicuously absent.

Emphasizing the continued threat of violence, 1,000 to 2,000 ultrarightist youths marched about the Right Bank again, accompanied among others by the lawyer Jean-Louis Tixier-Vignancourt, a nationalist leader. Some of them penetrated the Opera and the St. Lazare railroad station, which were occupied by employes. The police ultimately turned them away.

School Is Vandalized

A second group vandalized an office in the Institute of Political Science, a prestige school on the Left Bank, but was driven off by the students.

On the other side, there was wide apprehension about the day of protest called by farm organizations for Friday. These groups have in recent years marked their discontent by setting up barricades on highways and by sacking prefectures and town halls.

None of the nation's leaders appeared to offer a clear program for ending the spreading paralysis.

In a rather oblique statement, the Politburo of the Communist party stressed the limited nature of the workers' demands, and denied that their movement was an insurrectional strike. Instead, it said, it was "tending toward the elimination of the Gaullist regime and Government and the accession, with all the forces of the Left, of a veritable republican regime opening the way to Socialism."

The Communists and the Socialist bloc have jointly sponsored a motion of censure that could bring the Government down Wednesday night—though nobody now expects it. But the Socialists had nothing to say today on the Communists' call for a joint program of government.

Government members called at Elysée Palace one by one today, beginning with Pierre Messmer, Minister of the Armed Forces. Each was received for 20 minutes.

But the highest figure in the regime to make a public comment was Raymond Marcellin, Minister of Planning, and his statement did not discuss the demands of the workers and students. Instead, he recalled that the President and the Assembly were popularly elected, and said it was "the most imperious duty of the Government to make republican order prevail."

* * *

August 21, 1968

CZECHOSLOVAKIA INVADED BY RUSSIANS AND FOUR OTHER WARSAW PACT FORCES; THEY OPEN FIRE ON CROWDS IN PRAGUE

TANKS ENTER CITY

Deaths Are Reported—Troops Surround Offices of Party

By TAD SZULC
Special to The New York Times.

PRAGUE, Wednesday, Aug. 21—Czechoslovakia was occupied early today by troops of the Soviet Union and four of its Warsaw Pact allies in a series of swift land and air movements.

Airborne Soviet troops and paratroopers surrounded the building of the Communist party Central Committee, along with five tanks. At least 25 tanks were seen in the city.

Several persons were reported killed early this morning. Unconfirmed reports said that two Czechoslovak soldiers and a woman were killed by Bulgarian tank fire in front of the Prague radio building shortly before the station was captured and went off the air.

[Soviet troops began shooting at Czechoslovak demonstrators outside the Prague radio building at 7:25 A.M., Reuters reported. C.T.K., the Czechoslovak press agency, was quoted by United Press International as having said that citizens were throwing themselves in front of the tanks in an attempt to block the seizure of the city.]

Move a Surprise

The Soviet move caught Czechoslovaks by surprise, although all day yesterday there were indications of new tensions.

Confusion was caused in the capital by leaflets dropped from unidentified aircraft asserting that Antonin Novotny, the President of Czechoslovakia who was deposed in March by the Communist liberals, had been pushed out by a "clique." The leaflets said that Mr. Novotny remained the country's legal President.

At 5 A.M. the Prague radio, still in the hands of adherents of the Communist liberals, broadcast a dramatic appeal to the population in the name of Alexander Dubcek, the party First Secretary, to go to work as usual this morning.

The radio station said: "These may be the last reports you will hear because the technical facilities in our hands are insufficient."

The announcer said that Czechoslovaks must heed the orders of ina Presidium of the Central Committee, "which is in continuing session even though the building is surrounded by foreign units."

The radio said that it remained loyal to President Ludvik Svoboda and Mr. Dubcek.

While earlier this morning the radio appealed to the population not to resist invading troops from the Soviet Union, Poland, East Germany, Hungary and Bulgaria, small-arms fire was heard shortly after 5 A.M. in the Maala Strana district of Prague.

At 2:45 A.M., as part of this dispatch was being filed by telex, the city appeared calm, though the roar of aircraft and the broadcast, heard by many, had awakened the population.

Starting shortly after midnight veritable airlift of Soviet and other Warsaw Pact aircraft flew troops into Prague. Ruzine Airport had been secured earlier by Czechoslovak troops though it was not known under whose command they were operating.

At 5:15 A.M. aircraft were still heard landing and taking off.

Despite the Prague radio broadcasts, the whereabouts of Mr. Dubcek, Mr. Svoboda and their associates was not known.

In any event, the invasion that began at 11 o'clock last night when the Czechoslovak border was crossed from several sides evidently put an end to the Dubcek experiment in democracy under Communism that was initiated in January.

The expectation was that the occupying forces would sponsor the establishment of a new regime that would be more amenable to orthodox Communist views of Moscow and its partners.

There are about 5,000 United States citizens in Czechoslovakia at this time, of whom about 1,500 are tourists and 400 are delegates to an international geological congress.

Shirley Temple Black, the former actress, is among the Americans at the Hotel Alcron here.

The news broadcast early today said that Soviet troops had sealed all border exits to Austria. Trains were not running and airline operations were halted.

After 3 A.M., all city lights went out.

Appeal to Public

A broadcast at 1:30 A.M. had appealed to the population not to resist the advance and for officials to remain at their jobs.

Yesterday, as the tension mounted, the Czechoslovak leadership was reported to have been seriously concerned over renewed Soviet press attacks on Mr. Dubcek's liberalization program.

Last night the party Presidium met unexpectedly under Mr. Dubcek's chairmanship, presumably to discuss the new tensions.

At a confidential meeting Saturday with five progressive members of the Presidium, Czechoslovak editors were told that a successful party congress next month was the most urgent priority in the country and that, therefore, their cooperation was needed.

Internal Battle Continues

Internally, however, the political tug of war between the progressives and the conservatives continued.

Rude Pravo, the party's official organ, whose editor, Oldrich Svestka, is regarded as a leading conservative, published three articles today critical of the progressives' policies.

Another example of mounting political sensitiveness was an announcement by the Foreign Ministry, published in Rude Pravo and later distributed by the official press agency, that Henry Kamm, a correspondent of The New York Times, "will not be allowed to return to Czechoslovakia."

Mr. Kamm, who left Prague for the United States and a vacation Saturday, was charged by Rude Pravo with "slanderous information" and "fabrications" concerning its editorial staff.

Dispatches by Mr. Kamm published in The Times on Aug. 14 and 15 described a continuing struggle between Mr. Svestka and the progressive members of the staff. One dispatch said that Mr. Svestka, who is a member of the party's

Presidium, had curtailed coverage of the visit here earlier this month by President Tito of Yugoslavia, who is a backer of the Dubcek faction.

The newspaper said yesterday that "the management of Rude Pravo resolutely opposes this shameless provocation, which has become the pretext for a slanderous press campaign against Rude Pravo abroad," and that "it is indubitable that its aim is the unconcealed effort to interfere with our internal affairs."

Mr. Svestka, however, came under attack himself in the liberal weekly Reporter, which in its current issue reported that he had played down the Tito visit. The magazine said that Mr. Svestka "has set up a sort of internal police which watches over everything that goes into print."

A Rude Pravo's counterattack yesterday included a front-page article signed by Mr. Svestka, in effect defending the conservative position. He wrote that unless the Communist party regained its "antibureaucratic" character and returned to the aims of the workers, the new "demagogic slogans" could turn against the party itself.

In an allusion to the progressives' efforts to oust conservatives from key jobs, Mr. Svestka wrote that democracy was not served "by making life miserable for the honest officials and members who have not discredited themselves, by turning them away from political activity."

A second article took to tasks a television commentator, Jirl Kanturek, for what it said were attempts to discredit Mr. Svestka.

A third article charged that a "secret committee" had been established to attack the people's militia, a paramilitary organization widely considered to be controlled by the conservatives. The article referred critically to the signing of petitions in Prague last week for the abolition of the militia.

* * *

August 21, 1968

THE CRISIS IN PRAGUE RECALLS ANXIOUS DAYS IN 1930'S

By RICHARD D. LYONS

"Our state is the key to the whole postwar structure of Central Europe. If it is touched either internally or internationally, the whole fabric of Central Europe is menaced, and the peace of Europe seriously infringed. It would not be long before all Europe would be grievously conscious of the fact."

These were the words of a Czechoslovak leader—but they were not uttered yesterday—they were said a generation ago in the ominous years when the freedom of the little nation also was threatened.

Eduard Benes was the speaker and the time was November, 1935, one month before Mr. Benes was to take over the presidency of the small republic, which had been carved out of Central Europe with United States help.

While the cast of countries involved in the carving up of Czechoslovakia in the late nineteen thirties was almost the same, those friendly to the Czechoslovaks then are not necessarily those today.

Hitler Gave Secret Orders

The key then was Germany, which plays a role today also. Hitler was determined to smash the Czechoslovaks for their defiance of his aims at expanding into Central Europe.

Within two years, Hitler had secretely issued orders to his military chiefs for the occupation, by force or peace treaty, of both Austria and Czechoslovakia.

After Austria's turn on March 12, 1938, the pressure was put on Czechoslovakia and President Benes ordered a partial mobilization two months later.

The crisis escalated and war seemed inevitable, with the Western powers and the Soviet Union coming to Czechoslovakia's aid. But having failed to bluff the Czechoslovaks into surrender, Hitler turned the pressure from Prague to London and Paris.

While Prime Minister Neville Chamberlain of Britain was addressing the House of Commons on Sept. 28, 1938, he received from Hitler a telegraphed invitation to meet with Hitler, Mussolini and Premier Edouard Daladier of France the following day in Munich.

This was at a time when France, Yugoslavia, Rumania and the Soviet Union were reiterating their support for Czechoslovakia.

Without consulting Prague or Moscow, which had a military-assistance pact with the Czechoslovak, the British, French, Italians and Germans signed an agreement at Munich on Sept. 30 under which the Czechoslovakis would cede to Germany large chunks of territory.

The Poles and Hungarians then put in their bids for Czechoslovak territory and within five weeks Czechoslovakia lost about one-third of her population to the three nations.

President Benes resigned on Oct. 3, 1938, and fled the country. By the following March the Germans held sway over the remainder of the country and Hitler appeared in Prague to accept the take-over of Czechoslovakia.

Six months later Poland was invaded and the real war, which many had hoped to avert at the sacrifice of Czechoslovak independence, started. It was to be five more years before the Germans would start being ousted by the Russians.

* * *

August 29, 1968

HUMPHREY NOMINATED ON THE FIRST BALLOT AFTER HIS PLANK ON VIETNAM IS APPROVED; POLICE BATTLE DEMONSTRATORS IN STREETS

HUNDRED INJURED

178 Are Arrested as Guardsmen Join in Using Tear Gas

By J. ANTHONY LUKAS
Special to The New York Times.

CHICAGO, Thursday, Aug. 29—The police and National Guardsmen battled young protesters in downtown Chicago last night as the week-long demonstrations against the Democratic National Convention reached a violent and tumultuous climax.

About 100 persons, including 25 policemen, were injured and at least 178 were arrested as the security forces chased down the demonstrators. The protesting young people had broken out of Grant Park on the shore of Lake Michigan in an attempt to reach the International Amphitheatre where the Democrats were meeting, four miles away.

The police and Guardsmen used clubs, rifle butts, tear gas and Chemical Mace on virtually anything moving along Michigan Avenue and the narrow streets of the Loop area.

Uneasy Calm

Shortly after midnight, an uneasy calm ruled the city. However, 1,000 National Guardsmen were moved back in front of the Conrad Hilton Hotel to guard it against more than 5,000 demonstrators who had drifted back into Grant Park.

The crowd in front of the hotel was growing, booing vociferously every time new votes for Vice President Humphrey were broadcast from the convention hall.

The events in the streets stirred anger among some delegates at the convention. In a nominating speech Senator Abraham A. Ribicoff of Connecticut told the delegates that if Senator George S. McGovern were President, "we would not have these Gestapo tactics in the streets of Chicago."

When Mayor Richard J. Daley of Chicago and other Illinois delegates rose shouting angrily, Mr. Ribicoff said, "How hard it is to accept the truth."

Crushed Against Windows

Even elderly bystanders were caught in the police onslaught. At one point, the police turned on several dozen

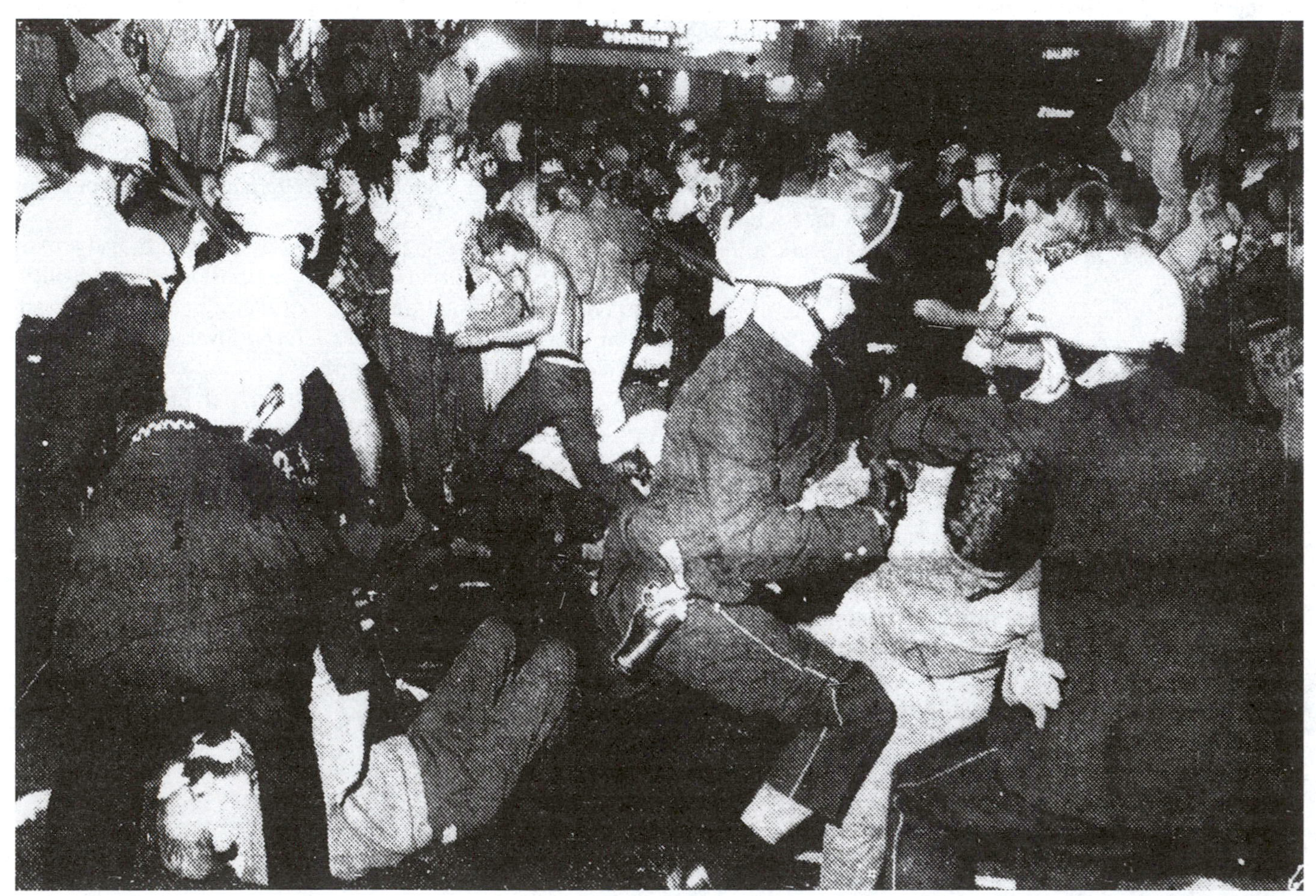

United Press International

IN STREETS: Police attempting to clear demonstrators on Michigan Avenue outside Conrad Hilton Hotel last night.

Associated Press

PRISONER: Police escorting demonstrator to van during fracas on Michigan Avenue outside Conrad Hilton Hotel.

persons standing quietly behind police barriers in front of the Conrad Hilton Hotel watching the demonstrators across the street.

For no reason that could be immediately determined, the blue-helmeted policemen charged the barriers, crushing the spectators against the windows of the Haymarket Inn, a restaurant in the hotel. Finally the window gave way, sending screaming middle-aged women and children backward through the broken shards of glass.

The police then ran into the restaurant and beat some of the victims who had fallen through the windows and arrested them.

At the same time, other policemen outside on the broad, tree-lined avenue were clubbing the young demonstrators repeatedly under television lights and in full view of delegates' wives looking out the hotel's windows.

Afterward, newsmen saw 30 shoes, women's purses and torn pieces of clothing lying with shattered glass on the sidewalk and street outside the hotel and for two blocks in each direction. It was difficult for newsmen estimate how many demonstrators were in the streets of midtown Chicago last night. Although 10,000 to 15,000 young people gathered in Grant Park for a rally in the afternoon, some of them had apparently drifted home before the violence broke out in the evening. Estimates of those involved in the action in the night ranged between 2,000 and 5,000.

Although some youths threw bottles, rocks, stones and even loaves of bread at the police, most of them simply marched and countermarched, trying to avoid the flying police squads.

Some of them carried flags—the black anarchist flag, the red flag, the Vietcong flag and the red and blue flags with a yellow peace symbol.

Stayed Defiant

Although clearly outnumbered and outclassed by the well-armed security forces, the thousands of antiwar demonstrators, supporters of Senator Eugene J. McCarthy and Yippies maintained an air of defiance throughout the evening.

They shouted "The streets belong to the people," "This land is our land" and "Hell no, we won't go," as they skirmished along the avenue and among the side streets.

When arrested youths raised their hands in the V for victory sign that has become a symbol of the peace movement, other demonstrators shouted "Sieg heil" or "Pigs" at the policemen making the arrests.

Frank Sullivan, the Police Department's public information director, said the police had reacted only after "50 hard-core leaders" had staged a charge into a police line across Michigan Avenue.

Mr. Sullivan said that among those in the charge were Prof. Sidney Peck, cochairman of the Mobilization Committee to End the War in Vietnam, the group that is spearheading the demonstration. He said Professor Peck had struck James M. Rochford, Deputy Superintendent of Police, with his fist. Mr. Peck was arrested and charged with aggravated assault.

As the night wore on, the police dragnet spread from Michigan Avenue and the area around the Hilton throughout downtown Chicago.

On the corner of Monroe Street and Michigan Avenue, policemen chased demonstrators up the steps of the Chicago Art Institute, a neoclassical Greek temple, and arrested one of them.

As in previous nights of unrest here newsmen found themselves special targets of the police action. At Michigan Avenue and Van Buren Street, a young photographer ran into the street, terrified, his hands clasped over his head and shrieking "Press, press."

As the police arrested him, he shouted, "What did I do? What did I do?"

The policeman said, "If you don't know you shouldn't be a photographer."

Barton Silverman, a photographer for the New York Times, was briefly arrested near the Hilton Hotel.

Bob Kieckhefer, a reporter for United Press International, was hit in the head by a policeman during the melee in front of the Hilton. He staggered into the UPI office on Michigan Avenue and was taken for treatment to Wesley Memorial Hospital.

Reporters Hampered

Reporters and photographers were repeatedly hampered by the police last night while trying to cover the violence. They were herded into small areas where they could not see the action. On Jackson Street, police forced a mobile television truck to turn off its lights.

Among those arrested was the Rev. John Boyles, Presbyterian chaplain at Yale and a McCarthy staff worker, who was charged with breach of the peace.

"It's an unfounded charge," Mr. Boyles said. "I was protesting the clubbing of a girl I knew from the McCarthy staff. They were beating her on her head with clubs and I yelled at them 'Don't hit a woman.' At that point I was slugged in the stomach and grabbed by a cop who arrested me."

Last night's violence broke out when hundreds of demonstrators tried to leave Grant Park after a rally and enter the Loop area.

At the Congress Street bridge leading from the park onto Michigan Avenue National Guardsmen fired and sprayed tear gas at the demonstrators five or six times around 7 P.M. to hold them inside the park.

However, one group moved north inside the park and managed to find a way out over another bridge. There they met a contingent of the Poor People's Campaign march led by their symbol, three mule wagons.

Chase Youths

The march was headed south along Michigan Avenue and the police did not disrupt it, apparently because it had a permit. But they began chasing the youths along Michigan Avenue and into side streets.

The demonstrators were then joined by several thousand others who had originally set out from the park in a "nonviolent" march to the amphitheatre led by David Dellinger, national chairman of the Mobilization Committee to End the War in Vietnam, and Allen Ginsberg, the poet.

The climactic day of protests began with a mass rally sponsored by the mobilization committee in the band shell in Grant Park.

The rally was intended both as a mass expression of anger at the proceedings across town in the convention and as a "staging ground" for the smaller, more militant march on the amphitheatre.

However, before the rally was an hour old, it, too, was interrupted by violence. Fighting broke out when three demonstrators started hauling down an American flag from a pole by the park's band shell where speakers were denouncing the Chicago authorities, the Johnson Administration and the war in Vietnam.

Four blue-helmeted policemen moved in to stop them and were met by a group of angry demonstrators who pushed them back against a cluster of trees by the side of the band shell. Then the demonstrators, shouting "Pig, pig," pelted the isolated group of 14 policemen with stones, bricks and sticks.

Grenade Hurled Back

Snapping their Plexiglass shields down over their faces, the police moved toward the crowd. One policeman threw or fired a tear-gas grenade into the throng. But a demonstrator picked up the smoking grenade and heaved it back among the police. The crowd cheered with surprise and delight.

But then, from the Inner Drive west of the park, a phalanx of policemen moved into the crowd, using their billy clubs as prods and then swinging them. The demonstrators, who replied with more stones and sticks, were pushed back against rows of flaking green benches and trapped there.

Among those injured was Rennie Davis, one of the coordinators for the Mobilization Committee to End the War in Vietnam, which has been spearheading the demonstrations in Chicago.

As the police and demonstrators skirmished on the huge grassy field, mobilization committee leaders on the stage of the baby-blue band shell urged the crowd to sit down and remain calm.

The worst of the fighting was over in 10 minutes, but the two sides were still jostling each other all over the field when Mr. Ginsberg approached the microphone.

Speaking in a cracked and choking voice, Mr. Ginsberg said: "I lost my voice chanting in the park the last few nights. The best strategy for you in cries of hysteria, overexcitement or fear is still to chant 'Om' together. It helps to quell flutterings of butterflies in the belly. Join me now as I try to lead you."

So, as the policemen looked out in astonishment through their Plexiglass face shields, the huge throng chanted the

Hindu "Om, om," sending deep mystic reverberations off the glass office towers along Michigan Avenue.

Following Mr. Ginsberg to the microphone was Jean Genet, the French author. His bald head glistening in the glare of television lights, Mr. Genet said through a translator:

"It took an awful lot of deaths in Hanoi for a happening such as is taking place here to occur."

Next on the platform was William Burroughs, author of "The Naked Lunch." A gray fedora on his head, Mr. Burroughs said in a dry, almost distant voice:

"I've just returned from London, England, where there is no effective resistance at all. It's really amazing to see people willing to do something about an unworkable system. It's not evil or immoral, just unworkable. And they're trying to make it work by force. But they can't do it."

Mailer Apologizes

Mr. Burroughs was followed by Norman Mailer, the author who is here to write an article on the convention. Mr. Mailer, who was arrested during the march on the Pentagon last October, apologized to the crowd for not marching in Chicago.

Thrusting his jaw into the microphone, he said: "I'm a little sick about all this and also a little mad, but I've got a deadline on a long piece and I'm not going to go out and march and get arrested. I just came here to salute all of you."

Then Dick Gregory, the comedian and Negro militant leader, took the platform. Dressed in a tan sport shirt and matching trousers with a khaki rain hat on his head, Mr. Gregory said, "You just have to look around you at all the police and soldiers to know you must be doing something right."

Many of the demonstrators in Grant Park had drifted down in small groups from Lincoln Park, where 300 policemen had moved in at 12:15 A.M. yesterday and laid down a barrage of tear gas to clear the area. About 2,000 young protesters had attempted to stay in the park despite an 11 P.M. curfew.

* * *

August 29, 1968

HUMPHREY AND HIS VIETNAM TRAP

The angry Democratic debate at Chicago yesterday concealed the fact that the differences between the majority and minority Vietnam planks were far fewer than the similarities. The efforts made by both sides to compromise the issue in the platform committee—and make it easier for the McCarthy, Kennedy and McGovern supporters to work for Nominee Humphrey—might even have succeeded, had Mr. Johnson not personally intervened to prevent it. He removed any freedom of action from the convention by giving it the impossible alternative of an outright repudiation of the President.

Nevertheless, a year ago the debate the country witnessed on television yesterday would have been unthinkable. A year ago there would have been proposals for extending the bombing of the North, or blockading Haiphong, or expanding the ground war into Laos, Cambodia and North Vietnam—all positions toward which the President himself seemed to be moving on the urging of the military and of Congressional conservatives in both parties.

Yesterday at Chicago both Administration and anti-Administration factions opposed escalation and urged a negotiated political settlement of the war. Both called for an end to the bombing of the North, a cease-fire and withdrawal of all foreign troops from South Vietnam. Meanwhile, both planks called for a shift of responsibility to the South Vietnamese for defensive operations.

The chief issues were not a war policy against a peace policy, despite the oversimplifications of yesterday's debaters. The issues were whether to halt the bombing before or after a Hanoi gesture and whether to encourage Saigon's leaders to negotiate with the Vietcong or to pressure them to do so by starting American troop withdrawals.

The differences are important. But the points of agreement were more important. The challenge that now faces Mr. Humphrey—if he is not rescued from his dilemma by progress in the Paris talks—is to emerge from the Vietnam trap by moving toward his critics. Events undoubtedly will create opportunities for him to do so in the coming months; his task will be to demonstrate that he has the will and freedom to make that move.

* * *

November 7, 1968

NIXON WINS BY A THIN MARGIN, PLEADS FOR REUNITED NATION

ELECTOR VOTE 287

Lead in Popular Tally May Be Smaller Than Kennedy's in '60

By MAX FRANKEL

Richard Milhous Nixon emerged the victor yesterday in one of the closest and most tumultuous Presidential campaigns in history and set himself the task of reuniting the nation.

Elected over Hubert H. Humphrey by the barest of margins—only four one-hundredths of a percentage point in the popular vote—and confronted by a Congress in control of the Democrats, the President-elect said it "will be the great objective of this Administration at the outset to bring the American people together."

He pledged, as the 37th President, to form "an open Administration, open to new ideas, open to men and women of both parties, open to critics as well as those who support us" so as to bridge the gap between the generations and the races.

Details Left for Later

But after an exhausting and tense night of awaiting the verdict at the Waldorf-Astoria Hotel here, Mr. Nixon and his closest aides were not yet prepared to suggest how they intended to organize themselves and to approach these objectives. The Republican victor expressed admiration for his opponent's challenge and reiterated his desire to help President Johnson achieve peace in Vietnam between now and Inauguration Day on Jan. 20.

The verdict of an electorate that appeared to number 73 million could not be discerned until mid-morning because Mr. Nixon and Mr. Humphrey finished in a virtual tie in the popular vote, just as Mr. Nixon and John F. Kennedy did in 1960.

With 94 per cent of the nation's election precincts reporting, Mr. Nixon's total stood last evening at 29,726,409 votes to Mr. Humphrey's 29,677,152. The margin of 49,257 was even smaller than Mr. Kennedy's margin of 112,803.

Meaning Hard to Find

When translated into the determining electoral votes of the states, these returns proved even more difficult to read, and the result in two states—Alaska and Missouri—was still not final last night. But the unofficial returns from elsewhere gave Mr. Nixon a minimum of 287 electoral votes, 17 more than the 270 required for election. Mr. Humphrey won 191.

Because of the tightness of the race, the third-party challenger, George C. Wallace, came close to realizing his minimum objective of denying victory to the major-party candidates and then somehow forcing a bargain for his support on one of them. Although he did not do nearly as well as he had hoped and as others had feared, he received 9,291,807 votes or 13.3 per cent of the total, and the 45 electoral votes of Alabama, Georgia, Louisiana, Mississippi and Arkansas.

Mr. Wallace's support ranged from 1 per cent in Hawaii to 65 per cent in his home state of Alabama, and his presence on the ballot in all 50 states unquestionably influenced the outcome in many of them. But there was no certain way of determining whether Mr. Nixon or Mr. Humphrey was the beneficiary of the third-party split offs.

Mr. Humphrey's narrow victory in states such as Texas was probably due to Mr. Wallace's strong showing there. Conversely, Mr. Wallace's drain-off in traditional Democratic strongholds, such as New Jersey, probably helped Mr. Nixon.

Strong in the Northeast

The Vice President, staging a remarkable and highly personal comeback drive in the last three weeks of the campaign, after the opinion polls showed him 10 and even 15 percentage points behind, ran extremely well in the northeastern industrial states, including New York, and in Michigan. And he profited from large urban majorities, including Negroes, Jews and Spanish-speaking communities, to take Pennsylvania, Texas and Maryland, and possibly Missouri.

Mr. Humphrey mounted a strong challenge in California, but his only other successes west of the Mississippi were in his home state of Minnesota, Hawaii and possibly Washington, with Alaska still in doubt.

Mr. Nixon's victory, therefore, though marginal in numbers, turned out to be well spread geographically.

He established the Republican party as a formidable and probably permanent political factor in the South and Southern border states, profiting from the Wallace inroads, but nonetheless running extremely well in such states as Kentucky and Virginia. Mr. Humphrey lost everything south of West Virginia and east of Texas to his two rivals, a result that should profoundly shake the Southern Democratic parties.

Hurt in Urban Areas

Yet the broad spread of Mr. Nixon's strength clearly did not extend into the great urban areas where he must perform his works of unity and redevelopment.

After receiving Mr. Humphrey's concession, congratulations and offer of cooperation at noon yesterday, Mr. Nixon replied before television cameras with a statement that implicitly recognized this possible obstacle to his rule. Of all the signs, friendly and hostile, thrust at him on the campaign trail, he said, the one that touched him the most appeared in the hands of a teen-ager one evening in Ohio, reading "Bring Us Together."

He had not campaigned very much in Negro communities and knew of the overwhelming opposition to him by black voters. His running mate for the Vice-Presidency, Gov. Spiro T. Agnew of Maryland, had become, rightly or wrongly, a kind of symbol of white annoyance with the restiveness of the Negro community. Mr. Nixon made no mention of Mr. Agnew as he thanked all these who had contributed to his success and vowed to restore peace between the races.

Yet another challenge before the Nixon Administration will be a Congress firmly managed by the opposition party. Mr. Nixon is the first man since Zachary Taylor in 1844 to be elected President without his party's also winning control of both houses of Congress.

With the net loss to the Republicans of only four seats in the House and four, possibly five in the Senate, the Democrats will organize the legislative agendas of the 91st Congress and command all its committees. By retaining control on Capitol Hill through a change of parties in the White House, they will be in a position to exercise a powerful restraint on Mr. Nixon's budgetary priorities, which in fact means his priorities of government.

President Eisenhower, too, had to deal with a Democratic Congress for six of his eight years in office but his personal and nonpartisan standing among the opposition legislators cannot be compared with Mr. Nixon's reputation on the Hill for tough and highly partisan combativeness. Perhaps because he anticipated some of these problems, the President-elect expressed the hope in his victory statement that he could cooperate with President Johnson as Mr. Johnson dealt closely with President Eisenhower.

The Republicans took only of the 390 contested seats of the 435 in the House, and lost five seats in return, for a final line-up of 243 Democrats and 192 Republicans.

In 34 Senate races, the Democrats gained two seats, in California and Iowa, and lost seats in Maryland, Florida,

Arizona, Oklahoma, Pennsylvania and Ohio, with the fate of Senator Wayne Morse of Oregon still in doubt.

The political complexion of the new Congress, however, may have shifted another few degrees from the innovative and liberal-minded spirit that prevailed in the first two years of the Johnson Administration. The concern about excessive spending on domestic social programs and about law and order that Mr. Nixon stressed in his campaign has been evident on both sides of the aisles in both Houses for some time.

Yet there was no clear ideological pattern in any of the voting, for President or Congress. Critics of the Vietnam war, for instance, lost some contests and won in others. Energetic Democratic incumbents were able to resist even strong tides to Mr. Nixon in some states while others fell victim to them elsewhere.

Survival for some created new opportunities for leadership of the now leaderless Democratic party. Mr. Humphrey indicated that he would not retire from public life, and his efforts to pay off campaign debts may in fact keep him talking for quite a while. But it will be in Congress that a new generation of Democratic leaders now begins to emerge.

Senator Edmund S. Muskie, Mr. Humphrey's running mate, became an exciting new national figure even in defeat, with a broad appeal that extended all the way from some of Senator Eugene J. McCarthy's young admirers to the hard-bitten party regulars of big-city Democratic organizations.

New Leaders Emerge

Senator Edward M. Kennedy, by loyally playing a key role in the revitalization of the Humphrey campaign, further extended his standing as a Democrat to be reckoned with in future years. Senator George S. McGovern's brief bid for his party's nomination after the assassination of Senator Robert F. Kennedy gave him new stature.

Gov. Harold E. Hughes' successful campaign for a Senate seat in Iowa will further add to his reputation as a formidable vote-getter in Republican regions and Alan Cranston of California, though a quiet and professional man, should gain stature from his defeat of the arch-conservative Superintendent of Public Instruction, Max Rafferty.

The Republicans, too, produced some vigorous new Senators such as Charles Mathias of Maryland and Richard S. Schweiker of Pennsylvania, who defeated two incumbents, Senators Daniel Brewster and Joseph S. Clark.

Of more immediate interest, however, was the question of where Mr. Nixon would turn for candidates for position in his Cabinet, his White House policy staff and other key positions. His choice of men and a few crucial appointments, such as a new Chief Justice, may well reveal how far to the right and left he intends to reach in the interests of unity and the "new coalition" of which he sometimes spoke during the campaign.

The old Democratic coalition that Franklin D. Roosevelt put together in the 1930s—united the South with the urban North, racial segregationists with Negroes, big-city machines, labor unions and the offspring of immigrants—was thought this year to be finally breaking apart.

Racial tension and the loss of interest in the economic bounty traditionally associated by the lower middle classes with the Democrats clearly threatened this political alignment, as did the physical shifting of populations out of the cities.

But Mr. Humphrey sang a vigorous last hurrah for the remnants of the New Deal and proved that the old economic arguments—or fears of Republican economic management—were strong enough to hold many Democratic voters from defection. Saddled from the start of the campaign with an unpopular President and an unpopular war in Vietnam, he also managed to wriggle loose from those burdens and held much of his party together at least one more time in opposition to Mr. Nixon.

The results suggest that in many of the big states, this remains a potent appeal. And where the Democrats remain well organized, as in Texas, Missouri or Illinois, or where the unions put their men and money to work, there was shown to be a political mechanism still worthy of the attentions of ambitious leaders.

Above all, the campaign demonstrated that the American political system as a whole could still adjust itself to the most violent strains. The bitter conflict over the war, the unexpected abdication of President Johnson in March, the shooting of the Rev. Dr. Martin Luther King Jr. and of Senator Kennedy in April and June, the riots in the Negro ghettoes and the turbulence, inside and out, at the Democratic National Convention, had spread disgust and disaffection through political ranks.

Yet the excitement of the closing days of the campaign appeared to kindle new emotions and Mr. Nixon pleaded in his victory statement with the young partisans in different branches of the Democratic party to remain within the system and to retain their enthusiasm, even if they felt compelled to continue to oppose him.

The widespread fear that neither Mr. Nixon nor Mr. Humphrey would win a clean victory and that weeks of bizarre maneuvering would result both in the Electoral College and in the House of Representatives persisted through the long night of return watching and analysis. The close escape at the end may now encourage the forces of reform who wish to alter or abandon the elector system, Mr. Humphrey among them.

But harrowing as the campaign proved to be and narrow as Mr. Nixon's margin unexpectedly came to be, the system held and turned, under the leadership of the retiring President and the defeated Vice President, to the swift and orderly passage of power.

PART VII

DÉTENTE AND CONFRONTATION

March 2, 1969

BERLIN ROAD SHUT 2D TIME BY REDS AS TROOPS MOVE

East Germans Close Main Autobahn in First Major Harassment Since '65

KIESINGER CALLS ENVOY

But He and Russian Make No Progress—Soviet and Ally Prepare for Maneuvers

By DAVID BINDER
Special to The New York Times.

BERLIN, March 1—Heavily armed Communist border guards sealed the main Autobahn access route to West Berlin this morning at Marienborn, the East German checkpoint on the West German border, for about two hours as large movements of Soviet and East German troops got under way preparatory to joint maneuvers.

[The road was closed Sunday for a second time, Reuters reported.]

It was the first major harassment of Berlin traffic since April, 1965, and the reason offered was much the same as before—reprisal for West German Government activities in this outpost city, 110 miles inside East Germany.

There was no sign that the Eastern side had carried out its threat of last night to begin selective long-term restrictions on traffic of passengers and goods in air, land and canal routes.

Further Action Implied

An American who works in the East Berlin State Opera was told not to try to cross through the wall Wednesday, the day of West Germany's controversial presidential election in West Berlin, implying that the restrictions on travel would be extended to the middle of the city.

[In Paris the traveling White House assured West Germany Saturday that the United States would "fulfill its responsibilities as one of the occupying powers in Berlin." At the same time Pravda, the Soviet Communist party newspaper, stirred speculation that the Soviet Union might conceivably be considering action in the Berlin air corridors by referring to West German politicians visiting Berlin as "contraband goods delivered by the aviation of the Western powers."]

Mayor Klaus Schütz of West Berlin and other Western officials dismissed the road hindrances as familiar.

They expressed much more concern about the long-range implications of the Soviet and East German threats to halt the movement of various vaguely described categories of goods and people on the access routes.

The Soviet-Union charged that West Berlin factories were producing weapons for the West German armed forces.

In Bonn during the afternoon, Chancellor Kurt Georg Kiesinger called in the Soviet Ambassador, Semyon K. Tsarapkin, to reject Soviet accusations that West Germany was creating mischief in Berlin. But apparently he did not try to resume the probing for a Moscow-Bonn compromise that had begun last weekend and collapsed Thursday.

Emerging from the Chancellery after almost three hours, Mr. Tsarapkin answered a reporter's query whether the "crisis" was continuing by replying in English: "Yes—there was no result."

A Government spokesman confirmed afterward that the talks had achieved "no progress."

An informed source said Chancellor Kiesinger had "gone to the extreme" by assuring the Soviet envoy that Bonn had "no burning interest" in staging further state events here beyond the session of the Federal Assembly, or electoral college, to elect West Germany's President.

Easter Pass Offer Stands

However, the source added, Mr. Tsarapkin was evidently acting under orders to stick by a limited Communist compromise offer to provide visiting privileges in East Berlin to West Berliners at Easter in exchange for a shift of the electoral assembly.

A Government spokesman said this was "an imposition." He also described the talk as having been "sober and objective," but without the wine that was served to the Ambassador last Sunday by the Chancellor.

The spokesman left the door open for further talks, but said West Germany was going ahead with the election plan as scheduled.

Chancellor Kiesinger went on television at night to tell the German people that he had done his best to make an acceptable deal with the Russians, "but there is a limit that nobody who values the dignity of his nation can exceed."

The Communist side is retaliating against West Germany's plan to hold its fourth consecutive presidential election in Berlin, the old imperial capital, contending that the election here is illegal.

Chancellor Kiesinger disclosed that he was keeping President Nixon posted on the developing East-West confrontation over Berlin by special bulletins to Paris.

Associated Press

STOPPAGE ON THE AUTOBAHN: With armed guards posted along barrier, vehicles stand still on highway through East Germany to West Berlin. Traffic was halted for about two hours yesterday. The city is 110 miles inside East Germany.

Foreign Minister Willy Brandt indicated in a television interview that West Germany would ask Mr. Nixon to intervene with the Russians to prevent a grave clash, a move considered earlier in the week by Bonn and rejected.

New Element Seen

Mr. Brandt said the new element in the present confrontation, which he called a "small crisis," was the involvement of the three Western allies responsible for West Berlin's security. This, he added, came about through Soviet warnings addressed to the allies—the United States, Britain and France.

The three allied embassies in Bonn isued a joint declaration this afternoon rejecting Soviet allegations of "illegal West German military activities" in West Berlin as "groundless."

Without noting that this was the 13th anniversary, accompanied by celebrations, of the East German National People's Army, they added: "It is only in the Eastern sector of Berlin that organized German military activity has taken place." The allies concluded with a plea for "reducing international tensions."

However, the three allied commandants who ultimately govern West Berlin protested in a joint declaration that the

People's Army ceremonies in East Berlin constituted a "flagrant violation" of the "demilitarized status of Berlin."

The Western allied military contingent numbers about 12,000 combat troops, mostly motorized in infantry and tank units. Their assignment in the event of a critical emergency is to try to break out of their West Berlin posts and harass Communist communication transport lines.

Mayor Schütz adopted much the same cool tone as the allies at a news conference here at noon. He refused to call the present situation "a crisis."

"It is not an airlift situation," he said. "It is very serious, but not comparable to previous occasions"—an allusion to the 1948 land blockade of West Berlin.

He condemned the Eastern side's threats and maneuvers as "absurd," "ridiculous" and "chicanery," but added:

"We must go the way of reason prudently, soberly. Miscalculations are in this situation and in these days the real danger."

The Mayor also emphasized that he was in close contact with the three allied commandants in West Berlin and that they were unanimous in the appraisal of the situation and their response to it.

The latest restrictions on the access routes included a four-hour closure of the highway to Hamburg from 1 A.M. to 5 A.M. and delays of drivers already under way on the western and southern Autobahns. Some drivers were halted by police units and directed to side roads while tanks and other military vehicles took over the highways. Some drivers were delayed up to 10 hours.

Travelers reported sighting as many as 200 East German tanks under way on the Autobahn beyond Helmstedt, while others reported seeing Soviet tank convoys to the south.

In voicing concern over the long-range implications of the Soviet-East German threats to halt the movement of goods and people, Mayor Schütz pointed out that last year West Berlin moved $3-billion worth of industrial products through the access routes to West Germany.

There could be very broad interpretations, the Mayor said, for the Soviet note to East Germany, which spoke of restricting the transport of weapons allegedly produced in West Berlin factories and restricting movement of "young recruits" of the West Germany Army.

The Communists have named dozens of West Berlin companies as purported manufacturers of arms for the West German Army, including the huge Siemens and Telefunken electronics plants.

Since more than 70 per cent of the 12.5 million tons of goods annually sent out of West Berlin to the West are moved by truck, the expectation here is that the pinch would come first and foremost on the three main roads to the city. About 11 per cent of the goods annually produced in Berlin is moved by rail, 19 per cent by canal barges and the remaining 25,000 tons by air.

* * *

April 16, 1969

U.S. SCOUT PLANE WITH 31 IS LOST, REPORTED DOWNED BY 2 NORTH KOREAN MIG'S

WIDE HUNT BEGINS

Navy Sights Debris—2 Soviet Vessels Guided to Area

By WILLIAM BEECHER
Special to The New York Times.

WASHINGTON, April 15—North Korea asserted today that it had shot down a United States Navy electronic intelligence plane. The Nixon Administration is said to believe that the plane, with a crew of 31, was attacked by two MIG jets off the Korean coast.

A broadcast by North Korea monitored here said that the four-engine EC-121 aircraft, based in Japan, had intruded into its airspace and was downed with "one shot" at 1:50 P.M. Tuesday, Korean time (11:50 P.M. Monday, New York time).

Pentagon spokesmen said that an air-sea search for survivors had begun in an area centered about 75 miles off North Korea in the Sea of Japan. Later, the Defense Department reported a sighting of debris that it said "could be associated with the missing aircraft." The debris was sighted by a Navy search plane about 120 miles southeast of Chongjin, North Korea. The search plane did not report any evidence of survivors.

Russians on Scene

The Pentagon reported at 10:15 P.M. that a Navy patrol plane had guided two Soviet destroyers that were on the scene to the area where the debris had been located. There was no report of the ships' findings.

The incident occurred 15 months after North Korea's seizure of the American intelligence-gathering ship Pueblo.

[In Prospect Heights, Ill., the head of the Remember the Pueblo Committee, citing a Government source, announced that possibly seven survivors of the plane had been picked up by North Korean gunboats.]

Unofficially, a high Administration official said the plane was believed to have been shot down about 100 miles off the Korean coast. Senator Everett McKinley Dirksen, the Republican leader, said two MIG's and the figure 60 miles had been mentioned to him at a White House briefing conducted by Henry A. Kissinger, national security adviser to the President.

A Pentagon spokesman said the plane had been on a routine reconnaissance flight similar to hundreds of missions flown in the area since 1950, when the Korean war started.

Particularly because of the recent border incidents between the Soviet Union and Communist China, the plane was believed to have been concerned with intercepting radio messages from those two countries. Its track carried it along the North Korean coast as well because of interest in picking up any information relating to possible sabotage missions against South Korea, the sources said.

The private comments here raised the possibility of another dispute between the United States and North Korea about the location of an attacked intelligence craft. That was the central issue in the seizure of the spy ship Pueblo last year and the detention of her crew of 82 for 11 months.

While the new incident presented the Nixon Administration with a difficult policy decision, one official said the President wanted to play it "low key—at least until we get all the facts."

One reason, the sources said, was an unconfirmed report that two North Korean destroyers were thought to be speeding toward the area. American warships also were racing there from Japan.

There was considerable concern that the Koreans might attempt to capture any survivors and hold them hostage against the possibility of retaliation, as was done in the case of the Pueblo. The United States said the Pueblo was about 25 miles offshore; North Korea says its air and sea space extends 12 miles from shore.

Pentagon planners were known to be preparing a list of possible retaliatory steps, but they conceded that any military action was fraught with risks.

The White House said Mr. Nixon had been watching the situation closely since he was awakened early by Mr. Kissinger. It was decided that no immediate Presidential response was required, the sources said.

Mr. Nixon discussed the crisis with Defense Secretary Melvin R. Laird and Secretary of State William P. Rogers. The matter was added to the agenda of a meeting of the National Security Council previously scheduled for tomorrow.

Daniel Z. Henkin, chief Pentagon spokesman, said the EC-121 had been operating under orders from the Commander in Chief, Pacific, with headquarters in Honolulu. The missions are approved by the Joint Chiefs of Staff. The plane's commander was identified as Lieut-Comdr. James H. Overstreet of McLaurin, Miss.

The propeller-driven craft, a modified version of the Lockheed Super-Constellation, was "flying a track which maintained it at a distance of at least 50 nautical miles from the coast of North Korea," he said, adding that it was in communication with its base at Atsugi, Japan.

The sources cautioned, however, against assuming the plane had been in direct touch with the base during the attack.

The plane has about six tons of electronics equipment. It carries two crews to enable it to remain on station for about eight hours, the crews working in relays. In addition to monitoring radio messages, it is equipped to determine the frequencies employed in air-defense radar.

The State Department spokesman, Robert J. McCloskey, disclosed that the United States had asked the Soviet Union, Japan and South Korea for any assistance they might render in helping to locate the missing crewmen. The requests were made in the capitals of the three countries, he said.

In addition, he said, Secretary Rogers talked for 15 minutes with the Soviet Ambassador, Anatoly F. Dobrynin. Mr. McCloskey said the talk was "not in any way a protest" but rather an appeal for assistance.

A North Korean broadcast said the plane was shot down at 1:50 P.M. Korean time (11:50 P.M. Monday, Eastern standard time) after having invaded Korean airspace.

The air-sea search was reported to be concentrating in an area 83 miles southeast of Chongjin and 72 miles due east of the North Korean coast.

Seas in the area were described as moderate, with waves of about four feet and winds of 10 to 16 knots. The air temperature was reported as 10 to 16 degrees above freezing, with water temperature slightly higher. The plane carried enough life-rafts for the crew.

Although there were no confirmed reports of survivors, the size of the rescue operation was being substantially expanded, the Pentagon said.

At the time of the Pueblo seizure, the United States had eight combat aircraft in South Korea within easy range, but they were unavailable for quick use since they had racks and other equipment for a potential nuclear mission. On this occasion the United States had 128 warplanes in South Korea and 50 more in Japan. The South Koreans have 175 jet fighters. North Korea has 440 jet fighters and 80 bombers.

Two F-106 fighters were dispatched from Osan Air Base in Korea, the search area to protect long-range planes from harassment, the sources said.

According to Pentagon sources, there have been three attacks on American aircraft by North Korea since the war ended in 1953.

On June 15, 1959, a Navy P-4 patrol plane was damaged by a MIG about 85 miles east of Wonsan, North Korea, but returned to Japan. On May 17, 1963, an Army helicopter strayed across the demilitarized zone in Korea and was forced down. On April 27, 1965, an RB-57 reconnaissance plane was attacked by two MIG's and damaged but returned to its base in Japan.

* * *

July 21, 1969

MEN WALK ON MOON

ASTRONAUTS LAND ON PLAIN; COLLECT ROCKS, PLANT FLAG

A Powdery Surface Is Closely Explored

By JOHN NOBLE WILFORD
Special to The New York Times.

HOUSTON, Monday, July 21—Men have landed and walked on the moon.

Two Americans, astronauts of Apollo 11, steered their fragile four-legged lunar module safely and smoothly to the historic landing yesterday at 4:17:40 P.M., Eastern daylight time.

Neil A. Armstrong, the 38-year-old civilian commander, radioed to earth and the mission control room here:

"Houston, Tranquility Base here. The Eagle has landed."

The first men to reach the moon—Mr. Armstrong and his co-pilot, Col. Edwin E. Aldrin Jr. of the Air Force—brought their ship to rest on a level, rock-strewn plain near the southwestern shore of the arid Sea of Tranquility.

About six and a half hours later, Mr. Armstrong opened the landing craft's hatch, stepped slowly down the ladder and declared as he planted the first human footprint on the lunar crust:

"That's one small step for man, one giant leap for mankind."

His first step on the moon came at 10:56:20 P.M., as a television camera outside the craft transmitted his every move to an awed and excited audience of hundreds of millions of people on earth.

Tentative Steps Test Soil

Mr. Armstrong's initial steps were tentative tests of the lunar soil's firmness and of his ability to move about easily in his bulky white spacesuit and backpacks and under the influence of lunar gravity, which is one-sixth that of the earth.

"The surface is fine and powdery," the astronaut reported. "I can pick it up loosely with my toe. It does adhere in fine layers like powdered charcoal to the sole and sides of my boots. I only go in a small fraction of an inch, maybe an eighth of an inch. But I can see the footprints of my boots in the treads in the fine sandy particles."

After 19 minutes of Mr. Armstrong's testing, Colonel Aldrin joined him outside the craft.

The two men got busy setting up another television camera out from the lunar module, planting an American flag into the ground, scooping up soil and rock samples, deploying scientific experiments and hopping and loping about in a demonstration of their lunar agility.

They found walking and working on the moon less taxing than had been forecast. Mr. Armstrong once reported he was "very comfortable."

And people back on earth found the black-and-white television pictures of the bug-shaped lunar module and the men tramping about it so sharp and clear as to seem unreal, more like a toy and toy-like figures than human beings on the most daring and far-reaching expedition thus far undertaken.

Nixon Telephones Congratulations

During one break in the astronauts' work, President Nixon congratulated them from the White House in what, he said, "certainly has to be the most historic telephone call ever made."

"Because of what you have done," the President told the astronauts, "the heavens have become a part of man's world. And as you talk to us from the Sea of Tranquility it requires us to redouble our efforts to bring peace and tranquility to earth.

"For one priceless moment in the whole history of man all the people on this earth are truly one—one in their pride in what you have done and one in our prayers that you will return safely to earth."

Mr. Armstrong replied:

"Thank you Mr. President. It's a great honor and privilege for us to be here representing not only the United States but men of peace of all nations, men with interests and a curiosity and men with a vision for the future."

Mr. Armstrong and Colonel Aldrin returned to their landing craft and closed the hatch at 1:12 A.M., 2 hours 21 minutes after opening the hatch on the moon. While the third member of the crew, Lieut. Col. Michael Collins of the Air Force, kept his orbital vigil overhead in the command ship, the two moon explorers settled down to sleep.

Outside their vehicle the astronauts had found a bleak world. It was just before dawn, with the sun low over the eastern horizon behind them and the chill of the long lunar nights still clinging to the boulders, small craters and hills before them.

Colonel Aldrin said that he could see "literally thousands of small craters" and a low hill out in the distance. But most of all he was impressed initially by the "variety of shapes, angularities, granularities" of the rocks and soil where the landing craft, code-named Eagle, had set down.

The landing was made four miles west of the aiming point, but well within the designated area. An apparent error in some data fed into the craft's guidance computer from the earth was said to have accounted for the discrepancy.

Suddenly the astronauts were startled to see that the computer was guiding them toward a possibly disastrous touchdown in a boulder-filled crater about the size of a football field.

Mr. Armstrong grabbed manual control of the vehicle and guided it safely over the crater to a smoother spot, the rocket engine stirring a cloud of moon dust during the final seconds of descent.

Soon after the landing, upon checking and finding the spacecraft in good condition, Mr. Armstrong and Colonel Aldrin made their decision to open the hatch and get out earlier than originally scheduled. The flight plan had called for the moon walk to begin at 2:12 A.M.

Flight controllers here said that the early moon walk would not mean that the astronauts would also leave the moon earlier. The lift-off is scheduled to come at about 1:55 P.M. today.

Their departure from the landing craft out onto the surface was delayed for a time when they had trouble depressurizing the cabin so that they could open the hatch. All the oxygen in the cabin had to be vented.

Once the pressure gauge finally dropped to zero, they opened the hatch and Mr. Armstrong stepped out on the small porch at the top of the nine-step ladder.

"O.K., Houston, I'm on the porch," he reported, as he descended.

On the second step from the top, he pulled a lanyard that released a fold-down equipment compartment on the side of the lunar module. This deployed the television camera that transmitted the dramatic pictures of man's first steps on the moon.

Ancient Dream Fulfilled

It was man's first landing on another world, the realization of centuries of dreams, the fulfillment of a decade of striving, a triumph of modern technology and personal courage, the most dramatic demonstration of what man can do if he applies his mind and resources with single-minded determination.

The moon, long the symbol of the impossible and the inaccessible, was now within man's reach, the first port of call in this new age of spacefaring.

Immediately after the landing, Dr. Thomas O. Paine, administrator of the National Aeronautics and Space Administration, telephoned President Nixon in Washington to report:

"Mr. President, it is my honor on behalf of the entire NASA team to report to you that the Eagle has landed on the Sea of Tranquility and our astronauts are safe and looking forward to starting the exploration of the moon."

The landing craft from the Apollo 11 spaceship was scheduled to remain on the moon about 22 hours, while Colonel Collins of the Air Force, the third member of the Apollo 11 crew, piloted the command ship, Columbia, in orbit overhead.

"You're looking good in every respect," Mission Control told the two men of Eagle after examining data indicating that the module should be able to remain on the moon the full 22 hours.

Mr. Armstrong and Colonel Aldrin planned to sleep after the moon walk and then make their preparations for the lift-off for the return to a rendezvous with Colonel Collins in the command ship.

Apollo 11's journey into history began last Wednesday from launching pad 39-A at Cape Kennedy, Fla. After an almost flawless three-day flight, the joined command ship and lunar module swept into an orbit of the moon yesterday afternoon.

The three men were awake for their big day at 7 A.M. when their spacecraft emerged from behind the moon on its 10th revolution, moving from east to west across the face of the moon along its equator.

Their orbit was 73.6 miles by 64 miles in altitude, their speed 3,660 miles an hour. At that altitude and speed, it took about two hours to complete a full orbit of the moon.

The sun was rising over their landing site on the Sea of Tranquility.

"We can pick out almost all of the features we've identified previously," Mr. Armstrong reported.

After breakfast, on their 11th revolution, Colonel Aldrin and then Mr. Armstrong, both dressed in their white pressurized suits, crawled through the connecting tunnel into the lunar module.

They turned on the electrical power, checked all the switch settings on the cockpit panel and checked communications with the command ship and the ground controllers. Everything was "nominal," as the spacemen say.

LM Ready for Descent

The lunar module was ready. Its four legs with yard-wide footpads were extended so that the height of the 16½-ton vehicle now measured 22 feet and 11 inches and its width 31 feet.

Mr. Armstrong stood at the left side of the cockpit, and Colonel Aldrin at the right. Both were loosely restrained by harnesses. They had closed the hatch to the connecting tunnel.

The walls of their craft were finely milled aluminum foil. If anything happened so that it could not return to the command ship, the lunar module would be too delicate to withstand a plunge through earth's atmosphere, even if it had the rocket power.

Nearly three-fourths of the vehicle's weight was in propellants for the descent and ascent rockets—Aerozine 50 and nitrogen oxide, which substituted for the oxygen, making combustion possible.

It was an ungainly craft that creaked and groaned in flight. But years of development and testing had determined that it was the lightest and most practical way to get two men to the moon's surface.

Before Apollo 11 disappeared behind the moon near the end of its 12th orbit, mission control gave the astronauts their "go" for undocking—the separation of Eagle from Columbia.

Colonel Collins had already released 12 of the latches holding the two ships together at the connecting tunnel. He did this when he closed the hatch at the command ship's nose. While behind the moon, he was to flip a switch on the control panel to release the three remaining latches by a spring action.

At 1:50 P.M., when communications signals were reacquired, Mission Control asked: "How does it look?"

"Eagle has wings," Mr. Armstrong replied.

The two ships were then only a few feet apart. But at 2:12 P.M., Colonel Collins fired the command ship's maneuvering rockets to move about two miles away and in a slightly different orbit from the lunar module.

"It looks like you've got a fine-looking flying machine there, Eagle, despite the fact you're upside down," Colonel Collins commented watching the spidery lunar module receding in the distance.

"Somebody's upside down," Mr. Armstrong replied.

What is "up" and what is "down" is never quite clear in the absence of landmarks and the sensation of gravity's pull.

As Mr. Armstrong and Colonel Aldrin rode the lunar module back around to the moon's far side, the rocket engine in the vehicle's lower stage was pointed toward the line of flight. The two pilots were leaning toward the cockpit controls riding backwards and facing downward.

"Everything is go," they were assured by Mission Control.

Their on-board guidance and navigation computer was instructed to trigger a 29.8-second firing of the descent rocket, the 9,870-pound-thrust throttable engine that would slow down the lunar module and send it toward the moon on a long, curving trajectory.

The firing was set to take place at 3:08 P.M., when the craft would be behind the moon and once again out of touch with the ground.

Suspense built up in the control room here. Flight controllers stood silently at their consoles. Among those waiting for word of the rocket firing were Dr. Thomas O. Paine, the space agency's administrator, most of the Apollo project officials and several astronauts.

At 3:46 P.M., contact was established with the command ship.

Colonel Collins reported, "Listen, baby, things are going just swimmingly, just beautiful."

There was still no word from the lunar module for two minutes. Then came a weak signal, some static and whistling, and finally the calm voice of Mr. Armstrong.

"The burn was on time," the Apollo 11 commander declared.

When he read out data on the beginning of the descent, Mission Control concluded that it "look great." The lunar module had already descended from an altitude of 65.5 miles to 21 miles and was coasting steadily downward.

Eugene F. Kranz, the flight director, turned to his associates and said, "We're off to a good start. Play it cool."

Colonel Aldrin reported some oscillations in the vehicle's antenna, but nothing serious. Several times the astronauts were told to turn the vehicle slightly to move the antenna into a better position for communications over the 230,000 miles.

"You're 'go' for PDI," radioed Mission Control, referring to the powered descent initiation—the beginning of the nearly 13-minute final blast of the rocket to the soft touchdown.

When the two men reached an altitude of 50,000 feet, which was approximately the lowest point reached by Apollo 10 in May, green lights on the computer display keyboard in the cockpit blinked the number 99.

This signaled Mr. Armstrong that he had five seconds to decide whether to go ahead for the landing or continue on its orbital path back to the command ship. He pressed the "proceed" button.

The throttleable engine built up thrust gradually, firing continuously as the lunar module descended along the steadily steepening trajectory to the landing site about 250 miles away.

"Looking good," Mission Control radioed the men.

Four minutes after the firing the lunar module was down to 40,000 feet. After five and a half minutes, it was 33,500 feet. At six minutes, 27,000 feet.

"Better than the simulator," said Colonel Aldrin, referring to their practice landings at the spacecraft center.

Seven minutes after the firing, the men were 21,000 feet above the surface and still moving forward toward the landing site. The guidance computer was driving the rocket engine.

The lunar module was slowing down. At an altitude of about 7,200 feet, with the landing site still about five miles ahead, the computer commanded control jets to fire and tilt the bug-shaped craft almost upright so that its triangular windows pointed forward.

Mr. Armstrong and Colonel Aldrin then got their first close-up view of the plain they were aiming for. It was then about three and a half minutes to touchdown.

The brownish-gray panorama rushed below them—the myriad craters, hills and ridges, deep cracks and ancient rubble on the moon, which Dr. Robert Jastrow, the space agency scientist, called the "Rosetta Stone of life."

"You're 'go' for landing," Mission Control informed the two men.

The Eagle closed in, dropping about 20 feet a second, until it was hovering almost directly over the landing area at an altitude of 500 feet.

Its floor was littered with boulders.

It was when the craft reached an altitude of 300 feet that Mr. Armstrong took over semimanual control for the rest of the way. The computer continued to have control of the rocket firing, but the astronaut could adjust the craft's hovering position.

He was expected to take over such control anyway, but the sight of a crater looming ahead at the touchdown point made it imperative.

As Mr. Armstrong said later, "The auto-targeting was taking us right into a football field-sized crater, with a large number of big boulders and rocks."

For about 90 seconds, he peered through the window in search of a clear touchdown point. Using the lever at his right hand, he tilted the vehicle forward to redirect the firing of the maneuvering jets and thus shift its hovering position.

Finally, Mr. Armstrong found the spot he liked, and the blue light on the cockpit flashed to indicate that five-foot-long probes, like curb feelers, on three of the four legs had touched the surface.

"Contact light," Mr. Armstrong radioed.

He pressed a button marked "Stop" and reported, "okay, engine stop."

There were a few more cryptic messages of functions performed.

Then Maj. Charles M. Duke, the capsule communicator in the control room, radioed to the two astronauts:

"We copy you down, Eagle."

"Houston, Tranquility Base here. The Eagle has landed."

"Roger, Tranquility," Major Duke replied. "We copy you on the ground. You got a bunch of guys about to turn blue. We are breathing again. Thanks a lot."

Colonel Aldrin assured Mission Control it was a "very smooth touchdown."

The Eagle came to rest at an angle of only about four and a half degrees. The angle could have been more than 30 degrees without threatening to tip the vehicle over.

The landing site, about 120 miles southwest of the crater Maskelyne, is on the right side of the moon as seen from earth. The position: Lat. 0.799 degrees N., Long. 23.46 degrees E.

Although Mr. Armstrong is known as a man of few words, his heartbeats told of his excitement upon leading man's first landing on the moon.

At the time of the descent rocket ignition, his heartbeat rate registered 110 a minute—77 is normal for him—and it shot up to 156 at touchdown.

At the time of the landing, Colonel Collins was riding the command ship Columbia about 65 miles overhead.

Mission control informed the colonel, "Eagle is at Tranquility."

"Yea, I heard the whole thing," Colonel Collins, the man who went so far but not all the way, replied. "Fantastic."

When the Apollo astronauts landed on the Sea of Tranquility, the temperature at their touchdown site was about zero degrees Fahrenheit in the sunlight, even colder in the shade.

During a lunar night, which lasts 14 earth days, temperatures plunge as low as 280 degrees below zero. Unlike earth, the moon, having no atmosphere to act as a blanket, is unable to retain any of the day's warmth during the night.

During the equally long lunar day, temperatures rise as high as 280 degrees. By the time of Eagle's departure from the moon, with the sun higher in the sky, the temperatures there will have risen to about 90 degrees.

This particular landing site was one of five selected by Apollo project officials after analysis of pictures returned by the five Lunar Orbiter unmanned spacecraft.

All five sites are situated across the lunar equator on the side of the moon always facing earth. Being on the equator reduces the maneuvering for the astronauts to get there. Being on the near side of the moon, of course, makes possible to communicate with the explorers.

* * *

July 26, 1969

NIXON PLANS CUT IN MILITARY ROLE FOR U.S. IN ASIA

Starting Tour, He Promises Respect for Commitments, but Under New Forms

ARRIVES IN PHILIPPINES

President, at Guam, Asserts Nation Won't Be Drawn Into More Vietnams

By ROBERT B. SEMPLE JR.
Special to The New York Times.

MANILA, Saturday, July 26—President Nixon declared yesterday that the United States would not be enticed into future wars like the one in Vietnam and would redesign and reduce its military commitments throughout non-Communist Asia.

Mr. Nixon promised, however, that the United States would continue to play a sizable role in the Pacific and would not forsake its treaty commitments.

This was the essence of views put forward by the President in an informal news conference before he set forth from Guam on the diplomatic leg of his global journey.

President Exhilarated

The President, who seemed exhilarated by the successful moon venture of Apollo 11, arrived here today for the first foreign stop of a tour taking him to Indonesia, Thailand, India, Pakistan, Rumania and, briefly, Britain.

During his short stop in Guam, Mr. Nixon set forth in considerable detail the purposes of his week-and-a-half trip and disclosed major points he would be making to the Asian leaders. He spoke for publication but asked that his words not be directly quoted.

The President defined his Asian policy in more specific and forceful terms than at any time since taking office. Some of his views had been expressed earlier in articles and in the political campaign last fall, but he went further today in emphasizing his intention of limiting United States commitments.

New Aid Is Hinted

Specifically, he said he might order a reduction of military operations in South Vietnam if that would help the negotiations to end the war.

The President also hinted that new forms of economic aid to the Asian nations might soon be forthcoming, but—perhaps mindful of growing ill will toward foreign aid at home and the constraints that inflation has placed on new Government spending—he carefully avoided promising an increase in aid.

The President spent the major part of his news conference, held at the naval officers' club in Guam, on questions relating to Vietnam and Asia, demonstrating that despite all the early publicity devoted to visit he will pay to Rumania Aug. 2, he himself was placing highest priority on the Asian part of the journey. Yet in the course of his unusually relaxed and unusually long session—it last 52 minutes, compared with his average news-conference length of 30 minutes—Mr. Nixon also made these points:

- He remains willing to participate in a top-level meeting with the Soviet Union to talk about the Vietnam war, the Middle Eastern crisis and the arms race, but only if such a meeting were to be preceded by lower-level consulations and held out some promise of success.
- While he most wishes for a summit meeting to enlist the Soviet Union in the search for an end of the war, he doubts that Moscow would work for a settlement, even if it wants one, in so public and highly visible a forum.
- There is no basis for what he called speculation that his visit to Rumania would be an affront to either the Soviet Union or Communist China; instead, it is designed to develop communication with Eastern European nations.
- Recent charges by some Senators that the United States had struck a secret defense agreement with Thailand are without foundation.

Mr. Nixon acknowledged at the outset his consuming interest in the future of Asia after the end of the war in Vietnam. He said further that the Asians were equally interested in whether the United States would continue to play a significant role in their area or whether, like the French, British and Dutch, it would withdraw from the Pacific and play a minor part.

He conceded that many Americans were extremely frustrated by the Vietnam war and, in their frustration, wished for a substantial reduction of America's Pacific commitments. He indicated by his tone that he understood these frustrations and to a certain extent sympathized with them.

But he argued that the United States could not withdraw from its Asian commitments, first because withdrawal might well pave the way for other wars; and second, because the United States itself is a Pacific power with a major stake in Asian stability.

In answering subsequent questions, however, Mr. Nixon sought more clearly to define the future dimensions of that commitment. He asserted, for example, that except when Asian nations were threatened by a nuclear power such as Communist China, the United States would insist that both internal subversion and external aggression be dealt with increasingly by the Asians themselves.

Collective Security Urged

He said it was foolish to believe that the non-Communist Asian nations could soon devise collective security arrangements enabling them to defend themselves against Communism. Collective security now is a weak reed to lean on, he said, and it will take five to 10 years for the non-Communist Asian nations to devise adequate collective security arrangements among themselves.

This blunt assessment of the prospects for collective security prompted a question on what the United States would do in the event of another Vietnam situation in the five to 10 years in which the Asian nations would be struggling to devise mechanisms for self-protection. The President replied that such incidents would have to be judged case by case.

But he will consider each case very carefully, he asserted, with an eye to avoiding what he called creeping involvements that eventually submerge a great nation, as, he said, the Vietnam conflict has submerged the United States in emotional discord and economic strain.

To illustrate his point, the President recalled a line from his election campaign that he said he had used in every speech, drawing loud applause each time. He said the statement had been made to him by Mohammad Ayub Khan, former President of Pakistan, in 1964.

"The role of the United States in Vietnam or the Philippines, or Thailand, or any of these other countries which have internal subversion," the statement went, "is to help them fight the war but not fight the war for them."

Mr. Nixon then declared, in answer to a question, that military assistance of all kinds, including the commitment of United States troops, would be reduced. He did not say how large such reductions would be, or how soon they would be carried out.

To compensate in part for the reduced military assistance, Mr. Nixon indicated that the United States would soon be suggesting initiatives on the economic side designed to add fresh momentum to what he said was the developing economic strength of non-Communist Asia. He promised that United States aid would be adequate to meet the challenge of Asian economic problems.

The President professed to see several hopeful signs that non-Communist Asia had recently become stronger, including rapid economic development. He rattled off an impressive list of statistics showing the economic growth of South Korea, Japan, Thailand, Indonesia, India and Pakistan.

Another sign, he said, was the dwindling capacity of Communist China to foment internal insurgencies in other countries. Early in the news conference, Mr. Nixon declared that China was the single biggest threat to stability in Asia, but later he expressed a conviction that the appeal of the Communist philosophy had dwindled in some Asian countries in the last 16 years. He cited Pakistan, India, Indonesia and Japan as examples.

The President returned to the same themes on his arrival at the Manila International Airport, where he was greeted by President and Mrs. Ferdinand E. Marcos and a large delegation of Filipino officials.

"I want to convey throughout the trip," he said, "the great sense of respect and affection which the people of the United States feel for their Asian neighbors and the readiness of my country to support the efforts of Asian nations to improve the life of their peoples. I will also offer the view that peace and progress in Asia must be shaped and protected primarily by Asian hands and that the contribution which my country can make to that process should come as a supplement to Asian energies and in response to Asian leadership."

* * *

August 16, 1969

RED CHINA CHARGES SOVIET IS MOBILIZING

By TILLMAN DURDIN

Special to The New York Times.

HONG KONG, Aug. 15—Communist China accused the Soviet Union today of mobilizing for war against China and continued to warn the Chinese people to prepare for conflict with the Russians.

The charges, made in a dispatch from Peking by Hsinhua, the Chinese press agency, were accompanied by reports from Urumchi, the capital of Sinkiang Province, of huge anti-Soviet demonstrations throughout the Central Asian territory.

Peking's stress on the prospects of armed struggle followed the clash Wednesday between Soviet and Chinese troops on the Soviet border with Sinkiang, in the Tiehliekti area. Each side has blamed the other, and both report that they had suffered casualties in killed and wounded.

The warnings from Peking were in keeping with the agitated tone that its propaganda has taken toward Moscow for some time, and it was therefore unclear whether they reflected a genuine increase in concern over the possibility of war.

The Peking dispatch asserting that there was an intensification of the Soviet military threat said that Soviet forces had increased their "anti-China deployment" and charged that Marshals Andrei A. Grechko and Ivan I. Yakubovsky had "openly threatened to start a nuclear war."

The dispatch said that such acts "can by no means intimidate anybody" and only revealed weakness.

Despicable End Predicted

"If the Soviet revisionist renegade clique is bent on following the old road of aggression taken by Hitler and the Japanese Fascists," Hsinhua said "then like them it will come to a despicable end."

The threat-of-war theme was prevalent in most of the radio broadcasts from Communist China heard here. The Wuhan radio, for instance, demanded that the people of central China "realize and prepare for the enemy to launch a major war," while the Hunan radio asked the people and the military of the province to "get rid of the false and deadly dangerous idea that fighting can occur only in border areas."

Hsinhua's report of the Sinkiang demonstrations said that Saifuddin, a Uighur who is vice chairman of the Sinkiang Revolutionary Committee, had addressed a rally of more than 80,000 civilians and military men in Urumchi and had asserted that Soviet troops, in their incursion Wednesday, had "beaten up and kidnapped many of our revolutionary people and frontier guards in the area."

* * *

October 29, 1969

BRANDT MAKES BID FOR IMPROVED TIES WITH EAST EUROPE

First Policy Declaration as Chancellor Also Proposes Wide Internal Reforms

BONN PRIORITIES LISTED

Socialist Leader Forecasts Approval of Pact Barring Spread of Atomic Arms

By DAVID BINDER
Special to The New York Times.

BONN, Oct. 28—Chancellor Willy Brandt made a low-keyed bid to the major powers of Eastern Europe today for improved relations. He also announced a program of extensive domestic reforms.

These made up the foreign and internal priorities in his Government's first declaration to the Bundestag, the lower house of Parliament.

Specifically, the Social Democratic leader offered to negotiate agreements with the Soviet Union, East Germany and other Eastern European states to renounce the threat and use of force. Such agreements would "acknowledge the territorial integrity of the respective partners," he added.

[In Moscow, a Soviet-Czechoslovak communiqué called on West Germany to grant "international legal recognition" to East Germany if relations were to be improved between Bonn and Eastern Europe.]

Surmounting Suspicion

The Chancellor and his coalition partners, the Free Democrats, led by Foreign Minister Walter Scheel, intend the formula to surmount two decades of suspicion of Bonn's policies by East Germany and Poland.

Mr. Brandt, who was sworn in last Tuesday, emphasized the "defensive principle" of the West German forces, adding that West Germany's common cause with the United States in the Western alliance made the country "strong enough to allow a more self-reliant German policy within a more active partnership."

He said Bonn would sign the treaty to halt the proliferation of nuclear weapons as soon as "clarifications" were received from Washington. [United States officials expressed optimism that the treaty could finally be brought into force as a result of West Germany's decision.]

Mr. Brandt made it clear that the international recognition frequently demanded by the East German Government was "out of the question."

Rather, he said, his Government, formed as a result of the Sept. 28 federal elections, would start from the assumption that two German states exist and that since both are parts of the same nation, "their relations with each other can only be of a special nature."

Chancellor Brandt, emphasizing that his was a "consistent continuation" of the German policy inaugurated three years ago by the coalition of Christian and Social Democrats in which he was Foreign Minister, said Bonn was prepared to work for "contractually agreed cooperation" with the East Germans.

He added that West Germany would no longer attempt to interfere in East Germany trade and cultural exchanges with the rest of the world, as it had in the past.

Almost since its inception in 1949, the Government has spent literally billions of marks, mostly in the underdeveloped countries, to purchase the favor of governments with the aim of encouraging them not to have dealings with East Germany. Both Mr. Brandt and Mr. Scheel feel it has largely been a waste of funds.

Right to Self-Determination

On the other hand, Chancellor Brandt twice emphasized that the right of the German nation to self-determination, saying:

"The Germans are one not only by reason of their language and their history in all splendor and misery—we all at home in Germany, and we still have common tasks and a common responsibility to ensure peace among us and Europe."

Listing "short-term decisions" that he would undertake in the next weeks and months, Brandt said his Government would start talks with the Warsaw Government aimed at reconciliation with Poland. He added that Bonn was seeking to "bridge the gulf" with Czechoslovakia—presumably an allusion to the Munich pact of 1938 under which Hitler dismembered the prewar Czechoslovak state.

Some of the remarks by the Chancellor, who was wearing a sober gray suit and black-rimmed glasses, drew mocking laughter and angry catcalls from the opposition benches, held by 242 deputies of the Christian Union parties. Their leader, Kurt Georg Kiesinger, Mr. Brandt's predecessor as Chancellor, sat in a front row.

'Continuity and Renewal'

The 55-year-old Chancellor, remarking that his was a policy of "continuity and renewal," said:

"We stress our basic readiness to have diplomatic relations and to increase existing trade relations with all states of the world that share our desire for peaceful cooperation. The Federal Government rejects any form of discrimination, oppression and foreign rule, which in our day is endangering the peaceful coexistence of nations again and again."

The bulk of his 90-minute declaration was devoted to domestic affairs.

Though he did not go into great detail, he promised legislation soon to promote educational television, the acquisition of private capital by employes, better educational opportunities for children from rural and industrial families, computerized governmental operations, town planning and sports.

In the view of listeners who know the Chancellor well, the real Willy Brandt came out only in the last few minutes, when he said:

"This Government will not fawn on anybody. It demands much, not only of others but also of itself. It sets concrete targets.

"In a democracy a government can only work successfully if it is supported by a democratic commitment of its citizens. We are as little in need of blind approval as of pomp and high and mighty aloofness. We do not seek admirers. We need critical people to think with us, to decide with us and to take responsibility with us."

* * *

January 20, 1970

THE 2 GERMANYS INDICATE READINESS TO START TALKS

By DAVID BINDER
Special to The New York Times.

BERLIN, Jan. 19—West Germany and East Germany indicated in separate statements today that political talks between them could be opened for the first time since the two states were established 20 years ago.

Tentative agreement to this effect emerged this afternoon after Walter Ulbricht, the East German Communist chief, announced here that his Government was "prepared now as before for negotiations on fundamental problems, to which questions of renunciation of force naturally belong."

Replying at a news conference to questions submitted in writing, the 76-year-old Mr. Ulbricht, looking dapper in an excellently tailored navy blue suit and gold-rimmed eyeglasses, said: "We have no preconditions."

'Waiting for a Reply'

"Each side makes its proposals," he declared. "We are waiting for an official reply."

This appeared to several East German newsmen who attended the crowded news conference in the State Council building in East Berlin to be a sharp reversal from Mr. Ulbricht's stance only last week. The controlled East German press at that time was adding additional items to an already large catalogue of demands on the Bonn Government that were described as "preconditions" for improved relations between the two Germanys. Although the two countries may be semantically and factually far apart on the issue of diplomatic recognition of East Germany, each appears ready now to test the other at a negotiating table without demanding preconditions in the form of ultimatums.

Last week, in a speech to the West German parliament on the state of the nation, Chancellor Willy Brandt called for talks between the two German Governments with an open agenda.

Less than three hours after Mr. Ulbricht's statement today, Conrad Ahlers, the chief spokesman of the Bonn Government, said that Mr. Brandt would respond this week by sending a letter to the East German Premier, Willi Stoph, outlining his proposals. It was not immediately clear whether the West Germans planned to send a draft treaty to East Berlin as a counterpiece to the draft sent by Mr. Ulbricht to Bonn on Dec. 17.

At his news conference, the first in nearly nine years that he has held in his capital with Western newsmen attending, Mr. Ulbricht reiterated that West Germany must accord "internationally legal recognition of the state existence of the [East] German Democratic Republic."

He added that if Mr. Brandt were really "sincere" about offering a pact renouncing the use of force in bilateral relations, he "must prove it in the very first place by recognizing the G.D.R. as a sovereign German state and take up equal, that is, internationally legal relations."

Bonn Ready for Treaties

Since he took power in Bonn last October, Chancellor Brandt has said West Germany was prepared to make treaties with East Germany "binding in international law," but has asserted that he would not recognize East Germany as a "foreign country" since both states are parts of the "German nation."

In his speech to the parliament last week, Mr. Brandt said he did not regard Mr. Ulbricht's draft treaty proposing an exchange of ambassadors between Bonn and East Berlin as a useful basis for negotiations.

East German newsmen at today's news conference said it was "evident" that Mr. Ulbricht felt he was under pressure from the Soviet Union and other Communist allies to make a conciliatory gesture in response to Bonn's offers of a dialogue on renunciation of force and other issues. "But he did not give away much," one Communist correspondent commented.

The only signs of infirmities of age shown by Mr. Ulbricht, who was ailing last year, were occasional lapses in speech while he paused to catch his train of thought and two brief coughing spells.

Ironic Humor Shown

After he had warmed up with a 52-minute speech and an hour more of answering questions, he began accompanying his remarks with lively gestures, smiles and flashes of ironic humor, saying, for example: "We are old hands at fighting German imperialism—you cannot play Little Red Riding Hood and the wolf with us."

He indicated repeatedly that East Germany was in no hurry to begin negotiations with West Germany, saying: "We are patient people—we will wait."

He also made it plain that his readiness to negotiate with Mr. Brandt would depend almost entirely on the outcome of Bonn's month-old dialogue with the Soviet Union on renunciation of force.

"It is understandable," he said, "that we will wait above all for the result of the negotiations between the Soviet Union and the Federal Republic before we conclude a treaty with the Federal Republic of Germany on the basis of the Soviet negotiations."

In reply to a question, he added that he had consulted with the Russians on this subject and that "we are for a renunciation-of-force pact on the identical basis."

* * *

April 30, 1970

U.S. AIDS SAIGON PUSH IN CAMBODIA WITH PLANES, ARTILLERY, ADVISERS; MOVE STIRS OPPOSITION IN SENATE

RISING PERIL SEEN

Nixon to Speak on TV Tonight—Action Is Termed Limited

By WILLIAM BEECHER
Special to The New York Times.

WASHINGTON, April 29—The United States announced today that it was providing combat advisers, tactical air support, medical evacuation teams and some supplies to South Vietnamese troops attacking Communist bases in Cambodia.

The South Vietnamese offensive, involving thousands of troops, began this morning.

Announcing an expansion of the nine-year-old active United States involvement in Indochina, Daniel Z. Henkin, Assistant Secretary of Defense, for Public Affairs, said that North Vietnamese and Vietcong troops operating from Cambodia had "posed an increasing threat" to American and allied troops in South Vietnam.

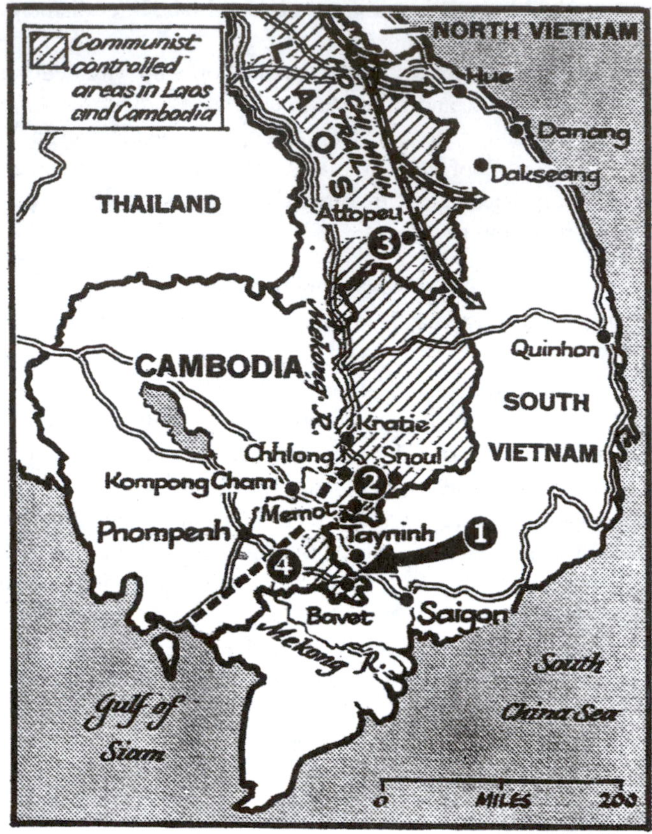

The New York Times

THRUST INTO CAMBODIA: The U.S.-backed Saigon force pushed to Bavet (1) in a Vietcong stronghold. Communist troops took Memot (2) in Cambodia and drove into Attopeu (3) in Laos in an apparently related action. Dotted line shows Cambodian area (4) where foe continued raids.

Move Is Unexpected

The Nixon Administration's unexpected move, which brought an immediate outcry in Congress, is to be discussed by the President in a televised address to the nation at 9 P.M. tomorrow.

The decision came after six weeks of intensive debate over the risks and opportunities of alternative courses of action against the Communist sanctuaries in Cambodia. The issue arose following the ouster of the neutralist Chief of State, Prince Norodom Sihanouk, on March 18, and the decision of the new Government to attempt to end the Communist forces use of Cambodian territory.

It was primarily an American decision that the offensive into Cambodia be staged, officials said privately, even though public statements stressed the South Vietnamese initiative.

Numbers Undisclosed

While Administration officials declined to say how many Americans would be involved or how long the South

Vietnamese offensive might take, some sources stressed in private the limited nature of the decision, estimating that the number of Americans would be "in the low hundreds."

They also said that the South Vietnamese troops and their American advisers were expected to stay on Cambodian soil only until enemy arms depots and bases could be destroyed, perhaps in a week or two.

A statement issued by the United States command in Saigon reported that Americans were also providing helicopters and artillery support.

The officials declined, in answer to questions, to give the legal basis for the Administration's support of the military action in Cambodia. They said it would be clarified by the President.

Mr. Henkin said that Washington had been fully consulted before the Saigon Government launched the offensive and that it had requested American support. To help foster the impression that the initiative was South Vietnam's it made the announcement both of the assault and of the United States role.

Ronald L. Ziegler, the White House press secretary, said the decision to provide American support should not be viewed as Mr. Nixon's answer to the request of Premier Lon Nol of Cambodia for military aid.

More than three weeks ago General Lon Nol appealed to the United States, as he had to other countries, to provide weapons for an expansion of his 35,000-man army to about 200,000 men. As an interim measure Washington agreed to supply several thousand captured AK-47 automatic rifles through the South Vietnamese.

There was some speculation that the President would announce a decision to provide American weapons to the shaky government. There was even some speculation that he might hold open the possibility of providing support to Cambodian troops in actions against enemy forces near the South Vietnamese border, giving as a basis that they were a common foe threatening the security of American forces and the viability of Cambodian's control over her territory.

Mr. Ziegler said Mr. Nixon would discuss "the entire situation in Cambodia as it relates to both Cambodia and U.S. forces in Vietnam."

Administration sources said the new South Vietnamese offensive might have the following effects:

- If it succeeds in destroying most of the enemy's combat supplies in the area of Cambodia known as the Parrot's Beak, which juts into South Vietnam, it should undermine enemy plans to launch a sustained offensive in the southern part of South Vietnam.
- It might shore up the Lon Nol Government by demonstrating strong outside support and by putting pressure on the enemy's rear areas.
- It might underscore Mr. Nixon's warning to Hanoi, issued last Nov. 3—and repeated three times since—that "if I conclude that increased enemy action jeopardizes our remaining forces in Vietnam, I should not hesitate to take strong and effective measures to deal with that situation."

The last point was underlined by officials concerned with the success of the Administration's strategy of withdrawal and disengagement, or Vietnamization of the war.

In the policy read by Mr. Henkin, the decision to support the offensive was explained as "a necessary and effective measure to save American and other free-world lives and to strengthen the Vietnamization program."

Military sources say the South Vietnamese offensive follows the pattern of search-and-destroy operations in enemy base areas in South Vietnam. Under these tactics, seldom employed any more in Vietnam, a large force moves in, searches for supply caches, headquarters, hospitals and base camps, destroying or removing anything of value to the enemy and then pulling out.

The American support, Mr. Henkin said, "will take the form of advisers, tactical air, air coordinators, medical evacuation, and some logistics assistance."

There are usually 100 to 200 American advisers, mostly officers of the rank of major to colonel, assigned to a Vietnamese division. They help plan operations and move into the field with commanders of subordinate units down to the battalion level.

The air support will be flown from bases in South Vietnam, the sources here said, with American "coordinators," or forward air controllers, operating from the ground and from small spotter planes to direct aerial attacks.

The officials say that the pace of American withdrawals from Vietnam, which has been averaging about 12,000 men a month since June, will probably be slowed temporarily until the enemy reacts to the latest move.

* * *

May 5, 1970

4 KENT STATE STUDENTS KILLED BY TROOPS

8 Hurt as Shooting Follows Reported Sniping at Rally

By JOHN KIFNER
Special to The New York Times.

KENT, Ohio, May 4—Four students at Kent State University, two of them women, were shot to death this afternoon by a volley of National Guard gunfire. At least 8 other students were wounded.

The burst of gunfire came about 20 minutes after the guardsmen broke up a noon rally on the Commons, a grassy campus gathering spot, by lobbing tear gas at a crowd of about 1,000 young people.

In Washington, President Nixon deplored the deaths of the four students in the following statement:

"This should remind us all once again that when dissent turns to violence it invites tragedy. It is my hope that this tragic and unfortunate incident will strengthen the determination of all the nation's campuses, administrators, faculty and students alike to stand firmly for the right which exists in this country of peaceful dissent and just as strongly against the resort to violence as a means of such expression."

In Columbus, Sylvester Del Corso, Adjutant General of the Ohio National Guard, said in a statement that the guardsmen had been forced to shoot after a sniper opened fire against the troops from a nearby rooftop and the crowd began to move to encircle the guardsmen.

Frederick P. Wenger, the Assistant Adjutant General, said the troops had opened fire after they were shot at by a sniper.

"They were under standing orders to take cover and return any fire," he said.

This reporter, who was with the group of students, did not see any indication of sniper fire, nor was the sound of any gunfire audible before the Guard volley. Students, conceding that rocks had been thrown, heatedly denied that there was any sniper.

Gov. James A. Rhodes called on J. Edgar Hoover, director of the Federal Bureau of Investigation, to aid in looking into the campus violence. A Justice Department spokesman said no decision had been made to investigate.

At 2:10 this afternoon, after the shootings, the university president, Robert I. White, ordered the university closed for an indefinite time, and officials were making plans to evacuate the dormitories and bus out-of-state students to nearby cities.

Robinson Memorial Hospital identified the dead students as Allison Krause, 19 years old, of Pittsburgh: Sandra Lee Scheuer, 20, of Youngstown, Ohio, both coeds; Jeffrey Glenn Miller, 20, of 22 Diamond Drive, Plainview, L. I., and William K. Schroeder, 19, of Lorain, Ohio.

At 10:30 P.M. the hospital said that six students had been treated for gunshot wounds. Three were reported in critical condition and three in fair condition. Two others with superficial wounds were treated and released.

Students here, angered by the expansion of the war into Cambodia, have held demonstrations for the last three nights. On Saturday night, the Army Reserve Officers Training Corps building was burned to the ground and the Guard was called in and martial law was declared.

Today's rally, called after a night in which the police and guardsmen drove students into their dormitories and made 69 arrests, began as students rang the iron Victory Bell on the commons, normally used to herald football victories.

A National Guard jeep drove onto the Commons and an officer ordered the crowd to disperse. Then several canisters of tear gas were fired, and the students straggled up a hill that borders the area and retreated into buildings.

A platoon of guardsmen, armed—as they have been since they arrived here with loaded M-I rifles and gas equipment—moved across the green and over the crest of the hill, chasing the main body of protesters.

The youths split into two groups, one heading farther downhill toward a dormitory complex, the other eddying around a parking lot and girls' dormitory just below Taylor Hall, the architecture building.

The guardsmen moved into a grassy area just below the parking lot and fired several canisters of tear gas from their short, stubby launchers.

Three or four youths ran to the smoking canisters and hurled them back. Most fell far short, but one landed near the troops and a cheer went up from the crowd, which was chanting "Pigs off campus" and cursing the war.

A few youths in the front of the crowd ran into the parking lot and hurled rocks or small chunks of pavement in the direction of the guardsmen. Then the troops began moving back up the hill in the direction of the college.

Students Cheer

The students in the parking lot area, numbering about 500, began to move toward the rear of the troops, cheering. Again, a few in front picked up stones from the edge of the parking lot and threw them at the guardsmen. Another group of several hundred students had gathered around the sides of Taylor Hall watching.

As the guardsmen, moving up the hill in single file, reached the crest, they suddenly turned, forming a skirmish line and opening fire.

The crackle of the rifle volley cut the suddenly still air. It appeared to go on, as a solid volley, for perhaps a full minute or a little longer.

Some of the students dived to the ground, crawling on the grass in terror. Others stood shocked or half crouched, apparently believing the troops were firing into the air. Some of the rifle barrels were pointed upward.

Near the top of the hill at the corner of Taylor Hall, a student crumpled over, spun sideways and fell to the ground, shot in the head.

When the firing stopped, a slim girl, wearing a cowboy shirt and faded jeans, was lying face down on the road at the edge of the parking lot, blood pouring out onto the macadam, about 10 feet from this reporter.

Too Shocked to React

The youths stood stunned, many of them clustered in small groups staring at the bodies. A young man cradled one of the bleeding forms in his arms. Several girls began to cry. But many of the students who rushed to the scene seemed almost too shocked to react. Several gathered around an abstract steel sculpture in front of the building and looked at a 30-caliber bullet hole drilled through one of the plates.

The hospital said that six young people were being treated for gunshot wounds, some in the intensive care unit. Three of the students who were killed were dead on arrival at the hospital.

One guardsman was treated and released at the hospital and another was admitted with heat prostration.

In early afternoon, students attempted to gather at various area of the Commons but were ordered away by guardsman and the Ohio Highway Patrol, which moved in as reinforcements.

Tarentum Valley Daily News via Associated Press

A girl screams as fellow student lies dead after National Guardsmen opened fire at Kent State.

There were no further clashes, as faculty members, graduate assistants and students leaders urged the crowd to go back to the dormitories.

But a bizarre atmosphere hung over the campus as a Guard helicopter hovered overhead, grim-faced officers maneuvered their men to safeguard the normally pastoral campus and students, dazed, fearful and angry, struggled to comprehend what had happened and to find something to do about it.

Students carrying suitcases and duffel bags began leaving the campus this afternoon. Early tonight the entire campus was sealed off and a court injunction was issued ordering all students to leave.

A 5 P.M. curfew was declared in Kent, and road blocks were set up around the town to prevent anyone from entering. A state of emergency was also declared in the nearby towns of Stow and Ravenna.

* * *

August 13, 1970

PACT WITH SOVIET SIGNED BY BRANDT IN KREMLIN PALACE

Kosygin Acts for Moscow—U.S. Hails Step, but Looks to 'Tangible' Results

By BERNARD GWERTZMAN
Special to The New York Times.

MOSCOW, Aug. 12—Chancellor Willy Brandt of West Germany and Premier Aleksei N. Kosygin of the Soviet Union signed a treaty today accepting the postwar European borders as inviolable and opening the way to closer ties between Bonn and the Communist nations of Eastern Europe.

The treaty, a result of months of negotiation, was signed in the ornate white and gold St. Catherine's Hall in the Great Kremlin Palace by the two chiefs of government and their Foreign Ministers, Walter Scheel and Andrei A. Gromyko.

United Press International

A NEW RELATIONSHIP: Chancellor Willy Brandt of West Germany, left, and Premier Aleksei N. Kosygin of the Soviet Union signing a treaty to improve German-Soviet ties.

The ceremony was televised in the Soviet Union and throughout Eastern Europe.

[In Washington, Secretary of State William P. Rogers hailed the treaty as a "first step" and called on the Soviet Union for "tangible evidence" of goodwill in improving the situation in divided Berlin.]

Two Premiers in Accord

After the signing, Mr. Brandt said to Mr. Kosygin:

"This is the end of an epoch but, it seems to me, a very good beginning."

"I'm completely of your opinion," Mr. Kosygin replied.

From the Soviet viewpoint the signing, 25 years after the end of World War II, represented Bonn's acceptance of the status quo in Europe. From Chancellor Brandt's point of view his presence in the Soviet capital represented his Government's attempt to break with precedent and deal with the realities of the European situation.

In a speech recorded in Moscow for West German television, Chancellor Brandt hailed the treaty as a success for his policies of seeking better relations with Eastern Europe.

'A Path Forward'

"The treaty endangers nothing and no one," he said. "It should help to open a path forward. And if it does this, it will serve peace, Europe and all of us."

Tass, the Soviet press agency, in an authoritative commentary on the treaty, called it "a milestone in Europe's postwar history."

"The significance of the treaty," Tass said, "by far transcends the boundaries of mutual relations between the two countries. It will facilitate an improvement in the political climate in Europe and may, to a certain extent, facilitate an improvement in the general international situation."

The treaty does not go into effect until it is ratified by the West German Bundestag and the Supreme Soviet. Mr. Brandt's Government has said that it will not offer it for ratification until the Soviet Union agrees to improve the status of West Berlin in talks with the Western powers, due to resume next month. According to Mr. Scheel, Mr. Gromyko indicated the Soviet Union would agree to some improvement in Berlin's status if the treaty was signed.

The treaty contains wording interpreted by Mr. Brandt and Mr. Scheel as leaving open the possibility of eventual unification of Germany on a peaceful basis, although this is not deemed probable for the near future.

Article 3 of the five-article treaty asserts that the two sides "regard the frontiers of all the states in Europe today and in the future as inviolable, as they stand on the date of the signing of the present treaty, including the Oder-Neisse line, which forms the western frontier of the People's Republic of Poland, and the frontier between the Federal Republic of Germany and the German Democratic Republic."

Mr. Brandt asserts that this wording does not rule out a future agreement by the two German states to merge into one, and the Soviet side, according to West German sources, does not contest this interpretation.

In return for Mr. Brandt's acceptance of the status quo in Europe, the Russians have in effect given their endorsement to his policy of seeking better ties with Eastern Europe without breaking Bonn's alliance with the Western powers.

It is expected that in coming months West Germany will take steps to establish diplomatic ties with Poland and other Warsaw Pact states as well as enlarge its economic relations with those countries.

Soviet Seeks Technical Ties

Soviet leaders made it clear to Mr. Brandt in private talks that they intended to take advantage of the paragraph in the preamble calling for improved "economic relations, as well as well as scientific, technological and cultural ties.

In a meeting this morning, Mr. Kosygin was reported by a Bonn spokesman to have emphasized the desire of the Soviet Union to establish long-range trade and technological ties with West Germany.

Mr. Kosygin was reported to have been frank in stating that the Soviet Union would seek Western help in exploiting its natural resources.

It was agreed that Karl Schiller, Minister of Economy, and Hans Leussink, Minister of Science and Education, would come to Moscow next month to discuss ways of improving economic and technological ties. West Germany is now fourth behind Britain, Japan and Finland in trade by non-Communist countries with the Soviet Union.

Mr. Kosygin reportedly asked Mr. Brandt about the possibility of a new Nazi-style government's taking power in Bonn. Mr. Brandt replied that the socioeconomic conditions that led to Hitler's rise could not be repeated today.

Leonid I. Brezhnev, the Soviet party leader, who was present at the signing, had a discussion with Mr. Brandt in the afternoon before a Kremlin dinner in the Chancellor's honor. Tass said the two leaders "expressed confidence that the treaty opens up possibilities for a further development of relations between the two countries and for the strengthening of European security.

* * *

October 23, 1970

GROMYKO MEETS NIXON TWO HOURS IN 'HELPFUL' TALKS

Discussion Is Described as Positive, but No Specific Progress Is Disclosed

MIDEAST SPLIT PERSISTS

Other Topics Are Indochina, Berlin, European Parley and Arms Negotiations

By HEDRICK SMITH
Special to The New York Times.

WASHINGTON, Oct. 22—President Nixon met for more than two hours today with the Soviet Foreign Minister, Andrei A. Gromyko, for talks that both sides described in positive terms. But no specific progress was disclosed on the wide range of issues discussed.

American officials later said the two sides had not broken the deadlock over the Middle East cease-fire and resumption of Arab-Israeli peace negotiations, nor did they see any compromise within reach at the moment.

In an apparent effort to tone down their public sparring, both the White House and Mr. Gromyko chose in public comments after the meeting to emphasize prospects for improving the climate of Soviet-American relations.

No Details Disclosed

Neither side would disclose the details and specific topics that included the Middle East, Indochina, Berlin, European security, strategic arms negotiations, and the landing of two American generals from Turkey in Soviet Armenia. Cuba, a recent point of contention, was not discussed.

The President evidently made the point that the two superpowers must refrain from trying to seize tactical advantages in such areas as the Middle East, Berlin or Cuba in the interest of the broader goal of maintaining world peace. Mr. Gromyko's response was not disclosed though American officials were understood to be somewhat encouraged.

"The meeting was conducted in a friendly atmosphere," Ronald L. Ziegler, the White House press secretary, told newsmen. "It is felt the meeting was helpful for laying the basis for improved relations between the United States and the Soviet Union."

In a brief statement distributed by the Soviet embassy, Mr. Gromyko echoed that cautiously positive assessment. He said he had found the discussions "interesting" and he hoped both the meeting and the talks "will be of positive significance for the development and improvement of Soviet American relations."

As if to emphasize the civil atmosphere despite substantive disagreements, American officials noted that Mr. Gromyko had been the highest Soviet official with whom President Nixon had met since taking office. The White

House noted that their meeting, which lasted 2 hours and 25 minutes, had been "one of the longest, if not the longest" Mr. Nixon has held with any foreign visitor.

The decision to emphasize the positive aspects of the session contrasted not only with the tart tone of Mr. Gromyko's speech to the United Nations General Assembly yesterday, but also with recent comments by American officials raising doubts about Soviet intentions.

After the session American officials discounted the tough tone of Mr. Gromyko's speech as typical public rhetoric. They said they had found his speech less harsh than last year's.

Mr. Ziegler said that a major part of President Nixon's address to the United Nations tomorrow would deal with Soviet-American relations. The President was reported to be working on the speech late today, but officials would not say whether his meeting with Mr. Gromyko had necessitated any revisions.

The President and Mr. Gromyko began their session at the Oval Room in the White House, joking and in apparent relaxation. They were joined by Secretary of State William P. Rogers; Henry A. Kissinger, Presidential adviser on national security affairs, and Ambassador Anatoly F. Dobrynin, and talked for roughly two hours through interpreters.

Then they went next door to Mr. Nixon's office at the Executive Office Building for a private, 15-minute discussion without aides or interpreters.

If today's talks went as planned, President Nixon emphasized the sincerity of recent proposals for a broadened Indochina peace conference and a cease-fire throughout the region. Mr. Nixon had also wanted to make clear that the American attitude toward the European security conference, which Moscow favors, would be largely determined by progress in the Berlin talks.

Earlier this week, in a meeting with Secretary of State Rogers, Mr. Gromyko reportedly told the Americans that they had misunderstood the Soviet line in the Berlin talks. He reportedly said that Moscow was not demanding that West Germany remove all its federal offices from West Berlin. The United States has taken a wait-and-see attitude toward this explanation.

Although the United States gave the impression in late September that it considered Soviet moves in Cuba, Berlin and the Middle East provocative, the White House today was playing down any such concern.

Officials disclosed that the United States had taken the initiative of encouraging Mr. Gromyko to call on President Nixon.

This contradicted the impression left by American officials earlier this week that Moscow had initiated the procedure and that the appointment had been granted only after Mr. Gromyko had taken a more conciliatory tone in his talks with Mr. Rogers on Monday.

* * *

November 15, 1970

SOVIET'S REMOVAL OF VESSEL IN CUBA IS AWAITED BY U.S.

Submarine-Support Ship Is Expected to Go as Result of an Understanding

NUCLEAR ARMS AT ISSUE

American Officials Hopeful Secret Talks Resolved Dispute Over Base

By BENJAMIN WELLES
Special to The New York Times.

WASHINGTON, Nov. 14—For seven weeks, the United States has been engaged in secret diplomacy to prevent the Soviet Union from basing nuclear-missile submarines or installing nuclear weapons in the Western Hemisphere. Now American officials believe that an understanding has been reached.

The officials said they would regard the departure of a Soviet submarine tender from the Cuban port of Cienfuegos in the coming days as proof that the Russians accept the understanding. The vessel normally carries spare nuclear weapons and such facilities as high-powered cranes for handling submarine nuclear arms.

Early Departure Likely

The officials disputed a report from another highly credible source that the tender would leave within the next two or three days.

Current discussions between Washington and Moscow over this issue are in such a delicate state, the officials warned, that the national interest might be impaired by anything that Moscow might misinterpret as an ultimatum, even through press reports.

They did confirm that the United States had warned the Soviet Union that anything resembling a permanent nuclear facility in Cuban or other Hemisphere waters would seriously jeopardize American-Soviet relations.

Heart of Understanding

Reliable American sources indicate that the heart of the understanding is an unwritten pledge by the Soviet Union not to base missile-carrying nuclear submarines, store nuclear weapons or install repair and servicing facilities anywhere in the Western Hemisphere.

In return, the American sources indicate, the United States will closely watch but not obstruct periodic visits by the Soviet fleet to Cuban or other Hemisphere ports for shore leave for crewmen and for routine ship maintenance.

Other sources, including some in the intelligence community, know enough of the facts to express considerable reserve over the understanding.

They say that recent aerial reconnaissance photographs of Cienfuegos show bulldozers still grading in the port's southeast section, which is reserved for Soviet use; a submarine net is still in place across this section of the harbor; two new barracks have recently been erected, capable of housing about 100 men each; recreation fields have been built and construction appears to be continuing on a communications center. Nothing has been dismantled up to the last 24 hours, the sources say.

Neither the Soviet Embassy nor the White House would comment today on the details of the understanding and officials at the State and Defense departments were under orders to say nothing.

The understanding is reported to have been reached after discussions between Henry A. Kissinger, President Nixon's adviser for national security affairs, and Foreign Minister Andrei A. Gromyko and Ambassador Anatoly F. Dobrynin of the Soviet Union.

Only a few officials beside the President and Mr. Kissinger are said to know the facts. They are believed to include Secretary of Defense Melvin R. Laird; Secretary of State William P. Rogers; U. Alexis Johnson, Under Secretary of State for Political Affairs; Richard Helms, Director of Central Intelligence, Adm. Thomas H. Moorer, Chairman of the Joint Chiefs of Staff, and a few subordinates.

The secrecy has been compounded by the fact that Premier Fidel Castro, normally quick to assail the United States as intervening in Cuban affairs, has refrained from any public mention of the American furor over Soviet activities at Cienfuegos.

Based on 1962 Accord

The Administration appears to be basing its understanding on the 1962 agreement between President John F. Kennedy and Premier Nikita S. Khruschev, under which the Russians removed the nuclear missiles and bombers they had implanted in Cuba and President Kennedy pledged that there would be "peace in the Caribbean" if the weapons were not reintroduced into the Hemisphere.

However, because the President tied the promise to "appropriate United Nations observation and supervision," which was not permitted by Premier Castro, some State Department officials and others believe the Kennedy-Khrushchev agreement to be inoperative. However, Mr. Kissinger and his immediate aides appear to be using it as the basis of the current understanding.

The 1962 declaration was mentioned on Friday by Robert McCloskey, State Department spokesman, in stating that the Nixon Administration believed it had an understanding with the Soviet Union over the limits "to their actions with respect to Cuba."

Mr. McCloskey was asked whether the understanding was based on negotiations in addition to a Soviet denial Oct. 13 that Moscow was building "its own military base" in Cuba and a reported private meeting in New York on Oct. 19 between Mr. Gromyko and Mr. Rogers.

The spokesmen conceded that there might have been unpublicized contacts, but added that he had no information on them.

"Even if there were," he said, "I'm not sure I would be in a position to discuss them publicly."

The basis of the United States concern stems from the presence of the 9,000-ton Ugraclass tender and two barges. Nuclear submarines are normally serviced by tenders, or support ships, that carry spare weapons and equipment for repairs and maintenance at sea.

The barges have aroused concern because they were transported on a tank-landing ship across the Atlantic from the Soviet naval base at Polyarny, near Murmansk, to Havana and then towed around western Cuba to Cienfuegos on Sept. 11. They have no power of their own and therefore, experts say, are intended as a permanent fixture. Their function is to store radioactive wastes discharged from a nuclear submarine's reactors.

The support ships service Soviet nuclear submarines bearing the Western code name "Y-class," which is the most modern type, carrying 16 missiles like the Polaris with a range of 1,500 miles.

Defense experts stress that the Soviet Union has at least three such submarines on station in the western Atlantic. Altogether 13 submarines of this type are said to be operational with 17 more nearing readiness. Eight to ten are said to be built each year.

The potential importance of Cienfuegos, according to specialists, would be to permit the submarines to avoid the 8,000-mile round trip from their West Atlantic stations back to Polyarny. Crew fatigue normally limits cruises to 60 to 90 days.

Affair Began in August

The Cuban affair came to the attention of American intelligence when agents and Cuban refugees last August reported Soviet construction activity around Cienfuegos. With the visit by a Soviet naval flotilla on Sept. 9-12, United States interest sharpened.

U-2 reconnaissance planes, which have been photographing Cuba about every fortnight, took pictures about Sept. 14.

The rolls of film were processed at the U-2 base in Texas and the negatives were flown to the National Photo Interpretation Center in Washington. There positives were ready about six hours after the actual photographing of the base.

The photo interpretation center is operated jointly by the Central Intelligence Agency and the Defense Department in a former Navy building in southeast Washington. Photo analysts work in shifts around the clock, studying film. They use optical equipment for detecting camouflage and eliminating distortion. Military experts are at hand to analyze the pictures.

Listed in C.I.A. Bulletin

The photographs of the two barges were mentioned in the C.I.A.'s 10-page morning bulletin of Sept. 15 and stimulated the interest of Secretary Rogers, Mr. Johnson and Mr. Kissinger. For the next eight days the Administration was absorbed with the crisis in the Middle East, where Israel had charged cease-fire violations by Egypt.

But on Sept. 23 orders from Mr. Kissinger's office forbade discussion of the new evidence that the Russians were preparing Cienfuegos to support nuclear-powered submarines. The Defense Department was permitted to discuss Soviet ship movements, but nothing else.

The first public report of what the Russians were doing appeared in The New York Times on Sept. 25 in a column by C. L. Sulzberger. Mr. Sulzberger said that the Soviet move was equivalent to the installation of missiles in Cuba in 1962, with the difference that the Russians now had nuclear submarines operating in the Atlantic.

Mr. Sulzberger linked Cuba with Chile, where a new leftist President, Dr. Salvador Allende Gossens, was about to take office. The columnist suggested that if Chile were backed up "even inferentially" by a Soviet base in Cuba, it might jeopardize present efforts to achieve a relaxation of tension between Moscow and Washington.

That day, Jerry W. Friedheim, Deputy Assistant Secretary of Defense for Public Affairs, in answer to questions raised by Mr. Sulzberger's article, said the United States did not know whether the Soviet Union was building a submarine support base, but mentioned the presence of barges among "the indications that make us feel" that the Russians want to establish a base.

Briefing at White House

Later that day, at a briefing on President Nixon's planned trip to the Mediterranean, a White House official told newsmen that the United States was watching developments at Cienfuegos.

The Soviet Union, he said, should not doubt that the United States would view the establishment of a strategic base in the Caribbean with the utmost seriousness.

He drew attention to President Kennedy's pledge of Nov. 20, 1962, that there would be peace in the Caribbean, providing the Soviet Union removed its nuclear weapons from Cuba and kept them out of the Hemisphere in the future.

"This remains the policy of this government," the White House spokesman said.

State and Defense department officials expressed private puzzlement about the high-level warnings. News reports of this perplexity in Government quarters were said to have irritated the White House.

On Oct. 10 the submarine support ship and a tug left Cienfuegos, apparently rounding western Cuba and heading northeast across the Atlantic as if for home. The two barges remained behind. Secretary Laird, appearing the next day with Secretary Rogers on the American Broadcasting Company's television program, "Issues and Answers," expressed concern over Soviet activity at Cienfuegos.

The next day, at a news conference, he said the activity "does not follow the under-standing that I believe was comprehended by both sides in 1962."

On Oct. 13, Tass, the Soviet press agency, issued a statement saying that the Soviet Union "has not been, and is not, building its own military base" in Cuba. The State Department spokesman said at a briefing that the United States considered the statement positive.

It was believed that the United States comment, prepared presumably at Mr. Kissinger's office, had been intended to signal to Moscow that Washington was satisfied with the Tass statement.

Tender Puts into Mariel

Daniel Z. Henkin, Assistant Defense Secretary for Public Affairs, noted the same day that in view of the departure of the tender and tug, it was now less likely that the Russians were building a submarine base.

However, four days later, on Oct. 17, the submarine tender and its tug turned around and put into the port of Mariel, 25 miles west of Havana. It was through Mariel that Soviet missiles and bombers were shipped in 1962 and later removed. Defense Department experts were unable to explain why the tender and tug were there.

On Oct. 19 Secretary Rogers talked privately with Foreign Minister Gromyko. They had met on the 16th but had not discussed Cuba. This time, Mr. Rogers told newsmen that he had raised the Cuban issue. He said the United States considered the matter resolved.

Mr. Kissinger then assumed a central role.

On Oct. 22 at about 4:45 P.M., Sam Jaffe, a United Press International radio reporter in front of the Soviet Union's mission on East 67th Street in New York, observed the arrival of Mr. Gromyko on his return from a United Nations meeting, followed four minutes later by Mr. Kissinger.

Mr. Jaffe tried to get the White House adviser to explain into a hand-held-microphone what brought him to the Soviet mission, but Mr. Kissinger, visibly startled, declined to answer and disappeared into the mission.

During the next hour and a half Maurice Schumann, the French Foreign Minister, also entered the Soviet mission, for an appointment with Mr. Gromyko. There were reports later that Mr. Gromyko had talked initially about Cuba with Mr. Kissinger but, because Mr. Schumann was waiting, had turned the White House official over to Ambassador Dobrynin to reach a mutually satisfactory agreement.

In any event, Mr. Kissinger left the Soviet mission at 6:27 P.M., with the ambassador showing him to the door, hurried past Mr. Jaffe, jumped into his car and was presumably driven to the airport. An hour and a half later there was a message for Secretary Rogers at the Waldorf Towers to call Mr. Kissinger in Washington. Observers suggested that the Secretary of State had been given instructions for a quiet talk with Mr. Gromyko during the evening at a dinner both were attending.

On Nov. 10 the submarine tender and the tug sailed out of Mariel, circled around the coast and back to Cienfuegos.

Some analysts believe that the Soviet Union may have agreed to remove facilities in Cienfuegos capable of supporting nuclear missile submarines, once world attention had died down. This, they say, may account for the secrecy imposed on the State and Defense Departments.

Yet these analysts also believe that the Administration will again claim victory through "strong but quiet diplomacy," as Herbert Klein, the President's director of communications did on Nov. 2 in a San Diego news conference. Mr. Klein said the "last of the equipment was pulled out over the weekend," a contention that intelligence photographs now refute.

Some intelligence and diplomatic experts feel that the removal of the submarine tender, even though important, will not be significant so long as the other installations for operations of a nuclear-missile submarine remains.

The Soviet Y-class submarine fleet is steadily growing, they say; the bulldozers are still working; the barracks are ready; the soccer field awaiting players; the submarine net is in its place, the communications center appears to be undergoing preparation and above all, the barges for the radioactive waste are still in Cienfuegos harbor.

"They may pull the tender out," said one source, "but I don't see anything to stop them from coming back in anytime they want. They have the legal right to. It's up to them and the Cubans."

Some officials believe, on the other hand, that Mr. Kissinger's display of quiet diplomacy may yet succeed in persuading Moscow to drop plans for a submarine base as a token of its desire for a relaxation of tension.

* * *

November 19, 1970

POLISH-WEST GERMAN PACT IS INITIALED BY MINISTERS

By JAMES FERON

Special to The New York Times.

WARSAW, Aug. 18—The Foreign Ministers of Poland and West Germany today put their initials to a treaty seeking reconciliation after the painful past of World War II.

The pact includes recognition of the Oder-Neisse line as Poland's western frontier, acknowledging the transfer of 40,000 square miles of prewar German territory to Poland.

It also calls for normal relations between Bonn and Warsaw. Their trade missions are expected to be raised to consular level and eventually embassies are to be established.

The treaty, drafted over a 10-month period, was initialed at noon in a downtown villa by Stefan Jedrychowski of Poland and Walter Scheel of West Germany.

Mr. Scheel indicated at a reception that the text of the nine-page document will be made public on Friday.

Mr. Jedrychowski, speaking first after the leatherbound pact had been initialed, said the accord "constitutes a lasting basis for normalizing relations between our two states."

"In closing the past," he said, "it will open a new propitious and fruitful era of relations between our two countries and between our two peoples."

Standing next to him was Premier Jozef Cyrankiewicz, who is scheduled to sign the document in a few weeks when Chancellor Willy Brandt comes to Warsaw.

Mr. Cyrankiewicz's presence added a poignant note to the gathering. He is a former inmate of Auschwitz, the Nazi extermination camp.

Mr. Jedrychowski, speaking Polish as an aide translated his words into German, said the treaty "settled difficult issues that derive from an exceedingly difficult past."

Mr. Scheel acknowledged what he characterized as the "painful past" and hinted at a possibly difficult near future as far as West German ratification of the treaty was concerned.

He told Mr. Jedrychowski that a "sharp struggle has yet to be waged for approval of the treaty by appropriate parliamentary bodies in the Federal Republic of Germany and by German public opinion."

Mr. Scheel said this struggle was a "normal and necessary process for real German-Polish reconciliation." He added that his Government would unswervingly continue its policy and would eventually win broad approval at home.

The allusion was to Chancellor Brandt's attempt to heal the wounds of the Nazi period by seeking new diplomatic and economic ties with the Soviet Union and its East European allies.

Mr. Scheel added that Poland could help the Brandt Government gain ratification by moving quickly on the ethnic-German issue, which loomed large in the negotiations.

The issue concerns Germans living in the territory acquired by Poland after the war. Although most Germans left soon after the area's annexation by Poland, Bonn contends that many of those remaining still want to emigrate. The Poles have apparently promised to examine individual cases in what they describe as a "humanitarian" problem.

The issue is important in West Germany where several million former residents of what is now Polish territory represent a serious political factor. Some of Chancellor Brandt's domestic opposition has focused on the question of the ethnic Germans remaining in Poland.

Mr. Scheel spoke of the "bitter struggle" that had been waged over some issues in the treaty, but he said both sides had been aware that it would represent a turning point in their relations.

The initialing took three minutes and the speeches ten. Then, almost with relief, those present reached for glasses of champagne and, smiling for the first time during the ceremony, toasted one another.

Mr. Scheel arrived by plane from Bonn an hour before the ceremony and left four hours later.

The pact was hammered out during seven negotiating sessions in Bonn and Warsaw. The final round, led by the foreign ministers, lasted nearly two weeks and ended last Saturday at dawn.

* * *

December 4, 1970

NIXON GIVES NATO PLEDGE ON TROOPS

Bars Unilateral Reduction—
East Germany Is Pressed by Bloc on Ties to Bonn

By DREW MIDDLETON
Special to The New York Times.

BRUSSELS, Dec. 3—President Nixon told the North Atlantic Alliance today that the United States would not reduce its forces in Europe "unless there is reciprocal action from our adversaries."

At the same time, the alliance's three main powers—the United States, Britain and West Germany—expressed opposition to the Soviet-bloc proposal for a European security conference now.

The United States, the President said, will maintain and improve its forces in an alliance "confronted by a formidable mix of a potentially hostile force which is constantly improving."

Read by Rogers

Mr. Nixon's statement was read by Secretary of State William P. Rogers at the opening session of the meeting of foreign ministers of the 15 members of the Western alliance.

[After a meeting in East Berlin on Wednesday, Soviet-bloc leaders indicated that East Germany had been forced to give ground in its reluctance to improve relations with Bonn. Wladyslaw Gomulka, the Polish leader, said that West Germany's treaties with Moscow and Warsaw should be followed by similar understandings with East Germany and Czechoslovakia.]

In his accompanying speech, Mr. Rogers opposed further movement by the alliance toward the conference on European security on the ground of insufficient progress in the Big Four talks over Berlin and the discussions between East and West Germany.

Secretary Rogers did suggest that the Soviet bloc be urged to agree to exploratory talks next year on "mutual and balanced" reduction of forces. But, as one European pointed out, the Soviet Union has opposed discussing such reductions before a security conference was held.

Allied delegates and NATO diplomats sensed a stiffening of the West's attitude toward the Soviet bloc in Mr. Nixon's statement and in the speeches by Mr. Rogers, Sir Alec Douglas-Home, Foreign Secretary of Britain, and Walter Scheel, Foreign Minister of West Germany.

To these three ministers talk of "détente"—so popular a concept at the Rome meeting in May—was secondary now to warnings about Soviet power from the Indian Ocean to central Europe and to proposals for a stronger Western defensive position.

Repeating his Government's opposition to a security conference now, Mr. Scheel emphasized that "a substantial withdrawal of United States forces would result in the collapse of the Western alliance." He also "warmly welcomed" President Nixon's message.

Mr. Scheel called the Berlin talks "a crucial test case in which the Soviet Union will have to prove its will for a balanced East-West relationship."

Sir Alec's view was that the West must be adamant about its security but should proceed with flexibility.

The North Atlantic Treaty Organization, Sir Alec said, should not commit itself to exploratory talks on mutual and balanced cuts in forces as long as the Soviet Union displayed a negative attitude in the Berlin discussions.

French Back Parley

Another speaker, Foreign Minister Maurice Schumann of France, said that a conference in European security would be the best possible starting point for renewed and improved Western relations with the Soviet bloc. A successful agreement on Berlin, he said, should be the only condition for such a conference.

The French minister took a position on West Berlin's future relations with West Germany that differed sharply from that of the United States and Britain. They believed that political, economic and cultural links between the city and the federal republic should continue unimpaired. Mr. Schumann, according to French officials, mentioned only economic and cultural links.

He also acknowledged Europe's military dependence on the United States in terms rarely heard since France ended her military integration with the alliance in 1966. Should United States forces depart, Europe would be almost defenseless, he said.

Luns Also Gloomy

Dr. Joseph M. A. H. Luns, the Foreign Minister of the Netherlands, took a gloomy view of East-West relations. Like his colleagues, he saw the Soviet attitude in the Berlin talks as the key to meaningful negotiations in a European security conference. But such a conference, he said, is still distant.

These speeches, taken with events Tuesday and Wednesday, give NATO a more militant aspect, diplomats said, than any seen since the December meeting two years ago after the Soviet-led invasion of Czechoslovakia.

On Tuesday, the so-called Eurogroup—the 10 European countries of the alliance—announced a package amounting to nearly $1-billion to be invested in organization, weapons and men during the next five years. Yesterday, the Defense Planning Committee put forward its proposals for a stronger alliance under the title "Allied Defense for the Seventies."

Consequently, many diplomats see the alliance returning to the militancy of the cold war years and only two of 14 interviewed appeared to be disturbed by this. The others maintained that this was the only road to realistic negotiation with the Warsaw Pact, the Soviet-bloc military alliance.

Nixon Speech Welcomed

In this spirit, President Nixon's affirmation of intentions to maintain United States forces in Europe was heartily welcomed by the foreign ministers. To many, Mr. Nixon's statement went beyond Secretary of Defense Melvin R. Laird's pledge on Monday that American troop levels, now at 285,000, would not be reduced through the fiscal 1972 fiscal year.

Few European diplomats believe the Soviet Union is prepared to take the "reciprocal action" that Mr. Nixon said might prompt American withdrawals.

According to United States officials, Mr. Rogers said at the meeting that recent events had shown that the Russians might be expected to assert their power in a crude way even if this worsened dangerous situations.

The official said, however, that he saw an element of prudence in Moscow's conduct, which sometimes leads to a real desire for negotiation leading to useful agreements.

* * *

December 7, 1970

BRANDT IN POLAND, SIGNS PACT TODAY FOR NORMAL TIES

Treaty Accepts Control by Warsaw of Lands East of Oder-Neisse Line

GREETING IS CORDIAL

Ethnic Germans Expected to Get Exit Permits Starting in Month

By JAMES FERON
Special to The New York Times.

WARSAW, Dec. 6—Chancellor Willy Brandt of West Germany arrived here tonight to sign a treaty opening normal relations with Poland.

The pact, negotiated and initiated here last month by their Foreign Ministers, will be signed tomorrow by Mr. Brandt and the Polish Premier, Jozef Cyrankiewicz.

It represents the second major stage in the West German Chancellor's "Ostpolitik" following a similar pact signed in Moscow last August with Soviet leaders.

The Warsaw treaty acknowledges Poland's acquisition of 40,000 square miles of prewar German territory by stating that the line termed by the Oder and Neisse Rivers represents Poland's western frontier with East Germany.

Exit Permits Expected

Poland was expected, meanwhile, to begin issuing exit permits to ethnic Germans still living in Poland to fulfill a diplomatic promise made to West Germany. West German Red Cross officials have disclosed that 90,000 ethnic Germans will be allowed to emigrate in 1971 and 1972.

West Germany reportedly has contended that 200,000 ethnic Germans have sought to join families in West Germany. They were among several million Germans living in the 40,000 square miles of Germany given to Poland after World War II.

For the West Germans, the treaty eliminates a border issue that had blocked normal relations with Poland and enables Mr. Brandt to continue his policy of restoring ties with Eastern Europe.

Negotiations with Czechoslovakia over a "normalization" treaty are expected to be next, followed by talks with Hungary. Discussions with East Germany also are in progress.

Krupp Man Present

Mr. Brandt arrived at Warsaw's military airport in a twin-engine Government jet, accompanied by a dozen leading West German personalities. Among them was Berthold Beitz, chairman of the supervisory board of Krupp, the steel company, whose trading activities in Poland and other East European states had paved the way for the restoration of diplomatic links.

Also in the German party were Henri Nannen, editor of the West German magazine Stern, and Klaus von Bismark, director of West German television and radio. Both have been advocates of a political settlement with Poland on the basis of the postwar status quo.

Günter Grass, the author, also was in the official party. Many of his stories are set in his birthplace, Danzig, now the Polish city of Gdansk.

The Germans stepped off the plane to a war greeting by Mr. Cyrankiewicz and then stood in the cold Warsaw night air as a military band played the German national anthem. It was the first time that this theme, which was formerly called "Deutschland Uber Alles" with verses no longer sung, had been heard at an official Communist reception in Poland.

The song may have recalled events long past for some of the members of the Polish welcoming party, especially Mr. Cyrankiewicz, a former inmate of Auschwitz, largest of the Nazi extermination camps.

The official party drove through Warsaw to Wilanow Palace on Warsaw's outskirt. The party will remain in Warsaw until Tuesday.

Brandt to Pay Tributes

Mr. Brandt, one of the few West German figures admired here, will lay wreaths at the Polish Tomb of the Unknown Soldier and at the memorial to the Ghetto uprising, an ill-fated but heroic attempt by Warsaw's Jews to forestall final destruction by the Nazis.

Mr. Brandt was the guest tonight at a dinner given by Polish officials, including Wladslaw Gomulka, chief of the Polish Communist party. The West German and Polish leaders will confer tomorrow.

A West German spokesman indicated after tonight's dinner that the procedures for one aspect of normal relations had already been decided. He said that diplomatic relations would be established between the two nations after the treaty had been ratified.

The spokesman indicated that the treaty probably would not be submitted for ratification to the West German Parliament until the largest possible vote had been assured.

Brandt Hails Treaty

Special to The New York Times.

BONN, Dec. 6—Before boarding his plane to Warsaw this afternoon, Chancellor Brandt declared that the Polish-German treaty he is to sign tomorrow is "an end and a beginning."

He said that the treaty "closes a disastrous chapter of European history which is connected with great suffering for both nations."

Mr. Brandt added that insofar as the treaty would clear the way for the return of almost 100,000 ethnic Germans from Poland to West Germany, it "will realize a strong element of humanity in our policy."

Airport police reported that two bomb threats were received before the jet carrying the Chancellor's party departed.

* * *

December 18, 1970

POLISH DISORDERS SPREAD; POLICE ORDERED TO SHOOT AT RIOTERS AS TOLL RISES

10 TO 20 ARE DEAD

Injured in Hundreds, Premier Reports in Talk to Nation

By JAMES FERON

Special to The New York Times.

WARSAW, Dec. 17—Poland declared a virtual state of emergency tonight as anti-Government rioting spread and the toll of dead and injured rose.

Premier Jozef Cyrankiewicz told a nationwide television audience that the police and other authorities had been ordered to shoot at demonstrators if necessary.

The order meant that control measures in force in the northern port city of Gdansk, swept by riots that began Monday, would now apply throughout Poland.

[East European Communist sources in Bonn voiced the opinion that the rioting in Poland would have grave personal consequences for Wladyslaw Gomulka as party leader.]

Mr. Cyrankiewicz said during his brief address that 10 to 20 persons had been killed, both civilians and policemen, and several hundred injured in three days of rioting in Gdansk and other coastal cities following weekend increases in food prices.

Troop Moves Reported

Polish authorities reported six dead and dozens injured in a communiqué issued yesterday. That report also said that order had been restored in Gdansk.

The Premier's speech made it clear that the disorders had spread to Gdynia, said to have been sealed off last night, and Szczecin near the German border, where a curfew was reportedly in force.

Other unofficial reports stated that troops were being moved into other Polish cities, but these seemed to be precautionary moves in a nation alarmed and excited by the disorders in the north.

The riots were touched off in Gdansk when a demonstration by dock workers over the price increases swept out of control. Buildings were burned and shops looted.

Premier Cyrankiewicz—the name is pronounced tseerahn-KEH-vitch—said in his speech tonight that some militia units had come under fire in the demonstrations. It was the first indication that the rioters had been armed.

Until tonight's broadcast, Polish authorities had insisted that the situation was returning to normal with stores and buildings being repaired in Gdansk.

Unofficial information from the area indicated that tanks were stationed 50 yards apart in some sectors of the city and that unrest continued in nearby areas. Some dock workers continued to stay away from work.

Gdynia Shooting Reported

Nearby Gdynia, part of a three-city coastal area that also includes the resort of Sopot, was said to be sealed even tighter than Gdansk. Shots were reportedly heard in Gdynia.

Telephone communication with both cities has been cut except for official calls. Flights to the three-city area were suspended on Monday and reporters trying to get in by road were turned back.

Airline officials said tonight that flights to Szczecin reportedly under curfew, had also been suspended.

The Polish Government blames what it calls hooligans and adventurers for the riots, saying that they "exploited the situation that had arisen among Gdansk shipyard workers."

Travelers said that the workers, frustrated in wage talks at the port and infuriated by the Government decree raising food prices, had marched into the center of town Monday morning.

Many wore the paper caps common in this country to workers in rough jobs. Accounts differ, but some of the men were said to be carrying chains and lengths of pipe.

They gathered before the local Communist party headquarters shouting slogans and demanding that some official come out to speak with them.

Eyewitness accounts differ widely, but the demonstration suddenly became violent. Some reports, including one from a Polish student who saw the incident, say that a number of people broke into liquor stores and turned a tense scene into a violent one.

Shooting then broke out and the confrontation spread. Ambulances were operating though Monday night and well into Tuesday, according to reliable accounts. Troops were eventually brought in.

The city was sealed off and it was only Mr. Cyrankiewicz's sober report to the nation tonight that indicated, in his reference to "three days" of disturbances, that disorders continued.

In discussing the death toll, Mr. Cyrankiewicz used a Polish word—"kilkanascie"—that means "in the teens," or specifically, 11 to 19.

The communiqué authorizing militia units to open fire on demonstrators came a few minutes earlier, issued under the Premier's name, at the end of the evening news broadcast.

It referred to "the looting of state, social and citizen's property, the burning and demolition of buildings and public establishments, as well as the killings and heavy assaults," and called on "organs of prosecution and public order" to take measures." To restore public order" and "prevent attempts at disturbing it."

It said the militia, security service and other cooperating organs are obliged to take up all legal means of enforcement, including the use of weapons against all persons committing violent attacks on the lives and welfare of citizens looting and demolishing property and public installations.

It also said state organizations were obliged to provide assistance where necessary and that all citizens were urged to obey all authorized orders.

20,000 Work in Yards

Only one of the four shipyards in the Gdansk area was reported to be involved in the initial demonstration Monday. This would mean roughly 6,000 of an estimated 20,000 workers were involved at first.

Later reports indicated that some of the workers remained isolated in the yards, with access to the city covered by military units.

Unofficial reports circulating in Warsaw tonight said that there were indication of unrest, including demonstrations, in the major industrial cities of Lodz and Poznan.

It was in Poznan in 1956 that workers in the Cegielski Machine Factory went on strike in protest against harsh conditions and later clashed with the police. The clashes developed into riots and before they ended 53 people had been killed and 300 injured.

The severity of the Stalin period gave way in Poland after Poznan to a more liberal era under the leadership of Wladyslaw Gomulka, now the Polish Communist party leader.

* * *

December 20, 1970

STRAIN IN U.S.-BONN RELATIONS REPORTED

By DAVID BINDER
Special to The New York Times.

BONN, Dec. 19—High West German officials say that Chancellor Willy Brandt and the Nixon-Administration are close to a crisis of confidence over the Chancellor's Eastern policy.

The West German leader has reported about what he sees as a deterioration of his relations with the United States in recent weeks because of Bonn's policy of contacts with the Soviet bloc.

He is said to attribute the deterioration to a "constellation" of leading American officials who have become increasingly suspicious of his attempts to seek normal relations with Communist Europe.

"While the constellation is not completely clear to us, it covers at least four groups," a Government source said this week. He named President Nixon's national security adviser, Henry A. Kissinger, Secretary of Defense Melvin R. Laird, the State Department expert of German affairs, Martin J. Hillenbrand, and, in the fourth group, the former United States High Commissioners in Germany, Lucius D. Clay and John J. McCloy.

General Clay, who is retired from the Army, is a senior partner in Lehman Brothers, the investment banking firm, and Mr. McCloy, a former diplomat, is a partner in the New York law firm of Milbank, Tweed, Hadley & McCloy.

[In Washington, Dean Acheson, the former Secretary of State, confirmed that he and other Americans with experience in United States-Soviet relations viewed Chancellor Brandt's policy "with great alarm," but qualified American sources disputed the contention that the Chancellor's policy was a maneuver to hold his coalition together.]

The West German source said, "What Brandt is worried about is the real estimate of our Eastern policy by these people who, in one fashion or another, have voiced reservations and worry themselves about where we are headed."

Asked, for example, about criticism of Mr. Brandt attributed last week to Mr. Acheson, one official here said:

"We feel this is only the tip of the iceberg. Our concern is that when we ask the Americans what we should think of such criticism we always get positive and approving declarations. Nevertheless these criticisms keep emerging, from Acheson and from many others. We can localize the sources of the criticism but we are unable to get precise definitions of them. It is never in the open. It has become an unknown factor for us and that is what oppresses us."

It is understood that Mr. Brandt is also concerned that he has not succeeded in making clear to skeptics in Washington that he regards his approach to the East as a policy fully in harmony with the interests of the Western alliance.

Moreover, he is said to believe that the Nixon Administration has failed to realize that his entire Eastern policy is rooted in firm support of the Western defense alliance.

May Go to Washington

Because of the depth of his concern, the Chancellor is considering whether he or Foreign Minister Walter Scheel might go to Washington next month in an attempt to straighten out these matters with the Nixon Administration.

In circles close to the Chancellor it is remarked that the United States is justified in objecting to the tempo of Bonn's Eastern policy insofar as the policy does not suit the timing needs of Washington's "global strategy" toward the Soviet Union.

"One could say this of our treaty with Moscow and perhaps also of our treaty with Warsaw," an official observed, "even though we believe that the content of these treaties harmonizes fully with the ultimate goals of U.S. policy."

Asked about the Berlin problem, the source said he felt that there had been maximum cooperation between Bonn and Washington on that issue and that as a result the West had attained "a very good joint negotiating position."

"But even in the Berlin question we have the same problem," he said. "We notice that the Communists are seeking to use the lack of harmony in other matters to drive us against the Americans. What bothers us is the thought that the Americans are mistrustful whether we really are on their side."

In Government circles it was disclosed that Chancellor Brandt wrote letters last week to President Nixon, Prime Minister Heath of Britain and President Pompidou of France suggesting a means for speeding agreement with the Russians on the perennial Berlin problem.

The Chancellor is said to have suggested that the four-power ambassadorial talks on Berlin, which began last March, be transformed into a permanent conference.

* * *

December 21, 1970

GOMULKA QUITS IN WAKE OF POLAND'S PRICE RIOTS; GIEREK NEW PARTY CHIEF

Shake-Up Is Seen in U.S. As Move to Control Crisis

By TAD SZULC

Special to The New York Times.

WASHINGTON, Dec. 20—Authoritative observers here expressed their belief today that Wladyslaw Gomulka had been ousted from power in an effort by the leadership of the Polish Communist party to control the crisis that engulfed Poland in the wake of last week's rioting.

The observers, basing their opinions on information obtained from intelligence specialists, Eastern European diplomats and other sources here and in Warsaw, said that the Polish crisis had reached the point of such danger that an immediate and drastic change in leadership had become inevitable.

The rise of power of Edward Gierek in Mr. Gomulka's place was interpreted here as the only possible compromise among various factions of the Polish Communist party, although not necessarily a permanent solution.

It was noted that Mr. Gierek, long an enemy of Mr. Gomulka, had triumphed as the leader of an unusual coalition that included Communist "hard-liners" as well as younger and more liberally inclined figures and the chiefs of the armed forces.

Observers considered it significant that Gen. Wojciech Jaruzelski, the Defense Minister, who never had held a party post, had been named alternate member of the party's Politburo.

Mr. Gierek was described by those who know him as a pragmatist identified with the Communist party's group of technocrats. But he was also said to be a man highly responsive to the problems and anxieties of Poland's new generations.

For this reason, qualified observers here, studying all the personality changes in the top Polish leadership, warned against "oversimplified" conclusions that the Gierek leadership represented a conservative or repressive force in tune with the trends in the Soviet Union.

Actually, few government and private experts in the West had been aware of the real magnitude of the crisis.

Mr. Gomulka's resignation as First Secretary of the Polish Communist party came as a surprise to most United States officials, even though as early as last Friday some observers here had said that the rioting against the increase in food prices was rapidly turning into a major political crisis, raising the question of Mr. Gomulka's survival.

While the exact role of the Soviet Union in the weekend drama in Warsaw remained unclear, most observers tended to agree that Moscow had become alarmed over the Polish rioting and related tensions and, most likely, decided that Mr. Gomulka's removal was essential to stability.

The Soviet concern, according to specialists here, was that last week's rioting might get out of control not only in Poland, but also affect the situations elsewhere in Eastern Europe.

The area had been politically quiet since the Soviet-led invasion in August, 1968, crushed the Communist liberalizing movement in Czechoslovakia. But the recent history of Eastern Europe has shown that anti-regime disturbance in one country may have an impact on the neighbors.

Troop Movements Reported

There have been reports of Soviet Army movements in East Germany and Czechoslovakia since the eruption of the Polish riots.

Washington observers assumed that Moscow had been consulted during the night on the plans to replace Mr. Gomulka with Mr. Gierek, or, at least, informed of it.

But the sources here said it did not necessarily follow that the selection of Mr. Gierek and his associates represented precisely the type of leadership the Russians may have wished to see in power in Warsaw.

Nevertheless, observers said, Moscow evidently had no choice but to go along, for the time being, at least, because no other options seemed possible.

Reconstructing the Warsaw events on the basis of information reaching here, specialists said that Mr. Gierek and his close allies forced the decision to oust Mr. Gomulka at a Politburo meeting during the night and then called the Central Committee into session today to ratify the changes.

They said that although Mr. Gierek's new Politburo included some hard-liners and conservatives—notably former

Interior Minister Mieczyslaw Moczar—other members are identified with a more liberal line.

This, they said, is particularly true of Jozef Tejohma, the outspoken Communist leader identified with the youth and intellectual groups, who kept his Politburo position, and Stefan Olszowski, who rose from the post of the Central Committee's organization secretary.

General Jaruzelski, the new alternate member of the Politburo, was inspector-general of the army and chief of staff of the armed forces until his appointment as Defense Minister less than three years ago.

Eliminated from the leadership were Mr. Gomulka's closest associates, such as President Marian Spychalski, the party ideologist, Zenon Kliszko, and Boleslaw Jaszczuk, the Central Committee Secretary responsible for the economic reform that caused the rioting.

Right-winger Is Ousted

But, observers noted, another victim of the internal party coup was Ryszard Strzelecki, a leading right-wing Communist, who was ousted from the Politburo.

Observers here said that with the survival of Premier Jozef Cyrankiewicz and a Politburo member, Ignacy Loga-Sowinski, both identified with the anti-Stalinist factions in the fifties, the new leadership might tend toward a more "realistic" and even progressive line.

The judgment here today was that Mr. Gierek is unlikely to embark on a repressive campaign at this stage.

* * *

May 15, 1971

BREZHNEV URGES THE WEST TO CONFER ON TROOP CUTS

NATO Proposals Similar

By BERNARD GWERTZMAN
Special to The New York Times.

MOSCOW, May 14—Leonid I. Brezhnev, the Communist party leader, called on the Western powers today to begin exploratory negotiations on reductions in military forces and armaments in Central Europe.

Speaking in Tiflis, the capital of Soviet Georgia, at ceremonies marking the 50th anniversary of Soviet control of that Caucasian republic, Mr. Brezhnev said the Soviet Union would do everything in its power "to achieve the strengthening of the peaceful coexistence of states, regardless of their social system."

He proposed troop reductions in his address to the 24th Congress of the Communist party on March 30. The move attracted some interest in Western capitals at the time because it was similar to proposals made by members of the North Atlantic Treaty Organization.

The timing of Mr. Brezhnev's remarks suggested that the Kremlin might have decided to press harder on the issue as a way of attracting flagging Western interest in the Soviet bloc's much-discussed idea of a conference on European security.

The Soviet leader, in the brief foreign-policy segment of his nationally televised speech, said he wanted to talk about one point in the Western reaction to his congress address.

"Some of the NATO countries show an evident interest, and even some nervousness, concerning the reduction of armed forces and armaments in Central Europe," he said.

"Their representatives ask: Whose armed forces, foreign or national? What armaments, nuclear or conventional, are to be reduced? Could it be, they ask, that the Soviet proposals encompass all this taken together?"

A Light Brezhnev Touch

Then Mr. Brezhnev, in one of his infrequent light touches—aimed this time at the Georgian audience, whose people are fabled for their wine-drinking exploits—added:

"In this connection, we too have a question: Don't those curious people seem like a person that tries to judge the flavor of wine by its appearance without tasting it? If something is not clear to somebody, we are quite ready to make it clear."

"All you have to do is muster resolve to try the proposals that interest you by their taste," he said. "Translated into diplomatic language this means: Start negotiations."

The Soviet leader's remarks follow a call by Mike Mansfield, the Senate majority leader, for a unilateral 50 percent cut in the 310,000-man American force in Europe.

At the party congress Mr. Brezhnev spoke in more conciliatory terms than usual about the United States, and since then senior Soviet officials have said they had been ordered to negotiate seriously on outstanding differences.

He listed a six-point package, wrapping up many old Soviet proposals. The fourth point said: "We stand for the dismantling of foreign military bases. We stand for a reduction of forces and armaments in areas where the military confrontation is especially dangerous."

Western diplomats have inquired, as Mr. Brezhnev indicated, whether the proposal envisaged only the reduction of foreign troops, which would weaken Western defenses the most because the Russians are close by.

There has been interest in whether Mr. Brezhnev was contemplating talks by the two military blocs—NATO and the Warsaw Pact—or among all states on the continent. The latter is assumed, but is not clear, nor did Mr. Brezhnev elucidate today.

His remarks about the Soviet domestic scene were largely ceremonial. Of interest was a prolonged 12-second burst of applause given by the Georgians in the audience on the mention of the name of Stalin as a leading Georgian hero. Though the dictator has been discredited elsewhere in the country, he remains something of folk hero where he was born.

* * *

May 15, 1971

U.S. WELCOMES THE MOVE

By BENJAMIN WELLES
Special to The New York Times.

WASHINGTON, May 14—The Administration welcomed today the Soviet proposal for negotiations on reducing troops and armaments in Europe.

Ronald L. Ziegler, the White House spokesman, added that the proposal underlined President Nixon's opposition to a Congressional move for a unilateral reduction in the United States forces assigned to the North Atlantic Treaty Organization in Europe.

Senator Mike Mansfield, Democrat of Montana, the majority leader, has proposed that a bill extending the military draft be amended to oblige the Administration to cut the 310,000 man force in half by Dec. 31.

As the Administration massed its resources to oppose the Congressional move, Secretary of State William P. Rogers told the Senate Foreign Relations Committee that a unilateral action would be a "mistake of historic proportions."

Citing the proposal by Leonid I. Brezhnev, the Soviet Communist party leader, made during a nationally televised speech today, for talks on mutual troop reductions in Central Europe, Mr. Rogers said: "It is clear if we do it unilaterally we would kiss that issue good-by."

A unilateral troop cut, he added, "could be detrimental to our foreign policy and very harmful to our national interest."

It was evident that the Administration regarded the Brezhnev suggestion for negotiations on mutual troop and armament cuts as a timely additional weapon in its domestic battle to stave off Senate moves to reduce American forces in Europe. The Senate moves are interpreted at home and abroad as humiliating to the President and his principal advisers on an issue they regard as essential in over-all United States relations with the Soviet Union.

Charles W. Bray 3d, a State Department spokesman, noted that the NATO members, including the United States, initiated proposals for mutual and balanced force reductions at the alliance's ministerial meeting at Rejkjavik, Iceland, in June, 1968, and had reiterated interest in exploratory talks to that effect at each meeting since.

"We will be studying this response from the Soviets with great interest," he said.

Mr. Bray said that the next step would be close consultations between the United States and its NATO allies both on their reactions and on follow-up steps. The alliance will meet in Lisbon on June 3 and 4.

Negotiations on security in Europe are the focal point of United States foreign policy, Mr. Bray said, because "we regard Europe as the corner of the entire structure of peace."

Like Mr. Rogers, Mr. Bray also said that Mr. Mansfield's proposal had a direct bearing on the proposed East-West talks since unilateral troop cuts would "vitiate the possibility of holding meaningful negotiations on truly balanced force reductions."

President Nixon told NATO in December, 1970, that the United States would maintain and improve its forces in Europe, Mr. Bray recalled, and would not reduce them unless there was reciprocity.

It would be "highly ironic, perhaps even tragic," he said, if, at a time when the Soviet Union was expressing renewed interest in force reductions in Central Europe, the United States should "throw away its trump card."

Other officials pointed to an apparent easing of Soviet policy on troop cuts in recent months. Until the Communist party congress in March, they noted, the Soviet Government consistently called for negotiations on eliminating "foreign" troops. However, in addressing the party congress on March 30, they added, Mr. Brezhnev narrowed the area under discussion to Central Europe.

Since then, they said, the United States has been conferring with its allies on the significance of this apparent shift. Mr. Brezhnev's speech today, they went on, reinforces the belief that Moscow is ready to negotiate on mutual and balanced reductions.

Senior officials scrutinizing Mr. Brezhnev's words particularly noted the following:

"Some of the NATO countries show an evident interest, and even some nervousness, concerning the reduction of armed forces and armaments in Central Europe. Their representatives ask: Whose armed forces, foreign or national? What armaments, nuclear or conventional, are to be reduced? Could it be, they ask, that the Soviet proposals encompass all this taken together?

"In this connection, we too have a question: Don't those curious people seem like a person that tries to judge the flavor of wine by its appearance without tasting it? If something is not clear to somebody, we are quite ready to make it clear," Mr. Brezhnev said.

"All you have to do is muster resolve to try the proposals that interest you by their taste. Translated into diplomatic language this means: Start negotiations."

Vice President Agnew, in a speech before the Armor and American Ordance Association at Fort Knox, Ky., sounded an Administration warning on the need to maintain credible conventional strength in dealing with the Russians.

"Strength is the central pillar of the Nixon doctrine," he declared. "Although our strategic nuclear power remains the essential backdrop to our total deterrent, shifting strategic realties could cause a potential foe to test our will by the threat or use of force below the level of general nuclear war."

Secretary Rogers's opposition to the Mansfield amendment was challenged by Foreign Relations Committee members.

Senator Stuart Symington, Democrat of Missouri, Secretary of the Air Force in the Truman Administration, said it was difficult to see how a reduction of 150,000 men would leave NATO vulnerable or defenseless, as Administration spokesmen suggested, given the "incredibly strong U.S. nuclear-defense umbrella."

Senator Frank Church, Democrat of Idaho, rejected Mr. Roger's views as the "same old refrain we've been hearing for a decade—namely that calamity will befall us if we withdraw troops from Europe."

* * *

May 20, 1971

SENATE BARS A REDUCTION IN AMERICAN NATO FORCE

COMPROMISES FAIL

Administration Scores Major Victory on Foreign Policy

By JOHN W. FINNEY
Special to The New York Times.

WASHINGTON, May 19—The Senate, in a major foreign-policy victory for the Nixon Administration, rejected today all proposals for a reduction in the American forces stationed in Western Europe.

The Senate defeated a proposal by Senator Mike Mansfield, the majority leader, that would have required that the 310,000-man force in Europe be halved by the end of this year. The vote was 61 to 36.

Before this climactic vote in a week-long debate over future policy toward the Atlantic alliance, the Senate, responding to Administration wishes, rejected all compromises for smaller reductions. It also rejected a pro-Administration resolution that would in effect have endorsed Nixon policies toward the North Atlantic alliance.

Phased Withdrawal Rejected

By a 63-26 vote, the Senate rejected a compromise that would have provided for a phased 150,000-man withdrawal over a three-year period, with the provision that the initial reduction would not take place if the North Atlantic Treaty Organization and the Warsaw Pact entered into negotiations this year on mutual troop reductions in Central Europe.

This compromise, offered by Senator Gaylord P. Nelson, Democrat of Wisconsin, and endorsed by Senator Mansfield represented the rallying point for the Senate forces demanding a reduction in the American military commitment to the treaty organization.

Its defeat by more than a two-to-one margin underscored the dominance of the Administration in the Senate debate.

Cut of 50,000 Barred

The Senate, by an 81-to-15 vote, also rejected a last-minute compromise offered by Senator Frank Church, Democrat of Idaho, that would have called for a 50,000-man reduction this year.

Contending that the time had come to "chip away at the glacier of frozen positions that has characterized our policy in NATO," Senator Church said, "Many of these troops are so comfortable in Europe that they wouldn't move out even if the Russians moved in."

The Senate, by a 73-24 vote, also rejected a pro-Administration resolution that had been put forward by a bipartisan group, headed by Senator Charles McC. Mathias, Republican of Maryland, as a substitute for the Mansfield amendment.

Instead of imposing a mandatory troop reduction, the Mathias proposal would have called upon the President to enter into negotiations with the NATO allies as well as with the Soviet Union on troop reductions.

The Mathias proposal—co-sponsored by Senators Jacob K. Javits, Republican of New York, Hubert H. Humphrey, Democrat of Minnesota, and Adlai E. Stevenson III, Democrat of Illinois—was advanced as a fallback position for the Administration.

But the White House, spurning any compromise in the debate with the Senate, sent out instructions to its Republican and Democratic supporters to oppose the Mathias sense-of-the-Senate resolution.

Senator Mansfield, Democrat of Montana, endorsed the Nelson proposal as a reasonable compromise, providing for troop reductions while protecting the President's position in negotiating with the Soviet Union on mutual reductions in force.

The margin of the defeat of the Nelson proposal, offered as an amendment to the bill extending the draft, surprised even Mr. Mansfield.

By an even larger margin, 81 to 13, the Senate rejected a compromise offered by Senators Birch Bayh, Democrat of Indiana, and William B. Saxbe, Republican of Ohio. It would have provided for a 150,000-man reduction by the end of 1972 if, by the end of 1971, the NATO allies had not agreed to assume a greater share of the dollar cost of maintaining American troops in Europe.

In an attempt to assert Senate foreign-policy prerogatives, Senator J. W. Fulbright, chairman of the Senate Foreign Relations Committee, proposed at one point an amendment that in effect would have provided that the 150,000-man reduction would not go into effect if Congress subsequently authorized a greater strength.

His purpose, he explained, was to place the burden of justifying the present troop strength in the Atlantic Alliance on the President. His amendment was defeated 69 to 28.

While there undoubtedly was majority sentiment for a reduction, there was reluctance to impose it by a legislative mandate. There was also widespread concern—which Mr. Mansfield attempted to counter by endorsing Mr. Nelson's proposal—that the majority leader was proposing too drastic a cut.

In the opinion of many Senators, what tipped the balance was the offer last week by the Soviet Communist party chief, Leonid I. Brezhnev, to enter exploratory negotiations with the United States and the NATO countries on mutual troop reductions in Central Europe.

Throughout the debate the Administration's supporters repeatedly emphasized that any unilateral reduction would undermine the bargaining position of the United States and the Atlantic alliance in negotiating with the Communist bloc.

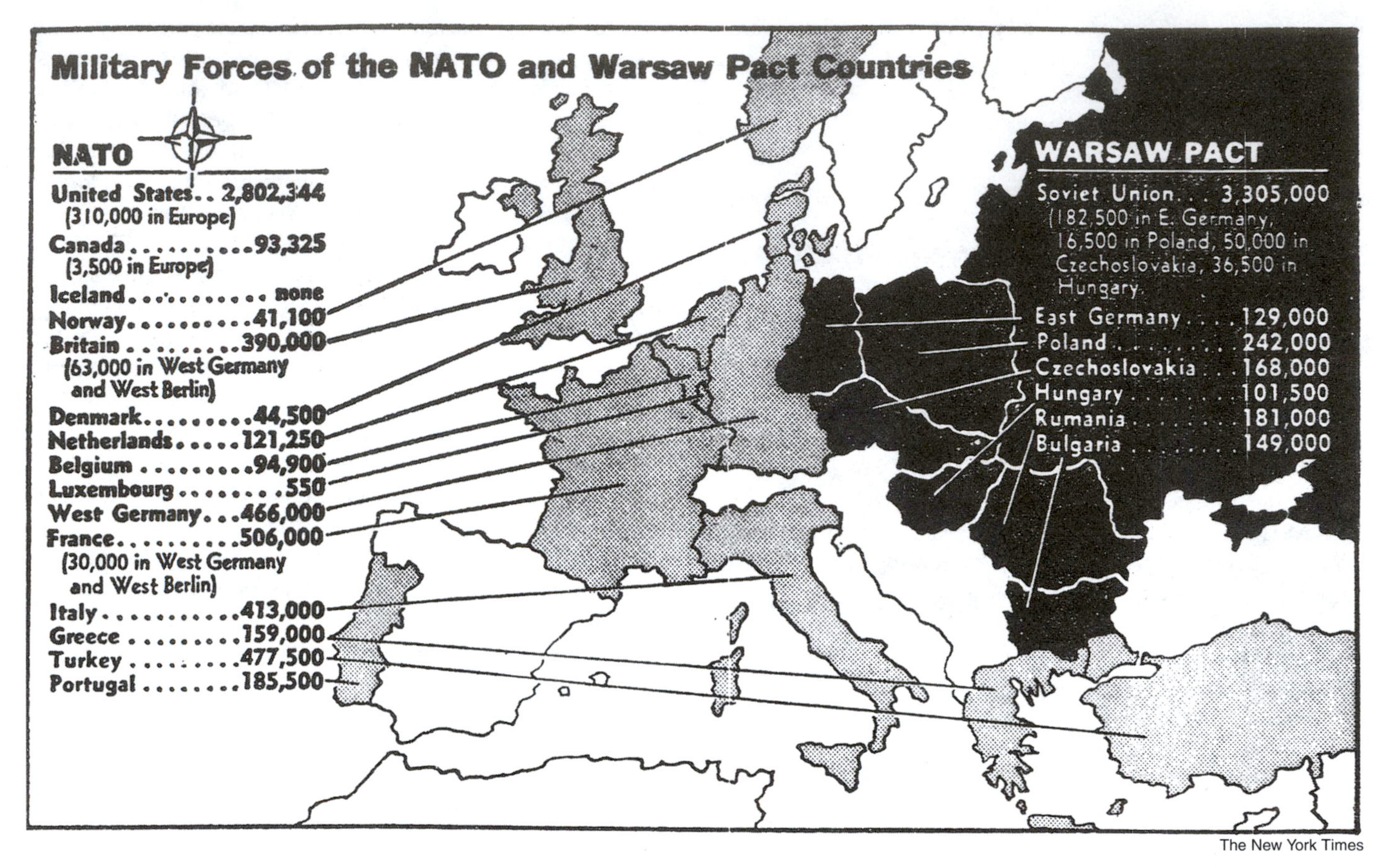

NATO has 1,105,000 troops in Western Europe, according to alliance sources, while Warsaw Pact has 1,235,000 on station in Eastern Europe. Thus, these two figures do not include all troops of the member countries of the two pact organizations referred to on map above. The U.S. total of 2,802,344 troops is the Pentagon's official figure as of last March 31. All the others are figures for 1970 furnished by Institute for Strategic Studies in London.

That argument was particularly used against the Nelson proposal, which would have provided for a reduction to 250,000 by June, 1972; 200,000 by June, 1973, and 150,000 by June 1974. It also provided that the initial 50,000-man reduction would be postponed if, before the end of 1971, NATO and the Warsaw Pact had entered into negotiations.

Senator John C. Stennis, chairman of the Senate Armed Services Committee, protested that the amendment would remove any incentive for the Russians to negotiate and would "hogtie" the President.

As the debate ended, Senator Stennis argued that the Senate should not go back on a "solemn commitment" that he said President Nixon gave to the NATO allies last December—that the United States would not reduce its force without a reciprocal reduction by the Communist side.

Shortly before the defeat of his amendment to a bill extending the draft, Senator Mansfield told the Senate, "It sometimes takes a sledge hammer to make an imprint and to place an issue on the table."

The issue of American troop contributions to NATO, he continued, "has been made, and regardless of the outcome it will not disappear or rest in the cobwebs where it has resided for the past ten years."

Protesting that the United States was "carrying a very one-sided burden" in the alliance, Senator Mansfield said, "I don't want to look over my shoulder and think that something that was good 10 to or 20 years ago should not be changed.

"I am not a member of the old guard," the 67-year-old Senator said.

* * *

June 16, 1971

JUDGE, AT REQUEST OF U.S., HALTS TIMES VIETNAM SERIES FOUR DAYS PENDING HEARING ON INJUNCTION

ARGUMENT FRIDAY

Court Here Refuses to Order Return of Documents Now

By FRED P. GRAHAM

United States District Judge Murray I. Gurfein yesterday ordered The New York Times to halt publication of material from a secret Pentagon study of the Vietnam war for four days. Argument on publication thereafter will be heard Friday.

The judge granted a request by the Justice Department for temporary relief, but he gave no hint as to how he would eventually rule. He also refused to order The Times to return the massive report immediately to the Government.

Declaring that the case could be an important one in the history of relations between the Government and the press, Judge Gurfein said that any temporary harm done to The Times by his order "is far outweighed by the irreparable harm that could be done to the interests of the United States" if more articles and documents in the series were published while the case was in progress.

Times Says It Will Comply

The Times, in a statement issued after the hearing, said:

"The Times will comply with the restraining order issued by Judge Murray I. Gurfein. The Times will present its arguments against a permanent injunction at the hearing scheduled for Friday."

Lawyers for The Times and the Justice Department told the judge, at the proceedings in the Federal District Court House at Foley Square, that this appeared to be the first time in the nation's history that a newspaper was being restrained by a court from publishing an article.

Meanwhile, the Justice Department disclosed in Washington that the Federal Bureau of Investigation was investigating possible violations of federal criminal laws in connection with publication of the secret documents.

The bureau was known to be checking all who had access to the document, of which Justice Department sources said there were 15 copies.

Judge Gurfein, in his first day on the bench after having taken his oath of office last week, acted upon the Justice Department's argument that the publication of further articles by The Times would cause serious injury to the nation's international relations.

The 63-year-old judge deferred until Friday's hearing a decision on the Government's request that The Times be ordered immediately to return the voluminous documents from which its Vietnam series has been drawn.

Order Expires Saturday

The temporary restraining order issued by Judge Gurfein yesterday expires at 1 P.M. Saturday.

His action came a day after Attorney General John N. Mitchell had requested that The Times cease publishing the documents and The Times had refused to do so voluntarily.

Yesterday afternoon, the Justice Department filed a civil suit seeking to permanently enjoin The Times and 22 of its officers, editors and reporters from going ahead with the series of articles and documents on the origins of the Indochina war. Three installments had been published and The Times had said that the series was to continue.

Word filtered through the city's legal community yesterday that the Government had requested an afternoon hearing on a temporary restraining order against The Times, and the courtroom was packed—mostly with young lawyers and spectators—when the mustached judge took his seat in Room 605 of the United States Court House.

The arguments pitted a 30-year-old staff member of the United States Attorney's office, Michael D. Hess, against Prof. Alexander M. Bickel of the Yale Law School, a 46-year-old constitutional authority who has been mentioned as a possible Supreme Court nominee. Prof. Bickel represented The Times and its personnel.

The gist of the Government's argument was that The Times had violated a statute that makes it a crime for persons having "unauthorized possession" of Government documents to disclose their contents under circumstances that "could be used to the injury of the United States or to the advantage of any foreign nation."

In his argument, Mr. Hess asserted that "serious injuries are being inflicted on our foreign relations, to the benefit of other nations opposed to our form of government." He told the judge that Secretary of State William P. Rogers had said that several friendly nations had expressed concern over the disclosures in the articles.

With the Government facing the prospect of "irreparable injury" in its international relations, Mr. Hess said, The Times should be required to suffer a "slight delay" in its publication schedule until the case could be heard on Friday.

Otherwise, he said, the case would be mooted by publication of the material before a decision could be reached.

Professor Bickel, a tanned, dapper man in a brown suit and blue shirt, replied that this was a "classic case of censorship" that is forbidden by the First Amendment's free-press guarantee. He also insisted that the statute being invoked by the Government was an anti-espionage law that had never been intended by Congress to be used against the press.

The law, Title 18 of the United States Code, Section 793, provides for a maximum punishment of 10 years' imprisonment and a $10,000 fine against:

"Whoever having unauthorized possession of, access, to, or control over any document . . . relating to the national defense, or information relating to the national defense which information the possessor has reason to believe could be used to the injury of the United States or to the advantage of any foreign nation willfully communicates . . . the same to any person not entitled to receive it, or willfully retains the same and fails to deliver it to the officer or employe of the United States entitled to receive it."

Mr. Bickel contended that to rely upon this wording to bar a newspaper from publishing certain matter "for the first time in this history of the republic" would set an unfortunate precedent. "A newspaper exists to publish, not to submit its publishing schedule to the United States Government," he argued.

During a final discussion in his chambers, Judge Gurfein heard brief statements from two civil liberties groups that asked to be heard as friends of the court. Norman Dorsen, general counsel of the American Civil Liberties Union, and Kristin Booth Glen of the Emergency Civil Liberties Committee made the statements and asked to be heard again on Friday.

Judge Gurfein instructed them to file briefs and reserved judgment on their request to be heard.

He urged The Times to consent to a restraining order, but Mr. Bickel refused, saying that to do so would invite future

Government efforts to curb news publications. The order was issued over Mr. Bickel's objections.

Order Not Appealed

The Times could have attempted to appeal the order to the United States Court of Appeals for the Second Circuit. However, such extraordinary appeals of temporary restraining orders are rarely granted, and The Times elected to have the issue tried on its merits before Judge Gurfein.

Mr. Bickel was accompanied in court by Floyd Abrams, a partner in the New York law firm of Cahill, Gordon, Sonnett, Reindel and Ohl.

The Justice Department named the following defendants in addition to The New York Times Company in today's injunction: Arthur Ochs Sulzberger, president and publisher, who will return today from a trip to London; Harding F. Bancroft and Ivan Veit, executive vice presidents; and Francis A. Cox, James C. Goodale, Sydney Gruson, Walter Mattson, John McCabe, John Mortimer and James Reston, vice presidents.

Also, John B. Oakes, editorial page editor; A. M. Rosenthal, managing editor; Daniel Schwarz, Sunday editor; Clifton Daniel and Tom Wicker, associate editors; Gerald Gold and Allan M. Siegal, assistant foreign editors; Neil Sheehan, Hedrick Smith, E. W. Kenworthy and Fox Butterfield, reporters; and Samuel Abt, a foreign desk copy editor.

* * *

June 16, 1971

BRANDT AND NIXON CONFER ON BERLIN

Agree in White House Talk Progress by Big Four May Lead to Troop Parley

Special to The New York Times.

WASHINGTON, June 15—President Nixon and Chancellor Willy Brandt of West Germany agreed today that continued progress in negotiations on the status of West Berlin might soon open the way for talks between the North Atlantic Treaty Organization and the Warsaw Pact on reducing military forces in Europe.

Following a one-hour-and-45-minute meeting between Mr. Nixon and Mr. Brandt in the White House, the Presidential press secretary, Ronald L. Ziegler, said that Berlin had been the principal topic along with the question of limiting conventional forces in Europe.

An accord on easy access to West Berlin, now the subject of negotiations with the Soviet Union, is a prerequisite from the West's viewpoint for talks on a mutual, balanced reduction of forces.

The growing indications that a Berlin agreement might be within reach after 15 months of discussions were reinforced when Secretary of State William P. Rogers said at a news conference today that he would meet this week with Ambassador Anatoly F. Dobrynin to determine when and under what circumstances Moscow would be ready to begin talks on a reduction of forces.

"I am going to talk to Ambassador Dobrynin in the next day or so to find out if they are prepared to have discussions on mutual and balanced force reductions, and find out what they are prepared to talk about, what they are thinking about in terms of time and place, et cetera," Mr. Rogers said.

Secretary Rogers, who conferred with Mr. Brandt at a luncheon at the State Department, is expected to meet with Mr. Dobrynin tomorrow afternoon.

The Secretary declined to enter into the details of the Berlin talks, but he said that "some progress had occurred recently in these discussions." Mr. Rogers added that "we are hopeful that an agreement can be reached, but there are still many differences."

Brandt Sees a Chance

In a speech this afternoon at the Woodrow Wilson International Center for Scholars, Mr. Brandt said:

"I do not know whether it will really be possible to achieve a satisfactory Berlin arrangement in the months ahead . . . but I do know that there is a chance."

The chancellor is in the United States on a five-day private visit. He is spending two days in Washington for policy discussions.

Mr. Ziegler, the press secretary, said the subject of troop reductions had been discussed by Mr. Nixon and Mr. Brandt in the light of "the most recent developments."

One of these developments, he said, was a speech in Tiflis on May 14 by Leonid I. Brezhnev, the Soviet party leader, urging the West to begin exploratory talks on the reductions of military forces in Europe.

Mr. Brandt said in his speech: "Now we see that the Soviet Union and the United States—and not only they—favor this idea in principle."

While until recently the Warsaw Pact powers had insisted that the troop reduction be discussed in the context of a broad European conference. Mr. Brandt emphasized that "there is basically no reason why we should not discuss this matter before such a conference is taking shape."

Speech Seen as Signal

Mr. Brezhnev's speech last month was considered by Western governments as a signal that the Soviet Union had changed its political strategy and was now willing to take up the question of reduction of forces.

Other topics covered at today's White House meeting included the new agreement between the United States and West Germany under which Bonn refunds to the United States a large part of the dollar cost of stationing American troops in West Germany. The current two-year agreement expires on June 30, and there have been problems in reaching a new accord.

Mr. Nixon and Mr. Brandt also discussed the relations between the United States and the West European Common

Market, after the expected entry of Britain, Denmark, Norway and Ireland.

The Chancellor was reported to have assured Mr. Nixon that the enlarged market would not threaten United States economic interests in Western Europe.

Touching on this point in his speech, Mr. Brandt said: "We in Germany belong to the vanguard of those who insist that the European Community, rather than isolate itself, must be outward-looking, above all in its relations with the United States."

* * *

July 16, 1971

NIXON WILL VISIT CHINA BEFORE NEXT MAY TO SEEK A 'NORMALIZATION OF RELATIONS'; KISSINGER MET CHOU IN PEKING LAST WEEK

MOVE A SURPRISE

President Says Action Is Not at Expense of 'Old Friends'

By JOHN HERBERS
Special to The New York Times.

SAN CLEMENTE, Calif., July 15—President Nixon said tonight that he would visit China before next May at the invitation of Premier Chou En-lai to "seek the normalization of relations between the two countries and also to exchange views on questions of concern to the two sides."

Mr. Nixon's brief and unexpected announcement was made on nationwide radio and television from Los Angeles.

Mr. Nixon disclosed that the arrangements had been made by Henry A. Kissinger, the chief White House adviser on national security, who secretly visited Peking during his recent worldwide tour.

Simultaneous Statements

The announcement was being made simultaneously in the United States and in Peking, Mr. Nixon said.

"Our action in seeking a new relationship with the People's Republic of China will not be at the expense of our old friends," he said in an obvious allusion to Nationalist China. "It is not directed against any other nation.

"We will seek friendly relations with all nations. Any nation can be our friend without being any other nation's enemy.

"I have taken this action," he continued, "because of my profound conviction that all nations will gain from a reduction of tensions and a better relationship between the United States and the People's Republic of China.

First Such Trip

"It is in this spirit that I will undertake what I deeply hope will become a journey for peace, peace not just for our generation but for future generations on this earth we share together."

Mr. Nixon's visit will be the first by an American President to China.

It had not been known that Mr. Kissinger was in China at all on his 11-day trip that took him to South Vietnam, India, France and other countries this month.

The President said Mr. Kissinger and Premier Chou conferred in Peking from July 9 to 11. That was when he was reported to be in Pakistan temporarily incapacitated by a stomach ailment.

Associated Press

The New York Times

President Nixon after announcing journey and disclosing that Henry A. Kissinger had met with Premier Chou En-lai.

Mr. Kissinger arrived at the Western White House Tuesday and has been in daily consultation with President Nixon since then. He was with the President tonight when he flew by helicopter from the Presidential compound to the National Broadcasting Company studio in suburban Los Angeles to make the announcement.

In a statement of fewer than 400 words, Mr. Nixon said he had requested the broadcast, at 7:30 P.M. Pacific time, to announce a "major development in our efforts to build a lasting peace in the world."

He said that he had pointed out on a number of occasions over the last three years that "there can be no stable and enduring peace without the participation of the People's Republic of China and its 750 million peoples."

"That is why I have undertaken initatives in several areas to open the door for more normal relations between our two countries."

Statement Read

He read this statement:

"Premier Chou En-lai and Dr. Henry Kissinger, President Nixon's assistant for national security affairs, held talks in Peking from July 9 to 11, 1971. Knowing of President Nixon's expressed desire to visit the People's Republic of China, Premier Chou En-lai, on behalf of the Government of the People's Republic of China, has extended an invitation to President Nixon to visit China at an appropriate date before May, 1972.

"President Nixon has accepted the invitation with pleasure.

"The meeting between the leaders of China and the United States is to seek the normalization of relations between the two countries and also to exchange views on questions of concern to the two sides."

President Calls Meeting

Earlier in the day, it became known that the President had called a meeting of the National Security Council for tomorrow at the summer White House here, where an intensive review of foreign policy has been under way for several days. This review, it was disclosed, had included extensive discussion of the seven-point Vietcong peace proposal put forward at the talks in Paris on July 1.

The President, who arrived here on July 6, is due to return to Washington on Sunday.

The arranging of a Presidential trip to China was by far the most dramatic development in the remarkably rapid thaw in relations between the two countries that has occurred in recent weeks. The United States has never had diplomatic relations with the Chinese Communist Government that came to power in 1949, and the United States has opposed entry of Peking into the United Nations.

President Nixon on several occasions recently has said that China had become so powerful and so energetic that it would be a mistake for it to continue in isolation from Western nations.

In a proclamation last week designating Oct. 24 as United Nations Day, Mr. Nixon pointed to a report by his commission for the observance of the 25th anniversary of the United Nations, headed by Henry Cabot Lodge, and commended it to the attention of all American citizens.

That report contained, among other things, the recommendation that the United States adopt a "two-Chinas policy"—that is, to recognize both mainland China and the Chinese Nationalist Government on Taiwan. The United States has recognized the Nationalist Government, which is represented in the United Nations.

The President's trip to China will have important political implications in this country.

President Nixon will presumably run for re-election in 1972. Much of the conservative wing of the President's Republican party is opposed to a thaw between the two countries. There is evidence that President Nixon agonized long over the decision but that he obviously feels the appearance of a President going forth in search of world peace will enhance his stature.

China's Interest in Settlement

The President spoke less than 24 hours after it had become known that Peking for the first time had expressed an interest in playing a part in a settlement of the Vietnam war by participating in a new Geneva conference on Indo-China. Premier Chou En-lai had expressed such an interest to Gough Whitlam, the leader of the Opposition Labor party of Australia, and the Australian Embassy in Washington quickly transmitted the development to the State Department.

Administration experts on China said in Washington this morning that they were taking the Chinese offer of participation seriously and saw it as a positive development.

* * *

August 16, 1971

NIXON ORDERS 90-DAY WAGE-PRICE FREEZE, ASKS TAX CUTS, NEW JOBS IN BROAD PLAN: SEVERS LINK BETWEEN DOLLAR AND GOLD

SPEAKS TO NATION

Urges Business Aid to Bolster Economy—Budget Slashed

By JAMES M. NAUGHTON
Special to The New York Times.

WASHINGTON, Aug. 15—President Nixon charted a new economic course tonight by ordering a 90-day freeze on wages and prices, requesting Federal tax cuts and making a broad range of domestic and international moves designed to strengthen the dollar.

In a 20-minute address, telecast and broadcast nationally, the President appealed to Americans to join him in creating new jobs, curtailing inflation and restoring confidence in the economy through "the most comprehensive new economic policy to be undertaken in this nation in four decades."

Some of the measures Mr. Nixon can impose temporarily himself and he asked for tolerance as he does. Others require Congressional approval and—although he proposed some policies that his critics on Capitol Hill have been urging upon him—will doubtless face long scrutiny before they take effect.

2 Tax Reductions

Mr. Nixon imposed a ceiling on all prices, rents, wages and salaries—and asked corporations to do the same voluntarily on stockholder dividends—under authority granted to him last year by Congress but ignored by the White House until tonight.

The President asked Congress to speed up by one year the additional $50 personal income tax exemption scheduled to go into effect on Jan. 1, 1973, and to repeal, retroactive to today, the 7 per cent excise tax on automobile purchases.

He also asked for legislative authority to grant corporations a 10 per cent tax credit for investing in new American-made machinery and equipment and pledged to introduce in Congress next January other tax proposals that would stimulate the economy.

Combined with new cuts in Federal spending, the measures announced by Mr. Nixon tonight represented a major shift in his Administration's policy on the economy.

Cuts Ruled Out Earlier

Only seven weeks ago, after an intensive Cabinet-level study of economic policy, the President announced that he would not seek any tax cuts this year and would hew to his existing economic "game plan," confident of success.

Eleven days ago, Mr. Nixon reasserted his opposition to a wage and price review board—a less stringent method of holding down prices and wages than the freeze he ordered—and said only that he was more receptive to considering some new approach to curtailing inflation.

The program issued tonight at the White House thus came with an unaccustomed suddenness, reflecting both domestic political pressures on the President to improve the economy before the 1972 elections and growing international concern therefore, the dollar would be devalued.

Mr. Connally said, "We anticipate and we hope there would be some changes in exchange rates of other currencies."

But this will depend on other countries. For 25 years non-Communist nations have maintained the international exchange value of their currencies by "pegging" them to the dollar. Their central banks would buy or sell their own currencies in daily trading in the foreign-exchange market to keep the value within one per cent either side of "par," expressed in a precise dollar amount for each unit of the other currency.

After Mr. Nixon's action tonight, they can still do so, if they so wish. But they are no longer obligated to do so under the rules of the International Monetary Fund. Their obligation to peg their currencies to the dollar was a counterpart of the United States's obligation to exchange dollars for gold. The United States has now renounced that obligation.

Referring to the 1944 conference in New Hampshire that established the I.M.F. and the present rules for monetary exchange, Arthur M. Okun, Chairman of the Council of Economic Advisers under President Johnson, said tonight, "We just ended the Bretton Woods system forever."

Mr. Okun said he could not say by what degree other currencies would rise in value relative to the dollar, but he was certain that they would rise.

Apparently more than 100 countries are going to have to make decisions within the next 48 hours as to what to do. In Europe, as it happens, most foreign-exchange markets will be closed tomorrow because of the Feast of Assumption, giving Governments and central banks a little more time to decide.

Although the President's unilateral action may cause difficulties in the nation's foreign relations, particularly with industrialized countries, he held out an olive branch. He said his action "will not win us any friends among the international money traders," but he added:

"In full cooperation with the International Monetary Fund and those who trade with us, we will press for the necessary reforms to set up an urgently needed new international monetary system. Stability and equal treatment is in everybody's best interest."

A Treasury statement said, "United States officials will promptly be meeting with their colleagues from other countries to explain the background and details of the President's program. They will develop United States proposals for both dealing constructively with the immediate repercussions of today's decision and employing (the opportunity opened by today's action for speeding the evolution in the international monetary system in directions that serve the common needs of trading nations."

The background of the President's action was a long series of deficits in the nation's balance of international payments, the trade balance of exports and imports, swung into deficit in the second quarter for the first time since an abnormal period in 1946 immediately following World War II.

Last week, the dollar was under heavy selling pressure in European foreign-exchange markets. Where it could weaken, it did—as in West Germany, which has a temporary "floating" exchange rate, following pressure last spring for an upward revaluation.

The President emphasized that, although imports might cost more as a result of his action, "if you are among the overwhelming majority who buy American-made products in America, your dollar will be worth just as much tomorrow as it is today."

Technically, the Treasury announced these steps:

- The United States "notified the International Monetary Fund that, effective today, the United States no longer freely buys and sells gold for the settlement of international transactions." This withdraws a commitment made in 1947.
- Use of monetary reserve assets, including gold and other assets such as drawing rights or "paper gold" on the International Monetary Fund, will be "strictly limited" to "settlement of outstanding obligations and, in cooperation with the

I.M.F., to other situations that may arise in which such use can contribute to international monetary stability and the interests of the United States."

• The President "requested" the independent Federal Reserve Board to cease the automatic operation of its system of "swaps" with other countries, which is a means of converting dollars into other currencies and temporarily averting conversion of foreign-held dollars into gold.

The statement said no "new decision" had been made regarding the present controls over the outflow of United States capital, such as investments by United States companies abroad and purchase by Americans of foreign securities, now subject to an "interest equalization tax." These restraints remain in effect, the statement said.

* * *

September 22, 1971

1945 PLEAS BY HO REVEALED BY U.S.

Censored Pentagon Papers to Be Published Monday

By NEIL SHEEHAN
Special to The New York Times.

WASHINGTON, Sept. 21—The Nixon Administration released to Congress today a censored 7,800-page version of the Pentagon papers. The text will be available to the public next week.

The decision to release the papers for publication by the Government Printing Office removed much of the remaining veil of secrecy that the Administration fought so hard to preserve through the courts after The New York Times and other newspapers began last June to publish articles and documents from the top-secret study of the Vietnam war.

The censored version contains previously unpublished material, including eight unanswered letters and cable-grams from Ho Chi Minh, then the Communist leader in Vietnam and later President of North Vietnam, appealing for help in his struggle against French colonial rule in 1945-46.

On the other hand, the Government deleted some material already published by The New York Times and other newspapers.

Among these deletions are five messages between Washington and the United States Embassy in Saigon in the fall of 1963, when the Kennedy Administration was encouraging a coup d'état against the Government of Ngo Dinh Diem.

Other deletions included several pages in the section on the Johnson Administration's covert military operations against North Vietnam and a number of key policy memorandums.

The four volumes on the secret diplomatic negotiations of the Johnson years, which none of the newspapers obtained, were withheld entirely. Rady A. Johnson, a Pentagon legislative aide, said in a letter to Congress that those volumes "deal exclusively with sensitive negotiations seeking peace and the release of prisoners" and "their disclosure would adversely affect continuing efforts to achieve those objectives."

A Pentagon spokesman said that 95 per cent of the material in the 43 other volumes had been released.

Jerry W. Friedheim, the Pentagon spokesman, said the decision to release the expurgated version had nothing to do with the forthcoming publication by The Beacon Press of Boston of a version of the papers obtained through Senator Mike Gravel, Democrat of Alaska. Beacon is to issue a 2,952-page, four-volume edition in mid-October.

Mr. Friedheim said the release was "solely in response" to an order last June from President Nixon to Secretary of Defense Melvin R. Laird that as much as possible be published as soon as possible. On June 22, he noted, Mr. Laird set up a group to declassify the study within 90 days.

The work of declassification, Mr. Friedheim added, was accomplished by about 100 State and Defense Department officials as well as by personnel from other agencies, apparently including the Central Intelligence Agency.

Some Congressional sources noted that the decision to publish the censored version came with unannounced suddenness.

Uniformed military personnel wheeled four sets, each of which fills two foot-square boxes, into the offices of the House and Senate Armed Services and Foreign Relations Committees this morning. The committees were told only this morning that the papers were arriving.

$60 a Set to the Public

Representative F. Edward Hebert, Democrat of Louisiana and chairman of the House Armed Services Committee, quickly sent a set to the Government Printing Office for publication.

A. N. Spence, the Public Printer, said that the unclassified version, in 12-volume clothbound sets printed by photo offset, would be published Monday. The price to the public will be $60, he added.

Mr. Spence said that he had thought at first of printing about 5,000 sets but had decided to print 2,500 to 2,700 because "we just found out that our competitor in Boston is coming out with them for $20."

Beacon will sell its set for $45 in cloth and $20 paperbound, according to Gobin Stair, its director.

Mr. Spence said he had already received telephone inquiries from several commercial bookstores, but he was quoted as expressing doubt that a large number of sets would sell because of the size and price.

"My aim is not to cut into the commercial market but just to make the documents available," he explained.

DUPLICITY LAID TO U.S.

By STEVEN V. ROBERTS
Special to The New York Times.

LOS ANGELES, Sept. 21—A lawyer for Dr. Daniel Ellsberg charged today that the Federal Government had "used duplicity and failed to honor an order of the court" in seizing 28 boxes of Dr. Ellsberg's personal papers and possessions.

The seizure took place late yesterday after an Assistant United States Attorney, David R. Nissen, had obtained a search warrant from a Federal magistrate.

The tangled legal battle began last week when the grand jury investigating the Pentagon papers case here issued a subpoena for several dozen boxes Dr. Ellsberg had stored with the Bekins Moving and Storage Company.

Dr. Ellsberg, now a research fellow at the Massachusetts Institute of Technology, has said that he gave the Pentagon papers to the news media. He was indicted here in June on two counts of stealing and possessing secret Government documents.

In fighting the subpoena, Dr. Ellsberg's attorney argued that the Government was conducting "a blanket fishing expedition" and could not use the grand jury to investigate Dr. Ellsberg further since he was already under indictment. Mr. Nissen replied that the Government was investigating persons other than Dr. Ellsberg and needed his property for that investigation.

Subpoena Was Quashed

Federal District Judge William Mathew Byrne Jr. took the case under submission and ordered Bekins not to release Dr. Ellsberg's property to anyone. He also ordered the Government attorneys to inform him if they obtained a search warrant to seize the property. Yesterday morning he quashed the subpoena.

Morse A. Taylor, lawyer for Dr. Ellsberg, asked if the Government attorneys to inform inform the court if it obtained a search warrant. Mr. Taylor came away feeling that the Government had agreed to inform the court, and so, apparently, did Judge Byrne.

When the transcript was reviewed later it showed that Mr. Nissen had agreed to only one thing: that he would not execute a search warrant before noon.

When Judge Byrne was informed of the situation he heard further arguments, reviewed the transcript and ruled that the Government attorney had violated no court ruling. He also said that any motion by Dr. Ellsberg's attorneys to quash the search warrant was premature and would have to be made after the evidence seized in the search was presented in court.

"What is so irritating," Mr. Taylor said, "is that the Government, by chosing a position of duplicity—which is the whole point of the Pentagon papers anyway—violated the spirit and intent of the courts' order."

* * *

October 26, 1971

U.N. SEATS PEKING AND EXPELS TAIPEI; NATIONALISTS WALK OUT BEFORE VOTE; U.S. DEFEATED ON TWO KEY QUESTIONS

SESSION IS TENSE

Washington Loses Its Battle for Taipei by 76 to 35

By HENRY TANNER

Special to The New York Times.

UNITED NATIONS, N. Y. Tuesday, Oct. 26—In a tense and emotion-filled meeting of more than eight hours, the General Assembly voted overwhelmingly last night to admit Communist China and to expel the Chinese Nationalist Government.

Moments before the vote, Liu Chieh, the Chinese Nationalist representative, announced from the rostrum that his Government would take no further part in the proceedings of the Assembly. He received friendly applause from most delegations, and then led his delegation out of the hall.

The vote, which brought delegates to their feet in wild applause, was 76 in favor, 35 opposed, and 17 abstentions. The vote was on a resolution sponsored by Albania and 20 other nations, calling for the seating of Peking as the only legitimate representative of China and the expulsion of "the representatives of Chiang Kai-shek."

Voting Is Sudden

Thus, the United States lost—in the 22d year—its battle to keep Nationalist China in the United Nations. This development, which came with dramatic suddenness, was denounced by the chief American delegate as a "moment of infamy."

The key decision that signaled the United States defeat came an hour and a half earlier, when the Assembly voted, 59 to 55 with 15 absentees, to reject the American draft resolution that would have declared the expulsion of the Nationalists an "important question" requiring a two-thirds majority for approval.

The United States had successfully used such a resolution since 1961 to keep the Chinese Nationalists in. Before that time, a simple majority would have admitted Peking but no majority could be mustered.

Pandemonium Breaks Out

Last night as the electrical tally boards flashed the news that the "important question" proposal had failed, pandemonium broke out on the Assembly floor. Delegates jumped up and applauded.

The American delegation, also in the front row, sat in total dejection. George Bush, the United States delegate, who had been leading the fight for Nationalist China with considerable energy, half turned away from the rostrum, looking silently at the turbulent scene.

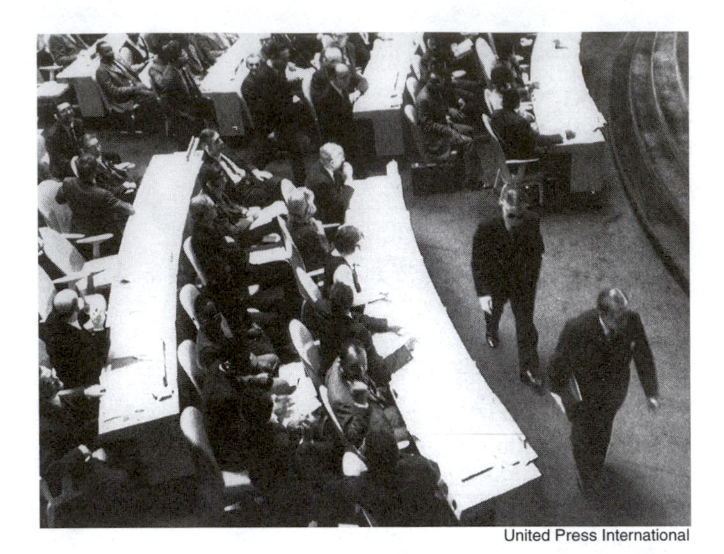

United Press International

Liu Chieh, right, Nationalists' chief U.N. delegate, and delegation walk out of the hall.

An analysis of the voting showed that the abstention of eight nations that had been thought almost to the last to be leaning toward the United States position had been fatal to the American cause. Had they voted with the United States, the American "important question" resolution would have been adopted, 63 to 59.

The eight nations were Belgium, Cyprus, Laos, Qatar, Senegal, Togo, Trinidad and Tobago, and Tunisia.

However, the 76 members who voted for the Albanian resolution to admit Peking and expel the Nationalists constituted a two-thirds majority of those voting. While this majority would have permitted the admission of mainland China even if the American "important question" motion had won, many observers expressed the opinion that the final vote had been swelled by the pattern of the earlier voting.

Meeting with newsmen shortly before midnight at the United States Mission across the street from the United Nations, Mr. Bush said he hoped the world organization would "not relive this moment of infamy."

"The United Nations crossed a very dangerous bridge tonight," he said. Expressing surprise at the vote, he added: "I thought we would win and it would be very, very close."

Mr. Bush said that he expected a very bad reaction from the American public.

When he was asked when he thought Peking's delegates would be arriving, he said: "It's hard to believe that a few hours ago we didn't think we had anything to worry about."

But Mr. Bush said the United States would "cross that bridge when we get to it" as he replied to a question as to how the United States would act regarding Peking's Security Council seat.

During last night's meeting, Adam Malik of Indonesia, who presides as this year's Assembly President, announced that he would notify the Peking Government immediately of its admission. Communist China had said repeatedly that it would accept a seat in the United Nations only if the Chinese Nationalists were expelled.

The suddenness of the voting came as a surprise to all. As late as the afternoon, as the long China debate was in its final phase, it had been expected that the vote would come sometime in the next day.

Time, many here believed, might have worked in favor of the American position. As late as the morning, it was reported, the 131-member assembly was close to being evenly divided. Therefore, the Albanian delegation, which for years has sponsored the resolution that would admit Communist China and expel the Nationalists, made it known that it would try to force a quick decision.

This precipitated an attempt by the supporters of Nationalist China to delay the proceedings. Jamil M. Baroody of Saudi Arabia proposed that all voting be postponed for one day, but his proposal lost, 53 to 56, with 19 abstentions.

In the parliamentary maneuvering that ensued, the United States experienced a short-lived victory. By a vote of 61 to 53, with 15 abstentions, the Assembly adopted an American proposal that priority be given to the "important question" resolution.

Earlier in the day, both Saudi Arabia and Tunisia had put forward compromise proposals for settling the China issue. The Saudi proposal included a call for a plebiscite on self-determination for the people on Taiwan.

Mr. Baroody, who made many trips to the rostrum during the eight-hour session, made his proposal for a delay in the voting so as to give time for the Assembly to study the American, the Albanian, the Tunisian and the Saudi Arabian resolutions.

The overwhelming vote for the Albanian resolution to seat Communist China and unseat the Nationalists contrasted with last year's bare majority—51 to 49. That was the first majority that advocates of admitting the Communists had obtained since the China item was first taken up by the Assembly in 1950.

* * *

December 4, 1971

INDIA REPORTS A FULL-SCALE WAR HAS BEEN STARTED BY PAKISTAN; BOTH CHARGE INCURSIONS IN WEST

Fighting Reported on Kashmir Line

By MALCOLM W. BROWNE
Special to The New York Times.

RAWALPINDI, Pakistan, Saturday, Dec. 4—Pakistan charged last night that the Indian Army had attacked at least four points along West Pakistan's border. The Pakistani Air Force and Army have been given orders to penetrate India as deeply as possible, a Government spokesman said.

The spokesman said that the first fighting in West Pakistan began about noon yesterday, with firing along the border, especially on the cease-fire line in Kashmir, where Indian and Pakistani forces fought a brief but bloody war in 1965.

"It's the 1965 war all over again," a military spokesman said.

He said incidents occurred almost simultaneously in Kashmir, in the Shakargarh salient, Poonch, Uri, the Kasur border, Hussein-i-Wala and at Chamb, between Jessar and Lahore, in Rajastan, and at Rahimyarkhan.

Cease-fire Rules Cited

According to Pakistan, the cease-fire rules in Kashmir require that when an incident has occurred the commanders of opposing Indian and Pakistani ranger forces immediately consult.

This time, the spokesman said, when the Pakistani commanders went to talk with their Indian counterparts, they were met by regular Indian troops, who fired on them. The Indian attacks were said to have been supported by artillery and fighter bombers.

The spokesman said the Pakistani Air Force retaliated during the afternoon and evening, bombing at least seven Indian airfields. He said the bombing was continuing.

Indian Targets Listed

He said the Indian airfields that were bombed were at Amritsar, Pathánkot, Avantipur, Srinagar, Uttarlai (in Rajastan State) and Agra and Ambala, both said to be Indian jet bomber bases.

He said no Indian interceptors had attacked the Pakistani planes, all of which returned to base.

"We will have to wait until morning to see whether the Indian bombers were knocked out," he said.

The spokesman added that Pakistan did not intend to bomb nonmilitary targets and did not plan attacks on Indian cities.

Pakistan's President, Gen. Agha Mohammad Yahya Khan, scheduled an address to the nation.

Various ambassadors called on the President to determine what was happening. Among them was the United States Ambassador, Joseph S. Farland.

The United States has repeatedly advised Pakistan to exercise restraint and avoid war.

A Foreign Ministry spokesman declined to say whether war would be declared. He also declined comment when asked what would be done about Indian diplomats posted in Pakistan.

During the 1965 conflict, war was never declared and there was never a formal break in diplomatic relations between Pakistan and India. The new fighting in West Pakistan appears to be in virtually the same places as in 1965.

The military spokesman said that Pakistan's offensive would extend to East Pakistan as well where, according to Pakistan, the army has been restrained from crossing the Indian frontier until now.

Under a full moon, army trucks and heavy artillery could be seen rolling toward their positions.

The Pakistani Government declared a blackout last night throughout West Pakistan and civilian flights were canceled, at least for the night. Radio and television alternated martial songs with instructions for air-raid alerts and civil defense and leading politicians made statements urging national unity in the coming war with India.

A leading politician told newsmen that Pakistan would probably announce the formation of a new civilian government in a day or two. Zulfikar Ali Bhutto, leader of the leftist Pakistan People's party, said there had been agreement that General Yahya Khan would continue as President, that the East Bengali politician Nurul Amin would be made Prime Minister and that Mr. Bhutto would be Deputy Prime Minister.

"Especially during wartime," Mr. Bhutto said, "a political base for the nation is essential—that means a civilian government.

"During the present emergency I have agreed to temporarily accept the second position in a civilian government with the understanding that wars do not last forever and things must be changed afterwards. After all, Mr. Nurul Amin represents only himself whereas I represent the people of West Pakistan."

During the last few days there have been increasing preparations for war in the west.

Civilian vehicles have been requisitioned, reservists and former servicemen have been called to duty, persons in essential positions have been mobilized and a civil defense corps has been organized.

Last week the dependents of Americans and other foreigners were evacuated from border towns in West Pakistan, most of them to Rawalpindi. Their men folk in Lahore and other border communities are expected to remain, at least for the time being.

Phone calls indicated that Lahore, 18 miles from the Indian border, was quiet, with no indication of approaching fighting. During the 1965 war the Indian Army nearly reached Lahore before the cease-fire took effect.

Pakistan maintained yesterday that India had made only "small tactical dents" in her territory, but Western military attachés, who admit that their information about the situation in the eastern wing is severely limited by the lack of observers, believe that the incursions have been much more serious.

* * *

December 4, 1971

MRS. GANDHI VOWS TO REPEL THE FOE

By CHARLES MOHR

Special to The New York Times.

NEW DELHI, Saturday, Dec. 4—India declared yesterday that Pakistan had launched "full-scale war" against her.

Prime Minister Indira Gandhi, making the announcement in a speech at midnight, pledged that "the wanton and unprovoked aggression of Pakistan would be decisively and finally repelled."

[Mrs. Gandhi told Parliament Saturday that Pakistan had declared war on India, but she did not say in what form any declaration had come, The Associated Press reported. The Indian Parliament unanimously approved the proclamation of a state of emergency.

[In Calcutta, the Press Trust of India reported that the Indian Air Force had carried out air strikes over Dacca, the capital of East Pakistan, and three other towns, Reuters reported.]

Indian spokesmen said that Pakistani jet fighter-bombers attacked 12 Indian airfields, the outskirts of Agra, a concentration of military vehicles and other targets. They said that four Pakistani planes had been shot down.

Incursion Charged

The Indian spokesmen also said that Pakistani troops in "substantial" strength had attacked Indian territory near Poonch in Jammu and Kashmir State. Pakistani artillery began bombarding Indian positions in the Punjab and in Jammu, they added.

The Indian President, V. V. Giri, declared a state of national emergency. The Indian Parliament was summoned to a special session this morning to approve a Defense of India bill that would give the Government wide emergency powers.

There was no report yet of full-scale Indian military retaliation aimed at the approximately 70,000 Pakistani troops in East Pakistan.

Such action, however, seemed inevitable. Indian leaders have made clear that their goal is the dismemberment of Pakistan and the creation of a "friendly" government in East Bengal.

Indian statements last night indicated that Pakistan had opened fighting on the western front where she was at less of a military disadvantage than in isolated East Pakistan.

According to Indian spokesmen, Pakistani F-86 sabrejet planes bombed and strafed forward Indian air bases at Armitsar, Pathánkot, Srinagar, Avantipur, Uttarlai, Jodhpur, Ambala and Agra and "heavy military vehicles" near Sadik in the Punjab.

Some 300 to 400 yards of the airstrip at Amritsar were damaged, but the field is still serviceable, the Indians said.

The Pakistanis used Mirage-III supersonic planes at Amritsar, the spokesmen said, and F-86 Sabrejets at most other locations. The Indians described the Pakistanis as coming in fairly small formations, such as six Sabrejets at Srinagar and four Mirages at Amritsar. This was, however, consistent with the way air strikes were conducted in the 1965 war between the two countries.

Pakistani artillery also began shelling seven Indian positions along the heavily defended Punjab border, a spokesman said.

The only ground attack reported so far by New Delhi was a Pakistani attack across the Kashmir cease-fire line—a legacy of an earlier war—near Poonch. But the coordinated air attacks on Indian airstrips was regarded as a prelude to major ground fighting.

The reported air attacks were said to have started at dusk and continued in various areas into the night as a full moon rose like a spotlight over the subcontinent.

Civil authorities in Agra, about 120 miles south of New Delhi, said that Pakistani planes bombed that area three times during the night and that one Pakistani plane was shot down.

Agra is the site of the Taj Mahal, a beautiful mausoleum built by a Mogul ruler and one of the world's architectural masterpieces. There was no report of damage to the Taj.

New Delhi was not attacked but, like most cities in North India, was blacked out.

India said that the Pakistani air strikes caused only minor damage. Air Marshal M. M. Engineer of the Western Air Command said the strikes had "not been able even to bruise, let alone hurt us." India did not report the loss of any planes in the Pakistani attacks.

The Pakistani radio charged that Indian ground forces had launched an attack upon West Pakistan on nine fronts.

India and Pakistan, born in the bloody religious rioting that accompanied the partition of British India in 1947, have been enemies ever since.

Relations have grown increasingly bad in the last eight months as West Pakistani soldiers have attempted to crush by force the move toward autonomy or independence by Bengali-speaking rebels in East Pakistan.

In recent weeks India dramatically increased her support of the insurgents in East Pakistan and sent units of her armed forces across the East Pakistan border in what she termed "defensive actions."

In an order of the day issued immediately after the reported attacks by Pakistani planes, Air Marshal Engineer told his pilots, "We owe it to posterity that we destroy the evil war machine" of Pakistan.

Official Indian spokesmen in New Delhi, however, were unable to say that Indian aircraft had scrambled to meet the attacking planes or had counter-attacked fields in Pakistan. It seemed possible that Indian forces were caught by surprise.

The official spokesmen also made no claim that Indian ground forces had promptly reacted. In fact, they indicated the reverse.

Citing reports by the Pakistan radio and Hsinhua, the Chinese press agency, that India had launched an attack in the western sector, an official statement said that such charges "are totally false" and that "our troops are in defensive position and there has been no offensive or defensive action along the western border by the Indian troops so far."

Later last night, however, the Indian Defense Minister, Jagjivan Ram, told newsmen that Indian forces would take "all necessary action."

Mrs. Gandhi, speaking in slow, grave and measured tones to her radio audience, said that "soon after 5:30 P.M. on Dec. 3, Pakistan launched a full-scale war against us."

"Today the war in Bangla Desh [Bengal Nation, the insurgent name for East Pakistan] has become a war on India," she said. "We have no option but to put the country on a war footing."

Mrs. Gandhi referred indirectly to the almost 10 million refugees from the turmoil in East Pakistan. The burden of the refugees was one reason India recently stepped up its political and military support for the East Bengali guerrillas.

She said that "since last March we have borne the heaviest of burdens and the greatest of pressures in a tremendous effort to ask the world to help in bringing about a peaceful solution and preventing the annihilation of an entire people whose only crime was to vote democratically."

"But the world ignored basic causes and concerned itself only with certain repercussions," she said, in an allusion to international suggestions that both India and Pakistan withdraw their forces from the borders of East Pakistan.

"The situation was bound to deteriorate," she said. "We must be prepared for a long period of hardship and sacrifice."

A Pakistan broadcast in the Urdu language said that "the enemy has finally aroused us to a jihad." Jihad is the word for a Moslem holy war. Pakistan is an Islamic state. India is constitutionally a secular state, but is predominantly Hindu.

A major preoccupation for Indian officials within the next few days will be the question of how China, which diplomatically supports Pakistan, will react and whether Chinese troops on the northern border will take any action.

Indian officials tonight said that the Chinese press agency's announcement of an attack by India was made almost simultaneously with the Pakistan radio report.

A sizable part of the Indian Army is tied down on the Chinese border.

India and Pakistan have fought two major but limited conflicts in the past. Both ended in stalemate and cease-fire—the 1947-48 struggle for Kashmir and the 22-day 1965 war in the Punjab and the Jammu area of Kashmir.

Early reports of the present conflict were sketchy and contradictory. The Indian spokesmen described shelling—but not a ground advance—by Pakistan along the Punjab border from Fazilka to Amritsar. This was a major battleground of the 1965 war.

In addition to the ground attack reported over the Kashmir cease-fire line near Poonch, the Indians later last night also reported that the town of Jammu was under artillery fire. This town straddles the only road from the northern Punjab to the Vale of Kashmir and is the lifeline of Indian troops in northern Kashmir. There is no rail line.

Before the dramatic announcement of the western attacks, India had asserted that Pakistani F-86 jets struck near the airfield at the Indian town of Agartala, close to the eastern border of East Pakistan.

According to officials, Indian troops crossed the border into East Pakistan at this point Thursday following a similar air raid and shelling. Pakistan denied the Indian version and said that the air strike was made on Indian troops within East Pakistan advancing toward the Pakistani railroad town of Akhura.

* * *

January 26, 1972

NIXON DISCLOSES A PEACE PLAN INCLUDING NEW SAIGON ELECTION; SAYS NORTH VIETNAM IGNORED IT

SECRECY IS BROKEN

Kissinger Visited Paris—Thieu Would Quit Under Proposal

By ROBERT B. SEMPLE Jr.
Special to The New York Times.

WASHINGTON, Jan. 25—President Nixon disclosed to the American public tonight a proposal to end the war in Indochina that he said had been offered in secret channels three months ago but ignored by the North Vietnamese.

The major new element of the plan would be a new presidential election in South Vietnam, with President Nguyen Van Thieu resigning one month before the election. This and other parts of the plan, Mr. Nixon said, were fully endorsed by Mr. Thieu when the proposal was set before the Communists in October.

[In Saigon, President Thieu, speaking on the radio Wednesday, offered to hold new presidential elections in which the Vietcong could participate, Reuters reported.]

An 'Accounting' to People

President Nixon also disclosed a series of 12 secret meetings in Paris between Henry A. Kissinger, his adviser on national security, and senior North Vietnamese diplomats. The meetings ended before Mr. Kissinger was able to present the new proposals personally, but they had been sent to the North Vietnamese negotiating team in a private communication from the President.

Mr. Nixon said he had decided to disclose the peace plan, as well as the private talks surrounding it, to give the American people an "accounting" of why negotiations to end the war had been disappointing, to put to rest charges that the Administration had not made its best efforts, and to demonstrate publicly "what we have long been demonstrating privately—that America has taken the initiative not only to end our participation in this war, but to end the war itself."

Other elements of the plan had been offered by Mr. Nixon in one form or another before, and were aimed at resolving both the military and political impasse in Southeast Asia. They included these points:

- An offer to withdraw all United States and allied forces from South Vietnam six months after the two sides had reached agreement in principle on the terms of a settlement.
- A general cease-fire throughout Indochina, to begin when the agreement is signed.
- A new presidential election, to be preceded by Mr. Thieu's resignation, along with that of Vice President Tran Van Huong, and to be organized and run by an "independent body" composed of all political forces in South Vietnam, including the National Liberation Front, or Vietcong.

In exchange, the North Vietnamese would agree to return all American prisoners of war and "innocent civilians captured throughout Indochina," and to remove their forces from South Vietnam, Cambodia and Laos. No timetable, however, was set for the removal of Communist forces.

Vietnamization Is Alternative

If the proposals are not accepted, Mr. Nixon said, he will proceed along the path of Vietnamization, which he defined as "withdrawing our remaining forces as the South Vietnamese develop the capability of defending themselves." In addition, he warned, if "the enemy's answer to our peace offer is to step up our attacks. I shall meet my responsibility . . . to protect our remaining troops."

"This is a settlement offer," Mr. Nixon said, "which is fair to North Vietnam and fair to South Vietnam. It deserves the light of public scrutiny by those nations and by other nations as well. And it deserves the united support of the American people."

Although Mr. Nixon said his main purpose tonight was to demonstrate the credibility of the United States as a "fair and generous negotiator" as well as to serve "the purposes of peace" by "bringing out publicly the proposals we have been making in private," additional compelling motives could be seen in his address.

Diplomatically, Mr. Nixon seemed to have given up on the private channels—principally, the secret talks between Mr. Kissinger and North Vietnamese diplomats. Not only has he received no response, but, as he suggested, private channels lose their effectiveness once they are given the sort of public notoriety Mr. Nixon gave his own paths of secret communication tonight.

At the same time, his disclosures suggested a level of personal diplomatic activity that few here had suspected. Mr. Nixon also protected himself against charges of "secret deals" with China by disclosing his latest and best overtures before embarking on his trip to Peking.

Politically, Mr. Nixon—without mentioning any of his critics or Democratic opponents by name—seemed to be trying to put an end to the divisiveness that he believes has hurt his efforts to reach a settlement, while defusing Democratic complaints that his offers to the enemy had been both tired and miserly.

Finally, in military terms, Mr. Nixon—by "going public" with his best diplomatic efforts—may have positioned himself for a stern response on the ground and in the air should the North Vietnamese launch heavy attacks in the coming weeks. Analysts here have been predicting such attacks, and Mr. Nixon may feel that he can more easily retaliate now that he has made his bargaining efforts clear.

General Settlement

Mr. Nixon treated the military and political issues of the war as inseparable elements of a general settlement—but only because, a White House official explained, the North Vietnamese had chosen to treat them that way. Should the North Vietnamese decide to solve the military problem first and leave political matters to later negotiations with Saigon, Mr. Nixon said, he is prepared to "withdraw all United States and allied forces within six months in exchange for an Indochina cease-fire and the release of all prisoners."

Neither the President nor an accompanying fact sheet handed reporters tonight before the speech mentioned United States aircraft stationed aboard carriers off the coast of Vietnam or based in Thailand. These aircraft represent the most powerful ingredient of the United States attack force left in Indochina, since by May Mr. Nixon will have reduced the authorized troop level in South Vietnam to a mere 69,000 men.

A White House official told newsmen at a briefing tonight that the cease-fire provision would cover all forces, including air attack forces. The eventual disposition of American aircraft based outside Vietnam was left unclear, although Mr. Nixon's plan calls for return to the Geneva accords of 1954 and for pledges on all sides of "no foreign intervention in the Indochina countries."

As part of the cease-fire, the fact sheet said, "there will be no further infiltration of outside forces into any of the countries of Indochina."

Last Meeting in August

Mr. Nixon said the negotiations between Mr. Kissinger and two key North Vietnamese—Le Duc Tho, with whom Mr. Kissinger met seven times, and Xuan Thuy, with whom he met five times alone—began Aug. 4, 1969, and ended Aug. 16, 1971.

During the course of these talks, Mr. Kissinger made several proposals which the President's Democratic opponents have accused him of not making.

Chief among these, the President said, was a proposal offered to the North Vietnamese on May 31, 1971, under which the United States would agree to a deadline for the withdrawal of all American forces in exchange for the release of all prisoners of war and a cease-fire.

That, in essence, has been the substance of a number of resolutions proposed by the Democratic majority in Congress—resolutions the Administration has systematically opposed.

Hanoi's Seven-Point Plan

At the next meeting, on June 26, the North Vietnamese rejected the American offer, responding with a counterproposal that—in Mr. Nixon's words—insisted that the United States overthrow the Government of South Vietnam.

Five days later, Mr. Nixon recalled, Hanoi's negotiators publicly unveiled a seven-point package that included the requirement that the United States abandon its support of the Thieu Government.

Although a White House official who briefed newsmen tonight would not expand on the differences between the enemy's private and public overtures, Mr. Nixon suggested that his was a somewhat broader proposal, covering all of Indochina. In any event, on July 12, at yet another private meeting in Paris, Mr. Kissinger agreed at North Vietnam's request to deal henceforth with the nine-point private plan.

On Aug. 16 Mr. Kissinger again offered the complete withdrawal of the United States and allied forces, but this time he said the United States would do so nine months after an agreement on over-all settlement. The North Vietnamese, according to the President, rejected that proposal too.

Despite accusations from the North Vietnamese that the United States had failed to respond to its public proposal, Mr. Nixon resolved in October to make another effort and sent what he described as a "private communication" to Paris that contained "new elements."

One major new element in that proposed package, a White House official said tonight, was the suggestion that President Thieu, assuming a settlement could be agreed upon, would resign his office one month before the new election. That suggestion was made public tonight as a firm proposal.

Mr. Nixon's speech followed weeks of criticism from some of his Democratic opponents to the effect that he had failed to make a clear public offer to the North Vietnamese to withdraw all American troops by an agreed date in exchange for the release of the American prisoners.

In a television interview with Dan Rather of the Columbia Broadcasting System on Jan. 2, Mr. Nixon said the possibility of a total withdrawal in exchange for the prisoners' release had been discussed with the North Vietnamese in Paris but that they had "totally rejected" it.

The next day Senator George McGovern, Democrat of South Dakota, who met with North Vietnamese officials in Paris last summer, asserted that a formal offer had not in fact been made and that the President was deceiving the public.

The day after that Administration officials conceded that the United States had never proposed a firm date but were convinced—on the basis of informal efforts to seek clarifications of Hanoi's attitude—that it would reject such a formula.

The basic reason for their pessimism has been Hanoi's insistence—outlined by Nguyen Van Tien, the Vietcong delegate in Paris, on Jan. 6 and again in a response to questions put to Hanoi by The New York Times—that the United States must not only withdraw its forces but also abandon support for the Saigon government before the prisoners would be released.

* * *

February 10, 1972

NIXON SAYS SOVIET AND U.S. DEFINED PACT ON MISSILES

Details of Interim Accord to Be Settled, Message on Foreign Policy Reports

A WARNING TO MOSCOW

President Declares He Will Increase Arms Outlays if Russian Build-Up Goes On

BY BERNARD GWERTZMAN
Special to The New York Times.

WASHINGTON, Feb. 9—President Nixon, in his third annual foreign policy message to Congress, said today that the United States and the Soviet Union had reached an accord on the outline—if not yet the details—of an interim agreement on the limitation of strategic arms. He said such an agreement could restrain the arms race without jeopardizing either side's security.

Mr. Nixon warned that if, in the absence of an accord, the Russians continued their intensified missile deployment and threatened to upset the current balance of power, he would not hesitate to increase spending on American strategic weapons.

The major focus in Mr. Nixon's 95,000-word State of the World report was on United States relations with the Soviet Union and China. The document also covered nearly every area of international life, sometimes with only a broad-brush approach but often in significant detail.

'Civilized Discourse'

Major points in the report, which bears the title "United States Foreign Policy for the 1970's: The Emerging Structure of Peace," included these:

- There are "serious grounds" for believing that a fundamental shift in Soviet-American relations may occur, but Mr. Nixon said it was unclear whether the Russians, engaged in a vast arms build-up, had undertaken a major policy shift or were making tactical moves for their own advantage.
- In the meeting with Soviet leaders in May, the President said, he hopes for concrete agreements beyond arms control and bilateral matters, including an understanding on limits on the arms flow to the Middle East and on curbs on big-power rivalry in such areas as South Asia, plus a discussion of measures to reduce tensions in Europe.
- The President conceded that Japan had every reason to be shocked by his unilateral economic and diplomatic initiatives last summer, but he did not apologize for the moves, which he said were necessary. He said that by the end of last year confidence had been restored and he applauded Japan's assumption of greater responsibility in Asia commensurate with her economic power.
- Mr. Nixon reported continued progress on all fronts—pacification, Vietnamization and economic reform—in Vietnam while noting that the enemy might be preparing for a major

offensive. He stressed the flexibility of his eight-point peace proposal, but insisted that he would not abandon the Saigon Government or prisoners of war to the enemy. He pledged to secure the return of the P.O.W.'s through negotiations or "other means."

Mr. Nixon said there were serious grounds for believing that "a fundamental improvement in the U.S.-Soviet relationship may be possible." But he said that it was unclear whether there had been a permanent change in Soviet policy "or only a passing phase concerned more with stactic than with a fundamental commitment to a stable internal system."

'Concrete Arrangements'

In his meeting with Soviet leaders in May, Mr. Nixon said, he hopes for "concrete arrangements of benefit," which, besides arms control and bilateral matters, would include an understanding on avoiding an inflammation of the situation in the Middle East, a curb on big power rivalry in such areas as South Asia and discussion of measures to reduce tensions in Europe further.

Summing up the "watershed year" that had just passed, the President said that the United States, despite sharp problems with Japan and with its Western European allies, had achieved "a more balanced alliance" with its friends. The forthcoming trips to Peking and Moscow are evidence of "a more creative connection" with America's adversaries, he added.

A sense of achievement pervaded the document—an attitude underscored in Mr. Nixon's brief radio address to the nation this morning on the message.

He said in the radio address that various "breakthroughs toward peace" took place last year because his Administration had consistently "stopped reacting on the basis of yesterday's habits and started acting to deal with the realities of today and the opportunities of tomorrow."

In an example of his rhetoric, he said that his current eight-point Vietnam peace plan was "the most generous peace offer in the history of warfare."

The report also contained a section on "disappointments" during the year. The most important, Mr. Nixon said, was the failure to end the Vietnam war. He also noted the inability to prevent the war between India and Pakistan, the continued tension in the Middle East, continued disagreements in Latin America, the diminishing foreign aid available for Africa and the inability of the United States to keep Nationalist China in the United Nations.

The report's discussion of the status of the 27-month-old talks on the limitation of strategic arms—the so-called SALT talks—was closely linked to the current balance of power in the world and to the determined Soviet effort to accelerate its deployment of land-based and submarine-launched missiles.

Crucial Milestone Foreseen

After noting that the Soviet Union had improved its forces "in virtually every category of strategic offensive and defensive weapons," Mr. Nixon said the United States was "approaching a crucial turning point in our strategic arms programs."

"If the Soviet Union continues to expand strategic forces, compensating United States programs will be mandatory," he said. "The preferable alternative would be a combination of mutual restraint and an agreement in SALT."

"But under no circumstances will I permit the further erosion of the strategic balance with the U.S.S.R." he added. "I am confident that the Congress shares these sentiments."

He said that the Russians were undertaking either "major improvements or the deployment of a totally new missile system" and that two new or greatly modified land-based intercontinental ballistic missile systems were being developed.

The Russians have built silos for additional giant 23-megaton SS-9 missiles that could destroy American offensive missile sites, the President said, also noting that in the near future they would have more missile submarines than the United States' current 41.

With this as a background, Mr. Nixon noted that "a consensus is developing on certain essential elements" of a strategic arms agreement.

He said both sides agreed that there should be a comprehensive limitation of the number of antiballistic missile (ABM) defensive systems. Deployments of ABM's should neither provide a defense for the entire country nor threaten the strategic balance, he said.

Agreement on a limitation on ABM's has not been reached, he explained, because the existing Soviet ABM defense network of 64 missile launchers surrounds Moscow while the initial American Safeguard program is geared to protect offensive missiles in less populated areas.

The Americans have proposed an asymmetric formula under which the Russians could have 100 missiles for Moscow's defense while the United States would have more for ICBM protection.

Mr. Nixon said that the two sides had agreed that once an accord was reached on details, the ABM agreement would be formalized in a treaty that would require Senate approval.

Throughout the talks the United States has pressed for a comprehensive limitation on offensive weapons as well, but Mr. Nixon indicated that a freeze was unlikely and that there should be only an interim arrangement on the halt of "certain offensive weapons."

Focus on Land Missiles

Informed sources have said that the two sides have decided to postpone action on submarine-launched missiles and are concentrating on land-based ones. Because of that, Mr. Nixon, in his budget, authorized further work on a long-range submarine-launched missile system to keep ahead of Soviet submarine construction.

In his report Mr. Nixon did not rule out an early submarine agreement, assuring that it was "still under intensive negotiation." In an apparent rejoinder to those in the Senate who have argued for a comprehensive treaty or none at all, Mr. Nixon said:

"We must weigh the advantages of prolonging the current stage of negotiations in order to reach agreements on every offensive system against the consequences of allowing the current Soviet build-up to continue, perhaps for a considerable period."

He said that an interim agreement would not impair American security, adding: "Moreover, Soviet willingness to limit the size of its offensive forces would reflect a desire for longer-term solutions rather than unilateral efforts to achieve marginal advantages."

Stressing his preference for the interim agreement, he said it "will be a major step in constraining the strategic arms race without compromising the security of either side." On the other hand, he said, if the negotiations are protracted, that would inevitably lead to an acceleration of the arms race.

"This is a reality of our competitive relationship," he said.

An Agenda for Moscow

On his proposed agenda for the Moscow talks in May, the President listed either an accord on the initial arms agreement or on the issues to be addressed in the second stage—a sign of confidence that an interim agreement would be worked out in the next three months.

Somewhat unexpectedly, Mr. Nixon placed Middle Eastern problems as the second most important item on the proposed agenda. Administration spokesmen have long expressed a desire to get an agreement with Moscow on limiting the flow of arms to the area. In his report Mr. Nixon gave an assessment of the scope of Soviet involvement in Egypt.

In 1970, he related, the Russians deployed some 80 antiaircraft missiles, several squadrons of Soviet-manned combat aircraft, 5,000 missile crewmen and technicians, and about 11,000 other advisers. Since then, he said, they have introduced mobile antiaircraft missiles, the advanced MIG-23 fighter and other aircraft. Most recently they have sent TU-16 bombers, equipped with long-range missiles, he added.

President Nixon said that the Soviet Union and the United States could encourage a Middle East settlement by furthering negotiation.

Tensions in Europe

Mr. Nixon said he also expected to discuss in Moscow the prospects for further easing of tensions in Europe. He said the United States favored participation in a carefully prepared European conference on security and cooperation, long proposed by the Soviet bloc. He reiterated that he opposed a unilateral cut in United States forces in Europe.

In summarizing the year's events, the President laid heavy stress on still-secret correspondence he had with Soviet leaders. He indicated that it helped facilitate the agreement on an improved status for West Berlin and the understanding on the arms talks announced last May 20.

* * *

February 28, 1972

NIXON AND CHOU AGREE TO RENEW CONTACTS; U.S. TO WITHDRAW GRADUALLY FROM TAIWAN

CHINA VISIT ENDS

President Presents a Pledge to Build Pacific 'Bridge'

By MAX FRANKEL
Special to The New York Times.

SHANGHAI, Monday, Feb. 28—President Nixon and Premier Chou En-lai concluded a week of unusual negotiations here today and parted with an American pledge to arrange a gradual withdrawal of United States forces from Taiwan and a joint pledge for a gradual increase in American-Chinese contacts and exchanges.

Mr. Nixon, contending that "This was the week that changed the world," headed home with a conviction that both governments were committed to "build a bridge" across the Pacific and 22 years of hostility. The President took off from Shanghai at 10:12 A.M. (9:12 P.M. Sunday New York time) and was scheduled to reach Washington, after a stopover in Alaska, at 9 P.M. Monday, New York time.

Chou at Airport

Premier Chou saw his guests off at the airport in an informal farewell, warm and high-spirited but without any ceremony. He held to the President's original vow to let their joint communiqué "speak for itself."

The communiqué alternated between statements of agreement and separate statements of divergent positions—a technique that is not uncommon in diplomacy but that was employed rather extensively by the two leaders.

The United States committed itself not to challenge the contention of both the Communist and Nationalist Chinese that "Taiwan is part of China." It reported Washington's desire for a peaceful settlement "by the Chinese themselves" and with that "prospect" in mind asserted the President's "ultimate objective of the withdrawal of all United States forces and military installations from Taiwan."

In the meantime, but without timetable, Mr. Nixon promised progressively to reduce the 8,000-man American contingent on the island "as the tension in the area diminishes." Almost all of the American forces in Taiwan are operating in support of the troops in Vietnam, but the Nixon Administration appears now to be earmarking their presence for diplomatic use in the developing relationship with China.

Taiwan Issue Held Crucial

American officials here insisted, however, that the United States would maintain the defense commitment to Taiwan that exists under the 1954 Mutual Defense Treaty. But this commitment was not mentioned in the communiqué.

On behalf of the Peking Government, the communiqué said that the Taiwan issue remained "the crucial question obstructing" normal relations with the United States. But it agreed to several steps, also without timetable, toward closer contacts.

The Chinese promised to stay in touch with the United States Government through various official channels, including the occasional dispatch to Peking of a senior American representative for diplomatic discussions. They agreed to "facilitate" further unofficial contacts in science, technology, culture, sports and journalism. And they agreed to permit the progressive development of trade with the United States.

These provisions on Taiwan and contacts formed the core of the bargain struck by Mr. Nixon and Premier Chou in 15 hours of formal talks last week, mostly in Peking. The two leaders, in their communiqué, touched on many other subjects, some of them concrete and some of them rather general. But the success of the collaboration they sought hinged on the central compromise.

The President had wanted an even faster pace of diplomatic and private communications and exchanges. The Premier had wanted a firmer recognition of Peking as the sole and legal government on Taiwan.

Movement by Both Sides

Both sides moved somewhat from past positions, but their concessions were in the realm of future action. Therefore, the degree to which they are actually carried out can be regulated to match the performance of the other side. The withdrawal from Taiwan and the contacts with China were not directly linked in the accord, but Henry A. Kissinger, the President's principal adviser, acknowledged that they could "become interdependent again" at any time.

Mr. Kissinger's use of the word "again" was the clearest indication of the trade-off that was arranged. But the President and the Premier had indicated their contending objectives on many other occasions, including the public toasts that they exchanged at alternately warm and restrained banquets through the week.

They parted in high spirits, at least outwardly. They downed a number of thimble-sized drinks in mutual tribute at a dinner here last night and stood to shake hands warmly on impulse when their host at the dinner, Chang Chun-chiao, the chairman of the Shanghai Revolutionary Committee, celebrated the agreement in his city.

The desire to cooperate in the search for stability in Asia after the Vietnam war was plainly a major impulse for the meeting in the first place. The communiqué said both sides had benefited from the candid discussions at a time of "important changes and great upheavals" in the world.

Look to the Future

Mr. Nixon said in his toast that the fact of agreement here and the future conduct of the two nations were even more important than the letter and the words of the communiqué.

Mr. Kissinger, commenting on the accord at a news conference, took the same approach. He said that the direction of the new relationship was more important than the accomplishments of the last week because the two sides had agreed to begin a process of coordinating when their interests converged and of reducing frictions when their interests differed.

A desire to help each other relieve the pressures generated by the Soviet Union was deemed to be another important stimulus toward agreement. On behalf of China and also as an expression of shared attitudes the communiqué twice vowed opposition to any effort to establish "hegemony" in the Asia-Pacific region.

It did not mention the Soviet Union, which Mr. Nixon will visit late in May, and Mr. Kissinger insisted that the language here was not aimed against any specific country. But this disavowal is widely described by American officials as merely a polite dodge for an effort to suggest to the Soviet Union that China and the United States would not let their relations with Moscow interfere with their own diplomatic prospects.

And presumably, the President and the Premier also found important domestic political advantages in the accord and in the elaborately televised public fellowship that accompanied the negotiations.

'Generation of Peace'

Mr. Nixon is returning home ready to argue that he had laid the basis for his "generation of peace." Premier Chou has re-enforced the moderate line by which he is trying to lead China from the convulsions of the Cultural Revolution toward more orderly and profitable development of industry at home and trade and contacts abroad.

The 1,800 word communiqué, issued last evening after two nights of intensive last-minute bargaining—presumably over the Taiwan issue—was divided into five separate but unmarked sections.

The first section was a straightforward account of Mr. Nixon's adjourn in China and his meetings with Mr. Chou and Chairman Mao Tse-tung. Mr. Kissinger said later that the one hour talk with Mr. Mao, the 78-year-old patriarch of Chinese Communism, had been general but not merely philosophical and that the American delegation had reason to believe that the Chairman was consulted by the Premier "at every step along the way."

The second section was made up of long and separate statements by the two sides of their divergent views on Indochina, Korea, Japan and South Asia. They offered statements of support for the rival positions of Hanoi and Saigon in the deadlocked negotiations for a settlement in Vietnam. They recited support for South and North Korea, with the United States stressing the need for "relaxation" of tensions and China stressing the aim of "unification." Neither mentioned its military defense commitments in Korea, where the two countries fought their only war, 22 years ago.

They recorded Washington's pre-eminent desire for "friendly relations" with Japan, and China's concern about Japanese "militarism."

And they reaffirmed their separate but overlapping policies in South Asia, alluding to their collaboration in support of a cease-fire during the recent war between India and Pakistan, a war in which both countries were seen to be leaning toward the defense of Pakistan. The Chinese also deplored "great power rivalry" in the subcontinent.

An agreement on general principles of international conduct made up the third section. Mr. Nixon subscribed fully to the Premier's long-standing definition of peaceful coexistence as first defined at the Bandung Conference of non-aligned nations in 1955, and Mr. Chou accepted an American statement that international disputes should be settled without threat or use of force.

This did not amount to a renunciation of the use of force against Taiwan, which Peking deems to be a province of China and therefore a strictly internal problem.

Statements on Taiwan

In the fourth section, separate Chinese and American statements were made concerning Taiwan, the first calling for an American withdrawal and the second promising withdrawal by stages, but conditionally. Mr. Kissinger would not specify the "tension in the area" that he said would delay the American force reduction for yet some time.

He had previously indicated that nearly all the troops on Taiwan were necessary mostly in support of war efforts in Vietnam. Before the build-up in Indochina, there were only a few hundred American troops in Taiwan, engaged in naval activities and on advisory and aid missions to the Chinese Nationalist Government.

But Mr. Kissinger avoided any suggestion today that an end of the fighting in Indochina would permit—or assure—the promised pullout. On the contrary, the Nixon Administration appears eager to extend the process of withdrawal to retain some leverage in the unfolding relationship with China. Its definitions of policy have already eroded the diplomatic position of the Nationalists—in the United Nations and in many other countries. This is expected to set in motion a form of political erosion on Taiwan and it is doubtful that Mr. Nixon will pull out American forces altogether until he has seen the pace of political change there and in Taiwan's dealings with Peking.

The United States had previously urged the Chinese sides to resolve the Taiwan issue by themselves and had promised not to interfere in this vestige of the Chinese civil wars. But in taking that step toward Peking, the President had also pledged to maintain diplomatic relations with and defense commitments to the Nationalists—pledges that were not mentioned in the communiqué.

Repetition Avoided

They were last made in the President's State of the World Message earlier this month and Mr. Kissinger said they remained active. But it was embarrassing on the Chinese mainland to repeat commitments with such an unpleasant ring to the hosts, he indicated, and so they were left out of the joint declaration. Mr. Kissinger asked that the issue not be raised further in this setting.

He also contended that the gradual withdrawal of American troops had been indicated on "innumerable" previous occasions by the Administration. He could not cite any precedents and reporters remembered only a statement to that effect by him last fall. And the pledge of an eventual total withdrawal of American forces had never been given before.

The fifth section of the communiqué consisted of expressions of agreement that the two nations would promote more exchanges of private groups, more trade and some continuous diplomatic link.

Mr. Kissinger indicated that the Chinese would refuse to send official representatives to Washington as long as the Chinese Nationalists maintained diplomatic status there. For the same reason, the Peking Government appears determined to move more slowly and in largely indirect ways on all forms of exchange and contact.

The communiqué did not mention it directly, but Mr. Kissinger said he thought a "contact point" between Washington and Peking would be established in the "reasonably near future," though not in the United States. He cited the precedent of the occasional and slow-paced ambassadorial talks between the United States and China in Warsaw over the last 15 years. He appeared to have in mind a more active channel, such as those he developed in Canada and elsewhere to arrange his and the President's trips here.

The official representatives who would be sent to Peking "from time to time" could have ambassadorial or even Cabinet rank, Mr. Kissinger indicated. Now that the President and the Secretary of State, William P. Rogers, and Mr. Kissinger have all been here, such a mission would obviously be well within the bounds of precedent.

Over all, however, Mr. Kissinger contended that the agreement took the two countries far beyond their positions of a year ago when the American table tennis team received its invitation to Peking and when Chairman Mao first indicated through Edgar Snow, the late American journalist, that the President would be received here if he wished to come.

At that time, Mr. Kissinger said, China envisioned only low-level people-to-people exchanges. China's decision to encourage much broader exchanges, to create a diplomatic mechanism for continuing contact and to join the United States in the definition of policy principles were all still "unthinkable" a year ago, he added.

Authority Limited

The talks here last week also ranged beyond his own conversations with Premier Chou, in July and October, Mr. Kissinger said, in that he had none of the President's ability to make commitments and to speak with authority on a variety of topics.

This defense of the value of Mr. Nixon's personal involvement was also offered by Ronald L. Ziegler, the President's press secretary, in a television statement before American cameras here. The very fact of the communiqué between the governments "is symbolic of the greater understanding produced" by the participation of Mr. Nixon, Mr. Ziegler said.

The President's concluding comment on the communiqué was an expression of gratitude for the "gracious hospitality" shown him by the Chinese Government. Encompassed in that remark was gratitude not only for the food and the comfortable quarters made available to the American visitors but also for the security and communications arrangements and the extraordinary efforts to facilitate live-color transmission of television coverage of many of Mr. Nixon's activities here.

The Chinese allowed hundreds of technicians and newsmen to run through their cities in every direction to manage this technological extravaganza, with the help of two ground stations that fed the television signals to a satellite over the Pacific for relay to New York.

Mr. Nixon's host thus provided him with a massive stage, from the Great Hall of the People in Peking to the Great Wall of China, 35 miles away, and other attractions in Hangchow and Shanghai. Apparently the Chinese understood Mr. Nixon's political desire for exposure at home in this election year and deemed it an accommodation that could be made without significant loss of control in their own territory. They may even have calculated that the vast coverage only further committed the President to a successful outcome here, thus easing their negotiating task somewhat.

No 'Scoreboard Mentality'

Mr. Kissinger insisted that the American delegation did not look upon the relationship here with a scoreboard mentality, registering points for or against one side or the other on various issues. But the Presidential aide, who has been the impresario for the entire undertaking, was unusually tense in addressing the news conference.

This was probably due in part to the inhibitions imposed by the need to address sensitive subjects on Chinese soil. But the nervousness appeared also to derive from a sense in the American delegation that some of its concessions might not be favorably received at home or in allied capitals.

As one diplomatic reporter observed, the negotiating side that feels it is coming out ahead does not usually disdain a look at the scoreboard.

Also appearing at the news conference was Marshall Green, the Assistant Secretary of State for East Asia, who will now fly to Tokyo, Taipei and other allied capitals in Asia to report on the discussions here and to avoid resentment or charges of diplomatic betrayal.

Mr. Kissinger was the principal "go-between" at the conference, negotiating difficult issues with Chiao Kuan-hua, a deputy foreign minister, on behalf of the principals. Secretary Rogers and the Chinese Foreign Minister, Chi Peng-fei, met for a total of 10 hours with their aides to consider more specific aspects of the same issues. They apparently dealt with the problems posed by more extensive contacts without diplomatic recognition and appeared to have concluded that easiest progress would come in places where unofficial groups such as academies of sciences or universities were available to deal directly with their counterparts and without Government involvement in China.

Some of the negotiators were up until 5 A.M. Saturday and again until 3 A.M. yesterday to prepare the final communiqué. At the very end they were juggling such minor issues as whether the Chinese view of some questions or the American view should be listed first. They decided in the end to run some paragraphs one way in the English version and in a different order in the Chinese text.

Premier Chou called on Mr. Nixon at his guest house for an hour before the departure, just reviewing their conversations and saying good-by.

Then at the airport, the Premier, in an obviously good mood and appearing to be very pleased with the outcome of the talks, dealt warmly with all the American officials. When Chou said good-by Marshall Green, who is flying out separately from Shanghai, the Premier, obviously aware of the Assistant Secretary's upcoming mission, said, "You have a difficult job."

After the President's plane took off, Mr. Chou surprised the American correspondents by remaining on the airport apron bantering with them for about 10 minutes.

Chou Fields Questions

There were some trivial exchanges. But there were also a couple of half-serious questions that he fielded alertly.

One newsman said that people hoped to see him at the United Nations or in the United States one day. He indicated that he had no plans to come to the United States, that this was work for his United Nations delegation.

Foreign Ministry officials at the airport would not talk much about the accord, but they did indicate that they thought the discussions a "positive" experience and they seemed happier than that with their outcome.

These officials clearly interpreted the communiqué and the week of talks as yet another step in American disengagement from involvement with Chiang Kai-shek and the Nationalists.

* * *

February 29, 1972

PRESIDENT HOME AFTER CHINA TRIP; REASSURES ALLIES

No Secret Deals, He Says, or Yielding on Pledges to Any Other Country

BIG WELCOMING CROWD

He Says He Has Returned With Beginnings of a New Relationship With Peking

Special to The New York Times.

WASHINGTON, Feb. 28—President Nixon returned here tonight from his journey to China and told a large and warm welcoming crowd that he had established "the basis of a structure for peace" without sacrificing America's commitments to any of its allies.

"We've agreed that we will not negotiate the fate of other nations behind their back, and we did not do so in Peking," he declared. "There were no secret deals of any kind. We have done all this without giving up any United States commitment to any other country."

Mr. Nixon mentioned no nation by name, but his assurance of continuing commitments was clearly and principally addressed to the Nationalist Government on Taiwan with which the United States has a defense treaty. That commitment was stressed by Henry A. Kissinger, the President's assistant for national security affairs, in responding to newsmens' questions in Shanghai yesterday.

Large Crowd on Hand

Mr. Nixon's plane, the Spirit of '76, arrived in front of a hangar at Andrews Air Force Base in Maryland at 9:15 P.M. after a seven-hour flight from Anchorage, where he spent part of the day resting and adjusting to the 13-hour time difference between Peking and Washington.

The crowd awaiting him inside the hangar, estimated by Air Force officials at more than 5,000, consisted of Cabinet members, Congressional leaders, the diplomatic corps, members of the White House staff who had not made the journey, and thousands of Government employes and their wives.

Army musicians greeted the President with "Hail to the Chief" when he and Mrs. Nixon emerged from the plane.

Vice President Agnew introduced him to the crowd and thanked him by saying: "We feel easier tonight because of the trip you took."

Returns to White House

As the Air Force band played spirited marches, Mr. Nixon boarded his Marine Corps helicopter for the flight home and his first night's sleep at the White House in nearly two weeks.

It was not immediately clear whether the President planned another, formal report to the nation on his voyage to Peking. But from the tone and content of his remarks tonight, he appeared to have intended them as a summation of the results of the trip as he viewed them.

Mindful, perhaps, of criticism not only from the Chinese Nationalists but also from members of his own party that he had traded away too much and gained too little, Mr. Nixon seemed to go to unusual lengths to say that he had not intended to sacrifice old friends even as he opened new channels to his enemies.

He also said that he had no illusions that the communiqué issued by the two Governments yesterday in Shanghai would "guarantee peace in our time."

No 'Magic Formula'

"We did not bring back any written or unwritten agreements that will guarantee peace in our time," he said. "We did not bring home any magic formula which will make unnecessary the efforts of the American people to continue to maintain the strength so that we can continue to be free."

In addition, the President described the communiqué as unique in the sense that it tried "honestly" to set forth differences between the two nations "rather than trying to cover them up with diplomatic double-talk."

Mr. Nixon wound up his remarks by saying that he had been reminded "of the greatness of our country" as he flew above it on the trip from Anchorage.

"Most of all," he said, "I thought of the freedom, the opportunity, the progress that 200 million Americans are privileged to enjoy. I realized again, this is a beautiful country."

Knot of Hecklers

While most of the large gathering was friendly, a small knot of hecklers clustered together in a far corner of the hangar and occasionally shouted hostile but largely inaudible words. Some of the demonstrators carried umbrellas by which they intended to link Mr. Nixon symbolically to Neville Chamberlain, the British Prime Minister who was accused of appeasement after he signed the Munich Pact.

Other demonstrators, who seemed equally opposed to Mr. Nixon's trip, carried signs supporting Representative John M. Ashbrook of Ohio, who represents Mr. Nixon's conservative challenge in the New Hampshire primary.

Tonight's gathering was clearly well planned. The White House staff had of course been urged to come, and tickets had been distributed in large blocks in the various Government departments. Meanwhile, the Air Force had turned the hangar in which the Presidential jet is normally serviced, into a model of spit and polish.

One conspicuous absentee was James C. H. Shen, the Chinese Nationalist Ambassador. A spokesman for his embassy here said the Ambassador had previously scheduled a dinner engagement but conceded that Mr. Shen wished also to reflect his Government's displeasure with the Nixon visit and with the joint communiqué.

Ambassador Shen entertained 14 people at a dinner to honor Alfred P. Chamie, the retired national commander of the American Legion, who received a decoration entitled "Cloud and Banner" on behalf of President Chiang Kai-shek.

Ambassador Shen said he and his guests watched the President's arrival on television and heard his speech, but he declined any comment on Mr. Nixon's remarks.

Prominent among the diplomatic corps was the Soviet Ambassador to the United States, Anatoly F. Dobrynin. He was the second diplomat greeted by Mr. Nixon after he shook hands with the dean of the corps, Ambassador Guillermo Sevilla-Sacasa of Nicaragua.

In his comments tonight, Mr. Nixon did not depart in terms of substance from what he had said earlier in Peking and what was said in the joint communiqué.

Agreements Are Listed

Among what he called "necessary and important beginnings" he listed agreements to expand cultural and journalistic contacts between the two nations; agreements to broaden trade; and an agreement that communications between the two Governments must be "strengthened and expanded."

More broadly, he insisted, both sides agreed that they were opposed to "domination of the Pacific area by any one power" and that international disputes should be settled by peaceful means.

He recalled also the part of the communiqué in which he had told his Chinese host that the United States would gradually reduce its forces on Taiwan "as tensions ease." But it was at this point in his remarks that he insisted that he had made "no secret deals of any kind."

Like much of the Presidential trip itself, tonight's arrival ceremony was carried live and in color during prime time hours.

The President will brief both the Cabinet and Congressional leader on details of his trip tomorrow.

* * *

April 27, 1972

NIXON TO WITHDRAW 20,000 MORE; EXPRESSES OPTIMISM ON VIETNAM; FOE BEGINS NEW QUANGTRI DRIVE

SPEECH TO NATION

President Is Expecting Progress in Paris—Air Raids to Go On

By ROBERT B. SEMPLE Jr.
Special to The New York Times.

WASHINGTON, April 26—President Nixon said tonight that he was continuing his troop withdrawal program despite the heavy enemy offensive in South Vietnam.

In a nationwide television and radio address, Mr. Nixon announced that 20,000 more troops would be withdrawn from South Vietnam by July 1, a move that would reduce authorized American troop strength to 49,000.

While sober and earnest in his presentation before the cameras, the President sounded a generally optimistic note about the military situation in Vietnam, and while not going into detail, he also said he was approaching the resumption of the Paris peace talks tomorrow with considerable hope. In Paris earlier, the Vietnamese Communists had agreed to attend.

Evaluation by Abrams

Mr. Nixon said that he had received this morning an evaluation of the fighting from his commander in Vietnam—Gen. Creighton W. Abrams—and that the general was convinced that despite four weeks of bitter fighting the South Vietnamese could contain the invasion "if we continue to provide air and sea support."

The President pledged to continue such support and to persist with air and naval attacks on enemy installations in North Vietnam "until the North Vietnamese stop their offensive in South Vietnam."

On the diplomatic front, Mr. Nixon offered no new negotiating proposals, asserting that the United States had already offered generous terms for peace. But he said that despite the enemy's refusal to accept these terms, or even talk seriously about them, "we are resuming the Paris talks with the firm expectation that productive talks leading to rapid progress will follow through all available channels."

Although the address was advertised in advance as a speech on troop levels and an evaluation of the military conditions in the field, Mr. Nixon clearly hoped to use the occasion not only to emphasize the distance he had come in winding down an inherited war but to explain the basis for his policies and appeal for public support for them.

He mentioned none of his opponents or other critics by name, but he said the enemy's "one remaining hope" was to weaken the fiber of the American spirit and "win in the Congress of the United States'' the victory "they cannot win among the people of South Vietnam."

For his part, he said, he intended to stand firm, and he pleaded to his audience to stand with him.

"The great question," he said, "is how we, the American people, will respond to this final challenge."

'We Have Evidence'

The President gave no reasons for his optimism about the peace talks. But his national security adviser, Henry A. Kissinger, who returned two days ago from a secret mission to Moscow, said, "We have evidence" suggesting that the appropriate moment had come to test Communist intentions at the negotiating table.

Specifically, Mr. Kissinger drew the attention of newsmen to reports that Le Duc Tho, a member of the Hanoi Politburo, might be returning to Paris. Mr. Kissinger said Le Duc Tho did not journey to Paris for "trivial" reasons.

The security adviser did not specifically say so, but he left the impression that during his visit to Moscow he had received hints that the talks might be productive.

He also recalled that the White House had consistently believed that the war would end by negotiations, and that the current major offensive might well be a prelude to negotiations.

Mr. Kissinger also shed a bit of light on what the United States would ask of the North Vietnamese when negotiations resume tomorrow.

Halt of Invasion Is Key

In his address, Mr. Nixon repeated the essence of yesterday's announcement that the United States would insist that the first order of business "will be to get the enemy to halt his invasion of South Vietnam." He listed one additional condition, that the enemy "return the American prisoners of war."

In a briefing with newsmen before the President's address, a text of which had been distributed, Mr. Kissinger was asked to expand on Mr. Nixon's remarks. He said he did not want to "negotiate at a press conference," but added that the Administration would ask Hanoi to withdraw those troops that had crossed the demilitarized zone straddling the border between the two Vietnams in apparent violation of a 1968 understanding.

When asked about the other North Vietnamese troops that entered South Vietnam via Cambodia and Laos, Mr. Kissinger said the Administration's position would be spelled out in detail at the negotiating table.

Asked to explain the purpose of the heavy bombing by the United States, he said it had two essential purposes: the first was to "defeat" the enemy offensive in South Vietnam by preventing enemy troops from either seizing control of "many" provincial capitals or gaining control of the countryside.

The second was to reduce Hanoi's capacity to mount a major offensive later in the year. This was the reason, he said, for the bombing of the Hanoi-Haiphong area.

As expected, Mr. Nixon devoted some of his speech to an explanation of his determination not to call a unilateral halt to American involvement in Indochina. He said, "We will not be defeated, and we will never surrender our friends to Communist aggression," insisting that to do so now would undermine America's diplomatic credibility throughout the world and encourage wars of aggression elsewhere.

"As we come to the end of this long and difficult struggle," he said, "we must be steadfast. We must not falter. For all that we have risked and all that we have gained over the years now hangs in the balance during the coming weeks and months. If we now let down our friends, we shall surely be letting down ourselves and our future as well."

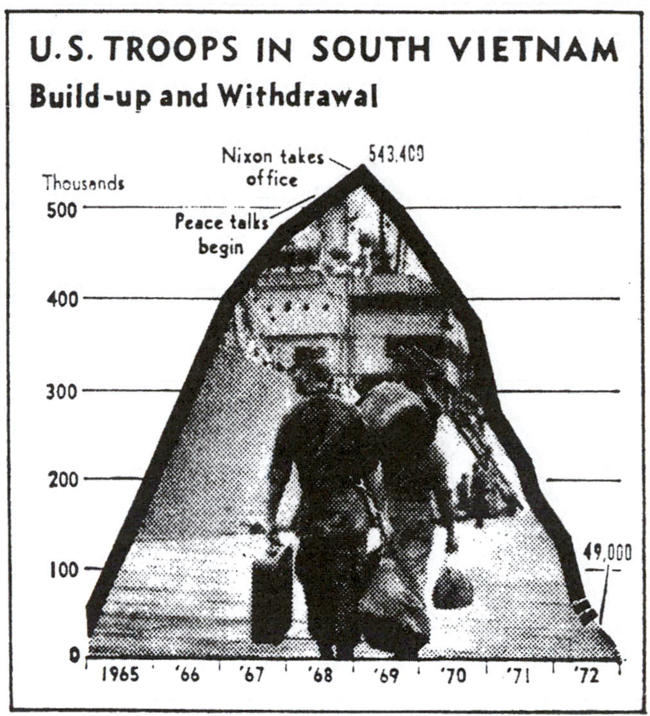

The New York Times

While highest authorized troop strength was 549,500, the peak that was reached was 543,400 in April, 1969.

Hope for Fruitful Talks

After his speech the President flew to Key Biscayne, Fla.

Earlier in the day the Defense Department volunteered a sanguine assessment of battlefield conditions, while the State Department expressed hopes that Mr. Nixon's decision to return to negotiations would lead to fruitful and serious talks.

The Pentagon spokesman, Jerry W. Friedheim, said he found cause for cheer in the fact that after four weeks of hard fighting the South Vietnamese had "acquitted themselves well" under adverse conditions.

"We are encouraged," he said, adding that "the enemy has taken very major casualties and is on his way to another set of losses similar to the 1968 Tet offensive."

According to "estimates and approximations," he said, the enemy—the North Vietnamese and the Vietcong—had "suffered half or more losses than he suffered in 1968."

At the State Department, meanwhile, officials said the United States had decided to attend the peace talks tomorrow to "explore" the possibility that Hanoi might be prepared to act in a more conciliatory manner.

The State Department officials also hinted broadly that the United States was prepared to resume secret talks with the North Vietnamese in Paris.

The State Department spokesman, Charles W. Bray 3d, refused despite intensive questioning to explain why the United States had agreed to return to the negotiating table after repeatedly saying that it would not do so while the North Vietnamese invasion continued.

However, speculation persisted here that the secret visit to Moscow by Mr. Kissinger had played an important role in Mr. Nixon's decision to resume the talks. Mr. Kissinger's mission was disclosed yesterday.

Privately, officials insisted that although there were encouraging signs on the military front, and elements of hope, however slim, on the diplomatic front, Mr. Nixon remained firm in his readiness to invoke additional American air and sea power to compensate for the dwindling number of combat troops and to help Saigon resist the enemy assault.

As evidence, Pentagon sources said that the United States was preparing to send 36 more F-4 fighter-bombers to Southeast Asia. The planes are expected, to leave Homestead and Eglin Air Force bases in Florida in a few days.

200 Planes for Asia

This move would bring to about 200 the number of heavy bombers and fighter-bombers flown to the war zone since the enemy offensive began late in March. In addition, the Navy has roughly doubled the number of its fighting ships off Vietnam.

The President's speech represented his first public assessment of the situation in Vietnam since the North Vietnamese offensive began.

It also represented his eighth public announcement on the numbers of United States troops in Vietnam since he assumed office on Jan. 20, 1969, when the authorized strength in Vietnam was 549,500 men.

Mr. Nixon began withdrawing troops from South Vietnam in June, 1969, with an announcement on Midway Island that 25,000 would come home by Aug. 31. During 1969 and 1970, Americans left Vietnam at an average rate of 10,000 to 12,000 men a month.

The monthly rate accelerated rapidly after Mr. Nixon's sixth withdrawal statement on Nov. 12, 1971. Under withdrawal timetables announced then and on Jan. 13, 1972—his last statement on troops before tonight—Americans have been leaving Vietnam at a rate of about 23,000 men a month.

Neither the President nor Mr. Kissinger promised that there would be any cuts beyond the 49,000 target on July 1. Mr. Nixon has said publicly that he intended to leave a residual force in South Vietnam until the prisoners of war were released. And this was the first of his troop-withdrawal announcements in which he did not promise to make another such announcement at some further date.

Mr. Kissinger said that the monthly withdrawal rate would now drop to 10,000 a month. But he said that to sustain the previous withdrawal rate of 23,000 a month would have meant that by Aug. 1 the United States would have given away to the enemy what Washington is trying to make Hanoi earn through negotiations.

* * *

May 27, 1972

U.S. AND SOVIET SIGN TWO ARMS ACCORDS TO LIMIT GROWTH OF ATOMIC ARSENALS; TRADE PACT DELAYED, TALKS TO GO ON

CEILINGS ARE SET

Nixon and Brezhnev Pledge to Abide by Treaty at Once

By HEDRICK SMITH
Special to The New York Times.

MOSCOW, Saturday, May 27—President Nixon and the Soviet Communist party leader, Leonid I. Brezhnev, signed two historic agreements last night that for the first time put limits on the growth of American and Soviet strategic nuclear arsenals.

In a brief televised ceremony in the Great Hall of the Kremlin, the two leaders put their signatures to a treaty that establishes a ceiling of 200 launchers for each side's defensive missile systems and commits them not to try to build nationwide antimissile defenses. The treaty, which is to run indefinitely, requires ratification by the Senate in Washington, but both sides pledged to abide by it at once.

Applause After Signing

They also signed an interim accord on offensive systems that freezes land-based and submarine-based intercontinental missiles at the level now in operation or under construction.

After signing the two accords, Mr. Brezhnev and Mr. Nixon walked toward each other, smiling broadly, and shook hands vigorously amidst applause from a gathering of senior officials, including negotiators who had worked through the day to put the final touches on the agreement.

Mr. Nixon then said:

"We want to be remembered by our deeds, not by the fact that we brought war to the world, but by the fact that we made the world a more peaceful one for all peoples of the world."

Can Improve Quality

Mr. Kosygin said in reply:

"This is a great victory for the Soviet and American peoples in the matter of easing international tension. This is a victory for all peaceloving people, because security and peace is the common goal."

Later, American officials reported that the two leaders had resolved several deadlocks in their talks here this week.

In a toast at a dinner he gave for the Soviet leaders at Spaso House, the American Ambassador's residence, the President hailed the agreements as "enormously important."

Gerard C. Smith, the chief American negotiator, told reporters that today's two agreements were "not the end of the road by any means, but they are a very solid step forward."

The agreements place no limitations on qualitative improvements in either offensive or defensive systems, no ceilings on the numbers of warheads that can be carried by offensive missiles, and no controls on the number of strategic bombers permited each side. Moderization of missiles, including the emplacement of new missiles in existing silos, would be allowed.

Moreover, during the five-year term of the agreement on offensive missiles, both sides are permitted to "cash in" some of their older land-based missiles and build additional missile submarines. In addition, the Russians would be permitted to replace some of their older submarines with new ones.

Henry A. Kissinger, Mr. Nixon's adviser on national security, said the two sides had agreed that, as of now, the Soviet Union has a total of 2,328 missiles, 1,618 intercontinental ballistic missiles and 710 on nuclear submarines, compared with 1,710 for the United States—1,054 ICBM's and 656 on submarines.

If the Soviet Union were to use all their options of replacing obsolete missiles and submarines, Mr. Kissinger explained in a post-midnight briefing, they could achieve a level of 950 missiles on submarines with a reduction to 1,408 on land, maintaining a numerical edge of about 600 missiles.

Mr. Kissinger also acknowledged that since Soviet warheads were larger, it had a 3-to-1 advantage over the United States in explosive tonnage.

Offsetting this, however, the United States has an advantage of 460 strategic bombers to 140 for the Soviet Union, and, more important, is expected by the end of this year to have a lead in nuclear warheads of 5,700 to 2,500 for the Soviet Union. This does not include any of the nuclear weapons available to the American forward air units based in Europe, which were excluded from the agreements, despite Moscow's previous desire to see this air power covered by the agreement.

Initial news briefings by American officials made it impossible to calculate the Soviet numerical advantage with preci-

United Press International

President Nixon and Leonid I. Brezhnev exchange treaty copies at Kremlin. In center, Soviet President Nikolai V. Podgorny.

sion. But in any case, the United States is expected by the end of 1972 to have a lead in nuclear warheads of 5,700 to 2,500.

In effect, the agreements match off the size of the Soviet arsenal against the technological superiority of the American arsenal, preserving the strategic parity that both sides feel they have achieved.

Despite the fact that neither agreement provides for on-site inspection to check against violators, American officials expressed satisfaction that other means of verification would be adequate.

In the agreements, both sides pledged "not to interfere with the national technical means of verification of the other party." In addition, the offensive-missile agreement states that neither side will use "deliberate concealment measures which impede verification."

Each side has the right to withdraw from either agreement by giving six months' notice, if it feels its supreme national interests are in jeopardy.

Critics have charged in advance that such agreements would merely divert the arms race from a competition in number to one in quality primarily by placing multiple warheads on the current force of offensive missiles.

The United States began this process with its Polaris submarine force and with some of its land-based Minuteman missiles, while the arms talks were under way and while the Soviet missile force was growing in size.

Without denying that point, Mr. Kissinger and other administration officials contended at briefings tonight that the agreements would serve to "arrest" the arms race.

The defensive missile treaty provides for establishment of a joint consultative commission to consider questions of compliance and the offensive missile agreement calls for "follow-on negotiations" to achieve a full-fledged treaty in that field.

None of the Soviet leaders had a direct comment on the agreement, but in their behalf, a spokesman declared Moscow's satisfaction with treaties that in its estimation accorded "non unilateral advantage" to either side.

Advancing the Administration's basic argument in anticipation of Congressional criticism that the Russians have been granted numerical advantages, Mr. Kissinger told newsmen that the Administration considered the combination of agreements signed today a major step toward stabilizing the arms race and international stability in general, toward creating

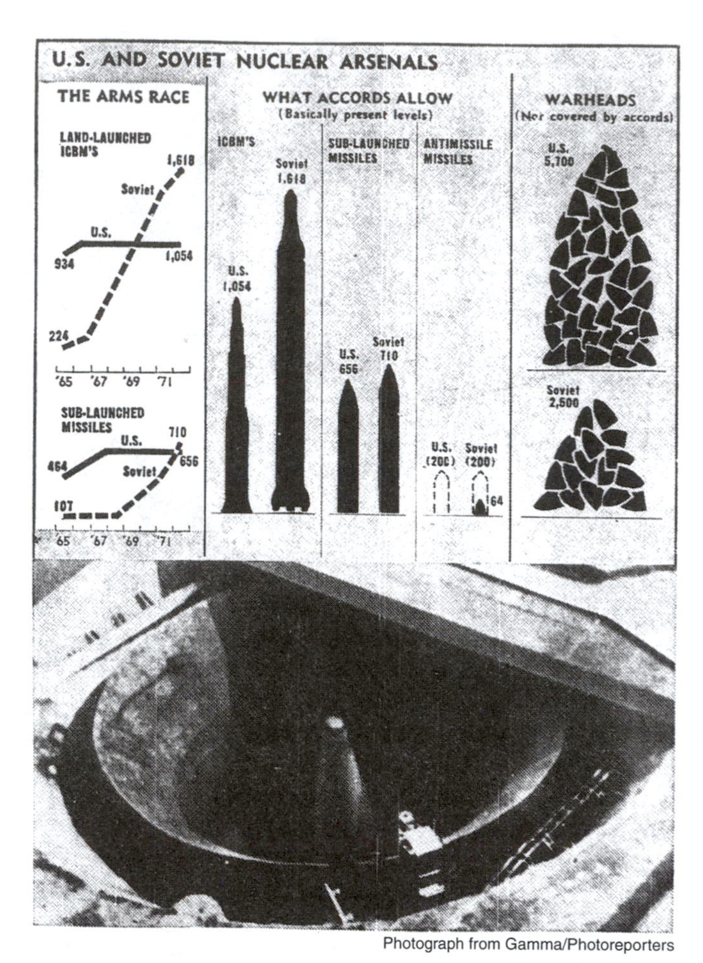

Photograph from Gamma/Photoreporters

MISSILE IN SILO: Above photograph, from a Czech source, is said to show a Soviet emplacement. Soviet arms totals on chart include weapons that are under construction.

mutual confidence and turning away from the old pattern of the postwar relations.

Specifically, he contended the agreement would slow the momentum of the Soviet arms build-up, which he said had been adding roughly 250 new nuclear-tipped missiles a year, on land and sea.

Mr. Smith, in a briefing for newsmen at the American Embassy, put greater stress on the curbs on defensive missiles. By forswearing an attempt to defend their populations or to try to defend more than a small portion of their own land-based strike forces, he said, both countries were deliberately leaving themselves vulnerable to the deterrent power of the other.

"This is an admission of tremendous psychological importance, a recognition that the deterrence force of either side is not going to be challenged," he said.

The essential reasoning behind the combination of agreements is that each side can now be confident that the other will not dare to attempt a nuclear attack because it does not have sufficient defenses to protect itself from retaliation, especially when large, mobile submarine-based forces exist on both sides.

The size of the submarine forces was one of the major points that was thrashed out this week by Mr. Nixon and Mr. Brezhnev and their aides. The United States, which has 41 nuclear-armed submarines, came into Moscow prepared to grant the Soviets a level of 42 nuclear, or Y-class, submarines in operation or under construction. But the Soviet leaders said they had 48, with 768 missiles. In the end, they compromised on 45 submarines with a total of 710 missiles.

Mr. Kissinger said the difference in Soviet and American figures was evidently due to varying definitions of what constituted a submarine under construction, whether it should be counted before or after its hull was completed.

There was an additional problem over how many obsolete G- and H-class Soviet submarines would be eligible for substitution by newer Y-class submarines with long-range missiles.

One of the major American aims was to obtain a limit on the number of giant Soviet SS-9 missiles, capable of carrying three five-megaton warheads apiece or many more smaller ones.

Throughout the negotiations, the United States insisted on a subquota for the SS-9's within the over-all missile ceilings and the agreement signed tonight included prohibitions on the Soviet Union putting in place more than "about 300" large SS-9's, a White House fact sheet stated.

Evidently with such provisions in mind, Mr. Kissinger told newsmen that the Joint Chiefs of Staff supported the agreements signed today. The military leadership had been particularly alarmed by the build-up of the Soviet SS-9 force over the last few years.

The antimissile agreement permits each country to have two ABM sites, each with 100 launchers. One is to defend the national capital, primarily against accidental attack or attack by third countries. The second complex would be established in a distant location to protect a portion of the land-based retaliatory force.

The United States specified that its second site would be at Grand Forks Air Base in North Dakota. The treaty requires the Soviet Union, which already has a ring of launchers around Moscow and in European Russia, to place its second site at least 800 miles from Moscow so that it cannot be hooked up with the Moscow system to provide continuous protection for a large percentage of the Soviet population.

* * *

May 30, 1972

NIXON AND BREZHNEV CLOSE TALKS WITH JOINT DECLARATION ON PEACE; 3 RUSSIAN LEADERS INVITED TO U.S.

A NEW ERA SOUGHT

2 Sides Pledge to Try to Avoid Military Confrontations

By HEDRICK SMITH

Special to The New York Times.

MOSCOW, May 29—President Nixon and the Soviet Communist party leader, Leonid I. Brezhnev, concluded their historic week of summit talks today with a declaration of principles intended to mark a new, more stable and constructive era of Russian-American relations despite continuing differences over such issues as Vietnam.

In the spirit of joint satisfaction that accompanied the end of Mr. Nixon's visit to Moscow, he invited Mr. Brezhnev, President Nikolai V. Podgorny and Premier Aleksei N. Kosygin to come to the United States. They accepted without setting a date but a White House official said a visit was unlikely before the election in November.

The joint declaration, initially proposed by the Soviet Union, was accepted by Mr. Nixon only after progress had been made during the negotiations last week.

Embraced in it are broad pledges that both sides will "do their utmost to avoid military confrontations," will "always exercise restraint in their mutual relations" and will refrain from efforts "to obtain unilateral advantage at the expense of the other" in tactical situations. The principles also commit them to promote favorable conditions for increasing economic and cultural relations.

After saying farewells in Moscow, President and Mrs. Nixon flew to the Ukrainian capital, Kiev, for an overnight stop before going to Iran and Poland on their way to Washington, where they are to arrive Thursday.

A joint communiqué issued before the Nixons left Moscow gave no indication that significant progress toward a Vietnam settlement had been made.

Publicly, each side restated its established position in the most cordial form, though a White House official characterized the private talks as "long, sometimes difficult and very detailed." Tonight, in a briefing for newsmen, Henry A. Kissinger, the President's adviser on national security, indicated that the mining of Haiphong harbor and the American bombing of North Vietnam would continue in the face of Soviet objections and he gave no clue on the timing of a new round of secret talks in Paris.

"We do not intend to take unilateral action," Mr. Kissinger said in answer to a question about whether the Moscow meetings might have persuaded President Nixon to change his military tactics against North Vietnam.

Despite the differences on Vietnam, the leaders took the extraordinary step of issuing the declaration of principles consisting of 12 points that Mr. Kissinger said "marked a departure in Soviet-American relations" from a period of "rather rigid hostility" to an era in which both sides would, hopefully, act with "a good deal of restraint and creativity."

Mr. Nixon and Mr. Brezhnev signed the declaration at 2 P.M. in the glittering elegance of St. George's Hall in the Great Palace of the Kremlin.

On other key issues, the following points emerged from the 1,100-word declaration, and the 3,500 word communiqué as amplified by Mr. Kissinger and other Soviet and American spokesmen:

• Force reductions in Europe—In the communiqué, the Soviet Union came closer to American language by endorsing the idea of "reciprocal reductions" of forces and armaments in Central Europe and by agreeing to hold talks "in a special forum." Unresolved were differences between the Soviet desire to negotiate primarily with the United States and the American desire to have negotiations conducted between the Atlantic alliance and the Warsaw Pact, an approach rejected by Moscow.

• European security conference—President Nixon fended off Soviet pleas to hold the conference this year. In the communiqué the two sides agreed that it should be held "without undue delay" but that it should be "carefully prepared." Multilateral preparatory consultations "could begin" after the four-power protocol on Berlin is formally signed, they said.

• The Middle East—The United States dropped public mention of its efforts to promote an interim settlement through the opening of the Suez Canal and through partial pullback of Israeli forces on the Sinai Peninsula. It joined the Soviet Union in a general offer to support the United Nations mediation effort for an over-all settlement, now nearing the end of its fifth year. The only concession from the Russians to the American desire for a curb on outside arms shipments was the observation that a settlement would permit "consideration of further steps to bring about a military relaxation in that area."

• Joint Agreements—About half of the communiqué was devoted to a summary of agreements signed during the past week, with the assertion that both sides attached "great importance" to the accord limiting the size of nuclear arsenals as "a major step toward curbing and ultimately ending the arms race." The importance of those accords, Mr. Kissinger asserted, "transcends the importance of individual restrictions" because it demonstrates the willingness of both sides to restrict their primary armament systems.

• Soviet-American trade—The documents asserted that both sides looked to negotiations culminating in a trade agreement this summer. They would also deal with such interlocking issues as payment on lend-lease loans to the Russians during World War II, American credits for Soviet imports from the United States, shipping costs and a new maritime agreement affecting long-term trade as well as a short-term American grain sale to the Soviet Union.

Differences over the terms of economic relations continued right up to Mr. Nixon's departure. As he was being seen off, Foreign Minister Andrei A. Gromyko remarked, "I hope this land-lease is settled," to which Mr. Nixon replied, "You're too tough."

* * *

December 20, 1972

3 B-52'S, 2 OTHER PLANES LOST IN RAIDS ON NORTH; FOE SHELLS A DESTROYER

2 SAILORS KILLED

3 Reported Wounded—15 Airmen Missing and 6 Are Saved

By JOSEPH B. TREASTER
Special to The New York Times.

SAIGON, South Vietnam, Wednesday, Dec. 20—Three heavy B-52 bombers and two smaller fighter-bombers have been lost since the United States resumed full-scale bombing and mining of North Vietnam Monday evening, an American military spokesman said today.

In addition to the bombing, which was believed to have been of unprecedented magnitude—and is still continuing—North Vietnam was bombarded by American gunships. One of the ships, the guided-missile destroyer Goldsborough, was struck by return fire from North Vietnamese coastal batteries. Two American sailors were killed and three were wounded, the command said.

However, the ship continued with combat operations, the spokesman said. He would not say precisely where the ship had been operating.

Crew Rescued

In the aircraft losses a total of 15 American airmen were listed as missing, joining the more than 1,800 other American servicemen who are either prisoners of war or who are missing in action in Indochina.

The six man crew and a military passenger were rescued from one of the B-52's, which managed to limp over northern Thailand before the men bailed out.

The two other B-52's crashed in the vicinity of Hanoi. One went down 30 miles west of the North Vietnamese capital. The spokesman said he could not immediately give the exact location of the second crash.

[In Hanoi, six American airmen, several of whom were said to be B-52 crewmen, were presented at a news conference, Agence France-Presse reported.]

First B-52 Downed in North

The spokesman said one of the fighter-bombers, an A-7 Corsair of the United States Navy, was hit by enemy fire and crashed at sea off the port of Haiphong. The pilot of the plane along with the two crewmen of the other fighter-bomber, an F-111 of the Air Force, which crashed 50 miles southwest of Haiphong, were among those listed as missing.

Before this, it was reported, no B-52 had crashed in North Vietnam, and the North Vietnamese had had no opportunity to study the plane's complicated electronic defensive systems.

The American military spokesman said that the two B-52's he reported down had crashed as a result of battle damage but that what had happened to the fighter-bomber was not known. He declined to comment on the report that a third B-52 had been lost.

The United States command was unusually uncommunicative about the new raids. It acknowledged in a terse statement that American planes were striking above the 20th Parallel in North Vietnam for the first time since Oct. 22. But, contrary to its daily practice for years, the command yesterday refused to disclose even in general terms the number of planes involved in the strikes or the general areas where the strikes took place, or to give any indication of the damage inflicted.

Informed American military officers estimated that more than 100 B-52's and several hundred fighter-bombers had participated in the raids.

The spokesman was reluctant to discuss any aspect of B-52 operations, including whether any of the eight-engine bombers had been used elsewhere in Indochina during the previous 24 hours or whether all of those available had been sent over North Vietnam.

American officials in the northern region of South Vietnam, where B-52 activity has been heavy in recent months, said that none of the big bombers were used in that area Monday or yesterday. Previously the biggest attack against North Vietnam had been mounted with 16 missions, or about 48 planes.

There are about 200 B-52's assigned to operate in Indochina, with three-quarters of them based at Guam in the Pacific and the rest at the Utapao air base in southern Thailand near Bangkok. They require a great deal of maintenance, and Air Force officers said that only a few more that 100 were available for combat at any time.

The planes routinely carry more than 20 tons of bombs each and drop them in a carpet pattern roughly half a mile wide and a mile and a half long. Most often they operate in flights of three.

The Hanoi radio, which made the first public disclosure of the raids Monday, said in a broadcast monitored here that all through Monday night and early yesterday American planes made repeated raids on "many areas" of Hanoi, the capital, and Haiphong, the chief port, and on six other provinces around the two major cities. The radio gave only sketchy details of damage.

Later in the day Monday it was officially announced in Washington that the United States had resumed the bombing and mining of North Vietnam above the 20th Parallel, and the White House warned that the attacks "will continue until such time as a settlement is arrived at" for ending the war.

Both here and in Washington, United States Government officials have also suggested that the latest raids were intended to disrupt North Vietnamese plans to mount a new offensive in the South. But military men here say they have seen no indication that the North Vietnamese are preparing for such a strike.

B-52's are bigger than Boeing 707 airliners, but they have only seven seats—six for the crew and a seventh that is sometimes occupied by a technician assigned to evaluate flight operations or even at times just an airman who goes along for the ride so as to meet the minimum requirements of time in the air set by the Air Force for collecting flight pay. The military spokesman said he did not know why a seventh person was aboard the B-52 that crashed in Thailand.

Although 11 B-52's had crashed in accidents since the big aircraft began flying over Indochina in 1965, American officers say none were lost to enemy fire until four weeks ago, when a bomber hit during a raid on North Vietnam on Nov. 23 crashed in Thailand on its way back to base.

The aircraft carry elaborate electronic jamming devices that work on several frequencies and had proved to be an almost foolproof defense against the radar-guided surface-to-air missiles of the North Vietnamese.

Recently, however, the B-52's have been flying over North Vietnam in greater numbers and the North Vietnamese, instead of aiming at a specific plane with a missile, as they used to, now often fire barrages—something like a hunter using a shotgun to kill birds. They hope for a lucky hit as the missiles explode into hundreds of pieces of jagged metal.

The B-52 that went down last month was damaged in that way, and that is most likely what happened to the two the spokesman reported lost today, although he said he had no immediate details on what battle damage they had suffered.

Now that a B-52 has crashed in North Vietnam, American officers believe the United States will be forced to devise new electronic defensive systems for the big aircraft. Despite its tactical role in Vietnam, they point out, it remains the principal strategic plane of the United States—the aircraft designed to deliver nuclear weapons in any all-out war.

The F-111 lost in the latest raids was said to be the fifth of the controversial fighter-bombers to be lost since they returned to combat in Vietnam nearly three months ago.

* * *

January 24, 1973

VIETNAM ACCORD IS REACHED; CEASE-FIRE BEGINS SATURDAY; P.O.W.'S TO BE FREE IN 60 DAYS

TROOPS TO LEAVE

On TV, Nixon Asserts 'Peace With Honor' Is Aim of Pact

By BERNARD GWERTZMAN
Special to The New York Times.

WASHINGTON, Jan. 23—President Nixon said tonight that Henry A. Kissinger and North Vietnam's chief negotiator, Le Duc Tho, had initialed an agreement in Paris today "to end the war and bring peace with honor in Vietnam and Southeast Asia."

In a televised report to the nation, a few hours after Mr. Kissinger returned to Washington, Mr. Nixon said a cease-fire in Vietnam would go into effect on Saturday at 7 P.M., Eastern standard time.

Simultaneous announcements were made in Hanoi and Saigon.

Mr. Nixon said that under the terms of the accord—which will be formally signed on Saturday—all American prisoners of war would be released and the remaining 23,700-man American force in South Vietnam would be withdrawn within 60 days.

Wider Peace Indicated

He referred to "peace" in Southeast Asia, suggesting that the accord extended to Laos and Cambodia, which have also been engaged in the war. But there was no direct mention of those two nations today, and it is not known if the cease-fire extends to them as well.

Obviously pleased by the long-awaited development, ending the longest war in American history, Mr. Nixon said the Hanoi-Washington agreement "meets the goals" and has the "full support" of President Nguyen Van Thieu of South Vietnam.

Earlier Mr. Thieu had expressed strong reservations about the draft agreement worked out by Mr. Kissinger and Mr. Tho in October.

Tonight Mr. Nixon sketched only the outline of the accord. The full text of the agreement and accompanying protocols will be issued tomorrow by joint agreement with Hanoi, he said.

It was not possible, for instance, to determine from Mr. Nixon's 10-minute address what changes had been made in the agreement since October.

In his brief description of the accord, Mr. Nixon said that the cease-fire would be "internationally supervised," a reference to the projected force of Canadians, Hungarians, Indonesians and Poles who will supervise the truce. But he did not say how large the force would be. The United States has wanted a highly mobile force of about 5,000 men. The North Vietnamese have suggested a substantially smaller force.

Mr. Nixon also said nothing about the controversial problem of the demilitarized zone that straddles the border between North and South Vietnam. Saigon has wanted this line reaffirmed to make sure, legally, that there are two Vietnams, and Hanoi had resisted this. All the President said on the subject was that the people of South Vietnam "have been guaranteed the right to determine their own future without outside interference."

Captive Issue Avoided

Nothing was said either about the release of the thousands of prisoners in Saigon's jails, many of whom were jailed on suspicion that they were Vietcong agents. At one point in the negotiations, Hanoi was seeking to make the release of American prisoners conditional on the release of Saigon's captives.

Some of these questions may be answered tomorrow when Mr. Kissinger holds a news conference at 11 A.M. It will be televised by the major networks.

Last fall, the President insisted that he would agree only to a "peace with honor," and tonight he insisted that the accord met "the goals that we considered essential for peace with honor."

Apparently in an effort to ease possible apprehensions in Saigon, Mr. Nixon pledged that the United States would continue to recognize Mr. Thieu's Government "as the sole legitimate Government of South Vietnam."

He also pledged—"within the terms of the agreement"—to continue to supply assistance to South Vietnam and to "support efforts for the people of South Vietnam to settle their problems peacefully among themselves."

The actual agreement is understood to provide machinery for the eventual reconciliation of the Saigon Government with the Vietcong. But officials here have expressed doubts in recent days that the two rivals for power would be able to resolve their hostility.

Calling on all involved parties to adhere to the agreement "scrupulously," Mr. Nixon also alluded to the Soviet Union and China, saying, "We shall also expect other interested nations to help insure that the agreement is carried out and peace is maintained."

It is expected that Secretary of State William P. Rogers will sign the agreement in Paris on Saturday at the former Hotel Majestic, along with the Foreign Ministers of North Vietnam, South Vietnam and the Provisional Revolutionary government, or Vietcong.

Mr. Nixon ended his speech with words to the various parties to the accord, their allies, and to the American people.

Cooperation in Future

To the South Vietnamese, who in the end listened to American entreaties and did not balk at the accord, he said, "We look forward to working with you in the future." He added that the United States and South Vietnam would be "friends in peace as we have been allies in war."

To the North Vietnamese, he said, "As we have ended the war through negotiations, let us now build a peace of reconciliation."

He said that the United States would make "a major effort" to help achieve that goal, but he stressed that Hanoi would have to reciprocate. Previously, Mr. Nixon has talked about a $7.5-billion program to rehabilitate North Vietnam and South Vietnam over a five-year period. Of that total, $2.5-billion would be earmarked for Hanoi.

Making a firm call for support from Moscow and Peking, Mr. Nixon said: "To the other major powers that have been involved, even indirectly, now is the time for mutual restraint so that the peace we have achieved can last."

U.S. Aid Believed Limited

Under the terms of the accord, it is believed, the United States is limited in the amount of military aid it can supply Saigon. But American officials have warned that if the Russians and the Chinese continue to supply Hanoi with extensive military equipment the balance of power could be upset.

Mr. Nixon said nothing about a key controversial item in the negotiations—the presence of 145,000 North Vietnamese in South Vietnam. But previously, Mr. Kissinger had said that the United States would not ask Hanoi to pull these forces back because they would be needed to protect the Vietcong enclaves permitted under the accord.

To the American people, he explained his silence of recent months about the situation in Vietnam. He said that if he had discussed the efforts to achieve an agreement, "it would have seriously harmed and possibly destroyed the chances for peace."

He ended his speech with some words about Lyndon B. Johnson, who died yesterday on the eve of the settlement. He said that no one would have welcomed this peace more than he.

Earlier, on Mr. Kissinger's return from Paris, the President set in motion a series of evening conferences before his televised report to the nation.

Mr. Nixon first met with his Cabinet officers to give them a report on the Vietnam situation, then conferred with the top Congressional leaders from both parties.

The White House said that Mr. Nixon had invited to that session the Senate majority leader, Mike Mansfield of Montana; the Senate Republican leader, Hugh Scott of Pennsylvania; the House Speaker, Carl Alpert of Oklahoma; the House Republican leader, Gerald R. Ford of Michigan, and the House Democratic leader, Thomas P. O'Neill Jr. of Massachusetts.

Throughout the day, despite the reports from Saigon and Paris about the initialing of the agreement, the White House refrained from any substantive comment.

Ronald L. Ziegler, the White House press secretary, met briefly with newsmen at about 1 P.M., after having spent much of the morning at a meeting with Mr. Nixon and White House sides.

Mr. Ziegler limited himself to announcing that Mr. Nixon would address the nation on the "status of the Vietnam negotiations," and that he would hold meeting with the Cabinet officers and Congressional leaders tonight. In addition, Mr. Ziegler said a larger session with members of Congress would be held tomorrow morning at the White House.

The substantive talks on a Vietnam settlement began in January, 1969, in the former Hotel Majestic in Paris, the same place Mr. Kissinger and Mr. Tho held their session today.

Meetings Around Paris

The negotiations that produced the actual agreement, however, took place in villas in and around Paris between Mr. Kissinger and Mr. Tho, beginning in August, 1969.

The holding of those negotiations remained a closely guarded secret until last Jan. 26 when Mr. Nixon disclosed them in a speech accusing Hanoi of delaying tactics.

After North Vietnam's offensive in South Vietnam last spring, the secret talks resumed.

A decisive breakthrough was achieved early in October when the United States and North Vietnam agreed to a nine-point draft agreement whose outline was made public by Hanoi on Oct. 26, and was confirmed by Mr. Kissinger that same day in his "peace is at hand" news conference.

Hanoi had originally insisted that the draft be signed by Oct. 31, but Mr. Nixon asked for further meetings to tighten the terms of the agreement and to meet some of South Vietnam's objections.

The talks resumed in Paris on Nov. 20 and recessed on Nov. 25. When they began again on Dec. 4, Hanoi objected to the proposals made by the United States in the previous round, and made counterproposals that Mr. Kissinger later called "frivolous." Those talks broke down on Dec. 13.

Reportedly angry over Hanoi's tactics, Mr. Nixon ordered the war's heaviest bombing of Hanoi and Haiphong—from Dec. 18 to 29. The raids, which included strikes by B-52 bombers, were called off north of the 20th Parallel on Dec. 29 with the announcement by the White House that Hanoi had agreed to resume "serious" talks.

Apparent Accord on Jan. 13

The negotiations opened on Jan. 8 and concluded with an apparent agreement on Jan. 13. Two days later all bombing, mining and shelling of North Vietnam ceased, and on Jan. 18—last Thursday—it was announced that Mr. Kissinger and Mr. Tho would meet again "for the purpose of concluding the text of an agreement."

Gen. Alexander M. Haig Jr., who until this month was Mr. Kissinger's chief deputy, returned to Washington on Sunday after a mission to Saigon to persuade President Thieu to add his agreement to the accord worked out by Hanoi and Washington.

Mr. Haig was with Mr. Nixon early this morning when first reports of the conclusion of Mr. Kissinger's Paris meeting were received here.

* * *

March 30, 1973

U.S. FORCES OUT OF VIETNAM; HANOI FREES THE LAST P.O.W.

By JOSEPH B. TREASTER
Special to The New York Times.

SAIGON, South Vietnam, March 29—The last American troops left South Vietnam today, leaving behind an unfinished war that has deeply scarred this country and the United States.

There was little emotion or joy as they brought to a close almost a decade of American military intervention.

Remaining after the final jet transport lifted off from Tan Son Nhut air base at 5:53 P.M. were about 800 Americans on the truce observation force who will leave tomorrow and Saturday. A contingent of 159 Marine guards and about 50 military attachés also stayed behind.

The fighting men were gone, but United States involvement in South Vietnam was far from ended.

When Gen. Frederick C. Weyand presided over the furling of the colors of the United States Military Assistance Command, Vietnam, this afternoon, he told a handful of American servicemen, "You can hold your heads up high for having been a part of this selfless effort."

In a second address later in the afternoon, delivered in halting Vietnamese, General Weyand declared: "Our mission has been accomplished. I depart with a strong feeling of pride in what we have achieved, and in what our achievement represents."

As the last American commander in Vietnam said good-by to the huge white tropical building that was sometimes called Pentagon East, a force of 7,200 American civilians employed by the Department of Defense was standing under the eaves.

A majority of these civilians are technicians who are already at work with the South Vietnamese armed forces, trying to fill the gap in special skills that the Vietnamization program has been unable to provide. Many are repairing helicopters, jet fighter-bombers, radar systems and computers, and some are instructing the Vietnamese in these tasks.

This afternoon at Tan Son Nhut, while waiting for his plane to take off, Col. Einar Himma, a naturalized American from Estonia, talked of his two tours in Vietnam. He had grown fond of the Vietnamese, he said, and he felt sad about their future.

"There's going to be a full-blown war starting up after we leave," he said. "The fighting has never stopped anyway."

As he spoke a Government officer downtown was reporting that more than 100 military incidents had occurred in the last day—almost double the number reported in the last weeks before the cease-fire was proclaimed on Jan. 28.

Across the airport, 20 coffins with the bodies of Government soldiers had just been unloaded from trucks. A Vietnamese woman knelt weeping beside her husband's coffin.

Colonel Himma's candid talk was unusual for a military man. Many of his colleagues refuse to admit that in eight years, with hundreds of thousands of soldiers, millions of tons of bombs, a panoply of deadly devices and billions of dollars, they had not won the war.

Many officers still contend that the Army never lost a battle in Vietnam; their reasoning is that, at whatever price, the troops always took or held the terrain in question. But now the places where some Americans consider that the greatest victories of the war were achieved—Khe Sanh, Dak To, Hamburger Hill, the Ia Drang Valley, the rises and hollows south of the demilitarized zone—are controlled by the Communists.

Army publications and some officers describe the Tet offensive of 1968 as an allied victory even though many others say that its impact on the American public triggered the beginning of the United States' disengagement from Vietnam.

Admiral Moorer's Regret

Still, one general said the other day: "The Army leaves with its chin out and its chest high. It's done a commendable job."

Today, there were congratulatory messages from Washington and the Pacific headquarters and a fleeting note of regret from Adm. Thomas H. Moorer, Chairman of the Joint Chiefs of Staff, that the war had not enjoyed "the full measure of support it deserved."

When the first big American fighting units began arriving in South Vietnam in 1965, there was a standard explanation for the United States presence.

"We've come here to stop the spread of Communism," the soldiers would say without hesitation. "If we don't stop them here we may be fighting them in San Francisco next." Sometimes the soldiers also mentioned giving the South Vietnamese the opportunity to live under a democratic system.

One officer who has been involved in Vietnam for several years conceded in an interview earlier this week that what the United States had achieved here was "certainly less than any of us planned in the beginning." He said that the United States had succeeded in giving the South Vietnamese "a reasonable chance to survive."

"Now," he continued, "it becomes a matter of will and determination on the part of the South Vietnamese."

To reach this point, the cost to the United States has been almost 46,000 men killed and more than 300,000 wounded. The military has become controversial, its self-confidence has been reduced and it has been forced into a new mold—a volunteer army spruced up to attract enlistees but anathema to many old regulars.

North Vietnam, South Vietnam and the Vietcong have lost a million men on the battlefield. No one on the allied side knows how many Communist soldiers have been wounded, but it is doubtful that the number is fewer than the 400,000 South Vietnamese hurt in combat.

American officials estimate that perhaps a million South Vietnamese civilians have been killed in the war and that more than 40 per cent of the 16 million survivors have been uprooted by the fighting, their homes and belongings lost, their families scattered.

From the beginning American military men felt that the fighting in Vietnam would be like the fighting in Korea. But there were seldom front lines or large formations of troops to assault.

"In this war," a colonel said, "a squad of 10 or 12 men was considered an excellent target for wings of aircraft and battalions of artillery."

The Americans used such tactics partly out of frustration, but also because commanders were under pressure from Washington to keep their casualties down in an unpopular war.

Many Vietnamese civilians became victims. Wide areas of territory used by the Communists were declared "free-fire zones." These were places where bombs could be dropped or artillery fired at any time without special clearance. Peasants living in the areas risked death if they did not leave.

Under Gen. William C. Westmoreland, the American commander in Vietnam when the troop build-up began, there were "search-and-destroy" operations, in which sometimes thousands of soldiers would push through an area, often in tanks and armored cars.

The ambush was the greatest enemy tactic and the booby-trap was his most effective weapon until last spring, when the Russians began supplying 130-mm. guns that could fire a shell 17 miles.

One way that the Americans tried to overcome the ambush tactic was to expose the enemy's hiding places. They did this by defoliating thousands of acres and plowing down great stretches of rubber plantations and forest land bordering the roads.

But the favorite weapon of the Americans was the helicopter. This, as one general liked to say, freed the men from the "tyranny of the terrain."

In the early days the most popular helicopter tactic was the air assault. A general would pick a trouble spot, soften it up with artillery and air strikes for 15 or 20 minutes and then load up 400 or 500 men in helicopters and set them down on the edge of the objective.

Toward the end of the American experience in Vietnam, helicopters were mainly used for armed reconnaissance in which they would scout a suspicious area and shoot at anything that moved. In Da Nang last June a couple of helicopter pilots bragged about how they had made a farmer "dance" in his rice field and how another time they had shot down a boney cow.

As United States troop strength moved downward from its 1969 peak of 543,400, the pressure increased to keep down American losses and the use of bombers increased. This added to the cost of the war and almost certainly led to more inadvertent casualties.

My Lai Most Damaging

The most painful memory for the Army was the My Lai massacre. But an incident in which eight Green Berets were accused of killing a Vietnamese double agent in the fall of 1969 hurt the Army too. The eight—six commissioned officers, a warrant officer and a sergeant—were arrested and charged with shooting Thai Khac Chuyen in June, 1969, and dumping his body in the South China Sea. A little later all Special Forces soldiers were pulled out of Vietnam.

Often when American military men talk about the mistakes of the war, they conclude that more force should have been used. Many think that North Vietnam should have been invaded. Failing that, they would have preferred to march deep into Laos to try to cut the Ho Chi Minh supply network.

Early Training of Vietnamese

There is general agreement that the United States should have started building the Vietnamese armed forces from the beginning, instead of assuming the main combat role until it became clear that the American public would no longer support the war.

There is little question that in four years the Vietnamese armed forces have made strides forward, but they still have shortcomings.

General Weyand declared today that the Government forces had proved "their readiness, determination and capability to defend their ideals" during the North Vietnamese offensive of 1972.

In that campaign, several South Vietnamese units broke and ran, others suffered devastating casualties and, in some cases, entire battalions were captured. American and South Vietnamese officers said that the massive use of American air power had saved the country.

Although American advisers to Vietnamese units and Special Forces soldiers often lived close to the Vietnamese, and often ate Vietnamese food, most American servicemen lived in isolation in compounds and barracks that were as much like home as they could make them.

Air-conditioners, soft drinks, beer, ice cream, the latest movies, television, tape recorders and pin-ups were standard. Most of the food was shipped from the United States. Generals prided themselves on elaborate messes.

Junior officers and noncoms took pride in building fancy clubs. The Air Force club in Pleiku was known for its huge crystal chandelier. One of the most popular clubs in Saigon used to be the top of the Rex Hotel, where the officers held barbecue cookouts every Sunday night. In the beginning there were slot machines everywhere, but they abruptly disappeared one day.

Heavy Ratio of Support

Men in support jobs outnumbered combat troops by more than 7 to 1. But there were line units with many helicopters, like the First Cavalry Division, where the "grunts," or fighting men, usually got two hot meals a day and sometimes had ice cream and soda in the field.

The tour of duty in Vietnam was one year. Its brevity made the separation from family more bearable but it created great turbulence in the armed forces. Many officers felt that this short tour weakened the services structurally and created a situation in which, as one officer said, "We didn't have 8 years or 12 years, or whatever it was of experience—we had one year of experience eight times."

Officers spent six months in combat duty and six months in administrative or support jobs. This gave everyone some exposure to the war and increased his chances for promotion, but it also kept everyone in unfamiliar jobs.

With all the amenities, though, morale began to fall in 1970 and 1971. Drug use became endemic. A few units refused orders to go into combat and enlisted men occasionally "fragged" their officers—throwing fragmentation grenades. Soldiers began to wear love beads and peace symbols and let their hair run shaggy. It was only after units had gotten down to a hard core of "lifers," specialists and technicians that the American forces in Vietnam regained some of the lost discipline.

Today, as the last men were heading home, a reporter asked whether they were happy or sad. Several majors, lieutenant colonels and colonels glared fiercely and snapped, "No comment!"

* * *

June 23, 1973

U.S., SOVIET SIGN PACT TO REDUCE POSSIBILITY OF NUCLEAR CONFLICT WITH EACH OTHER OR A 3D NATION

STRESS ON TRUST

Both Promise to Avoid Provocations That Could Bring War

By BERNARD GWERTZMAN
Special to The New York Times.

WASHINGTON, June 22—President Nixon and Leonid I. Brezhnev signed an agreement today to try to avert military confrontations that could lead the United States and the Soviet Union into a nuclear war either with each other or with any other country.

The accord, negotiated in secret for more than a year, was disclosed only this morning, shortly before the two leaders signed the eight-article document.

Under the agreement, both the superpowers pledge not to worsen relations with any country so as to provoke a nuclear war. This was immediately seen here as a further restraint on a possible Soviet nuclear attack against China. Peking has charged for some time that Moscow was contemplating a preemptive attack on its nuclear facilities.

Good Intentions Stated

The underlying significance of the accord, however, lay not in any specific detail but rather in the growing willingness of the United States and the Soviet Union to put on paper their trust in each other's good intentions.

This trend has been underscored by developments during the visit of the Communist party leader to the United States this week.

After the White House ceremonies, Mr. Nixon and Mr. Brezhnev flew to the California White House in San Clemente, where they will spend the weekend.

Call for Consultations

During Mr. Brezhnev's visit, eight formal Soviet-American accords have been signed. Mr. Nixon has accepted an invitation to visit Moscow again next year and Mr. Brezhnev told a group of businessmen today that he planned to return here in 1975.

Today's agreement "on the prevention of nuclear war" was broadly written and appeared to put into a formal document a number of practices already carried out by the two superpowers to avoid a direct confrontation.

Its most significant new element seems to be Article IV, which obliges Moscow and Washington to enter into "urgent consultations" if relations between them, or between one of them and some other country, "appear to involve the risk of nuclear conflict."

This would seem to mean that if the Soviet Union and China were on the verge of nuclear war, the United States would have to hold talks with Moscow to seek avoidance of a Chinese-Soviet war.

Henry A. Kissinger, Mr. Nixon's adviser on national security, was asked specifically if the document would "forestall any kind of military action against China."

He declined to answer directly, but said the agreement "will have the practical consciences of applying both to the situation you described as well as to many other conceivable situations."

No Solace for Peking

China has talked openly about fears of a direct Soviet nuclear attack, but Mr. Kissinger indicated that Peking would probably not welcome this Soviet-American accord because of its constant concern about Soviet-American "superpower" connivance to control the world.

Talking of the Chinese, Mr. Kissinger said, "I have no particular reason to suppose that they will necessarily approve a bilateral agreement between the United States and the Soviet Union, whatever its consequences."

At the signing ceremonies in the White House East Room, Mr. Brezhnev was again in the ebullient mood he has displayed all week.

He repeated his "game" with Mr. Nixon first played yesterday when they "raced" each other to see who would complete the signing of an accord on strategic arms limitation first.

'Truly Historic Ceremony'

In the champagne drinking period, after today's signing, Mr. Brezhnev clinked glasses with Mr. Nixon and other officials, then went to the microphone to thank the dignitaries assembled for coming to "this truly historic ceremony."

This was the only agreement that had not been discussed in the press before announcement. Apparently it had been negotiated in deep secrecy since last year's Moscow summit meeting, and discussed by Washington with only a few allies. Its main points are as follows:

- Both sides agree that they should eliminate the danger of nuclear war and the use of nuclear weapons, and to avoid creating situations that could lead to a military confrontation and a nuclear war between themselves or with other countries.
- The United States and the Soviet Union pledge to refrain from threatening the use of force against each other, against the allies of the other party, or against other countries. This is a clear restriction against the use of military threats, and would seem to have some relevance in Indochina as well as against China.
- Each side will consult with the other if they are faced with a risk of nuclear war between them or between one of them and other countries.
- The agreement permits each side to inform its allies, other countries and the United Nations of their consultations.
- Nothing in the agreement affects either nation's right to self-defense or its obligations toward its allies.

Mr. Kissinger, in his news conference, stressed that the agreement did not rule out nuclear war, but rather was aimed at preventing it.

Right to Retaliate

In other words, if, for example, the Soviet Union launched a large-scale attack in Central Europe with conventional forces, the United States would have the right to retaliate with nuclear weapons.

In the past, the Russians have sought an agreement in which each side would agree not to be the first to use nuclear weapons. This has been resisted by Washington to maintain a credible defense in Europe where the Russians have had an advantage in conventional forces.

To assure the allies, Secretary of State William P. Rogers met this morning with envoys from the 14 other members of the North Atlantic Treaty Alliance in Washington to point out that the agreement did not run counter to America's NATO commitments.

Three years ago the Soviet Union proposed to the United States a treaty calling for joint action against "provocative" actions by a third nuclear power. Washington interpreted this as an anti-Chinese proposal and rejected it.

Proposal by Russians

The current agreement arose, Mr. Kissinger said, when at the last session of the Moscow summit meeting, the Russians proposed an accord on how to control nuclear weapons beyond the ongoing talks on strategic arms limitation.

He said the talks were continued last fall when the Soviet Foreign Minister, Andrei A. Gromyko, visited Washington, and in messages between Mr. Nixon and Mr. Brezhnev. They were "extensively" pursued when Mr. Kissinger went to Moscow in May and in the last few days.

"This is an agreement which is designed to regulate the relations of the two great nuclear powers to each other and to other countries in time of peace," Mr. Kissinger said.

"It is an attempt to prevent the outbreak of nuclear war," he said, "and to the extent that it contributes to this task, it can be a significant landmark in the relationships of the United States to the Soviet Union and in the relationships of the two great nuclear countries towards all other countries of the world."

Mr. Kissinger said the agreement represented "a formal obligation" by the two nuclear powers toward each other and "equally importantly, with all other countries, to practice restraint in their diplomacy, to build a peace that is permanent."

The agreement has no enforcement machinery. As Mr. Kissinger said, "If either of the two signatories wants to find an excuse to go to war, it will find an excuse to go to war."

Mr. Kissinger seemed nettled by some questions about Article II, which obliges each side not to threaten the use of military force. He was asked whether it would rule out the current Cambodian bombing—he said it would not—and whether it would have barred the Soviet invasion of Czechoslovakia in 1968. He said the movement of forces to another country's territory "would not be in our view consistent with the spirit of this agreement, but I really do not want to go into a detailed analysis of every conceivable situation."

Earlier Crises Cited

Asked whether some previous crises might have been prevented with such an agreement, he cited the Cuban missile crisis in 1962, and past Berlin confrontations.

The agreement is not a treaty and does not require Senate approval. Mr. Nixon briefed some members of Congress about it today and the general response seemed favorable.

Senate Majority Leader Mike Mansfield of Montana said it was "a very good agreement." A similar view was expressed by Senator J. W. Fulbright, chairman of the Foreign Relations Committee

Senator Henry M. Jackson. Democrat of Washington, who had earlier called for a postponement of the summit meeting because of the Watergate scandals, said the agreement could be "a positive step toward lessening the dangers of war."

Jackson Is Hopeful

"If adhered to," Mr. Jackson said, "particularly with reference to the dangerous Sino-Soviet rivalry, it could help to dampen the concern that Soviet nuclear superiority vis-à-vis China could lead to military confrontation."

Last night, Mr. Brezhnev, in a toast at the Soviet Embassy, gave one of the strongest declarations yet of his desire for closer relations with the United States.

"I wish especially to emphasize," he said, "that we are convinced that on the basis of growing, mutual confidence, we can steadily move ahead. We want the further development of our relations to become a maximally stable process, and what is more, an irreversible one."

* * *

June 23, 1973

TALK BY BREZHNEV

He Tells Businessmen Trade Growth Will Aid Both Nations

By PHILIP SHABECOFF
Special to The New York Times.

WASHINGTON, June 22—Leonid I. Brezhnev delivered a 90-minute discourse to some of the most powerful businessmen of American capitalism today, telling them that the cold war is over and that expanded trade relations will be a boon to both countries.

After the meeting, held at Blair House, one of the businessmen who attended said, "Brezhnev could be one of the world's great supersalesmen."

According to accounts of the meetings by the businessmen, Mr. Brezhnev expressed regrets about divisions between the two countries created by the cold war.

'Was That a Good Period?'

"And I ask you, gentlemen," he said, according to a transcript of the meeting, "as I ask myself, Was that a good period? Did it serve the interests of the peoples? And my answer to that is no, no, no and again no."

Then the Soviet leader noted that there have been many political changes in recent years and departures "from old hidebound traditions."

Many things have changed in the world, Mr. Brezhnev said, including goods and merchandise and machinery. "And all this serves to raise advantageous exchanges, and mutually advantageous exchanges mean trade and cooperation."

A Word of Caution

One businessman, who has had long experience in dealing with the Soviet Union, had a word of caution after the meeting. "This kind of froth is typical when the Russians are establishing rapport," he said. "But when these guys sit down to do business with the Russians, they will find it is not so simple."

Although the Soviet leader did not discuss specifics, some of the businessmen interviewed later said that the meeting was valuable. They added they had been surprised by Mr. Brezhnev's warmth and humor and impressed by the sincerity of his desire to expand commercial and economic relations between his country and the United States.

"Everybody is convinced that this man is serious about improved relations and increased trade between our two countries—there is no doubt about it," declared Donald M. Kendall, chairman of Pepsico, Inc.

The Soviet leader's talk was punctuated by frequent bursts of laughter as the translator put the Russian into English. At one point he disclosed that he would probably again visit this country in 1975 and that his Foreign Minister, Andrei A. Gromyko, and the Ambassador to Washington, Anatoly F. Dobrynin, had asked if they could come along.

"To which I said, "I always take with me people who can really move things forward," Mr. Brezhnev said.

Burns Up Protocol

As the Soviet leader talked on, several of his protocol officers looked anxiously at their watches. Mr. Brezhnev, noticing their glances, picked up a piece of paper and set it afire with his cigarette lighter.

"If only I could burn up protocol like that. I would do it," he commented amid applause and laughter.

At the end of Mr. Brezhnev's talk, Nikolai S. Patolichev, the Soviet Minister of Foreign Trade, and George P. Shultz, the Secretary of the Treasury, signed two protocols—memorandums of their agreements—designed "to promote increased cooperation in U.S.-U.S.S.R. commercial relations and to expand and improve facilities for commercial purposes in both Moscow and Washington," according to a Treasury statement.

One protocol was an agreement to help establish a "U.S.S.R.-U.S. chamber of commerce" with membership from the American business and financial community. The other is an agreement that the two Governments will provide space for trade centers in each other's capital.

'Exceptionally Good'

After the meeting, Mr. Brezhnev was asked by a reporter for his assessment of his meeting with the American capitalists.

"In two words, exceptionally good," Mr. Brezhnev replied.

At a roast-beef-and-strawberry-shortcake luncheon given in his honor later by the National Association of Manufacturers, Mr. Patolichev emphasized the theme sounded by Mr. Brezhnev.

"I am a devout supporter of more contacts, contacts, contacts which would bring more contracts, contracts, contracts," the Trade Minister said, through an interpreter. The audience of major corporate executives applauded enthusiastically.

Mr. Patolichev told the businessmen: "We on our part will do anything and everything to help you develop your trade with us, and we hope you will do the same."

Long-Term Deals Sought

The Soviet Union has frequently expressed interest in developing long-term agreements with United States business to help develop the natural resources of Siberia and other unexploited areas.

The National Association of Manufacturers, meanwhile, announced today that it would work with other United States trade associations to gain approval by Congress of most-favored-nation status for the Soviet Union, which would give Moscow the same tariff-rates as the United States grants some non-Communist nations.

* * *

September 12, 1973

SOLZHENITSYN ASSAILS LIBERALS IN WEST

By THEODORE SHABAD
Special to The New York Times.

MOSCOW, Sept. 11—The novelist Aleksandr I. Solzhenitsyn has accused Western liberals of dual standards of morality in what he described as their quick readiness to denounce oppression in rightist countries but reluctance to criticize the Soviet Union.

In a wide-ranging commentary on world events, focusing on the basic issues of peace and war and "violence of the state," the 54-year-old author also called United States Senate leaders "hypocritical" in their charges of political misconduct in the Watergate affair.

He was critical of a visit last year by the British Labor party leader, Harold Wilson, to Czechoslovakia, of a trip made to North Vietnam by Ramsey Clark, the former United States Attorney General, and of what Mr. Solzhenitsyn described as Western silence at the time of the Communists' massacre of South Vietnamese civilians in Hue in 1968.

3,000-Word Statement

The dissident writer made these and other points about what he said was Western timidity in a 3,000-word statement, which also contained the nomination of Andrei D. Sakharov, the physicist and civil rights advocate, for the 1973 Nobel Peace Prize. The full text became available here today, a day after the nomination was disclosed.

Both Mr. Solzhenitsyn and Mr. Sakharov have been targets of official press attacks in recent weeks for interviews with Western newsmen that criticized the Kremlin's domestic and foreign policies.

Mr. Sakharov, in particular, has drawn the Government's anger by suggesting that there can be no genuine East-West reconciliation unless it is accompanied by democratic reforms leading to a more open society in the Soviet Union.

Mr. Solzhenitsyn took up the theme in his review of world affairs when he said that peace could not be assured by the absence of war, but required also an end of other forms of violence, including domestic political controls by governments.

Challenging the validity of the Soviet Union's policy of "peaceful coexistence," the novelist said: "Coexistence on this tightly knit earth should be viewed as an existence not only without wars—that is not enough—but without violence or anyone's telling us how to live, what to say, what to think, what to know and what not to know."

He was in part attacking Soviet residence restrictions that have kept him from obtaining an official permit to reside in Moscow at the apartment of his present wife, Natalya Svetlova. The novelist said in an interview two weeks ago that he would disregard the order.

Mr. Solzhenitsyn noted in his latest statement that railroad embankments in the Soviet Union were often decorated with stone mosaics spelling out the words "Peace to the World."

He commented, "That propaganda might be very useful if it meant that not only that there be no wars in the world, but that all internal violence cease as well."

A major theme in his statement was the danger of appeasement. It was in this context that he criticized some trips by Western public figures to Communist countries.

He also played with the notion that Neville Chamberlain, the prewar British Prime Minister, might have been awarded the Nobel Peace Prize after having signed the Munich pact with Hitler in 1938. Mr. Chamberlain described the treaty as assuring "peace in our time," but World War II began a year later with Germany's invasion of Poland. Mr. Chamberlain has since become a symbol of appeasement of the Nazis.

Charging that Western liberals were often reluctant to take a stand against Communist regimes, Mr. Solzhenitsyn said, "And yet, how they would close ranks if it were a matter of protesting the other way."

He mentioned the case of Pyotr G. Grigorenko, a Soviet dissident, who has been detained in a mental hospital for four years, and then asked whether world opinion would ever permit South Africa to detain a black African leader in this fashion.

"The storm of worldwide rage would have long ago swept the roof from that prison!" he said.

Comment on Watergate

He charged that the "hypocrisy of Western protests" extended even to such aspects of Western political life as the Watergate affair. Without pretending to defend President Nixon or the Republican party, he said, he is "amazed at the hypocritical, clamorous rage displayed by the Democrats."

Depicting American democracy as a system devoid of solid ethical foundations, he wrote: "Wasn't that democracy full of mutual deception and cases of misconduct during previous election campaigns, except, perhaps, that they were not on such a high level of electronic technology and remained happily undiscovered?"

The Watergate upheaval, he said, suggested to him similarities between the final years of Czarism in Russia, which he has been researching for his books, and the United States, which he said was "in what, I dare predict, are also its final years before the great breakdown."

* * *

September 12, 1973

ALLENDE OUT, REPORTED SUICIDE; MARXIST REGIME IN CHILE FALLS IN ARMED FORCES' VIOLENT COUP

JUNTA IN CHARGE

State of Siege Decreed by Military Chiefs—Curfew Imposed

By The Associated Press

SANTIAGO, Chile, Wednesday, Sept. 12—President Salvador Allende Gossens was deposed yesterday in a violent military coup, and the Santiago police said that he had committed suicide rather than surrender to the attackers.

Dr. Allende, a Marxist who was elected President in 1970, was reportedly found slumped over a blood-stained sofa in the presidential palace, a bullet through his mouth. The palace had been captured after a 20-minute assault in which the military used bombers and heavy artillery.

Proclaiming a mission of liberating Chile "from the Marxist yoke," a four-man military junta took control of the Government and declared a state of siege. Censorship and a curfew were imposed.

Noon Deadline Set

The coup followed weeks of nationwide strikes and economic chaos, with growing groups of workers and professionals joining in demands that Dr. Allende halt his attempts to bring socialism to Chile and resign. Yesterday morning, the chiefs of the army, navy, air force and national police

Associated Press

Gen. Augusto Pinochet Ugarte, left, the commander of Chile's Army, is a member of the four-man military junta that overthrew President Salvador Allende Gossens, at right.

sided with the anti-Marxist opposition and issued an ultimatum for the President to resign by noon.

But the President refused. In his last public statement, made by radio as two air force jets were making runs on the palace, he declared:

"I will not resign. I will not do it. I am ready to resist with whatever means, even at the cost of my life in that this serves as a lesson in the ignominious history of those who have strength but not reason."

Bombs Fell on Palace

Attacking only moments after the deadline set by the military had passed, the air force jets dropped bombs and fired rockets, severely damaging the fortress-like presidential palace. The President's official residence, about a mile away, was also bombed, the junta said, after guards there "resisted the armed forces and police."

A statement that the President had committed suicide was issued after the attack by Rene Carrasco, a police prefect. He said Augusto Olivares, a close Presidential adviser, had also killed himself.

Newsmen for the Santiago daily El Mercurio were allowed inside the palace and the newspaper's chief photographer, Juan Enrique Lira, said he saw the President lying dead on a blood-soaked sofa in the anteroom of the palace's dining hall. He said the President had apparently shot himself once in the mouth.

A series of orders was issued immediately after the coup by the junta, composed of Gen. Augusto Pinochet Ugarte, commander of the army; Gen. Delaire Gustavo Leigh Guzman, commander of the air force; Adm. José Toriblo Merino Castro, acting commander of the navy, and Gen. Cesar Mendoza Frank, chief of the national police.

A list of 68 prominent Socialist and Communist leaders was broadcast, and they were ordered to appear at the Defense Ministry or face arrest. More than 100 Communist and Socialist party members were reported arrested in Santiago and Valparaiso, a port city where naval units began the coup early yesterday.

Foreigners were ordered to report to the nearest police station to identify themselves.

The junta also broadcast an order freezing all bank accounts.

In a radio broadcast monitored after the coup, the junta said that it would soon name new ministers, including some civilians, but that Congress would remain in recess "until further order."

The new Government said it would maintain diplomatic relations with all nations except for Cuba and a few others.

In several monitored broadcasts the military junta made no mention of Dr. Allende. It said its aim was to "avoid violence and lead the Chilean people along the road to peace."

While the military attacks were under way yesterday, long-distance telephone and telegraph services in this city of three million people were shut down.

They were resumed late in the day, but communications were cut off again after a few hours.

What other casualties there might have been besides those at the presidential palace was not immediately clear.

A spokesman at the United States Embassy said no United States citizens were known to have been wounded.

The coup marked the first time in more than 40 years that the traditionally nonpolitical Chilean military had overturned a civilian Government. In 1931, a dictatorial President, Carlos Ibanez del Campo, was forced out during a general strike and other economic troubles.

Dr. Allende, a physician turned politician, took office nearly three years ago insisting that he would lead Chile to Socialism within a democratic framework, but growing opposition from Chile's large middle class made that impossible.

His leftist coalition, which succeeded the Christian Democratic Government of President Eduardo Frei, encountered political and labor turmoil, economic crises and strong opposition in Congress, which is controlled by anti-Marxist parties.

In October, 1970, Gen. René Schneider, then the army commander, was killed by right-wing extremists in an unsuccessful plot against the Allende Government. Last June, about 100 soldiers attacked the palace in a coup attempt that was crushed by loyal army units.

Warned of Coup

The 65-year-old President warned repeatedly in recent speeches that "fascists" were planning a coup against him. With unrest against him growing, he named military leaders to his Government in an attempt to keep them with him. The army and air force commanders now in the military junta that deposed him were appointed by Dr. Allende to his Government only two weeks ago.

Last week the military leaders left the Allende coalition, and he appointed lower ranking officers to succeed them.

The junta moved against him yesterday morning as a general strike by merchants went into the fourth day and 50,000 private truckers remained off the job for the 47th day.

In their first communiqué, the junta members said they were demanding Dr. Allende's resignation in the face of "the extremely grave economic, social and moral crisis that is destroying the country." The communiqué added that the armed forces and national police were united in "fighting for the liberation of the country from the Marxist yoke."

The communiqué, described as a "proclamation of the military Government junta," declared that, because the Government was unable to "stop the growth of chaos," the President "must proceed immediately to hand over his high office to the Chilean armed forces and national police."

"The workers of Chile may be certain," the declaration went on, "that the economic and social benefits they have achieved to the present will not suffer fundamental change."

The communiqué also warned that the Government's newspapers and radio and television stations must suspend their activities at once or "they will be assaulted by land and air."

First word of the revolt came from the port city of Valparaiso and Dr. Allende rushed from his residence to the palace. Shortly after 8 A.M. yesterday he made a brief statement over his Socialist party's radio station, saying "a sector of the navy" had rebelled and "I am awaiting now a decision from the army to defend the Government."

Bombs Strike Palace

Ten minutes later he went on the air again, saying "irresponsible elements" were demanding that he quit.

The heavy action centered at noon on the presidential palace, a fortress-like building that once was a mint and covers a block in the heart of the city.

Bombs and rockets smashed into the graceful interior patios and Dr. Allende's office was reported badly damaged. Several tanks opened fire at the front of the building when President Allende's guards refused to surrender.

Fires broke out and a column of black smoke rose from the building. Spectators gathered at intersections but then darted for cover as bullets struck near them.

Guests in the luxurious Carrera Sheraton Hotel fell to the floor as their windows were shot out. They were led to a relatively secure area at the rear of the second story.

The revolt left only four South American countries in the hands of civilians: Argentina, Colombia, Venezuela and Guyana. The other countries are directly ruled by the military, as in Brazil and Peru, or under heavy influence of military men, such as in Uruguay, which came under armed forces domination last May.

* * *

September 12, 1973

U.S. NOT SURPRISED

But Officials Are Wary of Any Comment on Santiago Events

By DAVID BINDER
Special to The New York Times.

WASHINGTON, Sept. 11—United States officials were not surprised by the Chilean armed forces' revolt today, but they declined to comment for the record, to avoid even a hint of commitment to the overthrow of President Salvador Allende Gossens or involvement in it.

According to information from the United States Embassy in Santiago, none of the 2,800 American citizens in Chile appeared to have been harmed in the rising, a State Department official reported. The embassy lies directly opposite the presidential palace, where Dr. Allende held out for a time this morning, and the official said the embassy building had been nicked by small-arms fire.

[Some of the American corporations whose properties in Chile have been seized indicated in the wake of the coup there that they might consider resuming operations if American investment was welcome.]

Expropriation Protested

Of the American residents of Chile about 2,300 live in and around Santiago, and half of those are United States Government employes and their dependents. The rest are mainly businessmen, students and missionaries.

The United States Government—which had a record of interfering in Chilean politics, principally with money, before Dr. Allende came to power in 1970—has maintained the position of a disinterested bystander since then, except for protests against his expropriation policy.

The expropriations, principally of United States-owned copper mines and International Telephone and Telegraph installations, have reduced United States investments from $750-million just before Dr. Allende came to power to under $70-million today.

Reports of the coup caused copper futures to rise about 3 cents to 78.25 cents on the New York Commodity Exchange, but an American official warned against the idea that a new regime might restore nationalized property.

"They haven't got any money anyway," he explained, "and all parties support nationalization. So any Anaconda shareholder who thinks he is going to get his money back is going to be disappointed."

The central element in Washington's attempt to be even-handed toward the Chilean developments is military aid and cooperation.

Four United States Navy vessels had been headed for Chile today from Peru as part of joint hemisphere naval maneuvers; they were redirected from Chilean ports as soon as news of the revolt came, the State Department said.

U.S. Aid Has Continued

The United States, which provided $1.7-billion in economic and military aid to Chile from 1946 through 1970, continues to give assistance in both fields.

In fiscal 1973 United States credits for Chilean military purchases and training totaled $12.4-million, while economic aid, including school lunches, amounted to about $3-million.

Six months ago the economic and military credits were justified by Washington as "an important means of demonstrating our continuing interest in the well-being of the Chilean population and of maintaining long-standing and friendly relations between the U.S. armed forces and their Chilean counterparts."

It is noted here that the Allende Government welcomed the military aid and rejected offers of Soviet arms.

"We have no vital interest in Chile," a Washington analyst observed. Privately, however, the Nixon Administration is distressed that Chile, with a long record of democratic constitutional practice, proved unable to resolve the current crisis by parliamentary means.

Military interference had been absent from Chilean politics since 1932. Officials here expect the military leaders to try to restore at least some parliamentary rule soon. "There is no Nasser, no colonel in the Chilean armed forces," another analyst remarked.

In conversations three weeks ago United States diplomatic and intelligence analysts predicted that a military coup would occur soon because of increasing nervousness in the armed services over the expansion of groups of armed factory workers in bases around Santiago. In the proclamation by the military junta that seized power today, the factory groups were cited as a reason for the revolt.

* * *

October 7, 1973

ARABS AND ISRAELIS BATTLE ON TWO FRONTS; EGYPTIANS BRIDGE SUEZ; AIR DUELS INTENSE

SYRIANS IN CLASH

Fighting Along Canal and Golan Height Goes On All Night

By ROBERT D. McFADDEN

The heaviest fighting in the Middle East since the 1967 war erupted yesterday on Israel's front lines with Egypt along the Suez Canal and Syria in the Golan heights.

Official announcements by Israel and Egypt agreed that Egyptian forces had crossed the Suez Canal and established footholds in the Israeli-occupied Sinai Peninsula.

A military communiqué issued in Cairo asserted that Egyptian forces had captured most of the eastern bank of the 100-mile canal. An Israeli military communiqué said the Egyptians had attempted to cross the canal at several points by helicopters and small boats and had succeeded in laying down pontoon bridge at two points. Armored forces were pouring across them into Sinai, it said.

Fighting All Night

A communiqué issued early today in Tel Aviv said fighting had raged all night along the canal's eastern bank and along the entire cease-fire line with Syria.

Each side accused the others of having started the fighting. But military observers posted by the United Nations reported crossings by Egyptian forces at five points along the Suez, and said Syrians had attacked in the Golan heights at two points.

Israeli and Syrian artillery dueled in the Golan heights, and on both battlefronts there were air clashes. The Cairo radio said Egyptian forces had shot down 11 Israeli planes and lost 10 of their own in battles over the Sinai and the Gulf of Suez. The Israeli spokesman did not comment on losses but said Israeli planes had shot down 10 Egyptian helicopters carrying troops into the southern Sinai.

Shelling by Syrians

In Damascus, the military command said that Syrian pilots and ground fire had shot down 10 Israeli aircraft in renewed action over the Golan heights this morning.

Syrian artillery was reported by the Israelis to have shelled a number of settlements in the occupied Golan heights and the Hula Valley area.

The Damascus radio said that Syrian forces had reoccupied Mount Hermon in the Golan heights for the first time since 1967, and said Syrian troops were fighting on the ground with Israeli forces along the entire cease-fire line.

An Israeli spokesman said today that Israeli planes had sunk an Egyptian vessel and that the navy had sunk three troop-carrying Egyptian craft during the night.

Gunboats Reported Sunk

As fighting continued into the night, Syrian and Israeli gunboats clashed in the Syrian harbor of Latakia, 110 miles north of Beirut. An Israeli communiqué said that five Soviet-built Syrian vessels were sunk by Israeli sea-to-sea missiles being used for the first time.

In Damascus, however, a military spokesman said that Syrian forces had sunk four Israeli naval vessels and shot down two Israeli helicopters in the sea battle.

No military action involving Jordan or Lebanon was reported, but King Hussein of Jordan placed his armed forces on full alert and conferred by telephone with President Anwar el-Sadat of Egypt and President Hafez al-Assad of Syria. Jordan was a belligerent in the 1967 war won by Israel.

The Government radio stations in Cairo and in Damascus accused Israel throughout the day of having started the fighting, but in a speech last night, General Assad appeared to concede something to the Israeli contention that Egypt and Syria had mounted coordinated attacks on Israel's southern and northern fronts.

After insisting that Israel had been massing her forces on the front for a week, General Assad said, "We did not allow the enemy to take us by surprise and our forces struck to repel this aggression at the right moment."

Israel's Defense Minister, Moshe Dayan, described the fighting last night as "all-out war." He conceded that Israel had lost several positions in the Sinai and at least one on the Golan heights, but he said that Arab advances on both fronts were being contained, and he predicted an ultimate Israeli victory.

Apparently trying to allay Israeli public concern over the Arab attacks in the Sinai, Mr. Dayan said more ground might be lost before Israel's mobilization was sufficient to counterattack successfully and hurl back the enemy forces. He said the Israeli aim would be to "inflict very heavy casualties" on the Arabs and to thwart any Arab effort to alter cease-fire lines.

The fighting erupted on both fronts at about 2 P.M. yesterday (8 A.M. Saturday, New York time) and the serenity of Yom Kippur, the holiest day of the Jewish calendar, was shattered across Israel with the wail of sirens. Thousands of reservists left homes and services in synagogues to report to military units as Israel declared a partial mobilization.

* * *

October 23, 1973

EGYPT AND ISRAEL BEGIN TRUCE AT U.N. CALL; SYRIA CONSIDERS TERMS BUT KEEPS FIGHTING

IRAQ REJECTS BID

Jordan Accepts It, but Says Her Troops Are Under the Syrians

By HENRY KAMM
Special to The New York Times.

TEL AVIV, Oct. 22—A ceases-fire in the fourth Middle East war since the creation of Israel went into effect today on the Egyptian front, about 12 hours after the United Nations Security Council called for an end to the hostilities.

Fighting continued, however, on the Syrian front.

[The Damascus radio said that Syria's leaders were considering the Security Council resolution, but subordinated this announcement to reports that Syrian forces were battling the Israelis.]

Meanwhile, Iraq, whose troops have been fighting alongside the Syrians, rejected the call for a cease-fire. Jordan announced acceptance but said her contingent in Syria was under Syrian orders.

Kissinger Visits Israel

With both Egypt and Israel agreeing to a cease-fire on the 17th day of the war, the truce went into effect officially at 6:52 P.M. (12:52 P.M. Monday, New York time).

Several hours before the official beginning of the truce, Secretary of State Kissinger arrived here for a brief visit on his way home from Moscow. He had conferred there with

Soviet leaders on the cease-fire resolution that the United States and Soviet Union introduced jointly in the Security Council last night and the Council adopted early today.

Neither the Israeli Government nor the American party commented on the visit, which involved talks with Premier Golda Meir and other Israeli leaders at a Government guest house near here. After less than five hours, Mr. Kissinger and his aides left for London.

[A military spokesman in Tel Aviv charged that Egyptian forces opened up with heavy fire on Israeli troops on the west bank of the Suez Canal at dawn Tuesday, Reuters reported. The report came after the spokesman said that the two sides fought numerous clashes during the night.]

All-Night Session

Israel announced her acceptance of the truce shortly before 7 this morning after Mrs. Meir and her Cabinet had been in session all night.

Neither she nor any member of her Government went on television to announce the partial end of the fighting. The decision was communicated in mimeographed press releases. The only public declaration was made at the regular military briefing by Maj. Gen. Shlomo Gazit before an audience made up mostly of foreign correspondents.

The reticence of the leaders reflected the somber mood with which the news was greeted by Israeli officials, military leaders and the public. The sudden halt in the fighting at a time when Israelis believed that the war had turned entirely in their favor caused a surprise not unlike the shock that beset Israel at the sudden outbreak of fighting Oct. 6.

The question why Israel accepted a cease-fire is widely discussed and little explained. Among suppositions put forward are desires to avoid being labeled as bellicose and opposed to accommodation and to reduce the damage done to Israel's reputation by her unwillingness to abandon Arab territories seized in the 1967 war.

Perhaps more profound, according to many Israelis, is a concern for holding casualties to the minimum. The loss of life appears to have a great demoralizing effect here.

General Gazit, asked at his briefing whether he would describe the military result as an Israeli victory, replied: "It was a very big victory, which could have been bigger."

The Other Wars

Confidants of Mrs. Meir recalled that she had always considered that her darkest moment came in 1957 when, as Foreign Minister, she had to announce that Israel had bowed to a United Nations call to evacuate the Sinai peninsula taken during the successful Israeli-British-French Suez campaign of the year before.

That 1956 campaign was the second Middle East war since Israel became a nation in 1948. The first came immediately in 1948 and ended the following year.

The third, in which Israel wrested the Sinai peninsula and the Gaza Strip from Egypt, the West Bank from Jordan and the Golan heights from Syria, was waged for six days in June, 1967.

The Israeli attitude now developing toward the cease-fire in the fourth Arab-Israeli war seemed to contain the seeds of bitterness over the halting of the army while it was advancing and while Egyptian troops remained in the Sinai in territory they had seized in the opening phase, two weeks ago.

Gains in Egypt Reported

As the fighting neared a halt, General Gazit said that Israeli troops had secured a salient about 20 miles deep and 33 miles long on the western bank of the Suez Canal, from the outskirts of Ismailia to about 9 miles from the city of Suez. The general said Israelis were blocking the two roads and the railroad line linking Suez and Cairo.

According to General Gazit, Egyptian forces continued to hold two strips about five miles wide on the canal's eastern bank. One, he said, is about 20 miles long from Qantara southward; the other, about 30 miles long from Suez at the southern end of the canal north to the Great Bitter Lake.

Asked whether these troops could be reinforced, General Gazit replied: "With whom?" He said that the Egyptian forces were not isolated, but were "definitely not in position to start offensive operations from there."

He said that the Egyptians on the eastern bank were the remnants of seven divisions and two armored brigades that had crossed the canal. Estimates of the number of troops ranged from 50,000 to 80,000.

The general said that the present disposition of forces on the canal, with Israelis in strength on both banks, prevented Egypt from reopening the canal to shipping without Israeli consent.

In Syria Israeli forces are on the main highway to Damascus at a distance of less than 25 miles from the capital. Military and political observers here reject the notion that Israel wants to seize either Damascus or Cairo.

Toll of Foe Cited

Describing the last days of fighting on the Suez front, General Gazit said that Israeli troops met with little resistance. He said that at least 100 Egyptian tanks and 11 aircraft had been destroyed, and a number of surface-to-air missile sites eliminated.

Summing up on the aircraft and tanks that Israel says her forces have destroyed, General Gazit put the numbers at 240 Egyptian planes and more than 1,000 tanks.

Arab losses on the Syrian front, he said, amounted to 212 aircraft and 1,000 tanks. He said those tanks included Iraqi, Jordanian and Syrian armor.

The general, adhering to Israeli policy of not announcing losses until an appropriate time, gave no comparable figures for the Israelis. They are believed to be significantly in excess of the casualties of the six-day war, in which more than 800 Israelis were killed.

Tel Aviv began the first night of the partial cease-fire as it had spent the 17 days of war—silent and blacked out. There was no celebrating, no rejoicing in the streets as the order to cease firing on the Egyptian front was made public. As night fell, the street lights and neon signs of Tel Aviv stayed out.

Families Are Apprehensive

The awareness of the number of casualties has created a mood of apprehension among those many families who have not been told their soldiers were casualties, but who have heard nothing else from them, either. Only the toll for the first eight days of the war—656 dead—has been announced.

As Mr. Kissinger's plane landed and he walked down the red carpet that stretched from the jetliner toward a specially prepared speaker's platform, he smiled, waved and shunned the microphones and the large number of reporters that awaited him.

He and his party went directly to the talks with the Israeli leaders. The secretary was accompanied by Joseph J. Sisco, Assistant Secretary of State for Near Eastern and South Asian Affairs, and his deputy, Alfred L. Atherton.

Besides Premier Meir, the Israelis participating in the talks included Deputy Premier Yigal Allon, Defense Minister Moshe Dayan, Foreign Minister Abba Eban, Lieut. Gen. David Elazar, the Chief of Staff, and Yitzhak Rabin, former Ambassador to the United States.

In the absence of any solid information outside the inner circle of the Government on the purpose of Mr. Kissinger's visit, various theories were mentioned by Israeli officials. There was speculation that the stopover here was scheduled as a show of support to balance the visit of Premier Aleksei N. Kosygin of the Soviet Union to Cairo last week, or as a personal report to Israeli leaders on the consultation with Soviet leaders, or as some possible "arm-twisting" to make Israel accept less than the full victory that many here think she could have achieved.

* * *

November 8, 1973

PRESIDENT ASKS CONGRESS FOR ENERGY-CRISIS ACTION; INSISTS HE'LL STAY ON JOB

FOR 50-M.P.H. LIMIT

Year-Round Daylight Time and Reduced Heating Urged

By EDWARD COWAN
Special to The New York Times.

WASHINGTON, Nov. 7—President Nixon asked Congress tonight to give him a variety of far-reaching powers to deal with the deepening shortage of oil.

Endorsing proposals made earlier by his energy policy director, Mr. Nixon asked in a television address that Congress pass an emergency energy act before it recesses in December.

The act would empower him to relax environmental standards, reduce automobile speed limits, regulate transportation schedules, impose daylight saving time the year-round and provide contingency plans for rationing gasoline.

The President appealed to the American people to help cope with the oil shortage by driving cars less and urged that the states reduce speed limits to 50 miles an hour.

6-Degree Cut Sought

He also asked Americans to lower temperatures in the home by 6 degrees, to a daytime average of 68 degrees.

And in the Administration's first acknowledgement that the fuel shortage could cause loss of sales, production and income, Mr. Nixon asked offices, factories and stores to achieve the equivalent of a 10-degree reduction by lowering the thermostat or curtailing working hours.

Mr. Nixon reiterated his plea for quicker construction and licensing of nuclear power stations and again called for creation of an energy research and development agency. And he asked Congress to enact, before its recess, several energy bills the Administration has sought for months.

Mr. Nixon made no new major policy proposals tonight. In the main, he asked Congress to enact proposals outlined in the last fortnight by John A. Love, the director of the Energy Policy Office.

The President said that the aim of his program was to begin to move the nation away from any dependence on Middle East oil by 1980. The current shortage has been worsened by reductions in production by Arab states and their total embargo on shipments to the United States.

Although his principal purpose was to stress the gravity of the shortage and the need for action by Congress and state governments, Mr. Nixon sought to reassure the country about what he called the prospect of "the most acute shortages of energy since World War II."

"The fuel crisis need not mean genuine suffering for any American," he said, "but it will require some sacrifice by all Americans."

Briefings for Officials

Mr. Nixon, whose popularity is at its lowest ebb because of the Watergate controversy, sought to rally politicians from both major parties to support his energy program. He invited members of Congress, Governors, Mayors and county executives to White House briefings today in advance of the address.

Returning to the theme of self-sufficiency that he articulated in his April energy message, Mr. Nixon said that the country must strive to meet its needs without relying on foreign countries.

Mr. Nixon spoke only in passing of the Arab oil embargo, which he said would cause a supply gap of 10 to 17 per cent in oil supplies this winter.

Oil accounts for about half the total energy consumed in this country. Of the 17 million barrels of crude oil and refinery products that have been burned every day, about two million have come, directly and indirectly, from Arab states.

Mr. Nixon spoke deliberately of "Middle Eastern" producers in what officials had said was a conscious attempt to avoid anything that might ring in Arab ears as a tone of rancor or retaliation. The President's strategy, the officials said, was to show the Arab producers that the United States cannot be crippled by the embargo and that it will adapt successfully.

"We have an energy crisis," Mr. Nixon said, "but there is no crisis of the American spirit." It was the first time he had called the fuel shortage a "crisis."

Appeal Is Repeated

The President renewed an appeal to Congress to authorize the five-year, $10-billion energy research and development program he proposed on June 29, and to create as a separate agency an energy research and development administration.

To dramatize the proposal, Mr. Nixon likened the push to develop new forms of energy to the World War II Manhattan Project to develop an atomic bomb and to the Apollo effort that put men on the moon.

Returning to his theme of energy self-sufficiency he suggested that the research effort be called "Project Independence."

Immediately after the President went off the air, Senator Henry M. Jackson, chairman of the Senate Interior Committee, said that he expected the committee to approve emergency legislation by Friday and the Senate to adopt it next week. The Washington Democrat's timetable was more optimistic than that of other Senate sources.

Less Discretion Seen

In any event, there was no expectation that the measure would cover the wide array of powers the President requested. It was thought certain to contain some authority to suspend environmental standards, if not so much discretion as Mr. Nixon sought. Authority for rationing also appeared probable, as did authorization to step up crude oil production at the Elk Hills, Calif., Naval Petroleum Reserve to the maximum rate, 160,000 barrels a day.

Mr. Nixon held out rationing as a future possibility if other actions to increase supplies and curb consumption proved inadequate.

At a White House briefing, Mr. Love emphasized his opposition to gasoline rationing because of the huge bureaucratic effort it would involve but he conceded that "it could come to that."

The White House said that a proposed plan to ration heating oil would be published in four weeks. That left open the possibility of weeks of public debate and appeared to reflect the Administration's known desire to scrape through the winter without consumer rationing.

15% Below Normal

Mr. Love said that, with heating oil supplies running 15 per cent below normal requirements, the Government's mandatory allocation scheme would assign to wholesalers and retailers not 100 per cent of last year's volume, as contemplated when the program started Nov. 1, but 85 per cent.

Mr. Nixon asked the public some weeks ago to lower the thermostat by 4 degrees. In going to 6 degrees he said the country should seek an average daytime indoor temperature of 68 degrees. Officials say it should be a half-dozen degrees lower at night.

In a half-humorous, half-serious interpolation in his prepared text, the President said, "Incidentally, my doctor tells me that in a temperature of 66 to 68 degrees you're really more healthy than when it's 75 to 78, if that's any comfort."

Mr. Nixon promised that the temperature would be reduced to 65 to 68 degrees in all Federal offices and in every room in the White House.

Mr. Nixon said he was asking states and communities to encourage car pooling and to stagger working hours so that more people could use mass transit.

Indeed, the only novel items in the entire program, as detailed in a White House fact sheet, was a proposal that states and localities discourage use of cars by "blocking off certain city sectors to cars with only one occupant" and by "providing preferential parking for car pools."

Looking beyond the winter's shortage, Mr. Nixon urged Congress, as he has done several times this year, to contribute to long-term energy supplies by passing the Alaska pipeline bill, by ending Federal regulation of natural gas prices, by enacting standards for strip-mining of coal and by creating a department of energy and natural resources in addition to an energy research agency.

Mr. Love said that the Government would put pressure on electric utilities to switch from oil to coal by cutting the utilities' fuel oil allocation.

Difficulties Foreseen

The White House produced an itemized list of conservation measures that it said could add up to 2,350,000 barrels of oil a day. Mr. Love conceded that this was "the top side of the estimates—they are not going to be easily achieved."

One difficulty in getting states to reduce speed limits on their roads, he said, is that few legislatures are sitting now.

The White House estimated that the present shortage of roughly two million barrels a day of crude oil and refinery products meant a 15 per cent shortage for heating oil, 13 per cent for residual fuel oil (burned by electric utilities, some factories and some apartment houses), 13 per cent for jet fuel and 7 per cent for gasoline.

Mr. Love, when asked about emergency exports of oil to Europe, appeared to rule it out, saying, "I do not now foresee we will be exporting."

* * *

June 30, 1974

NIXON, BREZHNEV IN TRADE ACCORD; THEY FLY TO YALTA

President Is Said to Demand Concessions From Soviet on East-West Contacts

ARMS TALKS CONTINUE

10-Year Commercial Pact Aims at Easing Conditions for U.S. Businessmen

By HEDRICK SMITH
Special to The New York Times.

YALTA, U.S.S.R., June 29—President Nixon and Leonid I. Brezhnev, the Communist party leader, today signed a 10-year economic agreement designed to promote Soviet-American trade and then flew to the Crimea, historic meeting place of the Big Three in World War II, to carry on their talks on arms control.

After the 720-mile flight from Moscow to the Crimean city of Simferopol, the two leaders motored through the lush coastal mountains to Oreanda, a beach resort near the center of Yalta, where Mr. Brezhnev often meets with his East European allies.

European Parley at Issue

During the 94-minute flight, a White House spokesman said, the two leaders discussed arms control over a light luncheon. When they reached Mr. Brezhnev's villa, in a setting much like the President's California home at San Clemente, Mr. Brezhnev took Mr. Nixon down to the beach.

In a session at the Kremlin this morning, the President was understood to have called for Soviet concessions on human contacts to gain Western agreement for a meeting at the heads-of-government level to conclude the European security conference.

An agreement on European security has been one of Mr. Brezhnev's cherished objectives and the Russians have been pressing for a wind-up of the conference. But the West has been adamant about getting the Communist nations to open up to easier movement between East and West as part of a détente.

Test Ban Discussed

Soviet and American spokesmen said negotiations on an agreement to impose limitations on underground nuclear testing had been conducted by Secretary of State Kissinger and Foreign Minister Andrei A. Gromyko and had been turned over to technical experts.

The crucial issue of imposing restraints on offensive nuclear weapons, especially on deployment of multiple warheads, has not yet been negotiated in detail, according to the White House press secretary, Ronald L. Ziegler.

"There have been some exchanges on the subject," Mr. Ziegler said at a midday news conference. "There are five more days and the leaders intend to have very intensive discussions on this question."

The most likely outcome was expected to be a general joint declaration stating that the arms negotiators in Geneva should concentrate on the issue of halting deployment of multiple warheads.

The trade agreement by President Nixon and Mr. Brezhnev this morning had been expected. Moscow has similar agreements with other Western trading partners like Britain, West Germany, France, Italy and Japan.

The White House said the American-Soviet agreement included provisions for exchange of economic information and commitments to facilitate working conditions for businessmen. They have often encountered bureaucratic delays in the Soviet Union. It was not clear what economic information was to be provided by the Russians beyond the limited data normally published by official Soviet agencies.

The 10-year agreement, signed by the two leaders in a ceremony in Vladimir Hall in the Great Kremlin Palace at 1:30 P.M., follows the original three-year trade accord signed in October, 1972, and does little more beyond providing some administrative machinery for trade and generally stated principles.

It totally avoids the issue of nondiscriminatory tariffs that had been written into the 1972 agreement and has been blocked in Congress by criticism of Soviet emigration restrictions on Jews and other citizens.

Mr. Ziegler asserted that the United States Government remained committed to obtaining equal tariff treatment to replace the higher tariffs that Communist nations normally have to pay on their imports into the United States.

In answer to a question on the Jewish issue, Leonid M. Zamyatin, the Soviet spokesman, declared that emigration "has no relation whatsoever to Soviet-American trade."

"I could put the following question to you: Would you agree to making United States trade with the U.S.S.R. dependent on the solution of the racial problem in the United States?" he added.

Luncheon on Plane

Almost immediately after the agreement-signing, the two leaders left for the Crimea aboard Mr. Brezhnev's Ilyushin-62 airliner, piloted by the same crew that flew him to the United States last year.

While they lunched over caviar and other light snacks, the President and Mr. Brezhnev, joined by their foreign ministers, talked over general East-West issues and arms control problems. Mrs. Nixon and White House staff members rode in another compartment of the plane.

The popular reception on the 64-mile drive through the winding mountain roads and past freshly painted white peasant cottages, evoking Mediterranean scenes, seemed warmer and more spontaneous than in Moscow on Thursday.

The motorcade reached Oreanda, three miles past the city center of Yalta, shortly after 6 p.m. and Mr. Brezhnev took his visitor to a spacious, buff-colored government villa used by Chancellor Willy Brandt of West Germany in 1971. It sits on a cliff overlooking the Black Sea and can be reached either by paths or by elevator.

The 67-year-old Soviet leader, relishing the role of host, took Mr. Nixon down to the Black Sea before sunset. The President and Mrs. Nixon spent a free evening tonight.

It was at near-by Livadiya that President Franklin D. Roosevelt met with Prime Minister Winston Churchill of Britain and with Stalin in February, 1945.

When the Russians originally proposed Yalta as a meeting place for Mr. Nixon's visit, the White House objected on the ground that Yalta had bad political connotations in the West from the wartime meeting.

Western Europeans regard Yalta as the site where the Big Three arranged the division of Europe, resulting in eventual Communist control of Poland and other East European countries. In the United States, political conservatives have associated Yalta with a sellout to Stalin.

But the Russians had evidently made too many preparations to change the meeting site. Communications lines had been installed and the Oreanda Hotel in Yalta, to be used by the White House staff, had been repainted.

In view of the extensive Soviet arrangements, the White House acquiesced, but officials emphasized that the President and Mr. Brezhnev were in Oreanda rather than Yalta. Reference books and maps show no administrative difference between the two because Oreanda is a suburban subdivision of the city of Yalta.

* * *

July 4, 1974

NIXON, BREZHNEV DECIDE TO SEEK A NEW ARMS PACT

To Aim at Another Interim Agreement on Offensive Missiles to End in 1985

MOSCOW MEETING ENDS

Kissinger Hints Military on Both Sides Still Oppose Permanent Limitations

By JOHN HERBERS
Special to The New York Times.

MOSCOW, July 3—President Nixon and Leonid I. Brezhnev, unable to make a breakthrough toward a permanent agreement on limiting offensive nuclear arms, signed a communiqué today committing their countries to negotiate a new interim accord extending to 1985.

With the ceremony, which was friendly but restrained, the two leaders ended their summit meeting, the third they have held, and President Nixon departed for the United States.

While agreements were concluded during the six days of talks here and in Yalta on limiting defensive missile complexes and underground nuclear tests, and on a number of economic, health and cultural issues, the failure to achieve a breakthrough on offensive weapons was a disappointment.

The communiqué, in calling for another interim agreement to follow the present five-year accord, represented the minimum progress that American officials said they hoped for. The present accord, signed in 1972, expires in 1977.

Permanent Pact Is Aim

The two leaders pledged at their meeting in Washington last summer to try to work out a permanent pact this year.

Secretary of State Kissinger indicated at a news conference today that even the less ambitious new interim accord was unlikely to be reached before next year at the earliest.

"Both sides have to convince their military establishments of the benefits of restraint, and that does not come easily to either side," he said, his comment apparently directed as much at Secretary of Defense James R. Schlesinger as at the Soviet Defense Minister, Marshal Andrei A. Grechko.

[At a news conference in Washington, Mr. Schlesinger rejected as unfounded the suggestion that the Pentagon had impeded progress on limiting nuclear arms.]

The announcements made here today at the end of the talks between Mr. Brezhnev, the head of the Soviet Communist party, and President Nixon said their achievements included the following:

- A treaty, which will require Senate ratification, prohibiting underground nuclear tests exceeding 150 kilotons (equivalent to 150,000 tons of TNT), effective March 31, 1976. The treaty does not cover tests for peaceful purposes of nuclear energy. American officials have said the level is far above what either side considers necessary for most tests.
- An unwritten agreement in principle by Mr. Brezhnev to permit on-site inspection of "peaceful" explosions. The actual accord on allowing such inspections—the Soviet Union has strongly opposed any inspection by foreign observers—is yet to be worked out.
- Two published protocols limiting both the Soviet Union and the United States to a single deployment area for antiballistic missiles, or ABM's. They would amend the defensive-missile treaty signed by the two leaders here in 1972 allowing each country two such areas. The amendments require Senate ratification.
- Two secret protocols, to be submitted to Congressional leaders, on the dismantling and replacement of missiles under provisions of the 1972 defensive missile treaty and interim accord on offensive arms. Mr. Kissinger said they were made secret at the request of the Soviet Union but that "they break no new ground, they change no provisions."
- An agreement to begin discussions on controlling the use of environment modification techniques as a means of warfare. Mr. Kissinger said the talks would begin in the near future because both sides felt this form of warfare, although in its infancy, "is not properly understood" and could "have profound consequences for the future of mankind."

The Secretary said the amendments to the antimissile treaty would require the Soviet Union to dismantle about 15 defensive missile launchers and associated radars at its test site. The United States would have to dismantle "some deployments that have taken place" in the Washington area, Mr. Kissinger added.

In discussing moves toward controlling offensive nuclear weapons, Mr. Kissinger said that if agreement was not reached well before the interim accord expires in 1977, there will be "an explosion of numbers and of technology."

"One of the questions we have to ask ourselves as a country," he declared, "is, 'What in the name of God is strategic superiority? What is the significance of it? What do you do with it?' "

The American and Soviet delegations at the arms talks will reconvene in Geneva around Aug. 1 to proceed with negotiations on the basis of instructions growing out of the summit meeting. Officials said that contrary to American hopes, the two leaders had not agreed on a common mandate to their negotiators.

Mideast Peace Stressed

On the Middle East, the two sides agreed on a general statement calling for initiatives for peace in that area. Any efforts, the communiqué said, must take into account "the legitimate interests of all peoples in the Middle East, including the Palestinian people, and the right to coexistence of all states in the area."

"As co-chairmen of the Geneva peace conference on the Middle East," it continued, "the U.S.A. and the U.S.S.R. consider it important that the conference resume its work as soon as possible, with the question of other participants from the Middle East area to be discussed at the conference."

On the subject of a European security conference to which the Russians attach a high premium, the communiqué said the two sides hoped the conference could be concluded at "an early date" with a meeting of heads of state.

The Americans extracted a pledge from Mr. Brezhnev that the Soviet Union would join in an effort to resolve "the remaining problems."

This is the first time in months that the Kremlin has conceded that any problems of significance remain. The West Europeans have refused to agree to a summit ending until the Soviet Union makes concessions in the field of East-West human contacts.

West to State Demands

Secretary Kissinger said the Russians had pressed for a coordinated position summarizing Western demands on this point. He added that while President Nixon visited Brussels on his way to Moscow, the Western allies agreed to work out a common position. But the entire lengthy procedure is a disappointment for Mr. Brezhnev, who has staked his prestige on a rapid, top-level conclusion of this conference.

On the continuing war in Southeast Asia, the communiqué expressed hope that all countries involved in the struggle would observe the truce accords. Both North and South Vietnam have been charged with violating the terms of those agreements.

North Vietnam and the Soviet Union have been pressing the Saigon Government to move forward with the formation of a national government of conciliation, including Communist and neutralist factions. But Saigon, backed in part by the United States, has insisted that North Vietnam has moved men and supplies into the South in violation of the military provisions of the cease-fire agreement.

Emigration Was a Topic

On trade, President Nixon affirmed American interest in granting the Soviet Union lower tariffs for its imports into the United States.

Secretary Kissinger said the two sides had discussed the question of emigration from the Soviet Union, which members of Congress have linked to easier tariffs and credits. But he would not disclose any details.

Secretary Kissinger has been trying to work out a compromise between the Soviet Government and Senator Henry M. Jackson, Democrat of Washington, among others, who oppose tariff concessions to Moscow until the Soviet Union allows unrestricted emigration for Jews and other citizens.

Secretary Kissinger left here separately from the President and Mrs. Nixon. He headed for Brussels, where he is to brief the West Europeans.

American officials said that the question of East-West force reductions in central Europe had not been dealt with in any significant detail. The Americans feel it is too early for hard bargaining.

The officials said the Soviet Politburo, or most of its members, held a meeting yesterday morning to review Mr. Brezhnev's talks with President Nixon.

The two leaders had a final personal session today before taking part in the 10-minute ceremony for the signing of the final documents. There was almost none of the personal levity that characterized the agreement-signing at the 1973 summit meeting.

The signing was followed by a reception in the glittering gilt-and-white St. George's hall of the Great Kremlin Place. White-liveried butlers served mushrooms julienne and other Russian specialties while a brassy band mixed "Moscow Nights" with "I Could Have Danced All Night" and "My Old Kentucky Home."

The airport departure ceremonies were more subdued than Mr. Nixon's welcoming last Thursday. Mr. Brezhnev seemed more tired today. His parting with Mr. Nixon was friendly but restrained.

* * *

August 9, 1974

NIXON RESIGNS

HE URGES A TIME OF 'HEALING'; FORD WILL TAKE OFFICE TODAY

The 37th President Is First to Quit Post

By JOHN HERBERS
Special to The New York Times.

WASHINGTON, Aug. 8—Richard Milhous Nixon, the 37th President of the United States, announced tonight that he had given up his long and arduous fight to remain in office and would resign, effective at noon tomorrow.

At that hour, Gerald Rudolph Ford, whom Mr. Nixon nominated for Vice President last Oct. 12, will be sworn in as the 38th President, to serve out the 895 days remaining in Mr. Nixon's second term.

Less than two years after his landslide re-election victory, Mr. Nixon, in a conciliatory address on national television, said that he was leaving not with a sense of bitterness but with a hope that his departure would start a "process of healing that is so desperately needed in America."

He spoke of regret for any "injuries" done "in the course of the events that led to this decision." He acknowledged that some of his judgments had been wrong.

The 61-year-old Mr. Nixon, appearing calm and resigned to his fate as a victim of the Watergate scandal, became the first President in the history of the Republic to resign from office. Only 10 months earlier Spiro Agnew resigned the Vice-Presidency.

Speaks of Pain at Yielding Post

Mr. Nixon, speaking from the Oval Office, where his successor will be sworn in tomorrow, may well have delivered his most effective speech since the Watergate scandals began to swamp his Administration in early 1973.

In tone and content, the 15-minute address was in sharp contrast to his frequently combative language of the past, especially his first "farewell" appearance—that of 1962, when he announced he was retiring from politics after losing the California governorship race and declared that the news media would not have "Nixon to kick around" anymore.

Yet he spoke tonight of how painful it was for him to give up the office.

"I would have preferred to carry through to the finish whatever the personal agony it would have involved, and my family unanimously urged me to do so," he said.

Puts 'Interests of America First'

"I have never been a quitter," he said. "To leave office before my term is completed is opposed to every instinct in my body." But he said that he had decided to put "the interests of America first."

Conceding that he did not have the votes in Congress to escape impeachment in the House and conviction in the Senate, Mr. Nixon said, "To continue to fight through the months ahead for my personal vindication would almost totally absorb the time and attention of the President and the Congress in a period when our entire focus should be on the great issues of peace abroad and prosperity without inflation at home."

"Therefore," he continued, "I shall resign the Presidency effective at noon tomorrow. Vice President Ford will be sworn in as President at that hour in this office."

Then he turned again to his sorrow at leaving. Although he did not mention it in his speech, Mr. Nixon had looked forward to being President when the United States celebrates its 200th anniversary in 1976.

"I feel a great sadness," he said.

Mr. Nixon expressed confidence in Mr. Ford to assume the office, "to put the bitterness and divisions of the recent past behind us."

"By taking this action, I hope that I will have hastened the start of that process of healing which is so desperately needed in America," he said. "I regret deeply any injuries that may have been done in the course of the events that led to this decision. I would say only that if some of my judgments were wrong—and some were wrong—they were made in what I believed at the time to be the best interests of the nation."

Further, he said he was leaving "with no bitterness" toward those who had opposed him.

"So let us all now join together in affirming that common commitment and in helping our new President succeed for the benefit of all Americans," he said.

As he has many times in the past, Mr. Nixon listed what he considered his most notable accomplishments of his five and half years in office—his initiatives in foreign policy, which he said had gone a long way toward establishing a basis for world peace.

Theodore Roosevelt Is Quoted

And, at the end, he expressed his own philosophy—that to succeed is to be involved in struggle. In this he quoted Theodore Roosevelt about the value of being "the man in the arena whose face is marred by dust and sweat and blood" and who "spends himself in a worthy cause."

After spending himself in a long political career, Mr. Nixon is scheduled to fly to his home in San Clemente, Calif., and retirement tomorrow while Mr. Ford is being sworn in in the Oval Office.

A White House spokesman said tonight that Mr. and Mrs. Nixon and their family would bid farewell to Cabinet members and staff personnel at 9:30 A.M. tomorrow in the East Room. Then they will board a helicopter at 10 A.M. for the short trip to Andrews Air Force Base, where they will emplane on the Spirit of '76, a jet aircraft, for their flight to San Clemente.

Ronald L. Ziegler, the Presidential adviser and press secretary, also said that Mr. Nixon's letter of resignation would be delivered to the office of Secretary of State Kissinger in the Executive Office Building adjacent to the White House by noon tomorrow.

Mr. Nixon's announcement came only two days after he told his Cabinet that he would not resign but would let the constitutional impeachment process run its course, even though it was evident he would be removed from office after a trial by the Senate.

In the next 48 hours the pressures for him to resign and turn the reins of the Government over to Mr. Ford became overwhelming.

His chances of being acquitted were almost hopeless. Senator Barry Goldwater, the Arizona conservative who was the Republican Presidential candidate in 1964, told him that he had no more than 15 votes in the Senate, far short of the 34 he needed to be sure of escaping conviction. Members of his own staff, including Gen. Alexander M. Haig Jr., the White House chief of staff, strongly recommended that he step down in the national interest.

In the end only a small minority of his former supporters were urging him to stay and pledging to give him their support. It was his friends, not his legions of enemies, that brought the crucial pressures for resignation.

Seventeen months of almost constant disclosures of Watergate and related scandals brought a steady attrition of support, in the country and in Congress, for what many authorities believed was the most powerful Presidency in the history of the nation.

However, a Presidential statement of last Monday and three transcripts of Presidential conversations that Mr. Nixon chose to make public ultimately precipitated the crush of events of the last week.

In that statement, Mr. Nixon admitted, as the transcript showed, that on June 23, 1972, he ordered a halt to the investigation of the break-in at the Democratic headquarters in the Watergate complex here six days earlier by persons in the employ of agents of Mr. Nixon's re-election campaign. He also admitted that he had kept the evidence from both his attorneys and the House Judiciary Committee, which had recommended that the House impeach him on three general charges.

Then came the avalanche. Republicans, Southern Democrats and others who had defended Mr. Nixon said that these actions constituted the evidence needed to support the article of impeachment approved by the House Judiciary Committee charging obstruction of justice. And it gave new support to other charges that Mr. Nixon had widely abused his office by bringing undue Presidential pressures to bear on sensitive Government agencies.

As the pressures mounted and Mr. Nixon held publicly to his resolve not to resign, the capital was thrown into a turmoil. A number of Senators anxious for a resignation began publicly predicting one.

At the White House yesterday, Mr. Nixon met in his White House offices with Mrs. Nixon and his two daughters, Mrs. David Eisenhower and Mrs. Edward F. Cox, and with his close aides. Members of his staff, acting independently of the Congressmen, sent him memorandums he had requested as to their recommendations. Most called for resignation rather than taking the country through a painful impeachment debate and vote in the House and a trial in the Senate.

Last night, Raymond K. Price and other speech writers were ordered to prepare a resignation statement for use tonight. Secretary of State Kissinger met with the President late in the evening and Mr. Nixon told him that he would resign in the national interest.

At 11 A.M. today, as crowds for the third day gathered along Pennsylvania Avenue outside the White House, President Nixon summoned Mr. Ford to his Oval Office and officially informed him that he would submit his resignation tomorrow to the Secretary of State, as provided by Federal law, and that Mr. Ford would become President.

Shortly after noon, Mr. Ziegler, the President's confidant and press secretary, his face saddened and weary, appeared in the crowded White House press room and announced that the President would go on national radio and television tonight to address the American people. As with most previous such announcements, he did not say what the President would talk about.

But by that time, other Presidential aides were confirming that Mr. Nixon planned to resign, and the tensions that had been building for days subsided.

At 7:30 P.M. Mr. Nixon met in his office in the Executive Office Building with a bipartisan Congressional leadership group—James O. Eastland, Democrat of Mississippi, President pro tem of the Senate; Mike Mansfield, Democrat of Montana, the Senate majority leader; Hugh Scott, Republican of Pennsylvania, the Senate minority floor leader; Carl Albert, Democrat of Oklahoma, the Speaker of the House, and John J. Rhodes, Republican of Arizona, the minority leader. The meeting was to give them formal notice of his resignation.

Among the White House staff today there was a sadness but there were no tears, according to those there. Mr. Nixon, who was described as wretched and gray yesterday while wrestling with his decision, was described today as relaxed. To some, he appeared relieved.

He ordered Mr. Price to begin drafting the resignation speech yesterday, even before he made his decision to resign, aides said. Five drafts of it were written before it was turned over to Mr. Nixon to make his own changes.

It was exactly six years ago last night that Mr. Nixon was nominated on the first ballot at the Republican National Convention to be the party's nominee for President, a note of irony that did not escape members of the President's staff.

That evening marked the beginning of an ascension to power that was to put the Nixon mark on an important segment of history. After a first term marked by innovations in foreign policy and a return of resources to the state and local governments in domestic policy, Mr. Nixon in 1972 won re-election with 60.7 per cent of the vote.

In early 1973, as he ended American military involvement in the Vietnam war and as he moved to strengthen the powers of his office in a multitude of ways, his popularity rating in the Gallup Poll registered 68 per cent. But as the Watergate disclosures broke his rating dropped quickly and was below 30 per cent before the end of the year.

Mr. Nixon made a number of counterattacks to win back his lost popularity. He campaigned from time to time across the country as if he was running for office. He disclosed information about his taxes and property. He hired a succession of lawyers to defend him in the courts and in Congress.

He made television and radio appearances. He ordered his subordinates to step up their activities to show that the Government's business was moving ahead. He made foreign trips to show he was still a world leader.

Cheered in Tour of Middle East

In the Middle East in June he was cheered by vast throngs, and he held a summit meeting with Soviet leader, Leonid I. Brezhnev, in Moscow.

Yet, when he returned to the United States, the Gallup Poll showed his rating at 24 per cent and the Watergate charges broke anew as the House Judiciary Committee stepped up its impeachment inquiry. His Administration was tottering when he made his remarkable statement last Monday, apparently in an effort to put his own interpretation on information that was expected to have been made public at the Watergate trials as a result of a Supreme Court decision upholding a court order for the information.

When the decision to resign came, Mr. Nixon moved to achieve an orderly transition of power to Mr. Ford. General Haig, who has had broad delegated authority in recent months, met frequently with the Vice President to brief him on policy, as did other Administration officials.

Mr. Kissinger gave a number of assurances that the nation's "bipartisan foreign policy" would remain firmly in place. The Defense Department announced that American military forces around the world would continue under normal status. And across this city thousands of Federal employes performed their chores as if nothing was happening.

* * *

November 25, 1974

FORD, BREZHNEV AGREE TO CURB OFFENSIVE NUCLEAR WEAPONS; FINAL PACT WOULD RUN TO 1985

A 'BREAKTHROUGH'

Kissinger Is Hopeful on Signing Accord Next Summer

By JOHN HERBERS
Special to The New York Times.

VLADIVOSTOK, U.S.S.R., Nov. 24—President Ford and Leonid I. Brezhnev, the Soviet leader, reached tentative agreement today to limit the numbers of all offensive strategic nuclear weapons and delivery vehicles through 1985.

Secretary of State Kissinger described the development as a "breakthrough" in efforts to halt the arms race. He said the agreement, which includes specific numbers for each side, would be subject to further negotiations in Geneva next year on technical questions.

The Secretary said, however, that he hoped the final agreement could be signed next summer, when Mr. Brezhnev visits the United States.

The numbers of nuclear weapons and delivery vehicles agreed upon in two days of talks here, Mr. Kissinger said, would be kept secret until President Ford briefs members of Congress, beginning Tuesday.

First Meeting as President

After exchanging toasts with Mr. Brezhnev and his party, President Ford left for Washington to end an eight-day trip that took him to Japan and South Korea before he came to Vladivostok for his first meeting as President with Mr. Brezhnev. They had met briefly when the Soviet leader visited Washington last year and Mr. Ford was House minority leader.

The Vladivostok meeting was first advertised as a get-acquainted session, but it provided the means for what officials called a significant step forward in Soviet-American relations.

> [President Ford arrived at Andrews Air Force Base in Maryland Sunday evening and told an airport audience that his meetings with Mr. Brezhnev had gone "very, very well." He said they had established "a sound basis for a new agreement that will constrain our military competition over the next decade," The Associated Press reported.]

Speaking in Vladivostok, Mr. Kissinger said the agreement, in the form of a joint statement by the two leaders, "marks the breakthrough with the strategic arms limitation negotiations that we have sought to achieve in recent years and produces a very strong possibility of agreement, to be signed in 1975."

If the agreement stands up, it would prevent over the next few years a scramble for newer and more sophisticated weapons and would save both countries a lot of money.

Although it would not extend beyond 1985, the agreement calls for further negotiations, beginning no later than 1980 or 1981, on further limitations and possible reductions after 1985.

Today's development, which was reached at a health spa on the outskirts of Vladivostok, was the most important between the two countries since May 26, 1972, when President Richard M. Nixon and Mr. Brezhnev reached an interim agreement on control of offensive arms. That agreement, which does not cover all nuclear weapons, expires in 1977.

Mr. Ford and Mr. Brezhnev, their agreement said, "are convinced that a long-term agreement on this question would be a significant contribution to improving relations between the U.S. and the U.S.S.R., to reducing the danger of war and to enhancing world peace."

A separate joint communiqué issued after their talks said:

"Both sides consider that based on the agreements reached between them important results have been achieved in funda-

Associated Press

President Ford and Leonid I. Brezhnev signing communiqué. Others are, from left, U.S. Ambassador Walter J. Stoessel Jr., Secretary of State Kissinger, Soviet Foreign Minister Andrei A. Gromyko, Ambassador Anatoly F. Dobrynin.

mentally reshaping American-Soviet relations on the basis of peaceful coexistence and equal security. These results are a solid foundation for progress in reshaping Soviet-American relations."

According to the arms agreement, further negotiations for a treaty in 1975 will be based on the following provisions:

- "The new agreement will incorporate the relevant provisions of the interim agreement of May 26, 1972, which will remain in force until October, 1977."
- "The new agreement will cover the period from October, 1977, through Dec. 31, 1985."
- "Based on the principle of equality and equal security, the new agreement will include the following limitations:

"A. Both sides will be entitled to have a certain agreed aggregate number of strategic delivery vehicles [including bombers].

"B. Both sides will be entitled to have a certain agreed aggregate number of ICBM's [intercontinental ballistic missiles] and SLBM's [submarine-launched ballistic missiles] equipped with multiple independently targetable warheads (MIRVS)."

Each Could Destroy Other

There was apparently no assurance that the degree of destructive force for the two sides would be equal. Each side now has the ability to destroy the other several times over.

The race for additional weapons has become more political and psychological than a race for superiority, in the view of many officials concerned. Mr. Kissinger said in a news conference that the proposed agreement would "mean that a cap has been put on the arms race for a period of 10 years."

"That cap is substantially below the capabilities of the other side," he said. "The element of insecurity, inherent in an arms race in which both sides are attempting to anticipate not only the actual programs but the capabilities of the other side, will be substantially reduced."

Achievement of today's accord and the apparent amity of the Ford-Brezhnev talks elated the President's party.

"The President will return home in triumph," said Ron Nessen, the White House press secretary.

In discussing with Mr. Nessen, in a reporter's presence, what kind of statement Mr. Ford should make upon returning home, Mr. Kissinger said, "I think the President should be modest. The agreement will speak for itself. The back of this thing has been broken."

The groundwork for the accord was laid in negotiations last month between Mr. Kissinger and Mr. Brezhnev. Mr. Kissinger attended all the talks here.

Arms control dominated them. Mr. Kissinger said that the Middle East, European security and other issues had been discussed but not at length. The Middle East occupied about one hour, he said.

"I think there is an agreement by both sides that the situation has elements of danger, that an effort should be made to diffuse it," Mr. Kissinger said, "The discussions on the Middle East, I think, may have contributed, and we hope will contribute, to a framework of restraint in enabling the two countries that have such a vital interest in the area to stay in touch with each other."

There was no indication that either side had sought to begin any new initiative on the Middle East.

Mr. Kissinger acknowledged that the negotiations for a treaty on arms control "could be difficult." He said there would be many "technical complexities, but we believe that the target is achievable."

He said that the tentative agreement did not include the American "forward base" planes that carry nuclear warheads. In the past the Soviet Union had insisted that these be included in any agreement. But Mr. Kissinger said that they longer pressed that point because they now believed that those weapons "are not suitable for a significant attack on the Soviet Union."

'The Freedom to Mix'

Included under the agreement, he said, is a "combination of missiles, of land-based missiles, submarine missiles, bombers and certain other categories of weapons." Within the total numbers to be assigned under the agreement, each side has "essentially the freedom to mix" in whatever way it wants, he said.

Mr. Kissinger said it was possible that the total arsenal of both sides would be reduced under the accord.

Under the Soviet-American agreement of 1972, the United States has 1,054 land-based missiles and 656 submarine-based missiles. The agreement permits the United States to have up to 710 sea-based launchers, but that total would require a reduction to 1,000 in land-based missiles.

The Russians are allowed 1,410 land-based missiles and up to 950 submarine-based missiles.

The 1972 agreement does not include limits on long-range bombers, of which the United States has about 400 and the Soviet Union about 125, nor does it encompass missiles with multiple warheads.

Mr. Kissinger said that two controversial American weapons—the Trident submarine and the B-1 long-range bomber—must fall within "the total number of the ceiling that will be established" by the new agreements.

Another agreement signed in 1972 permits each side two defensive sites of 100 missile launchers apiece, one protecting the national capital area, the other protecting an offensive-missile field.

* * *

November 25, 1974

A GAIN TOWARD DETENTE

Agreement in Summit Talks Is Seen As Surpassing Expectations by Far

By HEDRICK SMITH
Special to The New York Times.

MOSCOW, Nov. 24—Today's breakthrough by President Ford and Leonid I. Brezhnev toward a major agreement on strategic arms control appeared to exceed expectations by far. It will undoubtedly give a new impulse to East-West accommodations at a time of uncertainties on both sides.

The extent of the agreement and the speed with which it was achieved suggest also that the Kremlin might have been prepared last summer to move forward but held back in the belief that President Richard M. Nixon was too weak to get a complex arms agreement approved by Congress.

Trade May Be Linked

The Soviet Union may also have been persuaded to move ahead now by the start of Congressional action on the Administration's trade bill. The bill would grant Moscow concessions on trade and credit in return for more relaxed handling of emigration from the Soviet Union.

Whatever the causes, the success of the Far Eastern encounter is likely to bring political dividends for both the Soviet leader and the President and to give them better means for quieting domestic skeptics of détente.

More broadly, Mr. Brezhnev's emphasis on a need for long-term commitments on arms control and trade is a form of assurance to the West as a whole. The Brezhnev-led coalition in the Kremlin seems to be saying that it puts higher priority on accommodation than on trying to exploit the financial and energy problems in the West and thereby help Western Communist parties.

For the Russians, Mr. Ford's warm pledges to pursue détente and his ability and readiness to strike an accord with Mr. Brezhnev so quickly is reassurance that the change in the White House has not affected basic American policy toward the Soviet Union.

Amid the general amiability in Vladivostok, only here and there were there public indications of continuing problems.

In a dinner speech, Mr. Brezhnev hinted that he was somewhat impatient for Congress to approve the trade concessions. "Much has still to be done to really clear the way for the development of equitable trade and economic links between our two countries," he said.

On the Middle East, the two leaders were clearly still at odds though they voiced a common concern over the "dangerous situation" there.

President Ford refused to give Mr. Brezhnev the kind of endorsement Moscow wanted for an immediate resumption of the Geneva Conference on the Middle East and the moving there of all efforts for a settlement. The Arab-Israeli conference, with the Soviet Union and the United States as co-chairmen, has been in recess since just after it opened last December.

The vague wording of the Ford-Brezhnev communiqué on that matter indicated that Secretary of State Kissinger had retained full flexibility for his personal diplomacy despite Mr. Brezhnev's personal criticism of that approach.

On their cherished European security conference, the Russians received only a lukewarm endorsement from Mr. Ford that a "possibility" existed for its early conclusion. This was a more tentative stand than Mr. Nixon had taken last July.

It was strategic arms control, however, that the two leaders went to Vladivostok to discuss and on which they concentrated. And as the President's party indicated in parting, that is the issue by which the White House wants the Vladivostock meeting measured.

The final reaction of Congress will undoubtedly depend more on what was not disclosed today than on what was: the numbers of strategic nuclear weapons and delivery vehicles that each side tentatively agreed in Vladivostok to allow the other. The only clue given by Mr. Kissinger was that it would be under current Soviet strength.

The agreement would allow Moscow, however, to move fully into the deployment of multiple warheads for its missile forces, an area where the United States has held strong advantage.

Before the talks, the Administration was seeking to retain some advantages in multiple independently targetable re-entry vehicles—or MIRV's—to offset the Soviet advantage in numbers and power of launchers or the size of the warheads they could launch. Given Mr. Kissinger's reported optimism today, Washington appears to hope for an edge here.

The agreement today to limit strategic bomber forces, of which the United States has about 400 to 125 for the Russians, was an apparent gain for Moscow.

But the Americans appeared to gain when the Russians, according to Mr. Kissinger, dropped their firm insistence that about 500 forward-based American aircraft in Europe be considered part of the American strategic bomber force. This is expected to help in relations with Western European Allies, who regard that force as their nuclear umbrella.

Today's agreement suggests that the top political leaders on both sides believe that it is more important to find some loose formula for agreement on strategic parity than to argue too finely over numerical advantages.

If so, this is probably the most important reassurance from each side to the other on the full range of Soviet-American accommodations.

* * *

December 3, 1974

FORD SAYS ACCORD GIVES A BASIS FOR CUT IN ARMS

By BERNARD GWERTZMAN
Special to The New York Times.

WASHINGTON, Dec. 2—President Ford made public tonight the details of a tentative agreement on arms control that he and Leonid I. Brezhnev had reached in Vladivostok. He said the accord put a "firm ceiling" on the arms race and created a "solid basis" for future arms reductions.

"It's a good agreement and I think the American people will buy it," Mr. Ford said at a news conference.

Mr. Ford disclosed that both sides had put a ceiling of 2,400 each on the total number of long-range offensive missiles and bombers. Of that total, each side will be able to place multiple independently targetable warheads on up to 1,320 land-based and submarine-launched missiles.

Higher Than Reported

The over-all figure of 2,400 on strategic delivery vehicles had already become known, but the number of missiles able to receive MIRV's was higher than previously reported.

Earlier versions placed the figure on missiles that could be armed with multiple war heads at 1,200 to 1,300. The 1,320 total is sure to increase the criticism already voiced by both arms control advocates and those seeking cuts in military spending that the arms ceiling is too high.

Mr. Ford acknowledged that the United States would continue to spend at about the same level or higher as this year to keep American forces up to the ceiling permitted by the accord.

He said that because of inflation, the military budget proposed for next year would increase.

But he stressed, as Mr. Kissinger did at Vladivostok, that the agreement had put a "cap" on the arms race.

On the Middle East, Mr. Ford indicated that while the Soviet Union and the United States had a better understanding of each other's position, no substantial agreements were reached.

He said that he and Mr. Brezhnev had discussed the Middle East at some length and that both sides agreed to "make a maximum effort to keep negotiations going."

But Mr. Ford said the United States argued that the step-by-step approach, with Israel negotiating with Arab nations one by one "is the right one." The Soviet Union has pressed for a reconvening of the Geneva conference. Mr. Ford said that "we don't preclude a Geneva conference."

Mr. Ford, reporting on his recent trip to Japan, South Korea and the two days at the Soviet Far Eastern port city of Vladivostok, said that he and Mr. Brezhnev, the Soviet Communist party chief, went beyond their original purpose of reviewing Soviet-American relations.

"Building on the achievements of the past three years we agreed that prospects were favorable for more substantial, and I may say, very intensive negotiations on the primary issue of limitation of strategic arms," he said.

"In the end we agreed on the general framework for a new agreement that will last through 1985," he said.

Mr. Ford said that the accord worked out with Secretary of State Kissinger's assistance, put the total bomber and missile ceilings "well below the force levels which would otherwise have been expected over the next 10 years, and very substantially below the forces which would result from an all-out arms race over that same period."

'Long Step Forward'

"What we have done is to set firm and equal limits on the strategic forces of each side, thus preventing an arms race with all its terror, instability, war-breeding tension and economic waste," he said. "We have in addition created the solid basis from which future arms reductions can be—and hopefully will be—negotiated."

Critics such as Senator Henry M. Jackson, Democrat of Washington, have advocated arms reductions, not ceilings.

Mr. Ford said that the "framework" must now be negotiated in detail so that the final accord can be signed next year.

"It will take more detailed negotiations to convert this agreed framework into a comprehensive accord," he said. "But we have made a long step forward toward peace, on a basis of equality, the only basis on which agreement was possible."

His opening statement did not provide any details on other aspects of the accord, or what the American position was on verification procedures. Mr. Kissinger will presumably go into some of these details when he meets with the Senate Foreign Relations Committee in private on Wednesday.

Mr. Ford was asked about reports that the Soviet Union had violated terms of the five-year interim accord of 1972 that had put curbs on land-based and submarine-launched missiles.

Russians Criticized

These reports, apparently leaked by Pentagon officials, charged the Russians with trying to interfere with the American ability to monitor Soviet deployment through "national means" of surveillance. They also said the Russians were building missile silos not in accord with the agreement.

Mr. Ford said that "we know of no violations" by the Russians, but that there were "some ambiguities" and that the United States was asking for a meeting of the Standing Consultative Commission set up in Geneva to "to analyze any allegations as to violations."

The agreement was made known in outline form in Vladivostok Nov. 24 at the end of Mr. Ford's two days of talks with Mr. Brezhnev. Mr. Kissinger, who played a major role in negotiating the ceilings, called it "the breakthrough" that "we have sought to achieve in recent years and produces a very strong possibility of agreement to be signed in 1975."

If the two sides are able to work out all the remaining details, such as the verification procedures, they contemplate a formal treaty or agreement when Mr. Brezhnev visits Washington in the spring.

The numerical limits were not made public at first. Part of the reason was for each side to exchange memorandums of the agreement, setting forth on paper their respective understandings of what had been agreed to. This was done Saturday.

Mr. Ford did give a confidential briefing to some Congressional leaders last Tuesday and soon thereafter it was reported that the two sides had agreed to a ceiling of about 2,400 long-range missiles and bombers and that of that total, 1,200 to 1,300 missiles that could receive multiple warheads.

The size of the forces allowed each side came as a surprise to some disarmament specialists who were skeptical whether the agreement would slow down the arms race.

Heavy Cost Seen

Senator Jackson said that because the Russians have built heavier land-based missiles than the United States, the accord could permit them to have a much greater number of multiple warheads, and this in turn could threaten American missile sites.

He said that he was "astonished" by the large number of missiles that could be fitted with multiple warheads and he said that to keep the American deterrent strong the United States might have to spend billions to catch up with the Russians.

Mr. Ford, asked about the Jackson contention, said "it is recognized that the Soviet Union has a heavier throw weight"—a measure of the ability to deliver more powerful warheads—than the United States.

But he stressed that the Pentagon several years ago had decided on smaller missiles that were more accurate if less heavy.

Therefore, if the military now believes it needs heavier missiles, it can recommend building bigger missiles, and Congress can appropriate funds for them. Such a decision, however, would lead to a major increase in costs.

New Race Feared

Thomas A. Halsted, executive director of the Arms Control Association, a nongovernmental group, said he was afraid the accord would simply create a new arms race in qualitative improvements of existing weapons. He also was critical of the limits set.

The United States now has a total missile and bomber force of more than 2,200 and the Russians of more than 2,400.

Under the accord, the Russians would probably have to cut back, while the United States could build up to the ceiling.

Washington already plans to build 10 Trident submarines, with a total of 240 missiles, and more than 200 B-I bombers to replace the B-52 force.

The United States, ahead of the Russians in warhead technology, has already put multiple heads on about 800 land and sea-based missiles and has plans to go up to 1,200. The Russians have not deployed any multiple warheads but are testing them now and are expected to begin deployment in the next year or so.

* * *

December 3, 1974

VLADIVOSTOK PACT: HOW IT WAS REACHED

By LESLIE H. GELB
Special to The New York Times.

WASHINGTON, Dec. 2—The latest Soviet-American nuclear arms deal was worked out only after the Russians agreed to exempt American nuclear bombers stationed in and around Europe and to limit the total level of missiles, bombers and multiple warheads permitted on each side, according to authoritative Administration officials.

President Ford and Leonid I. Brezhnev, the Soviet leader, reached the accord in two days of bargaining at Vladivostok on Oct. 23-24.

American officials said that although Mr. Brezhnev appeared personally flexible in his bargaining, the announcement of details of the agreement had been delayed by his need to clear the terms with his colleagues.

The accord of Vladivostok would allow each country to have offensive nuclear arsenals of 2,400 long-range missiles and bombers and to place multiple warheads on as many as 1,320 land-based and submarine-launched missiles.

These figures were announced by President Ford this evening. The force ceilings worked out at Vladivostok are to be incorporated into a full-fledged agreement on the limitation of offensive strategic weapons to stay in effect until 1985.

At present the two countries are bound by the interim five-year accord that was signed in Moscow in May, 1972, by Richard M. Nixon, then President, and Mr. Brezhnev. That agreement, which is due to expire in 1977, called for a freeze on offensive missiles at 1,710 for the United States, and 2,360 for the Soviet Union. It did not cover bombers or multiple warheads.

On the American side, the last-minute give-and-take at Vladivostok was preceded by months of bargaining within the Ford Administration.

The debate pitted Defense Secretary James R. Schlesinger against Secretary of State Kissinger. Mr. Schlesinger favored either large mutual force reductions or, if the Russians did not agree, an all-out arms race. Mr. Kissinger argued for higher force levels now as part of a later step-by-step approach to reductions.

The Joint Chiefs of Staff backed Mr. Kissinger because his plan allowed for more new weapons than would Mr. Schlesinger's alternative. The Secretary of Defense finally agreed to Mr. Kissinger's offer of higher force levels, including more missiles with multiple warheads on both sides. The President then approved the plan.

As finally approved, the United States position offered the Russians two choices.

The first choice would give the Soviet Union and the United States the same numbers of missiles and bombers as well as the same numbers of missiles with multiple independently targetable re-entry vehicles, or MIRV's.

The second choice would give the Soviet Union a greater over-all total of missiles, bombers and multiple warheads but the United States would have a greater number of missiles with multiple warheads.

In Vladivostok, Mr. Brezhnev chose the first alternative—over-all equality—but then asked for, and got, equality with even higher force levels and an even larger number of missiles with multiple warheads than Mr. Kissinger had favored. The sources were not able to make clear President Ford's precise role in the Vladivostok talks.

Brezhnev Raises Levels

Administration officials say the agreement permits the United States to build weapons it planned to build anyway. But they say that the Russians are restricted to a lower number of weapons than United States experts believed they had planned.

In fact, the over-all ceiling of 2,400, the officials said, will require Moscow to eliminate about a hundred of its delivery vehicles.

The principal problems that remain to be negotiated, according to the officials, are the details of how to verify the number of missiles with multiple warheads each side actually has. Once deployed, it is difficult to distinguish missiles with single warheads from those with multiple warheads.

Administration officials expressed satisfaction at the new accord. Critics have attacked the agreement on the ground that it sets total force levels and the number of missiles with multiple warheads at much too high a figure.

Soviet Behind in MIRV's

The Soviet Union is far behind the United States in multiple-warhead technology, but is expected to deploy the weapons soon. United States officials say that in the absence of a new agreement the Russians could have had about 17,000 warheads. Now the number is expected to be significantly lower.

The 1972 agreement, signed by President Richard M. Nixon, sidestepped the issue of multiple warheads.

According to a number of United States officials, the starting point for the Ford Administration was the Soviet rejection of President Nixon's proposal last June in Moscow of a Soviet advantage in total delivery vehicles—missiles plus bombers—in return for a substantial American lead in numbers of missiles with multiple warheads.

The Russians wanted both a numerical advantage in delivery vehicles and almost as many missiles with multiple warheads as the United States. They also insisted that the American total include nuclear-capable American aircraft in and around Europe as well as British, French and Chinese nuclear forces.

The Russians also wanted the American totals to take account of geographical disparities in the servicing of submarines. American submarines can be serviced in allied ports, thus allowing them additional time on patrol. Soviet submarines must return to home ports to be serviced.

Mr. Kissinger and Mr. Schlesinger debated over what to do next in a series of National Security Council meetings in October, with Mr. Ford presiding.

Mr. Schlesinger contended that "we must face the Soviets down" on their desire to deploy a large number of missiles with multiple warheads or, failing that, "buckle down for a five-year, all-out arms race."

Ford Offered a Choice

Mr. Schlesinger told the President that if he wanted to postpone reductions in forces and controls on modernization, he had a choice of insisting either on over-all equality in force levels or on such a low ceiling for missiles with multiple warheads that neither side would be tempted to take advantage of the other.

Mr. Kissinger countered that Mr. Schlesinger was suggesting a tougher proposal than the ones that Moscow had already rejected. Unless Washington put forward a negotiable position, he said, a new arms race would indeed start, and might even jeopardize the 1972 treaty limiting defensive missiles on both sides.

He cited an intelligence study showing that the Russians were planning to deploy at least 3,000 delivery vehicles and 1,500 to 2,000 missiles with multiple warheads over the next five years, and suggested Washington could not outbuild the Russians.

Since, Mr. Kissinger maintained, Washington could not win an arms race and since Moscow was bound to reject the Schlesinger proposals, he favored a step-by-step approach of high ceilings now, followed by reductions and controls on modernization later.

Joint Chiefs' Position

The Joint Chiefs of Staff essentially side with Mr. Kissinger. They wanted a high ceiling on missiles with multiple warheads, since this would allow them to complete their modernization programs. Thus the Russian rejection of low multiple-warhead levels fit in with the Chiefs' own modernization plans.

The Chiefs also said that Mr. Schlesinger's alternative of an all-out arms race was not politically feasible because Congress would not vote the necessary funds.

At the last of these National Security Council meetings, Mr. Schlesinger began to soften his position, saying that perhaps Washington could educate Moscow to the view that land-based missiles were vulnerable to a first-strike attack and that both sides should move most of their new missile forces to submarines.

With the President playing a still undefined role, the following proposal was agreed to: An equal delivery-vehicle ceiling of about 2,000; an equal number of missiles with multiple warheads at about 1,000; and sublimits on big Soviet land-based missiles and American bomber-launched missiles.

If Moscow rejected this, Washington would then go back to the old proposal of a Soviet lead in delivery vehicles and an American lead in numbers of missiles with multiple warheads.

Mr. Kissinger said he would give the over-all equality in delivery vehicles "one more try."

In Moscow, beginning on Oct. 22, Mr. Brezhnev and Foreign Minister Andrei A. Gromyko reacted favorably to the proposal. They seemed to talk about American aircraft in and around Europe only rhetorically, and their stand on taking the nuclear capability of other nations and American geographical advantages into account also seemed to weaken. This was the basis for Mr. Kissinger's public optimism.

A week before the Vladivostok meeting, Moscow sent a message that seemed to confirm this shift, but gave little ground on the numbers of delivery vehicles and multiple warheads.

In Vladivostok, Mr. Brezhnev first responded to the American proposal with the following: equal delivery vehicles for both sides at some figure over 2,500; equal missiles with multitude warheads at some figure over 1,300; and a ban on American air-launched strategic missiles.

The Americans countered with a proposal to ban all mobile land-based missiles. The negotiators then agreed to sidestep such bans. At this point, they knew they were going to reach a simple agreement based on equality in numbers.

Terms of Accord

On the second day, the parties agreed to:

The following:

- An over-all delivery-vehicle ceiling for both sides of 2,400, up about 300 from the American proposal.
- About 1,320 missiles with multiple warheads, for both sides, up about 200 from the American proposal.
- If a missile has been tested with multiple warheads, every missile of that kind that is deployed will be counted against the ceiling of multiple-warheads.
- Land-mobile missiles and bomber-launched strategic missiles can be deployed, but are included within the over-all ceiling.
- A limit of 300 for the big Soviet land-based missiles, the SS-9 or the SS-18 when deployed, with no new silos to be built.

The agreement also permits both sides to increase missile throw-weight, the weight a missile can carry to the target.

Deployment May Be Open

In not pressing the ban on land-mobile missiles, the United States stated its understanding that if the Russians deployed these missiles, they would do so in the open—on railroad cars or trucks—where they could be counted, and not in concealed shelters.

The remaining issues concern verification of the agreement. The basic American point stated at Vladivostok was that neither side should now develop new missiles with multiple warheads that are indistinguishable from existing missiles with such warheads.

There are also verification problems associated with the deployment of land-mobile missiles and the destruction of existing silos.

The American intelligence community has frequently stated that any substantial cheating can be readily detected by satellite photography and other electronic means.

Mr. Ford and Mr. Kissinger were said to be impressed by Mr. Brezhnev's freedom to bargain in the absence of his principal Politburo colleagues. Their representatives were present, but Mr. Brezhnev seemed clearly in charge.

American officials said Mr. Brezhnev seemed to have more negotiating flexibility in Vladivostok than he would have had in Moscow. Nevertheless, the officials said, Mr. Brezhnev was not in a position to endorse the details of the agreement until after he returned to Moscow.

* * *

April 22, 1975

THIEU RESIGNS, CALLS U.S. UNTRUSTWORTHY; APPOINTS SUCCESSOR TO SEEK NEGOTIATIONS; EVACUATION OF ALL AMERICANS CONSIDERED

10-YEAR RULE ENDS

Vice President Huong, 71 Years Old, Takes Office in Saigon

By MALCOLM W. BROWNE
Special to The New York Times.

SAIGON, South Vietnam, April 21—President Nguyen Van Thieu, denouncing the United States as untrustworthy, resigned tonight after 10 years in office.

He immediately appointed his Vice President, the 71-year-old Tran Van Huong, to replace him.

He said that President Huong would immediately press the enemy to cease all acts of war and enter into peace negotiations. The Vietcong have said repeatedly that they would not negotiate while Mr. Thieu held office.

[A spokesman for the Vietcong delegation in Saigon said Tuesday the resignation of President Thieu "decidedly cannot change the situation," Reuters reported.]

Accuses the U.S.

In an impassioned address to the nation, President Thieu defended his character and the accomplishments of his regime while chronicling its collapse. He called for peace, but also said the successor government would fight on.

Speaking before assembled members of his Government and National Assembly at the Presidential Palace, President Thieu accused the United States of breaking its promises to support an anti-Communist Government in Saigon.

Mr. Thieu said that he had objected in October, 1972, to Secretary of State Kissinger's "acceptance of the continued presence of North Vietnamese troops in South Vietnam."

Pledge by Nixon

Mr. Thieu added that South Vietnam would fight on to defend the territory left to it. The armed forces chief of staff, Gen. Cao Van Vien, also spoke briefly, to say that his troops would continue fighting to "defend the homeland against the communist aggressors."

"I resign but I do not desert," President Thieu said in concluding his one-and-a-half-hour address. "From this minute I will put myself at the disposal of the President and people. I will continue to stay close to you all in the coming task of national defense. Good-by to you all."

His voice taut with emotion, President Thieu devoted most of his speech to a scathing criticism of the United States, saying:

"The United States has not respected its promises. It is unfair. It is inhumane. It is not trustworthy. It is irresponsible."

Mr. Thieu said that former President Richard M. Nixon had described all accords, including the Paris peace agreement, as "pieces of paper" unless they were implemented, and had therefore promised Saigon not only military and economic aid, but also "direct and strong United States military intervention" in the event the Communists broke the accord.

But then, Mr. Thieu said, Watergate undid American resolve in aiding Vietnam, and Washington deserted its ally. By the time former Vice President Spiro T. Agnew visited Saigon later, he said, Mr. Agnew spoke "coldly," referring only to "Vietnamization" of the war and continuing military and economic aid, but not of President Nixon's promise before the Paris accord to send American troops and B-52's if needed.

The State Department has said that there was no specific commitment by the United States to intervene militarily. And the White House noted earlier this month that any private assurance given by Mr. Nixon was no longer valid because of the Congressional ban on American combat activity in Indochina imposed in August, 1973.

"Let me say that we need at least $722-million, plus the B-52's" Mr. Thieu said today. "Let me say that we need immediate—I say immediate—shipment of arms and equipment to the South Vietnam battlefield."

"I would challenge the United States army to do better than the South Vietnamese army without B-52's," the President said.

President Huong was sworn into office immediately at the assembly and Government meeting tonight in the Presidential Palace.

Speech by Huong

In a brief speech, he praised the achievements of the outgoing President, noted that he was assuming a great responsibility, and called for national unity, saying: "United we live, divided we die."

President Thieu's resignation was one of two major demands the Vietcong have called prerequisites to any peace talks.

The other is that "all American military men and advisers disguised as civilians" leave Vietnam.

In a broadcast today, the Vietcong appeared to set a time limit for the latter demand as "two to three days, or in 24 hours even." The broadcast was strongly threatening in tone, and implied that if the conditions were not quickly met, a full-scale military drive would be launched on Saigon.

It was not immediately clear whether President Thieu's resignation and the current outflow of Americans would satisfy the Vietcong demands.

But it has been apparent in the last two days that the Communist side would now prefer a political finale to the war, rather than bald military victory.

President Thieu's decision tonight was clearly based on the desire of most of the people of this city to avoid the destruction and loss of life that a final battle would cause.

Presumably, the battered and demoralized Saigon troops commanded by General Vien will be ordered to fight only in a defensive way, to safeguard positions they hold until such time as peace talks of some kind end the war.

A senior Western diplomat said: "Military defeat always carries with it terrible political concomitants. We can only hope now that the physical suffering of the vanquished can be reduced as much as humanly possible under the circumstances."

Curfew in Saigon was advanced an hour tonight, to 8 P.M. But for the first time, policemen and soldiers stationed around the city seemed to be paying little attention to the many curfew violators in the streets.

The electric tension of recent weeks and days seemed a little relaxed, and soldiers were joking with each other.

One said with a laugh, "Well now how long will Papa Huong be able to look after affairs of state?"

Little Hope Offered

In his speech, President Thieu offered little hope that his resignation would bring better times.

Mr. Thieu said that it was popular now to blame him for everything "just as in 1963, everything was put on the head of the late Mr. Diem," a reference to President Ngo Dinh Diem, who was overthrown and assassinated that year.

"There now seems to be a formidable propaganda campaign the toxicity of which is even reaching some of our soldiers," Mr. Thieu said.

President Thieu asserted that simply because he was leaving office to another man did not suggest a basic difference in their viewpoints. And he added that President Huong would press Washington for more aid.

"President Huong, like myself, is a patriot," he said.

"Both of us want to negotiate—unconditional negotiations. Let them say anything, let them even tear up the Paris accord if they want, but let us have a dialogue. Let us have immediate, unconditional negotiations."

President Thieu recapitulated at length his political battles of the last 10 years, particularly those with the United States.

He said that when confronted with a draft Vietcong peace proposal on Oct. 26, 1972, "I told the Americans that if I accepted it, I would be a traitor to my country. I would be selling out South Vietnam to the Communists. So I protested against the proposed accord for three months."

He said his objection was to three main points.

The first was a demand that a tripartite coalition government be created, extending from the central government all the way down to hamlet level.

The second was Vietcong insistence that Indochina be considered to consist of three states—Laos, Cambodia and only one Vietnam, presumably a Vietnam led form Hanoi rather than Saigon.

"I said that if one Vietnam was not possible, it would be better to leave it divided at the 17th Parallel," he said.

The third point was "Mr. Kissinger's acceptance of the continued presence of North Vietnamese troops in South Vietnam."

In the end, a compromise was agreed to.

"Afterward," Mr. Thieu said, "President Nixon told me that all accords are only pieces of paper, with no value unless they are implemented. What was important, he said, was not that he had signed the accord, but that the United States would always stand ready to help South Vietnam in case the Communists violated the accord."

Mr. Thieu said that, to discuss this matter, the President had invited him to the United States.

"I asked that the United States should be ready to come back in force to help directly, not just Vietnamization, in case the Communists renewed their aggression against South Vietnam.

"The most important question in my view, at that time, was direct United States intervention.

"So I won a solid pledge from our great ally, leader of the free world, that when and if North Vietnam renewed its aggression against South Vietnam, the United States would actively and strongly intervene."

When Mr. Thieu visited Mr. Nixon in 1973 after the accord was signed, the American President reiterated the pledge, President Thieu said. But then, matters changed.

"Unfortunately, there was Watergate," he said, "and United States politics have greatly affected the volume of aid to South Vietnam, as well as Vietnamization."

The crucial test, Mr. Thieu said, came when Communist forces attacked and overran an outpost in 1973.

"By then, the United States did not intervene, and that encouraged the Communists to move on to attack other places," he said.

Generals Criticized

President Thieu assigned the major share of blame for recent events here to the United States, but he also had criticism for some of his generals.

"Recently the time came for us to take a decision. After the fall of Ban Me Thuot, I asked the generals whether they could hold Kontum and Pleiku and they said they could not.

"So we made the political decision not to hold Kontum and Pleiku, but would use our troops to retake Ban Me Thuot. That was the practical and political decision I took after consultation with the Prime Minister and commanding generals, but unfortunately, withdrawal is the most difficult of operations.

"The withdrawal from Kontum and Pleiku did not help us retake Ben Me Thuot."

The problem of the balance of forces, overwhelmingly in favor of the Communists, led to the fall of Hue, Da Nang, Nha Trang and the other towns lost in the last few weeks, he said.

The reduction in American aid "reduced our armed forces' war potential by 60 per cent," he said, and this was complicated by some mistakes by "some bad commanders."

Despite his plea for peace, President Thieu said:

"We will have to fight with sheer determination, regardless of how many troops and how much equipment we have left. I expect harder battles ahead."

In describing American political pressures on him, President Thieu spoke of the 1971 election, in which all opponents refused to run against him on the ground that the election was rigged.

Apparently referring to the United States, Mr. Thieu went on to say: "They plotted to create a power vacuum in Vietnam to impose a solution on us. I was determined not to let that happen, so I decided to run, even after other slates had withdrawn."

* * *

April 29, 1975

U.S. WITHDRAWING AMERICANS FROM SAIGON BY HELICOPTER UNDER MARINE PROTECTION; VIETCONG ATTACK ON AIRPORT FORCES MOVE

Saigon Defenses Attacked; Airport Under Rocket Fire

The following dispatch was written before Americans were ordered evacuated from South Vietnam.

By FOX BUTTERFIELD
Special to The New York Times.

SAIGON, South Vietnam, Tuesday, April 29—Saigon's airport came under the heaviest rocket attack of the war early this morning as North Vietnamese troops assaulted parts of the city's suburbs.

More than 150 rockets smashed into the sprawling Tan Son Nhut air base beginning at 4 A.M. Two United States marines guarding several thousand Vietnamese and Americans waiting to be evacuated from Saigon were reported killed in the attacks.

The rockets destroyed a United States Air Force C-130 cargo plane waiting near the runway to pick up refugees. The airlift was suspended because of the assault.

City Under 24-Hour Curfew

The city itself, which was not under attack, remained under 24-hour curfew this morning as rockets fired by the Communists continued to land sporadically around Tan Son Nhut airport and the nearby headquarters of the South Vietnamese joint general staff.

The two marines who were killed were part of a detachment of 140 here, most of whom have been sent from ships in the Seventh Fleet only during the last week to help in the evacuation. The men were said to have been on guard outside the United States Defense Attaché's Office, which formerly served as the United States military command in Vietnam. It was known as Pentagon East.

At least two Vietnamese waiting to be evacuated from Saigon at the airport were also said to have been wounded in the rocket attacks. United States officials said that about 2,000 Vietnamese were spending the night behind the Defense Attaché's Office after having been processed for flights to Guam.

Bright red flashes from the incoming rockets and long streams of red tracer bullets from Government helicopter gunships could be seen early this morning in downtown Saigon.

Witnesses said three South Vietnamese Air Force planes, including a C-119 gunship, were shot down by Soviet-made SA-7 Strella heat-seeking missiles as they tried to suppress the rocket fire.

At the same time Communist troops attacked the suburban towns of Hoc Mon, five miles northwest of the capital, Binh Chanh, six miles south of Saigon, and Phu Lam, situated on the southeastern edge of the city.

Other Communist commandos blew up a police station in the Eighth District of Saigon, a section situated across the Saigon River from the central area.

More heavy explosions were heard in Saigon at 11 A.M., apparently caused by further shelling.

The rocket and ground assaults followed an appeal yesterday for a cease-fire by the new South Vietnamese President, Gen. Duong Van Minh, who was installed after implied Communist demands that he be put in charge of the Saigon government or Communist troops would destroy the city.

Genral Minh took office yesterday during a tense, confusing day of fighting in and around Saigon in which unidentified planes bombed Tan Son Nhut, and North Vietnamese troops advanced to within a mile of the city's limits.

Shortly after 6 P.M., three A-37 light jet bombers struck the military side of the airport, causing devastating damage and explosions that rocked the city. A-37's are the mainstay of the South Vietnamese Air Force.

American officials expressed deep concern and mystification over the bombings. They said they tended to discount the possibility that the North Vietnamese were responsible and believed the attack must have been made by renegade Government pilots.

Former Air Vice Marshal Nguyen Cao Ky, reached by telephone at his home inside the air base, said that as far as he new the raids had not been carried out by members of the South Vietnamese Air Force. There had been speculation that the bombings were part of an attempted coup led by Mr. Ky, who was believed to be unhappy with the inauguration last evening of General Minh as President.

A spokesman for the Vietcong's Provisional Revolutionary Government, also reached by telephone, denied that Communist planes had taken part in the attack.

It was thought possible that the Communists might have used A-37's captured when they seized the former Government air bases at Pleiku, Da Nang or Phan Rang. A number of the small jet planes are known to have fallen into North Vietnamese hands.

According to military informants, three F-5 jet fighters, three C-47 transports, several helicopters and another military passenger plane were destroyed in yesterday's Tan Son Nhut bombing.

Downtown Saigon erupted into pandemonium as antiaircraft guns and soldiers with M-16 automatic rifles fired back at the planes all over the city. Heavy clouds of black smoke, apparently rising from the airport, were visible in downtown Saigon.

Several minutes after the first planes dropped their bombs, other aircraft swooped in low over the city heading for the base. A correspondent saw two other jets—fighters—flying at about 1,500 feet over the Saigon Cathedral. The planes, with delta-shaped wings and distinctive tail surfaces, strongly resembled MIG-21's, which are used by the North Vietnamese Air Force.

Strong explosions continued to shake the capital for more than an hour after the initial bombing.

In a statement read over the Saigon radio at 9 P.M., the military governor of the capital, Lieut. Gen. Nguyen Van Minh, said it was not known where the planes had come from.

North Vietnamese troops continued their inexorable advance toward Saigon, at one point yesterday morning moving to within sight of the city.

A small group of Communist commandos seized the far side of a bridge over the Saigon River at Newport, a large navy and port complex built by Americans on the northeastern side of town. Heavy clouds of black and white smoke rose throughout the day from an oil storage dump and a warehouse that the Communists blew up at the base.

Despite repeated strikes by South Vietnamese helicopter gunships firing rockets, the commandos held the far side of the bridge, only a mile from the city limits, until late in the afternoon.

Other North Vietnamese troops, who have been moving with blitzkrieg-like speed and daring over the last few days, continued to block all the roads leading into and out of Saigon.

To the northeast, Communist forces cut the main six-lane Saigon-Bien Hoa highway at Newport and three miles farther north at Cat Lai. To the west, Route 1, the road to Tay Ninh, was cut at Cu Chi.

And to the south, Route 4, the vital road that links Saigon with its major source of food in the populous Mekong River delta, was still severed around Ben Luc in Long An Province, 15 miles south of the city.

It was clear to nearly everyone in Saigon that the powerful North Vietnamese force assembled around the city, estimated at upwards of 10 divisions, had the capital in a strangle hold and could overrun it in a matter of hours, if the Communist leadership wanted.

Almost all the major towns around Saigon still under Government control also came under Communist attack.

North Vietnamese gunners shelled the capitals of four provinces—Tay Ninh, Hau Nghia, Bien Hoa and Long An—as well as four district seats, all within 50 miles of Saigon.

The worst hit was Tay Ninh city, where 30 122-mm. rockets landed, killing five civilians and destroying over 400 houses, reports from the scene said. In addition, informants said, North Vietnamese troops sneaked into a Cao Dai Buddhist temple in Tay Ninh and abducted 40 monks.

Tay Ninh is the seat of the Cao Dai sect, one of several militant and eclectic Buddhist groupings in South Vietnam.

Other North Vietnamese troops fought a series of battles with Government forces in Dinh Tuong Province in the center of the Mekong delta. Twelve civilians riding on a bus on Route 4 near Cai Lay in the delta were wounded when a mine blew up the vehicle.

The early evening bombing of Nhut caused an uproar in the city. People dashed for cover as the crash of bombs shook buildings and then dozens of antiaircraft guns opened fire.

An hour and a half later, Gen Nguyen Van Minh, the military governor, ordered a 24-hour curfew effective immediately.

Even before his order, many owners of shops and restaurants had pulled down their metal shutters and closed for the evening.

Rumors quickly spread that the North Vietnamese had attacked the city.

One angry or bewildered South Vietnamese soldier shot at a passing taxicab and, when he missed, turned his .45-caliber pistol on a CBS television newsman. The pistol misfired. He then hit the newsman on the head with the gun.

Although there was no way to confirm that Russian-made MIG-21 fighters had actually appeared over Saigon, the sighting accorded with two other sightings made by other newsmen on the road to Bien Hoa earlier in the day.

Intelligence officials have said for several weeks that the North Vietnamese had moved some of their MIG fighters into captured air bases in the south, at Da Nang, at Phu Bai, near Hue, and possibly at Pleiku.

The confusion surrounding the bombing of Tan Son Nhut was compounded by a severe thunderstorm that struck the area just as the bombs began to hit the base. Many people thought at first that the sound of the bombs was thunder.

A dark, menacing sky filled with lightning flashes hung over the city throughout the attack, which lasted more than an hour.

Saigon had been unusually hot, even for the height of the dry season, with the temperature hovering over 100 degrees.

When the Communist commandos occupied positions on the far side of the bridge at Newport, Government troops moved only very slowly to try to dislodge them.

As has often happened in the Vietnam war, most of the Government soldiers simply stood in the middle of the road, making no effort to dig in, an elementary infantry tactic. A National Combat Police truck brought up a mortar and crates of ammunition, but no one moved to unload the mortar or put it into action against the Communists.

A major in the South Vietnamese airborne forces stood by the side of the road smoking and chatting with an American correspondent. No one seemed in a hurry to assume leadership and advance against the Communists.

The commandos, on the other hand, were well dug in under the bridge, and when South Vietnamese helicopters fired rockets at them, they popped out of their foxholes and fired their AK-47 rifles back at the aircraft.

* * *

May 1, 1975

COMMUNISTS TAKE OVER SAIGON; U.S. RESCUE FLEET IS PICKING UP VIETNAMESE WHO FLED IN BOATS

'HO CHI MINH CITY'

Communications Cut Soon After Raising of Victory Flag

By GEORGE ESPER
The Associated Press

SAIGON, South Vietnam, April 30—Communist troops of North Vietnam and the Provisional Revolutionary Government of South Vietnam poured into Saigon today as a century of Western influence came to an end.

Scores of North Vietnamese tanks, armored vehicles and camouflaged Chinese-built trucks rolled to the presidential palace.

The President of the former non-Communist Government of South Vietnam, Gen. Duong Van Minh, who had gone on radio and television to announce his administration's surrender, was taken to a microphone later by North Vietnamese soldiers for another announcement. He appealed to all Saigon troops to lay down their arms and was taken by the North Vietnamese soldiers to an undisclosed destination.

[Soon after, the Saigon radio fell silent, normal telephone and telegraph communications ceased and The Associated Press said its wire link to the capital was lost at 7 P.M. Wednesday, Saigon time (7 A.M. Wednesday, New York time).

[In Paris, representatives of the Provisional Revolutionary Government announced that Saigon had been renamed Ho Chi Minh City in honor of the late President of North Vietnam. Other representatives said in a broadcast monitored in Thailand that former Government forces in eight provinces south of the capital had not yet surrendered, but no fighting was mentioned.]

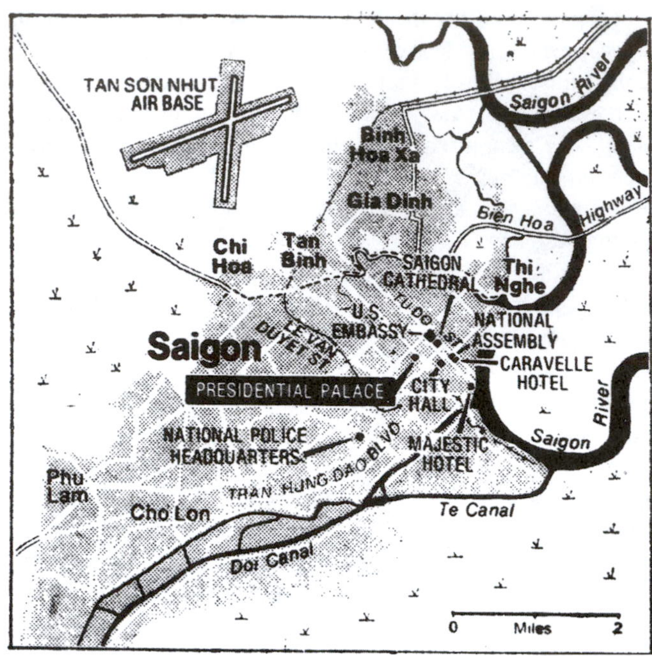

The New York Times

As the Communists took over Saigon, North Vietnamese tanks rolled into grounds of the presidential palace.

The transfer of power was symbolized by the raising of the flag of the National Liberation Front over the presidential palace at 12:15 P.M. today, about two hours after General Minh's surrender broadcast.

Hundreds in Saigon Cheer

Hundreds of Saigon residents cheered and applauded as North Vietnamese military vehicles moved to the palace grounds from which the war against the Communists had been directed by President Nguyen Van Thieu, who resigned April 21, and by President Ngo Dinh Diem, who was killed in a coup in 1963.

Broadcasting today in the early hours of the Communist take-over, the Provisional Revolutionary Government's representatives said:

"We representatives of the liberation forces of Saigon formally proclaim that Saigon has been totally liberated. We accept the unconditional surrender of Gen. Duong Van Minh, President of the former Government."

Colonel Shoots Himself

Meanwhile, many former soldiers sought to lose themselves in the populace. However, one police colonel walked up to an army memorial statue, saluted and shot himself. He died later in a hospital.

Shots rang out at one point around the City Hall. A North Vietnamese infantry platoon, dressed in olive-drab uniforms and black rubber sandals, took up defense positions in the square in front of the building. They exchanged shots with a few holdouts. Some people on motorbikes looked apprehensively to see where the firing was coming from. In a short while it subsided.

Coastal Ships Jammed

Between General Minh's surrender broadcast and the entry of the Communist forces into the city, South Vietnamese soldiers and civilians jammed aboard several coastal freighters tied up along the Saigon River, hoping to escape. They dejectedly left the ships as the Communist troops drove along the waterfront in jeeps and trucks, waving National Liberation Front flags and cheering.

As the Communist troops drove past, knots of civilians stood in doorways and watched without apparent emotion. Later, as more North Vietnamese troops poured into the city, many people began cheering.

Ky Nhan, a Vietnamese who had been submitting photographs to The Associated Press for three years, came to the agency's office with a Communist friend and two North Vietnamese soldiers and said, "I guarantee the safety of everybody here."

"I have been a revolutionary for 10 years," said Mr. Nhan. My job in the Vietcong was liaison with the international press."

This correspondent served them Coca-Cola and some leftover cake.

One of the soldiers, a 25-year-old sergeant named Binh Huan Lam, said he was from Hanoi and had been a soldier for 10 years.

"I have not married because it was not necessary during the war," he said.

Arrival Described

After smoking a cigarette, Tran Viet Ca, a 24-year-old private, told the Americans he had served seven years in the North Vietnamese Army.

"Two days ago we attacked Bien Hoa," he said. "Today we drove down the highway past the United States Army base at Long Binh. Our forces were led by a brigade of tanks. There was a little resistance, but most Saigon soldiers had already run away. Then we drove into Saigon."

Loud explosions were heard in the late afternoon in Saigon. They were said to have taken place aboard an ammunition barge burning in the Saigon River, but no damage was reported in the city except at the United States Embassy and other American buildings, which Saigonese looted. At the embassy they took virtually everything, including the kitchen sinks and a machine to shred secret documents.

A bronze plaque with the names of five American servicemen who died in a 1968 attack by Communist guerrillas was torn from the lobby wall. An Associated Press correspondent retrieved it.

Another memento from the embassy that was saved was a color portrait of former President Richard M. Nixon and his family, inscribed "To Ambassador and Mrs. Graham Martin with appreciation for their service to the nation. From Richard Nixon."

A French businessman who said he was taking refuge in the New Zealand Embassy grabbed the picture.

"I know the ambassador," he said. "I will personally deliver it to him in the United States some time in the future."

Outside the embassy, Thong Nhut Bouelvard was littered with burned cars.

* * *

May 9, 1975

CAMBODIA REDS ARE UPROOTING MILLIONS AS THEY IMPOSE A 'PEASANT REVOLUTION'

Old and Sick Included; Economy Is at Standstill

The writer of the following dispatch remained in Cambodia after the American evacuation and was among the foreigners who arrived in Thailand last Saturday. His dispatches were withheld, under an agreement among all the confined correspondents, until the remaining foreigners were transported to safety yesterday.

By SYDNEY H. SCHANBERG
Special to The New York Times.

BANGKOK, Thailand, May 8—The victorious Cambodian Communists, who marched into Phnom Penh on April 17 and ended five years of war in Cambodia, are carrying out a peasant revolution that has thrown the entire country into upheaval.

Perhaps as many as three or four million people, most of them on foot, have been forced out of the cities and sent on a mammoth and grueling exodus into areas deep in the countryside where, the Communists say, they will have to become peasants and till the soil.

No One Excluded

No one has been excluded—even the very old, the very young, the sick and the wounded have been forced out onto the roads—and some will clearly not be strong enough to survive.

The old economy of the cities has been abandoned, and for the moment money means nothing and cannot be spent. Barter has replaced it.

All shops have either been looted by Communist soldiers for such things as watches and transistor radios, or their goods have been taken away in an organized manner to be stored as communal property.

Even the roads that radiate out of the capital and that carried the nation's commerce have been virtually abandoned, and the population living along the roads, as well as that in all cities and towns that remained under the control of the American-backed Government, has been pushed into the interior. Apparently the areas into which the evacuees are being herded are at least 65 miles from Phnom Penh.

In sum the new rulers—before their overwhelming victory they were known as the Khmer Rouge—appear to be remaking Cambodian society in the peasant image, casting aside everything that belonged to the old system, which was generally dominated by the cities and towns and by the elite and merchants who lived there.

Foreigners and foreign aid are not wanted—at least not for now. It is even unclear how much influence the Chinese and North Vietnamese will have, despite their considerable aid to the Cambodian insurgents against the Government of Marshal Lon Nol. The new authorities seem determined to do things themselves in their own way. Despite the propaganda terminology and other trappings, such as Mao caps and Ho Chi Minh rubber-tire sandals, which remind one of Peking and Hanoi, the Communists seem fiercely independent and very Cambodian.

Isolation From World Seen

Judging from their present actions, it seems possible that they may largely isolate their country of perhaps seven million people from the rest of the world for a considerable time—at least until the period of upheaval is over, the agrarian revolution takes concrete shape and they are ready to show their accomplishments to foreigners.

Some of the party officials in Phnom Penh also talked about changing the capital to a more traditional and rural town like Siem Reap, in the northwest.

For those foreigners, including this correspondent, who stayed behind to observe the take-over, the events were an astonishing spectacle.

In Phnom Penh two million people suddenly moved out of the city en masse in stunned silence—walking, bicycling, pushing cars that had run out of fuel, covering the roads like a human carpet, bent under sacks of belongings hastily thrown together when the heavily armed peasant soldiers came and told them to leave immediately, everyone dispirited and frightened by the unknown that awaited them and many plainly terrified because they were soft city people and were sure the trip would kill them.

Hospitals jammed with wounded were emptied, right down to the last patient. They went—limping, crawling, on crutches, carried on relatives' backs, wheeled on their hospital beds.

The Communists have few doctors and meager medical supplies, so many of these patients had little chance of surviving. On April 17, the day this happened, Phnom Penh's biggest hospital had over 2,000 patients and there were several thousand more in other hospitals; many of the wounded were dying for lack of care.

Silent Streets, Eerie Lights

A once-throbbing city became an echo chamber of silent streets lined with abandoned cars and gaping, empty shops. Streetlights burned eerily for a population that was no longer there.

The end of the old and the start of the new began early in the morning of the 17th. At the cable office the line went dead for mechanical reasons at 6 A.M. On the previous day, amid heavy fighting, the Communist-led forces had taken the airport a few miles west of the city, and during the night they had pressed to the capital's edges, throwing in rockets and shells at will.

Thousands of new refugees and fleeing soldiers were filling the heart of the capital, wandering aimlessly, looking for shelter, as they awaited the city's imminent collapse.

Everyone—Cambodians and foreigners alike—thought this had to be Phnom Penh's most miserable hour after long days of fear and privation as the Communist forces drew closer. They looked ahead with hopeful relief to the collapse of the city, for they felt that when the Communists came and the war finally ended, at least the suffering would largely be over. All of us were wrong.

That view of the future of Cambodia—as a possibly flexible place even under Communism, where changes would not be extreme and ordinary folk would be left alone—turned out to be a myth.

Inadequate Descriptions

American officials had described the Communists as indecisive and often ill-coordinated, but they turned out to be firm, determined, well-trained, tough and disciplined.

The Americans had also said that the rebel army was badly riddled by casualties, forced to fill its ranks by hastily impressing young recruits from the countryside and throwing them into the front lines with only a few days' training. The thousands of troops we saw both in the countryside and in Phnom Penh, while they included women soldiers and boy militia, some of whom seemed no more than 10 years old, looked healthy, well organized, heavily armed and well trained.

Another prediction made by the Americans was that the Communists would carry out a bloodbath once they took over—massacring as many as 20,000 high officials and intellectuals. There have been unconfirmed reports of executions of senior military and civilian officials, and no one who witnessed the take-over doubts that top people of the old regime will be or have been punished and perhaps killed or that a large number of people will die of the hardships on the march into the countryside. But none of this will apparently bear any resemblance to the mass executions that had been predicted by Westerners.

> [In a news conference Tuesday President Ford reiterated reports—he termed them "hard intelligence"—that 80 to 90 Cambodian officials and their wives had been executed.]

Refugees Poured In

On the first day, as the sun was rising, a short swing by automobile to the northern edge of the city showed soldiers and refugees pouring in. The northern defense line had obviously collapsed.

By the time I reached the Hotel Le Phnom and climbed the two flights of stairs to my room, the retreat could be clearly seen from my window and small-arms fire could be heard in the city. At 6:30 A.M. I wrote in my notebook: "The city is falling."

Over the next couple of hours there were periodic exchanges of fire as the Communists encountered pockets of

Communists entering Phnom Penh from the North on Monivong Boulevard on morning of April 17. To the left, one uses portable communications set.

resistance. But most Government soldiers were busy preparing to surrender and welcome the Communists, as were civilians. White flags suddenly sprouted from housetops and from armored personnel carriers, which resemble tanks.

Some soldiers were taking the clips out of their rifles; others were changing into civilian clothes. Some Government office workers were hastily donning the black pajama-like clothes worn by Indochinese Communists.

Shortly before 9 A.M. the first rebel troops approached the hotel, coming from the north down Monivong Boulevard. A crowd of soldiers and civilians, including newsmen, churned forth to greet them—cheering and applauding and embracing and linking arms to form a phalanx as they came along.

The next few hours saw quite a bit of this celebrating, though shooting continued here and there, some of it only a few hundred yards from the hotel. Civilians and Buddhist monks and troops on both sides rode around town—in jeeps, atop personnel carriers and in cars—shouting happily.

Most civilians stayed nervously indoors, however, not yet sure what was going on or who was who. What was the fighting inside the city all about? they wondered; was it between diehard Government troops and the Communists or between rival Communist factions fighting over the spoils? Or was it mostly exuberance?

Some of these questions, including the nature of the factionalism, have still not been answered satisfactorily, but on that first day such mysteries quickly became academic, for within a few hours, the mood changed.

The cheerful and pleasant troops we first encountered—we came to call them the soft troops, and we learned later that they were discredited and disarmed, with their leader declared a traitor; they may not even have been authentic—were swiftly displaced by battle-hardened soldiers.

While some of these were occasionally friendly, or at least not hostile, they were also all business. Dripping with arms like overladen fruit trees—grenades, pistols, rifles, rockets—they immediately began clearing the city of civilians.

People Driven Out

Using loudspeakers, or simply shouting and brandishing weapons, they swept through the streets, ordering people out of their houses. At first we thought the order applied only to the rich in villas, but we quickly saw that it was for everyone as the streets became clogged with a sorrowful exodus.

Cars stalled or their tires went flat, and they were abandoned. People lost their sandals in the jostling and pushing, so they lay as a reminder of the throng that had passed.

In the days to follow, during the foreign colony's confinement in the French Embassy compound, we heard reports on international news broadcasts that the Communists had evacuated the city by telling people the United States was about to bomb it. However, all the departing civilians I talked with said they had been given no reason except that the city had to be reorganized. They were told they had to go far from Phnom Penh.

In almost every situation we encountered during the more than two weeks we were under Communist control, there was a sense of split vision—whether to look at events through Western eyes or through what we thought might be Cambodian revolutionary eyes.

Brutality or Necessity?

Was this just cold brutality, a cruel and sadistic imposition of the law of the jungle, in which only the fittest will survive? Or is it possible that, seen through the eyes of the peasant soldiers and revolutionaries, the forced evacuation of the cities is a harsh necessity? Perhaps they are convinced that there is no way to build a new society for the benefit of the ordinary man, hitherto exploited, without literally starting from the beginning; in such an unbending view people who represent the old ways and those considered weak or unfit would be expendable and would be weeded out. Or was the policy both cruel and ideological?

A foreign doctor offered this explanation for the expulsion of the sick and wounded from the hospital: "They could not cope with all the patients—they do not have the doctors—so they apparently decided to throw them all out and blame any deaths on the old regime. That way they could start from scratch medically."

Some Western observers considered that the exodus approached genocide. One of them, watching from his refuge in the French Embassy compound, said: "They are crazy! This is pure and simple genocide. They will kill more people this way than if there had been hand-to-hand fighting in the city."

Another foreign doctor, who had been forced at gunpoint to abandon a seriously wounded patient in midoperation, added in a dark voice: "They have not got a humanitarian thought in their heads!"

Whatever the Communists' purpose, the exodus did not grow heavy until dusk, and even then onlookers were slow to realize that the people were being forcibly evacuated.

For my own part, I had a problem that preoccupied me that afternoon: I, with others, was held captive and threatened with execution.

After our release, we went to the Information Ministry, because we had heard about a broadcast directing high officials of the old regime to report there. When we arrived, about 50 prisoners were standing outside the building, among them Lon Non, the younger brother of President Lon Nol, who went into exile on April 1, and Brig. Gen. Chim Chhuon, who was close to the former President. Other generals and Cabinet ministers were also there—very nervous but trying to appear untroubled.

Premier Long Boret, who the day before had made an offer of surrender with certain conditions only to have it immediately rejected, arrived at the ministry an hour later. He is one of the seven "traitors" the Communists had marked for execution. The others had fled except for Lieut. Gen. Sisowath Sirik Matak, a former Premier, who some days later was removed from the French Embassy, where he had taken refuge.

Mr. Long Boret's eyes were puffy and red, almost down to slits. He had probably been up all night and perhaps he had been weeping. His wife and two children were also still in the country; later they sought refuge at the French Embassy, only to be rejected as persons who might "compromise" the rest of the refugees.

Mr. Long Boret, who had talked volubly and articulately on the telephone the night before, had difficulty speaking coherently. He could only mumble yes, no and thank you, so conversation was impossible.

There is still no hard information on what has happened to him. Most people who have talked with the Communists believe it a certainty that he will be executed, if indeed the execution has not already taken place.

Soothing General

One of the Communist leaders at the Information Ministry that day—probably a general, though his uniform bore no markings and he declined to give his name—talked soothingly to the 50 prisoners. He assured them that there were only seven traitors and that other officials of the old regime would be dealt with equitably. "There will be no reprisals," he said. Their strained faces suggested that they would like to believe him but did not.

As he talked, a squad crouched in combat-ready positions around him, almost as if it was guarding him against harm.

The officer, who appeared no more than age 35, agreed to chat with foreign newsmen. His tone was polite and sometimes he smiled, but everything he said suggested that we, as foreigners, meant nothing to him and that our interests were alien to his.

Asked about the fate of the 20 or so foreign journalists missing in Cambodia since the early days of the war, he said he had heard nothing. Asked if we would be permitted to file from the cable office, he smiled sympathetically and said, "We will resolve all problems in their proper order."

Clearly an educated man, he almost certainly speaks French, the language of the nation that ruled Cambodia for nearly a century until the nineteen-fifties, but he gave no hint of this colonial vestige, speaking only in Khmer through an interpreter.

In the middle of the conversation he volunteered quite unexpectedly: "We would like you to give our thanks to the American people who have helped us and supported us from the beginning, and to all people of the world who love peace and justice. Please give this message to the world."

Noting that Congress had halted aid to the Phnom Penh Government, he said, "The purpose was to stop the war," but he quickly added: "Our struggle would not have stopped even if they had given more aid."

Attempts to find out more about who he was and about political and military organization led only to imprecision. The officer said: "I represent the armed forces. There are many divisions. I am one of the many."

Is Asked About Factions

Asked if there were factions, he said there was only one political organization and one government. Some top political and governmental leaders are not far from the city, he added, but they let the military enter first "to organize things."

Most military units, he said are called "rumdos," which means "liberation forces." Neither this commander nor any of the soldiers we talked with ever called themselves Communists or Khmer Rouge (Red Cambodians). They always said they were liberation troops or nationalist troops and called one another brother or the Khmer equivalent of comrade.

The nomenclature at least is confusing, for Western intelligence had described the Khmer Rumdos as a faction loyal to Prince Norodom Sihanouk that was being downgraded by Hanoi-trained Cambodians and losing power.

The Communists named the Cambodian leader, who was deposed by Marshal Lon Nol in 1970 and has been living in exile in Peking, as their figurehead chief of state, but none of the soldiers we talked with brought up his name.

One over-all impression emerged from our talk with the commander at the Information Ministry: The military will be largely in charge of the early stages of the upheaval, carrying out the evacuation, organizing the new agrarian program, searching for hidden arms and resisters, repairing damaged bridges.

The politicians—or so it seemed from all the evidence during our stay—have for the moment taken a rear seat. No significant political or administrative apparatus was yet visible; it did not seem to be a government yet, but an army.

The radio announced April 28 that a special national congress attended by over 300 delegates was held in Phnom Penh from April 25 to 27. It was said to have been chaired by the Deputy Premier and military commander, Khieu Samphan, who has emerged—at least in public announcements—as the top leader. Despite that meeting the military still seemed to be running things as we emerged from Cambodia on Saturday.

One apparent reason is that politicians and bureaucrats are not equipped to do the dirty work and arduous tasks of the early phases of reorganization. Another is that the military, as indicated in conversations with Khmer-speaking foreigners they trusted somewhat, seemed worried that politicians or soft-living outsiders in their movement might steal the victory and dilute it. There could be severe power struggles ahead.

After leaving the prisoners and the military commander at the ministry, we headed for the Hotel Le Phnom, where another surprise was waiting. The day before, the Red Cross turned the hotel into a protected international zone and draped it with huge Red Cross flags. But the Communists were not interested.

Order Hotel Emptied

At 4:55 P.M. troops waving guns and rockets had forced their way into the grounds and ordered the hotel emptied within 30 minutes. By the time we arrived 25 minutes had elapsed. The fastest packing job in history ensued. I even had time to "liberate" a typewriter someone had abandoned since the troops had "liberated" mine earlier.

We were the last ones out, running. The Red Cross had abandoned several vehicles in the yard after removing the keys, so several of us threw our gear on the back of a Red Cross Honda pickup truck and started pushing it up the boulevard toward the French Embassy.

Several days before, word was passed to those foreigners who stayed behind when the Americans pulled out on April 12 that, as a last resort, one could take refuge at the embassy. France had recognized the new government, and it was thought that the new Cambodian leaders would respect the embassy compound as a sanctuary.

As we plodded up the road, big fires were burning on the city's outskirts, sending smoke clouds into the evening sky like a giant funeral wreath encircling the capital.

The embassy was only several hundred yards away, but what was happening on the road made it seem much farther. All around us people were fleeing, for there was no refuge for them. And coming into the city from the other direction was a fresh battalion marching in single file. They looked curiously at us; we looked nervously at them.

In the 13 days of confinement that followed, until our evacuation by military truck to the Thai border, we had only a peephole onto what was going on outside, but there were still many things that could be seen and many clues to the revolution that was going on.

We could hear shooting, sometimes nearby but mostly in other parts of the city. Often it sounded like shooting in the air, but at other times it seemed like small battles. As on the day of the city's fall we were never able to piece together a satisfactory explanation of the shooting, which died down after about a week.

We could see smoke from the huge fires from time to time, and there were reports from foreigners who trickled into the embassy that certain quarters were badly burned and that the water purification plant was heavily damaged.

The foreigners who for various reasons came in later carried stories, some of them eyewitness accounts, of such things as civilian bodies along the roads leading out of the city—people who had apparently died of illness or exhaustion on the march. But each witness got only a glimpse, and no reliable estimate of the toll was possible.

Reports from roads to the south and southeast of Phnom Penh said the Communists were breaking up families by dividing the refugees by sex and age. Such practices were not reported from other roads on which the refugees flooded out of the capital.

Executions Reported

Reports also told of executions, but none were eyewitness accounts. One such report said high military officers were executed at a rubber plantation a couple of miles north of the city.

In the French Embassy compound foreign doctors and relief agency officials were pessimistic about the survival chances of many of the refugees. "There's no food in the countryside at this time of year," an international official said. "What will they eat from now until the rice harvest in November?"

The new Communist officials, in conversations with United Nations and other foreign representatives during our confinement and in statements since, have rejected the idea of foreign aid, "whether it is military, political, economic, social, diplomatic, or whether it takes on a so-called humanitarian form." Some foreign observers wondered whether this included China, for they speculated that the Communists would at least need seed to plant for the next harvest.

Whether the looting we observed before we entered the French compound continued is difficult to say. In any case, it is essential to understand who the Communist soldiers are to understand the behavior of some of them in disciplinary matters, particularly looting.

They are peasant boys, pure and simple—darker skinned than their city brethren, with gold in their front teeth. To them the city is a curiosity, an oddity, a carnival, where you visit but do not live. The city means next to nothing in their scheme of things.

One Kept, the Rest Given

When they looted jewelry shops, they kept only one watch for themselves and gave the rest to their colleagues or passers-by. Transistor radios, cameras and cars held the same toy-like fascination—something to play with, as children might, but not essential.

From my airline bag on the day I was seized and threatened with execution they took only some cigarettes, a pair of boxer underwear shorts and a handkerchief. They passed up a blue shirt and $9,000 in cash in a money belt.

The looting did not really contradict the Communist image of rigid discipline, for commanders apparently gave no orders against the sacking of shops, feeling, perhaps, that this was the least due their men after five years of jungle fighting.

Often they would climb into abandoned cars and find that they would not run, so they would bang on them with their rifles like frustrated children, or they would simply toot the horns for hours on end or keep turning the headlights on and off until the batteries died.

One night at the French Embassy, I chose to sleep on the grass outside; I was suddenly awakened by what sounded like a platoon trying to smash down the front gates with a battering ram that had bright lights and a loud claxon. It was only a bunch of soldiers playing with and smashing up the cars that had been left outside the gates.

Though these country soldiers broke into villas all over the city and took the curious things they wanted—one walked past the embassy beaming proudly in a crimson-colored wool overcoat that hung down to his Ho Chi Minh sandals—they never stayed in the villas. With big, soft beds empty, they slept in the courtyards or the streets.

Almost without exception foot soldiers I talked with, when asked what they wanted to do, replied that they only wanted to go home.

* * *

May 15, 1975

U.S. FREES CAMBODIAN-HELD SHIP AND CREW; MARINES STORM ISLAND, SUFFER CASUALTIES; PLANES HIT AIRFIELD, SINK 3 PATROL BOATS

FORD IS BACKED

Senate Unit Endorses His Right to Order Military Action

By PHILIP SHABECOFF
Special to The New York Times.

WASHINGTON, May 14—The White House said tonight that President Ford had consulted with Congressional leaders both before ordering the recapture of the merchant vessel Mayagüez and before ordering the sinking earlier today of Cambodian patrol boats.

At least some of the leaders later insisted, however, that they had not been consulted but merely informed of Presidential decisions already taken.

However, members of Congress generally expressed approval of the President's action and the Senate Foreign Relations Committee adopted a strong resolution of support this evening acknowledging the President's constitutional right to order military operations.

After a meeting at the White House tonight between the President and a bipartisan delegation of Congressional leaders, Robert C. Byrd of West Virginia, the Senate Democratic whip, reported that the President had been criticized by some of the leaders for his handling of the consultation process.

Senator Byrd said: "I certainly approve of the effort to take the ship and to land marines on the island."

Some Concern Voiced

There were "some expressions of concern" voiced by some of the leaders over the President's handling of the decision-making process, including the fact that the leadership of Congress had not been brought in on the process, Mr. Byrd told reporters. He said he shared in that concern.

Senator Byrd said that the concern was over what he characterized as "the failure to ask at least some of the leaders to participate in the decision-making process," even though the President was not required to take such action.

Late tonight, the White House reported that immediate public response to today's military action, including the marine assault, was overwhelmingly in support of the President. The White House said that by 10:30 P.M. 778 telephone calls approved the President's actions and 98 had disapproved.

President Ford will report in writing to Congress tomorrow at 6:15 A.M. on the military operation, under the War Powers Resolution of 1973, which requires such a report in 48 hours, Senator Byrd said.

Yesterday the White House press secretary, Ron Nessen, told reporters that President Ford would "consult" with Congress before ordering any military action to rescue the seized American freighter Mayagüez, or its crew.

He quoted the Congressional War Powers Resolution of 1973, which states, in part, that "the President in every possible instance shall consult with Congress before introducing United States armed forces into hostilities or into situations where imminent involvement in hostilities is clearly indicated."

Roderick Hills, a counsel to the President, told a questioner that Mr. Ford had acted under his Constitutional war powers to protect the lives and property of Americans. When asked to cite the specific authority in the Constitution, Mr. Hills said that he did not have the exact article in front of him.

But he insisted that the inherent right of the President to use war powers to protect lives and property had not been challenged. The only open question, he said, was the appropriate level of military response.

Mr. Hills, an assistant to Philip Buchen, the head of the White House legal department, indicated that the President believed that informing Congress of his actions satisfied the requirement of the War Powers Resolution that he consult with Congress before beginning military operations.

The resolution does not require prior approval of military action by Congress, he asserted.

At today's news briefing, Mr. Nessen said that the President, through his Congressional relations staff, "did consult" with Democratic and Republican leaders of the House of Representatives and Senate between 5:30 and 6 P.M. yesterday, "three hours before the fact." A statement issued by the Defense Department today indicated that the attack began shortly after 8:30 P.M., Eastern Daylight Time.

However, Senator Mike Mansfield, Democratic leader of the Senate and one of those listed by Mr. Nessen as having been consulted, said in a telephone interview today:

"I was not consulted. I was notified after the fact about what the Administration had already decided to do."

In a statement released later, Senator Mansfield said: "I did not give my approval or disapproval because the decision had already been made. My reaction at this point is that there are a lot of questions to which I want answers."

Senator James O. Eastland, Democrat of Mississippi and President Pro Tempore of the Senate, and Senator Clifford P. Case, Republican of New Jersey, the ranking Republican on the Senate Foreign Relations Committee, also said that they had not been consulted but had been informed. Mr. Eastland said he had been told after the attack.

Both, however, indicated that they strongly supported President Ford's action against Cambodian boats.

The majority leader of the House of Representatives, Thomas P. O'Neill of Massachusetts, also said he had not been consulted but only informed.

The House minority leader, John J. Rhodes of Arizona, was quoted by The Associated Press as having said that he had not been notified until after the Cambodian vessels were sunk. But a spokesman for Mr. Rhodes told a questioner: "He was notified beforehand. We are calling it a consultation. Mr. Rhodes has no complaint."

Senator Hugh Scott of Pennsylvania, the Republican head of the Senate, when asked if he felt he had been consulted by the White House replied:

"I am not going to play games with words. That is Mr. Nessen's word. That's not the President's word. It's not mine. We were informed. We were altered. We were advised. We were notified. We were telephoned. It was discussed with us. I don't know whether that's consultation or not. We were advised that certain action would be taken using the minimal force necessary."

A member of the White House Congressional liaison staff told a questioner that leaders of the Senate had been called about the President's planned action, starting with Senator Mansfield at 5:55 P.M. yesterday and concluding with Senator Eastland at 8:20 P.M. or shortly before the attack on the Cambodian vessels began. Memorandums of each call were sent to Max Friedersdorf, head of the Congressional relations staff, who had presumably passed the response along to the President, the staff member added.

This staff member said that about half the Senators had voiced approval of the President's action while the other simply "acknowledged" the information. Earlier today, Mr. Nessen said that the response of the Congressional leaders to the "consultation" was "a strong consensus of support and no objections."

The members of Congress were not given any legal basis for the President's order for military intervention when they were contacted by the White House staff. At today's briefings at the White House, Mr. Nessen said that "the President has authority to protect the lives of Americans and the property of Americans under the Constitution."

Although several members of Congress charged that the President had violated the War Powers Resolution by failure to consult Congress, there was little criticism of the military action itself.

The resolution adopted by the Senate Foreign Relations Committee, while it will not be voted on by the full Senate, was intended as a vote of Senatorial confidence. It was approved unanimously and said:

"Committee condemns an act of armed aggression on an unarmed U.S. merchant vessel in the course of innocent passage on an established trade route.

"The President has engaged in diplomatic means to secure its release and we support that.

"Third, we support the President in the exercise of his constitutional powers within the framework of the War Powers Resolution to secure the release of the ship and its men.

"We urge the Cambodian Government to release the ship and the men forthwith."

Even some of the most critical Congressional opponents of American involvement in Vietnam voiced support of the President's action. One was Representative Morris K. Udall, Democrat of Arizona, who said he had long opposed the Vietnam war and the conflicts in Cambodia and Laos, but added: "I feel compelled to state my support for the limited military action taken by President Ford after diplomacy failed to free the American crew and the ship illegally taken by the Cambodian Navy."

But Senator Henry M. Jackson, Democrat of Washington, who is regarded as one of the more hawkish members of Congress, said: "This is the time for cool heads. Because we are a strong and powerful nation we must exercise restraint in the use of force. A failure to show restraint could lead to a Tonkin Gulf situation." This was a reference to the 1964 incident that led to the vast build-up of United States forces in Vietnam.

Some members of Congress were totally opposed to the attack. Representative Bella Abzug, Democrat of Manhattan, said that American crewmen from the Mayagüez might have been on the Cambodian boats that were sunk and termed the military operation "sheer insanity."

* * *

May 15, 1975

3 COPTERS LOST

President, on TV After Midnight, Hails Valor of Servicemen

By JOHN W. FINNEY
Special to The New York Times.

WASHINGTON, Thursday, May 15—U.S. forces have recaptured the American merchant vessel Mayagüez, which the Cambodian Communists seized Monday, President Ford announced early today.

He said all 39 crew members had been rescued.

The President, who said he had ordered the operation last night, announced its results in a brief statement shortly after midnight. He praised the valor of the sailors and marines who took part. He said that some were still "under hostile fire" and indicated that they would be withdrawn from combat shortly.

As part of the operation, marines stormed Tang Island, where they suffered what were described as "light" casualties. No deaths were confirmed. Three helicopters were lost on the beaches, a Pentagon spokesman said, either from ground fire or mechanical failure.

Carrier-based fighter-bombers attacked the Ream airfield and a naval base in the area of Sihanoukville on the Cambodian mainland.

Confusion in Capitol

In the confused situation here this morning, it was not clear whether the bomb attack would have taken place had Mr. Ford known that the Cambodian vessel was prepared to turn over 30 of the Mayagüez crewmen.

The President met early last night with Congresional leaders. This morning the White House press secretary, Ron Nessen, said Mr. Ford would formally report to Congress today on the military operations.

Of the 39 crew members, 30 were delivered by a small Cambodian vessel flying a white flag to an American destroyer. How or where the other nine were found could not be learned at once.

The military operation was undertaken, according to American officials, about an hour before word of a Cambodian Government broadcast offering to release the vessel was received here. It began at 7:20 P.M. yesterday, Washington time and lasted about six hours.

Yesterday, the Defense Department announced that American aircraft had destroyed three Cambodian patrol boats in an effort to thwart a removal of the American ship's crew to the Cambodian mainland.

The operation to regain the Mayagüez was begun, according to American officials, about an hour before word of a Cambodian Government broadcast offering to release the vessel was received here. It began at 7:20 P.M. yesterday, Washington time, and lasted six hours.

First came the marine assault on the three-mile square island. About 135 marines went in by helicopter and searched the island for the crewmen.

An hour later, news services carried word of the Phnom Penh broadcast offering to free the ship. About the same time, Maj. Gen. Brent Scowcroft of the National Security Council passed to the President—with the attack well under way—a partial translation of the Cambodian broadcast.

With the marines already encountering hostile fire, the White House issued a statement, addressed to the Cambodians, stating: "As soon as you are prepared to release the crew members you hold, unconditionally and immediately, we will promptly cease military action."

Boarded by Marines

At 9 P.M., a contingent of marines boarded the Mayagüez. They had flown from Thaildan, according to Defense Department officials, to the Harold E. Holt, a destroyer escort, which then pulled alongside the Mayagüez.

No Americans or Cambodians were found aboard the container ship, which had been seized on Monday, although prior to boarding the ship marines had seen people on her decks. Dishes with warm food were found in the mess.

An hour and a half later, a small Cambodian craft with white flags flying approached the Robert L. Wilson, an

American destroyer. The destroyer reported this development at 10:30 P.M. but it was not until 11:14 P.M. that Defense Secretary James R. Schlesinger reported that 30 Mayagüez crewmen were coming aboard the Wilson from the boat.

In the interim, at 11:09 P.M., planes from the aircraft carrier Coral Sea struck the Ream airfield. According to one report, Cambodian troops had been observed massing there.

Both operations were carried out by a naval task force headed by the 52,500-ton Coral Sea, that had assembled in the Gulf. A battalion of 1,100 marines had been flown from Okinawa and the Philippines to Taphao Air Base in Thailand and then to the fleet.

The Administration had imposed unusually tight security on details of the attack on the Cambodian gunboats by American planes.

Initially, according to Pentagon officials, the military operations were limited to the rescue of the ship and its 39-member crew. But the officials said that Administration plans called, if necessary, for air raids in reprisal against military bases in Cambodia.

Message to Cambodia

The White House announced that the following "urgent message" was sent last night to Cambodian authorities:

"We have heard a radio broadcast that you are prepared to release the S.S. Mayagüez. We welcome this development if true.

"As you know, we have seized the ship. As soon as you issue a statement that you are prepared to release the crew members that you hold, unconditionally and immediately, we will promptly cease military operations."

Shortly after President Ford met with a bipartisan group of Congressional leaders last night, the White House press secretary issued the following statement to reporters in the White House briefing room:

"The President has directed the following military measures starting this evening, Washington time:

"U.S. Marines to board the S.S. Mayagüez.

"U.S. Marines to land on Koh Tang Island in order to rescue any crew members as may be on the island.

"Aircraft from the carrier the Coral Sea to undertake associated military operations to regain the vessel and the members of the crew."

The Defense Department reported that the marine assault force, which landed on the Mayagüez by helicopter, had found no one aboard the ship, anchored about a mile off Tang Island.

Shortly before the military operation was announced by the White House, the Phnom Penh radio broadcast a communiqué by the new Communist Government stating that it was prepared to free the ship and crew. The communiqué stated that the Government "will order the ship to withdraw from Cambodian territorial waters and will warn it against further espionage or provocative activities."

In preparation for the military operations, the Administration had assembled a naval task force, headed by the carrier Coral Sea, in the Gulf of Siam and had flown a battalion of 1,100 marines from Okinawa and the Philippines to U Taphao Air Base in Thailand. As dawn broke over Cambodia, the President—after a meeting of the National Security Council and a briefing of Congressional leaders—ordered the military operations to begin.

After announcing the marine attack, Mr. Nessen said that the White House was still trying to verify the reported offer by the Cambodian Government to release the Mayagüez.

In pledging to release the American ship, the Cambodian Government broadcast said in part:

"Based on the position that we are unwilling to provoke any dispute, and as a peace-loving people, we will release that ship.

"But we will not allow the U.S. imperialists to violate or spy in our territorial waters. We will not allow them to threaten us to release the ship at any specific time."

Mr. Nessen, briefing reporters at the White House, said that President Ford had authority under the Constitution to protect the lives and property of Americans.

It was unclear to Pentagon officials to what extent the patrol boats had acted on direct orders from the new Government in Cambodia in seizing the American ship and in the subsequent handling of the crew.

Pentagon officials reported there were only "skimpy" radio communications between Tang Island, where the American ship was taken, and the mainland, leading some to conclude that the local commander of the patrol boats had acted on his own rather than in response to direct orders from Phnom Penh.

The Administration imposed unusually tight secrecy on details of the attack by the American planes, leaving unanswered several crucial questions as to why the attack had been ordered. At the Pentagon, where officials were concerned over what they regarded as unauthorized "leaks" of information, plainclothes security officers were observed following reporters.

White House Meeting

As pieced together from various Administration officials the following sequence of events led to the President's decision following a National Security Council meeting last night at the White House:

Late Tuesday Washington time (and early in the morning Cambodian time) some of the Cambodian patrol boats, which had been gathered around the ship, anchored about one mile off the island, were observed by American surveillance planes to be moving toward the island.

On the basis of earlier sightings by the American planes, it was believed that some of the crew had been removed to the island, although the Administration could not be certain on this point.

Starting about 8:30 P.M. E.D.T., according to this account, the Cambodian vessels were observed moving, one at a time, toward the Cambodian mainland, presumably for the port of Kombong Som, or Sihanoukville.

The immediate presumption was that the boats were carrying some of the crew to the mainland, a development that Administration officials believed would greatly complicate rescue of the Americans.

With no United States ships yet on the scene, the President ordered Air Force planes in Thailand to take action to block the movement of the Cambodian boats to the mainland. The Administration premise was that as long as the ship and crew remained about 30 miles off the mainland, it would be feasible to carry out a military operation to rescue them.

The initial orders to the pilots were to take action to stop the patrol boats but not to sink them, the officials said. The orders, according to the officials, were later changed to tell the pilots to sink the craft if there was no other way to stop them.

It was not clear whether these revised orders came from the White House, the Secretary of Defense, the Joint Chiefs of Staff or the Commander-in-Chief Pacific, who was in direct charge of the operation.

* * *

June 21, 1975

U.S. SAYS RUSSIANS NOW HAVE DEPLOYED 60 MIRV MISSILES

By JOHN W. FINNEY
Special to The New York Times.

WASHINGTON, June 20—Secretary of Defense James R. Schlesinger said today that the Soviet Union in the last six months had deployed 60 intercontinental ballistic missiles armed with multiple independently targetable warheads.

Mr. Schlesinger, who said last Jan. 15 that the Soviet Union had begun deploying two new intercontinental missiles presumably armed with multiple warheads, told a Pentagon news conference today that he did not regard the deployment of the 60 missiles as particularly surprising or alarming.

Mr. Schlesinger provided the review of recent Soviet missile developments in a summary of a secret briefing he gave a group of defense ministers of the North Atlantic Treaty Organization earlier this month.

The Secretary also said that the Soviet Union was dismantling some of its older intercontinental missiles as it built up its number of submarine-launched ballistic missiles beyond 740. He said the new "milestones" reached by the Soviet Union served to underscore the Soviet effort to modernize its strategic force with larger, more accurate missiles.

The Soviet Union, he said, has made slightly greater progress than had been anticipated in improving the accuracy of its multiple warheads, known as MIRV's for multiple independently targetable re-entry vehicles. He said that it now appeared that some of the Soviet missiles had a "reasonable degree of accuracy" for attacking American missiles in their silos.

Since last fall Mr. Schlesinger has been cautioning that the Soviet Union was on the verge of deploying a new generation of missiles armed with multiple independently targetable warheads. His statements today provided an indication of the rate at which the Soviet Union was following the lead of the United States in moving toward MIRV missiles.

He said the Soviet Union had deployed 50 SS-19's, relatively large intercontinental ballistic missiles that are believed to carry six MIRV warheads of considerable accuracy. The Russians, he said, have also deployed 10 SS-17's, somewhat less accurate missiles that carry four MIRV warheads.

U.S. Has Wide Lead

While the Soviet Union has now deployed its first significant number of MIRV missiles, the United States has a wide lead in this area. The United States has 902 MIRV missiles—550 Minuteman III intercontinental missiles and 352 Poseidon submarine-launched missiles— and with weapons programs under way, will build up to a total of 1,286.

In addition, Mr. Schlesinger said the Soviet Union had deployed 10 SS-18's, its largest intercontinental missiles. It appears, he said, that the first operational SS-18 missiles carry single rather than multiple warheads.

The Secretary said, however, that the Soviet Union apparently had successfully concluded the testing of MIRV warheads for the SS-18. On a series of SS-18 tests earlier this month, he said, seven re-entry vehicles—the testing equivalent of warheads—were seen, with one of the vehicles falling about 100 yards from an American ship that was observing the impact area some 600 miles north of Midway Island in the Pacific.

Mr. Schlesinger said he found the Soviet missile developments "not helpful for stability" and expressed the hope that both sides could agree to exercise "mutual restraint" in developing so-called "counterforce weapons" capable of attacking the missiles of the other side. If such restraint is not agreed upon, he said, "we will not allow our position in this area to become secondary."

Shift in U.S. Policy

The United States is developing more powerful and more accurate ballistic missiles as possible "counterforce weapons." In addition, the Pentagon is developing long-range cruise missiles, which, when launched by submarines or bombers, could supplement ballistic missiles and bombers.

Mr. Schlesinger's willingness to distinguish between SS-18 missiles carrying single and multiple warheads provided an indication of a changing Administration position on how to verify an agreement establishing a limit on the number of MIRV missiles.

Last year's Vladivostok agreement, which the two sides are now trying to translate into a treaty, permits each side to have 1,320 MIRV missiles as part of an over-all total of 2,400 strategic weapons.

The Administration's original verification approach, which has been rejected by the Soviet Union, was that any type of missile that had been tested with MIRV's would be assumed to carry multiple warheads when deployed. Without elaboration, Mr. Schlesinger said a new verification method for counting the number of missiles with MIRV's was being discussed in the talks on the limitation of strategic arms.

This new approach is believed to be based on the concept of counting the MIRV missiles on the basis of the missile fields in which they are deployed.

Mr. Schlesinger said the Soviet Union had apparently stopped construction of the Yankee class of nuclear-powered, missile-firing submarines and was shifting to construction of the larger Delta class submarine.

The original Delta submarine carried 12 missiles with a 4,500-mile range. Mr. Schlesinger said the Russians were building a "stretched" version of the submarine carrying 16 missiles and might be moving toward an even larger version capable of carrying still more missiles.

Despite the expansion in the Soviet submarine programs, Mr. Schlesinger expressed doubt that the Soviet Union would reach the limit of 950 submarine-launched ballistic missiles established by the 1972 interim agreement on strategic weapons.

Under that five-year agreement, the Soviet Union was permitted an initial number of 740 submarine-launched missiles. To go above that number toward 950, the Soviet Union had to "trade in" some of its older intercontinental ballistic missiles.

Mr. Schlesinger said the Soviet Union was dismantling some of its older SS-7 and SS-8 intercontinental missiles as it builds up beyond a force of 740 submarine-launched missiles.

The Secretary said the Soviet Union was testing a new 2,000-mile missile designated SS-26. The missile, he said, is expected to replace intermediate range ballistic missiles aimed at targets in Western Europe.

On another issue, Mr. Schlesinger said the United States retained the option to use nuclear weapons or introduce more ground troops in the event of a North Korean invasion of South Korea. For the first time he provided official confirmation that the United States has tactical nuclear weapons in South Korea.

He also said that in the face of Soviet denials, U-2 reconnaissance photos "speak for themselves" in demonstrating that the Soviet Union was constructing a naval facility at the Somalian port of Berbera.

To suggest, as one Soviet commentator did, that the United States was seeing "mirages," he said, "is to put too much faith in the efficacy of hot air rising from the desert floor."

* * *

July 15, 1975

JULY 30 SUMMIT IN EUROPE SOUGHT

Ford and Brezhnev Would Be Among 35 Leaders Signing an East-West Charter

Special to The New York Times.

GENEVA, July 14—After nearly two years of negotiations, the 35 countries attending the European security conference decided today that they could set July 30 as the target date for a meeting to sign a charter on East-West relations.

The closing ceremonial session, which is expected to last three days, would bring together President Ford, Leonid I. Brezhnev, the Soviet Communist party chief, and 33 other leaders in Helsinki, Finland, where the conference opened on July 3, 1973.

The document they are to sign, consisting of about 100 pages, in effect ratifies Europe's postwar borders as inviolable. The Soviet Union, which had been pressing for a conference on European security problems since 1954 to win such an accord, had to accede in exchange to the West's insistence that frontiers "can be changed, in accordance with international law, by peaceful means and agreement."

The document also contains guidelines for improving political, military and economic relations between East and West and for easing the movement of information and human contacts across frontiers. But the pact will not have the force of a treaty. Nor will it contain binding legal commitments.

Nevertheless, Western representatives, who agreed to attend the conference to win some Eastern concessions on such matters as freer information and human contacts, believe that the document will have some moral force. They concede, however, that its actual value cannot be assessed until several years from now.

The negotiations have been conducted by representatives of all European countries except Albania, with the United States and Canada also participating [In Washington, Ron Nessen, the presidential press secretary, said that while no final agreement had yet been reached on holding the ceremonial session in Helsinki July 30, Mr. Ford would certainly attend if the meeting did take place then.]

The July 30 target date, which was proposed by Canada, was agreed to today after a major obstacle to completion of the document was removed. Both the Western and Eastern military blocs agreed to a Maltese proposal for a reduction of armed forces in the Mediterranean, though it took four days to work out a wording acceptable to all.

Malta's Prime Minister, Dom Mintoff, wanted the document to call specifically for the gradual withdrawal of United States and Soviet forces from the Mediterranean.

Language Watered Down

This was watered down to a statement saying that one of the aims of strengthening contacts between the countries at the conference and the "nonparticipating Mediterranean states" was the "reducing of forces" in the Mediterranean.

With the Mediterranean issue disposed of, two other important questions were also settled by the conference today.

Approval was given to the calling of a meeting of senior officials in 1977 to assess the results of the conference and to plan a possible future session to expand on them.

The conference was also able to record today its approval of a declaration of 10 basic principles that the participating nations recognize should guide their relations. The section of the document dealing with principles contains a phrase indirectly guaranteeing that the rights of the four occupying powers in Berlin will not be affected in any way.

The wording of this proved difficult, particularly because of Rumania's intention to avoid the possibility that the phrase could be interpreted as a recognition of the so-called Brezhnev doctrine, by which the Soviet Union is said to believe it has the right to intervene to did in Czechoslovakia in 1968.

The conference has yet to settle the details of a section that would call for advance notification of military maneuvers as a means of instilling confidence in relations between countries. Turkey, citing her geographical position—with only a small part of the country in Europe—wants less of her territory covered by such a section.

The only other major issue outstanding is the principle of nondiscriminatory tariff treatment in trade relations, which Moscow wants affirmed.

The difficulty when 35 countries negotiate in six languages on so many subjects is seen in the conference's decision to forego inserting in the final document the usual clause that all texts are equally authentic.

There were so many arguments over translations that it was not possible for the conference to agree that the same sentence in English, French, German, Russian, Italian and Spanish could be accepted as having the same shade of meaning.

* * *

July 29, 1975

POLISH CROWDS HAIL FORD; MILITARY DETENTE STRESSED

By JAMES M. NAUGHTON
Special to The New York Times.

WARSAW, July 28—Huge crowds of Poles greeted President Ford today as he proclaimed "Long live Poland" in their native tongue on a visit reaffirming a United States-Polish commitment to pursue military—not merely political—détente in Europe.

"Niech zyje Polska!" the President declared to a crowd at Okecie airport and a live television audience as he arrived for a visit that served as a prelude to an East-West summit meeting Wednesday in Helsinki. The police estimated generously that 250,000 or more people lined the streets of Warsaw to welcome Mr. Ford.

Edward Gierek, the Communist party leader, lavished praise on Mr. Ford as a partner in the search for world harmony. The two leaders issued a joint statement affirming their commitment to détente.

The President rode and walked through parts of the Polish capital rebuilt from the ruins of World War II, sampled a Polish-grown pear and placed a wreath at the Tomb of the Unknown Soldier in Victory Square as he undertook a visit that was largely symbolic.

Although Mr. Ford met privately for nearly two hours with Mr. Gierek, United States officials acknowledged that there were no "burning issues" outstanding and that cooperative agreements signed when Mr. Gierek visited Washington in October left little opportunity to "break new ground."

Officials accompanying President and Mrs. Ford on their five-nation journey across Europe characterized the stop in Poland, as well as later visits to Rumania and Yugoslavia, as opportunities to give visible encouragement to the three Eastern European nations least subservient to Moscow.

The President's appearance in Warsaw also created another occasion for Mr. Ford to assert that the European security agreement to be signed by him and 34 other leaders in Helsinki is a positive step toward international harmony. Domestic critics, including some in Congress and the press who urged Mr. Ford to turn back from Helsinki without agreeing to the security charter, have put the President on the defensive.

Thus the communiqué the two leaders signed with a flourish over champagne and while seated at an ormolu desk in the Polish Parliament building referred to the Helsinki meeting as "a genuine and strong stimulus for positively shaping relations" between East and West.

But Mr. Ford and Mr. Gierek, whose country has historically been a corridor overrun by armies from east and west, went on in the joint statement to declare that "efforts to strengthen political détente in Europe should be supplemented by a process of military détente."

They said that they would try to seek progress in the negotiations, thus far unproductive, at Vienna on a mutual, balanced reduction of military forces of both the Atlantic alliance and the Warsaw Pact nations.

The President went through a long day of sightseeing and meeting with no noticeable signs of fatigue.

He and Mr. Gierek rode for six miles in an open Soviet-made auto, waving to polite but undemonstrative crowds on the route from the Warsaw airport to Wilanow Palace, a remnant of 17th-century Polish aristocracy. The Fords stayed overnight there.

Onlookers waved plastic American and Polish flags as the auto passed, but there were few displays of emotion. The tone was almost one of nonchalance, in contrast with the exuberant reaction of the Poles when Richard M. Nixon stopped here three years ago. The Poles, whose fashionable clothing ranged from well-cut suits to blue-jean outfits, have progressed in trade and cultural access since bread riots in 1970 helped topple Mr. Gierek's predecessor, Wladyslaw Gomulka.

The theme of mutal cooperation was threaded through the public statements of Mr. Gierek and Mr. Ford on what was only the second Presidential visit to Warsaw since Poland became a Communist nation.

"The most profound desire of our people is peace," Mr. Gierek said. Recalling the devastation wrought on Warsaw in the war, he said that it had "impressed upon the hearts and minds" of Poles a central desire—"no more war."

After placing the wreath on the Tomb of the Unknown Soldier, which rests beneath the only remaining colonnade of a palace destroyed in the war, Mr. Ford wrote the following inscription in a guest book:

"In honor of all those who gave their lives for our freedom and yours."

Reporters who traveled aboard Mr. Ford's Air Force jet from Bonn this morning were told that the President was caught short by the outburst of domestic criticism of the European security agreement and that Mr. Ford felt he waited too long to counter the attacks.

In four days of meetings in Helsinki with the Soviet Communist chief, Leonid I. Brezhnev, and other leaders, Mr. Ford will attempt to emphasize the positive aspects of détente.

Before traveling there tomorrow, Mr. Ford will stop in Cracow and visit briefly at Auschwitz, the most notorious of the Nazi camps, where four million people, most of them Jews, died in gas chambers or from forced labor. The President's schedule calls for him to spend three minutes at the concentration camp, which the Polish government has preserved as a national memorial to the dead.

* * *

July 31, 1975

FORD, IN FINLAND, MEETS BREZHNEV ON ARMS ISSUES

They Describe Conversation as Very Constructive but Reach No Agreements

BUSY DAY OF DIPLOMACY

President Talks With Wilson and Caramanlis and Will See Demirel Today

By JAMES M. NAUGHTON
Special to The New York Times.

HELSINKI, Finland, July 30—President Ford and Leonid I. Brezhnev, here for the opening of the European security conference, held today what President Ford termed very constructive talks on strategic weapons but reached no specific agreements on means to limit nuclear arms.

Secretary of State Kissinger said at a news briefing that "it would be incorrect to claim any particular achievements" on arms limitations as a result of the two-hour meeting in the compound of the American Embassy.

But Mr. Kissinger said the meeting had provided a "very useful" opportunity for the United States to reply at the highest level to arms limitation ideas advanced two weeks ago in Vienna by the Soviet Foreign Minister, Andrei A. Gromyko.

A Long Day of Talks

The briefing by Mr. Kissinger followed a long day of diplomacy in which Mr. Ford also met privately with Premier Constantine Caramanlis of Greece and Prime Minister Harold Wilson of Britain.

Mr. Kissinger voiced cautious hope that Mr. Ford could persuade Premier Suleyman Demirel of Turkey, at a breakfast meeting tomorrow, to reopen at least some of the American military bases shut down last Saturday in retaliation against a Congressional ban on arms sales to the Turks.

The Secretary of State hailed Mr. Caramanlis as "one of the outstanding leaders of our period," lending weight to reports from Greek officials that the White House felt "provoked" by the Turkish action on the bases and in reaction was improving relations with Athens.

Meet Again on Saturday

President Ford and Mr. Brezhnev, who will meet again on Saturday, both described their discussions today as cordial and constructive at an impromptu news conference in the American Embassy driveway.

"It was businesslike, very friendly, and I am sure that when we meet again on Saturday further progress will materialize," Mr. Ford said.

The tone of the meeting was almost jovial as the Soviet and American leaders and their senior aides sat down around a small dining table. Referring to the recently completed Apollo-Soyuz space mission, Mr. Ford said that "the handshake in space was indicative of the progress we've been making."

Mr. Brezhnev, making light of Mr. Kissinger's penchant for diplomatic secrecy, smiled at the Secretary of State and said, "I know Kissinger's mind works that way. I take something and put it in my pocket and nobody knows about it." He gestured toward a pack of cigarettes on the table and pretended to hide it in his suit pocket.

Mr. Kissinger did not make public any details of today's discussions. But he said that they had included a United States reply on one of the most difficult of the issues holding up an arms agreement—verification of the fidelity of the two sides to a limit on nuclear tests.

Under a proposal reported to have been made by Mr. Gromyko in Vienna, on-site inspectors might be allowed to check on underground nuclear explosions that could possibly violate the so-called "threshold" accord. The accord would be broken if either side detonated a test device of more than 150 kilotons or conducted a nuclear test at other than an agreed site.

Mr. Kissinger insisted that "progress has been made" in the last month on an arms agreement, despite his acknowledgement that Atlantic alliance partners were not briefed after the Vienna meeting, as is customary when progress has been made.

The Secretary of State said that it took time to analyze the Soviet proposals and that American allies would be consulted before any positive steps were taken.

"I do not know that the discussion [of the strategic arms negotiations] now lends itself to a particular announcement, even on Saturday, he said. He continued to speak with optimism, however, about completing the negotiations in time for a planned Soviet-American summit meeting in the fall.

President Ford's conversations with Prime Minister Wilson and with Premier Caramanlis involved other issues that are preoccupying the private—and sometimes the public—dialogue among the leaders in Helsinki.

The suspension of the United States base agreement with Turkey cast a shadow over the meeting tomorrow between Mr. Ford and Mr. Demirel.

Mr. Kissinger, in effect using the Helsinki platform to lobby for a reversal of the Congressional decision last week to continue the embargo on arms aid to Turkey, said he held out little hope for a compromise solution in Washington. "Domestic developments in the United States have complicated our ability to play a useful role" in seeking an accord between Turkey and Greece over Cyprus, he said.

Asked whether Mr. Ford would try, at the first meeting with Turkish officials since the bases were taken over, to appeal for a reversal of Mr. Demirel's order, Mr. Kissinger said that would be futile because the Turks knew "very well that we wanted to keep them open."

Even so, Mr. Kissinger said the President would discuss "the sort of measures that might make it possible to put our relationship with Turkey on a new basis"—a basis that would in turn lead to "a reopening of all or maybe some" of the more important bases.

White House aides seemed to feel that Mr. Ford's luncheon had removed a good deal of the chill in relations between Athens and Washington. Mr. Ford, after the luncheon, said that the conversation had been very friendly and very deep and that it had involved not only Cyprus but also United States-Greek relations.

Later Mr. Kissinger added that the United States would do all it could to help Mr. Caramanlis. He said the United States wished the democratic Government of Greece well.

President Ford's breakfast meeting with Mr. Wilson was described by Mr. Kissinger as a general review of world issues with an old and valued ally.

Mr. Ford and Mr. Wilson will also meet together tomorrow with President Valéry Giscard d'Estaing of France and chancellor Helmut Schmidt of West Germany to discuss responsibilities in West Berlin as well as economic matters.

* * *

October 16, 1975

PACT WITH SOVIET ON MISSILE CURBS REPORTED IN PERIL

U.S. Officials, Differing With Kissinger, Doubt an Early Resolution of Issues

By LESLIE H. GELB
Special to The New York Times.

WASHINGTON, Oct. 15—Several authoritative Administration officials say the talks with the Soviet Union on strategic arms limitations are in trouble.

The officials said in interviews that the Administration was waiting for a response from Moscow to its latest proposal and expected that the response would not move the negotiations, now stalled, along very much.

This estimate stands in contrast to Secretary of State Kissinger's public remarks on Sunday that "about 90 per cent of the negotiation is substantially completed." The officials said Mr. Kissinger was trying to be upbeat.

Differ on Significance

Some officials agreed that 90 per cent of the important issues had been resolved, but said hard political decisions still needed to be made on secondary matters. Other officials contended that the unresolved issues, concerning the Soviet bomber called the Backfire, the air-breathing American cruise missile and the definition of a large missile, were of primary importance and that the talks might well fail over these issues.

The consensus among officials is that if there is no agreement before the Presidential election campaign next year gets into full swing, the odds against a final settlement will increase sharply. Many feel that Soviet-American détente could not survive failure.

Problems in Accord

The officials attributed the difficulty to the three following factors:

- The complexity of reconciling Soviet strategic forces, weighted with large land-based missiles, with a more balanced American land, sea and air posture, along with the different directions being taken by the two sides in the development of new weapons.
- The many misunderstandings that the officials said had been created by sloppy and hurried negotiations between President Ford and Leonid I. Brezhnev, the Soviet party leader, in Vladivostok last November coupled with several instances of Mr. Ford's and Mr. Kissinger's backing away from concessions previously made.
- Important philosophical differences between Mr. Kissinger and Defense Secretary James R. Schlesinger over the significance of the Backfire bomber and over how necessary it was to conclude this particular arms agreement with Moscow.

The officials also talked about what they would not say publicly, namely that Mr. Ford would link any future concessions to Moscow to the strength of conservative opposition to détente in his own party.

As a result of all these problems, the officials said, the National Security Council in September presented the President with nine alternative proposals, and Mr. Kissinger gave Foreign Minister Andrei A. Gromyko in New York a new proposal that he knew would be unacceptable.

At Vladivostok, it was agreed that neither side could exceed 2,400 strategic delivery vehicles, defined as intercontinental land-based missiles, long-range submarine-launched missiles and long-range bombers. Within this ceiling, neither side could have more than 1,320 missiles with re-entry vehicles equipped with multiple warheads.

Four major problems soon appeared on whether to count the Backfire and the cruise missile as part of the 2,400 ceiling, on the definition of a heavy missile and on how to verify whether a deployed missile contained multiple warheads.

The Backfire problem emerged because Mr. Kissinger never stated at Vladivostok that this new bomber should be included in the ceiling. When, at Pentagon insistence, he later raised the issue, Moscow contended that the Backfire was only a medium-range bomber and should not be included.

The issue of the cruise missile was left ambiguous in Vladivostok. The Russians subsequently contended that they assumed that any missile with a range of more than 600 kilometers (360 miles) would count. Washington said it had assumed that missiles would be counted only if they were ballistic, that is, traveled outside the atmosphere. Cruise missiles fly in the atmosphere.

In Helsinki last August, President Ford proposed to Mr. Brezhnev to include air-launched cruise missiles with a range of more than about 2,000 miles. This was not accepted. The United States has not offered any range limit on sea-launched cruise missiles.

The issue of how to define a heavy missile dates from the interim offensive missile agreement reached in 1972. Moscow then agreed to limit its deployment of large SS-9 missiles to 309.

Since then, Moscow has continued to emphasize heavy missiles and wants to retain this advantage. The Pentagon wants it stopped.

Brezhnev Wants Linkage

The fourth major issue, concerning verification of missiles with multiple warheads, has been settled in principle. Moscow has agreed that if a missile has been tested with multiple warheads, all missiles of that kind shall be considered as counting against the 1,320 ceiling.

However, Mr. Brezhnev told Mr. Ford that he would make this concession only if Mr. Ford made concessions on the Backfire and cruise missiles.

After the National Security Council meeting, on Sept. 17 had considered nine alternative proposals, Mr. Ford asked Mr. Kissinger and Mr. Schlesinger to work out a new proposal between them.

Mr. Kissinger presented this proposal to Mr. Gromyko on Sept. 21 in New York. Some officials said it sought a balance between the number of Backfires that Moscow could deploy above the 2,400 ceiling with a roughly equal number of American cruise missiles above the ceiling.

From Mr. Kissinger's point of view, it is not a matter of importance that the Russians be allowed 200 to 300 Backfires, given the thousands of delivery vehicles both sides already have. For him, the concessions are minor compared with the importance of having the agreement.

From Mr. Schlessinger's perspective, the benefits of détente are illusory and the advantages of concession suspect. Officials said he would not be alarmed if this agreement were not concluded.

* * *

December 24, 1975

KISSINGER INSISTS STAND ON ANGOLA WILL NOT CHANGE

Says U.S. Will Continue to Oppose the Imposition of a Soviet-Backed Regime

NEW TENSION FORESEEN

Secretary Asserts Senate Vote Hobbled Attempts to Find Diplomatic Solution

By BERNARD GWERTZMAN
Special to The New York Times.

WASHINGTON, Dec. 23—Secretary of State Henry A. Kissinger, warning that Soviet-American tensions might rise, said today that the Ford Administration would continue to oppose—through available military aid and diplomatic means—the imposition of a Soviet-backed regime in Angola by force.

At a news conference, Mr. Kissinger said the Senate vote last week against further secret financing in the Angolan civil war had "severely complicated" the Administration's efforts for a diplomatic solution. But he asserted that the Administration would use the $9 million left for military aid and take other steps to oppose Soviet "expansion," even at the cost of a setback in Soviet-American relations.

No American Forces

Pledging that no American forces would be introduced into the former Portuguese colony, Mr. Kissinger made a determined effort to rally support for the Administration's position. He also hardened the Administration's attitude toward Moscow.

Referring to Angola, where the Russians have reportedly sent in about $100 million in equipment and 200 advisers, and encouraged Cuba to send as many as 5,000 soldiers, Mr. Kissinger said:

"Unless the Soviet Union shows restraint in its foreign policy actions, the situation in our relationship is bound to become more tense, and there is no question that the United States will not accept Soviet military expansion of any kind."

Aims at Two Audiences

Mr. Kissinger clearly wanted to inform both Congress and the Soviet Union of the Ford Administration's determination to press for a solution acceptable to the United States in Angola.

He said the United States would make "every effort" militarily with the $9 million still left to it for covert aid to the Angolan factions opposing the Soviet-backed Popular Movement for the Liberation of Angola.

Diplomatic efforts would also continue, he said, primarily through the Organization of African Unity, the umbrella group for the continent, which will discuss the Angolan civil war next month. He said that if the situation in Angola had not improved by the time Congress reconvened Jan. 19, "We will go back to the Congress and present the situation as it then exists" in an effort to get more funds.

Later in the day, Mr. Kissinger met for 45 minutes with the Soviet Ambassador, Anatoly F. Dobrynin, and reportedly reiterated the American concern over Soviet involvement in Angola. Mr. Kissinger has over the last month had several discussions with Mr. Dobrynin about Angola, but so far there has been no agreement on what to do. The Russians have given support to the Popular Movement, which controls the capital, Luanda, and has, together with other Communist and some other third-world countries, extended diplomatic relations to that group, one of three fighting in Angola.

Link to Arms Talk

Mr. Kissinger, who has devoted much effort to putting relations with Moscow on a more normal basis, was ambiguous about the specific effects Angola might have on over-all Soviet-American relations, but he hinted that even the talks on limiting strategic arms could be affected.

With these talks deadlocked over a few key issues, Mr. Kissinger had planned to fly to Moscow in the second half of January to seek a breakthrough in the negotiations—something sought by both Moscow and Washington. But in answer to questions today, Mr. Kissinger for the first time raised the possibility that, because of Angola, his negotiating mission might be canceled.

"We are talking to the Soviet Union within the context of our over-all relationship, and there is no question that our over-all relationship will suffer if we do not find an adequate solution to the Angolan problem," he said. "Where it will suffer and in what ways, I am not prepared to say," he added.

As for the visit, he said, "we will have to look at the situation closer to the time of the trip before we can answer the question whether it is in jeopardy or not."

Up to now, the talks on strategic-arms limitation, which began in November 1969, have been insulated from other Soviet-American issues. Mr Kissinger, a leading proponent of an accord to limit offensive missiles and bombers, stressed that cancellation of his trip to Moscow would be a serious step.

"The question of strategic-arms limitations is a matter that is in our mutual interest and that should not be lightly discarded," he said. "It is not a favor we grant to the Soviet Union. It is an inherent necessity of the present period. Avoiding nuclear war is not a favor we do anybody. Avoiding nuclear war without giving up any interests is the problem that we face now."

Mr. Kissinger did say, however, that because of Angola the Administration would do nothing to revive efforts in Congress to grant the Soviet Union trade concessions.

Virtually the entire 45-minute news conference was taken up with Angola and problems in maintaining Soviet-American détente.

Mr. Kissinger said—as he had privately told Senators last week in vainly seeking support for $28 million in additional covert funds for Angola—that the United States did not oppose a Marxist faction's taking power, but only its being "imposed" by Communist intervention.

Imposition Called the Issue

"The issue is not whether the country of Angola represents a vital interest to the United States," he said. "The issue is whether the Soviet Union, backed by a Cuban expeditionary force, can impose on two-thirds of the population its own brand of government."

If the United States ends its support in Angola, he said, "we are practically inviting outside forces to participate in every situation in which there is a possibility for foreign intervention, and we are, therefore, undermining any hope of political and international order."

He said the funds sought from Congress were "trivial sums." By approving tens of millions of dollars, he contended, it did not mean that the country was automatically approving an unlimited involvement. Critics of the Angolan aid raised the precedent of Vietnam, where the American role escalated until billions of dollars and a half million troops were involved.

Mr. Kissinger said the money for Angola—$27 million has been spent this year—was arranged clandestinely "because we did not want to have a public confrontation if we could avoid it."

On détente, Mr. Kissinger said that the main American problem was to "manage" the emergence of the Soviet Union as a superpower in such a way as to avoid nuclear war "without sacrificing vital interests."

He said that the refusal of Congress either to approve "moderating" measures such as trade concessions to the Soviet Union, or to go ahead with Angolan military funds, had made it extremely difficult for the Administration to conduct a sophisticated foreign policy.

"I must stress again we are being deprived now of both the incentives for moderation and the capacity to resist, and this must lead to an extremely dangerous situation," he said.

* * *

March 17, 1976

U.S., ANGRY OVER ANGOLA, TO DELAY 3 SOVIET MEETINGS

By BERNARD GWERTZMAN
Special to The New York Times.

WASHINGTON, March 16—Because of Soviet military involvement in Angola, the United States has decided for the time being against participating in Cabinet-level meetings of various Soviet-American joint commissions set up in recent years when détente was in vogue, State Department officials said today.

There are nine such commissions, but the decision has so far affected only three, dealing in trade, housing and energy. The other commissions are not due to meet until late in the year, and, by then, the United States may decide to participate, officials said.

The United States decision not to take part in the energy commission was first indicated late last night by an Administration official.

Robert L. Funseth, the State Department spokesman, today announced the official decision on the commissions, when he said that "in light of the situation in Angola, we felt we could not conduct our business with the Soviet Union as usual."

At the very moment when the Administration was signaling its irritation with the Soviet Union, 10 Senators, including Henry M. Jackson, the Washington Democrat, introduced a resolution today in the Senate supporting efforts to improve Soviet-American relations.

The Administration's action was clearly a limited one and not meant to disrupt overall Soviet-American relations.

Secretary of State Henry A. Kissinger, testifying before the Senate Foreign Relations Committee, repeated that the Government's anger over Soviet involvement in Angola would not affect the talks on limitation of strategic arms and would not lead to any halt in the export of grain to the Soviet Union.

A State Department official said that, while Mr. Funseth was publicly linking the postponement to Angola, the Soviet Union was told through diplomatic channels only that further preparation was needed for the energy meeting due to have started in Moscow this week, and that the housing meeting, tentatively set for May, should be rescheduled. No date had been set for the trade commission.

Mr. Funseth also disclosed that the negotiations that have been going on since Jan. 26 for a Soviet-American oil agreement had been recessed because of failure to agree on the formula for shipping rates. He stressed that the oil talks were unrelated to the actions on the joint commissions.

Ever since a Soviet-backed Angolan faction was able to win the civil war in Angola with 12,000 Cuban troops and Soviet military aid of about $200 million, the Administration has been seeking to send "signals" that this would harm Soviet relations with the United States.

The Angolan Government has been recognized by most nations, including the West European countries, but not by the United States.

Since the Administration's détente policies toward the Soviet Union have come under attack during the current political campaign, the Administration has been cautious about its dealings with Moscow.

President Ford said he preferred to avoid the word "détente" while nevertheless still pursuing better relations. Government agencies and embassies abroad have been instructed not to use the word.

Mr. Kissinger has stepped up his attacks on the Soviet Union without going so far as to repudiate his own policies. He has called for support of what he called again today the "dual policy" of trying to "firmly resist and deter adventurism" while keeping open "the possibility of more constructive relations" with Moscow.

Alluding to the joint commissions set up as a result of meetings between President Richard M. Nixon and Leonid I. Brezhnev in 1972, 1973 and 1974, Mr. Kissinger said the United States favored enlarging bilateral cooperation "when political conditions permit it."

The decision to avoid Cabinet-level meetings with the Russians was calculated to avoid displays of cooperation during a period when the United States has not yet accepted the accession to power in Angola of the Soviet-backed forces.

The Senate resolution in favor of détente was the inspiration of Senator Alan Cranston, Democrat of California. His prime Republican co-sponsor is Senator Howard H. Baker Jr., Republican of Tennessee.

Among the sections of the resolution was one calling for a widening of relations in all spheres, taking into account "the risks and advantages" of such ties.

Mr. Cranston said his idea stemmed from his concern over "all the assaults on détente, the silence on Capitol Hill in defense of it, and the dropping of the word in the campaign by the President."

When told about the delay in the meetings of three joint commissions, Mr. Cranston said that was "sort of silly." He said it was foolish to expect the Russians not to support "anti-colonialism" in Angola.

The resolution was ostensibly aimed at such critics of détente as Senator Jackson, who is a Democratic contender for the Presidency and has been critical of some of the Administration's attitudes toward the Soviet Union. But the resolution was so broadly written that Mr. Jackson announced this afternoon that he had decided to co-sponsor it.

Officials said that while Cabinet-level meetings of the joint commissions were not contemplated now, working groups of experts and other officials were not affected.

Shumilin Visiting U.S.

For instance, a Soviet delegation headed by Boris T. Shumilin, Deputy Minister of Interior, was visiting the Department of Transportation today as part of a working group in the joint transportation committee dealing with highway safety.

Last week, an American team was in Moscow dealing with work on an artificial heart under the joint committee on health cooperation.

The joint commissions have never been regarded in Washington as very productive institutions. Within the Federal bureaucracy, many officials have regarded them as largely the deliberate creations of Mr. Kissinger.

Mr. Kissinger justified them in terms of getting officials from both sides involved in constructive relations. He said that if the Soviet bureaucracy became so involved in relations with the United States, the Kremlin would have to think seriously about taking political actions that would upset the United States.

The joint areas of activity include agriculture, ocean research, transportation, energy, housing, atomic energy, science and technology, health, and environment.

* * *

November 4, 1976

CARTER, IN VICTORY, HAILS 'NEW SPIRIT'; STARTS TRANSITION WITH FORD'S STAFF

President Concedes Defeat And Offers Support to Rival

By CHRISTOPHER LYDON
Special to The New York Times.

WASHINGTON, Nov. 3—President Ford, accepting his first political defeat, conceded victory to Jimmy Carter without reservation today and offered "my complete and wholehearted support" in the transition to a new national leadership.

Mr. Ford, who went to bed before 3:30 A.M. today with still a flickering hope of victory, learned at midmorning that the battle had been lost. Mr. Ford was told by Stuart Spencer, his campaign director, and Robert Teeter, his pollster, that he would still be short of an Electoral College majority even if Mr. Carter's hairbreadth margins in Ohio and Oregon at that point were erased. The next closest states in the voting, including New York, looked well out of range of recount reversals, they said.

Shortly after 11 A.M., red-eyed and hoarse, Mr. Ford telephoned his congratulations to Mr. Carter in Plains, Ga. Because his own voice was failing, Mr. Ford asked his chief of staff, Richard B. Cheney, to read Mr. Carter the message he was also sending by wire:

"Dear Jimmy," it read, "It is apparent now that you have won our long and intense struggle for the Presidency. I congratulate you on your victory.

"As one who has been honored to serve the people of this great land, both in Congress and as President, I believe that we must now put the divisions of the campaign behind us and unite the country once again in the common pursuit of peace and prosperity.

"Although there will continue to be disagreements over the best means to use in pursuing our goals, I want to assure you that you have my complete and wholehearted support as you take the oath of office this January.

"I also pledge to you that I and all members of my administration will do all that we can to assure that you begin your term as smoothly and as effectively as possible.

"May God bless you and your family as you undertake your new responsibilities."

'Characteristically Gracious'

The telegram that Mr. Carter would later in the day call "characteristically gracious," was signed informally, "Jerry Ford." About an hour later the 38th President, who said that he still had a lot to do in the final 78 days of his appointed term, made his first farewells to newsmen in the White House press lounge.

The President's immediate family stood with him in a brief and emotional ceremony, exchanging embraces, kisses and stricken looks. The President himself appeared uncommonly drawn but composed. Mrs. Ford, whom the President smilingly designated as "the real spokesman for the family," held back tears as she read two statements for her husband, including the telegram to Mr. Carter.

Their three sons, Jack, 24 years old, Steve, 20, Michael, 26, and Michael's wife, Gail, seemed silently shattered. Susan Ford, 19, looked as if she had cried all night. She was still inconsolable.

Prepared Text

"The President," Mrs. Ford began from a prepared text, "wants to thank all of those thousands of people who worked so hard on his behalf, and the millions who supported him with their votes. It's been the greatest honor of my husband's life to have served his fellow Americans during two of the most difficult years in our nation's history."

President Ford had said at the outset, "I think all of us, Betty, and the children and myself, would like to just come down and shake hands and express our appreciation personally" for "the friendship that all of us have had."

And so they did, in a sadly chatty family procession among about 200 newsmen, photographers and technicians jammed into the strangely subdued press quarters. For several minutes the loudest sound in the normally roaring room was the click of camera shutters.

"Looks like Ohio kicked a field goal in the last quarter," one reporter told the University of Michigan's most famous football center.

"But we came from way back," Mr. Ford said in a thick voice. "Nobody can say we didn't give it a hell of a try."

Mrs. Ford said that she had every intention of moving back to the house that the Fords still own in suburban Alexandria, Va.

Asked how he would spend his lame-duck days before Mr. Carter is sworn in on Jan. 20, President Ford replied eagerly, "We're going to keep working. It's the job. We've got a lot of things to do and we're going to keep doing them."

Mr. and Mrs. Ford will start a vacation in Palm Springs, Calif., this weekend, and Mr. Ford said today that the family would spend Christmas, as usual, in a working-and-skiing trip to Vail, Colo.

Mr. Ford, who was the most valuable player on the 1934 Michigan team that scored only 7 points and won only one game during the season, has a competitor's understanding of victory and defeat. And he was said to be in no mood for might-have-beens today.

He Was 'Very Strong'

"He was serious, disappointed and very strong," said Robert Teeter, who went over the numbers with the President at midmorning. "I think he genuinely had the feeling that we'd given it our best shot. There was nothing vindictive or maudlin about it. We kind of agreed not to second-guess it."

There was never any serious thought after daybreak today, Mr. Teeter added, of challenging the results. "There just weren't enough states worth recounting," he said. "In New York," where Republicans first filed and then withdrew a suit to impound ballots, "we knew there were irregularities but not enough to change 200,000 votes. We had given it our best shot, and it just wasn't there."

* * *

January 14, 1977

CARTER WILL PURSUE EARLY PANAMA PACT AND CYPRUS ACCORD

CONGRESSMEN GIVEN PRIORITIES

New Moves to Ease Soviet Curbs on Emigration Also Stressed in Nine-Hour Discussion

By BERNARD GWERTZMAN
Special to The New York Times.

WASHINGTON, Jan. 13—Jimmy Carter intends in the first weeks of his Presidency to press for a solution of the Cyprus dispute and to speed up negotiations for a new Panama Canal treaty, Congressional sources said today.

Members of Congress who participated yesterday in a nine-hour exchange of views with Mr. Carter, Secretary of State-designate Cyrus R. Vance and other aides said there was considerable discussion of ways to alter the so-called Jackson-Vanik amendment of 1974, which bars trade concessions to the Soviet Union until there is assurance that it will liberalize its emigration practices.

They said most participants agreed that the restrictions had not been effective in persuading the Soviet Union to increase Jewish emigration, which was 14,000 in 1976, compared with 35,000 in 1973.

Law Forces Confrontation

There was general agreement, they said, that the present law forces a confrontation on the issue and that a more indirect way had to be found to give Moscow an incentive to increase emigration in return for trade benefits.

It was agreed that there would be further discussion of this issue in coming weeks and it was cited as an example of executive-legislative cooperation.

Mr. Carter spent much of today in meetings on national defense and in telephone conversations with Prime Minister James Callaghan of Britain, President Valéry Giscard d'Estaing of France and Chancellor Helmut Schmidt of West Germany.

The President-elect and Mr. Vance underscored at yesterday's session the priority they want to give to achieving a new arms-limitation agreement next October and to laying the groundwork for a further accord with the Soviet Union on the reduction of force levels on both sides.

In recent days, Mr. Carter and Mr. Vance have discussed, in general outline, the priorities and approaches they intend to give to key foreign policy areas.

New Initiative on Cyprus

On the surface, the Carter Administration does not appear to be deviating significantly from the policies followed by President Ford and Secretary of State Henry A. Kissinger.

But a prominent West European ambassador predicted there would be shifts. Commenting on this apparent similarity, he said today: "Whenever there is a change, everyone says there will be no change, but there always are changes." He added that the only restrictions were those imposed by outside events.

On Cyprus, Mr. Carter has been urged by members of Congress to make a fresh effort to revive the deadlocked negotiations between the Greek and Turkish communities on the island and Greece and Turkey.

Participants in yesterday's closed-door session said today that Vice President-elect Mondale would discuss Cyprus on his European trip beginning Jan. 23, three days after the inauguration. Then, Mr. Vance told them, it is expected that a fact-finding mission will be named to go to Greece, Turkey and Cyprus and make recommendations for a new American approach.

Mr. Vance, who was deeply involved in negotiations over Cyprus during the Johnson Administration, told the Senate Foreign Relations Committee on Tuesday that "a just and durable solution is even more important than before." He said that "in weeks ahead" new ideas would be formed "to bring meaningful progress."

On Panama, which some participants viewed as the most interesting element of the discussions, Mr. Carter said with fervor that he intended to try to finish the negotiations by the end of the spring and that the Panamanian Foreign Minister, Aquilino Boyd, would come to Washington soon after the inauguration to resume the discussions.

'A Festering Sore'

Mr. Vance reportedly said that the canal issue was "a festering sore" and that it was necessary to conclude a treaty to avoid major trouble in Latin America and the third world.

When reminded of strong opposition in Congress to any ceding of control to Panama, Mr. Carter reportedly said he was ready to use a "fireside chat" on television to press the case.

Other areas discussed by Mr. Carter and Mr. Vance in the last few days include:

MIDDLE EAST—Both have noted excellent signs of progress but have urged caution. One Congressman said he got no new ideas on the Middle East from yesterday's session. Mr. Carter contended that the Israeli elections due May 17 made it unlikely that anything concrete would emerge before then, although preliminary talks could be held. The President-elect has already said that he wants to meet the various leaders here, and at some point a representative will probably go to the Middle East for initial discussions.

Cuba Ban Called Ineffective

CUBA—Mr. Vance told the Foreign Relations Committee that the trade embargo against Cuba had been ineffective and that if Cuba showed a willingness to live in the "system of states" ways could be found to remove the impediments to normal relations. It is assumed that if Cuba withdraws its 13,000 men from Angola, this could lead the way to talks.

ARMS TALKS—On the talks with Moscow on the limitation of strategic arms, Mr. Carter said at yesterday's session that he was accepting the 1974 Vladivostok formula for a ceiling of 2,400 on heavy bombers and intercontinental ballistic missiles. He said that he hoped to conclude the negotiations, deadlocked for almost a year, over whether a Soviet bomber, known in the West as Backfire, and the American subsonic cruise missile should be included in the total, before the current five-year freeze ends in October. Then, he said, he wants to move quickly to an accord for reductions of that 2,400 total.

CHINA—Mr. Carter and Mr. Vance both said they wished to normalize relations with Peking on the basis of the Shanghai communiqué of 1972, but to insure the security of the people of Taiwan. So far, it has been impossible to find a formula for reconciling those two points of view.

SOUTH KOREA—Mr. Carter and Mr. Vance repeated that in principle they favored a gradual, phased withdrawal of United States ground troops in South Korea, but stress was laid on the need to be careful and to do so only in closest consultation with South Korea and Japan. Mr. Vance made it clear in his appearance before the Foreign Relations Committee that the scandals involving South Koreans would not lead to abrogation of the security treaty with Seoul. He also said a withdrawal of land forces would not affect the continued presence of United States Air Force units in South Korea.

SOUTHERN AFRICA—Mr. Vance has strongly supported Britain's initiative in seeking a transition to black majority rule in Rhodesia. He told the Foreign Relations Committee that the Carter administration would also try to revive the diplomatic efforts to bring about the peaceful independence of South-West Africa from South Africa. On South Africa, Mr. Vance said the Administration would show by word and action its opposition to apartheid but he gave no details.

ARMS SALE—Mr. Carter, who has strongly criticized the Ford Administration for its arms sales to foreign countries, was reported to have said yesterday, "We're going to take the lead in attenuating dramatically arms sales levels." He said the United States would propose meeting with other producer countries. Mr. Vance said Tuesday that Israel would be protected and sales to Arab nations would depend on their security requirements and on maintenance of the overall balance in the region.

* * *

February 2, 1977

CARTER DISCUSSES HUMAN RIGHTS AND ARMS ISSUES WITH DOBRYNIN

By BERNARD GWERTZMAN

Special to The New York Times.

WASHINGTON, Feb. 1—President Carter told Ambassador Anatoly F. Dobrynin today that the United States would not back down on its commitment to strengthen human rights in the Soviet Union and elsewhere, the White House said.

According to an official statement, Mr. Carter, in a meeting devoted mainly to arms limitation matters, made a point of raising the rights issue by saying, "We are not attacking the Soviet Union, but we are expressing our commitment on human rights."

Later, White House officials said the President's comments had been expressed in a general way without direct reference to Andrei D. Sakharov, the physicist and human rights advocate, who had become the center of a Soviet-American controversy in recent days. The officials said the message was clear, however, and did not take up much time in the meeting.

The White House statement echoed comments that reporters earlier heard Mr. Carter make to Vice President Mondale aboard a helicopter carrying them from Andrews Air Force Base. It tended to refute some news reports that the Administration had been embarrassed by a State Department statement last week in defense of Dr. Sakharov.

The State Department statement was not cleared by either Mr. Carter or Secretary of State Cyrus R. Vance, and the President told reporters on Sunday that he was not happy with the way the department had handled the matter, although he supported the substance of the statement.

Mr. Vance and others have since said that the Administration was not trying to scale down its interest in the issue. Complicating the situation was a complaint on Thursday by

Mr. Dobrynin that the statement constituted interference in Soviet affairs.

Although the President raised the matter with Mr. Dobrynin in their hour-long session today, it appears that, initially at least, the White House intended to avoid mentioning it and to focus instead on strategic arms matters.

Reporters were allowed to witness Mr. Dobrynin's arrival in the Oval Office. On meeting the envoy, who has served here since 1962, Mr. Carter said: "I've heard great things about you and your service in Washington. I hope to have a great relationship with you and also with Mr. Leonid Brezhnev."

Mr. Dobrynin said the United States and the Soviet Union had mutual interests and "we must not let them go by." He handed over presents from Mr. Brezhnev, the Soviet leader-for the President, a miniature silver samovar and for Amy, his daughter, a set of hollow wooden "matryoshka" dolls, a traditional Russian peasant article in which smaller dolls fit into increasingly larger ones.

Carter's Comment to Mondale

After the session, which was attended by Mr. Vance and Zbigniew Brzezinski, the national security adviser, the White House issued a statement prepared by Mr. Brzezinski's office that did not mention human rights and said the participants had reviewed the whole range of United States-Soviet relations, with particular emphasis on the forthcoming negotiations for a limitation of strategic offensive weapons.

By that time, Mr. Carter had gone to Andrews Air Force Base to welcome Mr. Mondale on his arrival home from his round-the-world mission. As they flew back to the White House in a Marine helicopter with a small group of reporters aboard, Mr. Mondale asked Mr. Carter whether "the Sakharov flap had died down."

The President was quoted by the reporters as having replied:

"I told Dobrynin that we're not going to back down on that. We have a commitment on human rights and when statements like that are made it's not an attack on the Soviet Union but an expression of support for that commitment."

After the reporters aboard the helicopter had briefed their colleagues, the White House press office issued the following additional statement about Mr. Carter's session with the Soviet envoy:

"The President specifically raised the human rights issue. He told Ambassador Dobrynin that the United States will not back down on the human rights issue. We have a commitment on a position. We are not attacking the Soviet Union, but we are expressing our commitment on human rights."

* * *

February 9, 1977

PRESIDENT OUTLINES PROPOSALS FOR ARMS PACT WITH SOVIET, ASKS A HALT IN UNDERGROUND TESTING

QUICK ACCORD SOUGHT

Carter Would Defer Issue of Russian Bomber and U.S. Cruise Missile

By CHARLES MOHR
Special to The New York Times.

WASHINGTON, Feb. 8—President Carter offered today to reach a quick agreement with the Soviet Union on a ceiling for strategic weapons by postponing consideration of whether a Soviet bomber and the American cruise missile should be counted within the limits.

In his first formal news conference since taking office, Mr. Carter also asked the Soviet Union to agree to a mutual halt in the development of mobile land-based missiles and a mutual agreement to give prior notice of missile test launches.

The President offered to overcome an impasse on the question of a complete nuclear test ban by suggesting that the United States would agree to observe detonations by the Russians for civil engineering purposes in return for a stop to underground testing.

Strong Backing for Warnke

Mr. Carter not only strongly backed Paul C. Warnke, who has been nominated for the post of arms-control chief, but left little doubt that Mr. Warnke's views on disarmament were little, if any, more advanced than Mr. Carter's. Some critics feel Mr. Warnke is too willing to reduce the United States arsenal without reciprocal Soviet steps.

"There will be instances," the President said, in which it would be desirable for one side to take unilateral initiatives in reducing particular weapon systems. He said it was more important to work for an overall balance of mutual restraint.

Mr. Carter also indicated that, unlike former Secretary of State Henry A. Kissinger, he would not be inhibited in criticizing violations of human rights in the Soviet Union and elsewhere for fear that such statements would jeopardize progress on arms reduction.

The President said several of the arms proposals he outlined today had been communicated to the Soviet Union. He did not indicate whether a response had been received.

Mr. Carter spoke of the impasse in implementing the 1974 Vladivostok agreement, under which the Soviet Union and the United States agreed to a mutual limit of 2,400 long-range bombers and missiles, of which 1,320 could carry multiple warheads. Final agreement has been stalled by Soviet reluctance to include a bomber-designated Backfire in the West-and by American reluctance to include sea-launched drone cruise missiles in the total.

"I would be willing to go ahead with the Soviet Union to conclude a quick agreement, if they think it advisable, and omit the Backfire bomber and the cruise missile from the negotiations at this stage," the President said. He added that the two weapons systems could be discussed at a future stage.

This is similar to a proposal made a year ago by the Ford Administration. The Russians showed flexibility on the issue of cruise missiles carried in bombers, but they wanted sea-launched cruise missiles counted under the ceiling. Secretary of State Cyrus R. Vance is expected to pursue the arms question on a visit to Moscow next month.

Soviet-American progress in arms reduction would lead to broader agreements involving other nuclear countries, Mr. Carter predicted. He said that Huang Chen, Peking's envoy in Washington, said in a meeting earlier in the day that "the goal of the Chinese Government was to reduce dependence on nuclear weapons to zero." China lags behind both the United States and the Soviet Union in nuclear capability.

Several of the steps proposed by Mr. Carter to the Soviet Union have ramifications that were not fully discussed in the half-hour news conference.

He said he would like to see the Russians cease deployment of an intermediate-range missile-designated the SS-20 in the West-in mobile launching facilities. He said it was difficult to pinpoint the sites of such mobile launchers and to distinguish them from a larger, intercontinental missile called the SS-16. In principle, the mobile intermediate missiles being targeted toward West Europe could thus be converted to intercontinental weapons threatening the United States.

A refusal to cease deployment of the SS-20, Mr. Carter said, "would put a great pressure on us to develop a mobile missile of our own."

A symbolically important step, the President said, would be mutual agreement to give prior notice of test launchings. He said Soviet tests took place from operational silos while American tests were made from Vandenberg Air Force Base on the West Coast.

Mr. Carter said the Russians had been reluctant to agree to a total prohibition of nuclear explosions because they hoped to use such devices for engineering purposes such as canal excavation. He said that he felt an agreement could be negotiated to allow such civilian blasts, as in the case of a river in northern Russia, "and let us have some observers there to learn from them and vice versa."

The Soviet plan for a nuclear canal excavation is designed to divert water from the Pechora River in northern Russia southward to the Volga Basin, which is approaching a shortage of water.

Mr. Carter reiterated his determination to "speak out strongly and forcefully" when human rights are threatened, although not necessarily in every instance. Such action, he said, can "legitimately be severed" from diplomatic maneuvers in such fields as arms reduction.

* * *

February 19, 1977

U.S. STOUTLY DEFENDS LETTER THAT CARTER WROTE TO SAKHAROV

RESPONDS TO SOVIET WARNING

Administration Explains Position After 'Displeasure' Is Voiced on Comments About Dissidents

By GRAHAM HOVEY
Special to The New York Times.

WASHINGTON, Feb. 18—The Administration stoutly defended President Carter's letter to Andrei D. Sakharov today in the face of Soviet warnings that official American expressions of sympathy and support for Russian dissidents could damage relations between Moscow and Washington.

Anatoly F. Dobrynin, the Soviet Ambassador in Washington, called on Acting Secretary of State Arthur A. Hartman yesterday afternoon to deliver what a State Department spokesman called an expression of the Soviet Government's "displeasure" at the Administration's statements' on human rights in the Soviet Union.

The Soviet news agency Tass, which first announced Mr. Dobrynin's visit, said the Ambassador had informed Mr. Hartman that the Soviet Union "resolutely rejects attempts to interfere under a thought-up pretext of defending human rights, in its internal affairs." Such actions, Tass said, would complicate relations and make the solution of problems more difficult.

Dobrynin Asks Appointment

Ambassador Dobrynin telephoned to ask for an appointment with Mr. Hartman just hours after President Carter's letter, dated Feb. 5, was delivered by the United States Embassy in Moscow to Dr. Sakharov, the Soviet physicist and dissident leader.

"We shall use our good offices to seek the release of prisoners of conscience," Mr. Carter wrote. "And we will continue our efforts to shape a world responsive to human aspirations in which nations of differing cultures and histories can live side by side in peace and justice."

Mr. Dobrynin did not mention the President's letter, according to a State Department spokesman, Frederick Z. Brown. Mr. Brown added that the Soviet Ambassador did not characterize his verbal presentation to Mr. Hartman as a "protest."

The White House press secretary, Jody Powell, said today that the President, in sending his letter, "was not attempting to challenge the Government of the Soviet Union."

"The President was responding to a letter from a Nobel Prize winner," Mr. Powell said. Both Mr. Powell and Mr. Brown denied that the Carter letter and earlier Administration expressions of concern about human rights in the Soviet Union constituted interference in that country's internal affairs.

Mr. Powell said the Soviet Union had often commented on "domestic differences" in this country. He mentioned support voiced by the Communist Party newspaper Pravda for Angela

Davis, the American Communist, during her trial and the fact that Leonid I. Brezhnev, the Soviet party chief, had received Gus Hall, the American Communist leader, during Mr. Hall's visit to Moscow.

"I want to emphasize that it is our belief," Mr. Powell said, "that it is possible to work with any government to reduce the chances of war and nuclear holocausts, and to promote other common interests without sacrificing the commitment of our people and this country to the struggle for individual freedom."

In a State Department briefing, Mr. Brown emphasized the Administration's view that its expressions of concern for human rights should not impede progress on other issues of major concern to the American and Soviet governments. "We believe other aspects of our relations with the Soviet Union should go forward on their merits," he said.

In its commentary on Mr. Dobrynin's call on Mr. Hartman, however, Tass warned that to inject the human-rights issue in Soviet-American relations would make it more difficult to solve problems "that really can be and must be the subjects of interaction and cooperation between the two countries."

The warning was reminiscent of the "linkage" theory of Soviet-American relations of former Secretary of State Henry A. Kissinger: That it was necessary to make progress—or exercise restraint—in one area in order to move ahead on other fronts.

* * *

March 5, 1977

VANCE SAYS MOSCOW STILL SEEKS DÉTENTE

He Is Hopeful for New Arms Pact and Direct Talks With Cuba

By BERNARD GWERTZMAN
Special to The New York Times.

WASHINGTON, March 4—Secretary of State Cyrus R. Vance said today that Soviet leaders had shown "a continuing deep and abiding interest" in concluding further arms control and other agreements with the United States despite the strains that had arisen recently over human rights issues.

"I think that détente does exist today," Mr. Vance said at a news conference at the State Department. "And I believe and hope that it will continue to exist."

[In Moscow, the Government newspaper Izvestia accused several leading Jewish dissidents of working for the United States Central Intelligence Agency. In Sofia, Bulgaria, Soviet and other Communist Party representatives ended a two-day meeting with a call for a "decisive" battle against the human rights movement in Eastern Europe.]

Mr. Vance said that during his visit to Moscow later this month he looked forward to "fruitful negotiations" with the Soviet leaders on a new strategic arms limitation accord and other matters.

Seeks Definition of Détente

He said that during the visit he also hoped to begin discussions of "a clearer understanding of what the meaning of détente is as between the two nations."

"In a sense," he said, "it is a setting down, or arriving at, a set of ground rules which permit competition side by side with resolution of outstanding questions and it is not a simple task."

The Secretary also made the following points on other subjects:

- On Cuba, he said that the United States still hoped to begin direct discussions with Cuban officials leading toward normalization of relations. He said that the United States had informed Cuba of its desire for prompt discussions on fisheries questions and that he expected talks to begin soon.
- On China, he said a check by himself and others of former President Richard M. Nixon's papers had shown no sign of any secret agreement or understanding with Peking on when relations would be normalized.
- On Uganda, Mr. Vance said that he was unable on the basis of his intelligence reports to "nail down" that any Cuban troops were there, despite press reports. He also said that he did not see any weakening in the Administration's resolve on human rights in thanking President Idi Amin for his assurances that Americans in Uganda would not be harmed after earlier criticisms of him for the "horrible murders" in his country.
- On the Middle East, he said that the Administration was now reviewing the positions put to him by Israeli and Arab leaders during his recent trip and that it would present some ideas on how to narrow their differences during a series of meetings with Middle East leaders. He refused to give details.
- On southern Africa, he confirmed that the United States and British officials had agreed on a new initiative for getting Rhodesian negotiations restarted, but said he could not provide any information until it had been cleared at the highest British levels.

Soviet-American relations and human rights have been the subjects that have dominated the Administration's foreign policy and were again the key issues reporters asked about today.

Mr. Vance, in keeping with past statements, affirmed that human rights "is one of the fundamental values that is our heritage and it will be threaded through our foreign policy."

Détente, which is the French word for relaxation of tensions, was a hallmark of Soviet-American relations from 1972 to 1975. But last year, former President Gerald R. Ford, under attack during the presidential primaries from Ronald Reagan, ordered that it no longer be used since it seemed to imply that to be for détente was tantamount to appeasement.

Mr. Vance has had no hesitation about using the word, but he has also been seeking a formula to describe the Administration's policy toward the Russians.

He has seemed uneasy with the attention given the Administration's criticism of the Soviet Union over human rights, although he has endorsed the policy of speaking out.

In his news conference, he seemed to be trying to signal that he wanted the emphasis in relations to be on more substantive issues.

On Cuba, Mr. Vance stressed that the United States favored direct discussions without prior conditions.

He said that when Mr. Carter spoke at the Agriculture Department recently and stated certain moves that the Cubans should take, such as release of political prisoners, removal of troops from Angola and an end to the export of revolution, they might have been interpreted as preconditions for talks.

The President's comments, he said, produced "some misunderstanding," but he said Mr. Carter shared his desire for holding direct talks without preconditions.

* * *

March 18, 1977

CARTER URGES U.N. TO STEP UP EFFORTS FOR HUMAN RIGHTS

SAYS MACHINERY IS IGNORED

Suggests That Commission Meet More Often and Move From Geneva to New York

---

By BERNARD GWERTZMAN
Special to The New York Times.

UNITED NATIONS, N. Y., March 17—President Carter brought his campaign for human rights to the United Nations tonight, asserting that the world body had allowed "its human rights machinery to be ignored and sometimes politicized."

"There is much that can be done to strengthen it," the President said. He suggested that the United Nations Commission on Human Rights meet more often and that it transfer its activities from Geneva to New York "where its activities will be in the forefront of our attention."

These statements came in a wide-ranging speech to United Nations members in the General Assembly Hall, a speech that was intended to underscore the Administration's support for the organization. In it Mr. Carter also made a fresh appeal to the Soviet Union to join in greater efforts "to contain the global arms race."

Cites Georgian Background

Discussing the pressing economic issues involving both the developed and undeveloped countries, he said that since he, a Georgian, came from a poor region of the United States, he sympathized with the leaders of the developing countries and would do what he could to "bring greater prosperity" to the people of all lands.

Dozens of foreign delegates interviewed after Mr. Carter's speech said that they were favorably impressed by his remarks, particularly his stress on human rights.

After the speech, Mr. Carter attended a reception given by Secretary General Kurt Waldheim and shook the hand of the deputy observer of the Palestine Liberation Organization, but the President said nothing to him. Later, Mr. Carter reiterated that there would be no follow-up American contact until the P.L.O. changed the provisions in its charter calling for Israel's destruction.

Four Hours in City

Mr. Carter spoke during a four-hour stopover in New York that capped a day and a half journey from Washington. It took him to Clinton, Mass., for a town meeting last night, and to Charlestown, W.Va., for a seminar on energy earlier today. He suggested at the seminar that the fuel-conservation measures that he planned to offer Congress next month might be strict and painful enough to damage him politically.

The President, on his first visit to New York since his inauguration, flew to Kennedy International Airport from Charleston and then went by helicopter to Wall Street, where he was greeted by Governor Carey and Mayor Beame. He proceeded by motorcade to the United States Mission to the United Nations, where he had a light dinner with the American delegate, Andrew Young, and Secretary of State Cyrus R. Vance.

At about 7 P.M. he drove by limousine from the mission across First Avenue to the General Assembly building, where he told the delegates at an unofficial meeting—the Assembly is not in session—that "I have come here to express my own support, and the continuing support of my country, for the ideals of the United Nations."

Mr. Carter delivered his half-hour televised speech, reading from a teleprompter, in a relaxed voice, often gesturing to make a point. He was applauded four times during the address, his first formal speech on foreign affairs as President.

The speech itself did not contain any major surprises and Mr. Carter's aides said that it was intended as "an agenda" of the problems facing the world and the United States this year and his ideas about them.

"We can only improve this world if we are realistic about its complexities," Mr. Carter said. "The disagreements we face are deeply rooted, and they often raise difficult philosophical as well as territorial issues."

"They will not be solved easily; they will not be solved quickly," he continued.

"The arms race is now imbedded in the fabric of international affairs and can only be contained with the greatest difficulty. Poverty, inequality are of such monumental scope that it will take decades of deliberate and determined effort even to improve the situation substantially."

Discussing human rights, one of the most controversial aspects of his foreign policy, Mr. Carter called for more frequent sessions of the Human Rights Commission, which currently meets only once a year and has just completed its latest session. Moreover, he said, he would like to see the entire Human Rights Division returned to New York from Geneva, where it moved in 1974 at Arab and Soviet-bloc insistence.

If it was moved to New York, Mr. Carter said, its activities would be scrutinized more closely by the world press.

He also supported a 12-year-old proposal for a United Nations high commissioner for human rights.

As to criticism that the United States was interfering in the internal affairs of other countries by speaking out on human rights. Mr. Carter said that all signers of the United Nations Charter had pledged to support human rights.

"Thus, no member of the United Nations can claim that mistreatment of its citizens is solely its own business," the President said. "Equally, no member can avoid its responsibilities to review and to speak when torture or unwarranted deprivation of freedom occurs in any part of the world."

Mr. Carter promised that the United States would seek "to deal with our deficiencies quickly and openly" in the human rights field. He said that he would ask Senate approval of United Nations covenants in the field and would urge the Senate to ratify the Convention Against Genocide, which was signed by the United States more than 25 years ago but never approved by the Senate, despite several attempts.

Signals to the Russians

But despite his stress on human rights, Mr. Carter made it clear that the United States would not try to link it to other security or economic issues that had even higher priority, such as limitation of strategic arms. Human rights, he said, "should not block progress on other important matters affecting the security and well-being of our people and of world peace."

"It is obvious that the reduction of tension, the control of nuclear arms, the achievement of harmony in troubled areas of the world and the provision of food, good health and education will independently contribute to advancing the human condition," he said.

With Secretary of State Vance to leave for Moscow a week from tomorrow, Mr. Carter clearly wanted to send additional signals to the Russians about his sincerity in seeking further arms-control agreements. Mr. Carter has often spoken of his interest in ending the deadlocked talks on limitation of strategic nuclear arms.

A five-year interim agreement reached in 1972 to limit some offensive weapons expires this October, and Mr. Carter has stressed the need to reach a new accord, based on a framework agreement achieved in Vladivostok in November 1974 but not yet carried out.

In Vladivostok, Leonid I. Brezhnev, the Soviet leader, and President Gerald F. Ford agreed to set each side's ceiling of missile launchers and heavy bombers at 2,400. Of that total, each side could have 1,320 missile launchers with multiple warheads.

Impasse on Cruise and Backfire

But disagreements have brought the talks to an impasse over Soviet insistence and American refusal on including American sea-launched cruise missiles of more than 360-mile range, and American insistence and Soviet refusal on including the Soviet bombers known as Backfire in the total of 2,400.

The Ford Administration suggested putting the cruise missile and Backfire issues aside and signing an accord on other matters. Mr. Carter has since endorsed that approach, but the Russians have continued to reject it. Tonight Mr. Carter made another appeal on the issue.

He said that he would prefer strict controls and even a freeze on new types of weapons, with "a deep reduction" in the strategic arms of both sides. Such a move would be "a major step" toward arms limitations, he said.

He added that "perhaps more easily" the two sides could conclude "a more limited agreement based on those elements of the Vladivostok accord on which we can find complete consensus and set aside for prompt consideration and subsequent negotiations the more contentious issues and also the deeper reductions in nuclear weapons which I favor."

This was an effort to get the Russians to agree on the American formula with a promise of a quick follow-up negotiation.

Mr. Carter also asked again for a Soviet-American ban on all underground nuclear explosions without waiting—as Moscow insists—for the Chinese and others to agree to join in the accord. He also said that Mr. Vance would seek Soviet willingness to agree on "mutual military restraint" in the Indian Ocean and in arms exports to troubled areas of the world.

On other areas, such as Southern Africa, the Middle East and China, Mr. Carter spoke mostly in general terms.

Regarding southern Africa, he said that "fundamental transformation" to black majority rule could be achieved, and he noted with satisfaction Congress's repeal of the Byrd amendment, bringing the United States into compliance with the economic sanctions "against the illegal regime in Rhodesia."

He said he would sign the bill tomorrow, and this brought him his first round of applause.

Nothing Specific, Aides Say

He was much less specific on the Middle East than he was last night in Clinton, Mass., when he surprised Israelis by speaking of the need for "a homeland" to be provided "for the Palestinian refugees who have suffered for many, many years."

Some Israelis regarded this as a sign of sympathy for the idea of a Palestinian state, but Carter aides insisted that he had nothing so specific in mind and was merely referring to the need to solve the Palestinian question.

In Clinton, Mr. Carter seemed to suggest that the Palestinian issue was now up to the Arab countries to solve, perhaps meaning a link to Jordan, an idea favored by Israel.

Tonight aboard Air Force One, flying from Charleston to New York, Mr. Carter defended his use of the word "homeland," asserting that "I think what I said is appropriate."

"I think some provision has got to be made for the Palestinians in the framework of the nation of Jordan or by some other means," reporters on the plane quoted him as having said.

Mr. Carter's visit here already had ruffled some Israelis, because after first inviting only member nations to a reception in the President's honor, Secretary General Waldheim then received permission from the State Department to invite permanent observers, including the Palestinian Liberation Organization.

On the plane Mr. Carter said, "I didn't even know about it, as a matter of fact." He said that Mr. Vance, when pressed by Mr. Waldheim to invite observers, decided "to go ahead."

"I didn't know about it, but I don't object," he said.

On the issues between developed and underdeveloped countries, Mr. Carter said that the United States would consider with a "positive and open attitude" the negotiations of agreements to stabilize commodity prices, including common arrangements for financing buffer stocks where they are a part of individual negotiated agreements.

* * *

March 23, 1977

CARTER ENCOURAGED BY SOVIET ON ARMS; ADAMANT ON RIGHTS

INSISTS 2 ISSUES ARE SEPARATE

As Vance Prepares to Go to Moscow, President Bids Congress Step Up Broadcasts to Eastern Bloc

By BERNARD GWERTZMAN
Special to The New York Times.

WASHINGTON, March 22—President Carter told members of Congress today that he was not discouraged by Leonid I. Brezhnev's warning that criticism of human rights conditions in the Soviet Union could jeopardize relations between the two countries.

The President said he would not back down on his concern for human rights anywhere and, in a letter to Congress, he asked for funds to build additional transmitters for United States-sponsored radio broadcasts beamed into the Soviet Union and Eastern Europe.

Speaking with a Congressional group at a breakfast meeting, Mr. Carter chided those who had expressed concern over the effect that American actions in the rights field might have on arms control and other matters.

"Some people are concerned every time Brezhnev sneezes," the President gibed, according to Senator Alan Cranston, Democrat of California.

Brezhnev Notes Encourage Carter

According to Mr. Cranston, the President said he had found some "very, very hopeful signs" in Mr. Brezhnev's speech. Mr. Carter said he had also received encouraging private communications from the Soviet leader. The President was particularly pleased by Mr. Brezhnev's emphasis on the need for arms accords and a Middle East settlement.

Meanwhile, plans were being completed for Secretary of State Cyrus R. Vance's trip to Moscow this weekend. The President, Mr. Vance and other members of the National Security Council conferred on the position to be taken in Moscow in negotiations for a new treaty limiting strategic arms. This is the major topic, but not the only one, to be discussed during the three days of talks.

To Use American Interpreter

As part of his preparations, Mr. Vance has decided to break with a practice of relying on Soviet interpreters in sensitive negotiations. In recent years the interpreting at a high level has been done by Viktor M. Sukhodrev, the leading Soviet English-language interpreter, who first became known in the United States during Nikita S. Khrushchev's visit in 1959.

Some officials have considered it risky not to have a Russian-speaking American on hand, and Mr. Vance has decided to take along his own interpreter, William D. Krimer of the State Department. Mr Vance thus hopes to forestall a complaint lodged in the past against Secretary of State Henry A. Kissinger, that he was negotiating in secret by meeting privately with Mr. Brezhnev and the Soviet interpreter.

Yesterday's speech by Mr. Brezhnev saying that normal relations were "unthinkable" if the United States supported Soviet dissidents, received close consideration here.

Mr. Carter, who told the Congressional visitors that his remarks on human rights were not against the Soviet Union as such, went out of his way to stress those aspects of the speech that left open the possibility of progress in arms control and other matters. Jody Powell, the White House spokesman, said the speech reflected two aspects of concern to the Russians as the Vance visit approached.

"The first part stated quite forcefully their position on the debate about human rights," he said. "The differences between the United States and Soviet Union are well known, have been well publicized and existed for some time and are likely to continue to exist in the future. The second part dealt more directly with specific matters that will be under discussion."

Vance Due In Moscow Saturday

Mr. Vance is scheduled to leave Washington on Friday evening, stopping in Brussels in the morning and arriving in Moscow late on Saturday. Formal talks are due to begin on Monday.

"We saw absolutely no reason to change our own views that serious and constructive negotiations are indeed possible and in that spirit we continue to prepare actively for Secretary Vance's visit to Moscow," Mr. Powell said.

He added that the Administration had noted with interest and, indeed, with approval the statement by Mr. Brezhnev that the Soviet Union had its own negative ideas about conditions in the Western world and that it made no secret of that opinion.

"We agree with that statement," Mr. Powell said. "We do not fear open debate on the principles that guide our respective societies before the court of world opinion.

"But we frankly state that, for our own part, we will not allow this open and healthy debate to stand in the way of our strong and publicly expressed desire to negotiate seriously and in good faith to reduce the burdens of the arms race on the American and Soviet people and to reduce the threat of nuclear destruction."

Referring to Mr. Carter's recent speech on human rights at the United Nations, Mr. Powell said:

"I believe the President has made it quite clear—and he has certainly not changed—that he believes this issue to be important enough to stand alone without relation to other matters."

Mr. Vance is taking with him one of the largest American delegations in recent years. It includes:

Paul Warnke, director of the Arms Control and Disarmament Agency and arms negotiator; Philip C. Habib, Under Secretary of State for Political Affairs; Richard M. Moose, Deputy Under Secretary for Management; Arthur A. Hartman, Assistant Secretary for Public Affairs.

Also Anthony Lake, director of the Policy Planning Staff; Leslie H. Gelb, director of the Bureau of Politico-Military Affairs; William G. Hyland of the National Security Council staff; Lieut Gen. Edward L. Rowny, special representative of the Joint Chiefs of Staff; Marshall D. Shulman, consultant to Mr. Vance; Walter D. Slocombe, Deputy Assistant Secretary of Defense for International Security Affairs; Mark J. Garrison, Soviet desk officer at the State Department; and Ralph Earle 2d of the arms control agency.

* * *

May 21, 1977

U.S. AND SOVIET AGREE ON A FORMULA TO END ARMS PACT IMPASSE

Vance and Gromyko Finish 3 Days of Talks—Need for Further Negotiations Is Stressed

By BERNARD GWERTZMAN
Special to The New York Times.

GENEVA, May 20—Secretary of State Cyrus R. Vance and Foreign Minister Andrei A. Gromyko concluded three days of talks with an agreement on a formula for ending the impasse in the negotiations to limit strategic arms, United States officials said tonight.

The officials stressed, however, that further negotiations would be needed to complete agreement on the text of the new treaty limiting each side's offensive nuclear-armed missile launchers and long-range bombers.

The so-called "framework agreement," as described privately by American officials, was said to be a compromise based on previous American and Soviet proposals, opening the way to signing a new treaty before the October expiration date of the five-year interim accord.

Vance Schedules Briefing

There was no briefing for reporters tonight after the last Vance-Gromyko meeting, and both sides agreed to issue a formal communiqué tomorrow morning. Mr. Vance had also scheduled a press conference tomorrow, before his departure for Washington, to discuss the results of his discussions.

Reporters had expected some definitive word on the results of the Vance-Gromyko talks tonight after the two men conferred for an hour and 40 minutes at the Soviet mission. But instead, when Mr. Vance returned to the Hotel Inter-Continental, he told waiting reporters that he had concluded the talks and added that they "have been very useful as far as we're concerned and I believe that view is shared by the Soviets as well."

Lacking the details of the compromise, reporters were unable to tell what had happened in the weeks since Mr. Vance's mission to Moscow in March failed to produce progress toward resolving the impasse.

The breakdown of those Moscow talks produced a major strain in relations, and all signs now seem to point to a more relaxed atmosphere.

The first sign that the talks were making progress came yesterday when some American officials privately began telling reporters that a framework agreement was now likely. Before arriving here many officials had warned reporters not to expect any major achievement in these discussions.

It now seems apparent that the two sides, after three days of talks that were described officially by the Americans as "businesslike, good-faith, intensive, and worthwhile," had reached agreement on two aspects of the strategic arms picture.

They apparently have decided how to proceed in overcoming the remaining obstacles to putting into treaty form the 1974 Vladivostok agreement that set ceilings of 2,400 on each side's missile and bomber force.

The formula for this was not divulged tonight, although officials privately acknowledged that the two sides were in agreement. It is presumed that the formula will include some understanding on two weapons systems that had prevented progress in the last two years—the American cruise missile and the Soviet bomber known in the West as the Backfire.

* * *

May 27, 1977

CARTER DEFENDS PLAN TO REDUCE FORCES IN KOREA

By BERNARD WEINRAUB
Special to The New York Times.

WASHINGTON, May 26—President Carter, emphasizing the "staunch" commitment of the United States to South Korea, defended the Administration's plan to withdraw American ground troops there and expressed confidence today that it was strong enough to repel attack.

President Carter also said at his news conference that Maj. Gen. John K. Singlaub's criticism of plans to withdraw the 32,000 ground troops from Korea over the next four or five years was "a very serious breach" of his responsibility.

"I think to some degree it was an invitation to the North Koreans to believe that South Korea was not able to take care of themselves, which we think they are," said President

Carter. "I think it was an invitation to the world to expect an inevitable war, and I certainly don't agree."

General Singlaub was removed from his job as chief of staff of United States forces in Korea after publication of a newspaper article that quoted him as saying that the troop withdrawals would lead North Korea to attack. General Singlaub, who was ordered home by the President, left Washington this morning for Korea to pack his belongings and await a new assignment.

President Carter, who spoke at some length today about General Singlaub and Korea, said in reply to a question:

"General Singlaub was not fired. He was not being chastised or punished. He was being transferred to a new position at an equivalent degree of responsibility and stature."

Later in the news conference, Mr. Carter said that General Singlaub, the third-ranking United States Army officer in Korea, had been briefed on the plans to withdraw American troops from Korea.

By saying that the pullout would result in war, General Singlaub committed "a very serious breach of propriety that ought to exist among military officers after a policy has been made," President Carter said.

"I don't believe that General Singlaub could have effectively carried out this policy when he had been publicly identified as being opposed to it," the President added.

President Carter's comments came with the first substantial signs of Congressional unrest, especially among conservatives, over the troop withdrawal plans.

What apparently disturbed some Congressmen were the remarks of General Singlaub before a House subcommittee yesterday that most American military and civilian officials in Korea opposed the withdrawal, and that the United States military command had not yet received a clear explanation on the reasons for it.

Today, Senator Barry Goldwater, the Arizona Republican, said in a statement on the Senate floor that he was "disturbed" at the treatment accorded General Singlaub and was puzzled at the Administration's policy in Korea.

"I can't find a policy declaration," he said. "It has not been presented to the Senate Armed Services Committee, of which I am a member, and so far as I know it has not been presented to the committee on foreign affairs."

President Carter, who promised to withdraw American ground troops from Korea during the election campaign, made it plain at his news conference that the United States would maintain "adequate" numbers of Americans, including air and naval forces and intelligence personnel, in Korea.

"The essence of the question is: Is our country committed on a permanent basis to keep troops in South Korea, even if they are not needed, to maintain the stability of that peninsula," Mr. Carter said.

"I think it's accurate to say that the time has come for a very careful, very orderly withdrawal over the period of four or five years of ground troops, leaving intact an adequate degree of strength in the Republic of Korea to withstand any foreseeable attack and making it clear to the North Koreans, the Chinese, the Soviets, that our commitment to South Korea is undeviating and is staunch."

Mr. Carter said that South Korea's economy was buoyant. "They have massive, very healthy industry—in steel, shipbuilding, electronics, chemical industries—to make it possible for them to go into a position of defending themselves," he said.

"We have a complete confidence in the deep purpose of the South Koreans to defend their own country."

* * *

July 2, 1977

SOVIET SEEMS UNSURE ABOUT CARTER MOVES

Ignores Opposition to B-1 While Criticizing Cruise Missile

By CHRISTOPHER S. WREN
Special to The New York Times.

MOSCOW, July 1—When President Carter conceded recently that he had not anticipated the extent of Moscow's unhappiness with his human rights policy, he identified only part of a problem souring Soviet-American relations. More than five months after he took office, the signs are that the Russians still do not comprehend the President and their uncertainty has congealed into a sullen truculence that has increasingly left less room for accommodation.

Hopes that a personal encounter with the Soviet leader, Leonid I. Brezhnev, might help clear the air apparently prompted Mr. Carter yesterday to express his interest in such a meeting. Earlier, the Soviet press agency, Tass, replying to a previous White House statement, said that the proposal was an American idea and strictly preliminary.

Gesture on B-1 Ignored

Tass left it unclear whether the Soviet Union opposed a summit or just did not want to give the appearance of being rushed into one. Mr. Brezhnev has been reportedly anxious to take the measure of Mr. Carter, the third American President he has confronted in less than three years. Yet some factors that argue for the meeting also seem to be giving the Kremlin pause.

Even when Mr. Carter announced yesterday that he was opposed to the production of the controversial B-1 bomber, the Kremlin passed over the gesture. Instead, it focused upon his decision to deploy the cruise missile, a new weapons system that worries the Russians. Today, Tass asserted that "the implementation of these militaristic plans seriously complicated efforts for the limitation of the strategic arms race."

Thus far, Moscow has been unwilling to risk summit talks with the new Administration unless agreement had been reached or was near on a new strategic arms limitation agreement, something that would convey the impression of fresh momentum in détente. If the two leaders clash on differences over an unresolved arms pact or human rights, an unsatisfactory encounter in Moscow's view could prove worse than none at all.

The chill Soviet response to the idea of a summit meeting reflects the disparity in the perception of the malaise in Soviet-American relations. While Washington has tried to see the half-full glass, Moscow has persisted in viewing it as half-empty. After Secretary of State Cyrus R. Vance and Foreign Minister Andrei A. Gromyko ended their negotiations in Geneva in May, Mr. Vance worked hard to be optimistic about progress toward a new strategic arms agreement. But Mr. Gromyko was considerably more dour, contending that Washington's obstinacy had left a new accord "still a long way off."

Moscow's criticism of Mr. Carter seems largely self-serving. It amounts to a complaint that he has not been forthright enough on curbing the weapons spiral and has been too forthright in discussing human rights. But the President also seemed to catch the Kremlin off balance by moving too fast during his first days in office. One Soviet observer likened him to a revolutionary consolidating power, a style, he said, more appropriate to Nikita S. Khrushchev.

Russians Had Been Optimistic

Ironically, it was the Russians who were reflecting optimism before Mr. Carter took over. A Soviet official, summing up the prevailing mood, has noted that when Mr. Carter was still an enigma, it was reassuring that so many of his appointees, like Mr. Vance, were already familiar faces in Moscow.

Consequently, Moscow was unprepared to find the Carter Administration assailing its performance on human rights within days after taking office. The timing of the criticism was particularly sensitive in view of the coming Belgrade conference that would review compliance with the 1975 Helsinki accords. The Russians had already begun cracking down on organized dissent and viewed Mr. Carter's pronouncements as interference in their internal affairs or, more precisely, in its tidy-up of dissidents in advance of not only the Belgrade conference but also the 60th anniversary of the Bolshevik Revolution in November.

Some Western diplomats wonder whether the Kremlin, with total power over a nation that has never really known democratic freedoms, was in fact capable of believing that Mr. Carter's human rights stance might be based on more than some insidious political expediency. The President's contention that he had not singled out the Soviet Union for criticism did not seem to satisfy Moscow, which claimed to see each accusation from the West as part of a "noisy malicious campaign" masterminded by the Central Intelligence Agency.

Counting on an Arms Agreement

Already on the defensive about its treatment of dissidents, the Kremlin was jolted anew by another confrontation, this time over arms limitation. It had been counting on the Carter Administration to complete the tentative accord reached by Mr. Brezhnev and President Ford in late 1974 at Vladivostok.

When Mr. Vance visited Moscow in late March he brought what the Russians viewed as two other, unacceptable proposals. One called for concluding the Vladivostok agreement but deferring two new weapons systems, the American cruise missile and the new Soviet bomber known as Backfire in the West, for later negotiation. The second envisioned slashing by up to 25 percent the ceiling of 2,400 strategic bombers and missiles on each side and imposing other constraints.

The Soviet Union responded that the new Administration was trying to scrap the Vladivostok understanding, which Mr. Brezhnev had presumably worked out beforehand with his own military establishment. Because Moscow had called for inclusion of the cruise missile, it seemed to regard Mr. Carter's decision yesterday to go ahead with deployment as a further blow that would touch off fresh weapons competition and force a reassessment of Soviet nuclear strategy.

Last month, the party newspaper, Pravda, charged that the Carter Administration was using human rights as a pretext for justifying "a new dangerous spiral of the arms race." The fear that the President is bent upon outflanking and humiliating the Soviet leadership has been bolstered by other actions like his increased support of Radio Free Europe and Radio Liberty, which Moscow spends time and money jamming, and his pledge to "aggressively challenge" the Soviet Union in some regions where it enjoys influence.

Carter Seen as Unreasonable

The conclusion, sometimes privately expressed here, that Mr. Carter is unreasonable and therefore dangerous seems rooted partly in Moscow's concern that it cannot forecast what he will do. One Soviet intellectual observed that ex-President Richard M. Nixon projected a clearly defined policy, whatever its flaws. Mr. Brezhnev has valued stability above all in dealing with Western leaders and Mr. Carter has been far less predictable than Mr. Nixon or even Mr. Ford.

Mr. Carter's assertion yesterday that he did not believe relations were deteriorating seems at variance with a more strident tone in the Soviet press, which has periodically taken the President to task by name.

"The more the rabid anti-Soviet ballyhoo on human rights in the U.S.S.R. is whipped up, the more is the gold reserve of détente reduced in which all peoples, including the people of the United States, are vitally interested," Tass declared the other day.

Some Western diplomats feel that the impasse over arms control and new run-ins over human rights may send Soviet-American relations dipping further this year. A few have speculated that unrelated factors might have exacerbated the Kremlin's displeasure with the new administration.

Israel and China Are Complications

For instance, one senior diplomat observed, the conservative swing in Israel's election could delay the Middle East peace conference that Mr. Vance and Mr. Gromyko are seeking to convene at Geneva this fall and thus undermine an opportunity for potential cooperation.

Moscow's other foreign policy problems may have contributed to its petulance with Mr. Carter. Hopes for even cosmetic reconciliation with China have been dashed by a hostile new leadership in Peking. Soviet fortunes in the Middle East remain near rock bottom. In the Horn of Africa the Russians face a potential backlash in trying to accommodate two hostile neighbors, Ethiopia and Somalia.

Relations with other Western countries, such as Norway and Japan, are visibly cool. The independence of some Western European Communist Parties has given the Kremlin an increasing ideological headache. And Moscow is on the defensive at the preparatory session of the East-West conference at Belgrade, making it harder to give any ground to Mr. Carter on human rights.

More obscure are developments inside the Kremlin itself that might shed further light on the mood toward Mr. Carter. The refusal to respond to Mr. Vance's arms control options in March with any counterproposals suggested in some diplomatic quarters here that the present aging, cautious leadership was unable to respond quickly with any fresh ideas of its own.

Brezhnev Also an Unknown

The unknowns extend to Mr. Brezhnev himself. One ranking diplomat, taking note of reports about the Soviet leader's unhealthy appearance during last month's visit to France, wondered whether the Kremlin might be stalling on a meeting with Mr. Carter simply because Mr. Brezhnev was not physically up to it yet.

The technical arms control discussions that are continuing in Geneva and recent talks here on demilitarizing the Indian Ocean suggest that Moscow is as interested as Washington in maintaining some semblance of détente. Mr. Brezhnev himself seems genuinely anxious to reduce tensions with the United States and curb the arms race, although on terms acceptable to Moscow.

The Soviet position seems to contain an implicit assumption that if Moscow holds tight, the Carter Administration will have to make concessions sooner or later, whether on strategic arms or human rights. Tass reported not long ago that Americans increasingly "did not approve of the way President Carter handles practical affairs with the Soviet Union."

If the intractability extends to both sides, it may take more than a brief summit meeting to sort out the misconceptions.

* * *

July 8, 1977

U.S. AND SOVIET: TIME OF TESTING

Crucial Period Seen Ahead Amid Strains

By BERNARD GWERTZMAN
Special to The New York Times.

WASHINGTON, July 7—The Carter Administration, which concedes that it did not expect the sharp reaction its policies evoked in the Soviet Union, believes that it is entering a crucial period that will test the United States' contention that, despite continuing problems, the two superpowers can still make progress in a number of key areas.

An effort is under way to see where relations can be improved without doing violence to President Carter's human rights concerns or his desire for progress toward disarmament. As part of this, a speech by Secretary of State Cyrus R. Vance on East-West relations is being contemplated.

Mr. Carter, who told editors recently that Soviet criticism of his human rights policies had proven "a greater obstacle" to better relations than he had expected, nevertheless denied last week that overall relations had deteriorated.

But other officials interviewed in recent days acknowledge freely that the United States handled its relations with the Russians with a lack of finesse in the first months of the Carter Administration.

They said the Soviet Union was clearly angry over Washington's stress on human rights, which the Russians see as psychological warfare, and Mr. Carter's arms policies, which the Russians regard as aimed at gaining strategic advantage for the United States.

The State Department has been receiving many reports of Soviet discontent. Leonid I. Brezhnev put it directly to Ambassador Malcolm Toon on Tuesday; Soviet diplomats have emphasized it in talks with the French, West Germans and other American allies; and the Soviet press has been taking Mr. Carter to task for his policies.

One official said the atmosphere has been charged by what he called "a ticker war" in which actions and reactions resounded over news agency wires with Tass, the Soviet agency, quick to respond to Western statements.

The Soviet apprehensions have been mirrored to a certain extent in the United States. American officials seem perplexed about the refusal of the Russians to accept Mr. Carter's explanations and his efforts to calm the situation.

Shulman Has Meeting With President

Mr. Carter, who began his term with an exchange of cordial messages with Mr. Brezhnev, has been surprised by the turn of events although he continues to say that the situation is not as bad as it may seem. He believes that the Russians should be more willing to deal with him than with his predecessors in view of his desire to reduce arms spending and his refusal to see regional conflicts exclusively in East-West terms.

With a number of arms control issues coming up for negotiation, Mr. Carter is said by aides to look to Soviet cooperation rather than increased confrontation, even though his domestic support seems to have been rising with the strains in United States-Soviet relations.

In the State Department, it is felt that Soviet policy has not been enunciated in a clear enough fashion and Secretary of State Vance's planned speech is designed to do just that.

His adviser on Soviet affairs, Marshall D. Shulman, met with Mr. Carter today to present his analysis of Soviet-American relations. Mr. Shulman has advocated priority for arms control and has sought to bring about the liberalization in the Soviet Union through long-term accommodation with the West rather than through confrontation over human rights or other ideological issues.

The American effort to discern what is happening in Moscow has been complicated by uncertainty over what is happening in the Soviet leadership and by the conflicting information about Mr. Brezhnev's health.

The mood in Washington, while unhappy over the trend, has not been gloomy. Indeed, some officials believe that a more realistic era may be under way, without the euphoria and expectations of the early détente period, but also without the confrontations of the cold war.

Although many Americans are concerned about the Soviet military buildup, the official position seems to be that the United States will be able to maintain nuclear parity for the foreseeable future. This conclusion should have the effect of not aggravating relations and of helping arms control negotiations.

Indeed, both sides seem interested in maintaining the framework for relations that was established in recent years. High level communications continue. This week, for instance, Vladimir P. Kirillin, the Deputy Prime Minister who heads the State Committee for Science and Technology, has been in Washington and will sign a new scientific exchange agreement tomorrow. The talks on this level were described by a participant today as productive.

The more reliable barometer will come in the next weeks and months. The United States and the Soviet Union, together with Britain, will resume formal talks next week in Geneva for a comprehensive ban on nuclear explosions. Talks are also commencing in Geneva for an accord banning dangerous chemical weapons.

In early September, Mr. Vance and Foreign Minister Andrei A. Gromyko will resume talks somewhere in Europe on the strategic arms treaty and their discussions will continue in New York when Mr. Gromyko goes to the United Nations General Assembly. Progress in any or all of those negotiations will go a long way toward improving the atmosphere.

But officials here say they do not want to return to the Kissinger days when the two countries were in the habit of signing rhetorical statements of principles. They would prefer specific agreements that are verifiable and less likely to cause problems later.

One official said that, in the last few years, the United States and the Soviet Union have been in the habit of promising to show restraint around the world but in fact ended up arming parties in regional conflicts. It would be better, he said, if agreements could be achieved limiting the numbers of specific weapons sent to these areas.

* * *

July 10, 1977

U.S. NEUTRON BOMB CRITICIZED IN SOVIET

Tass Says Radiation Weapon Runs Counter to Human Rights Cause

By MALCOLM W. BROWNE
Special to The New York Times.

MOSCOW, July 9—A Soviet commentator today denounced a proposed American neutron bomb as inconsistent with President Carter's stand on human rights, and said that development of such a weapon could jeopardize Soviet-American talks on strategic arms limitation.

The comment, by Yuri Kornilov, was distributed by the Tass press agency. The neutron bomb, which has been tested underground, has so far been designed for tactical battlefield use rather than as a strategic warhead. It can destroy life without causing significant damage to structures. The radiation is short-lived, and the target area can be occupied within a few hours.

Mr. Kornilov said "development of this and other new types of weapons for mass annihilation can only complicate the international situation and bring about a new and extremely dangerous round of the arms race."

"It is pointed out by sober-minded analysts," he continued, that the development of these new weapons creates additional difficulties for further Soviet-American strategic arms limitation talks."

The current agreement on strategic arms limitation is due to expire Oct. 3. American diplomats describe the situation at the talks in Geneva as "complex." There has been some progress toward agreement since March, they assert, but not on substantial issues. It seems unlikely, they say, that agreement can be reached by Oct. 3, although failure to reach agreement is unlikely to have an immediate effect on the arms race.

Among the most difficult present issues is the development and production of American cruise missiles, pilotless aircraft that are guided at low altitudes precisely to their targets by terrain-recognizing computers.

In relating neutron bomb development to human rights, Mr. Kornilov said:

"It is well known what a tremendous effort is being made in Washington, to be more precise, by the new Administration in the White House, to portray America as a 'bulwark of peace,' a 'champion of the mainstays of democracy and humanism.' "

"The question naturally arises, how all this loud talk about love of peace and love of man by Washington be squared with the fact that it is the United States that is again creating and putting into production such a new weapon?

"How can one pose as a champion of human rights and at the same time brandish the neutron bomb that threatens the lives of millions of people? Washington is trying hard to do both. Its propaganda campaign about its 'love of man' is nothing more than rhetoric around a myth."

A comment today in Pravda, the party daily, discounted President Carter's decision against production of the B-1 bomber while endorsing further research and development. The Pravda commentator, Tomas Kolesnichenko, said the decision not to proceed with production would have little effect since more effective strategic weapons had already been approved.

* * *

July 27, 1977

U. S. WILL KEEP BULK OF COMBAT FORCES IN KOREA UNTIL 1982

RESPONSE TO PLEA BY SEOUL

Two-Thirds of Infantry Division to Stay Till Last Phase of Pullout—Brown Ends Talks

By BERNARD WEINRAUB
Special to The New York Times.

SEOUL, South Korea, July 26—The United States, responding to a plea by the South Korean Government, announced today that the bulk of the American combat soldiers stationed in Korea would remain here until the final year of the planned troop withdrawal.

A joint statement, issued at the conclusion of two days of talks on the pullout, said that "the headquarters and two brigades of the Second Division would remain in Korea until the final phase of the withdrawal." The troop withdrawal is scheduled to start next year when 6,000 American soldiers are to depart in the first phase of a pullout of four to five years ordered by President Carter.

The Carter Administration had announced plans to withdraw the 33,000 American ground troops in Korea, leaving behind 7,000 Air Force personnel and approximately 4,000 to 6,000 troops involved in communications, logistics and intelligence.

Park Is Reported Pleased

The key combat unit involved in the withdrawal is the Second Infantry Division—possibly the most highly trained unit in the United States Army—which is deployed on a corridor leading from the demilitarized zone toward Seoul. Elements of one brigade of the division are scheduled to depart next year, but the division's two other brigades and its headquarters—8,000 to 9,000 men—now are scheduled to remain until the last months of the pullout.

Pentagon officials said South Korea had urged that the bulk of the division remain until the end, and yesterday Secretary of Defense Harold Brown informed the South Korean President, Park Chung Hee, of the decision. An American defense official said that Mr. Park was "pleased."

"The South Koreans want to keep this deterrent to the very end," said one senior Pentagon official. "This is designed to maintain as much combat capability as possible."

Secretary Brown, leading the American delegation here at the annual security consultative meeting on Korea, strongly emphasized that, despite the withdrawal of ground troops, the United States "would respond promptly to aggression against South Korea."

Appearing at a news conference in the Ministry of Defense, Mr. Brown displayed rare public emotion when he denied a statement by an Asian journalist that it was difficult for South Korea to trust America's commitment after the collapse of Vietnam.

"That the United States observes its commitments to other countries is nowhere shown more clearly than in the case of the Vietnam War," said Mr. Brown in a trembling voice.

"It is testified to by the tens of thousands of American dead and hundreds of thousands of American wounded in that war," he said. "It is testified to by the deep, painful and not yet healed wounds on the American body politic from that war.

"So I think that as long as an American security commitment exists, no one should have any doubts about our willingness, our intention of honoring it." Mr. Brown sat beside the South Korean Defense Minister, Suh Jong Chul, as he spoke.

At the news conference today, following issuance of the seven-page joint statement, Mr. Brown hedged somewhat on a question about the deployment of tactical nuclear weapons in Korea. It is widely assumed that the United States maintains nuclear artillery shells and warheads here as well as nuclear bombs with its F-4 fighter-bomber squadrons.

Mr. Brown said, somewhat ambiguously, that South Korea "will continue to be protected by the U.S. nuclear umbrella." He added, however, that South Korea should be defended "by conventional means" and declared that "it is a mistake to depend on nuclear weapons to protect a country when non-nuclear weapons will suffice."

'Compensatory Measures' Planned

The communiqué today stressed that "Minister Suh and Secretary Brown agreed that in connection with the planned withdrawal of United States ground combat forces, compensatory measures will be implemented in advance of or in parallel with the withdrawals."

It also stated that the United States had agreed to provide "appropriate weapons on a priority basis to insure that the Republic of Korea is capable of deterring North Korean aggression."

Pending Congressional approval, the Carter Administration is planning a $2 billion program of military sales, credits and gifts to build up South Korea's defenses. The program includes $275 million a year for the next five years in military sales credits, or loans, to South Korea, as well as a "one-shot" $300 million credit and a gift of more than $500 million of military equipment to be left behind by the Second Division as it departs.

Although United States and South Korean officials had sought to draw up a "precise package" of the kinds of weapons and equipment to be left behind, some disagreements and friction evidently resulted. Mr. Brown and Mr. Suh then decided to work out a list of items that the South Koreans seek and that the United States is willing to sell or leave behind as a gift.

Disagreement About Tanks

It is known that sizable numbers of helicopters and armored personnel carriers will probably remain in Korea, but there is some disagreement about tanks. South Korea has indicated that it would like to buy some of the latest model M-60 tanks, to offset the North Koreans' sizable advantage in armor.

But the United States says it would be unwise for the South Koreans to assume the burden of another supply line for an additional weapon. United States officials told the Koreans that their M-48 tanks needed some upgrading but "are equivalent in capability and don't require a separate logistics line."

Mr. Brown and his party left Korea tonight for Tokyo and meetings with Japanese officials. The Defense Minister was accompanied by Richard L. Sneider, the United States Ambassador to South Korea, who said that the planned pullout was necessary for South Korea's self-sufficiency and self-reliance.

"Staying would have been anachronistic in terms of not only the American sense but also in terms of the Korean sense," said Mr. Sneider. "We're not pulling out of this place and we're not foolhardy and we're not about to commit hara-kiri here. It's obviously as much in our interest as it is in the Korean interest to do the job the right way and I'm convinced that we are going to do it the right way."

* * *

October 5, 1977

CARTER SAYS THE U.S. IS WILLING TO SLASH ATOMIC ARSENAL 50%

STEP WOULD DEPEND ON SOVIET

President Tells the U.N. Assembly That All Countries Should Share in Curbing the Arms Race

By KATHLEEN TELTSCH
Special to The New York Times.

UNITED NATIONS, N.Y., Oct. 4—President Carter, calling on all governments to share in curbing the arms race, told the General Assembly today that the United States was "willing now" to cut its own arsenal of nuclear weapons by as much as 50 percent if the Soviet Union would do the same.

Speaking of the present round of strategic arms talks, Mr. Carter declared that the United States and the Soviet Union were "within sight of a significant agreement" to limit offensive nuclear weapons.

Administration officials said later that the President, in suggesting a readiness to cut the United States arsenal by as much as 50 percent, was not putting forward a short-term bargaining offer. They said it was not meant to produce an immediate Soviet acceptance.

Putting U.S. on Record

Rather, they said, the President, who had previously spoken of a readiness to make deep cuts in the arsenal, was, as a matter of personal commitment, putting the United States on record before the United Nations that its objective was the reduction and eventual elimination of nuclear arms.

In Washington, meanwhile, Defense Secretary Harold Brown disclosed at a news conference that the Soviet Union had developed the "operational capability" to destroy some United States satellites in space.

The President expressed the hope that an accord on strategic arms would lead to better relations with Moscow "in other spheres of interest," saying the United States was ready to go as far as possible, consistent with its security needs, in reducing its stockpile of nuclear weapons. "On a reciprocal basis," he added, "we are willing now to reduce them by 10 percent, by 20 percent, even by 50 percent."

By emphasizing progress with the Soviet Union and the expectation of even wider agreements to come, Mr. Carter seemed to be answering critics in and out of government who had been saying that his Administration's human-rights campaign and open criticism of Soviet treatment of its dissidents was jeopardizing disarmament prospects and undermining relations with Moscow.

Domed Assembly Hall Filled

The address was generally well received by the diplomats, who filled every seat in the domed Assembly Hall and stood along the sides. He was interrupted once by a round of applause. This came when the President declared: "I hereby solemnly declare on behalf of the United States that we will not use nuclear weapons except in self-defense; that is, in circumstances of an actual nuclear or conventional attack on the United States, our territories or armed forces or such an attack on our allies."

According to Mr. Carter's advisers, this was the first formal renunciation by the United States of the right to attack with atomic arms. But they said it was a long-held position that was being enunciated now in the hope that it would induce others to follow.

However, the pledge was worded so it would not exclude the use of nuclear weapons to retaliate if, for example, an ally such as West Germany were to be attacked with even conventional arms.

"What it amounts to is a 'no-strike' pledge and that's a step in the right direction, but it is not a commitment to forgo the first use of nuclear arms even against a non-nuclear country," one disarmament specialist observed.

Disarmament was the main focus of the President's address—the second here since he assumed office in January—but he also gave weight to American efforts to promote a resumption of Middle East peace talks.

He sought to reassure Israel and its supporters in the United States that last Saturday's joint Soviet-American declaration of negotiating guidelines and its call for a new Geneva conference "to insure the legitimate rights of the Palestinian people" would not undermine Israel's interests. The commitment of the United States to Israel's security is unquestionable," he said.

The Soviet reaction to the speech was one of satisfaction. Oleg A. Troyanovsky, the chief Soviet delegate, described the speech as well-balanced and said it was gratifying that the problem of ending the arms race and preventing nuclear war was "in the forefront of the President's speech."

Mr. Carter also declared that the United States had now begun to reduce its exports of conventional weapons, but he did not mention that sales already contracted had brought the total higher in the last year. However, he promised to work with governments to limit their dependence on acquiring ever more weapons.

On southern Africa, he commended the efforts under way to bring a shift to majority rule in Rhodesia and in South-West Africa, and called for "outside nations" to exercise restraint in their actions regarding both situations.

In doing so, the President referred to Rhodesia only as Zimbabwe, the name used by the nationalists. He also spoke of South-West Africa, a territory controlled by South Africa, as Namibia, the name used by nationalists and by which it is known here.

On the issue of nuclear control, the United States and the Soviet Union have been indicating for at least a week that there has been a narrowing of differences as a result of the meetings in Washington between Foreign Minister Andrei A. Gromyko and Mr. Carter and Secretary of State Cyrus R. Vance.

Mr. Carter's statement was more explicit, however, in announcing that accord was "in sight" on an agreement limiting each side's strategic bomber and missile forces. This would replace a five-year interim accord, which expired yesterday.

For one thing, the President indicated progress had been made on the total numbers of weapons, and then said it also related to "certain categories of weapons of special concern to each of us."

Under a 1974 Soviet-American agreement, reached at Vladivostok, each side would be limited to 2,400 offense bombers and missile launchers. The United States has been trying to reduce that number and Mr. Carter's statement suggested this has been achieved. The new number is said to be about 2,200.

In addition, both sides have had a problem with the new systems being developed. The Russians are concerned with the American cruise missiles, while the Americans have been concerned about a new class of heavy land-based missiles as well as a new Soviet bomber known in the West as the Backfire.

Luncheon With Africans

After his address, Mr. Carter, who is also here for two days of consultations with foreign leaders, had a "get-acquainted" luncheon for African representatives leaders at which he expressed eagerness for closer ties with them. He said in effect that in the past there had not been enough understanding of their needs and wishes, and promised to do better "in a spirit of partnership and equality" to understand their "hopes and dreams and aspirations for the future."

In reply, President Samora Machel of Mozambique, a Marxist, said: "Perhaps, for the first time, a President of the United States is trying genuinely to understand the problems of Africa."

Mr. Carter in his address to the Assembly, also referred to new American initiatives to induce the Soviet Union to "stabilize" naval activity in the Indian Ocean saying an agreement on restraining the military presence of each might later lead to agreement to reduce military activity "in this whole area."

The President also spoke of the recently signed Panama Canal treaties as an illustration of how peaceful settlements can be reached but did not otherwise touch on the controversy which has been generated in the United States over the pacts.

Mr. Carter did not in this address give more than passing mention to human rights matters, which he has made a cornerstone of the Administration's foreign policy but which he plans to speak about here tomorrow when he signs two United Nations covenants, one dealing with political and civil rights and the other with economic rights.

* * *

October 12, 1977

U. S. BIDS NATO SHARE THE RESPONSIBILITY FOR NEUTRON WEAPON

Pentagon Chief, at Meeting in Italy, Places Burden on Alliance, Where Bomb Is a Political Problem

By BERNARD WEINRAUB
Special to The New York Times.

BARI, Italy, Oct. 11—The United States urged the Atlantic Alliance today to share responsibility with it for the neutron bomb and said that the controversial weapon would only be deployed if the Europeans wanted it.

"It's not our purpose to jam anything down anyone's throat," said a United States source, following a meeting here between Defense Secretary Harold Brown and members of the North Atlantic Treaty Organization's Nuclear Planning Group. "If it's not desired, it won't be produced. Outside the alliance, it has no utility."

The neutron bomb is a nuclear warhead designed principally to thwart a Soviet tank attack in Central Europe. The weapon restricts blast and fire damage to a relatively small area, a radius of 200 to 300 yards, but intensifies the radiation yield, killing enemy soldiers without destroying buildings or other structures in nearby civilian areas.

Allies Uneasy Over Weapon

In effect, Mr. Brown was placing the responsibility for the so-called "enhanced radiation weapon" on European nations, whose military leaders generally favor developing and deploying it but whose political leaders are reluctant to support it publicly because of uncertain reaction.

American officials said that the weapon, which has been under development for nearly 20 years, was first discussed five years ago by NATO, "and a consensus developed within the nuclear planning group when it was first described." But publicity about potential deployment of the American-produced weapon has stirred uneasiness in West Germany, Britain, Belgium and the Netherlands, nations that would be likely to have the weapons on their soil.

'Emotional Political Factors'

"It's not simply a military question," conceded an American official. "Emotional political factors have to be taken into account. These are battlefield weapons, useful against tanks and other battlefield armor. These are designed for allied use. There has to be substantial consensus about what ought to be done."

At this point it is unclear when President Carter will make a decision on whether to produce and deploy the neutron bomb. United States sources indicated that his decision depends largely on whether the Europeans want the weapon and publicly agree to it.

President Carter has received a sizable mandate from both Houses of Congress approving funds for the bomb's development. But actual production and deployment, American sources indicated, will not take place until the Europeans decide on it.

An important advantage of the warhead, which was developed for use on surface-to-surface missiles with a 75-mile range, is that it enables allied troops to move within hours, instead of months, into the nuclear blast area.

Opponents of the weapon, in the United States as well as Europe, say that because it has such a relatively small range of destruction and seems so effective, it invites use by making a "small" nuclear response that much more plausible, thus lowering the threshold between conventional and nuclear war.

A key nation involved in the decision is West Germany, where many of the weapons would be stationed. So far the West German Government has made no final decision on the weapon's stationing but officials have indicated that Bonn would not oppose the warhead's deployment.

The two-day meeting of the Nuclear Planning Group began this morning with remarks by Mr. Brown on the nuclear balance in Europe and latest strategic developments in the United States, including plans to create a new global missile called the MX.

The conference is being held at a heavily guarded downtown hotel in this pleasant Southeastern city on the Adriatic. The Nuclear Planning Group is a NATO consultative body established by the United States in the 1960's to discuss and develop joint nuclear strategy for NATO. Attending the meeting are defense officials of the United States, Belgium, Denmark, West Germany, Greece, Italy and Britain.

PLAN FOR CONSULTATIONS

Special to The New York Times.

WASHINGTON, Oct. 11—A White House source said tonight President Carter would make no decision on whether to produce and deploy the neutron bomb until after consultation with NATO allies, such as is now taking place in Bari, Italy. The source said Mr. Carter's position on the bomb's deployment had remained consistent throughout discussion of the issue.

Another source close to Administration thinking described as "a little harsh" the statement of an unidentified American in Bari that "it's not our purpose to jam anything down anyone's throat" and that if the bomb is "not desired it won't be produced."

The Administration is understood, however, to share the thinking of the American aide in Bari that if, because of allies' objections, the bomb cannot be deployed, there is no use in producing it.

PART VIII

COLD WAR II

April 7, 1978

CARTER SAID TO FAVOR DELAY IN PRODUCTION OF THE NEUTRON BOMB

ANNOUNCEMENT IS DUE TODAY

Aides Say Pressure From Congress and Allies Not to Scrap Weapon Contributed to Latest Step

By RICHARD BURT
Special to The New York Times.

WASHINGTON, April 6—Administration officials said today that President Carter was expected to announce tomorrow an indefinite delay in producing the neutron bomb.

Officials believe Mr. Carter will stick to his earlier opposition to going ahead with production, but they said he had agreed not to cancel the neutron bomb outright and had adopted a formula for leaving open the choice of producing the tactical warhead at a later date.

Officials said that a major factor in Mr. Carter's thinking was the pressure that has been brought to bear on the White House by European allies and members of Congress, critical of a reported decision to end the neutron bomb program.

Acceptable to Allies

"The announcement will be acceptable to the entire Western alliance because it will leave a number of options open," said a high-ranking Administration official.

Under the plan described by officials, the Administration could continue development work on the neutron bomb while it carried on discussions with European allies over its deployment in Western Europe and talks with Moscow over its possible limitation in an arms-control agreement.

However, this plan would mark a significant departure from the formula being discussed by allied governments early last month which would have led to immediate production of the weapon. But this plan was reportedly scrapped when Mr. Carter, in mid-March, decided against moving ahead with the system. Some officials say that a decision to postpone production would differ little from abandoning the neutron bomb outright.

Vance Says Decision Is Due

Indications that an announcement was imminent came on Capitol Hill today, when Secretary of State Cyrus R. Vance told the House International Relations Committee that Mr. Carter's final decision would be made very soon. "And when I said very soon I mean very soon," he added.

He also said there would be a meeting tomorrow of the Atlantic alliance's Council of Ministers, a session that officials said later would be used by American officials to explain Mr. Carter's plan. They said an announcement from the White House would follow the alliance meeting tomorrow or possibly Monday.

If Mr. Carter has agreed to keep the possibility alive of producing the neutron bomb in the future, this would constitute a victory of sorts for his top foreign-policy advisers as well as members of Congress who have strongly criticized any decision to cancel the weapon.

Officials said it would also relieve the anxieties of European allies, particularly West Germany, whose governments this week have expressed concern over a complete halt to the program.

On the other hand, most of Mr. Carter's top foreign-policy advisers were originally in favor of moving ahead with the system, and a decision to postpone production is viewed by many officials as tantamount to ending the program. Some officials also say they fear a compromise decision—neither producing nor scrapping the weapon—could lead to continuing discord within the alliance and is not likely to stop Soviet criticism of the weapon.

Appears to Be a Compromise

"What we seem to have here is a compromise," noted one official. "The President, in heading off production, is getting his way, but in keeping the weapon alive, the proponents of the neutron bomb have something to cheer about."

On Capitol Hill, members of Congress who earlier this week expressed concern over stopping the neutron bomb said a decision by Mr. Carter to defer production would also run into Congressional criticism.

One Senator, who declined to be identified, noted that the Administration had money in this year's defense budget to start producing the weapon and said that it was likely that Congress would vote to approve it. With such a development, he said, the Administration could be forced into a battle with Congress if the White House attempted to undo that approval.

Officials said that regardless of what form Mr. Carter's announcement took, the recent confusion over the Administration's intentions on the weapons had badly strained alliance relations. They said the West German Government was especially upset over how the question had been handled and they doubted that any decision in the near future would remove the suspicions that now characterize ties between Bonn and Washington.

Already, officials said, leaders on both sides of the Atlantic have begun arguing over who was responsible for scrapping last month's alliance plan for moving ahead with the weapon. White House officials contend that Mr. Carter's reported decision to halt production was primarily spurred by doubts over whether West Germany and other allied countries would allow the weapon to be deployed on their territory.

But West German officials, along with officials in the State Department, said that Bonn was fully prepared to go along with deploying the weapon in the context of the alliance-wide plan under discussion in Brussels last month. In this plan European countries were to accept the neutron bomb in the event that an effort at arms-control with Moscow proved unsuccessful.

* * *

April 7, 1978

NEUTRON WARHEAD HAS POLITICAL FALLOUT

By TERENCE SMITH

WASHINGTON—Of all the controversies that have swirled around Jimmy Carter during his first 15 months in office, several of the more sensitive and politically hazardous have dealt with nuclear policy. Whether he has been tilting with the French and West Germans about plans to sell nuclear technology to Pakistan and Brazil, or challenging the wisdom of the Clinch River Breeder Reactor at home, the result has been fierce argument and bruised feelings. The irony has been that the most heated debates on nuclear policy have been with allies rather than adversaries.

That was the pattern again last week, in the dispute over the production of the "Enhanced Radiation Weapon"—alias the neutron bomb. Again, intense passions were aroused, allies rather than adversaries were alarmed about the Administration's intentions and the President was under attack from Congress. Once Mr. Carter's decision to defer production had been announced, there were two schools of thought as to its impact.

- The view of his critics that it had been essentially a non-decision, the empty compromise of a vacillating President unable to follow a coherent policy.
- The view of his supporters, that the deferral combined the best of both worlds by holding open the possibility of future production of the weapon if Russia fails to show restraint in its weapons programs and troop deployments.

By week's end, the Administration's top policymakers felt strongly that they had fulfilled the old cliche about fashioning a silk purse from a sow's ear. It had been a difficult decision, they argued, compounded by premature disclosure, and bound to be unpopular with factions in Congress either way.

The plan to produce a neutron warhead first emerged publicly last summer as a one-line item in the budget of the Energy Research and Development Administration for fiscal 1978. "W70 Mod 3 Lance Enhanced Radiation Warhead," it read—sheer gobbledygook until a journalist and a few Congressional staffers spotted it for what it was, the intensely radioactive antipersonnel device that headline writers dubbed the "Doomsday shell."

The bomb quickly became an emotional issue in the United States and in Europe, where it would be deployed for use against advancing tank columns from Warsaw Pact forces. Some allies opposed it on moral grounds; others, such as West Germany, felt it was a useful weapon but were constrained from publicly agreeing to its deployment because of domestic politics. Nonetheless, after protracted and partially secret debate, Congress approved funds for development of the weapon last summer. The ball then passed into Mr. Carter's court. As a man morally and intellectually troubled by the specter of nuclear proliferation, the President was never a strong supporter of the weapon, but he conceded the wisdom of developing it as a bargaining chip in the Strategic Arms Limitation Talks.

The Soviet Union promptly launched a propaganda campaign against the weapon, asserting it could "only bring the world closer to nuclear holocaust." The campaign adroitly focused on objections raised by non-Communist critics, that the so-called "clean" aspects of the neutron warhead would make it all that more likely to be used.

Two other developments added weight to the debate. President Carter's decision not to proceed with development of the B-1 bomber intensified the criticism of him among Congressional hawks, and the SALT talks moved to a climactic phase.

European hesitation over the weapon continued and in October, Defense Secretary Harold Brown flew to Italy to warn the North Atlantic Treaty Organization defense ministers that the alliance must share responsibility for its production and deployment. "It's not our intention to jam anything down anyone's throat," an official said. By last month NATO officials began moving toward a compromise under which the United States would begin producing the weapon, but deployment in Europe would be delayed for two years to see if the Soviet Union would display restraint in developing weapons such as the SS-20 missile.

This satisfied some American officials, but evidently not President Carter. He reportedly felt it was pointless for the United States to produce the weapon if the Europeans would not publicly agree to deploy it. Such a move would be useless as a bargaining chip with Moscow if it felt that the weapon, even if produced, would not be deployed.

These reservations apparently came to a head in Mr. Carter's mind on the weekend of March 18–19, while he was fishing off St. Simon's Island in Georgia. He immediately directed that a NATO meeting scheduled for March 20 be postponed to allow further consultation on deployment. Returning to Washington, Mr. Carter reviewed the situation and then dispatched Deputy Secretary of State Warren Christopher to West Germany and Britain to explain that the United States couldn't go ahead with production without a commitment on deployment. Mr. Christopher reportedly was instructed to say this was the President's judgment, not a final decision, and to seek European reaction.

The Administration hoped this maneuver would elicit a public commitment to deployment from the West Germans, but it did not. Instead, Hans Deitrich Genscher, the Foreign Minister, flew to Washington to tell Mr. Carter that Bonn supported production of the weapon, but could not publicly endorse deployment, at least not alone. If another Continental ally, such as Belgium, would call for deployment, that might change the situation. By now, Mr. Carter no longer had the luxury of time. The news of his inclination not to proceed with production had been revealed in the press and Congressional criticism was rising.

Once his deferral decision had been announced, Administration officials found new merit in it by the hour. Not only did it leave open the possibility of future production, they argued, but the Russians would have to be convinced that if the United States did proceed it would be only with the full understanding from the allies that the weapon would be deployed. In addition, by tying that decision to future Soviet restraint, the Administration hopes to shift the onus for the eventual construction of the weapon to Moscow. Finally, they believe the debate has changed public attitudes about the neutron warhead. Joking about that, one Administration official observed. "A year ago it was anathema. Today, it's five percent more popular than peanut butter."

The President's critics will not be so easily mollified, however. To them the Administration has appeared weak in this episode, the NATO alliance divided and the future direction of its nuclear strategy uncertain. With Congressional election campaigns getting underway, the neutron bomb will be more in the news than out of it.

Terence Smith is chief White House correspondent of The New York Times.

* * *

April 30, 1978

FOR INDOCHINA, ENDLESS WARS

Old Enmities Revived After U.S. Departure

By HENRY KAMM
Special to The New York Times.

BANGKOK, Thailand, April 27—Three years ago it was all over. The National Liberation Front's red and blue flag with a gold star flew over Saigon's Doc Lap Palace. After 30 years, the war in Indochina had ended with the surrender of Saigon on April 30, 1975. Peace brought rejoicing, even among many of the defeated and their foreign backers. The killing had gone on too long.

The victory had been complete in Vietnam, Cambodia and Laos. Whatever the victors would make of their countries, their grip was sure, and so, at last and at least, there would be peace.

New Violence in Region

Now, three years after the last round was fired, the last village bombed, the last mother killed with her child in that war, Vietnam and Cambodia are fighting each other, Vietnamese planes are firing rockets at mountain villages in Laos. And Thailand, the only country of the Indochinese peninsula spared by the war, fights skirmishes against incursions across its borders with Laos and Cambodia.

To be sure, the fighting is minor compared to the horrors that preceded peace, but peace was illusory. The wars on which the United States had grafted itself are finished, but the unresolved struggle for Indochina continues, and Southeast Asia is ill at ease.

The accusations of barbarous misdeeds that have been exchanged by Vietnam and Cambodia would be widely written off as anti-Communist propaganda if they came from another source. Those who fled Cambodia after the Communist victory related the horrors of a vast number of murders, forced evacuation of cities and regimentation of life on an inhuman scale. Skeptics who thought the accounts were malevolent inventions of the right wing may revise their judgments when the Hanoi radio broadcasts them daily.

Decolonization Is Seen

During the war, some people rejected suggestions by hardliners in the Pentagon that Vietnam's goals might extend beyond its borders after the war. Now those people may wonder what to make of Phnom Penh's ritual allegation that Hanoi is determined to create an Indochinese federation under its domination.

A notion much discussed by Indochina watchers in Asia, both Westerners and Asians, is that the process of decolonization, delayed by the continuation of direct Western intervention until 1975, is now in full swing. They view the Vietnamese-Cambodian conflict, along with the unrest on the Thai-Cambodian border, in this context.

France, in this view, arrived on the Indochinese scene late in the last century and halted regional developments by imposing its dominant presence. When France established its hold over Cambodia and Laos, it put an end to a rapid erosion of Cambodian territory by Vietnam from the east and Thailand from the north.

Now, these experts assert, these conflicts over the survival of an independent Cambodian nation have resumed. Historical enmities, frozen but not forgotten during the French and American interventions, have once more come to the surface. Cambodia, fearing both its neighbors—Vietnam perhaps with more justification now than Thailand—is struggling fiercely against what it perceives to be a threat to its national existence.

Forces Now Released

The analysts do not necessarily believe all Cambodian charges of Vietnamese subversion and barbarities nor justify

Cambodia's actions. But they contend that the conflict should be seen in the light of a historical enmity submersed but not forgotten for a century. Forces restrained by colonialism and its American aftermath, they believe, have now been released to take their course in a strictly Asian context.

As for Laos, the view of most Indochina watchers is that as a viable country, it has always been a myth. There are 30,000 to 50,000 Vietnamese troops within its borders and its northern tip is under Chinese domination.

The Indochinese contestants are not, of course, acting out their policies without influence from the Communist world to which they all belong. China, with apparent reservations, supports Cambodia, while the Soviet Union has thrown its weight behind Vietnam and Laos.

Vietnam's Reaction to Raids

In this alignment, too, Indochina watchers believe that an ancient antagonism, that between China and Vietnam has played a role in drawing Vietnam much closer to Moscow than to Peking

Because of Cambodia's alignment with China, Vietnam is thought to be exercising great restraint in its military reaction to Cambodian border intrusions that have killed or maimed many civilians and ruined some towns and villages from the southern end of the border on the Gulf of Siam to Tay Ninh Province west of Saigon.

Vietnam is assumed to be unwilling to risk offending China by pushing its troops to Phnom Penh and overthrowing the regime of Prime Minister Pol Pot. But recent visitors to Hanoi, journalists and international officials, have come away with the impression that Vietnam has made the removal of the Prime Minister, who is also the head of the Cambodian Communist Party, its principal objective.

There are reports in Thailand that Vietnam appears to be organizing thousands of Cambodians, including some from the ethnic Cambodian minority in Vietnam, some of those Cambodians who fled the Pol Pot regime and some of those who were taken to Vietnam during the major military incursion at the end of last year, to form the nucleus of a pro-Vietnamese Cambodian movement.

The travelers assume that Vietnam intends to use this movement either to populate a "liberated zone" in the course of a renewed limited thrust into the neighboring country or as a "fifth column" to assist in the overthrow of the regime.

Neighbors Are Watchful

The non-Communist nations of Southeast Asia, particularly the five members of the Association of Southeast Asian Nations—Indonesia, the Philippines, Thailand, Malaysia and Singpore—watch Indochina with anxiety. While trying to maintain proper relations with Vietnam and indicating satisfaction with their progress, officials express concern, always specifying that their names not be printed, over Hanoi's long-term aims. "Thailand is our barometer," a ranking Indonesian security official said. He added that he hoped the United States would show its continuing concern for Southeast Asia by not yielding to Vietnamese demands for extensive economic assistance.

Thailand is confronted with the dilemma of suffering frequent incursions from Cambodia, mainly by combined Cambodian and Thai Communist forces based in Cambodia, while hoping that Cambodia will remain strong enough to resist Vietnam. No matter how difficult a neighbor Pol Pot's Cambodia is, in the Thai view, a Cambodia subservient to Vietnam would be even less desirable.

Thailand and the rest of the nations in the association view Vietnam as their principal potential adversary. And, while remaining concerned over what China's future intentions might hold for them, they look to Peking for the time being as their principal hope for restraining the ambitions for regional hegemony that they suspect Vietnam of harboring.

* * *

May 7, 1978

A PLEA FOR ACTION . . .

By PAUL H. NITZE

It is characteristic of the American political system that candidates for public office deal with ends rather than means—and, to some extent, continue to do so after being elected. One can always be warmer, more human and more sympathetic when discussing ends than when dealing with the allocation of the scarce means necessary to achieve those ends.

But there is an additional problem if the ends are inherently contradictory. One can't simultaneously favor the young, the old and the middle-aged of both sexes; the blacks, the whites, the Indians, the Mexicans and all other racial minority groups; the Jews, the Catholics, the Protestants and the nonbelievers; the workers, the farmers, the white collar workers and the business managers. One can't both achieve a rising standard of living and take environmental measures that deny one the means to achieve that standard. By the same token, unless one makes wholly unrealistic assumptions about the nature of Soviet policies, one cannot simultaneously favor abolition of all nuclear weapons, a substantial cut in the defense budget and a national defense second to none.

It was therefore a foregone conclusion that President Carter would not be able to achieve some of the contradictory ends he set for himself during the campaign. But that has been true of many Presidential candidates. The more serious question is whether, since his inauguration, he has adapted his position to a more realistic approach to an imperfect world—whether he has plotted courses of action designed to get some specific and necessary things done for the country as a whole. I will not attempt to deal with the choices he faces on inflation, energy, the environment or the unemployed young; my subject is President Carter and the Russians.

It was Mr. Carter's original intention, in comparison with the preceding Administration, to be firmer with the Soviet leadership, more understanding toward our allies and more successful in negotiating equitable agreements with the Soviet Union. These agreements were to cover a wide range of subjects, including a new strategic-arms treaty (SALT II), an agreement on mutual, balanced force reductions in Europe, a comprehensive nuclear test-ban treaty, a new codification of the Law of the Sea and an agreement concerning the Indian Ocean. At the same time, he proposed to put less emphasis on East-West relations and more emphasis on North-South relations and the global issues of food, population, energy, economic development and the environment. All this was to be carried out against the background of a vigorous campaign to foster respect for human rights throughout the world, including the Soviet Union.

Today, this agenda looks far less practicable than it did on Jan. 20, 1977. What have been the causes for disappointment?

In my opinion, the principal cause is the President's misreading of the Russians. He shared the view of his chief arms-control negotiator, Paul Warnke, that the Soviet drive for greater military power was a reaction to our programs—limited to catching up—and that it would be reversed if we did not take steps to challenge it. He thought it possible to find solutions that the Russians would find "fair" to themselves and that would also be "fair" to us. His March 1977 SALT proposal went so far to be "fair" to the Russians as actually to be unfair to the United States. As his advisers now concede, the proposal would have guaranteed that, under no circumstances, could we gain from initiating an attack on the Soviet Union's fixed land-based missile silos, while leaving us without any guarantee that the Russians could not gain from such an attack on our silos.

However, the proposal would have also placed restraints on modernization and technological developments that the Russians were not prepared to accept. They were confident that they could improve their position vis-à-vis the United States without such restraints, and subsequent developments have proved them right.

President Carter was shocked by the force of the Soviet rejection. He is still in search of a "fair" solution. But the concept of "fairness" to a potential opponent is simply not seen by Soviet negotiators as a serious approach; they believe that opponents should strive to gain as much as possible from the other side, and give as little as possible.

Mr. Carter had hoped to be able to concentrate on the defense of the NATO front in Europe and the security of Japan, and to downgrade areas of lesser danger such as the Middle East, Africa and Korea. He had also hoped to separate the North-South issues from the East-West issues and give them greater priority. On both counts, he ran up against a reality that did not conform to his hopes.

He found that an important line of Soviet strategy was to outflank the NATO center by putting pressure on Norway and Turkey—particularly Turkey, which is now the largest single recipient of Soviet aid. He also found that the Soviet Union was working toward a position of hegemony in the Middle East designed to outflank Europe and Japan, and a position in Africa designed to outflank the Middle East.

The President thus found that it was not possible to separate North-South issues from East-West issues. It was the North-South issues that were being exploited by the Russians to upset the East-West balance in their favor—and this exploitation was fostered by the Soviet Union's growing strategic nuclear capabilities and its increasing power to project military force, either directly or through client states, to positions distant from Soviet borders. Although Mr. Carter announced that we would "compete" with the Soviets for influence in the third world, he found that the tools of American influence needed for that competition were not strong. Our ability to grant economic assistance is not what it once was. Military aid has been limited both by the Carter Administration's policies and by Congressional restraints. And there is a limit to what words and diplomacy, not backed by the more substantive aspects of power, can accomplish.

With respect to the human-rights part of his program, he has found the world more responsive to this initiative than might have been expected. Those who have suffered under Soviet domination, and who, therefore, know the Soviet regime well, received the White House appeals on behalf of human rights with renewed hope. This audience includes the people of Hungary, Poland and East Germany, among many others. In the Soviet Union itself, the regime has found it necessary to tighten the measures of repression. The regimes in Egypt, Somalia and China have also known the Russians well, but have other reasons for being opposed to the Soviet Union, and emotionally so. But those emotionally opposed to the Kremlin's policies do not, separately or together, command organized power adequate to make their opposition effective. They tend to look to us for more support than we are in a position to give.

In short, I believe President Carter misjudged the current state of the world and the Soviet Union's role in it. It seems evident that he is now having to reassess his policy, and that the issues sketched out above are causing divisions among his advisers.

Clues to the opposing viewpoints may be found in statements being made available to the press. In The New York Times of April 17, for instance, a high-ranking State Department official is quoted as saying that Zbigniew Brzezinski, the President's national-security adviser, "believes that only by displaying backbone can the Administration achieve its goals with Moscow," whereas "most people around here [the State Department] think that tough talk and a threatening posture could ruin the chances for working out a more stable relationship."

That comment seems to me to miss the point. It is undeniable that tough talk and a threatening verbal posture not backed by the tools to make it stick are not going to accomplish much; they may, in fact, expose us to the humiliation of a rude rebuff (as the Russians say) or force us into dangerous actions for which we are psychologically or materially unprepared. But neither, in dealing with Moscow, can we achieve our goals without displaying backbone. Accommodation without backbone leads to appeasement. We should talk not "tough" but with constructive reason and with an eye to correcting the continual stream of erroneous and deliberately deceptive propaganda issuing from Moscow. And while speaking quietly, we should urgently be doing those things that need to be done to reverse unfavorable trends in the underlying practical factors of power and influence.

The New York Times news story also reports the suggestion of a close aide to Secretary of State Cyrus Vance that Mr. Brzezinski's unhappiness with second-level State Department officials resulted from "a lack of clear policy direction from the top down." "We don't have a consistent policy toward Moscow," the official is quoted as saying, "and when this is the case, people get into trouble. It's not that the State Department is trying to undercut policy; we are only trying to carry out what we think the policy is."

Normally, a President would replace a Secretary of State whose close aide tells the press that Presidential guidance is so unclear as to lead to serious confusion. Perhaps Mr. Carter does not do so because he himself finds the fundamental issue in Soviet-American relations confusing and difficult to resolve.

What *is* the fundamental issue? George Kennan, the author of the "containment" doctrine, has in recent years asserted with increasing conviction that our policy must be one of "accommodation" to the Soviet Union's growing new imperial position in the world. Others, including myself, believe that the United States, with backing throughout the world from the host of potential supporters of independence from Soviet direction—if not of national and personal freedom as we understand these concepts—can maintain an effective base for continued widespread autonomy from Soviet pressures. These pressures take the form of propaganda, political action, psychological warfare, K.G.B. operations and moves and threats of a military nature. Despite the rhetoric of détente and accommodation, I believe these pressures will continue to grow if we continue on our present course.

However one interprets it, there can be no doubt about the continuing and mammoth buildup of Soviet military capabilities. Every recent Administration, including the present one, has testified to the magnitude of this buildup, and most Government agencies with competence in the field have stated that it exceeds any imaginable defensive need. Some people, mostly those who were national-security advisers to Senator George McGovern during the 1972 Presidential campaign, assert that this buildup springs from Soviet anxiety, in response to American initiatives, and is basically defensive in character. My own view is that the situation is not that simple, and that one should give weight to what the Soviet leaders themselves say on this subject to their own people.

Their doctrine, which they take most seriously, is that "scientific socialism," as they call their system, will inevitably triumph throughout the world; that they are duty-bound to assist this historically determined process by every available prudent means; and that, before succumbing to this inevitable outcome, others will defend themselves and strike back. From that vantage point, everything the Soviet leaders do is basically defensive. As Clausewitz puts it, the aggressor never wants war; he would prefer to enter your country unopposed; those who could defend their independence appear to the aggressor to be the warmongers.

To one who is doctrinally dedicated to achieving world hegemony, anyone else who has or may have the capability to resist that hegemony is a cause for anxiety. In that sense, the United States is a cause for Soviet anxiety. And the shift in the military balance, particularly in the strategic nuclear balance, over the last 15 years, gives the Soviet leaders increased confidence in the validity of their doctrine—confidence that 10 or 15 years ago was badly eroding.

The Soviet leaders do not want a nuclear war with the United States. They do, however, want strategic nuclear superiority (they call it "preponderance"). If at all possible, they would like to have the *capability* to fight a nuclear war—and to win such a war, in the military sense of ending up in undisputed command of the battlefield and being in a position to dictate the peace. They also propose to survive such a war, whatever the personnel and property losses they suffer, and to emerge as the predominant state in a world of Communist states. I don't think they have, as yet, the capability of achieving those objectives, but it is my view that unless we take urgent measures at once—not next year or the year after—to reverse current trends, the Russians *will* have such a capability in a few years' time. At a minimum, the disparity between our force and theirs will be such that we will have no grounds for confidence that the capability is not theirs.

In the Soviet view, preponderance of capability at the highest level of potential violence is the best way to prevent a confrontation at a lower level from escalating to the strategic nuclear level. However, it is also their view that preponderance at the strategic nuclear level can be exploited at lower levels in many forms of political pressure and violence. Strategic nuclear preponderance, they believe, is the fulcrum on which all other levers of pressure and influence depend.

One of their underlying concepts is the "correlation of forces." By that they mean the balance of political, economic, ideological, propaganda and organizational forces, as well as the military balance, at any given time. When that correlation is favorable, their doctrine calls on them to exploit their advantage. When it is unfavorable, it calls on them to be cautious, to retreat if necessary, to buy time in order to regroup and improve the balance so that it again moves in their favor. Associated with this doctrine is the idea that all the forces they control—political, psychological, diplomatic and economic—should be coordinated against the background of the relevant military balance, so as to optimize their gains and minimize their risks and potential losses.

Regarding themselves as being on the historical offensive, the Soviet leaders believe they should use the minimum amount of pressure or violence necessary to achieve their immediate aims. In their view, tactical caution is necessary to assure that, over time, grand strategic aims can be achieved. They follow strategies and tactics aimed at achieving a world controlled by regimes fashioned on the "scientific socialist" model—a world in which they, because of their longer experience, their years of effort and sacrifice on behalf of the Communist movement, and their preponderant power, will be the unchallenged hegemonic leaders.

Their attitude toward the United States has not been one of hatred. They have viewed the United States as being the central power among those nations and peoples who have a different view of the future, who believe that cooperative international arrangements can be made to work, that one country's gains are not necessarily another country's losses, that the actions of government should be responsive to the public will, and that the elemental rights of individuals should be fostered and not suppressed.

They believe the United States must of necessity oppose their basic aims. Therefore, the power and influence of the United States must be diminished by whatever prudent means come to hand. All measures taken must be be aimed, directly or indirectly, at assuring that the United States, as the strongest of the Soviet Union's potential opponents, is denied any realistic possibility of frustrating their ultimate goals.

The Soviet view of the United States has, therefore, been one of cold and respectful opposition. In recent years the component of respect appears to have diminished. Why should this have been so? In part, the reason may be found in President Carter's very virtues.

President Carter has a way with words. His special talent tends toward simple formulations expressed in brief sentences. The results are akin to homilies. His press conferences, for which his skills are superb, abound with sayings fit to be embroidered for a bedroom wall. A companion trait is self-assurance. He is warmed by inner confidence. A third and closely related quality is determination. His amazingly successful thrust for the Presidency two years ago was an object lesson in perseverance, a quality that grows by being used.

Each of those characteristics, favorable as they are to success in politics, has its obverse side. Words, for example, can become addictive. At Notre Dame University a year ago, the President revealingly offered the thought that, "in the spiritual realm, words are deeds." If that were all there is to it, we could all attain salvation on the basis of our New Year's resolutions. A capacity to deal with practical matters, not merely with words, is vital—a point no policy maker should ever forget.

Even self-assurance can become a bad habit. In an extreme form, it may induce political leaders to attribute transformative powers to their own personalities—as if some mysterious radiation of their presence could resolve human differences in the way kings in ancient times were said to be able to alleviate physical infirmities by touch of hand. Many a political project has been undone by this delusion.

One must take pains to be precise. The faith that moves mountains is indispensable; I question only the attitude that classifies all mountains as movable objects, the perseverance that only redoubles its efforts when finding itself on the wrong course, the aspiration that indulges itself by defining every impediment out of existence.

To those of us who entertain more and more doubts about President Carter on these grounds, his shortcomings appear as virtues carried to excess. Has his way with words led him to confuse strength with occasional strong utterances on the necessity of being strong? Has he unconsciously translated equations of power in world affairs into terms more applicable to personal relationships—relationships susceptible of being improved, redeemed, and resolved by his setting an example of patience and grace? Is he too devoted to an array of moral equivalents? Does the President find the ideal ends of policy too congenial to his spirit—to the prejudice of the obdurate factors of means? Has he imaginatively reconstructed the Soviet Union with hypotheses that fit his own hopes?

The Russians appear to believe that they face a confused man; a man who, on the one hand, would like to see a world wholly without nuclear weapons, but who, on the other hand, knows that the Russians are not going to give them up. The Russians are determined that so long as anyone in the world has nuclear weapons, or even the possibility of acquiring them, they are going to have them, too, and more and better ones than anyone else. The President, on the other hand, does not seem to be clear in his own mind whether we can or should fully hold up our end of the nuclear deterrent. I regard that attitude as dangerous, and believe it is high time the United States got on with reversing current trends and assuring that we maintain a strategic posture that can give us confidence in our ability to deter the Soviet Union and avoid nuclear war.

It is my view that the position of that part of the world not dominated by Moscow is more precarious today than it has been for some time. We must move forward with great caution and prudence, but to make "accommodation" the touchstone of our policy is, as Peking never ceases to remind us, the road to appeasement.

This issue—whether our policy toward the Soviet Union is to proceed from accommodation leading to appeasement, or from a rallying of our forces for prudent resistance to any Soviet purpose of world hegemony—must be resolved by the President, and resolved correctly. It must be resolved in the direction of prudent resistance, and without delay.

Paul H. Nitze, former Deputy Secretary of Defense and member of the U.S. SALT delegation from 1969 to 1974, is director of policy studies for the Committee on the Present Danger.

* * *

June 8, 1978

CARTER CALLS ON SOVIET TO END CONFRONTATION OR RISK 'GRAVER' STRAIN

TOUGHEST STAND YET

But in Policy Talk He Sees Good Arms Prospects and Asks Africa Cooperation

By TERENCE SMITH
Special to The New York Times.

ANNAPOLIS, Md., June 7—President Carter called on the Soviet Union today to choose between confrontation and cooperation and said the United States was "adequately prepared to meet either choice."

In his toughest speech to date on Soviet-American relations, Mr. Carter attacked the Soviet interpretation of détente, which, he said, "seems to mean a continuing aggressive struggle for political advantage and increased influence."

Warning that "competition without restraint and without shared rules will escalate into graver tensions," he called on Moscow to conclude a new accord limiting strategic arms and to join in working toward black rule in Rhodesia and South-West Africa.

Personal Appeal to Brezhnev

Without such cooperation, he told the graduating class at the United States Naval Academy here, "our relationship as a whole with the Soviet Union will suffer."

"I do not wish this to happen," Mr. Carter told an audience of midshipmen and 16,000 relatives and guests, "and I do not believe Mr. Brezhnev desires it. And this is why it is time for us to speak frankly and to face the problem squarely."

Briefing reporters before the speech, officials stressed the conciliatory aspects of the President's remarks. They pointed to his pledge to continue to negotiate "constructively and persistently" for a fair arms agreement as well as his call for increased cooperation in scientific and cultural fields.

Strongest Attack on Policies

But compared to Mr. Carter's three previous speeches on Soviet-American relations in the last 13 months, this was by far his strongest attack on Moscow's policies.

At the University of Notre Dame in May 1977, at Charleston, S.C., two months later, and on March 17 at Wake Forest University, Mr. Carter touched briefly on the problems separating the United States and the Soviet Union in the search for détente.

Today, he spent much of the speech accusing the Russians of a military build-up, of exploiting regional conflicts in Africa, violating human rights and attempting "to export a totalitarian and repressive form of government, resulting in a closed society."

Commenting on Moscow's overall standing Mr. Carter said the Soviet Union's political and cultural ties outside its bloc were "few and frayed," its economic growth was sharply down, its standard of living well below that of other developed nations and its farm production inadequate to meet its needs.

This portrayal seemed to contain some of the thinking of Zbigniew Brzezinski, the President's national security adviser, although it was expressed in the more modulated language of Cyrus R. Vance, the Secretary of State. One man in the audience at Annapolis described it as "polite Brzezinski."

Officials said in advance of the speech that it was designed to specify United States policy and dispel any confusion that might have arisen from the public statements of Mr. Vance, Mr. Brzezinski and Andrew Young, the delegate to the United Nations.

Aside from being directed at the Soviet Union, the speech was also designed to send a message to the American public and press, which has focused on the recent strains between Washington and Moscow.

Comparing the overall position of the United States to that of the Soviet Union, Mr. Carter said that, economically, politically and militarily, the United States was in a "much more favorable position."

"There is certainly no cause for alarm," he said, adding that "the healthy self-criticism and free debate which are essential in a democracy should never be confused with weakness, despair or lack of purpose."

Carter Made Proposal to Gromyko

In Africa, he said, the United States seeks a continent "free of the dominance of outside powers." Adding that Soviet and Cuban involvement "could deny this vision," he called on Moscow to join in efforts to achieve a settlement in Rhodesia and South-West Africa.

Mr. Powell said the President raised this idea with Foreign Minister Andrei A. Gromyko in a meeting on May 27. No formal reply has been received so far. Since then, Phedesjan guerrilla leaders have confirmed that Cubans are helping train their forces, which oppose a British-American plan for a political settlement.

On the arms talks, Mr. Carter said that, despite other differences with Moscow, the prospects for reaching a new accord were good. The United States has no desire to link these talks to other issues, he said, "but we recognize that tensions, sharp disputes or threats to peace will complicate the quest for an agreement."

The President spoke from an open podium set up at midfield in the stadium. A glowering sky threatened rain as he began his address, but he finished in warm sunshine 31 minutes later.

After having flown here by helicopter from Washington, Mr. Carter took his wife, Rosalynn, on a 25-minute tour of his old haunts at the Academy, from which he was graduated in 1964. Their limousine stopped briefly at Bancroft Hall while Mr. Carter showed his wife the corner room he had shared with three other midshipmen as an undergraduate.

* * *

June 17, 1978

CARTER AND TORRIJOS CONCLUDE TREATIES ON CANAL'S TRANSFER

PRESIDENT HAILED IN PANAMA

He Addresses Rally in Spanish and Says Pacts Show World the Spirit of 'A New Era'

By MARTIN TOLCHIN
Special to The New York Times.

PANAMA, June 16—President Carter joined Brig. Gen. Omar Torrijos Herrera here today in ceremonies that formally concluded the new Panama Canal treaties, declaring that "a new era of inter-American understanding and cooperation" was at hand.

Speaking in Spanish later at a rally in a jammed midtown square, the President said:

"In the peaceful process of negotiating the treaties, we have shown the world a spirit which recognizes and respects the rights of others and seeks to help all people to fulfill their legitimate aspirations with confidence and dignity."

Crowd Is Enthusiastic

The Panamanian Government estimated that 180,000 people had turned out during the day to welcome the President, who arrived with his wife, Rosalynn, Congressional representatives and aides for a 23-hour visit. There were heavy security forces to guard against any recurrence of recent anti-treaty violence, and special arrangements included the construction of a platform 40 feet high from which Mr. Carter addressed an enthusiastic crowd in the square.

At the airport, after a welcoming embrace from General Torrijos, the Panamanian leader, President Carter said that he had made the trip not "as a stranger, but as a friend and a partner."

The two leaders embraced again after they had signed and exchanged five documents that put the final formal touches on the two treaties which provide for the neutrality of the canal and for its transfer to Panama by the end of this century. The 20-minute ceremony was held in the New Panama Coliseum in front of 4,000 people, among them a delegation of 12 United States senators, 4 members of the House of Representatives and five Latin American leaders who had played leading roles in reaching agreement on the treaties.

Differences in Attitude

President Carter smiled and waved at the spectators after signing the leather-bound documents, but General Torrijos maintained a serious mien.

At the rally, held at the Fifth of May Plaza, the President, speaking in Spanish, said the treaties "breathe new life into old principles—principles of peace, nonintervention, mutual respect and cooperation." But, he said, their significance went far beyond the special concerns of the two nations.

Calling for the application of these principles to hemispheric concerns about "peace, human rights and dignity and economic development," he declared: "Let us advance the cause of human dignity, build a hemisphere in which citizens of every country are free from torture and arbitrary arrest, free to speak as they please, free to participate in the determination of their own destiny."

At the ceremony in the Coliseum, the President and General Torrijos exchanged four instruments of ratification—one American and one Panamanian document each for the neutrality and canal treaties. A fifth document, called the Protocol of Exchange of Instruments of Ratification, includes an explicit Panamanian acceptance of the 24 amendments, conditions, reservations and understandings adopted by the United States Senate since the treaties were signed in Washington Sept. 7 after having received a two-thirds vote of approval in a Panamanian plebiscite.

By comparison, the United States has implicitly agreed to only two understandings added by Panama. The United States did not accept, moreover, a Panamanian declaration that rejected the right of any country to intervene in its internal or external affairs.

A Carter Administration official asked about the popularity of the treaties whose Panamanian opponents see little improvement over the 1903 treaty, said, "We have confidence that the views of the Panamanian people as expressed in the plebiscite continue to be their views."

A State Department official, noting what he called "an undercurrent of disapproval" of the treaties in Panama, said that he thought the President's visit would be "a stabilizing force" and undermine the treaties' opponents.

Help for Torrijos

The President's visit also has been widely interpreted as an effort to bolster the regime of General Torrijos and thereby insure survival of the treaties.

Although the treaties were concluded today, becoming binding at 5:12 P.M. Eastern Daylight Time, the effective date of the exchange of ratification instruments will not come until next March 1 unless Congress enacts implementing legislation before then. The treaties themselves will become effective six months later, or Oct. 1, 1979, at the latest.

Both President Carter and General Torrijos faced intense domestic opposition to the treaties, which were negotiated over 14 years. The general as well as the President said they signaled a new era in inter-American relations.

General Torrijos, however, said also that it was "the Panamanian people that have made possible the celebration to ratify the treaties."

"This victory," he said, "belongs to the Panamanian people."

'Day of Dignity'

Security was tight at the Coliseum, as it had been at the airport and along the motorcade route, where crowds were thin. The Panamanian Government, which had named this the

"Day of Dignity," sought to provide a triumphant welcome to the President and to prevent violence, such as the incidents that caused the death of two students here protesting against the treaties.

President Carter left Washington this morning and stopped first in Atlanta for a breakfast speech at a meeting of the Baptist Brotherhood before flying on to Panama. He was the fifth United States President to visit here.

Tomorrow, he plans to visit the canal and meet with United States civilians and military personnel who operate and protect it.

In important victories for the Carter Administration, the neutrality treaty was approved by the United States Senate in March by one vote more than the necessary two-thirds, and the second pact was approved in April by the same margin.

Among the 12 senators whom the President invited to accompany him here were John J. Sparkman of Alabama, the retiring Chairman of the Senate Foreign Relations Committee, and his successor, Frank Church of Idaho.

* * *

August 9, 1978

CARTER TO MEET BEGIN AND SADAT IN THE U.S. SEPT. 5

Talks at Camp David Will Seek to Break Mideast Stalemate

By TERENCE SMITH
Special to The New York Times.

WASHINGTON, Aug. 8—The White House announced today that President Carter would meet Prime Minister Menachem Begin of Israel and President Anwar el-Sadat of Egypt on Sept. 5 to discuss ways of breaking the Middle East deadlock. The meeting will be at Camp David, the Presidential retreat in the Maryland mountains.

In a brief statement at the White House, Jody Powell, the press secretary, said that the President's handwritten invitations to attend the extraordinary three-way meeting had been delivered personally to Mr. Begin and Mr. Sadat by Secretary of State Cyrus R. Vance, who is expected back from the Middle East tomorrow.

In Alexandria, Egypt, where he is meeting with Mr. Vance, President Sadat said he had agreed to attend the meeting with Prime Minister Begin because of an American commitment to become a "full partner" in the peace negotiations. In Tel Aviv, Prime Minister Begin said the meeting had been arranged without Israeli acceptance of earlier Egyptian preconditions for resumption of direct talks.

Duration of Talks Undetermined

Mr. Powell said that Mr. Carter was "gratified" by the prompt acceptances of the Israeli and Egyptian leaders. He added that no specific time had been set for the duration of the Camp David talks, but White House officials speculated later that the meeting might last two or three days.

The idea of summoning the two leaders to a Washington meeting has been under consideration ever since the direct Israeli-Egyptian talks broke down last January. Up to this point, however, the White House had been against it on the ground that such a dramatic, high-level encounter would inevitably raise expectations of an immediate solution.

Seeking to counter this notion today, a senior White House official told reporters that the President was under "no illusions that the meeting in Camp David would itself produce a settlement."

No Broad American Plan

Despite the Administration's concern over the current deadlock, no broad American peace plan is expected to be introduced at Camp David, White House sources said. They said the United States would continue to make procedural suggestions on how to keep the talks going as it has in the past, but that the White House still believed that the only lasting solution would be one negotiated by the parties themselves.

The President had decided to arrange the meeting, he said, "not because the chances for peace are right now so high, but because the stakes in peace are very high and because the risks, in fact, have risen."

The official, who under the ground rules of the briefing could not be identified, did not specify what risks he had in mind. But White House officials have expressed concerns in recent days about the possibility that the deadlock in the Middle East negotiations might lead to renewed fighting there as early as this fall.

Two hours before the announcement, Mr. Carter summoned a bipartisan group of Congressional leaders to the White House to brief them on the planned meeting.

Among other things, the President said, Mr. Begin and Mr. Sadat wanted to discuss the possibility of sending American troops to the Middle East in some peacekeeping function. At this, one Republican Senator reportedly asked Mr. Carter if he was talking about "500 soldiers, 5,000 or 10,000?"

Mr. Carter brushed this question aside, participants in the meeting said, saying that he wanted to wait to hear what the two leaders had in mind before reaching any decision on it.

In fact, the Administration has already expressed a willingness to contribute American troops to some sort of peacekeeping force if both sides wish it. Such a force presumably would come into being only to police a formal agreement. At present, American civilian technicians operate electronic surveillance stations in the Sinai buffer zone between Israeli and Egyptian forces.

Mr. Carter told the Congressional leaders that he had considered going to the Sinai himself but had decided against it after discussing it with his advisers. The Senate Republican leader, Howard H. Baker Jr., said that the President had told the Congressional leaders that he felt the situation was deteriorating rapidly, and that he had sent handwritten letters of several pages to each man proposing the meeting. He described Mr. Begin as "enthusiastic" about the talks.

Skepticism Is Reported

Senator Baker said that there was some skepticism among the Congressmen about how productive such a hastily arranged meeting could be, but that he and others felt that the President should be given a chance to do whatever he could.

Other Congressional sources reported that Mr. Begin and Mr. Sadat had indicated an interest in discussing the possible carrying out of some of the less controversial aspects of a proposed Sinai agreement. This could include partial Israeli withdrawals and some initial diplomatic and commercial contacts between Israel and Egypt.

Even these limited concessions would be highly controversial, however, and Mr. Sadat and Mr. Begin would be unlikely to proceed unless the Camp David talks went well on other, more substantive issues, White House officials said.

Meanwhile, officials of the State Department said there was deep concern in the Administration that a flareup of fighting in Lebanon between now and Sept. 5 could disrupt the meeting. If Syria and Israel were face to face in a confrontation over the situation in southern Lebanon for example, it would be politically difficult for Mr. Sadat to sit down with Mr. Begin in Washington.

Lebanon Described as Dangerous

Commenting on the "extremely dangerous" Lebanese situation today, a State Department spokesman, Tom Reston, said that "the fighting must be stopped and the cease-fire scrupulously observed by all." He added that the Administration was pressing the various parties in the conflict to "do all that is possible to insure that calm and stability are restored."

Mr. Reston said that the United States was hoping for a "breathing spell" in Lebanon so that the peace-seeking efforts could proceed.

Specifically, the Administration is concerned that Israel may begin resupplying the Christian forces in Lebanon with additional arms, officials said. They added that the United States had warned Israel in several recent diplomatic exchanges that this would be "inconsistent" with American policy.

The decision to invite Mr. Begin and Mr. Sadat to a Washington meeting was reached at a meeting of Mr. Carter and his top foreign policy advisers at Camp David on July 31. Mr. Carter had spent the previous weekend there. And on Monday he was joined by Vice President Mondale, Mr. Vance, Zbigniew Brzezinski, his national security adviser, and Hamilton Jordan, his top political aide, for an extended discussion on the Middle East.

An Atmosphere of Crisis

An atmosphere of gathering crisis permeated the meeting, officials recalled today. President Sadat had just announced that Egypt was not prepared to resume discussions with Israel at the foreign ministers' level until Israel committed itself to virtually complete withdrawal from the West Bank of the Jordan, Gaza Strip and Sinai, Arab territories occupied in 1967.

Negotiations of any kind seemed unlikely and other forces in the Arab world, including the influential Saudis, were calling for an end to the Sadat peace initiative and a new, hardline Arab policy. Concluding that some dramatic move was required to break the stalemate, Mr. Carter instructed Mr. Vance to go ahead with his planned trip to the Middle East and invite the two leaders to Washington. Both men accepted the Secretary's proposal readily, officials said today.

Next month's meeting will be President Sadat's third visit to the United States since Mr. Carter took office and his second to Camp David. He conferred there with Mr. Carter on Feb. 4-5 and visited Washington in April 1977.

Mr. Begin has met Mr. Carter in Washington four times in the last 18 months. He was here in July and December of last year and in March and May of this year.

* * *

December 16, 1978

U.S. AND CHINA OPENING FULL RELATIONS; TENG WILL VISIT WASHINGTON ON JAN. 29

LINK TO TAIWAN ENDS

Carter, in TV Speech, Says 'We Recognize Reality' After 30-Year Rift

By TERENCE SMITH
Special to The New York Times.

WASHINGTON, Dec. 15—President Carter announced a "historic agreement" tonight under which the United States and China will establish diplomatic relations on Jan. 1.

The President also said that Teng Hsiao-ping, the powerful Deputy Prime Minister of China, would visit this country on Jan. 29. The visit here will be the first by a high-level Chinese Communist official since the end of the Chinese civil war in 1949. It will end what Administration officials described tonight as "a 30-year anomaly in international affairs."

In a dramatic and unexpected speech on national television, Mr. Carter also announced that the United States would terminate diplomatic relations and its mutual defense treaty with Taiwan. But in remarks addressed especially to the people of the island, he pledged that the United States would remain interested in the peaceful resolution of the issue.

[In Peking, a simultaneous announcement was made by the Communist Party Chairman Hua Kuo-feng. An official Chinese statement repeated the Chinese position that a reunification of Taiwan with the mainland was "entirely China's internal affair."]

'New Vista of Relations'

"The United States of America recognizes the Government of the People's Republic of China as the sole legal Government of China," the President said, reading from a joint communiqué released in Washington and Peking.

Speaking to reporters in the White House press room after his speech, an ebullient Mr. Carter said that the new agreement would open "a new vista of trade relations with the almost one billion people of China."

He added his own feeling that "the security of Taiwan is adequately protected" under the agreement. The United States will withdraw its remaining military personnel from Taiwan within four months.

'Recognizing Simple Reality'

"We do not undertake this important step for transient, tactical reasons," Mr. Carter said. "In recognizing that the Government of the People's Republic of China is the single Government of China, we are recognizing simple reality."

The President conceded that the normalization of relations with China after nearly 30 years was a politically controversial act and said that it had received "mixed response" from Congressional leaders with whom he met earlier in the evening.

The move drew angry fire from moderate and conservative Republicans, however. Senator Barry Goldwater of Arizona denounced it as "a cowardly act," and charged that it "stabs in the back the nation of Taiwan."

Bill Brock, the Republican national chairman, accused the President of "callous disregard for a fine friend and a loyal ally."

Briefing reporters after the speech, senior Administration officials conceded that they had not obtained an explicit pledge from China not to use force to retake Taiwan.

But the officials maintained that it was implicit in the Chinese acceptance of the American statement, issued unilaterally to coincide with the speech that expresses the continued interest of the United States in the peaceful resolution of the Taiwan issue.

They also felt that recent public statements by Chinese leaders indicating that the Taiwanese situation could be peacefully resolved were an indication of their true intentions.

The officials also pointed out that the United States would retain the right to maintain a full range of cultural and economic ties, including the supply of defensive arms, after the formal termination of the mutual defense treaty at the end of 1979.

They also cited as a Chinese concession the agreement to exchange ambassadors in March, before the formal termination of the United States-Taiwan defense treaty. Previously, the Chinese had said they would never do this.

No Use of Force

The major United States concession in the agreement, however, was the willingness to sign without an explicit guarantee that force would not be used to retake Taiwan.

In his speech, Mr. Carter made special mention of the key roles played in the "long, serious negotiations" with the Chinese by his predecessors, Presidents Gerald R. Ford and Richard M. Nixon.

Earlier in the evening, Administration officials confirmed that Treasury Secretary W. Michael Blumenthal would go to China soon for a broad discussion of financial and trade matters. Among the subjects on his agenda will be the complex problem of the Chinese and American assets that have been frozen in the two countries since 1950. These would have to be freed as part of the normalization process.

The United States holds that some $200 million worth of American assets in China were seized at the end of the civil war. China is seeking some $80 million in blocked assets.

The President's speech followed a day of mounting suspense and curiosity in the capital. Rumors of an impending important announcement began to circulate in midmorning, but the President's foreign policy aides were giving out no information.

The regularly scheduled White House briefing was postponed from 2:30 P.M. to 3:30 P.M., when Mr. Carter's press secretary, Jody Powell, emerged to announce that Mr. Carter would make a televised speech "on a matter of national and international importance." Mr. Powell declined to specify even the subject of the address, except to say that "we are not talking about anything that would involve military action or things of that nature."

When reporters asked if a national crisis was involved, Mr. Powell said with a smile: "I don't think there will be any need to start evacuating large cities or anything like that."

Soviet Envoy at White House

Speculation intensified when the Soviet Ambassador, Anatoly F. Dobrymn, arrived at the White House shortly after 3 P.M. The envoy smiled and waved at reporters as he entered the office of Zbigniew Brzezinski, the President's adviser on national security.

Moments later, Energy Secretary James R. Schlesinger arrived and joined the meeting. Neither man would comment after conferring with Mr. Brzezinski for 15 minutes.

Mr. Schlesinger's presence at the White House earlier in the day to confer with Mr. Powell and Hamilton Jordan, the President's top political aide, led many reporters to conclude that Mr. Carter's announcement would concern China. The Energy Secretary recently returned from a visit to China where he discussed cooperation in oil exploration and other energy matters.

Later, members of the Democratic and Republican Congressional leadership and key members of the Senate and House foreign relations committees were summoned to a 6:15 P.M. special White House briefing. Several said before they went in that they had no hint of what would be discussed.

Indication Came in Jerusalem

The first indication that an important foreign policy announcement was to be made came on Wednesday in Jerusalem, where Secretary of State Cyrus R. Vance was conferring with Israeli leaders over the proposed language of an Israeli-Egyptian peace treaty.

At the conclusion of a meeting with the Israeli Prime Minister, Menachem Begin, Mr. Vance was told that the President wanted to speak to him on the telephone. The Secretary drove to the mansion that houses the offices and residence of the United States Consul General and spoke with Mr. Carter for 15 minutes. Mr. Vance emerged and told reporters later that it was imperative he be back in Washington by Friday night, regardless of how the Middle East talks were progressing.

The Secretary refused to tell the reporters accompanying him on his Middle East mission any more, except to assure them that it would all be clear by Friday night.

The impression that the speech would deal with China mounted as the day wore on. ABC television reported in the afternoon that the President would announce a meeting with Chinese leaders on United States soil sometime in the near future.

Last night, Mr. Carter discussed relations with China in an interview with Barbara Walters. Citing the "great improvements in our relationship with China in recent months," the President said that the United States was pursuing the normalization of relations with China according to the terms of the Shanghai Communiqué.

"Whenever the Chinese are ready to move, we are," Mr. Carter said.

The President added, however, that since President Nixon and President Gerald R. Ford had both gone to China without a reciprocal visit by the Chinese. "I don't intend to go to China until after the Chinese leaders come here."

* * *

December 17, 1978

U.S. OFFICIALS EXPECT CHINA MOVE TO RESULT IN A GLOBAL REALIGNMENT

New International Order Seen

By RICHARD BURT
Special to The New York Times.

WASHINGTON, Dec. 16—White House officials said today that the establishment of full diplomatic relations with China should lead to a fundamental realignment of global politics.

Officials in the White House and the State Department said in interviews that President Carter's decision would help move global politics away from a system dominated by two military giants, the United States and the Soviet Union, toward an international order composed of several major powers, including China.

Although Peking still insists that American arms exports to Taiwan are unnecessary and undesirable, it did not make this a prerequisite to formal relations with the United States.

Officials See Wide Approval

Evidently pleased with developments, officials said the decision had met with widespread approval abroad and the President had been congratulated by Richard M. Nixon and Gerald R. Ford, his predecessors, and by Henry A. Kissinger, the former Secretary of State.

However, on Capitol Hill, the move was seen by some as an abandonment of Taiwan, and others complained about the lack of consultation with the Congress.

There were suggestions, for example, by Senator Bob Dole, Republican of Kansas, that the announcement had been timed to offset new problems in the Middle East, but this was denied by White House officials.

Accord Had Momentum of Its Own

"The process of reaching an agreement had a momentum of its own," one aide said. "It was unconnected with domestic considerations and was brought about by the decision of the Chinese to accept our terms for the establishment of relations."

Officials said the main benefits for the United States were twofold: Normal relations will enable the United States to establish strong trade and technological links; they will also give the United States greater diplomatic flexibility in East Asia and around the world.

On the strategic aspects, a Defense Department official said the new relationship would enhance national security and the situation of American forces in the Western Pacific. This view is shared by the Joint Chiefs of Staff, he added.

The official said the United States felt that normalization would have been more difficult to accomplish at some future time if China's relations with the United States deteriorated or if China's relations with the Soviet Union changed. A convergence of Soviet-Chinese policy would complicate the security interests of the United States, he said.

Asked whether China had ceased to be an adversary, the Pentagon official said he would not go that far. But he said normalization meant that China had ceased to be a major military threat.

White House aides said the step would not worsen ties with the Soviet Union nor interfere with efforts to conclude an accord limiting strategic arms. They insisted that the timing of the decision was not connected with a possible meeting early next year between Mr. Carter and Leonid I. Brezhnev, the Soviet leader.

Brzezinski Denies Any Linkage

"This was a strategic development in its own right," Zbigniew Brzezinski, Presidential assistant for national security, said in an interview. "It was not directed toward the Soviets or anyone else, but was designed to accomplish our objective of shaping a more open, pluralistic international system."

The Carter Administration's desire to move foreign policy away from a preoccupation with its military equal, the Soviet Union, is similar to the strategy pursued by President Nixon and Mr. Kissinger in 1972 when the first steps were taken to open ties with Peking. But despite Mr. Kissinger's support for a "multipolar world," American efforts to establish formal ties with China faltered after 1972 and the Soviet Union gradually emerged as the central preoccupation during the Ford Administration.

While Mr. Carter has stressed the importance of good ties with Moscow, upon entering office he is said to have given the normalization of relations with China equal priority. The keenest supporter of putting relations with China on an equal basis has been Mr. Brzezinski, and officials said he had been the driving force within the effort to reach a compromise with Peking.

While the Chinese-American communiqué says that Taiwan will be considered part of China after Jan. 1, the United States has reserved the right to continue unofficial economic and cultural contacts with Taiwan.

Officials said the United States, in essence, was adopting the policy chosen by Japan toward Taiwan when it recognized China in 1972. This involved the continuation of contacts with Taiwan while acknowledging Peking's formal control.

Except for the withdrawal of about 700 American servicemen from Taiwan next year, officials did not anticipate any changes in the near future in patterns of economic investment or other forms of American involvement.

And while Peking has not formally pledged to refrain from invading Taiwan, a White House aide said the recent negotiations between Peking and Washington had demonstrated that Peking had no such intention.

Privately, State Department officials said that one of the chief factors driving Peking to complete talks on normalization was the likelihood of a Carter-Brezhnev meeting. They said Mr. Carter's invitation to Teng Hsiao-ping, the Chinese leader, which was evidently issued at a crucial point in the negotiations earlier this week, may have had a decisive impact on China's decision to accept the United States terms for normalization.

Brezhnev's Interest in Accord Cited

The officials said full relations between Washington and Peking would be bound to affect Moscow. But several aides said Mr. Brezhnev was more interested in completing an arms accord than in upsetting relations with the United States.

Although the President's decision to abrogate the mutual defense treaty with Taiwan has provoked criticism from conservative ranks, officials said nothing in either the joint Chinese-American communiqué or the unilateral statements jeopardized Taiwan's security.

They said that Mr. Carter had affirmed an interest in the peaceful resolution of differences between mainland China and Taiwan and that Peking's own statement, by Prime Minister Hua Kuo-feng, had not contradicted that view. They also said that Peking would allow the United States to maintain cultural, commercial and other unofficial relations with Taiwan.

According to officials, this means that the United States, after the defense treaty with Taiwan expires on Dec. 31, 1979, will still be able to provide Taiwan with some defensive weapons.

The officials said Peking's willingness to permit American arms sales to Taiwan after the defense treaty expired was the single most important concession by Peking. Although the Chinese had indicated earlier that they would be prepared to accept continued arms sales, White House aides said it was only this week that the position was made formal.

Officials suggested that the desire of the United States to bolster the present Chinese leadership also played an important role. Following a course advocated by Deputy Prime Minister Teng, Peking has moved in recent months to open new economic and political ties with the West.

However, the political situation in Peking continues to be fluid, and the United States is said to have viewed normalization as a means of showing support for Mr. Teng's moderate policies.

* * *

December 25, 1978

CAMBODIA-VIETNAM BATTLES SPUR U.S. CONCERN OVER 'PROXY' WAR

By DAVID BINDER

Special to The New York Times.

WASHINGTON, Dec. 24—The Carter Administration has become more concerned in recent days over increased fighting between Cambodia and Vietnam, which knowledgeable officials now characterize as full-scale war.

The Administration's concern focuses not only on the impact of the fighting on Indochina but also upon its potential for involving the major powers in the rivalry, specifically China on behalf of Cambodia and the Soviet Union for Vietnam.

Murder Called Politically Motivated

In Peking today, Cambodian officials were quoted by Reuters as having said that an attack yesterday on three western visitors to Phnom Penh was politically motivated, designed to show that Cambodia could not protect its friends. A British scholar, Malcolm Caldwell, was killed in that attack. Two American journalists in the same party, which was staying in a government guest house in the Cambodian capital, escaped injury in the attack.

Diplomats in Peking suggested that the attack on Mr. Caldwell, a London University lecturer, might have been staged by a new insurgency movement, whose establishment was recently announced by Hanoi radio.

It is 11 months since Zbigniew Brzezinski, the President's national-security adviser, described what was then a violent border conflict between Cambodia and Vietnam as a "proxy war," with the respective combatants acting as proxies for China and the Soviet Union. At that time none of the Indochina specialists in the United States' intelligence and defense communities accepted this definition, arguing that the rivalry between the two Indochinese neighbors was much too grave and deeply rooted in history to be explained in such terms.

The American officials said they also had the impression that neither China nor the Soviet Union was in a position to exercise decisive influence on the two Indochinese parties. They added that there were signs that China had become increasingly annoyed with the belligerent conduct of the Phnom Penh leadership.

They note, for instance, that in recent commentaries the Chinese press has emphasized the "strength of Cambodia forces" but has avoided any ringing endorsement of the Government headed by Prime Minister Pol Pot. "We have the impression the Chinese are less than happy with Pol Pot," one official remarked.

"The amount of leverage Peking has is not that great," another official declared. "They cannot dictate to Phnom Penh. Peking would prefer the situation of a year ago: tension, but not war."

While the analysts still do not accept Mr. Brzezinski's definition, they now acknowledge that the fierce fighting, if protracted, could well draw China and the Soviet Union more deeply into the confrontation.

China has supplied Cambodia with what Administration officials said was 99 percent of its current war matériel, including tanks and heavy artillery, through the port of Kompong Som on the Gulf of Siam. The Soviet Union is the principal weapons supplier for Vietnam. Both Cambodia and Vietnam also draw on large stocks of war booty that were left after the United States' withdrawal from Indochina in 1975.

American analysts, drawing on what they freely acknowledge is "a limited fund of information," as one put it, believe Vietnam has already begun a dry-season offensive aimed at establishing a large permanently occupied area along the 750-mile frontier with Cambodia.

'Alternate Homeland' for Cambodians

They have also concluded that Vietnam intends that this area serve as a kind of alternate homeland, with a puppet Cambodian regime, for thousands of Cambodians disaffected from the harsh Phnom Penh regime.

A political organization sympathetic to Vietnam has already been established in the frontier area in the form of a 14-member committee called the Kampuchean National United Front for National Salvation. Kampuchea is the Pol Pot Government's name for Cambodia.

An American official called the Kampuchean Front "totally a creation of the Vietnamese," though its leaders, including the chairman, Heng Samrien, appear to be of Cambodian origin. The declared aim of the organization, expressed in a manifesto issued earlier this month, is to bring down the Pol Pot Government.

Policy Shift Alarming to U.S.

A high-ranking State Department official said that Vietnam's policy shift over the last year from noninterference in Cambodia to an attempt to topple a neighboring Government was alarming to the United States, and "very unsettling" for the independent states of the region.

This alarm was expressed in a public statement by the State Department of "serious concern" about the growing conflict, coupled with a warning to Vietnam that its latest moves were prejudicial to the establishment of normal diplomatic ties between Hanoi and Washington. Talks between the two sides on relations were last held in September at the United Nations.

Japan has also indicated sharp concerns about the growing conflict, and has advised Hanoi that future Japanese foreign aid would be conditional on Vietnamese behavior in the conflict with Cambodia.

American analysts, worried as they are about the latest developments in the conflict, including the signing of a friendship and mutual-assistance treaty between the Soviet Union and Vietnam last month, voice skepticism about Hanoi's ability to crush Cambodia. They note factors such as the apparently excellent morale of Cambodia's ground forces, which they rate as higher than that of Vietnam's much larger and better-equipped army. They also point out the ruggedness of much of the terrain along the Cambodian border and the vulnerability of the Vietnamese to hit-and-run guerrilla attacks by the Cambodians.

4 Vietnamese Salients in Cambodia

As depicted by the analysts, the Vietnamese, fielding about 100,000 troops in 13 to 14 divisions, have developed four sizable salients into Cambodian territory. The first straddles Route 19 in the north opposite Ban Kheo, the second extends beyond Snuol, the third beyond the plantation town of Mimot and the fourth near Svay Rieng.

But the American officials also say that long-range Cambodian patrols have demonstrated the ability to strike deep into Vietnamese territory in recent months, and cite mortar attacks on towns in the Central Highlands region. "It is not a nice logical little war," one official commented, adding that even with overwhelming military superiority, Vietnam was not capable of sealing the entire frontier.

Remarking that it was the Pol Pot Government that began the hostilities by provoking border clashes three years ago, the American officials said they believed the Phnom Penh leadership had taken pre-emptive action out of fear that Vietnam intended ultimately to subjugate Cambodia, as it has Laos. Following the Cambodian rejection last spring of Vietnamese peace overtures and Vietnam's creation of the Kampuchean front on Dec. 3, this prophecy has fulfilled itself, they observed.

Hanoi Seen Seeking Dominance

They said an ominous aspect of these developments was that Hanoi, with Moscow's backing, now apparently seeks to become dominant in a region the Chinese view as vital to their national security. The analysts said they doubted that Vietnam would take the political risk of striking at Phnom Penh itself, though militarily such an attack would have a good chance of success. They also said there was no sign as yet that Vietnamese troops were poised to cut Route 4, connecting the capital to the harbor of Kompong Som.

* * *

January 14, 1979

IRAN'S EXILED MOSLEM LEADER PICKS COUNCIL TO FORM A RELIGIOUS STATE

Special to The New York Times.

PARIS, Jan. 13—Ayatollah Ruhollah Khomeini, the religious leader of Iran's opposition, stepped up his fight today for the ouster of the Shah and abolition of the monarchy, announcing that he had formed the equivalent of a shadow cabinet charged with preparing institutions for an Islamic republic in Iran.

The announcement said that cooperation with the Government of Prime Minister Shahpur Bakhtiar was illegal and would be considered a crime.

The 78-year-old Moslem leader said he believed that Shah Mohammed Riza Pahlevi would attempt a last-minute military coup in an effort to remain in power. The Ayatollah called on both the army and the people to thwart such an attempt.

Made Public at Exile Headquarters

The announcement was published at his exile headquarters in Neauphle-le-Château, 20 miles west of Paris. The Ayatollah has been living there since last fall, when he was expelled from Iraq, his previous place of exile. He has been issuing a steady stream of uncompromising declarations to his followers in Iran, asking for an end of the Shah's rule.

His announcement referred to the new body around him as the Council of the Islamic Revolution. The description of its functions made it appear to be a shadow cabinet. Council members, apparently chosen by the Ayatollah, were said to have been picked from among "competent Moslem militant individuals who are worthy of trust." No names were given.

The council has been charged with selecting and installing a "provisional government," which, in turn, is to name a provisional Parliament seen as the new republic's constituent assembly. The assembly will be asked to enact a constitution, under which democratic legislative elections can be held, with the ultimate transfer of power to those elected.

The announcement indicated, and a Khomeini aide confirmed, that the council was already in business. The announcement said its membership and location would be announced later.

In an interview with CBS News, broadcast in New York yesterday, the Moslem leader said that he expected an Islamic state to be formed in Iran within a few days and that he would be its ruler.

"I will appoint the new government," he said, indicating that Dr. Karim Sanjabi, an opposition leader in Iran, would be a member.

When an aide was asked what contacts there might be between the Ayatollah's provisional group and the Bakhtiar Government, he replied: "That Government is both illegal and illegitimate."

In the preamble of today's announcement, the Ayatollah invoked "the legal right and the vote of confidence of the majority of the Iranian people that has been given to me to accomplish Islamic objectives."

In warning about the Shah's intentions, the announcement said:

"It is possible that the traitor Shah, who will be forced to leave, will commit an even greater crime, that is, a military coup, his last weapon. But the valiant people of Iran know that the army, apart from a few bloodthirsty men in important posts and whom I know, will not let them perpetrate such a crime that goes counter to their religion and nationality.

"I warn the army and I ask the military, if such a plot exists, to thwart it and not to accept that a few bloodthirsty people should drench the country in blood.

"Soldiers obeying these officers will be responsible before God and humanity and will be cursed by the new generation."

The Ayatollah concluded by exhorting the people "not to abandon the fight before the final victory. The people must continue strikes and demonstrations and, if attacked by the corrupt, defend themselves, even if this may cause deaths."

There was no information about the Ayatollah's plans for returning to Iran, but the view was widely held here that he would be leaving in a matter of days.

* * *

January 20, 1979

WEST IS CONSIDERING MISSILE FOR EUROPE ABLE TO HIT SOVIET

A REPLY TO MOSCOW'S BUILDUP

Weapon, Discussed at Guadeloupe Parley, Seen as Response to SS-20 and New Bomber

By RICHARD BURT

Special to The New York Times.

WASHINGTON, Jan. 19—The leaders of the United States, Britain, France and West Germany are considering development of a new intermediate-range nuclear missile that would be based in Western Europe and be capable of striking the Soviet Union, Carter Administration officials said today.

They said the missile would be developed by the United States. The four Western leaders view it, the officials said, as a possible response to a new generation of Soviet nuclear missiles and bombers that are directed against Western Europe and are not limited by existing agreements.

The matter was discussed at the summit meeting in Guadeloupe earlier this month by President Carter, Prime Minister James Callaghan of Britain, President Valéry

Giscard d'Estaing of France and Chancellor Helmut Schmidt of West Germany. But, the Administration officials said, the leaders made no firm decision on the missile question.

Soviet SS-20 a Threat

The four leaders concluded, however, that a new Soviet intermediate-range weapon known as the SS-20 posed an unacceptable security threat to the West. Accordingly, a senior Administration official said, they agreed that the North Atlantic Treaty Organization "should explore very actively" its options for countering the Soviet missile, including the deployment of a similar weapon in Western Europe in the 1980's.

The discussions at Guadeloupe were said to have underscored what the official called "the bewildering array" of technical and political questions that must be resolved before a final decision is made.

Officials here reported that a consensus was growing within the Administration and the alliance that the United States would probably have to add a long-range nuclear missile to the arsenal of shorter-range ones now deployed in Western Europe if it was to maintain nuclear deterrence on the Continent over the coming decade.

3 Missiles Now Deployed

The United States now deploys three types of nuclear missiles there—the Pershing, the Lance and the Honest John—but none has a range exceeding 450 miles.

Pentagon aides said about $350 million had already been included in the defense budget for the 1980 fiscal year to speed development of several new weapons for possible deployment in Europe, including sea- and ground-launched cruise missiles, an extended-range Pershing and a new medium range ballistic missile.

Each of these would be able to travel about 1,000 miles, sufficient range from West Germany to strike key military installations in the western part of the Soviet Union. Defense officials said that the cruise missiles and the longer-range version of the Pershing could be deployed in the early 1980's but that it would take more than five years to develop a new intermediate-range ballistic missile.

According to officials, the question whether the West needs to field a new class of long-range missiles in Europe has emerged as a major issue in European-American relations because it is viewed as having enormous implications for the future of alliance unity as well as for prospects of further progress in Soviet-American arms control.

If a decision is made later this year to base a new American missile in Europe, it would mark a significant shift in Western strategy, for it would be the first time the United States deployed a weapon in Europe with the specific aim of attacking the Soviet Union. In the 1960's, the United States promoted the idea of an alliance-wide, "multilateral force" of nuclear missiles for Europe, but the concept was abandoned after it was sharply criticized on both sides of the Atlantic.

In an effort to avoid repetition of that controversy or of the more recent one involving the neutron or enhanced-radiation weapon, White House and State Department aides said that alliance governments were making a special effort to examine the implications of putting a new missile in Europe.

Alliance military analysts are weighing the pros and cons of each of the three missile systems being considered in the United States, and while no decision has been made, some officials indicated that the longer-range Pershing was the leading candidate.

The debate within the alliance over a new missile began in 1977 as alarm grew in West Europe over Moscow's decision to begin deploying the SS-20, a mobile missile equipped with three multiple war-heads. Although a Soviet force of some 500 intermediate-range missiles had been aimed against Western Europe since the early 1960's, the SS-20, together with a new Soviet bomber called the Backfire, was viewed in some quarters as an attempt by Moscow to make Western Europe a "nuclear hostage."

The concerns were reinforced early last year when West European governments learned that the proposed Soviet-American accord limiting strategic missiles and bombers would not hinder Moscow's ability to deploy either the SS-20 or the Backfire bomber.

Europeans Fear Neglect

In private conversations with Administration officials last year, several European governments expressed fears that in negotiating with Moscow the United States might neglect European security concerns.

In an attempt to allay these fears, the Administration set up special consultative machinery on problems posed by the SS-20, including a so-called "high-level group" of defense officials that met several times in 1978. In addition, delegations from Britain, France and West Germany quietly came to Washington last fall for discussions.

* * *

February 18, 1979

CHINESE TROOPS AND PLANES ATTACK VIETNAM; U.S. URGES WITHDRAWAL, HANOI IN PLEA TO U.N.

4 PROVINCES INVADED

***Thrust Reported All Along Border—
Peking Says Move Is Retaliatory***

By FOX BUTTERFIELD
Special to The New York Times.

HONG KONG, Sunday, Feb. 18—The Chinese Government announced last night that its troops had struck against Vietnam along much of their 480-mile border.

The Vietnam News Agency reported yesterday evening that Chinese troops, supported by aircraft and artillery, had attacked four Vietnamese border provinces earlier in the day from Quang Ninh in the east to Hoang Lien Son in the west.

There was no immediate word from either Peking or Hanoi on how far the Chinese had pushed into Vietnam. But Hsinhua, the Chinese press agency, called the action counterattacks. In a dispatch with the dateline "Kwangsi and Yunnan Border Fronts," the agency said "fighting is still going on" at the time of the transmission.

China Disavows Territorial Aims

Hsinhua asserted that Peking did "not want a single inch of Vietnamese territory" and that "after counterattacking the Vietnamese aggressors as they deserve, the Chinese frontier troops will strictly keep to defending the border of their own country."

The Chinese attack began at 4 A.M. yesterday Peking time (3 P.M. Friday, New York time). It followed by six weeks the Vietnamese invasion of Cambodia and seizure of its capital, Phnom Penh, and by 15 weeks the Vietnamese signing of a treaty of peace and cooperation with the Soviet Union.

China is still supporting Cambodian forces loyal to Prime Minister Pol Pot, whose regime was routed by the Vietnamese.

Vietnamese Ask Soviet Help

The Vietnamese news agency said last night that "the people and Government of Vietnam "urgently call on the Soviet Union, the fraternal socialist countries" and other friendly countries throughout the world to "support and defend Vietnam." A spokesman for the Vietnamese Foreign Ministry said a letter had been sent to the United Nations Security Council calling on China to cease its "invasion."

> [At the United Nations, Vietnam accused China of launching a "war of aggression" and asked the United Nations to take "appropriate measures" to force Peking's troops to withdraw from Vietnam.]

China appeared to be trying to limit the repercussions of its actions to prevent a long fight with Vietnam or retaliation by the Soviet Union.

Hsinhua said the Chinese Government proposed that "the two sides speedily hold negotiations at any mutually agreed place" to discuss "the restoration of peace and tranquillity along the border."

The Chinese attack, if Peking cannot bring a quick end to the fighting, could seriously damage China's ambitious drive for economic modernization, diverting scarce resources and frightening off foreign businessmen. It could also impair Peking's new relations with the United States, raising fears that China might also invade Taiwan rather than seek to reunify the Nationalist-held island with the mainland peacefully.

Until 1975 when the Indochina war ended, China supported Vietnam against the United States. sending $10 billion worth of aid tot he Vietnamese, much of it over the railroad that runs from the Chinese border to Hanoi in the area where the Chinese attacked today. If the Chinese push far along the western part of the front, they will soon come to Dien Bien Phu, the scene of France's climactic defeat in the first Indochina war in 1954.

That the Chinese chose to attack Vietnam despite these considerations suggests that Peking felt very deeply it had to respond to what it saw as a joint Soviet-Vietnamese strategy to encircle and humiliate it.

Peking's anxieties were greatly heightened when Moscow and Hanoi signed an alliance accord last November, with provision for mutual defense, and then Vietnam invaded Cambodia in December.

Hsinhua said today that China acted only after Vietnam had "ignored China's repeated warnings" and "continually sent armed forces to encroach on Chinese territory and attack Chinese frontier guards and inhabitants."

"The Chinese frontier troops are fully justified to rise in counterattack when they are driven beyond forebearance," the dispatch asserted.

The press agency said that its announcement, released shortly after midnight Peking time, had been authorized by the Chinese government.

Vietnamese Mission to Cambodia

The timing of the Chinese attack may be connected to the arrival in Cambodia Friday of a large segment of Vietnam's leadership. The Vietnamese delegation, headed by Prime Minister Pham Van Dong and the Army Chief of Staff, Gen. Van Tien Dung, reportedly was scheduled to sign an alliance with the new regime of President Heng Samrin, which Vietnamese forces installed in Phnom Penh last month.

The Chinese were deeply angered by the swift Vietnamese takeover of Cambodia, seeing it not only as an effort by a traditional enemy, Vietnam, to become a major regional power, but also as part of a maneuver sponsored by the Soviet Union to demonstrate China's inability to defend its friends.

The Chinese Communists have been very sensitive about threats to their borders, particularly when their warning signals have been ignored. In two earlier cases, when United States forces approached the Yalu River in the Korean War in 1950 and again in a dispute over frontier territory with India in 1962, Peking reacted by attacks.

Over the last few weeks China has reportedly evacuated a large number of civilians who live near the Soviet border in Sinkiang Province in the northwest. Analysts here say that the Russians have increased patrols by their warplanes in the area, where the Chinese have relatively fewer troops than along their northeast border, close to one of their major industrial centers.

Since Vietnam's takeover of Cambodia, China had reportedly moved about 100,000 troops, supported by tanks, artillery and up to one-third of its fighter planes, to the border with Vietnam. The Vietnamese are said to have about 60,000 to 80,000 troops in the frontier region, in well-fortified positions and heavily defended by Soviet-built surface-to-air missiles and the country's small but modern air force.

Ally of Teng Reported in Command

The Chinese forces are believed to be commanded by Hsu Shih-yu, a member of the Communist Politburo and close ally of Mr. Teng, and Yang Teh-chih, a former deputy commander of the Chinese troops during the Korean War. Mr. Hsu, a blunt man who was born a peasant, is head of the Canton military region, and Mr. Yang was transferred to command the Kunming military region along the border in Yunnan only last month.

Like most senior Chinese officials, they are both elderly. Mr. Hsu is 73 years old, Mr. Yang 69.

Although the attack began early Saturday morning, neither Peking nor Hanoi disclosed it until late last night.

Hsinhua, in its announcement, charged that over the last six months the Vietnamese had made over 700 armed "provocations" along the border and "killed or wounded more than 300 Chinese frontier guards and inhabitants."

The press agency said that "by such rampant acts of aggression the Vietnamese authorities have meant to provoke military conflicts."

"It is the consistent position of the Chinese Government and people that 'we will not attack until we are attacked—if attacked we will certainly counterattack,' " it said.

Analysts here are uncertain which side was actually responsible for most of the border incidents, though some diplomats feel there is evidence the Vietnamese had recently been acting provocatively, confident of Russian backing. In the past few weeks, for example, Vietnamese gunboats are said to have run in close to shore on China's Haman Island, well across the Gulf of Tonkin from Vietnam, without the Chinese firing at them.

Hsinhua said last night that the Chinese Government was ready to hold talks with Vietnam at "an appropriate level" to discuss both the fighting and a full settlement of the border issue.

* * *

April 24, 1979

NEW MISSILE IS PLACED IN EUROPE BY SOVIET; 2 MORE ARE EXPECTED

By RICHARD BURT
Special to The New York Times.

WASHINGTON, April 23—The Soviet Union has begun to deploy a new nuclear-armed missile in East Germany, a step that Carter Administration officials described today as raising the risk of a stepped-up arms race in Europe.

The officials said that the missile, designated the SS-21 by American intelligence analysts, was recently observed with Soviet forces in East Germany. It is described as the first new nuclear missile deployed in Eastern Europe in over a decade and as one of three short-range missiles that the Soviet Union has recently developed. A White House official foresaw the others showing up in Eastern Europe in the coming months.

The SS-21 is described as belonging to the class of so-called tactical nuclear missiles that the United States and the Soviet Union have deployed on the territory of their European allies since the mid-1950's. Both have several hundred short-range nuclear missiles there, as well as nuclear bombs that can be carried by fighter aircraft.

The Russians' evident decision to expand their shorter-range nuclear arsenal comes as Moscow and Washington are reaching the final stages of a treaty limiting strategic—that is, long range—weapons. The SS-21 would not be limited under the treaty, and Administration aides view the Soviet deployment as a worrisome sign that an accord covering strategic arms could have the effect of increased competition in shorter-range missiles in and around Europe.

With a range of about 75 miles, the SS-21 is believed to be similar in design to the American Lance missile, which was deployed in Western Europe in 1972. Also included in the Russians' effort to upgrade their nuclear capability directed against Western Europe is a new intermediate-range missile, the SS-20, which was deployed last year and is based in western areas of the Soviet Union.

Several Western European leaders, including Helmut Schmidt, the West German Chancellor, have expressed concern over new Soviet nuclear deployments and have privately urged President Carter to include the weapons in the negotiations with Moscow. So far the talks have not focused on nuclear arms deployed in Europe, but Mr. Carter has said that after the completion of the treaty he wants to make that category of weapons a prime subject of a new round of negotiations.

Secretary of Defense Harold Brown and the defense ministers of the major Western European countries are scheduled to meet at Homestead Air Force Base in southern Florida tomorrow for two days of secret talks on whether the North Atlantic Treaty Organization should modernize its short-range nuclear arsenal in response to the Soviet weapon. In particular, officials said, the ministers will address the sensitive subject of developing and deploying a nuclear missile that would be based in Western Europe and would be capable of striking targets in the Soviet Union.

Although senior Defense Department officials are pressing allied governments to agree to a plan for the missile by the end of the year, many Europeans are skeptical and are said to be asking that the Administration investigate the possibility of conferring with the Russians on a limitation on new tactical nuclear arms in Europe. Officials said that the appearance of the Soviet SS-21 in East Germany would be likely to intensify this issue by putting increased pressure on West Germany and other countries to approve American plans for modernizing NATO's tactical missile forces.

In addition, some Pentagon officials argued that it could raise once again the controversial question of the deployment of the American neutron weapon, an enhanced-radiation device designed for use against personnel. A year ago, after a long and divisive debate in NATO over whether to deploy it aboard short-range American missiles in Europe, Mr. Carter decided against production. However, he said that he would reconsider if the Soviet Union failed to exercise restraint in nuclear deployments.

The discovery of the SS-21 in East Germany has already led some military officials and aides in the National Security

Council to suggest that it might be timely to review Mr. Carter's decision. However, White House officials said that with a meeting between President Carter and Leonid I. Brezhnev, the Soviet leader, likely to be announced in the coming weeks, the chances of a review of the neutron decision were slim.

* * *

June 16, 1979

BREZHNEV ARRIVES IN VIENNA AND SEES CARTER FOR 1ST TIME

THEY ATTEND OPERA TOGETHER

Soviet Chief Seems Stiff but Spry—Brings High Officials With Him to the Arms Talks

By CRAIG R. WHITNEY
Special to The New York Times.

VIENNA, June 15—Leonid I. Brezhnev, the Soviet leader, met President Carter for the first time today.

Mr. Brezhnev, who is both Chairman of the Soviet Communist Party and President, looked gray, somewhat uncertain on his feet but spry. He led three other members of the party's ruling Politburo here to begin a weekend of meetings that will lead to the signing of a treaty limiting the deployment of strategic weapons by the world's two major powers.

It was the highest Soviet delegation of any recent East-West summit meeting, including not only the Foreign Minister, Andrei A. Gromyko, 69 years old, and the Defense Minister, Marshal Dmitri F. Ustinov, 70, but also a longtime political ally and close personal aide of Mr. Brezhnev, 67-year-old Konstantin U. Chernenko.

Brezhnev Lays a Wreath

The Soviet leaders touched down in an IL-62 jetliner at 9:40 A.M., almost exactly 12 hours after President Carter's arrival. The 72-year-old Mr. Brezhnev waved from the plane's ramp to the assembled crowd and was sped into the city in the front passenger seat of a black Soviet Zil limousine that had been flown in for the conference.

A few hours later, the Soviet leader, after some confusion about where he was to stand, laid a wreath to the memory of Soviet war dead at a monument in downtown Vienna. Soviet and other Allied troops occupied the city from 1945 until Austria was declared neutral in 1955.

He first met with President Carter late this afternoon, during a courtesy call the two leaders paid on the Austrian President, Rudolf Kirchschlager, at the Hofburg, the court of the Hapsburg emperors during Vienna's imperial age. They smiled broadly at each other and shook hands.

'He'll Start Jogging'

About an hour later, both went to the State Opera to see Mozart's "The Abduction from the Seraglio." The opera was conducted by Karl Böhm, who received more applause than did the two leaders.

Associated Press

President Carter and Leonid I. Brezhnev meeting at the Hofburg in Vienna. Their interpreters are behind them.

Mr. Carter and his wife, Rosalynn, wore evening clothes. Mr. Brezhnev wore the dark blue suit and maroon tie in which he had arrived. He was accompanied by Mr. Gromyko and Marshal Ustinov, who wore full uniform.

An aide to Mr. Carter, told that the custom in Vienna was for the audience to promenade in a circle around the Baroque opera house during intermissions, remarked, "If Jimmy hears that the promenade is oval-shaped, he'll start jogging." The President has recently taken up jogging for exercise.

Mr. Brezhnev and the President sat together in a box. They smiled at each other several times during the performance, but left at the first intermission, which came after the second act of the three-act opera. On the street, Mr. Brezhnev was heckled by relatives and friends of Soviet dissidents who have been demonstrating here for several days in an effort to secure the dissidents' release or emigration. The President left the opera house a few minutes after Mr. Brezhnev, and aides explained that he was tired.

Mr. Brezhnev's health, which has been failing in recent years, was the subject of intense speculation before his arrival. Unlike Mr. Carter, who is 54 years old, the Soviet leader did not make a speech on arriving. He walked carefully and slowly along a red carpet to review an Austrian Army honor guard in sunny, fresh weather, and stood stiffly at attention while the Soviet and Austrian national anthems were played.

Soviet Citizens Cheer

In recent months, Mr. Brezhnev's speech has been labored and slurred. His conversation with President Kirchschläger at the airport this morning was not audible to onlookers. He wore a hearing aid in his left ear and a different device in his right. For Soviet journalists and officials here, however, there is no doubt that despite his age and infirmity, he is the man in charge.

Defense Minister Ustinov and the Chief of Staff of the armed forces, Marshal Nikolai V. Ogarkov, came with Mr. Brezhnev to participate in discussions about the strategic-arms treaty the two sides are to sign on Monday. United States officials said today they believed the military leaders had been included because Mr. Carter brought Secretary of Defense Harold Brown and the Chairman of the Joint Chiefs of Staff, Gen. David C. Jones.

The Foreign Minister, Mr. Gromyko, met this afternoon with Secretary of State Cyrus R. Vance, and is expected to play a major role in the four sets of talks the two chiefs of state have scheduled at the Soviet and United States Embassies tomorrow and Sunday.

The main subject of speculation here, however, was the presence of Mr. Chernenko in the delegation. He became a deputy member of the Politburo in 1977, and a little more than a year later, last November, Mr. Brezhnev had him appointed to full membership. Mr. Chernenko has grown steadily in power and authority since that time, and his presence may indicate that the successors to the present Soviet leadership will continue to support the arms-limitation treaty.

* * *

June 18, 1979

CARTER'S OBJECTIVES IN VIENNA

His Long-Term Aim Is to Talk Beyond Brezhnev To Those Who Will Be Leading Soviet in the 80's

By HEDRICK SMITH
Special to The New York Times.

VIENNA, June 17—Relaxing on the flight here from the United States, President Carter fell to talking with his aides about charges made by Senator Henry M. Jackson, the Washington Democrat, that Mr. Carter was guilty of appeasement of the Russians. Somebody mentioned that the weather in Vienna was overcast.

"Would God that it doesn't rain," a presidential aide said, evoking memories of Neville Chamberlain and the umbrella that still symbolizes his appeasement of Hitler at Munich in 1938.

"I'd rather drown than carry an umbrella," the President declared firmly. He did not drown, but he did have to stand bareheaded through a drizzle at the welcoming ceremonies.

Within 48 hours, he was jousting readily with Leonid I. Brezhnev, the Soviet leader, over which country was increasing defense spending more rapidly, over Soviet-American competition in the third world, over the secrecy of the Soviet system and his own decision to go ahead with the MX mobile missile, showing that he could hold his own with the Soviet leader without provoking a blowup in relations.

They have been fundamental disagreements, voiced without reticence but also without rancor. The American eagerness to describe them in detail indicates how vital Mr. Carter considers this posture of realistic and unflappable firmness to be to his principal objectives at this summit conference, objectives forced upon him, in part, by political weakness at home and by the failing health of Mr. Brezhnev.

His first and most immediate goal is to have the prearranged arms control package signed by Mr. Brezhnev, while the 72-year-old Soviet party chief and President is still well enough, and to use this occasion to gain momentum for the drive to gain Senate approval of the arms treaty.

His long-term objective, perhaps the most subtle and most important of all, is to talk beyond Mr. Brezhnev to others in the Soviet leadership who will be around when Mr. Brezhnev is gone and who will have to deal in the 1980's with the complexities of the next phase of strategic arms negotiations and other intricate issues.

His medium-term objective, the one that so far has most eluded him, is to get across the message to current and future Soviet leaders that they are jeopardizing détente by their opportunistic strategy in the third world and to press them for specific steps of moderation.

To both Mr. Carter and the Brezhnev faction in the ruling Soviet Politburo, which wants "to restore détente," as one Russian put it, the atmosphere here is important. So far, both leaders seem pleased by what they have begun calling "the common sense" summit meeting they have created. They seek agreement but recognize their limits. And candor about disagreement helps both rebut skeptics at home who feel they may be going too far toward appeasement.

Ready to Face Congress

To capitalize on this carefully modulated easing of relations, Mr. Carter has assembled his forces for the next round—before Congress tomorrow night. He has reinforced his normal foreign policy team by bringing along such political aides as Frank Moore, his chief Congressional liaison specialist; Anne Wexler, his top domestic lobbyist; Gerald Rafshoon, his press and television adviser, and Hendrik Hertzberg, his favorite speechwriter, who has been working night and day on his report to Congress on the arms treaty and the Vienna meeting.

And with much longer-term objectives in mind, the Americans structured their own delegation to induce Mr. Brezhnev to enlarge his team to include three other Politburo members—Foreign Minister Andrei A. Gromyko, Defense Minister Dmitri F. Ustinov; Konstantin U. Chernenko, a potential successor to Mr. Brezhnev, and Marshal Nikolai V. Ogarkov, the Soviet Chief of Staff. Today, at American initiative, the Soviet and American Defense Ministers and military chiefs met in a separate session for the first time since World War II to follow up on the broader discussions between Mr. Carter and Mr. Brezhnev.

What Mr. Carter sought to do, his aides said, was to set out the intricate issues that lie ahead for the next era of arms control—tricky issues such as the vulnerability and survivability of strategic weapons, new types of verification, the complexities of cruise missiles with their shallow trajectories, the problems raised by civil defense and air defense systems.

Must Lead in Arms Control

The White House view is that the United States not only leads in arms technology but also must take the lead in introducing new concepts of arms control and must act as a catalyst for Soviet thinking for the 1980's, much as officials now believe President Johnson and former Secretary of Defense Robert S. McNamara did during their summit meeting in 1967 with the Soviet Prime Minister, Aleskei N. Kosygin.

In hindsight, the Americans are now crediting that summit meeting with setting out the framework for the first strategic arms treaty, signed in 1972. Similarily, Mr. Carter and his advisers hope that they have been able to lay the groundwork here for the structure of a third arms agreement. Today, they were especially pleased that Marshal Ustinov, the Defense Minister, seemed to have been so engaged in those discussions.

But in the third realm, this summit meeting has apparently struck upon a rock. The two leaders have not visibly narrowed their differences over competition in Asia, Africa and the Middle East. More forcefully than before, President Carter warned at dinner tonight that if the Soviet Union seeks "to exploit the turbulence that exists in various parts of the world," it will push the superpowers toward "the road of competition and even confrontation" and the United States "will protect its vital interests."

No Response in Other Areas

From what American officials have revealed, Mr. Carter has heard no encouragement from Mr. Brezhnev in response to persistent American concerns about gaining Soviet acquiescence for continuing the United Nations peace force in the Middle East, about getting Cuban troops out of Angola or Ethiopia and Vietnamese forces out of Cambodia, or about help in stemming the forced emigration of thousands of refugees from Vietnam.

Significantly, Mr. Brezhnev seemed to put compromise and concession in those areas on a backburner by ridiculing as "sheer invention" the Carter Administration's worry that the West, after the upheaval in Iran, faces "an arc of crisis" from West Africa through Central Asia. And he sternly put the United States on notice that there would be "grave and even dangerous consequences" if the Senate tried to amend and tinker with the arms treaty.

It was tough, straightforward talk amid what President Carter called the friendly and harmonious mood of the private dinners. As an Administration official observed tonight, the Americans have run into a still unbridgeable ideological gap that blocks real progress on most issues other than arms control and, as the two sides agreed at dinner tonight, "makes the dove of peace the hardest bird of all to hit."

* * *

June 19, 1979

PRESIDENT, WARNING OF ARMS RACE, SETS THEME FOR DEBATE ON THE PACT

By BERNARD GWERTZMAN
Special to The New York Times.

WASHINGTON, June 18—President Carter told a joint session of Congress tonight that the strategic arms limitation treaty he signed today in Vienna with Leonid I. Brezhnev, the Soviet leader, would help prevent "an uncontrolled and pointless nuclear arms race that would damage the security of all countries including our own."

In a nationally televised speech two hours after Air Force One landed at Andrews Air Force Base, Mr. Carter tried to seize the initiative quickly and set forth Administration themes for a national debate on the new treaty, asserting that it "will withstand the most severe scrutiny because it is so clearly in the interest of American security and world peace."

As Mr. Carter was flying home, opponents of the treaty were developing plans for the Senate debate on the pact.

A Struggle Awaits Carter

The President went before the Senators and Representatives knowing that his Administration faced a difficult struggle in coming months to win the necessary two-thirds margin for approval by the Senate.

Senator Alan Cranston, the Democratic whip from California, said today that at this moment he counted 58 votes for the treaty, 30 against and 12 undecided. To gain approval of the treaty, the Administration needs 67 votes.

Mr. Carter looked serious and unsmiling as he slowly delivered his 40-minute speech. The reaction was largely polite attention. He was interrupted six times by applause, but not for any of the statements specifically involving the treaty.

The applause came when he called for an end to cycles of war and peace, when be asserted that American strength was growing, for a pledge to keep strong military power, for a warning about Cuban involvement in Africa, for determination to defend. American intersts and for praise of freedom as against tyranny.

Danger of Nuclear War Stressed

As he has done in the past, Mr. Carter argued for the treaty by referring to the dangers of nuclear war inherent in an unrestrained competition. "In the age of the hydrogen bomb," he said, "there is no longer any meaningful distinction between global war and global suicide."

He said the world has been living in a "twilight peace" in which there is always the possibility of "a catastrophic nuclear war, a war that in horror and destruction and death would dwarf all the combined wars of man's long and bloody history."

Without the treaty, President Carter went on, there would be greatly increased spending on strategic arms, greater uncertainty about the strategic balance, increased dangers of a spread of nuclear weapons and heightened East-West tensions.

Such tensions, Mr. Carter declared, "could escalate into superpower confrontations."

As to his overall impression of his three days of talks with Mr. Brezhnev, the President said:

"We have moved closer to the goal of stability and security in Soviet-American relations."

Few Details of Talks Disclosed

He provided few details about the talks themselves, leaving intact an impression conveyed from Vienna that the two sides had failed to make much headway in resolving major international differences.

But he said that the "strength of America" militarily, economically, diplomatically and politically, gave him confidence when he and Mr. Brezhnev "discussed specific areas of potential or indirect confrontation around the world, including southern Africa and the Middle East."

"For instance, I made it clear to President Brezhnev that Cuban military activities in Africa, sponsored or supported by the Soviet Union, and the growing Cuban involvement in the problems of Central America and the Caribbean, can only have a negative impact on United States-Soviet relations," he said, according to the text issued in advance by the White House.

Exchange Called 'Useful'

Mr. Carter did not dwell on the differences, however, and said in fact that the exchange with Mr. Brezhnev "was useful because it enabled us to clarify our positions directly to each other, face-to-face, and thus to reduce the changes of future miscalculations on both sides."

He said that he and Mr. Brezhnev had "developed a better sense of each other as leaders and as men."

This is important, he added, because "the responsibility for many decisions involving the future of the world rests on me as the leader of this great country, and it is vital that my judgments be based on as much first hand knowledge and experience as possible."

A major theme of the speech was the dual nature of American policy—to seek arms control accords and to maintain a strong defense, so strong, he said, that "no potential adversary could be tempted to attack us."

Most 'Comprehensive Treaty'

The treaty he signed, the President said, is "the most detailed, far-reaching, comprehensive treaty in the history of arms control."

Anticipating complaints that the United States had made too many concessions in the long negotiations, Mr. Carter said, "Neither side obtained everything it sought."

"But the package that emerged is a carefully balanced whole, and it will make the world a safer place for both sides," he declared.

The details of the treaty are complex but the fundamentals "are not so complex," Mr. Carter went on. "When all is said and done, SALT II is a matter of common sense."

The treaty reduces the danger of nuclear war, he said, by placing equal limits on each side's nuclear arsenal; it makes future competition "safer and more predictable;" it slows and "even reverses the momentum of the Soviet arms buildup" and it allows the United States to concentrate on building up conventional and allied forces.

"The treaty enhances our ability to monitor Soviet actions," Mr. Carter continued, "and it leads directly to the next step in controlling nuclear weapons."

Speech Like Nixon's in 1972

Mr. Carter's appearance on Capitol Hill tonight followed a pattern set by President Richard M. Nixon on June 1, 1972, when he spoke to a joint session less than a half-hour after returning from a four-nation journey that included his first meeting with Mr. Brezhnev.

In that speech, Mr. Nixon said that his trip to Moscow had laid the basis for "a new relationship between the two most powerful nations on earth."

During his meetings in Moscow, Mr. Nixon signed the first strategic arms limitation agreement, consisting of a treaty putting a ceiling of 200 on the number of antiballistic missiles permitted each side, and an interim accord putting a curb on land-based and submarine-launched offensive missiles. The Senate voted 88 to 2 on Sept. 14, 1972, to approve that treaty.

Jackson a Critic in 1972, and Now

The treaty that Mr. Carter and Mr. Brezhnev signed this morning in Vienna in a sense continues the process that was begun in 1972. The leading critic in the Congress in 1972 is the same Senator who is likely to play a major role in opposing the new treaty. Henry M. Jackson, Democrat of Washington.

Mr. Jackson, who said yesterday that no treaty would be better than the latest one, remarked that Mr. Nixon's speech to Congress seven years ago was "a very clever campaign speech."

Mr. Carter began his day in Vienna by holding his first private meeting with Mr. Brezhnev. With only their interpreters present, the two leaders conferred for 90 minutes at the American Embassy.

'Lots of Things' Discussed

Apparently to preserve some drama for tonight's speech, Mr. Carter told reporters that he and Mr. Brezhnev had discussed "lots of things," but he declined to provide details.

After the 35-minute signing ceremony. Mr. Carter and Mr. Brezhnev flew home.

Washington was considerably less excited by Mr. Carter's meeting with Mr. Brezhnev than it was by Mr. Nixon's meeting with the Soviet leader.

The 1972 meeting gave impetus to a period of more cordial relations known as "détente," which began to deteriorate when the United States and the Soviet Union found themselves airlifting supplies to the opposing forces in the Middle East war in October 1973.

Mr. Jackson and two Republican conservatives, Senators Jesse Helms of North Carolina and Jack Garn of Utah, have accused the Administration of practicing policies that could produce "appeasement," like the policies of the British Government toward Hitler's Germany on the eve of World War II.

Summing up, Mr. Carter said that the new treaty was "not a favor we are doing for the Soviet Union" but was rather "a deliberate, calculated move we are making as a matter of self-interest—a move that happens to serve the goals both of security and of survival, that strengthens both the military position of the United States and the cause of world peace."

He said that he and Mr. Brezhnev had discussed other nuclear matters that will be taken up in the next round of strategic arms negotiations—such as "deeper mutual reduction" in nuclear weapon inventories, stricter limits on the production of weapons, enhanced "survivability" and stability of authorized missile systems and advance notification of missile tests.

* * *

September 23, 1979

BRZEZINSKI CAUTIONS SOVIET ON CUBA UNIT

He Says Brigade Reflects 'Pattern of Disregard' of U.S. Interests

By BERNARD GWERTZMAN
Special to The New York Times.

WASHINGTON, Sept. 22—Zbigniew Brzezinski, President Carter's national security adviser, says that the reported Soviet combat brigade in Cuba stems from a Soviet "pattern of disregard" for American interests and he warns of possible retaliation if the Russians fail to cooperate in finding a solution.

Mr. Brzezinski, in an interview with editors yesterday that was released today, gave no details on a United States formula to settle the problem, but the State Department said Secretary of State Cyrus R. Vance would meet with Foreign Minister Andrei A. Gromyko of the Soviet Union in New York on Thursday.

Senate approval of the arms treaty with Moscow has been imperiled by the issue. Senator Robert C. Byrd of West Virginia, the majority leader, said today that action on the treaty could be completed this year, but that delay till next year could result in its defeat. Others in the Senate consider it increasingly doubtful that the treaty can be brought to a vote this year or next.

In the interview, Mr. Brzezinski said the issue of the brigade was "a serious problem in Soviet-American relations," and he renewed the White House assertion that unspecified actions would be taken if its status was not altered.

He seemed to rule out a military response to the presence of the Soviet brigade in Cuba. In answer to a question, he also appeared to eliminate the curtailment of grain sales to the Soviet Union. "We do not think that the profitable response to the Soviet Union is one which involves shooting oneself in the foot in the same process," he said.

Administation officials said no decisions had been reached so far on how to respond in case the talks were unsuccessful. The Administration is awaiting a response to ideas given by Mr. Vance to Ambassador Anatoly F. Dobrynin on Thursday.

But officials said that Mr. Brzezinski and his aides had raised the possibility of taking actions that would be as upsetting to Soviet political sensitivities as the Soviet presence in Cuba is to the United States. These would include a closer American relationship with China, ending the policy of evenhandedness with both Moscow and Peking in trade and other matters. It might mean also encouraging West European countries to sell military equipment to China. At the moment, the United States is showing indifference to such sales.

Problem for Both Countries Is Seen

"We consider this to be a serious problem, which we want to solve because we think it is a problem both for us and for the Soviet Union, and we want to solve it in a way which is responsive to our genuine, and we feel, legitimate concerns," Mr. Brzezinski said.

"We feel that this respect for our genuine legitimate concerns has to be an integal part of any enduring relationship and, precisely because we feel that way, we respect the Soviet desire that we be respectful of their interests and sensitivities, but it is not going to be a one-way street."

On the issue of linking the issue of Soviet troops to Senate approval of the strategic arms treaty, Mr. Brzezinski said the Americans had to compete with the Russians and to reject the treaty would be "a cop-out from the world of competition."

"In rejecting SALT, we punish ourselves as much, if not more than we punish the Soviet Union," he said. "We do not impose a real cost on the Soviet Union for its disregard of our interests if we reject SALT."

Vance Has Limited His Comments

Mr. Brzezinski's comments were consistent with those made by President Carter to a group of Congressional leaders on Thursday and by the White House spokesman, Jody Powell. But Mr. Vance has carefully limited his few public remarks on the subject to concern over the brigade and has seemed to seek to limit the debate to that subject.

Mr. Brzezinski said the presence of a Soviet combat brigade in the Western Hemisphere "is not an acceptable arrangement for us."

"Moreover, that brigade is present in a country which itself is using force around the world to promote its own ideological aspirations and uses that force occasionally, directly or indirectly, against our interests," he said. "And finally that country is sponsored, supported by the Soviet Union and acts as a proxy for Soviet political and foreign policy objectives."

Mr. Brzezinski said the United States was not trying to humiliate the Russians but "we see this as a serious problem in American-Soviet relations which has arisen as a consequence of a pattern of disregard for our interests."

The Soviet Union says that the brigade, believed to be made up of 2,000 to 3,000 soldiers, serves only in a military training role, but Mr. Brzezinski said the force has "a definite combat character and capability." He left open the possibility that the force might have performed other functions, including acting as a demonstration unit for the Cuban military.

West European View Dismissed

He scoffed at reports that West Europeans were disturbed by the way the United States had handled the problem, saying that they would have been equally upset if the United States had sought a dramatic confrontation.

Mr. Brzezinski's tone and approach underscored the continuing differences of approach within the Administration. He regards the Soviet brigade as part of a larger problem of Soviet aggressive activity around the world, insensitive to American interests. The State Department tends to look at issues in greater isolation and to see the brigade question in less universal terms.

President Carter, in a separate interview with editors, repeated that the issue was "of great concern to us" and that "the status quo was not acceptable."

If the effort to achieve a diplomatic solution was unsuccessful, "then I would have to take appropriate action," he said, but he declined to be more specific.

* * *

October 3, 1979

SENATE DEEPLY SPLIT ON CARTER'S SPEECH

But He Feels Stand on Soviet Unit Breaks Logjam on Arms Pact

By CHARLES MOHR
Special to The New York Times.

WASHINGTON, Oct. 2—President Carter's words and actions on the issue of Soviet troops in Cuba left the Senate deeply divided today over what it should and would do about the strategic arms limitation treaty with the Soviet Union.

Despite a mixed reaction in the Senate, the President told visitors to the White House that be felt encouraged by what he described as a mild Soviet reaction to his television speech yesterday on the troop issue. He said he was confident that his own measures and reported assurances from the Soviet Union had broken the logjam over Senate approval of the arms pact.

Senator Howard H. Baker Jr., of Tennessee, the minority leader, said he opposed delay on the pact, as other Republicans had urged. But he called for drastic amendments and said that, unless they were adopted, the treaty "will not get 60 votes." If all 100 senators vote, 67 votes will be needed for approval.

Republicans Oppose Compromise

Senator Baker and other Republicans also indicated that they would not be satisfied by a suggested compromise in which the Senate might adopt a resolution stating the treaty could not go into effect until President Carter certified in writing that a reported Soviet combat unit had somehow been made harmless.

Senator Frank Church, Democrat of Idaho and chairman of the Foreign Relations Committee, which is handling the arms treaty, indicated yesterday that he would put forth such a reservation. Today he said that Senate approval of the treaty would require "a clear statement by the President that Soviet combat forces are no longer deployed in Cuba."

By agreement with the Senate majority leader, Robert C. Byrd of West Virginia and with the White House, Senator Church had postponed committee action on the treaty while President Carter engaged in negotiations with the Soviet Union on the troop issue.

With those talks ended for the moment, the President's public position seemed to open the way for the committee to act and to send the treaty to the Senate floor for debate and a vote this year.

However, it was not clear whether the Senate would consent to ratification. Some senators care little about the Cuban troop issue, but they do want greater military spending than Mr. Carter has been willing to support.

Except for a few liberals, most Senate Republicans condemned Mr. Carter's speech and what they regarded as largely symbolic actions on the troop issue. Senator Baker called the actions "inadequate" and said, "In a toe-to-toe confrontation, we blinked."

Several Democrats were lukewarm or hostile to the President's handling of the troop issue, but most liberal Democrats, together with Senator Byrd, supported the argument that the arms treaty was more important than the problem of the Soviet troops.

During an exchange on the Senate floor, today, Senator Baker told the Democrats that the Republicans had been "remarkably restrained" spectators and had not made the Soviet troop question a major issue in the debate over the arms-limitation treaty. It was Senator Church, Senator Baker said, who reported that there was a Soviet combat unit in Cuba and that the Senate would not approve the treaty until the issue was resolved.

There were several flashes of temper and of acrimony on the Senate floor. Senator Jesse A. Helms of North Carolina, one of the staunchest conservatives among Republicans, said Mr. Carter had failed to show leadership, had made the United States look "ridiculous" and had made what was "tantamount to an admission that Soviet superiority is so great that the United States cannot resist."

Senator Byrd, angered, rose to say that Senator Helms was implying that "we should have a nuclear exchange with the Soviet Union." When Senator Helms tried to protest that he had made no such implication, Senator Byrd became upset because the North Carolina Republican was addressing him in the first person, rather than in the third person as required by Senate rules.

Senator Alan Cranston of California, the Senate whip, rose to argue that the Soviet troops did not threaten the United States and added: "It's time to put aside childish things and childish ways."

"There was never any real relevance between Soviet troops in Cuba and the SALT treaty," Senator Cranston said.

That remark triggered Senator Baker's statement that it was the President and the Democrats who had made the troop issue a test of wills.

Senator Baker said at a news conference that, despite the Soviet assurances described by President Carter, the reported brigade was not in Cuba on a training mission and had "never engaged in training."

* * *

October 7, 1979

U.S. AIDES LINK MOVE TO MISSILES

By BERNARD GWERTZMAN
Special to The New York Times.

WASHINGTON, Oct. 6—Carter Administration officials said today that Leonid I. Brezhnev's speech in East Berlin seemed part of a concerted Soviet effort to persuade West European countries not to go along with allied plans to deploy 572 new nuclear-armed missiles in Europe.

The initial reaction of Administration officials was that they hoped the Soviet leader's announcement of a withdrawal of up to 20,000 soldiers and 1,000 tanks from East Germany was a harbinger of more meaningful negotiations in the future on reduction of armed forces in Central Europe.

But these conciliatory American comments were balanced by a strong rebuttal to Mr. Brezhnev's criticism of the plans for the new missiles, which are expected to be approved at this December's ministerial meeting of the North Atlantic Treaty Organization.

The new missiles, a State Department official said, are being planned as a response to an "accelerated nuclear buildup" by the Soviet Union, which includes the deployment so far of about 100 SS-20's, a highly accurate long-range mobile missile, with multiple-warheads targeted on Western Europe.

The United States had expected Mr. Brezhnev to use the occasion of his speech today to attack the new NATO plans but the withdrawal statement came as a surprise.

However, officials said the pullback announcement was more symbolic than anything else since the Soviet Union, with about 400,000 soldiers in Central Europe, has 100,000 more there than the United States.

The Soviet withdrawal might give some added impetus to the long-stalled negotiations on mutual force reduction in Vienna, which have just resumed.

The Russians have been urging that the Warsaw Pact and NATO countries agree to set ceilings of 900,000 military personnel for each side, in. Central Europe, of which 700,000 would be ground forces.

The allies agree in principle but the two sides differ sharply on just how many are there now. The Western countries say that the Soviet Union has 150,000 more troops than it acknowledges.

This issue, referred to as a "data-base problem," has held up progress in the negotiations.

Some officials believe that the Russians, out of concern over the new NATO missiles, might take more constructive steps in the negotiations at Vienna in the hope that signs of progress in those talks might deter the Western countries from going ahead with the new missiles.

An American official said that the Brezhnev announcement on the withdrawal of troops and tanks appeared to be "a carrot" to Western countries, a show of Soviet willingness to reduce forces and an inducement against going ahead with a new NATO missile force.

At present, preliminary plans are for the new NATO missiles to be based in the Netherlands, Belgium, Britain and West Germany. But the Dutch and Belgians are far from enthusiastic about the idea. The West Germans do not want to be the only country on the continent to deploy the new missiles.

Nearly 500 of the weapons would be ground-launched cruise missiles. The others in the total of 572 would be longer-range versions of the American Pershing rocket system now in West Germany.

The problem for the NATO countries is how to handle the political pressure that Moscow is expected to generate in coming weeks to influence individual governments not to accept the new missiles, American officials said.

American officials noted with satisfaction that Mr. Brezhnev did not allude directly to the latest strain in relations caused by the dispute over Soviet troops in Cuba.

Some officials expected that he might have some harsh words for President Carter's actions in response to the reported 'combat brigade,' but the issue was not mentioned.

This seemed to reinforce the view in Washington that the Kremlin was as eager as the White House not to let the Cuban problem upset the general trend in relations or otherwise jeopardize approval of the strategic arms limitation treaty.

* * *

October 27, 1979

PRESIDENT PARK IS SLAIN IN KOREA BY INTELLIGENCE CHIEF, SEOUL SAYS; PREMIER TAKES OVER, G.I.'S ALERTED

MARTIAL LAW IMPOSED

Government Lays Shooting to 'Accidental' Flareup— 5 Others Killed

Special to The New York Times.

SEOUL, South Korea, Saturday. Oct. 27—President Park Chung Hee, South Korea's ruler for more than 18 years, was fatally shot last night by the chief of the Korean Central Intelligence Agency at a restaurant near the presidential residence, the Government announced early today. It said the death of the President was "the result of an accidental argument" between the agency chief and Mr. Park's chief bodyguard.

According to the official version, the assailant, Kim Jae Kyu, a lifelong friend of the President and the host at the dinner, opened fire with his pistol during an "emotional outburst." It was not clear what the argument was about. One bullet struck the 62-year-old President, the Government reported, and the bodyguard and four other persons were also killed. The four were not immediately identified.

More than three hours after the President's death, the Cabinet met in emergency session and named Prime Minister Choi Kyu Hah, an administrator who has held no real political power, as acting President.

Signal to North Korea

Martial law was imposed all over the nation except the southern island of Cheju, and all airports were closed.

The 38,000 United States troops in South Korea were ordered by Washington into an increased state of alert as a signal to North Korea not to attempt military action against South Korea.

The Cabinet named Gen. Chung Seung Hwa, the army chief of staff, as martial law administrator, and he imposed a curfew from 10 P.M. to 4 A.M., decreed press censorship for the first time since 1972, closed all universities and banned all meetings and outdoor demonstrations.

The Government announced that the director of the Central Intelligence Agency, Mr. Kim, had been taken into custody for questioning.

It also announced that there would be a national funeral for Mr. Park.

President Park, who came to power after a military coup on May 16, 1961, had previously survived two attempts on his life. In the second attempt, in 1974, a Korean gunman from Japan tried to shoot the President while he and his wife attended a ceremony at the National Theater here to celebrate Korea's liberation from Japanese rule in 1945. The gunman missed Mr. Park but killed his wife.

The earlier attempt came in January 1968 when 31 Communist guerrillas slipped into Seoul and sought unsuccessfully to fight their way into his official residence, the Blue House, to assassinate him.

The President's death followed a series of political protests against his authoritarian rule, including rioting and vast demonstrations by tens of thousands of people in the southern port city of Pusan and the nearby industrial city of Masan. The outbursts there, in which hundreds were arrested, were the worst since student rioting in 1961 led to the ouster of President Syngman Rhee and the beginning of the Park regime.

Opposition Leader Ousted

The recent rioting was apparently touched off by the ouster on Oct. 9 of the leader of the opposition New Democratic Party, Kim Young Sam, a native of Pusan, from Parliament, with only the members of the President's Democratic Republican Party voting in favor. Subsequently all 69 opposition members of Parliament resigned.

The sudden death of the President, who for the last seven years has ruled South Korea under a Constitution that he drafted to give himself vast powers, has thrown this nation of 40 million people into political uncertainty. The question being asked here this morning is whether the army will continue to back the present Government if it continues under the highly criticized Constitution of 1972.

There were no immediate signs that Mr. Park's fellow generals had seized power.

The first official announcement of the change in administration came last night with a broadcast saying that the Prime Minister had been named acting President under a section of the Constitution allowing the replacement of the chief of state because of incapacity. Rumors that Mr. Park had been killed swept through the capital, but these were not confirmed until the official announcement made at 8:35 A.M. today [7:35 P.M. Friday, New York time] by Public Information Minister Kim Seong Jin.

Restaurant Within Compound

According to the Government account, the President was shot last evening at the Kungjong Restaurant, which is within a K.C.I.A. compound near the presidential mansion.

Rushed to a military hospital, he was pronounced dead at 7:50 P.M. [6:50 A.M. Friday, New York time]. He reportedly was taken to the hospital by his chief of staff, Kim Kye Won.

The Cabinet met at 11 P.M., and shortly after it was announced that Prime Minister Choi, who has also served as Foreign Minister, would take over.

Seoul was quiet at the time. Some troops were seen around the Government buildings, and there were two tanks near the presidential residence. But, despite the rumors, there were no indications that anything violent had occurred or that any anti-Government action was in progress.

Before going to the restaurant for dinner, President Park had officiated at a dedication of a dam near Taejon, 100 miles south of Seoul. He returned here by helicopter.

After the news of Mr. Park's death was announced, the national radio began broadcasting dirges, and flags were lowered to half staff. People expressed shock, but the crisis atmosphere that the first rumors had brought seemed to abate somewhat.

Reports from around the country said that the various units of the 600,000-member South Korean Army remained generally calm.

In a special statement to the nation, the 60-year-old acting President appealed for continued calm and order.

Focus on Rioting

Until last night, much of the talk here had been of the significance of the rioting in the southern part of South Korea. For some, the events there seemed to consolidate the authority of President Park as they allowed him to silence the traditionally restive universities by declaring martial law limited to that region. But to others the demonstrations seemed to be working toward strengthening those who were seeking to end his one-man rule.

The Government early yesterday appeared to feel it had the situation in the south well in hand as it announced the withdrawal of most of the troops and tanks it had poured into the area during the height of the demonstrations.

Since the summer, Mr. Park had maintained pressure on the opposition party, but his decision to drive its leader from the virtually powerless National Assembly spurred an American protest and the recall of Ambassador William Gleysteen to Washington.

This was said to be the first time an American ambassador had been recalled in protest under Mr. Park's rule. Some here thought that the key to Mr. Park's continued rule might be in Washington, but that was before the unexpected events at a dinner party given the President by his close friend.

* * *

November 5, 1979

TEHERAN STUDENTS SEIZE U.S. EMBASSY AND HOLD HOSTAGES

ASK SHAH'S RETURN AND TRIAL

Khomeini Said to Support Attack by Several Hundred Youths— No Casualties Reported

By Reuters

TEHERAN, Iran, Nov. 4—Moslem students stormed the United States Embassy in Teheran today, seized about 90 Americans and vowed to stay there until the deposed Shah was sent back from New York to face trial in Iran.

There were no reports of casualties in the takeover of the embassy building, although witnesses said some of the several hundred attackers were armed.

A student spokesman told reporters at the embassy that 100 hostages had been taken and that 90 percent of them were Americans. He said the embassy staff was being treated well.

Has Khomeini's Support

In the holy city of Qum, a spokesman for Ayatollah Ruhollah Khomeini said the occupation of the embassy had the revolutionary leader's personal support.

> [In New York City, a small group of Iranian students chained themselves to railings inside the Statue of Liberty for three hours and unfurled a banner from the monument's top demanding that the deposed Shah be returned to Iran.]

Iranian Revolutionary Guards at the embassy gates did not intervene during the attack, which came as tens of thousands of people marched through the streets of the Iranian capital on the first anniversary of the shooting of students at Teheran University by the Shah's security forces.

Western diplomatic sources said Bruce Laingen, the chargé d'affaires who heads the United States Mission here, was not among the Americans seized by the students. They said he was in touch throughout the day with Foreign Minister Ibrahim Yazdi, who had just returned from an official visit to Algiers.

The Iranian Foreign Ministry, in a statement reported by the official Pars news agency, said:

Embassy Files Captured

"Today's move by a group of our compatriots is a natural reaction to the U.S. Government's indifference to the hurt feelings of the Iranian people about the presence of the deposed Shah, who is in the United States under the pretext of illness.

"If the U.S. authorities respected the feelings of the Iranian people and understood the depth of the Iranian revolution, they should have at least not allowed the deposed Shah into the country and should have returned his property."

The students showed reporters embassy files captured in the raid. They said staff in the building had been trying to burn documents when the embassy was taken over.

The students who invaded the embassy compound wore badges with the portrait of Ayatollah Khomeini, and they put up a banner saying: "Khomeini struggles, Carter trembles."

They read a statement they said they had received from Ayatollah Hossein Ali of Ayatollah Khomeini, and they put up a banner saying: "Khomeini struggles, Carter trembles."

They read a statement they said they had received from Ayatollah Hossein Ali Montazeri, head of Iran's Constitutional Assembly of Experts, in which they quoted him as saying:

"A few days ago, the Imam said the Iranian nation must clean up its situation vis-a-vis the United States. This action is a kind of recognition of that situation. America must know it can't play with the feelings of the Iranian nation." The Imam referred to is Ayatollah Khomeini.

The embassy takeover followed a series of strongly anti-American speeches by Ayatollah Khomeini, who said recently he hoped reports that the former Shah, Mohammed Riza Pahlevi, was dying of cancer were true. The Shah, who was deposed in the revolution led by the Ayatollah last January, is being treated for cancer at New York Hospital-Cornell Medical Center.

United Press International

Iranian students putting up a poster of Ayatollah Ruhollah Khomeini on the wall of the U.S. Embassy after seizing it.

The official Iranian radio broadcast a statement by the Islamic Society of University Teachers and Students commending the embassy takeover. "We defend the capture of this imperialist embassy, which is a center for espionage," the statement said.

This was the second time the embassy has been taken over since the revolution. Gunmen believed to be dissident revolutionaries invaded the embassy last Feb. 14, killing one Iranian and taking 101 people hostage, including Ambassador William H. Sullivan and 19 Marine guards.

The takeover came when both the Iranian and United States Governments appeared to be seeking improved relations.

The students involved in the takeover quoted from a recent speech by Ayatollah Khomeini in which he said, "What do we need a relationship with America for?"

In the speech in Qum, the Ayatollah declared: "Those who support great powers like Britain, which has given asylum to Bakhtiar, and the United States, which has given refuge to that corrupt germ, will be confronted in a different manner by us if they continue." Shapur Bakhtiar was the last Prime Minister under the regime of the deposed Shah.

The newspaper Islamic Republic, which speaks for the ruling clergy, called on Prime Minister Mehdi Bazargan today to explain what was discussed in his 75-minute meeting with President Carter's national security adviser, Zbigniew Brzezinski, in Algiers last week.

"In these days when the leader of the revolution has launched the strongest attacks on the world predator imperialists led by the United States, at a time when the United States, the United Kingdom and their allies plan plots against our people and every day confront the revolution, you, Mr. Bazargan, sit and talk with Brzezinski in Algeria," the newspaper said.

* * *

December 1, 1979

U.S. INSISTS SHAH GO, BUT SEEKS A REFUGE FOR DEPOSED RULER

SOUTH AFRICA CITED

Direct Channel Is Set Up Between Iranian and State Department

By BERNARD GWERTZMAN
Special to The New York Times.

WASHINGTON, Nov. 30—The United States made it clear today that it expected Shah Mohammed Riza Pahlevi to leave this country despite the last-minute decision by Mexico to refuse to allow the deposed Iranian ruler to return there.

As a result of the unexpected Mexican action, the Carter Administration was involved in intensive behind-the-scenes activity today to find a new refuge for the Shah. Senator Frank Church, chairman of the Foreign Relations Committee, suggested that South Africa might be a suitable haven, noting that the Shah's father had died in exile in Johannesburg in 1944.

Sadat Renews His Offer

Sources close to the Shah said that for the first time since the Iranian's entry to the United States, a direct channel had been set up between the Shah and the State Department. It was through this channel, the sources said, that the Mexican Government was told yesterday that the Shah would like to return to Mexico on Sunday. It was that formal request that led to Mexico's decision to bar his reentry.

With Mexico no longer a refuge, President Anwar el-Sadat of Egypt told reporters today that his country was still prepared to offer the Shah a home and that he was not at all influenced by the Mexican action.

But a source close to the Shah described him as unenthusiastic about going to Egypt. At the same time, the source said, the Shah is grateful to the Egyptian leader for having renewed his offer.

Meanwhile, Iran announced that it would not send a representative to the meeting of the United Nations Security Council on the Iranian crisis scheduled for 9 P.M. tomorrow. The council, nevertheless, decided to go ahead with its session.

The State Department issued a strong statement calling on Iran to allow a neutral oberver to check on the condition of the 50 American hostages in the Teheran embassy, which has been under the control of militant students for 27 days.

Hodding Carter 3d, the State Department's spokesman, said that "all the hostages have not been seen and we have no way of knowing the condition of those people."

The statement was sparked by a report from a Western diplomat in Teheran several days ago that about 10 of the hostages had been moved to other places of detention. But other diplomats, when asked to confirm the report, told Washington that they were unable to do so. In addition, Iran's former Acting Foreign Minister, Abolhassan Bani-Sadr, gave assurances to diplomats on his last day in office that all the hostages were in the embassy and were being well-treated.

The problems of the Shah were of paramount concern to the Administration because it did not want to appear to be offering him asylum here. But the Administration also did not want to seem to be without compassion for the Shah, who was admitted to this country for medical treatment on Oct. 22. As a result, Administration spokesmen were circumspect in their comments.

But it was understood that through the channel to the Shah used by David D. Newsom, Under Secretary of State for Political Affairs, it had been made clear to the Shah and his entourage that the United States expected them to live up to their promise to leave the country when the Shah's treatment was over.

Caribbean Islands Ruled Out

When the Shah left Iran in January, he stopped in Egypt and then Morocco. When he was discouraged from coming to the United States, he went to the Bahamas, arriving in Mexico in the summer. The source close to the Shah said no Caribbean island looked like a promising haven and he refused to say which other countries were possibilities.

The Shah said through a spokesman in New York that he planned to leave the United States as soon as a haven was found.

Iranian authorities have demanded the extradition of the Shah as the price for the release of the American hostages, a demand that has been rejected by the United States.

South Africa a Logical Choice

South Africa, which was suggested by Senator Church, Democrat of Idaho, as a possible place the Shah might go, was regarded by State Department officials as a logical possibility, given the ties of the Shah's family to that country. When the Shah's father, Riza Shah, was forced into exile by Britain during World War II, he spent two years in Johannesburg. He died there in July 1944.

The South African Ambassador, Donald B. Sole, said in a telephone interview today that his embassy had not been contacted about the possibility that the Shah might go to South Africa. But he said he could not rule out the possibility that efforts on behalf of the Shah were being made in South Africa by the United States. The State Department had no comment.

Hodding Carter, when asked about the Shah's plans, avoided saying explicitly that the United States wanted the Shah to leave. Rather, he said that "the Shah says he wants to leave the United States and I have no reason to doubt it."

Anger at Mexico's Decision

Privately, a State Department official said he believed that the Shah would prefer to remain in the United States, but that the Shah understood that the Administration expected him to live up to his commitment to depart.

The Administration was angered by Mexico's reversal of its promise to allow the Shah to return.

The first word of the decision was conveyed to Washington about an hour and a half before the formal announcement by Foreign Minister Jorge Castañeda.

Former Secretary of State Henry A. Kissinger received a phone call from a Mexican official, and an aide to Mr. Kissinger, William G. Hyland, relayed the news to Peter Tarnoff, an aide to Secretary of State Cyrus R. Vance.

* * *

December 22, 1979

SOVIET BUILDUP SEEN AT AFGHAN FRONTIER

U.S. Estimates Three Divisions—1,500 Troops Near Kabul

By RICHARD BURT
Special to The New York Times.

WASHINGTON, Dec. 21—The Soviet Union has moved three army divisions to its border with Afghanistan and has recently sent at least 1,500 combat soldiers into the country, Carter Administration officials said today.

The officials, in line with a recent high-level decision to publicize Moscow's military role in the Afghan civil war, said that in the last two weeks the Soviet Union had significantly increased its support for the Marxist Government's drive against Moslem insurgents. They said that more than 30,000 soldiers had been placed on alert near the Afghan border and that three battalions of armored and airborne troops had been flown to an air base near Kabul. The number of Soviet troops and military advisers is now said to exceed 5,000.

Intelligence aides are unsure about Moscow's motives in building up forces along the Afghan border, but some officials suggested that it could be preparing for a full scale invasion. "Their preparations on the border show all the marks of a major military intervention," a White House national security aide said, adding, in reference to action by forces of the Soviet bloc, "We saw the same signs before the invasion of Czechoslavakia in 1968."

However, other officials said that they doubted that Moscow would begin a major invasion and that the buildup was part of a more gradual process of military intervention in the guerrilla war.

On the way to a meeting in the Pentagon, Secretary of State Cyrus R. Vance, asked by reporters if the Administration anticipated a Soviet invasion of Afghanistan, responded, "That would only be speculation on my part."

The State Department spokesman, Hodding Carter 3d, speaking to reporters, confirmed that a buildup was under way along the border but declined to provide details. Other officials said that an airborne division and two motorized rifle divisions had recently left their garrisons and had moved up near the Amu Darya River, which forms the border with Afghanistan.

Moscow is also said to have created a special headquarters unit close to the border, a development that is seen by some intelligence analysts as a sign that Soviet forces might soon be ordered into action.

Officials are unsure about the role of the three combat battalions recently flown into the air base at Bagram. Some analysts described the contingent as a "security force," possibly meant to provide protection for the thousands of Soviet military and civilian advisers in the country and for the embattled Government now headed by President Hafizullah Amin. The airborne and armored troops could also be used in combat with Moslem insurgents operating all over the country, they added.

Steadily Increasing Presence

Moscow has steadily increased its military presence in Afghanistan since the pro-Marxist coup in April 1978 that led to the assassination of President Mohammad Daud. The installation of a pro-Soviet government set off protests by Moslem groups throughout the country that generated widespread fighting early this year.

Since January Soviet military advisers are said to have taken over virtual control of the Afghan Army, and more recently Soviet pilots have reportedly flown helicopter gunships in missions against the insurgents. Soviet forces in the country are now said to be under the command of a Soviet lieutenant general.

The turning point in the Soviet role, according to intelligence aides, came last September with a visit by Gen. Ivan G. Pavlovsky, Deputy Minister of Defense. He is said to have laid the groundwork for Moscow's decision in recent days to introduce combat troops into the country and to build up forces on the border.

Officials, concerned about the regional impact of increased Soviet involvement, asserted that it highlighted the problems Moscow had in helping the Kabul Government consolidate its hold on the country. They said that intelligence reports from the area concluded that in recent months, over 100 Soviet citizens, most of them military personnel, were killed in fighting.

* * *

December 28, 1979

AFGHAN PRESIDENT IS OUSTED AND EXECUTED IN KABUL COUP, REPORTEDLY WITH SOVIET HELP

AN EXILE TAKES OVER

Ex-Deputy Premier Karmal Becomes Third Leader Under Marxist Rule

By BERNARD GWERTZMAN
Special to The New York Times.

WASHINGTON, Dec. 27—President Hafizullah Amin of Afghanistan was ousted from power and executed today in a coup reportedly supported by Soviet troops.

The Afghan radio announced in a broadcast monitored here that Mr. Amin had been sentenced to death at a revolutionary trial for "crimes against the state" and that the sentence had been carried out.

The broadcast said that Babrak Karmal, a former Deputy Prime Minister who had been living in exile in Eastern Europe, was the new President and Secretary General of the ruling People's Democratic Party.

Mr. Amin was the third Afghan President to be toppled in the last 20 months. All three were slain.

The Afghan broadcast was the first authoritative word received in Washington that tended to confirm earlier reports from Teheran and Moscow about the political change in Kabul.

Soviet Said to Favor Karmal

On the surface, the switch seemed to replace one pro-Soviet figure with another. But intelligence analysts said that Mr. Karmal has long been regarded as more to Moscow's liking than Mr. Amin, who seized power only three months ago.

Earlier, State Department officials said that they received accounts, shortly before noon Washington time, from persons in Kabul that heavy fighting had broken out in the Afghan capital.

The witnesses said that Soviet troops, part of a contingent of more than 6,000 flown to Afghanistan in recent days, had led an assault on the Afghanistan broadcasting center.

Moreover, Soviet combat troops were observed in armored personnel vehicles taking part in battles elsewhere in the capital. One report said there was fighting near the Presidential Palace and that Soviet troops had been seen capturing some Afghans.

Senior Administration officials said the best guess seemed to be that the Soviet Union, which has invested considerable military and economic assistance in Afghanistan, particularly since the takeover in April 1978 by a Marxist Government led by the late Noor Mohammad Taraki, was seeking a more compliant leader to calm the insurgents active in most of the country.

The Soviet Union, with a large Moslem population in Central Asia near or bordering on Afghanistan, has long been concerned about signs of instability in that remote mountainous country, which through the centuries served as a buffer between Russia and the Subcontinent.

United States officials had no official comment, but they said in private that the Russians were probably under extreme pressure to try to end the insurgency in Afghanistan.

President Carter is to discuss the situations in Afghanistan and Iran tomorrow at a National Security Council meeting, which was scheduled before the coup.

The overthown President, who had been denounced by Afghan insurgents as a symbol of oppression, assumed the Presidency three months ago after a gun battle in the Presidential Palace in which President Taraki was mortally wounded.

Mr. Taraki represented Afghanistan at the recent meeting in Havana of the nations calling themselves nonaligned. On his way home he stopped off in Moscow where he was warmly embraced by Leonid I. Brezhnev, the Soviet leader.

Because of the Brezhnev reception of Mr. Taraki, intelligence analysts here believed that the Soviet Union was unhappy over Mr. Amin's seizure of power.

But if Moscow had doubts about Mr. Amin, it did not reveal them publicly. There were reports in recent weeks, intelligence officials said, that the Russians were cool to Mr. Amin and were looking for someone able to end the civil war.

Leader of Communist Wing

In the last few weeks, the Russians began to increase their military forces in Afghanistan and along the Afghan border. In the last two days, officials said, more than 200 military transports landed at the Kabul airport with troops and supplies. In addition, five Soviet divisions have reportedly been deployed along the border with Afghanistan.

Mr. Karmal was the leader of the Parcham branch of the People's Democratic Party, which was behind the overthrow of President Mohammad Daud in April 1978.

But Mr. Karmal's group lost power to the wing headed by Mr. Taraki and Mr. Amin. Both groups were pro-Communist, although Mr. Karmal's wing was regarded as more orthodox and willing to accept Soviet leadership.

Mr. Karmal, during his stay in Czechoslovakia, was reportedly summoned home to face charges of plotting a coup but he stayed on in Eastern Europe, according to State Department officials.

His assumption of power was the first indication to American officials that he had returned to Afghanistan.

There was no question in Washington that the Soviet Union strongly favored Mr. Karmal's assumption of power.

The Soviet press agency Tass gave favorable attention to Mr. Karmal's statement: "Today is the breaking of the machine of torture of Amin and his henchmen, wild butchers, usurpers and murderers of tens of thousands of our countrymen, fathers, mothers, brothers, sisters, sons and daughters, children and old people."

According to Tass, Mr. Karmal said that Mr. Amin and "his stooges" were all "agents of American imperialism."

The presumption of some officials tonight was that Tass would only have issued the Karmal statement if it had certain word from Kabul that Mr. Amin had been toppled.

Rebels Are Anti-Communist

The Soviet Union has seemed deeply troubled by the inability of either the Taraki or Amin governments to put down the rebellions in Afghanistan, which have been largely tribal but also militantly anti-Communist.

Not only have the Russians supplied the Kabul authorities with military equipment and advisers but they have also sent more than 6,000 combat troops to augment the nearly 4,000 military advisers.

This was the first time that organized troop units were sent outside the Soviet bloc or Cuba since World War II, and the move underscored Moscow's concern.

Afghanistan, which borders on Soviet Turkmenia, has always had close ties to the Soviet Union. But until recently the Russians seemed content to let the Afghans follow an ostensibly neutral policy.

* * *

January 1, 1980

AFGHANISTAN'S IMPACT: A NEW U.S.-SOVIET FREEZE

By BERNARD GWERTZMAN
Special to The New York Times.

WASHINGTON, Dec. 31—Moscow's decision to intervene militarily in Afghanistan has deeply angered the Carter Administration and seems likely to send Soviet-American relations into another period of bitter recriminations, more reminiscent of the cold war years of the 1950's than of the détente years of the 1970's.

In addition to the sharp dispute between the two Governments, an extraordinary personal element has been added to the crisis. President Carter, whose Administration had resisted pressures to engage in anti-Soviet polemics or actions, said tonight that his perception of Soviet actions had been drastically altered for the worse by Soviet activity and by what he called Leonid I. Brezhnev's "misleading" response to a personal message he sent to Moscow three days ago.

Not since the U-2 spy plane crisis of 1960 have the heads of the two nations become so personally involved. And this means that there is a strong possibility that the two countries are about to enter into a major freeze in relations that could last well into the new year. Some experts believe that relations may not be restored to normal again until after the elections next November.

For a President who has been accused by his critics of being too soft toward the Russians and who faces a re-election campaign in which foreign affairs seems likely to play an increasingly important part, the comments by Mr. Carter in a televised interview tonight are all the more telling. He says that his view of the Soviet Union has changed more in one week than in all his previous time in office.

The events in Afghanistan, however, did not occur in a vacuum. Ties between Moscow and Washington had already undergone severe strains in recent months despite the successful conclusion of the treaty to limit strategic arms and the meeting between Mr. Carter and Mr. Brezhnev in Vienna last June. The treaty, in fact, now seems to be the first and most obvious victim of the deterioration in relations.

Even before the dispatch of the Soviet combat troops into Afghanistan, relations seemed to be going nowhere but down for a number of reasons. Neither side seemed to pay much attention to the political sensibilities of the other. Washington established diplomatic relations with China, gave it economic concessions ahead of Moscow and made an issue of human rights in the Soviet Union. The Russians seemed oblivious to American concerns about the presence of Cuban troops in Africa and other regional issues.

Marshall D. Shulman, the State Department's senior adviser on Soviet affairs and the Administration's leading voice for moderation in relations with the Russians, signaled the direction events were taking when he told a Congressional committee on Oct. 16 that the superpowers were at loggerheads on almost every issue and that these differences "are unlikely to be reconciled in the near future."

'Going to Be a Difficult Year'

When asked to look ahead by the committee chairman. Mr. Shulman responded gloomily: "It's going to be a difficult year."

The latest developments, coming at the start of the Presidential campaign and at a time when this country has been emotionally preoccupied with the crisis over the Americans held-hostage in Iran, have produced an outburst of anger that mirrors the reactions in the election years of 1956, when the Soviet Union crushed the Hungarian revolt, and of 1968, when it led the takeover of Prague.

Other experts compare the chill with that of another election year, 1960, when President Dwight D. Eisenhower's meeting with Nikita S. Khrushchev was canceled in the wake of the shooting down of an American U-2 spy plane over Sverdlovsk. Not until John F. Kennedy assumed office the next January did another period of normality begin, only to be set back by the miscalculation of the attack on the Bay of Pigs in Cuba and the Berlin Wall crisis that summer.

The mood then, as it is now, was aggravated by the frustration in Washington at the United States inability to respond militarily to the Soviet Union's use of force in countries along its borders. Neither President Eisenhower in 1956, President Kennedy in 1961 nor President Lyndon B. Johnson in 1968 could risk a military confrontation with the Soviet

Union over countries that were in effect within the Soviet spheres of influence.

Similarity to Previous Moves Noted

The Soviet decision to move about 40,000 troops into Afghanistan is believed here to be based on the same kind of considerations that led to the previous Soviet moves into Hungary and Czechoslovakia and to the building of the wall in East Berlin—a determination not to permit a pro-Soviet and Marxist regime to be toppled by insurrection and chaos.

The particular reasons for the intervention in Afghanistan were probably additionally compelling to the Kremlin because of a concern that if a conservative Islamic state were to emerge in Afghanistan, possibly linked to the fundamentalists in Iran and Pakistan, the situation in Soviet Central Asia, where most of the Soviet Union's 50 million Moslems live, might become dangerous for Moscow.

In Washington, there is considerable speculation by both supporters and critics of the Administration on whether the action in Afghanistan was linked in any way to Moscow's view of the United States. In other words, did the Kremlin calculate that in intervening in Afghanistan it would cause problems for itself with Washington?

Ambassador Anatoly F. Dobrynin, who first arrived in Washington on March 30, 1962, at a time of serious crisis in relations, left for consultations in Moscow in advance of the latest crisis, more than three weeks ago, after two long meetings with Secretary of State Cyrus R. Vance in which they discussed Soviet-American relations at length.

American officials felt at that time that an important review was going on in the Kremlin on overall ties because Mr. Dobrynin wanted to know the answers to such questions as how strongly the Administration would push for Senate passage of the strategic arms treaty in an election year; whether the United States would intervene militarily to free the hostages in Iran; what the outlook was for détente in general, and what the chances were in particular for an improvement in Soviet-American relations.

Clearly, Mr. Dobrynin, a full member of the Communist Party's Central Committee, was needed in Moscow to give advice on now the intervention would affect relations with the United States.

The estimate now, in hindsight, is that the Kremlin decided its relations with Washington were so poor anyway that the reaction in Washington, which could be expected to be sharply negative, could not stand in the way of the intervention in Afghanistan, which clearly was being put into its final stages at that time.

The Soviet Politburo had to believe that because of the problems facing Senate passage of the arms treaty, there was little chance of its being put into effect in 1980. Moreover, it had to note the generally low state of Soviet prestige in the United States, the inability of Moscow to win any trade concessions here and the scoffing at Mr. Brezhnev's appeal for holding off on a decision to go ahead with the positioning of new nuclear forces in Western Europe.

Few Options for U.S. Reponse

For Washington, the problem of how to respond now is aggravated by the lack of attractive options. There is no chance that the United States will act militarily in support of the Afghan insurgents. The Administration's instinctive response was to try to bring worldwide pressure on the Russians by urging Western countries and Moslem ones to complain loudly.

The United States and its allies will probably seek a Security Council debate on the intervention, thereby forcing the Russians to defend themselves in the glare of publicity and to use their veto.

This probably means, in the end, that the United States will have to react to the Soviet moves in its own way. At the minimum, this means that the strategic arms treaty is dead for the moment. Whether it is buried by the Administration or by the Senate is still to be decided.

It means that steps will probably be taken to cut back trade with the Soviet Union to nonessentials.

The chances of the Soviet Union's receiving any sophisticated technology will be more remote than before. Likewise, it is doubtful if high-profile cultural or other exchanges will be permitted.

* * *

January 1, 1980

U.N. COUNCIL, 11 TO 0, GIVES IRAN ONE WEEK TO LET HOSTAGES GO BEFORE DECIDING ON SANCTIONS

TRIUMPH FOR THE U.S.

Waldheim Flies to Teheran—

Plan in Resolution Could Be Undone

By BERNARD D. NOSSITER

Special to The New York Times.

UNITED NATIONS, N.Y., Dec. 31—The Security Council voted 11 to 0 today to give Iran one week to release the American hostages. If they are not freed by then, the Council agreed to meet on Jan. 7 to vote to impose economic sanctions against Teheran.

However, the next Council will have at least four new members and it is conceivable that what was done today could be undone next week.

Nevertheless, today's action was considered a major diplomatic triumph for the United States, particularly since China and five of seven third-world members voted for the American plan.

Waldheim Leaves for Teheran

Its first stage has already produced the mission that sent Secretary General Kurt Waldheim to Teheran today in an effort to negotiate the hostages' release.

There was, however, widespread skepticism among diplomats here about whether Ayatollah Ruhollah Khomeini would be moved, either by Mr. Waldheim or by the threat to cut off Iran's imports.

In today's action, four of the 15 Council members abstained. They were the Soviet Union and its ally, Czechoslovakia; and two predominantly Moslem nations, Kuwait and Bangladesh. Two nations who voted with the majority, China and Zambia, indicated that they did not regard themselves bound by the resolution's decision to adopt sanctions next Monday if Mr. Waldheim was unsuccessful.

Vance Says He Is Pleased

After the Council meeting, Secretary of State Cyrus R. Vance told reporters, "I'm very pleased at the vote. I join everybody else in wishing the Secretary General good fortune, and I hope and pray he will have a fruitful trip."

After he spoke, Mr. Waldheim left with two aides. He is to arrive in Teheran tomorrow for talks with Iranian officials through Thursday. But he had no guarantee that he would see Ayatollah Khomeini.

According to one of Mr. Waldheim's closest associates here, the Secretary General's parting words were: "I don't have any illusions that I will come back with the hostages. But I hope to start a successful turn, get it going in another direction, that they will start negotiating."

Waldheim's Theme

Mr. Waldheim, an aide said, will point out that some day Iran will want to rejoin the world community and that now it is totally isolated. The Secretary General is said to believe that it will be unnecessary to point out that Iran has much more to fear from the Soviet Union than from the United States and that the Russian move into Afghanistan makes this point clear.

The resolution asked Mr. Waldheim to report to the next Council meeting. If he has failed to win the hostages' freedom, the resolution says, the Council will "adopt effective measures" under provisions of the United Nations Charter that provide for an embargo on trade.

Two weeks ago, the United States could count only six certain votes for sanctions—its own and those of Britain, France, Norway, Portugal and Bolivia. Nine are needed to adopt a resolution. The acquisition of five more votes—by Nigeria, Jamaica, Gabon, Zambia and China—is regarded as a major coup for Donald F. McHenry, the chief American representative at the United Nations.

The key move was yielding to the third world's plea to give Mr. Waldheim more time to negotiate. Mr. McHenry did so, but insisted on both a time limit and a commitment to impose sanctions if the Secretary General failed. The crucial votes from Africa were fixed at a private meeting Sunday between Mr. McHenry and B. Aprokode Clark of Nigeria, an influential figure here.

If Mr. Waldheim fails, the next Council meeting is committed in theory to order sanctions. Apart from the fact that both Zambia and China suggest that they are not committed, sanctions could be balked by a Soviet veto.

But Mr. McHenry said he doubted Moscow would veto sanctions. He said, "I would think that any country which is engaged in the rape of another country would be ill advised to engage in a veto."

Has the United States then made a deal with Moscow to look the other way over Afghanistan in return for a Russian pledge not to veto moves against Iran?

Mr. McHenry rarely splutters, but he did at that. He began, "We have made no secret . . ." Then he broke off and said curtly, "That's an obscene suggestion."

The Council's action on Jan. 7 is further complicated by the fact that at least four new members will take part. Niger, the Philippines, Tunisia and East Germany replace Nigeria, Gabon, Kuwait and Czechoslovakia. Moreover, Cuba and Colombia are still struggling for Bolivia's seat and it may well be vacant at the next gathering. However, the four newcomers are thought likely to divide in the same fashion as those they replace, two in favor of the plan and two abstentions.

* * *

January 5, 1980

CARTER EMBARGOES TECHNOLOGY FOR SOVIET; LIMITS FISHING PRIVILEGES AND SALE OF GRAIN IN RESPONSE TO 'AGGRESSION' IN AFGHANISTAN

WARNS ON OLYMPICS

President Fears a Danger to Strategic Oil Areas in Moscow's Drive

By TERENCE SMITH
Special to The New York Times.

WASHINGTON, Jan. 4—President Carter, denouncing the Soviet military intervention in Afghanistan as an "extremely serious threat to peace," tonight announced a series of punitive moves against the Soviet Union, including a sharp curtailment of grain shipments.

Warning that the actions he was announcing would require "some sacrifice on the part of all Americans," the President said it was vital that the response of the United States and the international community "match the gravity of the Soviet action."

"A Soviet-occupied Afghanistan threatens both Iran and Pakistan and is a stepping stone to possible control over much of the world's oil supplies," Mr. Carter said in a nationally televised speech.

'A Contagious Disease'

"History teaches perhaps very few clear lessons." he said. "But surely one such lesson learned by the world at great cost is that aggression unopposed becomes a contagious disease."

Mr. Carter's speech drew praise and doubts from politicians.

The actions announced by the President included the following:

Seventeen million metric tons of American grain ordered by the Soviet Union will not be delivered. This does not include eight million tons the United States must sell to Moscow this year under the terms of a 1976 agreement.

A cutoff of sales of high technology, such as advanced computers and oil-drilling equipment, until further notice.

A "severe curtailment" of Soviet fishing privileges in American waters. White House officials said this would deprive the Soviet Union of about 350,000 tons of fish this year.

An indefinite delay in the scheduled opening of new American and Soviet consular facilities and a deferral of any new cultural and economic exchanges.

The President also warned the Soviet Union that "continued aggressive actions" could jeopardize the participation of American athletes in the summer Olympics in Moscow this year.

In addition, Mr. Carter said that the United States, along with other countries he did not name, would provide military equipment, food and other assistance to Pakistan to help that nation "defend its independence and national security against the seriously increased threat it now faces from the north."

The President stressed that all these steps had been discussed with the European allies. He also said he had consulted with Congressional leaders and been assured of their support for whatever legislation might be required to carry out the measures.

Taken together, the steps seemed designed not so much to force the Soviet Union to withdraw its forces from Afghanistan as to persuade the leadership in Moscow that such moves would meet a sharp response from the West.

Steps to Ease Blow to Farmers

Discussing the curtailment of grain shipments, Mr. Carter pledged to reduce the impact on American farmers by removing the undelivered grain from the market through Government storage and price-support programs, with the grain to be purchased at market prices. Later, White House officials said there would be "zero effect on inflation" since the actions would tend to cancel out each other.

The President said he had received assurances from other grain-exporting nations that they would not make up the difference by increasing exports to the Soviet Union. White House officials said specific assurances to this effect had been received from Canada and Australia, and that Argentina was "sympathetic."

The President made no reference to the possibility, raised by Administration officials earlier in the week, of American military aid to the Afghan rebels who have taken refuge in Pakistan and are expected to challenge the Soviet-backed Government in Kabul. But a White House policy-maker, in a briefing for reporters before the speech, declined to rule out the possibility.

Carter's Toughest Speech

The speech was by far the toughest Mr. Carter has delivered as President and reflected a fundamental reappraisal of United States-Soviet relations that was under way in Washington this week.

But Mr. Carter stopped short of giving an ultimatum or of provocative language that might close the door to an improvement in relations.

His warnings about the possible Soviet threat to Iran seemed to be designed to persuade the revolutionary authorities in Iran that their own interests could be best served by releasing the American hostages they have held since Nov. 4 and by reopening communications with the West.

The President, who met today with Thomas J. Watson Jr., the Ambassador to Moscow who was summoned home for consultations, said they were engaged in "an immediate and comprehensive evaluation of the whole range of our relations with the Soviet Union."

Mr. Carter reiterated his belief that the pending strategic arms treaty with the Russians was in the best interests of the American people, but said he had asked the Senate to defer action on its ratification until he could "assess Soviet actions and intentions." He added that "as circumstances change in the future, we will, of course, keep the ratification of SALT II under active review."

U.S. Will Seek to Evade Veto

Nothing that the Soviet Union might use its veto to block a resolution condemning its actions in Afghanistan in the United Nations Security Council, Mr. Carter said the matter would then be pursued in the General Assembly, where no such veto power applies.

"In the meantime," he said, "neither the United States nor any other nation which is committed to world peace and stability can continue to do business as usual with the Soviet Union."

Mr. Carter began his remarks by restating his concern for the American hostages being held in Iran. He said the United States would continue to seek their release, adding: "We hope to do so without bloodshed and without further danger to the lives of our 50 fellow Americans."

Speaks in a Calm Manner

Dressed in a dark suit and seated at his desk in the Oval Office, Mr. Carter spoke in calm and measured tones. He seemed inclined to let the weight of his warnings to the Soviet Union stand alone, rather than reinforce them by gesture or raised voice.

The first official word of the President's plans to address the nation came in a White House statement at 2 P.M. Anticipation over what he would say built through the afternoon as Congressional leaders and Cabinet members trooped up the snow-covered driveway to the West Wing for advance briefings.

Zbigniew Brzezinski, the President's national security adviser, spoke by telephone with former Presidents Gerald R. Ford and Richard M. Nixon. White House officials said both expressed support for the President's action.

Search for Suitable Responses

Consultations had been held all week within the Administration and with European allies to find appropriate responses to the Soviet troop move into Afghanistan.

It was a week in which Mr. Carter's Republican Party challengers broke a self-imposed silence and began criticizing his handling of the Iran situation, thereby making it an open campaign issue.

The first reports of the Soviet-backed coup in Kabul and of major Soviet troop movements across the Afghan frontier reached Washington Dec. 27. In the preceding 24 hours, there was a large Soviet airlift of troops and equipment to Kabul.

As soon as the Soviet role in the Kabul coup became evident, the White House issued a sharp condemnation and sent Warren M. Christopher, Under Secretary of State, to Europe for urgent talks.

Exchange of Hot-Line Messages

Over the weekend, Mr. Carter and the Soviet leader, Leonid I. Brezhnev, exchanged sharp messages on the hot line set up for urgent consultations. In his message, Mr. Carter demanded that the Soviet Union withdraw its troops from Afghanistan and warned that the future of relations between the United States and the Soviet Union would depend on Moscow's response.

Mr. Brezhnev's reply, which came clattering into the White House Situation Room at midday Saturday, contended that the Soviet move had been made in response to a request for assistance from the Afghan Government and that the troops would be withdrawn after the crisis there had been resolved.

Soviet's Reply Angered Carter

Incensed by this message, which he publicly described as "completely inadequate and completely misleading," Mr. Carter told Frank Reynolds of ABC Television in an interview Monday that the "invasion" of Afghanistan had brought about a fundamental change in his perception of the Russians and their role in international affairs.

"This action of the Soviets has made a more dramatic change in my own opinion of what the Soviets' ultimate goals are than anything they've done in the previous time I have been in office," he said in the interview.

* * *

January 24, 1980

CARTER WARNS U.S. WOULD USE ARMED FORCE TO REPEL A SOVIET THRUST AT PERSIAN GULF; CALLS FOR RENEWAL OF DRAFT REGISTRATION

THREAT TO OIL CITED

Aide Calls State of Union Address an Ultimatum on Area's Security

---

By TERENCE SMITH

Special to The New York Times.

WASHINGTON, Jan. 23—President Carter, asserting that the Soviet forces in Afghanistan pose a "grave threat" to the Middle East oilfields, declared tonight that the United States would use "any means necessary, including military force" to repel an attack on the Persian Gulf.

In a 31-minute State of the Union Message to a joint session of Congress that was interrupted 20 times with applause, Mr. Carter also announced that he would shortly seek authority to resume Selective Service registration to insure that the nation can "meet future mobilization needs rapidly if they arise." The President added, however, that he hoped it would not become necessary to reimpose the draft itself.

Mr. Carter delivered his third State of the Union Address in firm but subdued tones to a packed House chamber. In addition to the Supreme Court Justices, Cabinet members and foreign ambassadors attending, Mr. Carter's chief rival for the Democratic Presidential nomination, Senator Edward M. Kennedy, followed a prepared text of the speech.

Reaction Split on Partisan Lines

The initial reaction to the speech split along partisan lines, with Democrats generally approving the President's remarks and Republicans finding them wanting. Representative John J. Rhodes of Arizona, the House Republican leader, contended that the speech contained "a lot of saber rattling, but not much in the saber."

A White House official said that the President's statement about protecting the Persian Gulf oilfields amounted to an "unmistakable ultimatum" to the Soviet Union not to threaten the oil supplies of the Western world.

Implicit in the President's speech was concern that the Soviet military intervention in Afghanistan might lead to further Soviet moves in such countries as Pakistan and Iran.

The Russians have maintained that they intervened in Afghanistan at the request of the Soviet-backed regime there. They have said that once their mission is over the troops, now estimated at 85,000, will be withdrawn. Moscow has also said it has no designs on any of Afghanistan's neighbors, but this has not eased concern in Pakistan, a country with which the United States has a defense commitment dating from 1959.

The President announced in his speech that in providing requested military and economic aid to Pakistan, Congress would be asked to reaffirm the 1959 comment.

Mr. Carter charged that the Soviet invasion of Afghanistan constituted an attempt "to consolidate a strategic position that poses a grave threat to the free movement of Middle East oil."

Soviet Forces Near Key Strait

Noting that the Soviet forces in Afghanistan were now within 200 miles of the strategic Strait of Normuz, which guards the entrance to the Persian Gulf, Mr. Carter declared:

"Let our position be absolutely clear:

"An attempt by any outside force to gain control of the Persian Gulf region will be regarded as an assault on the vital interests of the United States of America. And such an assault will be repelled by use of any means necessary, including military force."

With this declaration, Mr. Carter in effect extended the American security umbrella to the Persian Gulf. Heretofore, it has been explicitly committed only to Western Europe, the Far East and Israel.

American officials said that there had been "some consultations" with other governments about the American security guarantee in the Gulf, but they did not specify which governments had been involved.

Mr. Carter reminded his audience that American hostages were still being held in the United States Embassy in Teheran as he spoke and repeated earlier warnings that if they were harmed, "a severe price will be paid."

Conciliatory Note Sounded

But the President also struck a concilatory note by repeating that the United States had no quarrel with Islamic nations, including Iran, and declared that "the real danger to their nation lies to the north in the Soviet Union and from the Soviet troops now in Afghanistan." Administration officials have adopted this approach in recent days in an effort to convince the Iranian authorities that it is in their interest to free the hostages.

A ranking Administration official, briefing reporters before the speech, stressed that the President's statements were not in response to an "acute crisis." Nor, he said, is there any threat of "an immediate confrontation." Mr. Carter's declaration is intended to signal "a long-term response" to potential Soviet actions, the official said.

The official, who could not be identified under the ground rules of the briefing, declined to specify the exact geographic limits of the Persian Gulf region. He explained that the President wanted to be flexible in responding to different situations that might arise.

'Some Basic Questions' Raised

In his address, Mr. Carter said that the Soviet Union must answer some "basic questions" in defining its relationship with the West in the 1980's.

"Will it help promote a more stable international environment in which its own legitimate, peaceful concerns can be pursued? Or will it continue to expand its military power far beyond its genuine security needs, and use that power for colonial conquest?" he asked.

The President cited the recent economic sanctions and grain embargo imposed against the Sovet Union in response to the military intervention in Afghanistan and appeared to toughen his language regarding the previously imposed limits on Soviet fishing in American waters. "I will not issue any permits for Soviet ships to fish in the coastal waters of the United States," he declared.

Focus Is Almost Entirely Foreign

Mr. Carter's speech was remarkable for a State of the Union Address in that it focused almost exclusively on foreign affairs. He took note of this in his opening remarks when he observed: "It has never been more clear that the state of our union depends on the state of the world."

A central theme in the speech was the prospect of turmoil and challenge facing the United States in the coming decade. Mr. Carter described it as a "time that tests our wisdom and our skills."

He linked his warnings about the Soviet threat to Middle Eastern oil with a renewed appeal to Congress to adopt his energy program. "To be strong abroad, we must be strong at home," he said, adding that the nation's dependence on foreign oil was "a clear and present danger to our nation's security."

Mr. Carter also reiterated the need to continue the fight against inflation, reduce Federal spending and eventually balance the Federal budget in order to strengthen the economy.

* * *

February 23, 1980

U.S. DEFEATS SOVIET SQUAD IN OLYMPIC HOCKEY BY 4-3

By GERALD ESKENAZI

Special to The New York Times.

LAKE PLACID, N.Y., Feb. 22—In one of the most startling and dramatic upsets in Olympic history, the underdog United States hockey team, composed in great part of collegians, defeated the defending champion Soviet squad by 4-3 tonight.

The victory brought a congratulatory phone call to the dressing room from President Carter and set off fireworks over this tiny Adirondack village. The triumph also put the Americans in a commanding position to take the gold medal in the XIII Olympic Winter Games, which will end Sunday.

If on Sunday morning the United States defeats Finland, which tied Sweden, 3-3, tonight, the Americans will win the gold medal regardless of the outcome of the game between Sweden and the Soviet Union later that day. If the United States ties Finland, the Americans are assured of at least a bronze medal.

The American goal that broke a 3-3 tie tonight was scored midway through the final period by a player who typifies the makeup of the United States team.

His name is Mike Eruzione, he is from Winthrop, Mass., he is the American team's captain and he was plucked from the obscurity of the Toledo Blades of the International League. His opponents tonight included world-renowned stars, some of them performing in the Olympics for the third time.

The Soviet team has captured the previous four Olympic hockey tournaments, going back to 1964, and five of the last six. The only club to defeat them since 1956 was the United States team of 1960, which won the gold medal at Squaw Valley, Calif.

Few victories in American Olympic play have provoked reaction comparable to tonight's decision at the red-seated, smallish Olympic Field House. At the final buzzer, after the fans had chanted the seconds away, fathers and mothers and friends of the United States players dashed onto the ice, hugging anyone they could find in red, white and blue uniforms.

Meanwhile, in the stands, most of the 10,000 fans—including about 1,500 standees, who paid $24.40 apiece for a ticket—shouted "U.S.A.," over and over, and hundreds outside waved American flags.

'Born to Be a Player'

Later, the orchestrator of the team, Coach Herb Brooks, from the University of Minnesota, took out a yellow piece of paper, displayed the almost illegible scrawl on it, and said, "I really said this to the guys. I'm not lying to you."

Before the game, Brooks had taken out that card in the locker room and read his remarks.

"You were born to be a player," he read. "You were meant to be here." Though only one of the 20 players in the room ever had competed in an Olympics before, they proved him right.

The Americans were seeded seventh in this tournament, but they went through the opening round of play undefeated, with four victories and one tie to advance to the final round, which will decide the gold, silver and bronze medalists.

From the opening minutes fans and players fed off one another in the festive atmosphere at the arena. The tempo and emotion of the game was established early, when a longtime Soviet star, Valery Kharlamov, wearing the traditional lipstick-red uniform, was sandwiched between two Americans.

Suddenly, he was lifted between them and, looking like a squirt of ketchup, sailed into the air and then flopped to the ice.

Russian-Based Attack

Beyond the constant pressure of intimidating body checks, though, were the intricate passing patterns of the Americans, who have derived many of their techniques from the Russians.

The Soviet system is based on attack. The Russians more than doubled the shots on goal of the Americans, 39-16, but almost every one that the Russians took was stopped, often dramatically, by Jim Craig, a former goalie for Boston University.

As a result of tonight's victory, the hockey players will be among the prouder contingents of the 150 American Olympians who will be honored at the White House on Monday morning at a two-hour session with the President.

Tonight, though, the Americans struggled until the final period, never leading until Eruzione's goal. They trailed by 3-2 going into the last 20-minute period.

No hockey game is played nonstop for 60 minutes, but this one came close. The Russians have been famed for their conditioning techniques. They also were considered the finest hockey team in the world.

The Soviet Union broke through first, with its new young star, Valery Krotov, getting his stick in the way of Aleksei Kasatonov's whistling slap shot. The puck changed direction and sailed beyond Craig's reach in the first period.

Midway through the period, the only American who has been an Olympian, Buzz Schneider, drilled a shot over the left shoulder of Vladislav Tretyak, the Soviet goalie.

The goal was Schneider's fifth of the series, giving him the team lead. That is a surprising performance for a player who once failed the tryout with the lowly Pittsburgh Penguins in the National League, and since has bounced around American leagues of less stature.

Holding Goes Unnoticed

But there were other highlights of that first period. The Russians had one when Sergei Makarov punched the puck past Craig while fans screamed in vain for Referee Karl-Gustav Kaisla of Finland to notice an American who was being held.

Only a few seconds remained when Ken Morrow, a draft choice of the New York Islanders, slammed an 80-foot desperation shot toward the goal. The puck caromed out to Mark Johnson, who struck it home with no seconds showing on the clock.

A goal cannot be scored with no time remaining. Actually, when the puck had sailed in there was a second left. It took another second for the goal judge to press the button signaling the score and stopping the clock.

The Soviet skaters left the ice, contending time was over, but after Kaisla spoke to other officials, the goal was allowed. The arena rocked with applause with the verification of the 2-2 tie.

Soviet Goalie Replaced

Back came the disappointed Russians from their dressing room, adjusting their shiny red helmets. They had a new player on the ice, too—Vladimir Myshkin had replaced Tretyak in goal for the final faceoff of the period. Later, the assistant Soviet coach, Vladimir Jursinov, explained the removal of Tretyak, saying through an interpreter, "He is not playing well and my feeling is he is nervous."

Myshkin kept the Americans at bay for the second period, although they tested him with only two shots. The Russians took a 3-2 lead when one of their veterans, Aleksandr Maltsev, scored with a man advantage.

But in the last period Johnson swatted home a shot that David Silk had gotten off while being hauled down, and the puck eluded Myshkin to tie the score. About a minute and a half later, with exactly half of the period over, Eruzione picked up a loose puck in the Soviet zone, skated to a point between the faceoff circles and fired a screened, 30-foot shot through the pads of Myshkin for the winning score.

The goal set off cheering that lasted through the remainder of the game, as the youngest team of all the American squads, average age 22, put itself in a position to win only the second gold medal for an American hockey team.

* * *

July 4, 1980

U.S. AND BONN: BUMPY MARRIAGE ENDURES

By DAVID BINDER

WASHINGTON, July 3—Periodically over the last three years acrimony has boiled up in relations between the United States and its most important ally, West Germany, over issues of arms control, economic policy, nuclear exports and, most recently, over basic perceptions of East-West relations.

As in a long marriage, to which the 30-year-old Bonn-Washington relationship has sometimes been compared, the quarrels have always been patched up.

So it was again this week after Chancellor Helmut Schmidt's meetings in Moscow with Leonid I. Brezhnev, the Soviet leader, an action initially viewed by the Carter Administration as not being in harmony with its own policy toward the Soviet Union since the December 1979 intervention in Afghanistan.

The latest patching-up occurred yesterday when Foreign Minister Hans-Dietrich Genscher told Mr. Carter that West German initiative had extracted a Soviet concession on future discussions with the West of the strategic arms balance in Europe. The President voiced his "admiration."

Enduring Changes in 12 Years

However exaggerated some of the recent disputes may have seemed and however much they may have derived, as many believe, from temperamental differences between Mr. Schmidt and Mr. Carter, there have been some more enduring changes over the last dozen years in the Bonn-Washington relationship. They have arisen in part out of a growing West German awareness of a national self-interest and in part from Washington's occasional inability to persuade Bonn that American policies were always right.

The most evident changes are in Bonn's emergence from relative political isolation and the loss of feeling like a client of the United States. The loss of that status is symbolized by the termination of Bonn's payment of funds to compensate for the cost of stationing American troops in West Germany in the early 1970's and the ascendancy of the West German mark.

But it was the normalization treaties with the Soviet Union and its allies that provided West Germany with the flexibility it had been denied. Nor should it be forgotten that those treaties were negotiated in harmony with the efforts of the United States to place East-West relations on a sounder footing.

The fact that West Germany had already established itself as the dominant economic power within the Common Market served to strengthen its freedom of action.

The short ups and long downs of the Soviet-American relationship since President Richard M. Nixon concluded his wide-ranging arms agreements in 1972 with Mr. Brezhnev have tended to highlight the divergency in views between Bonn and Washington on the central issue of how to deal with the Soviet Union.

Treated Like a Faucet

For Washington, particularly under President Carter, the relationship with Moscow has been treated almost as a faucet that could be turned off or on. For Bonn, in the decade of its treaty ties, the relationship with Moscow has become a permanent aspect of its foreign relations, augmented by sizable trade and other exchanges, including the repatriation of hundreds of thousands of ethnic Germans from Eastern Europe.

These divergencies in pespective derive quite naturally from differences of size and location as well as from history. Like them or not, Germans know that the Russians are near neighbors. Most Americans do not feel that about the Russians.

The differences in perspective, along with West Germany's relative growth in power and America's relative decline in influence, were embodied for an instant in Mr. Genscher's flying visit to Paris and Washington yesterday to brief French and American leaders on the details of the Schmidt-Brezhnev meetings.

The underlying changes have recently led, from time to time, to suspicions in Washington and Bonn that the other partner was somehow becoming unreliable, leading even to small episodes of distrust.

Sensitive to U.S. Charges

Mr. Schmidt has become acutely sensitive to such charges, taking special pains in the last three weeks to remind visiting Americans that West Germany has "kept all of its pledges to the United States over the last 20 years," as he said to a high-level group of Americans in Bonn.

One reason why elements of distrust will probably persist is that despite all the telephone and letter exchanges that continue between Mr. Schmidt and Mr. Carter, and despite the steady stream of West German officials visiting Washington, there has been a general decline in interest on the part of Americans in West German affairs during the last six years. The interest seems to have declined as divided Germany has become a region of relative peace and accord.

But moments of distrust or not, and despite the quarrels, the Bonn-Washington marriage seems likely to continue indefinitely without the help of counseling or the pressure of in-laws, simply because the two partners depend so heavily on each other for security.

* * *

July 20, 1980

AFGHAN REBELS: ZEAL AND COURAGE

By NICHOLAS GAGE

Special to The New York Times.

PESHAWAR, Pakistan—In a makeshift hospital, one of three maintained in rented houses here by Afghan insurgents, two wounded guerrillas lie on rope cots in a small room buzzing with flies.

In one bed is Ahmad Khazamar, 25 years old, whose right foot bears several gaping shrapnel wounds. He has been in 30 engagements with the Russians in six months, he said, and as soon as he is able he is going back. "As long as my mind functions I will fight," he said.

In the next cot is Malek Sawad, 50, one of two survivors of a group of eight mujahedeen, or Moslem guerrillas. "We have chosen the way of martyrdom," he said. "How can we be defeated?"

The words of the two wounded Afghans illustrate why the Soviet military intervention in their country seven months ago has turned into a standoff between one of the great powers and groups of mountain tribesmen sustained by 25 centuries of experience in guerrilla warfare and a belief that it is glorious to die in the name of Islam.

Most Western analysts here believe that the Russians intervened in Afghanistan in the hope that they could maintain enough security to allow the local Communist Party to take control of the country's institutions and build up the army. But they have failed, the analysts say, brought to a stalemate by the refusal of the Afghans to submit.

'They Can't Win,' Afghan Says

"The Russians are trying to annihilate us," said Maulvi Mohammed Yunus Khalis, leader of one of five insurgent groups in the Islamic Alliance for the Liberation of Afghanistan. "They use napalm and gas bombs. There is not a single day when they do not bomb villages full of civilians. But they still do not control the countryside and they are not even safe in Kabul. Despite their overwhelming firepower, they cannot win."

The standoff, according to most of the analysts, is so frustrating to the Russians that they are almost certain to pour in additional troops once the Olympics are over Aug. 3. It is generally felt by the analysts here that if the new forces do not prove any more effective against the mountain fighters, who can easily slip back and forth across the 1,300-mile border with Pakistan, the Russians may try to overcome the situation by moving into northern Pakistan.

"The more they get bogged down in Afghanistan, the more they feel Pakistan is the root of their problems," said an ambassador from a neutral country with close ties to Moscow. "If their present mood continues, it is inevitable that they will strike at northwest Pakistan because it provides a safety valve for the insurgents."

Hiding in a cave in Kunar Province, Afghan guerrillas wait so they can raid Soviet emplacements in the countryside.

At the moment the North-West Frontier Province of Pakistan contains 720,000 refugees, according to Robin McAlpin, representative of the United Nations High Commissioner for Refugees. Every night they come into Pakistan over the treacherous mountain passes at the rate of 60,000 a month. There are 900,000 Afghan refugees in Pakistan, housed in 80 camps.

Thousands Cross the Borders

Thousands of insurgents move freely back and forth across the border every week, fighting in Afghanistan, regrouping and bringing their wounded into Pakistan. Most are from the Pashtun tribe, the largest group in Afghanistan, numbering 7.5 million of the 16 million people.

There are 15 million Pashtunis in all; the others live in northwestern Pakistan, where they are called Pathans and are eager to help their tribal brothers.

Afghan tribesmen live by the code of "badal," or blood vengeance. "Every time a Russian helicopter gunship strafes a village, every man in it will not rest until he has drawn Russian blood," said Haji Mangal Hussain, an Afghan teacher now with one of the insurgent groups.

The Russians charge that Pakistan is being used as a conduit for aid to the insurgents in Afghanistan. The Pakistanis are nervously making every effort to appear blameless; they have carefully maintained the position that they are providing only humanitarian assistance to the refugees.

Pakistan Describes Its Role

"We are accepting refugees from Afghanistan, but we are not providing any military assistance, either in the forms of arms or training, and we are not funneling arms for other countries," said Riaz Piracha, the Pakistani Foreign Minister. "We are not prepared to be a conduit to the resistance fighters. We are not prepared to jeopardize our own security."

The Pakistanis, to avoid any appearance of intervention, even refuse to allow foreign doctors to treat the refugees. Mr. McAlpin, who coordinates help to the refugees, said: "We have 20 mobile dispensaries and have just opened a small hospital with six Afghan doctors handling 100 to 200 patients a day. We could bring in many volunteer doctors from Western countries, but Pakistan won't allow it because it is sensitive to Soviet charges that it is being used as a pipeline to aid insurgents. Therefore it wants a minimum of Westerners dealing with the refugees."

Pakistan Says It Isn't Worried

Publicly the Pakistani Government dismisses the possibility of a Soviet invasion, saying that while Soviet troops might cross the border in hot pursuit of insurgents, a prolonged Soviet incursion is improbable. Privately the Pakistanis express deep fears of a major invasion.

"Militarily, I can see the strong temptation for the Soviets to bring the war to Pakistan," said a retired general now in a high Government post. "Pakistan provides sanctuary for villagers who support the insurgents. If they had no place to go, the insurgents might knuckle under, the way the Russians see it. They are wrong because the Hazaras in central Afghanistan, the Uzbeks in the east, even the Tadjiks in the north near the Soviet border, are resisting successfully without such a sanctuary. But in their frustration Pakistan has to be a tempting target for the Soviets when they see all the Afghan activity on the North-West Frontier."

The insurgents, eager not to make the Pakistanis any more nervous than they are, dismiss the possibility of a Soviet invasion. "The Russians cannot risk invading Pakistan: the cost would be too high," said Hassan Gailani, a leader of one of the groups fighting in the mountains. "The international reaction would be even greater than for Afghanistan. The Russians would completely lose the support of the Moslem world, with which they've had generally good relations, if they were to invade a second Moslem country. It would be a stupid and futile move. It would not stop the insurgency in Afghanistan and it would be foolish because Pakistan is not helping us militarily."

Rare Unanimity: Sources of Aid

As for the origin of financial and military support, the half-dozen major groups of insurgents fighting in the northwestern province, who disagree on nearly every other matter, answer this question with rare unanimity and in almost identical language.

"We are getting financial help from individuals in many countries but not from governments," said Abdul Rasoul Sayaf, president of the Islamic Alliance for the Liberation of Afghanistan, which includes five of the insurgent groups. "Many Moslems send us money, including some American Moslems."

Nevertheless, some here who are familiar with the aid being supplied to the Afghan guerrillas say that Saudi Arabia and several of the Persian Gulf states are giving money directly and that the United States is providing arms on a limited basis.

"The Americans are trying to maintain a balance between having insurgents armed well enough to make it too costly for the Russians to want to stay in Afghanistan while not providing so many weapons that the Soviets will be provoked to attack Pakistan," a European ambassador commented.

Weapons Acquired From Russians

The guerrilla leaders say they steal nearly all the weapons they need from the Russians. "As long as the Russians are in Afghanistan we will not have a shortage of guns," said Gulbuddin Hekmatyar, who heads one of the largest and most active group of insurgents, which he describes as the oldest, the strongest and the best armed. He refuses to unite with the other factions under the umbrella of the Islamic Alliance, maintaining that he wants representation in the alliance to be based on strength of numbers, not equally divided among the factions.

Mr. Kehmatyar, who was interviewed in his Peshawar headquarters, a former school, is a magnet for the young religious fighters who are drawn by his single-minded determination to establish an Islamic state. His father and two brothers were killed by the previous Communist Governments of Noor Mohammad Taraki and Hafizullah Amin and he was been imprisoned by King Zafer.

In addition to weapons taken from the Soviet forces or brought by defectors from the Afghan Army, whose ranks have dwindled to 35,000 from 80,000 in the last year, the insurgents can buy cheap, meticulously hand-crafted weapons only 25 miles south of here in Durra, which has been a center for arms manufacturing for hundreds of years.

The Pathans there can copy any machine-made pistol or revolver perfectly, right down to the factory marks and serial number, and they sell in an open bazaar such refinements as antitank rocket-propelled grenades, "fountain pen" pistols and "walking stick" guns, all at bargain prices.

Insurgent leaders like Mr. Hekmatyar say that the only weapons they cannot easily obtain are antiaircraft and antitank guns.

Hitting Inaccessible Positions

Tanks can be defeated by retreating into the deep mountain paths or by blowing them up with gasoline bombs. But the lack of antiaircraft weapons is a constant problem because helicopter gunships can maneuver through the mountains and strike otherwise inaccessible positions. "The helicopters are the only Russian weapons that can hurt us badly," Mr. Khalis said.

While the Russians can pursue the insurgents with gunships, they cannot seem to stop them. "Helicopter gunships can strafe a mountain all day and then a platoon moves up the mountain at night and it is cut to bits," said a European military attaché here who is following the war in Afghanistan. "That's what's so frustrating to the Russians. The Americans learned the same lesson in Vietnam. Superpower technology in a guerrilla war is valuable only for reprisals, wasting villages. In the end the Russians may find that the only alternative to withdrawal is genocide."

Parallels between the Russians in Afghanistan and the Americans in Vietnam are unavoidable. The Americans underestimated the Vietnamese Communist soldiers' superior knowledge of jungle warfare and the Vietnamese tradition of defending one's land and the graves of one's ancestors. The Afghans are able to hold off superior numbers of wellarmed Russians at least in part because of their experience in mountain warfare and their tradition of blood vengeance.

Back to Alexander the Great

"The Afghans have always been the best resistance fighters in the world," said Brig. Mir Abad Hussam, director general of the Pakistani Foreign Ministry. "Alexander the Great encountered them on his trek east and decided to take a southern route back. The British never stayed there, although they occupied the rest of the region."

The insurgents' strong Islamic faith is another factor the Russians have not taken into consideration, just as the Americans underestimated the power of religion as a force for revolution in Iran. The Afghan insurgents believe that dying in the name of Islam is a glorious death, one that will insure their place in paradise.

"The Russians have never before fought a people who were fighting for their faith," said Haji Mangal Hussain, a 30-year-old teacher at an Afghan agricultural college who is a spokesman for an insurgent group.

"The Soviets cannot win because they cannot fight with our commitment," said Mr. Sayaf of the Islamic Alliance. "To us killing a Russian or dying in battle represents an equal victory. If a Moslem kills an enemy in battle, he is a ghazi, an Islamic warrior, and if he is killed, he is a shaheed, a martyr for Islam, and the rewards are great in paradise." He added: "They are a superpower and we are among the poorest of peoples, and in the six months we have been fighting they have grown weaker every day and we have become stronger."

Lack of Unity Among Tribes

Although united by religion and by experience as mountain fighters, the insurgents are hampered by a lack of unity among tribal groups that prevents them from coordinating their operations and, even more important, from being able to control a fixed area where they could establish a provisional government. If such a government existed, other countries might provide more military assistance without involving Pakistan.

The leaders of the insurgents say they are close to such a goal. "If we can expand the alliance, we could pool our weapons and defend an area where we can base a government," Mr. Sayaf said.

Many Westerners here feel that centuries of feuding will not be easily set aside. Even within the Islamic Alliance the rivalries are deep. When Sayed Ahmad Gailani, leader of the most all-inclusive group in the alliance, went to Western Europe to seek arms for the insurgents, Mr. Sayaf, the president of the alliance, criticized the effort and issued a statement dissociating the alliance from it. In a clear criticism of Mr. Gailani, whose group includes Westernized Afghans, Mr. Sayaf said: "Gailani went without consulting the rest of us. We believe Westerners never help true Moslems but only those who accept Western values."

European and Asian diplomats here believe that the United States should give more support to the Afghan rebellion even if it increases the risks of a Soviet move against Pakistan, basically because they consider such an invasion to be inevitable.

Three Options for Russians

In the view of these diplomats, the Russians have three options left in Afghanistan. The first is to try to crush the rebellion with sheer force through saturation bombing of villages that support the rebels and by bringing in more troops trained in anti-insurgency tactics.

The second option is to try to seal the border with Pakistan, which would require more than double the troops now in Afghanistan, estimated at 85,000. It would require the troops to maintain static positions, allowing the rebels to cut them off from supply centers.

If these options fail, the analysts say, the Russians are certain to turn to their final option, an invasion of northern Pakistan. The hope of the Pakistanis and most of their supporters is that before this comes to pass the Soviet leaders will realize the quagmire they are in and accept a political solution that would create a neutral Afghanistan.

Former King a Possibility

In diplomatic circles here discussion frequently turns to personalities who might be suitable to head such a government and gain enough support to make it work. One of the names mentioned is former King Zafer, now living in Rome.

But his prospects are not considered good because many Afghans blame him for starting the flirtation with the Soviet Union that led ultimately to the military intervention. A more acceptable prospect is Sher Ali, a member of the royal family, also living in Europe, who has a record that would make him more acceptable to a wider spectrum of Afghan groups as well as to the Soviet Union and the United States.

Most of the resistance groups here say they will not accept any political solution short of a fundamentalist Islamic government. They will continue to fight any other solution, they insist, even if it has the support of both the third world and the United States.

"We do not want to wind up like Vietnam and drive out one superpower only to become the puppet of another," said Mr. Hekmatyar, the insurgent leader. Said Mr. Sayaf, president of the alliance of five groups, "Our fight is not being waged to gain anyone's aims but our own."

Reminded that the Soviet Union had made it clear that it would not agree to an Islamic government in Kabul, he said: "Then we will go on fighting. Time does not concern us. We have been fighting for centuries."

* * *

August 25, 1980

POLAND'S PREMIER IS DISMISSED IN SWEEPING PARTY SHAKE-UP; GIEREK PLEDGES UNION BALLOT

By JOHN DARNTON

WARSAW, Aug. 24—Poland's Prime Minister and three other full members of the ruling Politburo, as well as two deputy members, were dismissed today in a major shake-up of the Communist Party.

The reorganization was the largest in a decade and one of the most sweeping in the party's 36-year rule. It was intended to stem the national crisis caused by the strike of at least 200,000 workers on the Baltic coast, now in its 11th day, and was seen as a last-ditch move by Edward Gierek, the party's First Secretary, to continue his 10-year reign.

In a speech at a six-hour meeting of the party's Central Committee, at which the Government changes were decided, Mr. Gierek said that the committee felt that the Central Trade Union Council, which the strikers oppose, should hold new elections in all factories, with secret ballots and an unlimited number of candidates.

Far Short of Strikers' Demands

The proposals did not indicate any structural change in the relationship of the council to the party or Government and fell far short of what the workers were demanding. The initial reaction by the workers' leaders indicated that the moves would not bring an immediate end to the strikes.

In his speech Mr. Gierek said: "We are ready to talk to the workers' representatives, but we cannot make promises that cannot be fulfilled or agree to demands striking at the basis of the state's existence."

Some of the strikers' demands are political and challenge the institutions that have helped keep the Communists in power. Among them are demands for an end to censorship, for the release of all political prisoners, and the right to strike and elect union representatives independent of party control.

Repudiation of Union Council

Among those dropped from the Politburo tonight was Jan Szydlak, the union council leader who said last week that "the Government does not intend to give up its power nor to share it with anyone else."

His dismissal was seen as a repudiation of the union council, as was Mr. Gierek's promise that new union represenatives would be elected. He said that if the "recently self-elected" representatives—the strikers' committees—were lasting and popular, their members should "find themselves" in the new organization.

The concession was unprecedented for any Communist government, since it seemed to acknowledge that the workers' interests had not been protected.

Key Offer Involves Candidates

It remains to be seen if fully "free" trade unions can develop. The significant change is not the promise of a secret ballot, which has always been the nominal practice, but the offer of unlimited candidates. Currently the outgoing union representatives have the right to propose about 85 percent of the candidates, virtually insuring their own re-election.

A Central Committee member commented privately that this new provision could produce independent unions, making them responsive to the rank and file rather than to the party leadership.

Looking drawn and tired after the Central Committee debate, which he described as "sharp and painful," Mr. Gierek admitted that the party had made grave mistakes and promised to make "a basic shift in party and Government policy," in the economy, including agriculture, and other areas.

He repeated his words of a week ago that "only socialist Poland can be a free country with unviolable frontiers"—an implicit warning that extensive changes threatening the social system could invite intervention by the Soviet Union.

Mr. Gierek came to power in 1970, after strikes in the same Gdansk region were quelled by troops who shot into crowds and killed more than 100 workers. The shock this caused brought down the Government of Wladyslaw Gomulka.

In today's changes Prime Minister Edward Babiuch was replaced by Jozef Pinkowski, the 51-year-old Secretary of the Central Committee. Mr. Babiuch became head of Government only six months ago, in a shift that was also caused by the country's persistent economic problems. It was his decision to raise meat prices that set off the strikes.

The party changes came after the Government's initial talks with the 19-member strike committee last night failed to achieve a breakthrough. The Government had previously refused to bargain with the committee.

A Deputy Prime Minister, Mieczyslaw Jagielski, spent two-and-a-half hours inside the conference building of the Lenin Shipyards, the strikers' headquarters in Gdansk. He outlined the Government's feeling about some of the 21 demands but substantive talks were recessed.

The strikers were angry that the Government had failed to live up to a precondition for the talks—the restoration of telephone links between the northern coast and the rest of the country.

For their part the strikers' committee refused a Government request to restore bus service in Gdansk, asserting that this would undermine their solidarity. About 400 factories and other enterprises are involved in the stoppage in Gdansk and about 100 more in Szczecin to the west.

It was not immediately clear what affect the changes and Mr. Gierek's speech would have on the strike movement itself. Mr. Gierek's speech was broadcast live over loudspeakers in the shipyard conference hall and prompted some laughter from the hundreds inside. Later the workers sang the national anthem and held up victory signs.

Many strikers seemed impressed with the extent of Mr. Gierek's concessions, however, and a bit dazed by their own newly discovered power.

But the strike leaders were critical. "It's a patching up of holes," said Lech Walesa, chairman of the strike committee. "We want something new."

"I am not interested in personnel matters," he said of the new leadership. "I don't know these people. Our main problem is free trade unions, and it is not important for us who will meet with us."

Anna Walentynowicz, another key figure in the strike, said, "We have to continue our struggle." And Bogdan Lis, who is also on the 19-member strike committee, said, "The new team may be more democratic but it changes nothing."

Those dropped from the Politburo, besides Mr. Babiuch, were Jerzy Lukaszewicz, Tadeusz Pyka and Zdzislaw Zandarowski. The Cabinet changes involved Foreign Minister Emil Wojaszek, who was replaced by Josef Czyrk; Finance Minister Henryk Kisiel, who was replaced by Marian Krzak, and the Minister of Machine Industry, Aleksander Kopec, who was replaced by Henryk Gawronski.

* * *

October 20, 1980

PRESIDENT SUGGESTS REAGAN'S POLICY COULD LEAD TO A NUCLEAR PRECIPICE

By STEVEN R. WEISMAN
Special to The New York Times.

WASHINGTON, Oct. 19—President Carter, moving further to make the strategic arms treaty with the Soviet Union a major issue of his re-election campaign, charged today that Ronald Reagan's attitudes toward arms control could push the United States closer to a "nuclear precipice."

In one of his lengthiest recent statements on the issue of war and peace, Mr. Carter said in a paid 15-minute radio address that "peace is my passion" and "peace is my pledge" and that the treaty, which Mr. Reagan opposes, should be viewed as a "secret weapon" that would improve American security.

"Over the last 20 years, we've taken some tentative steps away from the nuclear precipice," Mr. Carter said. "Now, for the first time, we are being advised to take steps that may move us toward it."

Prepares for Campaign Trip

The radio speech, broadcast live from the Oval Office in the White House at 12:10 P.M., came a day before Mr. Carter was scheduled to begin a three-day campaign trip.

The President was to campaign in Pennsylvania, Ohio and New York tomorrow, in Florida and Louisiana on Tuesday and in Texas Wednesday. Senator Edward M. Kennedy of Massachusetts, his challenger for the Democratic Presidential nomination, planned to be in New York with Mr. Carter tomorrow.

Mr. Carter and Mr. Kennedy appeared together tonight at a $1,000-a-plate fund-raising dinner here, holding their arms aloft in the gesture of unity that eluded the President last summer at the Democratic National Convention. The dinner is the first of several planned to help pay off the Senator's campaign debt as well as raise money for the President's re-election effort.

The broadcast today was the second of three Sunday programs, each costing about $20,000, designed to give Mr. Carter an opportunity to outline his views in broad fashion in a way that would defuse criticism that his campaign was too "negative" in its attacks.

Timing of Reagan Speech

The President's topic for his address today was scheduled more than a week ago, before Mr. Reagan also made plans to speak on the issue of war and peace on television tonight. The coincidence of the two candidates addressing the same subject on the same day was welcomed by the Carter campaign, which has long said that it believed the issue was one of the President's strongest.

As with his speech last week on the economy, however, Mr. Carter did not mention Mr. Reagan's name in his address today. But he did attack Mr. Reagan's positions, citing again a recent quotation from his Republican opponent recommending that the United States threaten the Soviet Union with "the possibility of an arms race" as a way of negotiating better terms on a nuclear treaty with the Russians.

"He also urges that we seek nuclear superiority," Mr. Carter said of Mr. Reagan. "His position, and I think I state it accurately, is that by abandoning the current agreement and suggesting an all-out nuclear arms race, we could perhaps frighten the Soviets into negotiating a new agreement on the basis of American nuclear superiority."

'A Very Risky Gamble'

Mr. Carter said that in his view, based on "four years of sobering experience in this life-and-death field," such an approach would be "a very risky gamble."

"It is most unlikely that it would lead to any new agreement," he said. "A much more likely result would be an uncontrolled nuclear arms race, and almost certainly, a new rupture in Soviet-American relations."

The President's ringing support of the treaty to limit strategic arms was reminiscent of the way he championed the treaty last year. Mr. Carter and Leonid I. Brezhnev, the Soviet leader, signed the treaty in June 1979, but the Senate put off the ratification vote after the Russians intervened in Afghanistan at the end of last year.

In the last nine months Mr. Carter has said that he believes the treaty is in the national interest, but only recently has he made it a central focus of his speeches. The President's campaign advisers regard the treaty as an important way of reinforcing the fears among some voters, as discerned by public-opinion polls, of Mr. Reagan's positions on nuclear arms control.

As he has repeatedly, Mr. Carter emphatically denied again today that American military power had declined in the last three years. He said the United States had improved defenses by stepping up production of long-range cruise missiles, new battle tanks and modern armored fighting vehicles, the MX mobile missile, jet fighters and attack aircraft.

Problem in Persian Gulf

"When I came into office, I found we had little capability for quick action in the critical Persian Gulf region," Mr. Carter asserted.

"Now we have prepositioned equipment for 12,000 marines and munitions for 500 aircraft," he said. "We have arranged for the use of five different sites in the region. We have deployed two carrier task forces in the Indian Ocean. They give us air and naval superiority to act instantly to keep open the Strait of Hormuz, through which much of the world's old trade flows."

Mr. Carter also said the peace treaty between Israel and Egypt had greatly increased American security in the Middle East.

* * *

October 22, 1980

THE HOSTAGES AND ARMS POLICY: 2 VITAL ISSUES HEAT UP

By RICHARD BURT

Special to The New York Times.

WASHINGTON, Oct. 21—The emergence of the strategic arms limitation treaty as a central issue in the 1980 Presidential campaign represents a major turnabout in American politics.

President Carter and his senior political and policy aides have clearly decided that highlighting Ronald Reagan's opposition to the arms agreement of 1979 with Moscow is the best way of suggesting that a new Republican Administration would plunge the nation into an expensive nuclear arms race and possibly even a war. In line with this strategy, Secretary of Defense Harold Brown asserted yesterday that if the treaty were scrapped, Moscow could deploy thousands of additional nuclear warheads and that the future of arms control talks with the Soviet Union would be delayed, "perhaps indefinitely."

Paradox in Political Debate

But there seems to be a significant paradox in the growing political debate over the treaty: While Mr. Carter is likely to meet tremendous problems in gaining approval for the existing treaty from the Senate, Mr. Reagan is just as likely to face huge difficulties in getting Moscow to agree to a better one.

Mr. Carter's apparent success so far in capitalizing on the arms control issue stands in contrast with the situation a year ago, when the treaty was a major political headache for the White House. With a two-thirds vote by the Senate necessary for ratification, only about 25 liberal senators firmly supported the accord.

At the same time, a powerful coalition of conservative Democrats and Republicans, including Henry M. Jackson, Democrat of Washington, and Howard H. Baker Jr., Republican of Tennessee, opposed the accord on the ground that some of its provisions favored Moscow and others could not be protected against cheating. Following Moscow's intervention in Afghanistan last December, support for the treaty dwindled further and the Administration was forced to ask the Senate to defer action on the treaty.

Capitalizing on the anti-Soviet mood set off by the Soviet-Afghanistan crisis, Mr. Reagan and other Republican politicians depicted the arms treaty as an example of Mr. Carter's inability to stand up to the Russians.

Attitudes toward Moscow have not appreciably changed in recent weeks, but polls and political observers indicate that Mr. Carter is effectively using Mr. Reagan's opposition to the arms treaty to sow doubts about the Republican's ability to keep the country out of war. In recent speeches, Mr. Carter and Secretary of State Edmund S. Muskie said that a failure to approve the treaty would lead to a massive buildup of Soviet and American nuclear arms in the coming decade.

Obviously on the defensive, Mr. Reagan said in a paid television address Sunday night that, while he was still opposed to the current treaty, if elected he would begin immediate talks with Moscow on reaching an accord that more effectively constrained both sides' missile arsenals.

Long Postponement Feared

In response, Secretary Brown charged yesterday that Mr. Reagan's position was one that called the "process itself, and not just one agreement," into question. "Even if that is not the intention," Mr. Brown said, "the almost certain outcome of the proposed policy of discarding SALT II would be to damage the process gravely, and postpone it for a very long time—perhaps indefinitely."

Mr. Brown went on to assert that without the existing treaty, Moscow would be able, in the 1980's, to add 1,000 missiles and 10,000 nuclear warheads to its arsenal, a buildup, he added, that could require Washington to spend as much as $100 billion to match.

But if Mr. Carter has seized the initiative on the arms control question, political and military experts in and outside of Government have started to raise questions about the Administration's drive to revive the treaty debate. Even before the Soviet invasion of Afghanistan, the treaty was in trouble on Capitol Hill, with senators questioning Washington's ability to verify the accord and provisions giving Moscow an advantage in certain categories of weaponry, such as "heavy" land-based missiles.

In recent months, other factors have increased skepticism on Capitol Hill over Soviet intentions. In addition to its involvement in Afghanistan, reports last spring on the outbreak of an anthrax epidemic near the Soviet city of Sverdlovsk raised doubts over Moscow's adherence to an international ban on biological weapons. Doubts about Moscow's compliance with arms accords were reinforced last month when officials disclosed that a Soviet underground nuclear test may have exceeded the limit laid down by a 1974 accord.

Prospects in Next Senate

Consequently, Senate aides believe that Mr. Carter would face a severe test if he sought approval for the treaty early next year. Noting that some of the most ardent supporters of the accord, such as Frank Church, Democrat of Idaho, and John Culver, Democrat of Iowa, are in tough re-election races, the aides said there was a good chance that a new Senate would be less favorable to the treaty than the existing one.

The possibility that the Senate, in 1981, would be unlikely to approve the agreement has led some officials to suggest that Mr. Carter could ask the Senate leadership to vote on the agreement in the forthcoming "lame duck" session after the election. Mr. Brown told reporters yesterday that when the Senate reconvened in November the Administration would consult the Senate leaders on the matter.

While there are doubts whether Mr. Carter could win approval for the treaty, either this year or next, there are also questions over Mr. Reagan's ability to negotiate a better accord. Mr. Brown and other Administration officials maintain that after nearly seven years of negotiations, Moscow would be unlikely to accept a bid from Mr. Reagan "to begin at square one."

Even if Moscow were willing to scrap the existing treaty and begin again, some specialists assert that the momentum of the Soviet nuclear buildup would put Russian negotiators in a superior bargaining position in new talks. Reporting that new American nuclear systems, such as the Air Force's proposed MX mobile missile, are not scheduled for deployment until the end of the decade, one Pentagon specialist contended that the existing treaty was the best that could be obtained in the near future.

"It sounds like an attractive idea to just go out and negotiate a better treaty," he said, "But, in reality, we would be lucky if we ended up with an agreement that was the equal of the existing one."

* * *

October 27, 1980

KREMLIN LEADERS SEEM TO CONCLUDE THAT CARTER IS PREFERABLE TO REAGAN

By R.W. APPLE Jr.
Special to The New York Times.

MOSCOW, Oct. 26—With little more than a week left before the American Presidential election, senior Soviet officials appear to have concluded that they would be better off if Jimmy Carter prevailed over Ronald Reagan.

It has not been an easy conclusion to reach, and it is by no means unanimous. But according to Western diplomats, who base their judgment on conversations with middle-level officials, the men in the Kremlin now favor the man whom they have spent the last year attacking.

The key element in their thinking is the strategic arms limitation treaty. During most of the campaign, Soviet officials have professed unconcern about Mr. Reagan's "cold warrior" image. We have dealt with Republican hard-liners before, they said; at least they are consistent, at least we will know where we stand.

Ten days ago, however, the Soviet leader, Leonid I. Brezhnev, seemed to signal a new line in talks with Armand Hammer, the chairman of the Occidental Petroleum Corporation. Mr. Brezhnev went out of his way, Dr. Hammer reported, to express his "warm feelings" and "high regard" for President Carter. In the context of the campaign, those phrases amounted almost to an endorsement.

Press for Senate Approval

Mr. Carter's sudden popularity stems from his commitment to the arms treaty, a commitment reinforced in recent days. Both Secretary of State Edmund S. Muskie and Defense Secretary Harold Brown have said that, despite the Soviet intervention in Afghanistan, a second Carter Administration would press hard for Senate ratification of the strategic arms limitation treaty, or SALT.

By contrast, Mr. Reagan has said that he would seek to renegotiate the treaty, which he finds unacceptable. "SALT is of overriding importance to these people," a Western analyst said, "not only because of the treaty itself, but because it gets to their fundamental view of the world. They think the U.S. and the U.S.S.R., as equals, should determine the strategic balance in the world.

"Other things—Poland, Afghanistan, American nuclear strategy—are decidedly secondary in their view, and mustn't be allowed to interfere with the major question. Carter seems closer to that world view than Reagan does."

Another element that seems to influence the thinking of Soviet officials is Mr. Reagan's inexperience. Experience is a quality they admire.

No Visits to Soviet Union

Furthermore, Mr. Reagan is a largely unknown quality. His political career has advanced outside Washington. None of his aides have visited Moscow to meet people and exchange ideas, as had associates of Presidential hopefuls in the past.

A member of the Communist Party Central Committee commented that the leadership originally preferred Senator Edward M. Kennedy of Massachusetts for President. The Kremlin, he said, was impressed by the fact that Mr. Kennedy came to Moscow while still in the race.

Mr. Brezhnev, who considers personal relationships very important in foreign affairs, has never met Mr. Reagan. But there is no disposition in Moscow to attack the former Governor of California. Soviet officials say that if Mr. Reagan comes to power and insists on a renegotiation of the arms limitation treaty, they will have to consider that possibility.

The probability is that they would insist on merging SALT-2, the present treaty, and SALT-3, a treaty yet to be negotiated. That is, the Russians might propose a single treaty covering theater nuclear weapons, such as the American cruise missiles and the Soviet SS-20, that are not covered by the present treaty.

Some Soviet officials, particularly those with backgrounds in American affairs, doubt that Mr. Reagan would insist on reopening negotiations. One such official remarked to an American acquaintance recently that "whoever is President always moves to the middle ground."

A long report last week in Izvestia, the Government newspaper, made a similar point. The paper's Washington correspondent, Malor G. Sturua, said that "the Carter Administration does in a practical way what Reagan promises in a theoretical way." He quoted a Washington Post editorial arguing that if Mr. Reagan had been President in the last four years, he would have acted much as Mr. Carter did.

In another commentary, the magazine New Times, which is published by the union newspaper Trud, described both Mr. Carter and Mr. Reagan as undesirable possibilities and spoke in relatively favorable terms of the independent candidate, Representative John B. Anderson of Illinois.

* * *

November 5, 1980

REAGAN EASILY BEATS CARTER

REPUBLICANS GAIN IN CONGRESS

D'Amato and Dodd Are Victors

By HEDRICK SMITH

Ronald Wilson Reagan, riding a tide of economic discontent against Jimmy Carter and promising "to put America back to work again," was elected the nation's 40th President yesterday with a sweep of surprising victories in the East, South and the crucial battlegrounds of the Middle West.

At 69 years of age, the former California Governor became the oldest person ever elected to the White House. He built a stunning electoral landslide by taking away Mr. Carter's Southern base, smashing his expected strength in the East, and taking command of the Middle West, which both sides had designated as the main testing ground. The entire West was his, as expected.

Mr. Carter, who labored hard for a comeback re-election victory similar to that of Harry S. Truman in 1948, instead became the first elected incumbent President since Herbert Hoover in 1932 to go down to defeat at the polls.

Concession by Carter

Despite pre-election polls that had forecast a fairly close election, the rout was so pervasive and so quickly apparent that Mr. Carter made the earliest concession statement of a major Presidential candidate since 1904 when Alton B. Parker bowed to Theodore Roosevelt.

At 9:50 P.M., Mr. Carter appeared with his wife, Rosalynn, before supporters at the ballroom of the Sheraton Washington Hotel and disclosed that an hour earlier he had telephoned Mr. Reagan to concede and to pledge cooperation for the transition to new leadership.

"The people of the United States have made their choice and, of course, I accept that decision," he said. "I can't stand here tonight and say it doesn't hurt."

At a celebration in the Century Plaza Hotel in Los Angeles, Mr. Reagan claimed his victory and said: "There's never been a more humbling moment in my life. I give you my sacred oath that I will do my utmost to justify your faith."

The Latest Tally

With 73 percent of the popular vote counted, Mr. Reagan had 31,404,169 votes, or 50 percent, to 26,295,331, or 42 percent, for Mr. Carter, with John B. Anderson, the independent, drawing 3,862,679, or 6 percent of the national total.

Mr. Reagan also suggested that enough Congressional candidates might ride the coattails of his broad sweep to give Republicans a chance to "have control of one house of Congress for the first time in a quarter of a century."

The Republicans picked up Senate seats in New Hampshire, Indiana, Washington, Iowa, Alabama, Florida and South Dakota and were leading in Idaho. Going into the election, the Senate had 58 Democrats, 41 Republicans and one independent. The Republicans also appeared likely to gain at least 20 seats in the House, nowhere near enough to dislodge the Democratic majority.

In the Presidential race, Mr. Carter managed six victories—in Georgia, Rhode Island, West Virginia, Maryland, Minnesota and the District of Columbia—for 45 electoral votes. But everywhere else the news was bad for him. By early this morning, Mr. Reagan had won 39 states with 444 electoral votes, and more were leaning his way.

In the South, the states of Texas, Florida, Mississippi, Louisiana, Virginia, South Carolina, North Carolina, Tennessee and Kentucky fell to the Reagan forces, an almost total rejection of the President by his home region. In the Middle West, the former California Governor took Ohio, Illinois and Michigan, three states on which Mr. Carter had pinned heavy hopes, as well as most others.

But Mr. Reagan's showing was even more startling in the East. He took New York and Pennsylvania, always vital bases for Democrats, as well as New Jersey, Connecticut and several smaller states.

A New York Times/CBS News poll of more than 10,000 voters as they left the polls indicated that the predominant motivation among voters was the conviction that it was time for a change. The biggest issue in their minds was the nation's economy, especially inflation.

"The Iranian thing reminded people of all their frustration," Robert S. Strauss, the Carter campaign chairman said. "They just poured down on him. I don't think there's anything anyone could have done differently."

"It was really a referendum on leadership," countered Richard Wirthlin, the Reagan pollster. "The Presidential debate did not have a tremendous influence on the vote, but it strengthened Reagan's credibility for taking Carter on as sharply as we did in the last five days and drive home the attack on the economy."

The Times/CBS News survey revealed a general collapse of the traditional coalition that has elected Democratic Presidents since the New Deal. It showed Mr. Carter running behind his 1976 performance not only in the South but also among such groups as blue-collar workers, Roman Catholics and Jews.

Pocketbook Issues Stressed

Although the President had tried to make foreign policy, especially nuclear arms control, the principal issue of the election, voters leaving the polls told interviewers that pocketbook issues had been more decisive in their voting. Thirty-five percent of those interviewed said their family financial situation was worse than a year ago, and in that group, Mr. Reagan led the President by 65 to 25 percent.

That kind of voting pattern was particularily damaging to the President in such crucial battlegrounds as Pennsylvania, Ohio, Michigan and Illinois. The dimensions of his defeat carried a number of other Democratic incumbents down with him, including prominent liberal senators like Birch Bayh of Indiana and George McGovern of South Dakota, as well as the House Democratic whip, John Brademas of Indiana.

In addition to the Presidency, 34 Senate seats, 13 governorships, all 435 seats in the House of Representatives and about 7,500 seats in state legislatures were at stake in the election.

G.O.P. Hopes in Senate

Riding Mr. Reagan's coattails, Republican candidates for Congress seemed likely to exceed their advance expectations of picking up 15 to 20 seats and half a dozen in the Senate.

Nationwide, Mr. Reagan's overall margin was greater than Mr. Anderson's vote and his sweep so extensive that he largely put to rest the Carter contentions that the Illinois Congressman was "the spoiler" depriving the President of winning margins in key states.

Mr. Anderson made his concession statement at the Hyatt Regency Hotel in Washington, about an hour after the President spoke, asserting that his campaign had contributed "a new realism" to American politics. His vote total seemed to guarantee him Federal subsidies to help repay his campaign debts. He needed a minimum of 5 percent of the vote to qualify for Federal funds.

All the indications were that Mr. Reagan's solid year of active campaigning had put to rest voter worries about his age. As expected, he was the solid favorite of men, holding close to a 5-to-3 advantage over Mr. Carter in that group, according to the Times/CBS News Poll. Despite earlier indications that the Californian might be penalized among women by his opposition to the equal rights amendment, he managed to run even with the President in that group. That was the only demographic category in which Mr. Carter ran even with his challenger.

The mood of the two men, as they voted, reflected their advance estimates of the balloting. Mr. Carter had been given a pessimistic overnight report by his pollster, Patrick H. Caddell, who cautioned that this year there had not been the kind of election-eve surge that lifted the former Governor of Georgia to victory in 1976.

Carter Pledge in Plains

Mr. Carter, his voice breaking and tears welling in his eyes, told well-wishers in his hometown of Plains, Ga., "I will not disappoint you." Some in the small crowd were crying.

"I've tried to honor my commitment," he went on, but he had to pause for a moment to regain self-control, "to you." "God bless you," he said in conclusion. Mr. Reagan, who has been jaunty and joking over the last several days as aides reported firm momentum since the Presidential debate on Oct. 28, voted at a neighbor's house near his home at Pacific Palisades, outside Los Angeles.

When reporters asked if he expected to win, Mr. Reagan replied: "You know me. I'm too superstitious to answer anything like that." But his wife, Nancy, nudged him and whispered, "Cautiously optimistic," and he echoed, "Yes, I'm cautiously optimistic."

The Carter camp had pinned its final hopes on a big voter turnout and a breakthrough in the Iranian hostage crisis, but Mr. Caddell said the Iranian situation had worked against the President in the last 48 hours.

Assessments of Outcome

His analysis was that after the debate, the President had fallen 5 percentage points behind Mr. Reagan but recovered by last Saturday night. On Sunday, Mr. Caddell said, Mr. Carter was once again down 5 points and 10 points behind by Monday. "It was all related to the hostages and events overseas," he said.

But the Republican pollster, Mr. Wirthlin, differed, saying that the President's credibility had been damaged and Mr. Reagan's strengthened in the debate, laying the basis for the final Republican attacks on Mr. Carter's economic record. His own polling showed a mounting Reagan lead since the day after the debate, he said.

Mr. Wirthlin also attributed the unexpectedly large Republican margins in state after state to extremely effective organizations that got out a heavy vote and to the collapse of the Democratic coalition. "We cracked the unions, blue-collar voters, ethnics, Catholics and the South, just as he had planned," he said.

In the Northeast, Middle Atlantic States and coastal regions of the South, there were showers through much of the day, but most of the country had clear weather, cool in the Northern states and warm and pleasant in the South and Southwest.

Voting officials in major states like New York, Ohio, Pennsylvania, Illinois, Michigan, Texas and Florida reported long lines and fairly heavy balloting early in the day. In Columbus, Ohio, polling officials had to add extra voting machines to handle the crowds.

Most experts had been expecting turnout to fall below the 54 percent of the eligible voters who cast ballots in 1976. Census estimates placed the number of eligible voters at 160,491,000 and the likely turnout at not more than 88 million.

Appeal to Anderson Backers

Low turnout and Mr. Anderson's pull among potential Democratic voters were major worries for Mr. Carter. With a low turnout, Mr. Carter kept warning, "We Democrats can beat ourselves."

"Don't waste your vote," he pleaded to Anderson supporters in a voice raspy from dawn-til-dusk campaigning in the homestretch drive. For the President, the election year has been an unpredictable roller-coaster. A year ago, before the American Embassy was seized in Teheran, he looked as though he was headed toward almost certain defeat and might not even be renominated. But after the American hostages were taken, patriotic support rallied to him, and he overtook his main Democratic challenger, Senator Edward M. Kennedy of Massachusetts, in the polls and took an unbeatable lead in the primaries.

In mid-summer he was once again far behind, this time trailing Mr. Reagan in the polls by 20 points. But when Senator Kennedy healed the Democratic rift and began vigorously campaigning for the Carter-Mondale ticket, Democratic voters began "coming home" and the polls see-sawed until the debate.

When surveys showed Mr. Reagan gaining from their confrontation in Cleveland, the President stepped up the frantic pace of his campaigning. But there was too much ground for him to cover. He had to divide time between fighting for the battleground states of the industrial belt from New Jersey to Wisconsin and protecting his crumbling southern base in Texas, Florida, Alabama, Mississippi and South Carolina.

The strain began to show in the final week. "I need you," Mr. Carter kept telling his rallies trying to energize a vigorous push from blacks, Hispanic-Americans and other traditionally Democratic voting groups. His right hand was red and bruised from endless handshaking and his face, puffy and lined from the relentless pace he had set.

At the same time, Mr. Reagan concentrated his efforts on the pivotal states, bolstered by increasingly confident projections from his own pollsters.

* * *

November 6, 1980

RUSSIANS ATTRIBUTE CARTER'S DEFEAT TO HARD LINE TOWARD SOVIET UNION

Special to The New York Times.

MOSCOW, Nov. 5—The Soviet leadership responded today to Ronald Reagan's victory with new attacks on the man he defeated, President Carter.

Tass, the Government's press agency, reported from New York that Mr. Carter had been driven from office because he "broke hundreds of promises he gave voters during the 1976 election campaign." The boycott of the Olympics hurt him, Tass said, but by far the most severe damage was inflicted on his Administration "by its turn from the course toward détente to the course toward heightening international tensions."

Soviet officials, in guarded conversations with Westerners, made it clear that they were not sure whether the election of Mr. Reagan presaged better relations with the Soviet Union. Many were particularly nervous about the composition of the new Senate, where any strategic arms limitation treaty negotiated by Mr. Reagan would have to be approved.

Loss of Senate Liberals Mourned

The Soviet officials, whose job it is to study the United States, said they were depressed by the defeat of such Democratic advocates of détente as Senators George McGovern of South Dakota, John C. Culver of Iowa, Birch Bayh of Indiana, Gary Hart of Colorado and Frank Church of Idaho.

The news of the Reagan victory reached Moscow at about 7 A.M. Well before noon, the two glass-fronted display cases on the facade of the United States Embassy were filled with pictures of Mr. Reagan, including a large color photograph of the former actor riding a horse at his California ranch. A caption in Russian said, "The new President."

In the days leading up to the election, the Soviet press condemned both Mr. Carter and Mr. Reagan as practitioners of "anti-Soviet" policies. But there were reports from diplomats that the Soviet leadership had privately concluded that the strategic arms limitation treaty signed last year in Vienna would have a better chance of approval in the Senate if Mr. Carter were re-elected.

There was no hint of that attitude today, either in the Tass dispatch or in a Soviet television commentary. The program included the reading of a terse biography of Mr. Reagan that mentioned none of his policy positions, and it said of Mr. Carter, "In practical terms, he derailed every agreement reached in the area of arms reduction."

"Military threats, aggravation of international tensions—that was Carter's line in foreign policy, now rejected by his own people," the commentator said.

But the Russians appeared to be prepared to do business with the President-elect, no matter what he has said in the past. Mikhail Bruk, a Soviet journalist who has translated the works of Gore Vidal and Norman Mailer, said in an interview that Mr. Reagan was "a serious politician" whose victory meant he "should be taken seriously."

Some Soviet officials said Mr. Reagan would prove no problem, arguing that they had had better luck with President Richard M. Nixon than with liberal Democrats. But one government specialist said that "it would be dangerous to extrapolate from the Nixon experience because Mr. Reagan is far less of a professional politician than Mr. Nixon."

Campaign Oratory Is Discounted

Like leaders in London, Paris and elsewhere, the Russians put little credence in campaign pledges and are eager to see what sort of men the new President will surround himself with.

Although some Soviet analysts believed before the election that Mr. Reagan, despite his campaign statements, might seek ratification of the arms accord negotiated by the Carter Administration, they said today that the size of Mr. Reagan's victory and the new conservative composition of the Senate had made that impossible.

Putting the best possible face on the election result, some officials made a point of mentioning Mr. Reagan's distaste for the regime in Peking—a plus from the Soviet point of view—and his opposition to President Carter's grain embargo against the Soviet Union following its intervention in Afghanistan.

The Russians appeared to be skeptical about Mr. Reagan's ability to do what he had promised. After some disparaging remarks about American campaign oratory, Valentin Zorin said in a television commentary from Washington:

"American presidents, including this new one, cannot indulge their personal preferences but must be guided by the realities of the modern world, such as the balance of forces."

* * *

November 9, 1980

60 DAYS THAT SHOOK POLAND

By JOHN DARNTON

The euphoria has evaporated. The inspiring belief that the 60-day worker's revolt which shook Poland to its foundations this summer might cleanse and transform what had for 35 years been a dreary national existence has been tempered recently by the sober realization that change does not come that easily. There is a sense that events are spinning out of control and heading for disaster. Many Poles feel they are living on borrowed time.

The slogan of odnowa, which means "rebirth," is still heard, but now it sounds more like a plea than a promise. In homes, as in Government ministries, the talk is not so much about workers' rights and reconstruction as about more strikes, confrontation and Soviet tanks.

It is a far cry from the hope and optimism of Aug. 31, when the all-powerful Communist state, in the person of Mieczyslaw Jagielski, a well-tailored, slightly bald First Deputy Prime Minister, who found the glare of the television lights disquieting because they reminded him of his years inside the searchlight-swept confines of a Nazi concentration camp, sat down to sign the agreement that ended the Baltic coast strikes with Lech Walesa, an unemployed electrician with a Pancho Villa mustache, who had scrambled over the wall of the Lenin Shipyard to lead a workers' insurrection that brought the Government to its knees. The strike, the Gdansk agreement, the two months of labor turmoil that preceded it and everything that has happened since, are the most significant events in Eastern Europe since Yugoslavia was expelled from the Soviet bloc in 1948. As Tito broke the myth of monolithic Communism with a "separate road to socialism," the Gdansk strikers have broken the myth—in Poland, at least—that the Communist Party speaks for the working class. The right to strike and to form independent trade unions could be as historic an advance for participatory socialism inside the Soviet bloc as the Magna Carta was for Western parliamentarianism.

But everything depends upon what happens now, during an unsettling interregnum. So far, the signs are not good. The strikes unleashed years of pent-up frustrations and anger, and an earlier mood for reform has given way to calls for more radical changes. There is a touch of feistiness in the air.

Many of the independent unions that are springing up all over the country like mushrooms after a rain are making it abundantly clear they have no intention of knuckling under to the state, nor are they willing to compromise, even a bit, to help the Government convince its worried allies that Poland is not really slipping down the dark road of socialistic heresy.

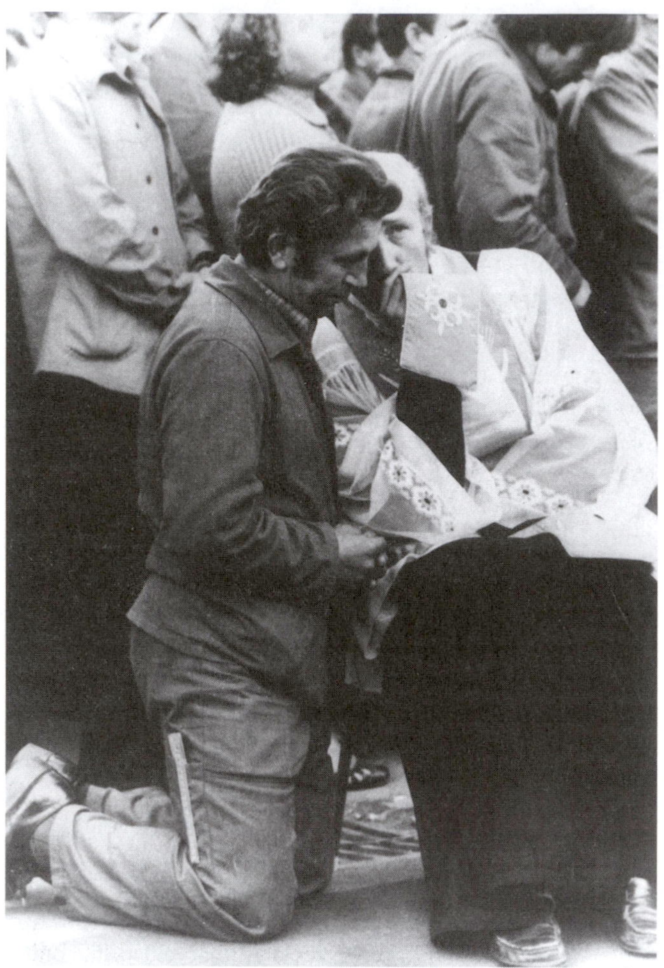

Lars Nyberg Pressens Bild—Photoreporters

Father Henryk Jankovski showed Church support for the strikers by hearing confessions prior to celebrating a shipyard mass in Gdansk.

Poland's neighbors, Czechoslovakia and East Germany, both "hardline" countries, were quick to join the Soviet Union in openly condemning the "anti-Socialist elements" inside Poland, a line now being replaced by intensified Soviet charges of subversive attempts directed from the West. East Germany has gone on to abandon its policy of rapprochement with West Germany, imposing new currency regulations to discourage visits across the border, and then, in a stunning rebuke to a fellow Socialist country, has slapped down travel restrictions to and from Poland. A cordon sanitaire has been raised along all of Poland's borders.

There is, however, a slim chance that Poland will emerge relatively unscathed, if only because all of the principals in the ongoing drama—the Government, the workers and the Soviet Union—realize that any kind of outside intervention would have regrettable consequences.

Stanislaw Kania, who replaced Edward Gierek as the Polish United Workers' (Communist) Party boss after the strike was settled, has been conciliatory and moderate in his pronouncements, at least to date. But, other than that he is an apparatchik from deep inside the party's bosom, nothing much is known about him.

The Polish Government may well try to honor the Gdansk accord, in spirit as well as letter, allowing the new unions to assume an autonomous role as collective bargaining agents for the workers and opening up such institutions of national life as the press and universities to nonparty voices. If this occurs in a peaceful, evolutionary way, without signficant outside interference, then Poland could became the first pluralistic society in the Communist world.

Unfortunately, other scenarios—all of them catastrophic—are equally likely: The new party leadership that came in with Kania, which really consists of old party faces in new positions, may try to renege on its pledges once the sense of crisis recedes, co-opting the unions, silencing the dissidents and halting the trend toward liberalization. The economy, already a shambles, may worsen even further so that discontent will erupt in new uprisings, this time coordinated and nationwide. The new unions could grow too big too fast and take on a political character that would threaten the party's "leading role" and engender a counterreaction.

Or the Soviet Union, deeply alarmed by the developments on its doorstep, may simply decide that enough is enough and send in its tanks. Such a move, many Western, Polish and some East European (other than Soviets, who don't talk) analysts feel, would trigger a full-scale Polish insurrection that would endanger world peace as much or more than the Berlin blockade, the Cuban missile crisis or the invasion of Afghanistan. Poland, with its tradition of heroic but futile uprisings against Russian rule during the 123 years in which it was partitioned off the map, is continually suspect in the Kremlin. But Poland matters more to Moscow than any other country in the Soviet bloc. Its population, approaching 36 million, makes it bigger by far than any other Soviet satellite. It has the 12th largest gross national product in the world. It is homogeneous, headstrong and inclined to romanticism. And it has a history on rabid, anti-Russian nationalism.

Its stubborn and resilient peasantry has assiduously resisted collectivization; three-quarters of the farm land remains in private hands. Its fervent Catholicism, practiced by 90 percent of the people, has meant that the church has always been a competing institution to the ruling Communist Party, with a far deeper hold on the national psyche.

Except by a handful of theorists, socialism is not taken seriously as an ideology. It has an alien caste to it, a stigma of having been forcefully imposed from the outside. There is a broad conservative belt in Poland, encompassing everyone from peasants to students to middle-level bureaucrats, that looks to the West and fantasizes about what life would be like under capitalism.

The only Soviet satellite never to build a monument to Stalin, Poland was the first to throw off the stultifying cultural doctrine of socialist realism. And in 1956, it was the first satellite to de-Stalinize (liberalize), and workers' riots in Poznan brought Wladyslaw Gomulka to power against the wishes of Nikita S. Khrushchev, who ordered troops dispatched to Warsaw but changed his mind at the last moment.

Moscow again contemplated intervention during the 1970 bread riots in Gdansk. But this time the Polish troops moved against the workers, and the violent suppression of the demonstrations later led to the toppling of Gomulka, who was replaced by Gierek.

After a temporary period of illusory prosperity, everything turned sour in the mid-1970's. Polish wage earners found that they had more money than ever before but few goods to spend it on. There was a stab at reform in 1976. But the general food price increase designed to reduce the burdensome system of subsidies was denounced by the workers, who rioted in Radom and Warsaw, burning down party headquarters and ripping up railroad tracks.

Gierek survived the next two years by striking an uneasy modus vivendi with the people: greater political tolerance to balance off the growing economic misery. But the benefits of this policy were felt primarily by the intellectuals; the workers remained apathetic.

In 1979, two things happened to change that. Poland's national income—the closest equivalent to the West's gross national product—declined, for the first time since World War II. The only other Soviet satellite to have reached a negative growth level was Czechoslovakia—there it led to economic reforms that culminated in the ill-fated "Prague Spring" of 1968. Then there was the visit by Pope John Paul II, an event that unleashed a flood of national and religious pride and cut through the cocoon of anesthetized indifference that had surrounded the workers. It is not surprising that the labor turmoil that rocked Poland last August should have exploded on the Baltic coast. There the sense of economic exploitation by the powerful neighbor to the east is markedly strong. The shipyards produce largely for a Soviet market, and the production is disadvantageous because Poland is required to equip the vessels with expensive equipment from the West, which must be paid for in hard currency.

The workers are rootless, volatile and prone to discontent, because they are first-generation proletarians who moved into the region to supplant the Germans in what had been Danzig and Stettin (now Gdansk and Szczecin). They are more given than most to anti-Soviet sentiment. Their fathers were peasants and laborers in the tiny villages and towns of the eastern territories gobbled up by Russia after the war.

They bitterly recall the brutal suppression of the 1970 demonstrations which caused hundreds of deaths. Many were politicized by that experience, which they refer to as a "war."

A handful of them began working with Poland's main dissident organization, the Committee for Social Self-Defense, known by its Polish acronym of KOR, which sprang up after the 1976 riots. KOR is the brainchild of Jacek Kuron, a former Communist who passed many of his frequent 48-hour detentions dreaming of forging an alliance for change between the intelligentsia and the workers.

Eleven months before the Baltic coast strikes, not many people noticed that KOR's samizdat newspaper, Robotnik (The Worker), had published a charter of workers' rights and a program for achieving them. Strikes, it said, are effective over the short run, but "in order not to waste the gains won," something more is required: free and independent trade unions. "Only they," the charter said, "can represent a power the authorities cannot ignore and will have to negotiate with on an equal footing." Among the 65 signatories to the document was Lech Walesa.

When Walesa climbed over the Lenin Shipyard wall on Aug. 14, the Gdansk strike was only a few hours old but Poland's labor turmoil had been going on for a month and a half, kicked off by surprise increases in meat prices on July 1.

What made the Gdansk strikers' action different was that instead of putting down their tools and walking off the job, they simply closed the shipyard gates and waited to see what would happen. What happened was that the Government floundered indecisively, the world press arrived, factories all across the country shut down in solidarity, and in no time at all the Gdansk strike leaders found themselves at the head of a burgeoning nationwide workers' revolt.

Walesa took a command role almost immediately because he was well known in the shipyard from previous activism there, is charismatic and had the courage to assume a frontline position. He also had nothing to lose, since he didn't have a job there.

Two days after the Gdansk strike began it was effectively "settled." Walesa had negotiated a package that included a 12 percent wage increase. When he presented it, he was denounced for having sold out. "We walked off for you," shouted a bus driver. "How can our buses stand up to tanks alone?" A tactical leader who knows how to shift directions to keep up with the rank and file, Walesa abruptly declared the strike still on.

From that moment, the strikers were challenging not local, but state authorities, and, by extension, Poland's Communist Party, which is supposed to rule all walks of life. The strikers formed a committee to promulgate a list of demands, which grew and changed but always centered on the right to strike and to form independent unions.

The strikes revealed the extent of worker discontent. Poles are economically worse off than any of their counterparts in Eastern Europe, except for the Russians. Luxury goods that appear in Prague and East Berlin are not to be found in Warsaw. The average Polish wage earner gets 5,100 zlotys, or $178 a month. He waits 8 to 10 years for a new apartment, 3 to 4 years for a car. Life is an endless series of lines, for meat, for shoes, for gasoline and, lately, for newspapers.

To journalists covering Gdansk, several impressions stood out. The strike delegates were noticeably young, in their late 20's and early 30's. These were not wizened workers, burdened with unspeakable memories of the war years. They were not peasants-turned-workers, innately conservative and awed by authority and the amenities of urban living. They were a new generation in the Socialist world—well educated, articulate and angry.

Publicly, the workers reaffirmed their commitment to Socialism, but the feelings they expressed privately were

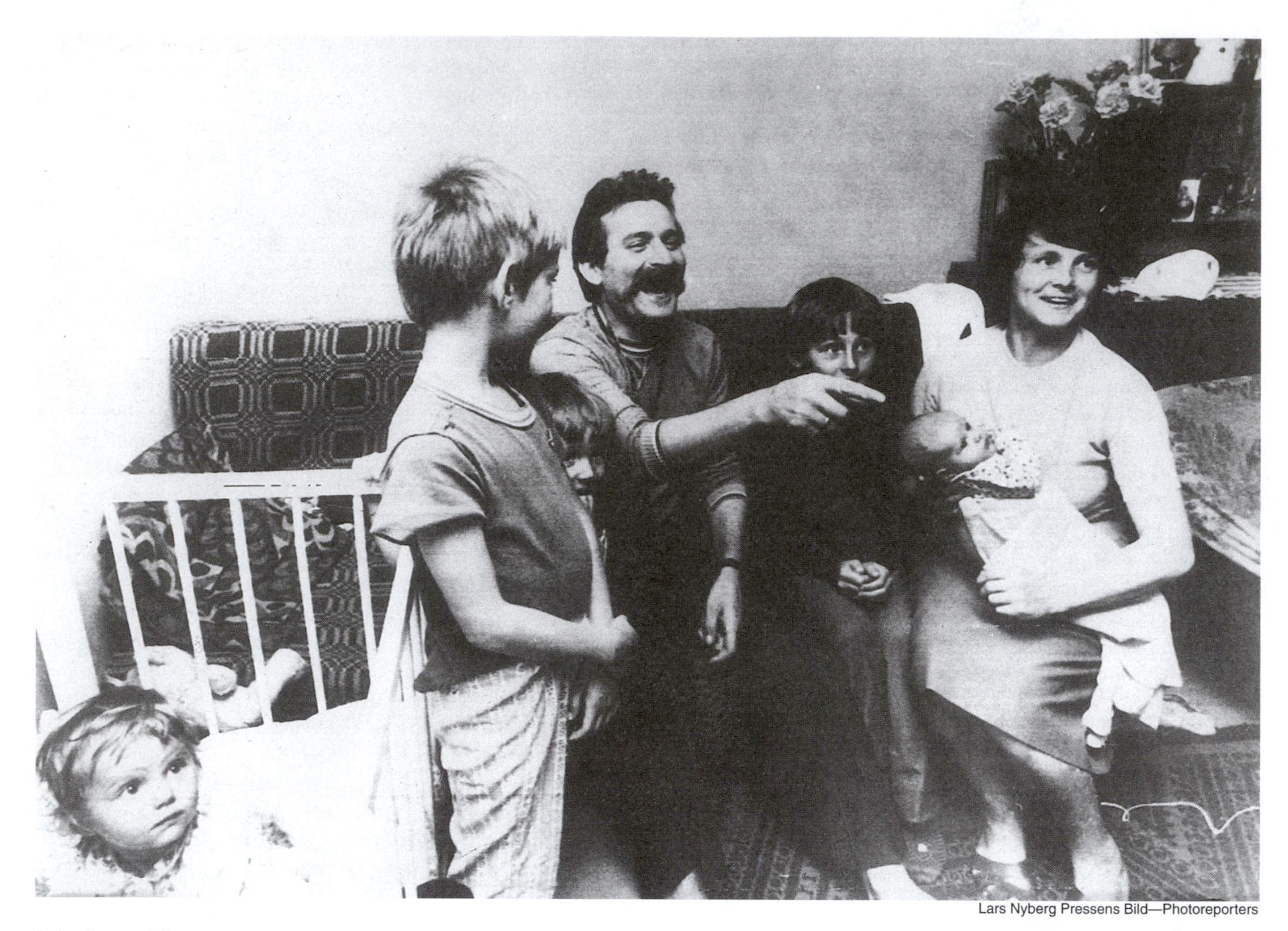

Lars Nyberg Pressens Bild—Photoreporters

Poland's new folk hero, Lech Walesa, relaxes at home with his wife, Miroslawa, and five of their eight children after leading strikers to victory.

reflected in a banner that read: "No Meat, No Bread, No Butter. All We Have To Eat Are the Words of Lenin."

Throughout, the call of nationalism and of the church was strong. It was no coincidence that the strikers' emblem was the national flag or that the Communist International, sung on the first day, gave way to the historic Polish national anthem, "Poland Has Not Yet Perished." Masses were celebrated in the struck yard and the church's right to broadcast them every Sunday became a demand.

The Government watched, virtually helpless. When Gierek's paternalistic plea for a return to work was met with derision, ominous warnings were issued: The country was headed for disaster, perhaps even dissolution.

The protesters held firm. Twelve days after the strikers had shut the shipyard gates, they reopened them to admit the Government negotiators. The negotiations were piped over a loudspeaker system so that all the workers could follow them. While this innovation hampered give-and-take, it made for collective bargaining in a literal sense. The strike leaders' statements made it clear that the new movement was not just concerned with free trade unions; it was grappling with a fundamentally different vision of national life.

"We should think what led to this crisis," declared Andrzej Gwiazda, the most eloquent strike leader. "We must remember Marx's criticism of capitalism—that it was owners exploiting workers. For 35 years, we invest, we invest, we invest and our society has practically nothing to show for it. For years, people asked how much steel was being produced, how much coal was being dug. But nobody looked at what it all meant for the life of the workers."

Hearing these words, a Polish diplomat told a friend: "This country will never be the same. It's a turning point. We are witnessing the birth of the working class."

Five days later, when the message from Gdansk had mobilized workers all over the country—even the coal miners, who had not struck in 1956, 1970 or 1976, began walking out—the Government capitulated.

For the signing of the historic accord, Lech Walesa produced a foot-long red and white pen, a souvenir of Pope John Paul II's visit last year. As he and First Deputy Prime Minister Jagielski scrawled their signatures, it towered over the bureaucrat's silver-plated ballpoint—a bit of lighthearted one-upmanship that delighted the victorious workers.

Lars Nyberg Pressens Bild—Photoreporters

Lech Walesa's foot-long Papal souvenir pen one-upped Deputy Prime Minister Mieczyslaw Jagielski's bureaucratic ballpoint as they signed the accord that ended the Baltic coast strikes.

And yet, afterward, not all the strikers were jubilant. While some were satisfied with the progress that had been made—"We've broken down a barrier of fear," said a nurse at the Lenin Shipyard. "It's a great psychological achievement."—others had clearly wanted more.

A scholar who was one of the team of "experts" advising the strike committee ran into a cluster of workers who asked him what had happened to the demand for an end to censorship. The exhausted adviser explained that both sides had agreed that a modicum of censorship is necessary for the social good, and that the whole issue would be settled in a bill to be introduced within three months. The workers stared at him hostilely. A playwright who witnessed the scene recalls blurting out, without even thinking what he was saying, "There was no victory." The continuing pressures for change are shaking almost all institutions. The Sejm (parliament), which has long been a rubber stamp, is now demanding real power. Research academies and universities are demanding greater autonomy. Students, a bit miffed that they missed out on all the action, are demanding an "independent" association to take the place of the party-dominated Socialist Students' Union.

Cultural life is changing. Journalists, writers, scholars and architects are forming a council that will challenge, among other things, the funding system by which the Ministry of Culture and Art hands out scholarships and stipends to party hacks. Polish films that had been blocked by the censors for years for being more political, graphically, than in their approved scripts, have started appearing on television. They are vivid portraits of the corruption, blackmarketeering and exploitation that had so angered the strikers. Movie goers have been shocked to see a never-before-released newsreel on the 1970 riots, showing tanks rumbling through the streets of Gdansk, militiamen advancing with drawn submachine guns, the Communist Party headquarters ransacked.

The press is gradually coming alive and fulfilling at least more of an informational role. But it is still carefully controlled by the Government, mindful, no doubt, that in Czechoslovakia in 1968 a runaway press alarmed the Soviet Union, which promptly stamped out the "Prague Spring." Some intellectuals fear plans to codify precisely what can and cannot be printed may actually make the situation worse, since the Government may use the censorship law now being promulgated as a pretext to crack down on illegal literature, which has been unofficially tolerated.

The church, now regularly broadcasting Sunday masses on radio, is flexing its muscle. A joint church-Government commission has resumed talks on the long-standing list of demands of the Polish bishops. The church is in a strong bargaining position because, at the official level, it counseled moderation during the strikes, for which the Government is grateful, but in the Lenin Shipyard it showed itself as the single greatest institutional force in Poland.

The Communist Party itself is in disarray. In some of Poland's 49 provinces, local first secretaries are bucking change; in others, they are pressing for it, and in still others, they are vascillating. Party boss Kania, who has not yet fully consolidated his hold on power, sees his first priority as rebuilding the party, but that is no easy task. A half-hearted purge against the corruption and privileges that accumulated in the Gierek era has begun, but because the abuses run so deep it is a tricky and almost self-defeating proposition; additional revelations would only further blacken the party's name.

To explain the August strikes, the evolving party rationalization is that "mistakes in policy," not theory, were to blame. Gierek had accumulated "too much power." The notion of independent unions is a Western one, but it is not incompatible with Socialism. This rationale has led to a Government propaganda campaign which by labeling political dissidents as "anti-Socialist elements" hopes to drive a wedge between them and the workers with whom they have struck up an alliance, the first such relationship in Eastern Europe. The new unions have made clear that any move against the dissidents would be unacceptable to them. For the time being, there is an uneasy standoff. Over the long haul, whatever happens in Poland will be determined by the economy. And the economy appears headed for disaster. The country has a $21 billion foreign debt (owed to the West) an amount so huge that 75 cents of every hard-currency dollar earned must go toward repaying it. Though the Poles have been insisting that they will repay on schedule, lately they have been giving out signs that they are not automatically against the idea of a moratorium.

What's more, the economic aspects of the Gdansk agreements, if carried out, will only make the situation worse. The wage and pension settlements will unleash a flood of new money at a time when there are few goods in the shops to absorb it—a classic recipe for discontent.

The effects of the agreement are already being felt in terms of declining production, brought on by such strike-won concessions as free Saturdays, longer maternity leaves and changes in the shift system in the mines. Most worrisome is the decrease in the excavation of coal, Poland's leading hard-currency earner. The Government is churning out figures to show that the manufacture of everything from machines to shoes is dropping, in an apparent campaign to switch the blame to work disruption caused by the unions. But because most people view the unions as instruments of constructive change, they are rejecting the Government's argument.

Under the weight of such practical dilemmas, the overriding theoretical question of whether independent trade unions are possible in a Communist country goes unnoticed. How can a command economy exist if the wage scales are not subject to command? How can central planners draw up five-year plans if officials must bargain year to year with Western-type unions? How can the party rule authoritatively if it doesn't rule in all spheres? One official, pressed on these questions, shrugged and said, "It almost sounds as impossible as a Communist Party existing side by side with the Catholic Church for 35 years." There are now three sets of unions competing for 13 million Polish workers. The new, independent unions, operating under a national council known as Solidatary, now account for about eight million of that number. The old party-sponsored Central Council of Trade Unions and its fictionally autonomous branch unions, which are suffering mass desertions by construction and metal workers, doctors and teachers, account for the rest. A fierce struggle is under way for control of the vast array of services and funds once administered by the old unions—everything from sports clubs to holiday camps and statutory payments made for the death of a spouse or the birth of a child—which are now up for grabs.

For all their thunder, the new unions' power base is still mostly regional, on the Baltic coast, and they are weak in certain important industries, like the textile mills of Lodz, but they are certain to continue growing. They fiercely defend their right to accept contributions from Western trade unions, without which they would be unable to organize. The Government construes this as the kind of "outside interference" that could lend a pretext for Soviet involvement.

But the unions have not had extensive, ongoing contacts with Western labor organizations for advice and they have been chary of approaching Western embassies for assistance. Some West European governments and organizations have tried to provide what the unions need most—printing presses—but these have been stopped at the border.

On Oct. 3, the new unions, charging the Government with delay in implementing wage promises and biased news coverage, launched a onehour strike. Its stunning success proved that the unions' strength was not a passing phenomenon. But some strikers felt the action was unnecessary and risky. A few began to question whether Lech Walesa—who has assumed the dimensions of a folk hero, but has also begun to show traces of demagoguery—has the intellectual capacity to lead the movement through a difficult phase of compromise, not combat.

Walesa has lost none of his zeal in moving from the role of an anonymous union activist to that of a worldwide media celebrity and, finally, at age 37, to being the undisputed leader of a burgeoning movement that while still rebellious is spawning its own bureaucracy. Solidarity is run by a staff of 20 and hundreds of volunteers out of a crumbly former hotel in Gdansk. Name and title cards—Chief, Propaganda Division, or Materials Division, or Press Division—run along a long corridor leading to the largest office, which is marked simply, "Lech Walesa, Chairman."

Walesa's organizing experience was gained in the streets, during the 1970 and 1976 riots. In 1976, when a delegate to the official trade union, he composed a list of workers' grievances and was fired from the Lenin Shipyard for being a political troublemaker. Two years later, he joined an underground committee to form free trade unions. In 1979, he was fired from a building company called Zremb, and last December, from an engineering firm called Elektromontaz, both times for political activities.

He is a complicated, private person, street smart, who rules by instinct. He openly enjoys such trappings of his high office as new suits and a new apartment, but draws the line at bigger benefits, which he considers corrupting. He claims to be put off by the adulation he receives but expects to get his way. He is deeply religious. A member of his entourage always carries a crucifix, to be fixed to the wall whenever Walesa addresses a gathering. His bodyguards carry Mace spray cans.

Because he has such a superstar following among the people, it is difficult to imagine someone rising up to challenge his leadership. His presence means that the tactics and direction of Solidarity depend to a considerable extent upon his own predilections, and this is unsettling because he is mercurial and constantly shifts between positions of moderation and militancy.

"He has good advisers," says Lech Badkowski, a member of the Gdansk union leadership, "but he doesn't listen to them—or rather he listens too much to them. Everything depends on who talks to him last."

During a remarkable campaignlike swing through the industrial south in mid-October, Walesa counseled moderation in declaring strikes. A week later, he was prepared to lead his organization in more sit-ins when the courts officially registered the new union but unilaterally rewrote its statutes to include a pledge to respect the "leading role" of the Communist Party. Under the influence of the Gdansk leadership, reluctant delegates from other parts of the country were pressed into proclaiming selective strikes on Nov. 12 if the Government doesn't override the court ruling.

Walesa's moderate side emerges after he has consulted with church officials, including Stefan Cardinal Wyszynski, the aging and powerful primate of Poland. The militant Mr. Hyde aspect of his nature becomes dominant after strategy sessions with Jacek Kuron, of KOR, a principal adviser.

Another possible showdown between the new unions and the authorities lies ahead. What it could produce in the shape of awful consequences was driven home to Poles by the coincidence of a Warsaw Pact Foreign Ministers meeting in Warsaw in mid-October, a reminder, not that any was needed, that Poland is inextricably bound in a military alliance to other bloc countries. For the moment, the Soviet Union has accepted the independent unions as the price its troublesome ally had to pay to extract itself from chaos. But Moscow clearly regards the union movement as a Trojan horse capable of spreading heresy throughout the Socialist empire, and it expects the Polish party to control it.

At a hurriedly arranged meeting in the Kremlin on Oct. 30, Polish Communist Party boss Kania appeared to have won Soviet backing for his handling of the labor crisis so far, but how solid that backing is and how long it will last is problematical.

The Kremlin's concern is that the contagion will spread beyond Poland's borders. Moscow has resumed jamming Western broadcasts but it can do little about the 600-meter-high antenna of Warsaw Radio One. The only dissident connection in the Soviet bloc is between Poland and Czechoslovakia, where activists have traditionally maintained sporadic clandestine contact. Czechoslovakia, which sarcastically called the Polish dissidents "godfathers of the new unions," has been arresting its own dissidents.

The strikes in Poland have set off unsettling ripples in other East European countries, whose economies are troubled by a rising inflation that puts consumer goods out of reach. Even before Poland's labor problems erupted this summer, there were reports of strikes in both the Soviet Union and Rumania, and the head of Hungary's official trade-union movement admitted recently that "work stoppages" had occured there, too. Strikes were also reported to have taken place early in October in Tartu, Estonia, a region of perennial discontent. The possibility cannot be ruled out that other strikes, unreported as of yet, have happened elsewhere in the bloc.

Erich Honecker, the East German leader, Nicolae Ceausescu, Rumania's party chief, and Vasil Bilak, a prominent Czechoslovakian Communist Party official, have all criticized developments in Poland in increasingly strident tones. Ominously, Czechoslovakia, the most doctrinaire Soviet satellite since its dissidents were quieted in 1968, offered to send "aid" to true-blooded Polish Communists fighting reactionary forces.

The Brezhnev Doctrine, as it was expounded by Pravda to justify the Warsaw-Pact invasion of Czechoslovakia, holds that no ruling Communist Party has the right to "damage Socialism in its own country, nor the fundamental interests of other Socialist countries, nor the worldwide workers' movement." The defining feature of the "Prague Spring" was that the Czech Party itself took a runaway turn deemed menacing by Moscow.

This is not the case in Poland. The party is not heretical; it continually reaffirms its loyalty to Moscow, and it is doing all it can to contain the situation. The question is: Is it strong enough? The single greatest fear of a long-experienced Polish journalist, who is no friend to the system, is that the party's prestige in the Kremlin has sunk too low. In the final analysis, he explains, only the party is a buffer against Soviet intervention. The same thought is captured in a popular new Polish saying that plays upon Vanya, the Russian diminutive for Ivan: "Better Kania than Vanya."

Since 1956, Poland has not been, properly speaking, a Soviet satellite; its orbit has been a bit too elliptical. The pull from the West is strong: from France, with its historical and cultural ties; from West Germany, the despised World War II occupier, now the major non-Socialist trading partner, and from the United States, where 10 million Polish-Americans constitute the largest group in the diaspora called "Polonia."

Despite Poland's strategic and industrial importance to the Kremlin, the Soviets have been reluctant to put to a test the extent of Polish loyalty to Soviet hegemony.

Only in Poland do Government officials take pains to draw elaborate distinctions between nationalism—construed as a negative, backward sentiment—and patriotism—the acceptable face of the same emotion—because only in Poland is nationalism so clearly seen as threatening the Soviet relationship. In East Germany, Soviet troops are as common as lampposts. In Poland, the 30,000 Soviet troops have to be garrisoned out of sight. When Leonid Brezhnev places an obligatory wreath on the Tomb of the Unknown Soldier in Warsaw's Victory Square, he is well aware that the soldier died during the Russo-Polish War of 1920.

Polish nationalism has grown, not diminished, under Communism. One reason is that it was plastered over with historical lies. The two greatest official taboo subjects are the secret Hitler-Stalin pact to partition Poland in 1939 and the Katyn Forest massacre, in which Stalin's secret police liquidated more than 10,000 Polish Army officers in 1940. These facts, taught in every Polish home, are kept alive because they are not acknowledged, and when the anniversaries roll around, they are commemorated.

A second reason is that Poles, more than Czechs or Hungarians or East Germans, are convinced that their economic ties to the Soviet Union are exploitative. To some extent, the conviction is outmoded, a memory of the postwar years when Poland was forced to deliver up various products at fractional "fraternal" prices. It ignores the fact that 80 percent of Poland's oil comes from the Soviet Union, at less than world-market prices. But the public perception is still there. Many Poles believe that there is a meat shortage because the best cuts are shipped off to Moscow, whereas most of the ham, pork and sausage that is exported goes to the United States and Western Europe, to obtain hard currency.

Whether the Polish leadership admits it or not, anti-Russian nationalism is its trump card. The Soviets will not invade, the theory goes, because the Poles, unlike the Czechs, would fight back. The international cost would simply be too high. What the theory ignores, and what some people fear, is Moscow's capacity for "soft" intervention, by making common cause with hard-line Polish party elements that now stand purged but could return to power with a vengence. The Soviet Union could easily destabilize any section of the country and use the pretext of social disorder for sponsoring a change in government.

Because the stakes are so high, few people doubt that Russia would use outright military force if she felt her own stability was truly threatened. This could happen if the Polish Communist Party lost all semblance of control or if the strikes spread to the nearby Soviet republic of Byelorussia or into the Ukraine, or to other Socialist countries. If force were used, Soviet troops would have to do much of the job on their own. East German soldiers, evoking war memories, would bring on an instant rebellion. Poland's armed forces (317,500 regular troops, 95,000 paramilitary) would certainly not fire upon Polish citizens, though they might very well turn their guns against any invaders.

The question then becomes: How would the West react? The United States has made it clear that it would not intervene because Poland, after all, is in Russia's sphere of influence. But the political pressures for some sort of response, if only covert arms supplies, would be considerable. The possibility of a major East-West confrontation would then be very large indeed. Poland is accustomed to compromise—no word better describes its national life since the end of World War II. In each of the three previous workers' revolts, the gains were short-lived and the promises broken, but never did the level of repression slide back to what it had been before. The current revolt has gone much further than any of the others. Suddenly, it seems to be all or nothing. There is a sense that a line has been crossed, an historic, exciting, but dangerous line.

"I am afraid in my bones," says a Polish writer, "that we shall have to pay dearly for those few days in August."

John Darnton is The Times's bureau chief in Warsaw.

* * *

December 3, 1980

U.S. CAUTIONING ON INTERVENTION IN POLISH CRISIS

By DAVID BINDER

Special to The New York Times.

WASHINGTON, Dec. 2—The White House said today that intervention by outside forces in the Polish crisis would severely affect East-West relations, especially Soviet-American relations.

A statement read by Jody Powell, President Carter's spokesman, said: "Intervention, or invasion of Poland, would be most serious and adverse for East-West relationships in general and particularly relations between the United States and the Soviet Union."

He said it would be a mistake to assume that the United States "lacks the will or ability to respond appropriately" in the transition period until President-elect Ronald Reagan takes office Jan. 20.

Richard V. Allen, Mr. Reagan's foreign policy adviser, made similar comments earlier in a television interview. In Luxembourg, ministers of Western Europe's Common Market issued a statement warning the Soviet Union of "serious consequences" in the event of an intervention in Poland.

The Washington statements, which represented the strongest yet since unrest began in Poland last summer, came on a day during which officials said intelligence reports showed an increase in activity by Polish internal security forces.

They said there was no indication of any heightened threat of a Soviet intervention or of any change in the deployment of regular Polish and Soviet forces in Poland or of Soviet-bloc forces along Poland's frontiers in the last 24 hours.

The intent of the activity of Polish internal security forces and of the jamming of communications among officials of the independent labor movement has been to create an atmosphere of isolation around the union leaders headed by Lech Walesa, an American specialist surmised.

The enhanced activity has been among some of the 18,000 border troops and 55,000 internal security troops under the Ministry of Interior and some units of the 350,000-member citizens' militia.

Administration officials said they had deduced from this and other information that the Soviet Union was still counting on the Polish leadership under Stanislaw Kania, the First Secretary, to deal with the unrest, even if it meant applying armed force.

Since the wave of strikes began in August, the Polish authorities have avoided mobilizing internal security forces as was done on a large scale to put down street demonstrations along the Baltic coast in 1970 and, on a smaller scale, in central Poland in 1976.

Kania Headed Security Affairs

The recommendation to avoid bloodshed this time was said by the Polish authorities to have come from Mr. Kania himself. He was a party secretary responsible for security affairs before he replaced Edward Gierek as the Polish party chief in September.

As for the potential for intervention by the Soviet Union together with one or more of its allies, Administration officials have not ruled out the possibility. However, an intelligence official said that even though Soviet troops along the Polish frontiers were placed on a higher alert status last month, they were still "not positioned to move within an hour."

Pentagon officials have monitored some recent mobilizations of Soviet reserves, but suggested that this might be connected with annual training exercises. Maj. Gen. Jerry Curry, a Pentagon spokesman, said at a news briefing that the United States had received advance notification of Soviet maneuvers in East Germany, necessitating the closing of areas along the Polish frontier from last Saturday to next Tuesday. The exercise, involving air defense units, had been on the agenda for some time and may be viewed as routine, military officials said.

Parallel to Afghanistan Doubted

Asked to assess the situation around Poland, an official said he doubted that there was a parallel with the buildup of Soviet forces in 1979 before the intervention in Afghanistan.

"From the sense of the signals, it is not a prelude to invasion," he said. "There are none of the signs, sounds or smells of the situation of Afghanistan in late September 1979, none of the logistics or traffic of a prelude to invasion."

Another official said the reports about a Soviet mobilization had been overstated in the press and that the situation was likely to end with "a compromise on law and order" in Poland.

"The Russians would prefer to have the Poles do it," he added.

* * *

December 21, 1980

HANGING IN WITH SALT II, BUT BY A THREAD

By RICHARD BURT

WASHINGTON—As a candidate for the White House, Ronald Reagan's position on arms control negotiations was unambiguous: The United States must scrap the 1979 strategic arms limitation agreement with Moscow and defer talks on any new agreement until progress had been made on building up the American strategic arsenal.

As President-elect, however, Mr. Reagan may be moderating that position. Senator Charles H. Percy of Illinois, who will become chairman of the Foreign Relations Committee, returned from Moscow reporting that the Kremlin was willing to begin new arms talks. Last week, Richard V. Allen, Mr. Reagan's top national security aide, added that "continuing the SALT process would be a good thing to do."

After Mr. Reagan designated Alexander M. Haig Jr. as Secretary of State, it seemed clear that both men would face hard questions on how to proceed. Members of Mr. Reagan's transition teams for the State and Defense Departments reportedly have urged him to hold off on arms control until basic defense policy is set, a process that could take six months or more. And, in a private session in Philadelphia with military experts with ties to the new administration, Georgi Arbatov, director of Moscow's U.S.A. Institute and a member of the Communist Party's Central Committee, said the Kremlin might not be willing to discuss a new treaty that was substantially different from the one negotiated by the Carter Administration.

Nuclear arsenals on both sides are still restricted by the accords reached by President Nixon and Leonid I. Brezhnev, the Soviet leader, in 1972. Antimissile systems were severely limited, while the SALT I agreement put a ceiling on the land-based and submarine-launched missiles each side could deploy. Scheduled to expire in 1977, that agreement was informally extended during further talks. In June 1979, SALT II was signed by Mr. Carter and Mr. Brezhnev. It set a ceiling of 2,250 on both sides' strategic arsenals of missiles and bombers and provided "subceilings" on weapons such as land-based missiles equipped with multiple warheads and the huge, Soviet "heavy missiles." In the Senate last year, both liberals and conservatives complained loudly about the treaty's failure to impose more severe reductions on both sides' arsenals. Republicans and conservative Democrats also voiced doubts about Washington's ability to monitor the

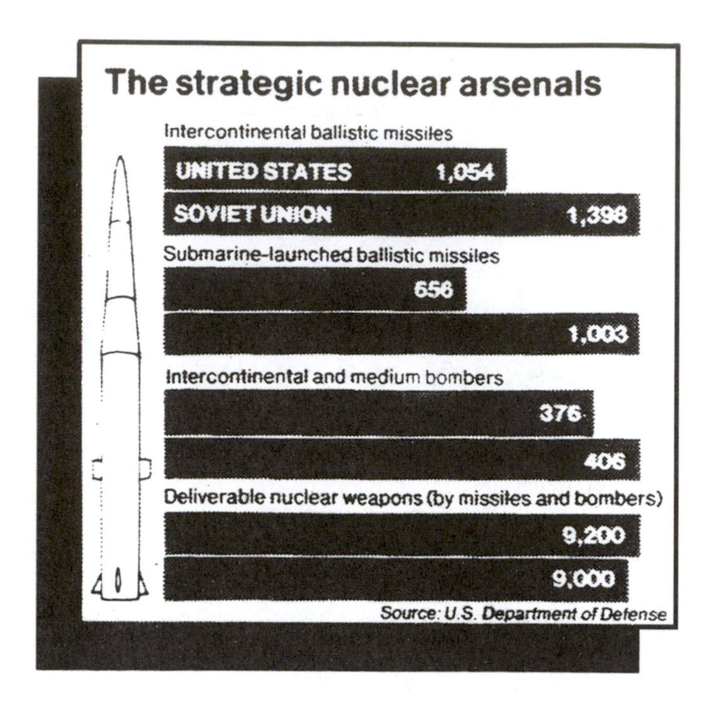

accord to prevent cheating and complained that only Moscow was permitted to deploy "heavy missiles."

Despite its drawbacks, some analysts have proposed that the two sides agree informally to adhere to the 1979 agreement while talks proceed. These analysts note that SALT II provides for more comprehensive restrictions on Soviet forces. The Republican transition team for the Arms Control and Disarmament Agency added an argument: Without new proposals to continue at least some elements of the earlier agreements, the Russians would have "specific options to accelerate their strategic programs, making it even more difficult for our defense program to match their extensive buildup." Pentagon aides fear that without a treaty covering multiple warheads, the Russians could double and even triple the number of separate nuclear weapons on their biggest missiles. Former Secretary of State Henry A. Kissinger reportedly believes that before negotiating an entirely new treaty, Moscow and Washington should agree to adhere to the most important SALT II provisions—to "bridge" the arms control gap.

However, Reagan advisers such as retired General Edward Rowny, who was the Joint Chiefs of Staff representative in the SALT II talks, assert that the treaty is too flawed to keep, even temporarily. Others question whether Moscow would put into operation aspects of the agreement desired by Washington without insisting on pro-Soviet provisions too. Accordingly, they believe, if talks do begin, negotiators should plunge ahead on devising a completely new treaty. Underlying and going beyond this important debate is a more far-reaching question: What sort of arms agreement should a Reagan administration seek? Senator Percy has suggested beginning by seeking Moscow's agreement to several technical amendments to the treaty that were proposed last year by the Foreign Relations Committee. Many of the amendments are meant to improve Washington's ability to monitor the treaty; however, none deal with the weapons ceilings which have been sharply criticized.

Other Republicans, unhappy with the treaty's overall design, favor a more radical strategy similar to President Carter's early proposal for "deep cuts" in both sides' strategic missile forces. The Carter Administration had called for reducing the overall size of Soviet and American arsenals to 1,800 missiles and bombers each and for cutting more than 50 percent of Moscow's land-based rockets. The Kremlin immediately rejected that. Many analysts contend that a Reagan administration revival of the proposal would receive a similar Soviet response. But Republicans who favor a Reagan initiative for "a real arms accord" argue that, in 1977, Mr. Carter should have dug in his heels, instead of quickly retreating to acceptance of negotiations that would not seriously dent Soviet strategic power.

Before deciding whether and when to renew the dialogue, Mr. Reagan and his aides must decide how seriously they regard campaign pledges to achieve "military superiority." Then, they must determine how arms talks would fit into their defense strategy.

In Phildelphia, Mr. Arbatov said that United States proposals to cut back Soviet capabilities would be met by equally ambitious counterproposals. Any effort by Washington to achieve "superiority" presumably would bring similar Soviet matching efforts. "Real" arms control would not be easy to obtain. An American nuclear buildup probably would be needed first, to give Moscow incentives to take American negotiating proposals seriously. Also, if Soviet troops were sent into Poland, all bets, of course, would be off. A change in the top Soviet leadership—former Premier Aleksei N. Kosygin's death last week was a reminder of its advanced age—also could cause delays. If it took almost seven years to conclude SALT II, a far-reaching SALT III treaty might not be obtainable for a decade, if ever.

* * *

January 19, 1981

U.S. AND IRAN SIGN ACCORD ON HOSTAGES: 52 AMERICANS COULD BE SET FREE TODAY

By BERNARD GWERTZMAN

WASHINGTON, Monday, Jan. 19—The United States and Iran reached formal agreement early this morning on the terms for releasing the 52 American hostages and returning to Iran billions of dollars of its assets frozen by American authorities.

The agreement was signed in Algiers by Deputy Secretary of State Warren M. Christopher on behalf of the United States. Behzad Nabavi, the chief Iranian negotiator, had signed it earlier in Teheran.

President Carter planned to fly to West Germany later today to be on hand when the hostages are flown there, with a stop in Algeria, after being released by Iran, presumably today.

Medical Examinations Planned

Algerian transport planes flew to Teheran to pick up the hostages, and a team of Algerian doctors left their hotel in Teheran to examine the Americans before their departure.

The announcement of the signing in Algiers ended hours of suspense that began yesterday when it became clear that both the United States and Iran had agreed on the substance of the agreement but that a formal announcement was being held up until the two sides accepted the detailed language in the various texts of the documents, which had been translated into English, Persian and French.

The Americans will stay for about a week in a United States military hospital at Rhein-Main Air Base, near Wiesbaden.

U.S. Completes Review

A senior White House official said that the United States had completed its review of the final agreement earlier yesterday and had been waiting since then for word from Algiers that the Iranians had also formally accepted it.

Late yesterday afternoon, explaining the delay in announcing an agreement, a White House official had said there were "no major problems" standing in the way of the accord.

"There are no hitches," he said. But he said, "There is the complex process of checking and translating and reviewing the specifics of complicated legal and financial documents."

Mr. Carter, who was in his office for most of the evening awaiting the signal from Algiers, spoke on the phone during the day with President-elect Ronald Reagan to discuss his plans to go to West Germany and personally welcome back the Americans, whose fate had been a preoccupation of his Administration's last 14½ months in office.

Under the terms of the arrangement with Iran, which took three months of intensive negotiations to achieve, the United States will transfer into an Algerian escrow account in the Bank of England more than $7 billion of Iran's frozen assets, in return for the release of the hostages.

This transfer of assets will begin shortly after the formal documents are signed in Algiers by Deputy Secretary of State Warren M. Christopher, who has been the chief American negotiator, and in Teheran by Behzad Nabavi, Iran's negotiator.

Doctors to Accompany Americans

The Iranians are expected to turn the hostages over to the custody of Algerian doctors now in Teheran. Once the hostages are in the air, the Algerians would turn the money in the escrow account over to Iran. The Iranians, however, are obliged to use a significant part of those funds to make payments on loans and clear up other debts with Western banks.

First word of the apparent breakthrough came from Teheran yesterday morning when Mr. Nabavi told Pars, the Iranian press agency, that the United States and Iran had "finally reached agreement" but that "several wholly trivial points" remained to be settled. Vice President Mondale and Zbigniew Brzezinski, the national security adviser, and other officials promptly denied that the accord had been reached, but they agreed that only minor issues remained.

Mr. Carter, who was spending the last weekend of his Presidency at Camp David, the Maryland retreat, flew back to the White House by helicopter yesterday afternoon to confer by telephone with Mr. Christopher in Algiers, and to spend several hours in meetings with Secretary of State Edmund S. Muskie, Treasury Secretary G. William Miller and other top aides on the remaining details.

It was evident all day that with Mr. Carter's term in office now being measured in hours, a major push was under way here and in Teheran to resolve the crisis before a new administration was in power in Washington. American officials interpreted Mr. Nabavi's comments yesterday morning as an effort to expedite even more the negotiations that had already been proceeding at a rapid pace ever since Iran produced a compromise to settle the assets question on Friday.

After consultation with Washington, Mr. Christopher exchanged several messages with Iran yesterday through the Algerian intermediaries. Late in the afternoon, Mr. Nabavi, in an interview over the Teheran radio, said that all differences had now been resolved.

Statement From Algiers Awaited

This created a sense of anticipation throughout the United States, but the White House said it would not confirm the conclusion of the negotiations until there was an announcement from Algiers that the necessary documents had been signed by the Iranians and Americans.

The delay was also part of an effort to reward the Algerians, who had served as intermediaries since November, by allowing them the opportunity to make the first announcement, officials here said.

Jack H. Watson, Mr. Carter's chief of staff, said earlier in the day that there were "two points of difference" that had delayed the agreement in the closing hours.

One dealt with the exact amount that would be placed in the Algerian escrow account by the United States. He said the discussions centered on an area "between $7 billion and $8 billion."

The other question, he said, involved the international arbitration arrangement to deal with American claims against Iran's assets on deposit in this country. Iran has agreed to the formation of an arbitration panel to handle the claims, but has wanted to deny the use of the arbitration mechanism to American companies that have contracts giving Iranian law precedence in disputes. This was opposed by many American companies.

Medical Team Off for Germany

In advance of the final agreement, a group of medical experts flew from Washington to Wiesbaden, West Germany, Saturday night to be ready for the expected arrival of the hostages. Another group, including former Secretary of State Cyrus R. Vance, was waiting for the official go-ahead to leave Washington for Wiesbaden.

When asked about the likelihood of Mr. Carter's going to West Germany, Mr. Watson, speaking on the NBC News "Meet the Press" program yesterday, said that with the inauguration of Mr. Reagan less than 48 hours away, "I think is is unlikely." But he added, "I cannot say for sure."

For the families of the hostages, the wide publicity given the reports from Teheran on the ending of the crisis produced considerable optimism, offset by their realization that they had had hopes dashed in the past.

"It's been a day of chills and thrills," Louisa Kennedy, wife of Moorhead C. Kennedy Jr., who was economics officer at the embassy in Teheran when it was seized by Islamic militants on Nov. 4, 1979, said to reporters at the State Department. "We have every expectation that an agreement will come tonight."

Translation Causes Delay

Katherine Keough, wife of William F. Keough Jr., who was the head of the American school in Islamabad, Pakistan, and was visiting Teheran at the time of the takeover, said that both Mr. Carter and Mr. Muskie had talked to her yesterday. They told her, she said, that the difficulties were not substantive but only the matter of rendering the agreement into three languages, English, Persian, and French.

French is the language used by the Algerians. When asked what she planned to do when her husband returned, Mrs. Kennedy said, "I am very superstitious about even mentally planning for days ahead."

"Let's take it day by day," she said. Mr. Carter broke off his discussions at the White House to drive to the State Department shortly before 7 P.M. to make a brief appearance at a dinner given in honor of Mr. Muskie and Mr. Christopher, in absentia, by other senior officials.

President Seems Confident

When asked by reporters if an agreement had been reached, the President only smiled as he entered the department. When he left 10 minutes later, he said he hoped to have something to say later in the evening.

Mr. Mondale, Mr. Brzezinski and Mr. Watson all said they were confident that the negotiations had gone so far that even if for some unexpected reason there was a delay beyond Tuesday Mr. Reagan would not break them off.

Mr. Reagan's choice for national security adviser, Richard V. Allen, and Secretary of State-designate Alexander M. Haig Jr. have both received detailed briefings on an hour-by-hour basis on the status of the negotiations.

Mr. Watson, in his television appearance, said, "I would anticipate that if we cannot close the matter finally between now and the inauguration on Tuesday, that what remains to be done will be picked up by then-President Reagan's administration and handled smoothly."

As Mr. Reagan moved around Washington today in a series of pre-inauguration events, he indicated that he shared the general optimism and had no problems with the projected agreement.

Under the terms of the agreement, the United States would also lift the economic embargo against Iran that was imposed as the result of the crisis and would ask dismissal of the International Court of Justice decisions against the Teheran regime.

Iran Could Buy From U.S.

This would permit Iran to buy industrial and some military equipment from the United States that has been barred. But it is not anticipated that the agreement on the hostages will lead to a resumption of normal relations between Iran and the United States. And American officials said that even though Iran had about $500 million in a trust fund for the purchase of military hardware, it was unlikely to receive any sophisticated equipment that could be used in its war with Iraq.

The United States has declared its neutrality in the conflict, but has warned Iraq against trying to destroy Iran politically. Mr. Brzezinski said that "it will take time for the American-Iranian relationship to recuperate." "We don't even have diplomatic relations now," he said yesterday on the CBS News program "Face the Nation." "They will not be reinstituted with the resolution of this issue," he said. "It will take time to resolve that. It will take time for the wounds to heal."

* * *

January 21, 1981

REAGAN TAKES OATH AS 40TH PRESIDENT; PROMISES AN 'ERA OF NATIONAL RENEWAL'

MINUTES LATER, 52 U.S. HOSTAGES IN IRAN FLY TO FREEDOM AFTER 444-DAY ORDEAL

By BERNARD GWERTZMAN
Special to The New York Times.

WASHINGTON, Wednesday, Jan. 21—The 52 Americans who were held hostage by Iran for 444 days were flown to freedom yesterday. Jimmy Carter, a few hours after giving up the Presidency, said that everyone "was alive, was well and free."

The flight ended the national ordeal that had frustrated Mr. Carter for most of his last 14 months in office, and it allowed Ronald Reagan to begin his term free of the burdens of the Iran crisis.

The Americans were escorted out of Iran by Algerian diplomats, aboard an Algerian airliner, underscoring Algeria's role in achieving the accord that allowed the hostages to return home.

Transferred to U.S. Custody

The Algerian plane, carrying the former hostages, stopped first in Athens to refuel. It then landed in Algiers, where custody of the 52 Americans was formally transferred by the Algerians to the representative of the United States, former Deputy Secretary of State Warren M. Christopher. He had negotiated much of the agreement freeing them.

They then boarded two United States Air Force hospital planes and flew to Frankfurt, West Germany early this morning. They will stay at an American military hospital in nearby Weisbaden, where they will be visited by Mr. Carter, as President Reagan's representative, later today. They will stay in Wiesbaden for a week or less to "decompress," as one official described it.

The 52 Americans were freed as part of a complex agreement that was not completed until early yesterday morning, when the last snags holding up their release were removed by Mr. Carter and his aides, in the final diplomatic action of their Administration.

Under the terms of the accord, as the Algerian plane left Iranian air space, nearly $3 billion of Iranian assets that had been frozen by the United States were returned to Iran, and many more billions of dollars were made available for Iranian repayment of debts.

The 52 Americans were freed only minutes after Ronald Reagan was sworn in as the 40th President of the United States. The concurrence in timing held millions of Americans at their radios and television sets, following the pageantry of Inauguration Day and the news of the hostages' release.

Negotiations Were Intense

The negotiators, who had worked around the clock for five days in an effort to bring the crisis to an end before Mr. Carter left office, said that they had no idea whether the Iranians had deliberately dragged out the talks so as to insure that the hostages were not actually in the air until Mr. Reagan was President.

Mr. Reagan was informed that the Algerian plane carrying the hostages had left Iranian airspace as he was about to have lunch with the Congressional leadership at the Capitol after the inauguration ceremony.

"With thanks to Almighty God, I have been given a tag line, the get-off line, that everyone wants for the end of a toast or a speech, or anything else," the President said after brief remarks.

"Some 30 minutes ago, the Algerian planes bearing our prisoners left Iranian airspace and they're now free of Iran." Ringing applause drowned out his final remarks and Mr. Reagan responded by lifting a glass of white California wine to his lips and drinking to the end of the crisis.

Drama Seized World's Attention

The end of the drama that has seized American and world attention for nearly 15 months evoked a jumble of emotions from the families of the 52, ranging from exhilaration to disbelief.

Anita Schaefer, wife of Col. Thomas E. Schaefer, who was the senior military officer in the embassy in Teheran when it was seized on Nov. 4, 1979, was told that the plane carrying the hostages had left Teheran by Mr. Carter at Andrews Air Force Base, only minutes before the former President boarded his plane for the trip home to Plains, Ga.

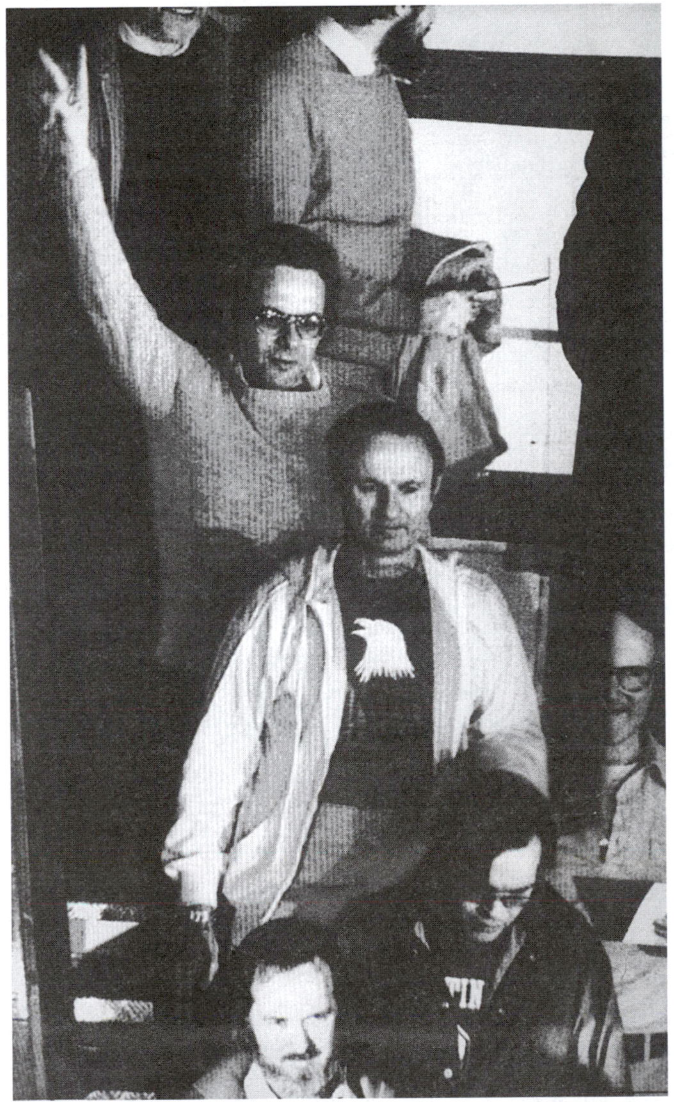

Associated Press

Former hostages leaving a plane in Algiers were tentatively identified, from the top, as: Malcolm Kalp; Col. Charles W. Scott, military attaché; Clair Cortland Barnes and William E. Belk, communications officer.

"Tom is in the air," Mr. Carter told her as they embraced, both crying. Mr. Carter, at Plains, said that while he was on Air Force One, "I had received word, officially, for the first time, that the aircraft carrying the 52 American hostages had cleared Iranian airspace on the first leg of the journey home and that everyone of the 52 hostages was alive, was well and free."

He had hoped to fly to West Germany Monday, his last full day in office. But at Mr. Reagan's invitation, Mr. Carter, together with other senior members of his Administration, will make the trip today. Former Secretary of State Cyrus R. Vance had already gone to Wiesbaden to be there when the Americans arrive.

"Throughout this time of trial, we Americans have stood as one, united in our prayers, steadfast in our concern for fellow Americans in peril," Mr. Carter said. "I doubt that at any time in our history more prayers have reached heaven for any Americans than have those given to God in the last 14 months."

Carter Administration officials have been very sensitive to allegations that the arrangement amounted to "ransom." This charge has been made by some Republicans and columnists—but not by Mr. Reagan—because the United States agreed to return Iran's frozen assets, to drop claims against Iran and to help Iran seek to recover the property of the late Shah in the United States.

Yesterday afternoon, four hours after they were out of office, former Secretary of State Edmund S. Muskie and former Treasury Secretary G. William Miller, as well as several other outgoing officials, took part in a news conference at the State Department that had been permitted by the Reagan Administration.

Mr. Muskie stressed that "the assets returned are Iranian property" and that the terms of the agreement "were determined to be fair and technically feasible."

Aides to Mr. Carter have maintained that Iran was "punished" for the seizure of the hostages by having had its billions of dollars worth of assets frozen for nearly 15 months, and by being isolated politically and economically as a result of the crisis.

The hostages themselves, a virtual cross-section of this country, ranging from Ivy League Foreign Service officers to teen-age enlisted men, and including two women and one black, were described by the Swiss Ambassador in Teheran, Eric Lang, as having been very emotional at the airport there prior to departure.

"They were laughing and crying and hugging each other," he said. "Many of them could not believe they were on their way to freedom." The Swiss have represented the United States in Teheran, but in recent weeks the most significant help given the hostages was provided by Algeria, which at the request of Iran became the intermediary in three months of protracted negotiations.

Americans Examined by Doctors

As part of the agreement, worked out through the Algerians, the American hostages were turned over to Algerian custody, and they and their belongings were flown out on two Algerian aircraft. A third, and smaller, Algerian plane carried six doctors who had examined the Americans before their release.

The Americans were taken to Algiers not only as part of the arrangement but to demonstrate the United States Government's gratitude for the Algerian efforts, State Department officials said.

The negotiations, which last month seemed on the verge of collapse when Iran demanded that the United States provide $24 billion in financial guarantees, picked up momentum in the last two weeks. The last five days were particularly active as diplomats and financial experts in Washington, Algiers, Teheran, London and New York worked around the clock to conclude the accord.

Early Monday morning, Mr. Christopher signed the formal agreement in Algiers and Behzad Nabavi, the chief Iranian negotiator, signed it in Teheran. That led to a sense of anticipation that the hostages would be freed late Monday.

But the Iranians objected to a document sent to Iran by the United States to allow the complex agreement to be put into effect. American officials said that there were several other snags in the final hours, as messages went back and forth through Algiers.

It was uncertain Monday night whether Mr. Carter would be able to bring about the hostage release during his Presidency, but at about 3 A.M. yesterday, Jody Powell, Mr. Carter's spokesman, told a crowd of reporters at the White House that a formula had been agreed upon by Washington and Teheran on removing the last obstacle to the carrying out of the accord.

Under terms of the agreement, the 12 American banks holding frozen Iranian assets funneled them to the Federal Reserve Bank of New York. At about 6 A.M. the Federal Reserve sent nearly $8 billion to the Bank of England for a special escrow account in the name of the Algerian central bank.

By 7 A.M. the Algerians were able to notify Iran that they had possession of the frozen assets and that Iran was now obligated to release the American hostages to them.

This happened in the morning hours Washington time, which is eight and a half hours behind Teheran time. The hostages were then put aboard one of the two Boeing 727's that Algeria had sent there Monday, and their belongings on the other.

* * *

April 19, 1981

U.S. SAID TO REVISE STRATEGY TO OPPOSE THREATS BY SOVIET

By RICHARD HALLORAN
Special to The New York Times.

WASHINGTON, April 18—The Reagan Administration has begun to fashion a military strategy that would prepare the armed forces for the possibility that some confrontation with the Soviet Union might lead to a protracted conventional war, according to senior Pentagon officials.

The concept, which is basically set but is still being refined, reflects the initial imprint of Defense Secretary Caspar W. Weinberger and his top associates on the nation's military thinking. It is part of the policy being drafted to guide the services as they shape their 1983 budgets.

The officials said the plan sheds the concept that any war with the Soviet Union would probably be of short duration and settled by negotiation or enlarged into a nuclear conflict. Instead, they said, it envisions the possibility of a long conflict with conventional weapons in several parts of the world at the same time.

An Expensive Strategy

The new strategy would require investing huge sums of money in weapons and ammunition, transport, equipment and supplies. It would also require a vast mobilization of manpower and revitalization of the defense industry, the officials said.

The Administration would retain the long-standing reliance on strategic and tactical nuclear weapons as a deterrence, the officials said, but would strive to make the military command and communications apparatus invulnerable to nuclear attack.

They said that the Administration would also retain the commitment to the North Atlantic alliance and continue to modernize its medium-range nuclear weapons, keep United States forces in South Korea and elsewhere in Northeast Asia and prepare for localized conflicts against adversaries other than the Soviet Union.

Skepticism on Détente

President Reagan and his senior advisors have not so far articulated an overarching concept of foreign and miliary policy comparable to the Truman Doctrine or containment; President Eisenhower's strategy of broad nuclear retaliation; the flexible response of President Kennedy, or the Nixon doctrine of détente. President Carter followed a policy of détente and, until nearly the end of his term, military restraint.

The new military strategy, which reflects Mr. Reagan and Mr. Weinberger's skepticism of détente, may lead to such an overall doctrine. In the immediate case, the President laid out the basic approach, Mr. Weinberger shaped it and Under Secretary of Defense Fred C. Ikle pooled recommendations from his staff, the military departments and senior military officers.

The strategy thus being formed shows strong influence from the Joint Chiefs of Staff and from the commanders in chief of the forces in the United States and abroad. In a recent extensive revision, Mr. Weinberger ordered that the Joint Chiefs and the military service secretaries be brought more into the planning and budgeting process.

Services to Adjust Budgets

Once the strategy has been decided, it will go to the Army, Navy and Air Force to guide them as they draw up budgets for the fiscal year 1983, which begins this Oct. 1. Their recommendations will be sent to Mr. Weinberger's office for coordination, then go to the Office of Management and Budget for revision. The military budget will be approved by President Reagan before he sends it, along with the rest of his budget proposals, to Congress next January.

The policy guidance instructs the military services to plan their forces, weapons and equipment to defend the nation's interests as far away from American shores as their resources will permit, the officials said.

These goals would add to expenses because transporting forces and sustaining them far away is costly. But the policy, the officials said, justified increasing the Navy's size to 600 ships from 450.

The threat of the Soviet Union to the West's sources of oil in the Middle East and around the Persian Gulf is emphasized, the officials said. The strategy calls for the direct introduction of American forces into the region if access to petroleum supplies is jeopardized.

Oilfields a Concern

This policy appears to solidify and extend the policy enunciated by Jimmy Carter, then President, after the Soviet intervention in Afghanistan in late 1979. At the time, Mr. Carter pledged to defend American interests in that region with military force if necessary.

However, Mr. Weinberger, in his initial appearance before a Congressional committee as Defense Secretary, criticized that Carter Administration policy as "extraordinarily clumsy and ill-advised."

The new policy, the Pentagon officials said, asserts that it is "essential" that the Soviet Union be confronted with the possibility of a far larger conflict if Russian forces try to deny the United States access to oil.

Spread of a Conflict

The officials asserted that such a geographic spread of a conflict would not necessarily escalate into a nuclear exchange because neither side could be certain of escaping devastating damage. Thus, the conflict could turn into a long conventional war for which the United States must be prepared.

To build up the total military force confronting the Soviet Union, the officials said, the United States would increase its military assistance to other nations, especially in the Middle East and particularly Egypt, Turkey and Saudi Arabia.

The new strategy calls for building up a strong apparatus to mobilize large numbers of men, including a military draft, and to train, assemble and transport them.

The policy also envisions revitalizing the defense industry to be able to double or triple production within a year after the onset of hostilities, as in the Korean War, and to produce eight times as much within three years, as in World War II, the officials said.

* * *

November 19, 1981

HOUSE VOTES FUNDS FOR THE B-1 AND MX AND BACKS REAGAN

By STEVEN V. ROBERTS

Special to The New York Times.

WASHINGTON, Nov. 18—In a strong endorsement of President Reagan's military strategy, the House of Representatives tonight passed a $197.4 billion military appropriation bill that included funds to continue development of the B-1 manned bomber and the MX missile.

Both systems are key elements of a strategic weapons package, announced this fall by Mr. Reagan, that would cost $180 billion over the next six years.

Before considering the full authorization bill, which they passed by a vote of 335 to 61, the lawmakers defeated an amendment by Representative Joseph P. Addabbo, Democrat of Queens, to strike $1.8 billion set aside for the B-1. The amendment lost by 263 to 142. They then turned back, by a vote of 264 to 139, a proposal by Mr. Addabbo to eliminate $1.9 billion for the MX.

'Excessive Spending' Assailed

By a margin of 202 to 197, the House also rejected an amendment by Representative Marge Roukema, Republican of New Jersey, to cut $1.65 billion meant for military procurement and research. Mrs. Roukema accused the Pentagon of "wasteful and excessive spending" and said, "We want to bring the Department of Defense into line with budget realities."

The bill's total spending figure was slightly less than $4 billion below the Reagan Administration's request, but about $25 billion more than was appropriated last year.

On a matter related to the military budget, Secretary of Defense Caspar W. Weinberger asserted today that "it just isn't correct" that the Pentagon is a "swamp" of waste and inefficiency, as the budget director, David A. Stockman, had contended in a magazine interview.

Several lawmakers said earlier that to vote against the MX would be "pulling the rug out from under the President" on the same day that he advanced a new proposal for talks on reductions of strategic arms with the Soviet Union.

Representative David F. Emery, Republican of Maine, called the missile system a "bargaining chip" in those talks, and Representative Jack Edwards, Republican of Alabama, added: "We've got to support our President. Any changing of course on this missile would be an extreme mistake at this time."

Speaking in opposition to providing funds for the missile, Representative Thomas J. Downey, Democrat of West Islip, L.I., maintained that it was "an extremely expensive bargaining chip." Representative Addabbo added that the Pentagon did not need the money now and that putting it in the bill would only add to the widespread waste in military spending.

Even some opponents of the Addabbo amendment, however, expressed reservations about the White House plan to base the first MX missiles in existing silos. Representative Elliott H. Levitas, Democrat of Georgia, termed the basing plan "naive, childish, and foolish," but added that it would be "unconscionable" to vote against the President right now.

The margin of defeat for the Addabbo amendment on the B-1 bomber was wider than expected, and after the vote, legislators said that they were convinced that the B-1 was needed, despite a price tag that could reach $300 million per plane and $40 billion for the whole fleet.

"I guess people were persuaded that you lead with the best that you can build," said Representative Jim Wright of Texas, the majority leader.

But political considerations were clearly important in the outcome. According to Mr. Wright, many members were concerned that if they voted against the B-1, they could be branded "weak on defense" by political opponents next year.

"The B-1 is a ribbon or a badge you can wear out there to prove you're tough-minded on defense," said Mr. Downey. "It's a lot easier to vote for them than defend a vote against them."

On Tuesday the Senate Appropriations Committee approved a $208.5 billion version of the bill, including funds for the B-1 and the MX.

A Bomber to Bridge a Gap

Proponents of the bomber project, which had been killed by President Carter, focused on the argument that the current flagship of the bomber fleet, the B-52, would not be able to penetrate Soviet airspace after 1985 and that a new and advanced bomber, the Stealth, would not be available until after 1990. Thus, the proponents argued, the B-1 was necessary to bridge the gap.

"A penetrating bomber is one of the bargaining chips the President should have" in future arms talks with the Soviet Union, said Representative Jack Edwards, Republican of Alabama.

Representative C.W. Young, Republican of Florida, held up a paper airplane and said to his colleagues, "We all have to admit, this is the Stealth bomber right now." He was alluding to general lack of common knowledge about the bomber, whose purpose is to evade detection by radar.

Opponents of the bomber focused on its enormous cost and limited useful life. "The American people want a strong defense," said Representative Geraldine A. Ferraro, Democrat of Queens, "but they do not want a boondoggle."

'Monument to Military Madness'

Representative Ronald V. Dellums, Democrat of California, said that going ahead with the B-1 was a "political decision" by the White House and "a monument to military madness."

Other opponents said the B-1 had come to symbolize the decision by the Reagan Administration to build up military spending while cutting back domestic programs.

* * *

December 13, 1981

POLAND'S LEADER PUTS MILITARY IN CHARGE AFTER UNION CHIEFS CALL A NATIONAL VOTE ON FUTURE OF THE COMMUNIST GOVERNMENT

By JOHN DARNTON
Special to The New York Times.

WARSAW, Sunday, Dec. 13—Gen. Wojciech Jaruzelski, the Polish leader, invoked emergency constitutional powers this morning to declare a "state of war" and impose what appeared to be a military Government on Poland.

General Jaruzelski, the Prime Minister and Communist Party leader, made the announcement at 6 A.M. (midnight,

New York time) in an emotional, 23-minute speech over the Warsaw radio.

Speaking just after troops had taken up positions and sealed off sections of the capital, he said the Government would be under the direction of an Army Council of National Salvation.

Army to Run Ministries

"We have to protect law and order, that's the only way to get out of the crisis," he declared. He said army commissars would be appointed to take over Government ministries.

(Tass, the Soviet press agency, said in a dispatch from Warsaw that General Jaruzelski "announced the introduction of martial law in the country and the setting up of a Military Council of National Salvation.")

His speech followed a night in which Solidarity activists were apparently rounded up and detained all across the country. The union's national leadership under Lech Walesa had been meeting in the northern port city of Gdansk. With all communications between Warsaw and the rest of the country cut off, there was no word on what had happened to them.

Riot Police Surround Office

The union's Warsaw office was surrounded by riot policemen shortly after midnight and journalists later saw occupants being escorted to police vans.

(United States officials, who spoke on the condition that they not be identified, said there were no indications of large-scale Soviet military moves around Poland. Mark Weinberg, a White House spokesman, said President Reagan was aware of the events in Poland and was being kept informed. A State Department spokesman said the department had established a special task force to monitor the situation.)

General Jaruzelski said in his speech that "extremists" from Solidarity had been taken into custody. He gave no further details. Hours before the speech, there were reports of unusual movements of military and police units around the country. There were also reports that at least one union leader, Krszytof Sliwinski, head of Solidarity's foreign section, had been arrested at his home in Warsaw.

In an attempt to balance off the move against the union and avert what is bound to be a strong reaction, he also announced that the authorities were detaining some "people who are personally responsible for leading the country into crisis"

He specifically mentioned Edward Gierek, the party leader ousted in September 1980; Piotr Jaruszewicz, his long-time Prime Minister; Zladislaw Grudzien, a former party leader from Katowice, and Jerzy Lukasziewicz, a former Politburo member in charge of party propaganda.

A New Role for Army

Never before has the army occupied such a role in the life of a Communist country in Eastern Europe. General Jaruzelski justified the change today to the Polish people by arguing that the situation had become too dangerous to be allowed to deteriorate any further.

"Our country is on the verge of an abyss," he said. "Our economy is a tragedy. The state structures no longer function. Everyone is on strike. They call for a confrontation with the Reds."

He said the Government had been "patient" and had offered to bring the unionists into a "front of national agreement." But at its current meeting in Gdansk and at a meeting last week in Radom, in which militant statements were aired, the union had "shown its real face," he asserted.

'We Had to Do Something'

The course of events had to change in Poland, the General said, or else it would lead to chaos and civil war. "We couldn't allow democracy to cause tragedy," he said. "We had to do something before they dragged our country into civil war. We are thinking about the future of our country."

Promising a new and more authoritarian rule, the general said that the military council, the duties of which otherwise remained undefined, would fight against hoodlums and law-breakers.

Appealing to patriotism, he added, "Polish soldiers always served the country well. He was always on the front lines. Our soldiers have clean hands."

The dramatic moves Saturday night and this morning culminated what some Western diplomats had called a coup in slow motion. The army's power, as the institution of last resort, had been growing since General Jaruzelski was appointed Prime Minister.

'A Temporary Measure'

Army rule, he promised, would be "a temporary measure" and not a substitute for civil government. "We are just a drop in the stream of Polish history," he asserted.

In his address he made a special point of speaking to Poland's Communist allies, promising no break in friendly relations and asking for "understanding" for the difficult conditions here.

He asked Polish workers to give up temporarily their right to strike, which was won at the Gdansk shipyard in the summer of 1980, and he appealed to Polish farmers not to "let the country starve to death."

He ended the speech with the opening words of the national anthem, "Poland has not yet perished as long as we live," and the music of the anthem dramatically arose in the background.

Stage Set for Crackdown

The Government has been paving the way gradually for its crackdown. For weeks, official press outlets have been emphasizing labor unrest, crime and conditions of "anarchy" in the country.

The Polish Consitution allows for a suspension of normal laws during a time of "state of war," which is not very well defined and has generally been interpreted as a state of emergency. During a "state of war" the Government is empowered to make summary arrests, try offenders before military tribunals and take other steps to ensure law and order. In effect it is martial law.

On Saturday, the union's national leadershp decided at a meeting in Gdansk to conduct a nationwide referendum on establishing a government outside the jurisdiction of the Polish Communist Party and defining Poland's military relationship with the Soviet Union.

The union's leaders also approved a resolution calling for an automatic general strike if the Government passed a law granting itself emergency powers.

Union Leaders to Be Interned

General Jaruzelski, who was named Prime Minister last February and became the Communist Party leader in October, opened his address with the playing of the national anthem.

"There is one thing that I want, peace," he said. "We have to come out of the crisis by ourselves by our hands. History would never forgive us if we failed."

Union sources said the police had detained the son of the political dissident, Jacek Kuron. While placing him under arrest, the sources said, the police informed him that his father, who was attending the union's leadership meeting in Gdansk, was also in police custody and being taken to Warsaw.

Shortly before the police and troops arrived at the union's Warsaw headquarters, the national leadership in Gdansk also voted to endorse the Warsaw chapter's Dec. 6 call for a nationwide day of protest on Thursday over "the use of force and the threat to use force."

The union vote on the protest defied the Government's demand earlier Saturday that the Warsaw branch cancel its plans for the demonstration in the capital and other cities Thursday.

The Warsaw chapter called for the protest after the storming of a strikebound fire cadets' academy by the police on Dec. 2. At that time, about 300 students occupying the building were removed without injuries.

A statement issued by Jerzy Urban, the Government press spokesman, said such a demonstration "may have unpredictable consequences in the present tense situation in the country."

It ended with the warning that "law enforcement agencies will oppose with determination any actions aimed against people's power, in the name of peace for citizens and public order." The reference to "people's power" meant the Communist Government.

Telephone Lines Cut

Telephones and telex lines in Warsaw were cut as the police descended on the Warsaw union offices. At least 11 trucks carrying riot policemen were seen on both ends of the block on Mokotowska Street, where the union headquarters is situated in an old school building.

(The London international telephone exchange reported that all telephone and telex links between Poland and the rest of Europe were cut off Saturday at 1 P.M. E.S.T., The Associated Press reported. Telephone communications between the United States and Poland were closed at 7:15 P.M. E.S.T., according to Wayne DuBois, a spokesman for the American Telephone & Telegraph Company.)

At 1 A.M. (7 P.M., New York time), a correspondent saw people coming out the building and entering a windowless police van. The van then pulled away.

Other Police Raids Reported

Solidarity sources said similar police raids took place in other cities, among them Rzeszow, Lublin and Radom. The proposed referendum, scheduled for Feb. 15, was to be conducted by Solidarity, presumably among nonunion people as well as union members, if General Jaruzelski's Government did not agree to a series of union demands by the end of the year.

The vote on the proposal, by far the most controversial that the union had ever considered, was conducted by the union's full 107-member national commission.

Unusual Troop Activity

The reports of unusual troop activity around the country came from six locations earlier Saturday. In Poznan, Leszno and Gostyn, union members reported that tanks with Soviet markings were moving eastward. They said there were formations of between 40 and 60 tanks on the roads.

Warsaw region staff members also displayed a telex message from a union official, Marek Zylinski, in Olsztyn, about 60 miles southeast of Gdansk, listing unusual movements in three nearby locations—Muszaki, Barto Szyce and Szczytno. Some of the movements were toward Gdansk, others toward Warsaw.

At least one such movement, a large concentration of troops with tanks and heavy weapons, was said to be Polish. The telex said the troops were asked where they were going, but said they did not know.

New Phase in 'Struggle' Urged

The Solidarity leaders, assembled inside the Lenin Shipyard where the union was born in historic negotations with the Government 16 months ago, were in a mood to display their militancy, sparked in part by a sense that the Government was pressing for a showdown.

The meeting hall rang with calls for new tactics, amendments to proposed referendums and speeches on the need to switch "the struggle" into a new phase.

'Whiff of Terror' Seen by Press

The Gdansk meeting has aroused critical reaction in the state-controlled press. Trybuna Ludu, the main organ of the Communist Party, officially known as the Polish United Workers' Party, said that the opening day Friday provided no grounds for optimism.

"So far, a whiff of terror has come from the meeting hall," the paper asserted. Among the demands Solidarity says must be met are such matters as access to the mass media, the creation of a special "social council" to oversee the economy, and free and democratic elections to local councils in the provinces.

According to a draft proposal the referendum would declare that "society cannot any longer tolerate the existing situation in the country," and would raise four questions:

- Are you for a vote of confidence in General Jaruzelski?
- Are you for establishing a temporary government and free elections?
- Are you for providing military guarantees to the Soviet Union in Poland?
- Can the Polish United Workers' Party be the instrument of such guarantees in the name of the whole society?

A Tactic for Pressure on Regime

Political observers pointed out that the mere threat to hold such a referendum could be seen as a pressure tactic against the Government.

* * *

December 13, 1981

A NEW STRATEGY FOR NATO

By STANSFIELD TURNER

There are times in the history of military alliances when some long-latent problem reaches a point where a decision, no matter how painful, must be made. Such a time has arrived for the North Atlantic Treaty Organization, the compact of free nations that for 32 years has been the framework of security for Western Europe and the United States.

The Soviet Union and its Eastern European satellites, banded together under the Warsaw Pact, have been growing stronger in military terms. Yet the Atlantic alliance cannot seem to agree on how best to respond. The Europeans have lost much of their old confidence in American leadership; they tend more and more to be preoccupied with narrow national concerns and to take independent positions on issues that demand a common allied strategy. This restiveness has even seeped down to the level of public opinion. In recent weeks, the political atmosphere in Western Europe has been roiled by mass demonstrations against allied plans for deploying new American missiles on European soil.

These bickerings and differences are symptomatic of a deeper problem. The military threat to Western Europe has changed—the result of new conditions inside the Soviet bloc that have changed Soviet perspectives. The Western alliance is organized around a strategy for yesterday's dangers. All these trans-Atlantic disagreements over force levels and weapons missions stem largely from inner doubts and plain confusion about their relevance to present needs.

The most likely threat to the Western alliance today is pointed not directly at Western Europe but, obliquely, across third-world areas like the Persian Gulf. What we need is a new strategy providing those regions with a defensive shield. This would best be done by the United States and Western Europe acting in concert. But if, as seems probable, the Europeans are unwilling or unable to increase their military potential for this purpose, the United States must act alone.

This will mean a smaller American contribution to the military defense of Western Europe, as we divert forces to the third world. The Europeans will be shocked, but the alliance will survive and emerge all the stronger for recognizing the realities of the 1980's. In fact, fear of facing up to reality will vitiate the partnership more surely than anything else.

It must be admitted, to start with, that, by and large, Western Europe and the United States bring differing viewpoints to the question of whether the times call for more détente or more defense.

Détente for Europe has meant new markets for trade with Eastern Europe and the Soviet Union, increased dialogue with the East and a chance to influence East-West relations independently of the United States. The Europeans have put emphasis on perpetuating détente despite the Soviet invasion of Afghanistan and Moscow's blatant pressures on Poland. The very fact that the Polish workers dared to rebel and the Kremlin has been holding back from military intervention is seen by Europeans as deriving partly from the attitudes of détente acquired in the 1970's.

Most Americans, on the other hand, see détente more as a desirable principle than a working basis of foreign policy. We have supported détente publicly but we question it privately, tending to see it as having led to Soviet gains in Angola, Ethiopia, Southern Yemen, Nicaragua and Cambodia. We look on East-West trade with much less enthusiasm than the Europeans, reasoning that, from the Western standpoint, the impetus for such trade is political rather than economic. (Western Europe's trade with Communist countries accounted for only 4.9 percent of its total foreign trade in 1980; alternative markets could easily have been found elsewhere.) The European view that the Soviet leaders are sincerely committed to détente, if only because of their concern with the Soviet bloc's internal political and economic difficulties, gets a skeptical hearing in the United States.

There is, nonetheless, something to be said for the European analysis. The Kremlin's current difficulties could well be having some inhibiting effect. The Soviet leaders must be increasingly worried about the satellites' political reliability. Poland is only the most dramatic expression of this endemic problem; there are long-term forces undermining the foundations of socialism across a much wider spectrum within the Warsaw Pact. Each Eastern European leader must feel that his fate hinges to some degree on the outcome of the Polish drama. Tension within the Communist alliance is bound to increase. And whatever makes the satellites even less reliable will tend to limit Moscow's freedom of action toward the West.

The economic malaise spreading across the Soviet empire is just as serious in its implications. The problems of the Soviet-style planned economy, with its lack of individual incentive, have assumed formidable proportions. Growth rates are declining both in output and productivity. The

Soviet leaders are caught between three competing needs—continued spending on the military, investment in plant and equipment, and a better break for the consumer—and there are no easy choices to be made.

But a different analysis of Moscow's difficulties could lead to a conclusion far different from the one espoused by most Europeans. As economic requirements push up against military spending, and as political tensions within the Warsaw Pact grow more serious, the Soviet leaders could be tempted to establish footholds around the world before their military advantages ebb and before our renewed defense program takes effect. The objective, according to this "lashout" theory, would be not only to win all they can while they can but to divert domestic attention from increased austerity at home.

The Russians could take military action in remote regions alone, but this would hardly achieve their objective. They could, as a second alternative, lash out on the central front in Europe, but that would be risky indeed. A third option, an attack on Europe's flanks, or on Iran or Pakistan, would also involve serious hazards. Thus, while the possibility of some desperate move of this nature cannot be ruled out entirely, it seems unlikely—at least during the next few years, when the Russians will almost certainly be faced with the unsettling difficulties of a succession to the aging leadership of Leonid I. Brezhnev and his men.

A fourth alternative seems more probable—a Soviet foreign policy not unlike the one we have seen for some years, combining aggressive opportunism in the third world with military intimidation and political-economic inducements in Europe.

There is now a question, however, about the European aspects of this policy. Except for the realm of strategic forces, the Russians' potential for intimidating Western Europe will lessen as their military buildup reaches the limits of their capacity and as the reliability of their East European allies becomes increasingly suspect. At the same time, Soviet inducements to Western Europe will look less appealing as the harshness of the Communist societies comes more to the surface in response to the buildup of internal pressures.

In the third world, on the other hand, the outlook for Moscow is more promising. In the wake of the Vietnam War, the United States offered no real opposition as the Soviet Union extended its influence over one third-world country after another. Our stiffer reaction to the invasion of Afghanistan took the Russians by surprise but is not likely to deter them in the future. They have seen little consistency in our foreign policy over recent years, and one grain embargo is hardly likely to persuade them that we will be as firm next time, especially since the embargo was lifted by President Reagan in response to pressure from the domestic farm bloc.

The Russians are likely to continue to seize opportunities to support and manipulate leftist factions in the third world. In some cases, these will be revolutionary elements seeking to take control, as in Angola in 1975. In others, they will be socialists in power who come under challenge from domestic opponents, as in Ethiopia in 1978. There will be blatant moves suggests selective and determined resistance in areas of to install power from outside the country, as the Vietnamese and Russians did in Cambodia in 1978.

There are, it is true, some inherent limitations to this Soviet technique. Moscow's aid to its political proteges is almost entirely military in character. Lacking sufficient reserves of materials, money and know-how for the kind of economic programs that could meet the recipient countries' needs for economic growth, the Russians have rarely been able to establish close, long-term relations with their new-found friends. In the past 20 years, they have been ejected from China, Indonesia, Egypt, Sudan and Somalia, losing out in most cases to strong forces of nationalism.

Yet the Russians have always been willing to make a stab at controlling selected parts of the third world and cutting their losses, if necessary. And today there are two new factors at work. In Angola, Ethiopia and Cambodia, the Russians have left behind sizable surrogate forces, Cuban or Vietnamese. It would be much more difficult for these nations to escape from the Soviet camp than it was for the Egyptians and others. And in Nicaragua, we may have recently witnessed a new Soviet technique—meddling based on Libyan financing. If the Russians can induce Libya to fill the economic void in selected underdeveloped countries, their capability for intervention could be significantly enlarged.

Look, for instance, at what they might attempt from their position in Southern Yemen. By destabilizing Oman, on one side of Saudi Arabia, and Yemen, on the other side, they could outflank the Saudi regime and generate considerable pressure on that Government to amend its pro-Western posture. Soviet prospects in Iran after the death or exit of the Ayatollah Ruhollah Khomeini are even brighter. If the Communist Tudeh Party emerged even temporarily as the dominant Iranian political force, and if the Tudeh "invited" a Soviet military detachment into the country, Iran could be brought under Soviet hegemony. A subsequent march to the northern shores of the Persian Gulf would intimidate Saudi Arabia and place the flow of oil to the West in jeopardy.

Look, also, at the exposed position of several other nations to which we have formal or implied commitments. Pakistan has Soviet troops just across its border with Afghanistan and is frequently accused by the Russians of aiding the Afghan resistance. Thailand's territory has been violated by spillovers from the fighting in Cambodia. South Korea must worry constantly about Moscow encouraging the North Korean leader, Kim Il Sung, into another act of aggression.

If the Russians continue to discern few risks in such third-world adventurism, they surely will continue to make use of their opportunities. It is for these areas, therefore, that a new policy must be forged by the Western alliance, and primarily by the United States.

It must be our common purpose to create unacceptable risks for the Russians—to make the costs of aggression unacceptably high wherever our vital interests are involved. This is not to advocate universal intervention in troubled areas or a return to total containment of the Soviet Union. It overriding concern.

Koussy/Sygma

Americans and Egyptians at a joint exercise in the Egyptian desert: "It must be our purpose to make the costs of Soviet aggression unacceptably high wherever our vital interests are involved."

Clearly, we have vital interests in the major oil-producing countries. There are many other suppliers of raw materials on whom we and our allies depend, and many of these countries are key markets for our exports. The Russians seek to drive a wedge between these countries and the West, to cut off our mineral supplies and to create strains within the Atlantic alliance by forcing each member to scramble to protect its own interests.

The Russians need not take direct military action to cut our supplies. They may influence a leftist-leaning government to do that; they may foment internal disorders or regional wars that will interrupt production and shipment. In anticipation of this kind of Soviet meddling, we must make sure they know that we are ready and capable of resisting their overtures and interventions.

Our resistance can take a number of forms—diplomatic, economic or military. In most instances in the third world, the tools of diplomacy and economic aid will be more applicable than military presence or combat. But diplomatic and economic leverage will be insufficent unless the Western alliance can present a united front and display a readiness to protect its interests with adequate military power.

In the Persian Gulf, clearly a nexus of the vital interests of the United States and its allies, it has become highly probable that we will need the capacity to at least threaten the use of force—and enough power in the region to make the threat credible. The Russians must be left with no doubts about our readiness to resist any attempt to alter the balance of power in this critical area. Only when they become convinced of our resolution and capacity will they see the costs and risks of overseas adventurism as being higher than in the past.

Our chances of drawing a line and holding it are good. In measuring risks against opportunities, the Russians will have to take their own lessening economic and political strength into account. The Russians are bogged down in Afghanistan; they are subsidizing Cuba, underwriting Vietnam's occupation of Cambodia and standing poised with 30 to 40 divisions on Poland's perimeter; surely they must think carefully before extending themselves further. A full range of responses to Soviet meddling in the third world has a better chance of success today than ever before.

We should encourage our European allies to participate in the development of new Western defenses in the third world. It will always be helpful politically to have a multinational force

Philippot/Sygma

Soviet troops in Afghanistan: "Our reaction to the invasion of Afghanistan is not likely to deter the Russians in the future."

rather than one that is strictly American. French and British naval forces, and the 4,000-man French Army contingent posted in Djibouti, are the best candidates. But the Europeans have only limited potential for projecting sizable military power over long distances. The transport and support of any allied forces carried into action would have to come from the United States.

The rub is that this is bound to affect our military posture in Western Europe. The United States cannot maintain two armies and two air forces, one for the plains of Europe and one for deployment around the world; neither the American public nor the Congress would support that expense. Difficult as the decision would be, a reduction of our forces in Western Europe is an unavoidable component of a new strategy that in the end would enhance the security of both Europe and the United States.

The change would, of course, pose a variety of problems. Some of them are technical. The military equipment we need for remote regions is quite different from what we now have in Europe. If we are to transport tanks, artillery, armored personnel carriers and other such hardware to remote areas, they must be light and compact. Since we can't have two armies and two air forces, our troops in Europe must adapt their tactics to lighter and more mobile equipment. This means less dependence on massive firepower and stoutly defended positions and more reliance on mobility and maneuver. Instead of holding fixed front-line positions by firepower and armored defense, American ground units in Europe would be trained to move rapidly to where Warsaw Pact forces have been positioned for a breakthrough.

There are those who believe that such tactics of maneuver are more suited, in any case, to tomorrow's technology and battlefield environment. In any event, the alliance's military tactics would have to change appreciably if the United States retooled its ground forces to acquire a dual capability for Europe and for the third world. The forces of our European allies would have to be similarly reshaped—or they would have to think through a new role for themselves, complementing a lighter, more flexible American force.

Similarly, land-based American air power must be easily transportable around the world. The problem is not with the aircraft themselves but with the cumbersome support elements of spare parts, computerized testing equipment, technicians, and so on, that must follow along to keep the sophisticated aircraft flying. Switching to less sophisticated aircraft with more sophisticated weapons could make a big difference.

It would take years to develop and deploy these lighter forces and apply these new tactics. In the meantime, we could improve on our ability to move quickly to unexpected trouble spots by drawing upon equipment and personnel in Europe whenever they are closer to the scene.

In the best of all worlds, our European allies would accept the argument that the United States must take these steps even at the cost of doing less in Europe, and that they should compensate by taking on a larger role themselves. If they did not, in view of their disinclination to increase their defense spending, our best course would be to proceed independently, though after full explanation and consultation. To ignore the problem of continued Soviet interventionism in the third world would be shortsighted. To take on this new responsibility without making the necessary adjustments in Europe would be unrealistic.

Some feel that our military capabilities can be extended to the third world without having any great impact on our commitments in Europe; perhaps a small Rapid Deployment Force, as initiated by President Carter, would do the trick. It could—where the Soviet Union is not directly involved. But it would be patently inadequate in cases of Soviet or Soviet-sponsored military adventurism. The Cuban presence in Ethiopia and Angola is sizable and well equipped; a Soviet thrust into Iran would be massive. A commando force big enough only for putting out "brush fires" in the third world does not constitute a serious enough commitment to have a deterrent effect on Moscow.

There are others who argue that if the Washington reduced its military effort in the defense of Europe, the Europeans could drift into neutralism and accommodation with the Soviet Union. Indeed, as we have noted, there are increasingly vocal leftist factions in Europe that may be willing to sell out their heritage of freedom in just this way, but it would be surprising if this minority view prevailed. There is also the argument that this is no time to raise such a difficult new issue—we have enough problems within the alliance as it is. That is a reasonable principle, but the problem is that the threat of Soviet subversion in vital areas like the Persian Gulf will not go away. The alliance cannot remain strong if it chooses to ignore a critical threat to its survival.

The basic fault with our present alliance strategy is that it confuses preparedness for the most serious possible threat with preparedness for the most likely threat. Our focus for all of these past 32 years has been on the danger of Soviet conquest of Western Europe. Naturally, adequate defense against this possibility must remain among our top priorities. But the most likely danger today is the indirect one of Soviet attempts to extend control over the West's supplies of oil and other minerals and over its political and economic relationships with the third world. The old saying that the road to Berlin is through Baghdad is worth renewed consideration.

The Soviet Union, as we have seen, is facing a set of conditions, internally and externally, that will make it tempting for the Soviet leaders to improve their world position while they still can. The perilous uncertainties of an attack on Western Europe would make that a very difficult choice, to put it mildly, for any Soviet leadership. Yet the impulse to do something may be very strong. An effort to undermine the alliance by way of the third world will be a compelling alternative.

Facing up to this new challenge will test the Atlantic alliance, but the process of testing can also be one of reinvigoration. It can establish new criteria for the sharing of effort, new ability to adjust to change and a renewed sense of commitment to our basic objectives. Yes, there are risks that the alliance will not measure up, but avoidance of necessary risk has never been a sensible policy in the defense of freedom.

Admiral Stansfield Turner, U.S.N., retired, is a former Director of Central Intelligence. Capt. George Thibault, U.S.N., head of the military strategy department of the National War College, helped him prepare this article.

* * *

December 14, 1981

POLAND RESTRICTS CIVIL AND UNION RIGHTS; SOLIDARITY ACTIVITIES URGE GENERAL STRIKE

By BERNARD GWERTZMAN
Special to The New York Times.

BRUSSELS, Dec. 13—Secretary of State Alexander M. Haig Jr. said today that the United States was "seriously concerned" about the imposition of martial law in Poland, and he renewed the West's warning to the Soviet Union not to interfere in the crisis.

After talking by phone with President Reagan, who was then at Camp David, Md., Mr. Haig said at a news conference here that the United States was urging the Polish Government to resume negotiations and to pursue a policy of compromise with the Solidarity trade union to prevent an outbreak of civil strife that could worsen the situation.

Mr. Haig said Polish authorities had assured the United States Embassy this morning that "there will be no return" to the situation that existed in Poland prior to establishment of the independent union in 1980. In addition, he said Western intelligence agencies had not detected any Soviet military moves "which would be a source of alarm."

"But we continue to watch the situation very carefully," he said.

'Very Serious' Consequences

If the Soviet Union intervened in Poland, Mr. Haig said, "the consequences would be very serious and long lasting." Western officials have previously said that, in that event, all trade with the Soviet Union would be suspended and political relations would be sharply curtailed.

President Reagan, arriving back at the White House, was asked about the danger of Soviet intervention and said that the United States had several times "made it plain how seriously we would view interference" by the Soviet Union. The Polish Ambassador and the Soviet Deputy Chief of Mission were summoned to the State Department for discussions on the situation.

Mr. Haig was scheduled to leave Brussels this morning for a seven-day trip to Israel, Turkey, Pakistan, India, Egypt and Morocco. But after talking by phone with Vice President Bush and with various foreign ministers, Mr. Haig decided at the last minute to scrap his travel plans. Reporters traveling with him were already aboard his Air Force plane when they were told to return to the hotel. Mr. Haig is to fly to Washington Monday to meet with Mr. Reagan and other officials.

In his news conference, Mr. Haig briefly appraised the overnight developments that he said had produced "what amounts to martial law" in Poland.

Assurances by U.S. Aide

"Of course, we have no way of predicting what the outcome of these developments will be," he said. Noting the assurances to the United States charge d'affaires in Poland, Herbert E. Wilgis Jr., that the reforms would be allowed to continue, Mr. Haig said, "That, of course, remains to be seen."

In the absence of more information, he said, it would be "unwise to say too much at this time." He added, "I must emphasize that we are seriously concerned about the decision to impose martial law."

"As we have said before," Mr. Haig went on, "the political experiment under way in Poland should be allowed to proceed unimpeded. The potential instabilities in Poland which could arise from the imposition of martial law are obvious to all."

What has worried American officials in previous times of tension in Poland has been that a crackdown by Polish authorities could lead to civil disobedience that might produce a breakdown in authority and a request by the Warsaw Government for Soviet troops to maintain order—events that could produce a situation similar to those preceeding the Soviet moves into Hungary in 1956 and Czechoslovakia in 1968.

Poland 'Should Find a Solution'

To avoid this, Mr. Haig said, "the United States Government reiterates that the Polish people should find a solution to their current difficulties through a process of negotiation and compromise among the parties involved.

"Above all, they should be permitted to do so without any outside interference," he said. The Soviet Embassy in Washington was told of the American concern, Mr. Haig said, and a similar message was expected to be sent to Moscow through the United States Embassy.

Earlier in the year Mr. Haig, in private comments, was almost fatalistic about Soviet intervention in Poland, but Mosow's apparent willingness to let the Poles handle their problems by themselves eventually produced a change in his mood. At the meeting of Western foreign ministers that ended here on Friday, Mr. Haig was optimistic in his comments about the possibility of progress next year in the Soviet-American dialogue.

Today, he said that Soviet statements about Poland in recent days had increased "quite noticeably" in stridency, but "as of this moment we do not see any signs of direct Soviet involvement in the events as they have unfolded."

No NATO Meeting Planned

Under Western contingency plans worked out in December 1980, the foreign ministers of the North Atlantic Treaty Organization nations were to meet here in the event of Soviet moves into Poland. But Mr. Haig said no such session was planned, only a lower-level meeting of political directors at NATO headquarters on Monday. Lawrence S. Eagleburger, Assistant Secretary of State for European Affairs, will represent the United States.

Mr. Haig also noted that no other Western leader had detected any Soviet moves. In fact, Foreign Minister Claude Cheysson of France said in Paris that the developments in Poland were strictly an internal matter and did not require French intervention.

With American officials aware of European caution about the situation, there was no effort to dramatize the crackdown in Poland, aides to Mr. Haig said.

When asked if he was surprised by the developments, Mr. Haig said, "I would say in general that all the Western parties were surprised."

Says U.S. Knew of Tension

"I know the United States was," he said. "In the context of immediately available information, that's not to suggest that we were not clearly cognizant of the growing level of tensions between Solidarity and the party.

"This had caused all of us to raise our level of concern about the internal situation in Poland," he added, "but we had no information suggesting that this sweeping imposition of martial law would take place the way as it did.

"I think the foreign ministers that I have spoken to today—and there have been a number—had no information either." According to the information available to the United States, Mr. Haig said that the arrests of dissidents and union leaders in Warsaw had been matched by similar actions in other Polish cities. He said Polish communications had been cut inside the country and abroad but that the United States Embassy was able to send messages.

He said that the crackdown was so far being carried out by Polish police and internal security forces and that military units were on "standby basis."

Poland has benefited from extensive Western financial and material aid in recent years. In the last year, the United States has supplied about $900 million in food at low credits or free through charitable organizations such as CARE.

* * *

February 7, 1982

REAGAN'S MILITARY BUDGET PUTS EMPHASIS ON A BUILDUP OF U.S. GLOBAL POWER

By LESLIE H. GELB
Special to The New York Times.

WASHINGTON, Feb. 6—The Reagan Administration will be asking Congress for authority to spend $1,640 billion in the next five years on the armed services, with special emphasis on building American capability to project power around the globe.

Funds for the European front and for strategic nuclear forces will rise, but the sharpest increases will go to equipment, supplies, military construction and airlift and sealift capability for the Rapid Deployment Force. The philosophy behind this, according to senior Pentagon officials, is that the United States must not simply be able to respond to an attack by the Soviet Union wherever it occurs, but also be able to strike back at areas of Soviet weakness.

This represents a growing shift in priorities to seapower and a global maritime strategy and away from land forces and the European theater.

Specifically, Defense Department officials said that if Soviet forces were to invade the Persian Gulf region, the United States should have the capability to hit back there or in Cuba, Libya, Vietnam or the Asian land mass of the Soviet Union itself.

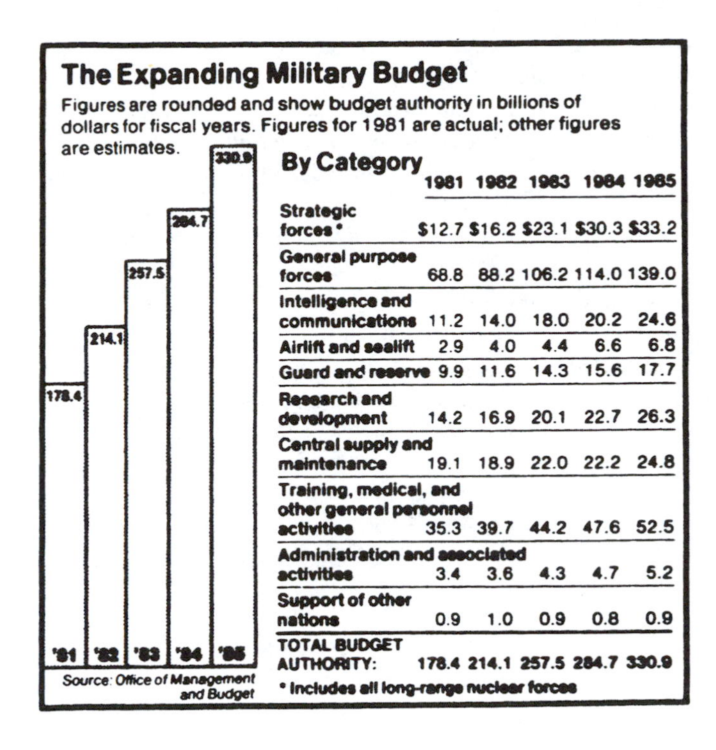
The Expanding Military Budget

Figures are rounded and show budget authority in billions of dollars for fiscal years. Figures for 1981 are actual; other figures are estimates.

Source: Office of Management and Budget

By Category

	1981	1982	1983	1984	1985
Strategic forces *	$12.7	$16.2	$23.1	$30.3	$33.2
General purpose forces	68.8	88.2	106.2	114.0	139.0
Intelligence and communications	11.2	14.0	18.0	20.2	24.6
Airlift and sealift	2.9	4.0	4.4	6.6	6.8
Guard and reserve	9.9	11.6	14.3	15.6	17.7
Research and development	14.2	16.9	20.1	22.7	26.3
Central supply and maintenance	19.1	18.9	22.0	22.2	24.8
Training, medical, and other general personnel activities	35.3	39.7	44.2	47.6	52.5
Administration and associated activities	3.4	3.6	4.3	4.7	5.2
Support of other nations	0.9	1.0	0.9	0.8	0.9
TOTAL BUDGET AUTHORITY:	178.4	214.1	257.5	284.7	330.9

* Includes all long-range nuclear forces

Congressional Challenge Likely

To support this strategy, the Administration wants to spend $216 billion in the fiscal year 1983, which starts Oct. 1, up from $183 billion this year. The Administration will ask Congress for military appropriations totaling $257.5 billion for the next fiscal year, an increase of $43.4 billion over the budget authority for the current fiscal year.

In presenting the budget today, Deputy Defense Secretary Frank C. Carlucci said that it was "fair to say we will find a challenge" to the military budget on Capitol Hill. But he added that the request was "fully justified when weighed against the military threat."

He also said the Administration considered this a "reform budget," with savings of billions of dollars resulting from new management techniques such as multiyear contracting.

The gap of more than $40 billion between appropriations, or budget authority, of $257.5 billion and actual expenditures, or outlays, of $216 billion is the largest in peacetime. It was exceeded only in the initial years of the Korean War and the Vietnam War. Its effect is to build up a bow wave of spending commitments in future years.

Worried Over Future Cutback

Officials in the Reagan Administration have made it clear that their intent is to get as much money for the military as possible, while support for these expenditures is high in Congress and in the public.

This is of great significance to Pentagon planners who are worried that economic pressures might cause the Administration to cut back military spending in future years, and that the only convenient place to reduce spending will be in what is called readiness—the capability of American forces to fight now. Readiness includes such accounts as operations and maintenance, training, spare parts and ammunition.

Administration officials note that the new military budget places heavy emphasis on readiness and will increase these accounts by 9 percent after discounting for inflation. But in years past, Congressional committees invariably slashed first those items that they considered unglamorous, such as operations and maintenance, in favor of procuring more ships and planes.

The sizeable increase in military spending proposed by Jimmy Carter last year at the end of his Presidency went almost entirely to increasing the readiness of existing forces. By contrast, the Reagan Administration's first military budget both adds to the capabilities of existing forces and places heavy emphasis on expanding forces.

Procurement of New Weapons

The new budget proposes an increase in the procurement of new weapons, to $55.1 billion in the fiscal year 1983 from $41.2 billion this year. Compared to other accounts, it is by far the largest proposed increase in outlays. For example, operation and maintenance would increase to $67 billion from $60 billion, manpower outlays would rise to $44 billion from $38 billion and research and development would reach $22 billion compared to $18 billion this year.

The budget calls for increasing spending on strategic nuclear forces to $23.1 billion from $16.2 billion. The big ticket items here are the new B-1B long-range bomber, a new submarine-launched ballistic missile called the Trident 2, new cruise missiles, defense against a bomber attack on the United States, a vast expansion of communications and control systems such as radars and radio links, and the new MX land-based ballistic missile.

This program reflects the decision to cancel the multi-billion-dollar mobile basing system for the MX missile. But a good part of the funds saved here would go to the B-1B bomber and the new strategic air defense programs.

Congressional opponents of the new bomber, an improved version of the B-1, are certain to ask again about the advisabililty of the program in the face of the new Stealth bomber program that also is under way. Similarly, questions will be raised about the wisdom of spending billions of dollars on defense against Soviet bombers when there is no defense against Soviet missiles that would strike the United States first.

Relative Imbalance Cited

In the budget document, President Reagan maintained that a review of American strategic forces "found that the relative imbalance with the Soviet Union will be at its worst in the mid-1980's and hence needs to be addressed quickly."

Spending authority on non-nuclear conventional forces, called general purpose forces in the budget, is planned to increase by 20 percent, to $106.2 billion from $88.2 billion. The Army will receive more money for the new M-I tank, other fighting vehicles and helicopters. The Air Force will be able to buy more tactical aircraft and additional Awacs radar surveillance planes.

Also scheduled for large increases are cargo ships and planes needed to deploy and sustain the Rapid Deployment Force. The budget calls for some $4.4 billion for a new fleet of improved C-5 giant cargo planes and KC-10A tanker and cargo aircraft, improving the SL-7 logistic ship and chartering additional ships to place equipment and supplies near potential trouble spots.

But the service that benefits most from the budget is the Navy. The President promised in his Budget Message to increase the number of ships from 513 to 600 by the end of the decade. For the next five years, he has proposed a $96 billion shipbuilding program for 133 ships, including six new Trident missile-firing submarines and two new nuclear-powered aircraft carriers.

Budget authority for the aircraft carriers is $6.8 billion. It would add to the present fleet of 13 carriers, only three of which are nuclear powered.

Funds for Cruise Missiles

The sea-launched cruise missile program also receives special attention. Two refurbished battleships and other vessels would be fitted with these new missiles, which would carry conventional warheads.

The $258 billion request for budget authority next year, when coupled with a projected average annual real, or after-inflation, growth in expenditures of 7.4 percent, leads to the five-year 1,640 billion total.

The $258 billion figure is solely for military expenditures made by the Department of Defense. It does not include $5.5 billion more spent by other agencies on nuclear research and the manufacture of material for nuclear warheads, nor does it include more than $1 billion in military aid to foreign countries.

In stressing the cost-saving programs that the Administration was implementing, Mr. Carlucci said that through such methods as the multiyear letting of contracts, the Pentagon would "save" $2.4 billion in the fiscal year 1983 and a total of $13.8 billion through the fiscal year 1987.

As an example, he offered the $6.8 billion full funding of the two new aircraft carriers. By building the two ships "in tandem" at the same shipyard so that work crews and equipment can move from one ship to another, he said, "we will be able to save $750 million and get delivery more than two years earlier."

Mr. Carlucci also said that the new procedures would give Congress a more accurate picture of military costs. In the past, he said, items were underpriced and inflation factors were too low.

* * *

April 3, 1982

ARGENTINA SEIZES FALKLAND ISLANDS; BRITISH SHIPS MOVE

By The Associated Press

BUENOS AIRES, April 2—Several thousand Argentine troops overcame 84 British marines today and seized the Falkland Islands in the South Atlantic.

The Argentine junta announced that army, navy and air force units captured the British-held Falklands, 250 miles off the southeastern tip of Argentina, and the South Georgia and South Sandwich Islands, British dependencies to the east.

President Reagan sought to persuade the head of the junta to call off the invasion, but his 50-minute telephone call was in vain.

Britain Assails 'Wanton Act'

At the United Nations, Britain called the invasion "a wanton act" and asked the Security Council to demand the immediate withdrawal of Argentine forces.

In London, the Government said "a substantial number of Royal Navy ships" were heading toward the islands, and a carrier task force was forming off the British coast.

Amateur radio operators in Stanley, the capital of the Falkland Islands, told the British Broadcasting Corporation that an Argentine aircraft carrier and four other ships put a large detachment of men ashore there with armored vehicles.

The radio operators said fighting lasted three hours, with heavy damage to buildings. One operator said the Argentine invaders were broadcasting communiqués in Spanish.

Islanders Are of British Descent

The vast majority of the 1,800 Falkland Islanders, who call themselves kelpers, are of British descent and want to remain under British control. They live off fishing and the production of mutton and wool.

The South Georgia and South Sandwich Islands have only a handful of inhabitants, mostly fishermen. Britain maintains an Antarctic research base at Grytviken on San Pedro, the largest island in the South Georgias.

The islands were discovered by a British explorer, Capt. John Davis, in 1592, and settled by the English, French and Spanish, mostly whalers. In 1770, Spain bought out the French and drove out the British.

Argentina claimed the islands after it gained independence from Spain in 1806, but Britain reclaimed them in 1832, declaring them a Crown Colony. Argentina never accepted the British move.

Many Inconclusive Talks

Argentina and Britain have held many talks, all inconclusive, on the future of the Falklands. Last year the islanders—and Argentina—rejected a British proposal that the Falklands be ceded to Argentina and leased back to Britain. Argentina insisted on control; the islanders insisted on remaining British.

Today, jubilant Argentines on the mainland cheered, waved flags, tooted horns, sounded sirens and tolled church bells, even though the Argentine military reported that one of its marine lieutenant commanders was killed and a lieutenant and a corporal were wounded by the British defenders. No British casualties were reported. Argentine military sources said that between 4,000 and 5,000 troops, led by a landing party of marines, took part in the capture of the Falklands, called the Malvinas by Argentina. The marines, put ashore by a naval vessel, seized the Stanley airport and secured it for use by C-130 troop transports.

The Argentine Government announced the appointment of Brig. Gen. Mario Benjamin Menendez as Governor of the islands, and said it would "guarantee the safety, lives, property and rights of British citizens and English-speaking Argentines in the islands."

About 200 people gathered outside Government House in Buenos Aires to wave flags and shout, "Argentina! Argentina!" Motorists honked their horns, sirens sounded and church bells rang in celebration in several cities.

The invasion came at a time of increasing domestic trouble for the Argentine regime. Last weekend, Argentines demonstrated against the junta's economic policies.

The issue of the islands' sovereignty has always been a patriotic rallying point for Argentines. But, also, valuable deposits of gas and oil are believed to be offshore.

'The National Honor'

The head of the Argentine military junta, Lieut. Gen. Leopoldo Galtieri, said in a nationwide broadcast, "We have regained the southern islands that legitimately form part of our national patrimony—safeguarding the national honor—without rancor, but with the firmness demanded by the circumstances."

He said the decision to take the islands was due "to a need to put an end to the interminable succession of British evasions and delays designed to perpetuate their dominion over the islands and their zone of influence."

Later, standing on a balcony of the Presidential Palace, he was cheered by some 5,000 flag-waving Argentines as small planes rained down leaflets declaring, "150 years of piracy ended," and "They're no longer the Falklands, now they're the Argentine Malvinas."

Events leading to the occupation of the islands were set in motion on March 19, when Argentine scrap-metal workers landed on San Pedro, reportedly to begin dismantling an abandoned whaling station purchased from a Scottish concern by an Argentine businessman.

Britain protested that the Argentines were on the island illegally and ordered them off, but the Argentines sent naval vessels to the area to "protect the interests" of Argentine citizens.

It was the first time since 1870 that Argentine military forces had been involved in a conflict outside their own mainland borders. In 1865, Argentina joined Brazil and Uruguay in a war against Paraguay. Paraguay held out for five years but in the end was devasted and a considerable part of its male population was killed.

BRITAIN APPEALS TO U.N.

Special to The New York Times.

UNITED NATIONS, N.Y., April 2—Britain said today that the invasion of the Falkland Islands was "a wanton act of armed force." It asked the Security Council to demand the immediate withdrawal of Argentina's troops.

Sir Anthony Parson, the British delegate, told the Council that Argentina had launched "a massive invasion" to force "unwanted control" over people who had chosen "to maintain their links with Britain and the British way of life."

Eduardo A. Roca, the Argentine delegate, replied that any charge of aggression was "absurd." His country, he said, has simply "recovered for its national sovereignty" islands that properly belonged to it.

Mr. Roca said Argentina was willing to negotiate any issue with Britain, "except for sovereignty." The Council tentatively plans to vote Saturday on the British resolution.

* * *

November 11, 1982

BREZHNEV IS DEAD IN SOVIET AT AGE 75; NO IMMEDIATE WORD ON A SUCCESSOR

U.S. FORESEES NO EARLY POLICY SHIFTS

By JOHN F. BURNS
Special to The New York Times.

MOSCOW, Thursday, Nov. 11—Leonid I. Brezhnev, the Soviet leader for 18 years, died yesterday, the state television announced this morning.

The announcement, carried simultaneously on radio and television and on the official press agency Tass, said: "The Central Committee of the Communist Party of the Soviet Union, the Presidium of the U.S.S.R. Supreme Soviet and the Council of Ministers of the U.S.S.R. inform with deep sorrow the party and the entire Soviet people that Leonid Ilyich Brezhnev, general secretary of the C.P.S.U. Central Committee and president of the Presidium of the U.S.S.R. Supreme Soviet, died a sudden death at 8:30 A.M. on Nov. 10, 1982.

"The name of Leonid Ilyich Brezhnev, a true continuer of Lenin's great cause and an ardent champion of peace and Communism, will live forever in the hearts of the Soviet people and the entire progressive mankind."

Cause of Death Not Given

The two-minute announcement was read twice on television by a dark-suited announcer. As he spoke the screen displayed a recent photograph of Mr. Brezhnev bordered by orange bands.

Mr. Brezhnev was 75 years old. The announcer gave no indication of the cause of Mr. Brezhnev's death. Nor did he give any suggestion of Mr. Brezhnev's successor as general secretary of the party or president of the Presidium of the Supreme Soviet.

Mr. Brezhnev had been in poor health for several years, apparently because of heart and respiratory problems. His last public appearance was on Sunday, when he stood for two hours atop the Lenin mausoleum in Red Square reviewing the annual military parade marking the 65th anniversary of the Bolshevik Revolution.

Later he spoke at a Kremlin reception attended by Soviet dignitaries and the diplomatic corps.

No Obvious Successor

Westerners at the parade were surprised that Mr. Brezhnev stayed so long in the subzero weather. Clad in a heavy overcoat and fur hat and with tinted sunglasses to shield the sun's glare, he stayed atop the mausoleum with other Politburo members more than twice as long as he did in 1981, when the weather was milder.

However, Soviet television offered few of the close-ups shots it had telecast of Mr. Brezhnev at past parades, and the Soviet leader appeared to be largely impassive. He rarely spoke to the generals and other political leaders alongside him.

Mr. Brezhnev's death left no obvious successor. The choice, to be formally made by the party's Central Committee, appeared to lie between a small group among the 12 surviving members of the Politburo.

3 in Line to Succeed

In recent months, public appearances by the leadership suggested that the effective second-in-command in the Kremlin was 71-year-old Konstantin U. Chernenko, a close aide to Mr. Brezhnev whose links with the party leader went back 30 years. At the Red Square parade on Sunday, Mr. Chernenko stood close to Mr. Brezhnev, separated only by Nikolai A. Tikhonov, the Prime Minister, who is not regarded as a likely successor.

Western diplomats believe that the strongest challenge to Mr. Chernenko is likely to come from Yuri V. Andropov, aged 68, who until this year was head of the K.G.B., the state security police, a post he held for 15 years. Like Mr. Chernenko, Mr. Andropov has dual membership in the Politburo and in another key group, the Secretariat of the Central Committee, which acts as a clearing house for all important party decisions.

Diplomats thought that some sort of contest between Mr. Chernenko and Mr. Andropov could develop. Although some analysts detected different shades of opinion in the speeches and writings of the two men, both were thought likely to follow the main lines of domestic and foreign policy under Mr. Brezhnev, including the pursuit of arms agreements with the United States.

A possible compromise candidate for the leadership in the event of a deadlock appeared to be Viktor V. Grishin, 68, a Politburo member who is head of the Moscow party apparatus. Mr. Grishin's position was enhanced last week when he was chosen to make a keynote speech in the Kremlin on the eve of the anniversary of the Revolution.

The speech followed closely the recent pronouncements by Mr. Brezhnev, attacking the Reagan Administration harshly for its arms policies but renewing the Soviet pledge to seek a relaxation of tensions.

Consensus Style of Leadership

The last time there was a change in the Soviet leadership, in October 1964, Nikita S. Khrushchev was ousted by his Politburo colleagues while he was vacationing in the Crimea. The previous shift occurred in 1953, on the death of Stalin. On that occasion, it took three years for Mr. Khrushchev to emerge from the jockeying for power as the pre-eminent leader.

As far as is known, the party leadership has made no arrangements since then that would ease the strains of succession. The situation now appears to be complicated somewhat by the fact that Mr. Brezhnev had developed what Western analysts described as a consensus style of leadership, which allowed for no clear successor to emerge.

Mr. Brezhnev died at a time when his policies had run into trouble at home and abroad. In the rare interviews he gave in the years before his death, he often cited détente with the West as his principal achievement. But the raft of accords on arms limits, human rights and trade that were reached with the United States and other Western countries in the early 1970's were placed under severe strain by the intervention of Soviet troops in Afghanistan and by the declaration of martial law in Poland in December 1981.

At home, Mr. Brezhnev was credited with establishing a period of stability that won him broad support among Soviet citizens traumatized by Stalin's terror and wearied by the erratic style of Mr. Khrushchev. In the early years, Mr. Brezhnev's policies led to considerable economic growth and a rising standard of living, reflected in the tens of millions of people who moved into new apartment blocks in the country's major cities. Many acquired private cars for the first time, and obtained modest country retreats, or dachas.

* * *

November 11, 1982

BREZHNEV ATTEMPTED TO ADVANCE SOVIET GOALS THROUGH DETENTE; SOVIET LEADER USED CONSENSUS IN POLITBURO ON DOMESTIC ISSUES

As the leader of the Soviet Union, Leonid Ilyich Brezhnev was a canny and careful Communist Party functionary who sought to make his country the military equal of the United States and promote its political influence around the world through the policy of détente.

In domestic affairs, as General Secretary of the Communist Party, Mr. Brezhnev (pronounced BRYEHZH-nyev) ruled as first among his equals on the Politburo, not as an autocrat, and professed to want economic development of his country of 265 million people spread over a sixth of the globe's land area.

Both his policy and his health faltered in these tasks in the last years of his life. Détente, which had seemed a necessity to many Western leaders after Soviet tanks moved into Czechoslovakia in 1968 to crush the liberalization of the "Prague Spring," lost much of its appeal in the United States after the Soviet invasion of Afghanistan in 1979, and President Carter imposed an embargo on grain sales and other trade curbs.

After the Polish military authorities ceded to pressure from Moscow and declared martial law in December 1981, President Reagan imposed further economic and political sanctions on the Soviet Union, though not an embargo on grain sales. The Western European allies remained more reluctant to cut back their important industrial trade with the Russians, and insisted on going ahead with the deal, creating a political rift within the NATO alliance that Mr. Brezhnev obviously sought to exploit.

But domestic economic stagnation had become an acute domestic problem by the end of the Brezhnev years. In this area, despite their recognition of the crisis, the aging Soviet leaders made no effective attempt to reform the rigidities of centralized economic planning. And as the standard of living declined, political repression increased. Dissidents, who had emerged openly in the mid-1970's to criticize violations of human rights, were later harassed until most had either left the country or were in prison camps by the early 1980's. Soviet Jews, who had been permitted to emigrate by the thousands a month in 1977 and 1978, found that by 1982 permission to emigrate was virtually impossible to get.

In his last years, Mr. Brezhnev's speech became labored and his features pale and bloated, apparently as a result of medical treatments for a disability that was never publicly revealed. At the height of his powers in the early 1970's, in contacts with Presidents Nixon, Ford and Carter and Secretary of State Henry A. Kissinger, he was a burly, gray-haired, black-browed figure of 5 feet 10 inches, gregarious and talkative, but powerful and very much aware of his power over associates and adversaries alike.

Then he had a reputation as a lover of good food and drink, fast cars—which he collected—and hunting. Mr. Brezhnev talked extensively about his weight, which he sought vainly to keep under control, and often joked about his excessive cigarette smoking, which was thought to have aggravated his health problems.

His smoking (Philip Morris Multifilters) was such a vexation that he used a box with a time lock to slow his pace. But he conceded to one visitor, "I keep a reserve pack in the other pocket." Ultimately he had to give up smoking altogether.

Long Part of Coalition

Mr. Brezhnev was long part of a coalition in the ruling Politburo of his party's Central Committee. Two other members of the coalition who for years were most visible to the West were Prime Minister Aleksei N. Kosygin, who died in December 1980, and President Nikolai V. Podgorny, who was ousted from the leadership group in 1977.

In the early years, after this coalition had ousted Nikita S. Khrushchev in a bloodless coup in 1964, it operated as a troika, with none of its members seemingly more authoritative than the others.

Prominent, first in support of Mr. Khrushchev and then as a member of the coalition that ousted him, was Mikhail A. Suslov, the party's ideologist. As Mr. Brezhnev encountered growing problems with his health, Mr. Suslov's authority, already enormous, seemed to grow to the point where many considered him the second-ranking figure in the hierarchy. But death removed the ascetic ideologist from the leadership on Jan. 25, 1982, at the age of 79.

In the fall of 1970 Mr. Brezhnev emerged from his post as the party chief to become the personal ambassador for détente. This occurred in his first meeting with Chancellor Willy Brandt of West Germany and in a subsequent conference with President Charles de Gaulle of France.

In these and in other meetings in 1971, the Soviet leader appeared stiff and uncomfortable, but he loosened up remarkably as his self-confidence grew.

On June 11, 1979, Mr. Brezhnev and President Carter, meeting in the ornate Hofburg Palace in Vienna, signed an arms control treaty that for the first time limited both sides to the same maximum number of long-range bombers and missiles.

For millions of television viewers around the globe, Soviet-Western rapprochement was symbolized when the two leaders embraced just after the signing and, to a crescendo of applause from onlookers, Mr. Brezhnev gave Mr. Carter hearty kisses, Russian-style, on both cheeks.

Despite the optimism expressed by the two men at the signing ceremony, the treaty came under criticism from a number of United States senators who believed it conferred a unilateral advantage on the Soviet Union in heavy land-based missiles. Mr. Carter withdrew the treaty from Senate consideration after the invasion of Afghanistan, and it was never approved by the Senate.

Détente Policy Set Back

Mr. Brezhnev's détente policy was further set back by the establishment of martial law in Poland in December 1981. With the intervention in Afghanistan began a hardening of attitudes in the West, including an American boycott of the Moscow Olympics in 1980 and the imposition of trade restrictions by the United States and other Western countries; Mr. Brezhnev criticized these steps as a return to the cold war, but never acknowledged the Soviet Union's responsibility for provoking them.

Instead, in his statements and speeches, Mr. Brezhnev sought to portray his country as still open to arms reductions talks and détente, not only with the West but also, with increasing emphasis as relations with the West deteriorated, with China.

In February 1982, the Soviet leader proposed a two-thirds cut by 1990 in both sides' medium-range nuclear arsenals in Europe. He said the Soviet Union was ready to reach agreement not only on the complete termination of all tests of nuclear weapons but also on ending their further production and on the reduction and subsequent elimination of their stockpiles.

Early in March he announced that Moscow was suspending its deployment of new medium-range missiles in the European part of the Soviet Union. He said this was intended to set "a good example."

But United States officials saw his moves as attempts "to convey the impression of restraint while diverting attention from the enormous growth of Soviet capability."

In a public appearance in Tashkent on March 24, Brezhnev issued a new appeal to Peking to revive the search for ways to end the Chinese-Soviet feud. "We remember well the time when the Soviet Union and People's China were united by bonds of friendship and comradely cooperation," he said. Negotiations with the Chinese did resume in the fall of 1982, and Mr. Brezhnev, in a speech to an audience of Soviet generals shortly afterward, said that while the prospects of a real improvement in relations were slim, the Soviet Union had an interest in pressing for them.

Regarding détente with the West, the still unratified arms control treaty with the United States entailed some Soviet concessions, but on several other issues, Mr. Brezhnev's approach to the policy—called "peaceful coexistence" under Mr. Khrushchev—accomplished much for the Soviet Union.

These accomplishments included strategic nuclear parity with the United States; an increase in conventional military strength on land and at sea; acknowledgment by West Germany and the rest of Western Europe of the division of Germany and of Europe; recognition of East Germany and its admission to the United Nations; increasing imports of Western technology to modernize the Soviet economy, and a growing role in the Middle East and Africa.

Concession on Emigration

These were attained with few concessions to the West. A major concession—or certainly the most publicized—was the Soviet willingness to permit some emigration, mostly for Jews, starting in the late 1960's.

The policy of allowing emigration for Soviet citizens was, however, a controversial one within the leadership, and there were periodic indications, especially from the police apparatus, of disquiet with this relaxation of traditional curbs. The most recent tightening came in 1981 in response to stiffening Western positions over the intervention in Afghanistan.

In addition, there was some evidence that Mr. Brezhnev's critics in Moscow felt that he had not gained sufficient trade and credit advantages in bargaining with the United States.

Efforts in Washington to make improved commercial ties dependent on further relaxation of emigration restrictions illustrated one of the practical problems of détente. Mr. Brezhnev could not explicitly lift emigration barriers because this might be construed as bowing to external pressures, and the United States could not do less than insist, owing to its domestic pressures.

Although Mr. Brezhnev and American Presidents were in accord on avoiding situations that might lead to armed conflict, there were world areas where the interests of the two superpowers clashed. In the Middle East, the Soviet Union supported Arab nationalism with arms and technical experts and carried on a campaign to discredit Israel. Syria and Iraq were among the main beneficiaries of Soviet backing.

When strikes and rioting in Iran in late 1978 began to build up into a revolution, Mr. Brezhnev issued a warning against "outside interference, especially military interference" by the United States. At about the same time, he cemented Moscow's ties with the new pro-Soviet regime in Afghanistan by signing a 20-year treaty of friendship and cooperation, binding the two countries to close economic and military links.

In the Horn of Africa, the power balance was reversed as Ethiopia, once a client of the United States, shifted to the Soviet camp, while Somalia, once close to Moscow, effected a rapprochement with Washington.

Invasion of Czechoslovakia

There was also an adversary conflict over India. In Southeast Asia, Soviet military aid helped North Vietnam to victory over American-supported South Vietnam. In Central America, the Reagan Administration charged that the Soviet Union, through its Cuban allies, was trying to expand Communist influence in Nicaragua under the Sandinista regime that came to power in 1979, and by supporting the leftist guerrilla movement in El Salvador.

In Europe, on the other hand, the superpowers were less at daggers drawn. One evidence of this was the change in Western attitudes toward Czechoslovakia after 1968. In that year, Soviet-led forces went into Czechoslovakia to depose Alexander Dubcek, the Communist leader who had become an apostate from Kremlin orthodoxy. Mr. Brezhnev, defending the incursion, found his name associated with "the Brezhnev Doctrine" —that the Soviet Union had a right to enforce by arms its control in Eastern Europe.

The bluntness of Mr. Brezhnev's interventions in Czechoslovak internal affairs was as much condemned then as the baldness of his doctrine. Ranged against him were not only a large segment of public opinion in the West, but also dissenters within two major Communist parties in Western Europe.

Both the French and the Italian parties rebuked Mr. Brezhnev, and their assertion of independence from Moscow developed into the separate line of Communist development known as Eurocommunism, though it also faded towards the end of his rule.

Despite the Czechoslovak episode, Mr. Brezhnev managed to maintain the cohesiveness of Eastern Europe, and only independent-minded Rumania was the odd man out in retaining cordial relations with China.

But the cohesion among Moscow's allies in Eastern Europe came under strain—more even perhaps than occurred over Hungary in 1956 and Czechoslovakia in 1968—as the rise of the Solidarity trade union movement in Poland in 1980 fostered a wide-ranging liberalization of Polish life that ended in December 1981 with the imposition of martial law.

Chinese-Soviet Dispute

With China, Mr. Brezhnev maintained strictly correct relations at the governmental level while hurling anathemas against the Peking leadership, both in the last decade of Mao Zedong's life and under Mao's successors. For a long time, the Chinese-Soviet dispute was both doctrinal and territorial, and it involved a struggle for hegemony over nationalist and revolutionary forces in the third world. Soviet policy toward the Chinese fluctuated in response to changes in the situation.

At first, Mr. Brezhnev made a number of efforts to convoke a congress of adherents to Moscow's version of Communism that would read China out of the world Communist movement, but he was unable to gather a sufficiently impressive alignment.

This failure was ascribed partly to an underlying distaste among Communists, even in the Soviet Union, to a formal splitting of the Communist movement; partly to Peking's stature in strategic areas of the third world, and partly to hope among substantial segments of pro-Moscow Communists that the Soviet Union and China could ultimately be reconciled.

The confrontation never escalated to the point of war. When China invaded Vietnam early in 1979, Mr. Brezhnev duly warned Peking to halt its "brazen bandit attack," but the statement was relatively subdued in tone. Tentative moves to improve relations betweeen the two countries followed; at the same time, Vietnam fell clearly into the Soviet sphere of influence.

Mr. Brezhnev's power within the Soviet Union derived from his position as the head of the ruling party rather than from his assumption of the nation's presidency—for the second time—in 1977. In the gradual loosening of the Soviet system of one-man rule, Mr. Brezhnev was not, however, the single dominant leader, as Lenin, Stalin and Khrushchev had been, and he sought, not always successfully, to reduce many of the trappings of "the cult of personality" that Stalin and then Khrushchev had nurtured.

Because Mr. Brezhnev's power was more circumscribed than that of his predecessors, he was obliged to come to terms with often competing interests.

Careful Arms Negotiator

One of the groups that Mr. Brezhnev had to take into account was the military establishment. Like their counterparts in Western countries, Soviet military leaders tended to favor large budgets, impressive displays of weaponry and conservative mentalities. But the Soviet leader was never so much at odds with his "military-industrial complex" as some Western politicians and analysts thought and hoped.

In the slow-moving negotiations on the limitation of strategic arms, Mr. Brezhnev bargained carefully with American Presidents, constantly checking during the negotiations with other Politburo members, including the representatives of the military. He always seemed careful to move in tandem with the military on all significant policy issues.

On the other hand, Mr. Brezhnev, by wheeling and dealing (how was never made public), altered the complexion of the Politburo over the years so that he was able to accumulate a large measure of personal power without arousing his colleagues' fears of a return to one-man rule. Shortly after the collective leadership was installed in 1964, he neutralized Aleksandr N. Shelepin, an ambitious Politburo member, by shifting him from control of the security police to the trade union leadership.

And in December 1965, he persuaded Mr. Podgorny to yield a key party secretary's post to become chairman of the Presidium of the Supreme Soviet, a ceremonial post equivalent to that of President of the Union of Soviet Socialist Republics. Mr. Podgorny was to hold the presidency for 12 years until Mr. Brezhnev himself assumed that post in addition to the party leadership.

In 1971 four new men, all Brezhnev supporters, were elected to the Politburo. And two years later he eased out

Pyotr Y. Shelest and Gennadi I. Voronov, both considered opponents of détente. Despite this seeming majority in the Politburo, which was further consolidated in subsequent years, Mr. Brezhnev was subject to scrutiny on such matters as the performance of the economy, the size of the grain harvest, corruption in the party machinery and the development of Siberia. In addition, of course, the détente policy was examined from time to time in terms of specific Soviet advantages, political and commercial.

One of Mr. Brezhnev's dreams was to oversee the rapid development of Siberia with the aid of outside credits and technology. Blocked by United States reluctance to commit substantial capital to the venture, he turned increasingly to Western Europe and Japan for partners in Siberian development projects.

Projected Air of Realism

The ebullience Mr. Brezhnev displayed abroad or to foreign visitors was in contrast to his staid and conservative deportment in Soviet public life. There he was very much the Communist in the gray flannel suit, proper and formal and serious. The air he projected was one of realism, calmness and stability.

He was not much in the public view, except on ceremonial occasions. Nonetheless, there seemed to be a conscious effort to humanize him in official photographs that showed him, for example, in shirtsleeve talks with Chancellor Brandt of West Germany, greeting women factory workers in Yugoslavia with a kiss on the lips, hoisting up young children in Poland, or wearing dark glasses and an open-necked windbreaker and leaning against the gunwales of a yacht.

Although Mr. Brezhnev appeared to enjoy the limelight, he was careful to let a share fall on his principal colleagues. Both Mr. Kosygin and—while he was President—Mr. Podgorny journeyed abroad from time to time, and Foreign Minister Andrei A. Gromyko, who was elevated to Politburo membership under Mr. Brezhnev, remained the principal Soviet spokesman abroad.

Mr. Brezhnev's attitude toward expressions of dissent in the Soviet Union was firm. A number of intellectuals, artists and scientists opposed the Kremlin's ideological policies in whole or in part, and there was restiveness among Soviet youth.

Outspoken dissidents in the Brezhnev years often found themselves committed to prison, mental institutions or deprived of their jobs. Some were deported to the West, notably Aleksandr I. Solzhenitsyn, the novelist. Those who remained, including Andrei D. Sakharov, were denounced as lacking in socialist consciousness, which meant a refusal to place their talents at the disposal of the ruling ideology.

Describes His Ideology

As Mr. Brezhnev described his views a couple of years ago: "People who fall for self-publicity, ready to make a name for themselves not through work for the homeland but by any politically dubious means—and not disdaining to praise our ideological opponents—sometimes fall into their net. The Soviet public harshly denounces the abominable deeds of these double-dealers.

"Renegades should not expect to get away unpunished. The country's enemies clutch with great tenacity at any manifestations of ideological immaturity or hesitation among the intellectuals."

Mr. Brezhnev left the formulation of ideology to others, chiefly Mr. Suslov, the party ideologist and Politburo member whose close association with the party leader grew in the years after the ouster of Mr. Khrushchev in 1964. Mr. Brezhnev's speeches were often more pragmatic than ideological, although earlier he had studded his remarks with Marxist references to the decline and corruption of capitalism. But he avoided the flourishes that were associated with Mr. Khrushchev, who once promised "to bury capitalism." Nor did Mr. Brezhnev contend, as his predecessor did, that the Soviet Union would become a wonderland of material satisfactions while the United States and other capitalist societies were developing into wastelands for their citizens.

Mr. Brezhnev and his colleagues displayed some uncertainties in handling Soviet public opinion, especially regarding Stalinism. Whereas Mr. Khrushchev had pursued a clear-cut policy of de-Stalinization after denouncing Stalin's excesses in 1956, the Brezhnev group tempered the policy on the ground that it was undermining the authority and unity of the Communist system.

The Stalin issue, with which the Soviet Union has not come fully to terms, was hushed up, but a nostalgia for some aspects of Stalin's rule was permitted to revive. His leadership in World War II was occasionally mentioned; his face reappeared on movie screens; and his bust was mounted on his grave behind the Lenin Mausoleum in Red Square.

The memory of Mr. Khrushchev was, on the contrary, long drowned in official silence. The anniversaries of his death were not noted, nor was his regime recalled in panegyrics.

But Mr. Brezhnev, in reminiscences published in November 1978 in the Soviet magazine Novy Mir, gave Mr. Khrushchev some credit as an administrator of agricultural policy—although he also described him as having been petulant, stubborn and apt to use strong language.

When Mr. Brezhnev came to power after Mr. Khrushchev's ouster, his hold on the Communist party seemed a little uncertain at first. In recent years, however, he appeared to accept greater deference as due his position as both the nation's President and the party's chief.

For Red Square parades, for instance, he usually mounted to the reviewing stand on the top of the Lenin Mausoleum ahead of other members of the Politburo. When the crowd applauded, he sometimes doffed his hat, waved and smiled in response. Mr. Kosygin and others looked at the throng but refrained from responding to its acclaim.

In contrast to the endless anecdotes illuminating Mr. Khrushchev's jaunty and unpredictable personality, little humor surrounded Mr. Brezhnev or his colleagues. But Soviet citizens quietly exchanged jokes about the Soviet leader, most of them unflattering.

He rode around Moscow in a ZIL limousine, modeled after the 1965 Lincoln Continental, and he was often observed riding out of the Kremlin on a Sunday afternoon through crowds of visitors. He was in the front seat beside the driver with only one security guard in the back and no escort vehicles. The crowd looked at him blankly, and he looked back in the same fashion.

Some Earthy Amusements

Because of his position, he had a choice of good housing, but he continued to live in his old apartment on Kutuzov Prospekt. In moments away from his office in the Kremlin, he seemed to enjoy earthy amusements and glad-handing.

Once at a circus performance, women performers in scanty costumes presented him with bouquets of flowers. He thanked the first few with kisses. Then a few more. And then he made certain that those at the rear were not omitted, for they, too, received hearty, full-faced busses. Finally, he donned his glasses and settled back to watch the performance, with the pleasure of one who finds a circus more entertaining than the ballet or an opera.

Mr. Brezhnev's broad face with its dominating eyebrows often lost some of its impassivity at cocktail parties, once he could down an impressive number of cognacs or straight vodkas. In the last few years, though, he was under physicians' orders to cut down on drinking.

Before he assumed the party leadership in 1964 and when he traveled abroad on good-will missions during a previous stint as President, he liked to unbend in toasts. On a visit to Iran in 1963, after toasting a seemingly endless list of worthy objectives, he lifted his vodka glass to exclaim: "Down with protocol! Long live freedom!"

In some private conversations he displayed a certain candor. In 1963, while talking with Glenn T. Seaborg, then chairman of the United States Atomic Energy Commission, he conceded that most Soviet buildings were hideous and suggested that the Soviet Union might profit by sending some of its young architects abroad to study.

Although Mr. Brezhnev did not have much time for hobbies, he was known to enjoy hunting, swimming and watching soccer. He also collected antique watches and was an ardent ornithologist, reputed to have one of the finest collections of live birds in Moscow. He had an interest in agriculture and land reclamation.

Born in the Ukraine

Before his rise to eminence as Mr. Khrushchev's protege, Mr. Brezhnev was not conspicuous in Soviet life. Of Great Russian parentage, he was born Dec. 19, 1906, in Kamenskoye, now Dneprodzerzhinsk, in the Ukraine. His father was a steelworker.

The boy began his working life at 15 in the local steel mill. Starting in 1923, he went to school nights and was graduated four years later from a land survey and reclamation school in Kursk.

In this period he joined the Komsomol, the Young Communist League, and at the age of 25 he was accepted as a member of the Communist Party. At the same time he entered the steel engineering school in his hometown. He was graduated in 1935 and worked as an engineer for two years.

In May 1937 he was elected deputy mayor of Dneprodzerzhinsk, his first post in government. Having impressed party leaders with his abilities, he was promoted the following year to a party secretaryship of Dnepropetrovsk Province at a time when Mr. Khrushchev headed the party in the Ukraine. Their friendship is believed to have begun at that time.

In World War II Mr. Brezhnev served with the Red Army as a political commissar with the 18th Army in a beachhead on the Black Sea coast of the Caucasus, in the Crimea and in the Ukraine. On his 60th birthday Soviet authorities reviewed his war record and said:

"In the period of severe trials during the Great Patriotic War against Hitler's aggressors, while directing the army's political department and the southern and fourth Ukrainian front's political boards, you played a direct part in devising and conducting combat operations; you experienced such historic engagements as the battle of the Caucasus, and the liberation of Crimea and the Ukraine. The fighting men and commanders of the Soviet Army know you as an outstanding political worker and a man of great spirit and courage."

Mr. Brezhnev's wartime exploits were also romanticized and effusively praised in biographical articles that began appearing in the late 1970's. By then, he also carried the honorific title of Marshal of the Soviet Union.

Mr. Brezhnev's war experience was the foundation for his many friendships among Soviet military men, who were one of the chief sources of his later influence in party and government affairs.

Mr. Brezhnev, returning to civilian life in 1946, was named to a series of responsible party posts in the Ukraine, supervising postwar reconstruction, and was then brought to Moscow in 1950 for further seasoning in the Central Committee's secretariat.

In the middle of 1950 he was sent to the Moldavian Republic as party leader, a post he held for two years. Simultaneously, he was elected a member of the national Central Committee and a candidate member of its Presidium, as the Politburo was then called. He was also named a national secretary, a position he occupied until the death of Stalin in 1953.

When the party leadership was reorganized after the dictator's death, Mr. Brezhnev was dropped from the secretaryship and from the Presidium, apparently because he was not in the confidence of Vyacheslav M. Molotov, Georgi M. Malenkov and others who took over from Stalin.

After a brief return to political work in the Ministry of Defense as the chief political commissar of the armed forces, Mr. Brezhnev resumed his rise in the party hierarchy in July 1957, when Mr. Khrushchev ousted some of his rivals from the leadership.

Supervised Virgin Lands

For his loyalty to Mr. Khrushchev, Mr. Brezhnev was rewarded with the leadership of the republic of Kazakhstan. His job was to supervise Mr. Khrushchev's virgin lands project, which brought vast acreage into productive use. In two years 87 million acres were placed under cultivation.

Mr. Brezhnev had proved the program a success, confounding experts who had forecast its failure. The project later ran into difficulties, but not until Mr. Brezhnev had earned a splendid reputation as an administrator, a man who could accomplish the impossible.

After being called back to Moscow, Mr. Brezhnev was made President of the Soviet Union in 1960, replacing Marshal Kliment Y. Voroshilov. As President, Mr. Brezhnev became a traveling salesman for the Soviet system, visiting Italy, North Korea, Finland, Morocco, Guinea, Ghana, Yugoslavia and Iran. His travels and his friendship with Mr. Khrushchev convinced many observers that he was being groomed as the party leader's successor.

That speculation increased in 1963, when Mr. Brezhnev combined his job as President with that of second national secretary of the party, in charge of personnel selection. Then, in the summer of 1964, he stepped down as President to devote full time to his party tasks.

Suddenly that fall, criticism of Mr. Khrushchev within the party councils came to an abrupt climax, and he was obliged to retire, ostensibly because of his age (he was in his 70's) and his health.

Although there was no official bill of particulars, it became known that he had been ousted on accusations of bungling the Cuban missile crisis with the United States in 1962, mishandling the Soviet rift with China, mismanaging the Soviet economy and supporting a cult of personality.

Although he defended his policies, his removal from office by the Central Committee's Presidium was confirmed by the committee itself. In his stead the collective leadership of Mr. Brezhnev, Mr. Kosygin and Mr. Podgorny took over.

Four days later Mr. Brezhnev and his associates appeared atop the Lenin Mausoleum at a celebration for three astronauts, the first to circle the earth in a multiseat spacecraft.

Speaking in a deep baritone and reading his address through darkrimmed glasses, Mr. Brezhnev promised to spur the economy, lift living standards and insure social democracy. In foreign matters, he said, the Soviet Union would continue efforts toward peaceful coexistence with capitalist states.

Seeking to assure the Soviet public, to which he was virtually unknown, he also promised that the party's new leaders would "constantly feel the pulse of the people's life."

Health Seemed to Decline

Mr. Brezhnev subsequently became, of course, well known to the Soviet public, and in recent years the state of his health became a continual subject of speculation in the Soviet Union as elsewhere.

A United States intelligence report, early in 1978, that he was suffering from gout, leukemia and emphysema was not officially confirmed, but by February 1979 it was evident that he was ailing.

He seemed to lack stamina, to have become unable to put in the long work days that his position required, to be leaning more heavily than in the past on such aides as Konstantin U. Chernenko, who became a full member of the Politburo in November 1978.

At the same time several other allies of Mr. Brezhnev were promoted to the inner circle of the Soviet leadership, but the shifts gave no hint of who his eventual successor might be.

Mr. Brezhnev's apparent ill health was in evidence during his meeting with President Carter in June 1979, which was the first Soviet-American summit meeting since late 1974.

While in Vienna, Mr. Brezhnev was seen to stumble on a couple of occasions, and he shut his eyes from apparent fatique while President Carter made a short public statement on the day the treaty was signed.

And in his trip to East Berlin in October 1979, Mr. Brezhnev's condition seemed to have deteriorated even further as he frequently slurred his words during his 35-minute address to the East German Parliament.

Mr. Brezhnev held a number of decorations. In 1961 he was made a Hero of Socialist Labor "for outstanding services in the development of rocket technology and in guaranteeing the successful flight of man into outer space in the Sputnik spacecraft 'Vostok.' " The citation did not elaborate on his contributions to that flight, nor did his official biography specify his role.

He also held five Orders of Lenin and was twice given the title of Hero of the Soviet Union, on his 60th and 70th birthdays. In keeping with Soviet practice, little of Mr. Brezhnev's family life was in the public domain. It was known that he and his wife, Viktoriya, had three children; two sons, one of whom, Yuri, is a First Deputy Minister of Foreign Trade, the other a student at Moscow University; and a daughter, Galina, who works as a journalist at Novosti, the Soviet news feature agency.

* * *

November 13, 1982

ANDROPOV IS CHOSEN TO HEAD SOVIET PARTY; VOWS HE WILL CONTINUE BREZHNEV POLICIES

By JOHN F. BURNS

Special to The New York Times.

MOSCOW, Nov. 12—Yuri V. Andropov was chosen by the Communist Party's Central Committee today to succeed Leonid I. Brezhnev as its General Secretary, making him the Soviet Union's principal political leader.

Until six months ago, Mr. Andropov headed the K.G.B., the Committee for State Security, and was in charge of the internal security police and foreign espionage operations. His appointment today came barely 48 hours after Mr. Brezhnev's death. The selection was said to have been unanimously approved by the Central Committee.

Mr. Andropov was nominated for the post by Konstantin U. Chernenko, a longtime lieutenant to Mr. Brezhnev who had been considered Mr. Andropov's principal rival for the top party job.

Supreme Soviet to Meet Nov. 23

There was immediate speculation that Mr. Chernenko would be named to the other post held by Mr. Brezhnev, the largely ceremonial one of chairman of the Presidium of the Supreme Soviet, the head of state. If this happened it could signify that Mr. Andropov shared power in a collective leadership in the Politburo, as Mr. Brezhnev did for a few years after he became General Secretary in 1964.

The new head of state is almost certain to be known by Nov. 23, when the Supreme Soviet, the country's nominal parliament, meets for its regular winter session.

In a speech just before his election, Mr. Andropov, who is 68 years old, pledged himself to the continuation of the domestic and foreign policies followed under Mr. Brezhnev, who died Wednesday at the age of 75. In a eulogy delivered immediately before the Central Committee ratified his appointment, Mr. Andropov called Mr. Brezhnev a "tireless fighter for peace" and praised him "for removing the threat of world nuclear war hanging over mankind."

Soviet's 'Invincible Might'

But Mr. Andropov did not specifically mention détente or disarmament, policies that his predecessor considered his greatest accomplishments and to which Mr. Brezhnev rededicated the Soviet leadership in his last speech, on Sunday. Instead Mr. Andropov appeared to emphasize what the Russians regard as the need to meet foreign threats by maintaining powerful armed forces.

"We know well that the imperialists will never meet one's pleas for peace," he said. "It can only be defended by relying on the invincible might of the Soviet armed forces."

The choice of the new party leader came at a specially convened Central Committee meeting that appeared to have lasted less than an hour. Mr. Chernenko, who is 71, indicated that the election was a formality by saying in his speech that the task of nominating Mr. Andropov had been "entrusted" to him by the Politburo, the inner cabinet of the Central Committee, which is the country's effective ruling body.

The swift designation of Mr. Andropov as party leader surprised many Western diplomats, who had thought that Mr. Chernenko's rival claim on the post could delay a decision. Since the effective withdrawal from political activity earlier this year of Andrei P. Kirilenko, 76, who was long favored as a possible successor to Mr. Brezhnev, Mr. Chernenko had played an increasingly prominent role as the party leader's principal deputy.

The Politburo's apparent success in averting a power struggle, at least for the time being, was taken by some analysts as a measure of increasing maturity in the Soviet system. The lack of a certain procedure for transferring authority and for securing a new party leader against challenge led in part to the traumas of Stalin's terror and led to a bitter struggle after his death in 1953 that was not resolved in Nikita S. Khrushchev's favor for several years.

Powerhouse in the Soviet System

But diplomats cautioned that the appointment of Mr. Andropov did not necessarily signal that he enjoyed unchallenged primacy. Although the General Secretary's job has been the principal powerhouse in the Soviet system since Stalin occupied it in the early 1920's, there have been several periods since 1917 when its occupant has had to share ultimate authority with several others.

In the struggle after Stalin's death the job went effectively to Georgi M. Malenkov, Stalin's choice, but he lost it within a week, and it was six months before Mr. Khrushchev was named to the position and another three or four years before he finally overtook Mr. Malenkov, Nikolai A. Bulganin and others. And when Mr. Brezhnev got the job after Mr. Khrushchev's ouster in 1964, he shared power for several years with the Prime Minister, Aleksei N. Kosygin, and the chairman of the Supreme Soviet, Nikolai V. Podgorny.

The speeches at the Central Committee meeting that designated Mr. Andropov underlined the careful path he must tread if he is to build up the sort of authority that Mr. Brezhnev had in the second half of his 18 years in power. Although Mr. Chernenko emphasized that he nominated Mr. Andropov at the command of the Politburo, both Mr. Andropov and Mr. Chernenko stressed the importance of "collective leadership" and unity.

Mr. Andropov made the point twice, once when he extolled Mr. Brezhnev's efforts to advance the "close-knit, collective work" of the "party headquarters," and again toward the close of his speech. His phrasing suggested that he was offering an assurance that he would not abuse his position to place others in the Politburo—some of them men in their 70's and older, with nearly a generation in the top Kremlin ranks—in subordinate roles.

'Unity of Our Party Ranks'

"We comrades have such a force which helped and continues to help us at the most difficult moments, a force which enables us to tackle the most complicated tasks," Mr. Andropov said. "This force is the unity of our party ranks, this force is the collective wisdom of the party, its collective leadership, this force is the unity of the party and the people."

Mr. Chernenko also spoke of the party and its 18 million members as being "united and close-knit," adding what could have been a warning to Mr. Andropov not to test his Politburo colleagues' loyalty. "All of us are obviously aware that it is extremely difficult to make up for the loss that was inflicted on us by the death of Leonid Ilyich Brezhnev," he said. "It is now twice, thrice more important to conduct matters in the party collectively."

Mr. Chernenko added, "Concerted, joint work in all party bodies will insure further successes both in Communist construction and in our activities in the international scene."

Mr. Chernenko described Mr. Andropov as Mr. Brezhnev's "closest associate" and said Mr. Brezhnev had "highly valued" Mr. Andropov's "dedication to the party, his broad vision, outstanding efficiency and personality."

'Safeguard and Strengthen Peace'

In addition, he said, "all members of the Politburo believe that Yuri Vladimirovich assimilated well Brezhnev's style of leadership, Brezhnev's concern about the interests of the people, Brezhnev's attitude to cadres, determination to stand up with all strength to the machinations of aggressors, to safeguard and strengthen peace."

In many respects, the speech must have been a difficult one for Mr. Chernenko. For 30 years, since he joined Mr. Brezhnev's staff at the party headquarters in Moldavia, a Soviet republic on the Rumanian border, it has been he, not Mr. Andropov, who has been considered to be Mr. Brezhnev's "closest associate." And events of recent months suggested that he was Mr. Brezhnev's choice for the succession.

As recently as Sunday, when Mr. Brezhnev appeared for the last time atop the Lenin mausoleum to review the annual military parade through Red Square, Mr. Chernenko was positioned next in order of precedence to Mr. Brezhnev after Nikolai A. Tikhonov, the 77-year-old Prime Minister, who usually stands beside the party leader on such occasions. Mr. Andropov was one place farther away.

At the time, this was taken as confirmation of a pattern that was repeated throughout the summer and fall. Mr. Chernenko, long regarded as a lackluster bureaucrat, began to speak out with increasing authority on matters of defense, foreign policy, ideology, culture and economic management. Last year he went to France for the Communist Party congress there, another signal of his stature.

The K.G.B. Position

For 15 years, until May of this year, Mr. Andropov was chairman of the K.G.B., one of the most powerful positions in the country but one with associations that in the past had been thought to disqualify its occupant from aspirations to the leadership of the party. Stalin's K.G.B. chief, Lavrenti P. Beria, was so feared by other Politburo members that he was executed in the struggle after Stalin's death.

In March there were reports that Mr. Brezhnev had suffered a heart attack while on a trip to Tashkent, in Soviet Uzbekistan. He disappeared from view for two weeks, and when he resumed his activities it was plain that he was fading. Shortly afterward, Mr. Andropov left the K.G.B. foreboding headquarters on Dzerzhinsky Square and was replaced as K.G.B. chief by Vitaly V. Fedorchuk, a career K.G.B. officer.

The move was heralded as Mr. Andropov's opening shot in the contest for the succession. Within days he was appointed to the Central Committee Secretariat, a group as exclusive as the Politburo that is headed by the General Secretary. Associates put out the word that he had assumed the responsibilities of ideological overseer that fell vacant when Mikhail A. Suslov, a 79-year-old survivor of the Stalin leadership, died in January.

In April, Mr. Andropov made an important speech at a Lenin anniversary rally in which he lashed out against corruption in the Soviet system and advocated a flexible carrying out of Marxist-Leninist doctrines, the formulation that implied that as leader he might favor a crackdown on laxity in Soviet life combined with greater degree of autonomy for factory and farm managers within the centrally plannned economy.

Out of Public View

After that speech Mr. Andropov fell from public view for most of the summer. Analysts began to think that he was ceding the succession contest to Mr. Chernenko, but an incident at a Politburo meeting in May apparently persuaded him that he could bide his time. According to a Soviet source who is thought to have contacts with Mr. Andropov, Mr. Chernenko opposed Mr. Andropov's return to the Central Committee Secretariat and, in a bitter debate that ensued, was overruled by a majority that included several key figures.

In what Mr. Andropov was said to have considered to be a preview of the vote on the succession to Mr. Brezhnev as party leader, the K.G.B. chief was said to have been backed by the Defense Minister, Dmitri F. Ustinov, and by one of the most powerful regional party figures, Vladimir V. Shcherbitsky, head of the party in the Ukraine.

Kremlin watchers have long believed that no Politburo figure could be elected party leader without the backing of the Soviet military. With Mr. Ustinov behind him, the Soviet source said, Mr. Andropov felt secure in attending to Secretariat matters, taking a summer vacation and leaving the limelight to Mr. Chernenko.

Mr. Andropov's speech today offered few clear insights into the policies that he will follow. A second speech, made after his choice as party leader was ratified, was summarized in a single paragraph by Tass, the official press agency, suggesting that he may have been more direct in off-the-cuff remarks than in his earlier, prepared text.

Faithfulness to Brezhnev Policy

The first address, mostly a paean to Mr. Brezhnev, was predictable in its pledge of collective leadership and faithfulness to Mr. Brezhnev's domestic and foreign line. But there were shadings, particularly when compared with Mr. Chernenko's longer speech, that suggested that the two men could have diverging approaches.

For example, Mr. Andropov spoke of Mr. Brezhnev's concern at the end of his tenure for tackling "the major tasks of economic, social and cultural development." This could be taken as an indication that Mr. Andropov feels the need to do something about the slump in the Soviet economy, particularly when it is placed against Mr. Chernenko's assertion that "we have a detailed, well-balanced socioeconomic program," a formulation that implied a satisfaction with economic arrangements as they are.

* * *

December 11, 1982

REAGAN HAILS POLAND'S EASING OF MARTIAL LAW

By STEVEN R. WEISMAN
Special to The New York Times.

WASHINGTON, Dec. 10—President Reagan welcomed today what he described as recent "partial steps" easing the military crackdown in Poland and promised to relax United States sanctions against Poland if "meaningful liberalizing measures" were introduced in the future.

In what an Administration official said was a "modification" of the United States position toward Poland, Mr. Reagan also omitted a specific reference to the Solidarity trade union when he listed the conditions Poland would have to meet before the sanctions could be lifted.

In the past, Mr. Reagan has said the sanctions would not be lifted until Poland lifted martial law, released Lech Walesa and other detainees and restored "dialogue and reconciliation" with both Solidarity and the Roman Catholic Church.

Today the President said the "dialogue" would have to be with "truly representative forces of the Polish nation, such as the church and the freely formed trade unions."

Solidarity Outlawed in October

Solidarity itself was outlawed by Poland in October. Mr. Reagan's statement thus appeared to raise the possibility of an easing of sanctions even if that action is not rescinded.

"The United States can only respond to deeds, however, and not words," Mr. Reagan said today. In recent weeks, Poland has released Mr. Walesa, the Solidarity leader, and announced that 317 citizens are still being detained, compared with 600 a couple months ago, and more than 10,000 at one time or another in the last year.

"Reports reach us that further steps in this direction may be taken by the Polish Government in the coming weeks and months," Mr. Reagan told a group of Polish Americans in the White House East Room.

He said that such moves would lead the United States to take "equally significant and concrete actions of our own." Mr. Reagan spoke as the Parliament in Poland prepared to meet Dec. 13, the first anniversary of the imposition of martial law. A State Department official said this week that the Government would probably lift martial law at that time and release additional detainees.

Among the sanctions against Poland imposed a year ago were suspension of guaranteed credits, Export-Import Bank credit insurance, civil aviation and fishing privileges, travel programs and export licenses for high-technology items.

'Not Intended to Be a Signal'

Last October, after Poland outlawed Solidarity, Mr. Reagan announced suspension of Poland's most-favored-nation trade status, which had the effect of raising tariffs on Polish exports of manufactured products.

Administration officials said Mr. Reagan did not intend to suggest today that he had made any judgments about what the United States would do if further "liberalizing" steps were taken in Poland.

"This is not intended to be a signal that we're about to make any changes," said one aide. But he said that "clearly" Poland probably would not meet all the conditions previously enunciated by the United States.

"But if they meet some of the conditions we have set forth, maybe we can do something," the official said. Today's ceremony, officials said, was put together only in the last few days: a signing in the East Room of proclamations declaring Human Rights Day and Week 1982, and declaring Sunday "A Day of Prayer for Poland and Solidarity with the Polish People."

In the "Human Rights Day and Week" proclamation, Mr. Reagan said that progress in this area was "darkened" by Poland's attempt "to extinguish the flames of liberty ignited by Solidarity."

In the "Day of Prayer" proclamation, he said "a genuine labor movement was suppressed by a Government of generals who claim to represent the working class."

* * *

December 21, 1982

DON'T PUSH MISSILES ON EUROPE

By JOHN W. DOUGLAS

WASHINGTON—The Soviet Union seems to recognize that medium-range missiles have long constituted a touchy political issue for Western Europe, but at present the Reagan Administration demonstrates no such understanding. Indeed, by misreading the cards, it is playing into Moscow's hand.

Originally, the so-called double track procedure papered over the divisiveness of the North Atlantic Treaty Organization's missile plan. It called for 572 United States Pershing II and cruise missiles to be installed in Europe starting in December 1983—unless Soviet-American arms talks produced an agreement. A year ago, Washington eased European concerns by advancing a "zero option" whereby the Soviet Union would dismantle its more than 600 medium-range missiles in return for Europe's foregoing all new American missiles. But as the impact of both the double-track and zero option initiatives fades, discord is rising again.

Anticipating West Germany's parliamentary election next March, the Soviet Union has signaled its intention to go public with a proposal cutting, over a period of time, its medium-range missiles by a substantial number in exchange for non-deployment of the American missiles. Although it contains loopholes, the idea represents a significant Soviet step. Nonetheless, the Administration has thrown cold water on the overture and gives every indication of holding fast to the zero option.

But when push comes to shove, Europe is less committed to installation of new missiles on its soil than the Soviet Union is to the exclusion of such missiles. Europeans can gain the dismantling of Soviet missiles only with Soviet agreement, but they can veto new American missiles whenever they so desire. Europeans can speak out against missile installations in their own countries but Russians cannot do so in theirs. All of this handicaps America in its negotiations and illuminates a structural flaw in the double-track process.

Leaving aside the bargaining-chip concept, the basic rationales for new missiles in Europe are not persuasive. One strategic theory, never acknowledged by the North Atlantic Treaty Organization, was to crowd the Soviet Union by bringing to Europe new missile technology and a capacity to reach targets in the western part of the Soviet Union not previously within range of American missiles in Europe. But such crowding is not in NATO's real interest. It would facilitate mistakes in a crisis, and accelerate the arms race.

The psychological theory was that Europe needed reassurance of American interest in its security. But this proposition, never convincing because of the more than 300,000 American troops in Europe, has lost further credibility as antinuclear sentiment in Europe has grown.

Beneath the official veneer of proclaimed North Atlantic Treaty Organization unity, cracks are widening. Denmark's Parliament has withdrawn its backing for the new missiles. Greece has declared its opposition. Norway's Parliament continued its support by a single vote. In Belgium and the Netherlands, the juries are still out. Even the British and West German defense ministers hint that they will part company with the zero option if it proves unacceptable to the Kremlin.

West Germany remains the key, and the first visit to this country of the Christian Democratic Chancellor, Helmut Kohl, was instructive. The Pentagon privately dusted off an old idea to double the Pershing II missile from 108 to 216. But Mr. Kohl turned it down and then, for obvious political reasons, publicized both the confidential request and his rejection of it, thereby underscoring the tenuous nature of Bonn's support for the missiles.

For their part, the opposition Social Democrats have moved away from the North Atlantic Treaty Organization missile plan. They have even decried a lack of West German influence in the American-Soviet talks, a striking turnabout for a party that had supported the NATO plan, had backed the double-track negotiation and had been out of power only 10 weeks. The triumph of the Social Democrats in Hamburg's state elections Sunday will solidify their adherence to this new policy.

As the missile-installation date nears, and antimissile demonstrations intensify, the West German Government, whether Social Democratic or Christian Democratic, will feel increasingly isolated if there is no American-Soviet agreement. Then, under heavy domestic pressure, the Government will likely finesse the issue, possibly by postponing the installation date pending further negotiations with Moscow. Of course, any such postponement would probably scuttle the NATO missile plan.

While Washington, nevertheless, still clings to the zero option, the Europeans show no stomach for remaining tied indefinitely to that mooring. Hence, a United States failure to move away from the zero option surely will result in the dismantling of fewer Soviet SS-20's than otherwise might be attainable as well as produce the most serious crisis yet for NATO. Since the NATO plan was drawn to assuage European anxieties, there is no point in pushing the missiles on the Europeans if they do not want them.

Certainly, the new missiles would not advance United States strategic interests. Every worthwhile Soviet target of such weapons can be covered by existing American missiles on our territory, submarines and planes.

John W. Douglas, a lawyer, is chairman of the board of trustees of the Carnegie Endowment for International Peace.

* * *

January 8, 1983

U.S. LIFTS EMBARGO ON MILITARY SALES TO GUATEMALANS

By BERNARD GWERTZMAN

Special to The New York Times.

WASHINGTON, Jan. 7—The Reagan Administration today lifted the five-year-old embargo on arms sales to Guatemala because of what it said were "significant steps" taken by the Government to end human rights abuses.

The State Department announcement allows Guatemala to buy from the Defense Department $6.3 million worth of spare parts and other equipment for its air force, mostly to rehabilitate American-made helicopters for use against guerrillas.

The move, while small in military terms, was viewed by the Administration and its critics as an important symbolic step signifying support for the Government of Gen. Efrain Rios Montt, who overthrew Gen. Romeo Lucas Garcia and seized power last March.

'Progress Has Been Made'

Guatemala has been accused by the United States and many human rights groups of repressive tactics and rights violations. But Administration officials have reported an improvement in recent months.

"While we want to see further progress in Guatemala in promoting respect for human rights, President Rios Montt has taken significant steps in this area," John Hughes, the State Department spokesman, said. "Progress has been made."

The move brought immediate criticism from some members of Congress who have opposed any resumption of military sales to Guatemala. Representative Tom Harkin,

Democrat of Iowa, introduced a bill, cosponsored by 76 other representatives, to block the sale.

More Muted Criticism

Representative Michael D. Barnes, Democrat of Maryland, the chairman of the House Foreign Affairs subcommittee on Latin America, who has been a strong critic of Guatemala, did not join in the Harkins bill and took a more cautious approach. He said in a statement that while the decision to sell military spare parts was unfortunate, it was necessary to "recognize that this sale is a fact" and make sure that it does not open "the floodgates" to more military aid.

"My staff and I spend a lot of time talking to Guatemalans who seek a humane, democratic government for their country, and I take their views very seriously," Mr. Barnes said. "I have found that they are not as concerned about this sale itself as they are about the possibility that it will open the floodgates that lead to more military aid. The Administration had felt the spare parts issue, which it inherited, was a lingering irritant in our relations with Guatemala that had to be put behind us. But we have no further commitment of this sort and none should be made."

The equipment that will be sold to Guatemala for cash has been sought by the Guatemalans since 1979. It includes $2.9 million for communications equipment; $1 million for spare parts for UH-1H helicopters; $1.35 million for inspection and repair of three of those helicopters; equipment for A-37B aircraft flown by the Guatemalans, and other items, including flight uniforms, technical catalogs and spare parts for earthmoving machinery.

How the Ban Began

Because of Guatemala's human rights record, the Carter Administration in 1978 banned the further sale of items by the Pentagon to that country through the foreign military sales program. Guatemala, angered over the Administration's human rights report of 1977, had already declined any further aid. In 1980, the Carter Administration banned the sale of military equipment even through commercial channels, although items previously approved could be delivered.

Mr. Hughes, in describing the reasons for the end to the embargo, said that since General Rios Montt took power last year, "political violence in the cities has declined dramatically; recently there are indications that the level of violence in the countryside has declined as well; villagers have been provided food and medical supplies along with the means to defend themselves; plans are under way for the election of a constituent assembly; the Indian population is increasingly participating in the country's political process, and President Rios Montt has been attacking corruption within the Government."

"The Government has declared its desire to cooperate with independent human rights groups and United Nations agencies and has permitted a number of private groups to visit the country," Mr. Hughes said. "These are steps which we feel should be recognized and encouraged."

The Critics' Explanation

Critics of the Administration decision have asserted that the relative calm in Guatemala today is the result of large-scale terrorist raids carried out by the army during the summer against villages.

Mr. Harkins said that "the 'quiet' the Administration cites as justification for the sales is the quiet of the dead." "We should not reward the Government of Guatemala for being particularly effective in its brutality nor for simply moving the Government's violence into the countryside where it may be more difficult to see but is still horribly real," he said.

Mr. Barnes said that only a few months ago, "according to the preponderance of the evidence, the Guatemalan army was systematically slaughtering the Indian population" and that helicopters and the A-37B's were both used.

He added, however, that he was "encouraged by reports I have received that the massacres are ending." The American people "are just not ready to resume a military relationship with Guatemala," he said. President Reagan signaled the decision last month after he met with General Rios Montt while on his stopover in Honduras. After the meeting, Mr. Reagan said that the Guatemalan leader had received "a bum rap" and that he was convinced that he was dedicated to making progress toward democracy.

* * *

January 18, 1983

GROMYKO WARNS GERMANS OF RISK IF NEW U.S. MISSILES ARE DEPLOYED

By JAMES M. MARKHAM

Special to The New York Times.

BONN, Jan. 17—Foreign Minister Andrei A. Gromyko of the Soviet Union said tonight that West Germany would be caught in a sharpened nuclear confrontation if a new generation of American medium-range missiles was stationed in Western Europe.

On the second day of his visit to West Germany, Mr. Gromyko repeated the offer of Yuri V. Andropov, the Soviet leader, for a reduction of Soviet medium-range weapons to the level of the existing independent nuclear forces of Britain and France, and spurned the Reagan Administration's public stance at the arms reduction talks in Geneva.

'Gamblers and Con Men'

Mr. Gromyko brought a new element to the standing Soviet proposal by saying Moscow was prepared to negotiate a reduction of its shorter-range SS-21, SS-22 and SS-23 nuclear weapons systems targeted on Western Europe on the basis of "mutuality" with the North Atlantic Treaty Organization.

According to disarmament experts, it was the first time that Moscow had publicly offered to consider negotiating its short-range ballistic missile systems. The comparable American weapons stationed in Western Europe are the Pershing 1A and Lance missiles.

Mr. Gromyko, who is on his first visit to Western Europe since the death of Leonid I. Brezhnev in November, said in a toast at a dinner given in his honor, "In the nuclear age the Federal Republic of Germany and the Soviet Union are, figuratively speaking, in one boat."

Apparently alluding to the Reagan Administration, the 73-year-old Foreign Minister said the danger of nuclear war could be overlooked only by "people who are not capable of seeing things as they are."

"If there are gamblers and con men who state that they are ready to plunge humanity into a nuclear catastrophe for the sake of their ambition," Mr. Gromyko said, "then the question is allowed: Why do they want to and who gave them the right to pull all of the people who want to live down the abyss with them?"

Mr. Gromyko's four-day visit to Bonn, coming just as an election campaign gets under way in West Germany, is from a Soviet viewpoint an important opportunity to urge the West German public to reject the deployment of cruise and Pershing 2 missiles.

"One would like to give expression to the hope that the federal Government, the political parties, independent of their current role in governing the state, and the entire West German public would soberly judge the present situation and do everything to avert the danger of a nuclear arms race in Europe," Mr. Gromyko said.

He said carrying out the NATO plan would mean "for the whole world an extended nuclear confrontation with all its consequences." He added pointedly, "We cannot ignore the fact that the Federal Republic is the only state due for the deployment of Pershing 2 rockets that can reach strategic targets deep inside the Soviet Union in a few minutes."

Mr. Gromyko met today with Foreign Minister Hans-Dietrich Genscher for four hours at his guest villa outside Bonn and paid a courtesy call on President Karl Carstens, whose position is largely ceremonial. Mr. Gromyko will meet Tuesday with Chancellor Helmut Kohl and other political figures and hold a news conference.

A West German Foreign Ministry statement said a two-hour session between Mr. Gromyko and Mr. Genscher this afternoon provided "welcome refinements" in the Soviet position at Geneva. It added that the meeting took place "in an extraordinarily factual, unpolemic and good atmosphere conducive to a genuine clarification of the questions touched upon."

The positive tone of the Foreign Ministry statement suggested that Mr. Genscher had extracted from Mr. Gromyko details of arms reduction proposals that Mr. Andropov has offered in recent weeks as part of a campaign aimed at Western European public opinion.

'Embedding' of Bonn in NATO

A Bonn statement on the two-hour morning session, which concentrated on relations between the two countries, sounded eager to reassure the United States and other NATO allies that the Gromyko visit did not signify the opening of a privileged negotiating channel between West Germany and the Soviet Union.

It said the "embedding" of West Germany in Europe and NATO was "a solid basis for our relations with the Soviet Union," and recalled that both Vice President Bush and France's Foreign Minister, Claude Cheysson, visited Moscow for Mr. Brezhnev's funeral.

The American approach to the Geneva talks has grown into a central issue in the campaign for the West German elections on March 6. Last week, Hans-Jochen Vogel, the opposition Social Democrats' candidate for Chancellor, returned from a visit to Moscow urging the Reagan Administration to modify its so-called zero option at Geneva.

Parity of Nuclear Warheads

Under the zero option NATO would forswear the deployment of 572 cruise and Pershing 2 missiles in Western Europe if the Soviet Union dismantled all its medium-range weapons aimed at Western Europe.

Mr. Vogel also said his conversations with Mr. Andropov and other Soviet officials led him to believe that Moscow was willing for the first time to negotiate a parity of nuclear warheads—not missiles. This idea was not voiced by Mr. Gromyko this evening.

The Social Democrats argue that the zero option, which Mr. Gromyko tonight called one-sided, is unrealistic. Mr. Genscher spoke last week of an "interim result" that would lead to a stationing of fewer than 572 American missiles in exchange for comparable reductions.

In his toast tonight Mr. Genscher defended the zero option, but in a radio interview earlier today he rejected the idea of an "all or nothing" approach in Geneva and insisted that a compromise was possible. This echoed his statements last week about an "interim result."

Tonight Mr. Genscher also praised the growing volume of Soviet-West German trade as a stabilizing factor in international relations. And he said an eventual meeting between President Reagan and Mr. Andropov would be "in the interest of all peoples."

* * *

March 4, 1983

THE QUESTION ABOUT SALVADOR: WHY A CRISIS NOW?

By BERNARD WEINRAUB

WASHINGTON, March 3—The Reagan Administration is in a mood of crisis over El Salvador. Salvadoran officials share Washington's concern about how the war against the guerrillas is going, but not the sense of urgency, which seems to have grown out of the Administration's way of reacting to a crisis some officials saw coming months ago. The military situation in El Salvador deteriorated in the guerrilla offensive of January and February, which provoked few public expressions of concern by the Administration at the time. However, a recent nine-day trip to the region by Jeane J. Kirkpatrick, the United States delegate to the United Nations, at President Reagan's request led to what officials said was anxiety in the White House.

Congressional critics say that, in dispatching Mrs. Kirkpatrick to El Salvador, Mr. Reagan received exactly what he expected to hear: that the military situation was deteriorating and that the Salvadorans needed more arms. Mrs. Kirkpatrick has a reputation within the White House as an articulate and shrewd diplomat with a hard-line approach against dealing with the left, especially in Latin America. But White House officials say even President Reagan was caught by surprise at the depth of Mrs. Kirkpatrick's concerns about possible guerrilla advances in Central America.

Guerrilla Takeover Feared

Mrs. Kirkpatrick told President Reagan and Congressional leaders that not only was the Salvador military situation bleak, but that Government officials, educators, journalists and businessmen in such nations as Venezuela, Costa Rica, Panama and Honduras were fearful that a guerrilla takeover in El Salvador would lead to stepped-up insurgent activity across all of Central America.

"Kirkpatrick came back with a different story than what people had been saying to the President," an Administration official said. "It may be that nobody ever talked to the President like this, but she did."

President Reagan and his national security adviser, William P. Clark, have been gloomy about the situation in El Salvador for the last year, officials said. There have been consistent reports from the Central Intelligence Agency and the Defense Department that the Salvadoran military leadership was largely failing to respond to the advice of American military advisers, who have advocated hit-and-run tactics and night maneuvers to defeat the insurgents. Moreover, officials said, the loss of weapons and the expenditure of bullets, artillery and helicopter spare parts were eating up United States aid far more quickly than expected.

Even before the most recent series of guerrilla attacks, Mr. Reagan and Mr. Clark, as well as State and Defense Department officials, had for months told Congressional leaders that the $26 million in military aid authorized for El Salvador for 1983 was inadequate. Administration officials noted that in 1982 the United States provided $82 million in such aid and that the request for 1984 is $86.3 million. This year, the Administration had initially requested $63.3 million, but under the interim funding measure known as the continuing resolution only $26 million was authorized.

Figure 'No Great Surprise'

"The Administration has known for several months that this was an inadequate level of funding, that they would have to ask for more," said a ranking House aide. "The fact that Weinberger let slip the $60 million figure came as no great surprise but it brought it out in the public and it started the ball rolling."

On Feb. 22, in an appearance before the House Foreign Affairs Committee, Defense Secretary Caspar W. Weinberger was asked about the Administration's plans for more military aid to El Salvador. "I understand it is $60 million," said Mr. Weinberger. Some Congressional aides said Mr. Weinberger's disclosure was a slip of the tongue and it revealed, for the first time, that the Administration was actually seeking an additional $60 million in military aid.

On the same day, President Reagan, having heard Mrs. Kirkpatrick's report, stepped to the rostrum at the American Legion's annual conference and said, "The specter of Marxist-Leninist controlled governments in Central America with ideological and political loyalties to Cuba and the Soviet Union poses a direct challenge to which we must respond."

According to Administration officials, the situation in recent days evolved rapidly because the White House sought to blunt opposition from members of Congress to the aid request. Mr. Weinberger had initially indicated that the additional funds would come from a special discretionary fund set up in 1961 for use by the President "to provide emergency military assistance to foreign countries." It was made clear at once to the White House that the use of these funds, which needs no Congressional approval, would provoke anger on Capital Hill, where lawmakers recalled that the fund was used in Vietnam.

Report Has Strong Impact

In an attempt to fend off Congressional opposition, Mr. Reagan called in a group of senior legislators from both parties on Monday. The first official called by Mr. Reagan to brief the visitors was Mrs. Kirkpatrick and her report—that the nations in the region were frightened about the deteriorating military situation in El Salvador and its impact on nearby nations—apparently had a strong impact.

According to White House officials, the dominant role in the handling of United States policy on El Salvador has shifted in recent months from Thomas O. Enders, Assistant Secretary of State for Inter-American Affairs, to Mr. Clark at the White House. With this change, officials say, has come a stream of gloomy reports about the military situation in El Salvador from Lieut. Gen. Wallace H. Nutting, the commander in chief of the United States Southern Command in Panama, which oversees Salvador operations.

Administration officials have been especially troubled by intelligence showing that guerrillas are now being supplied continually by helicopter and light aircraft from Nicaragua. The guerrillas, the officials say, have no shortage of weapons, mostly American-made M-16's, Soviet and East German demolition equipment and American-made mortars. There is concern that not only may some of the American weapons have been captured from Government soldiers, but that they may also have sold some on the black market.

Uneasy Over Pope's Visit

In addition to their nervousness about the military situation, White House aides are uneasy about the visit of Pope

John Paul II to Central America, including El Salvador, and the impact of his calls for reconciliation in the region.

Behind this concern is the persistent urging of European Socialists, Latin American officials and Congressional critics for some form of negotiation with the guerrillas. In recent months, Administration sources said, ranking officials have discussed various options, including the possibility of pressing for a "dialogue" with the guerrillas and dealing with the crisis in a "conciliatory fashion."

Officials say this option, offered by some State Department officials, has apparently been ruled out by Secretary of State Shultz as well as Mr. Clark and Mrs. Kirkpatrick. Mr. Shultz said two weeks ago that the Salvadoran insurgents were "creating hell" with Soviet-supplied weapons and that the United States would never support negotiations allowing them to "shoot their way" into the Government.

Publicly, the Administration says it opposes negotiations unless the guerrillas lay down their arms and enter the democratic process, or participate in elections, which the insurgents refuse to do. Privately, officials say the possibilities of a "dialogue" remain if, for example, Central American or European Socialists are able to participate in talks and attract anti-Government figures and some key political leaders of the guerrilla movement who may not be staunch Marxists into the "democratic process."

"Whether or not a crisis exists depends on your perception," said a Congressional aide involved in Salvador policy. "A crisis exists because enough people perceive a crisis exists. It could have been perceived a month ago. The military situation has been going downhill for a while and it's just right now, when the Administration, wants more aid, that we have this crisis."

* * *

March 9, 1983

REAGAN DENOUNCES IDEOLOGY OF SOVIET AS 'FOCUS OF EVIL'

By FRANCIS X. CLINES
Special to The New York Times.

ORLANDO, Fla., March 8—President Reagan, denouncing Soviet Communism as "the focus of evil in the modern world," today warned Protestant church leaders not to treat the arms race "as a giant misunderstanding and thereby remove yourself from the struggle between right and wrong, good and evil."

Appearing before a convention of evangelical Christians, the President delivered one of the most forceful speeches of his Administration on the subjects of theology and war, morality and government.

In what White House aides privately said was something of a rebuttal to recent criticism of Administration policy by church officials, notably the Roman Catholic hierarchy, Mr. Reagan delighted his audience by declaring:

"In your discussion of the nuclear freeze proposals, I urge you to beware the temptation of pride—the temptation of blithely declaring yourselves above it all and label both sides equally at fault, to ignore the facts of history and the aggressive impulses of an evil empire."

'Very Dangerous Fraud'

In an addition to his prepared text, the President used some of his strongest language in again rejecting as "a very dangerous fraud" calls for a nuclear freeze without additional Soviet arms reductions.

"That is merely the illusion of peace," he said. "The reality is that we must find peace through strength." He continued: "A freeze at current levels of weapons would remove any incentive for the Soviets to negotiate seriously at Geneva and virtually end our chances to achieve the major arms reductions which we have proposed."

The speech, to the National Association of Evangelicals, received a standing ovation in the Sheraton convention center as the orchestra played "Onward Christian Soldiers."

The President also issued renewed calls for Federal laws that would restrict abortions and permit organized prayer in public schools. But the strongest thrust of his address appeared to be his response to unspecified church leaders who have criticized his foreign policy.

"Simple-minded appeasement or wishful thinking about our adversaries is folly," Mr. Reagan said as he discussed the nuclear freeze issue. "It means the betrayal of our past, the squandering of our freedom."

The President argued, in effect, that his national security goals were parallel with the nation's founding spiritual values. He echoed a debating point of the past in praising as a "profound truth," a young father whom Mr. Reagan said he once heard discussing Communism with his daughters.

"I would rather see my little girls die now, still believing in God, than have them grow up under Communism and one day die no longer believing in God."

There was strong applause as Mr. Reagan the President delivered this line with dramatic emphasis, and an undertone of cheers could be heard in the hall, too.

"Let us pray for the salvation of all those who live in that totalitarian darkness," Mr. Reagan said, adding that Americans also must not forget that Communists "are the focus of evil in the modern world."

He then criticized unidentified people, individuals who, he said, would have the nation accept Communists "at their word and accommodate ourselves to their aggressive impulses."

"So I would urge you to speak out against those who would place the United States in a position of military and moral inferiority," Mr. Reagan continued.

Catholic Church Stands on Freeze

The National Conference of Catholic Bishops is scheduled to vote in May on a final draft of a pastoral letter on the arms race. Earlier drafts have endorsed a two-way bilateral nuclear freeze and the final version is expected to include such a statement. Many Protestant denominations have taken similar stands against nuclear arms.

United Press International

President Reagan at Orlando, Fla., meeting of National Association of Evangelicals. Others are, from left: Dr. Ray Hughes and Dr. Robert W. McIntyre, vice presidents of the group, and Dr. Billy A. Melvin, executive director.

Last month, in another major statement, the Synagogue Council of America, representing six leading groups of Conservative, Reform and Orthodox organizations, asserted that the United States was "morally bound" to reduce the danger of nuclear war. The statement further urged President Reagan and the Soviet leader, Yuri V. Andropov, to seek a "total cessation of production and deployment of nuclear weapons."

In discussing domestic issues that have been dormant induring the Administration's recent budget troubles, Mr. Reagan stressed a full list of social proposals being pressed in the Congress by conservative legislators, lawmakers and church leaders.

"No one seems to mention morality as playing a part in the subject of sex," Mr. Reagan said, asserting that "sexually active" had replaced "promiscuous" as a description for some girls. He defended the so-called "squeal rule," proposed by his Administration and enjoined temporarily by two Federal judges, under which parents must be notified when children receive contraceptive help from Federally-aided clinics.

Court Fight Pledged

"Is all of Judeo-Christian tradition wrong?" Mr. Reagan asked, drawing strong applause as he added: "We are going to fight in the courts. The rights of parents and the rights of family take precedence over those of Washington-based bureaucrats and social engineers."

In quick order, with his comments punctuated by the crowd's frequent applause, Mr. Reagan urged these steps:

- A renewed fight for a constitutional amendment for organized public school prayer. "Let our children pray," he said.
- A renewed fight to end "abortion on demand." He said, "You and I must never rest," he said, until abortion is outlawed.
- Congressional hearings on "infanticide" legislation to protect the handicapped against "mercy killing." Mr. Reagan said this was a growing problem directly related to "a decline

in respect for human life," caused by the growing prevalence of abortion.

'Enjoined by Scripture'

"There is sin and evil in the world," Mr. Reagan declared. "And we are enjoined by Scripture and the Lord Jesus to oppose it with all our might."

He called on the Christian preachers to use their pulpits to denounce "hate groups preaching bigotry and prejudice." The gathering applauded in approval.

The National Association of Evangelicals is the largest umbrella group for conservative Protestants. Formed in 1942, it is a loosely knit organization of 38,000 individuals and church groups from 40 denominations with a total membership of 3.5 million. While members affirm central religious beliefs common among evangelicals, the association has generally refrained from taking strong stands on social issues.

But an activist group has been gaining strength within the association in recent years. Many in the group, called Evangelicals for Social Action, have pressed the association to consider making an antinuclear statement. In May, the activists plan a large conference in Pasadena, Calif., on the subject of war and peace.

* * *

March 24, 1983

REAGAN PROPOSES U.S. SEEK NEW WAY TO BLOCK MISSILES

By STEVEN R. WEISMAN
Special to The New York Times.

WASHINGTON, March 23—President Reagan, defending his military program, proposed tonight to exploit advances in technology in coming decades so the United States can develop an effective defense against missiles launched by others.

In effect, Mr. Reagan proposed to make obsolete the current United States policy of relying on massive retaliation by its ballistic missiles to counter the threat of a Soviet nuclear attack.

In a television address from the White House, he coupled his proposal with his strongest appeal yet for his Administration's program to increase military spending.

Decades Away From Reality

Mr. Reagan declared that a new missile defense program presented "a vision of the future which offers hope," even though the necessary technological breakthroughs "may not be accomplished before the end of this century."

He called on American scientists "to turn their great talents" to the effort. As he spoke, a dozen nuclear scientists were having dinner and receiving briefings at the White House. They included Hans Bethe, a Nobel laureate in physics, and Edward Teller, known as the father of the hydrogen bomb.

White House officials said the new program might involve lasers, microwave devices, particle beams and projectile beams. These devices, most of which are in a very early stage of development, in theory could be directed from satellites, airplanes or land-based installations to shoot down missiles in the air.

Scientists have felt the beam defenses could revolutionize the concept of nuclear strategy because, up to now, the idea of shooting missiles down after they were launched has been deemed impractical.

Defends Arms Reduction Plans

Mr. Reagan also used his speech to defend his Administration's arms reduction proposals to the Soviet Union, but for the first time he hinted publicly that he might be ready to modify his "zero-zero" proposal for banning all Soviet and American medium-range nuclear missiles from Europe.

Administration officials said today that Mr. Reagan was prepared to recommend instead new and lower equal limits on Soviet and American missiles. The President said he would address the issue next week in a speech in Los Angeles.

Using charts, graphs and photographs—some of them recently declassified for tonight's speech—Mr. Reagan reviewed in detail what he said was the buildup of Soviet military forces in recent years, especially in Central America. His Administration's program, he said, is needed because of "our neglect in the 1970's."

On air reconnaissance photographs, Mr. Reagan pointed to Soviet installations in Cuba, Nicaragua and Grenada to show how the Russians had tried to project power in the Caribbean. The photographs, however, did not show anything new beyond what the Administration had previously said existed in the region.

"Sooner or later these bills always come due, and the later they come due, the more they cost in treasure and in safety," Mr. Reagan said. "This is why I am speaking to you tonight—to urge you to tell your Senators and Congressmen that you know we must continue to restore our military strength."

The speech tonight was aimed at defending his proposal to increase military spending by 10 percent in 1984. The proposal is under attack from Democrats and Republicans in both the House of Representatives and the Senate.

Just 33 minutes before the President spoke, the House approved by a vote of 229 to 196 the Democratic leadership's 1984 budget proposal, which the Democrats say provides an increase of 4 percent in military spending. In his address, the President contended that the Democrats had actually proposed a military program with growth of only 2 to 3 percent.

Most of the President's speech was devoted to a familiar litany of the Soviet threat as the Administration sees it. The most innovative part came toward the end, when Mr. Reagan said he had recently begun rethinking the foundation for the American strategic doctrine. That doctrine of massive retaliation is based on the United States ability to counter any Soviet attack with a nuclear attack of its own.

'Better to Save Lives'

He said the policy of deterring aggression through the promise of retaliation had worked in that "we and our allies have succeeded in preventing nuclear war for three decades."

Recently, however, Mr. Reagan said his advisers—especially the Joint Chiefs of Staff—had questioned the deterrence doctrine and persuaded him that "the human spirit must be capable of rising above" retaliatory threats. At the same time, he said recent technological advances had enabled the United States to rethink its "massive retaliation" policies.

"Would it not be better to save lives than to avenge them?" Mr. Reagan asked. "Are we not capable of demonstrating our peaceful intentions by applying all our abilities and our ingenuity to achieving a truly lasting stability? I think we are. Indeed, we must!"

At a White House briefing, senior Administration officials said the United States now spends about $1 billion a year on ballistic missile technology. They said the Administration would prepare a program for increasing this amount in the next several months.

More than a decade ago, the Soviet Union and the United States signed and ratified a treaty on "defensive" strategic weapons known as the Anti-Ballistic Missile Treaty.

At the time many scientists regarded ballistic missile systems as unworkable. The rationale for the treaty was seen as an acknowledgement by the two superpowers that there was essentially no defense against a nuclear attack. But many experts felt that if one side acquired such an ability, it might then be tempted to strike first against the other, believing that it could defend itself in return.

'No One Wants That'

Tonight Mr. Reagan made an allusion to this danger, saying he recognized that "defensive systems" lead to "certain problems and ambiguities" and that "they can be viewed as fostering an aggressive policy and no one wants that."

At the White House briefing, a senior Administration official said Mr. Reagan's proposal to embark on research on defensive missile systems represented no threat to the Russians. Nor did it violate the Anti-Ballistic Missile Treaty, he said, because that treaty barred the deployment, but not research and development, of such systems.

He said the United States would consult with its allies and with the Russians before deploying any such system. He and others thus emphasized that Mr. Reagan's proposal tonight should not be seen as an aggressive move. Rather he emphasized that it might lead to eventual arms reductions and less reliance on a policy of "basing your security on threatening others."

The official said Mr. Reagan was aware that the Russians might fear that the United States was seeking a "first-strike" ability by seeking a defensive system. "This is in no sense his intention," the official said. The commitment tonight, he said, was for research to be completed by "the turn of the century."

The bulk of Mr. Reagan's address was devoted to more familiar and less difficult to understand reviews of Soviet and United States military forces.

Although the recent debate in Congress has been over whether to subscribe to Mr. Reagan's 10 percent increase in military spending, Mr. Reagan said the debate should not be "about spending arithmetic."

He then challenged his opponents to name specific programs they would delete in reducing the military budget. Despite this challenge, he avoided some of the harsh oratory of the last week. He did not repeat his assertion that the Democratic proposals would bring "joy to the Kremlin," for example.

* * *

April 22, 1983

U.S. AIDES SEE NEED FOR BIG EFFORT TO AVERT REBEL VICTORY IN SALVADOR

By LESLIE H. GELB
Special to The New York Times.

WASHINGTON, April 21—A range of Administration officials say the United States must make a sustained, increased effort in El Salvador or lose the war to the guerrillas.

Even with such an effort, the officials believe, it will take from two to seven years before significant progress can be made toward bringing the situation there under control.

They also speak as if there is now agreement in the Administration that Cuba is "the source" of the problem in Central America, as Secretary of State Alexander M. Haig Jr. argued it was in 1981.

Making Cuba Pay a Price

Although there is apparently no agreement yet on what to do about it, some officials talk as if something is either going on or in the works to make Cuba pay a price.

The officials know they are running out of time. With few exceptions, officials say that if things continue as they are in El Salvador and if the United States does not do more to help "we will lose," as one high-ranking official put it.

Yet there is apparently no clear agreement on how much more aid or how many more advisers are needed in El Salvador, or on what actions should be undertaken against Nicaragua and possibly Cuba to prevent a defeat.

An Administration Consensus

Interviews with more than a score of officials in the White House, the State Department, the Defense Department and intelligence agencies show this consensus within the Administration:

- The Administration cannot step up direct United States military involvement and win a quick military victory, in view of Congressional constraints.

- The Administration will not seek a face-saving way of losing through negotiations, given its own view of El Salvador as vital in containing the spread of Communism.
- It cannot control the actions of its Salvadoran allies any more effectively than it could dictate to past dependents such as South Vietnam. Hence it cannot rapidly build a viable military force and a centrist government in El Salvador with the popular support essential to success.

Playing for Time

Thus the Reagan Administration, unable to win and unwilling to lose, is playing for time in the face of a messy situation in El Salvador. The real test, officials assert, is whether Congress and the people of the United States will give them that time.

During such a time, the Administration has to bring the Salvadoran right wing under control, build public support for the center through a program of elections, rebuild an economy shattered by the war, and transform the Salvadoran military into an effective fighting force.

Officials realize nothing is possible unless the security situation is brought under control, and United States military experts are not optimistic.

A special, high-level military report in 1981 found that even with increased United States aid the Salvadoran forces could not defeat the rebels without a major overhaul. According to two Pentagon officials, that overhaul is just beginning to get under way now, with uncertain prospects.

Many Striking Parallels

There are many striking parallels between the situation the Reagan Administration faces today in Central America and those the Johnson and Nixon Administrations faced a decade and more ago in Indochina.

But there is one major difference: Congress has already tied the Reagan Administration's hands on El Salvador in ways it took many years to do with respect to Indochina.

To get the necessary Congressional support for a sustained and increased United States effort in Central America, Mr. Reagan was told by top aides in February, he can no longer stand aside as he has done for more than two years, and he has to take his case to the public.

"He was told, in effect, that his policy could not be carried on the back of some assistant secretary of state," one high-ranking State Department official said. Mr. Reagan has taken this advice and is expected to address a joint session of Congress on the subject next week, a highly unusual step.

If Congress does not go along and the guerrillas win, officials make clear, Mr. Reagan intends to lay the blame on Capitol Hill and the Democrats.

'Not Being Done Cynically'

"This is not being done cynically," a key State Department official explained. "The senior people in this Administration are not prepared intellectually, politically and strategically to abandon El Salvador at all, and certainly not before the 1984 elections."

The Administration's secret policy is its public policy, as is clear from classified documents recently made available to the news media, and there is every sign that officials working on Central America strongly support the policy. This was not the case during the Vietnam War, except toward the end in 1975.

What there is of dissent is almost entirely over tactics—such as whether to ask for increases in United States military advisers and aid now or later, how much to stress negotiations without appearing weak, and the legality of covert military operations in Nicaragua.

So far Congress has dodged Administration thunderbolts. But Congressional objectives are far from clear. The majority of legislators has refused either to abandon El Salvador or give the Administration a relatively free hand.

'Tying Our Hands'

"They are forcing us to lose piecemeal by tying our hands," a Pentagon official said. "But they won't cut our hands off because that way they'd have to take the responsibility."

Some Congressional critics retort that they are trying to strengthen Mr. Reagan's hand. Congressional standards on human rights, they say, can be used by him to compel the Salvadoran Government to shape up. Others say they are trying to save the United States from falling into the Salvadoran quagmire. To this end, they are willing to support and share responsibility for a negotiated settlement with the guerrillas.

Senior Administration officials simply do not believe that civil wars are settled by negotiation, and the weight of history is on their side. To them, the kind of settlements proposed by critics are a disguised way of losing, and the Administration will not buy that.

The Administration is willing to negotiate left-wing participation in elections, including issues such as safety for candidates and access to voters and the news media. But officials make clear that they think there is little or no chance of the guerrillas' believing they can safely participate in elections.

The Administration is not prepared to go farther and grant the guerrillas a share of political power in advance of elections, as the guerrillas' political organizations have demanded. The Administration does not believe that left-wing guerrillas can be trusted to keep agreements and share power. Officials point to efforts by the Carter Administration to provide economic aid to Nicaragua on the condition that the Sandinistas allow a free press and political pluralism. The efforts did not work, they said.

A Propaganda War

Several officials make plain that the Administration sees the to-and-fro over negotiations essentially as part of a propaganda war. "The feeling never was that we could negotiate an agreement on El Salvador or Nicaragua," a high official said. "Notwithstanding, we decided in February that we needed to move on the diplomatic side to deflect the perception of our only going for a military solution."

On March 10 Mr. Reagan said the "defense of the Caribbean and Central America against Marxist-Leninist takeover is vital to our national security." That proposition is largely unquestioned within the Administration.

The belief is that if the left takes over in El Salvador the contagion will spread uncontrollably to the Panama Canal and up through Mexico to the border of the United States.

A Dissenting View

Some State Department officials are known to question the idea of inevitability and argue that what happens in the rest of the region depends on the specific situations in each of the countries. But there is no evidence that these doubters push their point very hard.

Prof. Robert Osgood of Johns Hopkins University analyzed the Administration's approach as a return to "the containment policy, pretty much as defined in the late 1940's, preventing the expansion of Soviet influence and control."

From the 1940's to the 1970's, Administrations regarded almost all revolutions as Communist-inspired and directed from Moscow. This sense waned in the 1970's.

But Administration officials are now convinced that the revolution in El Salvador would amount to little without external support from Nicaragua, Cuba and the Soviet Union.

Arms for the Guerrillas

Without exception, the officials maintain that there is no doubt that direction and supplies for the Salvadoran guerrillas come from Cuba and Nicaragua. They acknowledge that the guerrillas are now getting most of their arms from within El Salvador—by capturing them or buying them—but insist that the flow from Nicaragua is essential to the guerrillas' maintaining their current level of operations.

The officials say the United States' surveillance operation for Nicaragua is even greater than the one for the Soviet Union. "We can hear a toilet flush in Managua," an intelligence analyst said.

Asked why the Administration has not used this capability to shoot down one aircraft arriving from Nicaragua or capture one van coming over the mountains from Honduras, or present other evidence of the arms flow, the answers are sketchy.

One official said the guerrillas were now taking effective countermeasures to block United States intelligence-gathering. Another replied that shooting down an aircraft was "a good idea." Others said it would reveal our intelligence capabilities and thus jeopardize them.

Mexico Going It Alone

Administration officials also maintain that their view of a threat from Nicaragua and the Salvadoran guerrillas is shared by most of the Latin American countries involved in the area, with the exception of Mexico. To them, Mexican policy is short-sighted, intended to protect Mexico from revolutions at the expense of the rest of the area.

Administration officials are not impressed that almost all Latin American and Western European nations support more far-reaching negotiations than those backed by the United States. Most of these efforts, they contend, are being done primarily as domestic, political window dressing, and, in any event, will fail.

Matters such as these are discussed about twice a week by an interdepartmental group under the chairmanship of Thomas O. Enders, Assistant Secretary of State for Inter-American Affairs.

The group, which operates under the authority of the National Security Council, is regarded as the key policy group on El Salvador. Its meetings are seen as the place where day-to-day decisions are made, studies commissioned and broad policy choices are framed for the President.

Regular participants at the sessions in Mr. Enders's sixth-floor office include Alfonso Sapio-Bosch, a member of the National Security Council staff; Nestor Sanchez, Deputy Assistant Secretary of Defense for Inter-American Affairs; Lieut. Gen. Paul F. Gorman of the Army, assistant to the Chairman of the Joint Chiefs of Staff; Vice Adm. Thomas J. Bigley, Director of Plans and Policy for the Joint Chiefs; L. Craig Johnstone, Director of the State Department's Office of Central American Affairs, and a representative of the Central Intelligence Agency.

Several members of the group—Mr. Enders, General Gorman and Mr. Johnstone—were important middle level participants in Vietnam policy making, as are a number of other State Department officials and military officers working on Central America.

Richard Stone, a former Democratic Senator from Florida, often attends the meetings in his capacity as special representative of the President for public diplomacy in the area.

Mrs. Kirkpatrick's Influence

By virtually everyone's testimony, Jeane J. Kirkpatrick, the United States representative at the United Nations, is the central intellectual force behind the policy. But she does not participate in the group.

Mrs. Kirkpatrick recently wrote that the United States had "moral" stakes in El Salvador. This view is widely shared in the Administration. The feeling is that the United States is doing the right thing in trying to create a viable political center in El Salvador.

Most officials acknowledge that the center is weak and weighed down by the right wing. But the conviction is that what there is of a political center has values in common with those of the United States, and would be better for the people of El Salvador than either the left or the right. These officials believe that the effort to establish the center as a real political force must not be abandoned. This, they say, is the goal, and they bemoan public questions about their sincerity.

Many of those interviewed conceded that the Administration carried a great deal of ideological baggage about supporting right-wing dictatorships, and that the United States was bound by historical burdens in Latin America.

But they insisted that the Administration was trying to do things right this time—to build up the center—and that it deserved a chance.

Morality vs. Viability

To the Administration, the issue of right—as the officials see it—transcends questions of viability. Officials tend to construe questions about whether the policy can work as tantamount to arguing that the United States should abandon El Salvador.

Consequently, there are a number of questions that many officials do not want to talk about, or, in some cases, have not thought much about.

Will Congress wait two to seven years to see real progress toward eliminating human rights abuses, Salvadoran "death squads," economic and military stability? Will a majority of legislators vote for increasing aid packages for another war of indefinite duration and result? Is it really possible to build up the political center and wean the right wing away from power? Are not many members of the guerrilla front a part of what there is of a political center in Salvador? How far is the Administration prepared to go on whom it will negotiate with, up to but not including the Communists? If all else fails, and the Administration continues to believe El Salvador is vital to United States security, will it then advocate sending United States combat troops?

* * *

June 3, 1983

REAGAN AIDES LOOK TO A LARGER ROLE IN LATIN CONFLICTS

By PHILIP TAUBMAN
Special to The New York Times.

WASHINGTON, June 2—Senior Reagan Administration officials, convinced that the United States military presence in Central America is too small to realize the policy goals proclaimed by President Reagan, are considering an increase in American involvement.

No final decisions have been made, according to senior national security officials, but options under review include more military advisers for El Salvador, expanded military cooperation with Honduras and the renewal of military aid to Guatemala.

A senior Administration official said, however, that short of a provocative change in the balance of power in Central America, such as a large influx of Cuban forces or an invasion of Honduras by Nicaragua, the United States was unlikely to increase its military presence greatly. He said the Administration remained committed to keeping American combat forces out of the conflicts in Central America.

Choice as Envoy Named

Secretary of State George P. Shultz announced today that President Reagan intended to nominate Thomas R. Pickering, a career diplomat who is now Ambassador to Nigeria, as the new envoy to El Salvador. Mr. Pickering, if confirmed by the Senate, would replace Deane R. Hinton.

The announcement was made at a news conference at the State Department at which Mr. Shultz praised Mr. Hinton and the departing Assistant Secretary for Inter-American Affairs, Thomas O. Enders. One official said Mr. Shultz had been "irritated" over what several senior officials regarded as a deliberate effort by some White House officials over the weekend to denigrate the department and Mr. Enders and Mr. Hinton. Mr. Shultz announced last Friday that Mr. Enders would be replaced by Langhorne A. Motley, a political appointee who has been Ambassador to Brazil.

Reagan 'Given the Facts'

Mr. Reagan and his top national security advisers recently reviewed a proposal to expand United States military activity in Honduras, national security officials said. They added that the plan, which they declined to discuss in detail, went "substantially beyond" the previously announced agreement to send more than 100 advisers to Honduras, tripling the present number, and open a training camp for Salvadoran soldiers there.

An Administration official, asked about the national security officials' comments, said tonight that Mr. Reagan was "given the facts on certain countries" at White House meetings this week, but added, "There's no consideration at present of increasing personnel, funding, or the level of U.S. involvement."

The White House, meanwhile, confirmed that the Administration plans to send a team of up to 25 military doctors and medical corpsmen to El Salvador. President Reagan denied that this represented a deepening of American involvement in the Salvadoran civil war.

"If they say it," Mr. Reagan said of potential critics, "they will be as wrong as they've been on some many others things." Senior officials said a consensus had emerged within the Administration that the commitment of American resources in Central America needed to be increased to bring it into balance with the policy aims of Mr. Reagan.

Specifically, they said, the military assistance to El Salvador and Honduras has not been sufficient to reverse guerrilla advances in El Salvador or prevent the expansion of Cuban and Soviet influence in the region.

A More Assertive Stand

They said the Administration plans to be more assertive in opposing Congressional cuts in American aid to El Salvador and legislation in the House that would end the financing of insurgents in Nicaragua.

The dismissal last week of Mr. Enders as the State Department's senior official dealing with Latin America resulted in part from dissatisfaction with his efforts to negotiate a compromise with the House Foreign Affairs Committee on help for the insurgents, the officials said.

The Defense Department, according to White House officials, has taken the lead in advocating a tougher stand by the

Administration in its relations with Congress, frequently clashing with the State Department.

While Mr. Enders was negotiating with House Democrats last month, Secretary of Defense Caspar W. Weinberger, in a letter to the chairmen of the Senate and House intelligence committees, vehemently opposed the House bill to terminate covert assistance to the rebels in Nicaragua and provide $80 million in overt aid to Central American nations to intercept arms shipments to guerrillas in El Salvador, Defense Department officials said.

In the letter, which the officials said also reflected the thinking of the Joint Chiefs of Staff, Mr. Weinberger argued that the only way to shut off the flow of Soviet and Cuban weapons through Nicaragua to El Salvador would be an air and sea quarantine that would require large numbers of American troops, aircraft and vessels.

Mr. Weinberger, the officials said, maintained that it would be "totally unfeasible" for Central American nations, acting alone, to block the flow of weapons. By proposing that the United States commit itself to helping other nations prevent the arms shipments, he said, the House legislation could lead to the kind of increase in American military involvement that the bill's sponsors seek to avoid.

House Panel Postpones Vote

The House Foreign Affairs Committee today postponed a vote on the legislation until next week, the third time in 10 days that it has delayed consideration of the bill. A number of Democratic members are concerned that a favorable vote could leave them vulnerable to election campaign charges by Republicans that they had abandoned American allies fighting against Communists.

Senior officials at the White House, Defense Department and Central Intelligence Agency have grown impatient with Congressional resistance to Mr. Reagan's policies, according to White House aides. Instead of trying to work out compromises with Congress, as Mr. Enders did, these officials concluded it would be better for the Administration to hold out for what it wants and force Congress to accept or reject the Administration's requests.

In internal discussions, this position has been supported by William P. Clark Jr., the White House national security adviser, William J. Casey, the Director of Central Intelligence, and top Pentagon aides, including Fred C. Ikle, Under Secretary of Defense for Policy, and Nestor D. Sanchez, Deputy Assistant Secretary for Inter-American Affairs, the officials said.

Resistance in Congress

These same officials have pressed Mr. Reagan and other senior policy makers, including Mr. Shultz, to consider increasing the American military presence in Central America.

Any increase, Administration officials acknowledged, is likely to be opposed in Congress. The officials believe, however, that Congressional and public opinion is slowly growing more favorable to the Administration's policy.

A resumption of military aid to Guatemala, which was suspended by the Carter Administration, could be pushed through Congress, several senior Administration officials said, because human rights problems in Guatemala have decreased and the Government has made significant gains against insurgents.

The Administration lifted a ban on the sale of military spare parts to Guatemala this year, but has not ended the embargo on security assistance.

Any increase in the number of military advisers in El Salvador will be difficult to get through Congress, the officials said. The Administration has an agreement with Congress not to station more than 55 advisers in El Salvador.

But the Administration officials said that guerrilla gains have made it clear that the Salvadoran military cannot make headway without an increase in the number of American military advisers.

Larry M. Speakes, the White House spokesman, said today that the decision to send medical doctors and corpsmen to El Salvador "in no way conflicts with our self-imposed commitment to hold the number of military trainers" to 55.

"We have no plans to exceed this limit," he added. Mr. Speakes said that the doctors and medics were being sent at the request of the Salvadoran Government to help ease "a devastating situation" of weak and overextended medical facilities.

* * *

June 17, 1983

A CHILL AT THE KREMLIN

By JOHN F. BURNS

Special to The New York Times.

MOSCOW, June 16—The last three days have seen the largest flurry of political activity since Leonid I. Brezhnev's death in November, but two high-level meetings have ended with little sign that the Kremlin is any closer to bold initiatives that could shake up a sagging economy or ease tensions with the United States.

Doubts about Yuri V. Andropov's authority have been eased by his appointment as head of state as well as party leader. But his health remains in question and the speech that he delivered to the party's Central Committee Wednesday, together with an earlier one by Konstantin U. Chernenko, another major Politburo figure, bore a conservative stamp that suggested that the Andropov era may do more to reinforce the coercive aspects of Soviet life than to reinvigorate the increasingly exhausted Soviet system.

In foreign policy, too, there was little sign of new moves to reopen a dialogue with the United States, wind down the Soviet intervention in Afghanistan or encourage a growth of popular support for the Communist authorities in Poland. To the contrary, much of what Mr. Andropov and other leaders said implied that the Kremlin feels it is time to remind the West of Moscow's unyielding resolution to defend Soviet positions.

Acrimonious Attack on U.S.

The gulf was brought home today when Foreign Minister Andrei A. Gromyko spoke on the world situation before the Supreme Soviet, launching an acrimonious attack on the United States. In substance the address seemed in many ways like a mirror image of Secretary of State George P. Shultz's statement to the Senate Foreign Relations Committee Wednesday, with Mr. Gromyko depicting Washington as the cause of the impasse in arms control, of tensions in Poland and Afghanistan, and of local conflicts in El Salvador, southern Africa and elsewhere.

Like Mr. Shultz, Mr. Gromyko said improvement in the relationship was a major goal. But also like the Secretary of State, he left no doubt that it was up to the other side to make the first concessions. On Poland he reverted to the harsh formulations common before the martial law clampdown in 1981, attributing the problems there to Western "subversion" and warning obliquely that Soviet military might was the ultimate guarantee of Poland's loyalty to Communism.

Mr. Andropov implied that the climate in Soviet-American relations could deteriorate further. He hinted that the Kremlin was ready to increase arms expenditures still higher if the Reagan Administration continued to shun "peaceful coexistence." And while affirming that "the export of revolution is altogether impossible," he called for a stepped-up propaganda campaign against the United States to insure victory in what he described as "a struggle for the hearts and minds of billions of people in the world."

Mr. Chernenko, the party's ideological chief, marked his return to the center of power after a lengthy illness with a speech that had earmarks of earlier Soviet attitudes toward the United States. He, too, called for an intensification of "counterpropaganda," but he said that it should be directed at domestic life as well as foreign audiences, so as to combat Western efforts to "smuggle in" ideas and practices alien to Communism and to "poison the minds" of Soviet citizens.

Suggestions of Flexibility

Mr. Chernenko's predecessor as ideological overseer in the Kremlin, Mikhail A. Suslov, was also given to diatribes that attributed slack work habits and young Russians' affinity for Western styles in dress and pop music and other departures from Marxist ideals as the product of noxious Western influences. But Mr. Suslov's death last year at the age of 79 and the accession to the party leadership of Mr. Andropov, said by his associates to be more cosmopolitan than his predecessors, encouraged suggestions that policy on such matters would become more flexible.

Speeches to party gatherings have often been the occasion for a demonstration of Marxist austerity that has had little practical impact. But both Mr. Andropov and Mr. Chernenko insisted that there must be a tightening of ideological controls across a broad spectrum of Soviet life, including the arts, the area traditionally most sensitive to such drives. This followed a spate of articles in the Soviet press demanding that plays, books, films, radio and television broadcasts and even popular music abandon "bourgeois" and "nihilistic" themes for a celebration of Soviet ideals.

Mr. Andropov balanced the Spartan elements of his speech with remarks that were bound to be popular, notably his renewed calls for greater industrial efficiency, more food in the stores and better housing, an end to "formalism and triteness" in party pronouncements and more realism about economic goals. His condemnation of the use of public office for "personal enrichment," backed up by the expulsion from the Central Committee of Mr. Brezhnev's police minister on the ground of corruption, also struck responsive chords.

Hard Work and Innovation

But there was little to suggest that he is prepared to tackle economic problems head on with the sort of changes that many Soviet economists have urged, involving a relaxation of the centralized planning process and a shift toward market principles. These have been resisted by the powerful Soviet bureaucracy, backed by party leaders who fear an unraveling of political authority.

As before, Mr. Andropov's prescription for improved living standards was harder work, less managerial feather-bedding and greater leeway for technological innovation.

The party leader's accent on "discipline and order," his main theme since assuming office, found expression in the one major party appointment to emerge from the meetings, the transfer of the Leningrad party boss, Grigory V. Romanov, to Moscow, where he will combine his Politburo work with a position on the powerful party secretariat.

* * *

July 5, 1983

PREMIER OF SOVIET WARNS KOHL ON BID TO DEPLOY MISSILES

By SERGE SCHMEMANN

Special to The New York Times.

MOSCOW, July 4—Yuri V. Andropov canceled his first meeting with Chancellor Helmut Kohl of West Germany here today, but Prime Minister Nikolai A. Tikhonov, who took the Soviet leader's place, exchanged blunt remarks with Mr. Kohl.

In a dinner speech, the Soviet Prime Minister said that if the North Atlantic Treaty Organization went ahead with the deployment of new American missiles in Europe, "we and our allies will respond by taking without delay additional measures to strengthen our security and develop a counterbalance to NATO's new military potential."

The warning echoed previous threats by Moscow to station new nuclear weapons on the soil of its Warsaw Pact allies if the West goes ahead with its deployment, with the new statement that the countermeasures would come "without delay."

Kohl Responds to Russian

Mr. Kohl said in response that it was the Soviet Union's "vast superiority" in medium-range weapons that had prompted the Western alliance to take countermeasures. He insisted that his "numerous talks" with President Reagan had convinced him of Washington's dedication to resolving the missile dispute by negotiation.

However tough the talk, it was Mr. Andropov's absence and the manner in which it was announced that dominated attention among diplomats. A spokesman for the West German Embassy said that early today Foreign Minister Andrei A. Gromyko told Bonn's Ambassador, Andreas Mayer-Landrut, that for personal reasons Mr. Andropov "would not yet be available on Monday."

The Germans said it was "envisaged" that Mr. Andropov would reschedule today's private talks for Tuesday in addition to a scheduled meeting involving Foreign Ministers Gromyko and Hans-Dietrich Genscher.

Word of Andropov Illness

Mr. Kohl, in an interview with West German television, said he had been led to understand that Mr. Andropov missed today's meetings because of health. Neither he nor any Soviet or Western sources would identify the ailment.

Mr. Andropov has appeared weak, unsteady and haggard at recent functions, including a meeting with the President of Finland and a session of the Communist Party Central Committee last month.

Unconfirmed reports have circulated in Moscow that Mr. Andropov, who turned 69 last month, is suffering from a kidney ailment and was hospitalized earlier this year, and that he suffered a heart attack in the mid-1960's.

A few diplomats, however, saw evidence of a diplomatic snub in Mr. Andropov's absence, possibly linked to the hard positions Mr. Kohl had pledged to expound in Moscow. These diplomats noted that the Soviet press had remained most critical of Bonn's policies in the days leading up to the meeting and that arrangements for the visit remained unusually unsettled up to the last moment.

Only today, for example, the Germans said Mr. Kohl would return to Bonn from Kiev on Friday rather than continue on to a town where the Germans are helping build a steel mill. The Germans attributed the late arrangements to "technical difficulties" over the additional visits.

The majority of diplomats polled on the question expressed certainty that Mr. Andropov was indeed unwell. They added that he would not have thus undermined his first meeting with a head of government of a NATO member, especially one with a critical role in the debate over the medium-range missiles, to deliver an ambiguous slight. It was not considered likely that Mr. Andropov would willingly touch off another round of speculation about his health.

A Full Official Welcome

Even in the absence of Mr. Andropov, the Russians gave Mr. Kohl and Mr. Genscher a full official welcome. The visitors were greeted at Vnukovo Airport by Mr. Tikhonov, Mr. Gromyko and a full display of flags, anthems and honor guards. Defense Minister Dmitri F. Ustinov also attended the first round of talks.

Most diplomats said they believed that the dinner speech made by Mr. Tikhonov was the one Mr. Andropov had intended to read. It set out the Kremlin's position with unusually direct terms for a formal meeting of this sort.

Mr. Tikhonov declared that the international situation had become "very alarming" and that the United States was "preparing to turn Europe into an area of maximum military political tensions."

Under the NATO plan, the new American missiles will be deployed beginning in December only if no agreement is reached at negotiations now under way in Geneva. But Mr. Tikhonov said the United States was "only creating a semblance" of participation at the talks. He warned that deployment of the missiles "will inevitably result in a sharp deterioration of the situation in Europe and all over the world."

Specter of World War II

Taking a direct jab at the West Germans, Mr. Tikhonov raised the specter of World War II, saying the NATO deployments "would mean that for the first time in postwar history a military threat again stems from the German soil to the Soviet people." He added, "Needless to say what that would mean to us."

In his speech, Chancellor Kohl said his policy was to develop longterm relations with the Soviet bloc and to set up regular contacts at all official levels. But he went on to underline West Germany's fundamental ties to the West, the Atlantic alliance and specifically to the United States.

While endorsing a policy of "understanding, cooperation, détente and accommodation with the East," Mr. Kohl listed a number of goals and positions that Moscow opposes.

He stressed Bonn's commitment to the reunification of Germany, a position Mr. Tikhonov reportedly criticized at the earlier talks in the Kremlin as a challenge to East-West treaties signed in the early 1970's.

Criticism on Afghanistan

Mr. Kohl criticized the Soviet Union for its continuing intervention in Afghanistan; called for an improvement in the situation in Poland; demanded a relaxation of restrictions on the emigration of ethnic Germans, and implicitly criticized Soviet behavior in Indochina, the Middle East and Africa.

On other issues, the Chancellor urged an early meeting between Mr. Reagan and Mr. Andropov, which he said could help "eliminate a great deal of distrust and pave the way for a solution of urgent problems."

But Mr. Kohl stressed the issue of medium-range missiles, which has loomed over his visit from the time it was announced. He declared unequivocally that Bonn was committed to the NATO decision.

"I should like to make it clear at this point that, if concrete negotiated results cannot yet be achieved by the end of this year, deployment will start, as envisaged, in accordance with the commitments entered into within the alliance," Mr. Kohl said.

"The federal Government, which has the backing of the majority of the German people, will not be deflected from this."

* * *

July 22, 1983

PRESIDENT ASSERTS SANDINISTAS MAKE REGION UNSTABLE

By FRANCIS X. CLINES
Special to The New York Times.

WASHINGTON, July 21—President Reagan, defending plans for largescale naval maneuvers off Central America, said today that it would be "extremely difficult" to bring about stability in the region so long as the Sandinista Government remained in control of Nicaragua.

Denying that the United States was trying "gunboat diplomacy" in the area, the President said he "would hope" there would be no need to impose a naval blockade on Nicaragua to stabilize the region.

The President's remarks, delivered in response to questions at a brief news conference, were among his strongest suggestions thus far that more forceful action might eventually be considered to deal with what he characterizes as a Soviet-Cuban "war machine" in Nicaragua that threatens the hemisphere.

Nicaraguan Offer Welcomed

In discussing the Administration's plans to increase military and economic aid in the area, Mr. Reagan said he welcomed as a "first step" Nicaragua's offer this week to take part in regional peace talks. "But I don't think it goes far enough," he added, saying the Sandinistas must fulfill earlier promises to guarantee civil rights and democratic freedom to Nicaragua.

In saying that, the President appeared to claim at least marginal success in pressing the Nicaraguans to negotiate by supplying United States help to the "contras," or anti-Sandinista insurgents. Mr. Reagan's critics insist the Administration is seeking the overthrow of the Sandinistas, but the President contends his goal is limited to stopping Nicaragua's support of leftist insurgents threatening the Government of El Salvador.

"It could be assumed that maybe what is happening there with the contras who are opposing the Sandinista regime had something to do with this decision," President Reagan said, speaking of the Nicaraguan negotiation offer. He said calls from other Latin American nations for a negotiated settlement also were a factor.

Flotillas to Be Sent

Asked whether regional stability could be advanced while the Sandinistas ruled alone in Nicaragua, the President replied, "I think it'd be extremely difficult because I think they're being subverted or they're being directed by outside forces."

The President confirmed plans to send aircraft carrier flotillas to both the Pacific and Caribbean coasts of Central America. "There are going to be maneuvers of various kinds," he said, adding that others had been conducted in various parts of the world in the past without provoking suggestions that the United States was trying to "start a war."

"Showing the flag" is a classic naval mission that has often had dramatic results. When the Nixon Administration sent the carrier Enterprise to the Bay of Bengal during the India-Pakistan war in 1971, India took it as a sign that the United States was favoring Pakistan, and anti-American demonstrations followed all over India.

Sending a naval task force to Central America could be intended as a demonstration of United States resolve to its friends in the region as well as to countries the Reagan Administration has deemed unfriendly.

Asked about the possibility of a full-scale naval blockade, the President replied, "A blockade is a very serious thing and I would hope that there will, that eventuality will not arise."

Byrd Accuses President

Plans for maneuvers under consideration, besides the sending of aircraft carriers, include dispatching Army engineers and Air Force transports to Honduras and the battleship New Jersey through the Panama Canal, according to senior Administration officials.

The Administration's use of military maneuvers as a pressure tactic was questioned today by critics, including the Senate Democratic leader, Robert C. Byrd. He accused the President of "establishing more of a U.S. presence, attempting to intimidate Nicaraguans" before he even hears from the new Presidential commission that is to study the problem.

Aside from significantly increasing the presence of warships patrolling the waters between Central America and Cuba, the maneuver plans would allow military officials to speed the expansion of United States training bases in Honduras. They would also provide a means for the Administration to dramatize its resolve and to attract greater domestic attention to the problem.

The Nicaraguans have expressed fears that the exercises could turn into a quarantine of their waters by United States forces, since they say the United States is already at war with them.

Choice of Kissinger Defended

Mr. Reagan appointed a 12-member commission on Central America on Tuesday, ordering it to report by Dec. 1 with advice on how to deal with the region's economic, social and security problems. Administration officials concede that the major factor in the commission's creation was the failure thus far to rouse enough popular and Congressional support for the President's Central American policy.

Answering questions in the White House briefing room, the President defended his choice of former Secretary of State Henry A. Kissinger to head the commission.

"Here is a man with a distinguished record in diplomacy," the President said in minimizing his past criticisms of Mr. Kissinger. "I believe he is exceptionally well qualified to bring back the information that I think we all need and that would help the Congress make the decisions it needs to make about Central America."

The President said he wanted the commission to provide basic information so he could "sit down" with Congress and construct "an overall program for all of our neighbors here in the hemisphere," one that he said envisioned "equal allies" dedicated to economic and social progress.

"To achieve it, however, you've got to stop the shooting," the President continued. "You have got to let them proceed with these reforms without getting murdered by terrorists."

The Administration's immediate goal is to prevent Congressional critics from denying some of the more controversial requests for increased military support for Central America, including covert aid, that the President has pending in Congress. The White House has defended its proposals as a necessary blend of economic and military aid, but such Democratic critics as former Vice President Walter F. Mondale, a 1984 Presidential candidate, contend the Reagan Administration has been neglecting diplomacy and militarizing the region's long standing economic and social problems.

NICARAGUANS CHARGE QUARANTINE

Special to The New York Times.

MANAGUA, Nicaragua, July 21—The Nicaraguan Government newspaper Barricada said today that the United States Navy ships now steaming toward Central America were the beginning of a military quarantine.

The Government itself has made no official statement on the matter so far, but Barricada devoted several articles to it. "The new war fleet is part of a far-reaching plan of the Joint Chiefs of Staff that also includes the mining of Nicaraguan ports," a front-page article said.

In an editorial, the paper said the United States had reacted only with a "warlike attitude" to recent peace initiatives in the region and particularly to that of the Sandinistas.

* * *

September 2, 1983

U.S. SAYS SOVIET DOWNED KOREAN AIRLINER; 269 LOST; REAGAN DENOUNCES 'WANTON' ACT

By ROBERT D. McFADDEN

A South Korean airliner missing with 269 people on a flight from New York to Seoul was shot down in the Sea of Japan by a Soviet jet fighter near a Soviet island off Siberia, the United States said yesterday.

There were no known survivors of the attack, in which a heat-seeking missile was said to have been fired without warning at the airliner by an interceptor that had tracked it over Soviet territory for two and a half hours.

President Reagan expressed "revulsion" over what he called "a horrifying act of violence." He cut short his California vacation and called a National Security Council meeting in Washington today to discuss possible reprisals.

U.N. Meeting Requested

Members of Congress and other American officials erupted in a fury of outrage, and the United States and South Korea requested a United Nations Security Council meeting on the incident. The Council was expected to begin debate today.

There was no clear explanation for the reported attack, which occurred amid several puzzling circumstances. There was an unconfirmed report that the airliner had experienced radio trouble. Soviet officials said it was flying without lights. And United States authorities acknowledged that it was far off course, despite carrying what South Korean officials called sophisticated navigational equipment.

As American, Soviet and Japanese ships and planes searched frigid seas north of Japan and reportedly found traces of fuel where the jet apparently went down, Secretary of State George P. Shultz demanded an explanation from the Soviet Union and told reporters, "The Soviet pilot reported that he fired a missile and the target was destroyed."

Soviet Explanation Rejected

A Soviet explanation late yesterday was rebuffed by the State Department as "totally inadequate." The Soviet statement did not acknowledge that a Soviet plane had shot down the airliner and did not accept responsibility for the incident, the State Department said.

The State Department spokesman, John Hughes, said a message from the Soviet Foreign Minister, Andrei A. Gromyko, asserted only that a plane had been sighted flying without navigational lights, had not responded to signals by Soviet interceptors and had ignored efforts to direct it to a landing site.

South Korea's President, Chun Doo Hwan, accused the Soviet Union of "a barbarous act" that "deserves the censure of the entire world." People all over South Korea condemned the attack. Japanese officials said they, too, believed the airliner had been shot down by a Soviet jet fighter and called the incident "very regrettable." In capitals around the world, governments called in Soviet ambassadors to deliver outraged protests. The French Foreign Ministry expressed its "sharpest indignation." The British Foreign Office called the incident "deeply disturbing." The Swedish Foreign Minister said he was "deeply shocked." And Canadian airline pilots called it a "despicable, bloody criminal act" and threatened retaliatory steps.

Relatives and friends grieved for those on the plane—about 30 Americans, including Representative Larry P. McDonald, Democrat of Georgia; 72 Koreans, 22 Japanese, 34 Taiwanese and more than 80 people of other nationalities, in addition to a crew of 29.

Calls to Revoke Grain Agreement

"There were no circumstances that can justify the unprecedented attack on an unarmed commercial aircraft," Larry Speakes, the President's chief spokesman, told reporters at Mr. Reagan's ranch in Santa Barbara, Calif. Mr. Speakes declined to speculate on possible retaliation, but there were calls in Congress for revocation of the recent agreement to supply American grain to the Soviet Union.

A crisis atmosphere surrounded the incident, one of the most serious international aerial confrontations in years. In 1978, a Soviet fighter forced a South Korean jetliner down in northern European Russia, killing two passengers.

Mr. Shultz was grim-faced and his voice sometimes broke with emotion as he reconstructed the drama, which he said occurred in darkness some 32,000 feet over the Sea of Japan as up to eight Soviet fighters tracked the airliner.

He said the Soviet fighter that fired the missile was "in constant contact with its ground control" and flew "close enough for a visual inspection." He noted, however, that there was no evidence that the Soviet jets had signaled or warned the airliner and added, "There was no, apparently no, ability to communicate between the two aircraft."

Under international aviation rules, which are endorsed by the Soviet Union, an established procedure for an interceptor to warn a straying aircraft at night is to flash lights at irregular intervals while dipping its wings. The intercepted plane responds by flashing its navagational and landing lights. There was no indication whether any such exchange occurred.

"The United States reacts with revulsion to this attack," said Mr. Shultz. "Loss of life appears to be heavy. We can see no excuse whatsoever for this appalling act."

Flight Left New York on Tuesday

The Secretary of State's announcement in Washington ended nearly a day of uncertainty over the fate of Korean Air Lines Flight 7, a Boeing 747 jumbo jet that left New York at 11:50 Tuesday night, refueled in Alaska 10 hours later and vanished from Japanese radar screens less than 5 hours after that.

The Japanese news agency Kyodo said a Soviet radio communication had been monitored by Japanese military intelligence that gave this exchange, apparently between the Soviet fighter and its ground station just before the airliner's disappearance:

"Take aim at the target."

"Aim taken."

"Fire."

"Fired."

Mr. Shultz and other American officials said the airliner had apparently strayed off course over Sakhalin, the Soviet island north of Japan, and that it was on a course that would have taken it out of Soviet airspace. But, they said, it was shot down without warning by an air-to-air missile.

Explosion Called Possible

In Tokyo, a Japanese military spokesman said radar information supported the theory that the plane might have exploded in midair after having been hit by a missile. The spokesman said pulses received from a special device in all civilian and military planes stopped at the same time as the plane disappeared from the screens.

The airliner was lost at 3:38 A.M. Thursday, Japanese time (2:38 P.M. Wednesday, Eastern daylight time) in the Sea of Japan, between Sakhalin and Moneron Island, about 30 miles southwest of the southern tip of Sakhalin. The site is about 700 miles north of Tokyo and about 900 miles northeast of Seoul.

Sakhalin is part of the Soviet Far Eastern military network, with air bases, radar stations and other tracking installations.

Amid conflicting reports and in the absence of many specific details about what happened, there were numerous unanswered questions:

How and why did the airliner go off course? Why was there apparently no direct communication between Soviet air defenses and the airliner? Did someone order an attack and why? Finally, why would an attack be carried out when a warning signal might have sufficed to make a plane land?

The Soviet Union, which had earlier denied an erroneous Korean Government report that the plane had been forced by Soviet jets to land on Sakhalin, issued its only official remarks in the note to the State Department. But Moscow gave no public account.

A Brief Tass Statement

The Soviet press agency Tass said only that "an unidentified plane" had twice intruded in Soviet airspace, first over the Kamchatka Peninsula off the Siberian coast west of the Aleutian Islands and later over Sakhalin Island. "The plane did not have navigation lights," the Tass report said, and "did not respond to queries" from Soviet air defenses. The Tass report added:

"Fighters of the antiaircraft defense, which were sent aloft toward the intruder plane, tried to give it assistance in directing it to the nearest airfield. But the intruder plane did not react to the signals and warnings from the Soviet fighters and continued its flight in the direction of the Sea of Japan."

The Tass report did not mention any air attack and left numerous questions unanswered, including what action Soviet planes took and why.

Airline Officials Dubious

Korean Air Lines officials in New York contended that the airliner could not have strayed off course into Soviet airspace because of what they called "sophisticated" navigational equipment on board. They also said the pilot of the airliner would have landed if he had been ordered to do so.

The captain of another Korean Air Lines plane that crossed the path of Flight 7 over the Aleutians said in Anchorage yesterday that the airliner appeared to be having radio trouble. He said he had tried to radio the other plane to share weather information but had been unable to make contact.

"His radio was very garbled," Capt. S. S. Yang said.

"They did not understand each other," he said, referring to the radio operators of the two airliners. "I tried to relay, but he couldn't hear me. I tried to call him several times."

A spokesman for the United States Federal Aviation Administration said he knew of no such radio difficulties.

Flight Began at Kennedy

The flight of K.A.L. 7 began at Kennedy International Airport at 11:50 P.M. Tuesday. According to airline officials in New York, the plane carried more navigational equipment than is standard on such 747's.

"Since we skirt this area here very closely," said Ralph Strafaci, the district sales manager, "the equipment we have on board is very important and very technical. It's a very difficult thing for that aircraft to stray." He said he could not elaborate.

Flight 7 is one of five weekly flights from New York to the South Korean capital. A spokesman for Korean Air Lines said last night's Flight 7 was fully booked and left Kennedy Airport on time.

On Tuesday night's flight, the airliner, with 244 passengers and 29 crew members, first flew to Anchorage for a refueling stop.

Four passengers left the flight there, and the plane took off again at about 10 A.M. Wednesday, New York time. It was over the Aleutians shortly thereafter that the passing Korean Air Lines plane tried unsuccessfully to raise the airliner by radio, according to the captain.

Two hours after leaving Anchorage, according to Mr. Shultz's chronology, Flight 7 "came to the attention of Soviet radar" and was constantly tracked by the Soviet Union thereafter.

Said to Stray Over Kamchatka

It then apparently strayed into Soviet airspace over Kamchatka, a peninsula the size of Sweden that juts into the north Pacific between of the Bering Sea and the Sea of Okhotsk. It is believed to have many military installations.

Almost immediately, Soviet jet fighters scrambled, according to the American account. There were conflicting reports on whether the fighters were MIG-23's or 1960's vintage SU-15's.

The Soviet jets apparently pursued the airliner out of Soviet airspace and over the Sea of Okhotsk. Next, the planes re-entered Soviet airspace over Sakhalin Island, a mountainous 600-mile sliver of land north of Japan that has air and naval installations.

What happened next was apparently monitored by United States intelligence installations, although this was not made explicit.

At 3:12 A.M. Thursday (2:12 P.M. Wednesday, New York time), Mr. Shultz said, a Soviet fighter pilot reported visual contact with the airliner.

At 3:21, he reported that the airliner's altitude was 32,000 feet.

In the next two minutes, Japanese air-traffic controllers at Narita, a huge airport outside Tokyo, received the airliner's last radio transmissions. A transcript provided by the Japanese Transport Ministry showed this:

K.A.L.: Will climb to 35,000 feet. Leaving 32,000 altitude.

Narita: Roger.

K.A.L.: This is K.A.L. 7 . . . .

Narita: We can't hear you. Please change to 10.048 kHz. K.A.L. 7, this is Tokyo radio. How is 10.048 kHz?

There was no response.

At 3:26 A.M., Mr. Shultz said, "the Soviet pilot reported that he fired a missile and the target was destroyed."

Four minutes later, the Secretary of State said, the Soviet pilot reported the Korean aircraft at 15,000 feet. And eight minutes later, he said, the airliner disappeared from radar screens.

* * *

September 4, 1983

EUROPE FACES HOT AUTUMN ON HOSTILITY TO MISSILES

By W.R. APPLE

LONDON—For Western Europe, summer ended last week with the kind of traffic jams and chaotic airports that the United States will experience today and tomorrow. Among other things, the advent of fall marks the beginning of a politically testing season. First and foremost, it is to be the season of the missiles. Unless, by some miracle, American negotiators can wrest a last-minute agreement from the Soviet Union at Geneva, the next few months—the exact dates have not been made public—will see the deployment of United States cruise missiles in West Germany and in Britain. The consequences are hard for anyone to calculate. Chancellor Helmut Kohl disparages predictions of a "hot autumn" in West Germany, but he is all but alone in doing so; the general expectation in Bonn is that he will spend much of his time in the weeks to come dealing with a campaign of hunger strikes, protest marches and attempted blockades of NATO bases. The antinuclear movement gave a preview last week with a peaceful demonstration that featured Heinrich B"oll, the Nobel Prize-winning novelist, some members of Parliament and about 1,000 other people outside the gates of a United States Army base in Mutlangen where Pershing 2's are due to be installed. Base officials refrained from calling in the police, which helped keep things quiet. What Mr. Kohl must try to avoid, his aides say, is the creation of a martyr or the involvement of American soldiers in a violent incident, either of which could convince the German public that the missiles are more of a threat than the Soviet threat they are meant to neutralize. Most of all, the West German Government wants to avoid giving a pretext for another surge of radicalism and terrorism like that of the late 1970's. The anarchists have already demonstrated their intentions to capitalize on the missile controversy with a series of bombings at American bases and the disruption of Vice President Bush's visit to Krefeld last spring. In Britain, Prime Minister Margaret Thatcher will also have to cope with antinuclear demonstrations. Her position is considerably stronger; less than three months ago, her pro-cruise Tories trounced the Labor Party, which had promised to cancel the deployment of the missiles. Her hold on Parliament is solid, and she has no coalition partner like the bumptious Franz Josef Strauss of Bavaria, who conducts regular political guerrilla raids against Mr. Kohl. Nor is the British peace movement as strong as those in West Germany and in neighboring Holland. It will be vulnerable to the anti-Soviet backlash from last week's shooting down of a South Korean airliner. Nonetheless, Mrs. Thatcher, too, will have to guard against an incident that would bring into the open the often unstated but pervasive hostility toward President Reagan among British voters. The big domestic event of the fall in Britain will be the selection of a new leader of the opposition Labor Party at the party conference in Brighton at the beginning of next month. It appears almost certain that Neil Kinnock, a glib, red-haired Welsh left-winger, who has never held Cabinet office, will defeat his two more moderate opponents, Roy Hattersley and Peter Shore. So attention is turning to the fight for the deputy leadership between Mr. Hattersley and Michael Meacher, an even less experienced left-winger. Labor's status as the main party of opposition is precarious after its humiliating defeat this summer; a further lurch to the left, which is what a Kinnock-Meacher team would mean, might well convince the British public to turn to the Liberal-Social Democratic Alliance as the principal alternative to the Conservatives. Mrs. Thatcher, Mr. Kohn and President Francois Mitterrand of France (who has no American missiles to worry about, although he supports the cruise program) all face continuing economic difficulties. Mr. Mitterrand, the only Socialist in the trio, must confront the worst problems, including the possibility of further demonstrations like those of last spring by students, police, doctors and others against Government policies. In response to high interest rates and a large trade deficit, Mr. Mitterrand instituted an austerity program frankly designed to cut people's standard of living. The result, so far, gives the Government some cause for optimism. The latest statistics, released early last month, show a marked decline in the trade deficit, a slight decline in inflation (from 9.7 to 9.3 percent), and no increase in unemployment. But the shopkeepers and others are restive about increased taxes, and there appears to be no chance of delaying a surge in the jobless figures. The key to whether there will be trouble in the streets would appear to lie with the huge Communist-led trade union, the Confederation Generale du Travail. The Communist Party has been relatively quiet so far because it wants to retain its place in the Government, but it cannot afford to seem tame to its militant working-class backers, especially in the face of major layoffs in nationalized industries. Ultimately, the union may decide on the basis of Mr. Mitterrand's success with the economy. If things seem to be improving, the unionists will probably lie low. Socialist-led Governments in Spain and Italy also will face tough problems this fall with high unemployment and inflation. Like France, Britain is continuing to suffer from high American interest rates and a strong dollar. A modest recovery that helped Mrs. Thatcher to win in June now shows signs of petering out; fear of just such a development was a key reason in her decision to go to the country early. Unemployment, already at a record level well above three million, is widely expected to reach four million before starting to fall. But there is no threat of trouble in the streets or of any concerted action from the disoriented and divided opposition. In West Germany, the economic picture is a good deal brighter, with both the balance of payments and inflation under control. But the underlying trend of unemployment, now at 9 percent, is still upward, and there is no sign of a surge in export orders, traditionally the trigger of economic recovery for the Germans. At the moment, Bonn's best customers are broke. Meanwhile, the three big countries and their Common Market partners are trying to reach agreement on some means of putting that organization's finances, strained to the breaking point by mushrooming agricultural subsidies, back on a firm footing. That may be the toughest chore of all for Mrs. Thatcher, Mr. Kohl and Mr. Mitterrand in the months that lie ahead.

* * *

September 12, 1983

A NEW U.S. TRANSCRIPT INDICATES SOVIET PILOT FIRED 'CANNON BURSTS'

By BERNARD GWERTZMAN
Special to The New York Times.

WASHINGTON, Sept. 11—The State Department today issued a revised transcript of a Soviet pilot's remarks that quotes him as saying he fired "cannon bursts" nearly six minutes before launching two missiles that shot down the South Korean airliner with 269 people aboard.

The new version provides possible but inconclusive substantiation for the Soviet contention that the pilot of the SU-15 jet fired warning shots before eventually downing the Boeing 747 with rockets. But the department said the shots might have been aimed at the plane, and added that in any case, the new information had not altered the previous contention that the Korean airliner never received any warning, and that "the Soviets consciously made the decision to shoot down the aircraft."

As the revisions in the transcipt were being released, Representative Larry P. McDonald, Democrat of Georgia, one of the 269 people killed on the Korean airliner, was memorialized by more than 3,000 people at a service here in Washington. Many at the service, held at Constitution Hall, were critical of what they called a tame response by President Reagan to the Soviet attack.

The statement about firing "cannon bursts" was one of three passages from the transcript of the pilots' messages that were revised after an extensive review of the tapes by linguistic experts.

Transcript Released at U.N.

The Administration had maintained until today that there was no indication the Soviet fighter pilot who shot down the Korean 747 had fired tracer shells to warn the airliner to land on Sakhalin island, as the Russians have repeatedly said he did. For instance, at the United Nations Security Council Tuesday, Jeane J. Kirkpatrick, the chief United States delegate, said, "Contrary to Soviet statements, the pilot makes no mention of firing any warning shots—only the firing of the missiles, which, he said, struck the target."

The original transcript, which was released at the United Nations simultaneously with Mrs. Kirkpatrick's statement, traces the Soviet pilot, known by his flight number, 805, as he reported to ground control while he tracked the Korean plane and, at 1826:20 Greenwich mean time, fired his rockets. Two seconds later he said that the "target was destroyed." That transcript provided no indication that any other weapon was fired except rockets.

But the revised transcript reveals for the first time that at 1820:49, nearly six minutes before the firing of the rockets, the pilot reported to ground control: "I have broken off lock-on. I am firing cannon bursts." The second part of this statement had previously been termed unintelligible.

The State Department, in a statement that was released this morning along with the revised transcript, said, "The transcript does not indicate whether the cannon shots were aimed at the Korean Air Lines plane or were tracer rounds." A plane's cannon is a shell-firing gun.

The statement noted that according to a transcript made public by the Japanese Government, the Korean airliner made a routine radio transmission at 1823, Greenwich time, "over two minutes after the cannons were fired," and gave no indication that it was aware of Soviet aircraft in the vicinity or that cannons had been fired.

"The evidence indicates that the pilot was totally unaware of the fact that he was off course, that he was intercepted by Soviet fighters or that any warnings—visual, radio, gunfire—were given," the statement said.

'Hundreds of Replays of Tape'

In explaining the discovery of the remarks on the cannon shots, the department said its linguistic experts had "continued to review the poor quality transmission on the tape" that was played to the Security Council. It said that the review was now complete and that as a result of "electronic enhancement" of the tape and "hundreds of replays of the tape," the experts "were able to interpret three passages more clearly."

The most important of the changes in the transcript appeared to be the one raising the possibility that warning shots might have been fired, even though the State Department maintained, in its statement, that there was no evidence to suggest the Korean pilot was aware of any such warning.

Another segment that was revised occurred at 1819:08 Greenwich mean time. The pilot who eventually shot down the plane was originally quoted as saying at that time, "I have enough time." The department said the correct transcription of the sentence should be, "They do not see me."

The statement is transliterated from the original Russian given as "Oni menya ne vidyat." The original version offered by the State Department is transliterated as "A vremya ne vyidet."

No Explanation of Discrepancy

It was not clear from the context what meaning to place on the corrected version. Did it mean, for instance, that the pilot was concerned that the Korean airliner did not see him and therefore was not responding to possible warnings? That would be the kind of meaning the Soviet authorities would seem sure to place on the remark.

It could also mean the pilot was reporting that he was not being detected, and therefore was in a better position to shoot the airliner down. This would be the interpretation that American officials presumably would place on the phrase.

The third change was to clear up the question whether the Soviet pilot fired one or two rockets. In the original transcript, there was a seeming internal contradiction, with the Soviet pilot being quoted as saying at 1823:37 that he would try "a rocket," and later as reporting that he had fired "both rockets."

The State Department said that after rechecking the tape, the experts "were able to clarify that the plural was used." Therefore, according to the department, the translation of the remark at 1823:37 should be, "Now, I will try rockets." The change reflected the experts' decision that the Russian word used by the pilot was "rakety" rather than "raketu."

U.S. Sticks to Its Position

The department said it was issuing the clarifications "as part of the policy of the United States Government to develop full information on the tragic shootdown of Korean Air Lines 007 by Soviet forces on Aug. 31."

It said that "this additional analysis of the tapes reinforces our belief that the totality of the events remains exactly as stated by the United States and Japan."

"The Korean airliner was not aware of the Soviet fighters, nor was it aware that any warning was given," it said. "The Soviets consciously made the decision to shoot down the aircraft. The fact is that it was an unarmed, civilian airliner, and it cost the lives of 269 innocent people."

* * *

September 22, 1983

BUSH PROMISES AID FOR EAST BLOC STATES WITH INDEPENDENCE

VIENNA, Sept. 21 (UPI)—Vice President Bush blamed Moscow today for the East-West division of Europe and pledged American support for countries that stray from the Kremlin's line.

Mr. Bush, before flying home to Washington after a tour that included stops in Hungary and Rumania, specifically praised the two Warsaw Pact countries for their independent policies.

In a speech sponsored by the Austrian Association for Foreign Policy and International Relations, he denied that the Yalta conference at the end of World War II had divided the continent into "spheres of influence," instead blaming the split on Soviet distortions of the Yalta accords.

"We recognize no lawful division of Europe," he said.

He also said the United States rejected "the notion that the Helsinki accord endorses the status quo, the present division of Europe."

Mr. Bush said the United States was ready to respond to the Eastern bloc countries to the extent that they are meeting their own people's aspirations, are pursuing their own, independent foreign policy and are willing to open up to the rest of the world."

"The United States will engage in closer political, economic and cultural relations with those countries such as Hungary and Rumania which assert greater openness or independence," he said.

He stressed that Washington "does not seek to destabilize or undermine any Government" and is "not saying that countries must follow policies identical to those of the United States."

* * *

October 6, 1983

ABC FILM DEPICTING CONSEQUENCES OF NUCLEAR ATTACK STIRRING DEBATE

By SALLY BEDELL SMITH

The ABC-TV film "The Day After," which graphically depicts the consequences of massive nuclear attack against the United States, is not scheduled to appear for seven weeks, but already it is generating emotional controversy on both sides of the nuclear-arms issue.

Because of widespread support for the film among groups urging the limitation of nuclear weapons, there has been growing criticism of ABC among organizations that advocate a stronger nuclear defense. As a result, some ABC officials say they are becoming concerned that the film is being made a political issue.

Numerous antinuclear-weapons activists have seen copies of the $7 million film, which ABC says were made without the network's authorization, although organizations on the other side apparently have not. "It would appear that someone involved in the production of the film has decided that it is a tool to help one side of the argument and has set about attempting to do that," said Tony Makris, director of Congressional relations for the American Security Council, a Washington-based organization advocating increased national defense.

'$7 Million Ad Job'

Most of the weapons-limitations groups are planning an array of events—teach-ins, press conferences, and appearances on radio and television shows—surrounding the film's showing on Nov. 20 in an effort to attract support for some form of disarmament among the film's viewers.

"ABC is doing a $7 million advertising job for our issue," said Janet Michaud, executive director of the Campaign Against Nuclear War, a disaramament group based in Washington. "We couldn't begin to reach as many people as they reach if we pooled all our resources. We want to reach new constituencies."

Those who have seen the contraband copies of the film include representatives of many of the major groups advocating disarmament or a freeze of nuclear weapons at current levels as well as several members of the House of Representatives who have been active in the nuclear-freeze movement. Representative Edward J. Markey, Democrat of Massachusetts, said: "I believe it is going to be the most powerful television program in history. People will be irrevocably changed in terms of their attitude about nuclear war."

Some See a Danger

Mr. Markey, who sponsored the nuclear-freeze resolution in the House, is planning to introduce a Congressional resolution praising ABC for making the film. Because of the film, he said, "the cause of arms control will be advanced." "Anyone," he said, "who advocates limited survivable nuclear war is not going to be happy with this movie."

At the same time, advocates of a stronger defense have begun to attack the ABC film and to plan activities of their own—including demonstrations at ABC television stations and letter-writing campaigns to potential advertisers. They contend that the film is dangerous because it is an emotional rather than a reasoned approach to nuclear war. And they maintain that the film's presentation—several weeks before the scheduled deployment of the United States Pershing 2 nuclear missiles in Europe—could help the Soviet Union's efforts to prevent that deployment by stirring up public opinion against a buildup of nuclear arms.

William A. Rusher, publisher of The National Review, charges this week in an editorial—his second attacking ABC for planning to show the film—that it will "generate an ignorant public hysteria at a time when calm resolution to preserve a credible deterrent is called for." The conservative magazine Human Events, in its current issue, calls "The Day After" a "propaganda spectacular." Both Mr. Rusher and Cliff Kincaid, the writer of the Human Events article, said they had not seen "The Day After."

'Going to Arouse Passions'

ABC officials emphasize that the two-hour film is intended to be nonpolitical. "We specifically took painstaking care not to in any way make the film a political statement for either side on the issue of nuclear warfare," said Anthony Thomopoulos, president of the ABC Broadcast Group.

"A backlash is bound to come. This film is going to arouse passions, and we could pay a price for it," said one ABC official, who requested anonymity. Among the concerns are that conservative critics could dissuade advertisers from buying commercial time, pressure ABC affiliated stations not to carry the program and to discourage viewers from tuning in.

The film, which stars Jason Robards, John Cullum, Jobeth Williams and Steven Guttenberg, focuses on Kansas City and several outlying communities following a full-scale nuclear war between the United States and the Soviet Union. Although the film never makes clear which side initiated hostilities, two references are made to Soviet concern over the deployment of Pershing missiles. One, a fragment of a radio broadcast, quotes a Soviet official as saying that it was "the coordinated movement of Pershing 2 launchers that provoked the original Soviet" action.

Ads Cost $135,000 Apiece

Mindful of the film's controversial implications, ABC has scheduled a special edition of "Viewpoint," ABC's periodic forum for an exchange of ideas, for one hour following the conclusion of "The Day After" at 10:15 P.M. Participating in the program will be a panel of experts representing various views on nuclear issues. "We recognize that the film will stimulate debate, and part of our mission is to provide a court in which people with different opinions can play," said George Watson, executive producer of "Viewpoint."

ABC has been screening the film for potential sponsors for the last month. According to one ABC sales official, several advertisers have agreed to buy commercial time, which is being sold in 25 30-second spots for an average price of $135,000 apiece. However, ABC is keeping the names of its advertisers confidential for fear that critics of the film will try to pressure sponsors into dropping out. "We don't want to open them up to any kind of nonsense from pressure groups," said the official, who requested anonymity.

However, ABC officials are determined to show the film even if the network stands to lose money. "The film will air on Nov. 20 regardless of how many advertisers are in it," said Mr. Thomopoulos.

A number of antinuclear-weapons groups will sponsor activities keyed to the showing of "The Day After." Physicians for Social Responsibility, a national organization that claims a membership of 30,000, is organizing discussion groups around the country to follow the program.

Viewing Being Organized

In Kansas City and Lawrence, Kan., a town of 53,000, where the film was shot, candlelight vigils will be held immediately following the program, and the next day town meetings in both locations will explore the questions raised by the film. "Our purpose is to convey a message about nuclear war to take back to Washington," said Allan Hanson, the coordinator of Let Lawrence Live, the group organizing activities in Lawrence with funds from the physicians' organization. "We want the arms race brought to an end right away."

In Washington, Ground Zero, an arms-reduction group, is producing more than 100,000 copies of a pamphlet about nuclear issues and is attempting to organize thousands of viewing groups around the country in high schools, colleges and churches, according to Theo Brown, deputy director of Ground Zero. Its slogan: "The Day After": too frightening to watch alone, but every American should watch it."

Other groups, such as the Campaign Against Nuclear War, in Washington, are raising money to buy advertising time on television, radio and in newspapers offering a toll-free number for viewers to call after the program to learn more about preventing nuclear war. The Center for Defense Information, a Washington-based group headed by retired military officers that supports a nuclear freeze, is producing a 60-second commercial narrated by Paul Newman, the actor, offering viewers a "nuclear war prevention kit." The center has raised half of the $100,000 it needs to place these commercials at the end of "The Day After" in dozens of cities around the country, according to Arthur Kanegis, media director for the center. In addition, the center's half-hour documentary about the nuclear issue narrated by Mr. Newman, "War Without Winners," will be shown following the ABC film in 50 cities around the country—but in some cases not on the same channels that will be showing "The Day After," for example, in New York City, it is scheduled on WNEW-TV.

Concern Over Young Viewers

Many of these activities are being planned because antinuclear activists believe that they must counteract the film's despair. "The film is paralyzing," said Susan Alexander, associate director of Educators for Social Responsibility, a national organization representing teachers and administrators. "There is no hope offered. People could just walk away from the film and the issue altogether. So it is important to prepare people to get involved in a positive way," she added.

Many who have seen the film have expressed special concern about how it will affect children. "We are urging families to actively prevent anybody under 12 from watching it," said Miss Alexander. However, to assist teachers in helping older students with the film, the educators group is joining with several other organizations, including the Union of Concerned Scientists, in a series of symposiums at more than 500 high schools and colleges around the country during the week of Nov. 5.

In the New York City area, a special conference for educators will be held in Suffolk County on Nov. 5. It will be called "Nuclear Lessons: Teaching for 'The Day After.' " The conference is being organized by Representative Thomas Downey, Democrat of New York, who saw "The Day After" several weeks ago.

Campaigns Being Organized

So far, ABC says, it has not shown the film to any special-interest groups or politicians, although such screenings are planned for the coming weeks. Mr. Thomopolous said he was "horrified" by the wide circulation of contraband copies of the film. He said: "I have had no discussion with any of those groups. We will do nothing to politicize this film."

Though no "peace through strength" groups, advocating a nuclear buildup, say they have seen the film, several groups are nevertheless beginning to mobilize to present their views on the subject. Accuracy in Media, a conservative press-watchdog group in Washington, is sending letters to 450 potential advertisers. "We are pointing out that this movie is generating enthusiasm among people opposed to having NATO missiles stationed in Western Europe," said Reed Irvine, chairman of Accuracy in Media.

Young Americans for Freedom, a conservative youth group with 100,000 members nationwide, is planning a teach-in at the University of Kansas in Lawrence to promote nuclear deterrence. There will also be demonstrations outside ABC offices in New York, Washington and Los Angeles, as well as letters to advertisers contending that the show is "propaganda that is detrimental to our national interest," said Robert Dolan, national chairman of the group.

A number of advocates of a bolstered nuclear defense are particularly concerned that antinuclear groups could have the edge in influencing public opinion because they have seen the film so far in advance. John Fisher, president of the American Security Council, said: "By showing nuclear war and how terrible it is, you have repeated the only argument the nuclear freezers have. People get very emotional about that, and whoever is best organized will capitalize on that emotion."

* * *

October 18, 1983

GERMANS WANT THE MISSILES

By PETER PETERSEN

BONN—Unfortunately, it looks increasingly unlikely that the Soviet Union and the United States will meet the December deadline for reaching an agreement on intermediate-range nuclear missiles in Europe—and, therefore, increasingly likely that the first such missiles will have to be deployed in West Germany, Britain and Italy before the end of the year.

The approaching deadline has badly exacerbated tensions, both between the superpowers and within the Western alliance. Disruptive anti-nuclear demonstrations have erupted in West Germany, and the Soviet Union has threatened to walk out of the negotiations in Geneva.

In this climate, some people in both the United States and West Germany have advocated postponing the deadline in order to keep the Geneva talks going and, eventually, avoid the deployment of the Pershing II and cruise missiles. We West German Christian Democrats strongly reject their suggestion: If we give up the December deadline, we will never again be able to fix another and make it stick.

The parties that form the Government in West Germany are firmly committed to deployment on our soil if the negotiations fail. We are for deployment now as we were in 1979 when Helmut Schmidt, then the Chancellor, proposed it and the North Atlantic Treaty Organization committed itself to the "double-track decision"—committed itself to installing missiles if negotiations failed.

Postponing deployment would undermine any slim chance of reaching an agreement: To get any kind of result in Geneva, we must make it clear to the Russians that we will deploy unless they agree to take out the SS-20 missiles that they now have in place. Nor is there any reason to believe that a delay would be fruitful: The talks have gone on long enough for both sides to understand thoroughly each other's positions. There are no new arguments. Moscow could have an agreement in a week if it really wanted one.

A delay could only be to the advantage of the Soviet Union, which has deployed one new SS-20 per week since the two-track decision was taken. At the time, there were 110 SS-20's in place—they were the reason that the decision was made in the first place. Today, there are some 335.

Former Secretary of Defense Robert S. McNamara wrote recently: "Nuclear weapons serve no military purpose whatsoever. They are totally useless—except only to deter one's opponents from using them." To us, this is a baffling and contradictory statement—for in our view deterrence is a perfectly valid, even compelling, reason to deploy the new missiles. We don't see how Mr. McNamara could come to any other conclusion.

The only reason for the North Atlantic Treaty Organization to deploy any weapons is to deter our opponents from using force or blackmail against us. We West Germans recognize that any war, nuclear or conventional, limited or not, would destroy our country—no matter who "won" in the end—and we are therefore determined to do all we can to deter one.

Much attention is given lately to polls that seem to indicate that the majority of West Germans are against deployment. This is misleading: One can get any results one wants from a survey poll, depending on the way that the questions are framed. Besides, these polls directly contradict the results of general elections held in the last year in Britain, Italy, the Netherlands and West Germany. NATO and NATO plans for intermediate-range missiles were very much an issue in all the campaigns—and in each country the party or parties that stood for the double-track decision received a vast majority, defeating those that were ambivalent or opposed to deployment.

Since the Korean airliner incident, even some members of the West German peace movement are having second thoughts. Maybe, some are saying, it is not true that all it takes to secure peace is to be nice to the Russians. Maybe in the face of such an opponent, the way to assure peace with freedom is to be firm, always willing to negotiate the reduction of forces—any forces—but strong enough to send a clear signal to any potential aggressor.

We must be sure that the men in the Kremlin know that they cannot do to any part of the North Atlantic Treaty Organization what they did in Afghanistan. Why not? Because they cannot calculate the risk involved.

Yes, we West Germans fear war. But we also know from looking across the Wall into East Berlin that there is no real peace without freedom. For us, deployment is important not as an end in itself but as a means to peace with freedom.

Peter Petersen is a member of the West German Christian Democratic Union, a representative in the Bundestag and ranking member of its Armed Services Committee.

* * *

October 26, 1983

1,900 U.S. TROOPS, WITH CARIBBEAN ALLIES, INVADE GRENADA AND FIGHT LEFTIST UNITS; MOSCOW PROTESTS; BRITISH ARE CRITICAL

By MICHAEL T. KAUFMAN
Special to The New York Times.

BRIDGETOWN, Barbados, Oct. 25—An assault force spearheaded by United States troops invaded Grenada before dawn today and soon seized both of the island's airfields. But the advance of the invaders, who included contingents from seven Caribbean nations, was reportedly slowed in the afternoon by heavy fire in the capital.

According to military and intelligence sources in the Caribbean, the initial landings were made by helicopter. Fire from armed Cubans met those landing at a jet runway being completed by Cuban workers at Point Salines, four miles south of St. George's, the capital.

In the initial contact, 12 Cubans were killed and 24 captured, according to officials of the Barbados Government, one of the contributors of troops to the invading force.

Russians Reported Seized

The United States contingent consisted of marines and army rangers. At least one marine was reported here to have been killed; in Washington the Defense Department put the number of marines dead at two.

Radio stations here reported that 30 Soviet advisers to the Grenadian Government had been seized. But officials here said they could not confirm that report.

By this afternoon, a source who had returned from Grenada reported that the invading force had established a perimeter that included the southern half of St. George's. The part of the city held by the multinational force included the deep-water harbor, the Prime Minister's residence and the Grenada Beach Hotel, the former Holiday Inn, which had been occupied by Cuban workers and Cuban troops.

Prime Minister Edward P. G. Seaga of Jamaica, whose country also had troops in the invading force, told the Jamaican Parliament in Kingston in the afternoon that "all major objectives" had been secured. He identified these as the two airfields; the two campuses of the St. George's University School of Medicine, where about 500 Americans are enrolled; the power station, and the broadcasting station. He reported also that three civilians had been killed.

Military analysts here, however, said it was likely that Cuban troops, whose numbers have been variously estimated between 500 and 1,000, had retreated into the heavily populated northern sector of the city, where any combat would involve sniper fire and house-to-house fighting.

The assault force that landed at the Point Salines airstrip moved to the capital in armored cars and jeeps. But its advance was reported slowed in the afternoon when it came under fire from the area of the central post office, which lies across the half-moon harbor known as the Carenage.

Some fighting was reported at Fort Rupert, the Grenadian Army headquarters on a steep hill above the port. But reports received here conflicted on whether the installation had been seized from Cuban and Grenadian forces. Firing was also reported from Fort Cedric on the outskirts of the city.

A second part of the invading force was positioned at Pearls Airport, 13 miles north northeast of St. George's. This force was expected to advance toward the south.

Figures on Force Differ

According to information available here, the assault was staged by at least 500 United States marines and army rangers and 300 soldiers from Barbados, Jamaica, Antigua, St. Vincent's, St. Lucia, Dominica and St. Kitts-Nevis, with about 1,500 Americans in a backup force offshore. These figures differed from totals given in Washington by Government officials, who said that about 1,300 marines and rangers landed in Grenada and were later reinforced by 300 Caribbean troops. The officials said that 600 marines remained in reserve aboard the helicopter carrier and amphibious ship Guam.

The invasion force was reportedly assembled on short notice from bases more than a thousand miles apart. Some of the United States troops reportedly came from Puerto Rico, some from Panama. Trucks and armored vehicles as well as concertina tents were flown to the Grenada headquarters from both Barbados and Trinidad. Armored cars and jeeps were flown to Barbados in an almost nonstop shuttle beginning this morning from Fort Polk, La.

Jamaican troops arrived in Barbados aboard an Air Jamaica airliner.

Trinidadian Leads Force

The Grenada operation, which was set in motion Monday after consultations here between Prime Ministers Seaga of Jamaica, Eugenia Charles of Dominica and J. M. G. Adams of Barbados and the United States Ambassador, Millard Bish, was commanded by Col. Ken Barnes, a Trinidadian serving in the Jamaica Defense Forces.

At dawn today, Colonel Barnes was aboard the United States aircraft carrier Independence but soon shifted over to the Point Salines airfield on Grenada, which is now the headquarters for the multinational force.

Additional troops and equipment, including a portable radio station, were flown to the island early this morning. The United States is supplying most of the materiel as well as the bulk of the forces.

On Monday, hours before the invasion, a Cuban vessel, the Vietnam Star, which had been tied up in the St. George's harbor, pulled out to sea, and Western sources here speculated that it might have taken some Cuban troops as well as some of the hard-line Grenadian Marxists whose power struggle with the leftist Prime Minister, Maurice Bishop, precipitated the chaos on the island. Mr. Bishop and more than 40 other Grenadians, including most members of his Cabinet, were killed by Grenadian troops last Wednesday.

According to sketchy reports from Grenada being relayed here by Barbadian military spokesmen, the resistance to the invading force was conducted today mostly by Cubans. Mobilization orders have been broadcast over the last two days by the official Radio Free Grenada, but only a few Grenadian miltiamen reportedly have responded.

The station went off the air today after broadcasting the news that the island had been invaded. It came back on briefly on a new frequency, leading Caribbean broadcasters in Barbados to believe that it had moved to the Soviet Embassy, which is in the northern part of St. George's. But broadcasts halted again this afternoon. Today's invasion was applauded by officials of the Organization of Eastern Caribbean States, which had appealed for United States help in dealing with Grenada, and by groups of Grenadian exiles.

"All we have wanted was a free Grenada and it appears that we now have a Grenada that is free," said a spokesman for the Grenada National Democratic Movement who held a news conference here to discuss the island's eventual return to democratic and civilian rule.

Vaughan Lewis, the director general of the Organization of Eastern Caribbean States, said the military action had been taken because the countries of the region had grown alarmed "at the military buildup in Grenada" which he said posed a threat to the stability of the region. He said the countries had called for help from the United States in accordance with the terms of a treaty empowering them to organize their collective defense.

It was decided Monday to alert units for a possible invasion after United States diplomats who had visited Grenada returned with reports that the Revolutionary Military Council there appeared to have retreated from earlier pledges to facilitate the departure of those Americans, Britons and Canadians who wished to leave.

Change of Mind Reported

According to a source close to the Government here, the United States diplomats had been told over the weekend that foreigners would be free to leave on commercial flights. By Monday, the Grenadians had reportedly changed their minds and said that six-hour advance notification had to be given for any flights.

They also said that their forces would not be able to guarantee the safety of the foreigners during the 13-mile ride to Pearls Airport. According to the source, it began to appear to some Americans that because of the very weak hold of the Grenadian military, which had scant public support, the Grenadian officials were moving toward effectively keeping the foreigners as hostages, either to permit the Cubans and Soviet advisers time to extricate themselves or to shore up the faction-ridden and chaotic Government.

In his televised statement in Washington this morning, President Reagan alluded to the question of the thousand Americans on the island by saying the United States had moved to "restore order and democracy." He made it clear that there were political considerations in the American participation and that these had as much to do with the decision as the safety of the Americans, most of whom are students at the St. George's University School of Medicine.

Here in Barbados, the initiative has been received with great enthusiasm. All day, radio talk shows have been carrying messages of congratulations phoned in by people all over the Caribbean. Calls to people in Grenada, made at random and broadcast on the radio, drew invariably happy responses from people who said they looked upon the invasion as a rescue.

* * *

November 24, 1983

SOVIET BREAKS OFF PARLEY IN GENEVA ON NUCLEAR ARMS

By JOHN VINOCUR

Special to The New York Times.

GENEVA, Nov. 23— The Soviet Union broke off talks with the United States today on medium-range nuclear missiles, saying it would set no date for resuming the negotiations.

The Soviet action was described in an official statement from Tass, the official Soviet press agency, as a "discontinuation of the present round of talks."

The action was widely expected because the Soviet leadership had frequently said over the two-year course of the negotiations here that the talks could not be continued once deployment of American-manufactured Pershing 2 and cruise missiles began in European countries of the North Atlantic Treaty Organization.

West Germans Vote Approval

On Tuesday, the West German Parliament approved the immediate start of deployment of the Pershings. The first of the missiles began arriving in West Germany today.

A first shipment of American-made cruise missiles arrived at an air base in Britain on Nov. 14. They are scheduled to be operational by the end of the year.

Today's Soviet decision to interrupt the talks here was described as "unilateral" as well as "unjustified" and "unfortu-

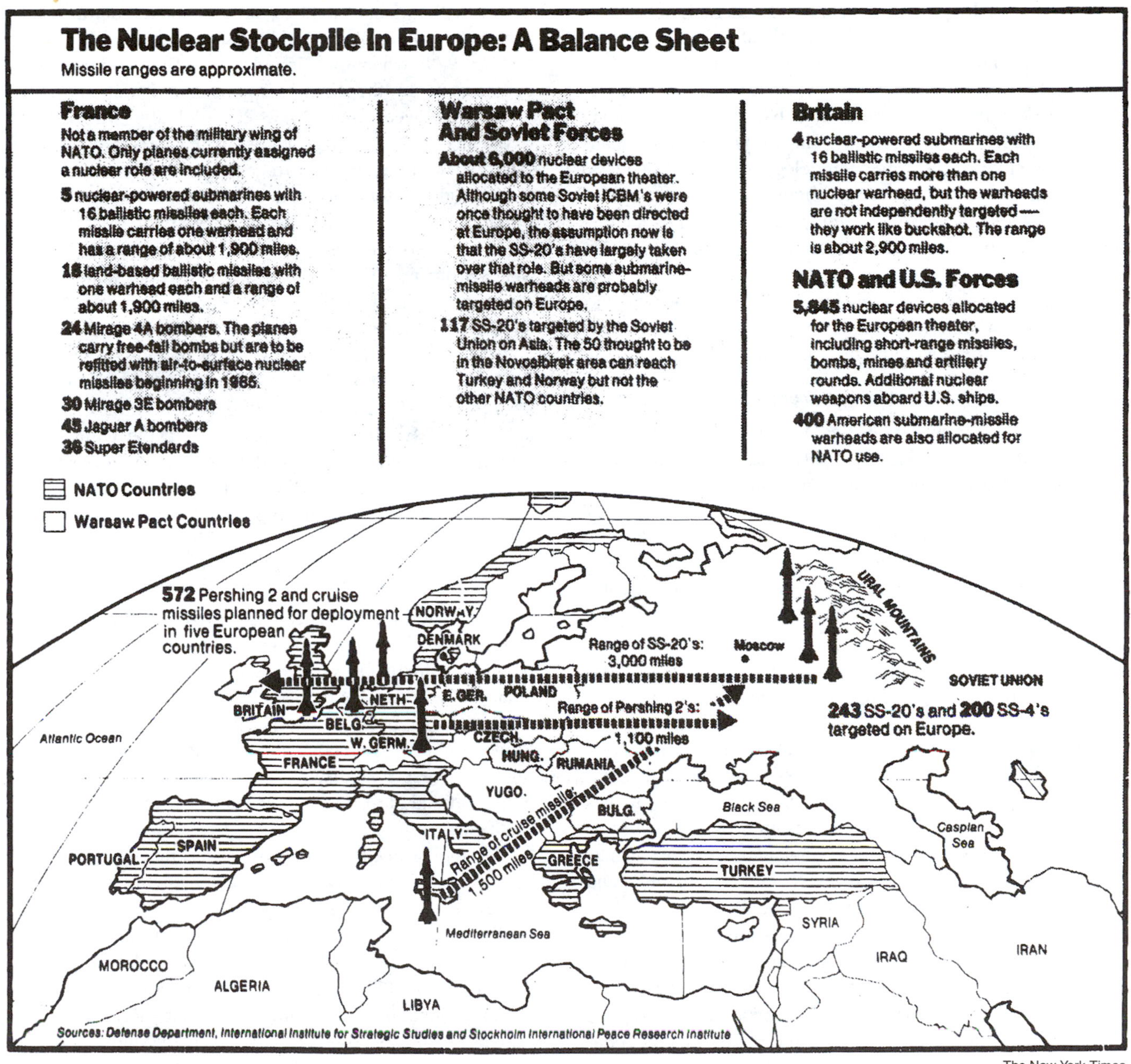

Source: Defense Department: International Institute for Strategic Studies and Stockholm International Peace Research Institute

nate" by the chief American negotiator, Paul H. Nitze. He said the United States deeply regretted the Soviet decision and was prepared to continue talking until an agreement was reached.

While avoiding predictions that the Russians would soon return to the talks here, Mr. Nitze called attention to the careful and apparently nondefinitive character of the Soviet announcement of the talks' interruption.

25-Minute Session Held

Mr. Nitze, who talked to reporters at a news conference, appeared to try to cast the Soviet step in the least dramatic light possible, stressing that today's 25-minute session had taken place in a businesslike manner and that the Soviet statement did not foreclose the possibility of future discussions.

"As you know," he said, "the Soviets did not say they were breaking off the talks absolutely. They declared they were discontinuing the present round without setting a date for resumption. So we are hopeful that the Soviet side will come to the conclusion that it is to their interest as well as to our interest and the world's interest that the negotiations resume."

One NATO analyst said the Soviet decision to halt the meetings was a logical move, with the Russians apparently hoping to limit or roll back the missile deployment by creating a period of heightened tension in Western Europe. The current series of talks ended without theatrics, although the mood in the conference room today was described as somber. The chief Soviet negotiator, Yuli A. Kvitsinsky, appeared at the entrance to the headquarters of the United States negotiating team where he shook hands with Maynard W. Glitman, the deputy chief of the American delegation. Mr. Kvitsinsky then issued a one-line statement announcing the interruption to reporters and drove off in a limousine. Afterward, according to one account, delegation members exchanged individual goodbyes.

"It was good knowing you," one of the Russians was said to have told an American counterpart. "It's been a pleasure and a privilege to work with you," another said.

Two Conflicting Standpoints

The interruption in the talks came at the 105th session of the series that began Dec. 1, 1981. The negotiations have essentially revolved around two conflicting standpoints—the position of the United States, holding out for equal levels of deployment, and that of the Soviet Union, which has adopted equal reductions as a bargaining concept in a way that would leave the United States without the deployment of any missiles in Europe.

The parallel talks on long-range, or strategic, nuclear weapons are still in session. The two sides in those negotiations met here Tuesday and agreed to meet again at the same time next week.

The NATO deployment schedule now calls for the stationing of 572 Pershing 2 and cruise missiles over a period running through 1986. The decision to deploy the weapons has been explained by the treaty organization as a measure to counter the 243 SS-20 missiles, each with three warheads, that are targeted on Western Europe by the Soviet Union, and the 117 mobile SS-20's it has aimed at points in Asia.

The NATO analyst described the Soviet departure statement as a "medium-line" document, placing it between possible formulations that he characterized as totally hard or rather more soft. If the Russians had sought a more definitive position, he said, they would have used the phrase "the negotiations have ended."

Instead, the analyst continued, they made a reference to the notion of the talks' being resumed, and chose a relatively imprecise word—"discontinuation"—to characterize their action today.

Mr. Nitze avoided predicting what the Russians might do in the next month, insisting that a resumption of the talks was entirely up to them.

In a statement issued after today's meeting, the United States negotiator described the Soviet decision as being "as unjustified as it is unfortunate."

Prior Soviet Deployment Cited

"The Soviet Union has rationalized the suspension of these negotiations on the grounds that approval by NATO parliaments of United States missile deployments and United States deployments of those missiles make continuation of such talks impossible," Mr. Nitze stated.

"In 1979, when the United States first proposed I.N.F. negotiations to the Soviet Union, the Soviet Union had already deployed some 140 SS-20's globally," Mr. Nitze said of the medium-range missile talks. The letters I.N.F. stand for intermediate-range nuclear forces.

"The global total of SS-20's is now 360, and this Soviet buildup continues," the American negotiator went on. "This continuing Soviet buildup has not prevented the United States from pursuing these negotiations and making every effort to reach an equitable agreement. These negotiations should continue until an agreement is reached."

"The United States stands ready to halt or reverse its deployments if an equitable agreement to reduce and limit, or eliminate, United States and Soviet I.N.F. missiles can be achieved," Mr. Nitze said. "For its part, the United States remains prepared to continue the I.N.F. negotiations until an agreement has been reached and our two countries have thus fulfilled their responsibility to contribute to the cause of peace."

Query on Merging of Talks

At his news conference, Mr. Nitze was questioned on whether he thought the talks on medium-range weapons would eventually be melded with those on intercontinental strategic weapons. He replied, "I do not think it's inevitable."

The Soviet position on this possibility remains unclear. Some official Soviet statements seem to have hinted at bringing the two sets of discussions together, but apparently no Soviet official has broached the subject with American negotiators here.

In rough terms, the United States has moved over the two-year period from a "zero option," involving no American deployment in exchange for the scrapping of all Soviet intermediate-range missiles, to a proposal that would allow the Russians 420 intermediate-range warheads in Europe and Asia. The United States, in turn, would deploy a lesser number, but an amount taking disparities in Asia into account.

The Soviet positions have successively suggested lowering the number of SS-20's targeted on Europe, each with three warheads, to 162, then 140, and most recently to a figure close to 120, but in each case on the condition that no corresponding American weapons are deployed.

Asked what the negotiations had achieved, Mr. Nitze said, "A great deal." He said both sides had moved, making progress "on almost all the issues."

"The one thing that has remained constant on the Soviet side," he said, "has been their demand that there be a continuation of the militarily significant deployment of SS-20's in Europe, and that there be absolutely no U.S. deployment of counter missiles on our side."

The American negotiators had been expecting the break-off since last month.

* * *

February 14, 1984

CHERNENKO IN TOP SOVIET POST; VOWS TO RETAIN ARMS BALANCE, WARNS AGAINST 'ADVENTURISTS'

By JOHN F. BURNS

Special to The New York Times.

MOSCOW, Feb. 13—Konstantin U. Chernenko was chosen by the Communist Party's Central Committee today to succeed Yuri V. Andropov as its General Secretary.

His assumption of the post automatically made Mr. Chernenko the Soviet Union's pre-eminent leader. At 72 years of age, he is the oldest of the men named to lead the party since the Bolshevik Revolution in 1917.

Mr. Chernenko immediately made a wide-ranging speech to the Central Committee in which he praised Mr. Andropov for the "tremendous prestige and respect" he had gained among the Soviet people and endorsed many of Mr. Andropov's domestic policies.

Selection Termed Unanimous

On relations with the United States, he said that while the Soviet Union remained committed to peaceful co-existence and elimination of the threat of nuclear war, it would insure that it had enough arms "to cool the hotheads of militant adventurists."

"We need no military superiority," he said. "We do not intend to dictate our will to others. But we will not permit the military equilibrium that has been achieved to be upset. And let nobody have even the slightest doubt about that: We will further see to it that our country's defense capacity be strengthened, that we should have enough means to cool the hot heads of militant adventurists."

An official announcement said that the 12 members of the ruling Politburo had unanimously recommended the appointment of Mr. Chernenko and that the Central Committee, which has about 300 members, had also been unanimous in approving the nomination.

An Aide to Brezhnev

The appointment marked what appeared to be a remarkable political comeback for Mr. Chernenko, a Russian peasant's son from Siberia who left school at the age of 12 and worked his way through party ranks to the Kremlin as an aide and protege of Leonid I. Brezhnev. He was the losing candidate 15 months ago when Mr. Andropov was named party leader in succession to Mr. Brezhnev and in the months after that he appeared to go into a partial political eclipse.

Public reaction to the appointment was muted. Russians, always wary of offering opinions of their leaders, found little to say to Western reporters who sought them out in the markets, standing guard at checkpoints around the Kremlin, and in rush-hour lines at bus stops. But some seemed disappointed at the choice of a man of Mr. Chernenko's age and reputation as a close ally of Mr. Brezhnev.

"I hope this does not mean a return to things as they were under Brezhnev," a merchant at the Central Market said. "Nobody wants to go back to the slack times anymore."

Appointment Widely Expected

Mr. Chernenko's appointment had been widely expected after he was named chairman of the funeral commission for Mr. Andropov, who died of a chronic kidney ailment last Thursday. But it came as a surprise to many Western analysts of the Soviet Union, some of whom predicted last spring that Mr. Andropov would ease Mr. Chernenko out of the Politburo to blunt resistance to his policies from Brezhnev allies.

Today, many diplomats acknowledged they were stumped for a ready explanation of Mr. Chernenko's appointment to a job that was widely thought to be lost to him forever after Mr. Andropov defeated him in November 1982.

Some thought that it meant the effective abandonment of Mr. Andropov's efforts to revitalize the party and the economy while others thought that Mr. Chernenko, as an experienced politician, would retain at least those elements of the Andropov legacy that were widely popular, such as the crackdown on sloth and corruption.

While these issues were debated, it was clear that the most powerful job in the Soviet political structure had passed to a man vastly different in character and background to Mr. Andropov.

While the former leader came to the post from 15 years as K.G.B. chief and was considered an intellectual by Kremlin standards, Mr. Chernenko has never ventured outside the ranks of the party bureaucracy and lacks Mr. Andropov's reputation for subtlety. His principal field of expertise in a 52-year party career has been ideology and propaganda, overall responsibility for which was assigned to him under Mr. Andropov.

Bush Arrives in Moscow

In his first public appearance as party leader, standing with other Politburo members before Mr. Andropov's bier, Mr. Chernenko appeared somber and preoccupied. He was absent from the Kremlin for several weeks last spring with what his office said was pneumonia, but Soviet officials said today that he had followed a regular work routine since then and was in good health.

The announcement of Mr. Chernenko's appointment coincided with the arrival here of the first of several dozen world leaders who will attend Mr. Andropov's funeral Tuesday in Red Square.

Among them was Vice President Bush, who was accompanied by Senator Howard H. Baker Jr., the Senate majority leader. The two went directly from Sheremetyevo airport to pay respects at Mr. Andropov's bier. After pausing for 20 seconds before the open casket, the Vice President approached members of the dead leader's family seated to one side of the bier and conversed briefly with Mr. Andropov's son, Igor, a diplomat.

In an arrival statement distributed to reporters, Mr. Bush said he was attending the funeral as President Reagan's representative to symbolize American "regard for the people of the Soviet Union" and to "signify the desire of the United States to continue to work for positive relations between our two countries."

The statement added: "We believe there are important opportunities ahead to help bring peace to regions torn by conflict, to achieve substantial reductions in nuclear weapons and to increase contact and cooperation between our peoples."

In his remarks to the Central Committee on domestic matters, Mr. Chernenko, a short white-haired figure with slightly hunched shoulders, voiced his support for the drive for greater responsibility from party officials, for more effort from the work force and for a "serious restructuring" of the economy, policies associated with Mr. Andropov.

But as befitted the closest political confidant of Mr. Brezhnev, whose political sponsorship over 30 years lifted Mr. Chernenko from the obscurity of a provincial propaganda chief to the inner circles of the Kremlin, the new leader also praised the country's past economic achievements and warned against "belittling" them.

Soothing Party Officials

In this and in other passages that blurred the distinction that Andropov supporters have made between the Brezhnev and Andropov periods, Mr. Chernenko appeared to be trying to ease the anxieties of party officials at all levels who felt threatened by Mr. Andropov's tough policies.

But while the tone of the speech was considered by some diplomats here to be conservative, they said it was too early to conclude that the new party leader intended to turn the clock back to the Brezhnev period, with its accumulation of bureaucratic privileges and relative immobility.

The diplomats said that more information was needed on how the decision on the leadership was made before reliable projections of Mr. Chernenko's course could be made.

Among other things, the diplomats said, it was important to know whether Mr. Chernenko's candidacy had faced opposition and if so on what basis and whether he had given undertakings to Andropov loyalists in the Politburo, a number of them younger men who were closely identified with Mr. Andropov's efforts to stimulate the party and the nation.

Although various accounts circulated in Moscow, none of these matters could be satisfactorily clarified. The Central Committee meeting appeared to have taken place in the Kremlin but even this had to be inferred from the movement of Zil and Chaika limousines that swept out of sight through the Borovitsky gate before 11 A.M., when Soviet sources had said the gathering was to begin.

Meeting Appears Brief

The meeting appeared to be brief. At 2 P.M. (6 A.M. New York time), the official press agency Tass and announcers on radio and television made simultaneous statements on Mr. Chernenko's appointment and followed with a formalized account of the proceedings, a biography of Mr. Chernenko and texts of the speeches made by the new leader and by Prime Minister Nikolai A. Tikhonov, who placed Mr. Chernenko's name in nomination.

Mr. Tikhonov's role in nominating the new party leader was one of several clues being sifted by analysts. Aged 78, he is the oldest member of the Politburo and had links with Mr. Brezhnev going back to the 1930's, when both were metallurgical engineers.

This and the fact that Mr. Chernenko was flanked by Mr. Tikhonov and other members of the Politburo in their late 60's and 70's on his appearances today and on Saturday at Mr. Andropov's bier suggested to some observers that an "old guard" had swung the leadership to Mr. Chernenko.

Some analysts inferred from Mr. Tikhonov's role in nominating Mr. Chernenko was that there had been no formal contest for the leadership. This inference was based on a party tradition, followed most recently when Mr. Andropov was nominated by Mr. Chernenko, that assigns the job of nominating the new leader to his defeated rival.

The procedure is intended to show unity, but since Mr. Tikhonov's age and other factors made him an improbable candidate for the leadership, analysts felt that there had to be another reason for his being given the task.

One theory was that there had been resistance to Mr. Chernenko, probably not in the formal Politburo meeting but in maneuvering that occurred in the four days that passed between the appointment today and Mr. Andropov's death.

When Mr. Brezhnev died, Mr. Andropov was named the new leader in only two days. Speculation about a possible power struggle focused on two men who seemed close to Mr. Andropov, Mikhail S. Gorbachev and Geidar A. Aliyev, and on a third who was thought to have a chance of succeeding Mr. Andropov, Grigori V. Romanov. These three form the core of the Politburo's younger members—Mr. Gorbachev is 52, Mr. Aliyev is 60 and Mr. Romanov is 61.

* * *

August 1, 1984

REAGAN AND PAPAL ENVOY TO DISCUSS MOVES AGAINST POLAND

By FRANCIS X. CLINES

SANTA BARBARA, Calif., July 31—The White House announced today that the Vatican's Apostolic Delegate to the United States would meet Wednesday with President Reagan at his vacation ranch to discuss the expected easing of American sanctions against Poland.

White House officials said privately that the unusual interruption of the President's vacation had some domestic political overtones of possible value to the President's reelection strategy of appealing to Roman Catholic voters.

But the President's spokesman, Larry Speakes, insisted that the sole reason for the visit was the President's interest in

Pope John Paul II's views on how well the Polish Government is fulfilling its promise to ease restrictions on political prisoners. Democratic critics have accused the President of trying to "pander" to Roman Catholic voters, a charge denied by the Reagan campaign.

'Views of the Holy See'

"The President believes it is important to have the views of the Holy See prior to making his final decisions on a number of Polish sanctions that were imposed over the last three years," Mr. Speakes said.

He added that the President valued the views of the Pope on a wide range of matters, including Central America and arms control, and particularly looked forward to his estimate of current affairs in Poland.

The Apostolic Delegate, Archbishop Pio Laghi, will have a private "working lunch" with the President at Mr. Reagan's mountainside ranch Wednesday. The President's national security adviser, Robert C. McFarlane, will also attend.

After the Polish Parliament approved an amnesty bill on July 21 that authorized the release of 652 political prisoners and some 35,000 common criminals, Administration officials said Mr. Reagan was likely to approved a further easing of sanctions. But they said the Administration would not lift the most damaging sanctions until there was more progress toward liberalization in the country.

The economic sanctions were first imposed after the declaration of martial law by the Polish Government in December 1981.

Views 'Under Advisement'

Mr. Speakes said the President would be taking the Vatican's views "under advisement" along with recommendations from Administration officials before making his final decision in the next several days. He said Administration officials had been looking for progress from the Polish Government in fulfilling its promise to release political prisoners from jail across a 30-day period this summer.

"We have always weighed the church's views on a number of subjects such as Central America, Eastern Europe, arms controls," Mr. Speakes said.

"These have been the discussions in the two meetings that the Pope has had with the Holy Father over the last two or three years," Mr. Speakes added, quickly correcting himself to refer to the Pope and the President.

Politically, Reagan strategists have been working hard to devise measures to counter the Democrats' nomination of Representative Geraldine A. Ferraro, a Roman Catholic, as Vice President and the challenge this poses to Mr. Reagan's relatively strong standing with Catholic voters.

Pope a 'Guiding Force'

Mr. Speakes said that seeking the Vatican's views on the Polish question was part of the Administration's policy in view of the Pope's strong interest in his homeland and the church's role as a "guiding force" in Poland.

"We have always consulted with the church on these matters," he said. Earlier this year, the Administration established full diplomatic relations with the Vatican.

The American sanctions include restrictions on Polish airline landing rights in the United States. The sanctions were partly relaxed earlier this year when Polish fishing boats also were allowed to re-enter American waters in response to an initial easing of conditions in Poland.

The Administration also reacted to the imposition of martial law by opposing new agricultural and trade credits for Poland, by restricting high technology exports and by opposing Poland's participation in the International Monetary Fund. Administration officials said the President's final decision would probably not relax the full range of economic sanctions.

* * *

August 10, 1984

'RED DAWN,' ON WORLD WAR III

By JANET MASLIN

Apocalypse Again

RED DAWN, directed by John Milius; screenplay by Kevin Reynolds and John Milius; director of photography, Ric Waite; edited by Thom Noble; music by Basil Poledouris; produced by Buzz Feitshans and Barry Beckerman; released by MGM/UA Entertainment Company. Running time: 114 minutes. This film is rated PG.

Jed .... Patrick Swayze
Robert C. .... Thomas Howell
Erica .... Lea Thompson
Matt .... Charlie Sheen
Daryl .... Darren Dalton
Toni .... Jennifer Grey

To any sniveling lily-livers who suppose that John Milius, having produced "Uncommon Valor," directed "Conan the Barbarian" and written "Apolcalypse Now," has already reached the pinnacle of movie-making machismo, a warning: Mr. Milius's "Red Dawn" is more rip-roaring than anything he has done before. Here is Mr. Milius at his most alarming, delivering a rootin'-tootin' scenario for World War III.

The place: a small, all-American town. The time: sooner than you think, mister. A history teacher is telling his class about Ghenghis Khan, when he looks out the window and sees enemy parachutists landing. We learn from a 15-second preamble that the United States has lost all its allies, and that the Soviet Union is badly in need of food. Soon enough, we see, beneath a bumper sticker that says "They can have my gun when they pry it from my cold dead fingers," the corpse of a American citizen, being relieved of his weapon by an invading soldier.

In Calumet, Colo., where the action takes place, a band of brave high-school boys heads for the mountains, taking with them bows and arrows and lots of Coca-Cola. They hide out for awhile, initiating themselves in the ways of the wild—drinking the blood of a deer they kill, for instance, or urinating into the radiator of their truck when it runs out of water. Eventually, they are ready to infiltrate Calumet's Main Street, and what they see there is horrible. The citizens have been rounded up in a detention camp, which used to be the local drive-in. The drugstore's supplies are so depleted that there's only one lone bottle of Charlie on the shelves. The movie theater is playing "Alexander Nevsky."

The band of teen-agers, calling themselves the Wolverines, after the town's football team, and joined by two girls whose grandfather refers to them as "my heirlooms," begins a guerrilla war against the invaders, some of whom are Cuban and Nicaraguan.

The rest of the film follows the course of this fateful struggle and is confined to Calumet, with only occasional news bulletins from "Free America," as much of the country is now known. An outsider the kids encounter tells them what's happening in Denver, for instance: "They live on rats and sawdust bread and, sometimes, on each other." This same outsider, asked "Who's on our side?" by one Wolverine, replies, "Six hundred million screamin' Chinamen."

"Last I heard there were a billion screamin' Chinamen," the Wolverine answers.

"There were" is the grim reply.

"Red Dawn," which opens today at the National and other theaters, may be rabidly inflammatory, but it isn't dull. Mr. Milius does know how to keep a story moving. He might well have turned this into a genuinely stirring war film, if he had not also made it so incorrigibly gung-ho. But the effectiveness of its chilling premise, from a story by Kevin Reynolds, is dissipated by wildly excessive directorial fervor at every turn. Those who consider the events set forth in "Red Dawn" to be probable are no more apt to find the movie credible than those who regard them as ludicrous.

The cast of "Red Dawn" has obviously been through a lot; the production notes quote John Early, technical adviser, as saying that the actors were taught military discipline and combat techniques, and that "we took them out into the hills and ran them from sunup to sundown."

They also had a lot to contend with in the screenplay, by Mr. Reynolds and Mr. Milius, which is hard-bitten enough to be virtually unplayable at times. Powers Boothe, who delivers those bulletins from the free zone, must also declare, when asked what his wife was like, "I met her in a closet at a party. Couldn't stand her at first, but once it took, I loved her so bad it hurt."

Mr. Boothe does a good job anyway, and so does Ron O'Neal as a Cuban commander leading the Calumet occupation. Ben Johnson and Harry Dean Stanton appear very briefly, Mr. Stanton to shout, "Avenge me! Avenge me!" from behind the barbed wire at the drive-in.

The younger players, among them Patrick Swayze, C. Thomas Howell and Lea Thompson, are adequate but less memorable. Their roles consist mainly of carrying out small-scale military maneuvers and reacting to such awful spectacles as the image of a band of Calumet citizens being executed by a firing squad. They sing "America the Beautiful" just before they're shot—but their patriotism is not in question, and the movie might have been a little less overbearing without the song.

"Red Dawn" is rated PG ("Parental Guidance Suggested"). It contains considerable violence, most of it not very explicit.

* * *

August 18, 1984

REAGAN CRITICIZES DIVISION OF EUROPE

By STEPHEN ENGELBERG

Special to The New York Times.

WASHINGTON, Aug. 17— President Reagan said today that the United States could not passively accept the "permanent subjugation of the people of Eastern Europe."

Speaking at a White House luncheon commemorating the 40th anniversary of the Warsaw uprising against Nazi forces, Mr. Reagan said the United States "rejects any interpretation of the Yalta Agreement that suggests American consent for the division of Europe into spheres of influence."

The 1945 Yalta agreement between the United States, Britain and the Soviet Union divided Germany into zones of occupation and set up a provisional government for Poland that included figures allied with both the West and Soviet Union.

The leaders agreed to free elections for the remaining countries in Europe liberated from the Nazis.

Critics have since contended that the Yalta accord set the stage for the cold war and Soviet control of Eastern Europe. American conservatives have criticized the terms as a betrayal of United States and European interests. In 1952, the Republican platform called for "repudiation" of the Yalta accord, saying that it aided "Communist enslavements."

In his comments, Mr. Reagan said he would "press for full compliance" with the Yalta agreement—specifically its stipulation of free elections. "We see that agreement as a pledge by the three great powers to restore full independence, and to allow free democratic elections in all countries liberated from the Nazis after World War II," he said. "There is no reason to absolve the Soviet Union or ourselves from this commitment." The President added: "Passively accepting the permanent subjugation of the people of Eastern Europe is not an acceptable alternative. In 1981, when it appeared Poland would suffer a similar fate to that of Hungary in 1956 or Czechoslovakia in 1968, we raised our voices in support of the Polish people. And we did not remain passive when under intense Soviet pressure, martial law was imposed upon them."

No New Policy, Aide Says

A White House official said the President's speech was not intended to set new Administration policy but was instead a means of underscoring President Reagan's concern about human rights issues in Eastern Europe.

He said several other Administration spokesmen had previously objected to "misinterpretation" of the Yalta agreement. Vice President Bush, for example, said in a speech last year in Vienna, "We recognize no lawful division of Europe."

In his luncheon speech to about 125 Polish-Americans and veterans of the Polish Home Army, the underground force that fought in Warsaw, Mr. Reagan once again attempted to use humor in his battle of words with Soviet Union.

Last week, the President's joke about outlawing and bombing the Soviet Union, made during a audio check for his weekly radio broadcast, provoked controversy in the United States and abroad.Today he told a story about an American and a Soviet citizen who were discussing freedom of speech. Mr. Reagan quoted the Russian: "Well, we're free to speak in the Soviet Union just like you are in the United States. The only difference is, you're free after you speak."

Mr. Reagan criticized people who "seem all too willing to turn a blind eye to Soviet transgressions, obstensibly to improve the dialogue between East and West." He added: "But those who condemn firm support for freedom and democracy—who in order to prove their sincerity would project weakness—are no friends of peace, human liberty or meaningful dialogue."

Targets of Criticism Unspecified

Larry Speakes, the White House spokesman, would not say whom the President had in mind.

Walter F. Mondale, his Democratic opponent, has said he would support a freeze on nuclear weapons and would immediately open arms talks with the Soviet Union if elected.

Mr. Reagan depicted economic sanctions, applied against Poland after the imposition of martial law in December 1981, as evidence that his Administration had not remained "passive" in the face of Soviet pressure.

Earlier this month, the Administration announced that it would authorize the easing of some of these sanctions in response to an amnesty for political prisoners.

Mr. Reagan has begun the process of restoring landing rights to the Polish airline and as well as resuming scientific exchanges. The Administration also said it would probably withdraw United States opposition to Polish membership in the International Monetary Fund.

A White House statement on Aug. 3 said the remaining sanctions, including a ban on direct Government credits, could be lifted if Warsaw fulfilled its pledge to release all political prisoners, particularly 11 protest leaders. They have been released.

An Administration official said no decision had been made on the sanctions but that Polish moves so far were "encouraging," in that the Government had kept its promise to release the prisoners.

Credits Are Still Blocked

The official said there has been no discussion of lifting the ban on credits, which prevents the Commodity Credit Corporation from guaranteeing American wheat sales to Poland. The Administration has also not yet taken up the question of whether to restore tariff preferences—called most favored nation trade status—to Poland.

At the luncheon today, President Reagan announced that he would ask Congress to appropriate $10 million as an American contribution to a farm improvement program administered by the Roman Catholic Church in Poland.

Others giving money to the fund include European and Canadian churches, Lech Walesa, who donated his $200,000 in Nobel Peace Prize money, and West European governments.

Mr. Reagan presented posthumous medals to three heroes of the Warsaw uprising: Maj. Gen. Leopold Okulicki, Lieut. Gen. Tadeusz Bor Komorowski and Lieut. Gen. Stefan Rowecki.

* * *

August 19, 1984

MOSCOW CRITICIZES REAGAN ON YALTA

By SETH MYDANS

Special to The New York Times.

MOSCOW, Aug. 18—The Soviet Union, reacting to President Reagan's remarks on the division of Europe, today accused him of distorting history and defaming both the Soviet Union and Poland.

Mr. Reagan, speaking Friday at a White House luncheon, said the United States rejected any interpretation of the 1945 Yalta Agreement "that suggests American consent for the division of Europe into spheres of influence," and added that the United States could not passively accept "the permanent subjugation of the people of Eastern Europe."

Tass, the official press agency, said Mr. Reagan's remarks, made in the framework of the election campaign, "challenge the postwar political setup in Europe."

It said that "no one, the White House included," has the right to call into question the decisions of the Yalta Conference or of the 1975 Helsinki Accords that confirmed the borders of Eastern Europe.

Fears of German Unification

It said Mr. Reagan's statements "strike the same notes" as demands it said are being made by some people in West Germany for a reunification with East Germany.

Moves toward better relations between the two Germanys have brought angry attacks from the Soviet press, which says attempts are being made to redraw the postwar German borders.

Plans for a visit to West Germany next month by the East German leader, Erich Honecker, have aroused particular criticism in Moscow of what it calls "revanchists" who seek a unified Germany. The Yalta Agreement, signed by the United States, Britain and the Soviet Union, addressed questions of the shape of the postwar world and included a statement of "the right of all peoples to choose the form of government under which they will live."

In Poland and in other Eastern European nations occupied by Soviet troops, Communist governments took control.

"We see that agreement as a pledge by the three great powers to restore full independence, and to allow free democratic elections in all countries liberated from the Nazis after World War II," the President said at the luncheon, which commemorated the 40th anniversary of the Warsaw uprising against the Nazis.

Tass said Mr. Reagan "used the occasion to call into question the decisions of the leaders of the three Allied powers" and "to defame People's Poland and the Soviet Union."

The Tass report referred to the President as "Mr. Reagan," a curt form of address in the protocol-conscious Soviet press that is reserved for occasions that do not call for niceties.

Jest Also Aroused Criticism

The comment on his remarks about Yalta followed days of agitated reaction to what the Soviet press has dubbed Mr. Reagan's "prank" in which the President, during a microphone test, jokingly said the United States was about to bomb the Soviet Union.

Soviet commentators have said Mr. Reagan was showing his true feelings in the off-the-record remark. The Communist Party daily, Pravda, said, "He blabbed out what is permanently on his mind."

The Tass article today was headlined, "President Reagan in his usual role."

"Distorting the history of Poland's liberation from the fascist yoke, the President did not utter a single word about the liberation mission played in the war by the Soviet and Polish armies," Tass said. "For what to President Reagan are 600,000 lives of the Soviet soldiers who died in the effort to liberate Poland?"

Tass said "all upright patriots of Poland remember and highly respect that contribution to the great battle against fascism. U.S. leaders should not forget about it either."

Sanctions Are Assailed

Tass added that President Reagan had shown what it called his true lack of concern for Poland's welfare by imposing sanctions against it and "by grossly intervening and continuing to intervene in the internal affairs of that sovereign state."

United States sanctions were instituted against Poland after the imposition in 1981 of martial law.

In a separate commentary today, Tass said Mr. Reagan's joke about bombing had aroused "indignation the world over" that extended to the President's "adventuristic policy" and "unwillingness to seek solutions to major political questions."

"It is emphasized in many pronouncements that Washington's recent attempts to improve Reagan's reputation, to present him as a sort of champion of peace, have flopped," Tass said.

"The whole world saw Reagan as a man who is saber-rattling, who conducts the policy directed against the cause of peace."

* * *

August 25, 1984

PRESIDENT ASSERTS DEMOCRATS CAUSED ERA OF SELF-DOUBT

By STEVEN R. WEISMAN

Special to The New York Times.

President Reagan pressed his attack on the Democrats today, saying they were responsible for a "dismal chapter of failed policies and self-doubt."

He likened their support for a nuclear freeze and cancellation of key weapons programs to the views of a "jackass."

Speaking to 1,500 applauding members of the Veterans of Foreign Wars, Mr. Reagan made his comments while suggesting "it would have been indefensible and immoral" to allow American military strength "to continue deteriorating as it was" before he took office.

He said that "some may insist they're just as committed to a strong deterrent even as they would cancel" production of the B-1 bomber and the MX missile. He said these people "may deny that a nuclear freeze would preserve today's high, unequal and unstable level of nuclear weapons."

He Is Reminded of Rayburn

"But that way of thinking only reminds me," he went on, "of what Sam Rayburn, a very wise Democratic Speaker of the House, once said: Any jackass can kick a barn down, but it takes a carpenter to build one."

The veterans responded with laughter and applause. Larry Speakes, the White House spokesman, said Mr. Reagan did not intend to apply the epithet "jackass" to Walter F. Mondale, but he said the Democratic Presidential nominee "represents the party of the donkey."

"It's just an old phrase out of middle America," Mr. Speakes added. "If the shoe fits, wear it."

Advisers Anxious on Stridence

Mr. Reagan made his comments despite the misgivings of some of his re-election advisers that his speech accepting the Republican nomination Thursday night contained too many partisan attacks on Democrats. These advisers are said to be concerned that an overtly strident approach could offend voters.

The President's advisers also counseled against overconfidence, with Senator Paul Laxalt, chairman of the re-election drive, said that he expected that the "exciting" poll results were soft.

Mr. Reagan has generally been attacking Mr. Mondale recently without mentioning his name, as he did today.

For example, he derided unspecified critics of the American invasion of Grenada last October.

"I seem to remember that it took critics weeks to decide whether it was a good idea to rescue our students," Mr. Reagan said. "They should have asked the students, for those students were already home."

Mr. Mondale was criticized last year for delays in taking a stand on the invasion, ordered after a coup appeared to endanger American medical students on the island.

The former Vice President initially withheld judgment about the invasion while asserting that the President failed to consult the Allies of the United States. He also said the invasion "undermines" the American ability to criticize Soviet actions in Afghanistan, Poland, Cambodia and elsewhere.

Later Mr. Mondale said the invasion might have been justified if the students' lives were in jeopardy or if Grenada was in danger of becoming a base for Soviet "subversion." He added that it was impossible to tell if this was the case because of a news blackout, and he said the Administration did not adequately explore alternatives to the use of force.

He Sees Proof of Buildup

Mr. Reagan said the performance of the military in seizing the Caribbean island and bringing out 600 American students demonstrated that his Administration's military buildup had paid off.

The military, he said, proved that it was "able to take on combat operations on short notice, get the job done, and get it done right." He said, "Because we were willing to take decisive action, our students today are safe, Grenada is free, and that region of the Caribbean is more peaceful and secure than before."

The audience cheered and shouted, "Four More Years! Four More Years!" Their reaction indicated that the invasion would become a major theme of Mr. Reagan's reelection drive. That theme brought substantial applause for Mr. Reagan's speech Thursday night at the Republican National Convention.

Mr. Reagan flew here from Dallas after meeting with members of the Republican National Committee this morning. After his speech to the veterans, he held a ceremony with Senator Charles H. Percy, a Republican who is in a tough reelection fight, to sign a bill establishing a federal commission to oversee development and preservation of a historic 100-mile canal from Chicago to La Salle, Ill.

He Did Not Wear His Cap

He then left for Washington, with plans to rest at Camp David, Md., after a busy week of politics.

The veterans have long been a receptive audience for Mr. Reagan. He has spoken before them several times, but usually he wears a V.F.W. cap. Today he did not, apparently because his advisers are these days trying to play down his identification with the military.

Indeed, White House officials noted that in this speech Mr. Reagan dwelt at length on the importance of arms control negotiations with the Soviet Union. One official said the speech could be seen as a contrast of sorts with the speech at the Republican convention of Jane J. Kirkpatrick, the United States representative to the United Nations, who spoke very little of the importance of arms control.

Only a few dozen demonstrators were outside the Conrad Hilton Hotel here, an unusually small number for Chicago. Inside the ballroom a single protester bore a sign that said, "Remember Lebanon."

Debate Negotiations Expected

In a related development, Mr. Reagan was asked by a reporter whether he was prepared to debate Mr. Mondale. His answer was inaudible, but Gov. James R. Thompson said he had answered yes. Campaign aides expect negotiations on the format and schedule of possible debates to begin shortly with the Mondale camp.

Mr. Reagan said he had proposed "seven different initiatives" to overcome the stalemate with the Soviet Union on nuclear arms. He said that the United States had to approach any negotiations from the position of military strength. "We're still not where we need to be, but we're getting there," he said. At another point, he contrasted the current situation with what he called the "halfway wishes" and problems of the past.

"Gone are the days when we abandoned principle and common sense," he said. "Gone are the days when we meekly tolerated obvious threats to our peace and security. Gone are the days when we either sought to achieve overnight grandiose arms control agreements that were bound to fail, or when we set our sights so low that the agreements permitted the numbers and categories of weapons to soar."

Volunteer Army Defended

The President also defended the all-volunteer Army before the group, which has called for a new draft. Mr. Reagan said that predictions that enlistment would drop once the economy started booming had proved wrong. Many people had predicted that the all-volunteer Army would deteriorate once the recovery began, he said.

"Well, forgive me, but those are the same people who were wrong on inflation, wrong on unemployment, wrong on interest rates and wrong on the recovery," he said. "And there they go again."

"It's hard to forget the mess America was in," the President said, "hard to forget the foolish talk of a malaise, the unfairness of runaway price increases, 21½ percent interest rates, weakened defenses, Americans held hostage, and the loss of respect for our nation abroad."

"It seemed that we woke up every morning wondering what new humiliation our country had suffered overseas, what disappointing economic news lay waiting for us on the front page," he said. "Well, I think we've come quite a long way together. In fact, I believe we've closed the books on that dismal chapter of failed policies and self-doubt."

PART IX

THE END OF THE COLD WAR

January 22, 1985

TRANSCRIPT OF SECOND INAUGURAL ADDRESS BY REAGAN

Following is a transcript of President Reagan's Inaugural Address in Washington yesterday, as recorded by The New York Times:

Senator Mathias, Chief Justice Burger, Vice President Bush, Speaker O'Neill, Senator Dole, Reverend Clergy and members of my family and friends, and my fellow citizens:

This day has been made brighter with the presence here of one who for a time has been absent. Senator John Stennis, God bless you and welcome back.

There is, however, one who is not with us today. Representative Gillis Long of Louisiana left us last night. And I wonder if we could all join in a moment of silent prayer.

Amen.

There are no words to—adequate to express my thanks for the great honor that you've bestowed on me. I will do my utmost to be deserving of your trust.

This is, as Senator Mathias told us, the 50th time that we, the people, have celebrated this historic occasion. When the first President, George Washington, placed his hand upon the Bible, he stood less than a single day's journey by horseback from raw, untamed wilderness. There were four million Americans in a union of 13 states.

Today we are 60 times as many in a Union of 50 states. We've lighted the world with our inventions, gone to the aid of mankind wherever in the world there was a cry for help, journeyed to the moon and safely returned.

So much has changed. And yet we stand together as we did two centuries ago.

When I took this oath four years ago, I did so in a time of economic stress. Voices were raised saying that we had to look to our past for the greatness and glory. But we, the present-day Americans, are not given to looking backward. In this blessed land, there is always a better tomorrow.

Meaning of New Beginning

Four years ago I spoke to you of a new beginning, and we have accomplished that. But in another sense, our new beginning is a continuation of that beginning created two centuries ago when, for the first time in history, government, the people said, was not our master. It is our servant; its only power that which we, the people, allow it to have.

The system has never failed us. But for a time we failed the system. We asked things of government that government was not equipped to give. We yielded authority to the national government that property belonged to states or to local governments or to the people themselves. We allowed taxes and inflation to rob us of our earnings and savings and watched the great industrial machine that had made us the most productive people an earth slow down and the number of unemployed increase.

By 1980 we knew it was time to renew our faith, to strive with all our strength toward the ultimate in individual freedom consistent with an orderly society.

We believed then and now there are no limits to growth and human progress when men and women are free to follow their dreams. And we were right. And we were right to believe that. Tax rates have been reduced, inflation cut dramatically and more people are employed than ever before in our history.

We are creating a nation once again vibrant, robust and alive. But there are many mountains yet to climb. We will not rest until every American enjoys the fullness of freedom, dignity and opportunity as our birthright. It is our birthright as citizens of this great republic.

Fruits of Meeting Challenge

And if we meet this challenge, these will be years when Americans have restored their confidence and tradition of progress; when our values of faith, family, work and neighborhood were restated for a modern age; when our economy was finally freed from government's grip; when we made sincere efforts at meaningful arms reduction by rebuilding our defenses, our economy, and developing new technologies helped preserve peace in a troubled world; when America courageously supported the struggle for individual liberty, self-government and free enterprise throughout the world and turned the tide of history away from totalitarian darkness and into the warm sunlight of human freedom.

My fellow citizens, our nation is poised for greatness. We must do what we know is right and do it with all our might. Let history say of us, these were golden years—when the American Revolution was reborn, when freedom gained new life and America reached for her best.

Our two-party system has solved us—served us, I should say, well over the years, but never better than in those times of great challenge, when we came together not as Democrats or Republicans but as Americans united in the common cause.

Two of our Founding Fathers, a Boston lawyer named Adams and a Virginia planter named Jefferson, members of that remarkable group who met in Independence hall and dared to think they could start the world over again, left us an important lesson. They had become, in the years spent in government, bitter political rivals. In the Presidential election of 1800, then years later, when both were retired and age had softened their anger, they began to speak to each other again through letters.

Lesson of 2 Founding Fathers

A bond was re-established between those two who had helped create this government of ours.

In 1826, the 50th anniversary of the Declaration of Independence, they both died. They died on the same day, within a few hours of each other. And that day was the Fourth of July.

In one of those letters exchanged in the sunset of their lives, Jefferson wrote, "It carries me back to the times when, beset with difficulties and dangers, we were fellow laborers in the same cause, struggling for what is most valuable to man, his right of self-government. Laboring always at the same oar, with some wave ever ahead threatening to overwhelm us, and yet passing harmless we rode through the storm with heart and hand."

Well, with heart and hand, let us stand as one today: one people under God determined that our future shall be worthy of our past. As we do, we must not repeat the well-intentioned errors of our past. We must never again abuse the trust of working men and women by sending their earnings on a futile chase after the spiraling demands of a bloated Federal establishment. You elected us in 1980 to end this prescription for disaster. And I don't believe you re-elected us in 1984 to reverse course.

The heart of our efforts is one idea vindicated by 25 straight months of economic growth: freedom and incentives unleash the drive and entrepreneurial genius that are the core of human progress. We have begun to increase the rewards for work, savings and investment; reduce the increase in the cost and size of government and its interference in people's lives.

We must simplify our tax system, make it more fair and bring the rates down for all who work and earn. We must think anew and move with a new boldness so every American who seeks work can find work; so the least among us will have an equal chance to achieve the greatest things—to be heroes who heal our sick, feed the hungry, protect peace among nations and leave this world a better place.

New American Emancipation

The time has come for a new American Emancipation, a great national drive to tear down economic barriers and liberate the spirit of enterprise in the most distressed areas of our country. My friends, together we can do this, and do it we must, so help me God.

From new freedom will spring new opportunities for growth, a more productive, fulfilled and united people and stronger America, an America that will lead the technological revolution and also open its mind and heart and soul to the treasuries of literature, music and poetry, and the values of faith, courage and love.

A dynamic economy, with more citizens working and paying taxes, will be our strongest tool to bring down budget deficits. But an almost unbroken 50 years of deficit spending has finally brought us to a time of reckoning.

We've come to a turning point, a moment for hard decisions. I have asked the Cabinet and my staff a question and now I put the same question to all of you. If not us, who? And if not now, when? It must be done by all of us going forward with a program aimed at reaching a balanced budget. We can then begin reducing the national debt.

I will shortly submit a budget to the Congress aimed at freezing government program spending for the next year. Beyond this, we must take further steps to permanently control government's power to tax and spend.

Must Protect Future U.S.

We must act now to protect future generations from government's desire to spend its citizen's money and tax them into servitude when the bills come due. Let us make it unconstitutional for the Federal Government to spend more than the Federal Government takes in.

We have already started returning to the people and to state and local governments responsibilities better handled by them. Now, there is a place for the Federal Government in matters of social compassion. But our fundamental goals must be to reduce dependency and upgrade the dignity of those who are infirm or disadvantaged. And here a growing economy and support from family and community offer our best chance for a society where compassion is a way of life, where the old and infirm are cared for, the young and, yes, the unborn, protected, and the unfortunate looked after and made self-sufficient.

Now there is another area where the Federal Government can play a part. As an older American, I remember a time when people of different race, creed or ethnic origin in our land found hatred and prejudice installed in social custom and, yes, in law. There's no story more heartening in our history than the progress that we've made toward the brotherhood of man that God intended for us. Let us resolve: There will be no turning back or hesitation on the road to an America rich in dignity and abundant with opportunity for all our citizens.

Let us resolve that we, the people, will build an American opportunity society in which all of us—white and black, rich and poor, young and old—will go forward together, arm in arm. Again, let us remember that, though our heritage is one of blood lines from every corner of the earth, we are all Americans pledged to carry on this last best hope of man on earth.

Safety and Security

And I have spoken of our domestic goals, and the limitations we should put on our national government. Now let me turn to a task that is the primary responsibility of national government— the safety and security of our people.

Today we utter no prayer more fervently than the ancient prayer for peace on earth. Yet history has shown that peace does not come, nor will our freedom be preserved, by good will alone. There are those in the world who scorn our vision of human dignity and freedom. One nation, the Soviet Union, has conducted the greatest military buildup in the history of man, building arsenals of awesome offensive weapons.

We've made progress in restoring our defense capability. But much remains to be done. There must be no wavering by us, nor any doubts by others, that America will meet her responsibilities to remain free, secure and at peace.

There is only one way safely and legitimately to reduce the cost of national security, and that is to reduce the need for it. And this we're trying to do in negotiations with the Soviet Union. We're not just discussing limits on a further increase of nuclear weapons. We seek, instead, to reduce their number. We seek the total elimination, one day, of nuclear weapons from the face of the earth.

Now for decades we and the Soviets have lived under the threat of mutual assured destruction; if either resorted to the use of nuclear weapons, the other could retaliate and destroy the one who started it. Is there either logic or morality in believing that if one side threatens to kill tens of millions of our people, our only recourse is to threaten killing tens of millions of theirs?

I have approved a research program to find, if we can, a security shield that will destroy nuclear missiles before they reach their target. It wouldn't kill people, it would destroy weapons. It wouldn't militarize space, it would help demilitarize the arsenals of earth. It would render nuclear weapons obsolete. We will meet with the Soviets hoping that we can agree on a way to rid the world of the threat of nuclear destruction.

We strive for peace and security, heartened by the changes all around us. Since the turn of the century, the number of democracies in the world has grown fourfold. Human freedom is on the march, and nowhere more so than in our own hemisphere. Freedom is one of the deepest and noblest aspirations of the human spirit. People worldwide hunger for the right of self-determination, for those inalienable rights that make for human dignity and progress.

America must remain freedom's staunchest friend, for freedom is our best ally, and it is the world's only hope to conquer poverty and preserve peace. Every blow we inflict against poverty will be a blow against its dark allies of oppression and war. Every victory for human freedom will be a victory for world peace.

So we go forward today a nation still mighty in its youth and powerful in its purpose. With our alliances strengthened, with our economy leading the world to a new age of economic expansion, we look to a future rich in possibilities. And all of this is because we worked and acted together, not as members of political parties, but as Americans.

My friends, we, we live in a world that's lit by lightning. So much is changing and we will change, but so much endures and transcends time.

Echoes of Our Past

History is a ribbon, always unfurling; history is a journey. And as we continue on our journey we think of those who traveled before us. We stand again at the steps of this symbol of our democracy, or we would've been standing at the steps if it hadn't gotten so cold. Now, we're standing inside this symbol of our democracy, and we see and hear again the echoes of our past.

A general falls to his knees in the hard snow of Valley Forge; a lonely President paces the darkened halls and powers, ponders his struggle to preserve the Union; the men of the Alamo call out encouragement to each other; a settler pushes west and sings a song, and the song echoes out forever and fills the unknowing air.

It is the American sound: It is hopeful, big-hearted, idealistic—daring, decent and fair. That's our heritage, that's our song. We sing it still. For all our problems, our differences, we are together as of old. We raise our voices to the God who is the author of this most tender music. And may He continue to hold us close as we fill the world with our sand, sound—in unity, affection and love. One people under God, dedicated to the dream of freedom that He has placed in the human heart, called upon now to pass that dream on to a waiting and a hopeful world.

God bless you and may God bless America.

* * *

March 3, 1985

THE EMERGENCE OF GORBACHEV

By SERGE SCHMEMANN

Official Soviet biographies make for specialized reading, somewhat in the style of classified ads: "Gorbachev, Mikh. Ser. (b. 1931), Sov. Part., Govt. Official. Mbr. CPSU 1952- . 1970 1st Sec'y Stavropol Kraikom CPSU. 1971 Mbr. CC CPSU. 1978 Sec'y CC CPSU. 1979 Cand. Mbr. Politburo CC CPSU. 1980 Mbr. Politburo CC CPSU . . ."

With practice, a message emerges from those stilted lines. The CPSU is the Communist Party of the Soviet Union. The CC is its Central Committee. And Mikhail Sergeyevich Gorbachev is the youngest of the 11 men who sit at the pinnacle of Soviet power, the Politburo.

Those few lines bracket a career that has become the focus of some of the most intensive speculation ever to have focused on the future of the Soviet state. The generation that led the Soviet Union from the ravages of Stalinism and World War II through the enormous expansion of power and might over the past three decades is approaching an end.

Now a new guard stands poised to take charge, a generation of men in their 50's and 60's, and the question is whether they will prove ready or capable of breathing new life into a system that seems to have followed its leaders into debility and fatigue. More than any other Soviet leader, Gorbachev has come to personify the new breed. At only 54 years of age, the peasant's son and career party official has emerged from the shadow of Kremlin politics to become No. 2 in the party hierarchy, and to be a major contender to succeed the ailing Konstantin U. Chernenko, a man 20 years his senior.

It was as if in recognition of his importance that a group of heavyset men in dark coats and heavy fur hats marched across the frozen tarmac to a waiting Aeroflot jetliner in December. At the foot of the forward ramp they bid goodbye to Gorbachev, who mounted the steps, pausing for the stiff wave required by the ceremony of a Politburo member setting off on a Kremlin mission. His wife, Raisa Maksimovna, unobtrusively mounted the back steps.

In London, the front door opened and the two popped out together, jubilantly waving to the welcoming officials and the banks of photographers.

It was a classic magician's trick: Put a Kremlin heavy into one end, quietly slip an attractive woman into the other, wave through the air and—Presto!—out comes a New Soviet Leader, smiling, charming, gregarious and complete with elegant, educated and cultured wife.

Few in Britain were disappointed. The Gorbachevs ooh'd and aah'd at Westminster Abbey and at Chequers. In the reading room of the British Museum, where Karl Marx once worked, he joked that "if people don't like Marxism, they should blame the British Museum." She ventured charmingly halting words in English and demonstrated a keen interest in literature and philosophy, which, it turned out, she had studied at Moscow State University. He suavely checked swarming photographers, saying, "Comrades, economize your supplies. That's enough." She captivated the gossip columnists: "What a chic lady is Mrs. Gorbachev!" gushed Peter Tory of The London Daily Mirror.

He wore business suits that made him indistinguishable from the Westerners he courted. She wore a dark suit one day, an executive pin-stripe with satin blouse the next, a white woolen suit with high- heeled patent-leather shoes the third, and, at a Soviet Embassy reception, a cream satin two-piece dress, gold lamé sandals with chain straps and pearl-drop earrings.

It was a measure of Gorbachev's success that he managed to generate excitement without diverging one whit from standard Kremlin lines. He faithfully pushed Moscow's current propaganda campaign against President Reagan's "Star Wars" space defense project, and he turned huffy at any mention of Moscow's repression of human and religious rights.

"I can quote a few facts about human rights in the United Kingdom," he fired back at one Member of Parliament who raised the issue in a private session. "For example, you persecute entire communities, nationalities." After some thought, his listeners concluded he probably meant Northern Ireland.

And, like any son of the Russian earth, he could not avoid a bit of classic Soviet bravado: "If you send us a flea, we will put horseshoes on it," he told a mystified Paul Channon, Trade Minister. The allusion was to a popular Russian tale whose moral is, in effect, that if you think you have done well, we can always top it.

That was hardly enough to darken the cheery glow of the visit. "A Red Star Rises in the East," declared The Sunday Times of London over a profile of Gorbachev. But it was Prime Minister Margaret Thatcher who provided the most fitting epitaph to the visit. "I like Mr. Gorbachev," said she. "We can do business together."

The scene of Mr. Gorbachev's return to Moscow, alas, is not recorded. He returned hurriedly on Dec. 21, six days into his visit, on learning of the death of Defense Minister Dmitri F. Ustinov. But given the immutability of Soviet civic ritual, it is safe to assume that she slipped out the back, while he gave a stiff wave up front to the dark men in fur hats gathered to welcome him back, and then stepped down to merge into their midst.

Who is the real Gorbachev? The Soviet politician poured from the same mold as his dark comrades, except for a bit more polish and pizzazz and a knack for public relations? Or the nice man who did the sights of London with his lady, bantered easily with the high and mighty, and charmed the British?

Kremlinologists are wary of spotting another "liberal" in the style of the late Yuri V. Andropov, and the debate over the real Gorbachev has gone back and forth. But if the outlines of the man remain a bit fuzzy still, what has emerged with startling clarity is that this stocky, balding peasant's son from southern Russia, with his pleasant style and calm face, has achieved one of the most dizzying rises in the annals of modern Soviet politics.

A scant three years ago, he was known to the West, where known at all, largely as the youngster of the Politburo, a farm boy two decades younger than most of his comrades, a competent and apparently smart politician whose no-win responsibility for agriculture would probably break his heart or his career. He presided, in fact, at a time when the perennially poor grain crop figures became a state secret. In May 1983, on the rise under his last and most powerful patron, Yuri Andropov, the young Agriculture Secretary toured Canada and was barely noticed by the rest of the world.

Yet by the time Chernenko came to power, Gorbachev was the acknowledged second in command of the Soviet Communist Party, an enormously powerful secretary charged with ideology, party cadres and most of the economy, as well, apparently, as agriculture. He has become the rallying point for an increasingly vocal portion of the white-collar elite that is convinced that the Soviet Union's solvency and credibility are at peril without a thorough overhaul of the economy.

Most important, he had emerged as a leading contender for the top job in the Kremlin, as the man who could lead a new generation to power in a leadership firmly gripped for 30 years by old Stalinists.

Why such a possibility excites, rather than alarms, the West is not always clear. It could be argued quite convincingly that a Kremlin in the hands of a bright new guard, not handicapped by the memories of Stalin or the insecurities of their war-scarred elders, could actually make the Soviet economy hum, making the Soviet Union a vastly more formidable and daunting adversary than it now is. One Western military attaché returned awe-struck from a recent voyage across the Soviet expanse and exclaimed: "My God, can you imagine what we'd be up against if they could make all that work?"

At a meeting of party workers last December, Gorbachev spelled out his program in unusually clear terms:

"We will have to carry out profound transformations in the economy and in the entire system of social relations. The process of the intensification of the economy must be given a truly nationwide character, the same political resonance that the country's industrialization once had."

Hyperbole, of course, is hardly new to Soviet rhetoric, and rare is the project not ranked with history's great exploits. But Gorbachev's words stood out for other reasons. He was not simply calling, like all Soviet leaders these days, for greater efficiency and managerial innovation. He was calling for a transformation of social relations in the Soviet system, for an upheaval that, as he indicated later in his speech, would lure the working man back into the fold. "Industrialization" was another word that made people listen. He seemed to be calling for a transformation of the nation as radical as the one wrought by Stalin in the brutal industrialization drive of the 1930's.

Snatching up the banner of his late mentor Andropov, Gorbachev argued that the Soviet Union would never achieve its global ambitions if it was unable to feed and clothe its own: "Socialism has exerted and continues to exert its main influence on world development through its economic policy and through its successes in the socioeconomic field."

The message was unambiguous: "Only an intensive, highly developed economy can guarantee the consolidation of the country's positions in the international arena, can permit the country to enter the new millennium as a great and flourishing state."

There is something in the notion of a young, educated and smooth leader advocating change and lambasting the bureaucracy that the West finds irresistible. It is a feeling based on far more than wishful thinking—it draws on a deep-seated conviction that anybody pragmatic enough to see the obvious flaws of Communist systems can only move his country closer to the Western world. A Gorbachev marveling at the stained-glass windows of Westminster Abbey evokes an image of the Soviet Union edging back at last from the paranoia and absurd claims that have kept it isolated from large parts of the civilized world for six decades.

There is, too, an instinctive identification with someone who in years, style and career seems so much more familiar than a Siberian peasant like Chernenko or a Ukrainian party hack like Leonid I. Brezhnev. Law school graduate, successful politician, foe of bloated bureaucracies and inefficiency, an advocate of change—these are elements dear to a Western heart, and it seems unduly callous to wonder whether the West should not, in fact, be hoping for someone more in the traditional mold, perhaps a coarse, gray functionary like Grigory V. Romanov, or an aging uninspired professional like Viktor V. Grishin.

That goes against nature. Beyond all the other reasons for Gorbachev's allure is a fatigue, in the West as in the Soviet Union, with a Kremlin whose public leaders are of interest only as indicators of the stage of their decrepitude, of old men who cling to scraps of paper for the simplest pronouncements, who have reduced leadership to ritual and tired slogans.

All Gorbachev had to do to impress the West, noted one Moscow cynic, was "to walk unaided and to talk without notes." It was a situation somewhat akin to Andropov's coming to power in November 1982. Never mind that he had been 15 years at the head of the K.G.B., or Ambassador to Hungary when Soviet tanks rolled through in 1956. After Brezhnev's long, tedious slide into senility, it was enough that he was ambulatory, that he seemed to be intelligent and to have a program, that he was someone with whom we could once again talk. It was hardly surprising when rumors spread that he even sipped whisky and liked jazz.

The image may have been a trifle overdone. But even in his few months in power, Andropov managed to live up to much of the advance billing. He set in motion extensive economic experiments, he kicked truant workers out of bathhouses, and he made inroads in the corrupt and ossified bureaucracy. The immediate results were marginal, but more important for Gorbachev and the future was the fascinating rise of an Andropov legend, of a posthumous image among common people and sophisticated intellectuals alike of a man who might have transformed his nation into a rich and powerful land had he only had time.

Gorbachev has inherited the legacy of Andropov and has emerged in the popular mind as the one man who might pick up where Andropov left off. During his trip to Canada in May 1983—in contrast to his December tour of Britain—Gorbachev was exposed to some tough public grilling by Members of Parliament, and he quickly let it be known that behind the affable visage lay a very quick temper and a keen sensitivity to perceived slights to his country. At one point, a Member of Parliament demanded to know why the Soviet Union stuffed its embassies abroad with so many spies. Gorbachev angrily fired back with charges of deliberate provocation, following Washington's practice, and similar charges.

If Gorbachev was guaranteed attention in the West, his prospects under Chernenko were never so sure. Shortly after his return from London, the banter at an embassy reception in Moscow was about his successes. The handful of Soviet officials and journalists who were there—members of the urbanized intelligentsia who naturally fall into Gorbachev's camp—listened to the reports with growing unease.

"Gorbachev is our only hope," one of the Russians explained in hushed tones. "But this kind of popularity is very dangerous. You've got to understand how it works here—a politician is not supposed to attract personal attention unless he's at the top. You're building up Gorbachev because you're not used to a Soviet leader who can talk for himself and act normally. But his enemies might seize on this and start saying, 'Why is it that the West likes him so?' "

It was a reaction that reflected the instinctive insecurity of Soviet politics and the fact that the qualities by which bright young men push to the top in the West are not at all the qualities that win in the brutal, Byzantine corridors of the Kremlin. Soviet politics, in a system stripped of most forms of public accountability, is a raw struggle for power. Succession is determined largely by the handful of men in the Politburo.

The fickleness and dangers of Soviet politics are best illustrated by the list of also-rans who litter Soviet history: Trotsky, Bukharin, Malenkov, Bulganin, Kirichenko, Kozlov, Kirilenko. What generated suspense around Gorbachev, however, was not only the question of whether he was destined for this list or for the shorter one of successful candidates. The larger anticipation was the transition to a totally new cast of characters on the Soviet stage, a new generation of men far better educated than the Brezhnevs and Chernenkos of yore, probably more secure, worldly and materialistic, and less puritanically or ideologically inspired.

We know tantalizingly little about these men. Official Soviet biographies generally consist, in addition to the dry chronological lists of positions held, of a set of speeches in the torturously boring prose of Communism and an airbrushed official photo—in Gorbachev's case, a prominent birthmark on his balding pate is carefully removed.

Kremlinology is largely a study of "formative" influences deduced from the few known facts. For men of Gorbachev's age, the dominant one is that they were in their teens when the Red Army sacked Berlin and laid the foundations for the Soviet Union as a global superpower.

Their youth was punctuated by proudly hailed coups: the Soviet atomic bomb; the launching of Sputnik, an event that jarred America from her postwar complacency; the launching of the first man into space. Their careers coincided with a growth of Soviet power undreamed of by the czars or even by Stalin, with rapid urbanization and the emergence of a new class of urban intelligentsia hungry for the good things of life, immune to the old slogans and impatient with the ossified party bureaucracy.

But if the world in which they grew up was powerful and assertive, it also remained obsessively defensive and secretive. It was a system that remained as intolerant as ever of any independence of spirit, that resolutely crushed dissidents and maintained the world's biggest political police force to hunt down any hint of defiance. If Moscow and Leningrad bred a new urban intelligentsia, then the rest of the Soviet Union remained mired in a dismal provincialism. And if younger Russians lost faith in Marxist-Leninist ideology, they remained enormously ignorant of the values and life styles of the West.

Zbigniew Brzezinski wrote at the time Andropov first came to power: "It's wrong to divide these people into conservatives or liberals, hawks and doves, Stalinists or non-Stalinists. The point is that they're all tough and brutal. The difference is that some are more intelligent, more sophisticated, more experienced and others are more parochial, narrow-minded and even stupid.

"Unless you expect the Soviet system to collapse under a stupid leader, it's probably safer for us all if our principal rival can be more intelligent."

Certainly nothing in Gorbachev's appearance betrays a radical departure. He is stocky and balding, and in public appearances he wears much the same dark suits and muted ties that his comrades do. Basically, he looks to be what he is, the son of Russian peasants.

He was born on March 2, 1931, in the village of Privolye, in the Stavropol region, a fertile, black-earth farming zone north of the Caucasus Mountains renowned for its sheep and grain. It was a region overrun by the Germans and one curious and unanswered question is whether Gorbachev lived as an adolescent through the occupation or whether he was evacuated to the east.

His official biography says that he worked at a machine-tractor station while still a student. Real advancement started in 1950, when at the age of 19 he entered the law school of Moscow University, a dramatic shift from the agricultural hinterlands to the most prestigious Soviet institution of higher learning. He is the only graduate of Moscow University in the Politburo, and the only member with legal training.

Moscow University's law school, of course, hardly paves a career path the way an Ivy League institution does. Even with his degree in hand, Gorbachev started his party career at the bottom, as the secretary of a Komsomol—Young Communist League—organization in Stavropol, and 10 years later, he still deemed it necessary to enroll in a correspondence course in agriculture.

On the other hand, Soviet law studies are highly politicized, and the record of Gorbachev's career in Moscow suggests that his real major was politics. Within two years of entering law school, Gorbachev joined the Communist Party and became Komsomol organizer for the school, a position that marked him as a promising politician.

These were particularly interesting years at the university. Stalin died in 1953, and the discontent and rumblings that eventually found expression in Khrushchev's secret speech attacking Stalin's "cult of personality" are said to have been strong at the law faculty. Russians who claim they knew of Gorbachev in those years say he was a critic of Stalin even before official de-Stalinization. That possibility is made moot, however, by the record, which shows Gorbachev to have been active in the Komsomol by 1952, when paeans to Stalin were still mandatory for any young Communist.

From Moscow, Gorbachev returned to Stavropol and began a classic rise through the party, advancing in steady steps from Komsomol secretary to first secretary of the regional party organization and a seat on the Central Committee by the age of 39.

Probably the most significant aspect of Gorbachev's 22-year service in Stavropol, however, was the patronage of Mikhail A. Suslov, the powerful ideologue and kingmaker in Brezhnev's Kremlin whose power base was in Stavropol. Gorbachev's election to full membership on the Central Committee in 1971—without the usual stint as a candidate member—was one sign of special favor. The major break came in 1978, when Fyodor D. Kulakov, the party secretary for agriculture and yet another Stavropol man, suddenly died. Gorbachev, 47,

Lenin's age at the time of the Revolution, was tapped to take over, and he moved to the center of power in Moscow.

In the waning years of the Brezhnev era, Gorbachev managed a program of massive investment in agriculture personally sponsored by Brezhnev as his "food program." He pushed through new ideas such as shifting control over agricultural operations from ministries in Moscow to regional agro-industrial authorities. He also moved to shift agricultural work to the "brigade method," giving groups of workers responsibility for a specific piece of land and paying them according to the results. The thrust in both these reforms was to restore some of the bonds that had once linked the peasants to the land, and which Stalin had so bloodily severed in the collectivization drive of the 1930's.

Gorbachev's experiments brought marginal improvement in some areas of agriculture, but not enough to offset a succession of crop failures.

What did work well for Gorbachev was the accession of Andropov.

The shrewd, tough former K.G.B. boss found in Gorbachev the perfect lieutenant to execute his ambitious efforts at sorting out the corruption and stagnation Brezhnev had left behind. Taking advantage of campaigns then under way in the party, Andropov and Gorbachev replaced one-fifth of the regional first secretaries and nine of 23 Central Committee department heads. They cracked down on corrupt officials and on laggard workers, and launched experiments to inject more incentives into industry and agriculture. As Andropov's health deteriorated, Gorbachev's role expanded, until, at the end, he was the sole link between the dying leader and the party hierarchy.

There is no evidence that Andropov meant for Gorbachev to succeed him. But to many in the party and in the white-collar intelligentsia, Gorbachev was the logical heir to Andropov's policies, the one man who could sustain the changes. Exactly what happened in the Politburo cannot be known, but the popular interpretation is that the old guard concluded it was not yet time for a man so many years their junior to seize the power they had wielded for some 30 years, and they opted to delay the inevitable with Chernenko, the oldest man ever to come to power and already ailing when he came there.

But Gorbachev emerged from the process the effective second in command, with more responsibility than any previous leader in a similar position.

Impressive as Gorbachev's rise has been, the evidence is inconclusive about his skills in political combat. Several times this past year, he seemed to slip. His speech nominating Chernenko after Andropov's death was never acknowledged in the Soviet press. At one awards ceremony in the Kremlin, he mysteriously shifted from the center of a Politburo lineup to the sidelines. At the October plenum of the Central Committee, his name was not mentioned even though the subject was agriculture, his field.

There is also the impression among Russians that he lacks an element of ruthlessness. His rise, after all, was due more to patronage than to brute force. Suslov and Andropov may have launched him into an orbit far higher than he could have achieved on his own, while less-celebrated but tougher members of the Politburo, like Grigory Romanov, the former Leningrad party chief, made it to the top by clawing their way up.

What he does have, probably to a greater degree than any previous candidate for Soviet power, is a platform. He is identified, more closely than any member of the Politburo, with calls for fundamental changes in economic, organizational and social thinking. He has the mantle of Andropov, whose memory has swelled into a legend of a man who combined the stick of tough discipline with the carrot of economic reorganization. He seems to have the backing of the brighter and younger minds in the Soviet leadership.

Nobody in the Soviet leadership is against economic change. The long lines outside stores alone make any other position politically untenable. But Soviet thinking on the issue has split roughly into two trends. On one side are the "hard-liners," men like Romanov and Prime Minister Nikolai A. Tikhonov, whose solution has been to cry out for more discipline within existing structures, for stronger centralized control, increased party supervision, for ruthless treatment of managers who don't achieve. Against these are ranged the "reformers," with Gorbachev at their head—men who advocate loosening of centralized controls, less party meddling, more self-management, greater use of market mechanisms and financial incentives.

Ardent as Gorbachev has been in crying out against "inertia, conservatism of thinking, inability or unwillingness to change established ways of work and shift to new methods," there are distinct limits to what he would, or could, do.

One telling incident was the furor that erupted after the journal Voprosy Istorii (Questions of History) published an article by Evgeny Ambartsumov, one of the leading advocates of reform, calling for more private enterprise in the Soviet economy. He cited as his authority the "new economic policy," the brief revival of private enterprise Lenin permitted in 1921 to repair the initial ravages of Bolshevism. Kommunist, the premier theoretical journal of the Communist Party, soon castigated Ambartsumov for his "shallow approach" and the editors of Voprosy Istorii for their lax controls. Several months later, Kommunist reported a special meeting at which the editors of Voprosy Istorii "recognized the justice of the criticism."

The greatest barrier before the "reformers" is the institutional resistance of a party bureaucracy that derives its power and privilege from things as they are. It is an elite, the defector Arkady Shevchenko wrote in his recent memoirs, that "will permit no one to transform that society or alter its foreign or domestic policy in any way that may affect their perquisites."

It was this ossified elite that smothered Aleksei N. Kosygin's attempts at reform in the 1960's, simply by doing nothing to implement them. Andropov, too, recognized its force, and parallel with his campaign to discipline and motivate workers he set about firing party secretaries and cracking down on the corrupt.

What makes the prospect of internal change more propitious now is a sense of crisis that seems to be spreading among Soviet economic managers, a sense that something must change and change fast. Oil production has fallen off, industrial output is climbing at a snail's pace and agriculture remains in dismal straits. The military is clamoring for more money to match President Reagan's military buildup, and consumers are becoming more vocal in their frustration.

On the political front, the 27th Party Congress, which is said to be scheduled for November, is expected to adopt a new party program and to name a new Central Committee. At least 15 percent of the current Central Committee membership is slated for replacement.

All this could give a new leader—Gorbachev or another member of his generation—some scope for action. Yet in setting up the centralized and overlapping system of bureaucratic control that still holds sway over Soviet life, Stalin insured that change could be imposed only from the top—and only by a leader who could gain control over the enormous apparatus of power. Accumulating such power could take years.

One lesson of Soviet history is that any real change is likely to be accompanied by increased repression. Change has always made Russians and their leaders nervous, and at such times the authorities have invariably become more authoritarian, less tolerant of debate or dissent.

It was so under Andropov, and Gorbachev would not be likely to act any differently. Nothing he has said or done suggests any greater degree of tolerance for unorthodox thinking than any of his colleagues, and it is wise to keep in mind that his two primary mentors were Suslov and Andropov, among the most stern of postwar Soviet leaders.

Foreign affairs is the field of Soviet endeavor least likely to change under a new generation. Gorbachev's public statements on foreign issues have demonstrated no marked originality, and his ideological discourses on differences between Communist and democratic systems have been dull and standard. He would likely favor détente, if only to give breathing space to domestic programs. But nothing suggests that he or any of his peers would react any differently from their predecessors to the insecurities, expansionist forces or sensitivity to loss of face that govern so much of Soviet behavior abroad.

A Soviet Union under Gorbachev or another of his ilk would not be radically different in the immediate future. Yet Gorbachev is a man Mrs. Thatcher found likable and possible to do business with. That and his youth and the pragmatism his statements reflect probably make him as good a Soviet politician as the West can expect.

Serge Schmemann is The Times's bureau chief in Moscow.

* * *

March 12, 1985

CHERNENKO IS DEAD IN MOSCOW AT 73; GORBACHEV SUCCEEDS HIM AND URGES ARMS CONTROL AND ECONOMIC VIGOR; TRANSFER IS SWIFT

By SERGE SCHMEMANN

Special to The New York Times.

MOSCOW, March 11— The Kremlin today announced the death of Konstantin U. Chernenko and, within hours, named Mikhail S. Gorbachev to succeed him as Soviet leader.

The announcement said Mr. Chernenko died Sunday evening after a grave illness at the age of 73. He had been in office 13 months, and had been ill much of the time, leaving a minor imprint on Soviet affairs.

The succession was the quickest in Soviet history, suggesting that it had been decided well in advance. Whereas the Central Committee had taken several days to name a successor to Leonid I. Brezhnev and Yuri V. Andropov, Mr. Gorbachev was confirmed in his new job 4 hours and 15 minutes after Mr. Chernenko's death was announced.

Youngest Leader Since Stalin

Mr. Gorbachev became, at 54, the youngest man to take charge of the Soviet Union since Stalin and the seventh to head the Soviet state.

"I am well aware of the great trust put in me and of the great responsibility connected with this,'' he said. "I promise you, comrades, to do my utmost to faithfully serve our party, our people and the great Leninist cause.''

In his acceptance speech on being named General Secretary, he showed his impatience to start working.

"We are to achieve a decisive turn in transferring the national economy to the tracks of intensive development,'' he said. "We should, we are bound to attain within the briefest period the most advanced scientific and technical positions, the highest world level in the productivity of social labor.''

Real Arms Cut Urged

In world affairs, he said he valued the "successes of détente, achieved in the 1970's.'' Referring to the Soviet-American arms talks starting Tuesday in Geneva, Mr. Gorbachev said the Soviet Union sought a "real and major reduction in arms stockpiles, and not the development of ever-new weapon systems, be it in space or on earth.''

The speech was one sign that the leadership intended to pursue business as usual despite Mr. Chernenko's death. The period of official mourning for Mr. Chernenko, who will be buried Wednesday in Red Square, is shorter than those of his predecessors.

The Geneva talks are to proceed as scheduled, and Prime Minister Nikolai A. Tikhonov and Foreign Minister Andrei A. Gromyko met today with Roland Dumas, the visiting French Foreign Minister.

The businesslike approach seemed to underscore the Kremlin's confidence in handling the third transition in two and a half years, this time to a new generation of Soviet leaders whose careers have been formed since the Stalin era.

The transfer of power was dramatized by the fact that Mr. Gorbachev was nominated in the Central Committee by Mr. Gromyko, 75, the most influential of the older leaders.

The loss of Mr. Chernenko brought the number of full members in the Politburo down to 10, half of them 70 or older.

His death was announced at 2 P.M. (6 A.M. New York time), although it had been signaled by the curtailment of several high-level Soviet missions abroad and the playing of somber music on radio stations.

Medical Report Is Issued

A medical report confirmed that Mr. Chernenko suffered from pulmonary emphysema and heart problems, and it revealed that he had also been afflicted by chronic hepatitis, which worsened into cirrhosis of the liver.

The first hint that Mr. Gorbachev had been selected as successor was the announcement of the membership of the funeral commission, with Mr. Gorbachev at its head. In the past the chairman has been the successor.

Mr. Chernenko will lie in state in the Hall of Columns of the House of Unions on Tuesday and Wednesday, and will be buried behind Lenin's Mausoleum.

The television news showed Mr. Chernenko laid out in the Hall of Columns. Politburo members led by Mr. Gorbachev stood a minute before the bier and then expressed condolences to Mr. Chernenko's wife, Anna, and other family members.

Mr. Chernenko was eulogized in terms reserved for senior officials, as an "outstanding party and state figure, patriot and internationalist, consistent fighter for the triumph of the ideals of Communism and peace on earth."

Stress Is on Uniting Ranks

The stress in the statements was on forming united ranks behind the Politburo and the party.

But beyond the familiar rites, the emphasis seemed on Mr. Gorbachev and the future.

Little known internationally as recently as three years ago and brought to the Politburo with the politically thankless task of overseeing the Soviet Union's problem-ridden agriculture, Mr. Gorbachev reached the forefront of Soviet politics through his association with Mr. Andropov.

Mr. Andropov had come to power determined to shake up the bureaucracy, discipline workers and jar the laggard economy into action. But as his health ebbed, he turned to Mr. Gorbachev for help.

On Mr. Andropov's death on Feb. 9, 1984, the Old Guard in the Politburo evidently chose to extend its hold on power a bit longer and picked Mr. Chernenko to be General Secretary. But Mr. Gorbachev emerged as the second-in-command of the party and as the heir to Mr. Andropov's unfinished program.

Although the pace of the experiments initiated by Mr. Andropov slowed under Mr. Chernenko, none was abandoned and some were actually extended, testifying both to the strength of Mr. Andropov's legacy and to Mr. Gorbachev's influence.

Pointed Reference to Andropov

In his speech today and in the hurry he demonstrated to get moving, Mr. Gorbachev made clear his legacy. While formally paying tribute to Mr. Chernenko's memory, he pointedly listed Mr. Andropov by name as architect of the strategy he would adopt.

He spoke of giving enterprises more independence and of increasing their interest in higher production. Sounding another theme raised by Mr. Andropov, Mr. Gorbachev talked of the need to provide people with more information. In foreign affairs, Mr. Gorbachev stressed the need for improved relations with China and with the West.

At the same time, Mr. Gorbachev took care to assure the military that it would receive "everything necessary" to maintain its defense capacity.

The shape of Mr. Gorbachev's program could become clearer next month, when a regular Central Committee meeting is scheduled. The session is expected to deal with science and technology, and could give the new leader an opportunity to bring new people into the Kremlin hierarchy.

Mr. Gorbachev also has more than eight months to plan for the next party congress, which is to approve a new party program, the next five-year plan, 1986 to 1990, and a new Central Committee, giving Mr. Gorbachev an opportunity to shape the ranks of the party elite to his taste.

Chernenko's Achievements

The rush to move ahead suggests that Mr. Chernenko will fade into relative historic obscurity. His achievements included a restructuring of education, to channel more students into vocational schools; an expansion of economic experiments, and a land reclamation program.

But Western diplomats believe he will be best remembered for keeping alive the changes initiated by Mr. Andropov, maintaining the campaign against corruption and the drive for labor discipline. In so doing, he may have supplied a smooth transition between the old generation and the new.

In foreign affairs, Mr. Chernenko presided over the return of the Soviet Union to negotiations with the United States after years of chill. The policies were associated more with Mr. Gromyko than with Mr. Chernenko, but, as in his economic policies, he was credited at least with not standing in the way of the revival of talks.

* * *

March 12, 1985

SUCCESSION IN MOSCOW: WHAT THE SPECIALISTS ARE SAYING

Experts on Soviet Differ on How Much of an Impact Gorbachev Will Have

The naming of Mikhail S. Gorbachev as the new leader of the Soviet Union was seen by some Soviet experts in interviews yesterday as a major event in Soviet history. Other experts, however, contended that the impact of Mr. Gorbachev's accession would be substantially limited by powerful and durable forces in the Soviet system. Following are excerpts from the interviews.

'Soviet people are happy'—Thomas J. Watson Jr.
Former Ambassador to the Soviet Union, chairman emeritus of I.B.M.

I don't think the United States should expect any real change in the Soviet Union as a result. The Government of the U.S.S.R. is a very solid, firmly-in-place, bureaucratic Government. We like to think that everyone there would like to revolt, but that is simply not the fact. Most of the Soviet people are happy; they may be unhappy about some things, but they are not about to revolt. Occasionally, there are some freedom moves, but such activity is very minimal. I think the impact of this change will be zero.

'Leader of the new generation'—William G. Hyland
Editor of Foreign Affairs magazine

He would never have reached the Politburo unless he had been loyal to the system and trustworthy in the eyes of the former President, Leonid Brezhnev, and Mikhail Suslov. It is therefore hard to think of Gorbachev as the new liberal.

But we are nonetheless dealing with a leader of the new generation. He is 54. It's difficult to believe he will be a carbon copy of the 73-year-old Chernenko. Gorbachev also inherits a vastly different situation than Brezhnev did in 1964: major economic problems that cry out for sweeping reform, a potentially inflammable situation in Eastern Europe, the continuing problems of Afghanistan, China and of an American adversary that seems to be gaining in self-confidence and assurance.

This kind of situation would suggest, as one option, that Gorbachev will play for time by reviving a semidétente with the West. If this is his choice, he has to be more forthcoming in the Geneva arms control talks and find some common ground even on such controversial issues as "Star Wars." At the same time, he has to consolidate his political position in the Politburo.

'Much higher order of vigor'—George F. Kennan
Professor emeritus at the Institute for Advanced Study in Princeton, N.J., and former Ambassador to the Soviet Union

The importance of Chernenko was often exaggerated. He was a compromise choice for the position and largely a figurehead. There is no evidence that he took any important part in policy making. The choice of Mikhail Gorbachev as his successor should produce a much higher order of vigor, flexibility and thoughtfulness in the leading position. But one should remember that the Politburo is a collective body. Even the first secretaryship does not of itself connote absolute personal power. It is not to be expected that the advent of Gorbachev will in any way affect Soviet positions at the arms control talks with the United States at Geneva.

'Change in form and style'—Arnold L. Horelick
Director of the Rand-U.C.L.A. Center for the Study of Soviet International Behavior

There is likely to be more of a change in the form and style of the Soviet leadership than in substance. The importance of this, however, should not be minimized. In foreign affairs, it is likely to make the Soviet Union a more formidable adversary. Merely because Mikhail Gorbachev contrasts with his frequently incapacitated, aged and only intermittently articulate predecessors, he will seem more energetic and will be able to present the Soviet case far more effectively than his predecessors.

On substance, particularly in the arms control area, there is no reason to believe in the short run that there will be any difference at all. Any Soviet leadership would try first to soften up the U.S. position, to explore the depth of the U.S. commitment to the Strategic Defense Initiative, the so-called "Star Wars," and if there is a Soviet fallback position, not to reveal it in the early stages.

'True post-Brezhnev succession'—Robert C. Tucker
Former director of Russian studies at Princeton University and author of "The Soviet Political Mind"

This is finally the true post-Brezhnev succession, a leader that has the actuarial likelihood of being in this position for some time. Inside the Politburo and outside among the political elites, a very serious struggle may be going on between the die-hard conservatives who had a representative in power and those like Gorbachev, who, however tough and loyal to the Soviet system, see that the country simply is in crying need of long-overdue internal change.

'Gorbachev will need a lot of time'—Arkady N. Shevchenko
Former Soviet senior diplomat and an Under Secretary General of the United Nations from 1973 to 1978. He is now living in the United States and is author of "Breaking with Moscow."

Mikhail Gorbachev may have been selected as General Secretary of the Communist Party, but that does not mean he has the authority to make policy, either domestic or foreign, except with the consent of key members of the Politburo. As far as Soviet-American relations are concerned, the Soviet approach to arms control will remain as it was before the death of

Chernenko. Foreign Minister Andrei Gromyko will retain his dominant position in foreign policy. As for the Soviet economy, Gorbachev will need a lot of time before he can make any substantial changes in that area. But after a long period of time when the old Soviet leadership was often sick and unable to function effectively, this man will be much more dynamic in style, if not in substance.

'Chairman rather than a dictator'—Adam B. Ulam

Gurney Professor of History and Political Science and director of the Russian Research Center at Harvard University

When it comes to Gorbachev's real views, we know very little about them for the simple reason that until they reach the position at the top, as General Secretary, members of the Politburo do not have, so to speak, distinct public personalities. So what he really would be like as the boss we do not know. So we do not know what Mr. Gorbachev might or might not do. Now, you also have to remember that whatever his views, he will be, in the beginning at least, chairman of the board rather than a dictator or boss, so general policies will be very likely still made by the collective of the Politburo members.

'Purely speculative to say'—Marshall D. Shulman

Adlai E. Stevenson Professor of International Relations at Columbia University and director of the W. Averell Harriman Institute for Advanced Study of the Soviet Union at Columbia

It would be purely speculative to say at this point what kind of leader Gorbachev will be. But those who have met him describe him as intelligent, thoughtful, knowledgeable, a good questioner and a good listener.

It is at least possible, although not assured, that he might be able to overcome the enormous resistance from the entrenched bureaucracy to modernizing reforms in the administration of the economy.

But in foreign policy, the problem he will face is that prospects for arms talks with the United States are not encouraging. This will mean that both countries will be putting still higher resources into the military sector and will be producing weapons that are less stable than the ones we have.

'Gorbachev has already had a year'—Jerry F. Hough

Professor of political science at Duke University and a staff member of the Brookings Institution

The speed of Gorbachev's election suggests that he was selected considerably earlier. In my opinion, the Soviet leadership decided on a two-stage selection after the death of Yuri Andropov. For this reason, I believe that Gorbachev has already had a year to begin consolidating power and that he will continue the consolidation very rapidly as the party congress approaches at the beginning of next year. The speed of Gorbachev's election also suggests that the Politburo is willing to facilitate this development in order to demonstrate to the West that it has a strong leader rather than leadership confusion.

* * *

August 18, 1985

REAGAN AIDES SEE NO POSSIBILITY OF U.S. ACCORD WITH SANDINISTAS

By SHIRLEY CHRISTIAN

Special to The New York Times.

WASHINGTON, Aug. 17—Reagan Administration officials involved in Central American policy say United States differences with Nicaragua cannot be resolved as long as the Sandinistas remain in power, and some indicate they favor the overthrow of the Sandinista leadership.

Robert C. McFarlane, President Reagan's national security adviser, said in response to a query that it was "absolutely not" the policy of the United States to overthrow the Sandinistas. But other officials, including some assigned to oversee and foster activities of anti-Sandinista rebels, said they saw no way to satisfy the concerns of the United States, the rebels and other Central American nations with the Sandinistas remaining in power.

In interviews in recent days, these officials described United States backing for the rebels in such terms as a chance to "win one for Reagan" and to "push Communism out of one country" or as a test case in what they called the global confrontation with the Soviet Union. All said they did not advocate using American troops for the purpose.

"The ultimate objective is to assure a democratic outcome in Nicaragua," said an Administration official who works closely with the rebels. "This goes beyond Nicaragua. If these people can stand up and throw off Communism, it goes beyond Managua. It goes to the gut of our national interest.

"The way to go after the Soviet Union is through the colonies," the official said. "We have to find ways to help democratic resistance movements without sending troops."

Force an 'Eventual Option'

There is nothing specifically on record from either President Reagan or Secretary of State George P. Shultz that calls outright for the overthrow of the Sandinistas. The President came close last February when he said that his goal was to "remove" the "present structure" in Nicaragua and that he wanted the Sandinistas to "say uncle."

In May, Mr. Reagan sent a classified report to Congress in which he said the use of United States military forces in Nicaragua "must realistically be recognized as an eventual option, given our stakes in the region, if other policy options fail."

Elliott Abrams, the new Assistant Secretary of State for Inter-American Affairs, said the Administration felt the Sandinistas would never abide by a commitment not to support insurgencies in neighboring countries. He said the only way to satisfy the security concerns of the United States was with what he called a democratic government in Nicaragua.

Mr. McFarlane, in an interview Wednesday, said American policies "remain to support the freedom fighters and in parallel to work for a diplomatic solution."

But in recent months diplomatic efforts have encountered many roadblocks. The Central American peace efforts of the so-called Contadora countries came to a standstill in June when Nicaragua demanded that the participants take up the issue of Washington's support for the anti-Sandinista forces. The United States refused last month to resume talks with the Sandinistas at Manzanillo, Mexico.

Meanwhile, the Administration's emphasis on support of the rebels, known widely by the Spanish term contras, has grown steadily.

Officials hedged their comments about whether and when the contras might be able to defeat the Sandinista army, estimated at 64,000 men including active reservists. Some said the rebels could not win an outright victory, but would have to rely on a combination of other factors, including internal dissatisfaction, to bring about the collapse of the regime.

"There is not much validity to the rationale for a specific timetable," said one man who has been a key Central America policymaker. "Nobody thinks about how long it will take to overthrow the Sandinista Front."

Gen. Paul F. Gorman, former commander of the Panama-based United States Southern Command, said in February in testimony to a Congressional committee just before finishing his assignment in Panama that the rebels were incapable of overthrowing the Sandinistas "in the foreseeable future."

Rebels Get New Help

The rebels have gone on the offensive in recent weeks, however, after an infusion of equipment and supplies made possible by as much as $25 million in private and foreign donations, plus the expectation of $27 million in nonmilitary aid from the United States Government.

They have penetrated deeper into Nicaragua than ever before. The main group, known as the Nicaraguan Democratic Force, has nearly doubled in size to about 16,000 in the last year, and its leaders predict it will double again in the coming year.

Officials said the Administration had gone through constant internal debate in recent years about whether to try to work out a "Yugoslavia" situation in Nicaragua, meaning an understanding that the Sandinistas would remain in power in exchange for not promoting insurgencies elsewhere or being a military threat to their neighbors.

"We go around 180 degrees on the subject all the time," said one participant in the debate, "but we always come out thinking that we'd be kidding ourselves if we thought we could solve our problems that way. One of the articles of faith in the Administration is that there cannot be a Yugoslavia solution. One reason is these guys are self-described revolutionaries."

Another Cuba, Another Vietnam

The parameters that have evolved for the policy, he said, are to avoid "another Cuba" in this hemisphere and "another Vietnam," that is, having American troops bogged down abroad. "Those parameters are like a chute," he said, "and you play for breaks as you go through. If the Sandinistas collapse internally, so be it."

The conceptual limits have developed over the last couple of years, he said, as the majority of members of Congress have become more critical of the Sandinistas. This has made it politically possible for the Administration to drop the argument that it was supporting the Nicaraguan rebels as a means of interfering with the supplying of the guerrillas fighting the Washington-backed Government in El Salvador.

Some Administration officials maintained that a negotiated settlement of the conflict in Nicaragua might be possible if it was acceptable to the Nicaraguan rebels and to the other Central American nations. But anything acceptable to those groups and governments, they said, would require so many changes in the Sandinistas' internal and external policies that the Sandinista Front would no longer be the same organization it is today.

They said any negotiated settlement would have to be a multilateral agreement, for instance through the Contadora talks, involving the Nicaraguan opposition, armed and unarmed, as well as the other Central American countries. They virtually ruled out any possibility of reaching a bilateral peace agreement with Nicaragua.

'Approximation' Is Acceptable

"We ought never to think a negotiated solution is not possible," one official said. "We accept the fact that any agreement that all those parties would agree to would be an approximation of what we would want. It is not going to be radically different. Honduras, for example, would want some agreement on the balance of arms with Nicaragua. That's their main concern. "It's true that you could solve the security issue without internal reconciliation, but what do you do then about 20,000 contras in Honduras?"

The Sandinista leadership has proposed agreements with individual Central American governments in recent months that would address some of the concerns of each of them, asking, in turn, that the other country abandon or soften its demand for internal changes in Nicaragua.

The strongest Sandinista offer was made to El Salvador informally in April. Salvadoran officials said that the Sandinistas had sent a mid-level official to El Salvador, and that he had said the Sandinista Front was willing to take several steps. They included expelling from Managua the leadership of the Salvadoran guerrilla organization, the Farabundo Marti National Liberation Front, other unspecified actions to halt or reduce support for the Salvadoran rebels and resettling permanently into Nicaragua a large number of pro-guerrilla Salvadoran refugees now in Honduras.

Contadora Is Emphasized

The vehicle through which El Salvador and other Central American nations would be expected by the Sandinistas to extend tacit acceptance to their Government is the proposed Contadora agreement, named for the Panamanian island on which discussions began among Mexico, Venezuela, Panama and Colombia. In all of the draft agreements that have so far emerged from the discussions, "internal reconciliation" has been a key element.

American officials said the Sandinista proposal to the Salvadorans was a variation on an offer Managua made to Washington after United States troops landed in Grenada in October 1983.

"I don't think these bilateral deals will sell to Central America," Mr. Abrams said, "basically because the Central Americans understand that the Sandinistas are Communists and that such agreements are lies and will be used to destroy the contras. After that, the Sandinista Front would be back at its historical mission of subverting these countries."

He and other Administration officials said the primary reason Nicaragua's neighbors might consider such arrangements is not so much that they really want to make separate agreements with the Sandinistas but that they fear the United States will abandon the anti-Sandinista cause at some point and leave them out on the limb.

A Message to Other Nations

The main reason for the economic embargo imposed against Nicaragua in May, according to an American source who took part in the decision, was to send a message to El Salvador, Honduras and Costa Rica, and, to a lesser extent, Guatemala, telling them that the United States was not abandoning the issue. It was always recognized, he said, that the economic impact amounted to "just a few bananas."

He added, "They want constant reassurance that we are with them."

High-level Administration officials who analyze statements on Nicaragua by the President said that despite his lack of a clear public stance, they are struck by the fact that he "keeps coming back to internal democratization and national reconciliation."

They interpret that to mean that the Sandinistas must go and that the United States cannot settle for anything like a "Yugoslavia solution." Several officials pointed out that those who favored exploring such an option have either left the Administration or fallen silent. Secretary of State Shultz is counted among the silent.

Trust Is Ruled Out

"I think there is interagency agreement on Nicaragua policy now," a senior official said. "The prevailing view in the Administration is that you cannot negotiate a deal with Communists that is based on good will or trust. You could negotiate only on the basis of a correlation of forces."

Mr. Abrams asked: "Why do we insist on internal reconciliation? Because the only guarantee that security agreements that are made will stick is internal democracy.

"The view that the democracy issue has been put on the table in order to trade it off is false," he added. "It is preposterous to think we could sign a deal with the Sandinistas to meet our foreign policy concerns and expect it to be kept.

"If, say, three months after such an agreement, the contras were disbanded, the guerrillas would begin to reinfiltrate into El Salvador within a month. What would we do about it then? Send in marines? One thing this Administration agrees on is that we are not going to sign a phony agreement."

* * *

November 22, 1985

REAGAN AND GORBACHEV OPTIMISTIC AFTER MEETING; PRESIDENT, BACK IN U.S., LOOKS AHEAD TO A 'NEW REALISM'

By BERNARD WEINRAUB

Special to The New York Times.

WASHINGTON, Nov. 21—President Reagan returned to the capital tonight from Geneva and told Congress that there would continue to be "enduring competition" between the United States and the Soviet Union.

But he said his meeting with Mikhail S. Gorbachev, the Soviet leader, had created "room for movement, action and progress."

He said the talks had opened the way for a "new realism" in relations with Moscow, although he conceded that they had failed to produce "a meeting of the minds."

Start of a Process

Confirming earlier predictions by White House officials, he said the conference marked the start of a process of discussion that he and Mr. Gorbachev had pledged to continue.

"It was a constructive meeting," Mr. Reagan said. "So constructive, in fact, that I look forward to welcoming Mr. Gorbachev to the United States next year, and I have accepted his invitation to go to Moscow the following year.

"We met, as we had to meet," he said. "I had called for a fresh start—and we made that start. I can't claim we had a meeting of the minds on such fundamentals as ideology or national purpose—but we understand each other better. That's the key to peace. I gained a better perspective; I feel he did, too."

While insisting that he and the Soviet leader had made a start toward agreements to reduce nuclear weapons, Mr. Reagan made it clear that they had had a "very direct" clash over the Strategic Defense Initiative, Mr. Reagan's plan to build a space-based missile defense. The President indicated that neither he nor Mr. Gorbachev had yielded any ground on the project, popularly known as "Star Wars."

"Mr. Gorbachev insisted that we might use a strategic defense system to put offensive weapons into space and establish nuclear superiority," the President said. "I made it clear that S.D.I. has nothing to do with offensive weapons, that instead we're investigating nonnuclear defense systems that would only threaten offensive missiles, not people."

Offers Soviet Inspection

Mr. Reagan said he was prepared "to permit Soviet experts to see firsthand that S.D.I. does not involve offensive weapons," adding that under a plan he had offered, American scientists would be allowed to see comparable Soviet research installations.

"Through reliance on defensive systems," Mr. Reagan asserted, mankind could "at long last escape the prison of mutual terror. "This," he said, "is my dream." Mr. Reagan began his address to Congress at about 9:15 P.M. after taking a helicopter to the Capitol from Andrews Air Force Base in suburban Maryland. He walked into a House chamber packed with legislators and Government officials, who welcomed him with thunderous and prolonged applause.

He opened his remarks with a warm tribute to his wife, Nancy, whom he termed "an outstanding ambassador of good will." Mrs. Reagan grinned and rose from her seat in the House gallery to acknowledge a standing ovation.

The President also expressed his appreciation to Senator Bob Dole, Republican of Kansas, the Senate majority leader, and Representative Thomas P. O'Neill Jr., Democrat of Massachusetts, the House Speaker, for their statements of support.

"You can't imagine how much it means in dealing with the Soviets to have the Congress, the allies and the American people firmly behind you," Mr. Reagan said.

A Look at American Policy

His 20-minute speech not only offered a review of the Reagan-Gorbachev sessions—the two leaders met alone for nearly five hours in Geneva—but also provided a glimpse of American policy toward the Russians in the aftermath of the first summit meeting since 1979.

Mr. Reagan's aides were especially concerned that the President's presentation to Congress would be hampered by the tiring day. But except for a slight huskiness in his voice, Mr. Reagan appeared relaxed and not especially fatigued. He delivered the speech in an almost conversational tone and was interrupted repeatedly by applause from both sides of the aisle.

Mr. Reagan said, "We discussed threats to the peace in several regions of the world.

"I explained my proposals for a peace process to stop the wars in Afghanistan, Nicaragua, Ethiopia, Angola and Cambodia, those places where insurgencies that speak for the people are pitted against regimes which obviously do not represent the will or the approval of the people."

'They Hit It Off Amazingly'

Beyond this, the Geneva summit meeting was framed by Mr. Reagan's apparent personal rapport with Mr. Gorbachev—"they hit it off amazingly," one White House aide said.

The meeting was also marked by the last-minute decision to issue a joint communiqué after considerable wrangling over language, and by a series of agreements that included cultural and educational exchanges, plans to open consulates in Kiev and New York and a North Pacific air safety pact to avoid incidents such as the shooting down of a South Korean airliner that entered Soviet airspace in 1983.

Mr. Reagan and Mr. Gorbachev concluded what the President called their "fireside summit" in Geneva without substantive agrreement, or even guidelines, on how to limit nuclear arsenals. "Serious differences remain on a number of critical issues," said the communiqué.

But standing on a podium in Geneva at a brief closing ceremony at the International Conference Center, Mr. Reagan and Mr. Gorbachev chatted amiably before separate departures—Mr. Reagan to Brussels, Mr. Gorbachev to Prague—to brief their allies. Before their departures, the two men toasted one another with champagne in a private ceremony.

Although Robert C. McFarlane, the White House national security adviser, said last week that a joint communiqué or statement was unlikely, a statement was issued today in Geneva that vaguely outlined the initiatives endorsed by the two leaders.

"While acknowledging the differences in their systems and approaches to international issues, some greater understanding of each side's views was achieved by the two leaders," said the statement.

"They agreed about the need to improve U.S.-Soviet relations and the international situation as a whole," it added.

'A Certain Momentum'

Mr. Reagan said in Geneva, "These two days of talks should inject a certain momentum into our work on the issues between us—a momentum we can continue at the meeting that we have agreed on for next year."

A United States official said the session was tentatively scheduled for June in Washington, with a follow-up meeting in Moscow the following year.

Shortly after the joint Reagan-Gorbachev appearance, the Soviet leader held a news conference at the Soviet Mission in which he reiterated his main point of contention with Mr. Reagan, the dispute over the "Star Wars" system.

If the United States proceeds with its space-based shield, Mr. Gorbachev said, "all restraint will be thrown to the winds." Privately, officials said that Mr. Gorbachev's discussion of "Star Wars" with Mr. Reagan was marked by anger.

In his remarks to Congress tonight, Mr. Reagan pointed out that the United States and the Soviet Union "remain far apart on many issues," such as the Soviet occupation of Afghanistan, human rights, arms limitation and the "Star Wars" project.

"We know the limits as well as the promise of summit meetings," Mr. Reagan said. "This is, after all, the eleventh summit of the post-war era, and still the differences endure."

A 20-Hour Day for Reagan

But the President, whose 20-hour day included a two-hour stopover in Brussels to brief allied leaders on the summit meeting, also made it clear that he was impressed with the Soviet leader, that he sought further meetings with him and that he wanted to hasten arms control negotiations.

"The world is waiting for the results," said Mr. Reagan.

He said that despite his differences with Mr. Gorbachev, the meeting had been worthwhile for both sides. "A new realism spawned the summit; the summit itself was a good start; and now our byword must be: Steady as we go," the President said.

An Administration official said that Mr. Reagan was essentially urging that the Russians "get on with it, get movement and positions," and start dealing solely with negotiations to limit offensive weapons. Such an approach has been hampered by the Soviet insistence that Mr. Reagan abandon his "Star Wars" program.

On the human rights issue, which the Administration has publicly muted in recent weeks, Mr. Reagan said, "Human rights is not an abstract moral issue—it is a peace issue.

"Those countries which respect the rights of their own people tend inevitably to respect the rights of their neighbors," Mr. Reagan said.

* * *

November 24, 1985

TWISTS AT THE SUMMIT: INSIDE THE GENEVA TALKS

The following article is based on reporting by Bernard Gwertzman and Bernard Weinraub and was written by Mr. Weinraub.

WASHINGTON, Nov. 23—In the predawn hours before President Reagan and Mikhail S. Gorbachev left Geneva on Thursday, American officials grew concerned about the outcome of the summit meeting and devised a "blow-up scenario" to limit political damage in case the meeting collapsed at the final ceremony.

"We had a nightmare vision with world headlines saying, 'Summit Breaks Up Over "Star Wars," ' " an American official said.

The specter of a collapse—and the resolution of this last-minute hitch with the agreement on a joint statement—were among accounts of the summit meeting pieced together from descriptions provided by officials of the White House, the State Department and the Pentagon who had been close to the negotiating sessions and the leaders' private talks.

The President described the private talks to Secretary of State George P. Shultz, Robert C. McFarlane, his national security adviser, and Donald T. Regan, his chief of staff. Details were provided to other officials, and their descriptions were used to reconstruct these episodes.

The exchanges between the President and Mr. Gorbachev ranged in tone from heated to humorous, shedding light not only on the personalities of the leaders but also on their efforts to avoid a collision while adhering to their conflicting policies.

Gorbachev Recalls a Cartoon

These are some of the twists of events at the summit meeting as described by the officials:

- At dinner at the Soviet Mission, Mr. Gorbachev, toasting Mr. Reagan, described a cartoon he had seen in a Western newspaper. It showed Mr. Reagan on one side of an abyss, Mr. Gorbachev on the other. In the caption, Mr. Gorbachev said, Mr. Reagan was saying: "We need a better relationship. You take the first step." As Mr. Gorbachev spoke, Mr. Reagan broke into laughter and applauded.
- The two sides threatened to leave without final statements if they did not achieve satisfactory wording, and an all-night battle developed. The United States, for example, insisted that a section on halting the spread of chemical weapons should also call for a ban on "use." The Russians refused, and the Americans finally dropped the word.
- The Americans decided not to denounce the Russians publicly on human rights, largely on the recommendation of former President Richard M. Nixon, who had said that public criticism would stiffen Soviet resistance.
- As the two leaders walked to a chateau pool house, Mr. Reagan told Mr. Gorbachev that he was miffed at a comment made the previous day by Georgi A. Arbatov, the Soviet expert on American affairs, who said Mr. Reagan had been a grade-B movie actor. "Tell Arbatov they weren't all B-movies," Mr. Reagan said.
- The negotiators struggled with two statements on arms control, and only the intercession of Mr. Reagan and Mr. Gorbachev late Wednesday made a compromise possible, hours before the final ceremony.
- The discussion on regional disputes was often sharp, but Mr. Reagan came away convinced that Mr. Gorbachev was looking for a diplomatic solution of the conflict in Afghanistan, where 100,000 Soviet troops have been bogged down since 1979.
- Nancy Reagan not only helped her husband select the room where he would first meet Mr. Gorbachev, but also suggested that the two men walk to the pool house for a private talk. "Reagan kept saying there are plenty of nice rooms, but Nancy insisted that a walk outdoors would be helpful," an official said. "She was right."
- As the two delegations were having coffee after dinner, Secretary of State George P. Shultz, normally mild-mannered, lost his temper at a Soviet official and, pointing his finger, told Mr. Gorbachev that the official, Georgi M. Korniyenko, a First Deputy Foreign Minister, was "an obstructionist" and was thwarting the possibility of a joint statement. "Mr. General Secretary," Mr. Shultz said, "this man is not doing what you want." Mr. Gorbachev whispered to an aide. The statement was agreed upon hours later.

One Topic: Human Rights

Officials said that, in the private talks, Mr. Reagan had raised the general issue of Soviet human rights violations, such as the problem of separated Soviet spouses of Americans, dissidents and Jews seeking to emigrate. But the officials said the President had not mentioned any specific cases.

White House officials said Mr. Gorbachev had responded by saying that Jews in the Soviet Union were not being discriminated against and that many Jews had risen to high positions. He also reportedly denied that there were still many Jews who wanted to leave the Soviet Union, as Mr. Reagan contended there were.

Officials were tight-lipped about this aspect of the discussions, adhering to Mr. Reagan's insistence that public condemnation of the Russians would be counterproductive.

Mr. Reagan was reportedly convinced that the personal assessments he and Mr. Gorbachev would make of each other at their first meeting, even in the first hour, would be crucial, not only to the outcome of the summit meeting, but also to relations between the two countries.

Mr. Reagan had told aides that he felt that in the 1961 meeting between President John F. Kennedy and Nikita S. Khrushchev, the Soviet leader "walked over Kennedy and Kennedy knew it."

That meeting, Mr. Reagan had said, led to the Cuban missile crisis, Mr. Kennedy's call-up of reserves in the Berlin crisis and an increase of American advisers in Vietnam.

This summit meeting, the first since President Carter and Leonid I. Brezhnev met in Vienna in 1979, began Tuesday at 10 A.M., when Mr. Reagan and Mr. Gorbachev walked up the steps of a 19th-century chateau outside Geneva and began an hour-long private talk.

According to a State Department official's account, Mr. Reagan said quietly to Mr. Gorbachev:

"You come from a modest background, and so do I. We are both family men. We are husbands, we have children. Here we are. The world is watching us."

Early on, during the formal sessions, the Americans and the Russians agreed not to disclose substance until the talks were over. American officials, however, painted a generally positive picture of the meetings, including the six hours of private talks. It was only in the last day that they revealed the intensity of disagreements.

"Was the tone belligerent between Reagan and Gorbachev?" a White House official asked, then answered himself, "No."

"It was very strong and categorical and positive but not angry," he said. "When Gorbachev wanted to make a point he would gesticulate but there was no table-pounding. They had good, frank, direct, let-it-all-hang-out exchanges."

According to officials, the two leaders argued both when alone and in the formal sessions. At times the exchanges were tense, as, for instance, when at one point in the formal talks the two sides were discussing the President's proposal to build a space-based missile defense.

A White House aide quoted Mr. Gorbachev as having said to Mr. Reagan, "Just answer, just answer, just answer."

Mr. Reagan, the official said, replied coldly, "I will if you will let me."

'Always Looking At the Soviets'

The following exchange also was reported: Mr. Reagan told Mr. Gorbachev, "You have no right to be in Afghanistan, Ethiopia, Angola. No right! This is Soviet aggression. It is destabilizing."

Mr. Gorbachev responded: "There is no basis for this! None at all. These are people struggling for national liberation."

Another White House official heard Mr. Gorbachev tell Mr. Reagan: "You Americans are always looking at the Soviets as the cause of all the problems in the third world. We are telling you this is not the case. There is not a Soviet aim in every crisis. But you perceive that and base your policies on that assumption. How do you explain Nicaragua? How do you explain Vietnam?"

Other exchanges were more lighthearted. As the two men, in a private talk, were discussing Mr. Reagan's movie career, Mr. Gorbachev reportedly said he had seen one of Mr. Reagan's movies but had forgotten the title. Mr. Gorbachev described it as a film in which Mr. Reagan portrayed a young man whose legs were amputated by a vicious surgeon.

Mr. Reagan beamed and said it was the best film he made, "King's Row."

On Wednesday, when Mr. Reagan met his aides for lunch to discuss the afternoon agenda on nuclear missiles, an aide said the encounter might be a tough one. The White House aide said Mr. Reagan grinned and then said: "I know what I will do. I will put my hands on my hips and say: 'What happened to that nice session we had this morning? Why are you doing this to me now?' "

The Schedule Was Negotiable

The original agenda for the talks was not followed, officials said. For instance, the first session on Tuesday morning was supposed to deal with an overview of Soviet-American relations, preceded by a 15-minute private meeting. But when the two leaders returned from their meeting, which had lasted a full hour, they found themselves locked in a debate over the space-based defense program.

While the two sides waited for the leaders to return from the private meeting, one of the President's assistants walked up to Mr. Shultz, looked at his watch and said: "They were supposed to meet for 15 minutes and they have been there for three-quarters of an hour. Shall I go in and break it up?"

Mr. Shultz later recalled: "I said: 'If you are dumb enough to go in and try to break it up, you don't deserve to be employed here. Let them break it up when they choose.' "

On Tuesday, before the group broke for lunch, Mr. Reagan outlined his concern about Soviet involvement in Afghanistan, Cambodia, Angola, Ethiopia and Nicaragua.

In the afternoon, when arms control was on the agenda, Mr. Gorbachev started off with a criticism of Mr. Reagan's views on regional issues. The same disjointed pattern was followed Wedneday.

Mr. Reagan told his aides that he was impressed with Mr. Gorbachev.

"It was Reagan's idea from the start to have extended one-on-one sessions," an aide said. "He was very conscious of the Soviet mentality that we have never given them credit as a superpower. They always feel we see them as inferior, as poorer, that they haven't kept pace with us technologically. He wanted to assure them, he wanted to put all that in perspective.

"In his talks with Gorbachev, he constantly referred to 'we two.' He kept saying that our countries are the only ones to

Associated Press

Mikhail S. Gorbachev and President Reagan before the first round of their summit meeting Tuesday morning in Geneva.

prevent a war and start a war. There was a chemistry between the two, but Reagan kept telling us: 'Look, this is our main adversary in the world. Let's not forget that.' "

The discussion of a final statement began when Mr. Shultz went to Moscow earlier in the month. The Soviet side had suggested a communiqué, and Mr. Shultz came with proposed language. There was "semi-agreement" in Moscow, a State Department official said, on some points, but the two sides were far apart on arms control.

In Washington, an interagency group headed by Robert C. McFarlane, the national security adviser, worked out a statement on control talks as a possible guide for a communiqué. Mr. Reagan handed the statement to Mr. Gorbachev on Tuesday.

Among the points were a commitment to continue to adhere to the 1972 treaty on antiballistic missiles and to form a joint program on space-based defense if American research proved successful.

The statement also called for early progress in the Geneva arms talks in areas where there was common ground, such as in the proposal for 50 percent cuts in comparable systems and the idea of an interim agreement limiting medium-range weapons. The United States wanted the medium-range weapons be limited to land-based weapons.

Another point was a statement about the need for strict verification and compliance.

Soviet Rejects Arms Proposal

On Wednesday morning, the Russians rejected the American draft and, instead, proposed a statement of their own calling for preventing an arms race in space and ending the arms race on earth, two points that had already been agreed to in a communiqué Jan. 8 preparing for the Geneva arms control talks.

In the Soviet interpretation, the stipulations of Jan. 8 in effect ruled out any research on a space-based defense program.

At a working lunch at the United States mission on Wednesday, Mr. McFarlane took the lead in working out a compromise, combing the Jan. 8 communiqué with the American points. But the Soviet side initially rejected that approach also.

Thus, by Wednesday afternoon, a deadlock seemed to cast a shadow over the summit meeting.

"I kind of felt it was like a football game, the fourth quarter and we were going in zero-to-zero," a White House official said. "Everyone was getting uneasy."

New complications arose when the Soviet side began insisting that it would not sign any cultural exchange accord or other agreement on Thursday if the arms control language was not worked out.

The Russians said they did not want to sign only "minor" agreements. The United States insisted it was ready to leave Geneva without a joint document if it was not satisfied.

"Shultz said that he did not believe Gorbachev had thrown the switch yet, had told his people what to do, but if there is no agreement and it all falls apart we should be prepared," a White House official said. "We created a blow-up scenario. We would make our statement. Our whole tone was: 'You guys don't want to agree, fine. We won't agree. We'll go home.' "

Through the night, the two sides labored in what one official called a "kind of chicken war," each refusing to make the major concession. The American group was led by Rozanne L. Ridgway, the Assistant Secretary of State for European and Canadian Affairs, and included Richard N. Perle, Assistant Secretary of Defense; Jack F. Matlock Jr. and Robert E. Linhard of the National Security Council staff; Robie M. Palmer, Deputy Assistant Secretary of State for European and Canadian Affairs, and Bruce G. Burton, an aide to Paul H. Nitze, the arms control adviser.

The Soviet team was led by Aleksandr A. Bessmertnykh, chief of the United States Department in the Foreign Ministry; Viktor P. Karpov, the arms negotiator, and Oleg M. Sokolov, the second-ranking diplomat at the Soviet Embassy in Washington.

Shultz Loses His Temper

It was that evening that Mr. Shultz was described as uncharacteristically losing his temper.

Mr. Reagan and his wife, Nancy, and Mr. Gorbachev and his wife, Raisa, were sipping coffee before a blazing fireplace with a handful of aides at the Maison de Saussure, the 18th-century gray stone chateau where the Reagans were staying. At that meeting, the two leaders agreed to make separate personal statements on Thursday.

"They agreed the statements should emphasize the positive and not the negative," a White House official said.

At that point, the question of a joint American-Soviet statement came up, but Mr. Shultz was called away on a phone call. It was from Miss Ridgway, who was in charge of the working group drafting the document. She told Mr. Shultz that, in the words of one official, there had been a Soviet "pullback" and a joint statement was running into difficulty. It was 10:40 P.M.

According to witnesses, Mr. Shultz returned to the room and, when the subject of a joint statement came up, arose and pointed his finger at Mr. Korniyenko, the First Deputy Foreign Minister. The witnesses said that Mr. Shultz remarked: "You, you, you are holding it up, we cannot do business with you."

Turning to Mr. Gorbachev, Mr. Shultz said, "Mr. General Secretary, we cannot do business with this man."

Afterward, Mr. Shultz told Mr. Reagan, "I apologize if you thought I was too hard."

Mr. Reagan replied, "Absolutely not."

By 4:30 A.M. the Russians had agreed to the compromise approach worked out by the United States, but won concessions from the Americans, who agreed to drop a reference to the space-based defense program and to eliminate "land-based" as the description of the medium-range weapons to be negotiated.

The Soviet side did not want the adjective "land-based" included because such a formulation would exclude American bombers in Western Europe as well as British and French submarine-launched missiles.

The compromise did not eliminate any differences in substance, but allowed each to assert that the wording backed its own arguments. The Americans said it helped their argument that progress in reducing nuclear arms should not be linked to a prior accord on not going ahead with space-based defenses. The Soviet side insisted that the Jan. 8 communiqué fortified its argument that the space-based defenses were intimately linked to arms reduction.

At least one result of the summit meeting was that tensions between the State Department and the Pentagon were, for the moment, smoothed over, in the aftermath of the disclosure of a letter by Defense Secretary Caspar W. Weinberger to the President. The letter, warning Mr. Reagan to take a hard line on arms control, was not issued officially, but The New York Times and The Washington Post obtained copies of it and published reports on its contents.

After the disclosure of the letter, one White House official told a reporter in Geneva that he felt it was designed to disrupt the summit meeting. Mr. Weinberger ordered an investigation into the disclosure.

Defense Department officials said they had been kept out of the talks on the first day, but that Mr. Shultz had included Mr. Perle in the second day of talks. At a Cabinet meeting on Friday, Mr. Shultz reportedly lauded the work of Miss Ridgway and Mr. Perle, saying that "they worked arm in arm together." Gorbachev, Public and Private One element of the summit meeting that especially interested Mr. Reagan and American officials was Mr. Gorbachev's leadership style and personality.

American officials noted that in the private talks between the two men, the Soviet leader referred to the space-based defense program by the Russian initials "S.O.I." which are also used in the Soviet press for "S.D.I.," for the Strategic Defense Initiative, the term Mr. Reagan prefers.

Publicly, Mr. Gorbachev called the program by the popular term "Star Wars," which Mr. Reagan resents.

"Clearly, he was the man in charge," one American said of Mr. Gorbachev's relations with other Soviet officials. "Others were a bit reluctant to make decisions without consulting him, but when the decision-making came to him, he made it and made it instantly without flinching, without asking for our position."

A White House official, for example, said that when Larry Speakes, the White House spokesman, and Leonid M. Zamyatin, the Soviet spokesman, decided to withhold reports on the substance of the talks, Mr. Zamyatin approached Mr. Gorbachev while photographers were taking pictures.

"Zamyatin said to him in Russian what the proposal was," the White House official said. "He never looked at Zamyatin. He just said instantly, 'We'll do it.' "

Mr. Gorbachev's decisiveness was also underscored at one point as Mr. Reagan escorted him to his ZIL limousine outside Fleur d'Eau, the chateau where the first round of talks was held.

"Reagan thought the moment was right as they stood there by the car, and asked him to come to the United States," a White House official said. "Gorbachev immediately accepted and said: 'May I ask you to come to Russia?' The President said, 'Yes.' "

Mr. Gorbachev is tentatively scheduled to visit the United States next June, and the President plans to go to the Soviet Union in 1987.

Mr. Regan, the White House chief of staff, said Mr. Gorbachev's attitudes differed between the formal, plenary sessions and the private talks "The vehemence was always in the plenary," Mr. Regan said. "Gorbachev was very quiet, more persuasive, more congenial, as the President described it to me, in his one-on-one."

Aide Says Reagan 'Learned a Lot'

Officials said Mr. Reagan had sought a summit meeting in part because he wanted to dispel the assertions of critics that he was more interested in a military build-up than in peace. At the same time, a White House official said, Mr. Reagan plainly "learned a lot."

"He comes away not having changed his view that fundamental differences exist between us and that this new leader is a very strong advocate of Soviet interests," the official said. "He came away with a certain amount of healthy respect for Gorbachev, respect for this leader who is a strong advocate and very good interlocutor.

"He also comes away with the knowledge that there is a hell of a lot left to be done, it is just the beginning now." Officials said that Nancy Reagan had played a pivotal role. "Her presence was felt in Reagan's mind," a White House official said. "She has an influence in terms of looking for accommodation. She is extremely anxious for success, anxious for him to accomplish something with the Russians, anxious for his place in history. She has more of a sense of history than he does. He plays his role every day, she looks to the future and how the future sees him."

Mr. Reagan himself told a group of editors on Friday: "We sat there in a room and I told him, here we are and between us we could come up with things that could probably bring peace for years and generations to come. And if we could erase these things that have made us suspicious of each other.

"I think I'm some judge of acting, so I don't think he was acting," Mr. Reagan said. "He, I believe, is just as sincere as we are in wanting an answer."

* * *

December 15, 1985

REAGAN URGES ARMS AID FOR NICARAGUA REBELS

By BERNARD WEINRAUB

Special to The New York Times.

WASHINGTON, Dec. 14—President Reagan, preparing to seek renewed military assistance next year for Nicaraguan rebels, denounced the Nicaraguan leadership today as "thugs" whose military units are increasingly dominated by Cuban military personnel.

Mr. Reagan said Nicaragua was emerging as "an international aggressor nation" and serving as "a breeding ground for subversion" by acting as a haven for more than 7,000 Cubans, Russians, East Germans, Bulgarians, Libyans, Palestine Liberation Organization members and "other bloc and terror groups."

The White House is canvassing members of Congress to see whether they will agree to revive military assistance to the Nicaraguan rebels, and a ranking Administration official said today that the President's address marked the start of a concerted White House and State Department effort to resume military aid to the rebels, or contras.

Combat Role for Cubans Denied

Nicaragua has denied that Cubans are taking part in combat. Mr. Reagan's remarks follow the recent approach taken by the State Department.

Last week, Elliott Abrams, the Assistant Secretary of State for Inter-American Affairs, testified in the House that Cubans were becoming increasingly involved in combat against rebel forces in Nicaragua. Mr. Abrams confirmed reports that insurgents shot down a Soviet-built helicopter on Dec. 2 and said two Cubans were among the 14 casualties.

Two days after Mr. Abrams's testimony, Secretary of State George P. Shultz first suggested a renewed effort on aid to the rebels. He applauded the downing of the helicopter and said there might be "further steps" taken on behalf of the rebels.

In especially strong remarks about Nicaragua's leaders and Cuban military involvement in the Central American nation, Mr. Reagan cited "recent disturbing events in a nation close to our borders: the Communist dictatorship in Nicaragua." "It is a nation condemned to unrelenting cruelty by a clique of very cruel men, by a dictator in designer glasses and his comrades drunk with power and all its brutal applications," the President said in a portion of his weekly radio speech.

Mr. Reagan asserted that Nicaraguans were now being trained in Iran, that Nicaragua was continuing border violations against Honduras and Costa Rica and that "Nicaragua's connection with the recent terrorist attack against Colombia's Supreme Court is now clear."

In that attack last month, about 100 people, including 9 judges, were slain in a guerrilla attack.

"What are we to do about such aggressions?" asked Mr. Reagan. "What are we to do about Cuba's willful disregard of the 1962 Kennedy-Khrushchev understanding, of which President Kennedy said, 'If Cuba is not used for the export of aggressive Communist purposes, there will be peace in the Carribean.' "

"Well, the answer is more than we are doing now," Mr. Reagan said. "If Nicaragua can get material support from Communist states and terrorist regimes and prop up a hated Communist dictatorship, should not the forces fighting for liberation, now numbering over 20,000, be entitled to more effective help?"

The senior official who described the remarks as part of a new initiative to provide funding to the contras said: "We've all been increasingly concerned and the President has been concerned about the growing Cuban combat role in Nicaragua, and as you get into the next session of Congress it's clear we have to think about the nature of support we will give to the democratic resistance."

The official added: "This issue is going to be addressed early next year. It has to be. What we're doing is giving people on the Hill and in the country something to think about over Christmas and over the recess. It's a way of getting the debate going again."

Last July, after a testy political battle, Congress approved $27 million for "humanitarian" or nonmilitary aid to the Nicaraguan rebels. Restrictions on the aid insured that the money was not to be spent on weapons or other military purposes, and was for clothing, food, medicine and other items for the United Democratic Opposition, the political umbrella group for the Nicaraguan guerrillas. The measure expires in March.

For nearly two years Congress has opposed direct Central Intelligence Agency involvement in the Nicaragua conflict, largely because of the agency's role in late 1983 and early 1984 in mining Nicaraguan harbors. Both the House and Senate denied Mr. Reagan's request last year for renewed C.I.A. funding of the guerrillas in fiscal 1986. Instead the humanitarian aid has been administered this year through an office in the State Department.

"I think that everyone on the Hill realizes that the current system—of an independent office administering overt humanitarian aid—is a difficult compromise between people who wanted to do more and people who wanted to do nothing," Mr. Abrams said in a telephone interview.

"I think Congress knows this is not a particularly brilliant setup," he added. "The question is now whether the balance in Congress is going to shift toward doing more or doing less."

Mr. Abrams recently completed a trip to Honduras, Guatemala, El Salvador, Panama and Costa Rica, accompanied by Adm. John M. Poindexter, the new national security adviser. A key reason for the trip, officials said, was to seek to end Honduran resistance to channeling United States aid through it to Nicaraguan rebels.

White House officials said no specific military aid proposal for the guerrillas had been set in the new legislative agenda.

* * *

April 29, 1986

SOVIET ANNOUNCES NUCLEAR ACCIDENT AT ELECTRIC PLANT

By SERGE SCHMEMANN

Special to The New York Times.

MOSCOW, April 28—The Soviet Union announced today that there had been an accident at a nuclear power plant in the Ukraine and that "aid is being given to those affected."

The severity of the accident, which spread discernable radioactive material over Scandinavia, was not immediately clear. But the terse statement, distributed by the Tass press agency and read on the evening television news, suggested a major accident.

The phrasing also suggested that the problem had not been brought under full control at the nuclear plant, which the Soviet announcement identified as the Chernobyl station. It is situated at the new town of Pripyat, near Chernobyl and 60 miles north of Kiev.

Heightened Radioactivity Levels

The announcement, the first official disclosure of a nuclear accident ever by the Soviet Union, came hours after Sweden, Finland and Denmark reported abnormally high radioactivity levels in their skies. The readings initially led those countries to think radioactive material had been leaking from one of their own reactors.

The Soviet announcement, made on behalf of the Council of Ministers, after Sweden had demanded information, said in its entirety:

"An accident has occurred at the Chernobyl nuclear power plant as one of the reactors was damaged. Measures are being taken to eliminate the consequences of the accident. Aid is being given to those affected. A Government commission has been set up."

Concern Is Reinforced

The mention of a commission of inquiry reinforced indications that the accident was a serious one.

United States experts said the accident probably posed no danger outside the Soviet Union. But in the absence of detailed information, they said it would be difficult to determine the gravity, and they said environmental damage might conceivably be disastrous.

The Chernobyl plant, with four 1,000-megawatt reactors in operation, is one of the largest and oldest of the 15 or so Soviet civilian nuclear stations. Nuclear power has been a matter of high priority in the Soviet Union, and capacity has been going into service as fast as reactors can be built.

Pripyat, where the Chernobyl plant is situated, is a settlement of 25,000 to 30,000 people that was built in the 1970's along with the station. It is home to construction workers, service personnel and their families.

A British reporter returning from Kiev reported seeing no activity in the Ukrainian capital that would suggest any alarm. No other information was immediately available from the area.

But reports from across Scandinavia, areas more than 800 miles to the north, spoke of increases in radioactivity over the last 24 hours.

Scandinavian authorities said the radioactivity levels did not pose any danger, and it appeared that only tiny amounts of radioactive material had drifted over Scandinavia. All of it was believed to be in the form of two relatively innocuous gases, xenon and krypton. Scandinavian officials said the evidence pointed to an accident in the Ukraine.

In Sweden, an official at the Institute for Protection Against Radiation said gamma radiation levels were 30 to 40 percent higher than normal. He said that the levels had been abnormally high for 24 hours and that the release seemed to be continuing.

In Finland, officials were reported to have said readings in the central and northern areas showed levels six times higher than normal. The Norwegian radio quoted pollution control officials as having said that radioactivity in the Oslo area was 50 percent higher.

Since morning, Swedish officials had focused on the Soviet Union as the probable source of the radioactive material, but Swedish Embassy officials here said the Soviet authorities had denied knowledge of any problem until the Government announcement was read on television at 9 P.M.

The first alarm was raised in Sweden when workers arriving at the Forsmark nuclear power station, 60 miles north of Stockholm, set off warnings during a routine radioactivity check. The plant was evacuated, Swedish officials said. When other nuclear power plants reported similar happenings, the authorities turned their attention to the Soviet Union, from which the winds were coming.

A Swedish diplomat here said he had telephoned three Soviet Government agencies—the State Committee for Utilization of Atomic Energy, the Ministry of Electric Power and the three-year-old State Committee for Safety in the Atomic Power Industry—asking them to explain the high readings over Scandinavia. All said they had no explanation, the diplomat said.

Before the Soviet acknowledgment, the Swedish Minister of Energy, Birgitta Dahl, said that whoever was responsible for the spread of radioactive material was not observing international agreements requiring warnings and exchanges of information about accidents.

Tass, the Soviet Government press agency, said the Chernobyl accident was the first ever in a Soviet nuclear power plant.

It was the first ever acknowledged by the Russians, but Western experts have reported at least two previous mishaps. In 1957, a nuclear waste dump believed related to weapons production was reported to have resulted in a chemical reaction in the Kasli areas of the Urals, causing damage to the environment and possibly fatalities. In 1974, a steam line exploded in the Shevchenko nuclear breeder plant in Kazakhstan, but no radioactive material is believed to have been released in that accident.

Soviet authorities, in giving the development of nuclear electricity generation a high priority, have said that nuclear power is safe. In the absence of citizens' opposition to nuclear power, there has been virtually no questioning of the program.

The terse Soviet announcement of the Chernobyl accident was followed by a Tass dispatch noting that there had been many mishaps in the United States, ranging from Three Mile Island outside Harrisburg, Pa., to the Ginna plant near Rochester. Tass said an American antinuclear group registered 2,300 accidents, breakdowns and other faults in 1979.

The practice of focusing on disasters elsewhere when one occurs in the Soviet Union is so common that after watching a report on Soviet television about a catastrophe abroad, Russians often call Western friends to find out whether something has happened in the Soviet Union.

Construction of the Chernobyl plant began in the early 1970's and the first reactor was commissioned in 1977. Work has been lagging behind plans. In April 1983, the Ukrainian Central Committee chastised the Chernobyl plant, along with the Rovno nuclear power station at Kuznetsovsk, for "inferior quality of construction and installation work and low operating levels."

U.S. OFFERS TO HELP

AGANA, Guam, Tuesday, April 29—Donald T. Regan, the White House chief of staff, said today that the United States was willing to provide medical and scientific assistance to the Soviet Union in connection with the nuclear accident but so far there had been no such request.

* * *

July 27, 1986

GORBACHEV'S DILEMMA

By HARRISON SALISBURY

There is an old Russian skazka (fairy tale) in which a wife must wash her hands into eternity, trying to remove the blood of the husband she murdered. All summer long the yellow water trucks have been flushing radioactive dust from the streets of Kiev and a cluster of towns surrounding the crippled Chernobyl nuclear reactor. By autumn, it is hoped, most of the dust will be gone. Not so the political fallout. That is a far different matter.

Ten days of talks in the Soviet Union and close monitoring of Soviet diplomatic and propaganda moves leave little doubt in this reporter's mind that the Chernobyl nuclear disaster has placed the "new politics" of the Soviet leader Mikhail S. Gorbachev at risk. He has counterattacked with spirit, but it may take all of his considerable political skill to protect and maintain his position as first among his Politburo equals.

Chernobyl, many high-ranking Soviet officials contend, has pushed Gorbachev into a hard-line stance to fend off moves by old-style Kremlin stalwarts to undercut him.

The problems of retaining power in the Kremlin, the toughest political arena in the world, are expected by these officials to dominate Gorbachev's thinking on both domestic and international issues—regardless of summitry, nonsummitry, White House maneuvers, propaganda offensives, arms negotations, Western unity or disunity.

Secrecy traditionally shrouds Soviet politics, but the trauma of Chernobyl has afforded an unusual occasion for some new assessments, the revision of clichés and the clearing away of wishful thinking on many issues. No one in Moscow is suggesting Gorbachev has been irrevocably damaged nor that a viable opposition coalition has yet emerged. What they are saying is that events have played into the hands of such figures as Andrei A. Gromyko, the last of the old guard in the Politburo, and military men, including the volatile Marshal Nikolai V. Ogarkov.

The following account is based almost in its entirety upon conversations conducted in Moscow in recent weeks. The talks, all held on a confidential basis, included four with high-ranking officials of the Communist Party Central Committee and Party Secretariat, each of whom has a direct relationship with Gorbachev. There were also talks with a half-dozen junior advisers, the kind who draft position papers and recommendations that may or may not be submitted by their superiors for Politburo consideration. There were talks with several people who understand the political and personal relationships within the Politburo.

Most of those canvassed expressed strong support for Gorbachev. Several, however, offered sharp (if strictly private) criticism. Under Gorbachev, one man said: "Nothing has changed. It's all boilerplate, propaganda, pretty words. It never will change." No other individual spoke with such pessimism.

All those interviewed, regardless of their politics or point of view, agreed on one point: the tragedy of Chernobyl has produced a season of internal crisis in Moscow. Most of those who expressed an opinion believed Gorbachev would retain his power—but at what cost? One recalled the U-2 incident of May 1, 1960, in which the shooting down of an American spy plane over Sverdlovsk derailed President Eisenhower's plans to visit the Soviet Union. The late Nikita S. Khrushchev held on for four years as Soviet leader but confessed to an American friend: "I never regained my political power. From that time on I was involved in an uphill struggle." Khrushchev was forced to scale down his plans for change in order to retain office; eventually, he was sacked.

Before may of this year, Chernobyl meant little to most Russians. Named for a dusty gray shrub that grows on the chalky soil at the nearby conflux of the Dnieper and Pripyat Rivers, Chernobyl was a sleepy town, set in a land of Russian sagas—of bogatyri, knights, of the Varangian from the north, of conflict between Goth and Slav. Near here Vladimir in 988 hurled down the heathen idols from the bluffs of Kiev and brought his people into Christianity with a mass baptism in the muddy Dnieper.

It was this dreamy, drowsy corner of Russia, now blistered with a formidable assemblage of atomic power plants, that riveted Moscow's attention during the "Six Days in May," a period from April 28 to May 4, during which, according to a Gorbachev associate, neither the Soviet leader nor anyone in the Politburo knew when, how—or whether—the nuclear disaster could be brought under control. In that time, a Gorbachev associate said, "Frankly, we felt we were on the edge." There was fear that the United States might seize the opportunity for an anti-Soviet maneuver and there was concern that Gorbachev's opponents might exploit the crisis.

These fears, some Gorbachev associates implied, underlaid the rally-round-the-flag tone of Gorbachev's television speech on May 14, with its strong patriotic appeal and its attack on the United States and the West. The speech was intended to push Soviet public opinion into the familiar defensive crouch of resistance against "capitalist encirclement," a cry first raised in the days of Lenin nearly 70 years ago and often reiterated since in times of crisis.

That President Reagan did not send Gorbachev a formal message of sympathy—as did British Prime Minister Margaret Thatcher and other heads of state—was cited by Gorbachev's associates as proof that Reagan is implacably hostile toward Russia, even in a time of a national tragedy.

According to one intimate, Gorbachev felt "personal outrage" over what he perceived as an American effort to repeat, in the Soviet adviser's words, "the propaganda triumph of the Korean 007 disaster." Another intimate said: "What do the Americans want from us? Gorbachev told me personally: 'I was ready to agree to everything at Geneva. How could Reagan let it all go? How do you deal with that? He just reads from cue cards that one of his aides has written out for him.' " If, in fact, Gorbachev was prepared "to agree to everything" at the Geneva summit, American negotiators got no such signal.

It must be noted that this negative image of Reagan contrasts with that offered in Moscow last November, immediately after the Geneva summit, by one of these same Grobachev advisers. The adviser then said that the Soviet side now understood and respected Reagan's "Star Wars" proposal—that is, they realized that the President truly believed "Star Wars" was a defensive plan. The same adviser said he felt both men now understood each other on a personal basis and got on well, particularly as a result of a long private chat during the summit.

No such coziness was reflected in Moscow in the grim post-Chernobyl atmosphere. Gorbachev's aides uniformly presented a mood of despondency and frustration. They seemed to feel that events had taken command. One of Gorbachev's younger advisers, a sandy-complexioned man in his late 30's who sports a blue windbreaker, tan chinos and loafers (looking more like the coach of a Glasgow soccer team than a dour Kremlin ideologue), made no secret of his feeling that neither of the superpowers any longer could control events.

He drew an analogy—one many sophisticated Soviet observers are coming to draw—between Soviet policy in Afghanistan and United States policy in Vietnam. "Neither power knew what it was getting into," he said. "And in the end, neither one knew how to get out."

Again and again, these highly placed specialists suggested that "we can no longer control technology"—defensively citing the Challenger disaster and Three Mile Island, along with Chernobyl. "What will be next?" one asked.

Gorbachev's advisers were bitter that the official American attitude on Chernobyl had inadvertently played into the hands of Gorbachev's domestic opponents. "We told you so," critics of Gorbachev's policies were saying of the General Secretary's effort to revive détente. Referring to the Americans, he said they "have just set a trap for you."

A cool-headed member of the Soviet elite, not a Gorbachev adviser, explained the Communist Party leader's problem in these terms:

"He was blind-sided by Chernobyl. It was not just that the local officials were stupid or tried to cover up. They literally did not know what had happened. They reported the accident but did not say it was a nuclear accident because they did not think it was an accident of that type. They thought it was a fire in the superstructure. Not for 48 hours, from the early hours of Saturday, April 26, until Monday morning the 28th, when Gorbachev sent Politburo members to Kiev did he know what he had on his hands. By that time, it was a nuclear reactor raging out of control."

Chernobyl, this Soviet official said, struck as Gorbachev was rapidly increasing his control of the party and state apparatus, but he was not yet firmly in the saddle. He came into office as a protege of the late Yuri V. Andropov, backed by a coalition that included the K.G.B., young party apparatchiks and military technocrats. Hard-liners, Brezhnev hacks and major industrial bosses opposed him.

Today only one of Gorbachev's major opponents, Gromyko, is in the Politburo. But there is still a three-way split in the Communist Party—the rapidly growing and more youthful group appointed by Gorbachev; the almost equally large group of loyalists to old ways and old leaders ("Stalin was right. You have to use the knout"), and sideliners waiting to see who comes out on top before joining the winner. "Gorbachev's job of taking control was still only half done at the close of the 27th Party Congress in February," one Russian told me. "Half the members of the Central Committee were not his men."

Gorbachev, this man said, moved swiftly and effectively at the start to put his own men into the Politburo and the Secretariat. He had taken control of the Leningrad Party apparatus by ousting his hard-line rival there, Grigory V. Romanov. He replaced the stodgy Moscow Party leadership after the November summit (when Gorbachev's prestige was high). But the Ukraine Party apparatus was still in place, and is still solidly in traditional hands.

The military also has been little changed during Gorbachev's brief tenure, remaining disdainfully aloof as it has watched the evolution of Gorbachev's "new politics." Soviet military leaders have seen campaigns for change before—under Nikita Khrushchev (they threw their weight against him and he was dumped) and Andropov. But Andropov was gone in little more than a year, his efforts to drag the Soviet Union out of the swamp of stale dialectic and dogma cut short by the onset of a fatal illness. Gorbachev has not yet mustered the strength to stand up to the military, and in the aftermath of Chernobyl, he must rely on them more than ever. There is not much sympathy for change among the beefy, medal-heavy marshals and generals. Their inclinations run toward a neo-Stalinist approach—bigger and bigger military budgets, no nonsense about "liberalism," guns not butter, tough talk to the United States.

One issue on which Gorbachev and the military do see eye to eye is Afghanistan. Many military men were reluctant to get involved in Afghanistan (although some welcomed the opportunity to test new weapons and tactics, feeling the United States had gotten ahead of them by extensive combat experience in Korea and Vietnam). And some Soviet military leaders share the concern of some young Gorbachev advisers about the cost-effectiveness of small-scale foreign involvements.

An issue that enrages the Gorbachev camp is the charge, made in the West, that the Kremlin deliberately withheld news of the Chernobyl disaster.

"It's true," one of Gorbachev's older advisers said. "The news was not well-handled at the beginning. Part of that was bungling, but mostly it was due to the difficulty at the top in finding out what had happened and what was going to happen."

There was fear of creating panic and there was panic in some quarters. One highly respected scientist reportedly threw up his arms and said: "This is the worst catastrophe of our times. I don't know what we can do." Some Chernobyl personnel just ran away. Two months later, they were still missing. In Kiev, the Ukrainian Minister of Health went on television during the accident to tell the population there was no need for alarm, and he outlined a series of precautions—take frequent baths, wash down sidewalks several times a day, don't let children play outdoors. Instead of calming the city, this set off an exodus. The problem, one Russian said, was that the population was not accustomed to hearing about disasters. When the health minister said there was no reason for concern, many people leapt to the conclusion that if the minister admitted this much, the situation must be far worse. They decided to get themselves and their children out of town.

In Russian terms, the reaction of the citizens made sense. Ashkabad, the capital of Turkmania, was leveled by an earthquake in 1948, taking the lives of half the city's population of more than 200,000. Only a paragraph or two about the disaster was published in the Soviet press days after the event. The first real details were contained in a poem in a literary magazine published years later. Tashkent, the largest city of Soviet Central Asia, was devastated by an earthquake in 1966. Little about that was ever published.

Nor has anything ever appeared in the Soviet press or on Soviet television about the great Kyshtym accident in 1957 near Chelyabinsk, the big industrial center in the Urals. A dump for radioactive materials exploded, devastating the area, causing hundreds of casualties and leaving behind vast pollution that still poisons the region. Some scientists, including the dissident Zhores A. Medvedev, who has done extensive research on the event, believe it was the worst nuclear accident in history. At the mention of the word Kyshtym, knowledgeable Russians pale and put a finger to their lips. More than a quarter century has passed, but Kyshtym is still too hot to discuss—much less mention in print.

It was in this atmosphere of secrecy that Mikhail Gorbachev took office in March 1985. One of the basic elements of his plan for reform was what the Russians call glasnost, openness. Glasnost was advocated not on a basis of principle but of pragmatism. In his effort to move the Soviet Union out of the economic, technological and creative slough in which it had been mired for nearly 70 years by the Russian version of Marxism-Leninism, Gorbachev was determined to shine the floodlight of publicity into the dark corners of the country, focusing on anachronisms, corruption, obsolescence, red tape, featherbedding and cronyism.

To do this he enlisted a new team of advisers. It is not accidental that high among them are specialists on America. Chief among them is Anatoly F. Dobrynin, whom Gorbachev summoned back from his lengthy term as Ambassador to Washington and installed in quarters close to his own in a relationship not unlike that of Henry Kissinger and President Nixon. To all intents, Dobrynin is Gorbachev's Secretary of State. Andrei A. Gromyko, sullen and skeptical, has been kicked upstairs to the ceremonial post of Soviet President. But he retains his membership on the Politburo, as much a pillar of political rigidity as his famous mentor, Vyacheslav (Old Stonebottom) Molotov.

The whole Soviet diplomatic corps has been shaken up as it has never been before. Orders went out that a new diplomatic style, more flexible, more realistic, less ideological, more innovative was to be the handmaiden of glasnost. New responsibilities went to Georgi A. Arbatov and his specialists at the Institute for the U.S.A. and Canada.

Gorbachev brought in Aleksandr N. Yakovlev, the unorthodox former ambassador to Canada, a one-time graduate student at Columbia University, an Americanist, an out-spoken opponent of Russian nationalist theories and neo-Stalinism. He was placed in charge of the drive for glasnost. Yakovlev is a strong believer in television. "The TV image is everything," he has been quoted as saying. Overnight, Yakovlev was installed as Party Secretary in charge of propaganda and information.

There are other far-reaching aspects of glasnost as conceived by Gorbachev: an end to writing history as propaganda; a cessation of publication of laudatory potboilers in the form of military memoirs and quasi fictional war novels.

Recently, a remarkable Congress of Writers was held in the Kremlin, marked by open and sometimes rowdy debate and the replacement of a stodgy, reactionary union leadership by younger, more free-thinking writers. This, it was said, had the personal encouragement of Gorbachev.

But glasnost and the ambitious ideas associated with it have been put on hold. How much will survive Chernobyl is unclear. Leaders under stress tend to jettison the controversial and the radical. When, after Chernobyl, Gorbachev raised the cry of "capitalist encirclement," it was a signal that he was moving to safer, more conventional ground. Experiments could wait.

A similar signal came from a senior foreign policy adviser who hauled out another longtime Soviet cliché—"equality." The United States, he said, echoing past generations of Soviet foreign ministers, was refusing to deal with Moscow on a basis of equality; it was trying to dictate to her as an inferior power.

For years, this argument had been thrown up by the Soviet Union as a barrier to productive diplomatic talks. In part, it stemmed from the days when the Soviet was an "outsider," begging for crumbs from the diplomatic table. In part, it was just a diplomatic bargaining chip. President Nixon and Kissinger went to great pains to emphasize that in their view the Soviet was an equal partner at the diplomatic table and, in their memoirs, both stressed that this attitude had played a major part in making effective great-power diplomacy.

The resurfacing of the "equality" argument suggested that Gorbachev did not want serious talks with Washington when his defenses were in disarray because of Chernobyl. The summit? Forget it for the near future. First things first, and the first priority for Gorbachev is damage control in the Kremlin.

A man in the second rank of Gorbachev's circle said he did not see how serious talks could be conducted "at the present time." He even scoffed at an unofficial exploration of presummit conditions.

It sounded very much like Gorbachev had drawn the wagons around the campfire. Yet, a day or two later, Pravda gave a clear hint that glasnost was not entirely dead. The newspaper published a blistering criticism of Soviet television, centering on the poor techniques and failures of Vremya, the Soviet equivalent of American network evening news. Pravda seemed to be saying that Vremya had not handled Chernobyl with an aggressive, forthright approach.

Certainly, whatever concessions he may have to make, Gorbachev is still in control. But neither he nor his associates seem to realize that perhaps their strongest move in buttressing their position at home and abroad would be to take the lid off Chernobyl itself, to make public a blow-by-blow, hour-by-hour, no-holds-barred account. And no harm would be done if, 29 years after it happened, the terrible secrets of the Kystym catastrophe were given to the Russian people—and the world. Therein may lie Gorbachev's way to securing Soviet credibility and the rout of the assemblage of bureaucrats, neo-Stalinists, and party and military elements with whom he must contend.

Harrison Salisbury is a former New York Times correspondent, associate editor and editor of the Op-Ed page who has specialized in Soviet affairs. His latest book is "The Long March: The Untold Story."

* * *

August 31, 1986

A U.S. JOURNALIST IS HELD IN MOSCOW

By PHILIP TAUBMAN

Special to The New York Times.

MOSCOW, Aug. 30—The Moscow correspondent for U.S. News & World Report was detained by the authorities today after being handed a package containing two maps marked "top secret" by a Soviet acquaintance.

The correspondent, Nicholas Daniloff, told his wife by telephone that he had been taken into custody by eight plainclothes agents after the meeting and was being held at a police or military detention center in Moscow.

It was not immediately clear whether Mr. Daniloff had been formally arrested or charged with criminal offenses. As of late evening, the Government had made no information available about the case.

U.S. Embassy Protests

The United States Embassy immediately protested the detention to the Foreign Ministry, American diplomats said. Richard Combs Jr., the deputy chief of mission, called the detention "an obvious provocation."

A State Department spokesman in Washington said that the allegations against Mr. Daniloff were unfounded and that efforts were under way to gain his release.

The incident seemed likely to disrupt relations between Washington and Moscow at a particularly delicate time, according to Western diplomats. The two sides have been trying to arrange a meeting later this year between President Reagan and Mikhail S. Gorbachev, the Soviet leader.

Mr. Daniloff, who planned to leave the Soviet Union next month after a five-year tour, told his wife that he did not expect to be freed soon and that the authorities appeared to be preparing to charge him with espionage.

"Nick said they kept asking him, 'Who do you really work for, who do you really take orders from?' " his wife, Ruth, reported. "It's a classic setup," she said. Western diplomats said the detention appeared to be in retaliation for the arrest in New York last weekend of a Soviet physicist assigned to the United Nations Secretariat. The Russian, Gennadi F. Zakharov, was charged with espionage against the United States.

A man identifying himself as an investigator for the K.G.B. told an Associated Press correspondent who telephoned the detention center that Mr. Daniloff was being kept there. The man said he did not know how long Mr. Daniloff would be held.

The United States Embassy was trying to arrange access to Mr. Daniloff, who told his wife late this afternoon that he would be permitted to meet with American diplomats. American diplomats said it appeared they would be unable to talk to or meet with Mr. Daniloff until Sunday at the earliest.

Western diplomats said it was possible that Moscow would threaten to try Mr. Daniloff on espionage charges in hopes of arranging an exchange of Mr. Daniloff for Mr. Zakharov.

Mr. Zakharov, who was arrested on a Queens subway platform a week ago as he gave $1,000 to an employee of an American defense contractor for three classified documents, did not have diplomatic immunity. Federal law enforcement officials said he could be prosecuted and might face life in prison if convicted.

Mr. Daniloff, who is 52 years old, worked here in the early 1960's for United Press International. He speaks fluent Russian and is considered one of the most knowledgeable foreign correspondents in Moscow.

Mr. Daniloff's wife said he left their apartment this morning to meet a Soviet citizen named Misha who called several days ago asking to see him.

First Contact Four Years Ago

Mrs. Daniloff said her husband first met Misha, who is in his mid-20's, four years ago during a visit to Frunze, the capital of the Kirghiz Republic, one of 15 constituent republics.

Mrs. Daniloff said Misha, whom she described as curious about the West, had stayed in touch with Mr. Daniloff, visiting him in Moscow several times in recent years.

"I think Nick and I have a pretty good sense for sinister Russians, and Misha never struck us that way," Mrs. Daniloff said. "I think the K.G.B. forced him to do this after they discovered he knew Nick."

Mr. Daniloff told his wife that he had met Misha near their apartment and walked with him in the Lenin Hills, a park area that rises along the Moscow River, offering a panoramic view.

He gave Misha two novels by Stephen King, one of Misha's favorite authors, according to Mrs. Daniloff, and in return was given a package that Misha said contained newspaper clippings from Frunze.

Mr. Daniloff said that not long after he took the package, he was surrounded by eight plainclothes agents, presumably from the K.G.B., who took him to the detention center.

Mrs. Daniloff said a Russian who refused to give his name called the Daniloff apartment about 1 P.M. and reported that Mr. Daniloff would not return home for several hours.

When he failed to show up for a 4 P.M. meeting with a friend, Mrs. Daniloff said, she became convinced that he was in trouble. Mr. Daniloff telephoned her from the detention center shortly after 5 P.M.

COMMENT BY U.S.

WASHINGTON, Aug. 30 (Special to The New York Times)—A State Department spokesman, Peter Martinez, said today: "Our embassy in Moscow has reported that Daniloff has been detained allegedly for accepting classified material from a Soviet citizen. Based on the information we have however, it is clear that the grounds on which he has been detained are contrived. We have thus launched strong protests at high levels here and in Moscow in which we have rejected any suggestion that Daniloff may have been engaging in activities incompatible with his status as a journalist and demanded his immediate release."

MAGAZINE IN TOUCH WITH REPORTER

WASHINGTON, Aug. 30 (Special to The New York Times)— A senior editor at U.S. News & World Report said Mr. Daniloff had been in touch with the magazine and had reported that he was being treated well.

According to the official, Henry Trewhitt, the magazine's deputy managing editor, Mr. Daniloff said he had not been charged with any offenses.

* * *

September 30, 1986

RUSSIANS SET DANILOFF FREE AND HE FLIES TO FRANKFURT; NOT A TRADE, PRESIDENT SAYS

By BERNARD GWERTZMAN

The Soviet Union yesterday freed Nicholas S. Daniloff, the American journalist who had been confined to Moscow for the last month on spying charges.

Mr. Daniloff was allowed to leave without standing trial. He flew to Frankfurt, West Germany, for an overnight stay on his way to the United States.

His release seemed to remove an obstacle to setting a date for a meeting between President Reagan and Mikhail S. Gorbachev later this year.

No Soviet Announcement

Reagan Administration officials said that as part of the arrangement on Mr. Daniloff worked out in talks in New York, Gennadi F. Zakharov, a Soviet citizen accused of espionage, would be allowed to plead no contest in court and be sent back to the Soviet Union in exchange for a group of Soviet dissidents.

Mr. Daniloff's release occurred suddenly, without public announcement, and appeared to end a dispute that had threatened to paralyze and worsen Soviet-American relations.

The breakthrough occurred after a three-hour meeting late Sunday in New York between Secretary of State George P. Shultz and Foreign Minister Eduard A. Shevardnadze at the Soviet Mission. It was their fourth and longest meeting in less than a week.

The first word of the release of Mr. Daniloff, who was in the Soviet Union for U.S. News & World Report, came in news reports from Moscow.

'Wonderful to Be Back'

"It is wonderful to be back in the West," he said on his arrival in Frankfurt. "All I know is that I am free, in the West, and delighted to see you."

President Reagan, on a campaign stop in Kansas City, Mo., made a brief mention of Mr. Daniloff's release.

"I have something of a news announcement I would like to make," Mr. Reagan said. "In case you have not heard it already, at 12 P.M., Central time, a Lufthansa airliner left Moscow bound for Frankfurt, West Germany, and on board are Mr. and Mrs. Nicholas Daniloff."

Details on the agreement, which came after a month of tension, were sketchy. Neither the Soviet Union nor the United States issued a statement on the apparent end of the crisis that had dominated relations for the last month. Mr. Shultz and Mr. Shevardnadze planned separate news conferences today.

In the absence of an agreed statement, the two sides proceeded to interpret what happened in their own way.

There were signs that steps might be taken as early as today to send the accused Soviet spy in New York, Mr. Zakharov, back to the Soviet Union in exchange for dissidents, in what appeared to be the second stage of the understanding. Both Mr. Daniloff and Mr. Zakharov had been released from prison Sept. 12 in the custody of their respective embassies pending trial.

A Soviet spokesman said the United States was also discussing a possible modification of the United States order expelling 25 members of the Soviet Mission to the United Nations.

Zakharov's Release Expected

The Soviet spokesman, Valentin G. Karymov, said that as part of the accord, he expected Mr. Zakharov, a Soviet employee of the United Nations, to be released soon. His arrest in Queens on Aug. 23 is believed to have led to the seizure of Mr. Daniloff in Moscow a week later.

The Soviet Union had sought a straight trade of the two. But the United States said it would never agree to a trade because it did not want to lend credibility to the charge that Mr. Daniloff had been a spy. It insisted that Mr. Daniloff, who is 51 years old, was a "hostage," while Mr. Zakharov was a "spy."

This debate continued yesterday, with the Soviet Mission talking of the Daniloff release as the first part of a "swap" and the Americans saying there had been no trade.

Reagan Denies Swap

Mr. Reagan said Mr. Daniloff had not been traded for Mr. Zakharov.

It was not the United States that gave in, the President told reporters on his campaign swing through the Middle West.

"They blinked," he said, referring to the Russians.

Administration officials said that if Mr. Zakharov was released, it would be after court proceedings and in exchange for Soviet dissidents who are in detention or have been refused emigration visas. Among dissidents whose names have been mentioned are Yuri Orlov, Vladimir Slepak, Ida Nudel and David Goldfarb.

Mr. Daniloff, speaking in Frankfurt, said:

"I think it is obvious to everybody what has happened over this past month. I was arrested without an arrest warrant, a case was fabricated against me with a narrow political purpose of giving the Soviet Union some political leverage over the case of Gennadi Zakharov in New York. The K.G.B. did not punish me. The K.G.B. punished itself."

He was referring to the Soviet Union's State Security Committee, the intelligence and internal security agency, which is generally known by its Russian initials, K.G.B.

Mr. Daniloff was welcomed in Frankfurt by the United States Ambassador to West Germany, Richard R. Burt, and spent the night at the home of the American consul general before traveling on to Washington today.

Explanations Expected Today

President Reagan promised that Mr. Shultz would provide more details today on the negotiations. There was no explanation why so little was said yesterday. One official suggested that the final arrangements concerning Mr. Zakharov had not been worked out and were contingent on Mr. Daniloff's leaving the Soviet Union in a manner that would allow the United States to say that his release was unconditional.

Aides to Mr. Reagan went out of the way to note that Mr. Daniloff had left the Soviet Union without being tried, and that Mr. Zakharov was still in New York, his status unchanged.

But Justice Department officials said his status could be changed quickly once the decision was taken on national security grounds to send him back to the Soviet Union. What was uncertain was whether Mr. Zakharov would stand trial.

Because of concern that Mr. Reagan not appear to have yielded to Soviet pressure, American spokesmen were sensitive to any suggestions of a trade.

Comment by Senator Dole

The Senate majority leader, Bob Dole, a Kansas Republican, said:

"Although all the information surrounding Daniloff's release is not yet available, it appears his release is unconditional. Implicitly, at least, the Soviets are admitting that Nick Daniloff was not a spy, and they are trying to find a way out of a colossal blunder."

If Mr. Zakharov is to be sent back to the Soviet Union, he may be handled in the same way as a Ghanaian agent last November. The Ghanaian, Michael A. Soussoudis, pleaded no contest on espionage counts. He was sentenced to 20 years in prison, but the judge promptly reduced this to time served, and turned him over to the Ghanaian Ambassdor on condition that Mr. Soussoudis leave the United States immediately.

The crisis over the Daniloff case began on Aug. 23 when agents of the Federal Bureau of Investigation arrested Mr. Zakharov, whom they accused of having asked a Guyanese working for a military contractor to provide secret data. The Guyanese had cooperated with the F.B.I. for the three years he had known Mr. Zakharov.

Custody Request Was Denied

Mr. Zakharov's lawyer requested that he be permitted to remain out of jail in the custody of the Soviet Embassy, but the United States Attorney's office did not support the request, and the court rejected it.

On Aug. 30, Mr. Daniloff, who had been a correspondent in Moscow for more than five years, was arrested by the K.G.B. after he had accepted a package from a Russian acquaintance. The package was said to have included secret documents. Mr. Daniloff said he had been set up to serve as a hostage for the release of Mr. Zakharov. On Sept. 7, Mr. Daniloff was officially charged with espionage, and two days later, Mr. Zakharov was indicted.

On Sept. 12, the two governments arranged to have Mr. Daniloff and Mr. Zakharov released from prison and remanded to the custody of their respective embassies pending trial. This touched off criticism from conservatives that Mr. Reagan had equated the two cases. The United States said the arrangement had been made for the sake of Mr. Daniloff's well-being.

The issue continued to dominate Soviet-American relations because Mr. Reagan had sent assurances to Mr. Gorbachev that Mr. Daniloff was not a spy and should be released. Mr. Gorbachev, in a public comment, said Mr. Daniloff had been caught "red-handed."

Shevardnadze Conciliatory

With relations tense, Mr. Shevardnadze arrived in Washington for previously planned talks on Sept. 19 and 20. To the surprise of the American side, he took a conciliatory tone, saying that the Soviet Union was ready for a summit meeting and wanted to resolve the Daniloff case.

Since the United States also wanted a summit meeting, the two sides were in agreement not to let the Daniloff case upset summit preparations. In addition, the two sides seemed to have made progress toward an accord limiting medium-range missiles.

The Americans, however, said that it made no sense to schedule a summit meeting so long as Mr. Daniloff remained in Moscow. In other words, the Soviet side was told that if it wanted a summit meeting, it would have to let Mr. Daniloff return home.

In a series of meetings between Mr. Shultz and Mr. Shevardnadze in New York, the Soviet side initially sought absolute equality in the treatment of the two men, but then bowed to American insistence that Mr. Daniloff not be tried, and be sent home first. Only then, the United States said, would it consider trading Mr. Zakharov for a group of dissidents and consider ameliorating the expulsion order.

Practice in Previous Cases

In arresting Mr. Daniloff after the seizure of Mr. Zakharov, the Soviet Union was following a practice it began in 1963 when a Yale professor, Frederick C. Barghoorn, was arrested on a Moscow street a day after a Soviet driver was jailed on espionage charges in New Jersey.

After the intervention of President Kennedy, the professor was freed. The driver was convicted of espionage, but allowed to live in the custody of the Soviet Embassy pending appeals. He eventually was allowed to return to the Soviet Union in 1971.

In 1978, two Soviet employees of the United Nations were arrested for espionage. An American businessman in Moscow, F. Jay Crawford, was arrested on currency violations. All three were then allowed out in the custody of their embassies. Mr. Crawford was tried on black market charges and expelled the same day. The two Soviet agents were convicted of espionage, sentenced to 50 years in prison, and while out on appeal, were traded for five imprisoned dissidents.

* * *

October 12, 1986

REAGAN-GORBACHEV MEETING OPENS WITH PLANS TO PURSUE ARMS PACT AND RIGHTS ISSUES

By LESLIE H. GELB

Special to The New York Times.

REYKJAVIK, Iceland, Oct. 11—President Reagan and Mikhail S. Gorbachev concluded two of their three scheduled meetings here today, and the two sides seemed to be crystallizing areas of agreement on arms control, human rights and other issues. At the same time they seemed to be heading toward setting a date for a full summit meeting in the United States, some time next spring.

The agreement today to establish two working groups, one on arms control and the other on human rights and other issues, was generally regarded as a positive sign.

The move seemed to indicate that the leaders would press for concrete results from their discussions.

The two meetings today were kept close to the schedule of two hours each, unlike their meetings in Geneva last November, when all sessions spilled well over the schedule.

Focus on Setting Next Talks

To officials on both sides, the principal test of the meetings is whether Mr. Reagan and Mr. Gorbachev will agree to meet again in the next several months in the United States.

Those officials continue to say that this will depend essentially on progress on arms control, which Moscow has emphasized, and only to a lesser degree on resolving regional and human rights issues, as Washington desires.

This seemed to be the case despite the agreement today to set up working groups in both general areas.

An Administration official said tonight that the Soviet leader had told Mr. Reagan that he would not set a date for a meeting in the United States unless prospects for signing a major arms control accord were good.

American officials were optimistic that the setting up of the working groups would help to narrow the two sides' differences.

At a minimum, the two sides are in a position to fulfill their stated goal of using the get-together here to seek new avenues of compromise for their arms negotiators in Geneva.

Officials on both sides, especially on the Soviet side, continue to speak positively about the prospects for a full summit meeting, perhaps in the early spring. That would provide time for the arms negotiators in Geneva to translate the generalities of Reykjavik into treaty language. This is said to be of particular concern to Mr. Gorbachev.

'Interesting Answers'

Key Administraton officials said here today that Mr. Reagan expected Mr. Gorbachev to raise these issues, and that the President was prepared to provide "interesting answers."

The most promising issue for movement here is said by both sides to be limits on medium-range missiles in Europe and Asia. Sources here said the Russians have come with two new concessions in this area, and the Administration is expected to respond in kind.

The key question to Administration officials is whether this will provide Mr. Gorbachev with what he needs to set a full summit meeting, or whether he will have to show progress on limiting space-based defenses and nuclear testing as well.

Space-Based Weapons a Concern

Administration officials expect the Soviet leader to press the issue of nuclear testing. Grounds for compromise are beginning to emerge, but it is not clear whether Moscow will settle for less than a total test ban.

But the area of central concern to both sides remains the future of space-based weapons and their relation to the prospects for deep cuts in long-range nuclear missiles and bombers.

The sides are still far apart on space-based systems, although each has recently taken the first tentative steps toward compromise. In particular, the Administration has been stressing its willingness to adjust the scope and timing of Mr. Reagan's plan to defend against missile attacks to account for cuts in strategic offensive forces.

Key Administration officials here said Mr. Reagan's own emphasis would be on strategic weapons.

Progress has been made on this subject in recent months, although major differences remain.

Officials in both capitals have also been alluding to the possibility of agreements in three other areas: risk-reduction centers in Washington and Moscow to manage accidents and crises, additional cooperation to prevent the spread of nuclear weapons and arrangements to prevent the spread of chemical weapons.

Hurdles Were Overcome

Perhaps the most striking thing to Soviet and American officials as they looked back over preparations for the Reykjavik meeting were the substantial hurdles they overcame to get here.

For one, American forces bombed Libya in April in reprisal for terrorist attacks. In response, Foreign Minister Eduard A. Shevardnadze canceled a meeting with Secretary of State George P. Shultz that was to have prepared for a summit meeting. In addition, preparations seemed to founder seriously when the United States arrested a Soviet employee of the United Nations on an espionage charge and Moscow retaliated by levying spy charges against an American news correspondent.

"Most experts were saying that these events showed the fragility of the relationship," a high-ranking Administration official said. "But the point is that the desire on both sides to improve relations was strong enough to surmount the difficulties."

By now, the explanations for this have a familiar ring. Mr. Reagan wants an arms agreement to enhance his stature in history. Mr. Gorbachev wants arms limits so he can concentrate on restructuring his ailing economy.

An Exchange of Letters

Whatever their motives, the two leaders took matters in hand this summer through an exchange of letters. The results were good enough by the end of last month for leaders on both sides to express some optimism. At the United Nations, Mr. Reagan spoke of "the beginning of serious and productive negotiation on arms reduction." Mr. Shevardnadze recently referred to "a breach in the wall."

The exchange of letters also led to a proposal from Mr. Gorbachev to meet in Iceland as preparation for the full-scale summit. Mr. Reagan then announced that the meeting would "take place in the context of preparations for the General Secretary's visit to the United States, which was agreed to at Geneva in November of '85." But Administration officials said that while Mr. Gorbachev had agreed to the phrase "in the context of," he pointedly had not agreed to a date for a summit meeting in the United States.

Pressure from Conservatives

The general Administration view is that Mr. Gorbachev is trying to use the absence of an agreement on a date as additional leverage on Mr. Reagan in Iceland, and that the Soviet leader will not renege on his pledge to meet Mr. Reagan in the United States. But a few officials, most of them in the State Department, are not quite as sanguine.

Over the last week, conservative counterpressures have been building in the United States against the prospect that Mr. Reagan would make new concessions in Iceland.

It also appeared that Mr. Gorbachev was facing similar problems.

In any event, Mr. Reagan began warning against "false hopes" about the Iceland meeting, and his aides have carried these lowered expectations with them to Reykjavik. By contrast, Soviet officials here continue to talk of compromises.

Whatever hope there is for a breakthrough here seems to center on medium-range missiles. It would not be difficult, as Administration officials pointed out, for the sides to work out a one-page agreement to agree. But such a document would obviously be exceedingly general and would still leave most of the thorny problems to the Geneva negotiators.

Elements of a Possible Accord

Such an "agreement" could contain the following elements:

- A limit of 100 missile warheads for each side in Europe.
- Limits on Soviet medium-range missiles facing Asia, with Washington retaining a right to deploy an equal number in the United States.
- A freeze on shorter-range missiles in Europe.
- Provisions for full verification of the terms.

On both sides, officials recognize that even a somewhat more detailed document would leave more problems unsolved than solved. For example, which shorter-range missiles would be covered, what number of missiles targeted on Asia would Moscow be allowed, and would the agreement last until it was replaced by a new one, as Washington desires, or would it last for only two or three years, as Moscow wants?

The second possible area of agreement here is on nuclear testing. Moscow has unilaterally refrained from testing for more than a year and insists on a total test ban. Washington, for a long time, simply suggested that the sides ratify the signed but unratified treaty limiting underground tests to no more than 150 kilotons, as long as Moscow would accept more intrusive verification of these tests.

Reagan Speaks at U.N.

There matters stood until Mr. Reagan's speech at the United Nations, in which he talked of a "step-by-step parallel program of limiting and ultimately ending nuclear testing."

Officials said that means he is willing to steadily reduce either the 150-kiloton limit on the size of permitted tests or the number of tests permitted or both.

Moscow has given some indications of interest, but nothing more.

Most interestingly to Administration experts, the Russians seem to have avoided emphasizing space-based weapons in recent weeks. These experts interpret this to mean that Mr. Gorbachev may be signaling a willingness to sidestep this issue in Iceland.

"He may understand that it's too hard to fix in Reykjavik, so he's avoiding setting himself up for a failure," one of them said.

But the Administration is still wary on this issue.

Mr. Reagan is now prepared to forgo deployment of space-based antimissile weapons for at least seven and a half years, under the terms of the existing antiballistic missile treaty, dating to 1972. Moscow is insisting on a longer period, perhaps 10 years.

And this is the least of the problems on this issue. It will be far more difficult to determine what kinds of testing and development would be permitted in the interim.

As the schedule for their meeting now stands, the leaders will discuss all of these issues plus some regional and human rights matters in about six working hours.

* * *

October 16, 1986

SUMMIT PUZZLES LINGER

Basic Questions About What Took Place at Reykjavik Talks Are Still Unanswered

By LESLIE H. GELB

Days after President Reagan and Mikhail S. Gorbachev parted company in Iceland after appearing to be on the verge of making an arms pact of historic proportions, Administration officials and critics alike are still looking for answers to key questions about that meeting.

How did a meeting designed, as both sides said, to give "impulses" to the arms talks explode into a full-fledged bargaining session?

Was the Administration prepared for this, what exactly was agreed to, and do the two sides now agree on what was settled and what was not?

Further, has the Administration shown that restricting tests of space-based weapons to the laboratory, as Moscow insists, would actually "kill" the Strategic Defense Initiative?

Interview with Shultz

Perhaps of the most elemental importance, has the Administration explained how it is prepared to maintain security for the United States and its allies in a world without nuclear weapons, in a world where Soviet conventional military superiority might then prove decisive?

Secretary of State George P. Shultz addressed some of these questions in an hourlong interview yesterday with senior editors of The New York Times. It was devoted entirely to Mr. Reagan's two-day meeting with the Soviet leader in Reykjavik last weekend.

Mr. Shultz and other senior Administration officials have spent the last two days trying, as their aides have acknowledged, to reshape perceptions of the Reykjavik meeting. Where Mr. Shultz and others initially called the meeting a deep disappointment, the Secretary spoke of it yesterday as a "watershed" event because "for the first time the two sides agreed to dramatic reductions in nuclear and strategic arms."

The Geneva arms talks resumed yesterday, and the chief American negotiator termed the Iceland meeting an unexpectedly successful "serious and positive step" in the direction of arms agreements.

Judging from the reactions of many strategic experts, legislators and Administration officials themselves, the answers from Mr. Shultz and other senior officials have not put basic questions to rest.

For example, in the interview yesterday, Mr. Shultz insisted that he and Mr. Reagan were prepared for the wide-ranging negotiations. Yet he acknowledged surprise that the Soviet leader had once again linked an accord on medium-range missiles in Europe and Asia to a resolution of the future of space-based defenses, commonly called "Star Wars."

He was asked if the elimination of medium-range missiles in Europe would only enhance Soviet conventional or non-nuclear superiority on the Continent. He answered that he thought American and allied conventional forces there could manage that situation well. This judgment put him at fundamental odds with virtually all of the military and intelligence estimates from the Administration.

Mr. Shultz and his senior colleagues have repeatedly stressed the dangers of Soviet cheating on an arms pact. They gave this as a principal rationale for Mr. Reagan's rejecting Mr. Gorbachev's proposal to limit testing of space-based weapons sharply. Yet, they expressed no discomfort with a situation where both sides would eliminate all ballistic missiles in 10 years, and where even a relatively small level of Soviet cheating—say, hiding 200 long-range missiles—could have profound consequences.

Soviet Demands on 'Star Wars'

Mr. Shultz repeated that the agreement on arms reductions foundered on Soviet insistence on confining space-based research to the laboratory. He reaffirmed Mr. Reagan's rejection of this on the ground that the United States would not "learn as much," and that "there are certain kinds of things that you can't really learn and feel comfortable about unless you see a demonstration." But he did not explain how what would be lost would actually kill Mr. Reagan's "Star Wars" effort or outweigh the immediate advantages of reductions in offensive nuclear forces.

Nor have senior Administration officials, including Mr. Shultz yesterday, fully rebutted the logic of Moscow's case against space-based defenses. Mr. Shultz and most of the others acknowledge that Moscow could have a point when it argues that a situation where both sides reduce their offensive nuclear forces by only 50 percent and also deploy a defensive system could be dangerous.

In this case, one side could think it might strike first and blunt a retaliatory blow. Thus, the Administration understands that space-based defenses with offensive forces could be dangerous.

By the same logic, the Russians argue that if all ballistic missiles were eliminated, as was tentatively agreed upon in Iceland, this should also eliminate the need for defenses against them. Mr. Shultz today reiterated the Administration's counterargument that the defenses were still needed as insurance against cheating.

But he did not deal with the fact that once ballistic missiles were gone, the space-based defense system would still be years away from deployment. Thus, if Moscow had cheated and stored away missiles, the system would not be in place to guard against them.

Focus Shifted at Reykjavik

All statements by both sides just before the Reykjavik meeting pointed to a session that would focus on medium-range forces and perhaps nuclear testing as well. The theory was that these would be sufficient for Mr. Gorbachev to declare he was ready to set a date for a full summit meeting in the United States within a few months. That line was essentially continued by both sides on Friday just before the meetings began.

According to accounts given during the meeting, the American side was surprised that Mr. Gorbachev quickly took discussions into the central questions of defenses and strategic forces. He even put forward a paper outlining his proposals.

By all accounts at the time, Mr. Reagan responded, and they were into a full bargaining session. Each altered positions throughout the two days, essentially in directions of their previous public statements.

But a number of Administration officials now acknowledge that their superiors are loathe to admit they were not ready for this. Doing so would indicate that the American side got into areas that had not been thoroughly prepared for beforehand.

In particular, the American side expected that medium-range forces could be agreed upon separately from other issues. But Mr. Gorbachev clearly backed away from this in Reykjavik.

Conflicting Soviet Statements

Even in the last few days, to add to the confusion, the Russians have been issuing conflicting statements on this. One Soviet negotiator has been touring Europe reassuring Western leaders that a separate deal can be struck on medium-range missiles in Europe. But in Moscow, the line remains that everything is tied to everything else.

On medium-range forces, the two sides agreed to having none for either side in Europe, and 100 for the Russians on their Asian territory equaled by 100 on American soil.

On intercontinental-range or strategic forces, there is no dispute about what was to be reduced in the first five years. All strategic forces—land-based and sea-based missiles, bombers, and air-launched cruise missiles—would be cut by 50 percent.

But over the next five years, the Administration says only ballistic missiles will be eliminated. Moscow says all strategic arms will be eliminated.

The difference is considerable. By the American interpretation, both sides would be left with bombers and cruise missiles, where the United States holds a demonstrable advantage. By the Soviet interpretation, all long-range and medium-range nuclear forces would be destroyed, thus leaving the Russians with conventional military advantages on the Eurasian landmass.

What Did Gorbachev Say?

Nor do Administration officials even agree among themselves over what position Mr. Gorbachev took and when on space-based defenses. Mr. Reagan said Mr. Gorbachev did not even raise the matter until the second day. Mr. Shultz said it happened on the first day, but he did not elaborate on what was said.

Richard N. Perle, a senior Defense Department official, told reporters that the Russians did not initially insist on restricting "Star Wars" testing to the laboratory. They did so, he said, only after Mr. Reagan changed his demand for cuts in offensive forces from 50 percent to all ballistic missiles over 10 years.

Administration officials at the working level and scientific experts generally remain split over what can be accomplished in development of space-based defenses over the next decade. But almost all agree that no system of any consequence could be deployed for at least 10 years or more.

How to Proceed with Research

In the meantime, scientists and technicians continue to argue about how to proceed with the research program. There is a strong body of scientific opinion that holds that the program would proceed on a sounder basis and would not suffer consequential delays if it were restricted to a broad definition of laboratory research. Mr. Shultz said yesterday, "Of course, it depends on what you decide you're going to call a laboratory."

In addition, from Mr. Reagan on down, the Administration has repeatedly said the program's purpose is only to conduct research to determine if the system is feasible at acceptable costs. That uncertainty has to be weighed against the reality of deep cuts in offensive forces over the next 10 years, and neither Mr. Shultz yesterday nor Administration officials on other occasions have elaborated on this.

But perhaps of greatest concern to strategic experts and a number of Administration officials are the effects on diplomacy and security of a world essentially without nuclear weapons. Both Mr. Gorbachev and Mr. Reagan have called for this for almost a year now. But experts in both countries have not treated the goal as fully serious or as a likely outcome.

There is little evidence, based on Soviet and American officials, that the two sides have studied the effect of a missile-free world on the conventional military balance, on whether spending on conventional forces would have to be increased, or on whether deterrence would be strengthened or weakened.

* * *

October 26, 1986

DID THE SUMMIT CHANGE ANYTHING?

By DIMITRI K. SIMES

WASHINGTON—The spirit of Reykjavik—if it ever existed—did not last long. The United States' expulsion of 55 Soviet diplomats and the Kremlin's retaliation, have delivered a powerful blow to the optimism. One reason for the renewed hostility is that the meeting was not handled well, either by the General Secretary or by the President.

Both Ronald Reagan and Mikhail S. Gorbachev were at their best. Both were bold and creative. Both were committed to their visions but prepared to seek compromises. And both were apparently sincere in their desire to eliminate or at least to drastically reduce nuclear weapons.

But the Reagan Administration and the Gorbachev Politburo also displayed some less commendable traits. The Russians lured Mr. Reagan to Reykjavik by creating the impression that the General Secretary was prepared to settle for an agreement in principle on such secondary arms control issues as intermediate-range nuclear weapons in Europe and nuclear testing. Instead, Mr. Gorbachev arrived in Iceland with sweeping proposals for cuts in strategic offensive arms and the de facto abolishment of the Strategic Defense Initiative. Some of his ideas were interesting and imaginative. Still, one does not build a foundation of trust by attempting to entrap the President.

Mr. Gorbachev was the victim of overconfidence and of an inadequate understanding of the West. He is a calculating statesman, and according to informed Soviet sources he came to Reykjavik with a fallback position. If Ronald Reagan would not take his bait of a "grand compromise" on strategic systems, Moscow was reportedly prepared to settle for a lesser deal—the general outlines of an agreement on a test ban and on intermediate-range nuclear missiles in Europe as a precondition for setting a date for a full-scale summit meeting in Washington. But the American delegation indicated such an interest in Moscow's more sweeping proposals that Mr. Gorbachev decided—unwisely—to play his everything-or-nothing game to the end.

The Russians had entertained the possibility that the meeting would fail. But they had expected that their dramatic proposals would have such a tremendous appeal for American and West European public opinion that Mr. Reagan would have to embrace them to avoid a major political setback. Instead, the President managed to turn the tables in the public-relations battle, as the public at home and in Europe rallied around his stand on strategic defenses. The Soviet leader is learning the hard way that Mr. Reagan has a unique talent for turning just about any political situation to his advantage.

The President has proved his willingness to give arms control an extra push by accepting the Soviet offer for an urgent meeting in Iceland. He was prepared to be broad-minded about Moscow's deceptive tactics and to respond to the Gorbachev initiative with flexibility and even enthusiasm.

Unfortunately, the enthusiasm of the American delegation was not always matched with expertise. It seems that Mr. Reagan unwittingly gave Mr. Gorbachev reason to believe that the United States was prepared to accept the elimination of all strategic arms by 1996. Such a agreement would have considerably amplified the advantage that the Russians already derive from their superior conventional forces. The American proposals also lacked coherence and rationale from the point of view of strategic planning. The President, who once campaigned on a platform of integrating arms control into an overall American defense policy, acted in Iceland as if cutting nuclear weapons was an end in itself.

The Administration remains unable to orchestrate anything resembling a coherent policy toward the Soviet Union. Excessive concessions are immediately followed by excessive belligerence, depending on which faction in Mr. Reagan's fragmented coalition has managed to prevail at a given moment.

The President, a man of vision with a talent for mobilizing public opinion, has three perfectly sensible beliefs about dealing with the Kremlin. First, America is confronted with a ruthless adversary and no full accommodation is possible unless there is a fundamental change in the Soviet Union. Second, no lasting peace is feasible unless Washington can deal from a position of strength. Finally, nuclear weapons are a threat to mankind, and reliance on them is unacceptable, both morally and politically.

Mr. Reagan's ability to build a consensus in the United States—and, to a degree, in Western Europe—in support of these sound ideas is precisely what persuaded the Politburo to negotiate seriously with America. My own conversations with senior Soviet officials in Reykjavik suggested that the people around Mr. Gorbachev view the President as a formidable rival; they have a grudging admiration for his political skills and see no alternative but to negotiate with him. His public-relations success in the last few weeks can only reinforce this assessment in Moscow.

Yet the United States team failed to exploit this leverage. The Reagan team is rich in both dedicated ideologues and pedantic technicians, but it had nobody close to the President with the sense of strategic purpose required to translate his vision into an effective foreign policy.

Clearly, then, there were errors of judgment in both capitals. But that is not the main reason why the parley did not lead to an accord. The real reason is that the President and the General Secretary got too ambitious. Their effort to accomplish too much was bound to be frustrated.

Today, both men blame the failure on political factors. Each side tends to accuse the other of its own shortcomings. Mr. Gorbachev claims that Mr. Reagan's refusal to accept the Soviet proposals proves that the President "is not free"—that he does not enjoy support even in his own Administration, which is dominated by the military-industrial complex. Surely that is more a problem in Moscow than in Washington. Meanwhile, Americans speculate about anonymous Soviet hard-liners attacking Mr. Gorbachev's arms control policies and threatening his ability to govern. Surely that is Mr. Reagan's nightmare, not Mr. Gorbachev's.

But it would be a mistake to attribute the differences between the two sides to mere political interference. Of course, both leaders have to operate in political settings and have to take the opinions of others into account. But there is something much bigger at issue here: their visions are hard to reconcile. Beyond personalities, it is conflicting American and Soviet interests—complicated by constrasting values and the bad chemistry produced by the clash of two political processes—that lie behind the rivalry. No summit conference could be expected to resolve that conflict.

Besides, while Mr. Gorbachev talks a lot about the need for "new thinking," his foreign policy does not depart significantly from that of his predecessors. Thus, his opposition to the Strategic Defense Initiative has less to do with fear of such defenses than with a traditional Soviet desire to retard American progress in new military technologies.

The meeting in Reykjavik may have come close to a breathtaking deal, but such a deal could have occurred only at Mr. Gorbachev's insistence and contrary to Mr. Reagan's promises not to focus on arms control at the expense of regional issues and human rights. It is no great tragedy that it proved impossible to paper over key differences in the name of a symbolic but ill-conceived arms control spectacular.

There has been no lasting damage to superpower relations. The Russians have once again learned that outconning Ronald Reagan is not an option. Nor do they feel that outwaiting him is appropriate, since nobody can be sure what his successor will be prepared and able to deliver at the bargaining table. Enough progress was made in Iceland to suggest to Moscow that negotiating arms control with the current Administration is not a hopeless task—even if it is extremely frustrating.

Still, to capitalize on the progress in Iceland, the Reagan Administration will have to establish modest arms control objectives considerably short of the elimination of ballistic missiles, to say nothing of strategic weapons. In the long run, Americans have to accept that the road to a non-nuclear world leads less through the Strategic Defense Intitiative or arms control than through a major modernization of the conventional capabilities of the North Atlantic Treaty Organization. If the President champions this cause with the same zeal and skill he has used to champion S.D.I., he may yet make a historic contribution to American security.

Dimitri K. Simes is a senior associate at the Carnegie Endowment for International Peace.

* * *

December 5, 1986

THE WHITE HOUSE CRISIS: 'NO INDICATION' TO DOUBT REAGAN

Ex-Aide To Reagan Is Said To Link Him To Early Iran Sale

By BERNARD GWERTZMAN
Special to The New York Times.

WASHINGTON, Dec. 4—Robert C. McFarlane, the former national security adviser, is said to have told the Senate Intelligence Committee that President Reagan gave advance approval to Israel's sale of arms to Iran, despite Administration assertions to the contrary.

Three people familiar with Mr. McFarlane's closed-door testimony disclosed that he took issue with assertions by Attorney General Edwin Meese 3d, who said last week that Mr. Reagan had been informed "generally" only after the first Israeli shipment took place in September 1985. A spokesman for Mr. Meese said the Attorney General stood by his original account.

Tonight, a White House official, when asked about Mr. McFarlane's testimony that Mr. Reagan had approved the Israeli shipment last year, said, "Documents prepared by other major participants in the Iran operation directly contradict that statement." The official would not elaborate.

Shipment 'Condoned'

They said Mr. McFarlane told the Senate Select Committee on Intelligence on Monday that Mr. Reagan informed the Israelis through Mr. McFarlane in August 1985 that he would "condone" the Israeli shipment and would sell Israel replacement parts for the antitank missiles sent to Iran.

The idea of supplying arms was raised by David Kimche, the director general of the Israeli Foreign Ministry, in the second of two meetings with Mr. McFarlane in July and August of 1985, the committee was told.

As a result of that shipment of missiles, one of the American hostages in Lebanon, the Rev. Benjamin F. Weir, was released in September, 1985. Mr. McFarlane told the committee that the sale of arms was opposed at the time by Secretary of State George P. Shultz and Secretary of Defense Caspar W. Weinberger, but that Mr. Reagan saw value in the operation, and gave oral approval.

Told of Diversion of Funds

According to the sources, Mr. McFarlane also confirmed that he had been told by Lieut. Col. Oliver L. North of the National Security Council staff, while they were on a mission to Teheran for Mr. Reagan last May, of the secret diversion to the Nicaraguan rebels of Iranian payments for weapons.

But under sharp questioning from some senators, Mr. McFarlane said he did not ask detailed questions about the diversion of funds to the rebels, known as contras, because he assumed that the decision had been approved at the highest levels of Government. Mr. Meese has said that only Mr. McFarlane, Colonel North, and Vice Adm. John M. Poindexter, who succeeded Mr. McFarlane as national security adviser, knew of the secret diversion to the Contras.

No One Told, McFarlane Says

Mr. McFarlane told the committee that he did not inform anyone else of the diversion to the contras.

The sources said other points developed in the hearing included these:

- A second Israeli arms shipment to Iran via Portugal was held up by Portuguese authorities in November 1985, while Mr. McFarlane was attending the Geneva summit meeting with President Reagan. As a result, Colonel North was asked to intervene with the Portuguese, and the Central Intelligence Agency was brought in to hire another plane to take the spare parts to Iran. The parts were returned to the Israelis three months later because they were not the ones that had been ordered.
- By the end of November, 1985, Mr. McFarlane had become convinced that the shipment of arms to Iran was a mistake, because instead of opening up channels to moderate Iranian leaders, it was simply becoming a ransom payment to Iran. At a White House meeting on Dec. 6, 1985, two days after Mr. McFarlane's resignation was announced, Mr. Reagan approved a recommendation by Mr. McFarlane, seconded by Mr. Shultz and Mr. Weinberger, to halt all further arms to Iran and to inform Israel and Iran of the decision.
- Mr. McFarlane met secretly in London on Dec. 8, 1985 with Mr. Kimche, the Israeli Foreign Ministry director, and with Manucher Ghorbanifar, the Iranian go-between, to inform them that while the United States was interested in pursuing political talks with Iran, it was ruling out any more direct or third-party arms sales. Both men opposed this decision, arguing that without arms, it would be impossible to make any progress with Iran.
- On Dec. 11, 1985, at another high-level meeting at the White House, with Mr. Shultz absent because of an overseas trip, Mr. McFarlane reported about his meeting in London and left the Government with the impression that the Iran operation had been closed down.
- On his mission to Iran in May, 1986, Mr. McFarlane was accompanied by Colonel North, George W. Cave, a retired C.I.A. expert on Iran, C.I.A. communications experts, and Amiran Nir, the Israeli anti-terrorist chief. Maj. Gen. Richard V. Secord, a former Air Force officer, was not on the mission, as had earlier been reported, but was in Israel monitoring the operation. General Secord, a friend of Colonel North, has been linked to the Iran and contra operations.
- Despite Iranian claims to have recorded "tapes" of Mr. McFarlane's conversations with the White House from his hotel in Teheran, the committee was told that the C.I.A. communications experts had set up secure communications.
- The talks in Teheran were with senior representatives of the Foreign Ministry and with the speaker of the Iranian Parliament, Hojatolislam Hashemi Rafsanjani. But because of the failure of Iran to live up to a commitment to obtain the release of all the hostages, the talks got nowhere and after four days, the mission returned to the United States.
- Mr. McFarlane recommended that no further arms sales go ahead, but some did anyway, the committee was told.

At the time of his trip to Iran, Mr. McFarlane had been out of Government for five months. He told the committee, the sources said, that he had been told by Admiral Poindexter that a deal had been arranged for all the remaining American hostages in Lebanon to be freed about the time he arrived in Teheran on May 28.

In return for the expected Iranian help in freeing the hostages, his Boeing 707 cargo plane carried spare parts for the Iranian Air Force, he told the committee.

The question of how the initial arms shipments to Iran began has been contentious, and a cause of disagreement between the Israeli and American Governments.

White House Statement

Mr. Reagan, at a press conference on Nov. 19, denied any knowledge of third-country involvement. But shortly after the conference ended, the White House issued a statement saying that an unnamed third country had facilitated arms shipments. It had been widely reported that Israel was the country.

On Nov. 25, Mr. Meese, in a press conference disclosing the unauthorized diversion of Iranian payments to the contras, was asked several times about the President's knowledge of Israel's role.

He said Mr. Reagan "did not have full details of all of the aspects of transactions that took place" before a formal decision by Mr. Reagan on Jan. 17, 1986, authorizing such shipments.

Statement by Meese

In particular, Mr. Meese said of the September shipment that "the President was informed generally that there had been an Israeli shipment of weapons to Iran some time during the late summer, early fall of 1985."

When informed by one reporter that Admiral Poindexter had said Mr. Reagan had authorized the September shipment, Mr. Meese said "our information is that the President knew about it probably after the fact and agreed with the general concept of continuing our discussions with the Israelis concerning these matters."

The Israelis have insisted that they sent arms to Iran from the beginning only with the approval of the United States.

Conversation with Kimche

In sorting out the discrepancies for the committee, Mr. McFarlane reportedly said that the idea for the arms shipments arose in his conversations with Mr. Kimche, who said that only by sending military equipment to the hard-pressed Iranians could the United States and Israel establish credible connections with moderate elements in the Iranian Government and that this might lead to the release of all the American hostages.

According to Mr. McFarlane's reported testimony, Mr. Kimche specifically asked whether, if Israel provided Iran with American-made arms, the United States would agree to sell Israel the necessary replacement parts.

The committee reportedly was told by Mr. McFarlane that he briefed Mr. Reagan and other top officials about his talks with Mr. Kimche, and that Mr. Reagan decided not to oppose the Israeli action, and to send assurances that Israel could buy replacements.

If he was an Israeli, Mr. McFarlane was said to have told the committee, he would reasonably assume that Israel had American backing for the arms sales.

Advised Against Shipments

Mr. McFarlane was said to have told the committee he was dubious about the idea of sending arms to Iran, and actively counseled against it in his last weeks in office at the end of 1985, because the focus was becoming increasingly on trading arms for hostages instead of opening wider discussions. The United States, in public policy statements, has long opposed the payment of ransom to free hostages.

According to this account, at the White House meeting on Dec. 6, 1985, all the senior advisers concurred that no more arms should be provided Iran. Mr. Reagan, according to the account, directed Mr. McFarlane to meet in London on Dec. 8 with Mr. Kimche and Mr. Ghorbanifar to convey two messages.

The first was that the United States was prepared for talks on a political agenda to discuss such subjects as the American opposition to state-supported terrorism, the Soviet threat to Iran, ways of ending the Iran-Iraq war, and getting Iran to agree not to promote revolutionary activity across its borders.

The second message was that the United States would no longer be party to transfer of weapons to Iran, directly, and would not encourage others to do so.

When Mr. McFarlane told this to Mr. Kimche alone, and later to Mr. Ghorbanifar, both men counseled the United States to be patient, and continue to supply arms through Israel, the committee was told.

The Iranian told Mr. McFarlane that without the arms, the dialogue with the moderate elements in Iran could not continue, the committee was told.

When he returned to Washington, Mr. McFarlane is said to have told the committee, he reported to Mr. Reagan and other officials on Dec. 11 that he had carried out his instructions. He told the group that he distrusted Mr. Ghorbanifar and that as far as he knew then, the Iran operation was over.

But on Jan. 7, at a later White House meeting, the issue of providing arms to Iran again rose, and Mr. Reagan has said that on Jan. 17 he approved a secret finding allowing such sales to take place, despite the continued opposition of Mr. Shultz and Mr. Weinberger.

* * *

December 7, 1986

PRESIDENT ADMITS FLAWS IN PURSUING SECRET IRAN POLICY

By GERALD M. BOYD
Special to The New York Times.

WASHINGTON, Dec. 6—President Reagan, adopting a highly personal and apologetic tone, said today that the execution of his secret policy initiatives toward Iran was "flawed," and that "mistakes were made."

The remarks by the President, made in his weekly radio address, marked a clear shift away from the defiant stand he had previously adopted in the face of continuing public and Congressional criticism.

Mr. Reagan did not abandon his repeated refusals to call the Iran policy a mistake, and he continued to express belief that the secret diplomatic initiative was proper. At the same time, he did not specify how the execution had been flawed, or who was responsible.

He Is 'Deeply Disappointed'

Even so, the approach was one of the most remorseful Mr. Reagan has ever offered the nation. He said he was "deeply disappointed" that the Iran initiative had caused such a controversy and "regretted" the concern and consternation it had caused the public.

But the President went on to say: "I pledge to you, I will set things right."

The House Speaker, Thomas P. O'Neill Jr., who delivered a Democratic statement recorded earlier, urged the President in sharp terms to acknowledge that the decision to sell arms to the Iran of Ayatollah Ruhollah Khomeini was wrong.

"The American people did not build this country to what it is today so that the arsenal of democracy would become the arsenal of the Ayatollah," said Mr. O'Neill, a Democrat from Massachusetts. "Paying tribute to terrorists is the one sure way to keep them killing."

'Terrible Decision,' O'Neill Says

"It is time for Ronald Reagan, our President, to say that sending the weapons of death to Iran was a terrible decision that must never be repeated," Mr. O'Neill said. Mr. Reagan began his address, which he delivered from the Presidential retreat at Camp David, Md., by saying he wanted to share "some personal thoughts" and "to speak to you, the American people, from the heart."

After discussing the effort to open contacts with Iran in the hope of curbing terrorism, he said: "But now I want to speak to you about something else—not the policies themselves, but how they were carried out. And while we're still seeking all the facts, it's obvious that the execution of these policies was flawed, and mistakes were made."

"Let me just say it was not my intent to do business with Khomeini, to trade weapons for hostages, nor undercut our policy on anti-terrorism," he said.

United Press International

WEEKLY ADDRESS: President Reagan delivering his radio address yesterday in which he stated "mistakes were made."

"I'm deeply disappointed this initiative has resulted in such a controversy," Mr. Reagan said, "and I regret it's caused such concern and consternation. But I pledge to you, I will set things right."

The President's tone and even some of his phrasing were similar to those used by Vice President Bush on Wednesday when he became the first senior White House official to admit publicly that "mistakes were made."

White House officials have said Mr. Reagan was pleased with the Bush speech, which was apparently a factor in the President's decision to make similar remarks.

In addition, some Reagan advisers have tried to convince the President to acknowledge publicly that a mistake had been made, expressing the belief that it would help to end the furor.

Mr. Reagan said on Nov. 25, when it was first announced that profits from the sale of arms to Iran had been diverted to a fund for Nicaraguan rebels, that the effort to carry out his Iran policy "was seriously flawed." But when asked if a mistake had been made in sending arms to Teheran, he responded emphatically, "No."

Today he sought to explain his policy goals, declaring that "much of our effort has been aimed at stopping terrorism, putting an end to the bombing of innocent civilians and the kidnapping of hostages, especially our own citizens, and bringing about an end to the bloody war between Iran and Iraq."

Describing how the secret contacts had begun, Mr. Reagan said word had come to him that individuals in Iran, including some in the Government, had asked through an intermediary in a third country for a meeting with one of his representatives. "I said yes," he said. "And even though these were responsible elements in Iran that might be able to assist us in stopping the violence and possibly helping us get back the hostages being held in Lebanon, there was a risk involved," he continued. "But I believed then, and believe now, there was a greater risk in doing nothing, of not trying. So I gave the order to proceed."

Purpose Not Explained

The President's explanation did not address why arms had been sold to Iran, although he has said previously that small amounts of arms were provided as a gesture of good faith.

In addition, Mr. Reagan did not explain what had prompted the contacts to be continued after his representative, Robert C. McFarlane, recommended they be ended because of a lack of progress. Mr. McFarlane, a former national security adviser, reportedly testifed to that effect to the Senate Intelligence Committee on Monday.

Mr. Reagan, asserting that the policy had generated "some notable success," said it had led to some reduction in terrorism and the freeing of three American hostages in Lebanon before the secret initiative was disclosed in a Lebanese magazine.

"This effort to establish a relationship with responsible moderates in Iran came to light and was broken off," he said. "But I think you can see the purposes behind our policy: to end the war in the Middle East, to prevent Soviet expansionism, to halt terrorism and to help gain the release of American hostages."

The President said that when he learned profits from the arms sale had been diverted to the Nicaraguan rebels, he had moved quickly to share the news with the public and the Congress and that he would cooperate fully with Congressional and other inquiries.

Vows Justice for Any Crimes

"If illegal acts were undertaken in the implementation of our policy, those who did so will be brought to justice," he said. "If actions in implementing my policy were taken without my authorization, knowledge or concurrence, this will be exposed, and appropriate corrective steps will be implemented."

His remarks drew a positive response from some Republicans in Congress, who said it would be important in ending the public furor.

Senator Bob Dole, the Republican leader, disputed Mr. O'Neill's assertion that Mr. Reagan needed to condemn the decision to sell arms to Iran and to condemn what the Speaker called "secret wars" being waged by United States Government officials.

"I believe when Ronald Reagan says, as he has now done publicly, that mistakes were made, that will go a long way in laying to rest some of the criticism," the Kansas Republican said.

* * *

December 22, 1986

GORBACHEV ON THE FUTURE: 'WE WILL NOT GIVE IN'

Special to The New York Times.

MOSCOW—Here are key passages from notes of a talk by Mikhail S. Gorbachev on June 19 at a closed meeting with a group of Soviet writers. The notes, taken by one of the writers, were translated by The New York Times. Although the note-taker's identity is not known, writers who attended have confirmed the authenticity of the material.

A very profound and serious movement has begun, and a very profound and serious struggle lies ahead.

Between the people who want these changes, who dream of these changes, and the leadership, there is a layer of officialdom—an apparat of ministries, a party apparat—that does not want changes and does not want to lose some rights associated with privileges.

Take Gosplan

For Gosplan there exist no authorities, no general secretaries, no central committees. They do what they want. The situation they like best is for someone to come into their private office and ask for a million, for 20 tractors, for 40,000—to beg them.

Today I was told that during smoke breaks they're getting the feeling that they will not manage to grind up the new leadership of the party, and will have to change something.

We have very many people who take advantage of their position. Nothing is exploited as much as official position. . . .

What two elements are at the basis of the work of the Politburo? First is not to walk away from problems that have piled up over the years.

You know, Brezhnev once said we need to hold a plenum on scientific-technological problems. I was shown sacks of documents prepared in this connection, all sorts of information and so forth.

When they began to sort this out, they suddenly saw that nobody knew where to take it, what to do with it. So they abandoned it. Everything remained in sacks.

We haven't walked away. Perhaps not all the decisions we make today are correct. Perhaps we err in some things. But we want to act and not to sit with folded arms, letting the process pass us by. . . .

Take the national tragedy—drunkenness. "Drunken budget." People want a "dry law." At the same time all kinds of epithets reach us from the queues: "Mineral secretary," all kinds of anecdotes about Gorbachev and others—"We'll keep drinking like before, we'll exhume Brezhnev once more."

No, we won't leave this path. I also like to drop into the Central Literary Club and have a drink. I know that letters reach us from the queues with threats, but we will not give in to these sentiments.

We will save the people, especially the Slavic people, because—even though it has spread to the Moslems and the Caucasus—but none of them suffer the way the Slavic part of the population suffers, that is, the Russians, Ukrainians and Byelorussians. The figures are frightening. We're not going to scare you, but we won't walk away from this. We will fight. . . .

Those who think that we can restructure in a month or two are naive! This has taken shape over years and will demand massive efforts and titanic labors. If we don't involve the people, nothing will come of it. All our plans depend on influencing the people.

The economy is very disordered. We lag in all indices. In 1969 we had a problem in Stavropol—what to do with meat and milk. We were awash in butter. Today there is nothing. The relations between money and goods, income and goods have been lost.

We have forgotten how to work. Not only that, we have forgotten how to work in democratic conditions. This is very difficult.

Not a few people are drunks, profiteers, embezzlers, but mostly, of course, bureaucrats, those people who do not want to part with their rights. . . .

Why do I constantly sit with volumes of Lenin, looking through them, looking for approaches? Because it is never too late to consult with Lenin.

The Central Committee needs support. You can't even imagine how much we need the support of groups like writers.

Don't think that all this is coming easily. Many directors write us: "We don't need rights or independence, let everything be as it was, it was easier for us then, easier to work." They don't want to, they don't know how. Generations must pass for us to really change. Generations must pass.

The restructuring is progressing with great difficulty. We have no opposition party. How then can we control ourselves? Only through criticism and self-criticism. Most important—through glasnost. We're learning here, too. We're restructuring everything, from the General Secretary to the rank-and-file Communist. Democratism without glasnost does not exist. At the same time, democracy without limits is anarchy. That's why it will be difficult. . . .

A restructuring is under way in the Central Committee, in the Council of Ministers. In the Council of Ministers we have completely changed the composition of the Government—one person remains.

A restructuring is under way at Gosplan, other agencies, but if only you knew how painfully it's going! Some are taking it very badly. The main thing is that the Central Committee helped out, concerned about how things were going. . . .

About meetings of the Politburo. There are clashes, arguments. For two, three years we postponed things, but now we want to act. The society is ripe for change. If we step away, the society will not agree to a return. The process must be made irreversible. If not us, then who? If not now, when? Our enemy sees us clearly. They are not frightened by our nuclear might. They will not start a war. They're worried about one thing: If democracy develops here, if we succeed, we will win. For this reason they have begun a campaign against our leadership using all means, including terror. They write about the apparat that broke Khrushchev's neck, and about the apparat that will now break the neck of the new leadership.

* * *

February 1, 1987

GORBACHEV'S GAMBIT

With Careful Cajolery, He Gets the Party To Budge

By PHILIP TAUBMAN

MOSCOW—Mikhail S. Gorbachev was at the Kremlin gate last week, tacking up another manifesto for fundamental change in the Soviet Union.

The Soviet leader asked the Central Committee of the Communist Party to consider introducing secret balloting and a choice of candidates in the election of local and regional party leaders.

It was quintessential Gorbachev: advancing an idea ahead of its time, then tugging at the Soviet establishment to accept it, seeking consensus but constantly agitating for more change in the face of stiff resistance. In this case, the Central Committee agreed to give voters more choice in the election of local officials, but pointedly did not approve changes that might have let a few rays of sunlight penetrate the party's secret process of choosing its leaders.

Western diplomats chalked up the long-awaited plenary session as a mixed success for Mr. Gorbachev, noting that he received a broad but imprecise endorsement for change and secured the promotion of several allies but not the appointment of a new voting member of the Politburo, which makes policy. "The outcome suggests that the Central Committee has reservations about the scope, pace and details of change," one diplomat said.

And so it has gone from the day Mr. Gorbachev assumed power in March 1985. Opposed at many turns by the party and Government establishment, but apparently facing no serious threat to his position as General Secretary, Mr. Gorbachev has combined the fervor of an evangelical preacher with the instincts of a riverboat gambler to cajole the Soviet Union toward a new day. Will his efforts produce permanent change, or, as some in the West believe, does the nature of the Soviet state, with its stultifying bureaucracy and repressive instincts, make lasting change impossible? While the moves so far have been well within the framework of socialism, they have touched many areas of Soviet life.

Arts and Literature

The most obvious change has been in the arts and literature, where the heavy hand of censorship has been lightened, and, in some cases, lifted. Long-suppressed works such as Boris Pasternak's "Doctor Zhivago" and Anatoly Rybakov's "Children of the Arbat," an unflinching look at Stalin's terror, are to be published this year. The novels of Vladimir Nabokov and the poetry of Nikolai S. Gumilev, who was shot for anti-Soviet activity in 1921, have also begun to appear.

A rebellion among directors that threw out the leadership of the main filmmakers' union also touched off a reassessment of previously banned movies. "Repentance," the first film to deal honestly with Stalin's purges and their chilling legacy, opened to the general public last month. "Is It Easy to Be Young?" a powerful film about disaffected young people and troubled Afghanistan veterans, is another current hit.

Change has come more slowly in other areas, but there are signs of a new tolerance for dissonant music, abstract art and experimental theater. Famous émigrés, who were once condemned, are now in demand. The Bolshoi Ballet recently invited Mikhail Baryshnikov and Natalia Makarova to perform in Moscow. Yuri P. Lyubimov, the former director of Moscow's Taganka Theater, has also been urged to return.

Press and Television

The Soviet press, while still tightly controlled and reverent toward top officials, has moved beyond traditional crusades such as environmental protection to become a testing ground for Mr. Gorbachev's drive for greater "glasnost," or openness. Now a forum for vigorous debate about foreign and domestic policies, the press has raised such long-ignored problems as prostitution, drug addiction, the alienation of youth and the disorientation of soldiers returning from service in Afghanistan.

Perhaps the high-water mark was a series in Pravda, the party newspaper, that exposed misconduct by K.G.B. officials involved in the illegal arrest last year of a Soviet reporter who uncovered corruption in a coal-mining region of the Ukraine. Several officials of the internal security agency were dismissed or reprimanded.

Coverage of the Chernobyl nuclear accident last year started out with a news blackout but eventually became quite extensive, and, in a recent example of candor, the press reported on anti-Russian rioting in the Soviet Central Asian city of Alma-Ata.

Even greater changes have occurred on television. News and entertainment shows have aired several favorable reports on Western life, including profiles of Michael Jackson and McDonald's.

The Economy

Change has been halting in the centrally managed economy with its aging industrial plant and lack of new technology. Apparently unsure how to attack an ossified system, Mr. Gorbachev has abolished a number of ministries, told central planners to get out of the day-to-day management of enterprises, improved incentives for workers, tinkered with subsidized prices and cracked down on alcohol consumption. Industries were given the right to negotiate their own deals with foreign companies. Mr. Gorbachev has also openly encouraged the cultivation of private plots by farm workers and given collective farms the right to sell some excess goods on the open market with prices set by supply and demand. These and other steps are credited with an improvement in national income, industrial productivity and other indexes, but most Western economists say the growth cannot be sustained without more fundamental reforms.

Government and the Party

Because he took office after a long period of stagnation, Mr. Gorbachev was able to put together a new team faster than any previous leader. He forced rivals off the Politburo and engineered the appointment of dozens of new Central Committee members. The party Secretariat, which carries out policy, is now almost completely in the hands of Gorbachev loyalists. But it has been harder to inject fresh leadership into the middle and lower ranks, and Mr. Gorbachev last week complained to the Central Committee about resistance at that level.

Rewriting History

For the first time since the Khrushchev era, the Soviet Union has begun a painful re-examination of the Stalin era. A Soviet journal recently published a long-censored poem by Aleksandr Tvardovsky, appealing to the nation to face the "rampage of evil" under Stalin. Mr. Gorbachev, addressing the period directly for the first time, told the Central Committee last week that "debates and creative ideas disappeared from theory and social sciences while authoritarian evaluations and opinions became unquestionable truths." Aleksandr Bovin, a well-known Soviet commentator, warned last week about opposition to Mr. Gorbachev's changes, noting that his generation watched "with bewilderment, pain and a disgusting sense of our own impotence" as Khrushchev's de-Stalinization efforts collapsed.

At the same time, the cult of Lenin has intensified, apparently to give some of Mr. Gorbachev's reforms a link to the revolution. Many Russians assume that the next step will be the rehabilitation of Nikolai I. Bukharin, an early leader who opposed Stalin's policies and was shot in 1938.

Dissent

The return of the physicist Andrei D. Sakharov to Moscow before Christmas and the many interviews he has since given to Western reporters are signs of a reversal in the handling of dissent. Hundreds of people remain in prison or exile because they challenged the state, but Mr. Gorbachev, if only to enhance Moscow's international image, has started the slow process of reviewing cases, freeing some prisoners and sending a message that some criticism of the system should be tolerated. Mr. Sakharov said Friday that he was told that two political prisoners, Anatoly Koryagin and Sergei D. Khodorovich, will be released and forced to emigrate. How much dissent Mr. Gorbachev will allow and whether he intends to curb the K.G.B. remain to be seen.

Meanwhile, in a reminder that some things stay the same, two American reporters watched last week as a dissident they had met in a Moscow park was pursued down the street by a plainclothes security agent.

* * *

February 17, 1987

GORBACHEV AVOWS A NEED FOR PEACE TO PURSUE REFORM

By PHILIP TAUBMAN

Special to The New York Times.

MOSCOW, Feb. 16—Mikhail S. Gorbachev said today that the Soviet Union was seeking world stability so it could concentrate on domestic concerns.

In a televised speech in the Great Kremlin Palace at an international forum on peace and disarmament, the Soviet leader said:

"Before my people, before you and before the world, I state with full responsibility that our international policy is more than ever determined by domestic policy, by our interest in concentrating on constructive endeavors to improve our country.

"This is why we need lasting peace, predictability and constructiveness in international relations."

Focus on Internal Renewal

Drawing a linkage between domestic issues and the Soviet Union's behavior abroad, Mr. Gorbachev said of his effort to revitalize the Soviet system:

"This is where we want to direct our resources, this is where our thoughts are going, on this we intend to spend the intellectual energy of our society."

He said that what he called the new Soviet approach to human rights "is there for all to see."

"And," he continued, "I must disappoint those who think that this has been a result of pressure on us from the West, that we want to gain someone's fancy in the pursuit of ulterior motives. We do not."

As he spoke, the family of the Jewish dissident Iosif Z. Begun said he was reportedly still in prison despite the assurance of a Soviet official on American television on Sunday that he had been freed.

ABM Change Is Criticized

On specific issues, Mr. Gorbachev said that any American effort to undermine the Antiballistic Missile Treaty of 1972 would violate the spirit of a broad agreement he reached with President Reagan in Geneva in 1985 to put a stop to the arms race.

Mr. Gorbachev said talk in the United States about a new interpretation of the 1972 pact that would allow extensive testing of the "Star Wars" space-based defense system "scorns the pledge" made in Geneva. He called for an international law banning the deployment of weapons in space.

Andrei D. Sakharov, the physicist and human rights advocate, was in the audience as Mr. Gorbachev spoke, rising and applauding with the other guests as the Soviet leader stepped to the podium.

Dr. Sakharov was seated prominently with the other guests, and television cameras paused momentarily on him in scanning the ornate meeting hall, in which the Supreme Soviet, the nominal legislature, usually sits.

Less than two months ago, Dr. Sakharov was living in exile in Gorky, where he had been confined in 1980 by Leonid I. Brezhnev for his public statements critical of Soviet policies. Mr. Gorbachev allowed him to return to Moscow on Dec. 23.

Mr. Gorbachev's speech appeared intended to provide a framework for Soviet foreign policy and to allay skepticism about Soviet intentions.

"It is often said—we still hear it—that there is some threat stemming from the Soviet Union, a Soviet threat to peace and freedom," he said.

There has been debate abroad whether policy changes under Mr. Gorbachev represent a change in style or in substance. Western leaders contend that the presentation of Soviet policies has become more polished, but that the underlying substance has not changed.

"We want to be understood," Mr. Gorbachev said, "and we hope that the world community will at least acknowledge that our desire to make our own country better will hurt no one, with the world only gaining from this."

He proposed no new initiatives in his hour-long speech, which was the main event of a three-day conference that brought together scientists, businessmen, doctors, writers and performing artists from dozens of countries, including the United States.

Mr. Gorbachev said the Soviet Union wanted to resolve regional conflicts, including the war in Afghanistan, and he reiterated Soviet pledges to help fight terrorism.

Repeating a theme that has been appearing with increasing frequency in his speeches, he talked about "diversity and increasing interconnections" in the world.

Western diplomats say that these references may signal a move away from Marxist-Leninist doctrine about the inevitability of conflict between capitalism and communism.

Among the Americans at the Moscow forum were Norman Mailer, Gore Vidal and Bel Kaufman, the writers; John Kenneth Galbraith, the economist; Gregory Peck and Kris Kristofferson, the actors; several scientists, including Frank von Hippel, a Princeton physicist, and more than a dozen businessmen.

Dr. Sakharov addressed the scientists over the weekend, the first time he had been given an officially sponsored public forum to speak his mind. He called for increased civil liberties in the Soviet Union and a relaxation of curbs on emigration while also urging deep reductions in strategic nuclear arms.

A participant at a business roundtable said it was the most practical of the gatherings, with Soviet trade officials pressing Western visitors to increase commercial links with the Soviet Union.

After Mr. Gorbachev's speech, the foreign guests attended a reception in the modernistic Palace of Congresses in the Kremlin, where they were greeted by Mr. Gorbachev; Yegor K. Ligachev, the second-ranking party leader; President Andrei A. Gromyko, and Prime Minister Nikolai I. Ryzhkov.

* * *

March 1, 1987

MOSCOW, IN REVERSAL, URGES AGREEMENT 'WITHOUT DELAY' TO LIMIT MISSILES IN EUROPE

Ready for Geneva

By BILL KELLER
Special to The New York Times.

MOSCOW, Feb. 28—Mikhail S. Gorbachev said today that the Soviet Union was willing to sign "without delay" an agreement to eliminate Soviet and American medium-range nuclear missiles in Europe within five years.

The offer, ending Soviet insistence that these missiles be considered part of a comprehensive package, was the first major arms control development since the Soviet-American summit meeting in Iceland in October.

Foreign diplomats said the Soviet proposal might help revive prospects for another summit meeting, in the United States.

Timing of Offer Is Noted

The Soviet arms offer came only two days after a Presidential review board in Washington issued a report critical of President Reagan and his advisers in the Iran-contra affair.

It was not clear whether the Soviet leader, by making his proposal, was trying to exploit Mr. Reagan's vulnerability or to help him out by holding out the prospect of an important arms accord. Such an agreement could benefit both Mr. Gorbachev and the President domestically.

Mr. Gorbachev said his offer was being put on the negotiating table in the Geneva arms talks. The current round is to adjourn Tuesday, and there was no indication whether adjournment would now be delayed.

Issued through Tass Agency

Mr. Gorbachev, who made his offer in a statement through the Government press agency Tass, said the Soviet Union was prepared to sign an agreement identical to one he and Mr. Reagan tentatively agreed on in Reykjavik, Iceland.

"The Soviet Union suggests that the problem of medium-range missiles in Europe be singled out from the package of issues, and that a separate agreement on it be concluded, and without delay," Mr. Gorbachev said.

"We were assured more than once that if the U.S.S.R. singles out the issue of medium-range missiles from the Reykjavik package, there would be no difficulty to agree to their elimination in Europe. A good opportunity is now being offered to prove that in practice."

After Mr. Reagan and Mr. Gorbachev had reached an understanding in Iceland on the elimination of medium-range missiles in Europe, the allies voiced misgivings. They saw the missiles as a symbol of American commitment to the defense of Western Europe and argued that they had invested political capital in inducing the public in their countries to agree to deploy American missiles in the first place.

Western diplomats said today that most of the misgivings had been removed. In December, the Defense Ministers of the North Atlantic Treaty Organization endorsed the elimination of Soviet and American medium-range missiles from Europe in five years.

"The primary governments are prepared to support it," a diplomat said.

Mr. Gorbachev said the two sides should sign an accord identical to an understanding reached with Mr. Reagan in Iceland, which the Soviet leader described as calling for the withdrawal of American and Soviet medium-range missiles from Europe in five years. Each side, under such an arrangement, would keep only 100 warheads outside of Europe—the Soviet Union in the Asian part of its territory and the United States within its territory, possibly in Alaska.

Western diplomats said some details would still have to be worked out before an accord could be signed, including problems of verification and the issue of limiting shorter-range nuclear missiles.

No Major Obstacles Seen

They said both issues had been discussed in Iceland, and neither was likely to pose a major obstacle.

"This is a real change of gears," a diplomat said.

Mr. Gorbachev said the Soviet Union was ready to begin negotiations immediately on the shorter-range missiles "with a view to reducing and fully eliminating them."

The Soviet announcement, coming when President Reagan is struggling to recover from the Iran-contra affair, offers him the prospect of a sorely needed foreign policy achievement. It would also keep alive the possibility of further arms-control agreements.

Mr. Gorbachev has expressed concern that Mr. Reagan had become so weakened or distracted politically that he could not focus on arms control.

From Mr. Gorbachev's point of view, an arms agreement would also help justify diverting financial resources to the domestic economy, which he has declared his first priority.

No Mention of Summit Talks

He made no mention of a possible summit meeting, but he has said that he would be willing to go to the United States if something concrete could be achieved at another meeting with Mr. Reagan. The two leaders have met twice, in Geneva in 1985 and in Reykjavik last year.

"Prior to Reykjavik, an agreement on medium-range missiles certainly would have been sufficient to get Gorbachev to go to the United States," a Western diplomat said, "and as far as the United States is concerned, the invitation is still open."

The Soviet Union and the United States have long proclaimed an ultimate goal of eliminating medium-range missiles from Europe, a modification of the so-called zero option first proposed by the United States.

But until the Iceland summit meeting, the Soviet Union insisted that the independent French and British nuclear forces be included in such a deal.

Gorbachev Dropped a Condition

In Iceland, Mr. Gorbachev dropped this condition. But when the meeting broke up over the issue of limiting the United States' space-based missile defense program, the Soviet Union insisted that henceforth medium-range arms would be curbed only as part of an overall arms accord that would also cover strategic, or long-range, nuclear weapons as well as space-based and other defensive systems.

Mr. Gorbachev said the offer of a separate agreement on medium-range missiles did not diminish Soviet interest in a more sweeping pact covering the other types of weapons as well. But he insisted a linkage between strategic arms and defensive space weapons "in view of the organic interconnection between these issues."

* * *

April 11, 1987

EXCERPTS FROM GORBACHEV TALK ON ARMS AND SOCIAL CHANGES

By REUTERS

PRAGUE, April 10—Following are excerpts from a speech here today by Mikhail S. Gorbachev, the Soviet leader, as translated and distributed by the official Czechoslovak press agency:

The Soviet Union responsibly declares that it tries to find mutually acceptable solutions to the whole complex of questions concerning nuclear disarmament. Radical cuts in strategic offensive weapons remain the basic issue.

In order to facilitate an early conclusion of an agreement on medium-range missiles in Europe, we suggest to start talks on the reduction and later elimination of missiles with a range of 500 to 1,000 kilometers sited in Europe and not to link with this the course or the result of the solution of the medium-range missiles issue.

Both sides would pledge not to increase the number of operational-tactical missiles during the talks. I emphasize: We favor a process toward a radical reduction and finally total liquidation of operational-tactical missiles in Europe, and regard as useless any inclusion in the future accord of various "possibilities" of an increase in their number and their improvement.

When an agreement on medium-range missiles is signed and irrespective of the course of the talks on operational-tactical missiles, the Soviet Union will remove, after agreement with the Governments of Czechoslovakia and East Germany, from these two countries the missiles sited there as a countermeasure for the deployment of Pershing 2 and cruise missiles in Western Europe.

Strict Control Favored

An agreement on operational tactical missiles would naturally be realized under strict control, just as an agreement on medium-range missiles and on strategic nuclear weapons.

Questions of verification of the observance of future agreements are gaining a qualitatively new significance in the case of reducing the level and the more so of liquidating whole classes of nuclear weapons in Europe. In these conditions, verification becomes one of the most significant means of safeguarding security. We shall thus strive for the elaboration of the strictest possible measures in this sphere. Naturally, our concern will not be verification for the sake of verification, but control of the fulfillment of obligations undertaken by the two sides in all stages of nuclear disarmament.

Much is now written and said in the West about the question of operational-tactical missiles. We are prepared to solve also this problem in a constructive manner but do it so as not to complicate the reaching of an agreement on medium-range missiles, which is of utmost importance today.

We regard the support for solving the problems of Euromissiles, expressed by Greece, the Netherlands, Spain, Italy, Finland and many other European countries, as a politically extremely significant fact. We call upon Paris, London and Bonn also to contribute toward clearing Europe of medium-range nuclear missiles and to finally embark on nuclear disarmament.

Consultations Taking Place

Reducing the state of the armed forces and weaponry in Europe requires the effort of all European states, the U.S. and Canada. Consultations between the countries of the Warsaw Pact and NATO are currently taking place in Vienna. However, the question arises whether it is not time for all foreign ministers of the countries participating in the Conference on Security and Cooperation in Europe to meet there and approve a decision on starting extensive talks with the aim to radically reduce the numbers of tactical nuclear weapons, armed forces and conventional armament.

The West speaks of disparity and imbalance. There naturally is an asymmetry in the armed forces of the two sides in Europe, but it stems from historical, geographical and other factors. We are in favor of removing the disparity which arose in some elements but not through their increase by the side which stayed behind but by reducing their numbers on the side which has a superiority in them.

Also such measures as the establishing of nuclear-free zones and zones free of chemical weapons would contribute toward the goals of strengthening European security. I want to say that we support the appeal of the Governments of East Germany and Czechoslovakia to the Government of West Germany proposing the establishment of a nuclear-free corridor in Central Europe.

An honest admission of one's own errors and mistakes and the determination to eliminate them strengthen the prestige of socialism.

Our effort is now focused on the reorganization of the entire social mechanism. In the economy, it is the transition from extensive to intensive methods, accelerated social-economic progress on a most progressive scientific-technological basis.

A Fundamental Turn

In short, a fundamental turn is necessary both in the organization of our entire activities and in social consciousness, in the psychology of people and their relationship to work, a turn revolutionary in its character.

The final aim of restructuring is to insure a better life for Soviet people, to introduce higher types of social organization and justice.

The main paths of progress in this direction have been fixed. It is the development of all forms of representative and direct democracy, a universal extension of autonomy, increase in the role of work teams, Soviets and social organizations, consolidation of the legal and economic guarantees of the rights of a person, legality, public information and people's control.

We are far from calling on anyone to copy us. Every socialist country has its specific features, and the fraternal parties determine their political line with a view to the national conditions. In addition, some problems which are now priorities in the Soviet Union have already been solved in other socialist countries or they are solving them in their own way.

At the same time, we do not conceal our conviction that the restructuring in the Soviet Union is in accordance with the very essence of socialism, the justified needs of social progress.

It can be said that the period of the formation of socialism as a world system has ended. A new stage has begun which requires that the entire system of our countries' cooperation be raised to a qualitatively different level.

No one is entitled to claim a special status in the socialist world. The independence of every party, its responsibility toward its people, the right to the sovereign solution of problems of the country's development—these are unconditional principles for us. At the same time, we are deeply convinced that the successes of the socialist community are not possible without the care of every party and country not only for their own but also common interests, without the relations of respect for friends and allies and without obligatory respect for their interests.

* * *

April 15, 1987

GORBACHEV OFFERS TO RENDER EUROPE CLEAR OF MISSILES

By DAVID K. SHIPLER

Special to The New York Times.

MOSCOW, April 14—Mikhail S. Gorbachev today proposed ridding Europe of all short-range nuclear missiles along with medium-range missiles, the Soviet press agency Tass said.

But in a sharply worded account, the agency said Secretary of State George P. Shultz had not accepted the offer, apparently because of objections from the Western European allies.

The rather harsh Soviet description of the talks seemed aimed at putting the onus on the United States for the continuing disagreements over arms control issues. The latest talks conclude on Wednesday with a final meeting between Mr. Shultz and Foreign Minister Eduard A. Shevardnadze.

'What Are You Afraid Of?'

Charles E. Redman, the State Department spokesman, refused to discuss the content of the negotiations. Virtually all the information came from the Soviet press agency, which disclosed details despite an agreement by the two sides not to discuss the substance of the meetings here.

"What are you afraid of?" Tass quoted Mr. Gorbachev as having asked Mr. Shultz. "After all, we are for a reliable agreement with the strictest and most comprehensive verification."

At another point, Tass said, Mr. Gorbachev asked: "What did Shultz bring? Is the Administration really ready to do something in the time that remains?"

Summit Issue Not 'Central'

Mr. Shultz began the meeting by delivering a renewed invitation from President Reagan to Mr. Gorbachev to visit the United States, but the Soviet leader indicated that he would like to have an arms agreement ready to sign before making the trip.

An American official said later that the summit meeting "was not a central issue in the discussions."

In Santa Barbara, a senior White House official said that the Administration had serious concerns about eliminating shorter-range nuclear weapons at a time that the Soviet Union had a sizable advantage in conventional forces. He said Mr. Shultz had made that point clear in his talks with Mr. Gorbachev.

Tass said the discussion between Mr. Gorbachev and Mr. Shultz, which lasted four and a half hours, "has borne out that the U.S. leadership is virtually unprepared to act vigorously, to go its part of the way."

Mr. Gorbachev also offered a concession on the testing of a space-oriented missile defense system, Tass said. It quoted him as having said that "research restricted to the laboratory" would be acceptable and as having proposed a relatively broad definition of laboratory as "research work on the ground—in institutes, at proving grounds, at plants."

"Let experts of the two countries take their time, ponder on the subject and agree on the list of devices which would not be allowed to be put into space in the course of this research," Mr. Gorbachev said. The Soviet Union has linked reductions on strategic offensive weapons to curbs on the "Star Wars" program. There has been uncertainty as to the forms of testing that would be acceptable to Moscow.

Iceland Accord Recalled

At the Iceland summit meeting in October, the Soviet Union and the United States agreed to bar all medium-range missiles from Europe. Later the United States insisted on limiting short-range missiles, which can travel 300 to 600 miles. The Russians have an advantage in such missiles, and the Reagan Administration has said that it wants to reserve the right to build up to the Soviet level.

Before leaving Washington, some American negotiators had speculated that the Russians might offer to scrap all the short-range missiles, as Mr. Gorbachev did in a speech in Prague on Friday and again today.

In anticipation of that possibility, Mr. Shultz was reportedly instructed to reply that he would have to consult with the Western European allies, who are afraid that without such missiles, they will be vulnerable to the superior Soviet conventional forces in Europe.

Since the issue has been aired publicly in Western Europe, Mr. Gorbachev undoubtedly knew of the concerns in the Atlantic alliance. But the Tass report had a tone of exasperation.

"No previous Administration had such chances," Tass quoted Mr. Gorbachev as having said, "yet we have not seen on the part of the U.S.A. the wish to use them for improving bilateral relations and the international situation."

Mr. Gorbachev also proposed barring from Europe all tactical nuclear weapons, those with ranges of less than 300 miles. But American officials have said that it would be impossible to verify such a treaty.

Positive Picture Given

Before the Gorbachev-Shultz meeting, the Soviet Foreign Ministry offered a positive picture of the mood.

"The atmosphere is businesslike, and therefore we are pleased with the atmosphere," Gennadi I. Gerasimov, the spokesman, said at a news conference. "But we are not pleased with certain positions of the American side, but evidently there is some reciprocity in that the American side is not pleased with certain positions of the Soviet side."

President Reagan's new invitation was contained in a letter handed by Mr. Shultz to the Soviet leader as they stood in the Kremlin's ornate Catherine Hall at the start of their meeting. A reporter asked Mr. Gorbachev whether there would be a summit meeting in Washington.

"This is precisely what we are going to discuss," Mr. Gorbachev replied. "We must continue the discussion and then answer your question.

"I have to be hopeful, and it just cannot be that I would avoid America in my travels. But generally, without a reason, I do not go anywhere, particularly to America. This cannot be just a stroll. When I will be nearing retirement, then I may travel just for pleasure, but now I need business."

Then he waved his arm toward Mr. Shultz, saying, "and the Secretary of State keeps silent."

"You are welcome to come," Mr. Shultz declared and pulled out an envelope. "I have a letter from the President, and it says so."

Tass later quoted Mr. Gorbachev as having said that even if the Reagan Administration did not have time to conclude treaties before its term ends, "key provisions" should be worked out on strategic arms, antiballistic missile systems and nuclear testing.

"I am ready to meet the President of the United States in order to reach agreement on these 'key provisions' and conclude a treaty on medium-range missiles," the Soviet leader said.

This morning Mr. Shultz met with Prime Minister Nikolai I. Ryzhkov, reportedly to discuss Soviet economic change and joint ventures with American companies. In the evening, Mr. Shultz met with Foreign Minister Eduard A. Shevardnadze to discuss regional issues.

President Reagan's initial invitation to Mr. Gorbachev to visit the United States was made at their meeting in Geneva in 1985. The trip was supposed to have been made in 1986, but in the absence of an arms accord to sign, the two leaders met instead in Iceland.

ALLIES' APPROVAL NEEDED

SANTA BARBARA, Calif., April 14—White House officials said today that the United States could not accept a Soviet offer to eliminate all nuclear weapons from Europe without the approval of the allies.

The officials voiced concern that elimination would lead to instability because of the Soviet Union's advantage in conventional forces.

* * *

November 1, 1987

UNCERTAIN SOVIET MARKS MILESTONE

By PHILIP TAUBMAN

Special to The New York Times.

MOSCOW, Oct. 31—The Soviet Union enters its eighth decade under Communism next week in a state of transition, wary of its past and uncertain about its future.

Unlike previous anniversaries, when the achievements of Communism were extolled in an atmosphere of ecstatic self-congratulation, this year's commemoration promises to be a time of introspection as well as celebration.

The commemoration is to begin Monday with what some diplomats and officials here say they expect to be a significant speech by Mikhail S. Gorbachev, the Soviet leader. It culminates on Saturday, Nov. 7, the actual anniversary of the Bolshevik seizure of power, with the traditional parade in Red Square, expanded this year to offer a recapitulation of Soviet history.

Unusual Self-Examination

Along with the usual signs of the approaching holiday—workmen festooning the capital with red bunting and immense portraits of Lenin, military vehicles rumbling through the streets at night rehearsing for the parade—there is an unusual mood of self-examination in Moscow as the country tries to come to grips with the legacy of seven decades of rigid rule.

Soviet officials said this was a moment when Mr. Gorbachev and his compatriots can pause to take stock not only of where they stand 70 years after the revolution, but also where they have come in the two years and eight months since he began a concerted effort to revitalize and reshape society.

The anniversary has been made particularly important for Mr. Gorbachev by the fact that it coincides with a pair of events: the announcement Friday that he will meet with President Reagan in Washington on Dec. 7, and a clash between party leaders at a Central Committee meeting on Oct. 21, described by Soviet officials this week. Soviet officials said Mr. Gorbachev needed to reassert his leadership and give his program renewed momentum. They said he should use the occasion to demonstrate that his political strength was not seriously damaged by the clash, in which Boris N. Yeltsin, the Moscow Communist Party chief and a nonvoting member of the Politburo who had been viewed as one of Mr. Gorbachev's firmest supporters, questioned his leadership and complained that change was moving too slowly.

Mr. Yeltsin's outburst, which led to a heated debate among party leaders, focused attention on the absence of any tangible improvement in the standard of living that many Russians have noted in recent months.

Several Gorbachev aides said the speech Monday, expected to last three hours, will deal with Soviet history, the current effort to restructure society and the role of the Soviet Union as a global power.

"He hopes to give the whole process a new impulse," a Gorbachev aide said.

The officials said Mr. Gorbachev, and a team of advisers working on the text with him, hoped to provide a historical and ideological framework for policies that until now have been presented without a binding purpose or statement of political philosophy.

Theory on Capitalism Dies

Aleksandr N. Yakovlev, a voting member of the Politburo and one of Mr. Gorbachev's closest advisers, told a group of scholars earlier this year: "The forecasts of the development of the capitalist system, of the boundaries of its viability and the reserves of its survival were found to be largely oversimplified. It all has to be abandoned, which is not at all easy."

Along with ringing praise of the scientific, industrial and military achievements of the Soviet Union, Mr. Gorbachev is expected to touch on sensitive historical periods, including Stalin's dismemberment of the party in the 1930's. He may talk about, if not rehabilitate, revolutionary leaders like Nikolai I. Bukharin who were executed by Stalin and excised from official memory.

The symbols of Moscow's success have not been forgotten. Mr. Gorbachev is almost certain to pay tribute to the Soviet Union's military power, its successful space program, the construction of housing for millions of citizens, and the transformation of a rural, largely illiterate country into an industrialized society.

Tass via Associated Press

Mikhail S. Gorbachev, the Soviet leader, visiting shipyard workers recently in Leningrad.

But Mr. Gorbachev, through the press, television and cinema and easing of censorship in literature, has made it possible to face failures and weaknesses like Stalin's terror, the evisceration of scholarship and literature, the chronic mismanagement of agriculture, the ossification of the economy and the neglect of consumer services.

He has created an intellectual climate more hospitable to new ideas and even to the possibility that drastic change may be necessary to pull the country out of stagnation.

Promises Outpace Change

But so far his promises of perestroika, or restructuring, have outpaced real revisions in the political and economic system.

There has been talk about decentralization of economic management. The party has given its approval in principle to price increases of basic goods like bread and meat, but the bureaucrats at the State Planning Committee, which has directed the economy with an iron hand for decades, seem not to be convinced that this is wise. Even a hint of rising prices sent consumers into a panic of hoarding this month.

The encouragement of individual enterprise has produced a few bright spots like cooperative restaurants, where the decor is pleasant, the food is good and the service is efficient, but the reintroduction of some personal incentives has barely made a mark on the economy.

The imposition of a rigorous quality-control program in major factories badly disrupted production without producing a visible improvement in the reliability of cars, home appliances and other manufactured goods.

Sakharov Is Hopeful

Andrei D. Sakharov, the dissident and physicist, said in a recent interview: "I have a great deal of hope in Gorbachev's policies and in him. I think perestroika is a historical necessity.

But he added: "There is a clear distinction between what Gorbachev says and what the Central Committee approves, and a still greater gap between what they approve and what happens in real life."

Mr. Gorbachev himself has grown impatient with the resistance to his program, recently appealing to party and Government officials to make an urgent effort to get more food into the shops, build more housing and increase the availability of consumer goods.

"We cannot live with hopes alone," he said at a party meeting on Oct. 20.

Direct Appeal to People

The 70th anniversary provides the Soviet leader with an opportunity to rekindle enthusiasm for his program by appealing directly to the people on an occasion that is likely to attract great national interest.

By reaching back to the past, he can also draw contrasts to periods of hardship, even terror, making the modest gains of the last three years and the improvement over the decades look more impressive.

The difficulty, underlined by the rebuke Mr. Yeltsin is said to have given, is that new ideological formulas, ambitious programs for change, and a more candid look at the past will not keep pace with aspirations that increasingly revolve around material possessions like cars and stereos, most still in short supply.

* * *

November 22, 1987

AFTER YELTSIN, GORBACHEV?

By MARSHALL I. GOLDMAN

CAMBRIDGE, Mass.—With Boris N. Yeltsin, the deposed Moscow party chief, tucked safely into a senior post in the construction industry, the Kremlin's spin-control artists are hard at work minimizing the affair. The West should not fall for their wiles.

"We are in the process of learning democracy and the culture of real debate," said Georgi A. Arbatov, a Government spokesman, of the 1930's-style public humiliation of Mr. Yeltsin. "It is sometimes hard to overcome old habits."

In fact, the Yeltsin affair may some day be seen as the first sign that Mikhail S. Gorbachev's efforts to reform Soviet society and economic life would end in failure.

A confrontation between the reformers and Moscow's enormously powerful and corrupt party bureaucrats—the so-called nomenklatura—had been brewing for some time.

It occurred in the Yeltsin affair and was won hands down by the reactionaries. The question now is whether Mr. Gorbachev himself can avoid a similar fate.

From the moment Mr. Gorbachev declared his intention to reform the economy, a confrontation with the nomenklatura was inevitable. That was only underscored with the 1985 appointment of Mr. Yeltsin, a strong proponent of reform.

The battle lines were drawn last April in a remarkably clear warning to Mr. Yeltsin and his fellow reformers from the wife of a senior party official.

"Don't snipe at us," the woman wrote in a Moscow newspaper. "We are the elite and you cannot halt the stratification of society. You are not strong enough. We will rip the puny sails of perestroika and you will be unable to reach your destination. So cool it." Earlier, others had warned Mr. Yeltsin to go back to his home base of Sverdlovsk, an industrial city in the Urals, while there was still time.

Under Mr. Yeltsin's predecessor, Viktor Grishin, Moscow officials, like their counterparts all over the Soviet Union, came to regard their niches in the state and party apparatus as personal fiefdoms.

For example, a Moscow food store manager built a personal fortune of $1.5 million by offering hard-to-buy goods in exchange for personal gifts. His partners included officials at the highest level of the Ministry of Light Industry. Such schemes exacerbated shortages and increased distrust of the system. No reform could take place until the system had been purged.

Mr. Yeltsin seemed the perfect manager to shake up and shake out the stagnant, corrupt and inept Moscow bureaucracy. After his appointment in 1985, Mr. Yeltsin moved immediately to flush out opportunists and misfits and to improve services.

In a memorable speech in April 1986, he announced that 800 trade officials had been arrested and he went on to attack certain bureaucrats by name. He challenged them to get out of their limousines and ride the buses, to forsake their special stores, restaurants, clinics and apartments, and live life as the ordinary masses did. Only then, he insisted, would they understand why the citizens of Moscow were alienated and unproductive.

Mr. Yeltsin went out among the people, standing in line at stores and listening to popular complaints. He also set out to make life a little cheerier by adding sidewalk cafes and more outside kiosks in the summer. No wonder he began to find favor among Muscovites while inspiring hatred among the bureaucracy.

The outcome might have been different if Mr. Yeltsin had produced a turnaround. While there was some improvement in the general atmosphere, food supplies, particularly vegetables, actually declined. Poor harvests and a lackluster response to new economic initiatives contributed to his problems. But he got no help from the nomenklatura, who set about sabotaging his efforts by restricting supplies of staples. The bureaucrats were determined to bring Mr. Yeltsin down before he brought them down.

In retrospect, it probably would have been better for Mr. Yeltsin to proceed more cautiously. His inability to produce immediate results was an obvious source of frustration for him. Reflecting his frustration, he complained in August, just as he did again at the fateful Central Committee meeting Oct. 21, that "there is evidently no need to report on achievements, especially and unfortunately since in terms of end results, not very much has been achieved."

Soviet conservatives bitterly oppose such criticism. In the words of Yegor Ligachev, the No. 2 man in the party, "People abroad and even some people in our country tried to denigrate the entire path of the building of Socialism in the U.S.S.R. and to try to present it as an unbroken chain of errors."

Viktor Chebrikov, the head of the K.G.B., is equally disturbed. He has focused on the call for glasnost. In September, he directed his wrath at those who seek "to install political and ideological pluralism" and plant "the virus of nationalism."

What is worrisome about all this is that while the ostensible targets of such attacks are foreigners and Mr. Yeltsin, there is no doubt that the attackers, especially when they rail against democratization, also target Mr. Gorbachev himself.

As recently as Oct. 13, Mr. Gorbachev complained that, "two and a half years, I think, for a revolutionary stage when everything is moving rapidly and developing is a long time: so why don't we have more to show?" Moreover, it was Mr. Gorbachev who had been complaining about the state of the economy and the fact that it "had gone downhill so that it stank."

Mr. Yeltsin was mercurial, unsophisticated and not particularly subtle. Yet his policies and actions were precisely those that Mr. Gorbachev was seeking to stimulate in others. In other words, he was Mr. Gorbachev's point man.

That is why it is disturbing that pressure from the conservatives and the nomenklatura was such that Mr. Gorbachev found it necessary to sacrifice one of his most outspoken supporters. If Mr. Gorbachev holds to his reforms, it is hard to see how he can escape a similar fate.

Marshall I. Goldman, professor of economics at Wellesley College, is author of a recent book on Soviet economic reform.

* * *

November 23, 1987

MIKHAIL S. GORBACHEV'S "PERESTROIKA"

By CHRISTOPHER LEHMANN-HAUPT

PERESTROIKA: New Thinking for Our Country and the World.
By Mikhail Gorbachev
254 pages. A Cornelia & Michael Bessie Book/Harper & Row. $19.95.

"New Thinking for Our Country and the World," is just what its title implies. It is the Soviet leader's account of what his planned perestroika, or "restructuring," of the Soviet system will entail, and what its presumed success implies for international relations, particularly those with the United States and the West.

Since the book addresses matters of monumental concern to all of us, readers will naturally be tempted to respond like Pavlov's dogs—to wonder, depending on their ideological persuasion, why his eloquent pleas for nuclear disarmament haven't been met by a more positive response in Washington; or why he never mentions his country's emigration policies, or why he wants perestroika to make it possible for women in the Soviet Union "to return to their purely womanly mission."

But these are ideological reactions to Mr. Gorbachev's book. And there seems good reason to respond in another way. According to the publicity material that came with "Perestroika," when the book's publisher, Simon Michael Bessie, first proposed the idea for the book to the Soviet Embassy in Washington, he said he was "not interested in speeches or propaganda, but in a real book." Since he has gone ahead and published the result, one assumes the publisher feels he got what he asked for. So one is emboldened to review "Perestroika" not as if it were a letter to the world (or an address to Congress) by the Soviet leader, but as nothing more, or less, than a book.

As such it is a distinct disappointment, especially coming from a man who in so many other stylistic respects has surpassed our expectations. Of course, one has to make allowances for the speed with which the book was prepared. Only haste to get it out in time for the celebration of the 70th anniversary of the Bolshevik Revolution can account for the number of typos, grammatical errors, repetitions and poorly translated passages. One surely has to allow also for the audience Mr. Gorbachev is addressing. It is not just his supporters who will read him carefully, but opponents of perestroika as well. To some degree he is probably compelled to write elliptically and to speak out of both sides of his mouth at once.

Still, the book is wooden and impersonal, and lacks the smallest ingredient of style or humor. Especially when he writes about domestic reform, his prose is dense, abstract and jargon-ridden: "The present economic reform envisages that the emphasis will be shifted from primarily administrative to primarily economic management methods at every level, and calls for extensive democratization of management, and the overall activization of the human factor."

Writing about the international scene, he blusters, strikes poses, cries crocodile tears and overstates the obvious. "Soviet-Indian relations have steadily developed over many years," he writes, as if some alternative form of diplomacy (unsteady? undeveloping? in an instant?) could just as likely be the case. Even when he tries to lighten up, he stumbles. "I recently talked with an outstanding Latin-American writer, Gabriel Garcia Marquez. A great mind indeed. His range of thinking is global: reading just one of his books shows this." Which one of his books? His last novel, "Chronicle of a Death Foretold," while profound and eloquent, was about as globally thoughtful as "The Catcher in the Rye."

Of course, learning to write well doesn't happen to be one of the requirements of becoming General Secretary of the Communist Party of the Soviet Union. Still, from the tone of his voice in "Perestroika," he could be Nikita S. Khrushchev or Leonid I. Brezhnev or any other Soviet leader of the past four decades. He could be a number of American leaders too, with his reference to "a meaningful lifestyle" and his repeated use of "perfectly clear" and "crystal clear."

But the most perplexing quality of "Perestroika" is its flaws of internal logic. The author seems wedded to a line of reasoning that holds that a condition and its opposite can be true at the same time. Most basic to his argument is his repeated insistence that perestroika, far from reflecting a weakness in the Communist system, is nothing but a return to revolutionary first principles, a reaffirmation of Lenin's vision of socialism as "the living creativity of the masses." The more Mr. Gorbachev celebrates the scientific inevitability of socialism, the more we are made to wonder why "restructuring" was necessary in the first place and what accounted for the "braking mechanism" he feels compelled to overcome.

In a similar vein: "Our achievements in education are universally known." Yet: "Now, after a nationwide discussion, we have adopted programs for a radical transformation of higher and secondary schools." Soviet law is also perfect yet flawed. "From the very beginning of Soviet rule Lenin and the Party attached paramount importance to the maintenance and consolidation of law." Yet: "Now that we have launched perestroika, and have resolved to do away with the negative phenomena of the past and to give a fresh impetus to the development of socialist democracy, we have seen the need for far-reaching transformation both in the sphere of our legislation, and in the perfection of socialist legality as a whole."

Even perestroika itself is ambiguous. On the one hand, its celebrant writes of the difficulties it faces both at home and around the globe. On the other hand, he speaks as if after only two and a half years it has proved a resounding success and demonstrated beyond doubt the resiliency and inevitability of the Soviet system.

Such double talk as this undermines the reasonableness of Mr. Gorbachev's text, and makes one doubt him even when he seems sincere, as he does most eloquently whenever he writes about the barrenness of nuclear diplomacy and the need for the superpowers to give up nuclear arms.

Of course one understands that he must sometimes speak in code, lest he nettle his political opponents at home and jeopardize what, for all his talk of inevitability, must necessarily be a delicate process of reform. Still, speaking in code is not for "real books." Mr. Gorbachev's "Perestroika" suffers from an excess of slogans, cant and elliptical hints at what the author really means.

* * *

December 9, 1987

REAGAN AND GORBACHEV SIGN MISSILE TREATY AND VOW TO WORK FOR GREATER REDUCTIONS

By DAVID K. SHIPLER
Special to The New York Times.

WASHINGTON, Dec. 8—With fervent calls for a new era of peaceful understanding, President Reagan and Mikhail S. Gorbachev today signed the first treaty reducing the size of their nations' nuclear arsenals.

The President and the Soviet leader, beginning three days of talks aimed at even broader reductions, pledged to build on the accord by striving toward what Mr. Gorbachev called "the more important goal," reducing long-range nuclear weapons.

In their White House conversations, the leaders were said to have reviewed their previous proposals aimed at furthering those negotiations, and they established an arms-control working group of ranking officials to hold parallel sessions.

'Mine is Mikhail'

An immediate mood of warmth was established as the two leaders agreed this morning to call each other by their first names, a White House official said. He quoted the President as telling Mr. Gorbachev, "My first name is Ron."

Mr. Gorbachev answered, "Mine is Mikhail."

"When we're working in private session," Mr. Reagan reportedly said, "we can call each other that."

The new treaty, which provides for the dismantling of all Soviet and American medium- and shorter-range missiles, establishes the most extensive system of weapons inspection ever negotiated by the two countries, including placing technicians at sensitive sites on each other's territory.

The Mood for Talking

The signing, the fruition of years of negotiation, set the mood for two and a half hours of talks between the leaders. The talks were "very serious, substantive discussions," Secretary of State George P. Shultz said tonight before a formal dinner in the White House.

The visit to Washington by Mr. Gorbachev was the first by a Soviet leader since Leonid I. Brezhnev was here 14 years ago, and it took on immediate drama as Mr. Reagan, who entered office with deep suspicions of the Soviet Union, welcomed Mr. Gorbachev on the South Lawn of the White House.

"I have often felt that our people should have been better friends long ago," he told his guest as they stood facing the Washington Monument across an array of full-dress military honor guards. Mr. Gorbachev received a 21-gun salute usually reserved for chiefs of state.

Mr. Gorbachev plunged energetically into a round of talks and public appearances. He met twice with the President, attended a formal dinner at the White House and met with a group of American public figures and intellectuals at the Soviet Embassy.

'Lively' Rights Discussion

The morning discussion, in which Mr. Reagan raised human rights issues, was "a very lively session," according to Marlin Fitzwater, the White House spokesman. He described Mr. Gorbachev as "animated" and Mr. Reagan as "forceful." Another official said there was "no give" by Mr. Gorbachev on Jewish emigration or other rights issues.

Mr. Reagan and Mr. Gorbachev both exuded warmth, with Mr. Reagan quoting Russian proverbs, Mr. Gorbachev quoting Ralph Waldo Emerson and both men exchanging frequent smiles in what seemed to be a spirit of satisfaction and expectation.

Seated side by side at a massive wooden table used by Lincoln's Cabinet, they signed English- and Russian-language versions of the treaty at a ceremony in the East Room of the White House, attended by about 250 invited guests, including the Joint Chiefs of Staff, the Cabinet, Congressional leaders, ranking Soviet officials and others.

"We can only hope that this history-making agreement will not be an end in itself," President Reagan said, "but the beginning of a working relationship that will enable us to tackle the other issues, urgent issues, before us: strategic offensive nuclear weapons, the balance of conventional forces in Europe, the destructive and tragic regional conflicts that beset so many parts of our globe, and respect for the human and natural rights that God has granted to all men."

The Road from Catastrophe

Mr. Gorbachev echoed some of those sentiments. "For everyone, and above all for our two great powers," he said, "the treaty whose text is on this table offers a big chance, at last, to get onto the road leading away from the threat of catastrophe.

"It is our duty to take full advantage of that chance and move together toward a nuclear-free world, which holds out for our children and grandchildren, and for their children and grandchildren, the promise of a fulfilling and happy life, without fear and without a senseless waste of resources on weapons of destruction."

If approved by the Senate, the accord would require the dismantling within three years of all 1,752 Soviet and 859 American missiles with ranges of 300 to 3,400 miles and their nuclear warheads. It also provides for stationing inspection teams at sensitive sites on each other's soil, with the right to make a certain number of short-notice inspections elsewhere each year for 13 years.

Although much debate is expected in the Senate, Republican and Democratic leaders there say they believe the treaty will be approved, perhaps with amendments, reservations or understandings attached. Senator Bob Dole, Republican of Kansas and the minority leader, who is running for President, has remained uncommitted.

Jesse Helms of North Carolina, the ranking Republican on the Senate Foreign Relations Committee, is strongly opposed to the accord. He declined an invitation to attend the signing ceremony, a White House official said.

Perplexed by Opposition

Mr. Gorbachev, meeting with a group of American intellectuals and public figures, expressed bewilderment at the opposition to the treaty. "I cannot comprehend those who have taken up the cudgels against the newly found elements of mutual understanding and cooperation that have appeared in preparation for the signing of the treaty," he said.

Mr. Reagan, who had some sharp exchanges with conservatives on the subject last week, laced his statements today with references to the need for realism and the avoidance of illusions, an apparent effort to allay the concerns of some conservatives that he is growing soft on the Russians.

"I have often felt that our people should have been better friends long ago," Mr. Reagan declared during the arrival ceremony on the South Lawn. "But let us have the courage to recognize that there are weighty differences between our Governments and systems—differences that will not go away by wishful thinking or expressions of good will, no matter how sincerely delivered."

At various times, both leaders referred to the Soviet-American alliance against Germany during World War II. And Mr. Gorbachev, at the arrival ceremony, also summoned the call of history to enhance the aura of this summit meeting.

The New York Times/Paul Hosefros

Mr. Gorbachev applauding after he and Mr. Reagan signed copies of the treaty. At rear, staff members exchanged the copies so that each could be signed by the other leader.

"History has charged the Governments of our countries, and the two of us, Mr. President, with a solemn duty to justify the hopes of Americans and Soviet people, and of people the world over, to undo the logic of the arms race by working together in good faith."

A choice was offered, Mr. Gorbachev declared: "Fears and prejudice inherited from the cold war and leading to confrontation, or common sense, which calls for action to ensure the survival of civilization."

At the signing ceremony, Mr. Reagan emphasized the extensive verification procedures that would enable both sides to monitor compliance with the treaty. "We have listened to the wisdom in an old Russian maxim," Mr. Reagan said. "Though my pronunciation may give you difficulty, the maxim is, 'Doveryai no proveryai,' 'trust but verify.' "

Mr. Gorbachev interrupted, laughing. "You repeat that at every meeting," he said. "I like it," Mr. Reagan replied. Mr. Gorbachev, who arrived in Washington on Monday afternoon, began his public day with a full-dress welcoming ceremony on the South Lawn. There were military honor guards, cannon salutes, trumpet fanfares and the playing of the two countries' national anthems.

Then Mr. Gorbachev and Mr. Reagan met privately in the Oval Office, each accompanied only by two note-takers and an interpreter. They were joined later by senior aides. Mr. Fitzwater, the White House spokesman, said they discussed human rights and arms control and reviewed the agenda, setting up two working groups.

One group, on arms control, is headed by Paul H. Nitze, special adviser to the President, and Marshal Sergei F. Akhrameyev, chief of the Soviet General Staff. Another group, to deal with regional conflicts, human rights and bilateral issues, is headed by Rozanne L. Ridgway, Assistant Secretary for European and Canadian Affairs, and a Deputy Soviet Foreign Minister, Aleksandr A. Bessmertnykh.

The two leaders held talks again this afternoon.

Although Mr. Reagan has said he would press the Soviet leader on human rights, the President made only brief public remarks on the issue.

"On the table will be not only arms reduction, but also human rights issues about which the American people and their government are deeply committed," Mr. Reagan said at the arrival ceremony. "These are fundamental issues of political morality that touch on the most basic of human concerns."

In a broadcast address after the treaty signing, the President declared: "Let us remember that genuine international confidence and security are inconceivable without open societies with freedom of information, freedom of conscience, the right to publish and the right to travel."

The missile treaty eliminates only a small percentage of weapons that are not very important to either country, and it leaves untouched the vast long-range strategic nuclear forces of each side. But the accord is widely seen as an important symbolic and psychological step. Some conservatives oppose it in the belief that Soviet compliance cannot be verified and that it leaves Western Europe exposed to a superior Soviet conventional force.

Mr. Gorbachev said today that he hoped to work toward agreements on reducing coventional forces in Europe, as well as a treaty eliminating chemical weapons.

"We have some real, legitimate concerns" about the arms treaty, Senator Dole said. "The bottom line for most Republicans is that we want to support the President; we will do our Constitutional duty, and we see no reason why the role must conflict."

Mr. Dole announced the formation of a Republican task force to coordinate "expeditious consideration" of the treaty.

At the East Room signing ceremony, with Nancy Reagan and Raisa Gorbachev looking on from the front row, the two leaders laboriously put their signatures to the parchment-quality paper on which the treaty is printed.

Then, with an impish smile, Mr. Gorbachev asked Mr. Reagan if he might like to exchange pens, so each could have the other's as a souvenir. They did, shook hands and walked from the room down a magenta-carpeted hallway.

* * *

December 11, 1987

REAGAN AND GORBACHEV REPORT PROGRESS ON LONG-RANGE ARMS; MUTE QUARREL OVER 'STAR WARS'; REAGAN TRIP IS DUE

By R. W. APPLE Jr.

Special to The New York Times.

WASHINGTON, Dec. 10—President Reagan and Mikhail S. Gorbachev concluded their three-day summit conference today with what they described as significant progress toward a treaty limiting strategic weapons. But they failed to conclude major new agreements on Afghanistan or the other key issues that still divide them.

Shielded from a drenching rain by black umbrellas as they stood on the South Lawn of the White House, the President said the two could "walk away from our meetings with a sense of accomplishment," and the Soviet General Secretary asserted that "a good deal has been accomplished."

Their main achievements, other than the signing of a treaty Tuesday on intermediate-range nuclear missiles, appeared to consist of better personal relations and a decision not to let "Star Wars" stand in the way of negotiating a new strategic missile pact.

'Lit the Sky With Hope'

"This summit has lit the sky with hope for all people of good will," the President said, reflecting the Administration's conviction that the sense of good will generated here will help to alleviate superpower tensions.

At a 1-hour, 50-minute news conference this evening, which ended not long before Mr. Gorbachev boarded his Aeroflot jet for the trip to East Berlin, where he will brief his Warsaw Pact allies, the Soviet leader described his visit to Washington as "a major event in world politics."

It had opened, he said, "a new phase in U.S.-Soviet relations," and because of a "deepening political dialogue" with Mr. Reagan, remaining differences were no longer insurmountable.

TV Report by President

The President spoke in a similar vein in a nationally televised summit report tonight, asserting that he and the Soviet leader had shifted the basis of Soviet-American relations. They are "no longer focused only on arms control issues," he said, but "now cover a far broader agenda, one that has, at its root, realism and candor."

"Mr. Gorbachev and I have agreed, in several months in Moscow, to continue what we have achieved in these past three days," the President declared. "I believe there is reason for both hope and optimism."

No date was set for the next meeting, but Marlin Fitzwater, the White House spokesman, said the President would travel to Moscow in the first half of next year, probably in the spring. The two leaders indicated in their communiqué that the meeting would take place whether a strategic arms treaty was ready for signature or not.

On the withdrawal of Soviet troops from Afghanistan, a topic that preoccuppied the leaders on Tuesday, no visible progress was made.

The outcome on strategic nuclear weapons was better, American officials reported. The two sides approached agreement on the outline of a treaty that could be signed in Moscow, though they remained sharply divided on the meaning of the 1972 Antiballistic Missile Treaty, the interpretation of which could provide the key to breaking the stalemate over the "Star Wars" program.

Negotiators reached a limited but nonetheless important agreement, arms-control officials said, on a limit of 4,900 ballistic missile warheads, a compromise between the previous Soviet figure of 5,100 and the United States demand for 4,800.

In addition, the team headed by Paul H. Nitze and Marshal Sergei F. Akhromeyev decided that for the moment negotiators in Geneva should work around "Star Wars," more formally known as the Strategic Defense Initiative. According to American officials, the negotiators will draft an agreement on strategic arms that would in no way preclude widespread "Star Wars" testing, which the Administration has said is permissible under its broad interpretation of the ABM treaty.

The Russians, who oppose such testing, apparently agreed to such an arrangement because the Administration has already been prohibited by Congress, through most of the remainder of Mr. Reagan's term, from carrying out any tests except those permitted under the narrow interpretation of the treaty that is favored by Moscow.

This method of skirting the "Star Wars" issue, on which the summit talks in Iceland last year foundered, amounts to an agreement to disagree that should allow for progress on the strategic arms treaty. The Soviet leadership had made it plain before arriving in Washington that it did not want the issue to block progress toward an agreement reducing long-range nuclear arsenals by up to 50 percent.

Little Movement on 'Star Wars'

In his news conference, Mr. Gorbachev acknowledged that there had been little movement on resolving the "Star Wars" issue.

In the last question of the two-hour session, he was asked, "Has your meeting here this week made it any less likely that the arms race will be extended into space?"

He answered: "I don't think so. I can confirm that it remains the goal of the Soviet Union to prevent the extension of the arms race into space. That's all."

One important question that must be settled in Geneva, in addition to limits on specific types of missiles, is how long the two nations would agree not to withdraw from the ABM treaty. The length of that period would determine, in part, when a "Star Wars" system could be deployed.

In the final communiqué, the matter was covered in this veiled language: "The leaders of the two countries also instructed their delegations in Geneva to work out an agreement that would commit the sides to observe the ABM treaty, as signed in 1972, while conducting their research, development and testing as required, which are permitted by the ABM treaty, and not to withdraw from the ABM treaty for a specified length of time."

The final hours of the meeting, the first between Soviet and American leaders in this country in 14 years, were cloaked in the same sort of mystery, and characterized by the same sort of furious last-minute activity, that marked the Reykjavik summit conference in October 1986.

Secretary of State George P. Shultz appeared, unannounced, at the Soviet Embassy at 8 A.M. for last-minute negotiations. Mr. Gorbachev left for the White House more than an hour late, and then he stunned everyone by leaping from his limousine to shake hands with people standing on the sidewalk along Connecticut Avenue.

No Surprise Proposals

But there were no surprise proposals here, as there were at Reykjavik, and the two leaders did not fall here, as they did there, over the hurdle of "Star Wars."

Today, moreover, they smiled at each other, if only intermittently, as they parted; they had departed from Iceland smothered in scowls.

Because both men needed for domestic political reasons to seem to do well, and because both want to encourage prompt Senate ratification of the treaty covering shorter- and medium-range missiles, they joined in putting the best possible face on things.

Almost up to the time of his departure, Mr. Gorbachev continued his remarkable campaign to sell himself, his policies and his country to the American people. Besides getting out of his limousine to meet with the crowds along Connecticut Avenue, he talked with 15 high school and college students, whom he urged to learn more about world problems, and met with American business leaders to whom he made a strong pitch for large American investments in joint ventures to develop Soviet natural resources.

Blinis for Bush at Embassy

While Mr. Shultz was conferring in another part of the embassy with Eduard A. Shevardnadze, the Soviet Foreign Minister, Mr. Gorbachev joined Vice President Bush and other guests for a breakfast of blinis—thin Russian buckwheat pancakes—and caviar. Mr. Bush said of his host, "This man has a good way about him, yet he's strong and he's tough in negotiations."

The Soviet leader's wife, Raisa, was also active, receiving a group of Armenian-Americans who expressed gratitude for permission granted to Armenians to emigrate from the Soviet Union, and talking with a small group of prominent women at the elaborate Georgetown residence of Pamela Harriman, the widow of W. Averell Harriman, the wartime American Ambassador to Moscow. Mrs. Harriman is a prominent fundraiser for Democratic candidates.

According to American officials who spoke at a background briefing on the condition that they not be identified, the Soviet Union refused to set a date for the start of their withdrawal from Afghanistan until agreement could be reached on what sort of transitional government would be formed in Kabul after a withdrawal. Mr. Gorbachev reportedly insisted upon a nonaligned regime while Mr. Reagan wants one elected by the Afghans.

There was also a disagreement, the officials said, about the timing of a cutoff of American aid to the guerrilla forces fighting Soviet troops. "It takes two sides to agree on something, and it just wasn't there," one of the officials involved commented later.

Long Talk by Gorbachev

At his news conference, Mr. Gorbachev talked for more than an hour, explaining and analyzing the agreements he reached with Mr. Reagan, before he began answering questions.

He put particular emphasis on the limit of 4,900 missile warheads. The 4,900 figure covers both intercontinental ballistic missiles and sea-based ballistic missiles, which have represented a particular problem because they are fired from naval vessels, whose movements make positive verification very difficult.

The Soviet leader said he agreed with American officials that the Geneva negotiators would have a difficult time between now and June working out the details of the strategic arms treaty. How to count certain categories of weapons, the Americans said, will present particularly thorny questions.

Mr. Gorbachev said United States officials had "displayed interest" in Soviet ideas about reducing conventional forces in Europe, in which the Soviet Union and its allies have considerable superiority. He urged urgent, early negotiations that would "cast aside all altercation" and said they would show "who is in earnest and who is, perhaps, trying to be too sly."

Some elements of the plan on strategic weapons were "resolved," the Soviet leader said, "while the participants in the official farewell ceremony" were waiting on the White House lawn. As a reult, publication of the joint statement by the leaders was delayed until late tonight.

Soviet Concession Seen

Asked at the end of his presentation whether he thought anything he had done here had reduced the chances that the United States would eventually have weapons in space, Mr. Gorbachev's "I don't think so" and his short answer suggested that he felt he had made a major concession to Mr. Reagan in agreeing to put aside the "Star Wars" question, at least for the time being.

On the more general question of how his relationship with Mr. Reagan had changed since their meetings in Geneva and Reykjavik, the Soviet leader replied, "It's more businesslike, we have more of a constructive approach, and I would even venture to say that we trust each other more."

In his televised speech, Mr. Reagan tried to rebut many of the criticisms that have been made of the shorter- and medium-range missile treaty. Using a map, he argued that removing those missiles would remove a major threat to Europe and Asia, and he also insisted that the verification procedures were more than adequate.

* * *

January 7, 1988

MOSCOW DECLARES ITS AIM IS TO LEAVE AFGHANISTAN IN '88

By BILL KELLER

Special to The New York Times.

MOSCOW, Jan. 6—Foreign Minister Eduard A. Shevardnadze said today in Afghanistan that the Soviet Union hoped to remove its troops from Afghanistan by the end of the year, and indicated that the withdrawal would not depend on creation of an acceptable transition government.

In an interview with the Afghan press agency, the Foreign Minister also said the United States had agreed to cut off aid to Afghan guerrillas as part of a withdrawal package.

"We would like the year 1988 to be the last year of the presence of Soviet troops in your country," the Soviet Foreign Minister said.

115,000 Troops in Country

Mr. Shevardnadze's remarks, and additional comments by Deputy Foreign Minister Anatoly L. Adamishin, were the most explicit public indication yet by Soviet authorities that removal of the 115,000 troops is not preconditioned on the makeup of the Government left behind.

Mr. Shevardnadze said that while the Soviet Union still hoped for a stable and neutral government in Afghanistan, that was something to be worked out after the superpowers' involvement had ended.

Western diplomats said the remarks of the two Soviet officials today appeared to be the first public confirmation of what Soviet negotiators have told American officials in private: that withdrawal does not hinge on creation of an acceptable coalition government.

Called Forceful Message

They said the the Soviet officials seemed to be trying to send a forceful message to the Afghan leader, Najibullah, that the Soviet leadership is serious about its plans to withdraw, regardless of Mr. Najibullah's fate afterward.

Under Secretary of State Michael H. Armacost, ending a visit to Pakistan today for talks on the next round of Afghan negotiations, said President Reagan had repeatedly said "we want to see such an agreement and the end of the Soviet occupation by the end of 1988."

Mr. Armacost, who apparently did not know of Mr. Shevardnadze's statements, added: "The Soviet leadership has stated that the political decision to withdraw has been made.

We hope this is so, and look for Soviet actions to match their words."

Hints of Impatience

Soviet officials have hinted strongly to Western diplomats and reporters that they were impatient with Mr. Najibullah's reluctance to lose his Soviet military backing and with his maneuvering to preserve his own place.

Diplomats said Mr. Shevardnadze's apparent optimism that Soviet troops could be gone by the end of 1988 also hinted strongly at a willingness to trim a few more months from the timetable.

Soviet officials have offered a 12-month timetable, while Pakistan, the major refuge and aid conduit for the rebels, has insisted on eight months.

"I wouldn't be surprised to see the Soviets say 10, and it would be hard for the Pakistanis to say no," one Western diplomat said.

Agreement Seen in February

Mr. Shevardnadze said his Government hoped to see an agreement signed at the next round of Afghan-Pakistani talks in February, with the Soviet withdrawal and American aid cutoff to take effect 60 days after the signing.

"Virtually the entire package of the necessary arrangements has already been agreed upon at the Afghan-Pakistani talks" mediated by Diego Cordovez, an Ecuadorean who is a United Nations Under Secretary General, Mr. Shevardnadze said. "There is an opportunity to conclude these talks at the next round in February."

He added, "It must be emphasized that the U.S. side agrees to be a guarantor and, consequently, to stop aid to armed groups conducting military operations against the people's power in Afghanistan."

Mr. Shevardnadze returned to Moscow tonight.

Officials Confirm U.S. Promise

Despite public professions of continued support for the rebels, American officials have confirmed that the United States has promised to stop supplying weapons to the rebels as part of an agreement removing Soviet troops.

But Soviet officials have never acknowledged the offer in public. By doing so in Kabul, one diplomat said tonight, Mr. Shevardnadze seemed to be announcing to both the Afghan and Soviet public that major obstacles have been removed and an agreement is at hand, and thus putting pressure on Mr. Najibullah "to face reality."

Closing the gap on a timetable and dropping the issue of a transition government would still leave some questions to be resolved.

American officials have said one remaining stumbling block is the question of what types of military units are sent home at what point during the withdrawal. They have expressed concern that large or elite Soviet units would remain long after weapons have been cut off to the rebels.

Nature of Peace Force

Another issue, described by a diplomat as "not insurmountable," is the nature of an international peacekeeping force, most likely from the United Nations, to oversee compliance with the agreement ending outside involvement in Afghanistan.

Soviet officials have also said they wanted a United States-Soviet agreement to respect Afghanistan's neutrality. A Western diplomat said tonight that the two superpowers had agreed on this in general and Soviet officials believe such an agreement could be achieved quickly.

Mr. Shevardnadze flew to Kabul on Monday for his first visit in a year, and for the first 48 hours the Soviet press imposed an unusual blackout on news of his activities.

Western diplomats read the silence as a sign of tense discussions with Mr. Najibullah, who has had himself declared President and proclaimed himself a devout Moslem in his efforts to strengthen his hold on power.

A Western diplomat said Soviet officials first indicated during the summit meeting last month in Washington that they no longer made the establishment of a stable coalition to rule Afghanistan a condition for troop withdrawal. This had once loomed as the largest obstacle to a pullout.

Interview in India

In an interview today in India, reported by the official Soviet press agency, Tass, Mr. Adamishin said national reconciliation of the Afghan factions "is not connected" with the withdrawal plan being negotiated with Mr. Cordovez's help.

At another point, asked specifically what the conditions would be for withdrawal, he cited the negotiations in Geneva and made no mention of the internal politics of Afghanistan.

When Mr. Shevardnadze was asked today by the Afghan interviewer whether there was a danger that fighting might go on after the Soviet troops withdraw, the Soviet Foreign Minister conceded that "armed struggle" might continue after the Russans leave. He repeated the Soviet desire for "a coalition government on the broadest basis," but made clear that this was a problem that would not stand in the way of troop withdrawal.

In what seemed to be a jab at Mr. Najibullah's ambitions, he added that anyone who refused to join in a broad political dialogue would be putting "some transient, circumstantial, personal considerations and aspirations above the interests of the nation."

U.S. SEEKS SHORTER TIMETABLE

WASHINGTON, Jan. 6 (Special to The New York Times)—American officials did not react immediately today to Mr. Shevardnadze's apparent willingness to separate the question of a Soviet withdrawal from Afghanistan from the composition of a transition government. But as for a timetable for withdrawal, 12 months is too long, a Reagan Administration official said.

American officials have stressed that the terms of the withdrawal must be acceptable to Washington before the entire package, including a cutoff of assistance to the Afghan guerrillas, can take effect. The Administration wants approval from the guerrillas before agreeing to a timetable, the official said.

Another question the Administration wants negotiated, officials said, is a cease-fire during the withdrawal.

* * *

April 9, 1988

ACCORD COMPLETED ON SOVIET PULLOUT

By PAUL LEWIS
Special to The New York Times.

GENEVA, April 8—Full agreement has been reached on a treaty under which the Soviet Union will withdraw its 115,000 soldiers from Afghanistan, the United Nations mediator announced today.

After nearly six years of negotiation, an accord was achieved on a four-part treaty that also provides for the safe return of Afghan refugees and the creation of a neutral and nonaligned Afghan state guaranteed by the United States and the Soviet Union.

In addition, Pakistan and Afghanistan promise to cease all interference in each other's internal affairs. A small United Nations military observer team will be sent to Afghanistan to monitor compliance with the treaty, which is to be signed next week.

"The documents are now finalized and open for signature," the mediator, Under Secretary General Diego Cordovez, said at a news conference here. Officially, the treaty will be signed by Afghanistan and Pakistan, which represents the Afghan insurgents. But, in addition, the United States and the Soviet Union will sign the document as "guarantors."

Shultz to Attend Ceremony

Reports from Washington said that Secretary of State George P. Shultz and the Soviet Foreign Minister, Eduard A. Shevardnadze, would probably attend the official signing ceremony later next week, along with the United Nations Secretary General, Javier Perez de Cuellar.

The agreement today between Afghanistan and Pakistan is meant to end a civil war that has cost at least one million Afghan lives and left five million homeless.

But both the United States and the Soviet Union, which arm most of the opposing forces in the civil war, have reserved the right to supply their allies with military assistance if the other side does so.

The United States-sponsored pact on the Soviet withdrawal from Afghanistan is a historic development, diplomats here say, because it is the first time Moscow has voluntarily abandoned territory conquered by its army since it withdrew from Austria after World War II in 1955.

Significantly, Moscow plans to start pulling out its troops May 15, the 33d anniversary of its withdrawal from Austria. Like Afghanistan, Austria agreed to become a neutral country in return.

To Wind Up in 9 Months

The withdrawal is to be completed in nine months with half the Soviet soldiers leaving during the first three months.

Radio Moscow carried a brief report today on a speech by Mikhail S. Gorbachev to party leaders in Tashkent, the Soviet Central Asian city where he met Thursday with President Najibullah of Afghanistan. The radio quoted Mr. Gorbachev as saying that the Afghan accord "should not be regarded as a sort of present to President Reagan on the eve of his visit to the U.S.S.R." and that the Soviet Union was "carrying out the plan outlined in our statement in February."

Reuters

Under Secretary General Diego Cordovez of the United Nations in Geneva yesterday as he announced agreement on Afghanistan.

As the agreement was announced in Geneva, all parties to it also issued a strong appeal to the warring factions in Afghanistan to bury their differences and form a broad-based government of national reconciliation.

The appeal, read by Mr. Cordovez, calls on "all elements of the Afghan nation, living inside and outside Afghanistan, to respond to this historic opportunity."

Help Is Promised

The parties further pledge they will do their best to help the Afghan people settle their internal differences in this way. "All concerned will therefore promote the endeavors of the Afghan people to work out arrangements for a broad-based government and will support and facilitate that process," the statement said.

This appeal for national reconciliation, diplomats pointed out, is intended to prevent the accord from merely opening a new phase in Afghanistan's long and bloody civil war, with the heavily armed insurgents intensifying attacks on the Communist central Government, which has been weakened by the progressive withdrawal of the Soviet troops fighting on its side.

The possibility that the agreement will do nothing to end carnage and suffering has been worrying negotiators. It is particularly upsetting for the United Nations, officials say, which is dedicated to advancing the cause of peace.

Leaders of the loose seven-party guerrilla alliance based in Peshawar, Pakistan, have consistently criticized the United

Nation's mediation efforts and many say they will refuse any compromise with the Communist Government in Kabul, pledging to overthrow it by force if necessary.

Moderates Favor Reconciliation

On the other hand, more moderate opposition groups, including those loyal to the exiled King of Afghanistan, Mohammad Zahir Shah, say they favor political reconciliation and the setting up of a new coalition government that could include Communist representatives.

In New York, Secretary General Perez de Cuellar also issued an indirect appeal to the two superpowers to cease supplying military equipment to their allies in Afghanistan and to strive to end the fighting. He asked all countries to refrain from actions "inconsistent with the spirit of the agreement."

In his news conference, Mr. Cordovez said, "The agreement has been negotiated in good faith and signed in good faith and I am convinced that all will exercise restraint in taking any action at variance with the letter and spirit of this agreement."

The United States and the Soviet Union have already told Mr. Cordovez and the Secretary General informally that they hope to arrange an informal agreement under which each side would cease supplying its ally with arms unless the other starts resupplying again, according to diplomats and United Nations officials here.

Sending Arms in Huge Quantities

But both superpowers have been rushing huge quantities of arms in recent months to beat the cutoff agreement. As a result, Kabul and the guerrillas are believed by officials here to have enough war materiel to carry on fighting for at least another year.

The Reagan Administration is said by these officials to have supplied the Pakistan Army with about $300 million worth of new arms which are to be passed on to the guerrillas as needed. The Soviet Union is reported to have sent over 1,000 truckloads of weaponry to Kabul in recent weeks.

Originally, Pakistan sought to bring the Afghan civil war to a swift conclusion by linking an agreement on Soviet withdrawal with the creation of a broad-based coalition government that would take over power in Kabul. It argued that without such an internal political settlement, the withdrawal agreement could lead to an intensified civil war inside Afghanistan that would delay the return of the Afghan refugees it is sheltering.

But in recent weeks Pakistan modified its demand, in part under American pressure, diplomats here say.

* * *

May 30, 1988

REAGAN AND GORBACHEV BEGIN SUMMIT PARLEY IN THE KREMLIN; 'STRIKE SPARKS' ON RIGHTS ISSUE

By STEVEN V. ROBERTS

Special to The New York Times.

MOSCOW, May 29—Opening his first visit to the Soviet Union, President Reagan quickly engaged Mikhail S. Gorbachev today in a heated discussion on human rights.

Mr. Reagan became the first American President to visit the Soviet capital since Richard M. Nixon came here 14 years ago to sign accords on nuclear testing and economic cooperation. He arrived on a bright spring day, and a pleasant breeze rippled the Soviet and American flags flying over Vnukovo Airport outside the city.

Mr. Gorbachev welcomed the President in a formal ceremony at St. George's Hall, an ornate ceremonial chamber in the Kremlin. The ceremony was filled with mutual praise and good cheer.

No Longer Polite

But when the two leaders then held the first of four scheduled private meetings, their strongly felt and divergent views on human rights broke the buoyant mood.

Howard H. Baker Jr., the White House chief of staff, said the two leaders could not be called "great pals" and added: "They strike sparks off each other pretty well, and did today."

The discussion today ranged over such issues as freedom of religion and the right to emigrate, and Soviet officials said, Mr. Gorbachev was irritated not so much at the specific points raised as by Mr. Reagan's insistence on discussing the issues at all.

Soviet Rejects Unsolicited Advice

Gennadi I. Gerasimov, the Soviet Foreign Ministry spokesman, accused Mr. Reagan of not understanding the improvement made in human rights policy here, and of trying to lecture the Soviet people about their failings.

"We don't like it when someone from outside is teaching us how to live, and this is only natural," he said at a briefing for reporters.

Disputes over human rights have punctuated the three previous meetings between the American and Soviet leaders, and as Mr. Gerasimov indicated, the Soviet Union is sensitive about what it considers intrusions into its internal affairs.

Today marked a remarkable moment in Mr. Reagan's Presidency. The tension over human rights illustrated the President's determination to use his four days here to reach out to the Soviet people and encourage changes taking place in Soviet life.

A Break for Gorbachev

The day was also a milestone for Mr. Gorbachev, who has made improved relations with the West a hallmark of his tenure.

Reuters

President Reagan and Mikhail S. Gorbachev as they met yesterday at the Kremlin in Moscow.

Reuters

Soviet security officers holding back a crowd trying to get close to President and Mrs. Reagan as they walked down the Arbat pedestrian mall.

But the visit was something of a diversion for Mr. Gorbachev, who is preoccupied with preparations for a Communist Party Congress next month that he hopes will ratify his sweeping proposals for political and economic change.

Soviet officials seemed uncertain and rather uneasy about the potential effect of Mr. Reagan's visit, and his discussion of Western ideals, on those who might see and hear him over the next four days. There was little advance publicity in the Soviet press, with only a brief official biography of the President appearing this morning on the front page of Pravda, the Communist Party newspaper.

Nevertheless, Soviet television provided more than an hour of live coverage today, from Mr. Reagan's arrival at the airport until he and Mr. Gorbachev began their private discussions at the Kremlin. It was the first time since Mr. Gorbachev came to power that there had been live coverage of a foreign leader's visit, although Soviet television did carry considerable live coverage of Mr. Gorbachev's visit to Washington in December.

A major part of the White House strategy for this summit meeting has been to place Mr. Reagan in colorful settings with Soviet citizens, and project television pictures around the world that show him talking to ordinary people.

Early this evening, the apparent Soviet uneasiness came to the surface when Mr. Reagan and his wife, Nancy, took a stroll on the Arbat, a popular shopping and meeting place near their quarters at Spaso House, the United States Ambassador's residence.

As the Reagans plunged into the enthusiastic crowd of Muscovites on a Sunday outing, a pushing match developed between Soviet security agents and American reporters and photographers trying to capture the event.

The President's visit began when Air Force One touched down at 2 P.M. (6 A.M., Eastern time), and the Reagans were greeted by a small group of Soviet officials headed by President Andrei A. Gromyko, the longtime Soviet Foreign Minister. Also present were Foreign Minister Eduard A. Shevardnadze and Anatoly F. Dobrynin, who was the dean of Washington's diplomatic corps until he was appointed the Central Committee's top official in charge of foreign affairs in 1986.

Greetings of a Casual Sort

About 100 members of the United States Embassy staff and their families, including many children in T-shirts and jeans, waved small American flags in greeting as the Reagans walked hand in hand down the ramp of the plane.

No ordinary Soviet citizens were allowed onto the airport grounds for the arrival, but military bands and drill teams performed for the President. Sunlight sparkled off the tubas and cymbals as the bands played the national anthems of the two countries, and the resounding thump of the marching units echoed in unison as they paraded past Mr. Reagan.

After a 30-minute trip into the city by a White House limousine—the President's own car had been flown here ahead of him—the two leaders met ceremonially in St. George's Hall.

It was a telling scene for the President, who has referred to the Soviet Union as an "evil empire" and built his political career as a hard-line anti-Communist.

For all the tensions produced by the rivalry between the two leaders, they stressed the positive, speaking of cordiality and cooperation.

In his opening remarks, Mr. Gorbachev seemed to be referring to the political history of his American guest when he said: "As this is our fourth meeting, we can already make some meaningful assessments. As we see it, long-held dislikes have been weakened; habitual stereotypes stemming from enemy images have been shaken loose."

After detailing the improved relationship between the two leaders, Mr. Gorbachev struck a cautionary note, saying: "But even more complex and important tasks lie ahead. And so, Mr. President, you and I still have a lot of work to do. And it is good when there is a lot of work to be done and people need that work."

In his remarks, Mr. Reagan echoed Mr. Gorbachev's call for hard work, saying, "I think the message is clear—despite clear and fundamental differences, and despite the inevitable frustrations that we have encountered, our work has begun to produce results."

Comfortable in 'Evil Empire'

When reporters asked the President how he felt being in the "evil empire," he replied, "Just fine."

But once the two leaders began their substantive private meeting in St. Catherine's Hall at the Kremlin, tensions began to emerge.

Mr. Reagan pressed the human rights issue and handed the Soviet leader a list of 14 cases he wanted to see resolved. They ranged, according to a White House official, from families seeking to emigrate to political prisoners.

Marlin Fitzwater, the President's spokesman, said Mr. Reagan felt human rights had "pride of place" on the summit agenda for two reasons: Americans place a high value on that issue, and many Americans who trace their roots to Eastern Europe are pressuring the Administration to raise the issue during the summit talks.

This argument struck sparks, as Mr. Baker put it. Mr. Gorbachev tried to deflect the President's criticism by pointing out that human rights was a "two-way street," according to his spokesman, who said the issue was not served well by a "sensational element and propaganda spirit."

The Russians have recently started giving Americans lists of their own regarding human rights cases in the United States, according to an American diplomat. And while Mr. Gorbachev apparently did not present such a list today, Mr. Gerasimov pointed out that a group of American Indians had arrived in Moscow and will hold a news conference Monday to dramatize their complaints against the American Government.

Mr. Reagan, the Soviet spokesman suggested, "does not have a concrete idea, an understanding of where the human rights issue stands within the Soviet Union." Accordingly, the spokesman said, Mr. Gorbachev proposed establishing a "regular seminar" on human rights issues between the two countries, perhaps at the parliamentary level.

Arms Talks in Other Forums

The President "responded that he would consider it," Mr. Fitzwater said.

While human rights dominated the top-level discussion today, working groups among top officials were established to discuss arms control and other issues, and met late into the evening.

One discussion is on regional conflicts, and Mr. Gerasimov repeated Soviet criticisms of Pakistan for continuing to aid rebels fighting the Soviet-installed Government of Afghanistan.

The Geneva accords that led to the withdrawal of Soviet troops from that country banned such help, according to the Soviet official. But Mr. Fitzwater said that the United States would continue to aid the rebels as long as the Russians helped Kabul.

As often happens at summit meetings, Soviet and American officials with common interests meet each other outside the framework of formal talks. One such meeting today took place between Secretary of Defense Frank C. Carlucci, and Gen. Dmitri T. Yazov, his Soviet counterpart.

In an interview on the the Cable News Network program "Newsmaker Sunday," Mr. Carlucci said that while "clearly there's a debate going on" in the Soviet Union about reducing the country's commitment to an offensive military force, the United States has yet to see practical effects of that changing doctrine.

The second face-to-face meeting on Monday morning between Mr. Reagan and Mr. Gorbachev will go on to other issues, including arms control, but human rights is again expected to dominate the day. At midday, Mr. Reagan will visit a monastery outside Moscow to dramatize his interest in religious freedom, and later in the afternoon, he will talk with political dissidents at Spaso House. The Russians have been irritated about that meeting.

In an interview on the NBC News program "Meet the Press," Mr. Baker looked forward to the rest of the summit conference this way: "Based on what we've seen so far, they're going to be tumultuous conversations, they're going to be energetic conversations, and I don't know what else will come out of it."

* * *

June 2, 1988

GORBACHEV CRITICIZES REAGAN, SEEING 'MISSED OPPORTUNITIES,' BUT CALLS VISIT A 'MAJOR EVENT'; SUMMIT TALKS END

By PHILIP TAUBMAN
Special to The New York Times.

MOSCOW, June 1—Mikhail S. Gorbachev complained today that his fourth and probably final summit meeting with President Reagan was filled with "missed opportunities" and impeded by contradictions in American policy.

But in a concluding two-hour news conference he balanced his criticism of Mr. Reagan by calling the President's visit to Moscow this week a "major event" that moved relations "maybe one rung or two up the ladder."

In a joint statement that recorded modest progress on a number of issues, the two sides expressed hope that the dialogue established by Mr. Reagan and Mr. Gorbachev in their four summit meetings since 1985 would endure, despite "real differences of history, tradition and ideology."

A President Proselytizing

This week's talks, which officially end Thursday morning with Mr. Reagan's departure for London, seem likely to be remembered less for any particular achievements than the symbolic spectacle of an American President in the Soviet capital proselytizing for change and expanded liberties.

After the tentative nature of the Geneva summit meeting in 1985, the volatility in Reykjavik, Iceland, in 1986, and the substantive accomplishments in Washington last December, the Moscow summit meeting seems to reflect a sense that the two men have all but exhausted the potential for advancing relations in the waning months of the Reagan Administration.

In separate news conferences, the two leaders said they were pleased with the gains recorded this week, but Mr. Gorbachev devoted a good portion of his remarks to criticism of Mr. Reagan, suggesting considerable frustration and irritation with the President.

Annoyance on Human Rights

Mr. Gorbachev's exasperation seemed to stem less from an absence of progress on central arms-control issues—the chance for that had never appeared great—than from Mr. Reagan's concentration on human rights issues and the President's refusal to endorse the general guidelines for Soviet-American relations proposed by the Soviet leader. The general guidelines included in the final joint statement were written by the Americans.

The Soviet leader also accused the American negotiators of trying to dodge issues on conventional arms, and he complained about unfavorable trade treatment.

Although he did not say as much, Mr. Gorbachev left the impression in his news conference that he had lost patience with Mr. Reagan and was ready to turn his attention to the President who will take office in January.

Nevertheless, the Gorbachevs and the Reagans seemed in good humor as they attended a special performance of seven dances by the Bolshoi Ballet. They sat in the royal box in the neo-classical, 19th-century Bolshoi Theater. They then drove to an official guest residence in the northwestern outskirts of Moscow for a private supper.

After supper, the Reagans returned downtown, stopping for a brief stroll around flood-lit Red Square shortly before midnight. "We're leaving tomorrow and I didn't want Nancy to miss it," Mr. Reagan said as they stood below the multicolored onion domes of St. Basil's Cathedral.

Earlier in the day, Mrs. Reagan and Raisa Gorbachev had inspected an exhibition of prized Russian icons at the Tretyakov Gallery.

At his news conference, Mr. Gorbachev seemed particularly irritated by Mr. Reagan's backtracking on including in the communiqué a proposed statement of principles for the management of Soviet-American relations.

The proposal included the traditional Soviet call for the renunciation of military force to settle disputes and praise for "peaceful coexistence." The phrase of Lenin's was widely used by Nikita S. Khrushchev and Leonid I. Brezhnev, former Soviet leaders, and is anathema to American conservatives.

Treaty Documents Exchanged

Mr. Gorbachev said Mr. Reagan tentatively endorsed the proposed statement on Sunday when the Soviet leader presented it to him, but rejected it this morning on the advice of his advisers. One American aide basically confirmed Mr. Gorbachev's account and said that Mr. Gorbachev was incensed at Mr. Reagan's apparent change of heart.

Mr. Gorbachev vented his anger just before the two men met in St. Vladimir's Hall in the Kremlin for a public exchange of documents that put into effect the treaty eliminating Soviet and American medium- and shorter-range land-based missiles.

Reporting that the two leaders argued intensely about the joint statement in their final meeting this morning, Mr. Gorbachev said, "I believe Mr. Reagan missed an important chance to take a step forward."

The President seemed to go out of his way not to criticize Mr. Gorbachev an hour later at his news conference in Spaso House, the American Ambassador's residence. He and the Soviet leader had accomplished "a good deal of important work," Mr. Reagan said.

He acknowledged that he had "liked the whole tone" of the five principles, but insisted that he had told Mr. Gorbachev last Sunday that he would have to let his advisers look them over.

The President said there were "certain ambiguities" that required that the American side rewrite the principles. It was the American version that was included in the statement issued today.

Mr. Reagan, who on Tuesday said he no longer thought the Soviet Union was "an evil empire," added today, "I think there is quite a difference today in the leadership and the relationship between our two countries."

'Propaganda Gambits'

The Soviet press has almost gleefully reported Mr. Reagan's retraction of the "evil empire" description.

During his news conference, at the Foreign Ministry press center, Mr. Gorbachev also sharply chastised Mr. Reagan for his treatment of Soviet human rights policies, saying the President's visit included "propaganda gambits and all sorts of spectacles and shows."

"I'm not filled with admiration for this part of the visit," Mr. Gorbachev said.

The comment was an apparent reference to Mr. Reagan's meeting on Monday with a group of dissidents, and his emphasis on human rights questions during the first two days of the visit.

Mr. Gorbachev also sharply criticized Pakistan, and by extension the United States, for continuing to aid Afghan guerrillas during the withdrawal of Soviet forces from Afghanistan. The Soviet leader warned that the assistance could lead to Soviet retaliation and could undermine the chances for resolving other regional conflicts.

The back-to-back news conferences offered a contrast in leadership styles, with Mr. Gorbachev plunging into policy details and repeatedly stabbing the air with a finger for emphasis.

'Common Ground' on Namibia

He was flanked by senior aides, including Foreign Minister Eduard A. Shevardnadze and Defense Minister Dmitri T. Yazov.

Mr. Reagan was more subdued and appeared to be uncomfortable with the discussion of specific issues, preferring instead to keep his remarks general and anecdotal.

One American official said that the two sides had found "important common ground on some aspects of the search for a Namibia-Angola settlement."

The official said Chester A. Crocker, Assistant Secretary of State for Africa, and Anatoly Adamishin, a Deputy Foreign Minister, had set Sept. 29 as the target date for resolving outstanding differences on a settlement that would lead to the withdrawal of Cuban troops from Angola, which is supported by Moscow, and independence for South-West Africa, the disputed territory also known as Namibia, now ruled by South Africa.

The New York Times erred in reporting today that Moscow and Washington had agreed in principle that Cuban troops should be withdrawn from Angola in the next 12 months and that South Africa, in turn, should relinquish control of South-West Africa.

Progress on Missiles

On arms control, the joint statement reported progress on verification of land-based mobile missiles and air-launched cruise missiles, though the two sides did not resolve all of their differences over these two weapons. They made no headway on limits on testing space-based defense systems and limits on sea-launched cruise missiles.

Although both leaders said they hoped a treaty to reduce strategic, or intercontinental, nuclear weapons could still be completed before Mr. Reagan leaves office, the prospects seemed remote. Mr. Gorbachev said a fifth summit meeting with Mr. Reagan was unlikely unless they were to get together to sign such a treaty.

On conventional arms, the two sides made no progress, an American official said. Mr. Gorbachev asserted at his news conference that the two sides were agreed on the basic principles for initiating new talks on reducing conventional arms. But a senior American official said that this was not true.

* * *

June 17, 1988

SECRET SOVIET PARTY DOCUMENT SAID TO ADMIT AFGHAN ERRORS

By BILL KELLER

Special to The New York Times.

MOSCOW, June 16—The leadership of the Soviet Communist Party has issued a secret circular admitting a series of errors and misjudgments leading to the Soviet military move into Afghanistan, according to people familiar with the document.

The circular, which was read aloud to party members, strongly implies but does not state explicitly that the original decision to send Soviet troops was wrong, people who discussed it say.

Although some Soviet journalists have argued that the 1979 decision to introduce troops was a mistake, Soviet officials have continued to defend the move in public.

Fundamental Errors

The document reportedly sides with critics who say the Soviet leadership erred fundamentally in believing that a tribal, Islamic country like Afghanistan was ready to make the transition to socialism.

Some who have been present at readings of the document said they were disappointed with its cautious tone and contents, including the failure to blame Soviet decision makers by name.

But others said the shift in the party line was important as a signal to Soviet journalists and political analysts to begin a deeper and more critical examination of the war.

In a commentary Wednesday in the Government newspaper Izvestia, Aleksandr Bovin, a prominent political writer, stated bluntly that the introduction of troops into Afghanistan reflected an excessive tendency to use military force in Soviet foreign policy.

Mr. Bovin also criticized the Soviet decision to deploy SS-20 missiles in Europe—missiles that are soon to be destroyed under an arms agreement with the United States.

"The deployment of SS-20 missiles and the introduction of troops into Afghanistan were, in my opinion, typical examples of subjective decisions oriented at the use of military force in foreign policy," he wrote. "In both cases we clearly overestimated our possibilities and underestimated what could be called the resistance of the environment."

Fyodor Burlatsky, a well-connected writer for Literaturnaya Gazeta, made similar comments about Afghanistan on Monday in a televised round-table discussion of current affairs.

Soviet scholars, in meetings with Western visitors, have recently begun freely describing the Afghanistan invasion as a mistake carried out by a narrow circle in the Politburo headed by Leonid I. Brezhnev, the Soviet leader who died in November 1982.

At least one leading Soviet publication is known to be preparing a more extensive and authoritative critique of the war, including the first criticism of the current Soviet-backed Afghan leader, President Najibullah.

"We are about to see a breakthrough in the political analysis of the war," a journalist said.

Public portrayal of the war as a mistake remains an extremely sensitive subject. Soviet officials say they are worried about offending the feelings of veterans and families of those who died in the war by abruptly declaring that they died in a misguided cause.

To Prevent Mistakes

Moreover, some Soviet officials presumably involved in the decision are still in prominent positions, most notably Andrei A. Gromyko, the longtime Foreign Minister who is now President.

Some Soviet journalists say a freer discussion of the subject is necessary both to prevent mistakes and to begin preparing the public for the possibility that the Soviet-backed regime in Kabul may be defeated by Moslem insurgents.

On May 15, Moscow began withdrawing the first of an estimated 115,000 Soviet troops from Afghanistan under an agreement worked out in Geneva. The withdrawal is to be completed within nine months. Soviet officials have since said that more than 13,000 troops have been killed and more than 35,000 wounded fighting the insurgents.

The new party line has been described to party members in the so-called propaganda sector, including newspapers, magazines and some academic institutes. Beginning about two weeks ago, they have been summoned to closed meetings at their workplaces to listen to a reading of the document, which is intended as a general guideline for publications on the subject.

Party members interviewed this week declined to provide details of the circular or to be identified by name, saying they had been warned of disciplinary action for violating secrecy.

Praise for Najibullah

They said the main point of the document was that Soviet leaders in 1979 had made their decision without fully understanding Afghanistan.

The new party line does not go nearly as far as some Soviet analysts would like, however. The document reportedly does not admit that the Soviet Union played a role in the coup that deposed the Afghan leader Hafizullah Amin in December 1979, setting off the crisis that the Soviet Union said it was seeking to end by sending in troops.

The document is said to have nothing but praise for Najibullah, the Afghan leader since 1986, although some Soviet experts on Afghanistan fault him for alienating the Moslem population and mismanaging the economy.

It also reportedly includes no criticism of the Soviet military for what some analysts here say was inadequate preparation for the war.

* * *

November 6, 1988

IN SEARCH OF THE GRAND COMPROMISE

By LAWRENCE FREEDMAN

THE MASTER OF THE GAME: Paul Nitze and the Nuclear Peace.
By Strobe Talbott
416 pp. New York: Alfred A. Knopf. $19.95.

Not long before the 1984 Presidential election, Strobe Talbott's "Deadly Gambits: The Reagan Administration and the Stalemate in Nuclear Arms Control" described in vivid detail the struggle within the Government to forge an arms control policy during President Reagan's first term. In "The Master of the Game," a sequel to "Deadly Gambits" and to "Endgame: The Inside Story of SALT II," Mr. Talbott, a senior correspondent for Time magazine, demonstrates his own mastery of bureaucratic drama, combining a gift for characterization and an eye for the revealing anecdote with a firm grasp of his subject. His sources are enviable, allowing him to offer an instant history that rings true throughout. For later historians of the President's Strategic Defense Initiative and the remarkable Reagan-Gorbachev summits, this will be a standard text.

"Deadly Gambits" conveyed a keen sense of what came to be described euphemistically during the Iran-contra affair as the President's "managerial style." The policy-making process had become a bureaucratic battle for the opportunity to play on the President's prejudices. With nobody at the Cabinet level proficient in the admittedly arcane details of arms control, the struggle was largely conducted by middle-ranking officials in the State Department and the Pentagon—between those who thought the Administration should try seriously to make a deal with the Soviet Union, even if that meant a degree of compromise, and those who engaged in arms control largely to legitimize a program of strategic rearmament and for whom about the worst thing one could say about an American proposal was that it was negotiable.

By 1984 the hawks had won the day, aided by a tired and petulant Soviet leadership. When in late 1983 the Kremlin had to come to terms with its failure to prevent the entry of cruise and Pershing missiles into Europe, it responded by walking out of the Geneva arms control negotiations. This did President Reagan a great favor; the lack of a superpower dialogue was not his responsibility but that of the ailing Konstantin U. Chernenko.

If the Soviet walkout and the consequent lessening of pressure on President Reagan to come up with an arms control agreement reduced the immediate political impact of "Deadly Gambits," the narrative still provided a disturbing portrait of a flawed policy-making process, although whether the flaw was "fatal" (as American political rhetoric requires all flaws to be) was a question left open for the President's return to office and the Russians' return to the negotiating table.

The cast of characters for the arms control drama in President Reagan's second term was similar to that in the first. Of the two Richards—Richard Burt of the State Department and Richard Perle of the Pentagon—who took starring roles in "Deadly Gambits," Mr. Burt moved to the periphery as Ambassador to Bonn, while Mr. Perle sustained his artful obstructionism until the retirement of his patron (Secretary of Defense Caspar Weinberger), together with the progress made possible by Mikhail S. Gorbachev's new and much more imaginative Soviet leadership, limited Mr. Perle's influence and he left the Government. The President continued to work his way through a stream of national security advisers, which means that "The Master of the Game" provides an interesting case study of the extent to which the attributes of the national security adviser can make a decisive difference in making nuclear policy.

Present throughout has been Paul Nitze as the supporting lead, admirably suited for the part of elder statesman. Mr. Nitze was in at the start of the nuclear age and has influenced its course ever since, in and out of the Government. His ideological credentials as a cold warrior are impeccable, yet his preferred battleground is the negotiating table. He takes superpower diplomacy seriously, which makes him something of an oddity in the Reagan Administration, and he derives satisfaction from its skillful practice. As chief negotiator in the intermediate nuclear forces (I.N.F.) talks, he went farther to achieve a deal than anyone else would have dared, using his reputation as protection from the inevitable backlash in Washington.

As the frustrations of President Reagan's first term gave way to the heady negotiations of the second, culminating in the 1987 Washington summit, Mr. Nitze remained in the thick of things, playing a creative and influential advisory role. Now in his early 80's, he is the great survivor—a symbol of continuity with the debates of the past and a driving force in shaping the debates of today.

Mr. Talbott has made Mr. Nitze the hero of this new book—the "master of the game" of the title—just as a character in a situation comedy who has demonstrated popular appeal in one series is then allowed to star in his own. To make this possible, the author uses flashbacks to establish Mr. Nitze's character firmly and explain his past before making him the central figure in the analysis of the development of arms control during President Reagan's second term.

Mr. Talbott's biography of Mr. Nitze provides a valuable potted history of the nuclear age. We start with American leaders' early appreciations of the atomic bomb, views that Mr. Nitze helped to shape through his participation in the official survey of the impact of strategic bombing, including the destruction of Hiroshima and Nagasaki. Then the cold war begins: in 1950 the sense of imminent confrontation is underlined in a historic policy document, drafted by Mr. Nitze at the State Department, that described the Soviet threat in stark terms.

From the cold war we move to the arms race and the fear that the Soviet Union was about to steal a lead. This outlook was reinforced by the Gaither Committee's 1957 report, drafted in part by Mr. Nitze, which concluded that American nuclear deterrence and the country's survival were in jeopardy. In the short term, it was the United States that surged ahead, strengthening its position during the crises of the early 1960's over Berlin and Cuba. In these Mr. Nitze took a hawkish position, although he resisted the suggestion that America might choose to make a pre-emptive nuclear first strike.

His role in the Government continued through Democratic and Republican Administrations. As strategic arms limitations talks were first mooted and then got underway, Mr. Nitze emerged as a key member of the team that negotiated the first strategic arms agreements in 1972. In 1974, alarmed at the weakness in the American bargaining position that resulted from Watergate, he resigned and became a severe critic of the process he had helped to shape. Having alienated President Carter, he remained out of the Government and gained his revenge through his successful efforts to sink the 1979 SALT II treaty as a leading light of the Committee on the Present Danger. This gave him the political credentials for a job with Ronald Reagan.

Despite Mr. Nitze's closeness to center stage for over 40 years, he never obtained the level of seniority in government he felt, with some justice, that his experience warranted. His intense involvement in the issues made him enemies and made his potential patrons nervous. This intensity was partly the result of a conviction developed early on that details mattered, that great political events could turn on the nuances of the military balance. Over a number of decades, he has been preoccupied with the threat posed by Soviet intercontinental ballistic missiles and has sought policies that could counter it.

The second half of "The Master of the Game" is the story of Mr. Nitze's attempt to use arms control to reduce this threat during President Reagan's second term. Mr. Talbott sees at the heart of the attempt the so-called grand compromise—essentially a trade of restrictions on S.D.I. for deep cuts in Soviet offensive arms and, in particular, for reductions in their specialty of heavy ICBM's, which carry large nuclear loads. Mr. Nitze had spent the Ford and Carter years offering gloomy analyses of the terrible ways in which the Soviet Union might one day exploit its advantage in this category of missilery.

The grandeur of the compromise derived largely from what it would require of the President. S.D.I. was his pet project. He insisted on describing it in utopian terms, was happy to be convinced by his acolytes that such descriptions were in the realm of the possible and expected S.D.I. to be protected from arms control. Indeed, he saw S.D.I. as the foundation of a new, cooperative, safer relationship with the Soviet Union.

With the Reagan Administration now drawing to a close, the grand compromise is not yet in place, but remarkable progress has been made on a strategic arms reduction treaty, so that the next Administration should be able to complete one reasonably quickly. S.D.I. no longer seems to be so much of a stumbling block. Mr. Talbott assigns to Mr. Nitze much of the credit for this state of affairs and thus declares him in the closing sentence of the book more than the master of the game, but "also a victor."

While Mr. Nitze has undoubtedly been of great importance in the drive for a radical strategic arms reduction treaty, it is by no means clear that this is being achieved through a grand compromise. Offensive arms may decline through arms control, but S.D.I. will not. It has already declined through its inherent political, technical and financial limitations.

Once Mr. Gorbachev realized this (and that the major factor working in favor of S.D.I. within the United States was his own hostility), S.D.I. became less important in the overall scheme of things. But Mr. Nitze helped to complicate matters by lending support to the so-called broad interpretation of the 1972 Antiballistic Missile Treaty. The orthodox, or narrow, interpretation inhibits S.D.I. by preventing serious development and testing of defensive missiles. Since Mr. Nitze helped negotiate the treaty's relevant clauses in the early 70's and had previously assumed that the narrow interpretation was correct, his conversion gave authority to what turned out to be a dubious and unconvincing proposition.

Unlike other supporters of the broad interpretation, who were largely content to use it as an argument for going full steam ahead with S.D.I., Mr. Nitze saw the broad interpretation as creating an ambiguity that had to be clarified for the grand compromise to work. The clarification could come, he suggested, with new treaty language that would distinguish, in technical detail, between permissible and prohibited developments. He failed to convince even his natural allies, such as Secretary of State George Shultz, of the wisdom and feasibility of this approach. If the broad interpretation had never been broached, S.D.I. would simply have been restricted by the 1972 treaty; now there is a lingering ambiguity, made worse by the growing recognition that the Soviet Union might be better placed to exploit it.

Apart from the fact that Mr. Talbott's conclusions do not quite tie the knot as neatly as he suggests, my other complaint with this book is the minimal space devoted to the arms control achievement of the Reagan Administration—the signing and ratification of the I.N.F. treaty that eliminates American and Russian intermediate range nuclear missiles. I was looking forward to the inside story on this remarkable agreement, yet I.N.F. appears almost as a side issue with barely a passing mention of the intense debates it occasioned within NATO on the future of deterrence.

Perhaps because Mr. Talbott is so fascinated by the struggle to influence policy in Washington he pays insufficient attention to the wider strategic environment. He therefore states that the almost unwitting legacy of the Reagan Administration has been to restore "the strange safety of mutual deterrence" as a means of keeping the nuclear peace. This view underestimates the lasting impact of the critique of mutual deterrence encouraged by the Administration; if the author's proposition is true, it is only because the Administration failed in a number of attempts to establish a convincing alternative.

Finessing The President

Between 1983 and 1988, the nation and the world watched the spectacle of a President who confused nostrums with policies and dreams with strategy. The drama was played out between him and members of his government, many of whom felt compelled to feign enthusiasm for an idea they considered extremely dubious. In the face of Reagan's stubborn attachment to S.D.I., his Administration became the scene of one of the most extraordinary episodes in the annals of American defense policy and diplomacy.

It was a bizarre instance of covert action carried out almost entirely within the executive branch. . . . Those conducting the clandestine activity were advisors to the President. Their target was the President himself. True to the spirit of covert operations, there was a large element of deception and dissembling in this struggle. . . .

This deception was deemed necessary largely because the President had his own objective in S.D.I., and it was compatible with neither of the competing ones that his advisors were trying, covertly, to impose on him. Ronald Reagan continued to believe very much in the original vision of March 1983: population defense so comprehensive and so close to being impregnable that the Soviet Union would have no choice but to cooperate in a transition to a new order in which defense would be the dominant, and eventually the sole, basis of Western security.

That was the President's sincere hope for S.D.I. Almost no one in his immediate employ shared that hope. So the objective of the game within the Administration . . . was to finesse the longer-term implications of S.D.I. while at the same time manipulating the shorter-term impact of the program in such a way as either to advance arms control or to stop it in its tracks.

Lawrence Freedman is a professor of war studies at King's College, University of London.

* * *

December 4, 1988

GORBACHEV GETS A CHANCE TO SIZE UP THE NEW MAN

By R. W. APPLE JR.

WASHINGTON—It won't be a real summit conference, they're saying in Washington, more a get-together to mark the changing of the guard, when President Reagan and President-elect Bush meet Wednesday in New York City with Mikhail S. Gorbachev.

Summit conferences have formal agendas, White House and State Department spokesmen explain. They last several days. They include subsidiary meetings among experts who discuss a wide range of issues.

All true, some of the time, and all essentially irrelevant. There have been short summit meetings and long ones, formal ones and casual ones, substantive ones and symbolic ones, since such get-togethers began after World War II. Now as then, the only real requirement is the presence of the leaders of the United States and the Soviet Union.

This time, Mr. Bush will be the American whom Mr. Gorbachev must now size up, both at the formal luncheon on Governors Island in New York Harbor and at a possible tête-à-tête afterward.

Eager to play down expectations, both the White House and the Bush camp have been saying that this will not be a negotiating session on anything. An aide to the President-elect said last week, for example, that Mr. Bush would be unable to set out "our detailed arms control formulations" because they were not complete and would not be until further talks with the allies.

But everyone expects Mr. Bush and Mr. Gorbachev to discuss Afghanistan and changes in the Soviet Union and "Star Wars." And most of the American planners half expect some flamboyant gesture from the man who startled Washington a year ago with his stroll down Connecticut Avenue. A second Bush-Gorbachev meeting in New York is not entirely out of the question.

To the degree that personal chemistry matters in superpower relations—and all but the most determinist experts assign it some weight—the meeting affords an opportunity for a rare continuity in the dealings between the White House and the Kremlin. Mr. Bush is at least as eager as Mr. Gorbachev to see that the baton is passed smoothly.

Reagan's Journey

It is, of course, notoriously difficult to predict the course of Soviet-American relations.

Who could have guessed, in the early days of the Reagan Administration, in those days of "evil empire" and tensions among the allies, that Mr. Reagan would hold four increasingly happy summit meetings with Mr. Gorbachev? Or that the old conservative crusader would actually sign an arms-limitation treaty with the Soviet Union? Who, indeed, could have guessed at the start that someone remotely like Mr. Gorbachev would become leader of the Soviet Union?

Nonetheless each leader must make strategic calculations in an environment where little can be taken for granted.

Mr. Bush, as the natural heir to the Reagan Presidency, might be expected to press hard for further arms-control agreements. Indeed, there were hints during his campaign that he might be somewhat more flexible on "Star Wars," an impediment to such agreements, than Mr. Reagan has been. He has chosen as his national security adviser a retired Air Force general, Brent Scowcroft, who takes a flexible position on the space-based antimissile defense system but who has also argued, in effect, that the United States should seek further concessions from the Soviets (and perhaps greater defense contributions from Western Europe) before negotiating reductions in conventional forces and strategic arms. Mr. Scowcroft also favors the development of a mobile missile system such as the much-debated Midgetman.

At the same time, some moderate Democrats of the sort Mr. Bush would need to win ratification of any new treaty as well as Republicans say that the United States should not appear too eager to court Mr. Gorbachev.

The new Administration will be under pressure from its friends in business to relax economic restrictions. Many business executives say they are eager to broaden trade with Moscow before the Europeans and the Japanese make all the big deals.

The Afghanistan Pledge

As the two men meet, Mr. Bush surely must ask himself about Soviet intentions in Afghanistan. Will the Russians go through with their pledge to withdraw all of their troops? And whether they come up or not, questions about the Middle East, Africa and Central America will hang in the air. But Mr. Bush must ask bigger questions as well. How widely shared is the impulse toward change in the Soviet Union? To use Margaret Thatcher's language, has Mr. Gorbachev really brought the cold war to an end and smashed the Iron Curtain? Were his promises last week to share some of the powers he had been gathering for himself a genuine gesture to those who fear overcentralization or a cynical ploy a la Brezhnev? With ethnic minority groups from Estonia to Armenia increasingly restive, with the Soviet economy responding sluggishly to the campaign of restructuring, and with elements of the party's old guard resistant to change, the survival of Mr. Gorbachev is a topic for Mr. Bush to weigh carefully.

The President-elect seems, to those most familiar with his thinking, predisposed to give the Soviet leader the benefit of the doubt, at least at the outset. He did not publicly demur from the hard-line policies of the early Reagan years. But he has tended to see relations between the two countries in terms of competition between great powers and not between good and evil.

Mr. Bush also has to consider superpower relations in the context of larger questions about the American role in the world. Some experts like William G. Hyland, the editor of Foreign Affairs, argue that the United States needs a whole new policy. "The desire to concentrate on America's own problems, even at the expense of international obligations and commitments, seems justified by a new wave of relief that the worst of the cold war is in the past," he wrote in an article in the journal Foreign Policy. "The American people are thus psychologically prepared for a new relationship with the Soviet Union, even if they are not necessarily eager for it."

* * *

February 16, 1989

LAST SOVIET SOLDIERS LEAVE AFGHANISTAN AFTER 9 YEARS, 15,000 DEAD AND GREAT COST

By BILL KELLER

Special to The New York Times.

MOSCOW, Feb. 15—The last Soviet soldier came home from Afghanistan this morning, the Soviet Union announced, leaving behind a war that had become a domestic burden and an international embarrassment for Moscow.

The final Soviet departure came on the day set as a deadline by the Geneva accords last April. It left two heavily armed adversaries, the Kremlin-backed Government of President Najibullah and a fractious but powerful array of Muslim insurgents, backed by the United States and Pakistan, to conclude their civil war on their own.

Lieut. Gen. Boris V. Gromov, the commander of the Soviet forces in Afghanistan, walked across the steel Friendship Bridge to the border city of Termez, in Uzbekistan, at 11:55 A.M. local time (1:55 A.M., Eastern time), 9 years and 50 days after Soviet troops intervened to support a coup by a Marxist ally.

'Our Stay Ends'

"There is not a single Soviet soldier or officer left behind me," General Gromov told a Soviet television reporter waiting on the bridge. "Our nine-year stay ends with this."

Associated Press

Lieut. Gen. Boris V. Gromov, the last Soviet soldier to leave Afghanistan, as he was greeted on his return yesterday by his son, Maksim.

Today's final departure is the end of a steady process of withdrawal since last spring, when Moscow says, there were 100,300 Soviet troops in Afghanistan. At the height of the Soviet commitment, according to Western intelligence estimates, there were 115,000 troops deployed.

This morning, as the last armored troop carriers rumbled home across the border, a Soviet newspaper carried the first report of atrocities committed in the war by the nation's military forces.

Massacre and Cover-Up

The weekly Literaturnaya Gazeta described the killing of a carload of Afghan civilians, including women and children, and the order by a commander to cover it up.

The article was a foretaste of recriminations expected in the months ahead.

The war cost the Soviet Union roughly 15,000 lives and undisclosed billions of rubles. It scarred a generation of young people and undermined the cherished image of an invincible Soviet Army. Moscow's involvement in Afghanistan was often compared to the American experience in the Vietnam War, in which more than 58,000 Americans died.

The Soviet intervention, which received international condemnation, cast a pall over relations with China, the Muslim world and the West. It led to an American trade embargo and a Western boycott of the 1980 Olympic Games in Moscow.

Western reporters flown to Termez to witness the finale said the ceremony at the border was one of festive relief at the homecoming. Today, there were no obvious second thoughts expressed about the venture.

"The day that millions of Soviet people have waited for has come," General Gromov said to an army rally in Termez, Reuters reported. "In spite of our sacrifices and losses, we have totally fulfilled our internationalist duty."

Token of Official Esteem

The official press agency Tass said the Defense Ministry presented all of the returning soldiers with wristwatches.

Yet in contrast with the joy at leaving Afghanistan, Soviet press reports told of insurgents massing outside Kabul, the Afghan capital, and other major cities, and of Afghan Army regulars deserting in droves. The reports seemed intended to brace the public for the possibility that defeat would follow retreat.

Vadim Perfilyev, a Soviet Foreign Ministry spokesman, described the situation in Kabul today as "relatively calm" but said the guerrillas continued to gather reinforcements around the main cities and along the highway to the Soviet Union.

Mr. Perfilyev said 160 trucks bearing food and fuel reached Kabul safely on Tuesday to relieve shortages in time for an expected siege. He added that aircraft were still ferrying supplies into airports at Kabul, Kandahar and Mazar-i-Sharif.

A Few Advisers and Guards

An estimated 250 Soviet civilians were believed to have stayed on at the Soviet Embassy in Kabul after the troops left. Mr. Perfilyev said he did know how many military advisers, "if any," were still in Afghanistan.

The official who negotiated the Geneva accords, Diego Cordovez of Ecuador, said at the United Nations today that he believed that fewer than 10 Soviet military advisers would remain in Afghanistan after the withdrawal, principally as embassy guards.

Western diplomats and Soviet journalists speculate that the guerrillas will attempt a quick victory, perhaps in the vulnerable eastern city of Jalalabad, to break the Government's morale. This would be accompanied by a slow-death blockade of Kabul.

But Soviet officials and some recent Western visitors say they believe that Mr. Najibullah's forces may prove sturdier than expected. They control vast arsenals of Soviet-supplied weapons, and are motivated by the fear of rebel reprisals if they lose.

A Government statement on the troop withdrawal said the responsibility for a blood bath in Afghanistan now would largely rest on the guerrillas' suppliers.

Onus for Further Conflict

"Whether the Afghan situation will develop along the lines of national accord and the creation of a broadly based coalition government," the statement said, "or along the lines of escalating war and tension in and around the country, depends to a large degree on those who have, over all these years, aided and abetted the armed opposition, supplying it with sophisticated weapons."

The Soviet Government renewed its appeal to Pakistan and the United States to join in a cutoff of military aid to the warring parties. The United States, which a year ago was pressing such an arrangement on the reluctant Soviets, now argues that it is too late.

The rebels insist that they will not take part in a coalition that retains Mr. Najibullah or his Communist political grouping, the People's Democratic Party of Afghanistan. But their own efforts to coalesce have faltered over issues of ideology and power sharing.

At home, the Soviet Government now faces a period of reckoning with the roots and consequences of the war.

In Pravda, the authoritative Communist Party newspaper, a commentator insisted today that the intervention was carried out with the best intentions—including maintaining the security of the Soviet Union's southern border. But he said that the war was characterized by the mistakes and misjudgments of previous leaders.

"One can question the Brezhnev leadership's assessment of the military threat," the commentary said. "One can say that in the future such vital issues as the use of troops must not be decided in secrecy, without the approval of the country's Parliament."

What Has Been Learned?

Other commentators, who have been constrained while Soviet soldiers were still fighting on Afghan territory, can now be expected to question more pointedly how the Soviet Union got into Afghanistan, what it did there, why it stayed so long and what lessons it has learned.

The account today in Literaturnaya Gazeta, a dark essay on the corrupting power of the war, was a sample of the gloves-off analysis that is likely to find its way into the press.

The article, by Gennadi Bocharov, who has written extensively from Afghanistan since 1979, told of Soviet troops firing on a carload of civilians after they refused to stop at a border checkpoint and ignored a warning shot.

The troops then opened fire on the vehicle, killing a young woman and wounding three others. An old woman and two children were not hurt.

When the soldiers radioed to their commander to ask for further intructions, he replied according to the account, "I don't need captives."

The commander, who was identified only as Rudykh, told them to eliminate the evidence.

"So they did," Mr. Bocharov reported. "The passenger car was smashed by an armored vehicle and buried in the earth."

The commander was reportedly sentenced to six years' imprisonment, but freed almost immediately in an amnesty.

History of the Struggle

The first Soviet troops parachuted into Kabul on Dec. 27, 1979, to assist Babrak Karmal, who had become President in a coup within the Communist leadership.

The Soviets have always insisted that they came in response to a plea for help from a legitimately constituted Karmal Government. However, most Western analysts say the Soviets engineered the coup as a pretext to replace the Afghan leader who had lost their trust, Hafizullah Amin.

The next day, four motorized rifle divisions crossed the Amu Darya River on pontoon bridges, and Moscow announced that its "limited military contingent" would stay as long as necessary to repel outside aggression.

This they did for years; along the way, in 1986, Mr. Najibullah, the former chief of the Afghan secret police, replaced Mr. Karmal in a purge.

The Soviet-backed Kabul Government has generally kept a firm grip on the cities, but throughout the war has been unable to rout the rebels in the countryside, where the conservative populace was antagonized at the outset by changes in social and land policies that offended Muslim tradition.

After 1986, the Soviet Air Force was rendered largely useless by advanced Stinger antiaircraft missiles supplied by the United States to the rebels.

Overture from East Bloc

Peace talks moderated by the United Nations bore little fruit until early last year, when Mr. Gorbachev and Mr. Najibullah offered a nine-month withdrawal timetable if Pakistan and the United States agreed to curtail their aid to the guerrillas.

The arms embargo never materialized, because President Reagan demanded that Moscow stop supplying Mr. Najibullah as part of the bargain, and the Soviets refused.

In the end, Moscow's withdrawal was in effect unilateral.

The Geneva accords introduced United Nations observers to watch the troops depart, but the agreements' other painstakingly negotiated provisions, promising an end to all outside intervention in Afghanistan, were generally ignored.

The Bush Administration has indicated that it plans to continue arming the rebels after the Soviet withdrawal.

* * *

March 10, 1989

POLAND'S SENATE TO BE RESURRECTED IN ELECTION PACT

By JOHN TAGLIABUE

Special to The New York Times.

WARSAW, March 9—Spokesmen for Poland's Government and the Solidarity union said tonight that they had reached broad tentative agreement on restoring Poland's second chamber of Parliament, with members chosen in open and free elections, and on instituting an office of president with broad powers for foreign and security affairs.

The second chamber, or senate, was abolished in referendums in 1946 that the Communists rigged to cement their control of power in postwar Poland.

Western diplomats and Poles agreed that the measures, if put into effect, would give Poland the most representational form of government in the Eastern bloc.

Free, Open Elections

Solidarity officials said many details of the plan remained to be settled in working groups under the broader Government-Solidarity talks on the shape of change in Poland, now in their fifth week. But if the agreement is carried out, it would be the first time in postwar Poland that a legislative body would be contested in free, open elections, serving to gauge for the first time the popularity of the Communist Party, which now controls the Government with its small allied parties.

The Communist Party has never permitted more than token opposition in Parliament.

As outlined by Solidarity, Communist negotiators agreed to establish a democratically elected senate, or upper house of Parliament, with powers yet to be defined, consisting of two delegates each from the 49 Polish administrative provinces.

President with Broad Powers

In Solidarity's view, the chamber might have responsibility for economic affairs and be a kind of control body for legislation passed by the lower house.

The new plan also includes more liberal regulations for the vote to the lower house, the 460-member Parliament, that Solidarity had demanded.

In exchange, Solidarity said it had agreed to accept a powerful office of the president, with sweeping powers in foreign affairs and domestic and foreign security. The president, who would be empowered to dissolve Parliament, would be elected to a six-year term, with the possibility of re-election to an additional term.

The Government's chief negotiator, Janusz Reykowksi, said he expected that elections to both houses would take place June 4 and June 18. Mr. Reykowski, who is also a member of the ruling Politburo, said at a news conference that the president, to be chosen by a national assembly that would consist essentially of the members of both houses of parliament, would be elected at the first session of a joint chamber.

Jaruzelski Expected to Be Named

He said a law incorporating the changes would be put before the Council of State, Poland's present collective presidency, and could go to Parliament as early as next week.

He said there were no plans to divide the seats in the upper chamber by quota, as has been agreed for the Parliament.

Solidarity members left little doubt that they expected the Polish leader, Gen. Wojciech Jaruzelski, who has ruled Poland since 1981, to be elected president.

Some Western diplomats said the arrangement appeared designed, over time, to ease the way to a parliamentary democracy in which the Communist party would have to share or even surrender Government power. They said the institution of the office of president appeared intended to allay security concerns of the Soviet Union and other Eastern-bloc allies by guaranteeing fulfillment of Poland's Warsaw Pact commitments.

'A Soft Landing for Democracy'

Others suggested the arrangements might be designed by the Communist leadership to curry popular favor, since many Poles link the start of Communist rule with the 1946 referendums in which Poles were asked to approve abolition of the senate, land redistribution and the nationalization of basic industries, and Poland's postwar frontiers with the West.

Referring to Communist officials, one Western European ambassador said the accord appeared to have been arranged "to pave the way for their own disappearance" and to "prepare, in the long term, for a soft landing in democracy."

Bronislaw Geremek, the senior Solidarity negotiator, said, "The arrangement affords grave risks for both sides." He noted that the senate would be elected through confrontational elections—a fact he said would "test the shape of the coalition."

At a news conference, Mr. Geremek said Solidarity also bore "considerable risk." He said Solidarity-backed candidates would suffer under the handicap that "after 45 years empty of politics," they would be forced to prepare election campaigns "within a very short time."

An Evolutionary Rebuilding

The Government, apparently confident that quick elections will guarantee it favorable returns, has insisted on moving up elections, originally planned for autumn, to June 4.

"One side is governing, with all the structures and all the means at its disposal," Mr. Geremek said. "The other side has no structures and no means."

On state television tonight, however, Mr. Geremek said, "A process has begun under which democracy is to be rebuilt in an evolutionary manner, not upsetting the political balance or stability."

Mr. Reykowksi, the Government negotiator, said the sides had agreed on allowing the opposition 35 percent of the seats in the next Parliament. But Solidarity said the Government had accepted the principle that the vote to determine who would sit in those seats would be open and free. The Government had been insisting that Solidarity agree, under patterns common throughout the Eastern bloc, to nationwide lists of candidates for each side.

* * *

April 6, 1989

POLAND SETS FREE VOTE IN JUNE, FIRST SINCE '45; SOLIDARITY REINSTATED

By JOHN TAGLIABUE
Special to The New York Times.

WARSAW, April 5—The leaders of Solidarity signed accords with the Government today restoring the banned union's legal status and providing for the first free and open elections in this country since World War II.

If carried out, the accords could markedly change the political system in this country, one of the first to be put under Soviet domination after the war. The political structure in Poland was more or less followed in the other countries that one by one were attached to the Soviet bloc in the late 1940's.

Poland was the first Soviet-dominated satellite to achieve a measure of independence in 1956, and it now appears that Poles, driven by economic disaster, have taken advantage of the changes wrought in the Soviet Union by Mikhail S. Gorbachev to forge new agreements that go well beyond anything current in the bloc.

Immediate Effects

These will be the most immediate effects of the accords:

- Restoration of Solidarity, the trade union that was formed in 1980 and then crushed after martial law was imposed in December 1981. The farmers union, Rural Solidarity, and the Independent Student Association, will also be restored to legal status.
- Elections in June for a two-house parliament, in which 35 percent of the 460 seats in the newly structured lower house will be allocated to delegates of the Solidarity-based opposition. The Communists will have another 38 percent, and parties formerly aligned with the Communists the rest.
- Restoration of Poland's upper house of Parliament, which was disbanded after World War II. It will have 100 members, who will be chosen in free and open elections. The upper house will be able to veto legislation of the lower house.
- Establishment of the post of president of the republic; the holder will be elected by the two houses of parliament for a six-year term. The president will have broad powers to dissolve parliament, and to veto laws passed by the lower house. The lower house can overturn vetoes by a two-third vote.
- Broad changes in the running of the economy, including the installment of a wage indexing plan, by which workers and retired people will receive compensation to 80 percent of any increase in the cost of living.

The announcement of the accords was broadcast on national television, a measure of the change already wrought since the Government began serious talks with Solidarity last August, after years of repression that culminated last year in two serious waves of labor unrest.

Parliament to Meet Friday

The current Sejm, or parliament, is expected to meet on Friday to make the agreements into law.

Today's developments came at a formal closing session of the round-table talks, which began eight weeks ago. The ceremony today involved the Interior Minister, Gen. Czeslaw Kiszczak, and Lech Walesa, the Nobel Peace laureate and leader of Solidarity.

Mr. Walesa endorsed the accords in a 10-minute speech after General Kiszczak addressed the round table.

For Mr. Walesa it was an almost dizzying moment of triumph: The union leader congratulating the Communist official who, together with Gen. Wojciech Jaruzelski, was one of the people who engineered the imposition of martial law on Dec. 13, 1981, and ordered the imprisonment of nearly all the union leaders, Mr. Walesa included.

A Parliament Revived

The most ambitious gains, after the union's legalization, appeared to have come in the political agreement. It announced that the authorities would cede 35 percent of the 460 seats of the lower house of parliament, leaving the Communist Party with only 38 percent, a minority for the first time since 1944. The remainder of the seats will fall to small parties that until now have been faithful allies of the Communists in a ruling coalition.

Perhaps the most startling concession, however, was the Government's agreement to restore Poland's upper house of Parliament with free and open elections. The upper house was abolished in 1946 in a rigged referendum, although some of the elections that year were free. The Government also agreed to create the office of president, who will be elected by a joint session of both houses. It is generally accepted that General Jaruzelski will be chosen the first president, for a six-year term, with the possibility of one more term.

To induce Solidarity to accept these arrangements the Government agreed to grant both the upper house and the president the right to veto lower house legislation. Their vetoes can only be overruled by a two-thirds majority of the lower house. The significance of this arrangement is that the Communists will be forced, for the first time in the postwar period, to rely on the opposition to override a legislative veto.

Access to News Outlets

The Government also agreed to make the state-controlled press available to Solidarity by allowing the union a half hour of air time weekly on television and one hour weekly of radio time. In addition the union will be allowed its own daily national newspaper and regional weekly papers. Government censorship is to be eased, though not abolished.

The agreements require the Government to make broad changes to assure the independence of judges and the courts, to assure that Poles can freely form associations and clubs, though not political parties, and to bring about an overhaul of the economy.

This aspect of the agreement was regarded as significant by Solidarity leaders because it allows the re-establishment of an independent farmers' union, and introduces a system of wage indexing to compensate workers and pensioners for rampant inflation.

Mr. Walesa, a 45-year-old shipyard electrician who in August 1980 founded Solidarity, said: "I have to emphasize that for the first time we have talked to each other using the force of arguments, and not arguments of force. It bids well for the future, I believe, that the round-table discussions can become the beginning of the road for democracy and a free Poland."

'Build Poland or Sink in Chaos'

"Either we'll be able to build Poland as a nation in a peaceful way, independent, sovereign and safe, with equal alliances," he said, "or we'll sink in the chaos of demagogy, which could result in civil war in which there will be no victors."

General Kiszczak seemed to be playing down the notion that the Government had surrendered substantial ground. "There's only one victor, the nation, our fatherland," he said.

The session was interrupted at one point for nearly three hours after arguing erupted over a demand by Alfred Miodowicz, the leader of the Government's official trade unions, to take the floor. The formal signing was imperiled briefly on Tuesday when the Government unions refused to accept a proposal to index wages to 80 percent of the inflationrate—an issue that Solidarity considered essential.

But in contrast with the turbulent days of August 1980, and the accords that gave birth to Solidarity, exuberance was short in a population apparently grown accustomed to broken promises. While thousands were jubilant in 1980, only several dozen braved unseasonable cold to greet the signers as they gathered for the final session.

WASHINGTON HAILS THE ACCORD

WASHINGTON, April 5 (Special to The New York Times)—The White House warmly welcomed the agreement today recognizing Solidarity, and indicated that "the historic step" will improve Polish-American ties.

"This is a great day for the Polish people and for freedom," said Marlin Fitzwater, the White House spokesman.

In response to a question about possibly expanding relations and providing economic credits to Poland, the White House spokesman said: "We are looking at various actions that could be taken. And hopefully, within the not too distant future, we'll have something to announce."

* * *

May 21, 1989

BIGGEST BEIJING CROWDS SO FAR KEEP TROOPS FROM CITY CENTER; PARTY REPORTED IN BITTER FIGHT

DEFY MARTIAL LAW

Democracy Rallies Held in Many Other Cities—Few Clashes

By NICHOLAS D. KRISTOF
Special to The New York Times.

BEIJING, May 20—Huge throngs, possibly amounting to more than one million Chinese, took to the streets today to defy martial law and block troops from reaching the center of the capital, effectively delaying or preventing the planned crackdown on China's democracy movement.

Troops approaching Beijing on at least five major roads were halted or turned back by the largest crowds to have gathered so far in a month of almost continuous protests. Students and ordinary citizens erected roadblocks or lay in the path of army trucks, while others let the air out of their tires.

Reports from around the country indicated growing support for the democracy movement. The city of Xian was reported brought to a standstill by 300,000 protesters, and rallies were reported in Shanghai, Canton and at least a half-dozen other cities and even small villages.

Mostly Peaceful Confrontations

A few clashed were reported, but the confrontations seemed to be mostly peaceful. More troops were reported to be making their way toward Beijing, however, and it was not clear that the people could continue to keep the soldiers out. So far, the troops have not tried very hard to enter Beijing, and a more concerted effort backed by the use of tear gas would almost certainly succeed. But after a full day of confrontation, questions were increasingly raised about the army's readiness to quell the protests.

Prime Minister Li Peng, who early this morning ordered the military crackdown on the nation's growing democracy movement, did not make an appearance or comment later today. Television stations repeatedly broadcast his speech calling for the military crackdown.

As the military crackdown seemed increasingly uncertain, there were signs that the Communist Party General Secretary, Zhao Ziyang, still had a chance of recovering his authority and elbowing aside Mr. Li and the senior leader, Deng Xiaoping, to become China's next leader in an intense and increasingly bitter power struggle within the Communist Party.

Communist Party officials with access to information at the highest level say that Mr. Deng has stripped Mr. Zhao of his powers while leaving him with his empty title. In addition, they say that a meeting of the Central Military Commission on Thursday effectively stripped him of his right to order troop movement.

Associated Press

Students continuing their protest in Beijing. "No government can survive by using the army against its own citizens," said a demonstrator.

Mr. Zhao submitted his resignation on May 17, after being outvoted 4 to 1 on the Standing Committee of the Politburo on his proposals to concede to most of the students' demands, the official said. The resignation was withdrawn the next day before it was formally acted upon.

Proposals Get Support

In the meantime, Mr. Zhao's bold proposals—including a plan to disclose the income and assets of officials at the level of Deputy Minister and higher—have subsequently received the support of a second member of the Politburo Standing Committee, Hu Qili. Now an intense effort is said to be under way to lobby the crucial swing vote of a Committee member, Qiao Shi, whose support would mean a majority for Mr. Zhao.

Mr. Zhao's future might also come up at a meeting of the full Politburo, which has not yet been scheduled, or at a meeting of the Central Committee, which originally had been expected at the end of this month. How the Politburo or Central Committee might vote is likely to depend on the success of the crackdown.

"Li Peng is now in charge of the party, so he'll be scheduling the meetings," an official said. "So if he thinks he might lose, he will delay holding a meeting." The harshness of Mr. Li's speech seems to have galvanized much of Beijing's population to support the student democracy movement, and Mr. Li and Mr. Deng are now openly referred to as public enemies.

Protestors in Shanghai today carried banners reading "Li Peng does not represent us" and "Li Peng, do not use the people's army against the people," Reuters reported.

In most parts of Beijing, neither the police nor the army troops could be seen today, but residents were in an exuberant frenzy to protect themselves from the threat of what is regarded as virtually an enemy invasion. All major intersections have been taken over by local residents who stand guard, waiting impatiently for the troops to arrive so that they can implement their careful plans to erect barricades and summon help.

"With the people behind us, we'll succeed," said Xu Shiyi, a student from Henan Province who has come to Beijing to support the democracy movement. "No Government can survive by using the army against its own citizens."

Not Much Work in Beijing

While proposals in the predawn hours for a general strike seem to have been little heeded, it was clear that even if workers did not call formal strikes they did not do much work. Beijing residents today had other things to occupy them, like how to keep the army out.

Reuters

Chinese Army troops on a truck that was halted Saturday by thousands of pro-democracy demonstrators.

As rumors spread about where troops might be arriving, citizens rushed by car, bicycle and foot to do their part to turn the troops back. The crowds were larger than those last Wednesday and Thursday that the official New China News Agency had estimated at more than one million.

Truck drivers drove their vehicles in front of military convoys to block their way, and ordinary citizens lay down on the ground in front of army trucks. Many seemed to remember these tactics from the Philippine military coup that ousted President Ferdinand E. Marcos. Television footage of the "people power" revolution of the Philippines was widely shown in China at the time and now workers delight in saying that people power will defeat Prime Minister Li.

The most serious of the scattered clashes reported today occurred on a road in western Beijing, according to students, who said about 150 police officers used cattle prods to beat about 45 students blocking military trucks.

Protests in the Provinces

Anti-Government demonstrations broke out in provincial Chinese cities and even rural towns today, witnesses said.

The ancient capital of Xian in northern China came to a standstill when 300,000 protesters, sympathetic citizens and onlookers packed the city's streets, a Western witness told Reuters.

On Shanghai's waterfront, 20,000 students flanked by thousands of sympathetic city workers protested for the fifth day running in support of 400 hunger strikers who have gone without food outside Government headquarters since Tuesday.

A large contingent of troops have been stationed in the European-style office buildings close to the waterfront but have not yet moved against the protestors, a reporter said.

Shanghai is also the host to a three-ship squadron of the American Seventh Fleet, which arrived for the second United States Navy visit to the port since the 1949 Communist takeover. Demonstrators have erected a 10-foot-high polystyrene replica of the Statue of Liberty in front of the Shanghai city government offices. The American sailors have been instructed to avoid the protests.

Waiting in Tiananmen Square

In Beijing, nearly 100,000 people seemed prepared this evening to wait all night in central Tiananmen Square to protect student hunger strikers from attack by troops. Even though there was no evidence of hostile troops within miles, many waited expectantly with clothes over their faces for the clouds of tear gas they have been told to expect.

The readiness to help has taken other forms. The Government today cut off the water supply to Tiananmen Square, but as word spread that the water fountains and taps in the area were no longer working, private business people from all over the capital contributed their motorcycles to carry buckets of water to the students.

There are still nearly 3,000 students engaged in a hunger strike on the square to back their demands for a dialogue with Government officials and for a reappraisal of the student movement.

The lengthening fast, which marked its ninth day today, puts further pressure on the Government because if a hunger striker happened to die or suffer serious injury, the result might be an explosion of rage against the authorities.

30,00 Troops Deployed

After the harshness of Mr. Li's speech, the lack of any strong military follow-through has raised questions about the extent to which the Prime Minister can force his will. About 30,000 troops from Inner Mongolia and Shanxi Province reportedly have been deployed, but they are vastly outnumbered by the more than one million people who took to the streets today.

Some of the troops today could be seen with tear gas canisters and some reportedly had guns, but they seemed decidedly pacifist. Most of the soldiers seemed unwilling to openly violate their orders to advance on Beijing, but they seemed quite happy to be blocked along the way.

There also were some signs of dissatisfaction from within the party and the Government at the hard line against the students. Officials in the central party organization today circulated among themselves an appeal for a party meeting to discuss the crisis and to consider the possible retirement of Mr. Deng, according to a person who has seen the letter.

The Communist Youth League Central Committee sent a delegation to protest in Tiananmen Square, and the People's Daily newspaper today seemed to offer an implicit endorsement of Mr. Zhao over Mr. Li. The newspaper printed a photo of Mr. Zhao that was not only higher than Mr. Li's on the front page but more than twice as wide. The accompanying article included excerpts from Mr. Zhao's comments to students, and was calculated to inspire sympathy.

Bitter Power Struggle

"Of course it's an endorsement," a senior party official said. "That's as clear as it gets."

The internal power struggle between Mr. Zhao and Mr. Li has taken a much more bitter turn in the last few weeks, partly because of furious disagreements over how to deal with the demonstrating students. But party officials say that perhaps the most important element was that Mr. Zhao took the unprecedented step of challenging his longtime patron, Mr. Deng.

While Mr. Zhao is said to have felt for some time that his patron should retire fully from politics, the conflict began after Mr. Deng reacted very harshly on April 25 to student demonstrators and organized a crackdown that later was aborted. When Mr. Zhao returned from a trip abroad he made a mild speech on how to deal with students. The speech won widespread support but was resented by Mr. Deng because it pursued a much more moderate strategy.

Zhao Attack on Deng

Then, as pro-democracy demonstrations grew increasingly large, Mr. Zhao seemed to think that they represented an important constituency that he could use to gain an advantage. According to an account by an official familiar with the struggle, Mr. Zhao made his attacks, in classic Chinese style, by purporting to praise Mr. Deng in his meeting Wednesday with Mikhail S. Gorbachev, the Soviet leader. Mr. Zhao hailed Mr. Deng as an indispensable leader who still must sign off on every important decision.

Without consulting Mr. Deng, Mr. Zhao also disclosed that the Central Committee had formally adopted a resolution saying that Mr. Deng should be consulted on important matters. While the comments were all "couched" in praise, the effect was to remind people that the 84-year-old Mr. Deng still makes all of China's important decisions.

The next day's demonstration was full of posters denouncing Mr. Deng, but Mr. Deng himself recognized the ploy, officials said. Mr. Li weighed in in the increasingly bitter fight by saying, in a televised meeting, that his sons were not involved in official profiteering—a clear slap at Mr. Zhao, whose two eldest sons are widely regarded as having been suspiciously successful in business.

Then last Thursday Mr. Zhao made an early morning trip to the hunger-strikers in Tiananmen Square and apologized to them for not coming earlier. "Things are very complicated," he said in what was widely taken as a reference to the difficulty of convincing Mr. Deng and Mr. Li of the need for compromise.

That was the last time Mr. Zhao has been seen in public.

* * *

June 1, 1989

BUSH URGES EAST TO JOIN IN ENDING DIVISION OF EUROPE

By BERNARD WEINRAUB

Special to The New York Times.

MAINZ, West Germany, May 31—President Bush called on the Soviet Union and its allies today to end the division of Europe.

In the major foreign policy speech of his European tour—and an effort to match and counter initiatives by President Mikhail S. Gorbachev of the Soviet Union—Mr. Bush outlined proposals "to heal Europe's tragic division, to help Europe become whole and free."

"The cold war began with the division of Europe," the President said. "It can only end when Europe is whole. There cannot be a common European home until all within are free to move from room to room."

Elections and Openness

Mr. Bush offered four steps for unifying Europe:

- The promotion of "free elections and political pluralism in Eastern Europe." Mr. Bush called on the political parties of the West "to lend counsel and support to those brave men and women who are trying to form the first truly representative political parties in the East."
- The tearing down of the Berlin wall. "It must come down," he said.
- An invitation to Western environmentalists and engineers to share knowledge with those in the East struggling to deal with acid rain and polluted rivers. "America has faced an environmental tragedy in Alaska," Mr. Bush said, adding: "Countries from France to Finland suffered after Chernobyl. Environmental destruction respects no borders."
- An appeal to the Soviet Union to join in Mr. Bush's new proposals to reduce conventional forces in Europe.

Publicity Courted

His speech, before a group of 3,500 Germans in a flag-draped auditorium in Mainz, was televised throughout West Germany and broadcast live by some American networks. White House officials said Mr. Bush was seeking to reach the widest possible audience in Europe as well as the United States.

White House officials said the speech was intended to serve as the political counterpart to arms initiatives the President offered to the North Atlantic Treaty Organization two days ago.

It was also designed to seize the public relations initiative from Mr. Gorbachev, and Mr. Bush used Mr. Gorbachev's own words against him, although the speech contained no direct criticism of the Soviet leader. "Glasnost may be a Russian word, but openness is a Western concept," Mr. Bush said. "Bring glasnost to East Berlin," he said at another point.

A Process That Has Begun

The President's remarks were framed in such a way that they did not take into account the growing movement of peoples already taking place between East and West in Europe. While West Germans would welcome the destruction of the wall dividing the two parts of Berlin as a symbolic easing of tensions, if the removal of the wall led to a vast influx of people from Eastern Europe into the West, this would cause severe problems for West Europeans already worried about growing numbers of East European refugees in their midst, He also skirted the issue of German reunification, saying he favored "self-determination for all of Germany and all of Eastern Europe," but without saying that he explicitly wanted a merger of the two states. The topic stirs passions in both East and West. Most West Germans favor unification with East Germany, but many other Europeans express concern over such a development.

Mr. Bush called his four proposals "the foundation of our larger vision—a Europe that is free and at peace with itself."

"Let the Soviets know that our goal is not to undermine their legitimate security interests," he said. "Our goal is to convince them, step by step, that their definition of security is obsolete, that their deepest fears are unfounded."

Propping Up Kohl

White House aides said that the President came to Mainz, an old wine port on the Rhine River, at the request of Chancellor Helmut Kohl of West Germany, whose popularity has been falling. Mr. Kohl is from the surrounding state, Rhineland-Palatinate, and Mr. Bush's visit to its capital was meant to stir support for the Chancellor's Christian Democratic Party in city and state elections on June 18.

"Kohl asked us to come, so we did a campaign swing through the Rhineland," an American official said.

The West German Chancellor, in his remarks before Mr. Bush, seemed to echo some of the President's views.

"For the first time since the end of World War II," he said, "we stand a realistic chance of escaping the shadow of the East-West conflict. Soviet policy is now more amenable to compromise, more open to dialogue and cooperation," he said.

After a Sail, Britain

After Mr. Bush's speech in Mainz, the President and his wife, Barbara, joined Mr. Kohl and his wife, Hannelore, for a nearly two-hour trip aboard an excursion cruise ship from Oberwesel to Koblenz.

Mr. Bush called it "an unforgettable day" as he left for London for meetings with Prime Minister Margaret Thatcher and a visit with Queen Elizabeth II. Earlier in the day in Bonn, the President met privately with Mr. Kohl for more than an hour, and then spoke briefly to several hundred American residents, including schoolchildren, in the backyard of the official residence of the U.S. Ambassador, Vernon A. Walters. Then he flew by helicopter to Mainz, a 40-minute trip.

Mr. Bush's speech, timed for delivery at midday to enable the American television networks to carry it on morning news programs, was enthusiastically applauded by a hand-picked audience of Mainz residents.

The President's theme was that demands for democracy in Communist countries, including China, had produced a "ferment" that demanded a response from the leaders of those countries. "The passion for freedom cannot be denied forever," he said.

"The momentum for freedom does not just come from the printed word, the transistor or the television screen," Mr. Bush said. "It comes from the power of a single idea—democracy."

Open Societies

"This one idea is why the Communist world, from Budapest to Beijing, is in ferment," said the President, who plans a visit in July to Hungary and Poland, where steps have been taken toward free and open elections.

"As President, I will continue to do all I can to open the closed societies of the East," Mr. Bush said. "We seek self-determination for all of Germany and all of Eastern Europe. We will not relax. We must not waver. Again, the world has waited long enough."

Although some of Mr. Bush's recent foreign policy speeches have been criticized, even within the White House, as lackluster, today's 30-minute address seemed pointed and finely tuned. The speech was written by Mark Davis, a former aide to then-Defense Secretary Frank C. Carlucci, who is now on the White House staff, and shaped two days ago in a late-night session in Brussels by Brent Scowcroft, the national security adviser; John H. Sununu, the chief of staff; David Demarest, director of White House communications, and several other officials.

Mr. Bush offered a veiled criticism of some German and other West European officials who have criticized his Administration for its tentative response to arms control.

"To those who are impatient with our measured pace in arms reductions," he said, "I respectfully suggest that history teaches us a lesson—that unity and strength are the catalyst and prerequisite to arms control."

* * *

June 4, 1989

CHINA ERUPTS . . . THE REASONS WHY

By NICHOLAS D. KRISTOF

Emperors and eunuchs, warlords and revolutionaries—all have presided over Beijing's Tiananmen Square. Last month was the turn of the hunger strikers.

Beginning in late April, 3,000 young people lay nearly comatose on the ground, feeble and sunburned, but galvanizing all of China with their threat to kill themselves rather than live without democracy.

Oceans of protesters, more than a million bobbing heads, jostled in and around the vast square, fighting their way forward to read more of the angry red banners calling for the resignation of the senior leader, Deng Xiaoping, and the Prime Minister, Li Peng.

When Mr. Deng and Mr. Li responded by imposing martial law, citizens flung themselves in front of army trucks and tanks, stopping and often reversing the long convoys. The soldiers retreated, some of them sobbing as they abandoned their orders to quell the uprising. "Our Government is too harsh to the students," snarled Sun Yong, an army engineer who marched against the Government. "The People's Liberation Army belongs to the people, and it is time for every Chinese to speak out."

The outlook for China's immediate future is murky, but most Chinese seem to expect that whatever the near-term setbacks, the nation has been set on the road toward less control by the Communist Party. The uprising of the last six weeks, whether it is renewed or repressed, seems to mark a turning point, and it happened with startling, and seemingly inexplicable swiftness. No one predicted that the convulsions would happen when they did, and not even China's most famous savants can safely predict what will happen next.

But if the timing and scale of earthquakes is uncertain, at least the fault lines can be mapped. In China, for most of the population, these fault lines—the immediate causes of public dissatisfaction—relate not only to vague yearnings for democracy but, more importantly, to profound economic frustrations and disgust over social inequities and corruption.

Before the turbulence, experts looked at China and saw an economic miracle—a society that in little more than a decade has managed to propel itself from the bland egalitarian poverty of Maoism to the new-found consumerism of color television sets, earrings and disco dancing. During the last 10 years, the average income in China has more than doubled.

But the expectations of the Chinese have risen even more. Foreign analysts see double-digit growth, but the Chinese tend to focus on the washing machine that they can now dream of but still can't afford, the rising prices that seem to cheat them out of their higher salaries, the bribes that they must pay in order to change apartments or, in defiance of official policy, to have a second child. The result is dissatisfaction and anger, mixed with bitterness at the advantages that high officials enjoy. In April and May, these subterranean pressures finally erupted in the volcano of protest that, whatever happens, has profoundly changed the way China will be governed.

If the proximate cause of the rebellion was this festering discontent, the underlying reason was that the Communist Party has been losing its grip on the country. This began long before the demonstrations, and it did not happen overnight; the party has suffered a prolonged erosion of its moral authority—and its ability to intimidate.

Throughout the country, the love, fear and awe that the Communist Party once aroused have collapsed into something closer to disdain or even contempt. Young people used to dream of joining the party; now they often speak condescendingly of their peers who join. "Me? A party member?" Cheng Lin, a 22-year-old woman who is one of China's best-known pop singers, responded to a reporter's question. "Nobody joins the party now, among young people," she cheerfully exaggerated.

But it is not only young people who disdain the party. Just as often it is ordinary working Chinese who undermine its authority, sometimes with an extra dash of daring, or even cruelty—people like Lei Xiding. A small-town peddler, Mr. Lei had tax evasion rather than rebellion on his mind when he took on the Government. Four officials went to his village to make him pay taxes on 46 pigs he had purchased, but Mr. Lei and his family tore up the men's legal papers, robbed them of their watches and locked them in cages with the pigs. Then, according to China's official press, Mr. Lei and his relatives beat the tax collectors for five hours, urinated on them, and paraded them blindfolded through the streets.

Eventually, the four men were released, alive—which makes them luckier than some of their colleagues. Since 1985, according to The People's Daily, 13 tax collectors have been murdered, 27 crippled and 6,400 beaten up.

Dissidents and student demonstrators have received most of the attention abroad, but among ordinary Chinese the practice of ignoring or defying the party has become nearly universal. For example, China propounds a "one couple one child" birth-control policy, but in 1987 and 1988, according to Beijing University's Institute of Population Research, Chinese couples could be expected to have an average of 2.45 children. The law also says women must be 20 and men 22 to marry, but as of 1986 (the last year for which the State Family Planning Commission has figures), more than a fifth of all marriages involved at least one partner who was underage; and in some remote areas these illegal marriages account for 90 percent of the total.

Though Chinese must have permission to move to another city, Shanghai officials acknowledge that fully 2.5 million of the city's 14.5 million residents have no permission to live there. Waves of illegal migrant laborers are sweeping across China, workers who search for new jobs without waiting to get permission. In February and early March, more than 2.5 million laborers flooded into Canton, ignoring sharp warnings from the Government. Suddenly, the city center was packed with sun-weathered peasants, huddled beside sacks of their belongings—mute testimony, two months before the demonstrations, to the diminishing control of the Government over the population.

Of course, during the last six weeks it was the students who were in the vanguard—as they have been so many times in recent Chinese history. But after they showed the way, many others flocked to follow. Workers defied their bosses to walk alongside the students, citizens from all over Beijing came out to help block the soldiers' entry into the city, and thousands of Chinese journalists signed their names to a petition calling for more press freedom.

"The students have shown that the will of the people can't be resisted," said Yan Jiaqi, one of the country's most prominent political scientists. "This is now a dominant idea in Chinese politics."

But even as exhilaration swept through the capital in May, among intellectuals and officials especially there was also a lurking tension, a fear that flits in the corners of the mind but takes no obvious shape. To some it is the specter of nationwide anarchy and the disintegration of China as a coherent unit, to others a vision of soaring crime and inflation that might finally shred China's social fabric, transforming the country into an oversized, Oriental Bolivia. It is these fears of spiraling unrest and chaos that seemed to inspire Mr. Deng and Mr. Li to crack down on the protests; even for many ordinary Chinese there is an apprehension of luan, or chaos.

Perhaps it is the pessimism of smart young Chinese, their obvious lack of appreciation for the regime that in the last decade has so palpably increased their opportunities and material comforts, that most strikes foreigners. Many Chinese hold the somewhat surprising perception that China is in the middle of an economic crisis.

True, China's annual inflation rate has passed 25 percent a year, and the country has seen such unfamiliar problems as bank runs and cash shortages. Bribes and abuse of power are no longer peripheral to the economy; they are the fuel that makes it run.

But all countries have graft and economic problems; indeed, some people who have lived on both sides of the Taiwan Strait say that corruption is even more massive on Taiwan. What is more worrying than the economy itself is the perception of crisis. Inflation and corruption have fueled a sense of economic frustration that lets people convince themselves that they are becoming worse and worse off financially. Statistically, this is nonsense; even after inflation, the economy is growing at 11 percent a year, and the overwhelming majority is better off than it used to be. In strict economic terms, China arguably is modernizing more successfully than any other undeveloped or socialist nation in the world today. But it is suffering a crisis of confidence.

The diminishing role of the Communist Party has exacerbated and magnified some of China's economic problems. There is neither a planned economy nor a market economy, but an economy that displays some of the vices of both. Growth is unplanned, so that investment in energy and infrastructure is inadequate; the result is power cuts and long delays in transporting goods.

The lack of planning has led to absurdities. During the last two years, for example, managers at a number of Chinese companies heard that because of the AIDS epidemic, there would be a huge growth in world demand for the disposable rubber gloves used by health-care workers. Though many other countries were already producing such gloves, companies all over China rushed to manufacture them. Today, China alone makes more rubber gloves than the world needs.

If there is no planning, neither is there much of a market. Raw materials do not go to the most efficient operator—the one that presumably would be able to pay the highest price—but to the enterprise with the best connections. Provinces have begun to compete with one another, refusing to allow their raw materials to be processed elsewhere. Xinjiang Province, for example, used to produce fine wool and cashmere for processing in Shanghai's mills, but now Xinjiang refuses to let the wool go, processing it in its own newly-opened, crude factories. Some provinces have stationed armed guards at their borders to prevent raw materials from leaving.

Even before the demonstrations, the party's decline had led to a marked expansion in what Chinese could openly say. People were still afraid, but far less so than before. "In China today, if you don't directly challenge the party authorities, you are basically left alone," said Joseph Y. S. Cheng, a senior lecturer at the Chinese University in Hong Kong. "You can condemn the party after a couple of glasses of wine and it's all right. As long as you don't take active steps, as long as you're not a threat to the Government, you're left alone."

Now, after the demonstrations have shown that massive numbers of people are willing to take on the Government, the difficulty in intimidating the masses may become more acute. "There will be a less-totalitarian society," Mr. Cheng predicts. "People will have more freedom."

As the party's power declines, some Chinese find historic parallels in the disintegrating dynasties of imperial China, such as the corrupt Qing Dynasty early in this century, which stubbornly refused to modernize until it was too late. Perhaps there is something to those parallels, but there are other scenarios: the rise of Taiwan just when its leadership was most discredited; the rise of Hong Kong just as the Korean War embargo of China seemed about to extinguish the colony's economy.

It is clear, in short, that, whatever the result of struggles at the top, the party is losing control, and many Chinese intellectuals despair that the worst is yet to come. But though such despair may well have its own consequences, it is not yet clear if it is warranted.

The withering of the party can be seen most poignantly in the generation gap that has emerged in China today. Many successful young Chinese business executives and Government officials are children of "old revolutionaries," men and women who joined the Communist Party in the 1930's or 40's and fought their way to power. The parents devoted their lives to the party, but the children are ideological atheists. Over dinner recently, in the company of an old revolutionary and his American-educated son, the son was asked if he was a party member. The son laughed, his expression a mixture of horror and astonishment. "Which party?" he asked. His father laughed too, but there was pain in his eyes.

It is not just the younger generation that sees things differently. Consider Zhang Hanzhi, a former English teacher and interpreter for Mao Zedong and the widow of former Foreign Minister Qiao Guanhua. In 1976, in a speech to the United Nations, Mr. Qiao earned fame for his stinging attack on the United States.

But Ms. Zhang surprises anyone expecting to meet a genuine fire-breathing Maoist. Behind the charming conversationalist is a thoughtful woman profoundly aware of the quandaries of Chinese Communism.

"My generation was very inspired by the revolution," Ms. Zhang recalled. "When my friends and I get together, we miss the good old days. Life then wasn't so comfortable, but there was a tremendous sense of honesty and pitching in for the common good."

Yet if Ms. Zhang can wax nostalgic for the exhilarating days in the early 1950's, when Communism really did seem to be the answer, not the problem, she also acknowledges that those days are past. Many Chinese, she says, now dream of a future that is not necessarily socialist, and they want a more democratic atmosphere. Looking at the state of Communism in China today, she has misgivings.

"I'm worried about whether all this corruption will lead to a rottenness that will be difficult to correct without big change," she said. And then she spoke most poignantly about the drift to America of many of China's young people. Her own daughter, sent to the United States in the mid-1970's by Mao Zedong to learn English and help the motherland, now lives in New York.

"To see them all settling down over there and not coming back is somewhat depressing," Ms. Zhang said. "My daughter, my niece, and the children of almost all my friends. Almost every time a young person comes by my house to say goodbye, I have the feeling they're not coming back."

Throughout Chinese history there has been an ebb and flow of central control. Typically, a vigorous leader proclaimed himself emperor and established a dynasty. He pulled the country together, strengthened central authority, eliminated rivals for power; but, just as typically, his descendants proved less adept at maintaining it and the nation gradually disintegrated again until—perhaps hundreds of years later—a new strongman emerged as emperor and founded another dynasty.

Some see the same process happening now. They liken Mao Zedong—who founded the People's Republic in 1949 and changed more people's lives in more ways than perhaps anyone else in this century—to the first man to rule unified China, the first Qin emperor.

Known as Qin Shi Huang Di, he was one of the greatest and fiercest of them all. He unified China in 221 B.C., protecting it by linking various short segments of a wall into the Great Wall that still stands. He standardized China's system of laws and of weights and measures, burned books, and buried Confucian scholars alive. According to legend, he defied his advisers and tried to build a bridge across the Pacific Ocean. The first Qin emperor predicted that his dynasty would last 10,000 generations; instead, less than four years after his death, his dynasty collapsed.

Mao Zedong was not opposed to comparisons with the first Qin emperor, and the similarities are indeed striking. Both were great, impetuous and brutal leaders, and the work of both men's lives began to be rapidly undone soon after their deaths. The question now is whether the Communist dynasty will crumble like the Qin or whether it will evolve into something more humane and practical.

Mao said that "political power grows from the barrel of a gun," but in Chinese history it has also grown out of the "mandate of heaven"—a kind of moral authority to rule. In the long run, the Communist Party relies not only on guns but also on some consensus that it provides a legitimate government.

In recent years this moral legitimacy dissipated, not only because ordinary people became embittered by the inflation, corruption and injustice around them, but because fewer and fewer people believed in Marxism. The Cultural Revolution of the late 1960's and early 70's turned much of the nation away from Communism, and though many were willing to give it a second chance when Mr. Deng took the helm in 1978, in China today there is remarkably little faith in Communism. Even party members do not usually believe in it in any traditional or meaningful way; rather, the believers talk about the need for social justice and equal opportunity and populist rule. They sound more like American democrats than communists. The result is an ideological vacuum.

Ironically, these are the same factors that led to the collapse of the Nationalist regime in 1949, when the Communists emerged victorious in China's civil war. It was also corruption and inability to modernize that doomed the Qing Dynasty, forcing the last emperor to abdicate early in 1912.

Many intellectuals see a common thread in the disintegration of the three regimes: "Absolute power corrupts absolutely," as a poster in a demonstration last month noted, quoting Lord Acton. China has never had any independent institution, such as a strong parliament or a free press, or even an organized church, that could dilute this absolute power, that could supervise the country's leaders and check their hubris. That is one reason intellectuals are so enthusiastic about freedom of the press: they see it as an independent mechanism that can restore some balance and control to the exercise of power in China.

The party's decline has been hastened by structural changes in the economy and society that have given people more room to maneuver. Before, every Chinese was under the strict supervision of the "work units" and "neighborhood committees" that regulated every aspect of life, to the point of charting women's menstrual cycles to get early warning of a pregnancy. Now, independent business people have no "work unit" to control them, and in the countryside the communes have been disbanded, so there is less authority over peasants as well. All this has fostered a new sense of freedom, a giddy sense of liberty; Big Brother is no longer peering over one's shoulder.

This break down of authority could worsen as a new generation takes power. Mr. Deng, the senior leader, was no longer regarded by most Chinese as a hero or savior, even before the declaration of martial law. But to many people that hardline step rendered him a tragic figure whose enormous achievements have now been undermined by his inclination to whim and hubris and repression. Even so, this 5-foot, 84-year-old bridge player, probably the only world statesman in recent years with a taste for dog meat, remains a giant, the last Chinese leader of the revolutionary generation, and the last civilian to have enjoyed unequivocal military support, although now he may have lost even that.

As events unfold, more and more young Chinese fear a return of the chaos and weakness that plagued China from the First Opium War in 1840 to the collapse of the Nationalist regime in 1949. Wu Jiaxiang, a prominent Communist Party theorist, is blunt about the risks:

"I think China is falling into chaos," he said during a recent interview. Mr. Wu's prescription to avoid the plunge is "neo-authoritarianism," a theory that many Chinese officials, including Mr. Deng, endorsed. Supporters of neo-authoritarianism emphasize the need for order and stability, and point to the economic miracles achieved by the authoritarian regimes in Taiwan and South Korea. Mr. Wu's version also emphasizes the need for the Government to respect individual human rights, but the style of government would amount to enlightened and benevolent despotism.

Mr. Wu and others prescribe such a system partly because they see a growing risk of urban unrest. As China's labor unions become more independent and workers more indignant, their discontent could boil over. One immediate challenge is the desperate shortage of cash in the hands of the central Government and state-owned companies. The official press has already acknowledged that some large state companies are unable to pay workers more than 40 percent of their wages. According to a People's Daily report in April, workers in a large Sichuan Province factory responded by beating their bowls in the factory cafeteria and singing the "Internationale," the song of revolution. During the May demonstrations, many workers went on strike to support the students, and it may be only a matter of time before workers stage walkouts to back their economic demands as well.

Further urban unrest might also be triggered by young workers and the unemployed who congregate in many cities, looking for trouble. On April 22, in the cities of Changsha and Xian, they took advantage of student protests to riot, burning and looting whatever they could find. A Shanghai diplomat said that city, too, was combustible, and noted that the authorities had recently moved hundreds of thousands of young migrant laborers away from the city to reduce the danger of clashes.

The risks of rural unrest are probably lower, but in a country with a tradition of peasant revolts, they cannot be ignored. The impoverished Government has recently been unable to pay peasants for their grain, pork and other products, and instead has been giving them white slips of paper as i.o.u.'s. Peasants in several areas have vowed that they will not sell their produce to the Government again, except for cash, and there could be confrontations during the summer harvest.

Some young Chinese expect the country to fragment, sometime during the next century, into competing provinces or military regions. Most foreign China watchers are not so pessimistic; they think it far more likely that China will thrive and become a strong and essential member of the international community.

"My problem is that I cut my teeth on China during the Cultural Revolution," says Harry Harding, a China scholar at the Brookings Institution in Washington. "There was tremendous social and political unrest in society, you had even stronger regional fragmentation, and yet it held together." Mr. Harding argues that many Chinese tend to overdramatize the risks, noting that the inflation rate of about 27 percent would inspire jealousy in Brazil, and that the student protesters are apple-polishing schoolchildren, compared to the South Korean militants.

Not everything is known about what Soviet President Mikhail S. Gorbachev discussed with Mr. Deng during their summit meeting in mid-May, but they could have commiserated with each other over the difficulties of opening up socialist systems. By any normal standard, Mr. Gorbachev's problems are greater: Russians number only half the Soviet population, several republics probably would like to go their own way, and the economy has been so numbed by state controls that it is scarcely responding to restructuring. In China, on the other hand, the economic problems are not those of stagnation, but of dynamism—overheated growth, to be more precise—and separatist tendencies are confined to peripheral regions, such as Tibet and Xinjiang.

Perhaps the most startling difference, however, is that the glasnost and perestroika in the Soviet Union seemed to trickle down mostly from above, but in China they bubbled up mostly from the grass roots. Beginning in the late 1970's, for example, peasants themselves divided up the vast communes before the Government could get around to the task. In recent years, entrepreneurs started up tens of thousands of small businesses even before it was clear that they were legal. In the Soviet Union, political change came at the initiative of Mr. Gorbachev; in China, such changes came at the initiative of intellectuals inside and outside of the party who forced the leadership grudgingly to retreat. This process will be extremely difficult to reverse.

It would be difficult for the party to get a grip even on its own scattered units. Today, the party central committee makes pronouncements in Beijing, and local party organizations look the other way. When people talk about the party losing power, in part what they mean is that the Communist Party as a coherent, centralized organ has lost power. Indeed, the local units have in some cases increased their power by snapping up the decision-making authority that Beijing was trying vainly to pass on to individual industrial companies.

China's leaders may try to recover a measure of their economic and political authority, but it will be extremely difficult. Wang Dan, a student leader at Beijing University, says that even if he is eventually arrested, others will take his place.

Perhaps he is right, for the student protests have exacerbated the sense of weakness in the party, while emboldening people throughout China who are embittered by corruption and lack of control over their own lives. During one recent demonstration, a young Government official emerged from his office to stand with the students and support them. He gazed at the endless river of young men and women, as mighty as the Yangtze and as central to the nation's future. "Now," he murmured, "the Chinese have minds of their own."

Nicholas D. Kristof is chief of The New York Times bureau in Beijing.

* * *

June 6, 1989

CRACKDOWN IN BEIJING; PRESIDENT SPURNS OTHER SANCTIONS

By BERNARD WEINRAUB
Special to The New York Times.

WASHINGTON, June 5—President Bush today ordered a suspension of American military sales to China in response to what he called the "violent and bloody" crackdown against demonstrators in Beijing.

After saying little during the weekend of bloodshed, Mr. Bush held a news conference this morning to take account of pressure which was mounting in Congress from both liberals and conservatives for a firm American reaction on behalf of the student "pro-democracy" movement.

While halting military sales and suspending visits of Chinese and American military delegations, the President resisted suggestions that he impose economic sanctions or withdraw the American Ambassador from Bejing.

'Bad Time to Withdraw'

Mr. Bush appeared to be seeking middle ground between Congressional calls for more severe penalties and his own instincts, based in part on his experience as head of the United States Mission in China, that Washington should not move abruptly to freeze relations with the Chinese leadership.

"I don't want to see a total break in this relationship and I will not encourage a total break," Mr. Bush said.

"When you see these kids struggling for democracy and freedom, this would be a bad time for the United States to withdraw," Mr. Bush said. He urged Chinese authorities "to avoid violence and to return to their previous policy of restraint."

Mr. Bush, in his opening comments, said: "In recent weeks, we've urged mutual restraint, nonviolence and dialogue. Instead, there has been a violent and bloody attack on the demonstrators."

But the President emphasized that he wanted to make "a reasoned, careful" set of steps "that takes into account both our long-term interests and recognition of a complex internal situation in China."

Other actions announced by Mr. Bush included a statement that the United States would engage in "a sympathetic review of requests" by any of the thousands of Chinese students in the United States to extend their stay.

White House aides said Mr. Bush's decision on military sales involved items in a package of more than $600 million ordered by the Chinese but not yet delivered. While not likely to damage China's military machine significantly, the move was meant to be a symbolic show of Washington's anger at elements in the Chinese military involved in the bloodshed that has left hundreds dead. In his press conference, Mr. Bush noted that not all of the Chinese military seemed to support the crackdown.

Disturbed by TV Film

In justifying his decision not to impose economic sanctions, Mr. Bush said he did not want to make "an emotional response" to the turmoil.

But Mr. Bush, whose closest aides said he was deeply disturbed at television news film showing Chinese citizens beaten and shot by security forces, told reporters, "I reserve the right to take a whole new look at things if the violence escalates."

Reaction from Capitol Hill was supportive, although some lawmakers urged stronger moves against the Beijing Government.

Mr. Bush's day was virtually consumed with the crisis in China. He received a stream of intelligence reports from

Beijing, phoned Prime Minister Margaret Thatcher of Britain to discuss the Western response, met Congressional leaders on the United States response and spoke to a group of Chinese students in the Oval Office.

Several ranking White House aides said, however, that information coming from Beijing was uncertain.

'A Very Murky Picture'

"He's monitoring the situation as it's reported by CNN and coming in from our embassy," said a ranking White House aide. "Quite frankly, we don't have very much information on what's happening on the scene or in the Government." Another senior official said, "We're watching a very murky picture."

Mr. Bush, who served as head of the United States Liaison Mission to China in 1974-75, in the years before there was full diplomatic relations, told reporters, "The United States cannot condone the violent attacks and cannot ignore the consequence for our relationship with China."

The President said that he sympathized with the Chinese citizens seeking a more open society and that the momentum toward democracy was unstoppable.

"You can't put the genie back in the bottle and return to total repression," Mr. Bush said. "It would be a tragedy for all if China were to pull back to its pre-1972 era of isolation and repression." That was the year President Richard M. Nixon visited China.

Growing Arms Purchases

Arms transactions between China and the United States have grown steadily since June 1984, when the Reagan Administration declared China eligible to make arms purchases.

Pentagon and State Department officials said China has purchased more than $600 million in gear or technology in four major transactions. The bulk of these transactions remain undelivered, and those already in the pipeline have been suspended.

The largest transaction, worth $502 million, was the sale of 55 avionics kits to modernize the electronic systems on Chinese F-8 jet fighters. Defense Department officials said the equipment—including radar gauges, computers and sensing items—had not yet been shipped to China, although State Department aides said a relatively small amount was already in the pipeline.

Another transaction included a $28.5 million sale of technology and assistance in October 1985 to build an artillery ammunition plant. The equipment had been shipped, but production lines have not been set up in China, officials said. A third transaction involved the sale of four MK-46 torpedoes in February 1986, valued at $8.5 million. These have not been delivered, Defense Department officials said.

Commercial Sales Included

A fourth transaction involved the $62.5 million sale of four artillery-locating radar sets. Two were delivered in March, Defense officials said. Two others are scheduled for delivery next year.

In addition, the United States approved commercial military sales to China last year totalling $85 million. These sales have also been suspended. Meanwhile, Secretary of State James A. Baker 3d told Congressional leaders in a private meeting that the fate of the senior Chinese leader, Deng Xiaoping, remained uncertain and that the United States did not know whether he was ill or even alive, a senior White House official said.

"It appears that somehow the continuity of control that had been exercised has unraveled," said another White House aide, who indicated that the bulk of his day was spent trying to determine the fate of the Chinese leader and who was actually in charge.

Mr. Bush also offered "humanitarian and medical assistance through the Red Cross to those injured during the assault."

Stronger Measures Urged

Lawmakers in both parties, liberals as well as conservatives, praised President Bush's decision to suspend Government and commercial military sales to China. But some, including Senators Jesse Helms, Republican of North Carolina, and Edward M. Kennedy, Democrat of Massachusetts, urged stronger measures.

Groups of lawmakers spoke to about 1,000 demonstrators, many of them Chinese students in black armbands, on the steps of the Capitol.

"I think he's taken the exact, appropriate steps," said Senator Alan Cranston, Democrat of California. "He has avoided taking extreme steps that would not contribute to the resolution of the problems."

Mr. Helms, ranking Republican on the Senate Foreign Relations Committee, said he would seek "contingency" legislation that would suspend trade, investment and other ties to China "if these brutal atrocities continue." The Foreign Relations Committee has scheduled hearings for Wednesday, and has asked Mr. Baker to testify.

Mr. Kennedy asked for further moves, including "a unified response with our friends and allies to block Chinese acquisition of any high-technology items with military applications."

In announcing the liberalization of immigration rules for Chinese students here, the President said American officials would look sympathetically on those who choose not to return to their homeland when their student visas expire.

The 40,000 Chinese students enrolled in the United States form the largest single foreign student group in the country, said Duke Austin, a spokesman for the Immigration and Naturalization Service.

Several students interviewed today expressed concern that if they went back now they might be subject to reprisals for joining demonstrations in the United States.

* * *

June 13, 1989

HUNGARIANS TO HONOR '56 UPRISING LEADER WITH HUGE FUNERAL

By HENRY KAMM

Special to The New York Times.

BUDAPEST—The Hungarian people are about to join in a commemoration that their leaders have denied them for 31 years. They will finally be allowed to hold a funeral for Prime Minister Imre Nagy, who was hanged on June 16, 1958, for heading the uprising that Soviet troops and tanks crushed in 1956.

Mr. Nagy (pronounced nudge) and the four other Communists who were condemned with him were thrown into unmarked ditches in a potter's field of Budapest's largest cemetery. Their wives and children were not told where.

In a concession to insistent public demands in these days of political thaw, the Communist leadership, as soon as a thaw in the weather made it possible, authorized the exhuming of remains in the field where about 260 people put to death for the revolt were buried and identified those of Mr. Nagy and his companions.

One man more than anyone else found himself in the unsought role of giving voice to the diffuse national yearning for a measure of justice to be restored in full view of the world. He is Miklos Vasarhelyi, the only survivor in Hungary of the Nagy trial. Sentenced to five years, Mr. Vasarhelyi, Mr. Nagy's spokesman and for many years a member of his inner circle, was freed in 1960.

In recent years, Mr. Vasarhelyi has played what is generally recognized as a quiet but vital role in furthering independent thinking and expression. He is the representative of George Soros, an American financier, who through a foundation called the Quantum Fund has subsidized a broad range of activities that Mr. Soros said were intended to "break the monopoly of dogma."

"The founder is really Miklos Vasarhelyi," Mr. Soros said. "It is his work more than anybody else's." Hungarians have called the foundation an "alternative Ministry of Culture." Although the modest 71-year-old former journalist would never admit it, the authorities and the opposition to this day see in Mr. Vasarhelyi the spokesman for Mr. Nagy and his cause of a more humane political system.

After the victims were exhumed and identified, the families were granted the right to carry out private reburials in the dignity of marked graves. But public pressure mounted to make the anniversary of the execution a day of national mourning for Mr. Nagy, a lifelong Communist and lover of the Soviet Union until the moment that his fellow Communists sent him to the gallows. He has now become a hero of legendary stature.

Work and Traffic Will Halt

It will be mainly to Mr. Vasarhelyi's credit when Budapest's largest square becomes the scene of a vast public—although unofficial—commemoration around five coffins and a symbolic sixth for all the others who were hanged. Church bells will chime throughout the nation; work and traffic will halt; special planes, trains and buses will bring mourners from all over, and national television will broadcast the ceremony live.

Mr. Vasarhelyi is the guiding spirit of the Committee for Historical Justice, a small group of those most directly involved—family members of the victims and himself, as a survivor of those who were judged.

As the funeral grew to the dimension of a highly political event, party and Government leaders at the Politburo level began to seek out the soft-spoken former comrade—expelled by the party even before the revolt, together with Mr. Nagy, for "anti-party activity"—to find a way of keeping the commemoration within bounds.

The leadership evidently fears the passions that may be released.

A still passion runs deep in Mr. Vasarhelyi, but not a yearning for revenge. The name of his committee denotes the persistent striving against all odds of a gentle man whose affability in manner and moderation in words cloak a burning determination to establish truth and justice.

'Don't Want Spilling of Blood'

"You know, I don't want trials," he said over coffee in his comfortable apartment in the leafy hills of Buda, not far from that of Mr. Nagy. "I don't want spilling of blood."

Mr. Vasarhelyi believes that in the democratization to which the Communist Party now subscribes, telling the truth about its own record of 44 years in power is indispensable.

"If this Communist Party wants to exist, if it wants to be competitive in free elections, it must change completely, not only in slogans but also in its whole political and historical judgment of Hungarian history," he said. "It must tell the truth, and not only of 1956 but on everything starting in 1945.

"The first thing it must do is detach itself clearly from everything in the party's past. A lot of people would have to go. An entire ruling class has to be peacefully dissolved. Peacefully, but they have to go. There can't be any real democracy and moral revival in Hungary with these people, who have absolutely no credit."

Ambassador Is Recalled

Last month, Foreign Minister Gyula Horn, announcing the recall of Ambassador Sandor Rajnai from Moscow, said this had nothing to do with a demand by the Committee for Historic Justice. Mr. Vasarhelyi smiled and, without rancor, spoke of the Ambassador's past.

He recalled how the leaders of the uprising and their families were seized by Soviet troops as they left their refuge in the Yugoslav Embassy, also on Heroes Square, with a safe-conduct guarantee and were taken to Rumania. They spent five months there as what Mr. Vasarhelyi ironically called "guests and prisoners."

"In April 1957, we were arrested personally by this man who was until recently our Ambassador in Moscow," Mr. Vasarhelyi said. "We spent three or four days in a Rumanian prison and then went all together in a plane, handcuffed and with black bands over our eyes, to Budapest."

The families—including Mrs. Vasarhelyi, a historian, and the couple's three young children—remained in Rumania, kept in ignorance of the men's fate.

No News for Families

"The trial lasted one week," Mr. Vasarhelyi said. "It began on Monday, the sentence was on Sunday and the executions Monday at dawn. The families learned two months later that they were dead. They received absolutely no news from the time we were taken to Hungary.

"The way they were told was typical. Rajnai arrived, called all the adults together and told them, 'Now I will tell you something, but please behave like Communists have to behave.' And he threw the party paper on the table and said, 'Please read this.' It was the paper of June 17.

"There was the communiqué on the trial, and so the woman knew from this newspaper whether she was a widow or the children that their father was dead. They were very caring, because at the door stood somebody with injections and gave sedatives to one or two women who fainted."

When they, like all the bereaved families, occasionally went to put flowers on one of the nameless mounds arrayed in rows in Plot 301, they did so in the hope that more or less official, whispered hints had led them to the right grave. But they never knew.

Mr. Vasarhelyi recalled as typical also that not even Mr. Nagy's farewell letter to his family was ever delivered. "They gave the family only a gold ring, but it was fake," he said. "It was not at all his ring; they stole everything."

Mr. Rajnai remains a member of the party's Central Committee, Mr. Vasarhelyi said drily.

"But I'm sure in the next few weeks he'll call on me to explain," he continued, with a laugh tinged with unaccustomed bitterness. "Others already did. The chap who was the president of our tribunal let me know through a friend that he was forced by the party to do this."

Correction: Because of an editing error, an article yesterday about plans for a funeral for Imre Nagy, the Hungarian leader executed in 1958, misidentified a foundation through which an American financier is subsidizing activities in Hungary. It is the Soros Foundation—Hungary, not the Quantum Fund.

* * *

July 8, 1989

GORBACHEV'S VISION

His Blueprint for European Amity Is Fuzzy And Tinged by Hints of His Own Problems

By JAMES M. MARKHAM
Special to The New York Times.

PARIS, July 7—Declaring that the postwar era is over, President Mikhail S. Gorbachev spent three days in France this week trying to sketch his seductive but elusive concept of "a common European home" stretching from the Urals to the Atlantic.

Yet his blueprint for bridging Europe's ideological divide was fuzzy, and he left his French hosts with several troubling questions about the structure he envisioned.

At a time of momentous political change in Poland and Hungary, Mr. Gorbachev indicated that the nations of Eastern Europe were free to seek their own destinies, and in a resonant speech in Strasbourg on Thursday, he implicitly renounced the Brezhnev doctrine of limited sovereignty for members of the Communist commonwealth.

If Mr. Gorbachev is to be taken at his word, Soviet tanks will never again roll into Eastern Europe to squash popular upheavals, as they did in East Germany in 1953, Hungary in 1956 and Czechoslovakia in 1968.

Warning to the West

Even so, on several occasions he reiterated his conviction that the countries of Eastern Europe would remain "socialist," and he sternly warned the West that any attempt to roll back Europe's ideological frontier could lead to catastrophe.

His insistence that an era of peace and cooperation was at hand was constantly counterbalanced by brooding and almost apocalyptic accents that hinted at the pressures and strains playing on the Soviet leader.

At a news conference Wednesday, he observed that Communist Europe confronted "a danger of destabilization, of a rupture that could be enormously harmful not only to the countries in question but to developments in the world, above all the European continent, where these processes appeared."

Worrying about Washington

While he spoke rarely of the Bush Administration, French officials said Mr. Gorbachev appeared concerned that Washington might be inclined to exploit the fluid situation in Eastern Europe, putting him in an even deeper predicament at home. President Bush sets off on visits to Poland and Hungary on Sunday.

Mr. Gorbachev's belief in the permanence of socialism in Eastern Europe seems remarkable in the light of elections in Poland, not to mention the Soviet Union, that have produced stunning repudiations of Communist barons. In Warsaw, Gen. Wojciech Jaruzelski appears to have been peacefully driven from the presidency as a consequence of the political opening he set in motion.

In one of his most intriguing assertions, Mr. Gorbachev predicted flatly that not just Hungary and Poland but all of what was once called the Communist bloc would ultimately be touched by "democratization." And his definition of "socialism" seemed to be an elastic one when he remarked that both Communists and Western European Social Democrats represented the aspirations of the working classes. Extending his guest's "European home" metaphor, President Francois Mitterrand expressed skepticism, saying that it would be going too far to say that a bedroom had been installed but that perhaps at this point inhabitants could meet in the kitchen and have a snack. In the end, he said, they would have to be free to come and go, chat around the dinner table over television, speak the same language.

"This is a vast enterprise," the French President cautioned. "We are only at the beginning."

Mr. Mitterrand's friendly but prudent handling of Mr. Gorbachev set the tone for the French press and television as they rated the Soviet leader's performance here, comparing it with his maiden visit to Paris in October 1985 and his triumphant trip to West Germany last month. The self-congratulatory verdict was that the clear-eyed French were not prey to Gorbymania, unlike their West German neighbors.

In an encounter with French academic and literary figures at the Sorbonne, Mr. Gorbachev disappointed many in the audience by failing, when pressed, to denounce the repression of the pro-democracy movement in China. At his news conference, he attacked the conservative newspaper Le Figaro for predicting that his days as leader were numbered, causing some here to recall Soviet attacks on the "bourgeois press" in the cold-war days.

These were perhaps small things in themselves, but they were regarded here as tests of Mr. Gorbachev's profession of sharing the kind of democratic values that would be the underpinning of a common European home.

Described as Preoccupied

At the human level, French officials who spent time with Mr. Gorbachev found him deeply preoccupied by the vast challenge of reviving a stagnant economy and holding the country's many ethnic groups together. Foreign Minister Roland Dumas observed that the Soviet leader was "very much under control of himself" but that "an enormous weight rests on his shoulders."

"He's like a driver on a slippery road," Mr. Dumas said. "He can't take the turns as if he were on a dry highway."

As the common European home depends importantly on the survival of one man, the almost existential anguish displayed by its would-be architect gave the French pause. At the same time, Mr. Mitterrand, Mr. Dumas and others concurred that it was the West's duty to help Mr. Gorbachev's restructuring succeed.

The French, however, were content with one apparently firm element in the foundation of Mr. Gorbachev's home: the continued presence of the United States in Europe. The American presence, it is clear, will be met by a continued Soviet presence. Both would seem to guarantee the continued division of Germany, which is a cornerstone of the European status quo.

* * *

July 11, 1989

BUSH, IN WARSAW, UNVEILS PROPOSAL FOR AID TO POLAND

By R. W. APPLE JR.

Special to The New York Times.

WARSAW, July 10—President Bush announced a six-part program of American aid to Poland today to help capitalize on what he termed the "unprecedented opportunity" presented by Poland's tenuous experiment in democracy. But the carefully limited package got a lukewarm reception from leading Polish political figures.

Mr. Bush, on his first visit to Eastern Europe as President, laid out the plan in a speech to a joint meeting of the Polish Parliament, with one house controlled by the Solidarity opposition and the other by the Communist Party.

He said he would urge the World Bank to move ahead with $325 million in new loans, ask the Western allies to support a rescheduling of debts that could amount to $5 billion this year and propose to Congress a $100 million fund "to capitalize and invigorate the Polish private sector."

Poles Say Package Falls Short

The President's program fell far short of the $10 billion, three-year infusion of foreign aid that Solidarity has asked for. Lech Walesa, the Solidarity leader, whom Mr. Bush will meet Tuesday in the Baltic port of Gdansk, said in a telephone interview that it did not provide the sort of "shock treatment" the country needs.

After describing today's events as "conciliatory, effective and successful," Col. Wieslaw Gornicki, the Government spokesman, said there was "very little concrete material" in what Mr. Bush had offered. He complained about the President's repeated emphasis on the need for further sacrifices by the Polish people and of excessive "rhetorical formulations."

"Nobody in this country had any illusions that the stream of gold would flow," the spokesman said. "We did not expect alms or handouts. But while we are very much satisfied with the political tone of the visit, the substance is somewhat limited."

'Symbolic of Our Support'

A senior American official, who asked not to be identified, said that Gen. Wojciech Jaruzelski, the Polish leader, had peppered the President with questions about the economic proposals this morning, an early sign of his dissatisfaction.

Tonight, in an interview with Cable News Network, Gen. Brent Scowcroft, the national security adviser, conceded that

The New York Times/Witold Jaroslaw Szulecki

President Bush addressing Poland's Parliament in Warsaw, where he announced an American aid program.

the $100 million in direct aid was largely "symbolic of our support for what it is the Poles are trying to do." But he argued that debt restructuring and new World Bank loans were substantive proposals which, if adopted, "will make a difference" here.

"I think the practical impact is as much political and psychological as it is substantive," he said.

On the first full day of his European trip, Mr. Bush also laid two wreaths and held several meetings, including a luncheon at the American Embassy for Communist and Solidarity leaders. Crowds of several thousand turned out to greet him, waving Polish and American flags, but the emotional outpouring that some American officials had predicted failed to materialize.

At one point, Mr. Bush jumped from his limousine to shake hands with a crowd near the Parliament. It was one of many moments of vivid contrast with the recent past; on the same spot only last week, the police clashed with opposition demonstrators who were calling for General Jaruzelski's ouster.

Secretary of State James A. Baker 3d said the Americans had not been "at all disappointed" by the relatively small crowds, because "this is not some election campaign."

As Mr. Baker acknowledged this evening, Mr. Bush adopted an almost conversational tone, making "no effort to divide or disrupt," as the secretary put it, and using "no hot rhetoric." Both the Americans and the Poles seemed eager to avoid offending President Mikhail S. Gorbachev of the Soviet Union, whose "new ideas" helped set in motion the changes here—indeed, Mr. Bush went so far as to quote Mr. Gorbachev in his speech.

Clearly, the President was walking a narrow line between raising expectations so high that failure to meet them would destabilize the country and giving so little that the Poles would lose heart and pull back.

Call for Sacrifices

Standing before a Polish eagle mounted upon an immense red-and-white banner in the neo-classical Senate chamber, the President said that "Poland is where the cold war began, and now the people of Poland can help bring the division of Europe to an end." But he warned that economic reform and recovery here "cannot occur without sacrifices" by every Pole.

"There can be no substitute for Poland's own efforts," Mr. Bush said as he outlined his program, which also included $15 million to fight rampant air and water pollution in the historic city of Cracow in southern Poland. "But I want to stress to you today that Poland is not alone."

He added, "The United States stands ready to help as you help yourselves."

Mr. Baker said that last phrase caught the attention of Prime Minister Mieczyslaw Rakowski. The Secretary reported that the Prime Minister told Mr. Bush at a later meeting, "I'd like to put that slogan on the wall with your name on it and mine, too."

Mr. Bush's offer of aid comes a month after President Francois Mitterrand, on a visit to Poland, announced that France had agreed to restructure $1.15 billion of Poland's $39 billion in foreign debt and provide new bank loans of nearly $100 million.

The United States, the International Monetary Fund and others are pressing the Poles to make major changes in the way they manage their debts and in the terms under which they permit private businesses to operate. The Government of General Jaruzelski is also under pressure at home and abroad to do something immediately about the country's inflation rate of almost 100 percent a year—so bad that "you can almost hear it whistling as it roars past," as one Warsaw working man said today.

Strings Attached to Future Aid

Without changes there will be no more aid, the Bush Administration has made clear.

"In the 1970's," Mr. Baker said at a briefing for correspondents traveling with him and with the President, "we and our allies and the Polish people made a mistake. We shovelled a lot of money into this country with no requirement for economic reform."

John H. Sununu, the White House chief of staff, made the same point in a much blunter way—too blunt, in the view of some Poles, who found his language patronizing—in an interview here with NBC News. It was important not to do "too much" for Poland, he said, adding the following explanation:

"The analogy that's almost appropriate is, you can't create the problem of a young person in the candy store, where there is so much there that they don't know which direction to take and don't have the self-discipline to take the right steps."

Despite the muted tone of the day, some of those in Mr. Bush's audience at the Senate building found his speech very moving. Zbigniew Mierzwa, a young Solidarity legislator from Przemysl, praised Mr. Bush for having made "a proposal that he can deliver" and for speaking "as if he were in his own Senate."

"You could see tears in some eyes," Mr. Mierzwa said. But even the limited measures proposed by Mr. Bush will require the cooperation of others—the Congress in the case of the private-enterprise fund, as well as the allies, whom he will ask to make further contributions. He needs the cooperation of the World Bank, too, and he will have to persuade the so-called Paris Club to back his plan for generous debt rescheduling.

To judge from the applause, the President's promise to help Cracow, while modest in terms of money, was perhaps the most popular element in his program. That city, once the political capital of Poland, remains its art capital, with a wealth of Gothic architecture, a much-loved Leonardo portrait of a young woman holding an ermine and the handsome buildings of the historic Jagiellonian University, where the astronomer Copernicus worked 450 years ago.

* * *

October 8, 1989

COMMUNIST PARTY IN HUNGARY VOTES FOR RADICAL SHIFT

By HENRY KAMM

Special to The New York Times.

BUDAPEST, Oct. 7—The Hungarian Communist Party voted today to transform itself into a socialist party and said it would strive to bridge the gulf between doctrinaire Marxism and European democratic socialism.

In a series of votes to change the party's name to the Hungarian Socialist Party and set general party direction, the delegates at an extraordinary party congress here greatly raised expectations that the reform-oriented leadership's entire program to overhaul the party would be adopted. Among the changes expected are more democratic procedures for choosing the leadership.

With Poland, Hungary is at the forefront of change in the Eastern bloc. But unlike Poland, where the Solidarity union has taken the reins of power with the Communist Party largely unchanged, Hungary is pushing through radical change from within its Communist Party.

Approval from the Floor

While decisive, tonight's vote totals were difficult to ascertain because some measures were approved by a show of hands of the large number of delegates and went uncounted.

In a news conference before the voting, Imre Pozsgay, a member of Hungary's collective presidency and a leader of those advocating major change, said an overwhelming majority of the delegates supported the leadership's program so that the party can better confront new, independently formed parties in free parliamentary elections due to be held by next June.

Mr. Pozsgay did not elaborate on the party's new path, but details of the nature of the renamed party and its prospective leadership were disclosed by an official close to Rezso Nyers, the party President.

Elections Ahead

The official said in an interview that by this morning, a majority of the more than 1,200 delegates to the congress had agreed on the new party structure, the leaders to be elected and the program to be adopted before the congress ends Sunday or Monday.

The official said Mr. Nyers would be chosen as party president. Mr. Pozsgay and Prime Minister Miklos Nemeth, another member of the presidency, are to be named vice presidents, and it is possible that a Politburo member, Pal Vastagh, will be elected to that same rank.

The post of General Secretary, now held by Karoly Grosz, is to be abolished. Instead, the lesser position of National Secretary is to be created. Jeno Kovacs, now a Central Committee secretary, has been chosen to fill the office, which is to manage the day-by-day work of the party.

Dispensing with the traditional Politburo and Central Committee, the new party is to be guided by a presidium of 15 to 21 members and a national committee of about 150.

Contrary to Communist practice, the national committee will not be chosen by the party congress, as the Central Committee is, but through balloting by all party members, a bow to greater democracy. Central Committee secretaries, the party's equivalent of government ministers, are to be replaced by presidium members assigned to specific tasks.

Faced with severe economic problems and declining popularity, as shown in recent losses in several parliamentary by-elections, the party has gradually introduced liberalizations in recent years, including the scheduling of next year's multiparty national elections, the country's first in more than four decades.

Another change came this year when, in an opening to the West, Budapest lifted restrictions along its border with Austria, setting off a mass migration of East Germans through Hungary and on to West Germany.

Defection of the Orthodox

The official close to Mr. Nyers said the leadership expects the Communist transformation to prompt as many as a third of the present membership of 725,000 to leave the party.

It is expected that some of those who leave will regroup in a new party. In expectation of such a move, the official said, the party has taken legal steps to secure its hold over such assets as the grandiose party headquarters on the Pest bank of the Danube.

In speeches, several delegates to the congress demanded that the party return to the Government many of its extensive assets throughout Hungary, including office buildings, hotels and resorts, and commercial properties.

The biggest loser in the creation of a new leadership is likely to be Mr. Grosz. Since unseating Janos Kadar last year, Mr. Grosz has seemed to be a reluctant reformer. As recently as Friday, he insisted in a toughly worded speech that reforms be limited and Communist ideals retained. And he aimed a sharp rebuke at Mr. Pozsgay, without mentioning him by name, accusing him of seeking to drive more orthodox Communists out of the party.

In a sharp rebuff to Mr. Grosz, the delegates tonight approved an amended text of a statement that specifically rejected a Grosz proposal. The General Secretary had strongly urged the Communists to simply declare a renewal of the party rather than the establishment of a new one. The amendment pointedly redrafted the declaration to make it clear that the old party was dead and that it considered itself a new party.

Mr. Nyers is said to have managed months of internecine disputes and maneuvers to prevent an open split in the congress while still securing the transformation of the party, which had been formally known as the Hungarian Socialist Workers Party. Although there is personal antipathy between Mr. Nyers and Mr. Pozsgay, both advocate change, as does Prime Minister Nemeth.

All three have stressed that their commitment to change does not mean that the party means to question Hungary's alliance with the Soviet Union in the Warsaw Pact.

Today, Mr. Nemeth sounded the clearest call yet for drastic change to prepare for next year's elections.

"We must be the most democratic of all Hungarian parties," he said to applause. "We need a new party, with a new form of organization, a new platform and a new name. We need a reformed membership. Our members should not be a flock of sheep following a bellwether. Those who don't feel at home in this party should form a new party."

Mr. Nemeth made evident the ultimate purpose of the reorganization, saying, "We don't want members, we want voters."

* * *

October 19, 1989

EAST GERMANY REMOVES HONECKER AND HIS PROTEGE TAKES HIS PLACE

By SERGE SCHMEMANN

Special to The New York Times.

WEST BERLIN, Oct. 18—Confronted with increasing demands for change, the East German Communist Party today ousted Erich Honecker, its hard-line leader of 18 years, and named his 52-year-old protégé to replace him.

The new leader, Egon Krenz, had been the Politburo member charged with security and youth affairs. He was named to Mr. Honecker's three positions—party chief, head of state and chairman of the Defense Council—granting him the broad powers Mr. Honecker spent years accumulating.

Though the youngest member of the Politburo, Mr. Krenz is generally regarded as a tough and conservative leader in Mr. Honecker's mold but 25 years younger, more sophisticated and probably better aware of the scope and sources of popular discontent.

Mr. Honecker, in his message of resignation, said that his illness and gall-bladder surgery "no longer allow me to devote the power and energy demanded today," and he proposed Mr. Krenz as his successor, describing him as "able and decisive."

Mr. Krenz underscored his difference in style from Mr. Honecker, who usually restricted his public appearances to stiff, formal rituals, with an appearance on television shortly after his appointment. Smiling, Mr. Krenz said: "My motto remains work, work, work and more work, but work that should be pleasant and serve all the people."

'A Great Loss of Blood'

In the evening, Mr. Krenz delivered an hour-long nationally televised address in which he reaffirmed the standing policy of "continuity and renewal," but added that "within these bounds, the door is wide open for earnest political dialogue."

"It is clear that we have not realistically appraised the social developments in our country in recent months, and have not drawn the right conclusions quickly enough," Mr. Krenz said. "We see the seriousness of the situation. But we also sense and recognize the major opportunity we have opened for ourselves to define the policies in dialogue with our citizens, policies that will bring us to the verge of the next century."

Mr. Krenz also spoke of the exodus of thousands of East Germans to West Germany as "a great loss of blood," and he referred openly to problems in industry, housing, productivity and elsewhere. Mr. Krenz also indicated that new travel regulations would soon be enacted, making it easier for East Germans to travel abroad.

And he insisted that "without the Communist Party, there is no German Democratic Republic." He gave no indication that the discussion he called for would include New Forum or other of the other unsanctioned new groups that have cropped up, demanding change.

Mr. Krenz did not directly criticize Mr. Honecker, but he used the phrase Mikhail S. Gorbachev had used two weeks earlier when the Soviet leader visited East Berlin: "We have to see and react to the times, otherwise life will punish us."

It is not known whether Mr. Gorbachev's visit in any way caused the change of leadership, which was made Tuesday in a Politburo meeting that Eastern European sources said was stormy. The full Central Committee was summoned to an extraordinary session today to ratify the changes.

Honecker Aides Are Retired

Retired with Mr. Honecker from the governing body were Gunter Mittag, the 63-year-old official in charge of the East German economy and a close associate of Mr. Honecker, and Joachim Herrmann, 60, the propaganda chief.

Mr. Mittag was believed to have been punished for his resistance to change in economic management, and even more for his proximity to Mr. Honecker. Mr. Herrmann was presumed to have fallen because of the inflexible propaganda approach that had the official press and broadcast outlets continue denying problems or the need for change until the storm broke.

The changes were the latest and most dramatic developments in the crisis that has seized East Germany in recent weeks, first with the flight of tens of thousands of citizens to West Germany through neighboring countries, then with the mass marches in major East German cities by people chanting demands for democratic change.

Seriously ailing through the summer, Mr. Honecker, 77, returned to preside over gala celebrations Oct. 7 commemorating the 40th anniversary of the East German state. But even as he read a defiant paean to his past achievements, the police struggled to contain spontaneous demonstrations in the streets.

Politburo Remains Intact

Meeting after the mass protests last week, the Politburo ordered a greater openness in the press and acknowledged the need to hold national discussions on political and economic change.

Western leaders and East German opposition spokesmen, however, were cautious in assessing the prospect for change under Mr. Krenz. They noted that all other members of the Politburo—including old-guard stalwarts like Erich Mielke, the 82-year-old Minister for State Security, or Hermann Axen, the 73-year-old party secretary for international relations—remained in place.

Mr. Krenz followed in his predecessor's steps first as head of the Communist youth organization and then as party secretary for security.

That, they said, suggested that the changes at the top could be more a jettisoning of ballast by a leadership bent on survival than a purge.

Visit to Beijing Leadership

On the one hand, they said they expected that Mr. Krenz was sufficiently aware of the scope of discontent in East Germany and that he would take urgent steps to defuse the tensions.

On the other hand, they noted that his image in the nation was of a hard-liner who earlier this month paid a well-publicized call on the Chinese leadership and who has never in the past spoken out on the need for change.

"Naturally we wanted somebody else for the job," said Michael Turek, a Protestant pastor and member of New Forum, the popular movement seeking changes that was formed last month, in a telephone interview from Leipzig. "He has never talked of reform, and has close connections with all the old hard-liners. We can only hope that he'll be intelligent enough to introduce a new program."

Willy Brandt, the former Social Democratic Chancellor of West Germany, said: "They are in a transitional phase, despite and even because of these personnel changes. I am skeptical about a genuine answer to the demands for real reforms."

Chancellor Helmut Kohl of West Germany said the new leader would be measured by whether he "takes the path of long overdue reforms or sticks to a defense of their monopoly on power."

* * *

November 10, 1989

EAST GERMANY OPENS FRONTIER TO THE WEST FOR MIGRATION OR TRAVEL; THOUSANDS CROSS

By SERGE SCHMEMANN
Special to The New York Times.

EAST BERLIN, Friday, Nov. 10—East Germany on Thursday lifted restrictions on emigration or travel to the West, and within hours tens of thousands of East and West Berliners swarmed across the infamous Berlin Wall for a boisterous celebration.

Border guards at Bornholmer Strasse crossing, Checkpoint Charlie and several other crossings abandoned all efforts to check credentials, even though the new regulations said East Germans would still need passports and permission to get across. Some guards smiled and took snapshots, assuring passers-by that they were just recording a historic event.

Politburo Announcement

The mass crossing began about two hours after Gunter Schabowski, a member of the Politburo, had announced at a press conference that permission to travel or emigrate would be granted quickly and without preconditions, and that East Germans would be allowed to cross at any crossing into West Germany or West Berlin.

"We know this need of citizens to travel or leave the country," Mr. Schabowski said. "Today the decision was taken that makes it possible for all citizens to leave the country through East German crossing points."

Mr. Schabowski also said the decision ended the agreement to let East Germans leave through Czechoslovakia and other countries. Some 50,000 East Germans have left through Czechoslovakia, and a 14-mile-long queue of East German cars was reported Thursday at the Schirnding border crossing on the Czech-West German border. Since September, thousands more have left through Hungary and Poland.

Flag Waving in the West

Once Mr. Schabowski's announcement was read on radio and television, a tentative trickle of East Germans testing the new regulations quickly turned into an jubilant horde, which joined at the border crossings with crowds of flag-waving, cheering West Germans. Thousands of Berliners clambered across the wall at the Brandenburg Gate, passing through the historic arch that for so long had been inaccessible to Berliners of either side.

Similar scenes were reported in Lubeck, the only other East German city touching the border, and at other border crossings along the inter-German frontier.

All through the night and into the early morning, celebrating East Berliners filled the Kurfurstendamm, West Berlin's "great white way," blowing trumpets, dancing, laughing and absorbing a glittering scene that until now they could glimpse only on television.

Many East Germans said they planned to return home the same night. The Mayor of West Berlin, Walter Momper, toured border crossings in a police radio truck and urged East Berliners to return.

East German radio announced that the uncontrolled crossings would be ended at 8 A.M. today, after which East Germans would be required to obtain a visa.

The extraordinary breach of what had been the most infamous stretch of the Iron Curtain marked the culmination of an extraordinary month that has seen the virtual transformation of East Germany under the dual pressures of unceasing flight and continuing demonstrations. It also marked a breach of a wall that had become the premier symbol of Stalinist oppression and of the divisions of Europe and Germany into hostile camps after World War II.

An Effort to Stem a Tide

The immediate reason for the decision was evidently a recognition by East Germany's embattled authorities that they could not stem the outward tide by opening the door a crack and hoping that rapid liberalization at home would end the urge to flee. They now seemed to hope that an open door would quickly let out those who were determined to leave, and give pause to those who had doubted the sincerity of the Government's pledge of profound change.

The Berlin wall—first raised on Aug. 13, 1961, to halt a vast hemorrhage of East Germans to the West—evolved into a double row of eight-foot-high concrete walls with watchtowers, electronic sensors and a no man's land in between. Frequent attempts to breach the barrier often ended in death, and the very sophistication of the wall became a standing indictment of the system that could hold its people only with such extraordinary means.

The decision to allow East Germans to travel freely came on a day when Egon Krenz, the new East German leader, was reported to have called for a law insuring free and democratic elections. In a speech to the Communist Party's Central Committee on Wednesday night that was published today, Mr. Krenz also called for new laws on freedom of assembly, association and the press. But he gave no details.

Mr. Schabowski's announcement about the unimpeded travel was greeted with an outburst of emotion in West Germany, whose Constitution sustains the hope of a reunited Germany and whose people have seen in the dramatic changes in East Germany the first glimmers of an end to division.

The West German Parliament abandoned a heated debate after learning of the new developments, and ended its session with a spontaneous singing of the national anthem.

"We demand of the responsible people in the German Democratic Republic that they start tomorrow to tear down the wall," declared Friedrich Bohl, the chief whip of the governing Christian Democrats.

In West Berlin, Eberhard Diepgen, the former Mayor, said: "This is a day I have been awaiting since Aug. 13, 1961. With this the wall has lost its function. It can and must be torn down."

Wall Will Not Come Down

Mr. Schabowski, however, said the wall would not be coming down. "There are other factors for the existence of the wall other than traveling," he said, suggesting that its fate depended on broader questions of relations between the two Germanys and between East and West.

In replying to a question, however, Mr. Schabowski abandoned the customary East German reference to the barrier as an "anti-fascist protection wall," and instead called it a "fortified border."

His statement underlined that the new regulations did not change the status of Berlin, which is still formally occupied by the victorious Allies of World War II, with East Berlin as the Soviet zone. There was also no change in the requirement that Westerners obtain visas for East Germany, or day passes to visit East Berlin.

East Germans began almost immediately to test the new measure. One couple crossed into West Berlin at the Bornholmer Strasse crossing with only their identity cards just two hours after Mr. Schabowski spoke. After a gleeful exchange with some West Berliners, they returned to their side of the wall, saying they had only wanted to test the new permeability of the barrier.

West German television showed curious East Germans flocking to crossing points at the wall, with some passing through with their identity cards.

Some Are Skeptical

Other East Berliners were more muted in their reaction, reflecting the skepticism forstered by the dizzying rate of change in East Germany in recent weeks. The Government had already allowed virtually unrestricted emigration to West Germany through Czechoslovakia, and on Monday it published the draft of a new travel law that went far beyond anything granted to before. The measure, however, was roundly condemned because it limited foreign travel to 30 days.

The new measures also raised some questions, including how much currency East Germans would be allowed to change into Western money. The East German mark is not freely convertible, and up to now East Germans have been allowed to exchange just 15 of their marks, about $8 at the official exchange rate.

Hans-Peter Schneider, a member of Democratic Awakening, one of the new opposition groups, said, "At the moment, I doubt that this is a step that will support our efforts to get people to stay in the country."

The official East German press agency, A.D.N., said the new measures took effect immediately. They provided that East Germans could apply for trips abroad without giving any reasons, as they had to do in the past, and that permission would be granted on short notice. A.D.N. added that permission would be denied only in exceptional cases, evidently concerning state security.

Emigration without Conditions

The new regulations also called on the authorities to grant emigration papers immediately and without condition.

The main novelty in the new regulations was that permission to travel to the West would be virtually automatic. Though millions of East Germans have traveled to the West in the past, the permission was always conditional and difficult to obtain.

The excitement over so momentous an opening failed to conceal a growing anxiety on both sides of the border over the swelling size of the exodus from East Germany.

More than 50,000 East Germans fled over only the last weekend. West German estimates have put the figure of East Germans yearning to settle in the West at up to 1.4 million, out of a population of 16 million.

The huge influx of East Germans and of ethnic Germans from the Soviet Union, Poland and other East European countries has already severely taxed West Germany's capacity.

525,000 Crossed This Year

In Bonn, Interior Minister Wolfgang Schauble said in Parliament that 225,000 East Germans had crossed into West Germany this year, plus about 300,000 other ethnic Germans. He said would-be migrants should consider the fact that they might be living in worse conditions in the West than they had in the East.

Chancellor Helmut Kohl of West Germany, starting a long-awaited visit to Poland, welcomed the East German decision. But he added: "It is hard to estimate what consequences this step will have. Our interest must be that our compatriots stay in their homeland."

Mr. Kohl said he was seeking an urgent meeting with Mr. Krenz. The Chancellor has repeatedly declared that he will give extensive aid to East Germany once it grants its citizens free elections.

The leader of the West German Social Democratic Party, Hans-Jochem Vogel, went on East German television to declare that he supported a public appeal made yesterday by Christa Wolf, a prominent East German writer, for East Germans to stay home.

Marked 40th Anniversary

The announcement of the travel measures was the latest in an extraordinary chain of events that has profoundly transformed East Germany since it marked its 40th anniversary on Oct. 7.

Shocked into action by the mass flights that gathered pace all through the summer, hundreds of thousands of East Germans have taken to the streets in the last months to press with increasing urgency for profound change in their society, which under Erich Honecker ranked among the most ironclad Communist strongholds in Eastern Europe.

The double pressures of the mass exodus and mass demonstrations has sent the Communist Party into headlong retreat. Mr. Honecker was ousted Oct. 18, and at the start of the extraordinary Central Committee session now under way, the entire Politburo resigned to enable Mr. Krenz, the new leader, to select a smaller and younger panel, including only five of the former members.

The Government had already resigned, and the presidium of the legislature announced on Thursday that it would call the full Parliament into session on Monday. Mr. Schabowski announced that the Central Committee would call a party conference on Dec. 15.

* * *

November 11, 1989

THE BORDER IS OPEN; JOYOUS EAST GERMANS POUR THROUGH WALL; PARTY PLEDGES FREEDOMS, AND CITY EXULTS

By SERGE SCHMEMANN
Special to The New York Times.

WEST BERLIN, Nov. 10—As hundreds of thousands of East Berliners romped through the newly porous wall in an unending celebration, West German leaders today proclaimed this the moment Germans had yearned for through 40 years of division.

At the same time, change continued unabated in East Berlin, where the Communist Party's Central Committee concluded a three-day session with the announcement of a program of radical changes. They included "free, democratic and secret elections," a "socialist planned economy oriented to market conditions," separation of party and state, parliamentary supervision of state security, freedom of assembly and a new law on the press and broadcasting.

'In the Midst of an Awakening'

"The German Democratic Republic is in the midst of an awakening," the Central Committee declared in the prologue to the newly adopted program. "A revolutionary people's movement has brought into motion a process of great change. The renewal of society is on the agenda."

Though the West Berlin police could give no estimate of the numbers of East Berliners who crossed over in the last 24 hours, the authorities said that only 1,500 so far had announced their intention to stay.

Beyond Berlin, only one of many points along the border between the two Germanys where people could cross, 55,500 East Germans crossed over the border between the two Germanys since the wall was opened on Thursday, and 3,250 remained in West Germany, the West German Interior Ministry said.

Chancellor Helmut Kohl, who interrupted a state visit to Poland to come to West Berlin, told an emotional crowd of East and West Berliners gathered outside the West Berlin city hall: "I want to call out to all in the German Democratic Republic: We're on your side, we are and remain one nation. We belong together."

Speaking on the steps of the city hall, from which President John F. Kennedy had made his "Ich bin ein Berliner" speech shortly after the wall was raised, Mr. Kohl declared: "Long live a free German fatherland! Long live a united Europe!"

Kurfurstendamm Is Packed

All through the night and through the day, East Berliners continued to flood into West Berlin in vast numbers, filling the glittering Kurfurstendamm until traffic came to a halt, forming long lines to pick up the 100-mark "welcome money"—about $55—that West Germany has traditionally given East Germans on their first time in the West, gaping at shop windows and drinking in the heady new feeling of freedom.

Reuters

An East German border guard handing a flower back to West Berliners who sat atop the Berlin wall.

A festival air seized the entire city. West Berliners lined entry points to greet East Berliners with champagne, cheers and hugs. Many restaurants offered the visitors free food. A television station urged West Berliners to call in with offers of theater tickets, beds, dinners or just guided tours of the "Ku'damm."

The Hertha soccer club, popular both in West and East, offered 10,000 free tickets to the game against Wattenscheid on Saturday.

Both West and East German television gave saturation coverage to the reunion, often under titles like "The End of the Wall," contributing to a widespread sense that a great moment was in the making.

In a development that gave further evidence of the figurative crumbling of the wall, East Germany announced the opening of five new crossings. One was at the Glienicke Bridge, famed as the site of past exchanges of captured spies between East and West, and another was at Potsdammer Platz, once the heart of Berlin.

The arrival of an army bulldozer at Eberswalder Strasse to drill another new opening quickly attracted a crowd on both sides and sent rumors through the city that the East German Army was breaking down the wall. When the machine finally

Agence France Presse

Thousands of Germans standing on the Berlin wall facing East German border guards near the Brandenburg gate yesterday, the first full day of the opening of the border.

broke through, West Berliners handed flowers to the driver and rushed to pick up pieces of the wall for souvenirs.

At the Potsdammer Platz crossing site, West Berliners mounted the wall to chip away pieces while East German workers laid paving stones in the no-man's land, watched by about 50 soldiers.

The East German authorities also announced that bus shuttles would connect East and West Berlin.

In the giddiness of the grand reunion, German reunification was in the air. "We've done it! The wall is open!" proclaimed the popular tabloid Bild in a giant headline. "This is the first step to unity."

The conservative Frankfurter Allgemeine tempered its excitement with caution: "Since Thursday evening that monstrous construction and barbed wire no longer divide the people. But with the joy over the end of the torment of German division, we must realize that faster German rapprochement needs a faster consideration of how politically to handle a situation changing by the hour."

A group of young men walked down the Kurfurstendamm with the two German flags, identical save for a Communist emblem at the center of the East German banner, sewn together.

The theme was there, too, in the emotional speeches from the steps of city hall. Willy Brandt, the former West German Chancellor who was West Berlin's Mayor in 1961 when the wall was raised, declared in a choked voice: "This is a beautiful day after a long voyage, but we are only at a way station. We are not at the end of our way."

"The moving together of the German states is taking shape in reality in a different way than many of us expected," Mr. Brandt said. "No one should act as if he knows in which concrete form the people in these two states will find a new relationship. But that they will find a relationship, that they will come together in freedom, that is the important point."

'Happiest People on Earth'

Walter Momper, the Mayor of West Berlin, raised cheers when he declared: "The whole city and all its citizens will never forget Nov. 9, 1989. For 28 years since the wall was built we have yearned for this day. We Germans are now the happiest people on earth. Yesterday was not yet the day of reunification, but it was a day of reunion."

The West German Foreign Minister, Hans-Dietrich Genscher, who returned with Mr. Kohl from Poland for the gathering, opened his address by recalling his roots in East Germany, from which he fled after the war.

"My most hearty greetings go to the people of my homeland," he said. "What we are witnessing in the streets of Berlin in these hours is that 40 years of division have not created two nations out of one. There is no capitalist and there is no socialist Germany, but only one German nation in unity and peace."

Evidently anticipating the anxieties of other countries, Mr. Genscher added: "No people on this earth, no people in Europe have to fear if the gates are opened now between East and West. No people have to fear that liberty and democracy have returned to the G.D.R."

Kohl Gets Loud Jeers

Mr. Kohl was met by loud jeers from the crowd, evidently reflecting his unpopularity among many West Berliners, as he declared this "a historic moment for Berlin and for Germany."

The Chancellor appealed to East Germans to stay in their country now that it was evidently firmly on the road to political and economic change. "We are sure that when these reforms come to pass, and if the G.D.R. goes forward on this path, our compatriots there who now think of leaving will stay in their homeland," he said.

Mr. Kohl flew from West Berlin to Bonn, where he will preside over an emergency Cabinet meeting on Saturday morning before returning to Poland to continue his official visit.

Krenz Addresses Party Rally

In East Germany, the conclusion of the Central Committee meeting was followed by a mass rally of Communist Party members that was addressed Egon Krenz, the new party leader.

"We plan a great work, a revolution on German soil that will bring us a socialism that is economically effective, politically democratic, morally clean and will turn to the people in everything," Mr. Krenz declared.

"That's why the Council of Ministers issued new travel regulations for all mature citizens in our country as an expression that we are serious in our policy of renewal and that we reach out our hands to everyone who wants to go with us," he said.

The "action program" adopted today, Mr. Krenz said, was "a program for our people to win back trust among the people."

"We want better socialism, we want free elections, we want our people to send their best representatives to Parliament," he said.

Mr. Krenz also reaffirmed his loyalty to Moscow, as he has taken care to do since he came to power. "Our close links to the Soviet Union make us strong, and give new meaning to our slogan, that to learn from the Soviet Union is to learn to win, especially in these days," he said.

Day Session a Turning Point

The action program outlined by the official press agency A.D.N. followed the proposals first made by Mr. Krenz on the opening day of the Central Committee meeting. The three-day meeting proved a turning point in the dramatic upheaval that has seized East Germany over the last month.

The Central Committee issued only broad directives for change. On the economic front, it called for making the planned economy sensitive to market conditions, though it did not elaborate how this would be done. With an eye to the most widespread complaints, it said the economy would concentrate on areas such as consumer goods, meat, beer and spare parts.

The proposed election law promised to be the most fateful of the new measures. The West German radio said Hans Modrow, the new Prime Minister, had discussed with Mr. Krenz the possibility of forming a coalition government with some of the small parties, including the Social Democrats and the Liberals.

Mr. Modrow said the action program of the Communist Party would not be enough without the input of the other parties, which have become more independent and vocal over the last month.

Ousted Leaders Censured

The Central Committee also strongly censured Erich Honecker, the fallen party leader, and two Politburo members ousted with him, Gunter Mittag and Joachim Hermann. "The Central Committee has learned that serious mistakes of the previous General Secretary and Politburo led the party and republic into deep crisis," the final communiqué of the session said.

The committee reserved its sharpest criticism for Mr. Mittag, who had been the secretary charged with the economy. "Comrade Mittag was excluded from the Central Committee because of the gravest violations of inner-party democracy, against party and state discipline and because of damaging the reputation of the party," it said.

The program also called for approval of freedom of assembly, legalization of new political organizations, a constitutional court and changes in criminal law to include independent juries. It also said the party would immediately take measures to lift privileges held by party leaders.

It declared, too, that military policy would be publicly discussed, and that military spending might be reduced.

The program is expected to come under more detailed discussion when Parliament meets on Monday.

* * *

November 13, 1989

U.S., ITS VISION BLURRED, AVOIDS CRISIS MENTALITY

By THOMAS L. FRIEDMAN
Special to The New York Times.

WASHINGTON, Nov. 12—Administration officials said today that in view of the recent events in East Germany they are studying every "way-out scenario" imaginable for Europe, NATO and the Warsaw Pact, but for the moment they intend to sit tight, let the dust settle and not do anything that will be regretted later.

Indeed, there was no sense of crisis in Washington today, no special "Berlin task force" to monitor events. Officials were home watching the Washington Redskins football team on television, just as they were last Sunday when the Berlin wall was still a real barrier.

At the State Department, more energy seemed to be devoted to monitoring the leftist guerrilla offensive in El Salvador than the drama in East Berlin.

This is not because Administration officials are indifferent to the events unfolding in East Berlin. It is rather that they evidently feel that the developments are generally in America's interests, and the product of American policies over the last 40 years, so there is little reason to get in the way.

Even if they wanted to put events on a different course, officials argue, they have few resources to accomplish this at the moment, and no clear, long-term vision of Europe yet that could guide them.

A top Administration policy maker, trying to explain the apparent contradiction between heavy American news coverage of Berlin and the absence of major activity in Washington, said: "It is natural that symbols take on great emotional meaning in international relations. And of all the symbols, the division of Berlin and the Berlin wall is one of the greatest.

"Both the apparent and real breaches in the Berlin wall naturally lead to a rush of speculation that a new order is in the offing," he said. "But it is not going to happen overnight.

"We are probably on the start of an era where American diplomacy can help shape the lines of a new international order," he added. "But what is important at this point is not crisis management, but considered thinking about the shape of that new order and how we get there, and that's what we're doing."

It appears that the only Administration decision has been to agree with the Soviet Union and West Germany to play down talk of any immediate reunfication of the two Germanys, and to refrain from doing anything that might inflame the situation.

Administration officials said that President Bush has an informal understanding with Chancellor Helmut Kohl of West Germany that Washington will continue to speak positively about the "principle" of German reunification, even though this is anathema to many allies in the North Atlantic Treaty Organization. In return, they said, Bonn must closely coordinate its activities with the United States and refrain from taking any immediate steps toward unification until a proper European security framework is established.

President Mikhail S. Gorbachev of the Soviet Union indicated a similar preference in his letter to President Bush on Friday, officials said.

These understandings rang through loud and clear in remarks by a variety of American, Soviet and German diplomats over the weekend.

When asked about German reunification on the ABC News program "This Week," Secretary of State James A. Baker 3d said, "In my view, it is at least premature to jump, to make the great leap—and it is a big leap—from right of free travel on the part of East Germans to the question of reunification.

"There are many things, it seems to me, that have to take place in between," he said. "One of those is fair and free and even multi-party elections in East Germany. Another is movement to a free economic system, free markets, free enterprise."

Earlier, Gennadi I. Gerasimov, the spokesman for the Soviet Foreign Ministry, was asked on the CBS News program "Face the Nation" whether the Kremlin was ruling out German reunification.

"Reunification is being talked about by people who are not in office, not in government," Mr. Gerasimov said. People in authority, he said, are not discussing it.

"We have two military organizations opposing each other, NATO on your side and the Warsaw Pact on the other side," he said, "and the German Democratic Republic is a very important member of the Warsaw Pact for us, and we have our troops there just as Americans have their troops" in West Germany. "So how can you reunify it now? So we must wait and let events take its own course."

When Mr. Gerasimov was asked whether Mr. Gorbachev and Mr. Bush might share a view that Europe's borders must be kept as they are, he answered: "I think that they may come to a common ground concerning that both countries, and actually everybody, is interested in stability, in not too much upheaval in Europe. I think this is in the common interests of both countries."

On the NBC News program "Meet the Press," Defense Secretary Dick Cheney made clear that for now, the Bush Administration sees NATO and the Warsaw Pact continuing to play important roles in Europe.

Asked what President Bush would say if Mr. Gorbachev proposed the dissolution of the two alliances, Mr. Cheney said: "Well, I think he should say that that's totally inappropriate at this time. It seems to me that what we're witnessing in the East is partly the triumph, if you will, of Western strategy for the last 40 years, and the NATO alliance has been the heart of that."

* * *

November 26, 1989

AS THE WALL CAME TUMBLING DOWN

By JOEL AGEE

The following is the record of a recent visit to East Berlin, at a time when the burst of freedom that greeted the opening of the borders to the West on Nov. 9 was still an anxiously held breath; when even the most optimistic could not imagine such a swift and fortunate denouement. The drama, of course, is just beginning. Already, its first great act is being credited to politicians whose only part, to this day, has been one of forestalling and then adapting to the inevitable. Here is a portrait of a few of the principal, though unknown, players—ordinary men and women whose passion and imagination are the real engines of revolution.

On a Saturday afternoon in October, I pass inspection by the East German border police at Bahnhof Friedrichstrasse, a big train station connecting West Berlin to East Berlin, and step out onto the street. Nothing has markedly changed in the look of things since I was last here eight years ago. Maybe the people are better dressed—I wouldn't be able to distinguish the local residents from their Western visitors. Of the recent extraordinary developments—not a sign. I look around for the shadow appointed to follow me, as was the case on my last visit. The streets are nearly empty: a leisurely bicyclist, a couple walking arm in arm . . . all stores and offices have closed for the weekend, as is usual in both Germanys.

There's the 22 streetcar, standing empty before it begins its round; the conductor is reading inside her glass booth. I step in, savoring the thrill of repetition: this car is the same as it was 30 years ago, and the ride still costs 20 Pfennig, a pittance you are invited to drop in a box before cranking a wheel for your ticket.

But is this really still the same line? My memory might be wrong. I'd better ask that fellow who's about to climb in.

"Sagen Sie mal, fahrt diese Bahn zum Kurt-Fischer-Platz?"

The man looks frightened and guilty, his whole body seems to be saying, "I mean no harm, and I'll leave if you want me to."

He opens his mouth, tentatively. "I'm sorry," he says, in American English, "I don't speak German." "Oh, I speak English," I say. He looks relieved. "I'd like to know if I can take a ride to the end of the line and back," he says. "Could you ask her that for me?"

I ask the conductor. She twists her body around, leans back, pulls her shoulders way up, spreads her hands and bulges her eyes, as if to say, "Don't ask me, I just drive this thing, but who knows, there may be danger lurking." My countryman needs no translation.

He steps in, we introduce ourselves, Jim and Joel. He's from Tampa, in West Berlin for a visit, just here to have a quick look around. I tell him I used to live here and want to visit my old house. He asks if I would mind if he joins me. Of course not.

He wonders at my accent: I don't sound German at all. I am not, I explained; I came here from Mexico in 1948, when I was 8 years old, with my American mother and my German stepfather. He was a Communist, and so had been in exile during World War II. I returned to live in America in 1960, the year before the wall went up.

There is an advantage, I notice, in traveling with this American. He is surprised by things that are too familiar for me to take notice of: that the city, block after block, is virtually deserted, for instance, while the few cars not parked by the side of the road are traveling so fast you'd be taking your life in your hands jaywalking.

And there seems to be only one type of car, the little Trabant (the word means "satellite"), in three or four colors, with a hard fiber and paper shell. Jim wonders if it's any good. "It obviously runs," I say, "but you'll have to wait 10 to 12 years for your turn to get one." And that reminds me of an East German joke: A rich American who collects fancy cars tells his friend in Texas about an amazing East German creation he has heard of, the Trabant. "You're put on a waiting list for 12 years—not even Rolls-Royce makes you wait that long, it must be a hell of a car." He orders one. The East German authorities are excited by the offer of hard currency and send the American his car right away. He calls his friend in Texas: "Remember that Trabant I told you about? It's got to be one hell of a car. They just sent me a beautiful cardboard model, and you can actually drive in it!"

We get out at Kurt-Fischer Platz. I'm disoriented: new buildings have gone up, ugly four-square embassy structures with outsized national emblems over their doors. Policemen patrol the street. I ask one of them how to find my old address: Kuchhoffstrasse 39-B. He obliges, looking a touch quizzical, and I explain my sentimental reason for being here.

A short walk down a narrow, familiar lane, and there is my house. I feel nothing but sadness: everyone who lived here with me—my mother, my stepfather, my brother—has died. Jim takes a couple of pictures of me with the house as background. The cop I talked to has followed us down the lane. Good thing I told him what we are here for, you never know how far afield their suspicion might take you, particularly when it attaches itself to your use of a camera.

Jim has some time to kill before going back to the West. We go to the Hawaii bar on Kurt-Fischer Platz, where my stepfather and I used to go for an occasional drink.

We order two beers. Jim takes a picture of me with my East German beer bottle, I take a picture of him with his. Suddenly a curly-haired, pudgy man at a table near ours—a worker, to judge by his appearance—stands up to inform Jim, in beer-slurred Berlin dialect but with unmistakable anger, that if he doesn't watch his step he'll throw him through the window along with his camera. Then he sits down again and resumes drinking his beer. Naturally, Jim is alarmed. I would like to know what the drunk's hatred of cameras is about. But I'm not sure I want to find out.

"Tell him I apologize," Jim says. "Tell him I don't know the rules here, and I'm sorry."

I stand up and convey Jim's apology to the drunk. He accepts with a gracious tilt of his head. "I don't care what he does with his camera, I just don't want him to point it at me," he says. "It's a personal matter, that's right, not a principle. I don't care much for principles. . . ." And as he rambles on, I notice that his words rhyme and scan.

"What was that you just said?" I ask. "That was beautiful." "It's a poem I wrote." He recites it. There is something very moving about it, though his tongue is so thick I can't make out all the words. I ask his permission to write it down. "My pleasure." The poem is about the end of the world; about the cruelty done to animals, about dried up rivers and flowers that are ceasing to bloom, about the broken sky, about man's slavish estate. It ends with the same line it began with: Ach Mensch, du Untertran. That line is a marvel. It subverts a whole species of German poetry that invokes the grandeur of man with the portentous words "Oh Mensch!"—"Oh Man!" But how to convey the meaning of "Untertan"? It is a quintessentially

German word. It means, roughly, "subject," "vassal," or "underling," but it implies voluntary, even grateful, subjection. You almost have to be German to feel the inward and outward stooping expressed by that word. "Ah Man, you underling!"

Now I feel safe to ask him what he has against cameras. It's hard to explain, he says. It has something to do with his having done time for "antisocial behavior."

"That's what they called it," he says. "I couldn't work. They didn't realize I was sick. I have asthma. See?" And he shows me a gray passport that identifies him as an invalid. "With this I can go back and forth to the West. Me and the old folks. I'm not valuable enough to lock in. That's about the only advantage. What I'd like is some certification that I'm not antisocial."

I tell him I think his poem proves he's not antisocial. This pleases him greatly, and he asks me if I could publish it in the West. "Not here," he says, "here everything you're allowed to say publicly loses its meaning."

"Don't you think things are changing? People are speaking out and it does mean something."

"You'll see," he says. "They'll find a way to shut everyone up or else make our words meaningless. They're masters at that." Jim looks at his watch—he has to leave. The poet asks me if I could give him a 5-Mark coin—a Funfer, he calls it. Jim gives him eight or nine West-Marks. I put my hand in my pocket and pull out an almost weightless handful of coins—the change I got for our beers. Is it an insult to give him this? Is it enough? Does he need it? "Say—you could use some Westgeld, am I right?"

"Ja, naturlich," he says, almost reproachfully. How could I have been so stupid?

After parting from Jim, I met with an old family friend, Jutte, a Danish woman who, like my mother, had married an exiled German Communist during the war and moved to East Germany with him in the late 1940's. She said I was lucky to have found her at home. She had just come out of the hospital to take care of some business, and had to go back the next day—heart trouble, nothing critical, but she had to be monitored.

She was in a room with another patient, "the wife of one of those awful public prosecutors," who was extremely upset by the goings-on in the churches and streets, by the masses of people running off to the West, and especially by that new political group, the New Forum, which wasn't even legal. She thought there was too much freedom in the country, and someone had better clamp down quick, before it all got out of hand, as it had in China. Law and order! "It's kind of hard to take, listening to her," Jutte said. "Not good for the heart," I replied. "Well, I'm hard to take for her, too. I'm a Gorbachev fan, and she hates and fears him like the devil. And her heart's worse than mine." "She needs reassuring," I said.

"I know, I've been tring to persuade her to stay away from the news, but she can't do that. Nothing this exciting has happened in a very long time. I tell her these young people need some kind of valve to release the pressure—that's coronary talk, she knew what I meant right away." "Did it calm her down?" "Yes, a little. And that's good for me, too."

I was surprised to find Jutte in such open sympathy with the protest movement. When I lived in East Germany as an adolescent, and on subsequent visits over the years, I had always had the impression that she was a firm supporter of the status quo—not because she was fond of dreariness and rigidity, but because she believed this was fundamentally the better of the two Germanys, the one that had made a clean break with Nazism; the one dedicated, at least in principle, to social justice; and that with all its flaws, it needed first to be defended, and only second to be improved.

Always, when her generation of socialists were questioned by the young about some of the system's absurdities—the Government's evident distrust of the working class, for instance, or the inequality that stared you in the face even as you were reading or hearing about the elimination of class differences—they would take refuge in densely armored arguments about the enmity of the West and the danger of giving too much autonomy to a population that was still under the impress of fascism and not yet politically mature. "The people are not ready"—that was the catch-phrase; or, in a slightly more noxious formulation, usually by political officeholders: "Our people are not ready." Now, to judge by the news, the people were more ready than their leaders could have wished in their most secret utopian dreams. And here was this old socialist, Jutte, in complete sympathy with demands that, 10 years ago, would have frightened her as symptoms of imminent collapse.

She prepared an omelette for the two of us, and poured out a good Bulgarian red wine. We watched the evening news while we ate. A Government official was talking to some workers in a factory. "Here's the new line," Jutte said, "its called 'dialogue.' Watch."

The workers and the official all wore hard hats, which made them look equal. A worker said: "If I as a comrade cannot work for change in my own company, I'm in the wrong place." This struck me as a very potent statement; for the implied right place, in the absence of a real possibility for change, was either outside the party or outside the country. The official appeared to be in full agreement. Three seconds of personal and political truth—I was amazed. But Jutte shrugged: "It's not enough."

The next item was an interview with a worker whose brigade had been exceptionally productive. "Notice his name," Jutte said. The name was Knebel, which means "gag." The man rambled on about percentage points and socialist initiative while the camera explored his nervous face and dutifully folded hands. "Here's where everyone switches to the West channel," Jutte said.

We talked for a while about personal matters. She was sorry she had not come to New York last year to see my mother before she died. And what was life in New York like these days? I told her: The streets are full of homeless beggars and crazy people. I can no longer take a walk in the evening, for fear of being assaulted; just recently, a young man in my building came home from basketball practice and was held up with a submachine gun; and the whole mess gets covered over with entertainment, the more glitzy and vapid the better, just so no one will have to bear the burden of thinking and feeling. "You sound bitter," she said. "I'm not usually that way. But there's not much hope for change at the moment."

"There is here," she said. "Lots of hope."

Back in West Berlin that evening, my friend Jan, with whom I was staying for the week, told me a story that cast some light on the way the East German leader and Communist Party boss Erich Honecker used to govern his country. Jan had heard it from an elderly East German woman who was visiting her son, a friend of Jan's, in the West. She was complaining about the inconvenience of being temporarily evicted from her home to make room for a construction crew. Construction? You don't mean maintenance, plumbing? No, there were structural problems, the whole building was falling apart. But those buildings went up in 1972, how could they be collapsing already? Well, this one was. And they had to open up the floors to put up a scaffolding. The floors? Aren't scaffoldings put up outside? Not here—what if Honecker found out? He would be upset. That street was his pride, luxury homes for the masses. He was driven past this house every day on his way to and from work. It had to be hidden. They even hung flags out the windows of the empty apartments on the Day of the Republic.

Jan, incidentally, has a special interest in stories from the East: he used to live there. Six years ago, he fled, via Hungary, and found himself an apartment that would be a five-minute walk from his previous home if the famous Wall with its sharpshooters didn't stand in the way. "What is the difference for you," I asked, "between one side and the other?"

"A different set of lies," he said, "a different style of hypocrisy. But there's more room for truth here. More oxygen. You can breathe better." Unfortunately, Jan could not come with me to test the new air on the other side. He was persona non grata there, excluded from the general amnesty for Republikfluchtige—"defectors from the Republic"—for reasons known only to the state security officer in charge of his dossier.

The next day, the border crossing is quick and almost friendly. The sun is out. It promises to be another mellow Indian-summer afternoon. I have an appointment at 11 with Petra, a costume designer. She's going to try to gain me admittance to a rally of theater people at the Deutches Theater.

I've forgotten the way to the theater. I ask a man for directions. "I'll walk with you. I've got some time." He is in his mid-60's, white-haired, pleasant-faced, and is carrying a bouquet of red carnations. It strikes me as almost too neatly symbolic: carnations are the traditional emblem of socialism in Germany. He says he is a metallurgist, but judging by where he says his offices are situated he is not an ordinary engineer, but a Government offical, most likely an industrial planner. I decide to ask him what he thinks of the new opposition. But I put it more vaguely: "What do you think about what's going on?"

I immediately regret the question—it feels indiscreet. "Come, let's cross over here first," he says, suddenly looking tense. He grips my arm and guides me across the street. We walk a few steps in silence.

"What I think?" he says then. "I think this was bound to happen, and it's a good thing, and what's more, I think it's irreversible. I'll tell you the truth: I was one of those people who raised unpopular questions and got into trouble. So I'm glad to see people finally calling a spade a spade. You can't spend 40 years telling your whole population that gray is white and black is red and expect them to just keep on pretending they see things your way. It doesn't work. It's a huge waste of energy."

The color symbolism is interesting. The meanings of gray, white, and red are fairly obvious, but black, in German political parlance, denotes reaction and counter-revolution, the dialectical opposite of red. This conversation could not have taken place a year or even a month ago. So the winds of change are blowing through the corridors of power, not just through the churches and the streets. Whatever the purpose of the man's bouquet, it seems to signal a celebration.

The Deutches Theater was packed with some 700 actors, directors, dramaturges, stage designers from theaters all over the country, along with a hefty handful of state security people. Petra and I found seats on the balcony. Many had to stand. On the brightly lit stage, two women and a man sat behind a table facing the audience. The man was the moderator: "The church and the theater," he said, speaking softly into a microphone, "are the only institutions where people are allowed to speak freely. We all know why we are here: to make fuller use of that freedom and seek out ways to make it available to all. Freedom of speech, then; but please, no speeches. . . ."

There was indeed no speechifying, none of the tedious ego-airing that normally accompanies political meetings anywhere in the world. The audience's impatient, sometimes angry, interjections saw to that. But of course it was not simply an audience and the speakers were not performers. Everyone here, including the secret police, must have felt himself at the dizzying edge of a truth whose day had come; and the fate of this truth, its ultimate consequence, lay in the hands of each person.

One of the two young women at the table read off a report about her detainment after the mass arrests on Oct. 7, the Day of the Republic. She would have done better to speak it impromptu, tears and all, because the involuntary quivers and catches in her voice, one week after the event, conveyed the horror more palpably than the bare facts she was trying to report impassively:

"We were shoved through a hallway into a big room while the police laughed at us and insulted us. We weren't allowed to go to the bathroom. Eventually, a few women had to urinate in their pants. The men in particular were tormented, some of them for two days straight. They had to stand naked facing a wall with their hands raised over their heads. If they lowered their arms or leaned against the wall, they were struck in the kidneys." A voice in the audience: "Faschisten!"

"Another game they played with the men was to make them hurry up and down a flight of stairs in the Haschen-Hupf (bunny-hop) position." I should add that I am citing from memory; it may be that I have omitted some details and included others from similar reports I heard subsequently of other detainments in other cities; the variations were frighteningly few.

The lawyer Gregor Gysi spoke next, a voluble, witty man who seemed barely able to contain his excitement at finally having the chance to speak his mind honestly in a public forum. He called for an investigation of the crimes that had just been described, and appealed to the victims and witnesses to assist him in preparing a public suit against the police. These events, he said, were symptomatic of a systemic malaise: "In this country we have a highly developed capacity for accusation, for condemnation, not just in the courts but everywhere; and virtually no consciousness of the need for defense, for mildness or amelioration." The crowd interrupted him with enthusiastic applause. "But," said Giesy, raising a cautioning forefinger, "but, this right to a defense must be granted also to those who want to deny it to us."

The director of a theater in Dresden warned the audience that his report would be rather depressing. His company had met with a man "on whom most of us have placed a great deal of hope"—Hans Modrow, the party secretary of Dresden (who has since been appointed Prime Minister). "He committed political suicide with his opening words, and from there things went from bad to worse. I wish I were mistaken. Perhaps I am. You had best make up your mind. I will read a transcript of the first five minutes of his opening remarks." He read them with a melancholy air—lifeless words about the need for restraint and moderation, cooperation with the responsible state organs, about the state needing directors too, just like the theater. A voice in the audience said "Selbsttor!"—a soccer term: it denotes a point lost by shooting the ball into one's own goal, the most shameful mistake a player can make. No one laughed at this witty remark, nor was it meant as a joke. Several people repeated the word with sad nods. The speaker broke off his recitation—no need for further comment.

I went to the foyer for a drink, then joined the crowd standing in the aisle of the orchestra. On the stage, a white-haired woman introduced herself as "a Communist since 1931, and I'm proud of it. I will never leave my party; they'll have to kick me out first." A smattering of uneasy applause. She just wanted to dream a little, she said, about some changes she'd like to see happening.

"Why do we have to watch soldiers parading by torchlight through the streets of Berlin? It brings up bad memories!" Surprised laughter, vigorous applause. I noticed a young man in front of me turning his head to exchange glances with another man in the rear orchestra: he looked miffed. "And what's the use of that stupid flag-raising ceremony in the schools?" Again that exchange of glances, with intensified displeasure. A few moments later, the two men left together. They didn't look like theater people to me.

Many demands were made at that theater meeting: a complete elimination of censorship in the press; a revamping of the school system, "so that our children are no longer taught to lie;" genuinely free elections; retirement of Erich Honecker and his aged associates in power; freedom to travel and emigrate, and to return unpunished from residence abroad; an economic restructuring along the lines of Perestroika; elimination of the Berlin Wall. The most urgent and immediate demand was to make public through all the communications media the brutal mistreatment of citizens by the police, and the prosecution of the guilty parties through the courts. A proposal for all the companies present to stage a nationally televised 12-hour matinee at the Deutsches Theater, on Stalin's birthday, Nov. 21, was accepted with laughter and enthusiastic applause.

At no point, at this rally or in any of my private conversations, was the socialist form of the economy put into question. Nor was the reunification of Germany so much as mentioned. With only one exception, the dozens of people I talked to were intent on staying in their country and helping to reform the system. They spoke of those who were leaving for the West not with disapproval, but with a certain sadness.

There was a moment in Petra's apartment that illustrates that point fairly clearly. The telephone rang. A friend was calling from West Berlin to say that he had arrived safely after crossing the border in Hungary. When she got off the phone, Petra said: "I'm finding it harder and harder to be nice to people who leave. It hurts too much. This guy, for example, he was a close friend. And what's almost worse, he's needed here badly. He's a doctor, one of the best heart specialists we have, and he happened to be treating another friend at the time he left. Now the doctor who has taken his place will have to consult with him by phone—and you know what the phone connections are like between East and West." "So why did he leave? For more money?" She shook her head. "I'll tell you what it is. He's fed up. He's sick of the lies and the regimentation—I mean really sick." She made the gesture of vomiting. "How can I blame him? I'm sick of it too. But I'm not leaving. All the problems I have here will be with me over there. Not just personal, but social problems, pollution, militarism, and all the rest of it. I'm staying."

Driving back to Jan's in a taxi after another visit to the East, I heard a familiar name being discussed on the car radio: Egon Krenz. It was the name of a Politburo member who one year ago had been the talk of the town on both sides of the border for insisting on the expulsion of four high-school students who had posted an antimilitarist article on their school's official bulletin board. So this was the nation's new headmaster. I saw him on East German television that night, addressing the people of East Germany with a dead-eye stare and a public-relations smile, his fists propped on the table before him. It was time, the new head of state said, for a change, a change in which the Communist Party would "recover the political and ideological offensive." He spoke of the need to re-establish trust between the party and the people, and went on to threaten "the outer and inner enemies of socialism." He spoke of the need for "mature, conscious, critical citizenship" and warned against "irresponsible actions." The communications media, he said, were important vehicles for the necessary "dialogue between the party and the people," but "our press cannot be a platform for directionless, anarchistic prattle."

I turned to a Western channel. It was showing interviews with East Berliners earlier in the day. Many had not heard the news and were incredulous. One old man said about Honnecker: "It's about time he retires. He'sz done his job, enough already, finish." His wife, asked if she was glad that Krenz was at the helm, replied: "No, I'm not glad." "Why not?" "Because I know something about him." "What do you know?" "That he's a lush"—a reference to rumors, according to which Krenz has undergone two treatments for alcoholism.

A young man said, "They're planning to dialogue us to death." Another: "When I hear the name Krenz, I think of Tienanmen Square." There followed an old news clip showing Krenz clinking glasses with a grateful Chinese diplomat after telling the press that the massacre on Tienanmen Square was a simple matter of re-establishing law and order.

Jan had gone on a business trip to Frankfurt. He called that night, and we talked about Krenz and his speech. "I don't have a TV set, here," Jan said. "Thank God I didn't have to see his face. But I heard him on the radio. I didn't realize who it was. I thought he was one of those awful actors from the Berliner Ensemble reading a Government communiqué, and I thought: 'You're lying, you son of a bitch, you're lying and you know it!' "

On the evening of Nov. 9, exactly three weeks after my return to New York, I saw the miracle on television; East and West Berliners cheering and dancing on top of the Wall. I immediately called Jan. He laughed. He had been drinking wine, he said, celebrating, when his 16-year-old son from the East called from a phone booth just around the corner. "He'll be here any minute. Can you imagine? I haven't seen him since he was 10!"

I told Jan I needed his help with my article: "It's going to press and I have to say something sensible about what just happened. I'm stunned."

"Joel, the only sensible thing is to celebrate. Please tell your readers that. Tell them that what we've just seen is greater than logic. 'The dance of the contradictions'—do you remember that wonderful phrase by Marx? This is it. The contradictions are dancing. The bell's ringing, my son is here, I have to hang up. Open a bottle and drink with us!"

Joel Agee, a freelance writer, is the author of "Twelve Years: An American Boyhood in East Germany."

* * *

November 29, 1989

PRAGUE'S UNLIKELY COLLABORATERS FOR CHANGE: PARTY STALWART AND EX-PRISONER

Havel, Often-Jailed Dramatist, Became Symbol of Dissent

By SERGE SCHMEMANN
Special to The New York Times.

PRAGUE, Nov. 28—If proof is needed that the pen is mightier than the sword, then Vaclav Havel is a veritable smoking gun.

In and out of prisons over the last 20 years, his plays banned in his native land, the playwright today accepted the figurative surrender of his tormentors at a meeting with Prime Minister Ladislav Adamec.

In a coincidence that seemed to close the symbolic circle, it was also today that Rude Pravo, the main party newspaper, announced that the Czech and Slovak ministries of culture had lifted 20-year-old bans on many works of art, including the writings of Mr. Havel.

Mr. Havel, to be sure, did not achieve his role in a vacuum. There is a tradition in this part of the world that intellectual integrity and independent art translate into raw political power.

Writers and artists have played major roles in dissident movements in the Soviet Union and throughout Eastern Europe. In Prague, the release of censored works also freed, for example, the writings of Milan Kundera, and among several prominent Czechoslovaks returning from exile was an actor, Pavel Landovsky.

Premier Symbol of Dissidence

"In our country there has been a tradition since the 19th century that social movements were always ignited by the intelligentsia," Mr. Havel said in an interview in the current issue of the West German weekly magazine Spiegel. "That was the case in 1968, and this time is no different."

But few writers or intellectuals have been thrust to the forefront of their nation's destiny quite as dramatically as Mr. Havel, the sardonic 53-year-old playwright and essayist. As uncompromising in his resistance to the totalitarian state as he is in his ironic plays, he withstood censure, prison and the muzzle to become the premier symbol of Czech dissidence in the years after the Soviet Union intervened to crush the Prague Spring of 1968.

Active in 1968 as chairman of an unsanctioned Club of Independent Writers, he subsequently helped found the Charter 77 dissident movement and through his clashes with the authorities was repeatedly sent to prison.

Mr. Havel was on one of his stints in prison only last May, this time for trying to lay a wreath at the grave of Jan Palach, a student who burned himself to death when the Warsaw Pact forces invaded in 1968. As recently as a month ago, the police dragged Mr. Havel from his sickbed to put him in detention on the eve of anticipated demonstrations marking the Oct. 28 National Day.

Symbolic Representatives

Now, at the huge demonstrations that have abruptly routed Czechoslovakia's neo-Stalinist regime, the crowds have chanted "Havel! Havel!" as the writer has proclaimed the demise of the system he fought with pen in hand and his willingness to join a government that would guide Czechoslovakia to democracy.

"If someone spends his life writing the truth without caring for the consequences, he inevitably becomes a political authority in a totalitarian regime," Mr. Havel said in the magazine interview. "I am willing, and may be able, to assume a role for a short time. This transitional phase may need symbolic representatives, who are not politicians but who represent the hopes of society."

What was good for democracy, however, was not conducive to his art. "I confess I'd like to arrange with the Interior Ministry to be free three days a week and to go to prison for two days a week to take a break from freedom," he said in the interview.

Vaclav Havel (pronounced VAHTS-lahv HAH-vell) was born on Oct. 5, 1936, in Prague, where his father was a well-to-do building contractor and restaurant owner. Legend holds that his father tried to evict the Soviet newspaper Pravda from one of his buildings. Mr. Havel stlll lives in a building built by his father.

The "bourgeois" background blocked Mr. Havel in his education, and his early postwar years included work as a taxi driver and study of traffic-control automation. But from his early years he wrote, and in June 1967 he caused a stir at a writers' congress when he criticized as absurd censorship and the Communist apparatus.

Work in a Brewery

After the 1968 invasion, he left Prague and settled in a remote farming village near Troutnova, where he worked in a brewery. His growing body of plays was banned across East Europe, but they rapidly gained him critical notice in the West.

In January 1977, Mr. Havel joined artists, former Communists and church leaders in forming Charter 77, a group devoted to human rights and civic freedoms. Mr. Havel was among the chief theoreticians of the movement, and his essay setting out his ideas on national resurgence in a totalitarian state, "The Power of the Powerless," was widely studied inside and outside Czechoslovakia. In it, he argued that citizens "living in truth" could successfully confront and overturn dictatorial rulers.

His involvelment with Charter 77 led to the first of Mr. Havel's several stints in prison. The longest was from October 1979 to February 1983, for founding a group called the Committee for the Defense of the Unjustly Persecuted and for "keeping up contacts with emigres." He later collected the letters he wrote from prison to his wife in a widely read volume, "Letters to Olga."

Last January, Mr. Havel was sentenced to eight months in prison for trying to lay the wreath at the tomb of Jan Palach. But after an international outcry, the sentence was reduced to four months.

'Parables for Human Life'

The authorities also tried to get Mr. Havel to emigrate, but he refused. He refused even to travel abroad to accept international drama prizes in the Netherlands and Sweden for fear he might not be permitted to return home.

At one point, the recently ousted Communist Party leader, Milos Jakes, privately admitted that the harassment of the playwright had only made him better known. The comment was secretly taped and further added to Mr. Havel's renown.

Mr. Havel's plays—the better-known include "Protest," "Temptation," "The Saviors" and "Audience"—are generally marked by strong irony, which sometimes strikes audiences as absurdist.

Many of these satirical comedies center on the dumb mechanization of man in a totalitarian world. In an interview last March, Mr. Havel said his satires should not be understood as "satire coined to some concrete conditions," but rather as "parables for human life itself."

* * *

December 11, 1989

4 POWERS TO MEET ON GERMAN ISSUES

By CRAIG R. WHITNEY
Special to The New York Times.

WEST BERLIN, Dec. 10—The Ambassadors of the United States, the Soviet Union, Britain and France will meet here on Monday to discuss the rapidly evolving relationship between East and West Germany, an Allied statement said today.

The four nations were prompted to hold the meeting, their first on the Berlin situation in 17 years, by the actions of Germans on both sides of the border. The Germans are rapidly taking practical steps that would make political and social unification possible while skirting political and legal technicalities and, in the view of several Western diplomats here, simply ignoring the prerogatives of the Allies.

The four nations, which occupied Germany after World War II, are still sovereign in both halves of divided Berlin and have not met formally together since 1972, when they signed the Quadripartite Agreement on the city's status that they had reached the preceding year.

A Modest Formal Agenda

The Allied statement today said the formal agenda would take up a suggestion made in 1987 by President Ronald Reagan when he was here to discuss improving the safety of air traffic routes through East Germany to the city, as well as the subject of sports and youth meetings.

But the background to the hastily called meeting is the growing concern by all four powers that the rapid change in

East Germany, whose Communist Party elected Gregor Gysi as its new leader on Saturday and will change its name next week, has set in motion a process of disintegration of the postwar European order that none of them can control.

Although Secretary of State James A. Baker 3d is to arrive here Monday night, American officials in Bonn said he would not attend the conference, which will involve the three Ambassadors to West Germany—Vernon A. Walters of the United States, Sir Christopher Mallaby of Britain and Serge Boidevaix of France—and the Soviet Ambassador to East Germany, Vyacheslav I. Kochemasov.

All four nations have occupation sectors on German territory and in Berlin. In practice, they have delegated much of their sovereignty in Berlin to German officials, though legally West Berlin is not part of West Germany.

But today the Germans are much more likely to act without consulting their allies than they were in the past.

The most significant instance of this recently was Chancellor Helmut Kohl's outlining of a 10-point plan for German unity in a speech he made to Parliament late last month without any prior consultation with the Western allies.

According to officials in London and Paris, both President Francois Mitterrand and Prime Minister Margaret Thatcher were considerably annoyed at the lapse. Mr. Kohl said after this weekend's European summit meeting in Strasbourg that his discussions with the other 11 leaders had been "complicated." They agreed on a statement recognizing the right of the German people to restore unity through self-determination, but within the context of existing alliances and state borders.

Regular Visits by Mayors

Since the East German border was opened on Nov. 9, hundreds of thousands of people have been pouring over to visit every day in what amounts to reunion, if not reunification, and between 1,500 and 3,000 a day decide to stay permanently in the West.

The changing realities are felt in ways big and small. Mayors Walter Momper of West Berlin and Erhard Krack of East Berlin have been visiting each other regularly since Nov. 9, and today they visited the outdoor Christmas bazaar near West Berlin's Kaiser Wilhelm Memorial Church together, signing autographs among the Christmas trees for a crowd that was half East Berliners, half West Berliners. On Saturday they will visit the Christmas market in East Berlin, off the Alexanderplatz.

Asked what the allies thought of such mayoral meetings, Mr. Momper looked puzzled and said: "They'd welcome it. They could come down and drink a little mulled wine with us."

The municipal authorities on both sides of the wall are now beginning to talk about ways to improve water and sewer service, increase the number of telephone lines, fight drug and currency smuggling, and cut sulfur dioxide emissions to reduce foul-smelling smog that repeatedly covers the city.

Allies Responsible for Berlin

But Allied diplomats in East and West say that legally the Germans cannot formally assert responsibility for Berlin as a whole. That is reserved to the Allies, who reaffirmed it most recently in the 1971 four-power agreement on the city's status.

Though they have delegated most of their rights to their respective German allies—West Berlin adopts West German law as its own, and East Berlin is recognized by the Soviet Union as the capital of East Germany—they jealously guard other privileges like sovereignty over airspace.

One Western envoy said privately that the United States was in danger of being dealt out of Central Europe if it did not soon assert a stronger interest in how things evolve here. "The Germans are going ahead without us," he said. "And in Washington we don't even seem to be aware of it."

The difficulty is that the Allies have often sought to assert that interest, intruding in petty ways that are beginning to offend West Berliners not old enough to remember the days of the Berlin airlift in 1948-49, which enabled West Berlin to survive a Soviet blockade.

British Helicopter Evicted

A few days after the Berlin wall was opened last month, the British authorities sent a helicopter to hover over the western side of the Brandenburg Gate, in their sector, to make sure crowds there did not get out of hand. A senior British diplomat was talking to a reporter on one of those days when the telephone rang. "It's the damned Germans," he said, "telling me to get my chopper off the Brandenburg Gate."

A Berliner flying into the city on British Airways the other day said: "When Lufthansa gets permission to fly here, these planes will be empty. We'll remember how British Airways treated us all these years."

Klaus Bolling, a journalist who lives in Berlin and formerly headed West Germany's diplomatic mission to East Germany, said: "The Allied military attachés all behave at times like representatives of their national airlines. The Allies are being shortsighted." Only airlines in the hands of American, British or French owners can fly in and out of Tegel and Tempelhof airports in West Berlin. Lufthansa, the West German airline, has suggested to the East German authorities that Lufthansa and Interflug, the East German carrier, start direct services to the West from Schonefeld airport on the outskirts of East Berlin. The two lines have initiated direct connections between Leipzig and Frankfurt and between East Berlin and Hamburg, but the allies, who control the air corridors over East Germany, have been reluctant to grant them long-term rights.

As an economic interest, the allied monopoly on commercial flights to West Berlin is small potatoes compared with the possibilities that may soon open up for West German business in East Germany.

Business Trip to Dresden

Today, for instance, Lothar Spath, the Governor of the West German state of Baden-Wurttemberg, flew to Dresden with a delegation of West German business leaders, to discuss cooperation agreements, joint ventures and other practical steps with their East German counterparts. They were greeted by Dresden's Mayor, Wolfgang Berghofer, who said, "The two German states will always remain the heart of the common European house."

On Thursday, Helmut Haussmann, the West German Economics Minister, will arrive in East Berlin for talks with his counterpart, Christa Luft. The agenda includes East German plans for economic liberalization, West German help in rebuilding East Germany's transport and communications networks, and insuring the security of investment and joint ventures involving Western companies. Chancellor Kohl, who promised a "completely new dimension of economic aid" to East Germany if it moved toward democracy, is to meet with Prime Minister Hans Modrow in Dresden on Dec. 19.

But, the daily Der Tagesspiegel pointed out today, West German business leaders are already way ahead of them.

"For most companies—on both sides—the German question no longer seems to be an obstacle," the paper said. "All of them have plans in the desk drawer for cooperation. Not arguments over technical terms but practical day-to-day steps will bring down the borders. 'Reunification' at the basic economic level has already taken place."

GORBACHEV CAUTIONS WEST

MOSCOW, Dec. 10 (Reuters)—President Mikhail S. Gorbachev, pledging that the Soviet Union will not allow harm to come to East Germany, has warned the West against taking advantage of the turmoil there.

In a speech to the Communist Party Central Committee, Mr. Gorbachev reaffirmed that Moscow would not interfere in the changes taking place in Eastern Europe and said all East Europeans had the right to decide their fate.

But he made clear that he considered any move toward German reunification destabilizing and that Moscow would resist Western attempts to push the issue. His speech was delivered on Saturday and published today in Pravda, the party daily.

* * *

December 13, 1989

BAKER, IN BERLIN, OUTLINES A PLAN TO MAKE NATO A POLITICAL GROUP

By THOMAS L. FRIEDMAN

Special to The New York Times.

POTSDAM, East Germany, Dec. 12—Seeking to give some American direction to the rapidly changing events in Europe, Secretary of State James A. Baker 3d today outlined proposals for transforming NATO from a primarily military organization to a political alliance.

Mr. Baker's proposal, made in a speech to the Berlin Press Club in West Berlin, was part of the most comprehensive and detailed set of ideas to emerge from the Bush Administration to deal with the upheavals that are reshaping the European political landscape.

Mr. Baker said he hoped that his ideas for recasting existing institutions like NATO, the European Economic Community and the Helsinki process could help channel the "peaceful revolution" under way in Europe into a stable, democratic new order.

Mr. Baker, in his speech, also proposed that the United States and the European Community work together to strengthen their ties. He urged support for changes in Czechoslovakia, Bulgaria and East Germany and suggested that the 35-nation Conference on Security and Cooperation in Europe be reshaped into a framework for "openness" between NATO and the armies of Eastern Europe. In addition, Mr. Baker repeated President Bush's views on German reunification.

Directly after his speech, Mr. Baker slipped into a Mercedes limousine and traveled to East Germany to deliver another message in a previously unanounced round of talks with East Germany's Communist Prime Minister, Hans Modrow, as well as with several East German opposition leaders.

Those talks were held in Potsdam, not far from the hall where Truman, Churchill and Attlee gathered to meet with Stalin in 1945 to frame Germany's postwar occupation, and they were made at the first visit of an American Secretary of State to East Germany. Potsdam lies just 20 miles southeast of Berlin.

While American officials would not say so explicitly, they left a clear impression that Mr. Baker's primary purpose in seeing Mr. Modrow was to do what he could to shore up his Government in the hope that it might survive long enough to conduct free elections now scheduled for May. In other words, after refusing to visit East Germany for 45 years because it was considered to have an illegitimate, unrepresentative regime, an American Secretary of State finally made such a trip. Officials also said that Mr. Baker wanted personally to urge the opposition to keep its movement nonviolent and to approach the issue of German reunification with sober restraint.

The Bush Administration seriously fears that the East German Government might collapse and force a disorganized, de facto unification with West Germany before either Germany's neighbors or the Soviet Union are prepared to accept it. Although he discussed the idea of visiting East Germany with the Soviet Foreign Minister, Eduard A. Shevardnadze, in a telephone call last Thursday, Mr. Baker only decided to go this afternoon after being assured by the American Ambassador to East Germany, Richard C. Barkley, that his visit would not provoke further instability.

Speaking to reporters after his one-hour meeting with Mr. Modrow, who is considered a leader of the liberal wing of the East German Communist Party, Mr. Baker said: "I felt it was important that we have an opportunity to let the Premier and the people of the German Democratic Republic know our support for the reforms that are taking place in this country. We also wanted to make it very clear that we support the process of reform in a peaceful manner, and we are very anxious to see the process move forward in a stable way."

Officials who attended the meeting said that Mr. Baker told the East German leader that if his country were to follow in the footsteps of Poland and Hungary, it could expect to receive a sympathetic hearing from the non-Communist industrialized nations should it seek economic assistance.

Modrow Is Reserved

Mr. Modrow was quite reserved when the two men emerged in a drizzle from their meeting at Potsdam's Interhotel, saying only that East Germany "tries in its relations with the United States to be a stable element." Tipping his hat to Moscow, Mr. Modrow added that East Germany was also "a building block in the common European home," which was how President Mikhail S. Gorbachebv describes his vision of a united Europe.

As dramatic as Mr. Baker's visit to Potsdam was—he made the 40-minute drive escorted by a bevy of West German and then East German motorcycle policemen, and crossed into the East over the famous Glienicke Bridge, scene of many East-West spy swaps—it was his Berlin speech which will likely have the more lasting impact.

In his speech, Mr. Baker emphasized that NATO would have to transform itself from primarily a military organization to more of a political alliance. It can do this by concentrating more on "arms control agreements, confidence-building measures and other political consultative arrangements."

In particular, Mr. Baker called for NATO to establish an "arms control verification staff" that would assist member governments in monitoring compliance with the conventional arms control agreement now being negotiated in Vienna by NATO and the Warsaw Pact, as well as future agreements that are bound to follow. NATO, Mr. Baker said, should also explore if it can play more of a diplomatic role in solving regional disputes.

On European Community

On the European Community, Mr. Baker said that as the 12 members of the E.E.C. became more political and economically intertwined after they merge into a single unified market in 1992, their organization will become the core of the new Europe. As such, it will be the main anchor insuring that any unified Germany remains in the Western camp, and the main magnet drawing Eastern Europe toward the free world.

Given that fact, Mr. Baker proposed that the United States and the community "work together to achieve, whether in treaty or some other form, a significantly strengthened set of institutional and consultative links."

American officials are increasingly viewing the new situation in Europe as an ideal way for them to get more of a foothold into the European Community and to get more of a say in its economic deliberations.

Mr. Baker also declared that if Czechoslovakia, Bulgaria and East Germany adopt changes similar to Poland's and Hungary's, the community and the non-Communist industrial nations should support them as well.

Helsinki Act Considered

The Secretary of State suggested that the 35-nation Conference on Security and Cooperation in Europe, which produced the 1975 Helsinki Final Act, consecrating Europe's postwar boundaries and establishing a common baseline for human rights, be transformed into a new framework for promoting greater openness and transparency between NATO and the armies of the East and, more importantly, into a vehicle for promoting free, multiparty elections throughout Europe.

The conference is the only organization that brings all of East and West Europe under one umbrella, said Mr. Baker, and, as such, it would be an ideal framework for providing practical technical advice to the East Bloc countries on how to make "the transition from stalled, planned, economies to free competitive markets."

Mr. Baker repeated that any process of German reunification should be consistent with the four principles outlined by President Bush in his speech in Brussels last week—specifically that reunification should emerge from a free vote in both East and West Germany, that it should come about gradually, that it should not involve any redrawing of German borders and that whatever new state might emerge would have to remain committed to both NATO and the European Community.

A Comprehensive Framework

While some of the ideas Mr. Baker laid out were not new, and others were not fully fleshed out, they nevertheless provided the first reasonably comprehensive framework for how the Bush Administration actually intends to go about trying to develop what the President has called "a Europe whole and free." Whether events in Eastern Europe will slow down, or remain stable enough to make implementation of this framework possible in the coming years, no one in the Secretary's delegation dared to predict.

Before Mr. Baker made his speech, he met in the morning with the West German Chancellor, Helmut Kohl, and the Foreign Minister, Hans-Dietrich Genscher. Mr. Genscher then escorted Mr. Baker for a visit to the Berlin Wall and Potsdamer Platz, once Berlin's equivalent of Times Square, which is where the East Germans first began to erect the barbed wire that eventually grew into a cement wall.

* * *

December 22, 1989

MITTERRAND, IN EAST GERMANY, CALLS FOR CAUTION ON UNIFICATION

EAST BERLIN, Dec. 21—President Francois Mitterrand of France today urged closer links between East Germany and Western Europe, but emphasized the need to avoid quick moves toward German unity.

Mr. Mitterrand met Prime Minister Hans Modrow of East Germany, other political leaders and students to express the West's concerns about the possibility of German unification.

The two countries signed six agreements, including an economic and industrial cooperation accord for 1990-94, as well as one on youth exchanges. The French President also discussed cooperation between his Socialist Party and the East German Communist Party.

At a meeting with 600 students at Karl Marx University in Leipzig, the birthplace of the democracy movement, Mr. Mitterrand said that "France set conditions but not a veto" on German unification. "German unity is first and foremost an affair for Germans," he said. "France will not stand in the way."

Importance of European Balance

"Only free, open, democratic elections will permit us to know exactly what the Germans on the two sides want," Mr. Mitterrand said in reply to questions asked by some of the students. "But the German people must take the European balance into account in its decision."

Since a peaceful movement forced the departure of the hard-line Communist leadership, a growing number of East Germans have called for quick German reunification. In recent weeks, demonstrators in Leipzig have carried West German flags and shouted for German unity.

But with memories of World War II still in many minds, European leaders have cautioned against quick unification and its consequences for stability in Europe.

Mr. Mitterrand said a written treaty could not wipe out "European realities created after World War II."

Kohl Urges Patience

He arrived in East Berlin on Wednesday, a few hours after Chancellor Helmut Kohl of West Germany had departed. Mr. Kohl and Mr. Modrow announced that the two countries expected to conclude a treaty in the spring broadly expanding bilateral cooperation. The treaty will provide for practical steps to establish close links between West Germany and East Germany in many areas.

Mr. Kohl also urged East Germans to be patient about unification, saying the process could not come overnight and that Germans had to consider the implications for other countries of such a move.

At the same time, a leader of the New Forum opposition group in East Germany warned that the movement, with 200,000 followers, faced a growing rift. Rolf Henrich, a co-founder of New Forum, said the group's members were divided over whether to constitute the movement as a political party or leave it as a loose organization.

* * *

December 23, 1989

CEAUSESCU FLEES A REVOLT IN RUMANIA BUT DIVIDED SECURITY FORCES FIGHT ON

By DAVID BINDER

Special to The New York Times.

WASHINGTON, Saturday, Dec. 23—After ruling Rumania as a dictator for a quarter of a century, President Nicolae Ceausescu was forced to flee Bucharest Friday when angry crowds of anti-Government demonstrators, backed by army units, took over large sections of the capital.

Reports spoke of fierce fighting in the capital between the army and the pro-Ceausescu security police, but by early today the army appeared to be gaining the upper hand.

Bucharest radio said the head of the security police changed sides and ordered his forces to support the army and the Rumanian people, Reuters reported Friday evening. The broadcast also said the Interior Minister and a Deputy Prime Minister had been arrested by anti-Ceausescu forces.

"The forces of democracy are in the ascendant," a State Department official who is following the situation said Friday evening.

4,500 Bodies in Open Graves

Loyalist forces also were reported Friday evening to be attacking Timisoara, the western city where the uprising began last Saturday. But the army said that it had repulsed that attack.

Early today, Maj. Gen. Stefan Gusa, the Army Chief of Staff, said regular army units opposing Mr. Ceausescu had taken control of almost the entire country from security police forces, Reuters reported.

Open graves were discovered in Timisoara Friday with what were believed to be as many as 4,500 bodies, many of them women and children, who were believed killed by security forces over the weekend.

Once Mr. Ceausescu and his wife, Elena, fled, the changes that took place in Rumania were more sudden and dramatic than any in Eastern Europe.

Prisoners Reported Freed

Early today, the Bucharest Radio reported that all Rumanian political prisoners had been freed.

The television and press, which yesterday had been the most rigidly controlled in Eastern Europe, declared their freedom. Viewers around the world saw live images of demonstrations and heard calls for freedom and change that had been inconceivable before. But shortly after midnight in Bucharest, the television station went off the air while heavy fighting was going on in the vicinity.

The anti-Ceausescu forces—a combination of army generals, veteran Communist politicians who had been placed under detention and student leaders—moved swiftly on Friday to form a provisional government under Corneliu Manescu, a former Foreign Minister who was put under house arrest in March for signing a letter urging Mr. Ceausescu to resign.

But with the Government in disarray and the opposition still organizing, reports were often sketchy and sometimes wildly contradictory. For example, there were initial reports Friday that Mr. Ceausescu and his wife, whom he had made his second in command, had fled Bucharest seeking to fly to a country like China or Iran, but that they had been captured in a car near a military airport. But later, the Rumanian radio said those reports were wrong, and that Mr. Ceausescu and his wife had apparently escaped capture.

Late Friday evening, the Soviet press agency reported that the Ceausescus were believed to have left the country.

But their son Nicu, who had been in charge of security forces in central Rumania, was captured and brought to a television studio and shown to the public.

Friday night, the old royal palace in Bucharest, which has served as the presidential residence, was on fire, and there were explosions in the Communist Party Central Committee headquarters. Before it went off the air, the Bucharest television station reported a gunbattle under way inside its building.

Flee by Helicopter

Mr. and Mrs. Ceausescu fled by helicopter, which lifted them off the roof of the Central Committee building and apparently flew them initially to the town of Tirgoviste, 45 miles northwest of the capital.

According to Rumanian and Yugoslav press reports, the trail of the escaping couple grew cold after Tirgoviste, as they raced away, changing cars at times.

The demonstrations in Timisoara started when the authorities moved to deport an ethnic Hungarian priest, the Rev. Laszlo Tokes, and crowds of his supporters came to surround his house and prevent his being taken into custody. Between 2,000 and 4,000 people were believed killed that day, including a number of children.

Then bloodshed began on Thursday in the capital of two million people as security troops opened fire on demonstrators in University Square, and again Friday on the vast square named for Gheorghe Gheorghiu-Dej, Mr. Ceausescu's predecessor.

Reports of Killings

Witnesses said several hundred residents of Bucharest had been killed by automatic weapons in that square. Friday evening, Bucharest television showed huge crowds in the square, against the backdrop of the burning royal palace, Mr. Ceausescu's official residence.

There was a large explosion in the Central Committee building and witnesses also reported that the National Archives, a few blocks to the west, had been set ablaze. There was a suspicion that that had been done by security troops to destroy damaging evidence about the Government.

Mr. Manescu, who is 73 years old, and Silviu Brucan, a former Ambassador to the United States, joined others to form a Committee of National Salvation Friday to organize free elections, according to a live broadcast of the television station, which was renamed Free Rumania Television.

Appeal From 4 Communists

They and four other veteran Rumanian Communists had been arrested last March when they issued a joint appeal to Mr. Ceausescu to end his tyrannical rule. They were relegated to dirt-floor dwellings on the edge of the sprawling capital and were forbidden contact with anyone but their police guards. An unidentified student leader appearing with Mr. Manescu and Mr. Brucan in an impromptu broadcast said young intellectuals had endorsed the men as brave patriots.

Other television broadcasts showed not only the dramatic scenes of a crowd of 120,000 celebrating their victory in Timisoara, but also the burning royal palace that had housed Rumania's kings until 1946.

Another broadcast showed Nicu Ceausescu, the favorite son of the presidential pair and lately considered the crown prince, being led into a television studio with his face severely bruised. The son, who is 39 years old, had been the party chief in Sibiu, in Transylvania, and was captured and disarmed after he tried to take command of a security police unit and to take hostages, the radio reported.

Nicu Ceausescu has been widely detested in Rumania since he ran over and killed a teen-age girl about 15 years ago on Aviator Square while driving fast under the influence of alcohol in his sports car in broad daylight. Well-documented stories of his debauchery have circulated for years in Rumania.

Other Family Members

But there was no word of the fate of the other 40 members of the extended Ceausescu family, many of whom, like Lieut Gen. Ilie Ceausescu of the Army and Lieut. Gen. Nicolae Andruta Ceausescu of the Interior Ministry, the president's brothers, acquired prominent posts in recent years.

The key to the revolution Friday appears to have been the defection of key army commanders to the side of the growing mass of civilian protesters.

One of Mr. Ceausescu's last official acts Friday morning was to declare a state of martial law. Evidently the Defense Minister, Col. Gen. Vasile Milea, refused to carry out the Ceausescu order.

Bucharest Radio, still in the hands of Ceausescu loyalists, reported that General Milea, whom it described as "a traitor," had committed suicide. Later, however, the radio station on Nuferilor Street, a mile north of the Central Committee building, reported that General Milea had been shot, apparently by security forces loyal to the President.

Battle at TV Station

The radio station had been invaded and taken over by students. Army tanks came to defend it against attacks by security troops during the afternoon. Similarly, the headquarters of Rumanian television next to Lake Floreasca had been taken over by rebels and then besieged for a time by security troops, who later fell back.

Leading the army commanders who rose up against Mr. Ceausescu after the death of General Milea was General Gusa, the chief of the general staff.

About 6 P.M. Friday, Bucharest time, the radio station broadcast the following "particularly important" communiqué:

"Upon the order of General Gusa, anti-terrorist army troops have to come urgently to Boteanu Street 3 at the basement exit, the cafeteria, whose entrance is from the Plenarelor Street. The second entrance is opposite a garage. Signed by General Gusa." The site on Boteanu Street is adjacent to the Central Committee building and opposite the palace.

General Addresses Rally

Shortly before, General Gusa, addressing a rally while standing next to Ion Iliescu, a former Central Committee member who had been denounced by Mr. Ceausescu as a rival in 1971, said over the radio:

"Brothers, the army throughout the country is at the side of the people. It is the people's army. All army units, all garrisons, and all our country's cities are quiet. Please, do understand that we have to put order into things in Bucharest as well. Therefore, you have to help the military to be able to go where they have missions to fulfill. The army will always be with us and with you. We swear, we swear, we swear."

The task facing the army in cleaning out the pockets of security forces appeared to be formidible. According to radio reports, security forces tried to occupy both Otopeni International Airport six miles north of the center of Bucharest and the nearby Baneasa airport, which handles domestic flights.

"The Otopeni attack was repulsed first," said Romilo Limonedis of Radio Free Europe's Rumanian service. Both assaults occurred about 6 P.M. Friday, Bucharest time.

Recruited from Peasantry

The security troops are mostly recruited from the Rumanian peasantry and were handpicked for their loyalty to Mr. Ceausescu, and are paid twice the wages of university professors, with starting pay of about $420 a month.

Asked to explain the forces that came together to bring about his downfall, one of the United States Government's leading analysts of Rumanian affairs said today:

"I think it was a people in despair of their physical survival under Ceausescu, facing at last the choice to die fast or die slowly."

The analyst, who asked not to be identified, said a combination of desires for "religious rights and wanting to live like human beings finally reached a stage where helplessness was replaced by rage."

* * *

December 26, 1989

ARMY EXECUTES CEAUCESCU AND WIFE FOR 'GENOCIDE' ROLE, BUCHAREST SAYS

By JOHN KIFNER

Special to The New York Times.

BUCHAREST, Rumania, Tuesday, Dec. 26—Nicolae Ceausescu, absolute ruler of Rumania for 24 years, and his wife were executed on Monday by the army that he once commanded, the Free Rumanian Television of the new provisional government said.

A first brief announcement said an "extraordinary military court" had tried Mr. Ceausescu and his wife, Elena, who was widely viewed as the country's second most powerful figure until widespread demonstrations forced the pair to flee the capital on Friday morning. They were reportedly captured on Saturday in Tirgoviste.

At 1:30 this morning, a few hours after the report of the executions, the television showed its first footage of the Ceausescus in captivity.

Evidence of Capture

Some of the footage appeared to be from Monday's trial. The words "condemned to death" were barely audible on the fuzzy sound track. At one point, Mr. Ceausescu slammed his fur cap on the table. At times he seemed contemptuous. His wife appeared frightened.

The film, which opened with a doctor taking Mr. Ceausescu's blood pressure, was the first solid evidence that he had indeed been captured. The sound track also referred to the billion dollars he was said to have secreted abroad.

"The sentence was death and the sentence was executed," said the television announcement. It was proclaimed in the name of a largely faceless revolutionary government, the Council of National Salvation, which took power after the Ceausescus fled.

Few Details on Execution

It has not been made clear exactly when, where, how or on whose authority the Ceausescus were put to death, and their bodies had not been shown.

The charges against the Ceausescus, according to the television announcement, included the "genocide" of 60,000 people, many of whom died in the last week of fighting; undermining state power; destroying the country's economic and spiritual values, and trying to escape the country to claim $1 billion reportedly hidden abroad.

The Rumanian television said this morning that fighting near its studios in the capital was preventing staff members from getting footage of the execution on the air, Reuters reported.

The television studio has been the focus of heavy fighting between the Rumanian Army, which has sided with the popular uprising, and the security police, which is loyal to the Ceausescu regime. It is not known whether the security forces will fight on after the death of their leaders, but the insurgents clearly hope to demoralize them by showing proof of the executions.

The announcement of the execution came as Rumanians celebrated a bittersweet Christmas, treasuring their newfound and tentative liberties but mourning the many hundreds and perhaps thousands slain in the uprising.

The capital was calmer on Monday, with Rumanians strolling the boulevards and only an occasional burst of gunfire. The army appeared to be consolidating control over the remaining bands of now-renegade secret policemen, the backbone of the old order.

A Christmas tree stood on the balcony of the Communist Party headquarters this afternoon. It was placed in the spot where only last Thursday Mr. Ceausescu was hooted into shocked silence, jeered by a crowd that had been summoned to hear him condemn protests in a western city, Timisoara.

Sightseers wandered where fighting took place over the weekend between diehard security forces, who had sustained the reign of the Ceausescus, and a spontaneous coalition that united army units and irate civilians. Among those who turned out were several hundred people who gathered in front of party headquarters early this morning chanting, "We want Ceausescu hanged here at the palace!"

Shrines for Slain Students

New newspapers have been printed in the last few days with names like Freedom, Liberty and Free Rumania. One paper that appeared as Spark when it was put under sanctions by Mr. Ceausescu renamed itself Truth. On Monday, when truckers drove by tossing out copies of the new papers, crowds rushed into the streets to grab them. "We had cold, hunger and terror," was the way one of the papers, Free Youth, described the past regime.

At a Christmas Mass at the Rumanian Orthodox Cathedral, the center of the major religion, Patriarch Teoctist Arapafu hailed "these brave young people, these young boys and girls who have died for freedom."

"They will live in our hearts forever," he said. At the same time, the Patriarch, who had cooperated with Mr. Ceausescu's Government, acknowledged that despite what he called shocking times, "I did not have the courage these children have shown."

Although orthodox, the Rumanian Church observes the same calender of holy days as does Catholicism, the next-largest denomination in the country. But under the old regime, observances of Christmas were celebrated in private or in secrecy.

Downfall of 'Leader for Life'

The reported execution of Mr. Ceausescu and his wife, along with the capture of his brother, son and daughter, ended nearly a quarter-century of absolute power. Mr. Ceausescu was routinely idolized as the "leader for life," with accounts of his daily routine dominating the local newspapers and the two hours each day that Rumanian television was on the air.

His harsh rule, enforced by a hated secret police and a system in which one in four Rumanians was said to be an informer, included drastic measures to pay off the foreign debt. Those included cutting off heat and electricity during the fierce Central European winter and exporting harvests of food while keeping citizens on meager rations.

But as in other Communist countries, a privileged inner circle of the party elite enjoyed amenities like ski and hunting resorts and special food shops.

The television made much of the luxurious circumstances in which Zoia Ceausescu, the ousted leader's daughter, lived, noting that $100,000 had been found in her home after she was captured over the weekend.

As in several other parts of the Soviet bloc, rigid and seemingly entrenched one-man and one-party rule has collapsed in the face of popular protest. Here the process was tougher and more violent both during the years of oppressive rule and in the days that have seen it toppled.

Accounts of extraordinary brutality that have been widely circulated included massacres by the secret police and confirmed reports of people buried in mass graves in Timisoara after they were shot for protesting 10 days ago. Still, no thorough accounting of the death toll has been made.

Thousands have died in the last two weeks, said Victor Ciobanu, the Health Minister in the old regime, as he appeared on television tonight. Mr. Ciobanu has given his support to the new but so far formless revolutionary leadership. But he rejected as grossly exaggerated the reports broadcast on Sunday by the Hungarian radio that as many as 60,000 had been killed. That figure would amount to more than twice the 30,000 who were thought to have died in the Hungarian uprising of 1956, crushed by Soviet force.

The membership of the new government has not been made public for what its spokesman says are security reasons. But it is known to include a number of members of recent governments, some of whom had fallen out with Mr. Ceausescu.

Those include Corneliu Manescu, a former Foreign Minister; Ion Iliescu, a onetime member of the Politburo who had quarreled with the former President; and two top military figures: the chief of the general staff, Gen. Stefan Gusa, and the Deputy Foreign Minister, Ion Stanculescu.

All along the main boulevard, named for Ana Ipatescu, a Communist heroine, thousands of people strolled today, pausing to look at handbills hailing the revolution that were posted in store windows. They barely flinched as bursts of gunfire sounded a few blocks away, although at one point a group took refuge in doorways when the gunfire sounded too close.

The demonstrators chanted "Arafat and Qaddafi, you have taken our bread!" reflecting a widespread resentment of Arabs, who had formerly received privileged treatment here.

There are constant rumors on the street that the security police is made up of Arabs and Iranians. A Rumanian television cameraman, racing from the television headquarters late Monday afternoon, said, "We are fighting four armies here: Palestinians, Syrians, Libyans and Iranians."

Correction: The main front-page article on Tuesday about Rumania misidentified Ana Ipatescu, for whom a street in Bucharest is named. She was a heroine of the 1848 uprising against the Turks and the Russians, not of the Communist takeover after World War II.

* * *

December 30, 1989

CZECHOSLOVAKIA: HAVEL, LONG PRAGUE'S PRISONER, ELECTED PRESIDENT

By CRAIG R. WHITNEY
Special to The New York Times.

PRAGUE, Dec. 29—Vaclav Havel, the Czechoslovak writer whose insistence on speaking the truth about repression in his country repeatedly cost him his freedom over the last 21 years, was elected President by Parliament today in an event celebrated by the throng outside the chamber as the redemption of their freedom.

In a speech formally nominating the 53-year-old playwright who until May 17 was serving a jail term, the country's Communist Prime Minister, Marian Calfa, praised Mr. Havel.

"He has won the respect of all," Mr. Calfa told the legislators assembed in the medieval Hradcany Castle high above the city. "He never accepted the suggestions of friends or foes that he go into exile, and bore the humiliation of a man oppressed and relegated by those in power to the margins of society. Your vote for Vaclav Havel will be a vote for insuring the human rights of every citizen of our country."

Mr. Calfa said Mr. Havel had insisted on free parliamentary elections next year as a condition for accepting the mostly symbolic post and would serve only until a new Parliament could be elected to choose a new President for a regular five-year term.

Alexander Dubcek, the country's Communist leader during the liberalizing Prague Spring of 1968 and now rehabilitated as the chairman of Parliament, called for other nominations. But there were none; Mr. Havel's election had been agreed to beforehand by the Communist leadership and the opposition Civic Forum.

Completing the formality, all 323 deputies in the heavily Communist legislature voted for Mr. Havel, Czechoslovakia's first non-Communist President since 1948.

Mr. Dubcek and Mr. Calfa left the 16th-century hall to fetch the new President, somber in a dark blue suit, and swear him in with an oath revised by Parliament on Thursday to delete a promise of loyalty to the cause of socialism.

After a 20-gun salute and a military parade, he addressed the joyous crowd that thronged the castle courtyard.

"Dear friends," he said. "I promise you I will not betray your confidence. I will lead this country to free elections. This must be done in an honest and calm way, so that the clean face of our revolution is not soiled. That is the task for all of us. Thank you."

After his short speech, Mr. Havel went into St. Vitus Cathedral, within the castle walls for a Te Deum Mass presided over by 90-year-old Frantisek Cardinal Tomasek, the country's Roman Catholic Primate and Archbishop of Prague. The Gothic cathedral was jammed with people of every age. The Czech Philharmonic Orchestra and choir performed Dvorak's "Te Deum."

Cardinal Tomasek, who celebrated the Mass, said, "We have come today to the cathedral to thank God for the great hope that has opened up for us in the last few days."

This evening, tens of thousands of people streamed into the center of Prague's Old Town in what amounted to a street celebration of Mr. Havel's election. He appeared along with the visiting Portuguese President, Mario Soares, and greeted them.

Students' Intellectual Hero

Mr. Havel, son of an upper-class civil engineer, was not allowed to go to university by the Communist Government after he finished his compulsory schooling in 1951, because of his class background. Today the students of Prague, many of them children of the Communist ruling class, have made Mr. Havel their intellectual hero, and they have been on strike since demonstrations on Nov. 17 sparked the peaceful revolution that overthrew the long repression.

"Havel is the only guarantee that the changes here will be of a permanent character," said one of them, Ludek Vasta, 21, an economics student.

The student strike was expected to end today with his election.

President Havel, whose most recent prison term was for participating in a demonstration last January in memory of a student who immolated himself in protest against the crushing of the Prague Spring of 1968, is expected to address the nation by television on New Year's Day. He has told friends he will not move into the splendid presidential residence in the castle as his retired predecessor, Gustav Husak did, but will remain in the flat in the center of town where he and his wife, Olga, have lived for years, and commute to work in his car.

Making Moral Judgments

He is a man who wrote, in a 1984 acceptance speech for a French university award that the Czechoslovak authorities would not allow him to pick up, "The slogan 'better Red than dead' does not irritate me as an expression of surrender to the Soviet Union, but it terrifies me as an expression of the renunciation by Western people of any claim to a meaningful life and of their acceptance of impersonal power as such. For what the slogan really says is that nothing is worth giving one's life for."

Through much of Mr. Havel's work runs the thread of what he calls "the absolute horizon"—the moral and philosophical judgments that give human life its meaning. He repeatedly warned his persecutors that by their repression of human freedom they were ultimately undercutting their own existence as well.

When the Soviet-led invasion began in August 1968, Mr. Havel took part in Free Czechoslovak Radio broadcasts. A year later, he signed a declaration condemning the post-Dubcek policy of "normalization." His published works were withdrawn from public libraries, and his new works were banned.

In April 1975, he sent a letter to the man he has now succeeded as President, Mr. Husak, warning that ultimately a repressed people would demand a price for "the permanent humiliation of their human dignity."

"I fear the price we are all bound to pay for the drastic suppression of history, the cruel and needless banishment of life into the underground of society and the depths of the human soul, the new compulsory 'deferral' of every opportunity for society to live in anything like a natural way," he wrote then, more than a decade before the facade crumbled in Czechoslovakia and elsewhere in Eastern Europe.

'The Lava of Life'

"No wonder, then, that when the crust cracks and the lava of life rolls out, there appear not only well-considered attempts to rectify old wrongs, not only searchings for truth and for reforms matching life's needs, but also symptoms of bilious hatred, vengeful wrath and a kind of feverish desire for immediate compensation for all the endured degradation," he wrote.

For writing that letter, and for organizing the Charter 77 human rights movement at the beginning of January 1977, Mr. Havel was arrested and charged with "subversion of the republic." Convicted that October, his 14-month sentence was conditionally deferred, but he was in and out of jail again until arrested in May 1979 for supporting the Committee for the Defense of the Unjustly Prosecuted. With Jiri Dienstbier, now Foreign Minister of Czechoslovakia, and four other defendants, he was tried again for subversion that October and sentenced to four-and-one-half years in prison, but he was released for health reasons in February 1983.

His refusal to break with the Charter 77 movement led to other brief periods of detention in jail. But in January of this year, defying police orders to stay away from a demonstration in memory of Jan Palach, the young man who burned himself alive in protest after the 1968 invasion, cost him four months' imprisonment.

After his release, Mr. Havel called for restraint in commemorating the invasion's 21st anniversary in August, but he had to hide from the police anyway to keep from being arrested. He and three associates organized a petition, called "A Few Words," which soon gathered tens of thousands of signatures, calling for the release of all political prisoners and an end to discrimination on religious and other grounds.

The presidency of independent Czechoslovakia was first held by Tomas G. Masaryk, from 1918 to 1935. Eduard Benes, his successor, resigned in 1938 when the Western Allies signed Czechoslovakia over to Nazi Germany in the Munich Pact, but served again from 1946 to 1948. After that all presidents had to be members of the Communist Party, and they were until President Husak resigned on Dec. 10.

* * *

February 7, 1990

A SINGLE CURRENCY FOR TWO GERMANYS IS SOUGHT BY KOHL

By FERDINAND PROTZMAN

Special to The New York Times.

BONN, Feb. 6—Seeking to bolster East Germany's collapsing economy, Chancellor Helmut Kohl of West Germany today called for immediate talks on creating a single German currency.

By proposing that East Germany move quickly to adopt the West German mark, Mr. Kohl is trying to give the people of East Germany confidence in their deteriorating economy. With his call for a monetary union, Mr. Kohl is holding out the prospect that the East German economy will soon be integrated into West Germany's strong capitalist economy. And an economic reunification, should it come, would represent a huge step toward political melding of the two Germanys.

The most striking sign of the East German public's lack of confidence in their nation's future is the daily flood of 2,000 or so East Germans to the West. Mr. Kohl's Government is under increasing pressure domestically to stem the flow of immigrants, which is straining West Germany's social services.

Ready for Negotiations

"The West German Government is prepared to enter into immediate negotiations with East Germany on a currency union with economic reforms," Mr. Kohl said after meeting with members of his Christian Democratic Union's parliamentary faction.

Even if Mr. Kohl's proposal was embraced in East Germany, Government officials in Bonn cautioned that obstacles remain and that it could be a few years before the two nations adopt a single currency.

But the Chancellor's proposal got a mixed response in both Bonn and East Berlin. Karl Otto Pohl, president of West Germany's powerful central bank, termed the proposal to introduce the West German mark as the official East German currency "a very fantastic idea." The East German Economics Minister, Christa Luft, said he opposed monetary union and is seeking a multibillion-dollar aid package from West Germany instead. Yet other East German politicians strongly supported a monetary union.

Warning from Economists

Private economists warned that moving to a single currency, without free-market reforms and possibly Western aid, would not by itself halt the weakening East German economy. Thus, some economists added, Mr. Kohl's call for talks on a monetary union would be unlikely to restore confidence among East Germans.

"Changing the currency will not do much unless there are goods to buy with it," said Gernot Schneider, an economist with the University of Cologne who was expelled from East Germany in 1984. "And those goods can only come from the West. East Germany cannot create a new economy alone."

The Chancellor will present the suggestion for talks to his Cabinet on Wednesday. Mr. Kohl said he knew a currency union is impossible before East Germany's first free elections, scheduled for March 18, but said the two Governments, should East Germany agree to talks, had to give East Germans a clear sign that their economy can be stabilized and revived.

Mr. Kohl, people in the Government said, will discuss the currency union with Hans Modrow, East Germany's Prime Minister, when Mr. Modrow begins a visit to Bonn on Feb. 14.

Government officials say steps toward a currency union could begin soon after the East German elections. "Time is pressing," said West Germany's Economics Minister, Helmut Haussmann, adding that the West German mark could achieve the status of a parallel currency in East Germany this year and that economic and monetary union with East Germany could be possible by 1993.

"A fixed timetable accelerates the reform process. The two Germanys could therefore set themselves the aim of achieving a common economic and currency union with the realization of the European Community internal market on Jan. 1, 1993," he said.

Opposed by Central Bank

The Government's position is opposed by the West German central bank, the Bundesbank, which says East Germany must first take steps to strengthen its currency, make it fully convertible and build up an efficient, market economy. Bundesbank officials are also acutely aware of the inflationary potential that currency union with East Germany carries, because it would require printing more money to satisfy East German demand for marks.

"It is an illusion to imagine that even one of the problems in East Germany would be solved by the introduction of the West German mark in East Germany," Mr. Pohl said.

Today, the East German economy is hampered by rising inflation and the continuing exodus of skilled workers to the West. Wildcat strikes, work stoppages and go-slow job actions are proliferating, East German economic experts say, as despair and disarray spread.

Domestic politics have lent an added urgency to the debate in West Germany over how to prop up East Germany's troubled economy. With East German elections just six weeks away, West Germany's political parties, with the exception of the opposition Social Democrats, are scrambling to form alliances with East Germany's opposition parties.

Preparing for Elections

But the parties are also positioning themselves for the West German national elections this December, where reunification will be the central issue. The push to play a leading role in molding reunification has released an avalanche of proposals from all West German political parties on what to do about East Germany.

The East German Government has rejected the calls for rapid currency union. Mr. Luft, the Economics Minister, said on Monday that what was needed was immediate economic aid of between 10 and 15 billion West German marks to shore up the battered economy. Bonn has rejected that idea.

Opposition More Receptive

But East Germany's opposition parties have been more receptive to currency union. Wolfgang Berghofer, the Dresden mayor who quit the Communist Party, called for union of the two currencies at an economics conference in Switzerland today.

"If something does not happen soon, the whole process of democratization will be endangered, not just in East Germany but also in the whole of Eastern Europe," he said.

Gregor Gysi, the East German Communist Party leader, said in an interview with Bildzeitung today that he urgently wanted monetary union with West Germany, but that state ownership should continue to dominate East Germany's economy.

"We need a monetary union fast and then an economic union," Mr. Gysi was quoted as saying. "But we have to succeed in retaining our dominance of state-owned property. A lot of things which our citizens have worked for must be saved. Our market economy must be designed so that social, ecological and cultural interests are taken into consideration. State ownership can also find a place in a market economy."

Exchange Rate in Question

A key question, if currency union proceeds, is what the exchange rate will be. The current, unofficial exchange rate in West Berlin is about six East German marks to one West German mark. The official rate remains one to one. Should the West German Government offer East Germans a favorable rate of exchange, it would effectively be a substantial subsidy to the East German economy without directly increasing West German aid, economists said.

"A generous rate will make the East Germans feel a lot wealthier, but they have nothing to buy," said Richard Reid, chief European economist with UBS Phillips & Drew in London. "An ungenerous rate means a substantial write-down of their wealth."

"The East German people feel like they have been paying for the war for the past 40 years," said Mr. Schneider, the Cologne economist. "Only now are they getting their chance at what West Germany has enjoyed."

* * *

February 7, 1990

U.S. BACKING WEST GERMAN'S UNITY IDEA

By THOMAS L. FRIEDMAN

Special to The New York Times.

PRAGUE, Feb. 6—The United States is backing a proposal by the West German Foreign Minister that a reunified Germany be part of NATO but that no NATO troops be based on the territory of East Germany, a senior Administration official said today.

The official, speaking to reporters after a meeting at Shannon Airport in Ireland between Secretary of State James A. Baker 3d and Foreign Minister Roland Dumas of France, said a majority of NATO members appeared to favor such a unification formula.

The official said Mr. Baker would raise the issue with President Mikail S. Gorbachev when he goes to Moscow on Wednesday. After his brief layover in Ireland, but before his trip to Moscow, Mr. Baker stopped in Prague for talks with President Vaclav Havel.

The Genscher Proposal

The remarks by the Administration official, who is in a position to speak authoritatively on behalf of the State Department, amounted to the first indication that the Bush Administration was ready to back the unification proposal, which was presented to Mr. Baker last Friday by the West German Foreign Minister, Hans-Dietrich Genscher.

Mr. Genscher, who is the chief of the Free Democratic Party in West Germany and who often floats ideas on foreign policy, has been discussing his unification idea with European officials.

The plan has not been endorsed by East Germany, which officially seeks a neutral and unified Germany sometime in the future. It has not been endorsed by the West German Chancellor, Helmut Kohl, who heads the Christian Democratic Union in the coalition government, or by the Government itself. But it has gained widespread support in Bonn, and Government officials there say it is likely to become policy.

American officials added that they were not wedded to the proposal, meaning that if it proves impossible to put into effect, or if a better idea comes along, they will also consider those.

'A Pretty Good One'

"Genscher has come up with one proposal, and we think that proposal, in terms of not having NATO forces move further east, is a pretty good one," the senior official said. "It maintains a NATO structure that will try to achieve not only the new missions we've talked about but the political purposes of the alliance. So we think that is a very positive contribution. This is the sort of thing that will have to be discussed among the various parties: NATO, the Germanys, the Soviets."

Asked what kind of support the proposal had in the North Atlantic Treaty Organization, the official said, "I think many of the other countries in NATO think that this serves the elements that we set and will help maintain stability." Up to last week, Bush Administration officials studiously avoided lending support to a detailed or concrete plan for German unity.

Four Conditions

Instead, whenever the President or the Secretary of State were asked for their preference on the unification question, they answered that they supported the basic principle, provided that it took place with four conditions. Those conditions were these:

- Unification must come about through the free voting and self-determination of East and West Germans. As Mr. Baker said in his speech in Berlin on Dec. 12, "We should not at this time endorse or exclude any particular vision of unity."
- Unification should occur in the context of Germany's continued commitment to NATO.
- For the sake of European stability, unification must happen step by step.
- There should be no enlargement of Germany's postwar borders, except through peaceful negotiations.

Administration officials said they were forced to move from those general principles to a more detailed blueprint two weeks ago, when the troubled East German Government announced that it was moving up elections from May to March 18.

'Takeover' or 'Merger'

Given the fact that the vast majority of East German parties running in the campaign urge unification, the voting is expected to be followed by the establishment of a new East German Government that will immediately take steps toward merging the countries.

As the Administration official put it, Washington recognizes that after the elections, "you can expect a very quick process dealing with the economic, political and legal aspects of unification between the two German states."

The question for the Administration became more immediate: on whose terms would unification take place? In Wall Street terms, would it be a "takeover" of East Germany by West Germany, or a "merger" between relative equals? The East German Prime Minister, Hans Modrow, weighed in last week with his own proposal, in which a "united fatherland" would cease to be a member of NATO or the Warsaw Pact and would set up its government in Berlin.

Brakes on Modrow Plan

It was in an effort to stop the Modrow proposal in its tracks, before it gained any momentum with the German public, that Mr. Genscher, encouraged by the Administration, came up with his own concrete proposal in a speech on Jan. 31. The hope in Bonn and in Washington is that by the time the vote takes place in East Germany, the West will have a formula for keeping a unified Germany in NATO and resisting calls for its neutrality.

The Genscher formula postulates that a united Germany remain in NATO but that NATO promise that its troops in

West Germany would not be extended into East German territory once the nations were merged.

The hope is that such an arrangement would make German unification less threatening to the Kremlin. Mr. Genscher has also proposed that the Soviets be allowed to continue maintaining some troops in East Germany, ideally in much reduced numbers, and that those troops could even engage in joint exercises, exchanges and other confidence-building measures with NATO troops so that Germany would be, as he puts it, a venue for East-West reconciliation, not confrontation.

Avoiding a Public Stand

To date the Bush Administration, unlike Mr. Genscher, has declined to take a position on Soviet troops. Officials traveling with Mr. Baker said, "We don't want to rule them in or out."

They do not want to rule them in so as not to appear to be sanctioning the presence of the Soviet Army in East Germany, the officials explained, and they do not want to declare that they must leave by a certain date because to do so would probably undermine hope of Soviet cooperation. The Soviets have about 390,000 troops in East Germany.

The Soviet position on the German question appears to be in flux. As to a meeting last week in Moscow between Mr. Modrow and Mr. Gorbachev, the Soviet President for the first time gave a cautious endorsement for a discussion of reunification.

But a day later, Foreign Minister Eduard A. Shevardnadze seemed to back away from that idea, saying that given Germany's Nazi past, unification was a concept that might be best put before an international referendum.

THOUSANDS RALLY IN PRAGUE

PRAGUE, Feb. 6 (AP)—Thousands of people filled Prague's Old Town Square today and demanded that 75,000 Soviet troops in Czechoslovakia withdraw unconditionally by May 31.

The crowd, estimated at 8,000 by a Western reporter and at 30,000 by the official press agency, applauded a speaker who demanded that Vasil Bilak and other former leading Communists be put on trial. Mr. Bilak and the others are deemed responsible for inviting troops into Czechoslovakia in 1968 to crush the liberalization movement known as the Prague Spring.

The new coalition Government, headed by President Havel, has demanded the withdrawal of the Soviet forces by the end of 1990.

* * *

February 14, 1990

WEST AND SOVIETS AGREE WITH 2 GERMANYS ON RAPID SCHEDULE FOR UNIFICATION TALKS; GORBACHEV ACCEPTS BUSH'S TROOP CEILING

By PAUL LEWIS

Special to The New York Times.

OTTAWA, Feb. 13—The four major World War II Allies and East and West Germany agreed today on a framework for negotiating German reunification after 45 years of division.

The agreement, announced at the end of an East-West conference of foreign ministers here, came as Moscow accepted President Bush's proposal last month on Soviet and American troop reductions in central Europe and elsewhere in Europe.

This represented a sudden reversal by President Mikhail S. Gorbachev of the Soviet Union, who only last Friday had insisted on absolute parity in troop strengths. Under the plan agreed to here, Soviet and American troop levels in central Europe would be limited to 195,000 but the United States could have an additional 30,000 troops in other parts of Europe, in accord with Mr. Bush's original proposal.

Difficult Issues Remain

Although some difficult issues remain to be negotiated, the swift pace of agreements suggested that the unification of Germany, once thought to be a remote goal, could be achieved much sooner than anyone had anticipated. It also suggested that the major powers were on the verge of an agreement to reduce conventional military forces in Europe after more than 15 years of fruitless negotiations.

The agreement on German unification set up a two-stage process by which West and East Germany would first discuss the domestic details of unification and then meet with the United States, Britain, France and the Soviet Union on more controversial questions relating to postwar security issues.

A central issue is whether a united Germany would remain a member of the North Atlantic Treaty Organization alliance, as West Germany and its allies want, or be neutral, as the East Germans and the Soviet Union prefer.

A Striking Turnaround

The turnaround on the issue of troop reductions was striking. Last week in Moscow, Secretary of State James A. Baker 3d was told by President Gorbachev that the two sides could each have 195,000 troops or 225,000 troops, but the United States could not have 30,000 more than the Soviet Union as Mr. Bush proposed.

The meeting of the foreign ministers here had originally been called to begin negotiations for an "open skies" agreement between the two alliances under which each side would open its airspace for aerial inspection by the other. But the talks quickly became dominated by Western efforts to negotiate German reunification.

Under the plan for reunification, the two Germanys would work out internal aspects of unification themselves as soon as a democratic government comes to power in East Germany after elections on March 18.

The Germanys would then start to negotiate their future security arrangements with Britain, France, the United States and the Soviet Union—the four World War II victors who still retain legal rights over Germany.

Brief Announcement

Despite the importance of the agreement, the announcement was brief. It said that the foreign ministers of West and East Germany would meet with their counterparts from the United States, the Soviet Union, Britain and France at an unspecified time and place "to discuss external aspects of the establishment of German unity, including the issues of security of the neighboring states."

It said that "preliminary discussions at the official level will begin shortly."

It is expected that if an agreement can be forged by the major powers and the two Germanys, it would be formally approved by an East-West conference of the 35 nations that originally met in Helsinki in 1975.

Remaining in NATO

The three Western powers and the Bonn Government want a united Germany to remain in NATO, but on terms that "satisfy the legitimate security interests of the Soviet Union and Poland," as the British Foreign Secretary, Douglas Hurd, put it today.

Mr. Hurd said at a news conference that non-German NATO forces would be barred from present-day East Germany. But he said the Soviet Union would be permitted to retain some of its troops stationed there for an agreed period.

In addition, a united Germany would "give a clear and binding agreement to respect Poland's present-day frontiers," which include land that was once German.

The West German Foreign Minister, Hans-Dietrich Genscher, said the four powers had made an "unconditional, formal commitment to the reunification of Germany." As a result, he said, whether Germany remains in NATO or become neutral is not a condition for its unification.

East Bloc Strains

Asked today whether a united Germany could remain in NATO, Foreign Minister Eduard A. Shevardnadze of the Soviet Union merely shrugged his shoulders and declined to reply.

On Monday, however, he said that "the most sensible way" to reunify Germany was to neutralize the country, although he acknowledged that this was "not the only way."

Throughout the meeting, the Soviet Union and its East European allies had appeared uncertain and divided over the Western proposals on German unification, their unity clearly under strain as a result of the political changes under way in Eastern Europe.

Western officials maintained that the Soviets had been less rigid in private than in their public stance.

'Useful Weight of Opinion'

During the talks here, the three Western powers said that they have told the Eastern Europeans in particular that a united Germany firmly anchored to the NATO alliance would be less threatening than if it is left on its own as neutral.

Today, the British Foreign Secretary said "a useful weight of opinion" against the idea of a neutral Germany had formed among Eastern Europeans during the conference. He cited Poland and Hungary as two leading opponents. The East German Foreign Minister, Oskar Fischer, he pointed out, was the only Eastern European minister to call openly for neutrality.

Mr. Genscher also sought today to reassure officials from the Soviet Union and Eastern Europe that they have nothing to fear from a larger and united Germany.

Echoing the German author Thomas Mann, he said, "We seek a European Germany, not a German Europe," adding that the two Germanys would unify themselves in consultation with the four Allies.

"We respect the rights and responsibilities of the four powers," he said, adding that "unification will not take place behind the backs of the four powers."

British and U.S. Claims

Both the United States and Britain were quick to claim authorship of the negotiating framework that the Soviet Union accepted today.

On Monday night a senior State Department official said the Bush Administration had been working on the formula for the last 10 days or so.

But today the British Foreign Secretary said it was "certainly a British Government initiative, though others were thinking along the same lines." Mr. Hurd described the plan as "a child the moment of whose conception is rather difficult to gauge."

The NATO and Warsaw Pact ministers also concluded their talks today with broad agreement that an open skies accord between the two alliances would play an important role in strengthening mutual confidence and reinforcing the process of disarmament under way in Europe.

"Open skies opens a new dimension of confidence building," Mr. Genscher said.

"Signing a treaty would give a boost to the Vienna conventional force reduction talks and would have an important impact on other arms control fora," the Hungarian Foreign Minister, Gyula Horn, said.

Call for New Talks

Many officials also called for a new round of disarmament talks to start as soon as the present Vienna negotiations produce a conventional arms reduction agreement later this year.

There was also support for developing the 35-nation Conference on Security and Cooperation in Europe into a more comprehensive mechanism for linking the continent's eastern and western halves.

"As the Warsaw Pact disintegrates, East European countries feel a need for something which brings them together," Mr. Hurd said. Foreign Minister Genscher called for "pan-European institutions" to foster the coalescence of Europe within the C.S.C.E. framework," suggesting human rights enforcement and environmental protection as possible areas for closer cooperation.

In a communiqué issued after their talks on an open skies agreement, the NATO and Warsaw Pact officials said such an understanding would "strengthen confidence among them, reduce the risk of conflict and enhance the predictability of military activities in participating countries, by allowing each side to inspect the other from the air."

The Warsaw Pact still favors an arrangement under which both sides would share all the information gathered from overflights, while NATO wants each alliance to provide its own planes and keep the intelligence they provide.

Discussions on an agreement will continue at a technical level here for another 10 days or so. The two alliances plan to meet again in Budapest in early May, when they hope to complete their agreement.

* * *

February 16, 1990

ACCORD ON EUROPE: ANATOMY OF A DECISION—A SPECIAL REPORT

Steps to German Unity: Bonn as a Power

By THOMAS L. FRIEDMAN
with MICHAEL R. GORDON
Special to The New York Times.

WASHINGTON, Feb. 15—Early Tuesday morning, as foreign ministers from the 23 NATO and Warsaw Pact nations milled around the main hall of the Ottawa Congress Center, the Soviet Foreign Minister, Eduard A. Shevardnadze and Secretary of State James A. Baker 3d stood off in a corner, whispering to one another through a Russian translator.

Mr. Shevardnadze reported that the Soviet Union would back down and accept President Bush's proposal for troop cuts in Europe, which would leave the United States with a 30,000-man advantage.

This conversation was the culmination of several days of diplomacy that was kept secret not only from the public but from many allied governments as well. The talks resulted in a new United States-Soviet understanding on troop levels in Europe.

But probably more important, they also resulted in an arrangement for how the four World War II Allies—Britain, France, the United States and the Soviet Union—would deal with the other major development on the continent: negotiations for a seemingly inevitable reunification of Germany.

Canadian Press

Secretary of State James A. Baker 3d and Foreign Minister Eduard A. Shevardnadze of the Soviet Union, right, conferring on Tuesday at closing session of meeting in Ottawa of NATO and Warsaw Pact ministers.

In these latter negotiations, the Big Four, once the undisputed overseers of Germany's fate, found themselves having to negotiate with Bonn as a real equal. West Germany used its weight in world affairs, as well as the political momentum of change within its borders and in East Germany, to help shape many of the terms of the Ottawa framework for determining how a united Germany will fit into a post-cold war European order.

How It Happened

A reconstruction of the negotiations, based on dozens of interviews today and in recent weeks, found these steps:

- Bush Administration officials consulted separately and in private with British, French and West German leaders to forge a consensus on dealing with German unification—before discussing the matter with Moscow.
- Britain, France and the Soviet Union initially preferred that the four Allied powers discuss the future of Germany among themselves—and not, at first, with the Germans—but Washington talked them into bringing the Germans in from the start.

• Once the Germans were brought into the process, Bonn insisted on excluding the other nations of the 16-member North Atlantic Treaty Organization from these discussions. The West Germans, in a bit of muscle flexing, wanted to make it clear that they would deal only with those Allied powers that had postwar legal rights in Berlin.

Setting the Stage: The Wall Falls, The Allies Respond

After the opening of the Berlin wall on Nov. 10, Administration officials assumed that the unification process would unfold gradually, and that no serious moves on their part would be required until the East German elections, then scheduled for May.

But on Jan. 28, with thousands of East Germans still flocking to the West every day, East German authorities announced that they were advancing the election date to March 18. They simply could not hold the country together until May. Since pro-unification parties were expected to sweep the elections, Administration officials realized that a unified Germany was no longer a possibility—it was all but a certainty.

So the Administration decided to come up with its own plan to manage reunification. President Bush consulted with his national security adviser, Brent Scowcroft, and the deputy adviser, Robert M. Gates, and Mr. Baker with his key aides—Robert Zoellick, State Department counselor; Dennis B. Ross, the department's Director of Policy Planning, and Raymond G. H. Seitz, Assistant Secretary of State for European Affairs. Mr. Seitz eventually produced a version of the plan adopted at Ottawa. It became known as the "two-plus-four" concept.

Sequence of Talks

Under this formula, after the East German elections were over the two Germanys would get together and discuss their economic, political and legal unification. After that, the United States, Britain, France and the Soviet Union would sit down with the two Germanys and discuss the size of the army their unified state might have, its relationship to NATO and security guarantees for its neighbors.

Mr. Baker and President Bush decided that they would keep the two-plus-four idea closely held and begin secretly polling the three other Allies, one by one. They would not tell the other members of NATO, until and unless there was an agreement among the four, plus the two Germanys.

The first serious discussion of the idea took place on Jan. 29, when the British Foreign Secretary, Douglas Hurd, met with Mr. Baker in Washington. Mr. Hurd, who had been thinking along similar lines, indicated that his Government's preference would be "four plus zero"—that is, the four Allied powers getting together to discuss the fate of Germany, at first without the Germans. Nevertheless, he gave London's backing to two plus four.

Bonn Wants Guarantees

Four days later, the West German Foreign Minister, Hans-Dietrich Genscher, flew to Washington for a private chat with Mr. Baker, during which the Secretary first laid out the two-plus-four idea to him. Mr. Genscher liked it, but he wanted to make certain that it was two plus four, and not four plus two. That is, he wanted to make sure that the two Germanys would first determine the nature of their unification on their own, and then deal with the other powers on external security issues.

Mr. Genscher also told Mr. Baker that his Government would have nothing to do with a "2-plus-15" arrangment—the two Germanys and the 15 other members of NATO deciding the German future. Nor would he accept "four plus zero." He also said that West Germany would not put its future in the hands of the 35 members of the Conference on Security and Cooperation in Europe. Two plus four, he said, was just right.

On Feb. 5, Mr. Baker began a trip to Eastern Europe and the Soviet Union. At the last minute, his schedulers added a stop in Shannon, Ireland, at 5 A.M. for a meeting with the French Foreign Minister, Roland Dumas. During the one-hour talk, Mr. Dumas also signed on to the "two-plus-four" concept, but only after saying that his first preference was also "four plus zero."

As the reunification negotiations progressed, pressure was building in the United States and in Europe for Mr. Bush to propose a deeper cut in Soviet and American conventional forces in Europe than he had presented to NATO leaders in May. At the urging of Mr. Scowcroft, Gen. Colin L. Powell, chairman of the Joint Chiefs of Staff, developed the plan to cut American and Soviet troops in Central Europe to 195,000, with the United States keeping 30,000 soldiers elsewhere in the European region.

Meetings in Moscow: Visit by Baker A Turning Point

On Feb. 7, Mr. Baker flew into Moscow. That night, he had a private meeting with Mr. Shevardnadze and tried to bring up Germany, but the Soviet official said that topic would have to be taken up with President Mikhail S. Gorbachev himself. The next morning, Mr. Baker presented the two-plus-four concept to the Soviet leader as they sat around a huge table in the Kremlin's Catherine Hall. Mr. Gorbachev was intrigued by the two-plus-four idea, but noncommittal. He too made it clear that he shared the British and French preference for "four plus zero."

"One of the things that is very striking about dealing with Shevardnadze and Gorbachev right now is that they will listen to your arguments," a senior State Department official said. "These are not stylized discussions. They tend to be very relaxed. When you make a case that they think is reasonable, they will come right back and tell you: 'Well, you know, that's reasonable.' And there was quite a bit of that in the discussion on the Germanys."

Distinction between Armies

But the German question was not the only issue Mr. Baker had to discuss with the Soviets. There was also the question of how they would respond to President Bush's troop proposal, with its insistence on American troop superiority in

Europe. This was to drive home the point that the Soviets, who were in Europe as occupiers, might have to leave at the behest of their allies, but that the Americans were there by invitation and would not be leaving entirely.

Mr. Gorbachev accepted the basic principle of lower troop levels, but gave Mr. Baker a counterproposal: both sides would go down to either 195,000 men or 225,000 men, but not 195,000 for the Soviets and 225,000 for the Americans. Administration officials say they believe that this idea may have been generated by the Soviet arms-control bureaucracy and that Mr. Gorbachev decided he had nothing to lose by seeing if he could bluff the Americans into accepting it.

Mr. Baker left Moscow without a Soviet answer to the German question, and with the troop proposal in limbo. Just as Mr. Baker was packing to leave, the West German Chancellor, Helmut Kohl, and his Foreign Minister, Mr. Genscher, were arriving for their own meeting with Mr. Gorbachev.

Mr. Baker decided that to avoid creating any impression of the United States and the Soviets—without the British and the French—deciding the fate of Germany, he would avoid any personal contact with Mr. Kohl in Moscow.

Instead, Mr. Baker sent Mr. Kohl a three-page, for-your-eyes-only note, laying out Mr. Gorbachev's reactions to the two-plus-four idea. Mr. Baker then took off for Bulgaria and Romania on his way to a conference in Ottawa on the "open skies" proposal for air missions over other nations' territories.

Success in Ottawa: A Deal Is Struck On Troop Cuts

While in Ottawa, Mr. Baker, Mr. Genscher, Mr. Hurd, Mr. Dumas and Mr. Shevardnadze, who were supposed to be dealing with "open skies," were in fact simply going from one meeting with each other, to another. Most of the other NATO and Warsaw Pact foreign ministers did not have a clue as to what they were talking about.

Mr. Baker's private secretary, Karen Jackson, carried around the schedules of each of the other ministers, which were constantly being updated. For instance, the Soviets would call to say that Mr. Shevardnadze was going to be at his embassy for 30 minutes, and then in his suite for an hour, and after that back in the conference hall, so that Mr. Baker could track him down at any moment.

A Baker aide mused that if anyone was tapping the phone calls between the ministers, they would have heard some of the most momentous issues in postwar politics being discussed with stunning frankness. At several points, Mr. Baker was jogging back and forth between meetings with Mr. Genscher and Mr. Shevardnadze.

On Tuesday morning, Mr. Baker, Mr. Hurd, Mr. Dumas and Mr. Genscher had breakfast at the West German Embassy in Ottawa and hammered out the proposed language of the two-plus-four arrangement. They decided then that if they could get Mr. Shevardnadze to sign on to it now, they should do it. Events in Germany were moving too fast, they reasoned, and if they broke up in Ottawa without an understanding, it would be that much more difficult later.

From that breakfast, Mr. Baker drove back to a full session of the open-skies conference. As ministers milled around the oval meeting table, Mr. Baker walked over to Mr. Shevardnadze with a scrap of paper in his hand. With Mr. Shevardnadze's translator standing between them, Mr. Baker, reading from the paper written in his own handwriting, whispered to the Soviet Foreign Minister the proposed language the Western Allies were suggesting for two plus four. Mr. Shevardnadze's translator wrote it all down in Russian, and Mr. Shevardnadze said he would have to call Mr. Gorbachev.

A Dizzying Speed: German Disunity, Other Loose Ends

It was at this juncture that Mr. Shevardnadze also informed Mr. Baker that Mr. Gorbachev was ready to accept Mr. Bush's original troop offer.

Mr. Baker was pleased but somewhat taken aback. No one had really expected Mr. Gorbachev to come around so soon. The Soviet leader was apparently playing from a much weaker hand than anyone thought. Mr. Baker walked out of the hall and telephoned President Bush with the news. Mr. Shevardnadze phoned President Gorbachev to get his reaction to the two-plus-four language.

Meanwhile, the President had been conducting his own telephone diplomacy on Tuesday morning, speaking twice with Chancellor Kohl. Mr. Bush—knowing that Mr. Genscher and Mr. Kohl, political allies of necessity in Bonn's governing coalition, dislike each other and often do not even tell each other what they are doing—decided that he had to personally make certain that Mr. Kohl approved of the two-plus-four deal that Mr. Genscher was striking with Mr. Baker. Mr. Kohl told the President that he was willing, and the President gave Mr. Baker his green light.

Concessions to Soviets

Two hours later, Mr. Shevardnadze and Mr. Baker met again in a private conference room. Mr. Shevardnadze said that Mr. Gorbachev supported the idea but that he needed some changes in the text. First, it could not mention the March 18 East German election date, or suggest that this was the event that would trigger the two-plus-four meeting. This was done to mollify his East German allies and to avoid treating unification, or the dissolution of East Germany, as a foregone conclusion.

Mr. Shevardnadze also insisted, apparently on behalf of the Poles, that the statement contain a line saying that the two-plus-four discussions would deal with "issues of security of the neighboring states."

Once this language was approved, news photographers were summoned for pictures of the two German Foreign Ministers and those of the four Allied countries standing together. No one was told why. Moments later, their two-plus-four announcement was released. Members of the press got it before most other NATO ministers. The Dutch, Italians and Belgians were incensed and began asking for some changes in the text, particularly for some reference not only to the security of states neighboring Germany, but also in the rest of Europe.

"They were told in no uncertain terms that this was a matter for the Allied powers with legal rights in Germany and nobody else," an Administration official said. "That is why the deal was cut this way, we told them, and if you don't like it, I'm sorry, but you have no legal rights."

* * *

February 26, 1990

BUSH AND KOHL TRY TO ALLAY FEARS OF A REUNIFIED GERMANY'S POWERS

By ROBERT PEAR

Special to The New York Times.

CAMP DAVID, Md., Feb. 25—Ending two days of talks, President Bush and Chancellor Helmut Kohl of West Germany declared today that there was no reason for anyone to fear the economic, political or military power of a united Germany.

Mr. Bush said they agreed that the nation being reborn in the middle of Europe should be a full member of NATO and take part in the alliance's military structure.

The two leaders played down fears of reunification expressed by some of the two Germanys' neighbors.

"I think we have learned lessons and we do not want to repeat the errors of history," Mr. Kohl said at a news conference with Mr. Bush.

"This is not 1945; this is 1990," Mr. Kohl said at another point.

The Chancellor declined again to say explicitly that he accepted the permanence of the existing Polish-German border. But he offered Poles somewhat more assurance than he has in the past, saying, "Nobody wants to link the question of national unity with changes in existing borders."

During World War II, Poland was occupied by both Nazi Germany and the Soviet Union. As a result of postwar negotiations, the Soviet Union kept most of the Polish territory it had occupied, compensating Poland by giving it control over eastern Germany.

Various agreements signed by European countries in recent years have confirmed the postwar boundaries. But Poland has been uneasy about sentiment voiced by right-wing parties in West Germany critical of the realignment of territory.

Border Question Delayed

Mr. Kohl said at the news conference that "the border question will be settled definitely by a freely elected all-German government and a freely elected all-German parliament," neither of which has yet been constituted. Many Polish officials want the current border to be confirmed before reunification by the separate Governments of East Germany and West Germany.

Mr. Kohl's critics say he is keeping the border question alive to satisfy rightist politicians who want the border to be an issue in the campaign leading up to the West German national elections in December.

On the border question, Mr. Bush was more categorical. He did not allow Mr. Kohl's comments to stand alone, but jumped in to say: "The U.S. respects the provisions of the Helsinki Final Act regarding the inviolability of current borders in Europe. And the U.S. formally recognizes the current German-Polish border." The Helsinki accords were signed in 1975.

Mr. Bush and Mr. Kohl discussed the future of Europe and the pace of German reunification, which has been faster than either leader had expected. Mr. Bush said nothing that would suggest he seeks to brake the rush toward reunification, which he described as "a golden moment in the history" of Germany.

On NATO Membership

In an opening statement, Mr. Bush said he and Mr. Kohl agreed that "a unified Germany should remain a full member of the North Atlantic Treaty Organization, including participation in its military structure." Mr. Bush thus seemed to rule out the possibility that a united Germany might have a special status in NATO like that of France.

France pulled out of NATO's integrated military commands in 1966, but otherwise remains a full member of the alliance.

Mr. Bush said he and Mr. Kohl also agreed that "U.S. military forces should remain stationed in a united Germany and elsewhere in Europe, as a continuing guarantor of stability." But the President said they also agreed that the land now constituting East Germany should have "a special military status that would take into account the legitimate security interests" of the Soviet Union and other countries.

Neither leader defined that special status. They were presumably referring to an arrangement that would exclude NATO troops from what is now East Germany. The Soviet Union has stated that it wants a unified Germany to be neutral.

The American Attitude

Mr. Bush said the American position was "not to be afraid of German reunification," but to welcome it. He said he looked forward to the day when the four major World War II Allies would not have to look "over the shoulders of a democratic unified Germany."

Similarly, Mr. Kohl said that "nobody needs to be afraid" of a united Germany. He said the new German state would have close ties to the United States and be embedded in a European Community moving toward economic union and closer political cooperation.

American and West German journalists posed more questions to Mr. Kohl than to Mr. Bush, who nevertheless volunteered his comments at several points. The West German leader smiled with apparent satisfaction while Mr. Bush spoke at the news conference. Mr. Bush often scowled and squinted while the Chancellor spoke.

The news conference was held in a recreation hall at Camp Greentop in the Catoctin Mountain park, just outside the gates of Camp David.

Timetable Not Discussed

Mr. Kohl and Mr. Bush said that the precise details and timetable for German reunification were not decided over the weekend.

Mr. Bush was asked to explain the "two-plus-four" formula, under which the two Germanys are supposed to negotiate the economic and political aspects of unification as a prelude to discussions with the four Allies on security issues.

"Those details have not been fully worked out in terms of timing of meetings and things of this nature," Mr Bush said. He said the formula was approved by the foreign ministers of the United States, Britain, France, the Soviet Union and the two Germanys on Feb. 13 in Ottawa, "and we simply have not tried to sit here in Camp David and fine-tune the procedures."

Mr. Kohl said that swift unification was needed to stem the flow of East Germans to the West. Since Jan. 1, he said, some 110,000 people have left East Germany for West Germany. Their exodus has accelerated the move toward reunification, he said.

Expects Separate Elections

Some West Germans have said that the union might be consummated in time for East Germans to vote in West German elections scheduled for Dec. 2.

But Mr. Kohl said he believed those elections would be held in West Germany alone. East Germans vote March 18 for a new government that will presumably negotiate the terms of union with Bonn.

The Chancellor sounded testy when a journalist suggested that other countries should receive assurances on "borders and security" before the two Germanys merge. "The question of German unity is a question of the right of self-determination, and all peoples of this earth have the right of self-determination," he said. He made no mention of the legal powers that the World War II Allies technically retain in Berlin and in Germany as a whole.

Mr. Kohl also bristled at the suggestion that a united Germany might drift away from NATO toward neutrality. "In 1983," he said, "I put my political existence at stake by agreeing" to the deployment of American missiles on West German soil, "so nobody has to tell me what a reliable partner is."

Dismisses 'Neutralism'

"Neutralism would be a very false solution for us," Mr. Kohl said. "I can't see that there would ever be any majority in the Federal Republic nor in a united Germany for a neutralized Germany."

Without mentioning the Nazis, Mr. Kohl acknowledged, "We have a certain history," and said, "We must understand that there are certain fears on the part of our neighbors," particularly Poland.

He said he was confident that in melding the two Germanys, "we will find ways and means of adopting solutions satisfactory to everybody."

Mr. Kohl was asked if a united Germany could have any ties to the Warsaw Pact or if it would allow the stationing of Soviet troops within its borders. "One thing is clear," he said. "A united Germany cannot belong to two different pact systems."

* * *

March 12, 1990

PARLIAMENT IN LITHUANIA, 124-0, DECLARES NATION INDEPENDENT

By BILL KELLER

Special to The New York Times.

VILNIUS, Lithuania, March 11—Lithuania tonight proclaimed itself a sovereign state, legally free of the Soviet Union, and named the leaders of a non-Communist government to negotiate their future relations with Moscow.

The Lithuanian parliament voted 124 to 0, with 9 abstentions and absentees, to restore the independent statehood ended by Soviet annexation 50 years ago. The Lithuanian Communist Party, which won only a minority of seats in parliamentary elections last month, joined the non-Communist majority in the vote, and in an outburst of songs and embraces that followed.

"Expressing the will of the people, the Supreme Soviet of the Lithuanian Republic declares and solemnly proclaims the restoration of the exercise of sovereign powers of the Lithuanian state, which were annulled by an alien power in 1940," said a resolution passed late tonight. "From now on, Lithuania is once again an independent state."

Full Implications Unclear

It was not immediately clear what the full implications of the Lithuanian action were. According to Lithuanian leaders, Mikhail S. Gorbachev, the Soviet President, has indicated a willingness to negotiate the conditions of independence. But there was no immediate reaction to the declaration of independence either from Mr. Gorbachev or the Soviet Government.

Tass, the Soviet press agency, issued a factual report of the Lithuanian action without comment. Reports on national television were similar. [The Bush Administration urged the Soviet Union to respect the Lithuanian move, but stopped short of an explicit statement of recognition of the newly declared government. Noting instead that the United States never recognized Soviet authority over the Baltic republics, officials urged nonviolence and said that only through talks with Moscow, not unilateral action, would Lithuanians achieve what they want.]

Hundreds of Lithuanians gathered outside the parliament building, singing national hymns and chanting independence slogans, as the legislators changed the name of the Lithuanian Soviet Socialist Republic to simply the Lithuanian Republic and ordered the hammer and sickle replaced by the old Lithuanian coat of arms.

At one point, people in the crowd outside used screwdrivers to pry the copper Soviet insignia from the front of the building, to a roar of approval.

But behind the united front, many legislators and ordinary citizens voiced deep worry about how Moscow would respond to this precedent-setting breach in the union. The most common fear was a wave of economic repraisals that could produce fuel shortages and unemployment, threatening the state with chaos.

Other legislators worried that such a dramatic act of defiance, especially on the eve of an important Soviet congressional gathering, would weaken President Gorbachev, who has so far generally acquiesced to Lithuania's drive for freedom.

Before approving the law completing the political break with Moscow, the parliament elected as Lithuania's new president Vytautas Landsbergis, a soft-spoken music professor who led the pro-independence movement called Sajudis from an eclectic band of dissidents to a legislative majority.

By a vote of 91 to 38, the Sajudis-dominated legislature elected Mr. Landsbergis over Algirdas Brazauskas, the Lithuanian Communist Party leader, whose personal popularity has soared since his party broke with the Soviet Communist Party in December, but not enough to overcome the Communists' association with decades of occupation.

New Leader Urges Calm

Mr. Landsbergis urged the 3.7 million citizens of the republic to be calm and united as they enter a period of tense negotiations aimed at persuading Moscow to treat them as a friendly neighbor. On Monday the parliament is to consider an appeal to Mr. Gorbachev asking for withdrawal of the more than 30,000 Soviet troops based in Lithuania and the speedy repatriation of Lithuanian men serving in the Soviet Army.

"We cannot ignore the interests of our neighbors, particularly our neighbors to the east," the new Lithuanian president said. "But we will not be asking for permission to take this or that step."

Mr. Brazauskas is an economist by training, and supporters said the Communist leader would be a more reassuring presence at the bargaining table where details of the disengagement are to be worked out. But Mr. Landsbergis represented a clean break with the 50-year period that Lithuanians regard as an armed occupation.

The neighboring Baltic republics, Latvia and Estonia, are also moving toward secession.

"It will be contagious for other republics," said Mr. Brazauskas, who voted for today's decision but had earlier argued for a more gradual separation. "Perhaps some will follow our example. But a great state like the Soviet Union will not collapse easily."

Although the Communists here voted for the declaration of independence, Mr. Brazauskas declined an offer to be vice president, and other party members said they were not interested in prominent positions in the new government.

Other Officials Named

Mr. Landsbergis appointed three deputies, one a Communist and two who have quit the party, and named as prime minister a market-oriented economist, Kazimiera Prunskiene, who has announced her plans to leave the party.

Ustas J. Paleckis, the Communist party ideology chief, said that the Communists were persuaded that Sajudis did not want to share power on a more equal basis and that some party officials had decided they would remain aloof from the government and let Sajudis take responsibility for the consequences.

In the corridors outside the parliamentary chamber, Mr. Brazauskas's Communists—about one third of the 133 legislators—and some non-Communists wondered aloud about the wisdom of moving so quickly to declare independence.

"Probably a third of the deputies think it is crazy to rush into this," said a local journalist sympathetic to Sajudis. "But anyone who speaks against it is sure to be branded a traitor."

No representatives of Moscow were evident in the hall.

Rights Advocate Applauds

Though there was no official reaction from the Kremlin, members of the parliamentary opposition in Moscow sent a message of congratulations, and Sergei Kovalyov, a human rights advocate and former political prisoner recently elected to the Russian republic's parliament, came here to applaud Lithuania's move.

"A lot of Russians will say, 'We liberated you from the Germans, we helped you industrialize,'

"Mr. Kovalyov said in a brief address to the parliament. "None of them will say that we deported half of the Lithuanian people to Siberia."

In recent days Mr. Gorbachev and other Soviet officials served notice that Moscow would make billions of rubles in financial claims on Lithuania if it secedes, and challenged Lithuania's boundaries, including its right to the Baltic seaport of Klaipeda, also called Memel. Mr. Gorbachev has also repeatedly cited security risks for Moscow in the loss of the republic, and promised to defend the rights of the republic's non-Lithuanian minority, 20 percent of the population.

There have already been some signs of stepped-up pressure, including a freeze by the Soviet Government-controlled banks on the assets of Lithuanian savings banks, that have led leaders of the republic to speculate about a possible economic blockade.

What Moscow Could Do

Annual trade between Lithuania and other Soviet republics is estimated at $24 billion at the official rate of exchange, including almost all of Lithuania's subsidized oil supplies.

Another fear is that Moscow could shut down centrally run industrial enterprises, throwing half a million Russian blue-collar workers out of jobs and raising ethnic tensions.

"My fear is that if we do not understand the progressive forces in Moscow, we can bring them a lot of danger," Mr. Paleckis added. "And it will be danger for us as well. If Mr.

Gorbachev loses, our declaration of independence will make moral sense, but. . ."

Mr. Landsbergis replied that "the people of Lithuania are not naive. Even after listening to frequent warnings about how difficult it was going to be, they voted all the same for the Sajudis platform. We consider that a kind of referendum." Mr. Landsbergis said he hoped for prompt recognition from foreign countries, including the United States, which has never formally acknowledged the annexation of the three Baltic republics but has been wary of undermining Mr. Gorbachev.

The vote was the climax of a campaign that began gathering momentum less than two years ago, with the creation of the Sajudis initiative group in June, 1988.

A year ago, the alliance proved its strength by capturing most of the republic's seats in a new Soviet Parliament.

Mr. Landsbergis and several other lawmakers said they would no longer participate as voting members of the Soviet Parliament, although they might come to Moscow as observers or as members of a bargaining team to work out the details of secession.

Correction: Because of a transcription error, an article on Monday about Lithuania's declaration of independence misidentified the new president of Lithuania in some editions, as did a picture caption in other copies. He is Vytautas Landsbergis. The article also misidentified the Communist Party ideology chief of Lithuania. He is Justas Paleckis. Because of an editing error, the article also referred incorrectly to the port city of Klaipeda. It was once called Memel; it is not known that way now.

* * *

March 25, 1990

A DEMOCRATICALLY EVOLVING HUNGARY HEADS INTO UNKNOWN AT POLLS TODAY

By CELESTINE BOHLEN

Special to The New York Times.

BUDAPEST, March 24—As they vote on Sunday to elect a government freely for the first time in more than four decades, Hungarians will continue a process that began here almost two years ago, long before the political whirlwind that swept through the rest of Eastern Europe last fall.

In recent months, changes have come more gradually than in neighboring countries, often with contradictory results. Even the returns in Sunday's vote for a new 386-seat Parliament are likely to be inconclusive, and require a second round of balloting next month.

Then, odds are that Hungary's new government will be a coalition, made up of parties that have spent months attacking each other.

But one outcome of the vote is expected to be clear. In overwhelming numbers, the 7.5 million Hungarians likely to vote are considered certain to reject any political choice that faintly resembles Communism, and to embrace those candidates and parties that promise to lead them further toward a Western-style economy.

In the final days of the campaign, political debate has been overshadowed by widespread emotional concern over the fate of Hungarians in neighboring Romania, where ethnic violence broke out last week in Transylvania. Some Hungarians say this may spur voters toward the more conservative, traditional parties, as they seek refuge from an outside world that suddenly seems strange and uncertain.

The Likely Front-Runners

Two parties are expected to dominate the voting, both newly formed but each representing strong trends in Hungarian political life.

The Alliance of Free Democrats is a party of liberals and free-market economists whose radical tactics have won it support among both urban intellectuals and disaffected workers. The Hungarian Democratic Forum, a coalition of center-right forces with a tinge of nationalism, is strong among the country's professional middle classes.

In the month since the official campaign began, a third party, the Independent Smallholders, which after the war won 58 percent of the vote, has surged too, buoyed by its promise to return land seized by the Communists.

These three parties have dominated recent opinion polls, including one by Gallup Budapest of 1,000 likely voters between Feb. 18 and March 1, which put the Free Democrats ahead with 23 percent of the vote, followed by the Democratic Forum with 21 percent and the Smallholders with 17 percent.

But after the failure of polls to fully predict elections in East Germany or Nicaragua, people here are reluctant to guess at the outcome. Some say other smaller parties, including the Federation of Young Democrats, several small Christian parties and even the Socialist Party, the successor to the Communists, could fare better than expected in the current volatile atmosphere.

What About Individuals?

A flaw in the polls is that they have tracked only party loyalities, and not gauged people's views of individual candidates including about 200 independents running in the 176 parliamentary constituencies. Here, name recognition, or local ties, or local issues, could overwhelm party affiliation.

The rest of Parliament's 386 seats will be filled under a hybrid proportional-representation arrangement, based on party lists compiled in Budapest and the country's 19 counties.

The complicated election law has added to the popular confusion created by the proliferation of parties. Although the Gallup Poll showed that political apathy in Hungary has waned, still 12 percent of those surveyed said they will not go to the polls, and 31 percent said they were not sure.

Without the catharsis of a popular revolution, as in Romania, or the issue of unification that overwhelmed last Sunday's vote in East Germany, Hungary's first step toward democracy has been relatively joyless.

City streets droop with political banners, posters line fences and walls, and evening television is filled with round-table debates. But popular participation—outside a few areas—has been low, and on buses and in wine bars here and in the provinces, people grumble that they do not know what it all means.

Life Getting Tougher

Part of the dissatisfaction comes from the timing of the election, which has coincided with a surge in inflation and a drop in living standards. Faced with a $21 billion foreign debt, the highest per person in Europe, the departing Government, made up of former Communists, has had to cut subsidies and take other steps that have clouded the future for many Hungarians.

And in Hungary, no personalities have emerged to guide people through their choices. Imre Pozsgay, a leader of the Socialist Party, was a popular reformer in the waning days of Communist rule, but since then, has lost much of his appeal.

Pictures of Jozsef Antall, the leader of the Hungarian Democrats and their candidate for Prime Minister, now hang from streetlamps around Budapest, but his sober demeanor and long-winded speeches have won him little personal popularity.

The darlings of the election may be the Young Democrats, whose bright, articulate candidates, all under 35, have brought a fresh, often humorous approach to the campaign.

The Free Democrats, many of whom had been dissidents in the Communist era, have been the most vigorous and visible politicians, pressing both the Government and its opponents on issue after issue.

In January, they and the Young Democrats cracked upon a scandal about the continued use of the secret police by the governing Socialists to spy on political opponents. They also have raised frequent protests about the continued control of television, a bitter battleground in the election campaign.

Holiday Becomes Controversial

But the Free Democrats' confrontational tactics have backfired on occasion. Recently, they were blamed—they say unfairly—for having failed to agree with their political opponents on how television should cover the celebration of March 15, a hallowed national holiday honoring Hungary's revolt against Austrian rule in 1848, which until last year had been suppressed and celebrated only by dissidents.

The quarrel over why a Government-named board canceled live television coverage of the March 15 celebrations became a dominant theme of the last days of the campaign, and was the subject of a two-hour televised debate and long newspaper articles.

For many voters, this was only further proof that political freedom means pointless debates about issues that have little direct effect on their lives. The fact that the parties' quarrel was over the March 15 holiday, a national symbol for Hungarians living in and outside the country, only irritated them further.

Since the beginning of the year, when events around Hungary proved that Communism was dissolving fast, the opposition's fight to push the Communists out of power turned increasingly into a battle between the different opposition parties.

But anti-Communism remains a compelling theme, and in the final weeks, all three leading parties have pledged that they will not form a coalition with any wing of the former Communist Party.

But because Hungarian reform Communists started on the road to democratic change two years ago—first with the ouster of the longtime leader Janos Kadar in May 1988, their leaders have proved more durable in office than their counterparts in Czechoslovakia, East Germany or Romania.

HUNGARY'S 12 MAJOR PARTIES

Parties qualified to be seated as national parties in the Hungarian Parliament, roughly in order of their popularity in recent polls. The first round of the election is today.

Hungarian Democratic Forum.

Leaders: Jozsef Antall, Geza Jeszenszky. Center-right, with Christian image and nationalist overtones. Favors a careful transition to a free-market economy, but as an early umbrella opposition group, includes a wide spectrum of opinion.

Alliance of Free Democrats.

Leaders: Janos Kis, Marton Tardos, Miklos Gaspar Tamas, Miklos Haraszti. Liberal with a social conscience, created from the base of the old dissident movement. Refused to compromise with the ruling Communists.

Independent Smallholders' Party.

Leaders: Vince Voros, Istvan Prepeliczay, Pal Dragon. A major party in the pre-Communist era. Agrarian and Christian. By promising to return the land to its 1947 owners, it has built a base in the villages, particularly among the elderly.

The Hungarian Socialist Party.

Leaders: Rezso Nyers, Imre Pozsgay. Legal successor to the Hungarian Socialist Workers (Communist) Party. Advocates social democratic policies, and argues for a strong "left" opposition. Membership has dwindled dramatically, but still strong among officials and workers.

Federation of Young Democrats.

Leaders: Viktor Orban, Tamas Dutsch, Gabor Fodor. A party with a membership limited to those under 35. Radical, iconoclastic, it is credited with running a sophisticated campaign, competing with the Free Democrats, its natural allies, for support of the younger intelligentsia.

Social Democratic Party of Hungary.

Leader: Anna Petrasovits, Gyorgy Fischer. A left-center party, which has revived its membership in the Socialist International. Has received support from foreign social democrats, but was badly hurt by an early split and has failed to carve out its own place.

Christian Democratic People's Party.

Leaders: Sandor Keresztes, Gyorgy Giczi. Right of center and Christian. Likely to get a boost from local Roman Catholic priests in village churches.

Hungarian People's Party.

Leaders: Csaba Varga, Janos Marton. Considers itself to be the successor of the prewar National Peasant Party. Populist centrist.

The Hungarian Socialist Workers Party.

Leaders: Gyula Thurmer, Karoly Grosz. A Marxist party that split from the main reformist wing of the old Communist Party last October. Advocates a renewed socialism, and warns workers of the dangers of uncontrolled capitalism. Supporters are mostly older members of the old Communist Party.

Entrepreneurs Party.

Leaders: Gyorgy Szucs, Imre Fejes. Promises economic rights and fair taxes to Hungary's emerging class of entrepreneurs.

Patriotic Election Coalition.

Leader: Istvan Asztalos. An ad-hoc alliance created for the elections, formed from the Patriotic People's Front, a grouping of mostly non-Communists that existed during the Communist monopoly.

Agrarian Federation.

A leftist coalition made mainly of cooperative farm presidents, who are in opposition to the Smallholders' Party in the debate over land ownership.

* * *

May 18, 1990

GORBACHEV MEETS WITH LITHUANIANS; 'BIG STEP' IS CITED

By BILL KELLER

Special to The New York Times.

MOSCOW, May 17—President Mikhail S. Gorbachev met with the Prime Minister of Lithuania in the Kremlin tonight and agreed to begin talks with the breakaway republic if the Lithuanian Parliament suspends its declaration of independence.

The official, Kazimiera Prunskiene, said tonight that the meeting, the first face-to-face encounter between Mr. Gorbachev and a leader of the Baltic republic, was a significant move toward negotiations that could lower the tension surrounding Lithuania's claim of sovereignty, made on March 11, and possibly end the limited economic blockade that Moscow has imposed in retribution.

Both the Lithuanian Prime Minister and the Soviet press agency Tass, reporting on the meeting tonight, said a serious hurdle remained in the way of beginning talks.

Status of the Argument

Lithuania has offered to suspend the application of its independence proclamation, including laws repealing the Soviet military draft and laying claim to national property, but the republic has previously insisted that suspending the act itself might jeopardize its status as an equal partner in talks with Moscow.

Mrs. Prunskiene indicated that this difference should not be insurmountable. She said she would offer a version of a new compromise that might be considered by the Lithuanian Parliament as early as Saturday.

She emphasized that she had told Mr. Gorbachev that independence itself was not negotiable, and said he did not dispute the point.

"He said the fact that we met, that we discussed the issues, that we made progress from our previous positions—this was a big step forward," Mrs. Prunskiene said.

Freer Hand for U.S. Talks

The meeting, which lasted an hour and 40 minutes, also appeared likely to ease the threat that the Lithuania conflict could overshadow Mr. Gorbachev's meeting with President Bush in Washington, beginning May 30.

Secretary of State James A. Baker 3d, reached tonight in Moscow, said that from what he had heard of the Kremlin meeting, "it would be a very encouraging step."

Mr. Baker is scheduled to see Mrs. Prunskiene on Friday after a meeting with Mr. Gorbachev, a session that tonight promised to be a bit more relaxed.

"One of the things we have wanted to see throughout this was the two sides talking face to face," said a senior American official who is here with Mr. Baker. "Here, you have them not only talking face to face, but at a high level."

The official added: "We're pleased. You don't want to get carried away with it, either. But it's a real positive step in the right direction."

The Lithuanian offer and Mrs. Prunskiene's mission to Moscow were timed to catch Mr. Gorbachev at a moment when he would be eager for progress toward a settlement. Unless Moscow eases its embargo on fuel and other supplies, Lithuania is expected to exhaust its oil supplies around the time of the Washington meeting.

Quickly Invited In

Mrs. Prunskiene had no assurance she would be welcomed in Moscow when she arrived this afternoon, bearing a compromise offer approved by the Lithuanian Parliament in a closed session on Wednesday.

But soon after her arrival, she said, Mr. Gorbachev telephoned and invited her to meet there this evening. They were joined by the Soviet Prime Minister, Nikolai I. Ryzhkov.

Mrs. Prunskiene said she got no firm commitment that Moscow would lift the economic sanctions that have caused an estimated 30,000 workers in Lithuania to be sent home from fuel-starved factories.

But she said the issue was discussed, and she left with an understanding that "there will be an appropriate decision" if the Soviet leadership is satisfied by the Lithuanian Parliament's next move.

Paris-Bonn Blueprint

The offer that Mrs. Prunskiene brought to Moscow closely resembled a compromise suggested last month by President Francois Mitterrand of France and Chancellor Helmut Kohl of West Germany. They proposed that Lithuania's sovereignty be accepted, but that the republic suspend any actions flowing from the decision as a basis for opening talks.

The meeting with Mr. Gorbachev was a significant step forward for several reasons.

First, the Soviet President has forsaken his earlier insistence that he would not meet with Lithuanian leaders until they had agreed to abide by Soviet law.

Second, it was the most explicit statement to date of the Kremlin's position, which has at times seemed deliberately ambiguous—at one point praising the Mitterrand-Kohl proposal, at other points insisting that Lithuania retreat all the way back to March 10, the day before it voted on independence.

How Moscow Views It

Tass confirmed tonight that if the declaration was not repealed but suspended, it would be sufficient.

Third, Mrs. Prunskiene got a clear and direct promise that if Lithuania agreed to those terms, this would lead to the long-sought talks.

Suspending the independence act, Tass said, "will immediately pave the way for the discussion of issues that worry peoples inhabiting Lithuania and that give rise to grave concern of Soviet republics, Soviet, and world opinion."

This promise, along with whatever message she takes home from her meeting with Mr. Baker on Friday, may be enough to ease suspicions on the Lithuanian side.

Effect on Neighbors

Lithuania's situation is likely to affect the two other Baltic republics, Estonia and Latvia. After Lithuania's declaration of independence, announced as a clean break with Moscow, Estonia said on March 30 that it would make a gradual withdrawal from the Soviet Union. On May 4, Latvia declared independence. In a move seemingly intended to reduce the possibilities for confrontation with Moscow, it established an open-ended transition period to independence, during which most Soviet laws would apply.

Mr. Gorbachev has insisted that any move to leave the Soviet Union must follow the procedures spelled out in a new Soviet law. These procedures include approval of independence by the republic's residents in a referendum, a transition period up to five years, and final approval by the Soviet Congress of People's Deputies.

But Lithuania, Latvia and Estonia have said that they were illegally incorporated into the Soviet Union and that therefore they will not submit to such laws. In 1940, Stalin annexed the three republics under a secret protocol to a pact with Hitler.

Freedom Is Another Matter

Mrs. Prunskiene, now a seasoned diplomat after her missions to the White House, Canada and European capitals, appeared buoyed by the Kremlin reception.

"Now we know to what the extent the other side has moved ahead, that there has been major progress, and what are the sticking points on the main issues," she told reporters tonight at the Lithuanian mission in Moscow. "We can say quite clearly that the desire and intentions to begin a discussion on the entire range of issues, within a framework of interests on both sides, have been expressed."

Mrs. Prunskiene said that while the Soviet leaders seemed eager to end the stalemate, they were far from enthusiastic about the idea of Lithuania actually getting its freedom from the Soviet Union.

"Do they want or welcome the independence of Lithuania?" she asked rhetorically. "I not only doubt this, but I am sure they have no such desire. I confirmed once again today that they have trouble with this kind of decision, when a people independently decides an issue without the involvement of the Kremlin."

* * *

May 21, 1990

FRONT IN ROMANIA SEEMS VICTORIOUS IN FREE ELECTIONS

By DAVID BINDER

Special to The New York Times.

BUCHAREST, Romania, May 20—The National Salvation Front, the group dominated by former Communists that has run Romania since the violent revolution last December, appeared to be headed toward a convincing victory today in the country's first free national elections in more than 50 years.

According to projections based on polls outside 252 voting sites across the country, Ion Iliescu, the head of the Front and the interim head of state, won 83 percent of the vote for a new President. The Front also won 66 percent in elections for the National Assembly and the Senate, according to the polls conducted by Infas, a West German political-opinion research organization. Most opposition parties had disappointing showings, far below their expectations.

No votes have been counted and scores of thousands of voters were still lined up outside polling stations in Bucharest at midnight, when the polls officially closed. Casting ballots was a tedious procedure in Romania's first free elections since 1937, with each voter expected to read through and stamp choices on a total of 37 pages of candidates.

Official Results Tuesday

The earliest official results are expected to be issued by the national election board on Tuesday.

Still, the polls projected a strong showing for the Front, which would snap a string of election victories by conservative political parties elsewhere in Eastern Europe, where Communist governments have been ousted in the last 12 months, in Poland, Hungary and East Germany.

Led by Mr. Iliescu, a 60-year-old former Communist Party secretary, the Front took power last Dec. 22 after President Nicolae Ceausescu fled from his office in the face of a popular uprising, ending a tyrannical reign of 24 years; Mr. Ceausescu and his wife, Elena, were executed on Christmas Day. The Front has enjoyed the powers of incumbency ever since, even though it has faced fierce criticism and rejection by many Romanians for being made up mostly of former Communist Party members who had served the Ceausescu Government.

Others Lack Resources

Opposition parties formed since the December revolution include revivals of the prewar National Peasants Party and National Liberal Party. But they lacked the resources and time to organize a truly effective alternative to the Front.

The Peasants Party's presidential candidate, Ion Ratiu, received only 6 percent of the vote, according to the Infas projections, and the party got only 4 percent in the National Assembly and 3.5 percent in the Senate races.

The Liberal presidential candidate, Radu Campeanu, like Mr. Ratiu long an exile until returning to Romania early this year, received 11 percent.

In the National Assembly races, the Liberals received 10 percent and for the Senate, 9.5 percent, according to the polling.

Those showings, if confirmed in the final count, appear to render moot the question of whether the the Liberals could offer themselves as coalition partners of the Front or accept a coalition offer from Mr. Iliescu.

Militants in Opposition

At the same time, such a gigantic endorsement may cause Mr. Iliescu further problems with more militant members of the opposition, many of whom were still out in the streets of the capital tonight shouting anti-Communist slogans against him and the Front.

His taking 83 percent of the vote might lend greater credence to charges of fraud; Mr. Ceausescu used to declare himself victor with 98 percent of the vote in his unopposed election races.

One of the election's surprises, judging by the Infas sampling of 16,000 voters, was the strong showing of a new environmental party, which gained 5 percent in both parliamentary races.

Apparently the exit polls were unable to take account of the thousands of independent candidates running by themselves or as candidates of one of the 80 other small parties registered in the elections. Their standings will become apparent only later.

Still, the elections would appear to be a personal victory for Mr. Iliescu, who has vowed that he has shed his Leninist past and wants to lead Romania on a path of social democracy. He himself had been relegated to minor posts in the 1970's after being deemed insufficiently loyal by Ceausescu.

An Offering of Stability

In interviews at polling stations, Romanians in and around Bucharest said they liked Mr. Iliescu and felt the Front would offer more stability in a country that is still fraught with chaos.

There were signs here and there that former members of the defunct Communist Party might attempt to manipulate the results in their districts in favor of the National Salvation Front.

As the evening wore on, reports coming in from some of the 500 foreign observers spread out through the country indicated a number of acts of intimidation and outright infractions—of missing ballots, missing rubber stamps for voting, and ballot-box stuffing.

In Election District 122 in the center of the capital, for example, the independent chairman of the election board, Florin Gloteanu, was suddenly replaced by a man identified with the Front named Mircea Carlin.

Protests from Engineer

When Mr. Carlin showed up with some toughs at his side, a district representative of the National Liberal Party demanded to know what was going on and who the extras were.

"I can bring my dog if I want to," Mr. Carlin told Bogdan Grigoroiu, the Liberal Party official.

A hot argument ensued. When Mr. Grigoroiu called the Mayor's Office to inquire what had happened to Mr. Gloteanu, the previous chairman, he was told, "Maybe he died."

Mr. Grigoroiu, a bearded young electrical engineer, protested the substitution and he also protested the arrival of an excessive and uncounted number of ballots and, stranger still, of the rubber stamps to be used by voters at the polling place. The rubber stamps were not supposed to arrive until 5 A.M. Sunday morning.

'Watching Like a Hawk'

"There still exists a possibility of manipulation," he said, "but I am watching like a hawk and so are representatives of other opposition parties. I fought Ceausescu in University Square on Dec. 21 and 22. We still have to fight these Communists."

Mr. Grigoroiu said he had made certain that the large ballot box with two slots for District 122 was empty when voting started at 6 A.M. in the schoolhouse on Mihai Eminescu Street.

He also pointed out that both Mr. Carlin and Mr. Gloteanu were present this afternoon, saying of the latter, "You see, he is not dead."

The dead of Romania may yet play a problematic role in the election, since, according to experts, roughly a million citizens have died since the last national census in 1977, while their names have remained on the voting lists.

Huge Turnout in Village

A few miles north of Bucharest in Tunari, a village of 4,000 inhabitants, 2,800 of them of voting age, there was a huge turnout as there seemed to be all over the country.

Inside the polling station, infractions of the election law passed in March by the provisional parliament could be observed, such as polling officials paging through the lengthy ballots for Parliament before they were cast by voters and voters going behind the yellow curtains of the balloting booths in pairs.

Outside the village clinic, the spirit was festive, with voters, a third of them of gypsy nationality, in Sunday best.

"It is not so important who wins," said Anton Chirita, a gypsy who is a radio parts maker. "The main thing is that we have democracy and freedom."

"Those who don't vote are their own enemies," said another Tunari voter.

Between Tunari and Balotesti, the next village, four miles north, a whole community of 3,000 houses was torn down several years ago as part of the Ceausescu "systemization" plan of eliminating thousands of Romanian villages and concentrating their inhabitants in large apartment buildings.

"It is an awful life in the flats," said a Tunari voter, "no running water and the toilets are outside!"

"We are happy that our own houses were not destroyed," said a Balotesti voter. "They were scheduled to go last March if Ceausescu had lived. We barely escaped." In fact those facing demolition had been told to level their own houses or face fines of 7,000 lei.

In the capital itself, Mr. Iliescu cast his ballot at 6:14 A.M.—early enough, he said, to avoid television cameras and a crush of news photographers. A crowd of 1,000 cheered Radu Campeanu, the Liberal candidate, when he went to vote later in the morning in the capital.

* * *

June 13, 1990

GORBACHEV YIELDS ON ALLIANCE ROLES IN A NEW GERMANY

By BILL KELLER

Special to The New York Times.

MOSCOW, June 12—President Mikhail S. Gorbachev today removed one of the main conditions that his country had imposed on German unification. He agreed for the first time that West German troops could remain in the North Atlantic Treaty Organization without a corresponding role for the East Germans in the Soviet-led Warsaw Pact.

His offer, made during a report to the Soviet Parliament on his talks with President Bush in Washington, falls short of Western demands that a united Germany be allowed to remain in NATO without conditions.

Mr. Gorbachev proposed that East Germany retain a vaguely defined "associate membership" in the Warsaw Pact, and that a united Germany "honor all obligations" inherited from the two Germanys.

Formula for Germany in NATO

But Mr. Gorbachev's remarks clearly showed that he was striving to find a formula that would allow a united Germany to join NATO, and to prepare his Parliament and public opinion for such an eventuality. [In Washington, Bush Administration officials assessing Mr. Gorbachev's statement said they were growing increasingly convinced that the Soviet leader was slowly reconciling himself to the idea that a united Germany would be in NATO, provided that Moscow's economic, political and security concerns are met.]

Before Mr. Gorbachev spoke today, Soviet officials had previously suggested various approaches intended to prevent German unification from tipping the military balance in NATO's favor. They had proposed a neutral Germany, joint membership for Germany in both alliances, and the dismantling of the alliances, all ideas rejected by the West.

Dual but Not Equal Roles

Today the Soviet leader renewed his call for a broad, general security structure to supplant the two alliances, but he conceded that the rival blocs would continue to exist "for longer than might be imagined."

He again called for "dual membership" for Germany in the competing alliances, but this time it was clear that he was not insisting on an equal membership. The West German Army, or Bundeswehr, would belong to NATO, he said, while the East Germany Army would answer only to the unified German government, not to either alliance.

"United Germany could declare that for this transition period, it would honor all obligations it inherits from the Federal Republic of Germany and from the German Democratic Republic," Mr. Gorbachev said. "For this period, the Bundeswehr would, as before, be subordinate to NATO, and the East German troops would be subordinate to the Government of the new Germany."

Troops to Remain in Germany

That proposal would evidently leave a united Germany free to use East Germany's Army any way it saw fit—including, as some West Germans have proposed, abolishing it.

The Soviet leader said he had proposed to President Bush that during that period, Soviet troops would remain stationed in East Germany, a condition the West has already accepted, and Moscow would agree to the continued presence of American troops in Europe.

"I told the President that I think that the American presence in Europe, since it fulfills a certain role in maintaining stability, is an element of the strategic situation, and does represent a problem for us," Mr. Gorbachev told his Parliament.

Mr. Gorbachev's carefully worded statement on the intricacies of the German question was so murky in places that many diplomats spent the day puzzling over it before recognizing the new elements.

Narrowing of Differences

Western diplomats here said Mr. Gorbachev's comments reflected a rapid narrowing of the conceptual differences between East and West on the future of Germany, although the negotiations on concrete proposals remain excruciatingly complicated.

"He is no longer insisting that united Germany can under no circumstances be a member of NATO, something he had said two months ago was absolutely excluded," said one European diplomat.

But the two sides remain mired in the complexities of such questions as the numbers of troops, the command structure, compensation of the Soviets for possible loss of East German trade, and the creation of new political organizations that would give the Soviets some say in European affairs.

"Given the circumstances, it would be unreasonable to expect him to show more of his cards now," the diplomat said. "He is still waiting to see some concrete proposals from us at the NATO summit," a meeting of the Western leaders scheduled for July, the diplomat said.

Threat of Hard-Line Assertions

Mr. Gorbachev's main concern is that German reunification not add to the threat—or the fear among his countrymen—of a decisive shift in the military balance, with NATO strengthened by the gain of a united Germany, while the Eastern alliance disintegrates.

If Mr. Gorbachev is not careful, his supporters say, hard-liners in the Government and military might use the loss of Germany to undermine the Soviet leader by asserting that his foreign policy is selling out Soviet security.

In the Communist Party Daily Rabochaya Tribuna today, Oleg Baklanov, the Communist Party official responsible for the military industry, warned that the Soviet Union was rushing into a position of disadvantage in Europe.

"In short, we are leaving and NATO is staying behind and, as far as I can judge, growing stronger every day," Mr. Baklanov said, in an interview reflecting the hard-line pressures on Mr. Gorbachev. "I think we should stop and look around for a moment to understand the disposition of forces in Europe, and it is not tending toward parity."

In a gesture apparently toward the hard-liners, Mr. Gorbachev today tersely rejected a written suggestion from one member of Parliament that Communist Party political cells in the military be abolished to make the army more independent of party contxrol. "No, I don't think so," he said. Mr. Gorbachev today also dismissed speculation that Moscow would welcome a united Germany that would be, like France, linked politically to NATO but not formally integrated into its military structure.

During the summit meeting in Washington, President Bush renewed the American insistence that Germany should remain in NATO, but offered a package of nine measures with a goal of alleviating Soviet security fears.

They included a promise not to extend NATO troops to East German territory, maintenance of 300,000 to 400,000 Soviet troops in East Germany at West German expense, revamping the NATO force structure to make it less threatening to Moscow, future discussions on limiting the German Army, and ways to institutionalize the 35-nation Conference on Security and Cooperation in Europe, which would give the Soviets a voice in general European security affairs.

Mr. Gorbachev today welcomed those proposals as a show of good faith and said that if NATO continued to remake itself into a more purely political alliance, the unification of Germany may be accomplished without bitterness.

* * *

July 17, 1990

EXCERPTS FROM KOHL-GORBACHEV NEWS CONFERENCE ON GERMANY AND NATO

Special to The New York Times.

BONN, July 16—Following are excerpts from a news conference today in Zheleznovodsk, U.S.S.R., at which Chancellor Helmut Kohl of West Germany and President Mikhail S. Gorbachev of the Soviet Union discussed the membership of a united Germany in the North Atlantic Treaty Organization. The news conference was broadcast on West German television and was recorded and translated by The New York Times.

KOHL STATEMENT

The . . . significance of our meeting lies in the results: We have agreed that significant progress could be made in central questions. This breakthrough was possible because both sides are aware that in Europe, in Germany and in the Soviet Union historic changes are taking place that give us a special responsibility.

That is true for the political work in the countries, but also for the developments of the mutual relations, and also the future of the whole of Europe.

President Gorbachev and I have agreed that we have to face this historic challenge and that we have to try to be worthy of it. And we understand this task out of a special duty of our own generation, which consciously saw and witnessed the war and its consequences, and which has the great, maybe unique, chance to durably create the future of our Continent and our countries peacefully, securely and freely.

It is clear to President Gorbachev and to me that German-Soviet relations have a central significance for the future of our peoples and for the fate of Europe.

We want to express this and have agreed to conclude an all-encompassing bilateral treaty immediately after unification, which shall organize our relations durably and in good-neighborliness. This treaty shall encompass all areas of the relations: political relations as well as questions of mutual security, economy, culture, science and technology, youth exchange and many things more.

Provisions of Accord

Today I can state the following with satisfaction and in agreement with President Gorbachev:

- The unification of Germany encompasses the Federal Republic, the G.D.R. and Berlin.
- When unification is brought about, all the rights and responsibilities of the Four Powers will end. With that, the unified Germany, at the point of its unification, receives its full and unrestricted sovereignty.
- The unified Germany may, in exercising its unrestricted sovereignity, decide freely and by itself if and which alliance it wants to be a member of. This complies with the C.S.C.E. Final Act. I have declared as the opinion of the West German Government that the unified Germany wants to be a member of the Atlantic Alliance, and I am certain that this also complies with the opinion of the Government of the G.D.R.
- The unified Germany concludes a bilateral treaty with the Soviet Union for the organization of the troop withdrawal from the G.D.R., which shall be ended within three to four years. At the same time, a transition treaty about the consequences of the introduction of the Deutsche mark in the G.D.R. for this time period of three to four years shall be concluded with the Soviet Union.
- As long as Soviet troops will remain stationed on the territory of the G.D.R., NATO structures will not be expanded to this part of Germany. The immediate realization of Articles 5 and 6 of the NATO treaty will stay untouched by this from the start. Non-integrated troops of the West German Army, which means troops of territorial defense, may be stationed on the territory of today's G.D.R. and in Berlin immediately after unification. For the duration of the presence of Soviet troops on former G.D.R. territory the troops of the three Western Powers shall, in our opinion, stay in Berlin. The Federal Government will ask the Western Powers for that and will arrange the stationing with the respective governments.
- The Federal Government declares its willingness to give a binding declaration in the current Vienna talks to reduce the army of a unified Germany within three to four years to a personnel strength of 370,000. The reduction shall start when the first Vienna agreement comes into effect.
- A unified Germany will refrain from producing, holding or commanding of atomic, biological and chemical weapons and will remain a member of the Non-Proliferation Treaty.

Contacts with Others

This joint agreement is a good starting basis to conclude now in time and successfully the external aspects of German unification within the framework of the two-plus-four talks.

On my return I will make the necessary contacts with the G.D.R. Government, and I take it that the Government of the G.D.R. shares our perception. I will also deliver today's reports to the three Western Powers immediately. Foreign Minister Hans-Dietrich Genscher will inform the three Western foreign ministers tomorrow.

At the end of this talk, may I thank you, Mr. President and you, Mrs. Gorbachev, for the great hospitality. This hospitality was essential for the understanding. I may say, the personal trust has grown further.

GORBACHEV STATEMENT

Chancellor Kohl has said a great deal about the great work we have done together, the work and the visit that I see as so important.

I want to give some concrete evaluations of some questions. First of all, I think that the work about such important and difficult points that we did does not only touch our two peoples, but all Europeans, and that it also touches the world public. . . .

We could work so fruitfully because, most of all, in the course of the past years we went our way. Our relations are already marked by a very high level of dialogue, and the meetings on highest levels, the telephone calls, the mutual visits have contributed to this intensive dialogue.

We have expected that there will be . . . changes, for example in the area of NATO. The Warsaw Pact has already, as you know, changed its doctrine at its last session. That was a challenge, a call to change the structures of the blocs, from military blocs to more political ones.

Impulse in London Talks

We have received a very important impulse from the conference in London, NATO's most recent conference, which brought very important positive steps, which were also understood as such by the socialist countries and other European countries.

If the . . . step of London had not been made, then it would have been difficult to make headway at our meeting. I want to characterize the two last days with a German expression: we made realpolitik. We have taken as a basis today's reality, the significance for Europe and the world.

We have reached agreement over the fact that the NATO structure is not going to be expanded to the territory of the former G.D.R. And if on the basis of our agreement the Soviet troops will be withdrawn in a time frame of, let us say, three to four years, then we take it that after this time period this territory will also be part of a Germany that has full sovereignity. We take it that no other foreign troops appear there; here we have trust and are aware of the responsibility of this step.

Mr. Chancellor, it was you most of all who developed this idea at this meeting. We cannot talk yet about a unified Germany, it is still an idea yet, but an idea that I welcome. . . .

QUESTIONS AND ANSWERS

Q. I can already see the headlines tomorrow, saying that the most powerful economic power and the superpower have edged closer together, evoking Rapallo. What do you have to say to that?

KOHL: You cannot prevent anyone from commenting or writing nonsense, and that goes for all walks of life. We have seen an outstanding example for that in London in recent days. Whoever knows something about history knows that the comparison with Rapallo is wholly off; it is a totally different historic situation.

Just look at what the Soviet Union was in the 20's and what it is in the 90's. This comparison is wrong, wrong in every way.

There is an even more convincing example: The reunified Germany is part of NATO and the E.C. and will also keep this course under an all-German government. We are still heading toward the date of the Dec. 31, 1992, when there will be the big single market in Europe. . . .

A reunified Germany does not want to go a way beside the Western community, but is an integrated part of this community.

The geopolitical situation of Germany determines that Germany is in a central position. We have been an area through which armies went from west to east. But it also has been a bridge for ideas and culture. . . . The development of German and Russian culture is not thinkable without this mutual fertilization. . . .

We have talked at length about how much we both feel the responsibility toward the generation of our grandchildren. . . . Why should we not, at the end of this century, have learned from some mistakes? That is our formula, and that does not threaten anyone.

Need for United Europe

GORBACHEV: When we laid down the wreaths at the war memeorial and we met the war veterans, they told us that it was necessary that there be a united Europe, and that our relations have to be peaceful, that what happened should not repeat itself. And these were people who themselves suffered under Hitler's fascism. . . . I think he [Mr. Kohl] is a responsible politician, and here the good will of the Germans was expressed, and it was satisfaction for our people.

Q. Is there a discrepancy in your attitudes with respect to the NATO status of a unified Germany?

KOHL: There is no contrast. For the short time in which Soviet soldiers will be stationed in a reunified Germany, there will be no NATO soldiers, but territorial defense units. After that, there can be every kind of troops; that is the decision of the united Germany.

We agreed that there will be no non-German troops on the territory of the G.D.R.

We have made it clear that with its full sovereignity, the unified Germany will conclude treaties about the presence of foreign troops in Berlin.

* * *

October 3, 1990

TWO GERMANYS UNITE AFTER 45 YEARS WITH JUBILATION AND A VOW OF PEACE

By SERGE SCHMEMANN
Special to The New York Times.

BERLIN, Wednesday, Oct. 3—Forty-five years after it was carved up in defeat and disgrace, Germany was reunited today in a midnight celebration of pealing bells, national hymns and the jubilant blare of good old German oom-pah-pah.

Associated Press

The German flag was unfurled in front of the Reichstag building in Berlin at midnight as the two Germanys were reunited.

At the stroke of midnight Tuesday, a copy of the American Liberty Bell, a gift from the United States at the height of the cold war, tolled from the Town Hall, and the black, red and gold banner of the Federal Republic of Germany rose slowly before the Reichstag, the scarred seat of past German Parliaments.

Then the President, Richard von Weizsacker, drawing on the words of the West German Constitution, proclaimed from the steps of the Reichstag: "In free self-determination, we want to achieve the unity in freedom of Germany. We are aware of our responsibility for these tasks before God and the people. We want to serve peace in the world in a united Europe."

Singing of Anthem

With that, a throng estimated at one million joined in the West German national anthem, now the anthem for united Germany: "Unity and justice and freedom for the German fatherland . . ." The words are from the third stanza of the prewar anthem, whose opening verses, now banned, began, "Deutschland, Deutschland uber Alles."

Associated Press

Berliners crowded the streets last night as unification neared. One carried an East German flag with its insignia crossed out.

The moment marked the return of a nation severed along the front line between East and West to the center stage of Europe, this time as an economic powerhouse vowing never again to bring grief to a continent it had so terribly ravaged in the past century.

It is the smallest unified German state to rise in the 119 years since Otto von Bismarck first gathered the Germans under the Prussian crown.

Beer and Revelry

Hundreds of German flags waved and firecrackers snapped in the chilly autumn night. Beer and sparkling wine flowed freely and the strains of divergent bands mingled in a rowdy cacophony. Soon bottles began smashing on the pavement and celebration turned to intoxication, and by early morning the center of the new capital was deep in smashed bottles and weaving revelers.

A force of about 5,000 police officers had been massed in case radicals tried to disrupt the festivities, and the police reported seven arrests. But what protests there were passed with no major incidents.

Unity essentially meant that the German Democratic Republic with its 16 million citizens acceded to the Federal Republic of Germany, which expanded to become a state of 78 million souls and 137,900 square miles. The accession meant that the name, anthem, Constitution and Government of the Federal Republic became those of all Germany, that Chancellor Helmut Kohl became the first Chancellor of the reunited state and Mr. von Weizsacker the first President.

Berlin Is Capital

Berlin, a city divided by the infamous wall into a gray Communist capital and a glittering capitalist enclave, became once again the political and spiritual capital of Germany.

"Everybody should know: Germany will not go it alone, there will be no unilateral nationalism and no 'restless Reich,' " vowed Mr. Kohl in an article written for the Frankfurter Allgemeine newspaper.

It was also a moment of poignant lasts. The German Democratic Republic, founded by Soviet occupiers as the "first state of workers and peasants on German soil," expired bankrupt but not entirely unmourned.

At the final session of Parliament, Jens Reich, a leader of the citizens' movements that led demonstrations a year earlier to bring down the Communists, assailed the first and only democratic legislature of East Germany for having done nothing but surrender the state to the West. "Unity must not become a memory of a stab in the back," he said.

'Farewell without Tears'

But a more prevalent note was struck by the East German Prime Minister, Lothar de Maiziere, at the final "state act" of the East German Government in the grand Schauspielhaus concert hall, attended by the political and cultural elite of the nation.

There, the first and last democratically elected leader of East Germany committed his state to history with the words: "In a few moments the German Democratic Republic accedes to the Federal Republic of Germany. With that, we Germans achieve unity in freedom. It is an hour of great joy. It is the end of many illusions. It is a farewell without tears."

Then Kurt Mazur, the conductor from Leipzig and a hero of the peaceful revolution last fall, rose to conduct Beethoven's Ninth Symphony, with the grand "Ode to Joy" in the final movement that for Germans stands as a spiritual hymn to hope.

Address by Kohl

Mr. Kohl, capping a year of political successes, addressed the nation on television several hours before unity.

"In a few hours a dream will become reality," Mr. Kohl said, his eyes turning misty. "After 40 bitter years of division, Germany, our fatherland, will be reunited. This is one of the happiest moments of my life. From the many letters and conversations I have had, I know the great joy also felt by the vast majority of you."

Many Germans, in fact, had spent the last several weeks complaining of the cost and dislocation of unity. But at the moment of unity, Mr. Kohl seemed correct in finding that it was a moment to celebrate.

'It Is Really Moving'

The Chancellor also made a point of thanking and reassuring Germany's allies and neighbors. "In particular," he said, "we thank the United States of America and above all President George Bush." Mr. Bush was among the first world leaders to abandon reservations about German unity and endorse Mr. Kohl's efforts.

In recent weeks, the process of unity had drawn growing grumbles from both East and West as Germans came to realize the huge cost of the undertaking. But for the hundreds of thousands who had gathered from across Germany and abroad, this was a night not to moan, but simply to celebrate.

"It is really moving," said Heinz Schober, a Berlin shopkeeper who had come with his wife. "We were here when the wall went up and we were here when it came down, and now we see something children will read about in history books."

Hundreds of stands along the Unter den Linden peddled everything from bratwurst and beer to "Day of Unity" T-shirts and chunks of the Berlin wall. Musicians ranging from rock bands to a Soviet military band to Wolf Biermann, a onetime East German dissident, blared from 16 stages set up among the beer and sausage stands, and all along the mile-long avenue the mood was festive and joyous.

At one point, revelers before the Reichstag pressed hard against the steps, where Chancellor Kohl and other political leaders were gathered, but no problems developed.

The most serious trouble was reported in Gottingen, a West German city near the former border, where about 1,000 radical youths went on a rampage, smashing windows and denouncing unity.

Year of Rapid Change

Unity came to the Germans barely a year after streams of East Germans began pouring out through newly porous borders in Hungary and Czechoslovakia, forcing the East German leader, Erich Honecker, to confront a crisis just as he prepared to preside over the celebrations of his state's 40th anniversary.

A year before unity came, on Oct. 3, 1989, a flood of East German refugees had all but overwhelmed the West German Embassy in Czechoslovakia, and the East German Government finally gave permission for the refugees to go west. It also closed its borders, touching off new discontent and disorders.

The celebration of East Germany's anniversary four days later marked the beginning of the state's undoing. The Soviet leader, Mikhail S. Gorbachev, gave the first indications that he was not prepared to prop up the East German Government, and waves of demonstrators clashed with the police in East Berlin and other cities.

The demonstrations rapidly grew, driving the Government into disarray until it took the fateful action on Nov. 9 of opening the Berlin wall a crack, touching off a rush to unity. By March 18 East Germany held its first democratic elections, and by July 1 its economy was merged into West Germany's. The pace accelerated through the summer, bringing formal unity up to Oct. 3 and setting the scene for the celebration.

The pace of events also required a rapid termination of the vestigial occupation under which both the Germanys and the Berlins existed, and the moment of unity was preceded by a flurry of final arrangements and actions to end the Allied controls.

The commanders of the Western Allied forces, the United States, Britain and France, which merged their occupation zones of the city after the war to form West Berlin and defended it against Communist encirclement in ensuing years, met for the last time and ceded authority over the city.

"I now close this final meeting of the Allied Kommandatura with a good, solid bang," said the British commander, Maj. Gen. Robert Corbert, pounding the gavel at the Allied headquarters with a solid thump.

* * *

November 15, 1990

POLAND AND GERMANY SIGN BORDER GUARANTEE PACT

By STEPHEN ENGELBERG
Special to The New York Times.

WARSAW, Nov. 14—Poland signed a treaty guaranteeing its border with Germany today, ending months of anxiety among Poles about the intentions of their neighbor to the west.

The ceremony, at a simple wooden table in the ballroom of a Government building, opened a new chapter in Polish-German relations in which the most important issues between the two nations will be economic, not political.

Hans-Dietrich Genscher, the German Foreign Minister, said the treaty was historic evidence of his nation's "responsibility for peace in Europe." Mr. Genscher pledged that Germany would help Poland and other Eastern European nations rebuild their shattered economies.

"Together we must insure that the frontier does not become a watershed between rich and poor," Mr. Genscher said. "We fully support Poland's request for association with the European community. The advantages that Western Europe can offer because of the large common market must also be shared by the nations of Central and Eastern Europe which have regained their freedom."

Plan to End Visa Policy

For much of the last year, Poland has been pushing hard for a formal treaty that would recognize the eastern borders set at the end of World War II. At that time, Poland lost large tracts of land to the Soviet Union, to the east, and received in compensation formerly German lands, from the west. Most of the German residents were expelled, although small pockets of ethnic Germans remain in Poland.

Poles' uncertainty about the border was heightened last year when Helmut Kohl, the German Chancellor, made a series of contradictory and ambiguous statements in which he declined to categorically recognize the existing frontier.

In his speech today, Mr. Genscher reaffirmed Germany's plans to lift visa requirements for Poles by the end of the year. That policy has been warmly greeted by Poland because it means that for the first time in postwar history, Poles will be permitted easy access to a country within the European Community.

The border treaty went into effect immediately, although it awaits ratification by the Polish and German Parliaments. The two countries are negotiating a separate pact to redefine their economic relationship.

Separate Meeting with Walesa

The treaty signed today by Mr. Genscher and his Polish counterpart, Foreign Minister Krzysztof Skubiszewski, is a potential issue in the national election campaigns in both countries. While the treaty could conceivably cost Mr. Kohl some votes in the German elections next month, from Germans who may still long for the land given to Poland, it is likely to be a boost for Tadeusz Mazowiecki, the Polish Prime Minister, who is a candidate in the presidential elections on Nov. 25.

In an attempt to dispel the impression that Germany had taken sides in the election, Mr. Genscher met separately this evening with Mr. Mazowiecki's chief rival, Lech Walesa, the head of Solidarity.

Zdzislaw Najder, a political ally of Mr. Walesa and an internationally recognized scholar on the works of Joseph Conrad, praised the treaty but said the Mazowiecki Government had spent far too much political capital on the border issue.

"We were so obsessed with the past, and the frontier, that we forgot about the future, which is economics," Mr. Najder said. "I don't see a danger in a German economic invasion of Poland. I see a danger that they won't come."

Forgiveness from Germans

Mr. Mazowiecki attended the ceremony for the treaty signing, and his speech, carried live by Polish television, touched on one of his basic campaign themes: the reintegration of Poland into Europe.

"The signing of this treaty closes the period when the problem of the border divided our two nations and created for us, the Poles, feelings of fear and threat," said Mr. Mazowiecki, who spoke of the immense suffering Germany inflicted on Poland in World War II.

Mr. Mazowiecki, making a statement unusual for a Polish political figure, also acknowledged that Germans had been hurt when the borders were forceably shifted in 1945.

"We ask for the forgiveness of the German nation for the sufferings which were caused by moving Poland from East to West," said Mr. Mazowiecki. "Remember that in the counting of victims, arithmetics have no value and the sufferings will remain, regardless of who inflicted them."

* * *

December 10, 1990

POLAND ELECTS WALESA PRESIDENT IN LANDSLIDE

By STEPHEN ENGELBERG
Special to The New York Times.

GDANSK, Dec. 9—Lech Walesa, the charismatic leader of the Solidarity movement for a decade, won a landslide runoff victory today in Poland's first direct presidential elections, according to exit polls and early returns.

In voting for Mr. Walesa, Poles chose a 47-year-old electrician with a vocational school education and a sure touch for mass politics to guide this formerly Communist nation through the next phase of its difficult transition to capitalism.

Mr. Walesa, the winner of the 1983 Nobel Prize for his role in the Solidarity labor union, soundly defeated Stanislaw Tyminski, a previously unknown émigré businessman from Canada and Peru whose pledge to improve Poles' lives within a month carried him into the runoff, ahead of the sitting Prime Minister, Tadeusz Mazowiecki.

Infas, a West German polling company which has accurately forecast every election in Eastern Europe this year, said Mr. Walesa would finish with 74.7 percent of the vote and Mr. Tyminski with 25.3 percent.

"I will do everything so that every Pole owns a share of Poland in his hands," a jubilant Mr. Walesa said at a news conference tonight at his headquarters here, a few blocks from the shipyard where the Solidarity movement was born a decade ago. "As far as Mr. Tyminski is concerned, I think as quickly as he was born he will fade out, because truly he did not propose anything tangible. They were just slogans."

Champagne and Firecrackers

Mr. Walesa called on his supporters to help him reach the significant minority who have lost hope in their Government. "People who live poorly, these people said, 'Enough.' These people don't trust Walesa," said the union leader. "I always sense the feelings of a society, and I feel they have their doubts."

"We need them," he declared.

The scene outside Solidarity headquarters was one of unabashed celebration. Hundreds of Gdansk residents came to cheer their most famous native son and listen to a brass band. They set off firecrackers, threw glasses against the wall of the headquarters and popped open champagne bottles.

With today's voting, Poles appeared to have solidly rejected a candidate whose message sought to capitalize on the pain and fears of a nation undergoing a wrenching passage to a free-market economy. An exit poll suggested tonight that Mr. Tyminski had made little headway since the first round, when he garnered 23 percent of the votes in a six-candidate field.

Mr. Walesa, who had been disappointed by his 40 percent showing in the first round on Nov. 25, tonight appeared close to realizing his pre-election goal of being elected with a mandate from 80 percent of the voters. The turnout was estimated tonight at 55 percent.

Walesa Attracts Older Voters

The exit polls showed that Mr. Tyminski ran strongest among young voters, who supported Mr. Walesa by a margin of 70 percent to 30 percent. Ninety percent of older voters backed the Solidarity chairman, as did 77 percent of the farmers.

Mr. Tyminski has hinted in recent days that he might challenge the election results, a move that could delay the presidential inauguration by two weeks or more.

The émigré entrepreneur had vowed to stay in Poland even if he lost the election and had been noncommital about whether he planned to have any role in next spring's parliamentary elections.

When Mr. Walsea takes up residence in the Belvedere Palace as the first Polish President ever chosen by direct elections, he will confront a host of difficult political and economic decisions. His first move will be to select a Prime Minister who can fashion a working majority in a Parliament which still has a majority of former Communists or their satellite parties.

Opponents Look to Assembly

He must also prepare for the parliamentary elections this spring in which his opponents from the once-united Solidarity movement will try to take control of the legislature.

The most significant issue facing the new President is how, if at all, to revive Poland's program for fostering a market economy. Mr. Walesa's critics phrased the question this way: Can he say no to the demands of millions of workers in the largely inefficient state-run industries? His supporters say he is the only politician who can do so.

International financial institutions like the World Bank view Poland's economic plan as the most ambitious effort of its kind in Eastern Europe. But its side effects include a sharp recession, a declining living standard and unemployment of one million workers, or 5.5 percent. The effort has stirred considerable apprehension among rural and working class Poles, as indicated by the startling first-round success of Mr. Tyminski.

Mr. Walesa took 40 percent of the vote in the first round, calling for "acceleration" of political and economic changes in Poland and declaring he would sweep the former Communists from posts in business and industry.

Same Economic Principles

His early criticism of the economic program adopted by the Mazowiecki Government upset foreign observers, prompting him to emphasize his intention to continue its guiding principles. Mr. Walesa even advanced the idea of choosing Leszek Balcerowicz, the Finance Minister under Mr. Mazowiecki, as his Prime Minister.

After Mr. Tyminski finished second, Mr. Walesa began stressing the need for "modifications" in the economic plan. At the same time, he moved to dampen public expectation about how much improvement Poles can count on in their daily lives.

In the runoff campaign, Mr. Tyminski became the target of a sustained attack by this country's leading institutions. The Roman Catholic Church abandoned its neutral stance and openly threw its support to Mr. Walesa. Poland's Primate, Jozef Cardinal Glemp, called Mr. Tyminski "impudent" and later referred to him as a "joke of history." Polish television broadcast a steady stream of negative stories about Mr. Tyminski, including reports that he beat his wife and abused his children. The businessman angrily denied the charges and threatened lawsuits.

Intense Scrutiny

His record as an entrepreneur in Canada, where he owns a computer systems company, and in Peru, where he introduced cable television in a remote mining town, drew intense scrutiny, as did his spiritual conversion in the Amazonian jungle and his belief in a "fourth dimension."

The runoff vote today had its beginnings in Gdansk this summer, when Mr. Walesa became restive with his role on the political sideline and began pressing for a "war at the top" among leading politicians.

Mr. Walesa demanded that the Solidarity movement split and that Poles, who were becoming dangerously disengaged from politics, be given a real choice about their futures.

Members of the Mazowiecki Government dismissed Mr. Walesa's statements as rationalization for a campaign to achieve high office.

Some critics even said Mr. Walesa had become jealous of Vaclav Havel, the Czechoslovak dissident who was elected President of his country this year. Many of the intellectuals in Solidarity opposed Mr. Walesa's candidacy, contending that he was unpredictable and had dictatorial tendencies.

* * *

August 20, 1991

K.G.B.-MILITARY RULERS TIGHTEN GRIP; GORBACHEV ABSENT, YELTSIN DEFIANT

West Voices Anger and Warns on Aid

By FRANCIS X. CLINES
Special to The New York Times.

MOSCOW, Aug. 19—The engineers of President Mikhail S. Gorbachev's ouster from power moved quickly today to reimpose hard-line control across the nation. The coup leaders, dominated by the military and the K.G.B., banned protest meetings, closed independent newspapers and flooded the capital with troops and tanks.

Boris N. Yeltsin, President of the Russian federated republic, who has often been at odds with Mr. Gorbachev, became one of his strongest supporters today, seeking to rally resistance to the Soviet leader's overthrow by climbing atop an armored truck and calling for a general strike on Tuesday to protest the move as an unconstitutional act, a coup d'etat.

By nightfall, Mr. Yeltsin had some of his own Russian republic troops and armored combat vehicles moving to his headquarters, and some positive responses were heard to his call for a strike, notably from coal miners and auto workers in Siberia. The scene was set for a possible confrontation between troops loyal to Mr. Yeltsin and those under the command of the national authorities.

Fatality in Latvia Reported

One death was reported, that of an unidentified driver said to have been killed in Riga, Latvia, one of the places under military control.

The nation was startled after Mr. Gorbachev, who had been on vacation in the southern Crimea since Aug. 4, was ousted from power the day before he was due to return to Moscow to sign a new union treaty. The landmark accord would have begun a program for speeding constitutional reforms and limiting the Kremlin's ability to dictate the life of the country.

Mr. Gorbachev has been increasingly unpopular at home, in large part because of the country's profound economic troubles, and has been sharply criticized even by many of his former supporters.

Still, there was general disbelief here in Moscow at the coup plotters' assertion that Mr. Gorbachev was ill and therefore had to be relieved of power.

Mr. Gorbachev's exact whereabouts were unknown. There was one report that he had been placed under house arrest in a naval hospital in Sevastopol in the Crimea.

The group now in charge is dominated by security and military leaders, and some top political figures, all of whom had strong disagreements with Mr. Gorbachev's democratization and economic-reform programs. This reform process had the further effect of doing away with the need for Communist Party supremacy.

The new ruling group calls itself the State Committee for the State of Emergency, or, in Russian, Gosudarstvenny Komitet po Chrezvychainomu Polozheniyu.

'To Get His Health Back'

"Over the years, he has got very tired and needs some time to get his health back," contended Vice President Gennadi I. Yanayev, who said he had taken over as acting president, and who directed a news conference at which he defended Mr. Gorbachev's overthrow and his assumption of presidential powers as necessary in the current state of economic and political crisis.

Mr. Yanayev (pronounced yuh-NYE-yeff) used the news conference, broadcast to the Soviet people, to also announce a series of measures aimed at winning popular support. These included stronger anti-crime moves and improved housing.

The group also said it would continue basic reform programs, but its first decrees—like imposing what amounted to martial law in Moscow, Leningrad and the Baltic republics, and closing the most independent press and television voices—contradicted the pledges to continue on the Gorbachev path.

Mr. Yanayev was asked what legal authority allowed the creation of the emergency committee, which is composed of eight Communist Party, military and intelligence figures noted for their hard-line inclinations.

He responded that "sometimes there are critical situations that call for immediate action" and that, in any case, the Soviet Parliament would eventually approve the action in a special session on Aug. 27.

Mr. Yeltsin, addressing a protest crowd of more than 20,000 Muscovites, decried the Gorbachev ouster as a lawless Kremlin putsch.

Yeltsin Is Warned

But the Yanayev committee, warning that it was prepared to "dismantle" agencies resisting its authority, cautioned him against carrying out his "irresponsible" resolve to lead a general strike.

Coal-mine leaders announced plans to begin closing pits in the major Ukrainian and Siberian coalfields.

A union spokeswoman said that half the mines in the Kuznetsk coal basin in Siberia stopped operating early Tuesday, Reuters reported from Moscow. But workers in the giant Tyumen oilfield declined to strike, the news agency quoted a trade union leader there as saying.

In Moscow, all of the major independent newspapers, which had been in the vanguard of the more open press typical of recent years, were ordered shut pending "reregistration." But printers at the Government newspaper Izvestia, though free to publish, announced that they would not work.

Throughout the morning, tanks and armored personnel carriers lumbered to critical crossroads of the city, four of them spinning wildly in a circle outside the Bolshoi Theater in a roaring display of force that left passers-by crying, "Shame!"

Several angry Muscovites ran into the road to retrieve chunks of the ripped-up macadam. "The final souvenirs of freedom," one man remarked.

Mr. Yanayev defended the necessity for the tanks, troops and a series of toughly worded orders aimed at overrruling, where necessary, the centers of insurgent political power that might contradict the Kremlin's new special orders.

The state of emergency would not be general throughout the nation, he said. The Emergency Committee spared such eastern republics as Uzbekistan and Kazakhstan, traditionally more obedient to Kremlin authority. But Leningrad and Moscow, centers of the opposition politics encouraged by six years of Gorbachev reforms, were among the first to receive state-of-emergency notices.

Reformist politicians in both cities, the Soviet Union's largest, sought to rally opposition. A large crowd began a night vigil outside Mr. Yeltsin's headquarters in the Russian republic headquarters building on the downtown bank of the Moscow River. Soviet tanks had been stationed there, with their crewmen leaning and watching casually through a long day, occasionally chatting with an angry civilian or joking with others.

Three of the tanks were suddenly turned around, as if in a nighttime lark, after Yeltsin loyalists said they had taken control of the vehicles. The Yeltsin supporters also claimed the defection of a score of Soviet paratroopers. But rumors abounded that the Kremlin forces might choose the time before dawn to make some confrontational move on the building.

Later, 30 more armored vehicles pulled up, and their crews turned out to be Russian troops loyal to Mr. Yeltsin. The crews, trailed by seven ammunition trucks, vowed to defend the building. The Soviets kept their distance.

Thus, ingredients of confrontation were gathering. A report from Leningrad said that Mayor Anatoly A. Sobchak told a crowd of about 2,000 outside city hall that the coup leaders first tried to press Mr. Gorbachev into signing his assent to his removal and, when he refused, placed him under house arrest in his dacha in the Crimea.

A close aide to Mr. Yeltsin reported that he sought to telephone Mr. Gorbachev at the dacha early Monday. The official said someone answered the phone and, when asked to summon Mr. Gorbachev for Mr. Yeltsin, responded: "We have been asked at this end not to disturb him."

In its first statements, the Kremlin special committee did not specifically comment on the strategic arms reduction treaty signed here earlier this month by Mr. Gorbachev and President Bush. But speaking in general terms, it declared that the Soviet Union was "a peace-loving nation and would unfailingly honor all assumed commitments."

It added, however: "Any attempts at talking to our country in the languages of diktats, no matter by whom, will be decisively cut short."

It was difficult to immediately gauge the nationwide effectiveness of the plotters' seizing of power. Journalists faced fresh censorship, and the public at large seemed stunned or passive. Here in Moscow, most people steered clear of both the tanks and opposition protest rallies, which went on only a block or two from shopping lines and casual cafe scenes typical of the city.

The fate of the union treaty slipped deeper into doubt with each statement by the Kremlin committee criticizing its provisions, particularly those that would have shifted power from Moscow to the republics. Mr. Yanayev insisted that the treaty had not been put aside, although he said there should be no rush to sign it now, so that "every citizen can assess the document at his leisure."

He appeared at his news conference with several members of the committee, but not with the two people considered critical in the overthrow—Vladimir A. Kryuchkov, chairman of the K.G.B., and the Defense Minister, Marshal Dmitri T. Yazov.

The former Soviet Foreign Minister, Eduard A. Shevardnadze, dismissed the talk of Mr. Gorbachev's ill health as a pretext for a coup provoked by hard-line officials fearful over the pending shift of power from Moscow to the republics, a change Mr. Gorbachev had negotiated with republic leaders.

The negotiations had produced a new treaty for a redesigned Soviet Union, and the first signatures were expected Tuesday at a Kremlin ceremony suddenly canceled in the wake of the coup.

'Not Inclined to Defend Him'

"We were expecting it to happen," Mr. Shevardnadze said of the coup. "Unfortunately, Mikhail Sergeyevich did not draw the necessary conclusions," he said, adding that there was confusion to be cleared up, including whether Mr. Gorbachev might have known of the looming plot.

"I'm not inclined to defend him," he said of his former mentor and friend.

The K.G.B. and defense chiefs stayed largely behind the scenes today, but the public did not doubt that they were the power behind the ouster. The other members of the emergency committee, besides the Vice President, are Oleg D. Baklanov, deputy chairman of the Soviet defense council; Prime Minister Valentin S. Pavlov; Interior Minister Boris K. Pugo, who commands the interior police; Vasily A. Starodubtsev, chairman of the Soviet farmers' union, and A. I. Tizyakov, president of an association of state enterprises.

At the news conference, Mr. Yanayev and other committee members insisted that they had an emergency program to deal with the nation's long-running crises. They spoke of attending immediately to the basic needs of food shortages and new housing, long the staples of traditional Soviet Communists' promises to do better.

As night fell across the nation, nervousness increased, and the Latvian republic's government reported that commando units—the so-called Black Berets—entered the Police Ministry in Riga and reportedly took control of the main television station.

The death in Latvia reported earlier was said to be that of a van driver who died at the hands of Interior Ministry troops, reports reaching Moscow said. Few other details were available.

In Lithuania, Soviet troops were also reported to have surrounded the main TV tower, in the city of Kaunas.

The top Soviet military leader in the Baltic region, Gen. Fyodor Kuzmin, declared himself the de facto ruler of Lithuania, Latvia and Estonia.

Soviet warships were reported to have blockaded the harbor at Tallinn, the Estonian capital.

Soviet citizens also returned in force to familiar sources in hard times for nonofficial news: the Voice of America, the British Broadcasting Corporation and Radio Liberty.

Outside the Kremlin near midnight, the main Manezh Square was deserted except for a few demonstrators and a column of soldiers that suddenly split into three parts of about 20 members each. They marched off in three directions, seemingly to guard the new leaders behind the Kremlin walls. A protester dogged them at a safe distance, reading aloud Mr. Yeltsin's announcement urging all soldiers to retreat from Kremlin intrigues.

* * *

February 2, 1992

BUSH AND YELTSIN DECLARE FORMAL END TO COLD WAR; AGREE TO EXCHANGE VISITS

By MICHAEL WINES
Special to The New York Times.

WASHINGTON, Feb. 1—President Bush and President Boris N. Yeltsin of Russia today proclaimed a new era of "friendship and partnership" as they declared a formal end to seven decades of rivalry, then agreed to exchange visits in Moscow and Washington by year's end.

Meeting in casual winter clothes under snowy skies at the Presidential retreat at Camp David, Md., the two leaders reviewed the prospects for further support for Mr. Yeltsin's program of reforms and for arms control proposals that could reduce the number of nuclear warheads that each nation deploys to as few as 2,500.

But they indicated at a news conference after their three-and-a-half-hour meeting that no agreements had been reached on either issue, and that the matters would be taken up this winter. Secretary of State James A. Baker 3d will visit Moscow this month to establish the basis for further arms talks, Mr. Bush said.

Restatement of Principles

The centerpiece of the meeting was a declaration signed by the two men that outlined general principles for relations between the United States and Russia. The declaration was largely a restatement of cooperative policies established between Washington and Moscow before the Soviet Union collapsed and Mikhail S. Gorbachev resigned as Soviet President at the end of December.

But by endorsing and signing the statement today, Mr. Bush lent prestige to Mr. Yeltsin as the leader of Russia, giving him a boost of the sort Mr. Gorbachev often gained in his trips abroad.

"Russia and the United States do not regard each other as potential adversaries," the declaration says. "From now on, the relationship will be characterized by friendship and partnership founded on mutual trust and respect and a common commitment to democracy and economic freedom."

Many Advisers on Both Sides

The two leaders were accompanied to Camp David by senior aides, including a roster of advisers to Mr. Yeltsin who are largely unknown to most Americans. They included the Russian Foreign Minister, Andrei Kozyrev; Marshal Yevgeny I. Shaposhnikov, who commands the combined military of the Commonwealth of Independent States; Yuli M. Vorontsov, chief Russian delegate to the United Nations; Yevgeny P. Velikhov, deputy chairman of the Russian Academy of Sciences, and Vladimir P. Lukin, the Ambassador-designate to Washington.

With Mr. Bush were Mr. Baker; Defense Secretary Dick Cheney; Treasury Secretary Nicholas F. Brady; Brent Scowcroft, the national security adviser; Robert S. Strauss, the American Ambassador to Russia, and Dennis Ross, the director of the policy planning office at the State Department and Mr. Baker's senior adviser on Russia.

The only new issue of substance to emerge from the sessionappeared to be an offer by Mr. Bush to set up a joint center in which American scientists would pursue research with some of the 2,000 or more Russian nuclear experts who are being displaced by Mr. Yeltsin's sharp military cutbacks.

Mr. Yeltsin said he enthusiastically supported the proposal, which is aimed at preventing the scientists from selling their services to terrorists or other nations seeking to develop a nuclear arsenal. Russia has already begun offering raises and other benefits to the scientists to keep them from leaving, he said.

At the news conference, the two leaders warmly praised each other's leadership.

The American President said he has "a very warm feeling in my heart about what he has done and is trying to do, and I

Jose B. Lopes/The New York Times

President Boris N. Yeltsin of Russia and President Bush at their news conference after meeting privately yesterday at Camp David, Md.

consider him my friend." In return, he received effusive praise from his guest.

'Tremendously Impressed'

"I consider I would be very lucky in life, both as a political person and just as a man, to have met George Bush," Mr. Yeltsin said. "I'm just tremendously impressed by his wisdom. I think he has incredible qualities not only as a political person but also as a person, as a really great political figure of the United States."

Later, perhaps with a measure of pride, he said: "We call each other on the telephone. We say Boris and say George. And already this says a lot."

Translating affability into substance, the two leaders said the enmity that had separated their countries over most of seven decades was ended.

As Mr. Yeltsin put it: "Today one might say that there has been written and drawn a new line, and crossed out all of the things that have been associated with the cold war.

"From now on we do not consider ourselves to be potential enemies, as it had been previously in our military doctrine. This is the historic value of this meeting. And another very important factor in our relationship, right away today, it's already been pointed out that in the future there'll be full frankness, full openness, full honesty in our relationship."

Mr. Bush said: "Russia and the United States are charting a new relationship, and it's based on trust; it's based on a commitment to economic and political freedom; it's based on a strong hope for true partnership."

Yet for Mr. Bush, the embrace sometimes remained at arm's length, especially when nuclear weapons came up.

Mr. Yeltsin discussed the possibility of cutting strategic and tactical nuclear warheads to 2,500 for each nation. That figure, which Mr. Yelstin proposed earlier this week, is roughly half the number that Mr. Bush suggested retaining in a proposal he made in his State of the Union address on Tuesday.

Mr. Bush said he had agreed only that further cuts in nuclear weapons would be taken up when Mr. Baker goes back to Moscow. "We didn't go into any agreements on categories or numbers, but we decided that we would let the experts talk about this in much more detail," Mr. Bush said. "But we saluted his very broad proposals."

He also refused to say whether the United States had reciprocated Mr. Yeltsin's decision, made public last week, to cease aiming nuclear missiles and bombers at American targets.

"We agreed all these matters will be discussed in Moscow," he said.

Similarly, Mr. Yeltsin said he and Mr. Bush had discussed developing a global space-based defense against nuclear missiles "on a mutual basis," perhaps in conjunction with other nuclear nations. But Mr. Bush said only that they had reached no decision and that their aides would take it up later.

Although President Ronald Reagan began research on a defense against incoming missiles with a pledge to share the technology with the Soviet Union, Mr. Bush has so far ruled out any transfer of missile-defense secrets.

Although he made no specific pledges, Mr. Bush was more positive in his support for Mr. Yeltsin's political and economic reforms, saying he was "totally convinced" of Russia's commitment to democracy and hoped to assist "in any way possible."

Money, and More . . .

Mr. Yeltsin said that his country needed far more than money if it was to make the transition to democracy, and that the cost of failure would be great.

"I didn't come here just to stretch out my hand and ask for help," the Russian President said. "No, we're calling for cooperation, cooperation for the whole world, because if the reform in Russia goes under, that means there will be a cold war. The cold war is going to turn into a hot war. This is, again, going to be an arms race."

Back in Washington after the Camp David meeting, Mr. Yeltsin met for an hour and 10 minutes with Congressional leaders, and the lawmakers said the conversation focused on economic reform and the assistance that Russia and the other former Soviet republics need. Representative Richard A. Gephardt, Democrat of Missouri, the House majority leader, said Mr. Yeltsin "delivered a loud, clear message that if there's going to be help, it needs to come now."

Senator Bob Dole, Republican of Kansas, the minority leader, said of Mr. Yeltsin: "He may be the last hope. That's the message he gave us. This may be the last chance."

While he was in Washington, Mr. Yeltsin also presented a medal to Mstislav Rostropovich, the Russian émigré cellist and conductor, who suggested that he would perform more and more in his homeland in the years ahead and live part of the time there.

Mr. Rostropovich left the Soviet Union after being barred from performing, and became conductor of the National Symphony here, vowing not to return while his homeland remained under Communism. He did return when Communism collapsed, and was on a visit to Moscow during the unsuccessful coup against Mr. Gorbachev last summer where he joined Mr. Yeltsin's supporters in defending the Russian Parliament.

Mr. Yeltsin left Washington about 4:40 P.M. to fly to Ottawa for a meeting with Prime Minister Brian Mulroney.

YELTSIN AND MULRONEY MEET

OTTAWA, Feb. 1 (Special to The New York Times)—President Yeltsin made the final stop of his three-day visit to North America in the Canadian capital today for talks with Canada's Prime Minister.

On arrival from Washington, Mr. Yeltsin broke away from Mr. Mulroney and other Canadian officials to talk briefly with spectators who had gathered at the airport to greet him in the sub-zero weather. "We're not here to quarrel, we're here to do business," Mr. Yeltsin said. "We come not as enemies, but as allies.

SUBJECT INDEX

BYLINE INDEX